Dictionary of World Biography

The Renaissance

Dictionary of World Biography

The Ancient World
The Middle Ages
The Renaissance
The 17th and 18th Centuries
The 19th Century, 2 volumes
The 20th Century, 3 volumes
Index

Dictionary of World Biography

Volume 3

The Renaissance

Frank N. Magill, *editor*

Christina J. Moose, *managing editor*

Alison Aves, *researcher and bibliographer*

Mark Rehn, *acquisitions editor*

FITZROY DEARBORN PUBLISHERS
CHICAGO • LONDON

SALEM PRESS
PASADENA • ENGLEWOOD CLIFFS

Dictionary of World Biography is a copublication of Salem Press, Inc. and Fitzroy Dearborn Publishers Ltd.

For information, write to:

SALEM PRESS, INC.
P.O. Box 50062
Pasadena, California 91115

or
FITZROY DEARBORN PUBLISHERS
919 North Michigan Avenue, Suite 760
Chicago, Illinois 60611
USA

or
FITZROY DEARBORN PUBLISHERS
310 Regent Street
London W1R 5AJ
England

The paper used in this volume conforms to the American National Standard for Permanence of Paper for Printed Library Materials, Z39.48-1992.

Library of Congress Cataloging-in-Publication Data
Dictionary of world biography / editor, Frank N. Magill ; managing editor, Christina J. Moose ; researcher and bibliographer, Alison Aves ; acquisitions editor, Mark Rehn.
v. cm.
A revision and reordering, with new entries added, of the material in the thirty vols. comprising the various subsets designated "series" published under the collective title: Great lives from history, 1987-1995.
Includes bibliographical references and indexes.
Contents: v.3. The Renaissance.
ISBN 0-89356-315-3 (v. 3 : alk. paper)
ISBN 0-89356-273-4 (set : alk paper)
1. Biography. 2. World history. I. Magill, Frank Northen, 1907-1997. II. Moose, Christina J., 1952- . III. Aves, Alison. IV. Great lives from history.
CT104.D54 1998
920.02—dc21 97-51154
CIP

British Library Cataloguing-in-Publication Data is available.
Fitzroy Dearborn ISBN 1-57958-042-4

First Published in the U.K. and U.S., 1998
Printed by Sheridan Books, Inc.

Cover design by Peter Aristedes.

Second Printing

CONTENTS

PUBLISHER'S NOTE

The *Dictionary of World Biography, Volume III: The Renaissance* is the third installment in a projected ten-volume series covering the lives of important personages from the ancient world through the twentieth century. This new series is a revision and reordering of Salem Press's thirty-volume *Great Lives from History* series. The contents of the various *Great Lives from History* sets have been integrated and then rearranged from a geographical perspective into a chronological one, combining biographies of important people from all over the world into individual titles each covering an era. The existing essays are enhanced by the addition of new entries, updated bibliographies, a new page design, and illustrations.

The Renaissance, volume 3 of the dictionary, gathers 185 essays from the *Great Lives from History* series and adds 26 new biographies, creating a total of 211 essays. The year 1400 was selected by the editors as the cutoff between the middle ages and the Renaissance; the year 1600 divides the focus of this volume from that of the next one, which is devoted to the seventeenth and eighteenth centuries. Biographies spanning two eras were moved into the period that best encompassed the subject's life's work or major accomplishments.

The articles in this series range from two thousand to three thousand words in length and follow a standard format. Each article begins with ready-reference listings, including a brief statement summarizing the individual's contribution to his or her society and later ages. The body of the article is divided into three parts. "Early Life," the first section, provides facts about the individual's upbringing and the environment in which he or she was reared, setting the stage for the heart of the article, the section entitled "Life's Work." This section consists of a straightforward account of the period during which the individual's most significant achievements were made. The concluding section, the "Summary," is not a recapitulation of what has been discussed but rather an overview of the individual's place in history. Each essay is supplemented by an annotated, evaluative bibliography, a starting point for further research.

The temporal and geographical scope of *The Renaissance* volume is broad. Represented here are figures as distant as Donatello, a Florentine artist of the early fifteenth century, and as recent as George Chapman, an English poet and playwright of the Elizabethan and Stuart eras; the selection spans the Eastern and Western hemispheres. The editors have sought to provide coverage that is broad in area of achievement as well as geography while at the same time including the recognized shapers of history. Major world leaders appear—emperors, conquerors, kings, and khans—as well as giants of religious faith: popes, priests, mystics, saints, and theologians who left their imprints on our political as well as spiritual institutions. Also included are scholars, philosophers, scientists, explorers, and artists—all of them architects of today's civilization.

While each volume in the *Dictionary of World Biography* has its distinctive qualities, several features distinguish this series as a whole from other biographical reference works. The articles combine breadth of coverage with a format that offers the user quick access to the particular information needed. For convenience of reference, this volume is indexed by area of achievement and by geographical location as well as by name. The tenth volume of the series will provide a comprehensive index to all previous volumes, allowing users access to the biographies of all the figures covered, from the ancient world through the twentieth century.

We would like to extend our appreciation to all those involved in development and production of this series. Each essay has been written by an academician who specializes in the area of discussion; without their expert contribution, a project of this nature would not be possible. A full list of contributors and their affiliations appears in the front matter of this volume.

CONTRIBUTING ESSAYISTS

Wayne Ackerson
Salisbury State University, Maryland

Patrick Adcock
Henderson State University, Arkansas

James W. Alexander
University of Georgia

Arthur L. Alt
College of Great Falls, Montana

J. Stewart Alverson
University of Tennessee at Chattanooga

Nancy Fix Anderson
Loyola University, New Orleans

Madeline Cirillo Archer
Duquesne University, Pennsylvania

Stanley Archer
Texas A&M University

Christopher Armitage
University of North Carolina at Chapel Hill

Dorothy B. Aspinwall
University of Hawaii at Manoa

Bryan Aubrey
Independent Scholar

Theodore P. Aufdemberge
Concordia College, Minnesota

Tom L. Auffenberg
Ouachita Baptist University, Arkansas

Barbara Ann Barbato
Webster University, Missouri

Michael Bauman
Northeastern Bible College

Graydon Beeks
Pomona College, California

S. Carol Berg
College of Saint Benedict, Minnesota

Robert L. Berner
University of Wisconsin-Oshkosh

Cynthia A. Bily
Adrian College, Michigan

Harold Branam
Temple University, Pennsylvania

Jeff R. Bremer
California State University, Bakersfield

J. R. Broadus
University of North Carolina at Chapel Hill

William S. Brockington, Jr.
University of South Carolina

Alan Brown
Livingston University

Kendall W. Brown
Hillsdale College, Michigan

Jeffery L. Buller
Georgia Southern University

Byron D. Cannon
University of Utah

Joan E. Carr
Washington University

Randolf G. S. Cooper
Florida State University

Daniel A. Crews
Central Missouri State University

Carol Crowe-Carraco
Western Kentucky University

Victoria Hennessey Cummins
Austin College, Texas

J. D. Daubs
University of Illinois at Urbana-Champaign

Ronald W. Davis
Western Michigan University

Thomas Derdak
University of Chicago

Reidar Dittmann
Saint Olaf College, Minnesota

Surjit S. Dulai
Michigan State University

Burton L. Dunbar III
University of Missouri at Kansas City

Bruce L. Edwards
Bowling Green State University, Ohio

David G. Egler
Western Illinois University

Mary Sweeney Ellett
Randolph-Macon Woman's College, Virginia

Robert P. Ellis
Worcester State College, Massachusetts

Thomas L. Erskine
Salisbury State University, Maryland

Clara Estow
University of Massachusetts, Boston

Barbara M. Fahy
Albright College, Pennsylvania

James J. Farsolas
University of South Carolina
Coastal Carolina Community College

Gary B. Ferngren
Oregon State University

Edward Fiorelli
Saint John's University, New York

Ronald H. Fritze
Lamar University, Texas

C. George Fry
Saint Francis College

Michael J. Garcia
Arapahoe Community College, Colorado

John Gardner
Delaware State College

Leonardas V. Gerulaitis
Oakland University, Michigan

Paul E. Gill
Shippensburg University, Pennsylvania

K. Fred Gillum
Colby College, Maine

Joseph A. Goldenberg
Virginia State University

Karen Gould
University of Texas at Austin

Gil L. Gunderson
Monterey Institute of International Studies, California

Surendra K. Gupta
Pittsburg State University, Pennsylvania

David B. Haley
University of Minnesota

Sheldon Hanft
Appalachian State University, North Carolina

Fred R. van Hartesveldt
Fort Valley State University, Georgia

Paul B. Harvey, Jr.
Pennsylvania State University

C. James Haug
Mississippi State University

Sharon Hill
Virginia Commonwealth University

Richard L. Hillard
University of Arkansas, Pine Bluff

Ronald William Howard
Mississippi College

Edelma Huntley
Appalachian State University, North Carolina

Raymond Pierre Hylton
Virginia Union University

Loretta Turner Johnson
Mankato State University, Minnesota

Richard W. Kaeuper
University of Rochester, New York

Donald R. Kelm
Northern Kentucky University

Robert W. Kenny
George Washington University, D.C.

Jean Moore Kiger
University of Mississippi

Ann Klefstad
Sun and Moon Press

James Kline
Independent Scholar

Grove Koger
Boise Public Library, Idaho

Jane Kristof
Portland State University, Oregon

Lynn C. Kronzek
Independent Scholar

Paul E. Kuhl
Winston-Salem State University, North Carolina

Eugene Larson
Pierce College, Washington

J. David Lawrence
David Lipscomb University, Tennessee

Harry Lawton
University of California, Santa Barbara

James Livingston
Northern Michigan University

Reinhart Lutz
University of California, Santa Barbara

Garrett L. McAinsh
Hendrix College, Arkansas

C. S. McConnell
University of Calgary

James Edward McGoldrick
Cedarville College, Ohio

Caroline McManus
University of California, Los Angeles

E. Deanne Malpass
Stephen F. Austin State University, Texas

Carl Henry Marcoux
University of California, Riverside

Elaine Mathiasen
Independent Scholar

Rose Ethel Althaus Meza
Queensborough Community College, New York

Robert E. Morsberger
California State Polytechnic University, Pomona

Terence R. Murphy
American University, D.C.

John W. Myers
University of North Carolina at Wilmington

Gregory Nehler
Indiana University, Bloomington

Edwin L. Neville, Jr.
Canisius College, New York

Frank Nickell
Southeast Missouri State University

Richard L. Niswonger
John Brown University, Arkansas

Charles H. O'Brien
Western Illinois University

Lisa Paddock
Independent Scholar

William A. Paquette
Tidewater Community College, Virginia

Susan L. Piepke
Bridgewater College, Virginia

George R. Plitnik
Frostburg State University, Maryland

Marjorie J. Podolsky
Behrend College of Pennsylvania State University

Ronald L. Pollitt
University of Cincinnati, Ohio

Dorothy Turner Potter
Lynchburg College, Virginia

Charles Pullen
Queen's University, Illinois

John D. Raymer
Indiana University at South Bend
Indiana Vocational College

Ann E. Reynolds
Independent Scholar

Betty Richardson
Southern Illinois University at Edwardsville

John O. Robison
University of South Florida

Carl Rollyson
Behrend M. Baruch College
City University of New York

Victor Anthony Rudowski
Clemson University, South Carolina

Joyce E. Salisbury
University of Wisconsin—Green Bay

Victor A. Santi
University of New Orleans

Stephen P. Sayles
University of La Verne, California

Daniel C. Scavone
University of Southern Indiana

Per Schelde
York College, Pennsylvania

William C. Schrader
Tennessee Technological University

R. Baird Shuman
University of Illinois at Urbana-Champaign

Roger Smith
Independent Scholar

Ronald F. Smith
Massachusetts Maritime Academy

Robert M. Spector
Worcester State College, Massachusetts

C. Fitzhugh Spragins
Arkansas College

S. J. Stearns
City University of New York,
College of Staten Island

David R. Stevenson
Kearney State College, Nebraska

Paul Stewart
Southern Connecticut State University

Gerald H. Strauss
Bloomsburg University, Pennsylvania

Donald D. Sullivan
University of New Mexico

James Sullivan
California State University, Los Angeles

Glenn L. Swygart
Tennessee Temple University

Nicholas C. Thomas
Auburn University at Montgomery, Alabama

M. J. Tucker
State University of New York at Buffalo

William Urban
Monmouth College, Illinois

Larry W. Usilton
University of North Carolina at Wilmington

Eric Van Schaack
Colgate University, New York

Anne R. Vizzier
University of Arkansas

Eric L. Wake
Cumberland College, Kentucky

William T. Walker
Philadelphia College of Pharmacy and Science

J. Francis Watson
Grace Lutheran Church

Martha Ellen Webb
University of Nebraska at Lincoln

Ann Weikel
Portland State University, Oregon

Allen Wells
Bowdoin College, Maine

Richard Whitworth
Ball State University, Indiana

Michael Witkoski
South Carolina House of Representatives

Diane Wolfthal
Brooklyn Museum, New York

Clifton K. Yearley
State University of New York College at Buffalo

Robert Zaller
Drexel University, Pennsylvania

LIST OF ENTRANTS

GEORGIUS AGRICOLA
Georg Bauer

Born: March 24, 1494; Glauchau, Saxony
Died: November 21, 1555; Chemnitz, Saxony
Area of Achievement: Geology
Contribution: Agricola was the forerunner of the new period of scientific investigation involving study and description of natural phenomena (especially geological in nature), preparation of metals from ores, and the development of mechanical procedures. He is regarded as the father of modern mineralogy.

Early Life

Born the son of a draper and named Georg Bauer, the young man Latinized his name, in the fashion of the time, to Georgius Agricola. Little of his life before 1514 is known, at which point he entered the University of Leipzig. In 1518, he was graduated, then went to Italy to continue his studies at the Universities of Bologna and Padua. His subsequent career began as a philologist, an expert in classical languages and the works of the classical writers. He then turned to medicine, took his degree at the University of Ferrare, and adopted medicine as a profession. While in Venice, he was employed for two years in the printing and publishing house of Aldus Manutius. At the Aldine Press, Agricola collaborated with John Clement, secretary to Thomas More. During this period, he also met and became friends with Desiderius Erasmus, who encouraged him to write and later published a number of his books. Coming home, Agricola began his medical practice in 1527 in Joachimsthal, in Bohemia, as city physician until 1533. In 1534, he moved to Chemnitz, another mining town, where he stayed for the rest of his life. In 1545, he was appointed Burgermeister.

Life's Work

As with his contemporary Paracelsus, Agricola's interest in mineralogy grew out of its possible connections with medicine and the diseases of the miners he treated. For more than two centuries, this combination of physician-mineralogist was to be prominent in the development of chemistry and geology. Agricola spent much time with the miners, in the mines and smelters, thus gaining an intimate knowledge of mining, mineralogy, and allied sciences. Most of his writings dealt with the geological sciences, although he wrote on many aspects of human endeavor. The beauty of his works lies in his use of illustrations, the woodcuts clear enough to let a modern builder re-create models of the ancient machines. His works were extremely difficult to decipher, particularly as they are written in Latin, a language ill equipped with appropriate terms for the mining trades. Since his ideas were based on German sources, he had to invent an entire new Latin vocabulary. As a result, some parts of the texts were difficult to understand even by contemporary readers. Only centuries after his death did Agricola get the credit he so richly deserved.

At Chemnitz, Agricola first became court historian, then city physician. Beginning in 1546, he published six works on mining and geology, a small work on the plague, and works on medical, religious, political, and historical subjects. It was a measure of his liberalism that, as a staunch Catholic, he served two Protestant dukes and worked dil-

igently with other men of the Reformation. He served his dukes on many diplomatic and military missions, and he dedicated his major work, *De re metallica libri XII* (1556; English translation, 1912), to them.

Abandoning inductive speculation as he had learned it through his classical studies, Agricola disregarded biblical beliefs about the nature of the world, expressed his impatience with the alchemists, and concentrated on exploring the structure of the world on the basis of scientific observation. Such observation led him to the first adequate description of the part played by erosion in the shaping of mountain ranges, the origin of ores, the filling of rock interstices by circulating solutions, and the classifying of minerals on the basis of special physical characteristics, such as solubility and hardness.

Working with the miners in the two cities in which he had settled, Agricola began accumulating a massive amount of information on mining, smelting, the characteristics of ore deposits, and chemical analysis. *Bermannus sive de re metallica dialogus* (1530) was his first contribution to geology. It covered the rise of the mining industry in Germany and the early development of the great mining centers in the region of the Erzgebirge. Agricola discussed topics in mineralogy and mining, and various ores, such as silver, copper, and other metals. He showed some of the prejudices of his time, however, by dealing with the demons that supposedly haunted many of the mines. This was really an introduction to his greater work.

In 1546, he published *De ortu et causis subterraneorum*, treating the origin of ore deposits. After critically reviewing the opinions of early writers, particularly Aristotle, he rejected them, specifically the notion that metals are formed from watery vapors, and the alchemic view that all metals are composed of mercury and sulfur. He also criticized the astrological belief that the stars influence the earth's interior. Two major ideas came from this work: the origins of mountains and the origins of ore deposits. For mountains, Agricola found five means of formation: the eroding action of water, the heaping of sands by winds, subterranean winds, the actions of earthquakes, and volcanic fires. For ores, he presented the theory of lapidifying juices, solutions carrying dissolved minerals that, when cooled, left the deposits in the cracks of the rocks, thus giving rise to mineral veins. Here he predates two of the modern theories of ore deposits, the theory of ascension and the theory of lateral secretion.

Agricola's next important work, published in 1546, was *De natura fossilium* (English translation, 1955), in which he introduced a new basis for the classification of minerals (called "fossils" at that time). Agricola reviewed and rejected the systems of Aristotle, Avicenna, and others. His system was based on physical properties such as color, weight, transparency, taste, odor, texture, solubility, and combustibility. He carefully defined and explained the terms he developed. He also discussed the medicinal properties of the minerals.

Agricola's problem was understanding what he called "mista," composed of two or more fossils so intermingled as to be inseparable except by fire. His problem was a result of the alchemy of the time, the lack of a microscope, and the lack of real chemical analysis. Even without that knowledge, however, Agricola managed to remove the tales of supernatural forces in minerals and the theories of thunderstones and rocks with crystal power.

Agricola wrote three other works before his great opus: *De natura eorum quae effluent ex Terra* (1546), on subsurface waters and gases; *De veteribus et novis metallis* (1546), dealing with creatures that lived underground; and *De animantibus subterraneis* (1549), sketching the history and geographical distribution of the various metals as far as they had been known to the ancients.

De re metallica, his greatest work, concentrated on mining and metallurgy and contained an abundance of information on the conditions of the time, such as mine management, machinery used, and processes employed. The book is still in print, having the unique distinction of being translated and edited (1912) by President Herbert Hoover and his wife, Lou Henry Hoover. Indeed, it was the leading textbook for miners and metallurgists for two centuries. At a time when it was customary to hold industrial processes secret, Agricola published every practice and improvement he could find.

In *De re metallica*, Agricola's interests are all-consuming. Tracing the history of mineralogy and mining, Agricola addressed the earliest Greek and Roman sources, using them as a springboard for a major study in the locating of mines and a classification of the types of liquids emanating from them. In part of his opus, Agricola covered the specific working of metallic veins and ores in mines. Original contributions by him include the idea that rocks containing ores are older than the ores themselves and that the ores are deposited from solutions passing through fissures in the rocks—revolutionary ideas. He also suggested the procedure of using a magnetic compass for exploring and charting underground tunnels and provided the first real assessment of the wealth available for the three richest mines of the area. The work also includes hundreds of informative drawings showing the mechanical aspects of mining.

Agricola benefited greatly from the period of tolerance during which he worked. The religious wars of the period eroded this tolerance. Well regarded by his contemporaries, Agricola died in Chemnitz on November 21, 1555.

Summary

Georgius Agricola has been considered one of the most outstanding figures in the history of geological sciences. Johann Wolfgang von Goethe compared him to Roger Bacon. Alfred Werner called him the "father of mineralogy," and Karl von Vogelsang addressed him as the "forefather of geology." His works became the most comprehensive source on mining and metallurgy, acknowledged as the true beginning of geological sciences. Equally important, however, was that, in publishing that which tradition had retained as family and guild secrets, such as the process of smelting, he brought alert and innovative minds into the field of geology. Among those contemporaries were Conrad Gesner, who classified minerals on the basis of the form of the stone, gem, or fossil, avoiding all references to magic and miraculous properties of minerals, and Lazarus Ercker, who amplified Agricola's descriptions for separating precious metals through smelting. The instructions and descriptions that Agricola, Gesner, and Ercker prepared were so accurate that they would be used as handbooks for the next two centuries.

Agricola's works also helped establish, at Freiberg, a central source of mining and metallurgy knowledge, leading to a formalized, definite curriculum emphasizing observation and information-sharing. Agricola's work and his determination to use observation as the basis of science led to the use of scientific theories based on observation and experimentation.

Bibliography

Adams, Frank Dawson. *The Birth and Development of the Geological Sciences.* London: Bailliere, and Baltimore: William and Wilkins, 1938. Traces the history of ideas and people contributing to the science of geology. Topics covered include the origins of metals, mountains, rivers, and oceans, and the nature of earthquakes.

Beretta, Marco. *The Enlightenment of Matter: The Definition of Chemistry from Agricola to Lavoisier.* Canton, Mass.: Science History Publications, 1993. Commended as a major contribution to the literature on this subject. The book covers many features of chemistry before 1800 and takes a scientific, rather than a sociological or political, approach. The author makes insightful use of both scholarly literature and original sources.

Dibner, Bern. *Agricola on Metals.* Norwalk, Conn.: Burndy Library, 1958. Concise treatment of Agricola's life, with special emphasis on his major work *De re metallica.* Contains a book-by-book explanation of topics of interest. Excellent reproductions of original woodcuts.

Faul, Henry. *It Began with a Stone.* New York: Wiley, 1983. A comprehensive work on the history of geology. Emphasizes people and their ideas, particularly as to how they arrived at their discoveries. Providing some of the original writings, the author shows how people such as Agricola thought.

Fenton, Carroll Lane, and Mildred Adams Fenton. *Giants of Geology.* New York: Doubleday, 1952. Details the thinking of the pioneers of geology, concentrating on the men who nurtured geological knowledge in exploring new areas of the world. Shows how ideas have altered over time, based on explorations and exquisite observations used to overthrow prejudices. Excellent references.

Geikie, Archibald. *The Founders of Geology.* London and New York: Macmillan, 1897. Tracing the slow growth of geology from ancient to modern cultures, the book deals with the controversies surrounding such geological ideas as volcanism, fossils, earth's origin, and geological succession.

Kranzberg, Melvin, and Carroll W. Pursell, Jr., eds. *Technology in Western Civilization.* Vol. 1, *The Emergence of Modern Industrial Society.* New York: Oxford University Press, 1967. This work portrays technology as one of the major determinants in the overall development of Western civilization. Attempting to integrate technological development with other aspects of society affected by it, the book deals nicely with the people and machines giving rise to modern society.

Singer, Charles, E. J. Holmyard, A. R. Hell, and Trevor Williams, eds. *A History of Technology.*

Vol. 3, *From the Renaissance to the Industrial Revolution, c. 1500-c. 1750*. Oxford: Clarendon Press, and New York: Oxford University Press, 1957. A superb overview of the development and emergence of modern science during the Renaissance and later periods. Chronicles the development of technology and the people involved.

Arthur L. Alt

AKBAR

Born: October 15, 1542; Umarkot, Sind
Died: October 17, 1605; Āgra, India
Area of Achievement: Monarchy
Contribution: As one of India's greatest Mughal emperors, Akbar conquered and unified northern India under his rule. In addition to military conquest, his most significant achievements include the development of an efficient bureaucratic structure, patronage of the arts, and enlightened policies of religious toleration.

Early Life

Abū-ul-Fath Jahāl-ud-Dīn Muhammad Akbar was born in the Kingdom of Sind, in what would become modern Pakistan. Of mixed Turkish, Persian, and Mongol ancestry, Akbar was a descendant of both Tamerlane and Genghis Khan. His grandfather, Bābur "the Tiger," a Muslim chieftain of a small state in Turkestan, invaded India in 1526 and within four years conquered Hindustan in northern India and Afghanistan. The Mughal (from the Persian word for Mongol) Dynasty, founded by Bābur, ruled northern India until the British took over in the eighteenth and nineteenth centuries.

Bābur was succeeded in 1530 by his weak son Humayun, who was unable to prevent the conquest of the empire by the Afghan chieftain Sher Khan Sur. Driven from his throne at Delhi, Humayun fled to Persia to seek support. During this flight, his Persian wife, Hamida, in 1542 gave birth to Akbar while in the Kingdom of Sind. In 1555, with the aid of Persian troops, Humayun reconquered the area around Delhi and reclaimed his throne. He died the next year, in January, 1556, as a result of an accident caused by the effects of opium.

Akbar was thirteen when he succeeded his father as the third Mughal emperor of India. He had been reared in the rough wilds of Afghanistan, where he developed a love of hunting and riding. Throughout his life, he sought reckless, dangerous activities, such as riding wild elephants and spearing tigers. Such risk-taking was probably the result of his recurrent bouts of depression, which caused him to take extreme chances in order, he said, to see whether he should die. A kindly person, he was also high-strung and had a violent temper.

Of only moderate height, Akbar was muscular and broad-shouldered. He had narrow eyes (reflecting his Mongolian ancestry), a dark complexion, a thin mustache, and long hair. Although his head drooped slightly toward the right and he suffered from epilepsy, he had an impressive commanding presence. He had a keen intelligence but never learned to read or write, even though he had been provided with a tutor from age five. He had, however, a deep love and knowledge of literature, which he learned through oral readings. He also enjoyed inventions and was skilled in mechanical arts.

When he became emperor, Akbar, despite his youth, was already serving as governor of the Punjab and had military experience. His claim to the throne, however, was immediately challenged by ambitious rivals, the most threatening of whom was a Hindu named Hemu. Akbar's rule was secured when his father's loyal and capable general Bayram Khan, on November 5, 1556, defeated Hemu's large army at Panipat, north of Delhi. Bayram Khan then ruled as the young emperor's regent for five years, until Akbar's ambitious nurse Maham Anaga had the regent deposed so that she could run the empire herself. In 1562, at age twenty, Akbar took personal control of his empire.

Life's Work

At the beginning of Akbar's rule, only a portion of the territory originally conquered by Bābur was under Mughal control. His reign characterized by successful military conquests, Akbar regained that territory and much more. With a large, efficient standing army that he himself often led, he extended Mughal authority over Afghanistan and all of India except the Deccan, in the south. The greatest resistance to his rule came from the fiercely independent Hindu Rajputs, who controlled the area west of Delhi known as Rajastan. The Rajputs were eventually subdued through both conciliatory and ruthless policies. In 1562, Akbar married the daughter of Raja Bihari Mal of Amber, one of the leading Rajput rulers. Although Akbar had a large harem, this Hindu princess was his favorite wife and mother of his heir Salim (later known as Jahangir). As a result of the marriage alliance, many Rajputs came to serve in the Mughal administration and army. The princes could continue to rule, but they had to acknowledge Akbar's suzerainty and supply him with money and soldiers. To facilitate Indian acceptance of Mughal rule, Akbar abolished the enslavement of prisoners of war and no longer forced those he conquered to convert to Islam. If rulers nevertheless resisted, they were mercilessly crushed. When the Rajput ruler of Mewar refused to follow his orders, Akbar, in 1568, captured the fortress of Chitor and ordered the massacre of thirty thousand prisoners.

Despite some episodes of draconian cruelty, Akbar's reign was generally marked by enlightened reforms promoting social peace. Most notably, he instituted a policy of religious toleration. In addition to his own sense of fairness and interest in unrestricted religious dialogue, Akbar believed that the conquering Mughals, who were Muslim, had to have the support of the native Hindu populace. Akbar therefore removed many of the penalties that had burdened Indian Hindus. In 1563, he abolished a tax, which dated back well before Bābur's invasion, on Hindu pilgrims who traveled to holy places. In 1564, he abolished the *jizya*, a tax on non-Muslims. He ended the destruction of Hindu temples and allowed new ones to be built. He encouraged Muslim acceptance of Hindu traditions, although he did try to eliminate the Hindu practices of child marriage and widow burning (suttee). Schools were founded under government sponsorship for Hindus as well as Muslims. Hindus served and advanced equally with the Muslims in the government and the army.

Akbar's economic policies were also fair and effective. Taxation was based on landed property, and one-third of the value of the harvest went to the royal treasury. (This was a lower taxation than before or after Akbar.) In times of poor harvest, taxation was reduced or suspended. Efficient tax collection, coupled with a sound currency and flourishing trade, created great prosperity. Most of the hundred million people under Akbar's rule were still very poor, but historians have suggested that peasants were probably better off then than in more modern times.

Akbar maintained centralized control over his empire by instituting an effective bureaucratic hierarchy based on standardized ranks and salaries. The higher administration was divided into thirty-three ranks, classified according to the number of cavalry the officeholder was expected to raise for the emperor. There was no distinction between civil and military ranks, and all were theoretically appointed by and responsible to the emperor. The empire was territorially divided into twelve provinces and further subdivided into systematic administrative units. The civil code was based on Muslim law, but local disputes that took place between Hindus could be decided according to Hindu law.

The prosperity of the empire allowed Akbar to amass a huge fortune, making him the richest king in the world. He had an elaborate court, which for many years he held at a magnificent new palace-city, Fatehpur Sikri (city of victory). Despite the grandeur of his public life, in which he assumed an almost godlike persona, Akbar in his personal life had simple, even austere habits. He maintained a very moderate diet, with usually only one main meal a day. Near the end of his life, under Jain influence, he almost entirely gave up eating meat. He did, however, drink liquor excessively and, like his father, was a regular user of opium. He slept very little, no more than about three hours a night.

During Akbar's reign, Mughal culture flowered, characterized by a distinctive, elegant blend of Persian and Hindu styles, with some European influence. Akbar employed more than one hundred painters at court who exhibited their work regularly to him. He himself was a gifted artist. He was also a musician, performing on a kind of kettle drum, and was skilled in Hindu singing. Although illiterate, he collected a large library and encouraged literary production. He created the post of poet laureate for Hindi, the northern Indian vernacular that became India's national language, and had Sanskrit works translated into Persian for his courtiers.

Akbar's primary interest was religion. He built at Fatehpur Sikri a house of worship in which to discuss theological questions. At first limited to Muslims, the debates were soon opened to Hindus and other faiths. He invited Jesuits from the Portuguese colony at Goa to come to his court, and he listened so intently to them that they thought he was about to convert to Christianity. He did reject Orthodox Islam, but, instead of becoming a Christian, he sponsored his own religion, known as the Divine Faith, a mystical blend of Hinduism and Islam. Akbar claimed that he was God's vice-regent, with authority to rule over spiritual as well as temporal matters. This new religion had little influence and disappeared after his death.

Akbar's last years were marred by his son Salim's attempts to usurp his throne. Salim may have caused his father's death in 1605 by poisoning him. When he succeeded Akbar, Salim took the Persian name Jahangir, meaning "world seizer." Akbar is buried in a mausoleum at Sicandra, near Āgra.

Summary

Known as "the Great Mughal," Akbar created an imperial government that lasted until the nineteenth century. His administrative system, efficient and open to the promotion of talent, was adopted by the British when they later conquered India. Although there were enormous disparities of income between the Mughal elite and the impoverished peasants, his reign was characterized by a level of general prosperity unmatched in later years. The contemporary of Elizabeth I of England and Philip II of Spain, Akbar surpassed both of them in wealth, power, and majesty. He enjoyed a semidivine status but nevertheless had a personal concern for the well-being of his subjects. He was humble enough to disguise himself sometimes in order to mix with his subjects and listen to their views.

Akbar succeeded in establishing internal peace within his empire, because he combined a realistic assessment of the limits of power with a humanistic concern and just administration. His system of taxation, for example, which brought great wealth into his treasury, was flexible enough to encourage rather than crush those suffering economic hardship. The glory of Akbar's reign included a cultural blending that produced the beautiful, distinctive Mughal style. This creativity was stimulated by the toleration for cultural and religious differences, a toleration which was perhaps Akbar's greatest achievement. With India later to be so torn apart by conflict between Hindu and Muslim, Akbar's policy of religious toleration and mixing makes him a model of enlightened rule.

Bibliography

Binyon, Laurence. *Akbar.* London: Davies, and New York: Appleton, 1932. A brief, readable biography of Akbar with emphasis on his personality rather than on his rule.

Burn, Richard, ed. *The Cambridge History of India.* Vol. 4, *The Mughal Period.* Cambridge: Cambridge University Press, and New York: Macmillan, 1937. This history of the Mughal Empire from the conquest of Bābur to the eighteenth century includes a detailed account of Akbar's rule, with emphasis on his military conquests and religious thought.

Du Jarric, Pierre. *Akbar and the Jesuits: An Account of the Jesuit Missions to the Court of Akbar.* Translated with an introduction and notes by C. H. Payne. London: Routledge, and New York: Harper, 1926. A translation and reprint of an early seventeenth century French account of Akbar and his rule, based on reports and letters by Jesuits in Akbar's court.

Malleson, G. B. *Akbar.* Oxford: Clarendon Press, 1891. An outdated, overly laudatory, but engaging short biography.

Moreland, W. H. *India at the Death of Akbar: An Economic Study.* London: Macmillan, 1920. A very critical account of Indian economy and administration under Akbar. Written to justify British rule in India. Contains very little information on Akbar himself.

Rudolph, Susanne Hoeber, and Lloyd I. Rudolph. "Modern Hate." *New Republic* 208 (March, 1993): 24. This article discusses the failure of once harmonious groups such as the Muslims and Hindus under Akbar, and the Serbs, Croats, and Muslims under Tito in Yugoslavia. Among other things, the authors explore different forms of nationalism and the media's effects on public perceptions of Hindus and Muslims.

Smith, Vincent A. *Akbar, the Great Mogul, 1542-1605.* Oxford: Clarendon Press, 1917. Still the most complete biography of Akbar. A balanced account that assesses the strengths and weaknesses of Akbar's personality and rule. Contains a lengthy annotated bibliography.

Wellesz, Emmy. *Akbar's Religious Thought, Reflected in Mogul Painting.* London: Allen and Unwin, 1952. A lucid account of how Akbar's eclectic religious interests and policy of religious toleration influenced the creation of Mughal painting. Includes forty black-and-white art plates.

Wolpert, Stanley. *A New History of India.* 5th ed. New York: Oxford University Press, 1997. The chapter on Akbar in this general history, written by one of the leading historians of India, provides an accessible introduction.

Nancy Fix Anderson

LEON BATTISTA ALBERTI

Born: February 18, 1404; Genoa
Died: April, 1472; Rome
Areas of Achievement: Architecture and philosophy
Contribution: Alberti is identified by Renaissance historians as an archetype of the universal man. He established a leading reputation as a theorist and practitioner of the visual arts, notably in the field of architecture. As a Humanist, he was the author of numerous moral dialogues.

Early Life

The prominent Albertis were known as textile merchants and bankers. In Florence they were associated with the Popular Party. Their decline began with the exile of Leon Battista Alberti's grandfather Benedetto, who left Florence with his son Lorenzo in 1387. Leon Battista was born in Genoa, the second natural son of Lorenzo and Bianca Fieschi, widow of a prominent Genoese family. On her death from the plague in 1406, Lorenzo moved to Venice, where he joined another brother, Ricciardo, in trade, shortly thereafter marrying a Florentine woman in 1408.

Leon Battista and his brother Carlo received the best Humanist education available. At Gasparino, Barzizza's academy in Padua, he studied with many who were to become major scholars in the world of Renaissance learning, such as Panormita and Francesco Filelfo. In 1421, Alberti went to Bologna, where he deepened his knowledge of Greek and Latin literature and began his studies of mathematics. Following the death of his father (1421) and his uncle Ricciardo a year later, the brothers were deprived of their legitimate inheritance by the machinations of their cousins, Ricciardo's sons. A combination of grief and academic pressure led to a serious deterioration of Leon Battista's health, in particular his eyesight. During his recuperation, he turned from the study of ancient texts to that of mathematics, an interest that profoundly affected his future researches. Alberti's friendship in Bologna with Tommaso Parentucelli da Sarzana—the future Pope Nicholas V—led to an appointment as secretary to a cardinal of Bologna. In 1428, the Florentine ban on the Albertis was lifted. It is most likely that Leon Battista made a brief visit to the city of his father that year, or early in 1429. These years coincide with the climax of the struggle between the Albizzi faction and the Popular Party, resulting in the eventual consolidation in Florence of Medici power under Cosimo de' Medici: Historically the Albertis had been closely allied to the Medicis.

Life's Work

As a papal secretary in the service of Eugenius IV, Alberti followed the pope to Florence, where he had been invited on the expulsion of the Papacy from Rome. Here he came into contact with all the major personalities responsible for the explosion of the new art and architecture of the Renaissance. In Florence, he established strong ties of friendship with the sculptor Donatello, the architects Filippo Brunelleschi, who had completed the dome of the cathedral, Michelozzo, who was to design the Palazzo Medici, and Lorenzo Ghiberti, who was working on the doors of the baptistery. The first fruits of this experience are the *De pictura* (1435; *Of Painting*, 1726) and *De statua* (possibly pre-1435; *Of Sculpture*, 1726), in both of which Alberti displays the fundamental principles of Renaissance art, in particular the relationship between mathematics and composition, the consequent rules of perspective, and the use of nature as a model. Alberti wrote both Latin and Italian versions of these treatises.

While the majority of his moral dialogues are in Latin, Alberti also turned to the vernacular in a conscious attempt to reach a wider audience and to restore to Tuscan the literary prestige it had enjoyed in the previous century as the result of the works of Dante, Petrarch, and Giovanni Boccaccio. *Theogenius* (c. 1440) and *Della tranquillità dell' anima* (c. 1442; of peace of mind) mark moments of deep reflection in Alberti's career: an internal debate on the relative merits of the active and contemplative life. The high point of these years came earlier, with the completion of the first three books of Alberti's most popular work, *Della famiglia* (1434; *The Family in Renaissance Florence*, 1969). In dialogue form, he details the moral basis of the family and its role in civic life, offering to the coming generation, in spite of the reverses he himself suffered at the hands of certain relatives, the example of the contributions made by their ancestors to the commercial expansion and intellectual vigor of Renaissance Florence.

Alberti's career as an architect was launched in Ferrara in 1442, when he was asked to judge the designs for an equestrian statue in honor of Nicolò d'Este. Alberti designed the minitriumphal arch for the statue's base. With the elevation of Parentucelli to the Papacy as Nicholas V, Alberti was named the pope's principal architectural adviser: the man he depended on more than any other in an ambitious program of restoration, street widening, and building projects designed to return to Rome the dignity it deserved as the seat of the Catholic church. The years that followed were to be the most productive of his career, and the achievements recorded between 1450 and 1470 were to give him his greatest satisfaction and ensure Alberti enduring fame. The buildings completed and designed were all the fruit of an experience that had ripened in the light of extensive theoretical meditation. Alberti's principles of architecture are detailed in the ten volumes of *De re aedificatoria* (1452; *The Architecture*, 1726), dedicated to his patron Nicholas V. In it Alberti acknowledges the contribution of the Roman theorist Vetruvius. His intention was to take the principles of harmony and proportion and apply them to the aesthetic and practical requirements of his own age.

Passing from theory to practice, he accepted a commission from Sigismondo Malatesta (1450) to transform the Gothic Church of San Francesco into the Tempio Malatestano, with its bold classical façade; divided into three triumphal arches. Also around 1450, he was called by the merchant Giovanni Rucellai to redesign the façade of his family's palazzo in Florence which, with its elegant pillars and flat beveled masonry, makes the building rather more inviting than the more fortresslike structures such as the Palazzo Medici-Ricciardi. During the reign of Pius II, one of the foremost Renaissance Humanists, Alberti accepted the invitation of Ludovico Gonzaga of Mantua to build the Church of San Sebastiano in that city. The same princely patron gave Alberti his final commission: to design the Church of Sant' Andrea in Mantua. The latter was only completed in the eighteenth century, following modified Albertian concepts. He did live to see the completion of a major project: the façade of Santa Maria Novella in Florence, again commissioned by his patron Rucellai. Here the addition of classical forms harmonizes with existing Gothic elements of the basilica, and the use of the characteristic black-and-white marble blends Santa Maria Novella with other major Florentine churches, including Santa Maria del Fiore. Alberti, who served popes and princes, also remained in touch with his allies the Medicis; in the tradition of the scholar advising civic leaders, he dedicated a small treatise on rhetoric (*Trivia senatoria*, c. 1460) to Lorenzo

de'Medici, who was still in his teens. Alberti died in Rome in April, 1472.

Summary

Leon Battista Alberti's writings in Italian, both on art and on social behavior, explore all the major themes of Renaissance Humanism. Scholars and editors of his works have asserted that he shaped and defined this movement in the history of ideas and that the Renaissance would not have made the intellectual advances it did without his contributions and prodding. In the introduction to *The Family in Renaissance Florence*, he expounds on the themes of virtue and fortune that so exercised the speculative curiosity of fifteenth century thinkers. In the decline of glory of his own family, he sees a parallel with the rise and fall of states. Against the thesis of inevitability and the stoic acceptance of a fate governing human affairs, Alberti juxtaposes the Renaissance idea of free will that allows men to shape an independent life for themselves in defiance of even the direst circumstances. This is what he means by virtue, which must never allow fortune to serve as an alibi for failure or incompetence. Virtue is also dedicated hard work and the determination to cultivate all the seeds of natural talents and curiosity with which one is endowed. The proclamation of these ideals makes Alberti a principal spokesman of the spirit of the active life that animates the mercantile ethic of civic Humanism in the first half of Quattrocento Florence. Man was born, he says, to be useful to other men.

While the impact of Alberti the moralist needs emphasizing, his dominant role as art theorist and architectural mentor is his most enduring achievement. Architecture in fact could be taken as a metaphor for the highest ideals of Renaissance culture, for it involves the most detailed knowledge of an infinite variety of activities, skills, and materials that must ultimately be synthesized into a harmonious whole. Granted his major achievements in so many fields, it is amazing to observe that Alberti's final significance was nearly overlooked. His original insights into art theory had been so integrated into practice and elaborated on by Leonardo da Vinci and others that the originator of the ideas had been largely forgotten.

Bibliography

Alberti, Leon Battista. *The Family in Renaissance Florence*. Translated by Renee Neu Watkins. Columbia: University of South Carolina Press, 1969. This modern translation includes a good introduction and bibliography of writings on civic Humanism in English.

Gadol, Joan. *Leon Battista Alberti: Universal Man of the Early Renaissance*. Chicago: University of Chicago Press, 1969. A very useful study detailing Alberti's contributions to the theory and practice of art and the development of architecture in the fifteenth century. Although mostly directed to his work in the visual arts (with reference to optics and perspective), the book places its subject firmly in the context of Humanism. The first chapter is biographical and includes a critical survey of views on Alberti's ultimate significance.

Garin, Eugenio. *Italian Humanism: Philosophy and Civic Life in the Renaissance*. Translated by Peter Munz. Oxford: Blackwell, and New York: Harper, 1965. This extremely lucid intellectual history of Renaissance Humanism includes some indispensable pages on Alberti in chapter 2 on the subject of civic life. Garin presents him as a major representative of the spirit of *negotium* (the active life) and thus a key figure in the intellectual life of the first half of the Quattrocento.

Grayson, Cecil. "The Humanism of Alberti." *Italian Studies* 12 (1957): 37-56. An essential synopsis of Alberti's thought and moral imperatives by the writer's most distinguished commentator and the major editor of his works. Grayson succinctly relates Alberti's thought to his family's commercial activity and the intellectual atmosphere of fifteenth century Florence.

Jarzombek, Mark. *On Leon Battista Alberti: His Literary and Aesthetic Theories*. Cambridge, Mass.: MIT Press, 1989. Jarzombek's thorough understanding of Alberti's writings on philosophy, ethics, aesthetics, architecture, and literature expand the bank of knowledge on this remarkable man. Jarzombek explores Alberti's views of the relationship between the writer and society, placing Alberti more accurately within the context of his times and clarifying the relationship among his works.

Lefaivre, Liane. *Leon Battista Alberti's* Hypnerotomachia Poliphili: *Re-Cognizing the Architecturial Body in the Early Italian Renaissance*. Cambridge, Mass.: MIT Press, 1997. The *Hypnerotomachia Poliphili* has long been considered the most legendary and enigmatic architectural book ever written and has received relatively little analysis. Lefaivre offers the closest critical-theoretical reading to date by using part fictional narrative and part scholarly treatise.

Mancini, Girolamo. *Vita di Leon Battista Alberti*. Florence: Sansoni, 1882. The definitive life in Italian by the nineteenth century's most distinguished Albertian scholar and editor of his Italian and Latin works. Mancini has added his authoritative voice to questions about Alberti's life.

Harry Lawton

AFONSO DE ALBUQUERQUE

Born: 1453; Alhandra, near Lisbon, Portugal
Died: December 15, 1515; at sea, near Goa Harbor
Areas of Achievement: Government and the military
Contribution: Albuquerque, called "the Great" and "the Portuguese Mars," conquered Goa in India (1510) and Malacca on the Malay Peninsula (1511), ended the Arabian trade monopoly in Asia, made Goa a center of the Portuguese colonial government and commerce in that area, and developed colonial administration using native officials. He served as the second Portuguese governor of India. His most lasting contribution was the foundation of the Portuguese colonial empire in the East.

Early Life

Afonso de Albuquerque was born the second son of Gonzalvo de Albuquerque, Lord of Villaverde. Through his father, he was related to the royal house of Portugal (through illegitimate descent), the males in the family having for several generations been confidential secretaries to Portuguese kings. On the maternal side, his grandfather had served as an admiral of Portugal. With these connections, it is not unexpected that Afonso's early education was at the court of King Afonso V. He served in the army of Portugal in North Africa, gaining military experience crusading against the Muslims. He fought in the conquest of Arzila and Tangier (1471), participated in the invasion of Spain (1476), and served in the expedition led by King Afonso against the Turks and in the Battle of Otranto (1480-1481).

On the death of King Afonso, Albuquerque returned to Lisbon and the court, where he was appointed chief equerry (master of the horse) under John II. He served again in military expeditions against the Muslims in North Africa (at the defense of Graciosa) and under King Manuel I in Morocco. During this period of Portuguese history, the court was continually concerned at home with the struggle of the king for dominance over the nobles. Albuquerque was little engaged in these affairs but did seemingly establish jealousy and make enemies among the nobles at court. He later fell victim to intrigues at court against him.

Life's Work

While his education had been at the Portuguese court and his military service for the most part crusading against the Muslims in Northern Africa and Europe, Albuquerque's fame was made in the East during the reign of Manuel. Here, again, he was engaged in battles against the Muslims, this time for trade dominance and empire. In a relatively short period of time (1503-1515), he secured Portuguese hegemony of the Deccan in India, Portuguese control of the spice trade through conquest and fortification of the Malay Peninsula and Sunda Isles, and the dominance of the waters through the Malaccan Strait. He governed the east-ern empire of Portugal (though he never received the title of viceroy).

After the history-making voyage of Vasco da Gama, in which he rounded the Cape of Good Hope to India (1499), the way was opened to the Portuguese to challenge the monopoly held by the Venetians and Muslims of the spice-trade routes between Europe and the East. Albuquerque, with his kinsman, Francisco de Albuquerque, sailed under Pedro Álvars Cabral (1503) to open relations and trade with the rulers of the East (India). During this first of his voyages to Asia, Albuquerque as-

sisted in establishing the Hindu ruler of Cochin in a bid for power against the native ruler, who was friendly to the Arabs, at Calicut. In return, the Portuguese were able to build a fortress at Cochin and establish a trading post at Quilon; thus began the Portuguese empire in the East.

Albuquerque returned in July, 1504, to Lisbon, where Manuel received him with honor. For a time, Albuquerque assisted in the formulation of policy at court. When Tristão da Cunha sailed from Portugal in April, 1506, with a fleet of sixteen ships, Albuquerque sailed with him as an officer in command of five of the ships. The object of the voyage was to explore the east coast of Africa and to build a fortress at the mouth of the Red Sea to block Arab trade with India. Admiral da Cunha's fleet successfully attacked several Arab cities on the African east coast, explored the coasts of Madagascar and Mozambique, and built a fortress on Socotra Island, effectively blocking the mouth of the Red Sea. On September 27, 1507, Albuquerque led his squadron in a successful siege of the island of Hormuz, which commands the Strait of Hormuz between the Persian Gulf and Gulf of Oman. Hormuz was one of the trade centers of the Arab monopoly. His ships' captains desired more to ply their trade on the seas than to be engaged in fortifying Hormuz, and Albuquerque temporarily was forced to abandon the project.

In 1505, Dom Francisco de Almeida was appointed the first governor in India with the rank of viceroy. In 1508, Manuel appointed Albuquerque to succeed Almeida at the end of his term. This commission did not, however, include the rank of viceroy though the distinction seemed never to have been made in the colonies or by Albuquerque.

Albuquerque proceeded to the Malabar Coast and arrived in December, 1508, at Cannanore, India, where Almeida refused to honor the commission and jailed Albuquerque. In previous skirmishes which Almeida had had with Arab forces from Egypt, his son had been killed and Almeida determined to remain in command in India until he had avenged his son's death. Almeida defeated the Muslims near Diu in February, 1509, and the Portuguese fleet arrived in November, 1509, confirming Albuquerque's commission. Albuquerque was then released from jail and subsequently assumed his position as governor. Almeida returned to Lisbon.

Albuquerque set out to control all the major sea trade routes to the East and to establish permanent colonial posts with fortresses and settled populations. He destroyed Calicut, which had continued hostilities, in January, 1510. He moved next to secure a permanent center for commerce and government on the Indian coast. Rather than moving to displace the Hindu rulers to the south, he attacked and captured Goa from the Muslims in March, 1510, with a fleet of twenty-three ships but was driven back by the Muslim army two months later; he regained the city permanently for the Portuguese in November. He executed the Muslim defenders of the city. This hard-won victory also established Portuguese acceptance by the Hindu rulers on the eastern coast of India.

Albuquerque was able then for a short time to turn his attention to administration. Using the government of Lisbon as a model, he established a senate for Goa, the first such senate in Asia, and gave financial and judicial responsibilities to native officials. He encouraged the intermarriage of his men with the population of Goa. He also developed a network of supply from interior villages for the coastal city.

In 1511, Albuquerque resumed his expeditions to break the trade monopoly of the Muslims to the Spice Islands (Moluccas). He established the Portuguese in Ceylon and the Sunda Isles. He attacked and sacked Malacca in July, 1511. He built a Portuguese fortress there, established control of the straits between the Malay Peninsula and the Island of Sumatra, and by these means guaranteed for Portugal the domination of the maritime route to the Spice Islands. While in Malacca, he established a colonial government with native officials (as in Goa) and developed trade relations with Pegu, Cochin (in what is now South Vietnam), China, Siam (modern Thailand), and Java.

Once more, in February, 1515, Albuquerque undertook a military expedition, this time with twenty-six ships, to the Red Sea. This early commission, from his first coming to the East, to establish Portuguese trade over the Persian Gulf region was yet unaccomplished. He laid seige to Aden (1513) unsuccessfully, led what is probably the first modern European voyage in the Red Sea, and retook Hormuz (1515). The retaking of Hormuz effectively established Portuguese dominance over the Persian Gulf trade. In September, 1515, Albuquerque became ill and set sail for Goa.

Whether his enemies at court succeeded in their jealous intrigues against him or whether Manuel was concerned about the state of Albuquerque's health, a successor to Albuquerque was appointed to govern the Portuguese holdings in the East. Albuquerque met the vessel from Europe carrying news of the appointment and learned, as he approached the harbor of Goa, that the post had been given to his enemy, Lope Soares. Manuel had recommended that Soares pay special deference to Albuquerque; weakened by illness and embittered by what he considered betrayal, Albuquerque died on December 15, 1515, while still at sea. Before his death, he wrote to the king giving an account of his service in the East and claiming for his natural son, Brás (later called Afonso the Younger), the reward and honor that he claimed as his own.

Albuquerque was buried in Goa in the Church of Our Lady, which he had built. For many years, Muslims and Hindus visited his grave to solicit his intercession against the injustices of their later rulers. A superstition held that the Portuguese dominion would be safe as long as Albuquerque's bones lay in Goa. These were, however, moved to Portugal in 1566. His natural son (Albuquerque was never married) was later honored by Manuel as befitted the accomplishments of his father.

Summary

Afonso de Albuquerque was one of those men distinguished in leadership, military achievements, and administration of which southern Europe seemed to have a bounteous supply at the end of the fifteenth century and through the mid-sixteenth. Facing long lines of supply and communication around the Cape of Good Hope, facing enemies by sea and by land, his enemies often as accomplished as the Europeans of the time in military organization and technology, Albuquerque was able to establish the basis for a Portuguese empire in the East. He was able to organize in the area colonial administration and trade practices that endured to times past Portuguese domination. He did not amass vast fortunes (that which he did have he lost through shipwreck early in his adventures in the East). He did not obtain enormous landholdings or accrue glorious titles. A loyal son of Portugal, his ambition was tied to its glory, wealth, and position; in Portugal's name, he gained control of all the main sea trade routes of the East and built permanent fortresses which, with their settled populations, were the foundation of Portuguese hegemony in the East.

Bibliography

Albuquerque, Afonso de. *Albuquerque: Caesar of the East*. Edited and translated by John Villiers and T. F. Earle. Warminster: Aris and Phillips, 1990. Selected text by Afonso de Albuquerque and his son.

———. *The Commentaries of the Great Alfonso Dalboquerque, Second Viceroy of India*. Edited and translated by Walter de Gray Birch. 4 vols. London: Hakluyt Society, 1875-1884; New York: Franklin, 1963. This resource includes Albuquerque's reports and letters compiled originally by his son Brás. It was first published by the Lisbon Academy of Sciences in 1576.

Armstrong, Richard. *A History of Seafaring*. Vol. 2, *Discoverers*. London: Benn, and New York: Praeger, 1969. The work is general in scope, designed for the general reader, and well illustrated with diagrams, maps, and reproductions. The short and vivid sketch of Albuquerque presents the major accomplishments of his career within the context of the history of discovery. Includes a good index and bibliography.

Boxer, C. R. *The Portuguese Seaborne Empire, 1415-1825*. London: Hutchinson, and New York: Knopf, 1969. A social history by one of Great Britain's leading Portuguese scholars. These tales of Portuguese sailing and trading and the transplantation of their social institutions to India are easy to read. Basing his research on original sources, Boxer contradicts the Portuguese myth of "no color bar" as the secret of successful governing of an empire vaster than its base. Good maps are included.

Neilson, J. B. *Great Men of the East*. 2d. ed. London: Longman, 1958. Neilson gives a glowing portrait of Albuquerque and his achievements.

Sanceau, Elaine. *Indies Adventure*. London: Blackie, 1936; Hamden, Conn.: Archon, 1938. Albuquerque's voyages and achievements in the East are vividly chronicled with emphasis on what made them remarkable.

Stephens, Henry Morse. *Albuquerque*. Oxford: Clarendon Press, 1892. In the Rulers of India series. This is a standard biography of Albuquerque and is one of the most complete available in English. It is the one found in most libraries of the United States and is a scholarly chronicle of and commentary on Albuquerque's achievements.

Barbara Ann Barbato

ALEXANDER VI
Rodrigo de Borja y Doms

Born: 1431; Játiva, Valencia
Died: August 18, 1503; Rome
Areas of Achievement: Politics, government, and religion
Contribution: Alexander VI's policies contributed to the growth of papal temporal power in the Papal States. A discriminating patron of the arts, he employed a number of noteworthy artists, including Pinturicchio and Michelangelo.

Early Life

Born Rodrigo de Borja y Doms (Borgia) in Játiva, Valencia, the boy who was to become Pope Alexander V1 was the nephew of Pope Calixtus III, who adopted him, showered him with church benefices, and sent him to the University of Bologna to study law. In 1456, Rodrigo was appointed a cardinal-deacon, and the following year he was made the vice-chancellor of the Church, a lucrative post that he held until his own elevation to the Papacy in 1492.

Rodrigo's many benefices enabled him to live in great magnificence and to indulge himself in such pastimes as cardplaying and merrymaking. His youthful indiscretions prompted Pope Pius II to send a scathing letter of reproof in 1460 for his alleged scandalous misconduct at Siena sometime earlier. His ordination to the priesthood in 1468 did not cause him to change his immoral behavior. Sometime in the early 1470's, Rodrigo entered into an illicit relationship with the beautiful Vannozza dei Cattanei, who was to be the mother of four of his children, Juan, Cesare, Lucrezia, and Jofré. In spite of these moral failings, Rodrigo was appointed Bishop of Porto in 1476 and made dean of the Sacred College in Rome. On August 11, 1492, he was elected pope by a bare two-thirds majority, amid charges, never substantiated, that he had bribed several cardinals to switch their votes in his favor. So worldly had the office of pope become by his time that there was little public criticism of his elevation to the See of Saint Peter, despite his reputation for moral irregularity. In fact, the Roman people held torchlight processions and erected triumphal arches to commemorate his election.

Life's Work

Described as a handsome and imposing figure, Pope Alexander brought considerable talent to his office. Francesco Guicciardini, a contemporary historian, noted that "in him were combined rare prudence and vigilance, mature reflection, marvellous power of persuasion, skill and capacity for the conduct of the most difficult affairs."

He began his pontificate by restoring order to Rome, which had been the scene of considerable violence, including more than two hundred assassinations, in the several years before Alexander's elevation. He divided the city into four districts, over each of which he placed a magistrate who was given plenary powers to maintain order. In the course of his pontificate, he subjugated the fractious Orsini and Colonna families, who had been troublesome elements in Roman politics for generations. In addition, he designated Tuesday of each week as a time for any man or woman in Rome to come before him personally to present his or her grievances.

As pope, Alexander advanced the interests of his own children, not only for their sakes but also as a means of strengthening papal political power. He betrothed his daughter Lucrezia to Giovanni Sforza in order to link the Borgia family with the powerful Sforza rulers of Milan. When this union ceased to be politically useful, Alexander annulled it and married Lucrezia to the son of the King of Naples. When Lucrezia's second husband was killed in 1501, Alexander arranged her marriage to Duke Alfonso I of Ferrara in the hope that it would further papal schemes in the Romagna. Favorite among his children, however, was his eldest son, Juan, the Duke of Gandía, and Alexander provided richly for him until Juan was murdered in 1497, whereupon the pope then placed his fondest hopes in Cesare. Alexander encouraged Cesare to establish a powerful principality in the Romagna, the most troublesome part of the Papal States.

Italy was subjected to two French invasions during the reign of Alexander. While the French kings had hereditary claims to both the Duchy of Milan and the kingdom of Naples, as long as the Triple Alliance powers of Naples, Florence, and Milan had been united, a French effort to make good these claims seemed remote. By January of 1494, however, the Triple Alliance had collapsed. Ludovico Sforza, the Duke of Milan, finding himself politically isolated in Italy, attempted to ingratiate himself to the French king, Charles VIII, by en-

The death of Pope Alexander VI, and his son Cesare Borgia, by food poisoning at a banquet

couraging him to invade Italy and claim the kingdom of Naples. Pope Alexander joined King Alfonso II of Naples, and Neapolitan troops were sent northward to block Charles's advance through the Papal States. Alexander's position worsened when two of his enemies, Cardinals Giuliano della Rovere (the future Pope Julius II) and Ascanio Sforza secretly went to the advancing Charles and tried to persuade him to call a council that would put Alexander on trial and depose him. Alexander met with King Charles, and an agreement was reached whereby Charles was allowed to enter Rome on December 31. A month later, Charles set out for Naples. In March of 1495, with Charles in possession of Naples, Pope Alexander formed the League of Venice, consisting of the Empire, Spain, and all the major Italian states except Florence. Its main purpose was to drive the French from Italian soil, a goal achieved by the end of the year.

When Louis XII succeeded Charles VIII as King of France in 1498, he quickly began planning an invasion of Italy to lay claim to the Duchy of Milan. Before executing this invasion, however, he dissolved the League of Venice by negotiating with Alexander, who agreed to remain neutral in return for Louis' assistance to Alexander's son Cesare in his efforts to conquer the Romagna. Louis invaded Milan in August of 1499, and by April of the following year he was firmly entrenched there. Louis then prepared for the conquest of Naples. King Ferdinand II also had claims to Naples, and Alexander arranged a settlement in November of 1500, whereby Naples would be partitioned between them, with Louis in control of the northern provinces and Ferdinand, the southern.

Meanwhile, Cesare, encouraged by the promise of the French king's friendship and assistance, waged vigorous war against the petty tyrants of the Romagna. His masterful and unscrupulous resourcefulness, coupled with his father's unstinting support, made Cesare remarkably successful. In April of 150, Alexander made his son Duke of the Romagna, and it appeared that a powerful state would soon be his. The death of Alexander in August, 1503, however, ended Cesare's successful course. Cesare was defeated by the forces of Pope Julius II, a bitter enemy of the Borgia family, and his lands were added to those of the Papacy. Julius would eventually make a modern Renaissance state of the papal holdings.

In 1495, Alexander first took official notice of the Dominican friar Girolamo Savonarola, when he ordered the latter to cease preaching in Florence. Savonarola's fiery sermons, in which he spared neither prince nor pope, had led to the expulsion of the Medicis from Florence, and he had begun to denounce the political machinations of Alexander. Savonarola had defied the pope, asserting: "You err; you are not the Roman Church, you are a man and a sinner." Pope Alexander excommunicated Savonarola in May of 1497 and again ordered him to cease preaching. While Savonarola had many supporters in Florence, and the pope had many enemies, in order to restore public order to the city thfe magistrates arrested the monk in April of 1498; after papal commissioners officially pronounced him guilty of heresy, Savonarola was ordered hanged and burned in May of that year.

Among the more positive acts of Pope Alexander were his efforts to preserve peace between Spain and Portugal by proclaiming the Line of Demarcation in 1493, whereby he allocated the New World to Spain, and Africa and India to Portugal for the purposes of exploration. Though he was generally preoccupied with worldly affairs, Alexander did, on occasion, assert religious leadership. He was the first pope to give strong support to missionary activity in the New World. The beginnings of *Index Librorum Prohibitorum*, or the Index, can be traced to his pontificate. The Sapienza was considerably augmented under his direction. He proclaimed the year 1500 a jubilee year, and pilgrims flocked to Rome. That same year, Alexander preached a crusade against the Turks, and, in a period of remorse and reflection after the death of his favorite son Juan, Alexander appointed a commission of cardinals that was charged with establishing proposals for extensive reform within the Church.

Despite the "moral miseries of the reign of Alexander VI," he was a splendid patron of the arts. Alexander employed architects and painters who beautified the region around the Vatican called the Borgo Nuovo. The artist Pinturicchio decorated many of the rebuilt and new Borgia apartments in the Vatican. His work included a famous portrait of Alexander kneeling in adoration of the miracle of the Resurrection. Churches and buildings were renovated, and new ones, such as the Tempietto, designed by Donato Bramante, were erected. It was under the patronage of Alexander that Michelangelo's *Pietà* was completed in 1499.

Pope Alexander and his son Cesare both became seriously ill at a banquet that they were attending in August of 1503. Although Cesare recovered, the pope died on August 18. While there were rumors that Alexander was the victim of poison that he had intended for certain of his enemies at the banquet, it is generally believed that he died as a result of a plague.

Summary

Nineteenth and twentieth century scholarship has tended to reject many of the more vicious moral crimes charged to Alexander VI. While few scholars have attempted and none has succeeded in exonerating him of corruption, immorality, and Machiavellian statecraft, it has been noted that many of the Renaissance popes were guilty of similar behavior. Although he did use the power and wealth of his office to advance the interests of his children, he was able to enhance papal power as well. The petty tyrannies in the Romagna that were destroyed by Cesare Borgia were never reestablished, and Julius II would be able to build a strong papal government in the Papal States on the foundation laid by Alexander's son. Although the political machinations practiced by Alexander hardly seem appropriate for the Vicar of Christ, the necessity to protect papal lands in Italy from encroachments by the Empire, France, and Spain led many medieval and early modern popes to practice a diplomacy characterized by capriciousness and deceit.

While some scholars might be willing to acknowledge that Alexander's failure as pope was in a measure counterbalanced by his patronage of the arts or that his encouragement of missions to the Americas more than compensated for his unwholesome example as a spiritual leader, most will not. Catholic scholars generally conclude, however, that "the dignity of Peter suffers no diminution even in an unworthy successor."

Bibliography

De la Bedoyere, Michael. *The Meddlesome Friar: The Story of the Conflict Between Savonarola and Alexander VI*. London: Collins, and New York: Hanover House, 1957. A good discussion of the early lives of the two men, with an explanation of the political events that led to the conflict. Dispels many of the legends that have surrounded both men. A well-balanced reassessment of the much-maligned Alexander. This book is based on extensive documentary research, although there are no footnotes and no bibliography.

Ferrara, Orestes. *The Borgia Pope, Alexander the Sixth*. New York: Sheed and Ward, 1940; London: Sheed and Ward, 1942. An attempt by a practicing lawyer to rehabilitate the character of Alexander and to refute the legends of his misdeeds and evil influence on the Church and the secular history of his time. While based on extensive research, the author's interpretation of evidence is often questionable. Must be read in conjunction with other works on Alexander.

Mallett, Michael. *The Borgias: The Rise and Fall of a Renaissance Dynasty*. New York: Barnes and Noble, and London: Bodley Head, 1969. Hailed as the best treatment of the Borgia family in any language. Presents Alexander as a representative personality of the Renaissance and places his achievements as well as his vices into a sound historical perspective. Discredits many of the legends concerning the Borgias. Includes extensive footnoting, an annotated bibliography, genealogies, and maps.

Pastor, Ludwig. *The History of the Popes from the Close of the Middle Ages*. 4th ed. Vols. 5 and 6. London: Kegan Paul, 1923; St. Louis, Mo.: Herder, 1949. Much of both of these volumes of this classic, monumental history of the modern Papacy is devoted to the pontificate of Alexander. In part based on archival material not available to earlier scholars, Pastor's account is well balanced and strongly documented. While acknowledging the merits of Alexander's cultural patronage, this account is critical of Alexander's failure as a spiritual leader. Includes an extensive bibliography, much of which is not in English.

Pazola, Ron "Who's Been Sitting in Peter's Chair?" *US Catholic* 58 (July, 1993): 34. The article evaluates different popes (including Alexander VI), their characters, the effects of their decisions on history, and the impact they had on society.

Portigliotti, Giuseppe. *The Borgias: Alexander VI, Caesar, Lucrezia*. Translated by Bernard Miall. London: Allen and Unwin, and New York: Knopf, 1928. Purports to be a historical and psychological study of the Borgias, their ancestry, characters, and crimes. Relies too much on gossip and suspicions and ignores the historical background of events and ideas. Also ignores the positive achievements of Alexander as statesman and pope. Should be read only in conjunction with more balanced accounts. Includes illustrations of Borgia family members.

Paul E. Gill

DUKE OF ALVA

Born: October 29, 1507; Piedrahita, Spain
Died: December 12, 1582; Lisbon, Portugal
Areas of Achievement: Diplomacy and military
Contribution: One of the greatest European soldiers and diplomats of the 1500's, Alva fought for and represented the Hapsburg emperor Charles V and his son King Philip II of Spain.

Early Life

Fernando Álvarez de Toledo, the third duke of Alva (also spelled "Alba"), was descended from one of the most illustrious Spanish families. Alva's father Garcia was killed in 1510 in Tunis in battle with the Moors. Alva's grandfather Fadrique, the second duke of Alva, gave him a humanistic education and nurtured in him a great fascination with the martial arts. By 1534, Fernando (the "great duke" of Alva, as he has commonly been called), had caught the eye of the Hapsburg emperor Charles V of Austria (Charles I of Spain), who had visited him in that year at the ducal palace in Alva de Tormes near Salamanca. The Alva holdings consisted of some three thousand acres, a considerable block of western Castile.

In 1535, the duke was chosen for military service by the emperor and participated with him in battles in Tunis. In the same year, Charles decided that he would have to take action against French invasions in Italy. In the ensuing campaign, in which Alva had his first independent field command, he revealed a mastery of the art of war that left an indelible impression upon the emperor. Thus by the age of twenty-eight Alva had developed a close working relationship with Charles, who increasingly called upon him for his advice and participation in military and diplomatic matters. In 1542, he brilliantly repelled an attempted French invasion of Spain at the Battle of Perpignan, and he was involved in the negotiations that led to the 1544 Peace of Crepy. Conflicts between the two countries had produced inconclusive results, and among the provisions of the treaty, Charles was to cede either Milan or the Netherlands to French control.

In view of his later experiences in the Low Countries, it is one of the great ironies of history that Alva presented cogent geopolitical arguments for maintaining Milan and ceding the Netherlands. Indeed, Alva advocated the complete abandonment of the Low Countries. Nevertheless, Charles, preoccupied with Germany, decided in favor of keeping the Netherlands.

Life's Work

By his late thirties, Alva had developed into a somber and forbidding man. Lean and tall, of sallow complexion and prominent nose, he dressed well but not ostentatiously, ate and drank moderately. Although of a fiery and arrogant disposition, he seems to have kept iron control of himself in dealing with others. Alva's only known sexual escapade occurred in 1527 and resulted in the birth of an illegitimate son, whom the Duke acknowledged and had educated as a gentleman. In 1529, Alva married his cousin Maria Enríquez de Gúzman. The couple had four children, three of whom survived to adulthood. Perhaps Alva's most striking characteristic was his fervent devotion to Catholicism and his distinct aversion to "infidels" and "heretics"—Muslims and Protestants.

In 1546, war broke out between Charles and the Protestants in his domains in Germany. He immediately called upon Alva to prepare for the coming battles. In 1547, the duke cemented his reputation as a military leader with his victory at the crucial Battle of Muhlberg. There was universal agreement that the triumph there, openly acknowledged by Charles, over forces led by John of Saxony was the result of Alva's brilliant tactical maneuvers. As a consequence, Alva became a powerful courtier at the imperial court, and Charles later counseled his son Philip II to honor and favor him—though circumspectly—and to consult him in matters of war and statecraft. He added that he considered the duke to be the best person available in such matters.

Sometime before his death in 1558, Charles retired and divided his empire between his brother Ferdinand and his son Philip. Ferdinand was awarded the imperial title of emperor and given the Hapsburg lands in Austria and Germany. Philip was given all the rest, including Spain, Italy, and the Low Countries. In 1554, French forces again posed a threat to Philip's inherited territories in Italy, and he dispatched an army under the command of Alva to defeat them.

The Italian Wars (1554-1557) began with Alva under severe disadvantages: unpaid and disaffected troops, lack of supplies, and scheming enemies at Philip's court. Alva surmounted all these difficulties. A devout Catholic, he eventually found himself in the position of having to invade the Papal Territories in Italy in order to achieve victory, but he was able to negotiate a face-saving peace for and with the pope. Thus, through a combination of military and diplomatic finesse, he solved a delicate situation with the pope without sacrificing Spanish interests. Alva was most active in negotiating the Treaty of Coteau-Cambreis, which ended the Italian Wars, delineated the Spanish relationship with the Papacy, and served to settle various issues there between Spain and France.

The most troublesome of the Spanish possessions was the Low Countries, particularly the northern part, the Netherlands. An underlying problem in dealing with the Low Countries was that they were not homogenous. They consisted of a patchwork of differing and conflicting religions, languages, and classes. Previous attempts by Charles to create a viable government had largely failed. Taxes were levied, but with poor results. Various Protestant denominations—Lutherans, Anabaptists, and Calvinists—found the busy mercantile cities of the north places of refuge and profit. The stronghold of the Catholic Church was located in the south, but the nomination and investiture of its hierarchy was effectively controlled by the great nobles. To devout Catholics such as Philip and Alva, the reform of both church and state in the Low Countries was an obvious imperative.

By the summer of 1566, overt opposition to Spanish authority constituted a serious rebellion. Alva counseled Philip himself to go to suppress it. At first Philip agreed, but he then reversed himself. He decided that a surrogate should suppress the revolt by harsh measures, directed particularly against Protestants, and that he would then follow, which he did not. A reluctant Alva, therefore, was sent on a fourfold mission: to establish a strong military presence; to punish those responsible for earlier disorders; to set up and enforce an effective system of taxation; and to restore and strengthen religious unity.

In 1567, Alva moved some fifteen thousand troops and auxiliaries—far fewer than he had requested—into the Low Countries. The garrisons in major cities were maintained and strengthened, and local militias were disbanded. Several rebel leaders were imprisoned or executed, and a "Council of Blood," as it was called by the insurgents, tried and ordered the execution of some one thousand people. Alva's attempt to impose a tax on

sales was a complete failure. Quite successful, however, was his reformation of the Catholic clergy in the Low Countries. Thousands, most notably the future leader of the Dutch struggle for independence, Prince William of Orange, fled to neighboring countries, where they proceeded to plot against Alva and his forces. It is against this background during the period 1567-1573 that a virtual civil war developed in which cities and towns were taken and retaken by the opposing forces. Meanwhile, back at the royal court, there were allegations that Alva's harsh policies had made the situation worse. In 1573, Philip replaced Alva as commander, and the duke was returned to Madrid.

On his return, Alva was put under virtual house arrest for months as the result of these events and continuing court intrigues against him. It is significant, however, that when the next important emergency in Spanish affairs arose—the conflict over Philip's claim to the Portuguese throne in 1580—he turned to Alva to mount and carry on a war to resolve the crisis. Although the duke is said to have complained at the time that he was being sent in chains to subjugate a kingdom, the by then seventy-two-year-old man took up his last campaign. Profiting from his experience in the Low Countries, where he had not been adequately supported, Alva asked for and was provided with forty thousand troops and ample supplies. More lenient in dealing with the Portuguese insurgents, probably in part because they were all Catholics, Alva by 1582 had reduced the countryside and captured Lisbon, the capital. The erstwhile claimant to the throne fled into exile, Philip was acknowledged as the Portuguese ruler, and Alva governed in his name. In December of that year, however, the old duke succumbed to an undiagnosed disease and died.

Summary

At an early age, the duke of Alva became a leading figure at the court of Charles V, and he continued to influence the policies of Philip II at the time when Spain was at the zenith of its power. He was relied on by both monarchs for advice and active conduct of military and diplomatic missions, often of a sensitive nature. For example, the duke played the leading role in the delicate arrangements leading up to the marriage of Philip to Queen Mary of England in 1554 and in 1559 to Elizabeth of Valois, daughter of Henry IV of France. In 1558, he single-handedly negotiated the seemingly impossible settlement whereby the city of Calais was transferred from English to French control.

Had Alva succeeded in resolving the problems facing Spanish rule in the Low Countries, the history of Western Europe would have been quite different. The failure was not completely his, however, as he was undermined by intrigues at the Spanish court, lacked adequate support, and from the outset was permitted and even encouraged by Philip to follow a harsh and repressive policy, particularly against Protestants. Still, at critical junctures he could have exercised more discretion and moderation, and he has been strongly censured over the years for the excesses of his governance of the Low Countries. On balance, though, Alva can truly be said to have been indispensable for more than half a century to two of the most powerful rulers of Renaissance Europe, and, with one exception, to have successfully advanced their causes and that of Roman Catholicism.

Bibliography

Elliott, John H. *Imperial Spain, 1469-1716.* London: Edward Arnold, 1963. A survey that provides considerable insight into the world in which Alva operated. Pays particular attention to warfare of the time.

Maltby, William S. *Alba: A Biography of Fernando Álvarez de Toledo, Third Duke of Alba, 1507-1582.* Berkeley: University of California Press, 1983. The best biography in English on Alva; an entertaining and objective account. Reflects exhaustive research on all aspects of Alva's life and career. Includes a "Notes on Sources" section that provides a fine description and location of all materials used in the work.

Motley, John Lothrop. *The Rise of the Dutch Republic: A History.* 3 vols. New York: Harper, 1871. A thoroughly researched and well-written history of the revolt in the Netherlands. Distinctly biased against Spain, however, and uncompromisingly harsh in its criticism of Alva's attempts to suppress the revolt.

Pierson, Peter. *Philip II of Spain.* London: Thames and Hudson, 1975. Concentrates on the political aspects of Philip's career and details Alva's diplomatic relationship to the monarch.

Thompson, I. A. A. *War and Government in Hapsburg Spain, 1560-1620.* London: Athlone Press, 1976. Describes the effect of wars upon the government in Spain and discusses Alva's role in the interaction of the two.

Jean Moore Kiger

PEDRO DE ALVARADO

Born: 1485; Badajoz, Spain
Died: 1541; northern Mexico
Area of Achievement: Exploration
Contribution: Alvarado was a key subordinate to Hernán Cortés in the sixteenth century Spanish exploration and conquest of Mexico and Central America.

Early Life

Pedro de Alvarado was born in the city of Badajoz in the Spanish province of Estremadura, an area that had furnished Spain with many professional soldiers in the country's centuries-long war to oust the Arab invaders from the Iberian Peninsula. He was descended from a family that belonged to the minor nobility, and he played an active role in Spain's battle against the Arabs. Like most of the nobles of his time, he learned little of such skills as reading and writing. Alvarado knew how to use a sword and was an excellent horseman, but he had few other marketable talents. The defeat of the Arab armies therefore left him, like many of his countrymen, unemployed.

The voyages of Christopher Columbus opened the Western Hemisphere to both exploration and exploitation by the Spaniards. Alvarado—in the company of his four brothers, Jorge, Gonzalo, Gómez and Juan—joined the flood of soldiers who saw this new frontier as an opportunity for both wealth and advancement. In 1510, the brothers emigrated to Cuba.

In 1511, Alvarado enlisted in an expedition headed by Juan de Grijalva; the expedition was sent from Cuba to explore the Yucatán. Although Grijalva had problems controlling his young lieutenant, he regarded him highly enough to send him back to Cuba carrying the spoils of the venture. Alvarado's tendency to go his own way without regard for his orders would prove to be a constant problem throughout his subsequent military career.

Life's Work

After his initial exposure to the newly explored territories of North America, Alvarado became one of the four chief lieutenants to Hernán Cortés during the conquest of central Mexico itself in the years 1518-1521. Subsequently, Cortés delegated to his subordinate the responsibility for bringing much of Central America into the Spanish colonial empire.

Alvarado joined Cortés' expedition in 1518 at the Cuban port of Trinidad, where Cortés had begun the process of recruiting followers. Cortés also undertook the acquisition of military stores and provisions and the overhaul of the ships that he planned to use in the voyage to the mainland.

The relationship between the two adventurers would remain a mercurial one throughout the many years of their association. Alvarado, headstrong and independent, was nevertheless an outstanding leader and soldier. Although Cortés regarded Alvarado as one of his top lieutenants, he would later have cause to regret giving command of certain undertakings to his undisciplined subordinate.

Alvarado often behaved unpredictably. On one occasion, he interfered with Cortés' scheduled execution of a condemned soldier, cutting the noose from the unfortunate's neck as he stood on the scaffold. He could also be generous; reportedly, he once forgave a debt of 20,000 ducats (equivalent to about $80,000) owed him by a fellow officer. His baser nature, however, led him to commit such heinous acts as burning prisoners alive, turning ferocious dogs on unarmed natives, and assaulting the new bride of an indigenous chief. Throughout his career, moreover, he regarded the property of conquered peoples as his for the taking.

Cortés' expedition consisted of eleven vessels, 110 sailors, 553 soldiers, and sixteen horses. With that force, Cortés launched a successful campaign that conquered all of Mexico and destroyed the Aztec Empire in the short span of three years. The Spaniards were ruthless in their dealings with the native peoples. They slaughtered those that opposed them through the use of their superior armament, and they exploited mercilessly those who sought to placate them. The invaders not only seized all the wealth that they could extract from the natives but also demanded that they abjure their ancient religions and accept Christianity.

Although the Spanish force was small, their firearms, body armor, horses, and fighting dogs gave them such an overwhelming advantage over the armies of the indigenous peoples that resistance proved futile. Moreover, the guileful Cortés succeeded in allying his troops with powerful native nations such as the Tlascalans, who hated the brutal Aztec regime. The Tlascalans feared and admired Alvarado. Because of his imposing physique

and flaming red hair, they called him Tonatiuh, or "child of the son."

Accompanied by his Tlascalan allies, Cortés marched on Tenochtitlán (now Mexico City), the Aztec capital, destroying the armies he encountered in the intervening countryside. The Aztec emperor Montezuma II, consumed by doubt about the origin of the Spanish forces and believing that perhaps they were gods, chose to bargain with Cortés, hoping to bribe the latter to leave the country. Once in the capital, the Spaniards pursued their usual policy of demanding both riches and the destruction of all the local deities. Moreover, the resourceful Cortés took Montezuma prisoner in order to better control the populace.

Although the Aztec capital was secure, Cortés faced a new problem. His enemy Diego Velásquez, the governor of Cuba, had organized an army three times the size of Cortés' forces to follow the latter into Mexico and take Cortés prisoner. The governor had become jealous of Cortés' success and planned to take over conquered Mexico himself.

Leaving Alvarado in charge in Tenochtitlán, Cortés not only defeated the superior pursuing force but also persuaded the majority of its soldiers to join his own army. Meanwhile, Alvarado had created a problem for his chief by slaughtering a number of Aztec nobles during a religious festival. The outraged natives began a massive rebellion.

Cortés, his army now strengthened by new recruits, marched quickly west once more, reentering the capital and rescuing the hard-pressed Alvarado and his small contingent. Nevertheless, the Aztecs continued their attacks despite heavy losses. Even Montezuma's appeal to his countrymen to lay down their arms failed, and they killed their emperor as he tried to address them. Recognizing his peril and running short of food and ammunition, Cortés decided to retreat to the coast.

What followed proved to be a harrowing adventure for the Spaniards. The night of the retreat came to be known as La Noche Triste ("the melancholy night"). Cortés, in a prodigious effort, managed to extricate his forces although the Aztecs killed and captured many. At one point, Alvarado, commanding the rear guard, found himself alone and surrounded by his enemies on the bank of a canal. He thrust his lance firmly into the water below and vaulted to the canal's opposite side. The jump that he made was so impressive that even today the spot is called *Salto de Alvarado* ("Alvarado's Leap").

Arriving once more at Veracruz, Cortés rested, rearmed, and assembled an even greater force for the recapture of the Aztec capital. He stopped short of the city and built several brigantines to ensure his control of the city's waterways. The Spaniards attacked the Aztec defenders and reconquered the city in the face of suicidal resistance. Estimates on the Aztec casualties from battle, hunger, and disease ranged from 120,000 to 240,000. Some 30,000 to 70,000 survived, and the victorious Spaniards allowed them to leave the ruined capital.

Spain's emperor, Charles V, named Cortés a marquis and granted him extensive holdings throughout New Spain, as central Mexico was known. At the same time, the emperor designated new civil authorities in the colony, and Cortés never again held the political power that he had achieved as a conqueror. Nevertheless, in his continued capacity as captain general, Cortés did authorize Alvarado to move south to subjugate most of Central America. Alvarado began the invasion of Central America in 1523. He adopted the same techniques employed by the Spaniards in the conquest of Mexico: the slaughter of any natives offering resistance and the exploitation of those that did not. He conquered what today is Guatemala, El Salvador, and northern Nicaragua.

Arriving at the kingdom of Cuzcatlán, now El Salvador, Alvarado emulated the behavior of Cortés at Tenochtitlán. Welcomed by the country's king, Atlacatl, and his nobles, furnished with sumptuous quarters and provisions, the Spanish leader repaid this hospitality by seizing the native leaders and holding them hostage. When forced to retrace his steps temporarily, Alvarado had Atlacatl and his contingent slaughtered. Although the Spaniards found some gold, the area offered merely a fraction of the wealth that they had acquired in Mexico. Only the Aztec Empire possessed such fabulous wealth.

Named governor and captain general of the kingdom of Guatemala by Charles V, Alvarado turned to other means to build wealth. Recognizing the value of native labor as a commodity, the new governor sought to stop their wholesale slaughter. Charles V granted Alvarado the right to build a fleet and explore the southern seas. The new governor also attempted to enter Peruvian ports with his ships and to share in the wealth of the Inca Empire, but he was denied entry by the Spanish authorities already established there.

His final campaign occurred in northern Mexico, at that time known as New Galicia. Asked by the king's viceroy in Mexico City to come to the aid of beleaguered Spanish forces in that territory, the irrepressible Alvarado moved north and launched an attack against the natives in mountain country during a heavy rain. During the engagement, his horse lost its footing and rolled over Alvarado, killing him. At the time, Alvarado was fifty-six years old.

Summary

The Spanish conquistadores, soldiers such as Pedro de Alvarado, Hernán Cortés, and Francisco Pizarro, invaded and conquered what is now Mexico, Central America, and Peru, for both wealth and prestige. Seasoned fighting men, they and their followers overcame tremendous odds to achieve their victories. In the process, they killed thousands of the indigenous peoples who opposed them. Thousands more died from the hunger and disease that resulted from the warfare itself. The Spaniards rationalized their behavior on the grounds that they brought Christianity to pagan peoples. Priests accompanied every expedition to convert the natives to the Christian faith. In their eagerness to spread the tenets of their religion, they also aided in the destruction of the existing indigenous cultures.

Pedro de Alvarado, a brave, accomplished, if somewhat erratic military man, personified the Spanish conquistador. His cruelty and rapaciousness helped to create the anti-Spanish "Black Legend," the reputation for brutality that the country earned not only in the eyes of the oppressed natives of the New World but also among other European nations.

Bibliography

Díaz, Bernal. *The Conquest of New Spain*. London: Penguin Books, 1963. An autobiography of one of the soldiers who accompanied the Cortés expedition, a brother-in-arms of Pedro de Alvarado.

Holmes, Maurice G. *From New Spain by Sea to the Californias, 1519-1668*. Glendale, Calif.: Arthur H. Clark, 1963. Covers the final years of Alvarado's military economic, and political career, including his attempts to open up new areas for trade overseas.

Kelly, John Eoghan. *Pedro de Alvarado, Conquistador*. Princeton, N.J.: Princeton University Press, 1932. One of the few complete biographies of Alvarado available in English.

Prescott, William H. *The Conquest of Mexico*. New York: Bantam Books, 1964. A complete, detailed history of the Cortés expedition and the role that Alvarado played in it.

Woodward, Ralph Lee, Jr. *Central America: A Nation Divided*. New York: Oxford University Press, 1976. Chapter 2, "The Kingdom of Guatemala," provides an overview of Alvarado's efforts to subjugate the inhabitants of Central America and add that area to Spain's empire.

Carl Henry Marcoux

ANDREA DEL SARTO
Andrea d'Agnolo

Born: July 16, 1486; Florence
Died: September 28, 1530; Florence
Area of Achievement: Art
Contribution: Andrea del Sarto is considered to be one of the most important Florentine painters of the early sixteenth century and is also a figure of great historical importance. In his own work, he was clearly inspired by the classical ideals of the central Italian High Renaissance, particularly by Raphael and Leonardo da Vinci, but his pupils were to become the creators of the anticlassical style later known as mannerism, which dominated Italian art from about 1520 until 1600.

Early Life

Andrea d'Agnolo, the son of Agnolo di Francesco Lanfranchi and Constanza, was born in Florence in 1486, probably one of twins, for the surviving documents indicate that Agnolo di Francesco's two sons, Andrea and Domenico, were both baptized on July 17, 1486, the day after their birth. Andrea's great-grandfather had been an agricultural laborer, his grandfather a linen weaver, and his father a tailor (*un sarto*), and for that reason Andrea was given the nickname of Andrea del Sarto. Andrea left school at the age of seven to work for a goldsmith before beginning his training as a painter, first in the studio of the little-known Andrea di Salvi Barile and later with Piero di Cosimo. It has also been persuasively argued by modern critics that Andrea must have studied with the technically accomplished Raffaellino del Garbo, or at least been strongly influenced by his work.

On December 11, 1508, Andrea was matriculated in the guild of Florentine painters. About two years earlier, he had entered into a partnership with Francesco di Cristoforo Bigi, known as Franciabigio. The two artists shared a studio and were later joined by the young sculptor Jacopo Sansovino, who had come from Rome.

Life's Work

Two fresco cycles in Florence are the major works of the collaboration of Andrea and Franciabigio. In the forecourt of the Church of Santissima Annunziata in Florence, they continued the fresco cycle which had been begun in the fifteenth century and which illustrated the life of Saint Filippo Benizzi and scenes from the life of the Virgin. The scenes from the life of Saint Filippo Benizzi, the chief saint of the Servite Order (of which the Santissima Annunziata is the mother church), were Andrea's first fresco commissions and show him experimenting with a variety of compositions. Two of the scenes are loosely organized and recall the pictorial ideals of the preceding century, but in the *Saint Curing the Possessed Woman*, *The Death of the Saint*, and the *Miracles Performed by the Relics of the Saint*, dated 1510, Andrea introduced rigidly organized, symmetrical compositions which reveal his debt to Leonardo da Vinci, while his handling of color, light, and shade shows how much he admired the work of Raphael. The finest work in this cycle is the last one that Andrea painted, the *Birth of the Virgin* (1514). In this remarkable work, which marks the beginning of his artistic maturity, the severity of the earlier scenes has given way to a more flexible and subtly harmonious type of composition. One can see in this work how completely Andrea had absorbed the pictorial ideals of the High Renaissance.

The two artists also collaborated in a commission which they received from the Florentine Compagnia dello Scalzo, a secular confraternity. The oratory of the compagnia was located not far from the Church of San Marco, and the frescoes by Andrea del Sarto and Franciabigio, which are still extant, are in what was once the cloister. The subjects are scenes from the life of Saint John the Baptist and the Cardinal Virtues. These frescoes are executed in girisaille, that is, in varying shades of gray. Although they were probably begun as early as 1511, Andrea continued to work on them from time to time until 1526. Ten of the scenes are by Andrea, who also painted *The Cardinal Virtues*, while two are by Franciabigio. The Scalzo frescoes are among the finest examples of the High Renaissance style in Florence. Each scene is elegantly composed, but with a naturalism of attitude and gesture that makes it completely plausible, a reality that is convincing but one that has become a realm of grace and beauty.

While he was working on these commissions, Andrea also had a hand in the preparation of the civic decorations in celebration of the return of the Medici family from their exile (February, 1513)

and for the ceremonial entrance of the Medici Pope Leo X into Florence in 1515. In 1517, he completed one of his most impressive paintings, the *Madonna of the Harpies*. In this, the characteristic elegance of composition and pose is enriched by startling innovations in color, intermittent passages of light and shadow, and a softness of modeling which create a richly atmospheric effect.

The work at the cloister of the Scalzo was interrupted by Andrea's departure from Florence to enter the service of Francis I of France. He accepted the invitation to go to Fontainbleau in the late spring or early summer of 1516 and remained there until 1519. Only a few paintings can be identified as having been painted in France, but one of these, the *Charity* (signed and dated 1518), is a masterpiece, one of his most completely realized works. Like the *Madonna of the Harpies*, it fuses the discipline of classical composition with a richly pictorial palette. The *Charity*, however, is enriched by a beautifully painted landscape background in which the idealistic transformation of nature echoes the visionary grace of the figures.

Andrea probably returned to Florence because he did not want to remain separated from his wife, Lucrezia del Fede, whom he had married shortly after her husband died in 1516. She was about four years younger than Andrea and, at the time of their marriage, was already the mother of a small child. Andrea's biographer Giorgio Vasari states that the French king gave him money to purchase paintings and sculptures for the royal collection after Andrea had solemnly promised that he would come back to France within a few months. Instead, he remained in Florence. While Vasari's account has been doubted, it is known that Andrea arrived in Florence with a large sum of money and that in October, 1520, he bought a plot of land on which he later built a large house and studio. He visited Rome about 1520 and in 1523 left Florence because of an outbreak of the plague. He went to the Mugello, north of Florence, where he worked for the nuns of San Piero a Luco for about a year before he returned to his native city. In November of 1524, he was back in Florence; very little is known about his activities from this point until his death in 1530 at the age of forty-four.

Andrea continued to work in the Scalzo until 1526 and produced a number of altarpieces for churches in and around Florence. The *Madonna and Child with Saints* of 1525-1526 is typical of his work during this period, with its soft modeling, strong color harmonies, and strong, simple grouping. Paintings such as this one made a great impression on the younger painters in Florence. Two artists who had studied with Andrea earlier, Jacopo Carucci da Pontormo and Giovanni Battista di Jacopo, called Rosso Fiorentino, had by this time evolved their striking anticlassical or early mannerist styles, but between 1520 and 1530 a new generation of painters turned to Andrea for inspiration. He strongly influenced the subsequent development of Florentine painting.

One of the finest of his late works is *The Last Supper* in the refectory of the former convent of San Salvi in Florence (1526-1527), a work of great pictorial interest that comes close to the dramatic intensity of Leonardo da Vinci's rendering of the subject. The *Madonna del Sacco* of 1525 in the Chiostro dei Morti of the Santissima Annunziata is another impressive example of his mature style, which shows the lack of emotional content seen in many of his last works.

Summary

Andrea del Sarto was an artist of great virtuosity. His surviving drawings, most of which are studies from life, are superb examples of draftmanship. He is equally skillful as a colorist and as a composer. He was also proficient at fresco painting and panel painting. Modern critics have noted that his work not only directly inspired a number of younger artists but also laid the foundations for some of the most exciting developments of Italian art during the seventeenth century. For Vasari, however, Andrea was an artist whose work was flawed because he lacked the moral strength to make the exertions required to achieve the highest results. There is a certain justice to this criticism, particularly in Andrea's late works, many of which are interesting for the virtuosity of their pictorial effects but are lacking in strong emotional content.

His frescoes in the Scalzo and the Santissima Annunziata, however, are some of the finest achievements of Florentine art. It is to Andrea's credit that while many of his contemporaries were able to imitate certain aspects of the style of Leonardo and Raphael, he was one of the few who were able to assimilate their styles without losing individuality.

Bibliography

Borsook, Eve. *The Mural Painters of Tuscany: From Cimabue to Andrea del Sarto*. 2d ed. Oxford: Clarendon Press, and New York: Oxford University Press, 1980. A detailed analysis of Andrea del Sarto's frescoes in the oratory of the Compagnia dello Scalzo in Florence. Includes much information on the relationship of the murals to the site and on the technique.

Freedberg, Sydney J. *Andrea del Sarto*. 2 vols. Cambridge, Mass.: Harvard University Press, 1963. A comprehensive study of all aspects of the artist's career. This book and the one by Shearman (see below) are the standard monographs on the artist. While Freedberg traces Andrea's development within the context of the classical style of the High Renaissance, Shearman shows the importance of Andrea's work, particularly his use of color, for subsequent developments in Italian art of the seventeenth century.

McKillop, Susan Regan. *Franciabigio*. Berkeley: University of California Press, 1974. The author publishes a number of new documents and includes a careful evaluation of the collaboration between Andrea del Sarto and Franciabigio.

Neufeld, Gunther. "On the Genesis of the *Madonna del Sacco*." *The Art Bulletin* 47 (1965): 117-118. A study of the preparatory drawings for Andrea del Sarto's *Madonna del Sacco* (1525) in the Cloister of the SS. Annunziata, Florence, and its derivation from a work by the Venetian artist Titian.

O'Gorman, James F. "An Interpretation of Andrea del Sarto, *Borgheriri Holy Family*." *The Art Bulletin* 48 (1965): 502-504. A study of the religious significance of Andrea del Sarto's painting of *Mary, Joseph, the Christ Child, and Young Saint John the Baptist* and its relationship to Florentine religious and political ideals of the late fifteenth and early sixteenth centuries.

Shearman, John. *Andrea del Sarto*. 2 vols. Oxford: Clarendon Press, and New York: Oxford University Press, 1965. One of the two standard monographs on the artist.

Vasari, Giorgio. *Lives of the Most Eminent Painters, Sculptors, and Architects*. Vol. 5. Translated by Gaston du C. de Vere. London: Macmillan and the Medici Society, 1912; New York: AMS Press, 1976. The standard translation of the second edition (1568) of the only contemporary biography of the artist. Although Vasari was only nineteen when Andrea died, he had access to reliable information about the artist when he was preparing his biography.

Eric Van Schaack

FRA ANGELICO
Guido di Pietro

Born: c. 1400; Vicchio, Tuscany
Died: February 18, 1455; Rome
Area of Achievement: Art
Contribution: Fra Angelico is best known for adapting the most advanced artistic techniques of his time (perspective and brilliant use of color and line) to extraordinary evocations of purely spiritual subjects.

Early Life

Not much is known about Fra Angelico's early life. His baptismal name was Guido or Guidolino di Pietro, but he was also named Giovanni da Fiesole. Il Beato Fra Giovanni Angelico is the name he was given after his death, even though he was never actually beatified. He was apparently an extremely devout man who, in or about 1425, took his vows in the Dominican Order. The first painting of his that can be confidently dated is the *Madonna Linaivoli Altarpiece* (1433), which is in St. Mark's Convent in Florence, Italy. It is speculated that he began painting perhaps ten years earlier, working on small pictures and miniatures, such as *Saint Jerome Penitent*, which is in the collection of Princeton University.

As Giulio Carlo Argon puts it, Fra Angelico was a man of "saintly habits, a learned and zealous friar." He seems to have turned to art not only as a way of glorifying God but also as a way of demonstrating the sacred contents of His world. This meant painting angels and holy figures in vivid color and specific detail; there is nothing abstract or stilted about Fra Angelico's human and divine figures. They are a recognizable part of the viewer's world, set off only by their brilliance and repose.

Fra Angelico may have achieved a significant place of authority among the Dominicans. One unverified account claims that the pope wished him to be Archbishop of Florence. What is certain is that Fra Angelico enjoyed the respect of the Vatican and worked for many years on papal commissions. From 1449 to 1452, he was prior of the convent of San Marco. Still, his fame as a painter far exceeded his accomplishments in the Church. His paintings reveal such skill, clarity, and intensity that many critics have presumed that the artist's aim was to combine Renaissance Humanism with an exalted portrayal of Christian doctrine.

Life's Work

Fra Angelico's main purpose was to give depth, resonance, and substance to his spiritual conception of existence. What separates his work from earlier medieval religious painting is his use of perspective, the portrayal of objects or people on a flat surface so as to give the illusion of three dimensions. In other words, Fra Angelico learned the technique of making his religious figures stand out, as though what he painted had an objective, concrete existence in the world of the senses. Perspective was a fifteenth century invention, and it is likely that Fra Angelico learned it from his contemporaries in Florence. At about 1420, the Florentine architects Filippo Brunelleschi and Leon Battista Alberti designed two panels depicting architectural views of Florence. For the first time, viewers of these panels could get a sense of the space in and around objects rather than having each object or image appear flattened out along the same plane. It was as if the viewer could look into a painting and not simply at it.

In *The Annunciation*, painted sometime in the 1430's, the Virgin Mary and the archangel Gabriel are framed by two arches that curve over them and create a coherent, concrete space which they can be seen to inhabit. This architectural detail is not merely decorative; it serves the function of creating a scene, a small drama that draws the viewer's attention to the entrance of the angel into the human realm. Gabriel is depicted leaning forward, with the tail ends of his golden wings and of his heavily ornamented pink-and-gold gown bisected by one of the pillars of an arch. Mary, on the other hand, is completely separate in her own panel, save for a small piece of her royal blue gown edged with gold that extends slightly into Gabriel's space. The Annunciation, Gabriel's announcement that Mary will bear the Son of God, is rendered in three streams of gold lines that penetrate the pillar that separates Mary's panel from Gabriel's. Visually, the two archways are linked by the representation of the Annunciation, yet their very solidity and the openness to the viewer suggests the simultaneous separation and unity of the human and divine worlds. Gabriel's index finger on his right hand points at Mary while his left hand is slightly raised, his fingers pointing upward. Mary, with her head inclining slightly toward him and her hands crossed on her breast, assumes the pose appropriate to receiving the Word of God. As Argon observes, "every line in the Virgin's figure is galvanized and taut, as she starts from her absorption in the prayer book on her knee." The delicacy with which these figures are profiled within the archways makes them intriguing, integral parts of a spiritual allegory.

In 1436, the Dominicans of Fiesole took up residence in St. Mark's Convent in Florence. Their protector, Cosimo de' Medici (1389-1464), the first of his noble family to rule Florence, made it possible for Fra Angelico to supervise the preparation of the frescoes of the building. One of the most ambitious projects was *The Presentation in the Temple*, a work renowned for its deeply receding perspective and its portrayal of interior lighting. As many critics have pointed out, the color schemes and lighting of Fra Angelico's paintings and frescoes account for much of his success, for they reveal his intense concern with natural and artificial environments, and the contrast between nature and architecture. The presentation of the Christ child, for example, is depicted in a scene of semidarkness. In three panels—the largest of which is set off by two archways with pillars—the artist assembles three figures in the foreground that emit the most light and that are naturally set apart from the dim interior. Slightly behind Jesus, Joseph and Mary are two votaries, a male and female, emerging from the archways and entering the center panel in prayerful and respectful poses. This arrangement of space was at the service of Fra Angelico's effort to show how God had proportioned the world, with the sight lines of the painting converging on the Christ child.

Other works, such as *Christ on the Cross Adored by Saint Dominic*, *The Crucifixion*, *Christ Scorned*, and *The Transfiguration*, all of which were completed after 1437, suggest the artist's growing concern with spiritual insight. They evince the effort of a devout man bent on creating objects of meditation. These paintings appeared in the Dominicans' cells, and they represent (much more than Fra Angelico's earlier work) an intimate concern with the relation of the individual soul to its Maker. There is, for example, Saint Dominic's contracted brows and the tightness of his jaw and pursed lips as he devoutly gazes upward at Christ, whose blood streams down the Cross. Saint Dominic is kneeling at the base of the Cross, his hands gripping it as

though to steady himself or to look directly at Jesus. This is the study of a man undergoing the agony of his own faith.

In painting after painting in the last ten years of his life, Fra Angelico concentrated on Christ as the very light of human life. In *The Transfiguration*, Jesus is depicted in his threefold aspect as martyr, creator, and savior. Enclosed in an oval light, with his arms outstretched and level with his shoulders, his hands, palms open, emerge from the light in benediction of the prophets and saints encircling him with expressions of supplication, yearning, thanksgiving, and contemplation. In *The Transfiguration*, the artist invokes the whole community of faith.

Summary

In 1445, Pope Eugenius IV called Fra Angelico to Rome to design the Cappella del Sacramento in the Vatican. Although he accepted other commissions in the late 1440's, his greatest work was accomplished in Rome during his final years with his rendering of episodes from the lives of Saints Stephen and

Lawrence, some of which was undoubtedly completed by his pupils. In 1449, Nicholas V was finally successful in healing the breach in the Catholic church known as the Schism, and that probably accounts, in part, for the themes of Fra Angelico's frescoes, which emphasized the unity of the religious community and the renewal of the faithful.

Although Fra Angelico continued to paint after his years in Rome, his return to Florence in 1449 as the Prior of San Marco evidently meant that he had much less time for his art. None of the works from his very last period of creativity amplifies in any significant respect the achievement of his mature years. He never painted a subject that was not religious. All of his work was suffused with the Humanism of the Renaissance. His religious figures are vibrantly alive with his age's growing interest in the human personality. An innovator in art, Fra Angelico sought to adapt the latest advances in painting to a depiction of the greatest spiritual subjects. The faith he professed had to be palpable and demonstrable, in vivid color and in space that had a sculptural clarity of form and depth. His Christianity took the shape of an art that made a union of seeing and believing and put religion in a realm of the senses that every human being could experience.

Bibliography

Argan, Giulio Carlo. *Fra Angelico; Biographical and Critical Study.* Lausanne, Switzerland: Skira, 1955. A biographical and critical study that skillfully places the artist not only in his times but also in the aesthetic traditions that influenced his work. Includes close analysis of several paintings, color plates, bibliography, index, and biographical notices for historical figures mentioned in the text. Somewhat difficult to follow for students not familiar with art terms.

Didi-Huberman, Georges. *Fra Angelico: Dissemblance and Figuration.* Translated by Jane Marie Todd. Chicago: University of Chicago Press, 1995. Fra Angelico, a Florentine painter who took Dominican vows, considered his work to be a theological project. Here, the author explores Fra Angelico's use of color to signal approaching visibility, of marble to recall Christ's tomb, and of paint drippings to simulate holy anointing. Didi-Huberman shows how the painter employed emptiness, visual transformation, and displacement to give form to the mystery of faith.

Douglas, Langton. *Fra Angelico.* London: Bell, 1902. Still informative as a general treatment of the artist's life and career. Douglas examines Fra Angelico's work, his influence on subsequent painting, and his use of architectural forms. The critic maintains a careful discussion of the differences between Fra Angelico's early and late work. Seventy-three plates, a bibliography, and an index of the artist's work, as well as a general index, make this a study worth consulting.

Hausenstein, Wilhelm. *Fra Angelico.* London: Methuen, and New York: Dutton, 1928. Useful primarily for discussions of individual paintings, although the criticism is sometimes marred by an excessively impressionistic and speculative style. Hausenstein often writes as an enthusiastic, not a discerning commentator. A list of sixty-four plates is included but no table of contents.

Hood, William. *Fra Angelico at San Marco.* New Haven, Conn.: Yale University Press, 1993. A stunning volume including 140 black-and-white and 140 color illustrations celebrating Fra Angelico at the convent of San Marco. Published with the assistance of the Getty Grant program.

LeClerc, André. *Fra Angelico.* London and New York: Hyperion Press, 1949. Concise introduction to the artist's importance, including a brief biography and a survey of his work. There is not much critical analysis of the painting, but the color plates present a comprehensive view of Fra Angelico's opus. Should be consulted for a clear, quick, summary of the artist's significance.

Phillemore, Catherine Mary. *Fra Angelico.* London: Sampson Low, Marston, Searle and Rivington, and New York: Scribner, 1881. Draws directly on late nineteenth century Italian scholarship on the early period of the Italian Renaissance. The study begins with a discussion of the precursors of Fra Angelico, then treats him in the context of Florentine oil painters and goldsmiths and Florentine artists in Rome. Useful index; illustrations in black and white.

Pope-Hennessy, John. *Fra Angelico.* Ithaca, N.Y.: Cornell University Press, and London: Phaidon Press, 1974. A systematic study of the artist's life, early works, panel painting and frescoes, period in Rome, and late works. Includes a catalog of works attributed to Fra Angelico. The index and black-and-white and color plates are presented with impeccable scholarship drawing on sources from both the artist's period and this century.

Schottmüller, Frida. *The Work of Fra Angelico Da Fiesole.* New York: Brentanos, 1921. A biographical introduction situates the artist's life and work in the context of the Middle Ages, the Renaissance, and Western art generally. Especially valuable for a discussion of Fra Angelico's contemporaries. Contains 327 black-and-white plates.

Carl Rollyson and Lisa Paddock

LUDOVICO ARIOSTO

Born: September 8, 1474; Reggio Emilia
Died: July 6, 1533; Ferrara
Area of Achievement: Literature
Contribution: Ariosto, although an accomplished Latin poet, made vernacular Italian the established language for serious poetry from lyrics and satires to drama and the epic.

Early Life

The life and works of Ludovico Ariosto, like those of his administrator-soldier father, are closely bound to the house of Este, the Dukes of Ferrara. In spite of the instability created by the almost-constant struggles between this city-kingdom and other rival city-states, the Estensi court in Ferrara was one of the finest in Renaissance Europe. It supported an army, a university, jousts and hunts, and many artists. Architects, painters, sculptors, musicians, and poets were an everyday presence in the life of this court, which was located on the main pilgrimage and trade routes of Spain, France, and Italian city-states such as Venice and Bologna. The young Ariosto was introduced to this center of gracious living in 1485, when his father, Niccol, after commanding citadels surrounding Ferrara for twelve years, was recalled. Ariosto had been born in Reggio, one such vast citadel, in 1474, the first of ten children.

Ariosto's love of literature only became a problem when Count Niccol, his father, enrolled him in the five-year law curriculum at the university about 1489. He completed slightly more than two uncongenial years toward his doctorate of law, while working with the court theater in his spare time, before his father relented and allowed him to study classical poetry in about 1494. Gregorio da Spoleto, who also taught the sons of the Strozzi and Este families, was a gifted and devoted teacher. Within one and a half years, Ludovico was the prize student, giving recitations at court and composing humorous poems about student life as well as lyrics and eclogues in Latin. It was not until 1503-1505, under Pietro Bembo, that Ariosto started composing serious poetry in the vernacular.

Ariosto's devotion to such work, however, was interrupted by family financial problems in 1498. That year, to lessen problems occasioned by his father's fall from ducal grace, Ariosto entered the service of Ercole I d'Este. Two years later, Niccol died, leaving Ariosto head of the family, with four younger brothers to educate and five sisters to support until their marriages, with only meager income from properties surrounding Ferrara. Duke Ercole appointed him to a more lucrative position as captain of a garrison in 1502. The next year, however, the last of his uncles died and Ariosto was forced to return to Ferrara to look after his family. He was then given a position in the household of Ercole's son, Cardinal Ippolito d'Este, which he kept until 1517. Ippolito's household, rather than being churchly, rivaled his father's and his brother Alfonso's in all aspects—art, women, hunting, feasting, and battling. Services demanded by a courtier might range from overseeing feasts to accompanying Ippolito on diplomatic or military missions. Ariosto's health declined, and stomach disorders, which would plague him all of his life, began.

Life's Work

The first written evidence of an inner conflict between Ariosto's art and his courtier occupation is found in two poems written at about the same time. One was in praise of Ippolito's purity and chastity, and the second was an epithalamium for Lucrezia Borgia, already twice married. These poems helped establish his position as the court poet and are, perhaps, the first evidence of what was to become his dominant tone as a poet—irony. His burdens were not lightened by the birth of his first illegitimate son, Giambattista, after a brief liaison, probably with a servant. It is also possible that during this time, in order to increase his income, he took minor Holy Orders, but he steadfastly refused the hypocrisy of the lucrative benefices of full priesthood. By 1507, his growing reputation as a poet relieved him from some of the least congenial aspects of his service. That year, he was sent to Ippolito's sister's court in Mantua to convey a poem celebrating the birth of Princess Isabella's first son. Isabella and her court welcomed him and especially admired a work in progress he read to them, a work all scholars agree must have been the first draft of the *Orlando furioso* (1516, 1521, 1532; English translation, 1591).

During the time between this visit and the poem's publication, Ariosto's time was doubly occupied. At court, he was in charge of many theatrical productions. In 1508, his own comedy, *La cassaria* (*The Coffer*, 1975), was elaborately produced and popularly received for *Carnivale*. He followed with another success, *I suppositi* (*The Pretenders*, 1566), in 1509, and prepared *Il negromante* (*The Necromancer*, 1975) for *Carnivale* in 1510, although its production was stopped because of the precarious political and military concerns of the city. Violence plagued Ferrara. In 1508, Ariosto's best friend, Ercole Strozzi, was assassinated, supposedly by Alfonso's men. Ariosto himself was mediating between Ferrara and the Papacy in Rome and France, with whom Ferrara had allied itself between 1507 and 1509, attempting to reassure each faction. He was on such a mission when Pope Julius' troops attacked Ferrara, and Alfonso was excommunicated. He rejoined Ippolito the next year, in time to witness the sacking of Ravenna in 1512. Later that year, when an attempted reconciliation between Alfonso and the pope suddenly failed, he accompanied Alfonso in a dangerous escape from Rome to Florence. In between, he worked on *Orlando furioso*. Probably in Florence, in 1513, he fell in love with a married woman, Alessandra Strozzi-Benucci.

Ariosto continued to travel on diplomatic missions for Ippolito and Alfonso, finding time to write between the assignments. Somehow, the first forty cantos of *Orlando furioso* were completed in 1515, the same year that Alessandra's husband died. Still, the couple did not marry. *Orlando furioso* was published in 1516, and all two thousand copies of the first edition sold within five years, making it the first best-seller of the Renaissance. Ariosto became famous throughout Europe.

His means of support still came primarily from his service at court. When Ippolito, who was also Primate of Hungary and Bishop of Buda, decided to move his court to Hungary in 1517, Ariosto chose to stay in Ferrara. Ippolito agreed but dismissed Ariosto from his services. Yet Alfonso almost immediately took Ariosto into service at his court in Ferrara at a better salary.

For the next three years, Ariosto's life was quite pleasant. He had time to finish and rewrite one of his earlier dramas, *The Necromancer*. He wrote his first three satires and started revising *Orlando furioso*. Its second edition was published in 1521, to be followed by multiple editions in the next seven years. By 1519, however, Ferrara was again rumored to be the target of a papal invasion.

Renewal of warfare drained Ferrara's resources and forced Alfonso to suspend pay to the professors and to many artists, including Ariosto. By

1522, Ariosto was forced to accept a post as commissioner of the Garfagnana district, which was controlled by Alfonso. He found himself temperamentally unsuited to deliver the severe punishment perhaps needed to establish peace and law in the area. Ariosto found the post beyond his powers and felt exiled rather than rewarded. When offered an ambassadorship to the court of Clement VII, he refused it and returned to his beloved Ferrara and Alessandra in June, 1525.

Finally, Ariosto had the leisure and enough money to live as he wished. Between 1526 and 1528, he composed *Cinque canti*, which was published posthumously in 1545. In 1528, the people of Ferrara elected him to be Judge of the Twelve Sages. Also in 1528, he was appointed to be director of the court theater, which Alfonso wanted restored to its former glory after the disruptions of the wars. Not only did Ariosto supervise construction of sets and productions but also he had a chance to revise his own dramatic works to fit his newer ideas of dramatic style. *La Lena* (1529; *Lena*, 1975) and a new version of *The Coffer* were both performed.

His prestige as a diplomat was the highest, and he was asked to make a few visits to Florence, Venice, and Mantua for Alfonso. Meanwhile, he worked on his final version of *Orlando furioso*, which was published in October, 1532. Weeks later, he was in Mantua with Alfonso to welcome Charles V, the Holy Roman Emperor, and give him a presentation copy. Most biographers also believe that Ariosto and Alessandra were secretly married between 1526 and 1530, but that they continued to live separately, perhaps to keep income from minor benefices conferred by Ippolito. By December, 1532, his lifelong stomach problems and later chest pains had taken their toll. Ariosto fell severely ill and died on July 6, 1533. Alessandra and his second son, Virginio, were by his bedside. He was buried by the monks of San Benedetto at their church, quietly, as he desired. His body was later entombed in the Biblioteca Ariostea of Ferrara beneath a marble tomb supplied by Napoleon.

Summary

Ludovico Ariosto is a prime example of the Renaissance man. An outstanding poet in all forms—lyrical, satirical, dramatic, and epic—he also was always involved in the active life of the courts of Ferrara as administrator and diplomat. He was always conscientious and loyal to family, friends, and patrons. He never sought great riches or titles but only enough to support himself and his family comfortably while he pursued his writing. Ariosto became the poet for whom Dante had called, one who would embody the greatest of Italian culture in a new form fit for the greatest of Italian vernacular poetry. *Orlando furioso* was a best-seller not only in Italy but also in France and in England, where Elizabeth I ordered an English translation. The almost picaresque structure of simultaneous multiple plots, the mixture of comic and tragic material, and the persona of a semidetached narrator were inventive strokes that allowed Ariosto to examine the form and values of the dying chivalric romance tradition while deeply investigating the problems of society in general and those of human nature. The *Orlando furioso* is great poetry, great fun for the reader, and full of great wisdom about man and his world. Because of a lack of readable translations, its American readership almost disappeared. Two translations, Barbara Reynolds' (Penguin, 1977) and Guido Waldman's (Oxford University Press, 1983) have again made the text widely accessible.

Bibliography

Brand, C. P. *Ludovico Ariosto: A Preface to the Orlando Furioso*. Edinburgh, Scotland: Edinburgh University Press, 1974. An excellent overview of Ariosto's life and works. Contains full chapters on life, lyrics, satires, and dramas while concentrating on a thematic study of the *Orlando furioso*. Emphasizes the opposition of love and war. Contains brief bibliographies for each chapter and two indexes.

Croce, Benedetto. *Ariosto, Shakespeare, and Corneille*. Translated by Douglas Ainslie. London: Allen and Unwin, and New York: Holt Rinehart, 1920. An extremely influential early modern essay on *Orlando furioso*. Rebutting the traditional criticism, Croce argues that the work achieves unity through the artist's control of point of view and style, a unity which ultimately reflects the rhythm and harmony of God's creation.

Gardner, Edmund G. *The King of Court Poets: Ariosto*. London: Constable, and New York: Dutton, 1906. Gardner's full-length biography contains a wealth of material and is easy to read. He includes a social, cultural, and political background of Ariosto's life and work. Contains a dated bibliography, a useful index, and three foldout genealogies of the houses of Ariosto, Este, and Pio.

Griffin, Robert. *Ludovico Ariosto*. Boston: Twayne, 1974. Good introductory work on Ariosto, beginning with a chapter on his life and ending with a survey of criticism. Also contains chapters on lyrics, satires, dramas, and a thematic analysis of *Orlando furioso*. Argues that the unity of the poem rests on man's inability to accept the will of fortune in a world beyond his limited comprehension. Contains chronology, notes, selected bibliography with brief annotations, and two indexes.

Rodini, Robert J., and Salvatore Di Maria. *Ludovico Ariosto: An Annotated Bibliography of Criticism, 1956-1980*. Columbia: University of Missouri Press, 1984. Contains 930 entries from journals, monographs, essays in books, North American dissertations, and books. Although meant primarily for scholars, the entry synopses are excellent and can easily be skimmed. Arranged by author but also contains detailed subject index and an index by works treated.

Sims, James H. "Orlando Furioso in Milton: Heroic Flights and True Heroines." *Comparative Literature* 49 (spring, 1997): 128. The author discusses the connections between characters and events in John Milton's biblical epics and the poem "Orlando Furioso" by Ariosto. Sims has a clear understanding and appreciation of the romanticism in Ariosto's work.

Wiggins, Peter De Sa. *Figures in Ariosto's Tapestry: Character and Design in the "Orlando Furioso."* Baltimore: Johns Hopkins University Press, 1986. Agreeing with Galileo's early comments on the psychological consistency of Ariosto's characters and his exact knowledge of human nature, Wiggins suggests that their complex inner lives are universal human types. This invisible interior world, at odds with an exterior world of folly and depravity, is a major theme of the work. Excellent index and notes for each chapter.

———. *The Satires of Ludovico Ariosto: A Renaissance Autobiography.* Athens: Ohio University Press, 1976. A bilingual text, using the Italian original edited by Cesare Segre with Wiggins' clear prose translations on the facing page. Each satire is placed in biographical and historical context with its own separate preface and notes. Argues that the narrator of the satires is an idealized poet courtier in typical situations rather than a factual mirror of Ariosto himself. Suggests that the satires share similarities with *Orlando furioso*: the theme of illusion and reality, the ironic humor, and the use of a dramatic persona as narrator.

Ann E. Reynolds

BĀBUR
Zahīr-ud-Dīn Muhammad

Born: February 14, 1483; Fergana
Died: December 26, 1530; Āgra, India
Areas of Achievement: The military and government
Contribution: Bābur, the first of the Mughal rulers in India, spread the Mughal Empire over most of northern India. He was a wise and kind king whose memoirs have revealed much about his life.

Early Life

Bābur, whose name is a Mongol word meaning tiger, was born in Fergana (modern Afghanistan), on February 14, 1483. A descendant of Genghis Khan and Tamerlane, Bābur became King of Fergana in 1494 at the age of eleven, when his father, 'Umar Shaykh Mīrzā, died. Along with the kingdom, Bābur inherited his father's struggles with his cousins for the kingdom of Transoxiana with its capital Samarkand. Bābur spent the first three years of his reign fighting his cousin Faisunqur, from whom he captured Samarkand in 1497 after a siege of seven months; yet he was soon forced to relinquish the city. Between 1498 and 1499, Bābur married, and he divided Fergana with his brother. In 1501, Bābur once again attempted to conquer Samarkand. Between April and May of 1501, Bābur suffered a defeat at Sar-i-Pul and retreated to Samarkand. After taking the city by surprise, Bābur and the inhabitants of Samarkand tried to repel the forces of Shaybānī Khān, chief of the Uzbeks, who had agreed to help Baisunqur Mīrzā fight his cousin, Bābur. Bābur was able to hold off Shaybānī Khān's men for four months but was finally forced to surrender the city. Bābur was released from his captivity, but only after he had agreed to give his sister's hand in marriage to Uzbek Khan.

Once free, Bābur spent the next three years in hiding at Tashkent, which had been given to him by his uncle, Sultan Mahmud Khan. Even though Bābur's uncle furnished him with a command of one thousand men, Bābur was defeated in 1503 at Arciyan by Tanbal, who had appealed to Shaybānī Khān for assistance. Having lost Fergana, Bābur spent the next year as a nomad in the remote territories of Sukh and Hushyar. In June, 1504, Bābur and his brother formed another army, composed of refugees from the Uzbeks, and secured Kabul, from which he would maintain himself until 1525. While at Kabul, Bābur came under the influence of Persian culture, traces of which can be found in his poetry.

From Kabul, Bābur conducted unsuccessful raids in central Asia and northwestern India. In January, 1505, Bābur made his expedition to Hindustan in search of badly needed supplies. Bābur, at the invitation of Husain Baiqara, who died soon afterward, marched on Herāt against Shaybānī Khān but returned to Kabul, because he was not prepared for the fierce winter. In June, 1507, Herāt surrendered to Shaybānī Khān. Meanwhile, Bābur's uncle, Muhammad Hussayn, had proclaimed Bābur's cousin Khan Mīrzā lord of Kabul in Bābur's absence.

After suppressing this rebellion by attacking the rebels without warning in the streets of Kabul, Bābur decided to gain possession of Qandahār, which was strategically important. Thus, when the Arghun princes in Qandahār asked Bābur for military assistance, he rushed to their aid. He had not traveled very far, though, before the Arghun princes changed their minds and decided to oppose Bābur. After defeating them in combat, Bābur learned that Shaybānī Khān was preparing to attack Qandahār. Instead of meeting Shaybānī Khān in combat, Bābur took a more prudent though admittedly less courageous course: He undertook his second invasion of India in 1507. During his return to Kabul, Bābur decided to change his title from *mīrzā* (prince) to *padishah* (emperor).

Three years later, Bābur conquered Samarkand for the third time by taking advantage of the political situation at the time. Shaybānī Khān's dispute with the Persian Shah Esmā'īl erupted into warfare. In 1510, Esmā'īl lured Shaybānī Khān from his refuge at Marv and slew him. As a result, the Uzbeks withdrew to Transoxiana. Elated by Esmā'īl's victory, Bābur sent Khan Mīrzā to thank him. Esmā'īl responded by returning Bābur's sister whom Bābur had given in marriage to Shaybānī Khān years before.

As a client of Esmā'īl, Bābur lost much of his popular support among the Mughals. Because Esmā'īl would not allow Bābur to break his pact, Bābur believed that the most expedient thing to do was to give lip service to the Shī'ite creed while remaining faithful to the Sunni doctrine. Years later, he was to prove the sincerity of his beliefs by writing a lengthy religious poem.

In 1511, Bābur once again invaded Samarkand and was pronounced king in 1511. Yet Bābur's reign as ruler of Samarkand proved to be short-lived. The Uzbeks, who were determined to remain in Transoxiana, encountered and defeated Bābur's forces at Kul-i-Malik. Bābur retreated to Hisar. He managed to solidify his hold on Badakhshān by placing his cousin, Khan Mīrzā, on the throne, but he relinquished all hope of reascending the throne of Samarkand. Instead, he occupied himself between 1515 and 1518 by waging wars in every direction in order to force the mountain dwellers of Kabul and Ghazni to fear and respect him.

Life's Work

The second phase of Bābur's career—his invasion and conquest of Hindustan—began only after he had finally relinquished his boyhood dream of conquering Samarkand. In a sense, Bābur decided to assimilate into his empire people who were not of Indo-Aryan stock because he considered the Hindu Kush to be his lawful heritage, passed down to him from his ancestor Tamerlane, who had established his rule in all the country between the Oxus and the Indus on his passage to India. One could also say that Bābur compensated for his failure to conquer Samarkand by turning his attention toward India. While it is true that Bābur prepared the way for the Mughal Empire in India, his forays into India were really nothing more than a military preparation for the more permanent rule that would be established years later by his grandson.

Before Bābur could become lord of India, he had to dethrone the five Muslim and two pagan rulers who governed Hindustan. Bābur initiated this campaign in 1519, when he cemented an alliance with the Yusufzais by marrying the daughter of one of their chiefs. He concluded what he considered to be his first expedition into Hindustan by conquering Bhera but winning the hearts of its occupants by sparing their lives.

Owing to the dearth of details in Bābur's memoirs concerning the second, third, and fourth expeditions, it is with his fifth expedition that the history of Bābur's Hindustani campaigns continues. Bābur agreed to assist Dawlat Khān Lodī in deposing Lodī's kinsman, who ruled most of northern Hindustan. In return for Dawlat Khān Lodī's promise to regard Bābur as his sovereign, Bābur utterly defeated the army of Ibrāhīm Lodī near Lahore, which Bābur claimed for his own. This impetuous decision on Bābur's part brought his alliance with Dawlat Khān Lodī to an abrupt end. Bābur quickly formed another alliance with 'Ālam Khān, the uncle of Ibrāhīm Lodī, who offered to cede Lahore to Bābur if Bābur helped him conquer Delhi. Bābur hoped that by substituting 'Ālam Khān for Ibrāhīm Lodī, he would not only be given the legitimate right to Lahore but also have control over 'Ālam Khān, who was old and feeble. Thus, Bābur ordered his soldiers to assist 'Ālam Khān in the assault on Delhi, but he decided that his presence was more sorely needed at Balkh, which Esmā'īl was defending against the Uzbeks. Dawlat Khān Lodī then seized the opportunity to recover Lahore by offering to help 'Ālam Khān conquer Delhi. After failing to take Delhi, Dawlat Khān Lodī's army scattered in disorder, so he and his son retreated to the fortress of Milwat, where they surrendered. Dawlat Khān Lodī died while being taken to the prison at Bhera.

Having secured Lahore, Bābur began his campaign to conquer Delhi. Aware of the political advantages of having the loyalty of an Afghan prince, Bābur gave 'Ālam Khān a command at Panipat and Khanua. Bābur then marched on Delhi with his eighteen-year-old son, Humāyūn, who led the forces that defeated the armies of one of Ibrahīm Lodī's emirs. Taking a defensive position at Panipat, Bābur's Mughals utterly defeated the vastly superior numbers of Afghan forces by flanking them with arrows and bombarding them with gunfire from the front. At the battle's end, Ibrāhīm Lodī was dead, and Bābur had reached his greatest goal: the conquest of northern India. As soon as he made his grand entrance into Delhi, he won the favor of the people by preventing his soldiers from looting and by taking the wives and children of the Rajah of Gwalior under his protection. On April 27, 1526, a week after his arrival at Delhi, Bābur was proclaimed Emperor of Hindustan in the Grand Mosque.

The founding of Bābur's vast empire in Hindustan, which began with the capture of Lahore in 1524, was completed in six years. With his victory at Panipat, most of the Afghan chiefs united under Bābur's rule. Bābur most likely restricted his conquests to northern India because of his reluctance to offend Esmā'īl by attacking Persian territory.

Bābur's death cannot be attributed to only one cause. From boyhood, he had suffered from a troublesome lesion, and throughout his adult life he was stricken with bouts of marsh fever. His body was further weakened by his intemperate ways, particularly his fondness for wine. He also became seriously ill as the result of an attempted poisoning by the mother of Ibrāhīm Lodī. His eventual death is enshrouded in mystery and legend. In the year 1530, when Bābur's son Humāyūn was attacked with fever, Bābur prayed that God would accept his life in exchange for that of his son. Coincidentally, Bābur was taken ill as his son slowly recovered, and he died three months later in Āgra on December 26, 1530. Several years later, his body was moved to its present location at Kabul.

Summary

Bābur is a prime example of a class of political entrepreneurs who vied with other seminomadic rulers from central Asia for revenues from the herdsmen and territory. Like his rivals and enemies, Bābur's kingdom was linked and sometimes divided by the loyalties of clan and family, not by treaties of national states. He was also typical of the rulers of that time in the savagery he displayed during battle.

Even though Bābur was born to the ruling class, he maintained and increased his kingdom as a result of his own adaptability and courage. He was a resourceful general who learned about musketry and artillery from the Uzbeks; he then applied these methods with great success against the lords of Hindustan. Thus, he became one of the first military commanders in Asia to realize the full potential of artillery. Bābur was a skillful diplomat, who prepared Hindustan for conquest by playing the emirs of Ibrāhīm Lodī against one other. He also performed the seemingly impossible task of molding an array of fiercely independent and competitive bands of Mongols into a nation by employing a prudent blend of force and kindness. In addition, he displayed moral courage as he risked the disapproval of other Sunni Muslims in his decision to appease Esmā'īl by adopting the Qizilbash headdress for himself and his soldiers. In addition, Bābur's custom of showing mercy to his defeated enemies endeared him to the people he conquered. While Bābur inherited some of the barbaric ways of the descendants of Tamerlane, he differed from most of the Mongol rulers of the sixteenth century in his love of beauty. An accomplished poet and diarist, Bābur composed works which rank with the best literature written at that time.

Bibliography

Bābur. *The* Bāburnāma*: Memoirs of Babur, Prince and Emperor.* Edited, translated, and annotated by Wheeler M. Thackston. Washington, D.C.: Smithsonian Institution, 1996; Oxford: Oxford University Press, 1997. Bābur left behind a memoir of his life and times—the central document most often quoted by historians and scholars of Mughal India. Thackston has provided a sparkling new translation of this intimate and truthful record in an exquisitely illustrated and produced edition that faithfully preserves the spirit and beauty of the original work. It is not only an extraordinarily detailed picture of life in Central Asia and India during the late fifteenth and early sixteenth centuries, but also the first real autobiography in Islamic literature.

Bābur. *The Bāburnāma.* Translated by Annette Susannah Beveridge. 2 vols. London: Luzac, 1921. An exciting and revealing firsthand history of Bābur's life and times in his own words. This is the primary source for most of the biographies that have followed.

Brown, F. Yeats. *Pageant of India.* Philadelphia: Macrae Smith, 1942. A brief biographical sketch of Bābur's life, heavily laced with quotations from Bābur's memoirs. Provides interesting anecdotes, especially regarding the assassination attempt by the mother of Ibrāhām Lodī.

Burn, Richard, ed. *The Cambridge History of India.* Vol. 4, *The Mughal Period.* Cambridge: Cambridge University Press, and New York: Macmillan, 1937. Chapter 1 is an excellent summation of Bābur's life. Although the chapter emphasizes his military campaigns, it also provides historical background, sketching the personalities who had an important influence on Bābur's life.

Dale, Stephen F. "The Poetry and Autobiography of the Babur-nama." *Journal of Asian Studies* 55 (August, 1996): 635. Dale explores the art and life of Bābur based on the prose memoir *Bāburnāma.*

Grenard, Fernand. *Baber: First of the Moguls.* New York: McBride, 1930; London: Lutterworth, 1931. Based entirely on Bābur's memoirs, this is a biased but highly readable account of his life. The fanciful story line is enhanced by the reproduction of sixteenth century paintings.

Lewis, B. "Bābur." In *Encyclopaedia of Islam,* edited by B. Lewis, Ch. Pellat, and J. Schacht. Leiden: Brill, 1959. This concise treatment of Bābur's life concentrates almost exclusively on his military conquests, paying little attention to his personal life.

Williams, L. F. Rushbrook. *An Empire Builder of the Sixteenth Century.* London and New York: Longman, 1918. A standard biography covering Bābur's entire life. Beautifully illustrated with paintings from the period. The book refrains from romanticizing Bābur's life, opting for the objective approach instead. Recommended for the serious student of Bābur's life and of this period of Mughal history.

Alan Brown

FRANCIS BACON

Born: January 22, 1561; London, England
Died: April 9, 1626; London, England
Areas of Achievement: Philosophy, science, and politics
Contribution: The first to use English instead of Latin for a philosophical treatise with his *The Two Bookes of Francis Bacon of the Proficience and Advancement of Learning Divine and Humane*, Bacon is credited with the formulation of modern scientific thought. His *Essayes* is widely admired for its worldly witticism and has become a classic of the form.

Early Life

Francis Bacon was born January 22, 1561, at York House in London, to Sir Nicholas Bacon, Lord Keeper of the Seal of England, and his second wife, née Ann Cooke, who was related to nobility through her sister, the wife of Sir William Cecil, the later Lord Treasurer Burghley. In 1573, at the age of twelve, Bacon entered Trinity College, Cambridge, which he left in 1576 for Gray's Inn, thus following in his father's steps and beginning a legal career.

After a brief visit to the French court in the entourage of Sir Amias Paulet from 1576 until his father's death in 1579, Francis Bacon stayed with the Inn and was called to the bar in 1582, two years before he began to complement his legal work with an ambitiously undertaken political career that commenced with his membership in Parliament.

After advancement to the position of Queen's Counsel in 1589, his career stalled under Elizabeth I, whom he seemed to have offended in a parliamentary debate regarding the implementation of regal subsidiaries in 1593; his enemies at court used the opportunity to bar his way to promotion, seeing in Bacon (not wholly unjustly) not only an ambitious, prolific writer of political advice but also an unscrupulous seeker of preferment. Again, on the personal level, his friendship with the young Earl of Essex did not bring him hoped-for political gain; in 1601, after Essex's ill-considered rebellion against the queen, Bacon's position required him to partake in the prosecution of his former friend.

Whereas *An Advertisement Touching the Controversies of the Church of England* (1589) had brought Bacon political advancement, his later work of political advice did not professionally benefit him. During a long period of arrested political development until Elizabeth I's death, Bacon showed himself stubborn and inclined to use the common practice of patronage and favoritism to lobby for a higher position. In his own office, he became a rather successful mediator of conflicts and tried hard but finally inefficiently to smooth the waves after Essex's insubordination preceding his open revolt against the queen.

A later painting shows Bacon as a tall, bearded officer wearing his regalia and insignia proudly; the picture suggests the reserved, somewhat unemotional yet nevertheless personally sensitive character which his later biographers have asserted on the basis of accounts from Bacon's chaplain and secretary William Rawley. At forty-five, he married Alice Barnham, daughter of a London alderman, who survived him; they had no children.

Life's Work

His long period of relative political inactivity under Elizabeth I gave Bacon time to write the first ten of his Essayes, which saw publication in 1597, and again, because of their popularity, in 1612 and in 1625, both times with significant enlargements which brought the total number to fifty-eight. A master of the essay form, which he helped to forge, Bacon here looks at men and their government realistically, free of passionate idealism and zeal for the betterment of man. What his critics have called his "Machiavellian" and "emotionless" coldness nevertheless facilitated a witty discourse on the world as it really is, and not as it should be in the eyes of reformers. With this was coupled political advice, as in "On Dissimulation" or "On Plantations," against the shortsightedness, greed, and abuses of his time.

The Twoo Bookes of Francis Bacon of the Proficience and Advancement of Learning Divine and Humane (1605) which he later enlarged into the Latin version *De Augmentis Scientiarum* (1623), represents his first step toward the formulation of a new method for looking at the natural world through the eyes of the experimenting and hypothesizing scientist who has purged his vision of religious allegory or Platonic metaphysics or Aristotelian dialectics.

Bacon's political fortunes changed in the reign of James I, which saw his ascension from his knighthood in 1603 through the office of attorney general (1613) to the high position of Lord Keeper in 1617, before he was made Lord Chancellor and Baron Verulam and ultimately created Viscount St. Albans in 1621, at the age of sixty.

During these years of success, Bacon wrote the *Magna Instauratio* (1620, "great instauration"), the planned preface, never completed, for six different works intended to describe a restoration of human knowledge; as is, it is a powerful model for radical change in the pattern of Western scientific thought, characterized by Bacon's clear sense of ordering and classification. *Novum Organum*, published in the same year, contains Bacon's argument for a "new logic," the discovery of a finite number of "natures" or "forms" lying at the base of the natural world, and an exhaustive description of natural history.

After he had reached the zenith of his power, Bacon's fall came when old enemies charged him with bribery; he admitted to the charges since he had indeed not only taken gifts from suitors, which was more generally acceptable, but also had accepted donations from individuals whose cases were pending with him as their judge (and in which he often decided against them despite the offerings given). Bacon resigned from his office, was fined forty thousand pounds, was briefly imprisoned in the Tower of London, and was banished from the court. He made slow progress at rehabilitation, but at the time of his death in the house of Sir Arundel in 1626, he had not yet received full royal pardon from the new king Charles II.

Summary

Although his public fall from grace as a result of misconduct in office linked Francis Bacon to his literary model Seneca, who showed similar excellence in thought and corruption in public life, the British naturalist and statesman must be remembered for his new, practical approach toward the natural environment; his proposed outlook at science bears the seeds of modern scientific thought.

In his last, unfinished work, *New Atlantis*, posthumously published in 1627, Bacon argues that there is no conflict between the free pursuit of scientific exploration and the dogmas of the Christian religion. He sums up the ancient Hebrew view of the natural world as there to use and explore rather than as the manifestation of sundry natural deities, and he connects this thought to the idea that scientific research is ultimately undertaken so that God (the final spiritual authority) "might have the more glory" in the "workmanship" of the scientists and men "the more fruit" in the "use" of their discoveries.

On a final note, Bacon's idea, in the utopian *New Atlantis*, for an organization dedicated to the free pursuit of all natural sciences which would collect and display its findings in central "houses," has been realized in the British Royal Society and the British Museum, two institutions which, founded in the spirit of Bacon, are thriving today.

Bibliography

Anderson, Fulton H. *Francis Bacon: His Career and His Thought*. Los Angeles: University of Southern California Press, 1962. Based on a series of lectures, his work attempts to link Bacon's philosophy with his politics and to relate his thought to contemporary problems.

———. *The Philosophy of Francis Bacon*. Chicago: University of Chicago Press, 1948. Influential book revealing Bacon's thoughts primarily through his own words. Somewhat dry and overinclusive, it makes up for the lack of critical discussion with its useful compilation of primary texts.

Bacon, Francis. *The Works, the Letters, and the Life of Francis Bacon*. Edited by James Spedding, R. L. Ellis, and D. D. Heath, 14 vols. London: Longman, 1857-1874. Includes William Rawley's *The Life of the Right Honourable Francis Bacon* (1657). Still the authoritative, standard edition of Bacon's complete work. Detailed biography with an impressive collection of primary sources such as Bacon's letters and notes. The standard against which all later works have to be judged.

Bowen, Catherine Drinker. *Francis Bacon: The Temper of a Man*. Boston: Little Brown, and London: Hamilton, 1963. Enjoyable biography which brings Bacon alive while not neglecting scholarly accuracy. Careful and perceptive; Bowen's favorable portrait forgives Bacon almost everything but his coldness toward women.

Bozeman, Theodore Dwight. *Protestants in an Age of Science: The Baconian Ideal and Antebellum American Religious Thought*. Chapel Hill: University of North Carolina Press, 1977. Traces the roots of modern fundamentalism to the antebellum Presbyterians, who used Bacon's idea to prove themselves right and all their pre-Darwinian opponents wrong. An interesting contribution to the history of ideas.

Church, R. W. *Bacon*. London: Macmillan, and New York: Harper, 1884. A nineteenth-century biography which has stayed amazingly fresh over the years. Church's readable, precise style provides an enjoyable encounter with Bacon, whose personality is emphasized.

Eiseley, Loren. *Francis Bacon and the Modern Dilemma.* Lincoln: University of Nebraska Press, 1963. Slim booklet emphasizing Bacon's achievements as a scientist; does not account for his deficient understanding of mathematics. Eiseley stresses Bacon's view of an integrated, responsible science.

Farrington, Benjamin. *The Philosophy of Francis Bacon.* Liverpool: Liverpool University Press, and Chicago: University of Chicago Press, 1964. Valuable discussion of Bacon's philosophical ideas; Farrington includes a fine translation of Bacon's minor Latin works and thus makes them accessible to a broader audience.

Fuller, Jean Overton. *Sir Francis Bacon.* London: East-West Press, 1981. Ingeniously relates events in Bacon's life to contemporaneous passages from Shakespeare's work. Lavishly produced reiteration of the generally discredited theory that Bacon was the true author of Shakespeare's oeuvre.

Maistre, Joseph de. *An Examination of the Philosophy of Bacon: Wherein Different Questions of Rational Philosophy Are Treated.* Translated and edited by Richard A. Lebrun. Montreal: McGill-Queen's University Press, 1998. This book is one of Joseph de Maistre's most important works. Lebrun's annotated translation includes de Maistre's complete text and an introduction that places the work in context. It also provides a critical exposition and assessment of de Maistre's criticisms of Bacon, biographical notes on persons cited or mentioned by de Maistre, and a bibliography. Differences between de Maistre's manuscript and the printed text, first published fifteen years after the author's death, are noted; his numerous citations have been identified, verified, and translated, making this the only authoritative and fully accurate edition of the work in either French or English.

Rossi, Paolo. *Francis Bacon: From Magic to Science.* Translated by Sacha Rabinovitch. London: Routledge, and Chicago: University of Chicago Press, 1968. Examines the European magical and alchemical tradition of science which Bacon rejected. Important bibliography.

Solomon, Julie Robin. *Objectivity in the Making: Francis Bacon and the Politics of Inquiry.* Baltimore: Johns Hopkins University Press, 1998. In any discussion of science or culture, Bacon figures prominently when assessing the capacity for objective analysis. In this work, Solomon shows how "disinterestedness" became a dominant principle of modern intellectual thought by examining Bacon's notion of scientific self-distancing against the background of early modern political ideology, socioeconomic behavior, and traditions of learning.

Reinhart Lutz

VASCO NÚÑEZ DE BALBOA

Born: 1475; Jeres de los Caballeros, Estremadura Province, Spain
Died: January, 1519; Acla, Castillo de Oro, Panama
Area of Achievement: Exploration
Contribution: Balboa was a Spanish conquistador who participated in the exploration and conquest of the Caribbean and the Central American mainland during the early sixteenth century. In 1513, he discovered the Pacific Ocean.

Early Life

Vasco Núñez de Balboa was born in 1475 in Jeres de los Caballeros in the Spanish province of Estremadura. Although part of the *hidalgo* class, Balboa's family was very poor. Thrilled by the reports of Christopher Columbus' voyages to the New World in 1492 and 1493, he drifted toward the vibrant atmosphere of Spain's port cities. He served eight years under Don Pedro Puertocarrero, Lord of Moguer, and acquired a reputation as an excellent fighter. In 1501, Balboa sailed to the New World under Don Pedro de Bastides, who discovered Barbados and sailed along the north coast of Tierra Firme (northern South America). The Bastides expedition terminated disastrously when his ships became infested with shipworms and eventually sank off the coast of Hispaniola (Haiti).

Balboa remained on Hispaniola to farm near Salvatierra, to mine for gold, and to fight Indians. He fell deeply into debt, and his creditors constantly harassed him for payments. As an Indian fighter, however, Balboa acquired great renown for his spirit and skill. Equally famous was Balboa's dog, the great "Leoncico" (little lion), that was noted for his ferocity in combat. Indeed, Leoncico was said to have been paid the equivalent of a captain's pay for his services.

Life's Work

At this time of his life (1510), Balboa was thirty-five years old, tall and well built, with red hair and blue eyes. He was charming and blessed with great energy and stamina. His presence on Hispaniola, however, had become untenable because of his creditors. Thus, in September, 1510, learning of an expedition bound for Tierra Firme under Martín Fernández de Enciso, Balboa arranged to have both himself and Leoncico smuggled on board in a large barrel. Once safely beyond Hispaniola, Balboa presented himself to an astonished and angry Enciso, who reluctantly allowed him to remain with the expedition.

Balboa became the key member of an extraordinary adventure in Latin American colonial history. In 1507, King Ferdinand V of Spain had given grants and powers to Diego de Nicuesa and Alonzo de Ojeda to explore and settle areas of Tierra Firme. Enciso was a lawyer and Ojeda's second-in-command, and he was expected to meet Ojeda at San Sebastian with supplies and reinforcements. At San Sebastian, Enciso learned that Ojeda, mortally wounded, had returned to Hispaniola, leaving behind forty-one near-starved survivors under Francisco Pizarro, later of Peruvian fame. San Sebastian was too difficult to hold in the face of Indian hostility, and Balboa suggested that they move to a more defensible site across the Bay of Urabá. Here, on the bank of the Darién River, Enciso established Santa María la Antigua del Darién, the first permanent settlement on the mainland.

Thereafter, Balboa's life was mired in political intrigue at Darién and the royal court. Enciso proved to be an arbitrary and unpopular leader, and settlers rallied behind the charismatic Balboa, who overthrew the petty tyrant. By spring, 1511, a three-way power struggle was under way. The Balboa-Enciso fight was complicated by the claims of Diego de Nicuesa, in whose grant Darién was mistakenly located. Nicuesa, however, was stranded and starving at Nombre de Dios. When supplies and news of the Darién colony arrived, he recovered and sought to impose his authority over the trespassers. Balboa led the resistance and sent Nicuesa away on a worm-infested vessel. Nicuesa was never seen alive again.

Balboa now moved aggressively on many fronts. He consolidated his authority over Darién and banished Enciso. He rescued the remaining survivors at Nombre de Dios, compelled settlers to grow crops and build homes, and pushed Spanish power into the interior. During these *entradas*, Balboa heard rumors of a great ocean to the south and of a great civilization in Peru. He also brought Franciscan priests to convert and baptize the Indians and to make them loyal subjects of the king.

Balboa discussed these events and other matters in an extraordinary letter to Ferdinand V in January, 1513. He provided a detailed description of the land and climate, and he defended himself against charges of usurpation of power and mistreatment

Balboa instructs the natives to set up a cross on the shores of the Pacific Ocean

of Indians. He noted the discoveries that he made, particularly gold mines, and rumors that a vast sea existed to the south. If he had only one thousand men, he wrote, he would bring the South Sea and all the gold mines under the dominion of the king.

In June, 1513, Balboa received contradictory news from Spain. He was made captain and interim governor of Tierra Firme, but he received stunning news that a new governor would soon replace him and that he would face arrest and trial for Nicuesa's death. Also, unknown to Balboa, Ferdinand sent a secret agent, Don Pedro de Arbolancha, to investigate affairs in Darién. Balboa's successor proved to be Don Pedro Arias Dávila (Pedrarias), an elderly, but iron-willed and cruel, military man. He left Apin in April, 1514, carrying *el requerimiento* (the requirement), a document designed to justify war with—and hegemony over—the natives.

To save himself, Balboa decided to find the South Sea. He left Darién on September 1, 1513, with 190 men. It was a grueling and arduous ordeal. On September 25 or 27, 1513, however, Balboa reached the crest of a mountain and sighted the South Sea. He promptly made a formal act of possession in the name of Ferdinand V. On September 29, 1513, he reached the ocean's shore at the Gulf of San Miguel. The party remained in the area for several weeks, found pearl beds, and learned more about the Inca civilization to the south. On November 3, 1513, they began their return to Darién, which was accomplished without major incident on January 19, 1514. Among the cheering throng was the secret agent, Arbolancha, who determined that he would endorse Balboa's continued rule over the settlement.

Events occurred too rapidly, however, for Balboa to rescue himself from his enemies. Pedrarias arrived at Darién with the crushing news that he was governor of the province, now called Castillo de Oro (golden castle). Balboa, bitterly disappointed, nevertheless sought to make the transition in leadership successful. Matters, however, soured almost immediately. Pedrarias quickly implemented his instructions to hold a two-month-long *residencia* (investigation) of Balboa's conduct. Then Darién was hit with a devastating plague, and Pedrarias' men made savage and bloody forays among nearby Indian tribes, killing, enslaving, and stealing gold, silver, and food. Pedrarias allowed these activities to continue well into 1515, undoing Balboa's earlier work to secure these tribes' friendship and loyalty.

Meanwhile, Arbolancha's report induced Ferdinand to appoint Balboa Adelantado of the coast of the South Sea and of Panama and Coiba. Although Balboa remained under Pedrarias' authority, the latter became embittered and alarmed over the former's restored reputation. Accordingly, Balboa was arrested on a charge of conspiracy to rebel against Pedrarias and was kept in a cage in the latter's home. Finally, Balboa was released on the condition that he marry Pedrarias' daughter in Spain by proxy; once Pedrarias had consolidated his position with the marriage, he allowed Balboa to go to the Pacific coast and erect a shipbuilding yard.

Summary

During subsequent years, Vasco Núñez de Balboa and Pedrarias were wary of each other. Balboa was far the more popular of the two leaders. He took the nearby Pearl Islands and seemed intent in moving south against Peru. By late 1518, Pedrarias had had enough of Balboa and ordered him to Acla, where he arrested Balboa on a charge of treason. In January, 1519, Balboa and several of his associates were beheaded, and Balboa's head was placed on a pike and put on display in Acla's plaza.

Thus died Balboa, one of the greatest conquistadores for *los reyes católicos*, a man of humble origins who possessed attributes of greatness: bravery, valor, humility, and a sense of fairness. He provided the inspired leadership that placed Spain on the mainland of Central America, setting the stage for the great conquests to the north and south. His greatest achievement was the discovery of the Pacific Ocean, which reinforced the growing realization that Columbus had discovered a great barrier to the Asian market. The temporal and spiritual power of the Spanish Crown was rarely served better in the New World.

Bibliography

Anderson, Charles G. *Vida y cartas de Vasco Núñez de Balboa*. Buenos Aires: Emece Editoriales, 1944. A biographical account and a collection of correspondence relative to Balboa's life and career. Oriented toward the specialist. No English translation accompanies the text.

Méndez Pereira, Octavio. *El Tesoro del Dabaibe*. Panama: Talleres Gráficos "Benedetti," 1934. Presents Balboa as having been fair in his treatment of the Indians. Méndez Pereira was a Panamanian diplomat and educator.

Ober, Frederick A. *Vasco Núñez de Balboa*. New York: Harper, 1906. A volume of the Heroes of American History series; a popular account of Balboa's life.

Romoli, Kathleen. *Balboa of Darién: Discoverer of the Pacific*. New York: Doubleday, 1953. The best account of the life and career of Balboa. Very readable and scholarly. Sympathetic toward Balboa while giving an objective analysis of the men who served with and under him.

Strawn, Arthur. *The Golden Adventures of Balboa: Discoverer of the Pacific*. New York: Brentano's, 1928; London: John Lane, 1929. Another useful though dated account of Balboa. Like Romoli, Strawn was a great admirer of Balboa as a warrior and as a diplomat.

Stephen P. Sayles

CHEVALIER DE BAYARD

Born: c. 1473; Chateau de Bayard, Pontcharra, France
Died: April 30, 1524; near Roasio, Italy
Area of Achievement: Military
Contribution: The ideal of chivalry, exemplified in Bayard, became a significant element in the education of young men of the upper classes.

Early Life

Pierre Terrail, lord of Bayard, was the son of Aymon Terrail and Hélène Alleman. The exact date of his birth is uncertain, but he was born sometime between 1473 and 1476. He received a rudimentary education under the eye of his uncle, Laurent Alleman, bishop of Grenoble. In 1486, he left home to serve as page at the court of Charles I, duke of Savoy, where he was expected to acquire the experience and skills of a young nobleman. That same year, he followed his master on a trip to Italy, where he observed the flowering of Renaissance culture without noticeable effect upon his medieval chivalric mind. Upon returning to Savoy in 1489, Bayard traveled with the duke to the court of Charles VIII of France, where he served the French king first as a page and then as a soldier. He took part in the king's expedition to Naples and, in 1495, was knighted for his valor in the Battle of Fornuovo.

In 1501, as Louis XII reasserted his claim to the kingdom of Naples, Bayard became one of the most celebrated knights in the French army, widely known for his horsemanship and swordplay. By July, 1502, the French were clashing with the Spanish, who also claimed Naples. Lack of supplies and adverse conditions made for small-scale operations that offered opportunities for Bayard to display courage and skill in individual combat. Encased in steel armor and wielding an enormous two-handed sword, Bayard led the charge of the French into the breach of the Spanish fortress at Canossa.

In the winter of 1503, Bayard joined ten other French knights in a duel with eleven Spaniards. Bayard saved the French cause from disaster, and the match ended in a draw. In another incident, the capture of a Spanish paymaster's hoard, Bayard distributed the treasure with characteristic magnanimity, half to a fellow captain and the rest to his men, keeping nothing for himself.

Bayard gained honor even as the campaign turned against the French. He killed the Spaniard Alonzo de Soto-Mayor in a famous duel. Despite fighting at a disadvantage—he was weakened by fever and on foot rather than mounted—Bayard dispatched his much larger opponent, then honored him by preventing a trumpeting of the victory. During the retreat from Naples, without armor and wielding a pike, he held the bridge over the Garigliano against hundreds of Spanish.

Life's Work

At his prime, about twenty-five years old, tall and slender, his eyes black, his nose aquiline, his beard shaved close, Bayard exuded energy and good humor. His loyal service to his king was rewarded with greater responsibility in the Italian campaign that began in 1509. Having earlier received the title of captain, he was given command of five hundred infantry and 180 horsemen in the War of the League of Cambrai, which pitted France, the Holy Roman Empire, and the Papacy against the Republic of Venice. Under his discipline, the infantry, little more than rabble, became an effective fighting force, distinguishing itself in the Battle of Agnadello on May 14, 1509. Subsequently, he fought in several skirmishes, leading his men in the thick of battle.

In September, 1510, as second in command, he defended the Duchy of Ferrara against Pope Julius II, now a Venetian ally, and nearly captured the aged, warlike prelate. To the astonishment of his Ferrarese allies, however, he rejected with horror a plot to have the pope poisoned.

The following summer, Bayard was given command of the duke of Lorraine's company of six hundred horse; he had risen to approximately the rank of brigadier general in a modern army, and he had a significant voice in councils of war. After campaigning in the Friuli during the summer and fall against the Venetians, he hastened to support French garrisons in the Duchy of Milan, which was threatened by the Swiss from the north, papal and Spanish armies from the south, and Venetians from the east. He was severely wounded in the thigh in the French capture of Brescia. Although the French brutally sacked the rest of the city, Bayard took nothing from the family with whom he convalesced, and he left large dowries for each of the family's two daughters.

He recovered well enough to participate in the French victory over the Spaniards at Ravenna in April, 1512. Deprived of their leader, Gaston de Foix, who died in the battle, and pressed by the

Swiss and the Venetians, the French largely abandoned the Duchy of Milan. Covering the retreat, Bayard was wounded in the shoulder.

Back in France, he recovered from a bout of typhoid fever in time to participate in a failed campaign in Spanish Navarre against the duke of Alva. Bayard again commanded the rearguard in the retreat under winter conditions over the Pyrenees back to France. By the midsummer of 1513, he was in Picardy with French troops awaiting an invasion by Henry VIII and Emperor Maximilian. In the ensuing rout of the French, Bayard was captured by Burgundians during rearguard action at the bridge of Guinegatte. He spent several weeks in imperial Flanders and is said to have met the English king and the emperor. After a ransom was paid for him, Bayard returned to France in October.

Following the death of Louis XII on January 1, 1515, his successor, Francis I, appointed Bayard lieutenant-governor of Dauphiné, his home province, where he was beloved and esteemed. He assembled a force of four hundred cavalry and five thousand infantry; his troops were to pave the way for the main body of the king's army in a confrontation with a new coalition of enemies—the Swiss, the new pope, Leo X, and the Spaniards. Francis would once more reconquer Lombardy. After a daring passage over the Alps, Bayard's men captured the papal commander, Prospero Colonna, and his supplies.

On September 13, 1515, Bayard shared in the French victory over the Swiss pikemen at Marignano, delivering Milan to the young French king. Exalted by the occasion and his own worthy contribution to it, Francis chose to be knighted by Bayard, the most highly reputed knight of the age.

By the summer of 1516, Bayard was back in Grenoble, tending to his duties as the king's representative in Dauphiné; his military skills were employed in running down marauding bands of ex-soldiers who ventured into his province. There were also opportunities for his legendary kindness and generosity. Urged by strong religious faith, he aided needy widows and comrades and helped others in distress, always with tact. By reason of this charity, and because he refused to profit by war, he remained throughout his life a relatively poor man.

In 1521, he left the peace of Dauphiné to assume command of the eastern frontier fortification of Mézières, which was threatened by an imperial army of thirty thousand. Beginning in August, Bayard, with fifteen hundred men, most of them raw

peasants, held out for several weeks until Francis raised an army strong enough to relieve them. Having saved the country's eastern provinces, Bayard received the gratitude of his king, who made him captain-in-chief, a rank for the command of an army corps. His reputation among his countrymen, borne with characteristic modesty, reached its zenith.

By year's end, he was en route to Genoa to shore up French control of that city. He could do little, however, to prevent first the Duchy of Milan, then Genoa from being overrun by imperial and papal forces. At the end of 1522, France was threatened by enemies on all of its frontiers. In the spring of 1524, Bayard, at the head of a company of fifteen hundred men, marched again with the French army toward Lombardy. It was an ill-fated expedition under an incompetent commander, the royal favorite Admiral Bonnivet. Though Bayard's force grew to comprise a third of the French army, it accomplished little in the face of a qualitatively superior and better-led enemy. Bayard retreated with the rest of the army to the west of Milan. Sick, his energy diminished, he was surprised in camp at Robecco, and his division was routed.

In the crossing of the Sesia River, April 29, Bonnivet was injured, and he turned his command over to a reluctant Bayard. Ill, entrusted with the wreckage of an army, the great captain resumed the retreat toward France, himself leading the rearguard. Near Roasio, April 30, in a skirmish with the enemy's vanguard, he was struck by a bullet that pierced his armor and broke his spine. Realizing the wound was fatal, he had himself laid against a tree, facing the enemy. The Spanish captain, Pescara, approached him with awe, placed him on a camp bed, raised a tent above him, and stationed a guard of honor around him. He lived eight hours while his enemies paid him respect. His body was carried to Grenoble, where he was buried.

Summary

The chevalier de Bayard was a man who lived out the knightly ideal of medieval Christianity, *sans peur et sans reproche* ("without fear or reproach"), a motto conferred on him by contemporaries. Like Joan of Arc, he became a great mythic figure, a national hero. Other less famous soldiers achieved as much or more, but Bayard's reputation was rooted in the personal qualities that he demonstrated so remarkably under adverse circumstances, often in defeat, fighting rearguard actions. In a pragmatic world of decaying chivalric ideals and amoral statecraft, he remained brave, loyal, sincere, and generous. His piety, sustained by regular prayer and devotion, informed his knightly ethos. Neither defeat nor the agnosticism or hypocrisy prevalent among his peers ever shook his simple belief in his calling by God to be a Christian knight. Neither a saint nor a prude, he enjoyed the pleasures of the flesh. A liaison with an Italian woman produced a daughter, Jeanne Terrail, to whom he gave his name and whom he lovingly supported. He never married.

The measure of Bayard's influence is evident in a vast body of writing that has grown around him, beginning in his lifetime and extending unbroken to the present, especially in France. His valor and sense of duty also can be detected in the lives of admirers such as Charles de Gaulle, Robert E. Lee, and many less well-known military men.

Bibliography

Baumgartner, Frederic J. *Louis XII*. New York: St. Martin's Press, 1994. Treats Bayard briefly in the context of Louis XII's Italian campaigns.

Garrisson, Janine. *A History of Sixteenth-Century France, 1483-1598: Renaissance, Reformation, and Rebellion*. Translated by Richard Rex. New York: St. Martin's Press, 1995. Provides political, social, and cultural background for an understanding of Bayard's life.

Guyard de Berville, Guillaume François. *The Story of the Chevalier Bayard*. Translated by Edith Walford. Edited, with notes and introduction, by James H. Friswell. London: S. Low and Marston, 1868. De Berville in 1760 amplified the memoirs of the Loyal Servant, most likely Bayard's steward, Jacques Jeoffre of Millieu.

Hale, John Rigby. *War and Society in Renaissance Europe 1450-1620*. New York: St. Martin's Press, 1985. Treats Bayard in terms of the transition from medieval to early modern systems of warfare.

Knecht, Robert Jean. *Renaissance Warrior and Patron: The Reign of Francis I*. 2d ed. London: Cambridge University Press, 1994. The most detailed study of French history for the last decade of Bayard's life.

Shellabarger, Samuel. *The Chevalier Bayard: A Study in Fading Chivalry*. New York: Biblo and Tannen, 1928. Reprint, 1971. The best study of Bayard in English separates facts from myths about the great captain.

Simms, William Gilmore. *The Life of the Chevalier Bayard*. New York: Harper & Brothers, 1847. Reflects the attractiveness of Bayard's chivalric ethos to the planter aristocracy of the antebellum South.

Wiley, W. L. *The Gentleman of Renaissance France*. Cambridge: Harvard University Press, 1954. This analysis of social attitudes uses Bayard to illustrate the qualities of a complete gentleman.

Charles H. O'Brien

BAYEZID II

Born: December, 1447 or January, 1448; Demotika, Ottoman Empire
Died: May 26, 1512; en route to Demotika, Ottoman Empire
Areas of Achievement: Government and the military
Contribution: Without being among the great sultans of the Ottoman Empire, Bayezid II filled an important transitional role. The fame of his father, Mehmed II, as well as the symbolic memory of his namesake Bayezid I, would have made it difficult for Bayezid to earn a reputation for strong rule or aggressive foreign policy. That much of Bayezid's time was spent trying unsuccessfully to respond to conflicts toward the East is probably the main historical significance of his reign.

Early Life

Little or nothing is known about Bayezid II's early life or education prior to his first official appointment to a key government training post. This appointment occurred a few years before the death of his father, Mehmed II, the more famous sultan who conquered the capital Istanbul in 1453, at about the time of Bayezid's birth. As governor of Amasya province (between Ankara and the Black Sea), Bayezid received important military experience, particularly at the distant Battle of Otluk Beli in 1473. This encounter marked a turning point in the long Ottoman struggle to subdue the Turcoman populations in the zone spanning western Iran and eastern Anatolia that had rallied around the famous tribal chief Uzun Hasan.

The most significant chapter of Bayezid's early life came when his father died in 1481. His younger brother Cem, Governor of Karaman, with its influential religious capital Konya, challenged Bayezid's right to succeed. This succession struggle would go on, in various forms, for some fourteen years. Bayezid's claims were apparently supported by the main imperial military forces and high officials of the "new" capital at Istanbul. Cem's challenge depended on a number of different sources of resistance, and even included attempts to establish alliances with influences far from the Ottoman imperial homeland. Thus, Cem first tried, but failed, to defeat Bayezid with the support of Egyptian/Syrian Mamluk forces lent by Sultan Ka;'it Bay of Cairo. He then sought refuge with the Knights of Saint John on their island fortress at Rhodes. The knights decided not to join in the succession fray but turned Bayezid's brother over to the French kingdom. Several Christian states' use of the Ottoman pretender as their possible preferred ally over the next ten years forced Bayezid to keep close surveillance over his army to avoid possible betrayals. This limitation on the sultan's power in the early years of his reign (at least until Cem's death in 1495) held the Ottomans back from carrying out the major yearly military campaigns that had characterized most reigns up to and including that of Mehmed II.

Life's Work

Bayezid scored some early successes in maintaining and even expanding Ottoman control over key Balkan zones (capture of Herzegovina in 1483, seizure of the lower Danubian fortress of Kilia in 1484, and increased control over the Dniester River approaches to Crimea on the north coast of the Black Sea). The new sultan did not possess for some years, however, sufficient strength to fortify his southeastern provinces against the threat of Mamluk Egyptian/Syrian forays into agriculturally rich Cilicia. By 1491, an inconclusive peace was signed that would leave this southeastern zone in an indecisive position until Bayezid's son and successor Selim I marched into the area with force.

Bayezid's main attentions prior to the rise of Safavid Iranian threats to his eastern imperial flank would remain tied to Balkan Europe and the Krim Tatar zone of the north Black Sea coast, where Poland's kings aimed at making Moldavia (now part of Romania) a Slavic dependency. This was a claim that Bayezid would only reverse militarily in 1499. During the same period, he became seriously engaged in the Aegean Sea itself, where the Ottomans faced a formidable trade and military rival in the powerful city state of Venice.

Perhaps to detract attention from rising heterodox religious discontent and sedition in the eastern provinces, Bayezid pursued an openly aggressive policy toward his closest Christian rival, Venice. The break began in 1491, when the Venetian *balyos* (the diplomatic representative recognized by his father after the 1453 conquest) was expelled from Istanbul. Political tensions turned to material frustrations when, in 1496 (one year after the death of his rebellious brother Cem), Bayezid closed Ottoman ports to Venetian trade. For the next four years, clashes with the ships of Venice occurred throughout the eastern Mediterranean and the Aegean zones.

This protracted war of maritime encounters, which Pope Alexander VI would have liked to expand into a full-scale crusade, had an important effect on Bayezid's priorities as ruler. First, it made it necessary for the Ottomans to spend money on the development of seaports in western Turkey. Also, a new supreme naval commander, Kemal Reis (a former pirate captain whose ships had raided as far west as France and Spain), was named head of a largely rebuilt and heavily armed Ottoman navy.

The peace that was finally signed in 1502 restored most of Venice's trading privileges but limited its physical control of key ports considerably: Only Albania on the Adriatic and the Morea (southern Greece) could be called Venetian preserves in Ottoman territory by the first years of the sixteenth century. A second major repercussion of these years of Ottoman emphasis on naval development was a gradual assimilation of Mediterranean renegade captains into Turkish service. In addition to Kemal Reis, Bayezid encouraged a number of other important raiders (*gazis*) to pledge loyalty to his sultanate. Among these would be some of the great captains of the next generation, whose home ports were in North Africa. These would, by the end of Bayezid's son's reign, play a major role in attaching the provinces of Algiers, Tripolitania, and, eventually, Tunisia to the Ottoman realm.

Bayezid himself, however, did not live to see the rebirth of expansive Ottoman military power under his son Selim or, especially, Selim's successor Süleyman the Magnificent. Many historians note that, after the Venetian peace of 1502, Bayezid tended to withdraw more and more from direct management of imperial matters. This decision to retreat from direct responsibilities of rule offered the possibility for Bayezid to live a contemplative life. He was himself interested in music and poetry, and invited a number of recognized scholars of history, science, and religion to frequent his court in Istanbul. One of these, Kemal Pasha Zade, wrote a commissioned history of the Ottoman Empire under Bayezid's auspices. There were, however, negative factors that stemmed from Bayezid's decision to let others take responsibility for key affairs of state. On the one hand, apparently the influence of certain less tolerant religious leaders who were protégés of the court rose. This even went to the point of allowing zealots to denounce violently their rivals with the tacit and sometimes direct support of the sultan. On the other hand, increasing social and religious ferment in the Ottoman eastern Anatolian provinces, spurred on by unorthodox proponents of Shi'a Islam under the banner of Safavid Shah Esma'il I, had spread considerably by the early 1500's. The sultan's lack of a determined policy of reaction nearly assured that a party of political opposition to him would emerge.

Bayezid's approach to the problem of Shi'a heterodoxy and its willingness to sponsor anti-Ottoman rebellions in far-flung provinces was to try to convince Esma'il to respect the integrity of a single unified community of Islam. By 1508-1509, the futility of expecting Esma'il to reason with the Ottoman sultan was apparent: Esma'il invaded Iraq and added it to the Safavid domains. Concerned Turkish military leaders feared that Syria and perhaps Ottoman Cilicia would be next. When an Ottoman army led by Grand Vizier 'Ali Pasha and Prince Ahmed only barely succeeded in expelling Esma'il's supporters from the southeast province around Kayseri (August, 1511), a party of militant opposition to Bayezid's rule began to plan his overthrow.

Although, as Bayezid's eldest son, Ahmed should have been considered the legal successor, military professionals most anxious to see a strong force dispatched to the East preferred the candidacy of Selim. Bayezid's appointment (in 1507) of Ahmed to the same Amasya provincial governorate that he had held prior to defending his claim to the succession in 1481 seemed to be a sign that the sultan was unaware of such preferences. Thus, Selim and his supporters decided not to await Bayezid's demise before claiming the throne. They revolted against Bayezid and divided the army against itself. Several incidents of open clashes occurred before Bayezid was formally deposed (April, 1512). Only a month later, while attempting to return to forced exile at his birthplace in Demotika, Bayezid died, presumably of natural causes.

Within a year after Bayezid's demise, his son Selim (the Grim) had begun to mount a major military reconquest of threatened Ottoman provinces in the East. In only two years, Esma'il would be defeated and a military route opened for Selim's conquest of the core countries of Arabistan: Syria and Egypt.

Summary

The reign of Bayezid II demonstrates that, despite the obvious imperial determination and military capacities of the Ottoman Empire, certain signs of internal dissension that would paralyze the political apparatuses of state in later centuries were already present in 1500. One of these is represented by the divisive influence of Cem's fourteen-year-long challenge to his brother's succession. Intrigues involving supporters of different scions of the Ottoman family as claimants to the throne had not been unknown before this date but had never affected so many different interest groups, both domestic and foreign.

Another negative characteristic of Bayezid's reign that would be repeated again and again in later centuries was his tendency to delegate active authority to govern. The sultan's retirement to the intellectually and aesthetically rarefied atmosphere of the imperial court left the field open for self-seeking politicians, military authorities, and religious zealots to play a larger role in high Ottoman affairs than had been possible under his predecessors. Although Selim's overthrow of his father in 1512 prepared the way for a reversal of these trends during the next two great reigns, the elements operating in Bayezid's period of rule would return to weaken many of the original bases of Ottoman imperial authority in the seventeenth century.

Bibliography

Brummett, Palmira Johnson. *Ottoman Seapower and Levantine Diplomacy in the Age of Discovery.* Albany: State University of New York Press, 1993. This work reframes sixteenth century history, incorporating the Ottoman Empire more thoroughly into world history. It analyzes the Ottoman Empire's eastward expansion as it relates to claims of universal sovereignty, Levantine power politics, and the struggle for control of the oriental trade.

Creasy, Edward S. *History of the Ottoman Turks.* New York: Holt, and London: Bentley, 1878. This detailed historical work is based on the massive mid-nineteenth century German classic by Von Hammer-Purgstall. The author states that he not only abridged Von Hammer but also incorporated a wide range of other sources, including memoirs of Europeans who witnessed the events described. For Bayezid's time, however, there were very few primary sources to be consulted. Thus, the historical accuracy of many of Creasy's subjective impressions must be accepted with caution.

Fisher, Sidney N. *The Foreign Relations of Turkey, 1481-1512.* Urbana: University of Illinois Press, 1948. This work covers the precise reign dates of Bayezid. It is therefore one of the most complete and detailed studies of Bayezid, even though emphasis is on relations with foreign powers, both European and Muslim.

Inalcik, Halil. "The Rise of the Ottoman Empire." In *The Cambridge History of Islam*, edited by P. M. Holt, and Ann K. S. Lambton, and Bernard Lewis, vol. 1. Cambridge: Cambridge University Press, 1970; New York: Cambridge University Press, 1978. The most concise survey of the entire early period of Ottoman expansion, with a specific section on Bayezid. The material on Bayezid is useful both for its cultural foci and for its discussion of social subgroupings, especially that of the Turcomans.

Inalcik, Halil, and Donald Quataert, eds. *An Economic and Social History of the Ottoman Empire, 1300-1914.* Cambridge and New York: Cambridge University Press, 1994. A detailed account spanning seven centuries of the social and economic history of the Ottoman Empire, from the origins of the Empire in approximately 1300 to the eve of its destruction during World War I. In four chronological sections the contributors provide valuable information on land tenure systems, population, trade, commerce, and the industrial economy as a basis for understanding contemporary developments in both the Middle East and the post-Soviet Balkan world.

Itzkowitz, Norman. *Ottoman Empire and Islamic Tradition.* New York: Knopf, 1972. This book contains a short but complete subchapter on Bayezid, placed in a general section entitled "From Emirate to Empire." More important perhaps than this chronological coverage of each sultanic reign is the fact that the three other sections of the book deal with various Ottoman institutions such as bureaucracy and provincial structure that shed light on conditions, either practical or legal, that Bayezid faced.

Shaw, Stanford J. *History of the Ottoman Empire and Modern Turkey.* Vol. 1, *Empire of the Gazis: The Rise and Decline of the Ottoman Empire, 1280-1808.* Cambridge and New York: Cambridge University Press, 1976. Of several general works on Ottoman history, this volume contains perhaps the most information on Bayezid's reign. Provides useful information on key cultural questions, including undercurrents of religious discontent and some elements of courtly literature from the late fifteenth and early sixteenth centuries.

Byron D. Cannon

FRANCIS BEAUMONT and JOHN FLETCHER

Francis Beaumont

Born: c. 1584; Grace-Dieu, Leicestershire, England
Died: March 6, 1616; probably Sundridge, Kent, England

John Fletcher

Born: December, 1579; Rye, Sussex, England
Died: August, 1625; London, England
Area of Achievement: Theater
Contribution: With their light, witty comedy and melodramatic tragicomedy, Beaumont and Fletcher introduced a new style and aristocratic outlook into Renaissance English drama.

Early Lives

Both Francis Beaumont and John Fletcher were products of the English upper class. Fletcher, born in 1579, was the second son (the fourth of nine children) of Richard Fletcher, a leading Anglican clergyman. His father served as president of Bene't College (Corpus Christi), Cambridge; was dean of Peterborough, officiating at the execution of Mary, Queen of Scots; and was successively bishop of Bristol, Worcester, and London, this last position making him Queen Elizabeth's chaplain. The background of Beaumont, who was born in about 1584, was even more aristocratic. As a member of an old Anglo-Norman family, Beaumont was related by blood or marriage to a large portion of the English aristocracy. Many of these aristocratic connections came through his mother, Anne Pierrepoint. His father, a Court of Common Pleas judge and owner of Grace-Dieu Manor, was also named Francis. Francis the playwright was the third son of four children. The families of both Beaumont and Fletcher had a number of poets, including Beaumont's older brother John and Fletcher's younger first cousins, the Spenserian poets Phineas and Giles Fletcher.

Thus, the social circle—educated, urbane, and artistic—in which they were reared gave Beaumont and Fletcher a running start as Renaissance playwrights. They grew up with clever, informed talk and, unlike fellow playwright William Shakespeare, did not have to imagine how the upper classes who populated Renaissance drama lived. Their educations were rounded off at Cambridge and Oxford and at the London Inns of Court, England's law school but also a center of literary and dramatic activity. Fletcher entered Bene't College, Cambridge, in 1591 and probably moved on to the Inns of Court in 1594 or 1595, after his father became bishop of London. It is uncertain whether he received a Cambridge degree. Beaumont entered Broadgates Hall (now Pembroke College), Oxford, in 1597, left without receiving a degree, and enrolled at the Inns of Court in 1600.

Neither Beaumont nor Fletcher completed his legal studies. In Fletcher's case, there were financial reasons. His father lost Queen Elizabeth's favor in 1595 and died in 1596, leaving the family in debt. Fletcher was forced to drop out, and there is no record of his activities for the next ten years. In Beaumont's case, the record is even more uncertain. Possibly he was not interested in law and gradually drifted into literary and dramatic endeavors. *Salmacis and Hermaphroditus*, an Ovidian narrative poem published anonymously in 1602 and in 1639 attributed to Beaumont, offers some evidence for this possibility. The next sure record, however, is in 1606, when Beaumont and Fletcher were practicing playwrights.

Life's Work

At first, each of the two playwrights apparently practiced on his own, experiencing the kind of uneven success typical of apprentices. Both wrote for the private theaters, indoor playhouses that drew a more exclusive audience than the outdoor public theaters, and their first plays were acted by boys' companies, then-popular offshoots of choir schools. Of the early plays attributed solely or mostly to Beaumont, *The Woman Hater* (c. 1606), a comedy, was fairly successful, but the masterful satire-burlesque *The Knight of the Burning Pestle* (1607) was a flop when it was first performed. An early tragicomedy attributed solely or mostly to Fletcher, *The Faithful Shepherdess* (c. 1608-1609), was similarly unsuccessful. The two young playwrights might have overestimated the sophistication of their audiences or the child actors.

When and why Beaumont and Fletcher began collaborating are not exactly known, but the two were probably drawn together by similar backgrounds and common ties. As their commendatory verses to Ben Johnson's *Volpone: Or, The Fox* (1606) make clear, both were "Sons of Ben." Johnson's satirical and critical inclinations undoubtedly influenced the two younger men; both socialized with Johnson's famous circle at the Mer-

maid Tavern. In the poem "Mr. Francis Beaumont's Letter to Ben Jonson," Beaumont described the circle's sparkling conversation:

> What things have we seen Done at the Mermaid! Heard words that have been So nimble and so full of subtill flame, As if that every one from whence they came, Had meant to put his whole wit in a jest, And had resolv'd to live a foole the rest Of his dull life . . . . We left an aire behind us, which alone,Was able to make the two next companies Right witty; though but downright fools, more wise.

In this situation, the idea for collaboration was not far off.

Beaumont and Fletcher not only became collaborators but also lived with each other, according to seventeenth century biographer John Aubrey in *Brief Lives* (1898): "They lived together on the Banke-side, not far from the Play-house, both batchelors; lay together (from Sir James Hales, etc.); had one wench in the house between them, which they did so admire, the same cloaths and cloake, etc., between them." It is uncertain how much of this colorful bohemian picture can be attributed generally to the Renaissance cult of friendship and specifically to the Castor and Pollux myth that grew up around the "twins of poetry." As a matter of fact, however, Beaumont and Fletcher do look somewhat like twins in the extant portraits (which might have been created with the myth in mind or might reflect typical idealization); both are depicted as Van Dyck cavalier types with wide poetic eyes, large, slightly aquiline noses, and reddish or light brown hair (curly in some portraits), mustaches, and beards (Beaumont's trimmed square, Fletcher's pointed).

Some of the performances of their collaborative plays were by the Children of the Queen's Revels, but most were by the King's Men, Shakespeare's company, with which Beaumont and Fletcher became associated when the company took over the private Blackfriars Theater in 1608. Their best collaborations are two tragicomedies, *Philaster: Or, Love Lies A-Bleeding* (c. 1609) and *A King and No King* (1611), and *The Maid's Tragedy* (c. 1611), in all of which Beaumont's hand predominates. Collaborative works in which Fletcher's hand predominates include the uneven tragedy *Cupid's Revenge* (1612) and three comedies, *The Coxcomb* (c. 1608-1610), *The Captain* (c. 1690-1612), and *The Scornful Lady* (c. 1615-1616). Other plays, such as *The Tragedy of Thierry, King of France, and His Brother Theodoret* (c. 1617), involved a third collaborator (or later, reviser), usually Philip Massinger.

Beaumont and Fletcher's collaboration tapered off or ended around 1612 or 1613, when Beaumont married an heiress, Ursula Isley. By himself, Beaumont wrote a final dramatic work, *The Masque of the Inner Temple and Grayes Inn* (1613), for a royal wedding. Apparently, Beaumont retired to his wife's estate in Sundridge, Kent. They had two daughters, Elizabeth and Frances, the latter born a few months after Beaumont died on March 6, 1616. He was buried in the Poets' Corner of Westminster Abbey in London.

After Beaumont's retirement, Fletcher continued to write plays for another dozen or so years, succeeding Shakespeare as the chief writer for the King's Men. Sometimes he wrote alone, but for the most part he worked in collaboration with other playwrights. His most notable collaborator was Shakespeare, with whom he and possibly other contributors wrote a play called *Cardenio*, which was lost, *The Two Noble Kinsmen* (c. 1612-1613), and *Henry VIII* (1613). Other collaborators included Nathan Field and William Rowley. Fletcher's primary collaborator during this period, however, was Massinger, with whom he formed a friendship and working association similar to that with Beaumont, except that Massinger was the junior partner. They collaborated on about fifteen plays, including the tragedies *Sir John Van Olden Barnavelt* (1619) and *The Double Marriage* (c. 1621), the tragicomedies *The Queen of Corinth* (1616-1617) and *The Knight of Malta* (1616-1618), both also involving Field, and the comedies *The Little French Lawyer* (1619-1623), *The Custom of the Country* (c. 1619-1620), *The Sea Voyage* (1622), and *The Spanish Curate* (1622). Plays written by Fletcher alone include the tragedies *Valentinian* (1610-1614), and *Bonduca* (1609-1614) the tragicomedies *The Mad Lover* (c. 1616), *The Humorous Lieutenant* (1619), *The Island Princess: Or, The Generous Portugal* (1619-1621), and *A Wife for a Month* (1624), and the comedies *Monsieur Thomas* (1610-1616), *Wit Without Money* (c. 1614), *The Chances* (c. 1617), *The Pilgrim* (1621), *The Wild Goose Chase* (1621), and *Rule a Wife and Have a Wife* (1624). Fletcher died in August, 1625, a victim of the plague, and was buried at St. Savior's Church in London.

Summary

Francis Beaumont and John Fletcher are considered the greatest collaborators in English literature, but the extent of their collaboration is something of a myth. Of the fifty or so plays attributed to the Beaumont and Fletcher canon, most are by the two playwrights working alone or in collaboration with other people. Fletcher's collaboration with Massinger, who typically receives little credit for his share in the canon, was actually more extensive than his collaboration with Beaumont, which lasted only six or seven years and involved a dozen or fewer plays. In these plays, one or the other's hand usually predominates; the plays best known today are those attributed solely or mostly to Beaumont, who is considered the better writer of the two. Still, Beaumont and Fletcher made the practice of collaboration fashionable among the playwrights of their time; even Shakespeare ended his career as a collaborator.

Of far more importance, Beaumont and Fletcher crystalized the turn of Renaissance English drama toward upper-class tastes, a trend already started by the private theaters and the satirical, classical bias of Jonson. They embodied this turn in their own social backgrounds. With their satire of bourgeois citizens, their light repartee, and their absolutist cavalier values, they gave the upper-class turn a definite form. The entertaining drama they created was highly regarded at the time—even ranked above that of Shakespeare's—but is virtually no longer produced. To modern audiences and readers, most of their work may seem somewhat juvenile; in fact, Beaumont was no more than a young-man-about-town—the writer as young gallant—when he penned his work, and Fletcher, repeating what had been successful, hardly advanced beyond Beaumont's attitudes.

Besides turning the drama away from the development of more serious themes, Beaumont and Fletcher helped split the Renaissance English audience, which in the public theaters had represented all social classes. Indeed, the English drama had begun in the Middle Ages with performances of religious mystery cycles by the town burghers, the very kind of people whom Jonson and then Beaumont and Fletcher satirized. From a negative standpoint, the damage Beaumont and Fletcher wrought on English drama is outweighed only by that of the Puritans, who on the other side opposed the theaters and finally closed them down in 1642. When the theaters reopened in the Restoration period, the upper class had absorbed the English drama, and its typical fare—the heroic play and the comedy of manners—clearly reflected the influence of Beaumont and Fletcher.

Bibliography

Appleton, William W. *Beaumont and Fletcher: A Critical Study*. London: Allen and Unwin, 1956; Folcroft, Pa.: Folcroft Press, 1969. This brief study of Beaumont and Fletcher's work also treats their influence in the Restoration and their later reputation; includes a useful checklist of plays with dates and collaborators.

Blincoe, Noel R. "Fury-Innocent as Used in *The Two Noble Kinsmen*." *Notes and Queries* 42 (September, 1995): 337. Blincoe studies the use of the word 'fury-innocent' in the play *The Two Noble Kinsmen* by Beaumont and Fletcher. The author discusses maiden love vs. married love in the play as well as the degeneration of the kinsmen's friendship.

Danby, John F. *Poets on Fortune's Hill: Studies in Sidney, Shakespeare, Beaumont, and Fletcher*. London: Faber, 1952; Port Washington, N.Y.: Kennikat Press, 1966. An excellent critical study that places these writers in their social and historical contexts. Sees Beaumont and Fletcher as the final, decadent stage of a great Elizabethan tradition.

Finkelpearl, Philip J. *Court and Country Politics in the Plays of Beaumont and Fletcher*. Princeton, N.J.: Princeton University Press, 1990. Although the dramas of Beaumont and Fletcher are now usually seen as epitomizing a decadent turn in theater at the end of the Jacobean period, Finkelpearl offers another view, revealing the subtle political issues in these plays. The book offers a wholly new conception of these dramatists and of the entire question of the relationship between the Crown and the theater of their time.

Fletcher, Ian. *Beaumont and Fletcher*. London: Longman, 1967. An introductory British Council pamphlet with a bibliography that sorts out the collaborators.

Gayley, Charles Mills. *Beaumont, the Dramatist*. London: Duckworth, 1914; New York: Russell and Russell, 1969. Somewhat dated but contains the fullest biography of Beaumont as well as considerable information on Fletcher and numerous miscellaneous topics. Digressive style with some fascinating trivia.

Hoy, Cyrus. "The Shares of Fletcher and His Collaborators in the Beaumont and Fletcher Canon." *Studies in Bibliography* 8-12 (1956-1962). The authoritative study on this subject but many details remain open to dispute and may never be settled.

Leech, Clifford. *The John Fletcher Plays*. London: Chatto and Windus, and Cambridge, Mass.: Harvard University Press, 1962. Perceptive analyses of Fletcher's main plays, with *The Humorous Lieutenant* seen as his masterpiece.

Squier, Charles. *John Fletcher*. Boston: Twayne, 1986. Concentrates on Fletcher but includes brief biographies of both Beaumont and Fletcher and introductions to all the plays in the canon. Contains useful notes and annotated bibliography.

Wallis, Lawrence B. *Fletcher, Beaumont, and Company: Entertainers to the Jacobean Gentry*. New York: King's Crown Press, 1947. Surveys critical opinions of Beaumont and Fletcher's work from their time to the modern period, then defends them as successful entertainers of their particular audience.

Harold Branam

GIOVANNI BELLINI

Born: c. 1430; Venice

Died: 1516; Venice

Area of Achievement: Art

Contribution: As the leading painter of the Republic of Venice over more than two generations, Bellini achieved a synthesis of major currents in art deriving from Italian centers such as Tuscany and Padua as well as from Northern Europe. His conquest of the poetry of light and color was the foundation of the greatness of Venetian painting in the sixteenth century.

Early Life

The year of Giovanni Bellini's birth is not known, but the approximate date of 1430 has been suggested. Sketchy evidence indicates that he was the second of two sons born to Jacopo Bellini and his wife, Anna Rinversi. Giovanni's brother, Gentile, was probably born about two or three years earlier, and a sister, Nicolosia, two or three years later. The close ages of the children is significant for Venetian art, as the brothers were frequently to work in close association, and a major artistic influence upon Giovanni was his sister's husband, the painter Andrea Mantegna, whom she married in 1453.

There is a scarcity of information about Giovanni's early life, but a few biographical facts do offer some insight. For example, it is known that Giovanni's mother was a native of the region of Pesaro, south of Venice on the Adriatic coast; Giovanni may have found it convenient to reside there while creating one of his early masterpieces, *Coronation of the Virgin* (c. 1473). The family connection with Pesaro suggests Giovanni's receptiveness to the world outside the city-state of Venice. Similarly, Jacopo Bellini's important early contact with the vibrant art of Tuscany is shown by his apprenticeship to Gentile da Fabriano.

During the early Renaissance, it became increasingly possible for a talented individual to transcend the status of craftsman to become an artist, a person endowed with intellectual as well as manual skills. Jacopo is this sort of transitional figure in the art of early fifteenth century Italy, and his sons—more particularly Giovanni—were to enjoy an even higher social position than their father. To Jacopo, however, goes the credit both for the technical education of his sons and for their introduction to Renaissance ideals, including the enthusiasm for antiquity and the respect for learning embodied in the concept of Humanism.

At an unrecorded date Giovanni married a woman named Ginevra Bocheta, and they later had a son, Alvise. His departure from his parents' household around 1459 may not indicate his artistic independence but only his move to new quarters. Gentile was the first of the brothers to win large public commissions, and it was in this field that he specialized, producing throughout his career many monumental decorations for the Venetian fraternal groups called *scuole*—literally, but not actually, "schools." While it is acknowledged that Giovanni was a more adventurous and accomplished artist than Gentile, the brothers' achievement has often been regarded collectively because of their joint dominance of Venetian art during their lifetimes and because they seemed to have esteemed each other very highly.

Giovanni's likeness is known from an anonymous and mediocre woodcut in the 1568 edition of Giorgio Vasari's famous work on the lives of painters as well as from a drawing (now in the Condé Museum of Chantilly, France) by one of Giovanni's students. This profile portrait shows the middle-aged Bellini as a handsome man with a well-proportioned face and a prominent but straight nose. Adjusting for the slightly different treatment of the face in the later woodcut, one might accept the argument of a prominent scholar that Giovanni pictured himself in a late work, *Feast of the Gods* (c. 1514), as the mythological figure Silvanus.

Life's Work

Bellini's independent career can be regarded as beginning around 1460. It is often impossible to determine the contributions of assistants to the collective work of a studio, and in the case of the Bellini family this is especially true in the production of the 1450's. There is also little basis for distinguishing some of the work of this period by Giovanni from that of his brother-in-law Mantegna, who may have studied with Jacopo and worked in his studio on the same basis as his sons. Thus, Bellini's earliest work can be conceived only in the general terms of a range of stylistic qualities and types of objects. Aside from preparatory drawings, it consists of small paintings of religious character, some executed on vellum and others on wooden panels of modest dimensions. The paintings on vellum have a delicacy befitting both their size and their derivation from the traditions of manuscript illustration, but the panels show added concern with the treatment of the human figure as a sculptural volume and with the placement of the figure in a natural landscape.

In Giovanni's early panels, the influence of Mantegna is believed to be manifest. A native of the region of Padua, Mantegna was an extremely precocious artist whose style is characterized by somewhat schematized and muscular linear forms rendered with tone to achieve an incisive sculptural effect. Bellini's debt to Mantegna may be seen in his firm contours and crisp detail as well as in his pictorial construction, but Bellini's adaptations are more sensitively observant of nature, as in his *Agony in the Garden*, dating from the early 1460's. The same subject as treated by Mantegna is more tautly composed, favoring drama over poetry; Bellini's landscape is almost pastoral, while Mantegna's represents, in one scholar's words, an almost "lunar ideal of natural landscape."

From Giovanni's studio in the 1460's came a remarkable outpouring of paintings of Christ, of the Madonna and Child, and of various saints. These show a mastery of form and a depth of feeling that place Giovanni, still only in his thirties, at the forefront of Venetian art. The works are freshly approached on both the technical and the emotional levels and show that, even at a considerable distance from sources of innovation in Tuscany and central Italy, Bellini is receptive to the more advanced artistic tendencies of his time. His *Pietà with Virgin and Saint John*, in the Brera gallery in Milan, is representative of the artist's fully developed early manner in the way it combines assurance of form with a powerful yet restrained rendering of its subject, the sorrow at Christ's death. Notwithstanding its relatively early date in Bellini's career, it is one of the great achievements of European art.

The next phase in Bellini's career is notable for the increasing use of the medium of oil paint and a growing affinity for Flemish art, within which oil techniques had been ascendant since the 1420's. Neither the oil medium nor the influence of Northern art were entirely novel in Venice in the early 1470's, but both were given prominence in Venice by the brief presence there of the Sicilian-born artist Antonello da Messina around 1475. It is evident that Antonello learned much of his technique from someone with close ties to Jan van Eyck or one of his contemporaries, because his style was formed

far less by Italian art than by the Northern tradition of rendering exact detail and effects of light. The influence of Antonello's Flemish orientation upon Bellini's work, and thus upon later Venetian painting, was lasting; the oil medium allowed for more fluid and colorful rendering of surfaces than did the traditional, fast-drying tempera paints, and provided Bellini and his successors with a material which was well suited to the Venetian artistic temperament, which was by nature more spontaneous and emotional than that of their central Italian counterparts.

During the 1470's, Bellini's appreciation of monumental form seems to have been enhanced by contact with the work of great Italian predecessors such as Donatello and Masaccio, though there is only indirect evidence of this. The influence of the frescoes of Piero della Francesca seems likely; Giovanni could have seen his work at Rimini, on the road between Venice and Pesaro. There is something of Piero's austere integration of form, light, and color in the large panel of Bellini's *Coronation of the Virgin*, part of the Pesaro altarpiece of the early 1470's. A small panel of the *Adoration of the Child*, part of the *predella*, or frame, of this altarpiece, shows Bellini's ability to create a convincing landscape environment for his solidly painted figures, but more particularly it reveals a poetic mastery of effects of light and atmosphere that was unmatched by his Italian contemporaries. Another panel (of disputed date, but perhaps painted as early as 1475), the *Saint Francis in Ecstasy* in the Frick Collection in New York, is considered one of Bellini's masterpieces. Conceived as an independent picture, this painting has a design that recalls the art of Mantegna, but its underlying character is more reflective. Bellini's art, increasingly receptive to the beauty of landscape, is in perfect harmony with the spirit of Francis of Assisi, of all the saints the one most devoted to nature.

In the following decade, Bellini continued with much the same range of subject matter as before, but he painted with increasing assurance. An *Enthroned Madonna and Child* of the late 1480's, also know as the San Giobbe altarpiece, is monumental both in size and in conception: It is more than fifteen feet high and eight feet wide and was originally installed in a Venetian church, where its pictorial space could be viewed as an extension of the actual interior space of the church. Another dimension of Bellini's work in this period was to meet the continuing needs of the *scuole* for large commemorative paintings, a task he often shared with his brother, but none of these has survived.

A continuous sequence of portraits by Bellini's hand—as distinct from works of his studio—cannot be established, but there are several portrait masterpieces that are unquestionably his own. His *Portrait of Doge Leonardo Loredan*, an exquisitely detailed rendering of Venice's leader, was probably painted following Loredan's election in October, 1501. In this work, Bellini gives a sense of the whole person in two senses: physically, by choosing a composition which shows more of the subject's attire, and psychologically, by means of rare human insight. Bellini's approach to portraiture soon became the norm with the new generation of painters, and his ability to keep abreast of the innovations of his younger contemporaries made him a sought-after artist into his final years.

Among Bellini's most important paintings is a work of his last years, the *Feast of the Gods*. Loosely based upon a subject taken from Ovid's *Fasti* (c. A.D. 8; feasts), the painting was commissioned by a knowledgeable patron, possibly Isabella d'Este of the Court of Ferrara. Isabella, a woman of decided tastes as well as strong intellect, had begun a project of decorating some study rooms in her private apartment with paintings of pagan subjects, and she may have engaged Bellini to paint a companion-piece to a work by Mantegna. *Feast of the Gods* is a painting that celebrates classical mythology while paying respects to the lively world of Italian Renaissance culture. One of Bellini's few paintings on classical subjects, its humor, lyricism, and mildly erotic content show that he could be moved by antique as well as Christian themes.

Summary

Giovanni Bellini's exceptionally long and productive career spanned more than six decades. The larger part of his work belongs to the 1400's, when Italian art evolved a unity of approach to pictorial organization and content within which local and individual styles are still strongly manifest. Bellini was Venice's foremost painter of this period, providing one of many regional inflections to the technical and expressive development of Italian art.

Like his great contemporaries, Bellini sought with success to enhance the sense of reality in his paintings through the study of space, volume, light, and color, but, among his varied achievements, art historians have credited him with a particularly astute understanding of atmosphere. Bellini learned to give his landscape-based compositions the reality of specific times of day and conditions of atmosphere, and he applied his discoveries to reinforcing the mood of his chosen subject.

Though Bellini developed his sense of light and color within the medium of tempera paint, his use of oil paint was particularly consequential for Venetian art, which increasingly exploited the brilliance and versatility of the oil medium. Bellini's mastery of oil was accomplished well before 1500, but his continuing conquest of its capabilities late in his career serves as a reminder that he not only survived into the new century but also was an active participant in it. Bellini remained extraordinarily vital in old age, perhaps spurred by friendly rivalry with a younger generation of painters that included Giorgione and Titian. It is likely that Giorgione was in some fashion Bellini's pupil, but the influence of pupil upon teacher is also suggested by scholars. Not long after Bellini's death, when the *Feast of the Gods* came into the hands of Alfonso d'Este in Mantua, the young Titian was engaged to revise it. Titian's kinship with Bellini—to an extent one of taste as well as of technical practice—is virtually the only explanation for the fact that Titian's alterations, though regrettable from the perspective of art history, are nevertheless quite successful in their own terms.

After a half century of work, Bellini achieved a style as unified and expressive as that of his greatest contemporaries. The German artist Albrecht Dürer, visting Bellini in Venice in 1506, had found him *optimo pytor* (a great painter) and *pest in Gemoll* (the very best). After hundreds of years, Bellini's achievement still places him in the highest rank of European artists.

Bibliography

Freedberg, S. J. *Painting in Italy, 1500-1600.* 3d ed. New Haven, Conn.: Yale University Press, 1993. This discerning guide to Italian painting of the fourteenth through the seventeenth centuries deals in proportion with the Bellini family, but it has a particular virtue in giving a sense of the proportion of one artist's achievement to another, when many belong in the category "great." A minor irritant is that illustrations are separated from the text.

Glick, D. "A Three-Handed Masterpiece." *Newsweek* 115, no. 5 (1990): 67. The author describes Bellini's painting "Feasts of the Gods" (1514) and the discovery during its restoration that it had been repainted in part and at different times by Titian and by Dosso Dossi.

Goffen, Rona. *Giovanni Bellini.* New Haven, Conn.: Yale University Press, 1989. Interpretation and criticism of the works of Bellini.

Hartt, Frederick. *History of Italian Renaissance Art: Painting, Sculpture, Architecture.* 4th ed. London: Thames and Hudson, and New York: Abrams, 1994. This standard survey of the field discusses the Bellini family very extensively. An excellent prelude to specialized reading, it retains its value for convenient reference to artists and works referred to in scholarly works. The illustrations are integrated with the text.

Hendy, Philip, and Ludwig Goldscheider. *Giovanni Bellini.* Oxford: Phaidon Press, and New York: Oxford University Press, 1945. This volume consists of more than one hundred illustrations of Bellini's works with an introductory essay by Hendy. The text is aimed at a general audience and contains comparative information useful to the student without an extensive background in Renaissance art. Color reproductions are given of five key works.

Meiss, Millard. *Giovanni Bellini's "St. Francis."* Princeton, N.J.: Princeton University Press, 1964. This short monograph on one of Bellini's most beautiful and celebrated paintings shows that scholarship in art history can be graceful as well as illuminating. The excellent illustrations (only the title painting is shown in color) include many works by Bellini and others that help place the St. Francis work in context.

Robertson, Giles. *Giovanni Bellini.* Oxford: Clarendon Press, 1968; New York: Hacker Art Books, 1986. Robertson's full-length study has the advantage of later scholarly research to differentiate it from Hendy and Goldscheider's monograph. The author negotiates a quantity of detailed information with surprising clarity. The absence of color plates may be accounted for by the extent of the black-and-white illustrations, of which there are 120.

Wind, Edgar. *Bellini's "Feast of the Gods": A Study in Venetian Humanism.* Cambridge, Mass.: Harvard University Press, 1948. Despite its many erudite references to issues in ancient literature and Renaissance Humanism—many of which appear only in Latin or Italian—this excellent small monograph is directed to nonspecialists as much as to scholars. Both the text and the plates give a broad sense of Bellini's later career and his cultural environment, and, though Wind's conclusions are questioned by later scholars, his observations are unfailingly interesting.

C. S. McConnell

SIR THOMAS BODLEY

Born: March 2, 1545; Exeter, Devon, England

Died: January 28, 1613; London, England

Areas of Achievement: Diplomacy, philanthropy, and education

Contribution: Bodley founded the Bodleian Library at Oxford University, which quickly became one of the world's great research libraries.

Early Life

Thomas Bodley was born on March 2, 1545, at Exeter in Devon. His father was John Bodley, a successful merchant of that city, and his mother was Joan, the daughter of Robert Hone of Ottery St. Mary, Devon. The family was staunchly Protestant and went into exile during the reign of the Catholic Mary I. In May, 1557, the Bodleys moved from Frankfort to Geneva. There, the twelve-year-old Thomas Bodley studied divinity from John Calvin and Theodore Beza while he learned Greek from Philip Beroaldus and Hebrew from Antoine Chevallier, later a professor of Hebrew at Cambridge.

The death of Queen Mary on November 17, 1558, brought the Protestant Elizabeth to the English throne and ended the Bodley family's exile. They returned to London, and in 1559 the now fifteen-year-old Thomas began his studies at Magdalen College, Oxford, under Lawrence Humphrey, a friend of his father and a fellow Marian exile. Bodley received his bachelor of arts in 1563 and in the same year became a probationary Fellow of Merton College. The next year Merton granted him a full fellowship.

During his time as a senior member of the university, Bodley was moderately successful. He began lecturing without fee on Greek at Merton in 1565 with such success that the college voted him a stipend and made the lectures a permanent institution. After receiving his master of arts degree in 1566, he began giving university lectures on natural philosophy, was elected a university proctor in 1569, and served as deputy public orator. It was during these years that he matured into a square-built, distinguished man with close-cropped dark hair and beard. Then, in 1576, Merton granted him a leave of absence to go abroad and study modern foreign languages. Four years of travel in Italy, France, and Germany allowed him to achieve proficiency in a number of foreign languages, particularly Italian, French, and Spanish.

Life's Work

When Bodley left Oxford in 1576, he had little intention of returning. Instead, he hoped ultimately to enter the service of the English government. By the early 1580's, he appeared to have secured the patronage of Sir Francis Walsingham and Robert Dudley, the Earl of Leicester. One of them probably obtained for him a seat as a Member of Parliament for Portsmouth in 1584. His first diplomatic mission came in the next year, when he traveled to Denmark to obtain support for Henry of Navarre and the French Protestants.

After his return from Denmark, Bodley scored the greatest triumph of his life and married Ann, the daughter of Richard Carey (or Carew) of Bristol and the widow of the wealthy merchant Nicholas Ball of Totnes, Devon, on July 19, 1586. It was Ball's fortune that allowed Bodley to refound and endow the library that bears his name. Ball had died in March, so his wife had remained a widow for a mere four months. Yet even then, Bodley was not Ann's first suitor. Another man was on the verge of winning her when Bodley arrived. Examining the situation, he persuaded the hapless man to play his hand in a card game. With his rival thus occupied, Bodley sought out the widow Ann in the garden, wooed her, and won her promise of marriage. In this way he acquired a wife, a fortune, and seven stepchildren who would later receive little benefit from their natural father's wealth as a result of its philanthropic diversion by their stepfather. Bodley and Ann had no children of their own.

Bodley's marriage quickly proved its value. Ann's contacts in Devon and Cornwall gained for Bodley a place in the session of Parliament called on September 15, 1586, for the borough of St. Germans, Cornwall. During 1588, the Elizabethan government sent him on a confidential mission to the fugitive King Henry III of France. Almost as soon as he returned home, he found himself appointed to replace Henry Killigrew as the resident English envoy on the Netherlands Council of State. Bodley served in that difficult post from 1589 to 1596. Queen Elizabeth complicated relations with the Dutch by insisting that they pay for the full cost of English military assistance in the war with Spain. Again and again, Bodley found himself thwarted by the uncooperative Dutch or placed in an impossible position by his own government. By 1592, he was hoping for recall, and in 1594, he quarreled with William Cecil, Lord

Burghley, the queen's chief minister, and asked to be relieved. That did not occur, but the incident was probably a big step in Bodley's progress toward deciding to abandon government service altogether.

Still unable to accomplish Queen Elizabeth's diplomatic bidding by 1596, Bodley returned home to discover that in his irascible queen's opinion he deserved hanging. Furthermore, the mutual animosities of Robert Devereux, the Earl of Essex, and Lord Burghley had recently cost him a promotion to be secretary of state. At that point, he decided to retire. Never again would he resume his career of government service and diplomacy. A mission was offered but refused in 1598 and James I's government tried one last time to coax him out of retirement during 1604 and 1605. This effort gained for him a knighthood but it did not change his mind.

The weary and disillusioned Bodley desired a project for his labor and talents that would bring him peace and satisfaction. After some thought, he settled on the refounding of a university library for Oxford. The original had disappeared in the middle of the sixteenth century during the turmoil of the Edwardian Reformation. Thus, on February 23, 1598, Bodley wrote to the vice chancellor of Oxford University offering to refurbish the library, to secure books for it, to hire a staff, to attract other benefactors, and, above all, to establish a permanent endowment which he believed was essential to the library's long-term survival.

Work and planning for the new library proceeded quickly. From the first, Bodley persuaded the university to appoint six delegates to oversee the library. These included his trusted friends Thomas Allen and William Gent, Fellows of Gloucester Hall, and John Hawley, the principal of the same college. By the end of 1599 at the latest, a librarian had been found, although the university did not officially confirm his appointment until April, 1602. Thomas James of New College practiced scholarship with a deeply antipapal thrust and proved to be an able head for the new library. Meanwhile, the work of refurbishing the library approached completion in June, 1600. It was a source of great relief to Bodley, since he could now begin to solicit in earnest the books and money needed to build up the library's collection.

Bodley took great interest in collecting books for his library. His house at Fulham, in London, continued to be his principal residence, and it was there that he collected the books he sought or solicited until they were dispatched in yearly batches to Oxford. Even the most casual offers of gifts were followed up. Potential donors were never allowed to forget what exactly they had offered. Thomas Allen, the library delegate, and Thomas James, the librarian, both significantly assisted Bodley in his efforts to attract donations of books, manuscripts, and money. In fact, James made the suggestion that resulted in the Stationers' Company agreeing in 1610 to deposit one free copy of every book that they printed in the Bodleian. Thanks to these efforts, between 1600 and 1605, seventeen hundred pounds were raised to buy books. By 1605, the collection contained fifty-six hundred volumes, for which James had compiled an up-to-date printed catalog. Growth continued so that by Bodley's death in early 1613 the library housed about seven thousand volumes or about fifteen thousand titles along with eight hundred manuscripts. The Bodleian Library had quickly grown to be one of the significant research collections of its day.

Bodley believed that it was his library's purpose to preserve the entire range of human knowledge. This attitude is reflected in his continuing efforts systematically to acquire Hebrew and Arabic books. As early as 1603, the Bodleian purchased its first Chinese books, although there was no one who could read them. Policies concerning admission to the library also reflected a broad-minded philosophy. Almost any member of the university could use the library, if he fulfilled certain conditions. Furthermore, students from foreign universities were also admitted if their subject of research met the approval of university authorities.

The library's rapid growth caused it to overflow quickly its original quarters. Bodley's last years and large amounts of his treasure were spent getting the Arts End extension built during 1610-1612. This building marked the first use of wall-shelving in a public library in England. His other final worry was to secure the permanent endowment to the Bodleian from challenge by any of his disgruntled heirs. He therefore produced a will on January 2, 1613, that gave his endowment firm protection with powerful overseers such as William Abbot, the Archbishop of Canterbury, and Edward Coke, then Chief Justice of Common Pleas. Although Bodley remembered most members of his family and his servants in his will, their portions were much reduced by the immense endowment of seven thousand pounds that he gave to his library. Many criticized his lack of generosity to his family and stepchildren (Ann had died in 1611). After his death, his brother Lawrence Bodley

and a niece, Elizabeth Willis, unsuccessfully contested the will. In the meantime, Bodley died on January 28, 1613, at his home in London after a lingering illness. He was buried with great pomp in the Merton College chapel.

Summary

Sir Thomas Bodley was a man of great ability, immense pride, and sensitive ego. If he had not possessed those traits, his energies would probably not have been redirected from a reasonably successful diplomatic career into the role of library benefactor. His premier achievement of refounding Oxford's university library has overshadowed his state service. Although battered and frustrated, Bodley survived the rigors of diplomatic service in the Netherlands. A close association with the ill-fated Earl of Essex did not permanently taint him in the eyes of the English government, which continued to seek his valuable skills long after he had lost any desire to offer them. Voluntarily forgoing the disconcerting world of diplomatic service, Bodley secured his place in history by benefiting scholarship. The Bodleian Library became the best academic library in England during his lifetime and remained in a class by itself until the British Museum and the Cambridge University Library began to catch up in the nineteenth century.

Bibliography

Bodley, Thomas. *Letters of Sir Thomas Bodley to the University of Oxford, 1598-1611*. Edited by G. W. Wheeler. Oxford: Oxford University Press, 1927. An edition of fifteen letters from Bodley to the various vice chancellors of the university concerning his library. These letters are also available in the *Bodleian Quarterly Record*, volume 5. Wheeler has also edited the correspondence between Bodley and his librarian Thomas James.

Chamberlain, John. *The Chamberlain Letters: A Selection of the Letters of John Chamberlain Concerning Life in England from 1597 to 1626*. Edited by Elizabeth McClure Thomson. New York: Putnam, 1965. A selection of extracts from Norman Egbert McClure's two-volume *The Letters of John Chamberlain* (Philadelphia: American Philosophical Society, 1939). Includes Chamberlain's description of the Bodleian's buildings and his critical comments concerning Bodley's vanity in leaving a fortune for a library named after himself while neglecting his legitimate heirs and family.

Mallet, Charles Edward. *A History of the University of Oxford*. 3 vols. London: Methuen, and New York: Longman, 1924-1927. Mallet's work is to be superseded by the projected multi-volume "Oxford History of Oxford University." Ian Philip's account of the foundation of the Bodleian is superior, but Mallet has some unique information.

Morris, Jan, ed. *The Oxford Book of Oxford*. Oxford and New York: Oxford University Press, 1978. An anthology of extracts of documents and anecdotes relating to Oxford. Includes several items relating to Bodley and the early years of his library. Bodley's letter of February 23, 1598, offering to refurbish and restore the university library is in this collection.

Philip, Ian. *The Bodleian Library in the Seventeenth and Eighteenth Centuries*. Oxford: Clarendon Press, and New York: Oxford University Press, 1983. A scrupulously researched and well-written account of the Bodleian Library from 1598 to 1800 by a retired member of its staff who is also a recognized library historian. The best work available on the subject.

Wernham, R. B. *After the Armada: Elizabethan England and the Struggle for Western Europe, 1588-1595.* Oxford: Clarendon Press, and New York: Oxford University Press, 1984. An excellent account of English foreign policy and military relations during a time of great international turmoil. Provides a context for Bodley's diplomatic efforts in the Netherlands and gives a good indication of why he found his service there to be so frustrating.

Wood, Anthony. *Athenae Oxonienses: An Exact History of All the Writers and Bishops Who Have Had Their Education in the University of Oxford.* 2 vols. London: Thomas Bennet, 1691-1692; New York: Franklin, 1967. A collection of biographical sketches of famous Oxford men starting with 1500 and including most of the seventeenth century. Originally published in 1691 and 1692 by one of Oxford's most famous antiquarians. Bodley's entry is located in volume 2 and its eulogistic tone shows the deep gratitude that his library benefaction inspired in the scholarly community by the late seventeenth century.

Ronald H. Fritze

ANNE BOLEYN

Born: c. 1500-1501; probably at Blickling in Norfolk, England
Died: May 19, 1536; London, England
Areas of Achievement: Church reform; government and politics
Contribution: The desire of England's King Henry VIII to marry Anne Boleyn led to the establishment of the Church of England.

Early Life

Future English queen Anne Boleyn was born into an ambitious family at a time when ambitions were realized through interactions with the court and marriage into the nobility. Young women from such families were expected to marry as their families dictated. Anne's great-grandfather, Geoffrey Boleyn, a tradesman lacking in social status, rose to become lord mayor of London in 1457 but improved his position further through marriage; Sir William Boleyn, her grandfather, made an even more impressive marriage to Margaret Butler, daughter of an Irish earl. Thomas Boleyn, Anne's father, was the eldest of their four sons. A highly successful courtier and diplomat, he married Elizabeth Howard, daughter of Thomas Howard, earl of Surrey; Elizabeth Howard was descended from King Edward I, thus bestowing a touch of royal blood upon her children.

While Elizabeth Howard was frequently pregnant, only Mary, Anne, and George survived to adulthood. To prepare Anne for an advantageous marriage, she was sent abroad, first, in 1513, to the court of Margaret of Austria, regent of the Netherlands. When Mary Tudor, sister of Henry VIII, married King Louis XII of France in 1514, Anne was moved to their court, where she joined her sister Mary. When Louis died, the sisters remained at court serving Claude of Valois, wife of the new king, Francis I, whose court was conspicuously vice-ridden. Mary Boleyn's reputation became tarnished; Anne remained aloof, although she developed the charm, wit, and love of French manners and fashions expected of her in that sophisticated environment.

She returned to England in 1521 or 1522, gaining a place in the household of Henry VIII's Queen Catherine of Aragon, where her social skills brought her immediate attention. Her sister Mary was then mistress of the king, which may have facilitated Sir Thomas Boleyn's ennoblement as Viscount Rochford. During this period, Anne attempted to marry Henry Percy, heir to the earldom of Northumberland. Her desire to arrange her own marriage was itself shocking; her plans were thwarted by Cardinal Thomas Wolsey, archbishop of York and lord chancellor of England. Anne temporarily left court.

Life's Work

Anne returned to court in 1524 or 1525. His affair with her sister ended, King Henry VIII was attracted to Anne. She resisted his approaches, either because she was genuinely repelled or because she was unwilling to settle for a role as a mistress. Since 1509, Henry had been married to Catherine, daughter of Isabella of Castile and Ferdinand of Aragon, rulers of Spain, but the king was increasingly frustrated by Catherine's inability to bear a male heir. A series of pregnancies had resulted in only one child, Mary, who survived infancy. While miscarriages and high infant mortality rates were common, Henry was concerned that he have a legitimate successor to protect England against a recurrence of the previous century's civil wars. Moreover, the birth of his illegitimate son to Elizabeth Blount had proved to his satisfaction that he could sire sons. In 1527, Henry sought a "divorce"—essentially a modern annulment, since rather than dissolving the marriage, it would show that a legitimate marriage had never taken place. The king's argument was that despite the papal dispensation for his marriage to Catherine, his marriage was forbidden by the Bible, specifically by Leviticus 20:21, which forbids marriage with a brother's wife. In November, 1501, Catherine had married Henry's elder brother Arthur, who died in April, 1502, probably without consummating the marriage. Catherine's failure to bear a son was proof, Henry believed, of divine displeasure with the marriage.

Such divorces were frequent. The duke of Suffolk, who had married Henry's sister Mary in 1515, had secured two; Henry's older sister, Queen Margaret of Scotland, similarly secured one and remarried in 1527. Henry expected the process to be rapid, entrusting Cardinal Wolsey with what came to be called the "King's Great Matter." In 1527, however, the troops of the Holy Roman Emperor Charles V had invaded Rome; the emperor was Queen Catherine's nephew. Pope Clement VII was now his prisoner and was unwilling to take steps

against the emperor's aunt. He began a series of delaying actions.

Anne's role as rival with Catherine for Henry's affection was known by early 1526. Flirtatious, volatile, outspoken, arrogant, and sophisticated where the queen was grave, mild-mannered, modest, and restrained, Anne was intelligent in an age that rarely acknowledged the value of female intelligence. Anne gained few friends. Many could not understand Henry's attraction to her. She was no beauty. She was dark-haired; the ideal of the day was blond. She was thin, and her skin was sallow. She was said to have a rudimentary extra nail on one hand. To much of the court and the public, she became a stereotypical image of the temptress, although her frequent absences from court may have been serious attempts to avoid the king's attentions. Anne was blamed for Wolsey's fall from power. Henry, accustomed to having his way, replaced Wolsey with Thomas Cromwell, a man more in sympathy with Anne. Anne was accused of avenging herself for Wolsey's earlier interference in her romance with Henry Percy. By 1529, however, she could not have saved herself from the king's plans had she chosen to do so.

Henry was not in sympathy with the Protestant movement, which had swept through northern Europe since Martin Luther had posted his designs for church reform on a church door at Wittenberg in 1517. Henry considered himself a good Catholic and had been given the title "Defender of the Faith" for his opposition to Luther. Nevertheless, in 1529, determined to impose his will and gain a male heir, Henry convened a Parliament that was to bring about a religious revolution, as Pope Clement continued to thwart Henry's plans. In 1530, Clement told Henry to dismiss Anne from the court; in 1531, he banned the king's remarriage while the divorce case was being heard, apparently indefinitely, in Rome.

Anne, however, had allowed Henry increasing intimacy, and by the end of 1532 they had become lovers. By December, 1532, she was pregnant, and, probably sometime in January, 1533, Anne and Henry were secretly married. Henry's logic, apparently, was that he had a right to this second marriage because the marriage to Catherine had never been valid. On June 1, 1533, Anne Boleyn, visibly pregnant, was crowned queen of England in an elaborate ceremony that was to be the high point of her life. Despite the public pageantry, crowds were quiet and occasionally hostile as the new queen passed. Queen Catherine's many charities and conventional domesticity won for her friends that the new queen could never possess.

In July, Pope Clement VII ordered Henry to renounce Anne and declared any child of the new marriage illegitimate. That child, the future Elizabeth I, was born on September 7, 1533. She was the wrong sex for an heir, but Henry and Anne assumed that Anne would continue to bear healthy children, although Anne by then was about thirty-three years of age, well into middle age at a time of low life expectancy. In 1534, Anne gave birth to two stillborn infants. Understanding the importance to her well-being of a healthy son, she continued to become pregnant. The increasing insecurity of her position did not improve her disposition.

Bent on having his way, Henry, via an Act of Royal Supremacy, made himself, not the pope, the spiritual father of the English people, thus separating England from the Roman Catholic Church. From February, 1535, it would be high treason to deny Henry's supremacy. He had already begun the series of executions that would taint his reputation for the remainder of his reign. He purged those who defied him, including his old friend the humanist scholar Sir Thomas More, who was beheaded in 1535, and the aged John Fisher, bishop of Rochester. They and many others could not accept the Act of Supremacy. Unwilling to accept any challenge to his will, he was also tiring of Anne's quick tongue and her apparent unwillingness to accept his unfaithfulness as had Catherine; like Catherine, Anne also failed to provide him with a son.

In January, 1536, Catherine of Aragon died. Henry was unlikely to marry for a third time while Catherine and Anne both lived, but he was pursuing Jane Seymour by November, 1535. Catherine's death freed him to rid himself of Anne and start anew. He maintained that Anne had bewitched him into marriage; he claimed she was a sorceress and was guilty of adultery. He also claimed that she had discussed what would happen when the king died, and such discussions constituted high treason. On May 2, Anne was arrested and taken to the Tower of London. There, where she had been received on the eve of her coronation three years before, she was made a prisoner.

Despite public hatred of Anne, few believed she was guilty. According to the case prepared by Thomas Cromwell, she had committed incest with her brother, George Boleyn (Lord Rochford). Three prominent courtiers, Sir Henry Norris, Sir Francis

Weston, and William Brereton, as well as her musician, Mark Smeaton, were arrested as her partners in adultery. Smeaton was not a nobleman; as a commoner, he could be and apparently was tortured into a confession. Charges included conspiracy to murder the king.

The duke of Norfolk, Anne's uncle Thomas Howard, presided over the trials of Norris, Weston, Brereton, and Smeaton on May 12; all were condemned to death. Anne and her brother were tried separately on May 14; again, Anne's uncle presided. Actual evidence against them was lacking, and the case was poorly prepared, but the results were foreordained. Both were condemned. On May 17, Archbishop Thomas Cranmer convened a court at Lambeth to annul Henry's marriage to Anne, thus preparing the way for Henry's marriage to Jane Seymour on May 30 as, essentially, his first valid marriage. Anne Boleyn was beheaded on May 19 at the Tower of London; her remains were buried in the Royal Chapel of St. Peter ad Vincula of the Tower.

Summary

Scholars have argued over the degree to which Anne Boleyn was a Protestant rebel against the Church of Rome. She encouraged individual reading of the Bible and the reading of works banned by the church, but there is little other evidence that she was a conscious Protestant. Nevertheless, because she was, willingly or otherwise, a pawn in the King's Great Matter, she was at the heart of the separation of England from the Roman Catholic Church and of the despoliation of convents and monasteries that was to follow. Her independence of spirit and attempts at autonomy, despite the great powers that controlled her destiny, seem to ally her with the Protestant movement, whatever her intent, and cause modern feminist historians to view her with sympathetic eyes.

Bibliography

Chapman, Hester. *The Challenge of Anne Boleyn.* New York: Coward, McCann and Geoghegan, 1974. Places Boleyn in the context of a politically ambitious family in an age of melodramatic excess; pays particular attention to the courts in which Boleyn was trained.

Erickson, Carolly. *Mistress Anne: The Life and Times of Anne Boleyn.* New York: Summit Books, 1984. In one of a series of Tudor biographies that include *Bloody Mary* (1978) and *Great Harry* (1980), Erickson vividly re-creates the world in which these people lived; her work is scholarly, but her style is popular. Her portrait of Anne is not generally sympathetic.

Fraser, Antonia. *The Wives of Henry VIII.* New York: Knopf, 1993. Originally published in London as *The Six Wives of Henry VIII* (1992). Fraser balances anti-Boleyn propaganda with information from other sources to achieve a convincing portrayal, in part sympathetic.

Lindsey, Karen. *Divorced, Beheaded, Survived.* Reading, Mass.: Addison-Wesley, 1995. A feminist interpretation of Boleyn's life, this work emphasizes Boleyn's role as victim of an all-powerful monarch determined to conquer her. Cites as evidence a poem by Sir Thomas Wyatt, who knew Anne well.

Warnike, Retha M. *The Rise and Fall of Anne Boleyn: Family Politics at the Court of Henry VIII.* Cambridge: Cambridge University Press, 1989. Focusing on the Anne's society and its conventions, Warnike argues that Anne's failure to produce a male heir doomed her.

Weir, Alison. *The Six Wives of Henry VIII.* London: Bodley Head, 1991. Heavily dependent on the virulently anti-Boleyn commentary of Spanish ambassador Eustace (or Eustache) Chapuys, Weir presents an almost totally unsympathetic portrait of Boleyn as manipulative seductress.

Betty Richardson

HIERONYMUS BOSCH
Jeroen van Aeken

Born: c. 1450; 's-Hertogenbosch, North Brabant
Died: 1516; 's-Hertogenbosch, North Brabant
Area of Achievement: Art
Contribution: Bosch produced strikingly original paintings, whose brilliant style, flickering brushstroke, and fantastic, nightmarish visions influenced twentieth century Surrealists. Bosch's message, however, is rooted in the preoccupations of the early sixteenth century. His obsessions—sin, death, and damnation—reflect orthodox Christian concerns.

Early Life

Hieronymus Bosch is the most fascinating early Netherlandish painter, in part because he is the most puzzling. Little is known about his life. Like most northern Renaissance artists, he left no self-portraits, letters, diaries, or theoretical writings. Contemporary sources mention several works by him, but none of these survives. Conversely, the paintings that are attributed to him are all undocumented. Hundreds of works bear his name, but few of these signatures are authentic.

The two principal archival sources for Bosch are the city records of his hometown, 's-Hertogenbosch, and the account books of one of the town's confraternities, the Brotherhood of the Blessed Virgin. These documents reveal that Bosch's family had settled in 's-Hertogenbosch by the year 1426 and that Bosch entered the family business: His grandfather, three uncles, his father, and his brother were all painters, and Bosch was probably trained by a family member, most likely his father. Since Bosch's name does appear with regularity in the 's-Hertogenbosch archives, he must have lived there throughout his life. His family name was van Aeken (possibly a reference to the city of Aechen), but by 1504 he adopted Bosch as his surname, to refer to the town where he lived and worked.

Bosch, like his grandfather, uncles, and father, was a member of the Brotherhood of the Blessed Virgin, a large and wealthy confraternity devoted to the worship of the Virgin Mary. Much of Bosch's activity for the brotherhood was created for their new chapel in the cathedral of 's-Hertogenbosch. He painted a panel of living and dead members, offered advice on gilding and polychroming a sculpted altarpiece, and designed a crucifix, a chandelier, and a stained-glass window. None of this work survives.

Sometime between the years 1479 and 1481, Bosch was married to a wealthy woman, Aleyt Goyaerts van den Meervenne, the daughter of pharmacists. It has often been noted that alchemical equipment appears to underlie many of the forms in Bosch's most important work. Bosch could have become acquainted with such apparatuses through his in-laws.

There was no active court life in 's-Hertogenbosch, but documents show that the nobility elsewhere were patrons of Bosch. In 1504, Philip the Handsome, Duke of Burgundy, commissioned an altarpiece of *The Last Judgment*, now lost, and Henry III of Nassau owned *The Garden of Earthly Delights* by 1517. Margaret of Austria's inventory of 1516 includes paintings by Bosch, and in the middle of the sixteenth century Philip II, King of Spain, favored his works.

Life's Work

Bosch's art stands outside the mainstream of early Netherlandish painting. While Bosch's holy figures are plain and at times awkward, most Netherlandish artists, such as Jan van Eyck, Rogier van der Weyden, and Hans Memling, idealize and dignify the Holy Family and saints. While Bosch tended to paint thinly and rapidly, most Netherlandish painters used a painstaking technique of multilayered glazes and meticulous brushwork. Whereas Bosch shows little interest in the individual, portraiture is a hallmark of the early Netherlandish school. In addition, Bosch depicts themes that are new to large-scale painting, such as the *Haywain* and *The Ship of Fools*, and interprets traditional themes, such as *Hell* or *Christ Carrying the Cross*, in a strikingly original way. More fundamentally, evil and corruption dominate Bosch's world. Hermit saints, such as Saint Anthony, strive to resist temptation through the contemplative life, but, as Max J. Friedländer observes, with Bosch, "innocence was pale." God is small and passive, mankind weak and sinful, and the Devil powerfully seductive. The disturbing quality of Bosch's works is far from the grace, beauty, and serenity that typify early Netherlandish painting.

Bosch's obsession with sin, death, and corruption expresses an undercurrent that is easily detected in northern Europe. Some in the North accepted new ideas, such as the humanistic belief in the dignity of man; however, for others, the time around 1500 produced only fear, conflict, and uncertainty. Millennial fears were widespread; the *Malleus malificarum*, a handbook on witchcraft, was a best-seller. The disturbing quality sensed in Bosch's paintings can also be found, for example, in the contemporary work of German artists such as Matthias Grünewald, Hans Baldung Grien, and Hans Burgkmair and in sculptures of Death, alone or with a lover.

Dating early Netherlandish paintings is notoriously hazardous. None of Bosch's works can be dated with certainty. Scholars generally agree that the early works, generally dated before 1485, such as the *Adoration* in Philadelphia, are characterized by an uncertain sense of foreshortening and perspective, timid brushwork, and simple, traditional compositions. As Bosch matured, his brushwork became freer, more painterly; his perspective and foreshortening improved; and his paintings achieved a power, an immediacy not seen earlier. The *Landloper* in Rotterdam, the *Adoration Triptych* in Madrid, and *The Crowning with Thorns* in London are generally viewed as late works, dating after 1500.

Scholars have suggested varying theories to explain Bosch's art. Some explanations, such as one that holds that Bosch was a member of a heretical sect, must be rejected as totally lacking in evidence. Others are more convincing. Astrology, alchemy, and Netherlandish folklore have been shown to be among the sources to which Bosch turned for his imagery. The widespread use of Nertherlandish proverbs in Bosch's oeuvre has also been noted.

Bosch uses a pictorial language that is largely lost to modern viewers. For example, his *Saint John the Baptist* shows an upright bear beneath a tree, a well-known symbol of the desert, used, for example, by Andrea Pisano on the Campanile and by the Limburg brothers (Pol, Hermann, and Jehanequin) in the *Belles Heures*. The saint's pose seems at first glance inappropriate; he seems to lounge on the ground. Yet his recumbent position, head in hand, refers to his dreamlike state, favorable for visions.

Modern scholarship has tried to place Bosch's art in its historical context. His images of Saint Anthony should, in part, be seen against the large numbers of victims suffering from Saint Anthony's Fire, a disease that produced hallucinations. Walter S. Gibson suggests that Bosch's works may have appealed to members of the societies of rhetoric and to the rich intellectual community of 's-Hertogenbosch.

Most scholars agree that Bosch held traditional, orthodox Christian views. For example, some of his works, such as the Philadelphia *Adoration* and the Madrid *Adoration Triptych*, show Eucharistic symbolism. In the interior of the latter work, Bosch uses Old Testament prototypes and alludes to the Virgin as altar; on the exterior, he depicts *The Mass of Saint Gregory*. Many of his works moralize against sin, specifically lust (*The Ship of Fools* and *The Garden of Earthly Delights*) or avarice (*The Death of the Miser* and *Haywain*). Others point the way to a devout life. The numerous images of *Christ Carrying the Cross* suggest that one should imitate Christ, as the writings of Thomas à Kempis had advised. Bosch recommends the contemplative life through his depictions of hermit saints such as Saint Anthony.

Bosch's work remains, to a great extent, a puzzle. The meaning of two wings in Rotterdam, for example, remains a mystery. No literary or visual precedents are known. There is also considerable disagreement as to the interpretation of individual motifs. For example, the letter "M" that appears on the knives in Bosch's *The Garden of Earthly Delights* had been explained alternately as referring to the painters Jan Mandyn or Jan Mostaert; to Malignus, the Antichrist; to the word "mundus," meaning "the world"; to the male sex organ; and to a cutler of 's-Hertogenbosch.

The Garden of Earthly Delights, Bosch's most famous work, reveals the artist's variety of sources, fertile imagination, brilliant style, and moralizing message. The title dates from a later time; the contemporary title is unknown. The interior left wing shows Adam and Eve in the Garden of Eden. Bosch makes their identity clear by their nudity, the apple orchard behind, the serpent coiled around the palm tree in the left middle ground, and the animal-filled garden. The moment depicted is rare in large-scale painting: the introduction of Adam to Eve. Adam's position, seated on the ground, seems inappropriate, but it refers to an earlier incident, his creation from the earth. Adam gazes eagerly at Eve, who modestly casts down her eyes. The rabbit to her right refers to her fertility.

This is clearly not the typical Garden of Eden. Creepy, slimy animals crawl out of the pool in the foreground. Animals fight, kill, and devour one another. Monstrous animals and bizarre rock formations further indicate that this is a corrupt earth. The central panel shows hordes of naked young men and women frolicking in an outdoor setting. Both blacks and whites are included to suggest all of mankind. Bosch indicates their lust in several ways; directly, by depicting embracing couples; metaphorically, through oversize strawberries and fish; and by association, through references to fruits, animals, gardens, dancing, and bathing.

Bosch condemns these amorous activities. Genesis I:28 had advised: "Be fruitful and multiply and replenish the earth and subdue it and have dominion over the fish of the sea and over the fowl of the air and over every living thing that moveth upon the earth." Clearly, mankind has disobeyed God. No children are shown, and the oversize fish and birds overwhelm the people. The mouse about to enter the bubble that holds an embracing couple suggests that their act is unclean. The owl, which was thought to be evil in contemporary Dutch folklore because it attacked day birds, is embraced by a lustful youth. The hollowness and fragility of earthly things are indicated by the numerous egg shapes, glass tubes, shells, and bubbles, as well as by such motifs as the figures standing on their heads, precariously balanced on a narrow ledge encircling a cracked globe that bobs in the water.

The right interior wing depicts Hell, a nightmarish vision with fire and ice, monstrous devils, and countless tormented souls. A literary source for this wing is known. The anonymous *Vision of Tundale*, which was published in 's-Hertogenbosch in 1484, describes a monster who ingests and excretes damned sinners. Bosch also illustrates traditional punishments for specific vices. The glutton vomits; the avaricious excrete coins; the proud woman admires her reflection in the polished rear end of a demon.

Another traditional motif is the world upside down: The rabbit, dressed in a hunting jacket, blows a hunter's bugle as he carries, hanging by the feet from a pole, his booty: a man. Bosch reflects a popular Dutch saying with the woman whose arm is burned by a candle (the modern equivalent is "burning the candle at both ends"). The man who coasts on an oversized skate into a hole in the ice suggests the saying "to skate on thin ice."

Summary

Although much of the content is traditional, Hieronymus Bosch's work stands apart, to some extent because of his wide variety of sources. Yet, more important, Bosch was able through his technical skill to translate his strikingly imaginative visions into visual form. His ability, for example, to express textures convincingly, whether ice or fire, metallic sheen or watery bubble, the strings of a lute or the smoke of Hell, made his visions believable. Bosch convinces one of the impossible. One accepts as reality, for example, the Tree-Man with barren trunks for legs, a broken eggshell body, and a face that wistfully directs its gaze at the viewer. Irrational visions haunt and frighten because they seem so real. Bosch's message is moral: Beware the consequences of sin. His worldview is pessimistic: Mankind goes straight from a corrupt Eden to a world full of sinners, to a nightmarish Hell. No alternative is offered; the power of his art is overwhelming.

Bosch had a tremendous impact on his age. Hundreds of works dating from 1500 to 1530 show the imprint of his style. His nightmarish visions continue to haunt later generations. The Surrealists were his children; indeed, even as late as the 1980's a play based on *The Garden of Earthly Delights* was performed in New York.

Bibliography

Bosch, Hieronymus. *The Complete Paintings of Bosch.* Edited by Gregory Martin and Mia Cinotti. London: Weidenfeld and Nicolson, 1969; New York: Abrams, 1971. A comprehensive catalog of the contemporary documents that mention Bosch. This thorough catalogue raisonné includes more than seventy paintings attributed to Bosch. Martin's introduction emphasizes Bosch's pessimism. Numerous color photographs, some detailed, as well as black-and-white reproductions of all cataloged works.

De Tolnay, Charles. *Hieronymus Bosch.* London: Methuen, and New York: Morrow, 1966. An expanded edition of De Tolnay's 1937 monograph. Bosch's paintings are divided into three chronological periods. His work is interpreted in the light of the dream theories of Sigmund Freud and Carl Jung. Abundantly illustrated with high-quality details of Bosch's works. Somewhat dated.

Friedländer, Max J. *Early Netherlandish Painting.* Vol. 5, *Geertgen tot Sint Jans and Jerome Bosch.* Edited by G. Lemmens. Translated by Heinz Norden. New York: Praeger, and Leiden: Sijthoff, 1969. The English translation of the 1927 edition. This is the fundamental discussion of Bosch's style and character. Includes a section on Bosch's drawings and engravings. Contains high-quality photographs of many works by Bosch and his school. Extremely well written.

Gibson, Walter S. *Hieronymus Bosch.* London: Thames and Hudson, and New York: Praeger, 1973. A thoughtful, balanced survey of Bosch's life and art.

———. *Hieronymus Bosch: An Annotated Bibliography.* Boston: Hall, 1983. This comprehensive annotated bibliography includes more than one thousand items, many little known and inaccessible. A concise introduction places the literature on Bosch in its historical context and evaluates the varying interpretations of Bosch's art and the sources for his unusual style. Extremely useful.

Mulazzani, Germano, and Caterina Limentani Virdis. "Bosch or Metsys at Chiaravalle." *FMR: The Magazine of Franco Maria Ricci* vol. 12, no. 57 (1992). The discovery of a fresco in the Flemish style at the Milanese abbey of Chiaravalle created quite a stir in the art world. Its discoverer, Germano Mulazzani, attributed the work to Hieronymus Bosch—a controversial stand. In the final stages of restoration Mulazzani reiterates his hypothesis while Caterina Limentani Virdis, a well-known teacher of Flemish art, opposes with a strong counter-hypothesis, attributing the fresco to another northern artist, Quentin Metsys.

Snyder, James. *Northern Renaissance Art.* New York: Abrams, 1985. Includes one chapter on Bosch. Less cautious than Gibson. Good introductory text, meant for college undergraduates.

Diane Wolfthal

SANDRO BOTTICELLI
Alessandro di Mariano Filipepi

Born: c. 1444; Florence
Died: May, 1510; Florence
Area of Achievement: Art
Contribution: Botticelli has been celebrated for the linear flow of his paintings and for the graceful and thoughtful cast of so much of his work. One of the greatest colorists of Renaissance painting, Botticelli created idealized figures that suggest great spirituality and somewhat less interest in humanity than was depicted in the works of many of his contemporaries.

Early Life

Sandro Botticelli was born Alessandro di Mariano Filipepi. Not much is known about his childhood or family life, except that, like many Florentine painters, he came from the artisan class. He grew up in an international city, already renowned for its art and commerce, for its wool and silk products, and for its bankers and princes—the Medicis, who determined much of the city's politics and art and who would become his patrons. Around 1460, Botticelli was apprenticed to Fra Filippo Lippi, one of the greatest Florentine painters of the early Renaissance. Known especially for his coloring and draftsmanship, he was to exert a lifelong influence on Botticelli's work. Lippi conveyed enormous human interest in his religious paintings, a characteristic Botticelli emulated while expressing a much more exquisite sensitivity to the devotional aspects of his subjects.

Botticelli's earliest commissioned paintings date from about 1470. The figure of *Fortitude*, now in the Uffizi in Florence, reveals many of his mature qualities and interests, as well as details he learned to apply in Lippi's workshop. *Fortitude* is portrayed as a full-figured woman with a characteristically swelling midsection and delicately featured face. The small head, angled toward her left shoulder, and her eyes, following the line of her left arm, suggest a contemplative, even melancholy, figure, whose thoughts are drawn together as tightly as her tiny closed mouth. The only expansive part of her face is her forehead, which is high and wide, and decorated with a pearl-studded crown (a touch borrowed from Lippi). This is a monumental work, which suggests both great volume and extraordinary finesse.

A companion piece from this period, *Judith and Her Maid*, depicts the characters walking through a beautiful landscape, returning to the Israelite camp after Judith has severed the head of Holofernes with a sword. Sword in one hand, and olive branch in the other, the picture of Judith with her head inclined toward her right shoulder resembles the figure of *Fortitude*. Although the sword is bloody, her expression is contemplative and in marked contrast to the maid, whose head juts forward under the strain of carrying Holofernes' head. Judith, in the foreground of the painting, seems to inhabit a space of her own, a spirituality to which the maid and the background landscape must be subordinated. Judith's face resembles Lippi's Madonnas, and the utterly composed quality of her expression is starkly contrasted with the battling troops, just visible on a plain below the path of Judith's progress. In this painting, Botticelli first seems to grasp the division between the realms of the mystical and the natural that is characteristic of his later work.

Life's Work

Botticelli is renowned for painting several versions of *Adoration of the Magi*, which can be studied as evidence of his artistic development. There is, for example, a painting (1482) in the National Gallery of Art, Washington, D.C., that is remarkable for its vivid color and for its striking portrayal of individual figures—all of them arranged in highly distinctive reverential positions. At the apex of the painting are the Madonna and Child, framed by a monumental yet open-ended and airy architectural structure; its triangular roof (through which the blue sky can be seen) is paralleled by the human triangle of the Magi presenting their gifts to the Christ child. This is a beautiful painting which reads like a moment of suspended time. It also has a subtlety and suggestiveness to it that is less apparent in a version at the Uffizi (c. 1475), in which the portraits of figures at the Adoration are more individualized and realistic but also somehow less important, because they contribute less to the meaning of the whole composition. In a recent restoration of this picture, however, it was discovered that the painting had been cropped, so that earlier comments by art historians on the painting's restrictiveness have had to be revised. As in the earlier painting of Judith, the restored Uffizi *Adoration* shows Botticelli employing an open landscape in the background to give perspective to the spiritualized content of his enclosed space.

The power of spirit over space is evident in Botticelli's painting *Saint Augustine in His Cell* (c. 1495). Augustine is presented as a massive, robed figure, holding a book in his powerful left hand while his right hand, with open tensile fingers, is stretched diagonally across his upper body. That he is in the grip of intense thought is also indicated by the lines of concentration on his forehead and his strongly focused eyes. While he is surrounded by the implements of the scholar and the churchman, his gaze is clearly heavenward, for he transcends all earthly instruments, which are merely the means to a spiritual end.

In such paintings, Botticelli retains enough objects and pays enough attention to the human body to create a sense of realism, but in comparison with his contemporaries it is evident that he is more concerned with the spiritual presence of his subjects. Thus, they are less individualized in terms of their clothing or bodily structure. For all of his massiveness, Augustine has none of the muscularity associated with Renaissance painting. Similarly, the details of a scholar's study are kept to a minimum and the sense of a domestic scene is not emphasized, especially when compared with the paintings of Saint Jerome by Domenico Ghirlandajo, Jan van Eyck, and Petrus Christus, which served as models for Botticelli's Augustine.

As significant as his religious painting is Botticelli's treatment of classical subjects. Two of his most famous paintings, *Primavera* (c. 1478) and *The Birth of Venus* (c. 1480's), reflect his concern for line and form rather than for story or for close copying of his Greek models. The central figures of *Primavera* has been taken to be Venus, surrounded by the dancing Graces of spring. The figure's expression suggests much of the same pensiveness of his Madonnas, as does her oval-shaped, tilted head and rounded body. Although an allegorical scene is being illustrated, which includes Flora (the figure of spring), Mercury, Zephyr, and Cupid in order to suggest the arousal of passion in the new season, most commentators have been struck by the elegant choreography of the setting, in which the Graces appear to be dancing while lightly touching one another and entwining their hands. There is a dreaminess, a magical lightness to this locale that evokes the feeling of spring.

For sheer elegance, Botticelli never surpassed *The Birth of Venus*. She stands in the nude on a seashell, blown to shore by the entwined allegorical figures of the winds at her left. Like so many of his female figures, Venus has soft lines—narrow, rounded shoulders and breasts and an upper body that swells out gracefully to wide hips and a rounded stomach. It is the continuity and fullness of his figures that constitutes beauty, not muscle tone or bone. Venus's attendant, at her left, moves toward her with billowing clothes, while the serene goddess stands perfectly poised with knees slightly bent, her hair flowing in the wind. Botticelli had classical sources for this rendering of Venus, but as in *Primavera*, the overwhelming impression of the painting is of the arrival of beauty and perfection, of an aesthetic ideal that is meant to be treasured in and for itself and not particularly for what it represents in myth.

Summary

Ethereal feminine beauty is so much a part of Sandro Botticelli's classical and religious paintings that it has been speculated that he was deeply influenced by the Neoplatonists, who equated the concept of

Beauty with Truth. Botticelli's Venus and his Madonnas could have the same expression, these critics argue, because their perfection was emblematic of the divine. Clearly the unity of his paintings and the way they minimize narrative in favor of tableaux suggests a Platonic bias. The softness of his colors, the vagueness of his landscapes, and his lack of interest in the structure of the human form are reflective of a sensibility that yearns toward some deep, inner mystical sense of the origins of things.

Although Botticelli was viewed as a technically resourceful painter in his time, he was eventually eclipsed by Leonardo da Vinci, whose range of human gestures, dynamic compositions, and use of light and shade made Botticelli seem old-fashioned. Not until the late nineteenth century, when he was taken up by the English Pre-Raphaelites, was Botticelli reinstated. To them, he represented the simplicity and sincerity of early Italian art. Similarly, the English art critic John Ruskin used Botticelli as an example of an artist who presented nature and human figures as expressions of a divinely created world. Art historians still marvel at the refinement, purity, and poignancy of Botticelli's painting. His figures have an otherworldly aura that is attributed to the artist's own faith. His paintings are not so much illustrations of his subjects as they are the subjects themselves—as though the apprehension of eternal beauty and perfection were itself a matter composed of his rhythmical lines, soothing colors, and elongated shapes.

Bibliography

Baldini, Umberto. *Primavera: The Restoration of Botticelli's Masterpiece.* London: Sidgwick and Jackson, and New York: Harry N. Abrams, 1986. Although this book concentrates on one painting (it includes several essays by different art critics), it also provides important criticism of Botticelli's other works and a helpful description of his period in history. A useful bibliography, an index, and handsome color plates make this an indispensable volume on the artist.

Dempsey, Charles. *The Portrayal of Love: Botticelli's "Primavera" and Humanist Culture at the Time of Lorenzo the Magnificent.* Princeton, N.J.: Princeton University Press, 1992. Botticelli's "Primavera" is widely acknowledged as a prime manifestation of Florentine humanist culture under Lorenzo de' Medici. In this work, Dempsey examines the poetry written by Lorenzo and his literary clients in order to give definition to the cultural context in which the Primavera was created.

Ettlinger, Leopold D., and Helen S. Ettlinger. *Botticelli.* London: Thames and Hudson, 1976; New York: Oxford University Press, 1977. An excellent introduction to Botticelli's oeuvre, including 138 illustrations, eighteen in color. An annotated bibliography and an index make this a particularly useful resource.

Hatfield, Rab. *Botticelli's Uffizi "Adoration": A Study in Pictorial Content.* Princeton, N.J.: Princeton University Press, 1976. As the subtitle indicates, this is a specialized study, aimed at developing a vocabulary to describe the pictorial content of Botticelli's paintings. All plates are in black and white. Essentially a book for advanced scholars, this might prove useful to students concentrating on one aspect of the artist's career.

Lightbown, Ronald. *Sandro Botticelli.* 2 vols. London: Elek, and Berkeley: University of California Press, 1978. This is a superb study, with individual chapters on the artist's early life, his early works, his relationship with the Medicis, his period in Rome, his religious and secular paintings, and his drawings. An appendix of documents, notes, an annotated bibliography, and an index make this an essential and accessible scholarly work.

MacGregor, Neil. "I Sandro Painted this Picture." *Spectator* 275 (December, 1995): 80. MacGregor presents his analysis of the symbolism in Botticelli's "Mystic Nativity" and discusses the popularity of the painting at the National Gallery in England.

Venturi, Lionello. *Botticelli.* London: Phaidon Press, 1949. A competent introduction to Botticelli's life and work, with helpful references to his place in the history of art criticism. Forty-eight large color plates make this an especially good volume for studying the paintings.

Carl Rollyson

TYCHO BRAHE

Born: December 14, 1546; Knudstrup Castle, Scania, Denmark

Died: October 24, 1601; Prague, Bohemia

Area of Achievement: Astronomy

Contribution: Brahe realized early that the existing means for observing and measuring celestial bodies and their motions were inaccurate. His great achievements are to have significantly improved existing instruments, to have invented some new instruments, and to have made amazingly accurate observations.

Early Life

Tyge Brahe Ottosøn was the eldest of ten children born to Otto Brahe. The Brahes were an old and noble family with both Danish and Swedish branches. Tyge's father was privy councillor to the King of Denmark at the time of Tyge's birth and ended as governor of Helsingborg Castle in Scania—then part of Denmark. Tycho was not reared with his parents and younger siblings. His father's brother Jørgen, who was childless, stole him while he was still a baby. Initial turmoil in the family was stilled when Otto's second son was born. It was therefore in the home of his uncle that Tyge was reared, showing so much early scholarly promise that, in addition to the requisite training for a young nobleman in horseback riding and swordsmanship, he was allowed to learn Latin in the hope that he would become a statesman and counselor to the king.

At thirteen, he entered the University of Copenhagen, head held high above a piped collar and small rapiers by his side. Thirteen was not an unusual age for university entry at the time. He studied, as did most of his colleagues, philosophy, rhetoric, and law. The curriculum was in Latin. His academic career was planned for him: After finishing his studies in Denmark, he would go to one of the more famous German universities and study law, still in preparation for a career in government. The problem was that young Tyge (he took the name Tycho upon graduation) was not interested in law. An event that took place on August 21, 1560, when he was nearly fourteen, came to fascinate him so deeply that it, in effect, determined his choice of career. He heard that an eclipse of the sun had been predicted for that day. The fact that the prediction proved to be correct and that the sun was indeed eclipsed seemed to him divine.

It was not considered good form for a man of Brahe's social station to become a mere scientist, and his fascination with astronomy was greeted with far less than enthusiasm by his uncle and father. His astronomical studies were performed in secrecy and at night. When he went to Germany, a tutor accompanied him to ensure that he did not stray from his legal studies. The two arrived in Leipzig in 1562, when Brahe was not quite sixteen. Anders Sørensen Vedel, the tutor, kept a rapt eye on his charge, and Brahe studied law by day and reserved his nights for gazing at the stars. He also managed to study mathematics, which would be necessary for him in his further astronomical studies, and he met two of the more famous astronomers of his day, who happened to reside in Leipzig—Bartholomaeus Scultetus and Valentin Thau. The instruments he used for his observations were quite crude: a globe, a compass, and a radius.

Life's Work

The tutor eventually became aware of his charge's illicit nightly activities, and the two of them were called home to be under Jørgen Brahe's intense scrutiny. Yet Jørgen died not long afterward, leaving the nineteen-year-old Brahe a wealthy and independent man. Brahe could embark on his life's work. For a while, out of a sense of duty, he performed his responsibilities as a nobleman and oversaw the Tostrup estate in Scania which was part of his inheritance. In 1566, however, he decided to make his scientific studies the center of his life and activities. To the accompaniment of his family's scorn, Brahe moved to Wittenberg and worked with Kaspar Peucer, a then-famous astronomer, until an outbreak of the plague forced his return to Denmark. Later, he went to Augsburg because of its famous instrument makers; he wanted new, more precise, better designed instruments made for his observations. He had a new globe, sextant, and radius made. His fame in the scientific community began to grow.

Brahe concentrated his early studies on the apparent movements of the planets and the fixed stars. His father's death and an appointment as cantor of the Roskilde Cathedral devoured much of his time, but he steadfastly continued his work. His growing fame changed the attitudes of his family and peers toward his work: His uncle Steen Brahe had a lab outfitted for him. His first major break-

through was the observation of a new star, first seen on November 11, 1572. The star, which he appropriately called Stella Nova in a book entitled *De nova et nullius aevi memoria prius visa stella* (1573; about the new star), appeared in the Cassiopeia constellation. Large and bright, the new star remained visible until 1574. The accuracy of the observations, down to the minute details, caused a sensation in the scientific community, and Brahe was established as a great scholar.

Brahe, by now a grown man, cut quite a striking figure. Bejeweled and flamboyantly dressed, he was stocky, with reddish-yellow hair combed forward to hide incipient baldness, and he sported a pointed beard and a flowing mustache. When he was a young man in Germany, Brahe had been in a duel, and his opponent sliced off a large piece of his nose, for which Brahe had a substitute made of gold and silver and painted to look natural. He always carried a box with glue and salve.

Brahe's plan was to settle abroad and continue his studies, but the king changed his plans by donating to him the small island of Hveen, in the channel between Denmark and Sweden. The position of the island was perfect for his purposes, and Brahe accepted the generous offer. On Hveen, he built his famous observatory: the architecturally beautiful Uraniborg (after the muse of astronomy Urania), which contained a chemistry lab, his famous mural quadrant, and observatories in the attic. He also built the smaller, but equally famous, Stellaburg, which, except for a cupola, was built underground. This building contained many observational instruments, including his renowned revolving quadrant. It also had portraits, in the round, of the greats of astronomy: Timocharis, Hipparchus, Ptolemy, Nicolaus Copernicus, and himself.

On the official front, Brahe became royal mathematician and lecturer at the University of Copenhagen. Little is known about his private life. He married a bondwoman, Kirstine, by whom he had eight children, five girls and three boys. Brahe did not reveal this part of his life in his own writings, and his contemporaries restricted themselves to expressing disapproval of this alliance. In his observatories, he continued his work, making surprisingly accurate observations of celestial bodies. He always had a number of students living with him, who helped him in his observations.

By 1582, Brahe had reached a point at which he could propose his own astronomical system. He rejected both the static Ptolemaic system with the sun and planets moving around Earth in individual orbits and the Copernican system, which has Earth and the other planets moving around the sun. Brahe's system is an amalgam. For reasons involving both the laws of physics and the Bible, he could not accept a system that makes Earth simply one of the planets that revolve around the sun. In Brahe's system, Earth is static and the moon and the sun revolve around it, with the other planets revolving around the sun. It remained for Brahe's student Johannes Kepler to reinstate the correct Copernican system reinforced by Brahe's minutely correct measurements and observations.

On Hveen, Brahe had his own printing press and published, besides his own works, calendars and horoscopes for the king and other high dignitaries. Like many of his contemporaries, Brahe did not distinguish sharply between astronomy and astrology, but he apparently did not think highly of horoscopes and only made them under duress. Many kings and dignitaries from around Europe visited the island to see the famous observatories.

At Hveen, Brahe did the bulk of his scientific work. He made accurate observations of the sun, moon, and planets. Many scholars find that his greatest achievement, besides his introduction of the use of transversals on the graduated arcs of astronomical instruments and his improvements of existing instruments (such as the equatorial armillae, which are spheres used to establish differences in longitude and latitude), was his catalog of fixed stars, which stood until such improved instruments as telescopes and clocks of precision came into use.

Unfortunately, Brahe did not adhere to his scientific studies. As he grew older, his idiosyncrasies became more obvious and he became involved in some petty suits that alienated the king, who had been one of his staunchest supporters. Brahe's intransigence finally caused the king to confiscate land that had been bequeathed to him, leaving Brahe without an adequate source of income.

Finally, in July, 1597, Brahe left native shores and moved to Rostock, Germany. He sent a submissive letter to King Christian IV, in which he asked the king to take him back into his good graces. The letter elicited a direct and angry response from the king, who said that until Brahe came to his senses, admitted his faults, and promised to do as he was told, he should not return.

Brahe, determined not to give in, decided to find a new mentor. He approached Emperor Rudolph II in Prague. Rudolph had a reputation as a patron of the sciences and indeed took Brahe and his collaborator Kepler under his wing. The two famous astronomers had, at times, a stormy relationship, and, after several years, Kepler had a nervous breakdown and left Prague. Brahe died on October 24, 1601, in Prague.

Summary

Tycho Brahe was a transitional figure in the history of astronomy. His theoretical work was flawed and actually a step back from the work of Copernicus. His great achievements were in the areas of practical and spherical astronomy. He devised new and more sophisticated instruments for observations and recorded an astounding body of observations that represented a quantum leap forward in knowledge about the movements and relative positions of celestial bodies.

Brahe's observatories on the island of Hveen represented the state of the art in sixteenth century astronomical observations. Here he gazed at the stars, recorded his observations, made his mathematical computations, and had his most famous instruments built and installed: three equatorial armillae; a mural quadrant, which he used to determine time; and sextants with transversals on the graduated arc and improved sights that allowed for pointing the instrument with great precision to measure distances and angles.

Brahe's legacy, which has made him, in one biographer's somewhat hyperbolic phrase, "a king among astronomers," is his large body of accurate observations and measurements performed by means of instruments and methods devised by him.

Bibliography

Dreyer, J. L. E. "The Place of Tycho Brahe in the History of Astronomy." *Scientia* 25 (March, 1919): 177-185. A concise outline of Brahe's scientific achievements, including descriptions of his most important instruments. Places Brahe in the history of astronomy, trying to assess his importance relative to other greats such as Ptolemy, Copernicus, and Kepler.

———. *Tycho Brahe: A Picture of Scientific Life and Work in the Sixteenth Century*. Edinburgh: Black, 1890; New York: Dover, 1963. The most detailed work on Brahe in terms of his work and studies. Early in the book, Dreyer sets the general scientific and astronomical stage Brahe was to enter. While somewhat technical, the book gives a thorough and minute description of Brahe's instruments and observations.

Gade, John Allyne. *The Life and Times of Tycho Brahe*. Princeton, N.J.: Princeton University Press, 1947. Gade gives the social and political backdrop to Brahe's life and work. His emphasis is not so much on technical descriptions as on Brahe the man and the community member. Gade writes amusingly of Brahe's childhood and youth and gives a fairly complex psychological profile of the adult scientist and nobleman. The most personal portrait of Brahe extant.

Gray, R. A. "Life and Work of Tycho Brahe." *Royal Astronomical Society of Canada Journal* 17 (1923). Starts with a careful statement of the Ptolemaic and other theories current before the advent of Brahe. Lists among Brahe's achievements his statement that comets are not, as previously believed, within Earth's atmosphere. Also mentions Brahe's improvements on existing instruments.

Parsonby, Arthur, and Dorothea Parsonby. *Rebels and Reformers: Biographies for Young People.*

London: Allen and Unwin, 1917; New York: Holt, 1919. Takes the reader into Brahe's physical world at Hveen, describing the buildings and instruments in great but nontechnical detail. Mentions Brahe's difficult personality. Outlines his major scientific contributions, listing as the most important his catalog of fixed stars. Very didactic.

Shackelford, Joel. "Tycho Brahe, Laboratory Design, and the Aim of Science: Reading Plans in Context." *Isis* 84 (June, 1993): 210. Shackelford attempts to study the scientific aims and laboratory designs of Tycho Brahe within the context of his adherence to the occult Paracesian philosophy.

Thoren, Victor E. *The Lord of Uraniborg: A Biography of Tycho Brahe*. Contributions by John R. Christianson. Cambridge and New York: Cambridge University Press, 1990. This is a scientific biography of the famed astronomer, alchemist, and litterateur of the sixteenth century Danish Renaissance. At Uraniborg he constructed astronomical instruments, cast horoscopes, concocted medicines, composed Latin verse, and almost completely renovated the science of astronomy. Thoren's biography offers new perspectives on Tycho's life and new analyses of virtually every aspect of his scientific work.

Per Schelde

DONATO BRAMANTE
Donato di Pascuccio d'Antonio

Born: 1444; Monte Asdruvaldo, near Urbino, Papal States

Died: April 11, 1514; Rome

Area of Achievement: Architecture

Contribution: One of the greatest architects of the Italian Renaissance, Bramante stands out for the pure classicism of his buildings. His influence extended throughout Europe. Except for the long nave, St. Peter's in Rome is basically his design.

Early Life

Donato di Pascuccio d'Antonio took his father's nickname "il Bramante" ("the dreamer") as his cognomen. At first a painter, he may have studied at Mantua with Andrea Mantegna and with Piero della Francesca at Urbino. Their influence is visible in Bramante's interest in the science of perspective. At Mantua, he may have met the architect Leon Battista Alberti, designing there his noted church of S. Andrea.

In the 1470's, Bramante primarily designed architectural decorations for interiors and façades. In the new ducal palace at Urbino in about 1476, he helped decorate the *Studiolo* of the Duke of Urbino. In this small office, the walls are covered with pictures formed by inlaid wood of different tones so as to create an atmosphere both of intimacy and of illusionary space. Bramante also made illustrations of illusionistic perspective in the duke's chapel and library.

At Urbino, Bramante had access to the graceful architectural plans of Luciano Laurana, patronized by the Duke of Urbino along with Piero della Francesca. Alberti may have contributed to the design of the new palace, influencing Bramante, who would soon become an architect. Alberti's classically inspired treatise on architecture, as well as those of Filarete and Francesco di Giorgio, were certainly available as manuals for Bramante. In the Palazzo del Podestà in Bergamo in 1477, Bramante created the illusion of "opening" a wall by painting on it a loggia or corridor, with philosophers seated between the columns.

From about 1479 to 1499, Bramante was in Milan. His first project there was to construct the three-aisled, barrel-vaulted, domed church of S. Maria presso (near) S. Satiro, a diminutive ninth century Carolingian church. About this same time (1481) can be dated the large print prepared by Prevedari. It contains fanciful classical architectural themes and is signed by Bramante.

Commissioned by Cardinal Ascanio Sforza, Bramante's plan for the cathedral of Pavia in 1488 foreshadowed in boldness his future conception for St. Peter's. A high dome was to rest on eight massive piers, creating a large central space. The choir was to be cruciform, its three arms ending in apses, the whole arranged in a harmonious hierarchy of proportions. In 1492, Bramante left the project, which was completed after his death and much altered by later architects.

Bramante designed the loggia (or *ponticella*) of Ludovico Sforza and decorated some rooms in Castello Sforzesco, of which all that remains is his painting of mythical Argus. The Brera Pinacoteca contains paintings certainly by Bramante: *Christ at the Pillar* and eight frescoes of artists and warriors which, with his *Heraclitus* and *Democritus*, once decorated a room in Milan's Palazzo Panigarola. In these, Bramante painted shadows which reflected the actual light source and give the figures an impression of three-dimensionality.

Leonardo da Vinci came to Milan in 1482, and his writings manifest a respect for Bramante. The latter may have learned to appreciate the "central space" concept from Leonardo's sketches of Greek-cross type churches. Both worked for the monks of S. Maria delle Grazie, where Leonardo painted the *Last Supper* and where, from 1492 to 1497, Bramante constructed a choir and transepts. The crossing of nave and transepts here is a spacious open square surmounted by a dome-on-pendentives spanning sixty-five feet. Outside, this interior dome appears as a sixteen-windowed cylinder or drum with sloping roof and a lantern. The crossing was planned as a crypt area for the ducal Sforza family of Milan, Bramante's employers.

During these same years, Bramante designed, for Cardinal Sforza, Duke Ludovico's brother, several cloisters for the Abbey of S. Ambrogio (1492-1497), some additions to the ducal palace at Vigevano, where he resided while in Milan at least until 1495, and a west façade for the abbey church at Abbiategrasso (1497). He also designed a partial city plan, whose main feature was a large square like that of S. Marco in Venice, but here

NL.

serving as a court area between palace and cathedral. The work was interrupted by the French invasion of Milan in 1499, which relieved Bramante of several unfinished projects.

Life's Work

Also in 1499, Bramante arrived in a Rome electric with building activity in preparation for the coming jubilee year. The popes had even authorized the use of the Colosseum and other ancient monuments as stone quarries. Bramante received immediate employment to design a cloister for S. Maria della Pace, a two-storeyed arcade or loggia that on the ground level appears as a wall in which round arches have been cut. Its Ionic pilasters continue above, supporting a horizontal architrave. Between these, slender columns ride directly above the centers of the arches below, creating twice as many openings above as below.

Bramante's famous *Tempietto* absorbed him in 1501-1502. As a sort of monumental reliquary built upon the spot where Saint Peter was reputedly crucified, it had the round design and central plan customary for churches commemorating martyrdom. It is a two-storeyed drum of only fifteen feet in diameter, with a dome and a lantern. Around it is a Doric colonnade supporting a classical triglyph-metope architrave. Above, the drum is pierced by alternating windows and shell-topped niches. It achieves perfectly the avowed Renaissance aim to imitate the dignity of classical antiquity.

Appalled by the wholesale destruction of ancient Rome in the interests of Holy Year, Bramante campaigned for preservation of the past, or at least of an exact plan of imperial Rome. His first years there saw him devoted to drawings and three-dimensional projections of ancient monuments (his own new technique). His study of antiquity taught him much about Roman building secrets, most notably that of inserting brick ribs into walls before filling them with concrete. The new St. Peter's, built on a scale many times greater than normal, would depend on this knowledge.

Bramante's career in Rome (1500-1514) is closely tied to the regime of Pope Julius II (1503-1513). The architect rearranged the streets of Rome for this pope, receiving the nickname "Ruinante" because of his destruction of old streets and of so much of old St. Peter's. Julius invited the congenial, well-read architect to accompany him on military campaigns so that they could enjoy evenings of Dante together. In 1504, Bramante designed the courtyard of St. Damasus with three levels of columned arcades, to ensure papal privacy.

In 1505, he won the competition to design and supervise the construction of the new St. Peter's, to be the crowning glory of Christendom. Fund-raising for the project would destroy Christian unity. The fourth century Constantinian edifice was falling apart, and under Pope Nicholas V (1447-1455) a major restoration was begun. Julius decided on a complete reconstruction, the domed choir of which would contain his own massive tomb carved by Michelangelo with forty figures (the *Moses* is the masterpiece of a much-reduced monument in the church of St. Peter in Chains).

Bramante's concept was a Greek-cross design with a gigantic central hemispheric dome flanked by four equal naves ending in apses. Each corner would have a chapel surmounted by smaller cupolas, and, farther out, four towers would give the building the form of a perfect square with the four apsidal projections. This original design can be seen in the Uffizi Gallery, Florence, and in Caradosso's official souvenir medal. Though finally altered into a Latin cross, the present basilica retains Bramante's spirit and his entirely new massive scale. At his death, only the central piers for supporting the dome were in place. Significant but largely unnoticed is Bramante's bedrock substructure for this colossal edifice. Remarkable, too, is his sculptural modeling of walls. This awareness of the "plastic potentiality" of a wall, also used by Filippo Brunelleschi, was late Roman in origin and important in subsequent Baroque development.

Nicholas V also began the refurbishment of the papal residence into the imposing Vatican palace. Bramante's last important design (1514) was the Palazzo Caprini, planned as his own private residence. It is better known as the House of Raphael, since it was bought in 1517 by the painter.

Summary

Otto H. Förster, a scholar of Donato Bramante, has urged the theory that Bramante in 1510, and not Raphael, was the author of a treatise on the architecture of imperial Rome addressed to Julius II. It is full of confidence that the dome of St. Peter's could rival that of the Pantheon, the scale of which Raphael and others found impossible to contemplate. In it the author is critical of the Palazzo della Cancellaria, a building often attributed incorrectly to Bramante. It is, in fact, difficult to verify Bramante's part in many structures because of the damage and reconstructions of the centuries.

Despite his reputation for magnanimity, Bramante did not get on well with Michelangelo, who in a letter of 1542 voiced the suspicion that the older artist had enviously persuaded Julius to pull him away from the precious sculptural project for the great tomb in order to paint in the Sistine. Still, in a letter of 1555 the sculptor remarked, "Bramante was as gifted an architect as anyone from antiquity until now. . . . His plan for St. Peter's was clear and pure, full of light. . . . Whoever departs from Bramante's plan departs from the truth." Thus, one may assert Bramante's influence over Michelangelo the architect. Sebastiano Serlio imitated Bramante's use of columns; Andrea Palladio's S. Giorgio Maggiore in Venice manifests Bramantean influence.

In 1517, Bramante was satirized as arriving at the Gates of Heaven and immediately proposing improvements. He would replace the difficult road to paradise by a spiral ramp so that Heaven could be attained on horseback; "and I would tear down this Paradise and build a new one with finer accommodations for the blessed. If you agree, I'll stay; if not, I'll head for Inferno." Thus were perceived the confident assertiveness and integrity of Bramante at about the time of his death in 1514.

Bibliography

Baroni, Constantino, ed. *Bramante*. Bergamo: Istituto Italiano d'Arti Grafiche, 1944. In Italian, a fifty-page biography. Useful for its 134 excellent black-and-white photographs.

Burckhardt, Jacob. *The Architecture of the Italian Renaissance*. Translated by James Palmes. London: Secker and Warburg, 1984; Chicago: University of Chicago Press, 1985. Offers a useful organization into genres but the book's style is difficult. Excellent illustrations and bibliography.

Durant, Will. *The Renaissance*. New York: Simon and Schuster, 1953. Views Bramante in the context of Renaissance Italy. A very readable appreciation.

Förster, Otto H. *Bramante*. Vienna: A. Schroll, 1956. The best book on Bramante, in German. Useful for its numerous illustrations.

Hersey, George L. *High Renaissance Art in St. Peter's and the Vatican: An Interpretive Guide*. Chicago: University of Chicago Press, 1993. Hersey describes the complicated rebuilding and expanding of the Basilica of St. Peter, a project in which Bramante, Raphael, and Michelangelo took part. He explores the Vatican's magnificent Renaissance art and architecture, providing the story behind the works and outlining the significance of their themes for the artist, the papacy, and the Church.

Pevsner, Nikolaus. *An Outline of European Architecture*. 7th ed. London and Baltimore: Penguin, 1963. A good survey of major architectural achievements and theory. Bramante is seen in a wider European perspective.

Rossiter, Stuart, ed. *Rome and Environs*. London: Benn, and Chicago: Rand McNally, 1971. Thorough description of art and architecture in Rome for the scholarly traveler. Bramante's buildings receive generous and detailed coverage. Identifies all buildings in which Bramante may have had some role.

Daniel C. Scavone
Per Schelde

PIETER BRUEGEL, THE ELDER

Born: c. 1525; near Brée, Brabant
Died: September 5, 1569; Brussels
Area of Achievement: Art
Contribution: In an era when portraiture dominated, Bruegel teamed his subjects with their larger environment, greatly elevating landscape art. Bruegel's miniaturist style also chronicled the many facets of everyday sixteenth century Flemish life.

Early Life

Pieter Bruegel, called the Elder, hailed from the Brabant region, the Flemish countryside which straddles the southern part of the Netherlands and northern Belgium. Little can be ascertained about his early life, or when and where it exactly began. Although 1525 is often cited as the year of Bruegel's birth, scholars have hypothesized various dates ranging from 1520 to 1530. When the artist arrived in Antwerp to commence his career, he was listed as Peeter Brueghels. Since country-born Flemings often lacked surnames, one near-contemporary, the early seventeenth century biographer Carel van Mander, states that the artist adopted "Bruegel" or "Brueghels" from his place of birth. Other scholars speculate that it was a family name, although such a nomenclature often was preceded by "van." The artist's origin also remains unclear. Three Flemish towns bore some form of the name Bruegel, and at least the same number of families shared the appellation. Since two of the towns are close together, near the city of Brée in modern Belgium, this area frequently has been cited as Bruegel's birthplace.

Excepting the folktales which come from each of the artist's alleged hometowns, his biography begins in 1545, when he first apprenticed with Pieter Coecke van Aelst, a successful painter, architect, and ornamental/tapestry designer. Bruegel's master maintained operations in both Brussels and Antwerp, and subscribed to the Italian Renaissance style then dominating art. It remains difficult to trace Bruegel's creative evolution during his apprenticeship because guild rules dictated that students could not sign or sell any of their work; they were totally under the direction of the masters. Yet some very tangible benefits resulted from Bruegel's association with Coecke. The master's wife, Mayken Verhulst, was a talented miniaturist who may have imparted some of her skills to Bruegel. The apprentice also married the Coeckes' daughter, Mayken, some years later, in 1563. After the death of both Bruegels, Mayken Verhulst instructed the couple's young, artistic sons, Pieter and Jan.

Life's Work

Coecke's sudden demise in December, 1550, led his apprentice to Hieronymus Cock, a copperplate engraver who became less known for his personal artistry than for a rare ability to capitalize on the spirit of the day. Antwerp at mid-century was Europe's most active commercial center, attracting traders from all over the Continent and spawning a cosmopolitan, consumer-oriented existence. Art proved to be a major beneficiary of the economic climate. Realizing the public's increasing desire for affordable creations, Cock opened the Four Winds publishing house. The owner/ entrepreneur successfully marketed prints of popular artists, such as Hieronymus Bosch, and used a broader approach to fulfill the demand for art: Cock engaged young, local talents to execute new works.

Bruegel thus arrived at Four Winds. Within several months, he became a master in the Antwerp chapter of the Guild of St. Luke, a brotherhood including painters, graphic artists, ornamental and interior designers, glass-workers, and others. Most craftspersons of the era proved to be extremely versatile. Bruegel himself was to draw and paint in oils; he also skillfully engraved at least one of his own works, though print-related processes usually were reserved for other craftspersons.

One advantage of Bruegel's association with the publisher Cock was that his employer dispatched him to Italy in 1552, possibly in search of new subject matter or because the trip might yield popular Italian-style art. During the journey, Bruegel witnessed the burning of the Calabrian seaport, Reggio, by Süleyman's Turks. The scene is later documented in *Sea Battle in the Straits of Messina*, Bruegel's only real historic painting.

Besides the exposure to Italy—which inspired several seascapes—the artist gained much from his trip across the Alps. Mountain vistas often appear in his work, with results that never could have been attained had he not ventured forth from the Flemish flatlands. It also is said that Bruegel acquired a new perspective: His paintings frequently seem to be executed from a higher ground, looking down.

This approach, perhaps a manifestation of his Alpine travels, was rather uncommon during the mid-1500's.

Returning to Antwerp in 1553, Bruegel continued his employment with Four Winds, creating drawings largely for public consumption. Some of his earlier works, such as the *Seven Deadly Sins* series (1556-1557), show elements of fantasy. Scholars thus debate whether Bruegel was creatively motivated by Bosch (1450-1516) or whether he imitated the established artist to satisfy public demand. Many factors may explain Bruegel's attraction to fantasy: a possible escape from politics, particularly Catholic Spain's harsh rule over the Reformist-leaning Low Countries; the superstition and magical beliefs which sometimes dominated daily life; or the artist's inclination toward social commentary and satire. Yet, as one expert notes, Bruegel rendered *The Temptation of Saint Anthony* without signing it. A previous Bosch engraving bore the same title and a similar style. Commercial factors therefore could have prevailed in some of Bruegel's earlier drawings.

Although association with the publishing firm perhaps muted the artist's powers of self-expression (at least through 1557), the connection served him well in other ways. Four Winds, complete with coffeehouse, became an intellectual center and mecca for art dealers. The atmosphere netted Bruegel excellent contacts, including a string of patrons who supported his best-known work—the oil paintings created from 1557 until the end of his life.

The biographer van Mander describes Bruegel's steadfast friendship with one patron, Hans Franckert: With this Franckert, Bruegel often went out into the country to see the peasants at their fairs and weddings.

> Disguised as peasants they brought gifts like the other guests, claiming relationship or kinship with the bride or groom. Here Bruegel delighted in observing the droll behavior of the peasants, how they ate, danced, drank, capered or made love.

Perhaps the artist derives his greatest twentieth century renown from these rustic scenes. Combining peasant life with miniaturist technique, he produced his acclaimed *The Blue Cloak* in 1559. The painting illustrates anywhere from seventy-five to one hundred sayings common during the sixteenth century. Some, such as a variation on the "he speaks from both sides of his mouth" theme, continue to be used. *The Battle Between Carnival and Lent* (1559) and *Children's Games* (1560) give further substance to this Bruegelian genre. The two paintings reveal literally hundreds of adults and youths, respectively, amusing themselves. Given the abundant activity and immense cast of characters illustrated, it is interesting to note that each of the three works only measures about four feet by five feet.

Later paintings concentrate more on smaller-scale activities. *Peasant Wedding* (1568) and *Peasant Dance* (1568) are well-known examples of Bruegel's ability to make the everyday, bucolic life-style of sixteenth century Flanders accessible to modern viewers. *Parable of the Blind* (1568) and *The Cripples* (1568) hold additional virtues. With its theme of "the blind leading the blind," the former painting depicts six men, each suffering from a different form of eye disease. Similarly, *The Cripples* shows various implements used by the era's handicapped. These subjects also sport foxtails, a sign of the Beggars, a political order seeking independence from Spain.

Indeed, scholars debate the level of sociopolitical commentary found in Bruegel's work. Some say that he moved from Antwerp to Brussels in 1563 partly to escape the volatile atmosphere pervading the port city. The primary reason for the relocation, however, remains simple: marriage. According to van Mander, Bruegel was permitted to marry Mayken Coecke only on the condition that he move to Brussels. The artist had previously been living with a servant girl, and apparently his new family wanted him to forget the relationship.

Subsequent to his marriage and move, Bruegel became a more prolific painter, perhaps because of his distance from the commercial lure of Four Winds. His work included landscapes populated by lively peasants, as well as biblical scenes. Some of the religious themes, however, may have masked political intentions. Soldiers garbed in sixteenth century regalia, marching through Alpine paths and snowy fields far from the Holy Land, dominate *The Road to Calvary* (1564) and *The Massacre of the Innocents* (1566). Artists of the era sometimes placed historical figures in contemporary surroundings, but Bruegel's inspiration remains subject to speculation. With orders from King Philip II of Spain, the Duke of Alba raised twenty thousand soldiers to invade the Low Countries during the mid-1560's, just as Bruegel executed his somber themes.

Arguments about Bruegel's politics notwithstanding, the last years of his short life proved to be the most successful. A wealthy patron, Niclaes

Jonghelinck, offered the artist his first commission: a series of six "seasons" paintings to be used for the decoration of a mansion. Out of this endeavor came *Hunters in the Snow* (1565), perhaps Bruegel's finest work. Public recognition soon followed. Shortly after 1569 commenced, the Brussels City Council advanced the artist money for a series of paintings commemorating the opening of a new canal. The paintings remained unfinished: Bruegel died on September 5, 1569.

Summary

Pieter Bruegel, the Elder, left behind approximately 150 drawings, fifty oil paintings, various prints, and a legacy: his two sons, Pieter, the Younger (1564-1638), and Jan (1568-1625). His namesake largely became known as an imitator of his father's work; Jan, however, helped to usher in a new creative era with his elaborate, Baroque nature subjects. Nicknamed "Velvet" Brueghel (both sons reinstated the "h" in their family nomenclature), he also developed a lifelong friendship and collaborated with one of the era's most outstanding painters, Peter Paul Rubens. The Bruegel art dynasty, in fact, survived for about two hundred years.

The reputation of Pieter, the Elder, outlived him, too, but not by more than a few decades. Changing trends—some spawned by the heated political events occuring during the mid-1500's—rendered his work unfashionable. Interest in Bruegel only resurfaced at the dawn of the twentieth century, with the very first exhibit of the artist's work in 1902. Perhaps nostalgia for a diminishing peasant life-style fostered this revival. Surely one of Bruegel's major contributions was in replacing elite faces with those of the rural lower classes. Yet, while Bruegel painted people, he refused to confine himself to the then-dominant portraiture. His crowded street scenes do not so much depict individuals as a social landscape. Bruegel also forced his vibrant peasants to share attention with the wheat-covered fields and steep Alpine paths which offered the essence of human activity.

Bibliography

Delevoy, Robert L. *Bruegel.* Translated by Stuart Gilbert. Lausanne, Switzerland: Editions D'Art Albert Skira, and New York: Crown, 1959. Using an advanced approach, this book explores Bruegel's artistic techniques as well as the content of his work. A biographical chapter debates various theories about the artist's life. Also included are an extensive bibliography, a list of major Bruegel exhibitions, translated documents, and color plates.

Denis, Valentin, ed. *All the Paintings of Pieter Bruegel.* Translated by Paul Colacicchi. London: Oldbourne, and New York: Hawthorn Books, 1961. A catalog of Bruegel's works containing 160 plates, this volume cites lost paintings and those which may not have been created by the artist. An introductory chapter presents Bruegel as one who withstood prevalent artistic influences and only gradually introduced his concepts into the mainstream. Also featured are selected criticism, biographical notes (timeline), and a brief bibliography.

Foote, Timothy. *The World of Bruegel c. 1525-1569.* New York: Time-Life Books, 1968. Portrays the artist as an innovator who, nevertheless, reflected—rather than attempted to comment on—social conditions. Also explores Bruegel's predecessors, peers, and successors; contemporary artistic trends; and the politics and religious attitudes of the sixteenth century. Contains a bibliography, a listing of other European masters, and both color and black-and-white plates.

Glück, Gustav. *Peter Brueghel, the Elder.* London: Commodore Press, and New York: George Braziller, 1936. Depicts Bruegel as having been a nonjudgmental, realistic painter of a chaotic world. Emphasizes the master's artistic progression and increasing ability to convey nature accurately. Glück also argues that Bruegel defined later genres of Dutch painting. This oversize book features forty-nine superb color plates and a bibliography.

Klein, H. Arthur, and Mina C. Klein. *Peter Bruegel, the Elder: Artist of Abundance.* New York: Macmillan, 1968. Bruegel appears as a social critic in this general biography. Details of the artist's environment and contemporary life-style are explored. Heavily illustrated in black and white, the book uses both Bruegel's works and those of his peers. Also contains a short color section and list of American museums housing Bruegel paintings.

Sullivan, M. "Bruegel's Proverbs: Art and Audience in the Northern Renaissance." *Art Bulletin* 73 (September, 1991): 431. Sullivan's study questions the scholarly consensus that Flemish "folk" proverbs are the only ones relevant for the historical interpretation of Bruegel's proverb art.

Lynn C. Kronzek

FILIPPO BRUNELLESCHI

Born: 1377; Florence

Died: April 15, 1446; Florence

Areas of Achievement: Architecture, art, and engineering

Contribution: Brunelleschi's architectural accomplishments, as well as his dedication to the principles of perspective, established a vigorous new classical Renaissance style that influenced building design for centuries.

Early Life

Filippo Brunelleschi was born in Florence in 1377, the second of three sons of Ser Brunellesco di Lippi and Giuliana degli Spini, the daughter of an established Florentine banking family. His father was a notary and middle-level public official frequently employed in various capacities by the republican government. Young Filippo thus grew up in a household heavily involved in the complex politics of Tuscany's leading city. His elder brother, Tommaso, became a goldsmith and died in 1431, while his younger brother, Giovanni, entered the priesthood and died in 1422.

As a child, Brunelleschi received the traditional education of boys of his class. Although his father may have wished him to follow him in a notary career, young Filippo early exhibited a penchant for art and mechanics. The elder Brunelleschi consequently apprenticed his second son to the Silk Guild for training as a goldsmith. His training there included a study of literature and the abacus as well as rigorous mathematical instruction. In 1398, Brunelleschi applied for registration as a goldsmith with the Silk Guild and was admitted as a full master six years later.

Even before this last event, the young artist had established a reputation for himself as one of the most promising figures in the Florentine artistic community. In the early 1400's, he made several silver figures for the altar of the cathedral in Pistoia. Two busts of prophets and two full-length figures of saints survive from this endeavor.

One of the turning points in Brunelleschi's early career concerned his participation in the 1401 competition sponsored by the Signory and Guild of Merchants for the commission to do a series of relief sculptures for the north doors of the Florence cathedral baptistery. Brunelleschi was one of the two finalists, but in 1402, the judges selected a panel submitted by his fellow goldsmith Lorenzo Ghiberti as the winner. Brunelleschi's competition panels on the theme of the sacrifice of Isaac have been preserved in the National Museum of Florence. Brunelleschi's defeat in the competition had important consequences for his future. Virtually the rest of Ghiberti's long career was consumed by the task of the north doors and a subsequent set for the eastern entry. Brunelleschi found himself free for other endeavors, and he increasingly became more interested in architecture in preference to sculpture.

Life's Work

Although he was active in many artistic and engineering projects, Brunelleschi's main contribution during the last four decades of his life was in the field of architectural inventiveness. He most probably left Florence shortly after his 1402 defeat and spent several years in Rome with his fellow Florentine, the sculptor Donatello. In Rome he studied ancient buildings in minute detail, making careful drawings of classic arches, vaulting, and other architectural features.

The Florence to which he returned in the early 1400's provided a fertile field of opportunities for the energetic and talented young Brunelleschi. The city's wealthy elite had an increasing thirst to commission city palaces, country villas, and burial chapels. Even more important, the civic Humanists dominating the Florentine government were eager to employ painters, sculptors, and architects to make Florence the premier city in Italy. The most important project to the city fathers was the completion of the great cathedral of Santa Maria del Fiore, an undertaking that gave Brunelleschi his most challenging and famous commission.

Begun in 1296 and designed in the traditional Tuscan Gothic style, the cathedral essentially stood finished by the late fourteenth century except for the dilemma of constructing a dome to cover the 140-foot octagonal space created by the crossing at the east end. No previous architect had found a solution to the technical problems and expense entailed by this problem. It remained for Brunelleschi, who had been involved with various facets of the cathedral's construction as early as 1404, to provide the answer.

In 1418, the cathedral's officials announced a competition for a workable design for the dome. Based on his studies of ancient Roman and Byzan-

tine vaulting, Brunelleschi proposed an innovative solution that entailed constructing the cupola without the traditional costly wooden centering or exterior scaffolding. After two years of feasibility studies, the commission finally jointly awarded the prize to Brunelleschi and his rival Ghiberti, but the latter soon largely retired from the project.

Brunelleschi personally invented much of the machinery necessary to erect his revolutionary dome. His eventual plan utilized a skeleton of twenty-four ribs (eight of them visible from the exterior) that enabled the cupola to be self-supporting as it rose from its base 180 feet from the ground. The ribs soared some one hundred feet and converged in an oculus meant to be topped by a lantern tower. To keep the weight of the structure to a minimum, Brunelleschi designed the first double shell in architectural history and placed the brickwork in herringbone patterns on the framework of the stone beams. When completed in 1436, his masterpiece was by no means a mere copy of classical patterns, but a unique and daring creation notable for its visual impressiveness from the outside, unlike such Roman structures as the Pantheon. It became the single most identifiable architectural landmark in the city. In 1436, Brunelleschi won yet another competition, this one for the design of the lantern that anchored the top of his cupola. This lantern was not completed until 1461, fifteen years after his death. He also designed the lateral tribunes that graced the structure.

Despite its overwhelming importance, Brunelleschi's work on the Florentine cathedral was not representative of the main thrust of his architectural style. Much more typical were his plans for the Ospedale degli Innocenti (foundling hospital), a building commissioned by the Silk Guild in 1419. His most important contribution to the project was a graceful portico of rounded arches that extended across the façade. The entire exterior reflected Brunelleschi's dedication to proper geometrical proportions, symmetry, and classical detail.

Classical elements also dominate the two basilican churches which Brunelleschi designed in his native city, San Lorenzo and Santo Spirito. Although neither was completed before his death and each was somewhat modified from his original plans, both reflected his dedication to mathematical proportion and logical design to provide visual and intellectual harmony. Their interiors of Roman rounded arches and pillars became hallmarks of the Renaissance style.

One of the Florentine master's greatest undertakings in church architecture was the Pazzi Chapel, a chapter house for the monks of the cloister of Santa Croce. Although his commission came in 1429, actual work did not begin until 1442 and continued into the 1460's. In this chapel, Brunelleschi again produced an edifice noted for harmonious proportions and clarity of expression, breaking with Gothic mystery and grandeur in favor of restraint and geometrical harmony. The interior, dominated by a dome-covered central space, became a highly influential model for future architects. Brunelleschi employed darkly colored pilasters against lightly colored walls to create a harmonious and peaceful atmosphere notable for its simplicity and classical beauty.

Churches were by no means Brunelleschi's sole architectural preoccupation. Despite the proliferation of palace-building in Florence during this time, only one such structure—the Palazzo di Parte Guelfa—was definitely designed by him. His model for a palace for Cosimo de' Medici was rejected as too ostentatious and imposing. Florence and other cities throughout Tuscany frequently employed him as a consultant to design fortifications and bridges and to supervise other public works projects. In 1430, for example, he became involved in an unsuccessful scheme to divert the Arno River in order to turn the city of Lucca into an island.

Brunelleschi did not completely abandon sculpture after his loss in the competition of 1401. His polychrome wood statue of the Virgin for the Church of Santo Spirito perished in a 1471 fire, but several other works have been attributed to him, including the terra-cotta evangelists in the Pazzi Chapel.

A lifelong bachelor, in 1417, Brunelleschi adopted five-year-old Andrea di Lazzaro Cavalcanti, more commonly known as Il Buggiano, as his heir. This foster son became his apprentice in 1419 and eventually collaborated with his mentor on many projects. Brunelleschi continued working actively on his numerous projects until his death on April 15, 1446. In 1447, city officials authorized the interment of his remains in the same cathedral which had played such an important part in his long and productive career.

Summary

At the time of his death, only a few of Filippo Brunelleschi's designs had been completed. Most, such as the great basilicas of San Lorenzo and Santo

Spirito and the lantern for his great dome, were finished only many years after his death. Nevertheless, during his active career of nearly half a century, Brunelleschi established himself as the premier architect in Florence and the first architect of the new Renaissance style. Unlike his younger contemporary Leon Battista Alberti, he never produced a book about his architectural theory, but his landmark buildings served as textbooks by themselves for numerous future architects such as Michelangelo.

With his profound respect for classical values, Brunelleschi personified the self-confident optimism of the early Renaissance Humanists. Much like Leonardo da Vinci later in the century, he was interested in a wide variety of subjects, including hydraulics, watchmaking, and practical mechanics. Sometime between 1410 and 1415, he drew two panels, now lost, which effectively rediscovered the principles of linear perspective. This had a profound impact upon painters of the era, such as Brunelleschi's young acquaintance Masaccio. Linear perspective helped revolutionize the style of fifteenth century Italian painting.

It is through his architectural accomplishments, though, that Brunelleschi made his major contribution. He was undoubtedly the pivotal figure in assuring Florentine supremacy in the field throughout the fifteenth century. Works such as his great cathedral dome and the Pazzi Chapel revived admiration for classical styles without resorting to slavish imitation of Greco-Roman forms. Brunelleschi thus created a vibrant, self-confident classical Renaissance style that profoundly influenced architecture for centuries.

Bibliography

Battisti, Eugenio. *Filippo Brunelleschi: The Complete Work*. London: Thames and Hudson, and New York: Rizzoli, 1981. A translation and revision from an earlier Italian version, this scholarly study thoroughly examines Brunelleschi's life and career, including such aspects as his military engineering, theatrical machinery, and verse. Contains a detailed documentary chronology of his life and times and a chronological bibliography from 1568 to 1980.

Fanelli, Giovanni. *Brunelleschi*. London: Summerfield, and New York: Harper, 1980. Briefly discusses Brunelleschi's career and major buildings and is chiefly useful for its lavish and detailed color illustrations of his major works. It particularly focuses upon his great dome.

Goldberger, Paul. "Challenge to the Origin of a Florentine Chapel." *New York Times* 146 (January, 1997): 30. Goldberger presents information on the Pazzi Chapel in Florence, Italy, and its architect. The author covers the claim by Marvin Trachtenberg that Brunelleschi did not design the chapel and provides comments from Trachtenberg himself.

Hyman, Isabelle, ed. *Brunelleschi in Perspective*. Englewood Cliffs, N.J.: Prentice-Hall, 1974. A useful monograph divided into two sections. The first is a collection of fifteenth and sixteenth century documents and writings about Brunelleschi; the second consists of twelve articles written by nineteenth and twentieth century authors. Contains a useful chronology of his life.

Manetti, Antonio di Tuccio. *The Life of Brunelleschi*. Edited by Howard Saalman. Translated by Catherine Enggass. University Park: Pennsylvania State University Press, 1970. Manetti was the probable author of the *Vita di Filippo Brunelleschi* that appeared in the 1480's. As a young man, Manetti had known and idolized Brunelleschi, and this work is a laudatory treatment that despite its inaccuracies and biases remains the best early source of information about the great architect. This particular edition, with texts in both English and Italian, contains an introduction discussing the problems of authorship, chronology, and reliability.

Murray, Peter. *The Architecture of the Italian Renaissance*. New York: Schocken, and London: Batsford, 1963. A standard survey that contains a useful chapter on Brunelleschi, showing his influence on architects of the fifteenth and sixteenth centuries. Contains a critical bibliographical essay on early treatises and more recent works.

Prager, Frank D., and Gustina Scaglia. *Brunelleschi: Studies of His Technology and Inventions*. Cambridge, Mass.: MIT Press, 1970. A brief monograph which discusses Brunelleschi's machines, innovative construction methods, and masonry work. Contains useful illustrations of his machines and problems concerning the construction of his dome.

Tom L. Auffenberg

LEONARDO BRUNI

Born: c. 1370; Arezzo, Republic of Florence
Died: March 9, 1444; Florence
Areas of Achievement: Historiography, literature, and politics
Contribution: Bruni was a leading Italian Renaissance figure, a Humanist scholar whose work was important in the development of historiography.

Early Life

Leonardo Bruni was the son of Cecco Bruni, a small grain dealer in Arezzo. As a result of civil war, Bruni and his father were imprisoned in 1384, with the young Bruni held apart from his father in a castle room on the wall of which was a portrait of Petrarch. Bruni would later write that his daily viewing of the painting of this famous Italian poet and Humanist inspired him with an eagerness for Humanist studies. The years following the war and his imprisonment were difficult for Bruni. His father died in 1386, his mother in 1388; family resources declined sharply.

In spite of the family hardship, Bruni moved the forty miles to Florence, perhaps to live with relatives, and began his studies. From 1393 to 1397, he studied law in Florence and came to the attention of the medieval scholar Lino Coluccio Salutati. In 1396, another scholar, Manuel Chrysoloras, moved to Florence and did much to broaden Bruni's career and education. In 1397, Bruni shifted to the study of Greek, in which Chrysoloras educated and then inspired him to complete a series of translations of several classical literary items from ancient times, many of which had been overlooked for centuries. These included works by Xenophon, Saint Basil, Procopius, Polybius, Demosthenes, Plutarch, Thucydides, and Aristotle. Before he was thirty-five, Bruni's achievement in this work led to his stature among contemporaries as the leading authority on the subject of ancient literature.

Life's Work

As a result of his recognition as a literary figure and because of his proficiency in Latin and Greek, Bruni received an appointment in 1405 as a secretary to Pope Innocent VII. Except for a brief period in 1410 and 1411, he would spend ten years with the papal court in Rome. In 1411, when he was forty-one years of age, he married. While little is known about his wife or her family, it is known that she brought to the marriage a dowry that reflects a family of wealth and status. Bruni also became a close acquaintance of Baldassarre Cossa, who became Pope John XXIII during the Schism of the Papacy until the famous deposition in 1415 at the Council of Constance. As a result of the loss of power by his patron, Bruni returned to Florence, where he settled into an active life in historical study and writing, Florentine politics, and personal investments.

It was as a historian that Leonardo Bruni became a great Renaissance scholar. Through translations, dialogues, biographies, commentaries, and his monumental *Historiae Florentini populi* (1610; history of the Florentine people), Bruni changed historical writing and thought so significantly that he was referred to as the "father of history" for at least two centuries after his death. Numerous Italian historians were influenced by his methods and style, and his impact extended into other disciplines. Although there is no complete chronology of Bruni's historical works, the list is impressive. It begins with his *Laudatio Florentinae urbis* (in praise of the city of Florence) and the *Dialoghi ad Petrum Paulum historum* (dialogues dedicated to Pier Paolo Vergerio), both produced between 1401 and 1405.

Laudatio Florentinae urbis is an attempt to present a thorough view of the Florence city-state in its geographic and historical perspectives, a total view of the city. The work is based, in part, upon the model of Aristides' eulogy of Athens in ancient Greece. Bruni sought to explain how Florentine institutions and politics evolved from the Italian past, in itself a new historical method. It was also in this work that Bruni's civic Humanism emerged. He expressed the view that the health of the state must ever be based upon the educated and ethical sense of the citizenry, factors which, in his view, had contributed much to the glory and fame of Florence. *Dialoghi ad Petrum Paulum historum* was a combination of two dialogues that served as reproductions of conversations between scholars from two Florentine generations. Here Florence is presented as the preserver of the best features of republican Rome and classical Greece. Together the two works are credited with marking the beginning of a new Humanism, a new civic sentiment, and a new view of the past.

Bruni's greatest work was his *Historiae Florentini populi*, the first and, as some would argue, the greatest achievement of Renaissance historical writing. Bruni intended this work to be a complete history of Florence to 1404 in order to explain the greatness of this Italian city-state. He concluded that the civic virtue of its citizens and the republican form of its government were key explanations for its greatness. In his view, Florence was the shining example of what men living in political freedom could accomplish. The setting for much of his history was the conflict between Florence and Milan. Although some scholars have criticized Bruni's continued use of the rhetorical methods of Greek and Roman historians and his heavy emphasis upon the symbols of the classical age, the work served as a model for historians for many years. Bruni's research was in response to clearly articulated questions and in pursuit of relevant causal relationships. He became more than a chronicler and instructed those who followed him that history must be true, utilitarian, documented, instructive, readable, thematic, respectful of the past, viewed in epochs or eras, and focused upon those matters which human beings can control, specifically politics. Finally, *Historiae Florentini populi* is important for the significant narrative techniques it introduced.

There are other writings for which Bruni received recognition. These include his *De militia* (1421; on knighthood), in which he advanced the establishment of the idea of a citizen-army for Florence; his 1427 funeral oration for a Florentine general, Nanni degli Strozzi, who had fought successfully against Milan, thus serving to promote the interests of freedom and humanity; his *De studiis et litteris* (1421-1424; *Concerning the Study of Literature*, 1897), one of the first treatises to advance a program of education based upon the humanities that offers a demonstrated concern for women as well as men. In his later years, he published his memoirs, *Rerum suo tempore gestarum commentarius* (1440-1441; commentary on the history of his own times), a perspective on contemporary history that substantially departed from the work of previous chroniclers.

The success of his literary career led Bruni into a prominent political role in Florence by the middle of the 1420's. He became a member of a number of prominent trade and professional guilds, served as an ambassador to Pope Martin V in 1426, and in 1427 became the Chancellor of Florence. In the latter position, he would play a major role in the political and military affairs of the state, an influence he would continue until his death in 1444. Tax records indicate that by 1427 he was one of the wealthiest persons in Florence, possessing a series of farms, houses, and investments. In 1431, his son Donato married into a prominent family and would himself occupy a visible place in the affairs of Florence for many years. Clearly Bruni spent a considerable amount of time promoting his personal political power and personal wealth.

The important role of Bruni in the affairs of Florence is borne out by the elaborate public funeral given upon his death in 1444. This proved to be an event of major importance, attended by figures of prominence from a wide area. His funeral oration was given by a leading statesman, and one of the most gifted sculptors of Florence prepared a marble tomb for him. Niccolò Machiavelli, the famous author and statesman of the Italian Renaissance, was buried beside Bruni upon his death in 1527.

Summary

Leonardo Bruni was one of the outstanding figures of the Italian Renaissance. In the first half of the fifteenth century, he was the leading figure in the development of Humanism, history, and political thought. His translations of ancient Greek texts from Aristotle and Plato made a major contribution to European scholars for centuries. He was clearly the greatest authority on ancient literature for his time. His own biographies, dialogues, histories, and commentaries created a virtual revolution in historical writing and thought. He divided the past in new ways, placed a new emphasis upon sources, developed new narrative forms, and established Humanism as a political necessity in the struggles among the Italian city-states. He is the most important example of civic Humanism in the early Renaissance.

Bibliography

Baron, Hans. *The Crisis of the Early Italian Renaissance: Civic Humanism and Republican Liberty in an Age of Classicism and Tyranny.* 2 vols. Princeton, N.J.: Princeton University Press, 1955. An outstanding study of the Italian Renaissance with Bruni as the central figure. Contains one volume of text and one volume of notes. Includes detailed analyses of Bruni's major works. Baron is the leading scholar of Bruni.

———. *From Petrarch to Leonardo Bruni: Studies in Humanistic and Political Literature.* Chicago: University of Chicago Press, 1968. An extension of the above work. Baron subjects Petrarch's and Bruni's writings to critical analysis based upon additional sources made available and upon the large amount of interest and reinterpretation of

Humanism and the Renaissance in the 1960's. A superb analysis of the evolution of Humanism from its Renaissance origins to the middle of the twentieth century.

Bondanella, Peter, and Julia Conaway Bondanella, eds. *Dictionary of Italian Literature*. Westport, Conn.: Greenwood Press, 1979. A brief but excellent summary of the major contributions of Bruni. Primary emphasis is upon his writings, with clear understanding of the influence of his *Laudatio Florentinae urbis* and *Dialoghi ad Petrum Paulum historum.*

Cochrane, Eric. *Historians and Historiography in the Italian Renaissance*. Chicago: University of Chicago Press, 1981. A superb study of the emergence, growth, and decline of Renaissance historiography. Places Bruni in historical perspective. References are made to several hundred historical writings of the period. An outstanding work on an important period in the development of historical writing.

Hankins, James. "The 'Baron Thesis' after Forty Years and Some Recent Studies of Leonardo Bruni." *Journal of the History of Ideas* 56 (April, 1995): 309. Hankins evaluates the studies of Bruni in relation to Renaissance historian Hans Baron's view of the nature and significance of "civic humanism" in Florence, Italy. Includes criticism of Baron's works.

Ianziti, Gary. "Bruni on Writing History." *Renaissance Quarterly* 51 (summer 1998): 367. The author examines the evolution of Bruni's writings during the period between 1404 and 1443, in particular the *Cicero novus*, *Commentarii de primo bello punico*, and the *De bello italico*.

Martines, Lauro. *The Social World of the Florentine Humanists, 1390-1460*. London: Routledge, and Princeton, N.J.: Princeton University Press, 1963. An excellent social study of the early Renaissance. This is an analysis of the social position of the Humanist scholars in Florence primarily in the first half of the fifteenth century. Provides insight into the political and financial position of Bruni. An unusual examination of the social lives of a number of prominent scholars.

Wilcox, Donald J. *The Development of Florentine Humanist Historiography in the Fifteenth Century*. Cambridge, Mass.: Harvard University Press, 1969. A study of the influence of Leonardo Bruni upon the writing of history in the fifteenth century. Much of the emphasis and analysis is based upon *Historiae Florentini populi*. The method and manner in which later historians were shaped by and reacted to this work is given attention. The role of moral commitment in Bruni's writing is clearly identified.

Frank Nickell

GIORDANO BRUNO

Born: 1548; Nola, near Naples
Died: February 17, 1600; Rome
Areas of Achievement: Philosophy and astronomy
Contribution: With his daring and speculative theories in astronomy and philosophy, Bruno anticipated many of the achievements of modern science, but his stubborn personality and arcane interests brought him into inevitable conflict with the authorities of his time.

Early Life

Giordano Bruno was born in 1548 in Nola. He was the son of Juano Bruno, a professional soldier, and his wife, Fraulissa Savolino. As a child, Bruno was named Filippo; he took the name Giordano when he entered the Dominican Order. He was sometimes known as "the Nolan," after the town of his birth, and he often referred to himself in this fashion in his works.

From contemporary records and his own writings, Bruno seems to have been a particularly intelligent and impressionable child. He left several accounts of odd, almost visionary experiences in his youth, including an extended, quasi-mystical dialogue with the mountain Vesuvius which first revealed to him the deceptiveness of appearances and the relativity of all material things. These were to become two dominant themes in his philosophy.

As a youth, Bruno was sent to Naples, where he attended the Studium Generale, concentrating in the humanities, logic, and dialectic. It is clear that Bruno had a thorough grounding in Aristotle and his philosophy and also was well acquainted with the works of Plato and the writings of the Neoplatonists, who were then creating considerable intellectual activity and controversy, especially in Italy.

In 1565, when Bruno was seventeen, he entered the Dominican Order, moving within the walls of the monastery of San Domenico in Naples. There he took the name Giordano. Bruno's decision to enter the Dominican Order is puzzling, for in retrospect it clearly stands as the major mistake in his often-turbulent life. Although he was well suited for the intellectual studies of the Dominicans, he was quite unfit for the accompanying intellectual discipline and submission required for the monastic and clerical life. His thoughts were too wide-ranging and innovative to be restrained within traditional confines, a situation which eventually placed him in mortal conflict with the Church.

Bruno spent eleven years in the monastery of San Domenico. He studied Saint Thomas Aquinas, Aristotle, and other traditional figures, but at the same time was reading in the mystical doctrines of the Neoplatonists, the new works of Desiderius Erasmus, and other reformers and seems to have become suspiciously well acquainted with the works of heretics such as Arius. These unorthodox diversions brought him into conflict with the Dominican authorities, and reports were made that Bruno was defending the Arian heresy. Arius had taught that God the Father and God the Son were not the same in essence. When the Dominicans learned that Bruno was suspected of defending Arianism, charges were prepared against him. Learning of this, he fled the monastery in 1576. He was age twenty-eight, and he would spend the rest of his life in exile or in prison.

Life's Work

When Bruno fled the monastery, he embarked upon twenty-one years of wandering throughout Europe. Many of his stops lasted merely a matter of months, and the most productive, for only three years. Controversy and conflict dogged him on his travels—much of it a result of not only his daring and speculative thought but also his unrestrained attacks on those who opposed him in any degree and his innate lack of common sense or practical judgment. Employment was difficult, and income was insufficient and insecure. Yet, during this period, Bruno wrote and published an enormous body of work whose content far outpaced even the most advanced thinkers of his time.

Bruno's first extended sojourn was in Geneva. There, safe from the power of the Church, he soon plunged into local intellectual conflicts. In 1579, he published a scathing attack on Antoine de la Faye, a noted professor of philosophy at the University of Geneva. Bruno's assault was more than an academic exercise, for he seemed to undermine de la Faye's theories, which were the basis for the quasi-theological government of Geneva. Bruno, the renegade Dominican on the run, had put himself in disfavor with the Calvinists of Switzerland. He was arrested, then released; he soon left Geneva, moving first to Lyons, then to Toulouse, France. In 1581, Bruno went to Paris, where he found his first real success. He lectured on his own techniques of memory, and the results were so impressive that King Henry III summoned Bruno to court to explain his methods. As a result, the king appointed Bruno to the College de France. Bruno held the post for two years, lecturing on philosophy and natural science and publishing a number of books, many of them on his art of memory.

Still, he managed to alienate many fellow professors and intellectuals in Paris. Some were outraged by his arrogant and self-proclaimed superiority, while the more conventional were troubled by his unorthodox views and desertion of his monastic vows. In 1583, Bruno left for London, with a letter of recommendation to the French ambassador Michel de Castelnau.

The London period, from 1583 through 1585, was the most productive of Bruno's career. Perhaps he was stimulated by the intellectual climate of England, for not only did he deliver a series of lectures at Oxford, explaining the Copernican theory, but also he had among his acquaintances men such as Sir Philip Sidney, Sir Walter Raleigh, and Sir Fulke Greville, noted figures of the English Renaissance. In 1584, Bruno produced a series of six dialogues expounding his philosophy; three of these dealt with cosmological issues, and three with moral topics.

In *Cena de le Ceneri* (1584; the Ash Wednesday supper), Bruno laid the foundation for his scientific theories. He began with the view of Nicolaus Copernicus that the sun, rather than the earth, was the center of the solar system. Bruno recognized that the sun was itself a star, and he concluded that other stars must have their attendant planets circling them. He came to the conclusion that the universe was infinite, and that it therefore contained an infinite number of worlds, each world capable of having intelligent life upon it. Such a theory ran counter to the traditions of both the Catholic church and the newer Protestant faiths.

Bruno continued the development of his theories in *De l'infinito universo e mondi* (1584; *On the Infinite Universe and Worlds*, 1950). He systematically criticized the prevailing Aristotelian cosmology, and in its place put forth a precursor of the modern theory of relativity later developed by Albert Einstein. Bruno maintained that sensory knowledge could never be absolute, but only relative, and it is this relativity that misleads humans in their attempts to understand the universe. Human perceptions are incapable of truly and completely comprehending the universe, and that universe itself can be accurately comprehended only as a total unity, rather than in isolated parts. Therefore, neither senses nor imagination can be fully trusted, but only reason, which allows humans to penetrate to the divine essence of creation.

Bruno also developed a theory that the universe was composed of "minima," extremely small particles much like the atoms proposed by the ancient Roman philosopher Lucretius. Like Lucretius, Bruno thought that certain motions and events were inevitable and that the universe develops inexorably out of inherent necessity. In order to resolve the conflict between this deterministic view and free will, Bruno postulated that the universe itself was divine; he projected a universal pantheism in which the Creator manifests Himself through and within creation.

Finally, Bruno resolved the difficulty of the relationship of human beings to God, of the finite to the infinite, or ignorance to knowledge. These were long-standing puzzles to theologians and philosophers, for it seemed impossible that the limited mind of man could comprehend or understand the perfect and infinite attributes of divinity. Bruno believed that there was an identity of opposites at work in which the essential elements of creation and divinity are found in all parts of the universe. Opposition is only relative and illusory; on the most fundamental level, everything is the same, and everything is therefore divine.

In 1585, Castelnau was recalled to Paris, and Bruno, left without a patron, was forced to leave England. For the next six years, he wandered through Europe, accepting and losing posts at a number of universities in Germany and the Holy Roman Empire. He continued to write and publish prolifically, including his special area of memory, and, in the fall of 1591, he received an invitation from a Venetian nobleman, Zuane Mocenigo, to come to Venice and teach him the art of memory.

Bruno accepted, believing that he would be safe in Venice, which was at that time a fairly liberal and independent state which carefully guarded its freedom from the Papacy. There was a dispute between Bruno and his patron, however—apparently the nobleman believed that he was being cheated and that Bruno planned to flee to Germany—and on May 23, 1592, Bruno was arrested by the Venetian Inquisition. He was questioned through September, but no decision was made.

On February 27, 1593, Bruno was delivered into the hands of the Roman Inquisition, and for the next seven years he was held in prison, repeatedly

questioned and examined, and urged to recant his heresies and confess his sins. Bruno tried to play a crafty game, willing to admit minor infractions, but pretending not to comprehend how his cosmological and philosophical writings could run counter to the teachings of the Church. Finally, in February, 1600, the Inquisition found him guilty and delivered him to the secular authorities for punishment. When Bruno heard the decision, he replied, "Perhaps you who pronounce my sentence are in greater fear than I who receive it." On Saturday, February 17, 1600, Bruno was burned in the Square of Flowers in Rome.

Summary

Giordano Bruno was a philosopher of great insight and imagination, yet a thinker who could link science to magic and yoke philosophical understanding to mnemonic tricks. He was poised amid the thought and traditions of the Church, the mystical teachings of the Neoplatonists, and the rapid advances of the sciences, especially astronomy. From the combination of these three traditions, he forged a new and highly individual vision of the cosmos and mankind's place in it.

Bruno's influence was recognized by both scientists and Humanists in the years following his death. Scientists, even to modern times, admire the startling insights which he drew concerning the infinite number of worlds in an infinite universe. Bruno's early recognition of the concept of relativity and the place which it must play in humanity's conception and understanding of the universe is also a prime legacy which Bruno left to science.

Humanists of the period were profoundly influenced by his insistence on the need for tolerance in matters of religion and belief. Perhaps because Bruno himself was so often a victim of the intolerance of the age, he was especially eloquent in his plea for patience and understanding.

Finally, Bruno combined the sense of infinite expansion and relativity of all things with a new approach to human knowledge and culture. He refused to divide the world into the sacred and the profane, the Christian and the heathen, the orthodox and the heretic. Instead, he saw human life and culture as a single strand and the universe as a divine manifestation which carried with it all knowledge and truth. To Giordano Bruno, the cosmos was God's creation and therefore all good, and man's role was not to judge but to understand.

Bibliography

Boulting, William. *Giordano Bruno, His Life, Thought, and Martyrdom.* London: Kegan Paul, and New York: Dutton, 1916. As indicated by its title, this biography is a highly favorable account of Bruno's life and thought. On the whole, it presents his philosophical and scientific views in a fair and unbiased light.

De Santillana, Giorgia. *The Age of Adventure: The Renaissance Philosophers.* New York: New American Library, 1956. An introductory survey of Bruno and his work, with particular attention paid to his influence upon later scientists and writers.

Feingold, Mordechai. "The Occult Tradition in the English Universities of the Renaissance: A Reassessment." In *Occult and Scientific Mentalities in the Renaissance: A Reassessment,* edited by Brian Vickers. Cambridge and New York: Cambridge University Press, 1984. An enlightening study of Bruno's 1584 visit to Oxford and the state of learning at that time, with special emphasis on which areas of knowledge were believed to be beyond the boundary of conventions.

Kristeller, Paul Oskar. *Renaissance Thought and Its Sources.* New York: Columbia University Press, 1979. Does not have an extended treatment of Bruno as an individual, but is an excellent source for understanding the intellectual climate of his times and how it developed.

León-Jones, Karen de. *Giordano Bruno and the Kabbalah: Prophets, Magicians, and Rabbis.* New Haven, Conn.: Yale University Press, 1997. This book represents a significantly new interpretation of the works of heretical philosopher Giordano Bruno. According to the author, Bruno's interest in and study of mysticism and the Kabbalah were not merely intellectual or satiric, but rather the work of a practicing believer.

Ordine, Nuccio. *Giordano Bruno and the Philosophy of the Ass.* Translated by Henryk Baranski in collaboration with Arielle Saiber. New Haven, Conn.: Yale University Press, 1996. In this highly original study, Nuccio Ordine uses the figure of the ass as a basis for analysis of the thought and writings of Bruno. Ordine offers the first analysis of Bruno's use of this complex symbol, which encompasses contradictory characteristics ranging from humble and hardworking to ignorant and idle. The result is a deeper understanding of Bruno the philosopher.

Singer, Dorothea. *Giordano Bruno: His Life and Thought*. New York: Schuman, 1950. A sympathetic but generally unbiased biography of Bruno, with emphasis upon his thought and theory. The volume contains several helpful appendices and an excellent annotated translation of the dialogue *On the Infinite Universe and Worlds*.

Yates, Frances. *Giordano Bruno and the Hermetic Tradition*. London: Routledge, and Chicago: University of Chicago Press, 1964. By one of the most distinguished scholars of Renaissance thought. Yates's account of Bruno's place is invaluable. Particularly good in situating him within the confines of a broad philosophical stream.

———. *Lull and Bruno*. London and Boston: Routledge, 1982. The section "Essays on Giordano Bruno in England" is particularly valuable for its studies of Bruno's lectures on Copernicus at Oxford and his views of religion and the established church.

Michael Witkoski

MARTIN BUCER

Born: November 11, 1491; Schlettstadt, Alsace
Died: February 28, 1551; Cambridge, England
Areas of Achievement: Church reform and religion
Contribution: During the Reformation, Bucer served as mediator between Huldrych Zwingli and Martin Luther and attempted to reconcile the Roman Catholic Church and the Protestants. He made lasting contributions to the liturgy of Protestant sects, particularly in England.

Early Life

Born on November 11, 1491, to Nicholas Butzer, a shoemaker, and his wife, an occasional midwife, Martin Bucer lived in Schlettstadt, in the Alsace region, until he was ten years old. By the time he had moved to Strasbourg and was put under the care of his grandfather, also a shoemaker, Bucer had already acquired the religious and scholarly zeal that characterized his entire life. At fifteen, however, he had to decide whether to follow family tradition and become an apprentice shoemaker or to continue his education by the only means available to poor young men, service in the Church. Although he did not really want to become a monk, he joined the Dominican Order and spent the next ten years in the monastery at Schlettstadt. There he was subjected to medieval Scholasticism, embodied in the works of Thomas Aquinas, and deprived of the new learning of the Humanists, notably the reformer Desiderius Erasmus.

The turning point in Bucer's life occurred ten years later, when he was transferred to the Dominican monastery at Heidelberg, a university town. There he was caught in the conflict between the medieval Scholasticism advocated by the Dominicans and the Humanism taught by the university professors. Bucer, a voracious reader, soon became a devoted follower of Erasmus, and his liberal leanings were strengthened by his meeting with Martin Luther, who came to Heidelberg in April of 1518 to defend his views. When he received his bachelor of theology degree and was made master of students in 1519, Bucer also received permission to read the Bible; he subsequently wrote biblical commentaries and grounded his own religious beliefs in Scriptures, not in the writings of the Church Fathers.

After joining the local literary society and meeting other religious insurgents, Bucer, whose models were Luther and Erasmus, became convinced that his views were incompatible with his life as a Dominican and attempted to win his release from his monastic vows. That first step in his break from the Catholic Church occurred in 1521; after brief stints as a court chaplain to Count Frederick of the Palatinate and as a parish priest, he married Elizabeth Silbereisen. While his marriage did not result in his immediate excommunication, Bucer's fervid defense of Luther's teachings, particularly the primacy of the Bible and the emphasis on faith rather than good works, eventually and inevitably brought him to the attention of his church superiors. Bucer was regarded as a threat because he used his preaching ability and debating skill to challenge conservative theologians who were reluctant to engage him in religious disputations. When, in 1523, he refused to go to Speier to meet with his bishop, Bucer was excommunicated. He was left virtually homeless when he lost his religious and political supporters and the Council of Wissembourg requested that he leave the city in May of 1523.

Life's Work

When he arrived, uninvited, in Strasbourg in 1523, Bucer found a city congenial to his Reformation views and strategically located between the warring strongholds of the Swiss Reformer Huldrych Zwingli and Martin Luther. In the eight years between his first sermon and his appointment in 1531 as official head of the Strasbourg clergy, Bucer brought his adopted city to prominence as a theological center. Under his unofficial leadership, ties were established between the church and the state; a public school system, with a religious emphasis, was inaugurated; and religious tolerance of a sort was established, though that tolerance was repeatedly tested by the Separatists and Anabaptists.

For the most part, Bucer's biblical commentaries were written during this period—a commentary on Romans, written in 1536, was the exception. Rather than using the traditional grammatical approach, he relied on close readings of the passages, which were placed in their historical context and compared to similar passages from elsewhere in the Bible. This comparative approach was especially helpful in his commentaries on the Gospels, but some critics believe that his best exegesis is contained in his work on the Psalms. (Unfortunately, this work was published under a pseudonym, Aretius Felinus, in order to gain for it an objective

reading in Catholic France, but the stratagem left him open to charges of duplicity and earned for him the ire of both Luther and Erasmus.)

Shortly after Bucer arrived in Strasbourg, the Supper Controversy, the conflict over the meaning of the Eucharistic phrase "This is my body," between Zwingli and Luther threatened Reformation unity. Zwingli's followers—and Bucer must be included among them—maintained that the bread and wine were merely symbols of Christ's body and blood, not His actual body and blood, as Luther's followers, and the Roman Catholic Church, believed. Although he sided with Zwingli, Bucer attempted to reconcile the two factions, who became engaged in pamphlet wars, by glossing over the real doctrinal differences and by attempting, through ambiguous language, to effect an apparent compromise where none was, in fact, possible. Bucer's conciliatory efforts were, unfortunately, hampered by his own writings, which revealed his own theological beliefs and which were attacked by Lutherans, Zwinglians, and Catholics: The middle ground was treacherous territory.

From 1524 until 1548, when he was exiled to England, there was hardly a religious conference in Germany or Switzerland that Bucer did not attend in his role of theological conciliator. The first significant conference, the Marburg Colloquy of 1529, established a tenuous peace between Luther and Zwingli on all religious doctrine except for the Supper Controversy, but the real differences between the two opponents kept surfacing. Working with Wolfgang Capito, another Strasbourg Reformer, Bucer drafted in 1530 at the Diet of Augsburg the Tetrapolitana, or Confession of the Four Cities—Strasbourg, Zurich (Zwingli's stronghold), Basel, and Bern—but the ambiguous language concerning the Eucharist resulted in its rejection by Luther and Zwingli, both of whom wanted changes of a more specific kind. After Zwingli died in 1531, Bucer renewed his efforts at establishing concord, and the resulting Wittenberg Concord of 1536 did effect a consensus, if not a lasting peace, primarily because of Bucer's gift of obscuring meaning through ambiguous wording. While Philipp Melanchthon secured Luther's approval of the compromise, Bucer's efforts with the Zwinglians, already suspicious because of Luther's endorsement, effectively brought the moderate Zwinglians into the Lutheran fold while permanently alienating the ultra-Zwinglians.

The Protestant cause, already adversely affected by the Luther/Zwingli hostilities, suffered another setback when Philip of Hesse, a supporter of the Reformers, sought their religious sanction for his bigamy. Appealing to Scripture, the authority for the Reformers, Philip approached Bucer through an intermediary. Although he had not sanctioned Henry VIII's earlier divorce from Catherine of Aragon and although his initial response to Philip's request was negative, Bucer weighed the religious and political factors and reluctantly acquiesced to Philip. In fact, Bucer wrote a defense of bigamy, but his ultimate response was typically equivocal: He sanctioned Philip's secret bigamy. Unfortunately, Bucer's attempts to keep the marriage a secret were thwarted by Philip, who made it public and who also sought approval from the Catholic Church.

Although the Reformation was an accomplished fact, the Catholic Church was intent on returning the Reformers to the fold, and Bucer himself participated in several councils whose ostensible purpose was to unite all Christians. In 1540, the year of Philip's bigamous marriage, the Colloquy of

Worms was convened, but no real progress was made, despite Bucer's efforts, which included secret meetings with liberal Catholic reformers. The following year, Bucer attended the Diet of Regensburg, which was called by Emperor Charles V, who had two aims: religious unity and military assistance against an impending Turkish invasion of the Holy Roman Empire. The authorship of the Regensburg Book, which served as the basis for the ensuing discussions, was unknown; the material, however, was drawn from the secret meetings conducted at the earlier Colloquy of Worms. At these secret meetings, Bucer had made compromises which, when they were made public, brought criticism from the Protestants, especially the Lutherans. When both sides rejected the Regensburg Book, Bucer apparently despaired of effecting a Protestant/Catholic reconciliation, and he became very anti-Catholic. Subsequent meetings, which were also futile, were held, but they were conducted, as Bucer suspected, more for political than for religious reasons. Charles V, who had been conducting secret negotiations with the pope, the French, and the Turks, finally attacked the Protestant German princes in 1546 and quickly defeated them. After the defeat of the Smalkald League, Charles V instituted the Augsburg Interim, which reflected not only his ideas but also some of the articles of the Regensburg Interim, which had been drafted in part by Bucer. Despite the similarities between the two documents, Bucer adamantly opposed the Augsburg Interim because it was the product of force, not negotiation, and because he had become more intolerant of the Catholics. Bucer resisted Charles V until 1549, when he was officially requested to leave Strasbourg.

Although he had various options, Bucer chose to accept Archbishop Thomas Cranmer's invitation to aid the Reformation effort in England. After all, his Cologne Ordinances had been included in the First Book of Common Prayer, and he had many friends and supporters in that country. Soon after his arrival at Cambridge, where he taught, he was again embroiled in the Supper Controversy, this time, however, with Catholic opposition.

In his service to Edward VI, he refuted the Catholic elevation of good works over faith, resisted the radical views of the Scottish Reformers, wrote *De regno Christi* (1557), a design for converting England into the Kingdom of Christ, and aided in the development of the English Books of Prayer. For his efforts he received the doctor of theology degree from Cambridge before he died on February 28, 1551. Even in death he was involved in controversy: English Catholics under Mary tried and condemned him posthumously for heresy, then exhumed and burned his body in 1555; Elizabeth, the Protestant queen, atoned for the Catholic desecration in 1560.

Summary

Unlike his more famous Reformation contemporaries—Luther, Zwingli, and Calvin—Martin Bucer was a mediator occupying the middle ground in most of the religious controversy of the sixteenth century. Rather than establishing his own sect, he sought to reconcile the intransigent extremes within the Reformation movement. His ecumenical efforts with such divergent groups as the Anabaptists and Catholics led him to make concessions, although for the goal of church unity, that undermined his credibility with his colleagues. Though he never abandoned the essential tenets of his faith, he did appear occasionally too willing to compromise, even to surrender, on the details that preoccupied other Reformers. Though he was inevitably unsuccessful in mediating what were irreconcilable differences, he did succeed in negotiating the reform of several German cities which were attempting to resolve questions about the disposition of church property and the use of images in worship services. Under his leadership, Strasbourg became an influential Reformation city which attracted young Reformers, most notably Calvin, who incorporated some of Bucer's ideas in his *Institutes of the Christian Religion* (1536).

Because he occupied the middle ground on theological disputes, Bucer is not a theologian whose influence is readily traced. His theology, because of his wide reading, was eclectic and drawn from many sources, some of them—Anabaptist and Catholic—inherently contradictory. Bucer's contribution was in his synthesis of theology, not in his creation of it. Centuries later, his ecumenical approach to theology seems more appropriate to the times than the dogmatic intransigence of his more famous contemporaries.

Bibliography

Eells, Hastings. *Martin Bucer*. London: Oxford University Press, and New Haven, Conn.: Yale University Press, 1931. The definitive biography of Bucer, this lengthy book contains valuable information about the historical context, theological differences between the Reformers, and the personalities of the major figures. The book is well organized, well indexed, and very readable. Though his sympathies are clearly with Bucer, Eells is fairly objective in his discussion of Luther, Zwingli, and the Roman Catholic Church.

Höpf, Constantin. *Martin Bucer and the English Reformation*. Oxford: Blackwell, 1946. A thorough review of Bucer's influence on the English Reformation. Höpf, who includes copious illustrations, original correspondence, and a comprehensive bibliography, extends Bucer's influence beyond his *Censura* (wr. 1550) of the First Edwardian Prayer Book and details how Bucer's psalms were printed in the English primers. Bucer, for Höpf, was more influential in England than either Zwingli or Luther.

Pauck, Wilhelm, ed. *Melanchthon and Bucer*. London: SCM Press, and Philadelphia: Westminster Press, 1969. Pauck includes his translation of Bucer's *De regno Christi*, which he introduces by discussing Bucer's substantial contribution to the Reformation and explaining how Bucer's Strasbourg experiences affected his recommendations for England in *De regno Christi*. Of particular interest are Pauck's comments about the relationship of church and state.

Stephens, W. P. *The Holy Spirit in the Theology of Martin Bucer*. Cambridge: Cambridge University Press, 1970. A close examination of the Holy Spirit in Bucer's theology. Stephens provides an introduction establishing Bucer's theology in the context of his times and summarizes the various influences that affected the development of his religious thought. There is also an excellent bibliography.

Wendel, François. *Calvin: The Origins and Development of His Religious Thought*. Translated by Philip Mairet. London: Collins, and New York: Harper, 1963. Although the book concerns the many sources of Calvin's theology, Wendel establishes Bucer as being particularly influential. Bucer's influence is especially prominent in the predestination material found in Calvin's *Institutes of the Christian Religion*, and Calvin's theology is regarded as being aligned with the theology of the Tetrapolitan Confession of 1530.

Thomas L. Erskine

WILLIAM BYRD

Born: 1543; possibly Lincoln, Lincolnshire, England

Died: July 4, 1623; Stondon Massey, Essex, England

Area of Achievement: Music

Contribution: Byrd was the outstanding English composer of the Renaissance, notable both for the variety of forms and styles in which he composed and for the outstanding quality of the individual pieces within each genre. He was apparently the first English composer to understand fully the new technique of imitative polyphony as developed in the Netherlands, and he passed this understanding on to his students, who included the composers Thomas Morley, Thomas Tomkins, and, almost certainly, Orlando Gibbons.

Early Life

Nothing definite is known of William Byrd's early life. The year of his birth is assumed to have been 1543, since he described himself in his will of November 15, 1622, as being in his eightieth year. He may have come from Lincoln, but he must have been reared in London because he was reliably reported to have been a student of Thomas Tallis, composer and organist of the Chapel Royal. He may have been a Child of the Chapel Royal, but the records from this period are incomplete and the names of many of the boys are lost. Thomas Byrd, Gentleman of the Chapel Royal in the 1540's and 1550's, may have been his father.

Byrd probably began composing music while still in his teens, and several compositions attributed to him are, if genuine, likely to have been student works. The motets "Alleluia, Confitemini Domino," and "Christus resurgens," the latter published in 1605, are to texts from the Sarum liturgy and could possibly have been written before the death of Queen Mary in 1559, when Byrd was sixteen. Both are cantus firmus motets with extensive use of canon in the older style of Tallis and his contemporaries. Several works for viol consort and for organ may also come from this period, although the exact dating of most of his compositions has not been established.

The only portrait of Byrd comes from the early eighteenth century and is not reliable. He seems to have been a man of strong convictions and of a tenacious character. He was a staunch Roman Catholic at a time when this was strongly discouraged, and he repeatedly paid fines for his own and his family's recusancy. That he retained his Chapel Royal position to the end of his life is a tribute to his skill both as an organist and as a composer. He was a man of some courage, willing to publish settings of the forbidden Mass Ordinary carrying his own name on each page. He was also a diligent and not altogether sympathetic litigant in numerous cases involving property during his later years. From his own compositions one derives the impression of a man of great energy and organizational skills, imbued with both a sense of artistic purpose and deep personal convictions.

Life's Work

In March, 1563, Byrd was appointed Organist and Master of the Choristers at Lincoln Cathedral, a post which involved teaching the boys as well as composing and directing music. In 1568, he married Juliana Birley, who died around 1586, and the first of his five children from two marriages was baptized in 1569. Byrd was given an unusually large salary, and the cathedral continued to pay him at least a portion of it until 1581, when he had been in London for more than a decade, in return for his continuing to send occasional compositions to Lincoln.

During his time at Lincoln, Byrd seems to have set out to master a variety of musical styles and forms. He looked principally to Tallis, Christopher Tye, John Redford, Robert White, and Alfonso Ferrabosco the Elder for models, sometimes borrowing specific musical ideas from their works. He composed settings for organ based largely on Latin hymns and began his lifelong interest in writing music for the virginals (an early smaller form of the harpsichord). He wrote a number of "In nomine" settings for instrumental consort, presumably intended for viols, and these seem to have been widely circulated in manuscript copies. He also wrote the first of his so-called consort songs for solo voice and viol consort, of which some are settings of metrical psalms and others of the sort of alliterative poetry popular at the time. Some of these pieces have simple choruses at the ends of stanzas and prefigure the development of the verse anthem, a form developed fully by Byrd's students Orlando Gibbons and Thomas Tomkins, in which music for solo voice or voices alternates with that for chorus, to an accompaniment of organ or viol consort.

Most of Byrd's music for the new Anglican liturgy seems to have been written at Lincoln and includes anthems, litanies, preces, and suffrages, two Evening Services and the so-called Short Service, based upon a similar work by Tallis. Ironically, this music, which formed only a small portion of Byrd's output, survived in the repertoire after his death and carried his fame into the eighteenth century.

His Latin motets from this period appear to have been attempts to master both the older style of cantus firmus writing and the newer style of pure, imitative polyphony as developed in the Netherlands by such composers as Josquin Desprez in the early sixteenth century and only just being imported into England. Cantus firmus motets such as "Libera me, Domine, de morte aeterna" and purely imitative ones such as "Attollite portas" are unlikely to have been sung at Lincoln in the 1560's, but they probably served as good advertisements for the young composer by demonstrating his grasp both of various styles and of large-scale formal planning.

Byrd was sworn in as a Gentleman of the Chapel Royal in February, 1570, and as joint organist with Tallis in December, 1572. This necessitated a move to London, where he occupied himself both with his Chapel Royal duties and with acquiring influential patrons. In 1575, Queen Elizabeth granted Byrd and Tallis a monopoly on the printing and selling of both part-music and lined music paper. In the same year, they published their *Cantiones Quae ab Argumento Sacrae Vocantur*, a collection of Latin motets—seventeen by each composer—for from five to eight voices. The volume was dedicated to the queen, and it is possible, but by no means certain, that some or all of the contents had been sung in her Chapel Royal, where the singing of Latin texts was still permitted.

Byrd's contributions to the 1575 collection give the impression of being an anthology of what he considered to be his best work to that date, together with several newly composed pieces. The newer works, primarily penitential in character, demonstrate Byrd's mastery of the Netherlands style and his debt to Ferrabosco. The most famous of these works is the motet "Emendemus in melius." At this time, Byrd also continued writing instrumental music, his most famous works being his Browning variations for five-part consort, the Walsingham variations for keyboard, and a series of dances (pavans and galliards), also for keyboard.

Beginning in 1581, with the discovery of a Jesuit plot to kill the queen and the subsequent brutal executions of Father Edmund Campion and other Jesuits, life for English Catholics became more difficult. Byrd maintained his Chapel Royal position and even composed works for official celebrations, including *Look and Bow Down* to words by the queen herself, written to celebrate the defeat of the Spanish Armada in 1588. He seems to have reacted to the persecution of his Catholic brethren by composing a series of deeply personal penitential motets, some lamenting the Babylonian captivity of Jerusalem, others petitioning for the coming of God and the deliverance of the faithful. The most famous of these works is the motet *Ne irascaris*, printed in the first of his two retrospective collections of Latin motets titled *Cantiones Sacrae*, published in 1589 and 1591, respectively. Whether these motets were meant to be sung in a liturgical context or merely circulated in support of Roman Catholicism is not clear. The penitential texts seldom have a specific liturgical function and seem to have been chosen, by Byrd or his patrons, to make a religious and political point—one, however, which was not so obvious as to warrant their suppression.

In 1588, Byrd published his first collection of settings of English texts titled *Psalmes, Sonets, and Songs of Sadness and Pietie* for five voices. This work contained mostly earlier consort songs, slightly reworked and with words added to the original accompanying parts in an attempt to capitalize on the new vogue for the Italian madrigal. The most famous piece from this collection was "Lullaby," while the most striking was perhaps "Why Do I Use My Paper, Ink, and Pen?" a setting of the innocuous first verse of a well-known seditious text concerning the execution of Father Campion.

In 1589, Byrd published *Songs of Sundrie Natures* for from three to six voices. This contained, in addition to material similar to that in the 1588 volume, a consort song in its original form ("And Think Ye, Nymphs"), two carols, and the verse anthem "Christ Rising Again." Byrd then contributed two madrigals to Thomas Watson's *First Sett of Italian Madrigalls Englished* (1590), but was in general not much influenced by the newer Italian style which so permeated the music of his student Morley and that of the other composers of the younger generation, especially John Wilbye and Thomas Weelkes.

Byrd's second collection of 1591 was the manuscript of keyboard music entitled *My Ladye Nevells Booke*, which preserved the best of his virginal music to that date. It included pavans and galliards, two new settings on a ground bass, some newly composed fantasias, and a number of earlier works, some of them extensively revised. Byrd's so-called Great Service, his largest and most outstanding contribution to the Anglican liturgy, may also date from around 1590.

Beginning at about this time, Byrd's attitude toward English Catholicism and the role in it of his own music seems to have changed. In 1593, he moved to Stondon Massey, Essex, near the seat of his patrons, the staunchly Catholic Petre family, at Ingatestone. After this date, he seems to have spent progressively less time in London and instead to have immersed himself in the life of the recusant Catholic community which surrounded the Petres. Instead of highly personal nonliturgical and penitential texts, Byrd began to set purely liturgical texts in a more emotionally restrained and less grandiose style. This music was apparently designed to be sung at clandestine Catholic services at Ingatestone Hall and elsewhere.

Byrd eventually gathered together this body of liturgical settings and published it in two collections, each entitled *Gradualia*, in 1605 and 1607; they were reissued together in 1610. The more than one hundred items included in these two volumes can be recombined in a variety of ways to provide the Mass propers for all the major feasts of the Catholic liturgy, including Marian feasts and votive masses. To provide the Mass ordinary texts, Byrd created settings for three, four, and five voices, of which the one for four voices is the most remarkable and that for five voices the most immediately accessible. These settings he had printed in the early 1590's, without title pages but with his own name clearly printed on each page.

Byrd's last published collection, the *Psalmes, Songs, and Sonnets of Sadness and Pietie* of 1611, was a miscellany, including both full and verse anthems to English texts, consort songs, madrigal-like songs for three to five voices, and instrumental fantasias. He subsequently included a number of his keyboard pavans and galliards in *Parthenia: Or, The Maydenhead of the First Musicke That Ever Was Printed for the Virginalls* (1613), a joint publication with the composers John Bull and Orlando Gibbons, both of whom were probably his students. His last published works were four sacred songs included in Sir William Leighton's *Teares or Lamentacions of a Sorrowfull Soule* (1614). His works continued to circulate in manuscript, the most famous collections being those of the Catholic Paston family of Appleton Hall, Norfolk, and the three volumes complied between 1609 and 1619 by Francis Tregian, the first popularly known as *The Fitzwilliam Virginal Book.*

Byrd continued to live at Stondon Massey, his last years increasingly troubled by lawsuits over his various property holdings. His second wife, Ellen, died sometime around 1606 and he, himself, died there on July 4, 1623, and is presumably buried in the churchyard, according to his own wishes. The *Old Cheque-Book: Or, Book of Remembrance of the Chapel Royal, from 1561-1744* (1872), noting his passing, called him "a Father of Musick." His son Thomas, also a musician, survived until about 1652.

Summary

William Byrd was one of the four greatest composers of the High Renaissance, the others being Orlando di Lasso, Tómas Luis de Victoria, and Giovanni Pierluigi da Palestrina. He surpassed all except Victoria in the emotional fervor of his music and all but Lasso in his variety of forms and styles. If Byrd was less able than Lasso and Palestrina to come to terms with the new style of the Italian madrigal, he surpassed them both in his command of instrumental forms.

Byrd is that rare example of a composer who was at once the consolidator of older traditions and the instigator of new ones. If Byrd's initial efforts in various genres are based more directly on earlier models than had previously been thought, his achievements are not lessened thereby. He appears to have been the first English composer to understand and successfully employ Netherlands imitative polyphony, and he thereby established the dominant style for his successors. Although he wrote comparatively little Anglican church music, his Great Service was the crowning achievement of the Elizabethan period; many of his smaller works survived the Commonwealth and, together with English *contrafacta* of some of his Latin works, formed the basis of the Tudor style as copied by such Restoration composers as Henry Purcell and William Croft and eulogized by eighteenth century writers on music.

Byrd made only a few fleeting efforts at writing in the new and popular style of the Italian madrigal. Instead, he developed the older, more sober form of the secular consort song to its full maturity and created from it the form of the verse anthem, initially either secular or sacred, which was to dominate English church music for nearly two hundred years. He essentially created a genre and repertoire of keyboard music from the slimmest of beginnings, polished it over a period of some fifty years, and bequeathed it to his successors Bull and Gibbons. His compositions for viol consort are more conservative in character and were overshadowed by the newer Italian fantasias at the turn of the seventeenth century, but they were still influencing native composers some twenty years later.

Byrd was the most influential musical composition teacher of his time, producing such disparate pupils as the forward-looking Morley, the brilliant émigré composer Peter Philips, the keyboard virtuoso John Bull, and the conservative and essentially serious Tomkins and Gibbons. The teaching style employed in Morley's *Plaine and Easie Introduction to Practicall Musicke* (1597) can probably be taken as Byrd's own. He appears as quite a modern figure, both in his attitude toward composition and in his tendency to revise his own works, collect them into anthologies, and then carefully supervise their publication.

Throughout his life, Byrd's consuming passion was his faith, and it is in his Latin church music that his greatest works are found. His early works are notable for their size and scope, his works of the 1580's for their penitential intensity, and his later works for their formal sweep and inner confidence. Although Byrd was capable of writing pedestrian music, his best works are unsurpassed, displaying a sense of technical command and personal conviction which set him apart as a great composer.

Bibliography

Andrews, H. K. *The Technique of Byrd's Polyphony.* London and New York: Oxford University Press, 1966. An extremely detailed technical discussion of Byrd's musical style and compositional techniques.

Fellowes, Edmund H. *William Byrd.* 2d ed. London and New York: Oxford University Press, 1948. A pathbreaking biography by the editor of the twenty-volume *The Collected Works of William Byrd* (1937-1950). Especially strong on biographical details, including many documents not printed elsewhere; it is necessarily somewhat dated.

Harley, John. *William Byrd: Gentleman of the Chapel Royal.* Aldershot: Scolar Press, and Brookfield, Vt.: Ashgate, 1997. The first comprehensive study of Byrd to appear in 660 years, Harley's work provides a detailed account of the composer's life based on a fresh examination of original sources, as well as several previously known documents which have now been identified as being of Byrd's creation. A number of questions have been resolved including his parentage and date of birth.

Howes, Frank. *William Byrd.* Edited by Landon Ronald. London: Curwen, and New York: Dutton, 1928. Pioneering biography, useful but outdated, with a brief but solid discussion of the music.

Kerman, Joseph. *The Music of William Byrd.* Vol. 1, *The Masses and Motets of William Byrd.* Berkeley: University of California Press, 1980. The most detailed discussions of Byrd's music, with special attention to sources, style, and compositional techniques.

Le Huray, Peter. *Music and the Reformation in England, 1549-1660.* Edited by Erik Routley.

New York: Oxford University Press, and London: Herbert Jenkins, 1967. An excellent survey of the entire period. Chapter 8 is especially relevant.

Mateer, David. "William Byrd's Middlesex Recusancy." *Music and Letters* 78 (February, 1997): 1. Mateer investigates Byrd's recusancy in Harlington, Middlesex, at the receiving end of anti-Catholic legislation. This ironically coincided with the most productive portion of his life as a composer.

Neighbour, Oliver. *The Music of William Byrd.* Vol. 3, *The Consort and Keyboard Music of William Byrd.* London and Boston: Faber, 1978. Volume 1 is by Joseph Kerman (see above). Volume 2 is in preparation.

Graydon Beeks

ÁLVAR NÚÑEZ CABEZA DE VACA

Born: c. 1490; Jerez de la Frontera, Spain

Died: c. 1560; Spain

Area of Achievement: Exploration

Contribution: Cabeza de Vaca's capture by Native Americans in Texas gave him the chance to explore the region in detail and write an invaluable account of the people and topography of Texas and northern Mexico that stimulated further exploration.

Early Life

Álvar Núñez Cabeza de Vaca was born at the end of the fifteenth century in a town near Cadiz. Sources differ about the exact year of his birth, with estimates ranging from 1490 to 1500. He was the oldest of the four children of Francisco de Vera and Teresa Cabeza de Vaca. The young man used his mother's surname because of its honored association in Spain with the struggle against the Islamic Moors. At a battle in 1212, an ancestor used a cow's head to designate an unmarked pass for Christian soldiers against the Moors. As a result of this action, which helped to win the victory, the ruler at the time gave the name "Cow's Head" to the ancestors of Cabeza de Vaca's mother.

Cabeza de Vaca's parents died when he was young, and he lived with an aunt and uncle until he launched his career as a soldier. He began as a page while still in his teens and was involved in fighting in Italy. He received serious wounds at a battle near the Italian town of Ravenna in 1512. During the next fifteen years, Cabeza de Vaca fought in battles with the armies of the Spanish king against rebels and also in struggles with the French in Navarre.

In 1527, Cabeza de Vaca joined the expedition of Pánfilo de Narváez that had been established to conquer Florida for Spain. The Spanish king, Charles I, designated Cabeza de Vaca as the treasurer and what was called the chief constable of the expedition. Five ships carrying six hundred people left for America in June, 1527. The expedition soon encountered obstacles. More than one hundred of its members elected to remain at Santo Domingo. A significant number then perished in a hurricane in Cuba. By the time Narvaez and his men had sailed from Cuba in April of 1528, there were only four hundred men left in his command. A few days later the expedition made landfall in Florida and claimed the territory for Spain.

Then the expedition began to fall apart. Narváez decided to explore the interior and left his ships and supplies. Eventually he and his men found themselves running low on food. Attacks from the natives put the Spaniards in even greater danger. Narváez had his men build some crude barges, and he decided to head for Mexico, which he believed was not far away. In fact, it was hundreds of miles distant.

The flotilla of five barges made good progress for a month and passed by the mouth of the Mississippi River. Then a violent storm scattered the vessels, two of which came to rest on an island near the Texas coast on November 6, 1538. Eighty men survived, including Cabeza de Vaca. However, they were alone in a wilderness at a great distance from any settlement of their European comrades.

Life's Work

Cabeza de Vaca's primary concern now was his own survival and eventual journey to Mexico to rejoin his countrymen. He later recalled that "the cold was severe, and our bodies were so emaciated the bones might be counted with little difficulty, having become the perfect figures of death." He had no way of knowing that it would be seven years before he found his way back to Mexico and his own civilization.

For four years until 1532, Cabeza de Vaca lived among the Indians of the Texas coast and ventured inland to trade goods with other tribes. He became a kind of medicine man to the Indians in the area. Since he had no real medical skill, all he could do was to pray over the sick and sometimes blow on their injuries. Cabeza de Vaca saw a great deal of the land because the Indians ranged widely to find the prickly pear fruits and pecan nuts that formed the major part of their diet.

Throughout this part of his adventure, Cabeza de Vaca thought constantly of escape, and he often considered his chances of making a break for freedom. Finally, he persuaded three other Spanish captives to go with him, though he would have made his expedition alone if necessary. By the autumn of 1534, he and his companions, Andrés Dorantes, a black slave named Estevanico (Estebán), and Alonso del Castillo Maldonaldo, fled southward in the direction of Mexico.

The exact route that they traversed has been the object of controversy. Because he was the first European to cross many Texas landmarks, Cabeza de

Vaca has become a part of Texas nationalism or state identity. Modern efforts to trace Cabeza de Vaca's steps through Texas and Mexico have indicated that "the four ragged castaways," as Cabeza de Vaca's party became known, spent twenty-two months on their route to Mexico. The final thirteen months saw the most sustained and purposeful travel. Their trek began in what is now known as southeast Texas near the Guadalupe River. They then moved southward toward the Rio Grande River. They crossed that waterway near the location of what is now the International Falcon Reservoir.

At the Rio Grande, they turned northwest and went in the direction of the present-day city of El Paso. Thinking that they could reach Spanish settlements on the Pacific Coast and eager to discover new lands, Cabeza de Vaca and his colleagues moved through northern Mexico and then headed south and east down the Pacific Coast of Mexico. This detour added two thousand miles to their journey.

During this phase of Cabeza de Vaca's trip, he once again practiced the medical skills he had used among the Indians. He came upon a man who had an arrow lodged near his heart. With a cauterized knife, Cabeza de Vaca removed the arrow and closed the incision that he had made. The success of this rough operation added to the four Spaniard's fame among the Indians. Cabeza de Vaca has become known as the "patron saint" of the Texas Surgical Society for having performed the first such operation within Texas.

Cabeza de Vaca and his associates encountered a band of Spanish slave hunters on April 11, 1536, the date when their ordeal in the wilderness came to an end. They then went on to Mexico City, arriving in July, 1536. Cabeza de Vaca wanted to leave for Spain immediately, but circumstances delayed his departure until the spring of 1537.

After he returned to Spain, Cabeza de Vaca prepared a detailed account of his years in the wilds of Texas and Mexico. His narrative, written during the three years after he came home and published in 1542, became known as *La Relación*, which later appeared in subsequent editions under the title *Los Naufragios* (the shipwreck). Another source, written by Cabeza de Vaca and two of his companions on the trek, was prepared in Mexico in 1536. These two versions became classics of the period of Spanish conquest and are the basic sources for any understanding of Cabeza de Vaca as an explorer and historical figure.

Once back in Spain, Cabeza de Vaca was given the post of governor of the province of Rio de la Plata (what is now Paraguay) in 1540. There he tried without success to apply some of the lessons he had learned with the Indians in Texas. His humane treatment of the natives there aroused political opposition among the Spanish settlers and he was returned to Spain in chains to face charges of misrule. The legal proceedings against him resulted in his banishment for a time to North Africa. Eventually, he was cleared of the charges and returned to Spain, where he died in poverty, probably around 1560.

Summary

Cabeza de Vaca's experience is one of the great sagas of the period of Spanish conquest, and it won for him an enduring historical fame. His work was also important to the future course of Spanish activity in North America. Because of the clarity of Cabeza de Vaca's account of his journeys, the Spanish in Mexico obtained a better sense of the geographical extent of Texas and northern Mexico. The information that Cabeza de Vaca provided also served to stimulate interest in the area north of where Cabeza de Vaca had traveled. Perhaps that region might contain the gold that animated so much of the Spanish impulse to conquer territory and subdue the Indians in the Americas.

To verify what Cabeza de Vaca had discovered, the Spanish authorities sent a priest, Friar Marcos de Niza, northward, along with Cabeza de Vaca's companion, Estevanico, the black slave. During this expedition, Marcos de Niza viewed a Pueblo Indian settlement and saw what he believed to be the glitter of silver and gold. He interpreted his findings as specific evidence of the legendary Seven Cities of Cíbola that would contain the gold that the Spaniards had long sought. From this report stemmed the expedition of Francisco Vásquez de Coronado that led to Spanish penetration of the interior of North America. In that sense, Cabeza de Vaca's wanderings and subsequent reports of his adventures proved a significant turning point in the history of the Spanish presence in what would become Texas and the United States.

Bibliography

Cabeza de Vaca, Álvar Núñez. *The Account: Álvar Núñez Cabeza de Vaca's Relacion*. Houston, Tex.: Arte Público, 1993. A translation of Cabeza de Vaca's account of his captivity and return.

Campbell, T. N., and T. J. Campbell. *Historic Indian Groups of the Choke Canyon Reservoir and Surrounding Area, Southern Texas*. San Antonio: Center for Archaeological Research, University of Texas at San Antonio, 1981. Despite its title, this work is a valuable interpretation of Cabeza de Vaca's route in Texas and the information that his account offers about Indian life and customs during the sixteenth century.

Chipman, Donald E. "Álvar Núñez Cabeza de Vaca," in *The New Handbook of Texas*, edited by Ron Tyler et al. Vol. 4. Austin: Texas State Historical Association, 1996. The best brief biography of Cabeza de Vaca, with a good review of the issue of his route to Mexico and his historical significance.

———. "In Search of Cabeza de Vaca's Route Across Texas: An Historiographical Survey." *Southwestern Historical Quarterly* 91 (October, 1987): 127-148. An excellent survey of the longstanding controversy about the route that Cabeza de Vaca took to return to Mexico during the mid-1530's.

Hedrick, Basil C., and Carroll Riley. *The Journey of the Vaca Party: The Account of the Narvaez Expedition 1528-1536, as Related by Gonzalo de Oviedo y Valdes*. Carbondale: Southern Illinois University Press, 1974. A good translation of the so-called Joint Report of the expedition of which Cabeza de Vaca was a part.

Howard, David A. *Conquistador in Chains: Cabeza de Vaca and the Indians of the Americas*. Tuscaloosa: University of Alabama Press, 1997. A biography of Cabeza de Vaca that sees his Texas experience as a key influence in his change from exploiter to protector of the Native Americans in the Rio de la Plata province.

Wallace, Ernest, David M. Vigness, and George B. Ward. *Documents of Texas History*. Austin, Tex.: State House Press, 1994. Contains a brief excerpt from Cabeza de Vaca's narrative.

Lewis L. Gould

JOHN CABOT

Born: c. 1450; Genoa?, Italy
Died: c. 1498; place unknown
Area of Achievement: Exploration
Contribution: Cabot persuaded Englishmen to explore new lands beyond the western horizon and laid the foundations of England's claim to and eventual control of the North American continent.

Early Life

Juan Caboto (John Cabot) was probably born in Genoa around 1450. By the early 1460's, he had moved to Venice, and in the late 1470's he became a citizen and married a Venetian named Mattea. Venice was then the center for Asian goods, especially spices, entering the European market. Thus Caboto became a merchant in the spice trade. He learned what he could about the trade by reading Marco Polo. A desire for direct knowledge and a willingness to venture his life prompted the young merchant to disguise himself as a Moslem and make the pilgrimage to Mecca. Whether the knowledge he gained through reading or travel helped him is doubtful. He was only one man in a city of wealthy merchants engaged in a trade that was already beginning to diminish, thanks to the Turkish control of the eastern Mediterranean.

Seeking broader economic opportunity, Caboto and his family settled in Valencia in 1490. Juan Caboto, the Venetian, as he became known, developed a reputation as a cartographer and navigator. In 1492, Caboto presented local officials with a proposal for harbor improvements. The project material was forwarded to King Ferdinand, then residing in Barcelona—two hundred miles along the coast above Valencia. Caboto had several audiences with the ruler to discuss the harbor proposal. That royal approval followed suggests how persuasive the arguments and the plans of the foreign expert could be. Unfortunately, the project was later abandoned. What is important about this incident is that it brought Juan Caboto to Barcelona at the time when Christopher Columbus entered to announce that he had reached the land of the Great Khan.

Caboto was skeptical. There was no evidence that Columbus had reached the densely populated and highly cultivated lands described by Marco Polo. Caboto tried to persuade potential backers in Seville that Columbus had reached only an island partway to his destination. Thus the wealth of the Indies could yet be attained by organizing an expedition under Caboto. While some Spaniards shared the doubts of Caboto, King Ferdinand and Queen Isabella did not. Besides, given the choice between two men from Genoa, it made sense to support the one who had already crossed the Atlantic Ocean and had returned with gold. Like Columbus, Caboto decided to move to where support for his project might be found.

In the late fifteenth century, Bristol was, after London, England's most active port, and its venturesome spirit was unmatched anywhere. Its ships carried local wool to Iceland and returned with dried codfish. Bristol merchants dominated the wine trade with Spain and Portugal. Always ready to try new trades, the merchants had sent ships to the eastern Mediterranean and to the islands of the Atlantic—especially Madeira. From the 1480's, Bristol ships made voyages of discovery seeking the legendary Isle of Brasil in the western Atlantic. The men of Bristol, both merchants and mariners, had more experience in the waters of the Atlantic than any men in any country. Naturally, John Cabot, as he was known thenceforth, selected Bristol as his new home and base of exploration.

Life's Work

Soon after his arrival in 1495, Cabot persuaded several Bristol merchants to try the westward route to Asia. A westward course in the high latitudes would bring a ship to the northeast part of Asia, which, Cabot argued, was much closer to Europe than the tropical region reached by Columbus. Cabot constructed a globe to demonstrate the advantages of his route. Like Columbus, Cabot reduced the size of the earth and increased the eastward limits of Asia to shorten the western route. The Cabot proposal was sent to King Henry VII.

Henry Tudor of England was famous for persuading reluctant subjects to make large contributions to the royal treasury. To such a ruler, Cabot's proposal was quite attractive. It was a second chance for the ruler who had rejected, in 1489, a similar scheme by Bartholomeo Columbus on behalf of his brother Christopher. Still, Henry VII was not about to risk his own money in a doubtful venture. He granted a patent to Cabot in March, 1496, to discover islands in the world unknown to Christians. Cabot would govern and receive the revenue (minus one-fifth for

John and Sebastian Cabot discover North America

Henry VII) of the towns and islands he could "conquer, occupy and possess."

With the royal patent and the financial backing of some Bristol merchants, Cabot put to sea, only to return a short time later. Officially he returned because of a shortage of provisions. Unofficially, the crew probably lacked confidence in the foreign expert and decided to end the voyage. Masters of ships at this time had limited powers and generally acceded to the wishes of their crew. On his next voyage, for example, Cabot followed the wrong course and made his landfall on the French coast because his crew did not trust the more northerly (and correct) heading proposed by Cabot.

In May, 1497, Cabot tried again. His small ship was named *Matthew*—probably an Anglicized version of his wife's name, Mattea. Cabot and his crew of eighteen men sailed toward the southwest tip of Ireland and then headed directly west. The passage was swift, thanks to smooth seas and fair winds. Land was sighted on June 24, only thirty-three days after leaving Ireland. As late as the eighteenth century, ships might take three or four months to make the same passage. Some scholars believe that Cabot's speed is attributable to the fact that he timed his departure and course to coincide with favorable weather patterns learned by earlier voyagers from Bristol. Cabot probably made landfall at the northern tip of Newfoundland. That particular site had been settled briefly by Vikings nearly five hundred years earlier. The crew of the *Matthew* went ashore and raised the standards of Henry VII, the pope, and Venice. Cabot claimed possession of the land but wisely kept his men near the water's edge; they had found evidence of local inhabitants. This brief ceremony was the only time that the men ventured ashore.

For the next month Cabot coasted along the foreign shore. Circumstances suggest that the *Matthew* sailed along the eastern coast of Newfoundland and then headed southwest past Nova Scotia to Maine. The southwest heading of the land mass matched the one Cabot had predicted for the easternmost area of Asia. The ship then turned home, crossed the Atlantic in fifteen days, and arrived at Bristol on August 6, 1497.

Cabot wasted no time. He left Bristol within hours of his arrival bound for London and Henry VII. Four days later the king received Cabot and presented him with honors and a pension (the latter to be paid by the Bristol Customs House). There was general agreement that Cabot had reached the northwest corner of Asia and that the next voyage would reach the Indies and the much-desired spice trade. Bristol merchants were also excited over the vast quantities of fish reported off the "new found land." Whatever became of the western passage, Bristol now possessed a new source of fish to replace the declining trade with Iceland. Thus Cabot's brief voyage of 1497 promised rich returns to merchants prepared to risk the trade with Asia and fish to men of more modest means and ambitions.

There was no shortage of backers for the follow-up voyage. Henry VII outfitted a large ship, and London and Bristol furnished four more vessels. This was not a voyage of exploration. Cabot expected to establish an island base to service British ships making the long passage to the Indies. If Cabot failed to build and hold such a base, then he possessed nothing and lacked a claim to any revenue from the Asian trade. Discovery entailed more than simply finding a site: One had to inhabit the site. (Columbus met this requirement when his flagship was wrecked and its crew built a camp ashore to await their leader's return from Spain.) Cabot's fleet departed in May, 1498. A storm struck the fleet, and one damaged ship entered an Irish port. There was no further news of the fleet.

There have been many guesses about the fate of Cabot's fleet. The discovery by Portuguese explorers in 1501 of Newfoundland Indians with several items of Italian origin provides a possible clue. Perhaps Cabot did establish his base during the mild Newfoundland summer. If so, then no one would have been prepared for the Arctic winter conditions common to the northern part of the island.

Summary

John Cabot, whose activities gave Great Britain its claim to North America, remains almost unknown to this day. There are few references to him. Unlike Columbus, Cabot left no journals to detail his work. Whereas Columbus had sons who preserved and enlarged their father's claim to fame, Cabot had Sebastian, a scoundrel who claimed his father's work as his own.

Cabot was not the first European to set upon the North American continent. The Vikings certainly came earlier, and in turn they may have been preceded by Romans and Greeks a thousand years before. Cabot's arrival, however, was different. He was the first of a constant stream of European explorers. Cabot ended the ancient isolation of the North American continent. The charts he made during the voyage of 1497 have long since disappeared. His contemporaries, however, made use of the charts. Juan de La Cosa's famous world map of 1500 shows a series of Tudor banners along the coast visited by Cabot.

It is customary to note the similarities in the lives and careers of Cabot and Columbus. Both were born in the same Italian city at about the same time (although in Cabot's case, place of birth is not certain); both convinced foreign monarchs to back a search for a westward route to Asia. While Columbus achieved greater fame and fortune, he lived long enough to suffer greater disgrace. Cabot the explorer simply disappeared and left all controversy behind. He died an explorer's death.

Bibliography

Beazley, Sir Charles Raymond. *John and Sebastian Cabot: The Discovery of North America*. London and New York: Unwin, 1898. With the people of the United States and Italy engaged in many celebrations over the four hundredth anniversary of Columbus' voyage to America, there was an attempt by English historians to commemorate John Cabot and strengthen his claim as the discoverer of North America. This biography was part of that effort. Although many of the author's conclusions are now questioned, the work does contain useful details about John Cabot.

Craig, Simon. "Mistaken Identity." *Geographical Magazine* (May, 1997): 30. This is the story of John Cabot's journey from Bristol on the voyage that would help open mainland North America to Europeans.

Davis, Ralph. *The Rise of the Atlantic Economies*. London: Weidenfeld and Nicolson, and Ithaca, N.Y.: Cornell University Press, 1973. Although only the first chapter of this book deals with fifteenth century exploration, the author's description and analysis of the maritime trades that used the Atlantic Ocean is unequaled.

Harrisse, Henry. *John Cabot, the Discoverer of North America, and Sebastian, His Son*. London: Stevens, and New York: Dodd Mead, 1896. Like the Beazley biography, this volume is best viewed as part of the late nineteenth century effort to make Americans aware of the role of England in the discovery and exploration of North America.

Morison, Samuel Elliot. *The European Discovery of America: The Northern Voyages, A.D. 500-1600*. New York: Oxford University Press, 1971. The most famous maritime scholar and the leading authority on Columbus presents detailed chapters on all known explorers. The book is distinguished by excellent charts and photographs of the possible landfalls of the various explorers.

Parry, J. H. *Discovery of the Sea*. New York: Dial Press, 1974; London: Weidenfeld and Nicolson, 1976. The preeminent maritime historian discusses the development of skills and technologies that opened up maritime exploration in the fifteenth and sixteenth centuries.

Penrose, Boies. *Travel and Discovery in the Renaissance*. Cambridge, Mass.: Harvard University Press, 1952. A fascinating study of how scholars and navigators, from the time of ancient Greece to fifteenth century Europe, viewed the world.

Pringle, Heather. "Cabot's Trail." *Canadian Geographic* vol. 117, no. 4 (July, 1997). Five hundred years ago, John Cabot crossed the Atlantic Ocean in search of the Orient; instead, he found Newfoundland. This article explores the journey.

Quinn, David Beers. *England and the Discovery of America: 1481-1620*. London: Allen and Unwin, and New York: Knopf, 1974. Though working with very limited sources, the author presents a strong case for the discovery of North America by English seamen before Columbus.

Skelton, R. A. *Explorers' Maps: Chapters in the Cartographic Record of Geographical Discovery*. London: Routledge, and New York: Praeger, 1958. An outstanding description of how the discoveries of explorers were incorporated into the rapidly changing world maps of sixteenth century cartographers.

Williamson, James A. *The Cabot Voyages and Bristol Discovery Under Henry VII*. Cambridge: Cambridge University Press, and Cambridge, Mass.: Harvard University Press, 1962. In addition to presenting the best balanced account of Cabot's work, the author has assembled all known documents about the explorer so that the reader may draw his own conclusions.

Joseph A. Goldenberg

JOHN CALVIN

Born: July 10, 1509; Noyon, Picardy
Died: May 27, 1564; Geneva
Areas of Achievement: Theology and religion
Contribution: Calvin was one of the most important theologians of the Protestant Reformation of the sixteenth century. The Reformed church that he established in Geneva became a model for Calvinist churches throughout Europe. Calvinism itself became the most dynamic Protestant religion of the seventeenth century.

Early Life

John Calvin was born in Noyon, Picardy, on July 10, 1509, the second son of Gérard Cauvin and Jeanne le Franc Cauvin. His father was the secretary to the Bishop of Noyon and fiscal procurator for the province, and his mother was the daughter of a well-to-do innkeeper. The young Calvin was tutored for a career in the Church, and in 1523 he entered the Collège de la Marche at the University of Paris. It was there that he Latinized his name to Calvinus for scholarly purposes. Next, he attended the Collège de Montaigne, an institution of great importance in the Christian humanistic tradition of the day. After having received his master of arts degree, he studied law at the University of Orléans. He returned to Paris in 1531, where he furthered his studies with some of the greatest Humanists of the period.

Sixteenth century Europe was in ecclesiastical ferment. The Roman Catholic Church had long been under attack because of its weaknesses and abuses. Religious reformers had, for more than a century, called for a thorough cleansing of the Church. In 1517, Martin Luther had initiated the action which ultimately became the Protestant Reformation. Given this environment, Calvin was soon affected by these ideas of protest and of reform. During this period of transition, Calvin published his first book, a study of Seneca's *De Clementia* (c. A.D. 55-56; *On Clemency*), which revealed him to be a forceful and precise writer.

Soon after the publication of this work, Calvin was converted to Protestantism. Fearing for his safety, he fled Paris and went first to Angoulême and later to Basel. He devoted himself to a study of theology, concentrating on the Bible, as Luther had done. In 1536, he published the results of his study in the first edition of his most important work, *Christianae religionis institutio* (*Institutes of the Christian Religion*, 1561). This work was to be refined, expanded (quadrupled in size from this edition to the final, 1559 edition), and developed over the course of his life. It quickly won for him a reputation as a Protestant authority. Indeed, most scholars agree that it is the single most important work produced during the Reformation.

The *Institutes of the Christian Religion* provided the foundation for a different form of Protestantism. Calvin's training as a lawyer helped him to produce a work which was well organized, clear, and logical. There were two primary themes within the work: the absolute majesty of God and the absolute depravity of man. On the one hand, God is omnipotent and omniscient, and therefore He knows all that was, is, and will be. Man, because of his corrupt nature, cannot determine his salvation; only God can do so. Indeed, because of God's omniscience, He has predetermined who is to be saved and who is to be damned.

The doctrine of predestination, while it did not originate with Calvin, made good works useless. While this may seem fatalistic, to Calvin it was not. A member of the elect would most assuredly perform good works as a sign that God was working through him. Hence, one of the elect would work hard and strive for earthly success in order to prove himself as having received God's grace. Calvin also stated that Christ is present in spirit when believers gather prayerfully; priests are not necessary, for they have no special powers. He also rejected all sacraments except for baptism and the Eucharist.

Life's Work

Shortly before the *Institutes of the Christian Religion* was published, Calvin left Basel for Ferrara, Italy. There, he visited the Duchess of Ferrara, a sympathizer who had protected a number of reformers. Calvin made a strong appeal to her for further financial support of the Reformation. This was the first of many of his efforts to acquire aristocratic support, which was essential in an age when aristocrats still controlled much power and wealth. Calvin returned to Basel, traveled to France, and, in 1536, stopped in Geneva, a city-state which had just become Protestant.

At this time, everyone in a given place had to be of the same religion. Geneva had revolted against its bishop, but the city had not determined which

Protestant ritual it would follow. Calvin, thus, stepped into a religious vacuum. He held public lectures on the Bible, and he printed a tract to prepare the Genevese for his concept of the Reformed faith. His dour version of Christianity, however, was met with antipathy by many less austere Genevese. In 1538, Calvin and his associate, Guillaume Farel, were ordered to leave Geneva.

Calvin went to Strasbourg for the next three years. There he developed a liturgy in French, created an organization for running a parish, and attended many religious debates on the Holy Roman Empire. He debated with Lutheran theologians, especially Philipp Melanchthon, and with Catholic theologians as well. During the debates, he became convinced that Roman Catholics could never be negotiated with and that there would never be a reunion with the Roman church. He also became convinced that Lutheranism had not resulted in enough reforms within its church. In 1540, he married Idelette de Bure. They had one child, who died in infancy. Idelette died in 1549, and Calvin never remarried. A naturally reticent man, Calvin rarely permitted outsiders a glimpse of his personal life.

In 1541, Calvin was asked by the Genevese council to return. He was promised total cooperation in building the religious state that he wanted. His first activity was to propose a series of ecclesiastical ordinances, which were ratified on January 2, 1541. The ordinances were to become the cornerstone of Reformed church (Calvinist/Presbyterian) polity throughout Europe. The ministry was divided into four categories: doctors, pastors, lay elders, and deacons. The doctors were to study the Bible and to develop theology; Calvin was the only doctor at that time. Pastors were to proclaim the word of God; elders were to oversee the carrying out of the Reformed church's dicta, that is, they were to be moral policemen; deacons were to help those who could not help themselves, that is, to perform benevolent works. The Company of Pastors was the official governing body of the Reformed church. Under the leadership of Calvin, the Company of Pastors determined religious assignments, worked with Protestants in other countries, and determined theology. The Company of Pastors also worked with the elders to control Geneva.

There were occasional sharp conflicts with the city council, but Calvin won absolute control of the city by 1555. All Genevese were forced to accept the moral laws of the Reformed faith or to suffer the consequences. From 1555 until his death in 1564, fifty-eight people were executed and 786 were banished in order to preserve the morals of the community. The most celebrated case was that of Michael Servetus, a somewhat eccentric Spanish theologian, who wished to debate Calvin on the doctrine of the Trinity. Calvin warned him not to come to Geneva. Servetus ignored the warning, came to Geneva in 1553, was arrested and convicted of heresy, and was burned. Calvin was not a believer in religious toleration.

With Geneva under his absolute control, Calvin devoted more time to the spread of his Reformed church to other areas. He created in 1559 a religious academy, which ultimately became the University of Geneva. Protestants from all over Europe were encouraged to come to Geneva to study. As his native land was his particular area of interest, hundreds of refugees were trained in the new theology and then were assisted in their return to France. Calvin also established an underground network throughout France to bind these French Reformed, or Huguenot, parishes together. Representative assemblies of pastors and elders were also encouraged. Drawing upon his earlier experiences in France and elsewhere, Calvin appealed to sympathetic French nobles for protection for the Huguenots. His most notable convert was the King of Navarre, although this ultimately resulted in the French Wars of Religion.

The last years of Calvin's life were spent in dominating Genevese theological issues, in working with Calvinists everywhere, and in developing the *Institutes of the Christian Religion* further. In the 1560's, he had serious health problems, and he permitted his heir apparent, Theodore Beza, to take over most of the responsibilities of managing the affairs of the Reformed church. On May 27, 1564, Calvin died. Throughout his life he had devoutly believed that he had been called by God to reform His church; this he had done. His powerful intellect and his unswerving devotion to his theology do much to explain Calvin's enormous impact on Western theology and on Western religion.

Summary

John Calvin's intellectual talents, quick mind, forceful writing style, and precise teaching skills enabled him to become one of the most important figures in Western religious history. While in Geneva, he created a religious dictatorship which became a model for Reformed church/Calvinist churches throughout Europe. His *Institutes of the*

Christian Religion became one of the most important documents in Western theology. Even during his lifetime, his significance was well recognized, and Geneva itself was called a Protestant Rome.

Calvinism, as this second-generation Protestantism came to be called, quickly became the most dynamic theology in a Europe wracked by religious debate. Although Calvinism was austere in the extreme, its success may be explained. First, the Roman Catholic Church was so corrupt and so filled with abuses that a thorough purging was viewed as absolutely necessary by most religious reformers of the day. To many, Luther had simply not gone far enough; Calvin, on the other hand, created an absolutely cleansed church. Second, Calvin's rules for a godly life were clear and succinct in comparison with those of the Roman church, and this clarity was appealing to those who hoped for salvation. Third, Calvin's tenet of predestination, while on the surface appearing to be fatalistic, came to be a rationale for the behavior of the middle class. While Calvin had stated that no one could know whether one was a member of the elect, it was believed that God's grace could be measured by one's success. Although this conclusion is much debated by historians, it is nevertheless true that the Calvinist areas of Europe were to be the most economically successful over the next several centuries.

Following Calvin's death, Calvinism became the dominant Protestant theology in the religious wars that occurred over the next century. Calvinist leaders played major roles in a number of European wars. Calvinism became the dominant religion of the Low Countries, southwestern France, Scotland, central Germany, and southeastern England. In each of these areas, strong economic growth took place, an educated middle class emerged, and demands for political power developed. Indeed, the period from 1550 to 1700 and afterward cannot be understood without an awareness of the impact of the theology of John Calvin.

Bibliography

Barnstone, Aliki, Michael Tomasek Manson, and Carol J. Singley, eds. *The Calvinist Roots of the Modern Era*. Hanover, N.H.: University Press of New England, 1997. Multidisciplinary views of Calvinism's dynamic, diverse, and persistent influence on modern American literature and thought. This collection of essays traces Calvinism's presence in twentieth century literature and demonstrates its impact on psychological construct, cultural institution, and the socio-political model. The editors conclude that, rather than being a monolithic force, Calvinism has "instead been dynamic, as different writers redefine and restructure it to fit their purposes and beliefs."

Bouwsma, William J. *John Calvin: A Sixteenth-Century Portrait*. New York: Oxford University Press, 1988. This work by a distinguished historian has been acclaimed as the best modern biography of Calvin. At the same time, as the subtitle indicates, Bouwsma uses Calvin's experience "to illuminate the momentous cultural crisis central to his century." Includes sixty pages of notes, a bibliography, and an index.

Calvin, John. *Institutes of the Christian Religion*. Edited by John T. McNeill. 2 vols. London: SCM Press, and Philadelphia: Westminster Press, 1960. These volumes are an annotated edition of Calvin's work and include a lengthy introduction and an extensive bibliography.

Haller, William. *The Rise of Puritanism*. New York: Columbia University Press, 1938. While his prose is at times turgid, Haller offers insight into the spread of Calvinism into England. His study is useful for understanding why Calvinism spread so rapidly.

Kingdon, Robert M. *Geneva and the Coming of the Wars of Religion in France, 1555-1563*. Geneva: Librairie E. Droz, 1956. Important for understanding Calvin's methods of exporting his theology to other areas of Europe.

McNeill, John T. *The History and Character of Calvinism*. New York: Oxford University Press, 1954; London: Oxford University Press, 1976. A carefully balanced source that offers an excellent interpretive discussion of the theory and practice of Calvinism. Includes a lengthy biography of Calvin, followed by a series of chapters on the spread of Calvinism throughout Europe and to the United States.

O'Connell, Marvin R. *The Counter Reformation, 1559-1610*. New York: Harper, 1974. Places Calvin and the spread of Calvinism in perspective. Includes an excellent bibliography.

Parker, Thomas H. L. *John Calvin: A Biography*. London: Dent, and Philadelphia: Westminster Press, 1975. Parker's work is a concise, single volume on the life of John Calvin. Particularly useful for a study of the impact of university life on Calvin and upon Calvin's scholarship. Well written and easily understood. Useful bibliography.

Wendel, François. *Calvin: The Origins and Development of His Religious Thought*. London: Collins, and New York: Harper, 1963. First published in French in 1950, Wendel's work is essential for an understanding of the evolution of Calvin's theology.

William S. Brockington, Jr.

LUÍS DE CAMÕES

Born: c. 1524; probably Lisbon, Portugal
Died: June 10, 1580; Lisbon, Portugal
Area of Achievement: Literature
Contribution: Camões is the author of *Os Lusíadas* (1572; *The Lusiads*, 1655), the national epic of Portugal. Celebrating the voyage of Vasco da Gama, the poem recites the heroic history of the Portuguese nation.

Early Life

Luís de Camões (sometimes written Camoëns) was born in 1524, the year Vasco da Gama died. He was probably born in Lisbon, although by 1527 his family was living with Luís' grandparents in Coimbra; most likely they fled from Lisbon to escape the plague, which reached the capital in that year.

Luís' father was Simão Vas de Camões, a gentleman of no great power or wealth. Little is known of Anna de Macedo or Sá, Luís' mother, beyond her name. When his father returned to Lisbon to take a position in the king's warehouse, Luís remained in Coimbra with his mother in the home of her family, who were influential people there.

As Luís grew into manhood, Coimbra was undergoing its own development into the educational center of Portugal. Under the guidance of John III, a great university was permanently established. In or near 1539, Luis entered the university and must have read Vergil, Ovid, Lucan, and Cicero in the original Latin. He learned to speak Spanish fluently and was also exposed to Italian, Greek, geography, history, music, and many other subjects. During this period, he developed many friendships with young aristocrats, from whom he learned courtly tastes and manners. He also suffered his first taste of love, leading to some of his earliest, most tragic lyrics. After the conclusion of his studies, he left Coimbra for Lisbon, never to return.

Life's Work

When Camões traveled to Lisbon to make his fortune, in or near 1543, he began a life of adventure and accomplishment as exciting as any legendary hero's. He started quietly enough: Camões took a position as a tutor to the young son of a count. During these years, he learned all he could of his country's history and culture. Camões was considered charming and attractive. Surviving portraits from this time show a handsome man with reddish-gold hair and blue eyes. In 1544, in church, he saw a young girl, Catarina de Ataíde, and fell immediately and passionately in love with her. For the rest of his life, Camões would consider Catarina the great spiritual love of his life; many of his most beautiful lyrics are dedicated to her.

While still in Lisbon, Camões also wrote three well-received comedies: *Auto del-Rei Seleuco*, performed in 1542, *Enfatriões*, performed in 1540, and *Filodemo*, performed in 1555. As he became more widely known as a writer, Camões was drawn deeper into the inner circles of the court, where he found many who admired his talents and charms, and many who despised his smugness and sharp tongue. Never one to feign modesty, he dedicated impassioned poetry to a series of lovers, in spite of his devotion to Catarina. Finally, his brashness led to his disgrace at court, though the actual sins committed are uncertain. Because of the scandal, he enlisted, under duress, in the army in 1547, served two years in northern Africa, and lost the use of his right eye in a battle at Ceuta in Morocco.

Camões returned to Lisbon no wiser than he had left; his wild living soon earned for him the nickname *Trincafortes*, or Swashbuckler. His absence had done nothing to restore his favor with the court, but he found himself equally capable of carousing with a lower class of companion. For the next two years, the poet earned a meager living as a ghostwriter of poetry and did all he could to enhance his reputation as a scalawag. On June 16, 1552, the intoxicated poet was involved in a street fight with a member of the royal staff, whom he stabbed. Camões was promptly arrested and sent to prison, where he languished for eight months.

When the stabbed official recovered, Camões' friends obtained the poet's release, but under two conditions: He was to pay a large fine and to leave immediately on an expedition to India. On March 26, 1553, he set sail on the São Bento, playing out the dangerous existence of the warrior-adventurer described in his epic. The voyage to India took six months, and the seafaring life was not an easy one. Boredom, hunger, scurvy, cold, seasickness, and storms—Camões and his companions had suffered it all before the ship rounded the Cape of Good Hope.

In September, 1553, the ship reached the Indian city of Goa, the Portuguese seat of power and wealth. During his residence there, Camões observed the local people and their exotic costumes, manners, and traditions, and began writing *The Lusiads*. He took part in several expeditions up the Malabar Coast, along the shores of the Red Sea, and through the Persian Gulf.

Camões continued to write poetry and satire, and to work on his epic; his play *Filodemo* was performed for the governor. The success of his play nearly brought him advancement and a return home, but it was not to be. A satire mocking local officials was wrongfully attributed to him, and the officials concerned goaded him into an intemperate display of public indignation. To restore order, he was sent to a new position as trustee for the dead and absent in Macao, China.

In Macao, Camões was happy for a time. He enjoyed the company of a woman he loved, and he continued to write new poems and to polish his epic. The silks, jades, porcelains, and teas of China provided him with new material, and he spent much time alone dreaming and writing. After three years in Macao, he was accused, apparently falsely, of misappropriating funds. Camões was forced to sail again for Goa to stand trial.

On the voyage to Goa, fate intervened. A typhoon struck the ship off southern Indochina, and the ship was wrecked. Camões grabbed the box containing his manuscripts before he was swept off the ship; when he recovered his wits, he was floating on a scrap of wood, and the manuscripts were still in his hand. He struggled to shore and was taken to a fishing village on the Mekong River. In 1561, he somehow was able to return to Goa. Yet his troubles did not end there. He learned that Catarina, his great inspiration, had died, and a few days later he was again cast into prison to face the misappropriation charges. No evidence was produced against him, and he was released. Camões remained in India for several more years, living again a life of poverty.

In the spring of 1567, he arranged passage to Mozambique, and in 1569, after an absence of seventeen years, he set sail for home, arriving in Lisbon in 1570 with the completed manuscript of *The Lusiads* his only possession. He dedicated his time to finding a publisher for his greatest work. Finally, in 1572, the poem was published, and he was granted a small royal pension. Of the next several years of the poet's life little is known, but he appears to have written almost nothing after his return to Lisbon. In 1580, he died of the plague, and his body was placed in an unmarked mass grave.

Summary

Had he written only the three comedies and his large variety of *Rimas* (1595; *The Lyrides*, 1803, 1884), Luís de Camões might be acknowledged as one of the finest European poets of the sixteenth century. With *The Lusiads*, however, Camões was able to capture the passion and nobility of a nation, and it is as the creator of the national epic of Portugal that he will always be remembered.

The Lusiads tells the dramatic story of Vasco da Gama's discovery of a sea route to India, but in the process, da Gama as narrator relates virtually the entire history of "the sons of Lusus," or the Portuguese. *The Lusiads* relies heavily on Camões' classical learning, especially his reading of Vergil (for its structure and tone) and Ludovico Ariosto (for its ottava rima). Yet Camões brought much that was new to the epic. Of the epics written before his, none is grounded so heavily in actual events; Camões demonstrated how actual historical figures could be given the stature of mythical heroes. Unlike Homer or Dante or others, Camões described countries, peoples, and storms at sea that he had witnessed at first hand.

The Lusiads was immensely popular when it was published and has never been out of print since. Schoolchildren throughout the Portuguese-speaking world still memorize its opening stanzas, and the poem has been translated into English many times. English poets such as John Milton, Lord Byron, William Wordsworth, and Elizabeth Barrett Browning have treasured and praised *The Lusiads*, which has been called "the first epic poem which in its grandeur and universality speaks for the modern world."

Bibliography

Bell, Aubrey F. G. *Luis de Camões*. London: Oxford University Press, 1923. This is a brief treatment that includes a biography of the poet, a description of his moral character as revealed by the poetry, an analysis of *The Lusiads*, and a chapter entitled "Camões as Lyric and Dramatic Poet." A difficult book, its approach assumes that the reader is familiar with previous biographies and with the major Romance languages.

Bowra, C. M. "Camões and the Epic of Portugal." In *From Virgil to Milton*. London: Macmillan, and New York: St. Martin's Press, 1945. An explication of *The Lusiads* as an epic poem, a poem of the ideal in manhood, demonstrating Camões' indebtedness to classical tradition and especially to Homer, Vergil, and Ariosto. The discussion of how the poet reconciles his use of pagan divinities with his Christian message is particularly illuminating.

Burton, Richard Francis. *Camoens: His Life and His Lusiads*. 2 vols. London: Bernard Quaritch, 1881. This is a commentary on *The Lusiads* in five sections: biography; bibliography emphasizing English translations; history and chronology of Portugal through the death of the poet; geographical study of the world as it was understood by da Gama and Camões; and annotations of specific passages in the poem. Appendix includes a table of important episodes in the poem and a glossary.

Freitas, William. *Camoens and His Epic: A Historic, Geographic, and Cultural Survey.* Stanford, Calif.: Institute of Hispanic American and Luso-Brazilian Studies, Stanford University, 1963. A historic and geographical study using *The Lusiads* as a source for information on Portugal's clashes with other nations. The final chapter traces the poem's roots of nationalism through the next four centuries of Portuguese history. Includes a bibliography of biographical, critical, and historical works in several languages as well as twenty illustrations, including portraits and maps.

Hart, Henry H. *Luis de Camoëns and the Epic of the Lusiads*. Norman: University of Oklahoma Press, 1962. A comprehensive, readable biography, filled with colorful detail of the scenery, culture, and history through which the poet walked. Appendices provide several examples of Camões' poems and a listing of books on the Orient which he may have read. Includes a generous bibliography and eight illustrations.

Monteiro, George *The Presence of Camões: Influences on the Literature of England, America, and Southern Africa*. Lexington: University Press of Kentucky, 1996. Analysis of Camões' influence on the literature of England, America, and Southern Africa.

O'Halloran, Colin M. *History and Heroes in the "Lusiads": A Commemorative Essay on Camoëns*. Lisbon: Commissão Executiva do IV Centenário da Publicação de "Os Lusíadas," 1974. A short book examining the use Camões made of the history of Portugal in the creation of the heroes and kings in his poem. Discusses the poem as a record of and tribute to Portugal's national drive to conquer new lands and convert the people there. It is interesting and accessible, but all quotes from the poem are in Portuguese.

Pierce, Frank. "Luis de Camões, Epic and Lyric." *Bulletin of Hispanic Studies* 69 (July, 1992): 303. A review of the works of Camões.

Cynthia A. Bily

THE CARRACCI FAMILY

Ludovico Carracci

Born: April 21 (baptized), 1555; Bologna, Papal States
Died: November 13, 1619; Bologna, Papal States

Agostino Carracci

Born: August 16, 1557; Bologna, Papal States
Died: February 23, 1602; Parma

Annibale Carracci

Born: November 3, 1560; Bologna, Papal States
Died: July 15, 1609; Rome
Area of Achievement: Art
Contribution: From the mid-1580's onward, the paintings and frescoes of the Carracci family of Bologna made their city one of the major centers of reaction against the so-called mannerist style, an elegant and often overrefined style that had dominated Italian art for sixty or seventy years. When Annibale went to Rome in the early 1590's, his work laid the foundation for the magnificent pictorial accomplishments of the Baroque period.

Early Lives

The Carracci family came to Bologna from Cremona, and Ludovico's father was a butcher named Vincenzo. Agostino and Annibale were his second cousins, the sons of Antonio Carracci, who was a well-known tailor. Ludovico began his artistic studies with Prospero Fontana. According to the Carracci's seventeenth century biographer, Carlo Cesare Malvasia, his work was so laborious that Fontana nicknamed him "the ox" and advised him not to continue with his studies. Ludovico then went to Florence. For a time he worked with Domenico Passignano and later traveled through northern Italy, where he saw at first hand the works that were to be so important in his artistic development, which were by Correggio and Parmigianino, the great sixteenth century masters of Parma and of the region known as Emilia, and by Titian and Paolo Veronese in Venice. By 1578, he was back in Bologna and was a member of the local painters' guild.

Agostino initially received some training as a goldsmith and also studied with Fontana. His real master, though, was Domenico Tibaldi, from whom he learned the art of engraving. His engravings, after works by Michelangelo and Baldassare Peruzzi, brought him some success, and he later went to Venice, where he produced engraved copies of works by Veronese and Tintoretto.

Annibale's training was much less formal, and it is possible that his cousin Ludovico was his only teacher in painting and that he learned engraving from his brother Agostino. In the spring of 1580, Annibale went to Parma in order to see and to paint copies of the works that had made such a deep impression on Ludovico a few years earlier. By late 1580 or early 1581, he was in Venice with Agostino; by about 1582, the brothers had returned to Bologna.

Life's Work

In the early 1580's, all three of the Carracci were involved in the development of a unique combination of artistic workshop and art academy, which they called the "Academy of the Eager Ones" or the "Academy of the Progressives." Considerable emphasis was put on drawing from life, but there were also lessons in anatomy and perspective as well as in architecture. What the Carracci developed at their "academy" was a program of practical and theoretical instruction aimed at reforming the art of painting, which, as they saw it, had deteriorated into a vapid and boringly repetitive set of formulas, devoid of life and energy.

In the early 1580's, the Carracci began to emerge as individual artists, but they also often worked together. By 1584, they had completed their first major joint commission, which was the series of frescoes illustrating the *History of Jason* in the Palazzo Fava, Bologna (modern Società Majestic Baglioni). Unfortunately, the frescoes are not in good condition, but their strong illusionism and richness of color can still be appreciated, and there is a remarkable lack of artifice in the easy and naturalistic poses of the figures. This was the first major public manifestation of their doctrine of artistic reform. The fresco cycle in the former Palazzo Magnani was also a joint production, and, when asked to tell which parts each of them had painted, they are said to have replied: "It's by the Carracci. All of us made it."

For the next ten years, the Carracci were actively engaged in creating altarpieces for Bolognese churches, many of which can now be seen in the Pinacoteca Nazionale, Bologna. While Agostino devoted much of his time to engraving and to

Annibale Carracci

teaching, he was also a painter of note, and *The Last Communion of Saint Jerome* (1591-1593) is his masterpiece of the period, admired by artists as diverse as Nicolas Poussin and Peter Paul Rubens. Ludovico's painting of the *Madonna of the Bargellini Family* (1588) is one of his strongest early paintings, and critics have recognized the qualities of his work. Yet it is clear that by the end of the 1580's, Annibale had emerged as the most important artist of the three, a painter of great power whose richness of color is matched by his masterful drawing. His *Madonna with Saint John Evangelist and Saint Catherine* (1593) reveals his brilliant synthesis of the formal order of the High Renaissance with the colorism of Venice and Parma. Annibale also had a lighter side. He was one of the first artists to produce caricatures in the modern sense of the art of caricature, and in his early twenties he painted a number of genre paintings. *The Bean Eater* (c. 1585) in the Colonna Gallery, Rome, is one of the best—a small-scale scene of everyday life rendered with an astonishing boldness and naturalism.

In the mid-1590's, the Carracci were invited to go to Rome to work for Cardinal Odoardo Farnese, the brother of the Duke of Parma and Piacenza. Annibale accepted the cardinal's invitation, and Agostino later joined him; Ludovico chose to remain in Bologna, where he continued to direct the Carracci's academy, and, in order to ensure that the academy would continue, he tried to have it officially incorporated into the professional association of Bolognese artists. Ludovico's own late work is uneven, and it is unfortunate that the fresco cycle that he and his pupils executed in San Michele in Bosco (about 1605) is lost and is known only from engravings. Two of the finest works from Ludovico's later period are the enormous paintings *Funeral of the Virgin* (1606-1607) and *Apostles at the Tomb of the Virgin* (c. 1612). He died in Bologna in 1619.

After Annibale's arrival in Rome in 1595, he developed into an artist of great historical importance. In the Palazzo Farnese, he was first asked to decorate the ceiling and upper walls of a room, now known as Camerino Farnese (Farnese's little room), with scenes illustrating the adventures of Hercules and Ulysses. In 1597, he began work on a fresco cycle in one of the principal rooms of the palace, the so-called Farnese Gallery.

The Farnese Gallery is Annibale's masterpiece, and subsequent generations considered it worthy of comparison with Raphael's frescoes in the Vatican Palace and Michelangelo's Sistine Chapel ceiling. A fictive architecture provides the framework for what appears to be framed easel pictures moved up the ceiling. There are bronze medallions, simulated marble statues, and naturalistic figures of youths sitting on pedestals—all painted with such convincing illusionism that distinctions between the real and the painted worlds seem to vanish. The theme is the power of love, and incidents illustrating the loves of the gods and goddesses of antiquity fill the ceiling and the upper walls. Many of the frescoes' stories are drawn from *Metamorphoses* (c. A.D. 8) by the Roman poet Ovid; yet behind this joyous and lighthearted exuberance, Annibale's contemporaries discerned a serious moral allegory.

In the execution of the Farnese Gallery, Annibale had been helped by Agostino, but about 1600 Agostino left Rome and went to Parma, where he remained until his death in 1602. His principal work there was a fresco cycle for the Palazzo del Giardino, but it was not finished when he died and was completed much later by other artists. Annibale continued to work on the Gallery, whose lower walls were probably not finished until about 1604. Among his surviving easel paintings from the Roman period are some religious works of great power, such as the *Mourning of Christ*. His late landscapes were also of great importance for the subsequent history of painting. The finest of these landscapes are the ones that he and his pupils painted for the chapel in the Aldobrandini Palace (modern Galleria Doria-Pamphili, Rome).

In the early part of 1605, Annibale suffered a breakdown, at least partially caused by his bitterness over the small sum of money he was paid for the Farnese Gallery. For the next four years, he was unable to work, and in the summer of 1609 he died in Rome. He was buried in the Pantheon, an unusual honor and one which had also been accorded to Raphael.

Summary

The three Carracci had a major role in the reformation of the mannerist style, and, while they often worked together, they were distinct and highly individual artists. Ludovico was a gifted teacher, and several of the younger men who were trained by him in the Carracci's academy after Annibale left for Rome went on to become important artists. Two of these students, Guido Reni and Domenichino, later became major figures of the Baroque era; yet there were many others of lesser distinction but considerable talent whose work provided the basis for the flourishing seventeenth century schools of painting in Bologna and Emilia.

Agostino was more interested in art theory than were the other Carracci, and, according to one of his biographers, he was a student of mathematics and philosophy. He also composed verses and was a musician. To some extent, his posthumous fame has been dependent upon his reputation as a theorist and an intellectual, but his qualities as an artist should not be discounted. He was a fine engraver, and his engravings after Venetian masters such as Veronese helped to spread the fame of their art. Yet he was also an excellent painter, although not as productive as his brother or his cousin.

Annibale's work gave new life to the tradition of monumental art in the grand manner. In Rome, under the influence of the work of Michelangelo, Raphael, and the sculpture of antiquity, his art matured and his combination of idealism and illusionism provided the greatest inspiration for the younger generation of painters. The Farnese Gallery was the first great fresco cycle of the Baroque era and set a precedent for the fresco cycles of the next two centuries.

Bibliography

Bellori, Giovanni Pietro. *The Lives of Annibale and Agostino Carracci*. Translated by Catherine Enggass. University Park: Pennsylvania State University Press, 1967. Giovanni Pietro Bellori's book was first published in Rome in 1672. This translation of the portion devoted to the Carracci is the only contemporary biography available in English. Most of the work is devoted to a description of the Farnese Gallery and an explanation of its symbolic meaning.

Boschloo, Anton Willem Adriaan. *Annibale Carracci in Bologna: Visible Reality in Art After the Council of Trent*. Translated by R. R. Symonds. 2 vols. The Hague: Government Printing Office, 1974. A detailed study of Annibale's work in Bologna and its relationship to the art of his contemporaries and predecessors.

Carracci, Ludovico. *Ludovico Carracci*. Edited by Andrea Emiliani; essay and catalogue by Gail Feigenbaum. New York: Abbeville, 1994. This book was published in conjunction with the Ludovico Carracci exhibition at the Museo Civico Archeologico-Pinacoteca Nazionale in Bologna, Italy, September 25-December 12, 1993; and at the Kimbell Art Museum in Fort Worth, Texas, January 22-April 10, 1994.

Dempsey, Charles. *Annibale Carracci and the Beginnings of the Baroque Style*. Locust Valley, N.Y.: Augustin, 1977. An extensive review of the critical evaluations of Annibale's work and a discussion of the Carracci academy and its role in the reform of painting.

Freedberg, Sydney J. *Circa 1600: A Revolution of Style in Italian Painting*. Cambridge, Mass. and London: Harvard University Press, 1983. Three lectures given at Cornell University in 1980 and dealing with Annibale and Ludovico Carracci and Caravaggio. Excellent exposition of the nature of the artistic accomplishments of the Carracci. The final lecture dealing with Ludovico is particularly illuminating.

Martin, John Rupert. *The Farnese Gallery*. Princeton, N.J.: Princeton University Press, 1965. The basic study of Annibale's work in the Palazzo Farnese. Richly illustrated and fully documented.

Partridge, Loren, and Michel Hochmann. "The Cardinal's Olympus." *FMR: The Magazine of*

Franco Maria Ricci vol. 15 (April, 1995). A tribute to the house of Farnese in their role as sixteenth and seventeenth century art collectors and patrons. This piece offers a glimpse of the superb pictorial project commissioned by Cardinal Odoardo Farnese to the Carracci family for the Galleria of his princely Roman abode.

Posner, Donald. *Annibale Carracci: A Study in the Reform of Italian Painting Around 1590*. 2 vols. London and New York: Phaidon Press, 1971. The standard monograph on Annibale. Contains excellent plates and detailed catalog entries of extant works.

Wittkower, Rudolf. *Art and Architecture in Italy, 1600-1750*. 3d ed. London and New York: Penguin, 1982. Still the basic study of the period. The chapter on the Carracci is an admirable summary, and there are excellent bibliographies for all the major artists of the period.

Eric Van Schaack

JACQUES CARTIER

Born: c. 1491; St. Malo, Brittany, France
Died: September 1, 1557; St. Malo, Brittany, France
Area of Achievement: Exploration
Contribution: Cartier explored the St. Lawrence River and the Gulf of St. Lawrence, claiming the area for France, and wrote a detailed account of his travels.

Early Life

Jacques Cartier was probably born in 1491 in St. Malo, France, but the date is uncertain and could be some time between 1490 and 1494. Nothing is known about his early years, although it is likely that he sailed to the waters near Newfoundland on fishing trips. His only known early voyage was in a Portuguese ship that crossed the South Atlantic to Brazil.

In 1519, Cartier married Marie Catherine, the daughter of Messire Honoré des Granches, chevalier and constable of St. Malo. Stocky, with a sharp profile and high, wide brow, Cartier dressed as a hardworking man in an unpretentious cloak and tunic. He was religious but strong-spirited and showed himself to be capable, courageous, and fair to his crew. His methodical nature was shown by the detailed journals he kept daily on his voyages.

Life's Work

Intrigued by the stories of earlier explorers, King Francis I commissioned Cartier to sail to Newfoundland to look for gold and to search for a waterway through the New World to India. On April 20, 1534, Cartier left St. Malo with two small caravels, not weighing more than sixty tons each.

The ships sighted Newfoundland within twenty days but, because of the bad weather, took shelter in a harbor south of Bonavista Bay. Choosing to investigate the Gulf of St. Lawrence, Cartier sailed through the straits of Belle Isle, entered the Gulf of Chaleurs, and landed on the Gaspé Peninsula. There he erected a cross, claiming the area for France. At Gaspé he met the Iroquois and their chief, Donnacona. When Cartier left, he took with him Donnacona's two sons. It may be that Cartier persuaded the chief to allow him to take the young men, but more likely Cartier tricked the chief and kidnapped the two brothers. As the autumn storms were beginning, the two ships headed back toward St. Malo.

Although Cartier had not found a northwest passage or riches, he convinced the king of the possibilities of the new land. One of these was the opportunity to convert the heathen Indians to the Catholic faith, thereby recouping the Church's losses to Calvinism and Lutheranism. Because of this and the potential for riches, King Francis sent Cartier on a second voyage in 1535 to explore further.

Leaving St. Malo with three ships and 110 men, Cartier entered and named the Gulf of St. Lawrence. The ships passed Anticosti, and then, with Donnacona's sons as guides, they sailed up the St. Lawrence River to Saguenay and on to the village of Stadacona, near the site, later, of Quebec. There, Donnacona welcomed back his sons and received the gifts the French had brought.

The Indians used trickery and false warnings to prevent Cartier from going to the next village, as they did not want their rivals to receive any of the French trinkets. Despite the Indians' protestations, Cartier and about thirty of his men traveled farther up the river to the village of Hochelaga, where Montreal was later established. The natives there indicated that up another river were great stores of

silver and copper, a story that would impress the King of France.

The men returned to Stadacona, where hostility between the Indians and the explorers had grown. For protection, a stockade had been built and fortified with cannons. Cartier had not expected the severity of the winter, and for five months the fort and ships were buried under snow. In addition to enduring subzero temperatures, the men were stricken with scurvy because no fresh foods were available. At least twenty-five had died before the Iroquois showed the French their remedy—the bark and needles of white spruce boiled in water.

Eventually, the weather warmed, and Cartier prepared to return to France. Since he thought that only the Indians could convince King Francis of the riches in the land, Cartier took Donnacona and several of his tribesmen prisoner. Promising to return them in a year, he sailed downriver and back to St. Malo, reaching it on July 16, 1536. Despite Cartier's words, he did not return in a year, and the Indians never again saw their homeland; all died in France.

Cartier's and Donnacona's stories intrigued the king, but war with Spain prevented Francis from sending out another expedition until 1541. This expedition was not only to explore the land and find the precious metals but also to establish a permanent colony in Canada.

The commander would be a Protestant nobleman, Jean-François de La Rocque de Roberval, and Cartier would serve on the ship as his subordinate, his captain-general and master navigator. The king provided funds for ten ships, four hundred sailors, three hundred soldiers, skilled tradesmen, a few women, and all kinds of supplies and livestock. It was difficult to recruit artisans and laborers, however, so criminals were taken from prison to become Canada's first settlers.

Cartier sailed with five ships in May, 1541, but Roberval was delayed until the following year. Cartier reached Stadacona on August 23, four years after he had promised to return with the kidnapped Indians. When the Iroquois asked about them, Cartier admitted that Donnacona was dead but then lied, saying that the others were well, enjoying France so much they did not want to leave. The truth was that only one young girl was alive; the others had already died.

Since the natives did not seem especially friendly, Cartier proceeded up the St. Lawrence to Cap Rouge. There, the men built two forts, planted a garden, and named the settlement Charlesbourg. While these preparations were being made, samples were found of what appeared to be gold and diamonds. Two of the ships were sent back to France to report on these discoveries and Roberval's nonappearance. The rest of the explorers wintered in Charlesbourg, and while scurvy was not a problem this time, the Iroquois were. In June, 1542, after enduring months of severe weather and threatening harassment from the Indians, Cartier set sail for France.

On the way, Cartier met Roberval at St. John's in Newfoundland and was ordered to turn back. For reasons known only to himself, Cartier disobeyed and slipped away in the night to continue his voyage to France. Once there, he discovered that his gold chips were iron pyrites and the diamonds worthless quartz.

Inexperienced and with little leadership ability, Roberval spent a tragic and unsuccessful winter at Charlesbourg. Disease, lack of food, and probably violence killed many before the winter was over. In 1543, Roberval returned to France, and the first effort to found a French colony in Canada ended.

Little is known of Cartier's remaining years except that he spent them on his estate near St. Malo. He wrote an account of his travels in 1545, which was translated into English by Richard Hakluyt in 1600. Mapmakers and geographers occasionally consulted him, and he sometimes served as a Portuguese interpreter. Cartier died at St. Malo on September 1, 1557.

Summary

Although Jacques Cartier is known as the discoverer of the St. Lawrence, historians differ as to the importance of his explorations, and most believe that Cartier's travels primarily covered areas that other men had already discovered. He left the first detailed account of voyages up the St. Lawrence, however, and this was valued by later explorers and historians. Although he explored that waterway as far as anyone had gone, he did not proceed farther when he had the opportunity. He did discover that the river was not a passage to India and claimed the gulf and valley of the St. Lawrence for France.

One significant discovery, which no one appreciated at the time, was that furs could be obtained from the natives at bargain prices. When beaver hats became popular, traders went to the tribes near the St. Lawrence.

Cartier's fame as an explorer is marred by his dishonest and treacherous dealings with the Indians. When he first met with them, the Iroquois were friendly and helpful; after they experienced French betrayal, they became hostile and uninviting to the French.

Cartier's vision and first voyage awakened a spirit of discovery among the French, and this produced maps and information not known before. Although colonization would not occur for years after his death, Cartier did establish the future center of the French effort in North America.

Bibliography

Cartier, Jacques. *The Voyages of Jacques Cartier with an Introduction by Ramsay Cook*. Buffalo, N.Y.: University of Toronto Press, 1993. This is a new edition of the well-known 1924 work, originally translated and edited by Henry Percival Biggar. Includes an extensive introduction by York University historian Ramsay Cook that places Cartier in the context of his time. Cook has also included twenty brief historical documents from Biggar's collection, some of which provide eyewitness accounts of incidents that occurred during Cartier's travels.

Costain, Thomas B. *The White and the Gold: The French Regime in Canada*. New York: Doubleday, 1954. This history of early Canada, written by a popular historical novelist, re-creates the lives of the people who helped to shape the nation. Detailed yet easy to read, it begins in 1490 and continues to the end of the seventeenth century.

Creighton, Donald. *Canada: The Heroic Beginnings*. Toronto: Macmillan, 1974. Readable history of Canada's settlement and development to the middle of the twentieth century. Written in cooperation with two government agencies, it contains many pictures of individuals and scenes in Canadian history.

Eccles, William J. *The Canadian Frontier, 1534-1760*. New York: Holt Rinehart, 1969. In this history of the Canadian frontier, Eccles captures the spirit of the times as he describes the hardships, adventures, and rewards experienced by the early explorers and pioneers. He also gives background to the explorations and discusses the reasons for them.

Lower, Arthur R. M. *Colony to Nation: A History of Canada*. New York: Longman, 1964. Lower examines topics such as Indian-French cultures, exploitation of peoples, and imperialism and colonialism. He also includes material on the governments of Canada and how the wars affected those governments.

McInnis, Edgar. *Canada: A Political and Social History*. 4th ed. Toronto: Holt Rinehart, 1982. Comprehensive history of Canada written in terms of politics and government. McInnis discusses Canada's periods of economic and social difficulties and how these difficulties have been overcome and followed by progress in independence, unity, and economic growth.

Parkman, Francis. *France and England in North America*. Vol. 1. Boston: Little Brown, 1865-1892; New York: Macmillan, 1899. Depicts the struggle between France and England for possession of the North American continent. Includes some Spanish history and covers in detail the years between 1512 and 1635.

Pendergast, James F., and Bruce G. Trigger. *Cartier's Hochelaga and the Dawson Site*. Montreal: McGill-Queen's University Press, 1972. Scholarly examination of the possible locations of Hochelaga, and Iroquoian village which Cartier visited and described. Much of the research used in this study is based on Cartier's data and account of his travels.

Winsor, Justin. *Cartier to Frontenac*. Boston: Houghton Mifflin, 1894. Describes the explorations of North America from 1492 to 1698. Maps and charts of the voyages are included to expand the geographical descriptions of the area. Includes a brief history of Cartier and discusses the results of his explorations.

Elaine Mathiasen

CATHERINE DE MÉDICIS

Born: April 13, 1519; Florence
Died: January 5, 1589; Blois, France
Areas of Achievement: Government and politics
Contribution: Catherine de Médicis contributed to maintaining a strong centralized monarchy in spite of challenges from noble and religious factions. Her attempts to balance Roman Catholic and Calvinist interests in France also encouraged at least a minimum of toleration in the seventeenth century.

Early Life

Catherine de Médicis' father, Lorenzo de' Medici, was *capo dello stato* in Florence, *gonfalonier* of the Church, and, after a victorious expedition, Duke of Urbino. His uncle, Pope Leo X, hoping to restore the Medicis to their earlier status, arranged a marriage between Lorenzo and Madeleine de la Tour d'Auvergne, a distant relation of Francis I, King of France. The young couple were married at Amboise in 1518, and within a year their daughter was born. Two weeks later, Madeleine was dead of puerperal fever, and five days later Lorenzo also died.

The baby Catherine was the last legitimate heir of the family. Immediately, she became a tool in the hands of her guardian, Pope Leo X, and of his half brother Giulio, later Pope Clement VII, to recoup the Medici fortune. Catherine's childhood was spent in Rome and Florence, where she was at times ignored and at other times the center of attention. In 1527, during a Florentine revolution, she was the hostage of anti-Medici forces and handled her desperate situation with great diplomacy. At the age of ten, she returned to Rome, where Pope Clement VII negotiated a marriage between Catherine and Henry, the second son of Francis I.

On October 26, 1533, Catherine and Henry, both fourteen years of age, were married at Avignon. Small and thin, with strong rather than beautiful features and the bulging eyes of the Medicis, Catherine was vivacious, self-assured, witty, bright, and eager to learn. As a new wife, she traveled everywhere with the French court and joined a group of young women, protégées of her father-in-law, to study Latin, Greek, French, mathematics, science, astronomy, and astrology. She hunted, danced, and rode using a sidesaddle she invented. Still a child when she married Henry, she had to call upon all of her habits of diplomacy to handle two major crises. The first was her husband's attachment to his mistress Diane de Poitiers. Catherine handled this problem by being a patient and loving wife and by making an ally of her rival. The second difficulty was more critical and became especially important in 1536, when Henry's older brother died and Henry became the heir to the French throne. That difficulty was her inability to bear children and the possibility that Henry would obtain a divorce to marry a fertile bride and leave Catherine without resources. Catherine's charm and vivacity saved her from this fate, and, after ten years of marriage, she presented Henry with an heir.

During the next thirteen years, Catherine bore ten children, including four sons, and settled into a mutually respectful relationship with Henry and Diane de Poitiers. When Francis died in 1547, Henry arranged a coronation ceremony for Catherine, an unusual innovation for sixteenth century French kings. In 1551, when Henry went to war in Burgundy, he left Catherine as his regent, and, although Diane was his chief adviser, he also consulted with his wife. In 1559, Catherine was one of the architects of the Treaty of Cateau-Cambrésis, which temporarily calmed the Franco-Spanish rivalry. The new amity was sealed with the marriage of Philip II of Spain and Catherine's daughter Elizabeth. A tournament was held to celebrate this alliance, and, during one event, a splinter from a broken lance pierced the French king's eye and he died.

Life's Work

Although she did not know it at the time, Catherine's life's work began with the death of her husband. Francis became king at the age of fifteen. A year earlier, he had married Mary Stuart, Queen of Scotland and niece of the Guises, a prominent French noble family. Mary's relatives assumed responsibility for advising the young king. If Francis had lived, Catherine would not have become an important political figure in France. When Francis died, Charles IX, aged ten, assumed the throne. After observing the arrogant despotism of the Guises, Catherine determined to become regent to her son.

During her years as regent, Catherine responded to two major crises in the face of four significant enemies. One struggle was to preserve royal authority against two noble families—the Guises and the Bourbons—who were determined to dominate the king and the royal family. The Bourbons were the hereditary kings of Navarre and the next in line to inherit the throne after Catherine's sons. The other major crisis for Catherine was the religious conflict between Roman Catholics and Protestant Calvinists, called Huguenots, in France. To complicate her task, the Guises became associated with the Roman Catholic position and often looked to the Spanish for assistance, while the Bourbons, at least the Queen of Navarre and her brother-in-law the fiery Prince of Condé, openly adhered to the Protestant faith. Even before Francis II's death, the Prince of Condé had mobilized Huguenot support against the Guises in a conspiracy aimed at kidnapping the king and executing his Guise advisers. His efforts failed, but the lines of conflict were drawn. Catherine also faced a powerful Spanish king, Philip II, who would act in his own dynastic interest even though he was Catherine's son-in-law. Finally, she had to deal with an inadequate treasury and the imminent bankruptcy of the Crown. As a woman and a foreigner, Catherine's task was doubly difficult.

The queen mother's response to the religious difficulties was to organize a national religious council to mediate between French Protestants and Catholics. The Colloquy of Poissy, which met in 1561, succeeded in getting the French religious parties to talk together, but it also polarized them. The Guises and other staunch Roman Catholics united and sought help from the Spanish king to challenge royal efforts at mediation. Religious passions intensified. In January, 1562, when Catherine issued the Edict of Toleration granting government protection to the Huguenots, the Catholics left the royal court, and the first of the French religious wars began.

During the next ten years, France was torn by three major civil wars motivated by religious and noble rivalry. Catherine tried desperately to maintain a balance among all of these forces, but she failed. The third and most savage of the first set of religious wars ended in August, 1570, with the Peace of Saint-Germain and a backlash against the Guises and their Spanish allies. A new party, the Politique Party, grew out of this disgust with foreign influence. Composed of Roman Catholic and Huguenot moderates who believed that the integrity of the state was more important than religion, this party reflected Catherine's own position.

Catherine's diplomatic expertise became especially important in 1572, in negotiating defense treaties with the English and the Ottoman Turks against Philip II and in gaining the throne of Poland for her third son, Henry. As Henry departed for Poland, Europe was rocked by news of the Saint Bartholomew's Eve Massacre. The occasion was the wedding of Catherine's daughter Marguerite to Henry, King of Navarre, heir to the French throne after Catherine's sons. All the important nobles of France were gathered in the capital, including the Huguenot leaders. Whether Catherine and Charles IX intended to kill all the Protestants in Paris on August 23, 1572, or whether Catherine only meant to kill one or two of the Protestant leaders, the result was a massacre of Protestants by Catholics in the capital city and in other cities throughout the nation. War broke out again and, in spite of their losses, the Huguenots managed to retain several key fortresses. When Charles IX died in 1574, and Henry III returned from Poland, the new king was also unable to seize the Protestant strongholds and to subdue the opposition. In 1576, peace was negotiated on the basis of the status quo. Henry III, Catherine's favorite son, was an adult when he came to the throne, and Catherine no longer played an important policy-making role. Since the king was unmarried and preoccupied with war, his mother continued to direct the ambassadors and to send and receive letters from agents and diplomats throughout Europe.

In June of 1584, Catherine's youngest son died of influenza. Thus, the Protestant Henry of Navarre would inherit the throne if Henry III were to die. War raged, and, fearing the Spanish king would send in troops, Henry III was forced to put himself at the head of the Catholic League in order to control its excesses. The Estates General refused to grant the government more money to fight the wars they did not want. On December 23, 1588, Henry III summoned the Cardinal of Guise to the royal chamber, where armed guards killed him. Shortly thereafter, Henry had the Duke of Guise assassinated as well. Catherine was in the castle at Blois that evening on her deathbed, when Henry carried the news of the Guises' deaths to her. She was not pleased; by destroying one faction, Henry had put himself in the hands of the other; he no longer had a weapon against the Bourbon and Protestant nobles. The collapse of Spain would give Geneva and the Calvinists the victory.

Catherine died less than two weeks later on January 5, 1589, and her son was assassinated before the end of the year. Henry IV, the Protestant King of Navarre, officially inherited the throne, but the war continued until 1595, when he had reconquered the north and converted to Catholicism. Henry was able, however, to protect his Huguenot

friends and relatives by issuing the Edict of Nantes that granted the Huguenots several armed cities and freedom to worship.

Summary

Catherine de Médicis set out to destroy the resistance to royal power, to secure for her sons the French throne, to build a government with a centralized power in the hands of the French monarchy, and to limit the authority of the nobles. She succeeded in gaining those ends even as she failed to achieve them peacefully and permanently. Accused by contemporaries and historians of being a Machiavellian, Catherine must at least plead guilty to being a realist in her exercise of power. She changed sides, made secret agreements, and even sent ambassadors to the infidel Turk to negotiate a treaty against the Spanish in 1570. She met with all parties and used every means available to achieve her ends. She condoned war and murder in the interest of her duty as the regent of France.

It may have been her failure to balance the dynastic and religious conflicts that brought on the civil wars, but it was her success at identifying the factions in the conflict and her attempts to balance them that allowed Henry IV to obtain his throne intact with Huguenots alive to tolerate. The religious civil wars were horrible, but some of the changes as a result of the wars moved France closer to the centralized, bureaucratic state that was more nearly modern than was the sixteenth century dynastic structure. The wars served to redistribute the land from the hands of a few large noble families to those of a number of smaller families who were loyal to the monarchy. The most significant result of the civil wars, however, was the creation of the Politique Party, a party that recognized the need for a strong monarchy regardless of religious affiliation and regardless of noble demands for power. Catherine's contribution to French government in the sixteenth century was the principle of centralized power in the hands of the monarchy.

Bibliography

Héritier, Jean. *Catherine de Medici.* Translated by Charlotte Haldane. London: Allen and Unwin, and New York: St. Martin's Press, 1963. Long biography of Catherine as a great national and moderate leader who preserved for Henry IV a kingdom which was battered but intact.

Neale, J. E. *The Age of Catherine de Medici.* London: Cape, and New York: Barnes and Noble, 1943. Short and colorful presentation of Catherine's rule as foolish, misguided, and middle class.

Roeder, Ralph. *Catherine de Medici and the Lost Revolution.* New York: Garden City Publishing, and London: Harrap, 1937. Presents the problem of sixteenth century France as the inability of Catherine to balance the dynastic and religious conflicts of the age.

Sichel, Edith. *Catherine de' Medici and the French Reformation.* London: Constable, and New York: Dutton, 1905. Presents Catherine as the evil nemesis of the political problems of France, never quite in control of her plans. Sichel also relates the art and literature of the period of the French Reformation to Catherine's reign.

Strage, Mark. *Women of Power: The Life and Times of Catherine de' Medici.* New York: Harcourt Brace, 1976. A conventional rehash of the story focusing on Catherine's relationship with Diane de Poitiers and Margaret of Valois.

Sutherland, N. M. "Catherine de Medici: The Legend of the Wicked Italian Queen." *Sixteenth Century Journal* 9 (1978): 45-56. An analysis of the attitudes of historians about Catherine de Médicis and her role in history from her contemporaries to the present day.

Van Dyke, Paul. *Catherine de Médicis.* 2 vols. London: Murray, and New York: Scribner, 1923. General study of Catherine within the context of her time. Catherine is held responsible for not solving the religious and political problems but not through inherent malice.

Loretta Turner Johnson

CATHERINE OF ARAGON

Born: December 16, 1485; Alcala de Henares, Spain

Died: January 7, 1536; Kimbolton, Huntingdonshire, England

Areas of Achievement: Church reform, monarchy

Contribution: Twice married to English princes, Catherine, the first wife of Henry VIII, refused to accept a royal divorce, which led to Henry's expulsion of the Roman Catholic Church and the establishment of the Protestant church in England.

Early Life

Born Catalina (Catherine), an Infanta of Spain, to their Most Catholic Majesties Queen Isabella of Castile and Leon and King Ferdinand of Aragon, this fifth surviving child and youngest daughter was named for her maternal English great-grandmother, Catherine of Lancaster. Catherine was twice descended from English kings: maternally from Edward III and paternally from Henry II.

For the first fifteen years of her life, Catherine remained under the tutelage of her mother, Queen Isabella, who considered her own education so deficient that Catherine was tutored by scholars Peter Martyr and Antonio and Alessandro Geraldini. Catherine was instructed in the Bible, Latin histories, and Roman and Christian writers. She spoke fluent classical Latin, in addition to Spanish; studied heraldry, genealogy, and civil and canon law; and gained proficiency in music, dancing, drawing, and the domestic arts of spinning, weaving, and embroidery.

Contemporary accounts describe the young Catherine as having naturally pink checks, white skin, a fair complexion, and fairly thick hair with a reddish gold tint. Catherine's features were neat and regular in an oval face. Lacking in height and usually described as short, tiny, and plump, with a low voice, Catherine appeared to be a young infanta who would be a healthy producer of children.

The unification of Spain led Ferdinand and Isabella to use their children as marital pawns on the chessboard of European diplomacy. Their first- and third-born daughters wed Portuguese kings. The second daughter and the only son wed Austrian Habsburgs. Marriage negotiations between Madrid and London for Catherine to wed Prince Arthur of Wales, the eldest son of Henry VII, were opened in 1487 and formalized by the Treaty of Medina del Campo in 1489. A dowry settlement committing Spain to a payment of 200,000 crowns, plus plate and jewels valued at 35,000 crowns, formalized the Spanish-English alliance. Catherine (by proxy) and Arthur were first engaged in 1497 and then married in 1499.

Catherine's London arrival on November 12, 1501, and her official marriage to Prince Arthur two days later were greatly acclaimed by the English people. The usually parsimonious Henry VII gave Catherine and Arthur a lavish wedding at St. Paul's Cathedral. For Henry VII, the Spanish marriage publicly legitimatized the Tudor dynasty in England, contributed to the encirclement of England's enemy, France, and provided King Henry with a substantial dowry to use for his own political purposes.

Unfortunately, at Ludlow Castle in the Marches of Wales, the physically frail Arthur succumbed to illness on April 2, 1502. The cause of death remains unknown, but speculation has centered on tuberculosis or an undetermined plague. Catherine herself was too ill to attend her husband's funeral and burial at Worcester Cathedral. In widowhood, the young Catherine, now princess dowager of Wales, confessed to the bishop of Salisbury, Cardinal Lorenzo Campeggio, that her marriage had never been consummated. The couple had shared the marital bed only seven times.

Life's Work

During her years of her widowhood, 1502 to 1509, Catherine found herself a political pawn used by both her father and father-in-law. Catherine was first pledged in marriage to and then repudiated by both her widower father-in-law, Henry VII, and Henry VII's second son, Prince Henry. At issue was whether or not Catherine was still a virgin. If Catherine's marriage to Arthur had been consummated, an impediment of affinity prevented her from marrying another member of Prince Arthur's family. In 1506, Pope Julius II granted a dispensation and waived the issue of affinity, even if the marriage had been consummated.

Catherine's status remained unclear, however, because 100,000 crowns of her dowry remained unpaid by her father, who continuously pleaded poverty, and because her father-in-law repeatedly reevaluated Catherine's value as a future English royal bride in comparison with royal princesses in France and Austria. Increasing poverty forced Catherine to

live in reduced state at Durham House, where she supported her household from her partial dowry and the sale of her plate and jewelry and suffered from frequent fevers.

Catherine's ambiguous status ended within two months of Henry VII's life when she wed her former brother-in-law, now Henry VIII, on June 11, 1509. Later, witnesses claimed that Henry VIII boasted his wife was a virgin when he took her to the marriage bed. Henry VIII's change of attitude toward Catherine was probably caused by his desire to retain her dowry and to keep Spain allied against France, and his need for an adult wife to found a dynasty. The possibility that Henry VIII actually loved Catherine should also not be discounted.

As queen, Catherine encouraged the arts, established her own library open to scholars, and befriended English writers. Queen Catherine contributed money to lectureships, supported poor scholars, and endowed the colleges of Ipswich and Oxford. She actively corresponded with leading humanists Thomas More, Erasmus, and Juan Vives. Catherine's greatest contribution to learning was as a pioneer of women's education. Catherine sponsored the publication of five handbooks on humanist instruction for women, including Vives's *The Instruction of a Christian Woman*.

Henry VIII appointed Catherine regent of England during his absences fighting the French on their territory. This action certainly demonstrates his appreciation and trust of Catherine's intelligence and diplomatic ability. While Henry was in France, Catherine gave the military orders launching an English army that defeated the invading Scots and killed their king, James IV (Henry's brother-in-law), at Flodden Field in 1513. Yet Catherine's promotion of a Spanish alliance and her continued involvement in policy making led her into conflict with Henry's lord chancellor, Cardinal Thomas Wolsey. Catherine would later blame Wolsey for Henry's desertion of her and his demands for a divorce.

The more important issue facing Catherine was her failure to produce a living male heir. The number of pregnancies and miscarriages suffered by Catherine has been the subject of much debate. Sir John Dewhurst, who has provided the best analysis of the existing period documents, concluded that there could have been only six pregnancies between the years 1509 and 1525: four stillbirths; a son, Henry, born January 1, 1511, who died seven weeks later; and their only surviving child, Mary, born February 18, 1516.

Exactly what caused Henry to announce his intention to divorce Catherine remains a topic of considerable debate. It seems that Henry's attitude toward Catherine changed abruptly after 1525, when the intended betrothal of their daughter Mary to Catherine's nephew, Charles V, king of Spain and Holy Roman Emperor, was broken by Charles so that he could marry an older Portuguese cousin. The termination of this marriage plan ended Henry's dreams of an Anglo-Spanish alliance dominating Europe. It is also true that Henry was involved with Anne Boleyn by 1526.

Henry's May, 1527, decision to challenge the validity of his marriage to Catherine is known as the "King's Great Matter." Using the biblical passages Leviticus 20:21 and Deuteronomy 25:5-7, Henry claimed that a man marrying his brother's wife did so against God's will. Henry further argued that the papal dispensations granted by Julius II to remove the issue of affinity and allow the marriage were invalid.

Henry's actions divided the Roman Church in England. He failed to anticipate Catherine's refusal to go quietly and Charles V's seizure of Rome and imprisonment of Pope Clement VII. On March 6, 1529, Catherine appealed to Rome, asking the pope to take her case. Her only appearance before the Blackfriars Court on May 31, 1529, witnessed a queen defending the legality of her marriage and intent on saving it.

Both Clement VII and his English representative, Cardinal Campeggio, delayed clerical action, hoping for reconciliation. After 1530, Catherine's health began to decline. Henry last saw Catherine at Windsor on July 11, 1531, whereupon she was removed to increasingly remote locations and finally to Kimbolton. Pressure from the Boleyn supporters, Henry's increasing desire for a legitimate male heir, and clerical resistance to an annulment forced the king to begin the process of disestablishing the English Roman Church.

Attempts to encourage Catherine to lead a rebellion against her increasingly unpopular husband and the Boleyn party were rebuffed by the queen. Wars in northern Italy, Germany, and France prevented military intervention in support of Catherine by Charles V and the pope. Finally, almost five years after Catherine's initial appeal to Rome, on March 24, 1534, the pope declared the marriage valid in the eyes of God and the Church. By that time, however, Henry had taken matters into his own hands. The English Roman Church was disestablished (1532), Parliament annulled Henry's marriage to Catherine (1533) so that he could legalize his marriage to an already pregnant Anne Boleyn, and the king was enthroned as the head of the English Church (1534).

Increasing ill health led to Catherine's death on January 7, 1536. Henry celebrated with a ball at Greenwich. Although rumors circulated of Catherine's having been poisoned, she probably died from either cancer or a coronary thrombosis. In violation of Catherine's instructions, she was buried at Peterborough Cathedral with the honors of princess dowager.

Summary

First as an infanta of Spain, then as princess of Wales, and lastly as queen of England, Catherine of Aragon was sacrificed to diplomacy and statecraft by her parents, Ferdinand and Isabella of Spain, her father-in-law, Henry VII, and her husband, Henry VIII. In all her titled positions, Catherine represented the emerging Renaissance woman who was educated, spoke several languages, and was lauded by contemporary scholars for her support of humanism and culture.

Although contemporary and later historians have praised Catherine's virtue, trust, and high-mindedness, they have faulted her for her inability to use her popularity with the English people, the nobles, and the Church to maintain Catholicism in England or to lead an army into battle against Henry VIII in order to make their daughter, Mary, queen of England. Catherine's obedience to her husband, her willingness to accede to all of Henry's royal commands during the "King's Great Matter," and her absolute faith and devotion to the institutions of marriage and the Church enabled her to defend her marriage and keep her daughter in the Roman faith and in the line of succession, but those characteristics ultimately contributed to England's Protestant Reformation.

Bibliography

Albert, Marvin. *The Divorce*. New York: Simon and Schuster, 1965. A detailed study of the events leading to the divorce of Catherine of Aragon by Henry VIII. The reader becomes a participant in one of history's most celebrated divorce trials.

Dewhurst, John. "The Alleged Miscarriages of Catherine of Aragon and Anne Boleyn." *Medical History* 28 (1984): 49-56. The best medical analysis of historical documents to determine the number and outcomes of Catherine's pregnancies.

Dowling, Maria. "A Woman's Place? Learning and the Wives of Henry VIII." *History Today* 41 (June, 1991): 38-42. Dowling reintroduces the reader to the wives of Henry VIII as promoters of education, religion, and scholarship.

Fraser, Antonia. *The Wives of Henry VIII*. New York: Knopf, 1992. Fraser's careful analysis and reevaluation of archival and published works produces a thoughtful reinterpretation of Catherine's role in shaping England's entrance into the modern age.

Kipling, Gordon. *The Receyt of the Ladie Katheryne*. Oxford: Oxford University Press, 1990. A scholarly analysis of sixteenth century documents describing Catherine of Aragon's arrival in England, her entry into London, her marriage to Prince Arthur, and her subsequent widowhood.

Mattingly, Garrett. *Catherine of Aragon*. Boston: Little Brown, 1941. Mattingly's access to extensive archival material provides a detailed analysis of Catherine's character, the dynasties of Spain, England, Scotland, and France, and the politics of the Papacy in the turbulent sixteenth century. Still the definitive biography of Catherine.

Roll, Winifred. *The Pomegranate and the Rose: The Story of Katherine of Aragon*. Englewood Cliffs, N.J.: Prentice-Hall, 1970. A highly readable study of a young woman whose fate was determined by the statecraft of Spanish and English kings and the Roman Church.

Scarisbrick, J. J. *Henry VIII*. Berkeley: University of California Press, 1968. British historian Scarisbrick's extensive access to French, German, Latin, Spanish, and English primary sources and his careful analysis of Henry's character and relationship with his wives, ministers, and church officials reveals a king whose achievement fell below his potential greatness.

William A. Paquette

THOMAS CAVENDISH

Born: September 19, 1560 (baptized); Grimston Hall, Suffolk, England

Died: c. May, 1592; at sea, near Ascension Island

Areas of Achievement: Exploration, navigation, and privateering

Contribution: A boldly enterprising voyager, Cavendish was the second Englishman to circumnavigate the globe; in the course of his expedition he captured one of the richest prizes in the history of English privateering against Spain.

Early Life

Thomas Cavendish was born in 1560 at his family's estate of Grimston Hall, near the town of Harwich, in Suffolk, and he was baptized on September 19. He was the heir of William Cavendish and his wife, Mary Wentworth, sister of Lord William Wentworth. William Cavendish died when his son was only twelve, leaving a reduced estate. Thomas and his mother went to live with Lord Wentworth at Nettleshead, Suffolk. At the age of fifteen, he entered Cambridge University, attending Corpus Christi College; he left in 1577 without taking a degree. In the next years he may have spent some time at the Inns of Court in London, studying law. In 1580, he went to the court of Queen Elizabeth I, where his sister Anne became one of the queen's ladies-in-waiting. Through his family he had easy access to important figures at court; he became a friend of Sir George Carey, son of Lord Hunsdon, of Lord Chamberlain, and of George Clifford, Earl of Cumberland, who became the most active aristocratic privateer in the country. Through the patronage of the Earl of Pembroke, he was elected to Parliament from Shaftesbury, Dorset, in 1584 and for Wilton, Dorset, in 1586.

Life's Work

As part of an ambitious and venturesome court circle, Cavendish was soon drawn into naval enterprises. When Sir Walter Raleigh organized a fleet of seven ships to send his first colony to Virginia in 1585, Cavendish contributed a ship of his own, the *Elizabeth*, and was high marshal for the expedition. The fleet under Sir Richard Grenville left from Plymouth in early April and sailed first to Puerto Rico, where, under the cover of building a pinnace to enlarge their fleet, they planned to attack Spanish shipping. Two well-laden Spanish vessels were captured and their crews held for ransom, an action that whetted Cavendish's appetite for further privateering. The fleet sailed on to Haiti, the Bahamas, and Florida before arriving on the Virginia coast near the end of June, 1585. In the next weeks, Cavendish became one of the party, including also Grenville and the artist John White, who conducted an exploring foray into what is now North Carolina. They came upon three Indian villages, one of which they burned after an Indian stole a silver cup. Their reprisal may have generated some of the hostilities suffered by the ill-fated colony. In August, Cavendish was one of those who accompanied Grenville back to England, leaving 108 men behind under the governorship of Ralph Lane. En route, they were able to capture another rich Spanish prize.

The privateering success of the voyage, apart from the misfortunes of the colony, stimulated Cavendish to organize a much more ambitious enterprise. The example he chose to follow was that of Sir Francis Drake, who, eight years earlier, had won wealth, reputation, and honor in a plundering voyage around the world. Many English believed that the Spanish claims to monopoly on the territories of Latin America and the East Indies were invalid and that the riches being drained away from overseas possessions were legitimate targets for sailors bold enough to take them. The Spanish considered what they did to be piracy, but their own government favored them unofficially. Queen Elizabeth and her officers often took shares in the major voyages and always absorbed much of the profits.

His preparations must have begun almost immediately after he returned to England, since he was ready to sail the following summer. He had one major ship, the *Desire*, at 140 tons, and two small ones, the *Content* and the *Hugh Gallant*, with a crew of 123 men. A joint expedition with the Earl of Cumberland may have been planned, since Cumberland was preparing a fleet at the same time, but Cavendish finished his preparations and sailed nearly a month before Cumberland was ready. He went first to Sierra Leone, then crossed to Brazil, where he paused to replenish his supplies and to build a small pinnace. Continuing southward, he stopped to slaughter thousands of penguins and take them on as food for the passage through the difficult and dangerous Strait of Magellan. Cumberland had followed him as far as Brazil but then turned back because of inadequate supplies.

Entering the strait, Cavendish came upon a party of Spanish survivors from a failed colony; he took one of them with him and left the others to try to make their way to the Rio de Plata. Later, he found the remains of their settlement and took the cannon they had abandoned. After waiting a month for favorable weather, he was able to proceed through the straits without incident. The next eight months he spent cruising up the Pacific coast as far as Baja California, raiding Spanish ports and pillaging and burning some twenty ships.

On the coast of Ecuador, Cavendish learned from a captive of the expected arrival of a great ship from Manila; the capture of that ship became Cavendish's principal aim and most striking achievement. The ship was the *Santa Ana*, which was bringing to Mexico the yield of gold mines in the Philippines. He waited off the tip of Baja California, his men occupying themselves by pearl fishing, until November 4, when the *Santa Ana* appeared, its crew ready for the end of their long transpacific voyage and its cannon put away in the hold. The first two English attacks were repulsed, but the third forced a surrender. The Spanish aboard were put ashore at San Lucas, and then the English spent two weeks sorting out their winnings. The ship carried gold worth seventy thousand pounds and great quantities of pearls, silks, and other goods.

Loss of the *Santa Ana* was a serious blow to the Spanish—it represented much of the year's profits from the East Indies. Now, however, it presented Cavendish with a problem of surfeit. He did not have a crew big enough to man the ship and take it home, and he could not even unload its cargo into his own vessels. He had been forced to abandon the *Hugh Gallant* on the South American coast, and he already had much of the cargo space in the remaining ships filled. In the end, he took what was most valuable and most easily portable and burned the rest, probably ninety percent of the cargo, along with the ship itself (it burned to the water line, but the Spanish were later able to salvage and rebuild it).

After the capture of the *Santa Ana*, the rest of the long voyage was anticlimactic. With the aid of a captured Spanish pilot, he crossed to the Philippines, arriving in January, 1588, but having lost the *Content* on the way. The pilot was hanged after trying to warn Spanish authorities, but without him Cavendish proceeded to the Sulu Sea, along the western shore of Mindanao, through the Banda and Flores Seas to Java. At every opportunity, he collected information about Spanish fortifications and apparently encouraged the Filipinos to resist the Spanish; conspirators arrested in Luzon the next year said that he had promised English support for their resistance. In March, he left again for England, arriving finally at Plymouth in September. The goods he brought back were officially valued at nearly ninety thousand pounds, a tremendous fortune for the time, but it is not known how much Cavendish kept after the queen and other officials took their shares. Cavendish made a great show of bringing his ship into the Thames, his crew in silk and golden chains, the ship itself rigged with sails of blue damask.

Cavendish was only twenty-eight years old when he returned to the acclaim of England. He was, for the moment, rich and famous, but his good fortune did not last. He expected to be knighted by the queen but was not, and the two-thousand-pound bond he had posted before the voyage was forfeited, possibly because of a skirmish with some Newfoundland ships or because he tried to conceal part of his prize. In the next years, he spent most of his new wealth, and by 1590 was ready to try the exploit again. This time, however, he was plagued with misfortune. He left Plymouth in August, 1591, with five vessels and sailed for the Straits of Magellan, his fleet including John Davis in command of the *Desire*. The fleet was separated in heavy storms in the straits, however, and Cavendish turned back toward Brazil. He made unsuccessful attempts to land at Santos and Espírito Santo, then tried to reach Ascension Island. He died en route, believing that he had been deserted by his other ships.

Summary

Thomas Cavendish's great voyage was one of the most daring exploits of Elizabethan seamanship. It inflicted a heavy economic blow and a more damaging psychological blow in demonstrating the vulnerability of Spanish trade even in the Pacific. Even more bitterly than the loss of the *Santa Ana* itself, the King of Spain is said to have mourned that it was taken by "an English youth . . . with forty or fifty companions." On the remainder of the voyage, Cavendish collected useful information to supplement what Drake had learned about not only the Straits of Magellan and the Pacific Coast of America but also the Philippines and the Indonesian islands.

Bibliography

Andrews, Kenneth R. *Elizabethan Privateering*. Cambridge: Cambridge University Press, 1964. The most complete and careful study of how privateering worked, who took part, and who shared in the proceeds. Cavendish can be traced in the context of Cumberland, Drake, and the other privateers.

Hakluyt, Richard. *The Principal Navigations, Voyages, and Discoveries of the English Nation*. London: Dent, and New York: Dutton, 1907. One of the most important early achievements of English scholarship, a massive and exhaustive compilation of narratives of English voyages. Includes a lengthy account of the 1586-1588 voyage around the world based on the description of Francis Pretty, one of the members of the expedition.

Quinn, David Beers. *The Last Voyage of Thomas Cavendish, 1591-1592*. Chicago and London: University of Chicago Press, 1975. A contemporary account, believed to be Cavendish's own, of the voyage on which he died. Includes an excellent biographical and textual introduction.

———. *The Roanoke Voyages*. Vol. 1. London: Hakluyt Society, 1955; Chapel Hill: University of North Carolina Press, 1985. A narrative of the 1585 expedition that incorporates all the major documentary sources. With careful and scholarly explanatory notes.

Sinclair, Andrew. *Sir Walter Raleigh and the Age of Discovery*. London and New York: Penguin, 1984. An attractive and highly readable description of the world that Cavendish shared with Raleigh at court, at sea, and in the colonies.

Robert W. Kenny

WILLIAM CAXTON

Born: c. 1422; the weald of Kent, England, possibly in the village of Hadlow
Died: c. 1491; London, England
Areas of Achievement: Printing and publishing
Contribution: In 1476, Caxton set up the first printing press in England, and before he died, around 1491, he had published some hundred items, many of them his own translations, at the same time helping to determine the variety of English in which printing would be done.

Early Life

Little is known of William Caxton's early life, and both the date and place of his birth (somewhere in Kent) remain uncertain. He was apprenticed in 1438 to Robert Large, a successful mercer. This suggests a birth date between 1422 and 1424, because apprentices usually began their work between fourteen and sixteen.

Presumably Caxton's father was the William Caxton buried in St. Margaret's churchyard at Westminster in 1478. Whether Oliver Cawston, buried at St. Margaret's in 1474, Richard Caxston or Caston, a monk there from 1473 until his death in 1504, or John Caxston, known to have belonged to the church from 1474 to 1477, are related to the William Caxton who became a printer in Westminster remains uncertain.

When Robert Large, who became Lord Mayor of London in 1439, died in 1441, Caxton went to Bruges, the hub of the brisk European wool trade, settling into the comfortable life of an English tradesman in the Lowlands. He remained there about thirty years, in the course of which he became wealthy, influential, and highly respected.

By 1453, Caxton was a member of the livery of the Mercer's company. Ten years later, he held the enormously influential position of Governor of the English Nation of Merchant Adventurers. During this time, the British government often called upon him to transact delicate trade negotiations for the Crown.

Indirect evidence suggests that Caxton married a woman named Mawde around 1461 and that she died in England in 1490. In that year, the vestry accounts of St. Margaret's Church record the cost of torches and tapers for the burial of a Mawde Caxston. In the same year, Caxton left off the printing of *Fayts of Arms* (1489) to turn his attention to completing *The Arte and Crafte to Know Well to Die* (1490), a piece of circumstantial evidence that suggests that the Mawde Caxston who was buried in 1490 was his wife and that as a result of her death he was preoccupied with death.

Caxton apparently had one child, a daughter. The Public Records Office has a copy of a document recording the separation of Elizabeth Croppe from her husband in Westminster on May 11, 1496. This document identifies Elizabeth as William Caxton's daughter and refers to her late father's will.

Resigning his governorship around 1470, Caxton entered the service of Margaret, Duchess of Burgundy, who was the sister of King Edward IV of Britain. Although Caxton continued in governmental service until 1475, around 1469, Caxton became extremely interested in literature.

Life's Work

A man of energy and perseverance, Caxton did not begin his life's most significant work until he was nearly fifty. Already distinguished as a mercer and as a royal servant, Caxton, around 1469, turned his energies to translating compiler Raoul Le Fèvre's *Recueil des histoires de Troye* (1464; *The Recuyell of the Historyes of Troye*, 1475), which he finally completed at the behest of Margaret of Burgundy, on September 19, 1471, in Cologne, where Caxton lived from 1470 until 1472.

Caxton, complaining that his pen had become worn from copying, now bought a printing press and two fonts of type. Colard Mansion of Bruges helped Caxton set up his press, and in 1475, Caxton printed in Bruges his translation of *Recueil des histoires de Troye*, the first book ever printed in English. He followed this book with his translation of a French allegory, *The Game and Playe of the Chesse*, in 1476, the same year that he printed two or three books in French. (The original work, which Caxton translated, was itself a translation of 1360 by Jean de Vignay of Jacobus de Cessolis' *De ludo scaccorum*, c. 1300.)

In 1476, Caxton returned to England, where he spent the rest of his life. At an age when many people of his position would have retired, Caxton embarked on the demanding new career that assured him his place in history. In the city of Westminster, in an area behind and to the right of the transept of Westminster Abbey, William Caxton set up the first printing press in England. From it was to issue

the first document known to have been printed in England, an indulgence from Abbot Sant dated December 13, 1476.

The first book from Caxton's press, *Dicteis or Sayenges of the Phylosophers* (1477), was translated from the French by the Earl Rivers, who commissioned Caxton to print it. The only extant copy of this book, which exists in two later printings, has been dependably dated as being issued before November 18, 1477.

Scholars have questioned Caxton's reasons for setting up his press across the Thames in Westminster rather than in London, the hub of cultural and mercantile activity of his day. Church records indicate that numerous Caxtons (Caxstons, Cawstons, Caustons, Castons) were associated with St. Margaret's Church in Westminster during the fifteenth century, suggesting that Caxton had family connections there. Also, Westminster was then inhabited by people of means who had the leisure to read, so that Caxton could sell his output more easily there than he might have elsewhere.

Caxton was probably also attracted by the royal court of Westminster, to which he had easy entrée because of the favor in which he was held by the royal family, whom he had served well. Certainly Caxton realized that being close to the Abbey would assure him regular printing jobs because of the volume of written material that issued from the Abbey regularly in manuscript form. That Caxton was in the good graces of John Esteney, the Abbot of Westminster, is indicated by the fact that the abbot provided choice space near the Abbey for Caxton to set up his press, today marked by a commemorative plaque. Members of the Commons, who met in the Abbey, passed Caxton's printery when they left to go to the Chapter House, as did members of the royal family, who usually entered the Abbey through the south door. Caxton was assured that those in the best position to use his services would be reminded frequently of his availability.

The humanism that had earlier ignited in Italy now spread through much of Europe and began to be felt in England. The demand for writing in Latin and Greek was substantial, but Continental printers, who exported their books to England, met this need. Caxton realized that his best market was in original works or translations in the vernacular. It was in this field, as a precursor of Martin Luther and other Humanists who called for works in the vernacular that common people could read, that Caxton made his most significant contributions.

In 1481, the first illustrated book in English, *The Myrrour of the Worlde* (1481), came from Caxton's press. Caxton's books found a ready market among the nobility and the rich merchants who flocked to London during Caxton's later life. Because his books were printed in the vernacular, however, and because many of them were illustrated, it is clear that Caxton reached a broader audience than merely the nobility and rich merchants.

Caxton's press ran at capacity most of the time. When it was not in use printing books, it was fully engaged printing shorter documents for the Church or the Crown. Printing was a profitable commercial enterprise, but Caxton's motives were not strictly financial. He felt keenly his responsibility to provide useful reading material to a public hungry to read.

Caxton was meticulous in his editing. He issued Geoffrey Chaucer's *The Canterbury Tales* (1387-1400) around 1478, but, in 1484, when deficiencies in the earlier edition were pointed out to him, he printed an improved version of the work from a more reliable manuscript. From Caxton's press came editions of most of the important literature of England—in 1485 Thomas Malory's *Le Morte d' Arthur*, in 1483 John Gower's *Confessio Amantis* (1386-1390), and most of the writings of John Lydgate.

Caxton translated twenty-four books and was actively engaged in translating from French, Dutch, and Latin until the very day of his death. He was a careful editor of the books his press printed, often writing prologues or epilogues for them. Modern critics regarded his editing of Malory's Arthurian legends as remarkably sensitive. Caxton's prologue to Malory's *Le Morte d' Arthur* is knowledgeable and intelligent.

In his fifteen years as a printer at Westminster, Caxton published more than one hundred titles. In so doing, he helped to preserve and promote the canon of early English literature. Although the exact date of his death has not been established, Caxton probably died in 1491, a year after the death of the Mawde Caxston who, supposedly, was his wife. Church records at St. Margaret's similar to those mentioning Mawde Caxston's burial expenses contain a bill for torches and tapers for the burial of William Caxton in 1491. Although some books with his imprint are dated as late as 1493, presumably those are editions he left behind that his faithful assistant, Wynken de Worde, printed and published after Caxton's death.

Upon Caxton's death, his printing shop, which had been expanded in 1483-1484 to the almonry adjacent to Westminster, did not pass to his heirs, suggesting that no son survived him. The press was instead taken over by Wynken de Worde, who continued to run the operation.

Summary

William Caxton's greatest contribution to later generations is twofold. By printing most of the notable English literature that existed in his day, he established and preserved the canon that constitutes early English literary studies. As important as that achievement was, however, there was perhaps even greater significance in Caxton's conscious determination of the level of English usage to be employed in printed books.

A year before his death, in the prologue to *Eneydos* (1490), a paraphrase of Vergil's *Aeneid* (first century B.C.) that Caxton had translated from the French, Caxton commented on the problems that face translators and printers. Acknowledging that he could not please everyone, Caxton explained that he would employ in his books an English between the "rude and curious." In doing so, he helped to establish a standard for English and to fix that standard so that the broad regional variations in the language that he observed during his lifetime would eventually be minimized.

Caxton tells of a merchant who, when he was traveling, "came into a house and asked for food; and asked especially for egges. The good wife answered that she could speak no French, and the merchant was angry, because he also could speak no French. And then another said that he would have eyren. The good wife said that she understood him well." Caxton asks, "What should a man in these days now write, egges or eyren?"

By grappling with such problems, Caxton determined for all time the level of usage that would predominate in printed works. For this contribution he will be longest remembered.

Bibliography

Baugh, Albert C., and Thomas Cable. *A History of the English Language*. 4th ed. London: Routledge, and Englewood Cliffs, N.J.: Prentice-Hall, 1993. The portions on Caxton are excellent. They help define his contributions to English literature and language. A good starting point for those unfamiliar with Caxton.

Blades, William. *The Biography and Typography of William Caxton, England's First Printer*. 2d ed. London: Trübner, and New York: Scribner, 1882. Updates Blades's *The Life and Typography of William Caxton* (1861, 1863); was the standard work on Caxton and until Blake's biography (below).

Blake, N.F. *Caxton and His World*. London: Deutsch, and New York: House and Maxwell, 1969. A thoroughly researched biography of Caxton, written in lively prose and organized well. Certainly the best full-length work on Caxton since Blades's pioneering work in the nineteenth century.

———, ed. *William Caxton: A Bibliographical Guide*. New York: Garland, 1985. The most comprehensive bibliography to date of Caxton's publications and of publications relating to him. Blake is exhaustive in his coverage and has presented a guide of immense use to Caxton scholars. Clear, succinct annotations.

Childs, Edmund. *William Caxton: A Portrait in a Background*. London: Northwood, and New York: St. Martin's Press, 1976. Reads well but is not always accurate or shrewd in its judgments. Should be used with caution and checked against Blake (1969) for factual accuracy.

De Ricci, Seymour. *A Census of the Caxtons*. Oxford: Oxford University Press, 1909. An indispensable book for serious Caxton scholars. Lists all extant copies of works known to have been printed by Caxton, including fragments.

Gill, Louise. "William Caxton and the Rebellion of 1483." *English Historical Review* 112 (February, 1997): 105. Gill highlights William Caxton's career as a mercer and diplomat, which earned him a pardon from the Crown under Richard III following the abortive gentry rebellion in England in October 1483. The article provides family background and information on his success as a printer and publisher, and also outlines how Caxton gained royal patronage as a result of his reputation as an entrepreneur and financier.

Seymour, M.C., ed. *Authors of the Middle Ages. Vol.s 1-4, English Writers of the Late Middle Ages*. Aldershot and Brookfield, Vt.: Variorum, 1994. This volume is designed to provide biographies of medieval authors (the fifteenth century is included) with all the information needed for further research. Experts on their subjects give accounts of the facts known about a particular author's life in historical context, together with a review of subsequent scholarship. This is supported by a dated and classified list of manuscripts and editions and a bibliography of secondary sources.

R. Baird Shuman

WILLIAM CECIL
Lord Burghley

Born: September 13, 1520; Bourne, Lincolnshire, England

Died: August 4, 1598; London, England

Area of Achievement: Government

Contribution: Combining his enormous capacity for work with his dedication to Elizabeth I, Cecil effectively managed the affairs of the English government for forty years, from 1558 to 1598.

Early Life

William Cecil was born on September 13, 1520, at Bourne in Lincolnshire. His father, Richard, was a minor officeholder (Groom of the Wardrobe) in the court of Henry VIII. William's grandfather, David Cecil, was a Welshman who assisted Henry Tudor (Henry VII) in his defeat of Richard III at Bosworth Field in 1485. Through his rewards from Henry VII, which included Stamford, and his marriage alliance with a wealthy family, David Cecil initiated his family's ascendancy in English society.

William Cecil attended schools in Grantham and Stamford and served as a page at court. At fifteen, Cecil entered St. John's College, Cambridge, to study the classics. At Cambridge, he came under the influence of the renowned humanist, John Cheke. Cecil fell in love with Cheke's sister, Mary. Despite family opposition, William married Mary in 1541. Before her untimely death in 1543, Mary bore William a son, Thomas. It was also during the early 1540's that Cecil studied law at Gray's Inn, London.

While at Cambridge, Cecil became a Protestant and, in 1542, was rewarded for his advocacy of Henrician policies by being granted a position within the Court of Common Pleas. In 1543, Cecil entered Parliament. During the last years of Henry VIII's reign, Cecil associated with Protestants both politically and socially; he married Mildred Cooke, a devout Protestant, in 1545.

Upon the succession of Edward VI in January, 1547, Cecil served as an assistant in the regency government to Edward Seymour (known also as Lord Hertford and Duke of Somerset). After Seymour's fall from power in 1551, Cecil aligned himself with the Duke of Northumberland. His allegiance to Northumberland, however, was short-lived; when Cecil learned of Northumberland's plans to change the line of succession as prescribed by Henry VIII's will, Cecil abandoned Northumberland in 1553 on the death of Edward VI. The Protestant Cecil served Catholic Mary Tudor's government in a variety of minor posts and gained considerable knowledge of and experience with the workings of the English government, and both Mary and Cardinal Reginald Pole, the papal legate, recognized his contributions and integrity. Cecil's commitment to his Protestant faith did not prove to be a barrier to his continuing service to the government. During the Marian period (1553-1558), Cecil maintained his contact with Princess Elizabeth, and it was upon her accession to the throne in 1558, that Cecil began his four decades of power in English politics.

Life's Work

Upon her accession to the throne in 1558, Elizabeth named Cecil as her secretary. During the next several years, Cecil assisted his queen in resolving a long-standing conflict with the Scots (in the Treaty of Edinburgh, 1560), in implementing the Protestant Elizabethan religious settlement (1559), and in administering the recoinage scheme (1561) developed by the Marquess of Winchester. The recoinage program resulted in curbing inflation and providing a sound financial basis for the government.

Throughout the early decades of Elizabeth's reign, Cecil supported the movement to have her marry and produce an heir, although he did not support the candidacy of Robert Dudley. (Dudley was Elizabeth's primary romantic interest during the 1560's.) Indeed, Cecil's position was threatened by Dudley's popularity. In 1564, Dudley was named Earl of Leicester and became a royal councillor. In response, Cecil brought Thomas Howard, the Duke of Norfolk, into the council. The principal issue which dominated political concerns during the late 1560's was the problem of Mary Stuart, the Catholic former Queen of France and Queen of Scotland who fled to England for protection in 1568. It was in this atmosphere that Leicester and Norfolk joined in an effort to remove Cecil, but a rebellion of northern Catholic earls (1569) resulted in a situation which strengthened Cecil's position at court. In 1571, Elizabeth named him the first Baron Burghley and in the following year, he was named Lord Treasurer.

During the 1570's and 1580's, the primary problems confronting the queen were the tenacity of the English Catholics (the Recusants), the rebellion in the Netherlands against Spain, and the rather chaotic relations with Valois France. The English Recusant cause gained momentum and focus after the establishment of the English College at Douai (1568) by William Allen, the papal bull (*Excelsis Regnans*) on the excommunication of Elizabeth in 1570, and the creation of the Jesuit Mission to England in 1575. The issue was complicated further by the continuing presence of Mary Stuart: She provided a Catholic alternative to Elizabeth. Conspiracies were frequent, and Cecil responded to the threat by escalating the measured response of the government. During the early 1580's, the Jesuit Edmund Campion was executed, and later, in 1587, Mary Stuart was beheaded as a traitor. Throughout this experience, Cecil did not seek to produce Catholic martyrs; rather, he sought to maintain the unity of church and state. In *The Execution of Justice in England* (1583), Cecil advanced his contention that both law and theology demanded the enforcement of the Elizabethan Settlement. A vi-olation of the religious code was comparable to a violation of the civil code, and if serious, it constituted a treasonable offense.

In the 1570's, Protestants in the Netherlands under William of Orange mounted a rebellion against Catholic Spain. After some initial reluctance, Cecil joined Leicester in convincing Elizabeth to support the rebels in 1576. For a decade, the issue would place an increasing strain on Anglo-Spanish relations, and ultimately it led to the War of the Spanish Armada. By 1588, Cecil had prepared England militarily, financially, and diplomatically to defeat the Spaniards.

Political instability was the primary characteristic of French society during the 1570's and 1580's. From the St. Bartholomew's Day Massacre (1572) through the War of the Three Henrys (1580's), France was in the grip of a dynastic, political, and religious crisis, which would be resolved with the victory of the Protestant Henry of Navarre (Henry IV) in 1589. When possible, Cecil manipulated the French situation to benefit England at Spain's expense. At best, the French were unpredictable and arrangements with them were short-lived.

Cecil's principal rival, Leicester, died in 1589, but he was replaced soon by the Earl of Essex. Cecil prevented the ambitious Essex from gaining substantive power during the mid-1590's. Cecil's son, Robert, became secretary to Elizabeth in 1596 as a result of his father's efforts.

Cecil's domestic accomplishments as secretary and Lord Treasurer were based on his conservatism, honesty, and dedication to his duty. He exposed and eliminated corruption, required public officeholders to work, and opposed increased taxation. When the long war against Spain threatened the solvency of the Treasury, Cecil only considered the curtailment of expenditures rather than seeking innovative measures to increase income. Cecil maintained that enhanced efficiency would result in cost reductions.

Privately, Cecil led a quiet life. He possessed an extensive library and was interested especially in cartography and genealogy. From 1557, he served as chancellor of Cambridge University, but his tenure in that position did not result in any significant contributions. Cecil involved himself in the detailed design and construction of his three houses: Burghley House at Stamford, Cecil House in the Strand, and Theobalds in Hertfordshire. Cecil died on August 4, 1598, at Cecil House; he was still in office and at work on negotiations to end the war with Spain.

Summary

During an extremely volatile period in English political history, William Cecil contributed competent political management and continuity of policy. Cecil's management skills, combined with his political wisdom, enabled him to retain his position of prominence though challenged by Leicester and Essex. Cecil did not possess the charm, boldness, or personal attractiveness of these two ambitious men, but he did pursue consistent, well-formulated policies which were based on elementary tenets of English national interest. In doing so, Cecil not only retained the support of Elizabeth I but also established a model for subsequent advisers and ministers of state.

Cecil refined and manipulated the centralizing procedures which were established earlier by Thomas Cromwell, who served as Henry VIII's principal adviser during the 1530's. His administration of the Elizabethan Settlement and the later problems associated with the English Recusants and the Puritans, serves to document his effective and, at times, restrained use of power in the interests of the state. During the turbulent days of the Rising of the Northern Earls (1569), the Ridolfi Plot (1571), the Throckmorton Plot (1583), the Babington Plot (1586), and the Spanish Armada (1587-1588), Cecil's management of the Elizabethan regime was firm, and his responses to these crises were within the law. In each of these instances, England prevailed and English interests were enhanced as a result of Cecil's actions.

Cecil's contributions to English politics went beyond these specific achievements. Along with Thomas Cromwell, Cecil provided a historic base for early modern political management. Cecil and Cromwell influenced the evolution of the English constitution through their use of power at the ministerial level. Cecil was a Royalist who served his monarchs and worked with, and not for, Parliament. Nevertheless, much of his substantive contribution survived not only his tenure but also the crises which dominated English political history during the seventeenth century. During the 1590's, Cecil's administration came under increasing criticism for not being in touch with the problems which confronted the country. Essex, among others, accused Cecil of providing uninspired and often inadequate advice to Elizabeth. Yet Cecil, not Essex, has been vindicated by later generations of national leaders and scholars.

Bibliography

Axelrod-Contrada, Joan. "William Cecil, Advisor to the Queen." *Calliope* 8 (May, 1998): 18. The author profiles William Cecil, providing background information and outlining his role in the queen's service.

Dickens, A. G. *The English Reformation.* 2d ed. London: Batsford, 1989; University Park: Pennsylvania State University Press, 1991. In this general review of the Anglican Reformation, Cecil emerges as an able and dedicated Protestant who provided Elizabeth with significant assistance in the establishment and maintenance of the Elizabethan Settlement. While sympathetic to Cecil, Dickens does not consider Cecil as an individual primarily motivated by religious considerations.

Elton, G. R., ed. *The Tudor Constitution: Documents and Commentary.* 2d ed. Cambridge and New York: Cambridge University Press, 1968. In this collection of primary sources from archival depositories, the work and impact of Cecil is mentioned in passing. The sources support the interpretation that Cecil was close to being the ideal public servant.

Erickson, Carolly. *The First Elizabeth.* London: Macmillan, and New York: Summit Books, 1983. This biography of Elizabeth portrays Cecil as a tireless, knowledgeable, and astute public servant who conducted the bulk of governmental business personally. Cecil is also interpreted as a man motivated by principles, faith, and a strong sense of duty.

Haigh, Christopher, ed. *The Reign of Elizabeth I.* London: Macmillan, 1984; Athens: University of Georgia Press, 1985. A scholarly collection of essays by such notable historians as G. R. Elton, Penry Williams, Patrick Collinson, J. D. Alsop, Norman Jones, and others. The interpretations on the impact of William Cecil on the reign and on English government are sympathetic.

Levine, Joseph M., ed. *Elizabeth I.* Englewood Cliffs, N.J.: Prentice-Hall, 1969. This book consists of excerpts from both primary and secondary sources. Cecil's personal relationship with Elizabeth is highlighted and her growing dependence on Cecil is documented.

Lockyer, Roger. *Tudor and Stuart Britain, 1471-1714.* London: Longman, and New York: St.

Martin's Press, 1961. In this authoritative study of the period, Cecil's substantive contributions as Elizabeth's adviser and as bureaucrat are applauded and documented.

MacCaffrey, Wallace. *The Shaping of the Elizabethan Regime*. Princeton, N.J.: Princeton University Press, 1968; London: Cape, 1969. Cecil's impact on English political history during the second half of the sixteenth century is considered throughout this important study. Cecil emerges as an efficient and durable administrator who was a master of court intrigue and factional politics.

Read, Conyers. *Mr. Secretary Cecil and Queen Elizabeth*. London: Cape, and New York: Knopf, 1955.

———. *Lord Burghley and Queen Elizabeth*. London: Cape, and New York: Knopf, 1960. This two-volume biography on Cecil constitutes the most scholarly and detailed study of Elizabeth's chief adviser. Cecil is viewed as the force of continuity within the regime—an able, intelligent, and loyal servant of his queen.

Rowse, A. L. *The England of Elizabeth*. New York: Macmillan, 1950; London: Macmillan, 1951. In this volume, Cecil is interpreted as Elizabeth's partner in running the government. While differences between them emerged on occasion, their mutual respect for each other prohibited such differences from escalating into major conflicts.

Youings, Joyce. *Sixteenth-Century England*. London and New York: Penguin, 1984. In this social history, Cecil is mentioned on several occasions. The general impression of Cecil is that of a political problem-solver rather than of an individual who addressed the underlying causes of the social and economic problems of the period.

William T. Walker

BENVENUTO CELLINI

Born: November 3, 1500; Florence
Died: February 13, 1571; Florence
Areas of Achievement: Art and literature
Contribution: Cellini is acknowledged as perhaps the finest goldsmith in Renaissance Italy. His sculpture, represented by his bronze *Perseus*, was also superb. He is, however, best known for his lively and spirited autobiography, which transmits his spirit and that of his age.

Early Life

Benvenuto Cellini was born in Florence at the beginning of the Cinquecento. He was the son of Giovanni Cellini, an architect and engineer, who was also a passionate amateur musician, and of Elisabetta Granacci, the daughter of a neighbor. Cellini describes his parents' marriage as a love match: Elisabetta married without a dowry. Benvenuto was born to them after some twenty years of marriage, during which time they had one daughter. Cellini's father dearly wished him to become a musician, a flutist, while Benvenuto himself wished to study art. This struggle, a friendly one, continued between the two for many years. When Benvenuto reached the age of fifteen, he apprenticed himself, against his father's will, as a goldsmith in the studio of Andrea di Sandro Marcone. He was not paid wages and so was not compelled to do much of the menial labor that fell to paid apprentices. He used his extra time to study drawing, a study he continued all of his life and one of the things that made him much more than a mere craftsman.

About a year into this apprenticeship, he became involved in a duel in support of his younger brother; the duel rapidly developed into a brawl. In this year, 1516, Benvenuto was banished from Florence for six months. He went to Siena and worked for a goldsmith there, until he was recalled to Florence by the Cardinal de'Medici at the elder Cellini's request (the Cellinis were Medici adherents through all the changes in Florentine government; Benvenuto continued this tradition, although his vigorous sense of *amour propre* meant that his relations with the great were always rather testy). Benvenuto was then sent by his father to study music in Bologna, but the youth also worked with a goldsmith there. He returned to Florence after several months and eventually made peace with his father on the art or music question.

Leaving for Rome at about age sixteen, Benvenuto ended up in Pisa for a year. While in Pisa, he worked as a goldsmith and studied the local antiquities. Returning to Florence, he studied the work of Michelangelo, whom he regarded as the greatest modern sculptor. Finally, in 1519, he did travel to Rome but returned, after two years, to Florence, from where in 1523 he had to flee under sentence of death for fighting.

Benvenuto fled to Rome and soon began to receive important commissions from the Bishop of Salamanca, Sigismondo Chigi, from his wife, Porzia, and from Pope Clement VII. At this time, he was artistically mature; he began to work for himself and not for other goldsmiths and established a shop of his own in Rome. What would be the pattern of his life had taken shape: a peripatetic habit, often set in motion of necessity, because of his terrible temper and tendency to violence; many important commissions; a great reputation for his work coupled with frequent disputes with his patrons; and much trouble with the law.

Life's Work

In Rome, Cellini's fine work in drawing, jewelry, and larger pieces such as serving plates and candelabras very soon caught the notice of rich and influential patrons. He was a musician, briefly, in Clement's orchestra; he did many drawings in the style of Michelangelo and Raphael; he made jewelry and set and estimated the value of jewels; he made cast and carved plate and ornamental silver; and he designed and struck medals and coinage. He was also drawn to military life during this period and participated in the defense of Rome in 1527, during the invasion of Italy by the Holy Roman Empire. He claimed to have shot the Constable of Bourbon and the Prince of Orange during the defense, and there is some evidence that his claims could be true. At this time, his sculptor's knowledge of structure and spatiality, translated into engineering, was useful in ordering the pope's artillery. Later he would design fortifications in Florence. (It was common for sculptors in this period to be called on to use their engineering skills to design weapons, fortifications, and buildings for their cities of residence.)

While in Rome, Cellini was often distracted from his art by his music and also by romantic dalliance. His ambition to excel in all branches of

goldsmithing, coinage, and sculpture also served to distract him from the relatively single-minded pursuit of one medium which was the norm then and now, for craftsmen. Most artists specialized in certain aspects of their art. Cellini was an endlessly ambitious and curious student of many arts and always was a leader in technical innovations in sculpture and goldsmithing.

After the invasion of Rome, Cellini left for Florence, intending to raise a company and become a captain under the famous condottiere Orazio Baglioni. On hearing this, Cellini's father sent him to Mantua so that he would not be called on to fulfill his obligation to Baglioni. Cellini went to Mantua, executed some small works for the duke there, quarreled with him, and returned to Florence, where he discovered that his father and sister Cosa had died of the plague. His brother and another sister remaining, he stayed in Florence until Clement declared war on the city and requested Cellini's presence in Rome.

In danger of being arrested as a traitor or spy because of these communications from Clement, Cellini traveled to Rome in 1529. He received at this time the commission from Clement for the famous morse (a clasp or button for a cope), now lost. Its design is recorded in three eighteenth century drawings in the British Museum: God the Father, in half relief is over a large diamond in the center of the morse, and the diamond is supported by three children. At this time also, Cellini began to make the steel dies for the pope's coinage and was appointed *maestro della stampe* at the papal mint.

After Clement's death in 1534, Cellini seized the opportunity of the resultant civic disorder to kill a rival goldsmith, Pompeo; he was absolved of this murder by the new pope Paul III, partly because of the support of influential friends such as Cardinal Francesco Cornaro and Cardinal Ippolito de'Medici, and partly because the new pope wished to retain him as master of the mint.

In 1536, Holy Roman Emperor Charles V arrived in Rome for his triumphal entry as conqueror of the city. Cellini had been commissioned by Paul to make the gifts for the emperor and empress: a crucifix in gold and a jeweled golden case for a richly illuminated Book of Hours. The works were not finished at the time of the arrival of the emperor (April 6, 1536), and the pope told Cellini to offer himself along with the gifts in order to see the work to its conclusion. By the time this was done, an enemy of Cellini (of which he always seemed to have a good supply) had slandered him to the pope, who became angry at Cellini, underpaid him for his work, and refused to send him with the book to the emperor, who had requested his presence.

At this point, Cellini decided to travel to France (he left April 1, 1537). He met at this time Ippolito I, Cardinal d'Este of Ferrara, who commissioned a basin and a jug from him; this friendship later proved to be his entrée with the King of France, Francis I. Becoming ill, Cellini returned to Rome. He was soon recalled to France by Francis through the Cardinal d'Este but, before he could leave, he was arrested by the pope and imprisoned in the Castle Sant'Angelo for allegedly stealing the papal jewels, entrusted to him at the time of the invasion of Rome in 1527. Pier' Luigi, the pope's natural son, was apparently behind this plot; Cellini writes that Pier' Luigi wanted to obtain Cellini's property. Francis requested Cellini of the pope but was refused.

During Cellini's long prison stay, which severely impaired his health, he survived poisoning attempts and political maneuvering; he was finally extracted from the papal clutches in 1539 by means of the deft diplomacy of the Cardinal d'Este, at the behest of Francis. Cellini brought out of prison a long poem he had composed there, which he reproduced in his autobiography, *La vita di Benvenuto Cellini (The Life of Benvenuto Cellini*, 1771), which was not published until 1728. The Cardinal d'Este brought Cellini back to France, where he arrived in 1540. Soon after his arrival, Cellini became dissatisfied with his treatment by the cardinal and tried to leave France on a pilgrimage to the Holy Sepulchre. This near loss made the cardinal more attentive and drew the attention of the king, who gave Cellini a large salary and a small castle in Paris in which to work. In 1542, Cellini was granted letters of naturalization by the king, and in 1543 he completed for the king the great saltcellar.

This saltcellar, one of Cellini's most famous works, has two figures in gold: a male representing the sea who holds a small ship (which holds the salt) and a facing female figure representing the land. Her hand rests on a small temple (which holds the pepper). The legs of the figures are intertwined as they halfway recline on an oval base. The piece is beautifully ornamented and enameled, and can be seen in any illustrated collection of Cellini's works. Cellini created many other works for Francis. Among these was a silver candlestick: a life-size figure of Jupiter, mounted on rollers, holding a (functioning) torch in one hand. Several pieces he did in France do survive: the *Nymph of Fontainebleau* (1545) and an accompanying satyr are among them. He began to make models for a monumental figure of Mars and accompanying smaller allegorical figures for a fountain at Fontainebleau, but this work never reached completion. Cellini had incurred the ire of the king's mistress, Madame d'Étampes; he apparently did not realize the extent of her power, especially in the realm of art commissions. She resented Cellini's obliviousness to her power and bitterly opposed his projects; her opposition was sufficient to prevent any new projects of his from coming to fruition.

Frustrated in his work, in 1545 Cellini asked leave to travel to Florence. The king denied him permission while the Cardinal d'Este told him he could leave; he left on what was meant to be a brief trip, but he never returned. In his autobiography, he often regrets his departure from France. In Florence, he visited Cosimo I de'Medici and described for him all that he had done for Francis. Cosimo asked Cellini to make, for the piazza of Florence, a statue of Perseus, symbolizing Cosimo's own victory over the Gorgon of republicanism. The *Perseus* would be in grand company—Michelangelo's *David* (1501-1504) and Donatello's *Judith and Holofernes* (1456-1457) already stood in the piazza. This was Cellini's chance to make his name as a sculptor in his home city, a city renowned for sculpture. He regarded the commission as an honor but received only about a third of the money he requested for the piece. The piece was finally finished and revealed fully to the public on April 27, 1554. It was greeted with great public acclaim; art criticism was a democratic activity in the Florence of those days. Cosimo, standing half-hidden at a window of the palace, heard the praise of the crowds. He apparently wanted to know the sentiments of the crowd before he expressed his own. The acclaim of the public allowed him to be equally pleased with the piece.

During his stay in Florence, Cellini had begun to work in marble. He restored an antique Ganymede for Cosimo and did a life-size Christ in white marble on a cross in black marble; this was to be for his own tomb (the piece is now in the Escorial). At this time, he induced Cosimo to have a competition among the Florentine sculptors for a beautiful block of marble, meant for a statue of Neptune, that had been quarried for Bandinelli (a hated rival of Cellini who had since died). Cellini did not get this commission, he thought, because of the opposition of Cosimo's wife, who thought him too haughty. At the end of his autobiography, he portrays himself as involved in rather acrimonious negotiations with Cosimo for making the *Neptune* from a different block of marble. This task was never accomplished.

Soon afterward, Cellini left Cosimo's service and established his own shop again, doing goldsmith's work for many clients. His life is poorly documented after this time, because it is not included in his autobiography and because he had fewer dealings with influential people. The writing of his autobiography is his most important work of this period, during which he also wrote his treatises on sculpture and on goldsmithing, *Trattati dell'oreficeria e della scultura* (1568; *The Treatises of Benvenuto Cellini on Goldsmithing and Sculpture*, 1898), which he published himself much later.

In 1557, in Florence, Cellini was condemned to four years in prison for sodomy, though this sentence was reduced to four years of confinement in his own house. During this time, he dictated his autobiography to a fourteen-year-old boy, while working at projects in his studio. In 1559, a version of his autobiography was completed, and Cellini gave it to the famed Benedetto Varchi, a Florentine writer and scholar, for criticism. Varchi liked the colloquial style and told Cellini to retain it. Cellini continued work on his autobiography until 1562. He died in Florence in 1571.

Summary

Benvenuto Cellini's life represents what is meant by the phrase Renaissance man. He was an immensely able, curious, and active practitioner of many civilized arts: drawing, music, sculpture, goldsmithing, swordplay, military strategy and architecture, conversation, and literature. His appearance was apparently pleasing, though no contemporary likenesses exist. He was social, well connected, and confident, and felt himself the equal of any by virtue of his skill. His directness and enthusiasm in *The Life of Benvenuto Cellini* seem to represent the spirit of his age.

As an artist, Cellini was both an excellent craftsman and a technically innovative and formally inventive sculptor. He could combine the Renaissance virtues of beautiful form and new technologies into works that can stand with the best of his day. It is unfortunate that, because of his temperament, the circumstances of his life, and the occasional uncooperativeness of patrons, his skill was not generally allowed the scope it needed. It is also unfortunate that, because many of his works were executed in precious metals, few of them survive, many having been melted down.

His greatest work, however, is not so much a work of art, perhaps, as of personality. His autobiography provides a most vivid picture of life in the Renaissance; it is undoubtedly tainted by exaggeration and boasting, but even these characteristics reveal aspects of an age of great energy. Cellini was an extremely subtle observer; through his description, figures that would otherwise be little more than names are revealed in detail. His own personality is revealed without caution and a thoroughly charming self-portrait of a fascinating man appears.

Bibliography

Avery, C. "Benvenuto Cellini's Bust of Bindo Altoviti." *The Connoisseur* 198 (May, 1978): 62-72. An unusual look at one of Cellini's portrait bronzes. Not very penetrating, but it does give some account of a mode of work in which the sculptor excelled and for which he is little remembered.

Cellini, Benvenuto. *The Life of Benvenuto Cellini.* Translated with an introduction by John Addington Symonds. London: Phaidon Press, and New York: Doubleday, 1960. This is the standard English translation of Cellini's autobiography. It is faulted on several counts, largely for its tendency to clean up and standardize Cellini's vigorous and colloquial Italian, yet it is coherent and very readable. Includes footnotes that put into context the many characters in Cellini's story.

———. *The Treatises of Benvenuto Cellini on Goldsmithing and Sculpture.* Translated by C. R. Ashby. London: Arnold, 1898; New York: Dover, 1967. This work by Cellini describes his beliefs about the trades to which he devoted his life.

Pope-Hennessy, John. *Cellini.* London: Macmillan, and New York: Abbeville Press, 1985. This magnificent work contains full photodocumentation of Cellini's surviving works and drawings, and the casts of some that have been lost. Pope-Hennessy has written an absorbing and readable essay on Cellini's life and works for the book. Contains much information not in Cellini's autobiography. His descriptions of Cellini as an accountant, record-keeper, and litigant are especially fascinating, revealing Cellini's nonswashbuckling side. The book is probably the best source on Cellini next to the autobiography and makes good use of many contemporary sources. Includes a good index, notes, and a bibliography.

Vasari, Giorgio. *Lives of the Painters, Sculptors, and Architects.* Translated with an introduction by William Gaunt. London: Dent, 1963. This four-volume work is a trove of biographical information on Renaissance artists, compiled and written by a fellow artist and contemporary. Although there is no separate entry on Cellini, he is mentioned in many of the other artists' biographies. Includes an index.

Ann Klefstad

GEORGE CHAPMAN

Born: c. 1559; Hitchin, Hertfordshire, England
Died: 1634; London, England
Areas of Achievement: Literature; theater and drama
Contribution: Best remembered because his translations of Homer's *Iliad* and *Odyssey* inspired John Keats to write a well-known sonnet, George Chapman also was a poet and dramatist whose tragedies reflected his classical background.

Early Life

George Chapman was born about 1559, probably in or near Hitchin, Hertfordshire, England, where his well-connected family had lived for decades. His father, Thomas Chapman, was a local landowner; his mother Joan was the daughter of George Nodes, sergeant of the buckhounds to King Henry VIII and later monarchs. On his mother's side, Chapman was related to Edward Grimeston, whose family served the English government in France and who wrote *A General Inventory of the History of France* (1607). The Grimeston relationship probably nurtured Chapman's interest in France and may explain why most of his tragedies are based on French history.

Little is known of his formal education. There is some evidence that he attended both Oxford and Cambridge Universities, but without taking a degree at either. A late seventeenth century account says that at Oxford, Chapman "was observed to be most excellent in the Latin and Greek tongues," but his contemporaries did not consider him much of a classicist. They claimed he accomplished his translations of Homer only with considerable dependence upon the works of continental Hellenists, and indeed his work is closer in style to the Elizabethan manner than to the Greek.

In about 1583, Chapman entered service in the household of Sir Ralph Sadler, a member of the Privy Council and chancellor of the Duchy of Lancaster, who had an estate in Hitchin. In the late 1580's or early 1590's, Chapman volunteered to fight in the Netherlands, and during this period he may have visited France. Upon his return to England in 1600, he was arrested and imprisoned for alleged nonpayment of an old debt, the first of his occasional financial problems. Prince Henry, whom he tutored and who became an early patron, promised Chapman a pension for the Homer translations, but the prince died in 1612, four years before the works were completed, so no money was forthcoming. Probably to escape debtors' prison, Chapman left London and his successful career as a prolific playwright. Retiring to Hitchin, he lived there in obscurity from 1614 to 1619, working on his translations.

Life's Work

Chapman's first published work was the long 1594 poem *The Shadow of the Night*, followed the next year by Ovid's *Banquet of Sense*. Aside from these pieces, his translations of Homer's epics, and the completion of Christopher Marlowe's unfinished poem *Hero and Leander* (1598), Chapman's major work was for the London stage. He became a dramatist at about the age of forty, at first writing for Philip Henslowe, the leading theater owner and producer of the time, but he soon left Henslowe's Admiral's Men and became an independent playwright. He wrote comedies and tragedies for other companies such as the Children of the Chapel (later called the Children of the Revels).

Many of his early plays for Henslowe are not extant, but what may have been his first work for stage does survive: *The Blind Beggar of Alexandria*, a 1596 comedy featuring a cynical quick-change artist who, living by his wits, assumes different identities and attains money, power, and sex through a complexity of intrigues. The comic hero may be a burlesque of Marlowe's Tamburlaine and other larger-than-life tragic figures. Chapman's second play, *An Humorous Day's Mirth*, done by Henslowe the following year, foreshadows Ben Jonson's comedies of humors in its focus upon universal human foibles. The 1599 *All Fools*, which balances romance and intrigue, was based on two plays by the ancient Roman playwright Terence; it has as its main character a young man who aims to make his fortune by tricking others but who in the end is gulled by one of his victims. The jealous husband subplot of *All Fools* would become a commonplace in Jacobean comedy. In his early years as playwright, Chapman must have written other comedies as well as tragedies that have not survived, because Francis Meres in *Palladis Tamia* (1598) labels him among the leading dramatists in both genres.

Though he wrote mainly tragedies after the turn of the century, Chapman continued to write comedies, including *The Gentleman Usher* (1606), *Mon-*

sieur D'Olive (1606), *May-Day* (1611), and *The Widow's Tears* (1612). The first of these is notable for its blending of serious and comic elements in the manner of Francis Beaumont and John Fletcher's tragicomedies, and it portends Chapman's increasingly sardonic attitude toward people's flaws. The last is the most serious of his comedies, presenting a society beset by chaos and corruption, quite the antithesis of the Homeric virtues Chapman celebrates in his translations, but similar to the world he presents in the tragedies. One other comedy warrants mention: The 1605 *Eastward Ho!*, a far-ranging portrait of London citizenry, on which Chapman collaborated with Ben Jonson and John Marston. Because King James I was offended by some incidental anti-Scottish satire in it, Chapman, Jonson, and Marston were imprisoned for a while.

The satire in his comedies foreshadows Chapman's didacticism in the tragedies, and he correctly has been described as the most deliberately didactic tragic playwright of his time. In the dedication to *The Revenge of Bussy D'Ambois* (c. 1610), Chapman wrote that "material instruction, elegant and sententious excitation to virtue, and deflection from her contrary [are] the soul, limbs, and limits of an authentic tragedy." Some critics believe that a key aspect of his development as a tragedian is the progressive exclusion from his plays of elements that did not advance his ethical goals.

His first tragedy, *Bussy D'Ambois*, is a melodrama of the Elizabethan Senecan type and probably was written about 1604, perhaps for the Children of the Chapel soon after Queen Elizabeth I died. One of at least four tragedies he wrote based on French history, it was often revived during Chapman's lifetime and later in the century, and he revised it at least once. Like his other tragic plays, it dramatizes the interaction between its hero and society, primarily his morality in conflict with social corruption.

The play is set in Paris in the late sixteenth century after a war has ended. Bussy D'Ambois, a soldier at loose ends, is introduced to the court by the king's brother, a Machiavellian opportunist who aims to usurp the Crown. Bussy is an anomaly at court, an apparently honorable man who eschews political intrigue and sexual hypocrisy, but while striving to remain an outsider, he gains the king's admiration and thus the disfavor of his sponsor, who sees his protégé as a threat. In spite of himself, Bussy becomes entangled in the political and romantic rivalries, kills rival courtiers, engages in adultery, and finally is murdered by assassins engaged by his rivals. Dying, he compares himself to a thunderbolt that "Look'd to have stuck and shook the firmament." These last words suggest the complexity of his character: courageous, self-reliant, unspoiled at the start, but also a braggart who, in a world without order and justice, cannot control his passions and falls victim to them. This first of Chapman's tragedies anticipates the pessimism that prevails in subsequent Jacobean drama, partly because of the difficulty the playwrights had in resolving the moral conflicts they confronted in their society.

The Revenge of Bussy D'Ambois, while not a sequel to the earlier play, represents a continuum. Its main character is Clermont, Bussy's brother, a stoical, virtuous, and self-sufficient man who believes he has a mandate to avenge his brother's death; instead of restoring natural law to the corrupt society, however, he ends up committing suicide when a friend and admirer dies. The static play is often labeled a "revenge tragedy" in the manner of Thomas Kyd's *The Spanish Tragedy* (c. 1587). It is mostly composed of moralizing, and the standard revenge-tragedy machinery appears only in the fifth act.

Chapman's other tragedies deserve only passing mention. *Caesar and Pompey* (c. 1605) is an undramatic collection of introspective homiletic speeches and has three main characters who are either too static or too inconsistently developed to be credible. *The Conspiracy and the Tragedy of Charles, Duke of Byron* (c. 1607), a play in two parts, is nothing more, according to one critic, than Chapman's rewriting of the Achilles story "in terms of Christian ethics and the Elizabethan stage" and shows the tragic danger of unbridled egotism. Chapman's last play, *The Tragedy of Chabot, Admiral of France* (c. 1621), is of interest because its main character resembles William Shakespeare's Coriolanus; both are military men who suffer from pride and try to deny their common humanity. Any merits the play has as a stage piece probably derive from James Shirley's revisions, done after Chapman's death.

Little is known about Chapman's later years. He no longer was active as a playwright and may have been too preoccupied by financial and legal difficulties to engage in literary work. He died in London in 1634 and was buried in St. Giles-in-the-Fields. Inigo Jones, the architect who designed masques (court entertainments) by Chapman, did a Roman-style monument.

Summary

Chapman's translations of the classics were his primary literary focus through much of his career, but they have been superseded by later versions and remain useful only because of his infusion of Elizabethan style and sensibility into the ancient works. His comic drama, respected though it was by contemporaries, is understandably forgotten, of interest only because the plays foreshadow humors comedy and other Jacobean stage motifs. Of his tragedies, only *Bussy D'Ambois* retains a place among the major non-Shakespearean plays of the period, primarily because of its hero. The tragedies as a whole merit attention, however, because they differ strikingly from others of the period, with the exception of the Roman plays of Samuel Daniel and Ben Jonson, which also examine the effect of greatness upon the political order, how a man's inner and outer selves often are at war, and how ethical and moral men sometimes betray their beliefs. Heroic ideals are central forces in Chapman's plots and characters, leading occasionally to major dramatic conflicts, but also slowing the pace of a play to that of a moral interlude or Senecan closet drama. Regrettably, Chapman the philosopher, classicist, and intellectual often got in the way of Chapman the playwright.

Bibliography

Ide, Richard S. *Possessed with Greatness: The Heroic Tragedies of Shakespeare and Chapman.* Chapel Hill: University of North Carolina Press, 1980. Shakespeare and Chapman, who shared an interest in the epic tradition and military heroism, individually wrote a number of tragedies with soldiers as protagonists: *Othello*, *Bussy D'Ambois*, *Antony and Cleopatra*, *The Conspiracy and Tragedy of Byron*, and *Coriolanus*. In each, the soldier's self-conception and aspirations lead him into fatal conflict with society.

MacLure, Millar. *George Chapman: A Critical Study.* Toronto: University of Toronto Press, 1966. Valuable for MacLure's discussion of Chapman's intellectual development, this book has a useful biographical section and offers balanced assessments of the poetry and plays. MacLure shows how Chapman's preoccupation with integrity affected his works, particularly the plays.

Rees, Ennis. *The Tragedies of George Chapman: Renaissance Ethics in Action.* Cambridge, Mass.: Harvard University Press, 1954. Rees suggests that Chapman's pattern in his heroic tragedies was to "juxtapose a reprehensible tragic hero . . . against the ethical code of Christian humanism" and to develop his plots and conflicts from that starting point.

Ribner, Irving. *Jacobean Tragedy: The Quest for Moral Order.* London: Methuen, 1962. Chapman is one of six playwrights Ribner considers in this examination of how playwrights in an irreligious age strove to find a moral order. The analyses of the tragedies are enlightening and useful for placing Chapman and his works in their moral and religious milieu.

Spivack, Charlotte. *George Chapman.* New York: Twayne, 1967. An admiring study accessible to the nonspecialist, the book begins with a biographical section and then reviews Chapman's literary work. Spivack considers him an important poet, a great playwright, and a consistent philosopher—a more favorable assessment than that of other critics.

Waddington, Raymond B. *The Mind's Empire: Myth and Form in George Chapman's Narrative Poems*. Baltimore: Johns Hopkins University Press, 1974. Distinguishing Chapman's verse from metaphysical poetry, to which it often is compared, Waddington sets forth what he sees as Chapman's poetic identity, grounded in classical philosophy and myth. He examines both the nondramatic verse and *Bussy D'Ambois*, which "exhibits a close thematic and mythic bond to the early poetry."

Gerald H. Strauss

CHARLES V

Born: February 24, 1500; Ghent, Burgundy
Died: September 21, 1558; Yuste, Spain
Areas of Achievement: Politics and religion
Contribution: Charles V initiated 150 years of Habsburg dynastic hegemony in Europe, stopped the Turkish advance in Europe, promoted reform, and expanded Spanish colonization in America.

Early Life

Charles V was born in Ghent, the ancient capital of Flanders and the heart of the Duchy of Burgundy. In 1477, Burgundy escheated to the Holy Roman Emperor, Maximilian I of the house of Habsburg. Maximilian's rivalry with the French over the Burgundian lands led to an alliance with Spain that resulted in the marriage of his son, Philip, to Joan, daughter of Ferdinand II and Isabella. Charles, as the eldest son of the couple, became Duke of Burgundy in 1506, King of Spain in 1516, and Holy Roman Emperor in 1519.

When Charles entered Spain in 1517, he could not speak the native language and was surrounded by a Flemish court that sought to monopolize high offices in the Spanish church and state. Physically, Charles appeared rather awkward, a lanky teenager with the jutting Habsburg jaw. After two years of ineffective kingship in Spain, Charles was elected Holy Roman Emperor to the dismay of many Spaniards, who believed that Charles would relegate their country to a peripheral province to be drained of wealth for imperial ambitions. Thus, almost immediately after Charles left Spain for his coronation, the Castilian cities initiated the Comunero Revolt (1520-1521) to force Charles's return and a reform of political administration.

The imperial election brought Charles problems outside Spain as well. Since the Investiture Conflict of the twelfth century, the powerful German princes, especially the seven imperial electors, had limited the emperor's power through the Germanic Diet, the major representative and administrative institution of the Holy Roman Empire. In addition, Germany's political weakness meant that its church was more directly under the control of the Papacy and, therefore, paid a disproportionate amount to the papal treasury. The desire of some of the princes to end papal taxation, obtain vast church lands, and maintain a decentralized political administration quickly merged with Martin Luther's call for a doctrinal reform of the Church following his attack on the sale of indulgences in Germany in 1517.

Charles held a diet of the Holy Roman Empire at Worms in 1521 to determine the fate of Martin Luther and his princely supporters. After listening to Luther speak, the emperor had the diet condemn the reformer with an imperial ban, though by that point most Protestant princes had left the meeting and, therefore, considered the ban unbinding upon them. Charles could not take action against the Protestants because of the Comunero Revolt and a simultaneous French attack in Italy that aimed to regain Naples from Spain.

Life's Work

In 1522, Charles returned to Spain and began his life's work, the forging of Habsburg hegemony in Europe based upon Spanish wealth and power. At Worms, he had received reports from Hernán Cortés about his conquest of Mexico. From that point, Charles's new empire in the Americas contributed its silver to the protection of his European inheritance. Cortés would be followed by Francisco Pizarro, conqueror of the Incas, and a host of lesser-known conquistadores. Charles reformed his court and from then on Spaniards predominated in high offices throughout his empire. His residence in Spain led Charles to appoint his brother Ferdinand as regent in Germany. Charles's decision to make Spain the center of his empire contributed to a resounding victory in Italy over the French king, Francis I, at the Battle of Pavia in 1525.

Charles could not enjoy his victory long, as a new and more dangerous enemy appeared to threaten his empire, Süleyman the Magnificent, Sultan of the Ottoman Empire. The Ottoman Turks mounted the greatest Muslim attack on Christendom since the eighth century. In 1529, Süleyman led a huge army into Austria (personal lands of the Habsburgs) and laid siege to Vienna; only inclement weather prevented the fall of the great city. Sensing an advantage, Francis renewed his attacks, forcing Charles to fight in Italy and Burgundy as well as southern Germany. The French and Turkish cooperation led to their formal alliance in 1535.

The Franco-Turkish War forced Charles to adopt a more conciliatory policy in regard to the religious conflict in Germany. (He was influenced as well by his own reform inclinations, which were similar to

those of Desiderius Erasmus, the famous Humanist and counselor to the emperor.) Charles sanctioned a series of diets in Germany to reach a settlement on the religious conflict in order to meet the Turkish threat. The diets of Speyer (1526) and Augsburg (1530) failed to achieve agreement, but they recognized the legal existence of the Lutheran religion pending the convocation of a general church council that Charles pledged to convene. In return, the German princes, Protestant and Catholic, rallied to Charles's war against the French and the Turks. As a result, the Turkish advance into Central Europe was finally halted during a decisive campaign in 1532.

Pope Clement VII sided with France during the war in order to avoid the emperor's pressure for a general council that might reduce the pope's authority. This proved disastrous as a combined German-Spanish army marched on Rome and sacked it in 1527. Clement agreed to call a general council, though it failed to materialize because of the renewal of war between Charles and Francis over Milan in 1535.

As the Franco-Turkish Alliance became operative during the war, Charles decided to deliver another blow against the Turks. In 1535, he organized a massive armada and captured Tunis, the base of Turkish power in the western Mediterranean. Following his victory, Charles triumphantly marched through Italy and appeared at the papal court, where he spoke in Spanish condemning the French for their alliance with the Turks and preventing the convocation of a general council. Charles finally secured a favorable peace with the Franco-Turkish Alliance in 1544 and gained the support of Francis for a general council. Charles then turned his attention toward resolving the religious conflict in Germany.

Pope Paul III recognized the urgent need to reform the Church but wanted to avoid any diminution of papal authority and any doctrinal compromise with Protestantism that might result from a general council. He sanctioned the Jesuit Order (founded by Saint Ignatius of Loyola), whose schools cleansed humanistic studies of paganism and used them to reinforce Catholic doctrine and improve the quality of the clergy. Having earned the reputation of a reformer, Paul agreed to call a general council in the city of Trent on terms that ensured papal domination of the council.

Charles tried to create a sympathetic atmosphere for a religious compromise at the pending council by convening the German Diet in Regensburg in 1541. Papal and Lutheran representatives agreed on several points, including a compromise position on faith and justification (double justification) but failed to settle issues surrounding the role of the Sacraments. In the end, even the agreement on double justification met with condemnation by the pope and Luther.

Charles abandoned his policy of peaceful negotiation in 1545 for three reasons: The Lutherans refused to participate in the Council of Trent because they correctly believed that it would be dominated by the pope; the French and Turks were no longer threatening; and Charles feared that the spread of Lutheranism among imperial electors would lead to the election of a Protestant emperor. Charles believed that with a victory over the League of Schmalkald, the alliance of Protestant princes, he could force the Lutheran princes to cooperate with the Council of Trent and reunite the Church.

The Schmalkaldic War, 1546-1547, ended with a dramatic victory for Charles at the Battle of Mühlberg. Yet the fruits of victory were spoiled at the

Council of Trent, where the pope, fearing an overpowerful emperor, rejected Charles's demands to move slowly, saving doctrinal issues for later discussion with Lutheran representatives. Instead, Paul enumerated and condemned Protestant doctrines and clarified traditional Catholic orthodoxy. The initial decrees of Trent meant that Charles would have to pacify the religious conflict in Germany himself.

The result was the Augsburg Interim of 1548, which provided for clerical marriage, communion in two kinds, and the half-Protestant doctrine of double justification. Otherwise, the interim reimposed the rites of the old religion. The interim applied only to German Protestants and was almost universally hated: The pope believed that it was a usurpation of his authority; the Lutherans viewed it as the reimposition of a foreign (Roman) church; and it failed to bring about the religious reunification of Germany sought by moderates. The breach was irreconcilable.

Even princes who were neutral during the Schmalkaldic War grew impatient with Charles's German policies. Political concerns loomed as large as religious ones. Charles had humiliated great princes with arrest and imprisonment. Following the war, his attempts to create an Imperial League and to make the imperial office hereditary threatened the princes' traditional predominance in the Holy Roman Empire. In order to regain their religious and political liberties, Protestant princes struck an alliance with the young French king Henry II in 1552. In return for helping to secure Protestant liberty, France gained the strategic fortress cities of Metz, Toul, and Verdun in the Rhineland; thus, the gates into Germany were opened to French influence. In order to defend his lands from French attack, Charles quickly made peace with the Protestant princes. The final religious settlement for Germany was the Peace of Augsburg of 1555, which stated that each prince in the Holy Roman Empire would determine whether his state would be Catholic or Lutheran. The settlement also ended Charles's attempts to create strong monarchical power in the Holy Roman Empire.

Charles did not sign the Peace of Augsburg, as he began divesting his authority in Germany to Ferdinand. He divided his lands between Ferdinand and his son Philip: Ferdinand was given Germany and the imperial title, while Philip received Spain, Naples, the American Colonies, Burgundy, and Milan. Following the territorial division, Charles abdicated the Spanish throne in 1556 and retired into a Spanish monastery, San Jeronimo de Yuste, where he studied religious works and contemplated his failure to maintain the religious unity of Christendom. He died two years later.

Summary

At Yuste, Charles V considered his reign a failure. Yet his moderate policy toward the Protestants prior to 1545 was essential for the defeat of the Turks and the reform of the Catholic Church. He led Spain into its Golden Age (1500-1650), when it became, for the first time in its history, the dominating political and cultural power in Europe. Philip II became the sword of the Counter-Reformation, while Spanish spirituality, exemplified by the Jesuits, was its soul. The Council of Trent represented a crucial turning point for Catholicism, as internal reform was essential for the reversal of Protestant gains in France, Poland, Hungary, and southern Germany.

If Charles was depressed for having lost part of Europe to Protestantism, he could take comfort in his opening of two new continents to Western influence. The colonial enterprise represented more a drain than a boon to Spain's resources prior to the 1530's. Given Charles's European commitments, he might have stalled the conquests rather than encouraged them. Mexico, Central America, and most of South America were all conquered during Charles's reign. He began the institutionalization of the colonial empire by creating the Council of the Indies and formulating the New Laws of 1541, which aimed to make the assimilation of Native Americans more humane.

Charles was both the end of one chapter in European history and the beginning of another. He was the last Holy Roman Emperor to dominate Europe and the last monarch to adhere to medieval ideals of chivalry. On the other hand, the division of his empire and development of Spain encouraged the emergence of the European state system and began the process of global Westernization that has continued into the twentieth century.

Bibliography

Brandi, Karl. *The Emperor Charles V: The Growth and Destiny of a Man and a World Empire.* Translated by C. V. Wedgwood. London: Cape, and New York: Knopf, 1939. This is a standard biography though somewhat slanted toward Charles's German concerns. Contains a detailed account of Charles as a classic Renaissance monarch who ruled each realm through traditional institutions but integrated them through dynastic policy. The thesis that Charles desired a world empire has long been contested.

Fernández-Santamaría, J. A. *The State, War, and Peace: Spanish Political Thought in the Renaissance, 1516-1559*. Cambridge and New York: Cambridge University Press, 1977. An excellent analysis of the impact Charles V's imperial policies had on the evolution of Spanish political thought. Argues that Charles's elevation of Spain led to a modern theory of state and empire. Also provides a detailed analysis of debates arising from American conquests over the legitimacy and extent of Spanish authority in the New World.

Fischer-Galati, Stephen A. *Ottoman Imperialism and German Protestantism, 1521-1555*. Cambridge, Mass.: Harvard University Press, 1959. A survey of Charles's relations with the Turks and how they influenced his policies toward the Lutheran princes. Argues that early Protestant success was dependent on Turkish advances. Temporary guarantees of security granted in 1526 and 1532 could not be revoked because of the continued pressure of the Franco-Turkish alliance.

Koenigsberger, Helmut B. "The Empire of Charles V in Europe." In *The New Cambridge Modern History*, vol. 2, *The Reformation, 1520-1559*. Edited by G. R. Elton. 2d ed. Cambridge and New York: Cambridge University Press, 1990. A good, short survey of political administration in Charles's heterogenous empire. This is the best place to begin a study of how Charles governed his empire: the type of institutions he had to work through in each area and the amount of revenue they contributed. This is also a good insight into Charles as the model Renaissance monarch, neither an absolutist nor a feudal monarch.

Lynch, John. *Spain Under the Hapsburgs*. Vol. 1, *Empire and Absolutism*. New York: Oxford University Press, 1964. A topical survey of Spain during the reigns of Charles and Philip. Particularly good on economic and social developments that contributed to the decline of Spain in the seventeenth century. Also demonstrates the impact of the American Colonies on the Spanish economy and Habsburg military campaigns. Good synthesis of a vast amount of secondary scholarship.

Wallerstein, Immanuel. *The Modern World-System: Capitalist Agriculture and the Origins of the European World-Economy in the Sixteenth Century*. New York: Academic Press, 1974. This book argues that Charles's empire and the impact of American silver contributed to the shift of Europe's economic axis from the Mediterranean to a Northwestern European core, which fostered the development of capitalist nation-states and an international division of labor based upon peripheral reaction to core demands. An intriguing argument but difficult reading for the novice in history and economics.

Daniel A. Crews

CHARLES THE BOLD

Born: November 10, 1433; Dijon, Burgundy
Died: January 5, 1477; near Nancy, Lorraine
Areas of Achievement: Government and politics
Contribution: Charles the Bold attempted to build the Duchy of Burgundy into a unified kingdom. He was considered a serious threat to the stability and centralization of the French state.

Early Life

Charles was born on November 10, 1433, at Dijon, the son of the immensely popular Duke of Burgundy, Philip the Good, and his third wife, Isabella of Portugal. Perhaps because Charles was the only son of three to survive, Isabella zealously protected the infant. She tended to his needs personally, refusing to relinquish him to wet nurses, as was the normal custom of the age. As a youth Charles received the education properly fitting for a future military leader and political ruler. Charles became a skilled horseman, having received his first lessons at the age of two on a specially constructed wooden horse. Charles avidly pursued knowledge of military affairs as well during his early years.

The future duke was familiar with Latin, although he was by no means a Humanist. He read Sallust, Julius Caesar, and the deeds of Alexander the Great, although he was more interested in their martial activities than their literary style. Charles had an aptitude for languages and could conduct himself in Italian and Flemish as well as in his native French. He had limited knowledge of English as well. In appearance, he was tall, fleshy, and well proportioned. His hair, eyes, and coloring were dark, favoring his mother over his father.

Charles was most revealing in his character traits. Like his mother, he was always suspicious, was slow to embrace friends, and seldom had confidantes. He possessed an enormous ego and reveled in excessive flattery. Above all, as his name, Charles the Bold, indicates, he was an impulsive and rash man, who followed courses unrelentingly without accepting or listening to prudent advice.

Life's Work

Charles became the Duke of Burgundy upon the death of his father in June, 1467. He inherited a large network of territories that consisted of Franche-Comté, Nevers, Bar, Luxembourg, the Netherlands, Artois, and Picardy. His domain lacked cultural, linguistic, and geographic unity. Charles governed his regional conglomeration through a complex feudal system of political, ecclesiastical, and military appointees. Much depended on personal loyalty to the duke on the part of his underlords and his subjects.

Charles was a product of his age and his culture. He believed in the feudal concepts of chivalry. Chivalric virtues emphasized military prowess, personal loyalty to one's overlord, courtesy to one's peers, generosity, and intellectual gentility. Charles and his court at Dijon reflected a chivalric society. Burgundian dukes patronized the outstanding artists of the fifteenth century, including Claus Sluter, Jan van Eyck, and Rogier van der Weyden. Their generosity as patrons was well-known. Tapestries depicting heroic feats of Alexander the Great, Caesar, and Charlemagne lined the walls of Dijon. Charles continued this benevolent tradition by supporting the historians Georges Chastellain, Olivier de La Marche, and Philippe de Commynes.

Unfortunately, early in his reign he learned that reality was less pleasant than the courtly activities at Dijon. Urban centers, in particular, had little time for chivalry. Their citizens preferred practicality, and they resented excessive taxation and deprivation of privileges. With an eye toward independence, the cities Ghent and Liège rebelled in 1468. Charles responded quickly and forcefully with an army that brought both cities to heel. Because he suspected that the citizens of Liège had conspired against him with the French King Louis XI, Charles planned ruthless punishment for the city. Louis, in the meantime, had come to Peronne, which was within the duke's lands, in October, 1468. The king hoped to negotiate with Charles. The French monarch found himself a virtual prisoner at the castle of Peronne after Charles had received what he regarded as evidence of the king's treacherous complicity with Liège. Louis was forced to watch the systematic pillage, carnage, and burning at Liège at the hands of the fully enraged duke. Louis witnessed Charles's impetuosity, a lesson he learned to put to good use in his future dealings with the duke.

Events at Peronne and Liège merely provided the necessary impetus for descent into formalized warfare between the ambitious Duke of Burgundy and his natural rival, the equally acquisitive Louis, correctly labeled the "universal spider." In order to outwit the monarch, his legal overlord, Charles activated his political design. In 1468, Charles was married to Margaret of York, the sister of Edward IV, the King of England. Through his marriage, Charles hoped to keep the English alienated from any potential alliance with the French. With the English federation under his control, the duke actively pursued his grander plan. Charles embarked upon his dream of creating an independent Burgundian kingdom as a buffer state between France and Germany. This conceptualized kingdom would extend from the North Sea to Switzerland.

Alsace and Lorraine, the heart of the old Carolingian Lotharingia, were to become the nucleus of the future Burgundian realm. In 1469, under the conditions of the Treaty of Omer, Charles happily received the mortgage of Upper Alsace from the impoverished and improvident Duke Sigismund of Austria-Tirol. The fifty thousand Rhenish florins loaned to Sigismund permitted Charles to take a firmer step toward further aggrandizement.

At his next juncture, he negotiated with Frederick III, the Holy Roman Emperor. These transactions were seriously conducted from 1469 to 1471. His goal was to secure the emperor's promise that Charles would receive the imperial coronation upon the abdication or the death of the old emperor. Part of the diplomatic arrangements ensured the hand of Mary of Burgundy, Charles's only child, to Frederick's son, Maximilian. A planned meeting between the emperor and the duke in November, 1473, at Trier was intended to seal the negotiations as far as Charles was concerned. Charles may have expected the coronation on November 18, 1473. The emperor delayed and then slipped away from Trier, almost secretly, on November 24, without crowning Charles and without finalizing the marital arrangements between Mary of Burgundy and Maximilian.

Charles was disappointed, and gravely so, but did not sulk for long. He proceeded to expand his territory in Alsace and then to secure Lorraine by force toward the end of 1475. His aggressive movements alarmed the Swiss, who were neighbors of Alsace and Lorraine. The "spider" king, Louis, managed to spin a web of intrigue around the oblivious Charles. Louis fed the fears of the Swiss and, simultaneously, managed to ally them with Sigismund of Austria-Tirol in 1474, after the transactions with the emperor and Charles had failed and before Charles's final aggression against Lorraine. Then Louis added René II of Lorraine to the federation. René was a willing cohort since his territory had been snatched by the duke in 1475.

Open warfare erupted between the German and Swiss league on one side and Charles the Bold on the other. Charles was soundly defeated at Grandson, Morat, and, finally, Nancy. The Battle of Nancy, fought in freezing cold on January 5, 1477, claimed Charles's life.

Charles's page later reported that the duke's horse had come to the edge of a ditch, stumbled, and unseated his rider. The duke died during the carnage of battle. His body was found several days later. It was an ironic and cruel trick of fate that the last of the proud and glorious house of Burgundy should come to an ignoble end, lying nude, stripped of clothing, weapons, and jewels, mutilated, and partly eaten by animals in a land that he coveted.

Summary

The political situation in Europe during the last half of the fifteenth century was in a process of rapid change. The balance of power between the monarchs and their magnates teetered in a precarious manner. Both sides battled furiously for control within and outside geographical boundaries. Louis and Charles the Bold were locked in such a conflict.

Charles, in some ways, was a Janus-like figure. He idealized the chivalric virtues of military prowess and personal obligations. Yet he combined these with the Renaissance characteristics of fame and glory. He looked back to the Carolingian middle kingdom of Lotharingia with nostalgia as he tried to remold it into a new state. Yet he hoped that this new kingdom would balance the power between Germany and France. At the beginning of his reign, it seemed quite possible to political observers (including Louis) that Charles might very well succeed.

He reached his peak with the submission of Ghent and Liège. The acquisition of Alsace and Lorraine represented an anticlimax since rapid defeats in Switzerland and Lorraine caused the death of the duke and the collapse of the Burgundian state in 1477. Charles was to blame, in part. He often acted rashly and consistently refused to follow the advice of his seasoned advisers, a fact that writers such as Niccolò Machiavelli and even Desiderius Erasmus would find troubling.

Fortune turned against him as well. He had no sons. The male line, consequently, ended with Charles. His daughter, Mary, was married to Maximilian I, the German emperor's son, in 1477. While this seemed a prudent move at the time, Mary died five years later, and the entire Burgundian inheritance disappeared into the domain of either Germany or France.

Two significant historical developments resulted from Charles's career and his ambitions, neither of which was intentional. First, Charles provided the setting for the last stage of the Franco-Burgundian struggle with the monarch winning over the magnate. Centralization of France was completed with the fall of Burgundy. Second, a more remote event was the eventual independence of the Low Countries from German and French competition. The seeds of discontent were orignally sown during Charles's era but did not fully blossom until the seventeenth century, when the Netherlands attained the formal status of independence.

Bibliography

Calmette, Joseph. *The Golden Age of Burgundy: The Magnificent Dukes and Their Courts.* Translated by Doreen Weightman. London: Weidenfeld and Nicolson, 1962; New York: Norton, 1963. Places Charles in the environment of the age of Burgundian power. Calmette is the only historian to treat the Burgundian court within the context of its intellectual and artistic milieu.

Gunn, Steven. "Henry VII and Charles the Bold—Brothers Under the Skin?" *History Today* 46 (April, 1996): 26. The author explores the surprising similarities in the style of governance of Henry VII of England and Charles the Bold of Burgundy, including their attitudes toward war and taxation policies, and their priorities.

Kirk, John Foster. *History of Charles the Bold, Duke of Burgundy.* 3 vols. London: Murray, and Philadelphia: Lippincott, 1864-1868. A detailed and straightforward account of the life of Charles. Generous quotes from letters, reports, and treaties. Strictly conforms to the nineteenth century historiographical emphasis upon factual information. Would be most useful as a source for an in-depth study of the duke, even though its interpretation is dated.

Putnam, Ruth. *Charles the Bold, Last Duke of Burgundy, 1433-1477.* New York: Putnam, 1908. Standard biography that is part of a larger series dealing with heroic individuals. A lively account of the duke's life and an equally vivid portrayal of the mores of the fifteenth century. The author stresses the role of the individual as hero in history.

Vaughan, Richard. *Charles the Bold: The Last Valois Duke of Burgundy.* London and New York: Longman, 1973. An excellent interpretation of Charles and his complicated relationship with his lands. The author penetrates the political motives of Charles, Louis, and other major figures. Ample quotes from diaries, dispatches, histories, and letters. Contains a full and detailed bibliography.

———. "Chasing a Sphinx: Charles the Bold's Burgundy." *History Today* 37 (May, 1987): 24-29. A good, brief overview that points out the lack of cultural and linguistic unity that prevented Charles from making Burgundy a modern state.

Barbara M. Fahy

CLEMENT VII

Born: 1478; Florence
Died: September 25, 1534; Rome
Areas of Achievement: Church reform and religion
Contribution: While Clement's pontificate was marred with failures, especially with regard to halting the spread of the Protestant Reformation, he did manage to encourage reforms within the Catholic Church through newly established religious orders and did much to enrich the art treasures of the Vatican.

Early Life

Guilio de Medici, who would become Pope Clement VII, was born in 1478 in Florence, the illegitimate son of Giuliano de Medici. Giuliano was the brother of Lorenzo de Medici, ruler of the powerful city-state of Florence. Within a year of Guilio's birth, his father was killed by an assassin, and the boy was left in the care of his uncle Lorenzo. Lorenzo died when Guilio was only fourteen, and guardianship of the boy was then assumed by Lorenzo's second son, Giovanni, himself only three years older than his cousin Guilio.

Giovanni became Pope Leo X in 1513. As pope, he quickly promoted his cousin Guilio to the rank of cardinal and also made him his personal vice-chancellor. Guilio proved an able administrator, serving his cousin Leo until the pope's death in 1521. He continued in this same capacity during the short reign of Leo's successor, Pope Adrian VI, who became pope in 1522 but who died in 1523.

Adrian's short papacy left the church facing another papal election in 1523. After nearly six weeks of deliberations among the cardinals, Guilio de Medici emerged from the Vatican's Sistine Chapel as Pope Clement VII on November 17, 1523. The election had been marred by deceit and trickery on the part of factions among the cardinals, including Clement himself. Subsequently, as Clement VII, Guilio de Medici was to face some of the most serious challenges yet to befall the Papacy—challenges that would end in the destruction of Rome and a weakening of papal influence.

Life's Work

Pope Clement VII began his papacy caught between the political ambitions of King Charles V of Spain (who was also emperor of the Holy Roman Empire) and King Francis I of France. Both kings wanted control of the duchy of Milan as well as other parts of northern Italy. Fearing he might end up under the complete domination of Charles, since the Spanish already ruled the entire southern part of Italy, Clement threw his support to Francis and entered into an alliance with the French in December, 1524. Siding with Francis meant a greater possibility of papal independence and the likelihood that France would leave Clement's home city of Florence under Medici rule. Upon hearing of Clement's alliance with Francis, Charles became furious and sought revenge.

On February 25, 1525, Charles's troops met the French army at Pavia. After a tremendous battle, the Spanish army emerged victorious, taking Francis I as prisoner. Upon receiving news of the victory, Clement, now fearing for the future of the Papacy, sought an alliance with Charles, which when finalized essentially placed all of Italy under Spanish protection.

In time, dissatisfied with the imperial rule, the duke of Milan, Francesco Sforza, conspired to overthrow his Spanish conquerors by bribing the commander of Charles's imperial troops, the marquis of Pescara. The plot called for offering Pescara the kingdom of Naples, already under Spain's control, in exchange for leading a revolt against Spanish forces in Italy. Clement was told of the plan and agreed to endorse it despite his previous alliance with Charles, but Pescara, loyal to the Spanish king, informed his sovereign of the plot and arrested Sforza. In the meantime, Charles, who knew of Clement's subversion, was content to leave the pope wondering what the future held for the Papacy.

After nearly a year, Charles agreed to release Francis on condition that the French king, under oath, renounce all claims to the Burgundy region of France as well as all northern Italian territories. Francis agreed and was released. Hoping to reunite in an alliance with the freed French king and thus regain more autonomy for the Papacy, Clement pursued Francis, offering to absolve him from breaking his oath to Charles on condition that Francis ally himself with the Papacy, Venice, and Milan against the Spanish. This alliance, the League of Cognac, was formed May 22, 1526.

The league, though, proved ineffective. Francis had neither the money to support the military needs of his allies nor the funds to ensure an adequate defense of Rome. Likewise, Clement's Italian allies, Milan and Venice, never delivered the support necessary to mount a strong opposition force. With little to stop the advancing forces under the command of Pompeo Colonna, a pro-Spanish cardinal, from attacking the Vatican, Clement, fearing for his life, fled the city to the safety of the papal Castle of Sant' Angelo.

Colonna's attack was followed by another attack by a united force of German mercenaries, known as landsknechts, and Spanish soldiers. The attackers made their way to the gates of Rome determined to take the city. In a panic, Clement attempted a hastened treaty with the Spanish ambassador to the Vatican, but it was too late. Angry because they had not been paid sufficiently for their services, the German mercenaries saw the spoils of war as a much more enticing reward than soldiers' pay and advanced on Rome, scaling its walls the morning of May 6, 1527. The sack of Rome had begun .

The siege and subsequent five-month occupation of Rome were chronicled in vivid detail. Captives were held for ransom, and those who could not pay were executed. Drunkenness and debauchery abounded. The German mercenaries, primarily Protestants, rejoiced in the open desecration of Catholic churches and religious objects. Nuns were raped, tortured, and killed. The Tiber River, which ran through the heart of Rome, was filled with the dead bodies of so many murdered victims that by mid-summer a plague had overrun what was left of the city. The inhabitants of Rome blamed the destruction of the city on Clement's clandestine treaties and broken promises.

With Rome in ruins and the papal treasury empty, Clement had no choice but to sign yet another treaty that subjugated the pope to the Spanish king's dominion. In return, Charles agreed to remove his troops from Rome on the conditions that the Vatican refrain from future political entanglements and plots against the Spanish sovereign and that Clement call for a Vatican council to discuss reforms within the church. Clement agreed, but in doing so, he relinquished much of the Vatican's political and religious influence to Charles.

The final crisis to face Clement was the matter of England's King Henry VIII's divorce from Catherine of Aragon. Catherine, the aunt of Charles V, had previously been married to Henry's elder brother, Arthur, who had died shortly after their marriage. According to Catherine, her marriage to Arthur had never been consummated. Henry argued that it had and asked for an annulment on that basis, although his real motive in seeking the annulment involved Catherine's inability to provide the king a male heir. The annulment controversy put Clement, once again, in the middle. If the pope granted Henry a divorce, he would certainly incur the wrath of Charles. On the other hand, Clement's uncle, as Pope Leo X, had previously praised Henry as "Defender of the Faith" for Henry's defense of the Church against the attacks of Martin Luther. The pope was thus faced with a difficult choice.

At first, Clement agreed to support Henry if the king could prove that Catherine's marriage to Henry's brother had been consummated. Then, within months, Clement reversed his offer before the king could substantiate his case. The pope's propensity for indecision and vacillation soured Henry's view of the Papacy, and he decisively put away Catherine to pursue his own resolution of the matter. In 1533, Henry installed Thomas Cranmer as archbishop of Canterbury. Cranmer subsequently proclaimed Henry's marriage to Catherine invalid, allowing Henry to marry his second wife, Ann Boleyn. The next year, Henry established himself as head of the Church of England. Henry's break with Rome further strengthened the progress of Protestantism and represented yet another loss for the Catholic Church.

Despite the criticism leveled against Clement VII's papacy, he might be better viewed as a victim of his times. Bred in an environment that was focused on the maintenance of political power, he knew that people and institutions could survive only by pursuing the advantages of power. As a Medici, Clement knew this particularly well; his family excelled in the art of political deal-making. While his indecisive character may have benefitted Protestantism to the detriment of the Catholic Church, the religious reforms that were to follow Clement's reign may well have come about only at the point at which the Catholic Church reached the crisis of the Protestant Reformation.

Summary

Despite its many failures, the papacy of Clement VII did produce some achievements. Clement's deep appreciation for the arts inspired him to devote considerable attention to enriching the interior of the Vatican. He commissioned Michelangelo to paint the famous *Last Judgment* in the Sistine Chapel, and he enabled the talented goldsmith and sculptor Benvenuto Cellini to begin his career in the papal court. Clement also encouraged church reforms, particularly by endorsing the establishment of reform-minded religious orders such as the Jesuits, the Capuchin Franciscans, the Theatine Fathers, and the Ursuline order of nuns.

On the other hand, Clement's propensity for indecision gave strength to the progress of the Protestant Reformation. Had Clement agreed, for example, in 1526 to call a reformation council to address the growing protests of the German states about conditions in the Catholic Church, he may have been able to halt the total loss of Germany and Scandinavia to Lutheranism. Likewise, his indecisiveness on the matter of Henry VIII's divorce from Catherine of Aragon left Henry enough time to deliberate his own decision to marry Ann Boleyn and subsequently to part with the Catholic Church.

Bibliography

Chamberlin, E. R. *The Bad Popes*. New York: Dorset Press, 1981. An informative discussion of seven medieval popes who reigned between 955 and 1534 and whose papacies were marred by elements of political intrigue and corruption.

John, Eric, ed. *The Popes: A Concise Biographical History*. Vol. 2. New York: Hawthorn Books, 1964. Briefly chronicles the lives of the popes. Volume 2 covers the Papacy from Boniface VIII (1294) through Paul VI (1963).

Knecht, R. J. *Renaissance Warrior and Patron: The Reign of Francis I*. Rev. ed. New York: Cambridge University Press, 1994. The most comprehensive coverage of Francis I and his times. Contains an excellent account of Francis' interactions with Pope Clement VII as well as the king's response to the Protestant Reformation.

McBrien, Richard P. *Lives of the Popes*. San Francisco: HarperCollins, 1997. Provides a complete listing of brief papal biographies. The appendices contain informative articles explaining how popes are elected and how they can be removed from office.

Maxwell-Stuart, P. G. *Chronicles of the Popes*. London: Thames and Hudson, 1997. A good reference source on the Papacy. Includes time lines, data files, and illustrations, many with sidebars that provide anecdotal information on the personalities and times of the popes.

Spitz, Lewis W. *The Protestant Reformation, 1517-1559*. New York: Harper, 1985. A comprehensive narrative by a noted historian about the causes and impacts of the Protestant Reformation. Provides a good discussion of the dynamics of the Reformation in England and Henry VIII's break from Rome.

Michael J. Garcia

JOHN COLET

Born: Probably 1466; London, England
Died: September 16, 1519; Sheen, Surrey, England
Areas of Achievement: Education, theology, and ecclesiastical reform
Contribution: As the founder of St. Paul's school and dean of St. Paul's Cathedral, Colet wrote, preached, and led other humanists in educational, social, and religious reform.

Early Life

Little is known of John Colet's early life. That he was born in London to a privileged position, probably in 1466, is clear. His father, Sir Henry Colet, a respected member of the Mercers' Company (an ancient guild of textile merchants of considerable prestige), was twice lord mayor of London. His mother, Christian Knevet, had important connections through marriage to some of the greatest families of England. John was the oldest of twenty-two children born of this union and the only one who reached maturity. No explanation of this astounding mortality exists. Contemporaries believed that the tragic family history may have accounted for the serious, almost austere, cast of Colet's personality and his frequent statements of preference for the celibate life.

Colet probably attended St. Anthony's Hospital, Threadneedle Street, for his early schooling. It was supported by the Mercers' Guild and would have been a likely choice for a boy of his social class. It is thought that he went to Oxford in 1483 and enrolled in Magdalen College. His work there would have been shaped by the tradition of the liberal arts. The trivium—grammar, rhetoric, and logic—required two and a half years of effort. The quadrivium—arithmetic, astronomy, geometry, and music, later broadened to include natural and moral philosophy, and metaphysics—required another five and a quarter years. The curriculum led to a master of arts degree.

In 1493, Colet left England for an extended period of study on the Continent, a sojourn in France, and a longer period in Italy. The Italian Renaissance, with its emphasis on the arts and the revival of the classical languages and literature, was at its height. In Florence, the young Colet met and studied with Marsilio Ficino, who directed the Platonic Academy in Florence. Greek, Platonic, and Neoplatonic studies filled these years. Colet returned to England in the spring of 1496. In the fall of that year, Colet gained international prominence among the coterie of humanists by a series of lectures on the Pauline epistles. Although he was not yet a deacon and had no credentials from theological courses, his use of humanist scholarship established his reputation and began his distinguished career. At the same time, he determined on his vocation, becoming deacon in December of 1497 and ordained a priest on March 25, 1498.

Life's Work

Colet remained at Oxford until 1504, where he completed his theological training. His theological and scriptural lectures were well attended and widely discussed. Yet no stipend was paid him. He received no academic honors or titles. He lived on the income from several ecclesiastical preferments which he had held since his youth. A long-standing custom of support for young men to pursue educational goals, benefices, and church offices were sometimes heaped together to bring in considerable revenue. The practice led to widespread abuse, and Colet came to be highly critical of the practice. He resigned all of his preferments but one (it was supported by family) when he was appointed dean of St. Paul's Cathedral. The revenue he had saved was expended for charitable enterprises.

The Oxford years were also important to Colet for the study of patristic literature, his continued work in Greek, and the many important contacts made with other humanists. Erasmus, whom he met in 1498, may have been his most important friend. The relationship continued to Colet's death, and Erasmus became Colet's first biographer and publicist.

In 1504, Colet's appointment as dean of St. Paul's Cathedral began the most public and the most productive part of his life. His first effort was reform at St. Paul's. He reviewed the discipline of the Chapter and Canons, those forty or so religious appointed to serve in various capacities at the cathedral. He cleared the nave of sleeping beggers and the ambulatories of businessmen plying their trade within the sacred precincts. He set the tone of dedication by the simplicity and the abstinence of his own life and household.

Colet also became a powerful and effective preacher, attacking abuses in the Church and speaking out on issues he considered immoral or menacing to the human condition. He preached

against war before the young king Henry VIII on Good Friday in 1513, as that monarch was about to embark on an expedition to France. Yet Colet retained the king's favor.

It was education, however, that was Colet's greatest concern. In 1509, he founded a new St. Paul's School, supported by his private fortune. It was to teach 153 boys, in the tradition of the "new learning." The curriculum was liberal and centered in sound training in the Latin and Greek languages. The hours were long and the demands many on the young scholars, their lives shaped by the dean's love of neatness, order, and simplicity. Taught by the best masters available, they were to fill the professions and the Church with a new leadership.

Colet authored a new Latin grammar with William Lily, his first headmaster and a notable grammarian. Generations of English schoolboys used it. Nothing was overlooked in Colet's plans for the school. While Colet knew many moments of satisfaction, his tenure as dean also brought problems. His denunciation of abuses in the Church incurred suspicion, and charges of heresy were brought against him. Exonerated, he continued as dean of the cathedral, admired by the circle of friends who shared his interests.

Late in his life, Colet seriously entertained the notion of retirement from the world to take up residence in a cloister. What caused him to change his plans is unknown. His last two years were also troubled by illness. In August of 1519, he made his will, disposing of his worldly goods by endowing boys who showed academic promise but were too poor to attend St. Paul's without assistance. Helpless, shortly after these efforts, he lingered on until September 16, 1519. At his death, he was buried in a simple sepulcher on the south side of the choir. William Lily wrote his equally simple epitaph.

In the seventeenth century, old St. Paul's was destroyed in the Great Fire of London, and the final resting place of the remains is unknown. A bust and several portraits have survived. Each of these depicts a serious, dignified face, sensitive and thoughtful, befitting one of the sixteenth century's most important Christian humanists.

Summary

John Colet, perhaps the most neglected member of a distinguished group of English humanists, became the subject of considerable scholarship in the nineteenth century. If one reads the correspondence of Erasmus, Thomas More, or the Flemish jurist Franciscus Cranevelt, the influence of Colet on his contemporaries is evident.

Part of a group, laymen and clerics, who sought the improvement of society, Colet believed that good education informed by Christian principles could lead to a better world. Characteristic of his circle, he recognized that the world was changing. The Church, he believed, must provide leadership in such a world. It must offer help to the poor and advice and admonition to monarchs, help to outlaw and curtail war, and enhance moral values in every class. It should provide assistance in material ways so that rehabilitation of the disadvantaged could be achieved.

Colet's sermons, tracts, and commentaries all manifest this optimistic view that with God's help, human beings can promote these lofty goods. A grammarian and linguist, he sought the purest interpretation of Scripture, although he did not believe in literal interpretation. His criticism of popular religious practices has led to a modern debate as to his loyalty to the Church of Rome which he served. His death in 1519 precludes an answer as to what might have been his role had he lived into the period of the Reformation. A moderate, his works did not manifest viewpoints at odds with historic doctrines but called for reform within the Church. His service to his peers and endless search for improved conditions of life place him high in that distinguished group known as the Christian humanists of the Northern Renaissance.

Bibliography

Adams, Robert P. *The Better Part of Valor*. Seattle: University of Washington Press, 1962. The author's stated purpose is to present the reader with a study of the men and ideas of the Renaissance period. Specifically deals with the thoughts and writings of Colet, More, Erasmus, and Juan Luis Viven on war and peace. Excellent source.

Colet, John. *John Colet's Letters to Radulphus*. Translated by J. H. Lupton. London: Bell, 1876. A short treatise on the Mosaic account of the Creation. Students or general readers will gain a sense of Colet's explanation of biblical texts.

Jayne, Sears. *John Colet and Marsilio Ficino*. Oxford: Oxford University Press, 1963; Westport, Conn.: Greenwood Press, 1980. A specialized study which ambitiously attempts to analyze the influence of the Italian scholar and philosopher on Colet's work. It is useful to the general reader in establishing the general background of Colet's work and lists a full bibliography of Colet's works.

Lupton, Joseph Hirst. *A Life of John Colet*. London: Bell, 1887; New York: Franklin, 1974. A sympathetic and searching biography by a nineteenth century headmaster of St. Paul's School, one of Colet's greatest admirers and scholars. Lupton discovered twenty-eight of Colet's writings. The fullest and most satisfactory biography despite its date.

Miles, Leland. *John Colet and the Platonic Tradition*. LaSalle, Ill.: Open Court, 1961; London: Allen and Unwin, 1962. One of a projected series of three volumes examining the relationship of the Platonic tradition and the work of Colet, More, and Erasmus; a somewhat easier work on an intellectual problem.

Seebohm, Frederick. *The Oxford Reformers*. London: Longman, 1897; New York: Dutton, 1914. An old work first written in 1867 and updated as a result of Lupton's work and discoveries, it retains much that is useful by describing the "fellow-work" of Colet, Erasmus, and More. Especially good in placing the writers in the framework of their times.

Sweeney, Patricia James. "Explorers with a Mission." *Momentum* 22 (November, 1991): 38-40. This article offers brief summaries of the achievements of several of Christopher Columbus's contemporaries, including Colet, Nicholas Cusa, Leonardo da Vinci, Michelangelo Buonarroti, Nicholas Copernicus, Johannes Gutenberg, Sir Thomas More, and Desiderius Erasmus; Sweeney urges modern Catholic educators to learn from these risk-takers and visionaries.

Anne R. Vizzier

CHRISTOPHER COLUMBUS

Born: Between August 25 and October 31, 1451; Genoa
Died: May 20, 1506; Valladolid, Spain
Areas of Achievement: Navigation and exploration
Contribution: Columbus' discovery of America was the first recorded transatlantic voyage. It led directly to Europe's colonial settlement and exploitation of the New World, and it altered the course of history.

Early Life

Christopher Columbus' father, Domenico, was a wool weaver and gatekeeper in Genoa. In 1470, he moved his family to nearby Savona, where he worked as an innkeeper. Christopher Columbus (in Spanish, Cristóbal Colón) was the eldest of five children, of whom Bartolomé and Diego played a large part in his life. Christopher had little formal education, having become an apprentice at sea at about age ten, not entirely surprising in the great port city of Genoa. His knowledge of mathematics, astronomy, and Latin came with experience.

Columbus' early days at sea brought him as far as Tunis and Chios, a Greek island that was then a Genoese possession. He next traveled to Ireland, Iceland, and Madeira, where, in 1478, he married Felipa Perestrello e Moniz of a noble Portuguese family with a hereditary title to govern Porto Santo, one of the Madeira islands. They had a son, Diego, and Columbus resided in Porto Santo for perhaps three years and worked as a seaman or merchant.

In the early 1480's, having sailed in either capacity to São Jorge da Mina on Africa's Gold Coast, then the southernmost point in the known world, Columbus gained experience of the south Atlantic. By 1484, his hair prematurely white, he had conceived the plan for a great *empresa de las Indias* (enterprise of the Indies). In that year, the Portuguese king John II rejected Columbus' idea of reaching Cathay, the islands of Japan, and India by sailing westward. Portugal was deeply committed to its search for an African route to India.

The concept of sailing westward was not new; indeed, it did not even originate with Columbus. A mathematician from Florence, Paolo Toscanelli dal Pozzo, had articulated this idea in a letter with a map sent to Prince Henry the Navigator in 1474. It was, moreover, widely accepted that the world was round. Columbus had researched his plan well. Perhaps he had seen Toscanelli's letter in the archives. Certainly he had read Marco Polo and Ptolemy. These books and Pierre d'Ailly's *Imago Mundi* (c. 1483; shape of the world), which Columbus had studied—he made hundreds of marginal notes in his copy—were authoritative at that time, though filled with errors tending to understate the size of the earth. The miscalculation of the journey's length by about two-thirds nearly destroyed Columbus' project.

By 1486, Portugal's repeated failure to cut through the Congo or to attain the southern tip of Africa allowed Columbus' plan a second hearing. In 1488, however, Bartolomeu Dias rounded the Cape of Good Hope, and Columbus was again disappointed in Portugal. Henry VII of England entertained the offer of Columbus' agent, brother Bartolomé. Yet it was Ferdinand II and Isabella of Spain who, after shunting his proposals into committee for four years, finally, in the flush of victory over Muslim Granada early in 1492, awarded him his chance. The Franciscan friar and astronomer Antonio de Merchena had helped him gain an interview with Isabella in about 1490, and court treasurer Luis de Santangel finally gained for Columbus Isabella's support by pledges of Jewish investment in the project.

During his pursuit of the Spanish royal court, Columbus had acquired in Córdoba a mistress, Beatriz Enríquez de Harana. She bore him a son, Fernando, who wrote an affectionate and thorough biography which is a chief source for modern knowledge about Columbus.

Life's Work

Fernando relates the exorbitant terms by which the Spanish monarchs agreed to grant Columbus 10 percent of all the gold or other goods acquired in the lands he might discover; he and his heirs were to hold the titles of Admiral of the Ocean Sea and viceroy of such lands. He was provided with two ships of the caravel type, the *Niña* and the *Pinta*, procured by Martín Alonso Pinzón of the port city of Palos; the round-bellied neotype *Santa Maria* was chartered from its owner by Columbus. For his efforts in raising money and crews numbering ninety men in all, mostly from Palos, and for his skill in commanding the *Pinta*, Pinzón would later claim a share in the credit and glory of Columbus' discoveries. The two smaller vessels were about fifty feet long, and the *Santa Maria* was about eighty-two feet long. They were equipped for any contingency with weapons, a translator of Hebrew and Arabic to deal with Marco Polo's Kublai Khan if found, and goods to sell for gold.

The first voyage of Columbus left Palos on August 3, 1492. After a stopover at Spain's Canary Islands, the tiny fleet began its ocean trek on September 6. Constantly favorable trade winds caused the sailors to despair at ever gaining a wind to aid their return home. The southwesterly flights of birds persuaded Columbus to accept Pinzón's advice to change his course to the southwest. A *Niña* lookout was the first to sight land. Columbus named the land San Salvador, landed, and, thinking he had reached an outlying island of Japan, claimed it for Spain.

Japan, and Cathay itself, he thought, must be only ten days distant. The search brought him to what are modern Haiti and the Dominican Republic, which together he named Hispaniola (little Spain). The native Arawaks were simple hunter-fishers who wore almost no clothes. Columbus was charmed by their courtesy. The native Cubans were equally friendly to their future enslavers. Arawak references to the *caniba* people (cannibals) and Cuban allusions to gold in the interior at Cubanacam further conjured images of Marco Polo's khan in Columbus' mind. Establishing the Hispaniola settlement of Navidad, the first in the New World, to organize gold-mining operations, Columbus departed for Spain before a favorable west wind, carrying six Arawak captives and news of the discovery of tobacco.

Having lost Pinzón with the *Pinta*, which departed on November 21, and the *Santa Maria*, on a reef on Christmas Day, 1492, Columbus had only the *Niña* for his return. He suspected Pinzón of trying to precede him to the khan, or to the sources of the gold, or back to Spain to claim the honor for his own discoveries. Therefore, their meeting at sea on January 6, 1493, precipitated a quarrel between the two captains. It was not until January 16 that the transatlantic return voyage commenced. Storms blew the *Niña* first into the Portuguese Azores on February 18 and then into Lisbon on March 9, causing King John II to charge Spain with illegal explorations of the African coast and to claim Columbus' discoveries for Portugal. This litigation was later settled in Spain's favor by the pope. Columbus' arrival in Palos on March 14 and subsequent reception by Ferdinand and Isabella at Barcelona at the end of April, accompanied by American natives in full ceremonial dress, was the admiral's greatest moment.

The royal announcement of a second voyage was met with numerous volunteers. A fleet of seventeen ships and fifteen hundred men departed Cádiz on September 25, 1493. On board were animals, seeds and plants, and tools for the establishment of a colony. Among Columbus' discoveries were Dominica Island (spied on Sunday), the Virgin Islands, and Puerto Rico. He found Navidad, however, destroyed by the natives and its settlers slain. Farther east on the north coast of what is now the Dominican Republic, he built the first European city in the New World, which he named Isabella. Leaving his brother Diego in charge there, he himself led the exploration of Cibao, the inland mountainous region of Hispaniola. There he founded the fortress settlement of Santo Tomás. He had still not seen the khan, but Columbus did discover Jamaica on May 5, 1494.

Convinced that Cuba was indeed the Asiatic mainland, Columbus forced his crew to sign an agreement to that effect. Back in Isabella, Columbus found the settlers angry and the natives in rebellion. Diego had been inadequate to the task of governing. Columbus' response was to ship five hundred natives to the slave market at Seville. Those who survived the journey, however, were returned to Hispaniola by the monarchs, who may have had in mind a more humane program of Christianization and agricultural exploitation for the colonies.

Columbus left Hispaniola again on March 10, 1496, leaving his brother Bartolomé to build a settlement at Santo Domingo. In the short space of four years since the coming of the Europeans, a flourishing Native American population had been decimated by exploitation, massacre, disease, and famine. Charges of misgovernment and cruelty greeted his arrival in Cádiz on June 11.

For Columbus' third voyage in six ships there were no volunteers. Indeed, the two-hundred-man crew had to be shanghaied or bribed by release from prison. Departure was from Sanlúcar, near Cádiz, on May 30, 1498. Sailing a more southerly route, the fleet was becalmed eight days in unbearable heat. On July 31, Columbus named three-peaked Trinidad, and the next day the fleet first spied the South American mainland. The first Europeans landed in the Paria Peninsula of Venezuela on August 5. Noting the fresh water flowing from the Orinoco River and the pearls worn by the wom-

Columbus, upon landing in the New World, claimed it in the name of Spain

en, Columbus believed that this was one of the four rivers of the Garden of Eden.

Arriving to find violence and syphilis in Hispaniola, Columbus was returned to reality. He only came to terms with his rebellious governor, Francisco Roldán, by means of the infamous *repartimiento*, or distribution of native serfs among the settlers as laborers and miners. On August 23, 1500, Francisco de Bobadilla arrived, sent by Ferdinand to replace Columbus as viceroy. In response to the admiral's resistance, Bobadilla sent Columbus and Diego back to Spain in chains.

Yet Columbus won the sympathy of the royal couple. On May 9, 1502, with brother Bartolomé and son Fernando, age thirteen, Columbus left on his "high voyage" (*alto viaje*) to find a way through Hispaniola to the Indian Ocean and restore his reputation. He was specifically prohibited, however, from landing at Hispaniola, where Nicolás de Ovando now governed with twenty-five hundred men.

Fernando records Ovando's flotilla making for Spain, and ignoring Columbus' warnings of a storm at sea; twenty of twenty-four ships were lost. Fernando also relates the discovery of Martinique in the Lesser Antilles, the exploration of the coasts of Nicaragua and Costa Rica, and the acquisition of gold from the natives of Honduras. The Isthmus of Panama blocked all access to an "Indian Ocean." Ovando could not have known that he was only forty miles from the Pacific Ocean.

Columbus ultimately fared little better. His entry into the unexplored western Caribbean Sea cost him more than a year at sea and the loss of his ships to storm and sea worms. Ovando waited another year before extricating the marooned men from Saint Ann's Bay in June, 1504. Sick in body and mind but rich with gold and new maps, Columbus reached Sanlúcar on November 7, 1504. The queen would die on November 26. He only saw a disinterested Ferdinand the following spring at Segovia.

Summary

Christopher Columbus spent his last years in vain demands for his rights and titles under the original royal charter and back pay for his men. Nevertheless, his share of the wealth of the "Indies" allowed him to live comfortably. His son Diego did retain the titles of admiral and viceroy after a long litigation. Columbus' library fell to Fernando, who bequeathed it, as the Biblioteca Colombina, to the Cathedral of Seville, where it remains. Columbus' body was eventually buried in the Cathedral of Santo Domingo (Hispaniola), but its specific site is uncertain.

He believed himself guided by Providence and biblical prophecy in all of his undertakings, a faith that made him intolerant of opposition and capable of great brutality in the name of God. His instincts at sea were regarded by his sailors as divine. He found winds and currents and reckoned directions as if inspired. His achievements were immense. European economic and political power would leave the Mediterranean lands and focus forever on the Americas.

Bibliography

Colón, Fernando. *The Life of Admiral Christopher Columbus by His Son, Ferdinand.* Translated by Benjamin Keen. London: Folio Society, and New Brunswick, N.J.: Rutgers University Press, 1959. An intimate and affectionate biography by Columbus' son. Fernando's book is the basis of all the extremely favorable accounts of Columbus' career.

Fuson, Robert H., trans. *The Log of Christopher Columbus.* Southampton: Ashford, and Camden, Maine: International Marine Publishing, 1987. This translation is based on the abstract of Columbus' log made by Bartolomé de Las Casas, with additions from his *Historia de las Indias* (1875-1876) and from Fernando Columbus' history of the Columbus family.

Landström, Björn. *Columbus.* London: Allen and Unwin, and New York: Macmillan, 1967. Ample illustrations, especially maps and ship designs, are extremely useful for illuminating the background, life, and voyages of Columbus. This is an interestingly written biography.

Madariaga, Salvador de. *Christopher Columbus: Being the Life of the Very Magnificent Lord Don Cristóbal Colón.* London: Hodder and Stoughton, 1939; New York: Macmillan, 1940. An engrossing biography of immense scholarship. Its extensive notes support a thorough discussion of debated Columbian issues. This book must be read by anyone serious about Columbus.

Morison, Samuel Eliot. *Admiral of the Ocean Sea.* London: Oxford University Press, and Boston: Little Brown, 1942. This is an eminently readable biography. Emphasizes Columbus as a seaman more than as an administrator. Does not stop at the "water's edge," as Morison claims other biographies do.

———. *The European Discovery of America: The Southern Voyages A.D. 1492-1616.* New York: Oxford University Press, 1974. Devotes eight chapters to Columbus, viewing him in the larger context of his southern voyages. This volume, by a lifelong student of Columbus, features photographs of coastlines as Columbus might have seen them. Includes forty-two pages of maps.

Russell, Jeffrey Burton. *Inventing the Flat Earth: Columbus and Modern Historians.* New York: Praeger, 1991. This book is Russell's attempt to set the record straight concerning the belief that the earth is flat—a belief still held by some today. He begins with a discussion of geographical knowledge in the Middle Ages and Renaissance, examining what Columbus and his contemporaries actually did believe, and then moves on to examine how the error was first propagated and how later historians followed the original mistakes.

Daniel C. Scavone

NICOLAUS COPERNICUS

Born: February 19, 1473; Thorn (Toruń), Prussia
Died: May 24, 1543; Frauenburg (Frombork), Prussia
Area of Achievement: Astronomy
Contribution: Copernicus discarded the Ptolemaic system and introduced the theory that the planets, including the earth, revolve around the sun. He defended the right of learned men to discuss scientific theories, even when they differ from currently accepted beliefs and contradict religious dogma.

Early Life

Nicolaus Copernicus' family origins and the commercial interests of his hometown, Thorn (modern Toruń), reflect the dual claim which Germans and Poles alike have upon him. His father, Mikołaj (Nicolaus) Kopernik, was an immigrant from Kraków who married a daughter of a prominent burgher family, Barbara Watzenrode, and, like other Thorn merchants, prospered from the exchange of Hanseatic goods for the wheat, cattle, and other produce of Poland. Thorn burghers were subjects of the Polish king, but Polish tradition allowed associated lands such as Prussia to govern themselves autonomously. Consequently, they made their political wishes felt through their representatives in the Prussian diet rather than directly to the king.

Had Mikołaj not died in 1483, his sons, Andreas and Nicolaus, would probably have entered upon careers in commerce. The guardianship, however, fell to their uncle, Bishop Lucas Watzenrode of Ermland (Warmia), who was best able to provide for them a future in church administration. A university education being indispensable to holding church offices, Bishop Lucas sent the boys to study first in Kraków, then in Italy. Nicolaus not only became a master of mathematics and astronomy but also acquired knowledge of medicine, painting, and Greek. Upon his return to Prussia in 1503, Nicolaus followed the contemporary practice of Latinizing his name, Copernicus, and became one of the canons in the Ermland cathedral chapter. As his uncle's physician, assistant, and heir apparent, Copernicus was present during inspection tours, provincial diets, and royal audiences. For several years he managed the diocese efficiently but without enthusiasm—his uncle was a hard taskmaster who lacked a sense of humor. Eventually, Copernicus announced that his interests in astronomy were greater than his ambition to become a bishop. From that time on, like most of the other canons, he lived according to clerical rules but remained a simple administrator who had no thought of becoming a priest.

The first of several portraits made during his lifetime show Copernicus to have been a dark, handsome man dressed in simple but elegant clothing, with nothing of either the cleric or the dandy about him. He was so utterly unremarkable in other respects that few anecdotes about him exist, leaving relatively little information about his personal life and intellectual development. Yet two facts stand out. First, Copernicus was a Humanist whose closest friends and associates were poets and polemists. His translation of an ancient author, Theophilactus Symocatta, from Greek into Latin was the first such publication in the Kingdom of Poland, and he dedicated the work to his humanistically trained uncle, Bishop Lucas. Later Copernicus used Humanist arguments to defend his astronomical theories. Second, Copernicus must be seen as a bureaucrat whose busy life made it difficult for him to make the observations of the heavens on which his mathematical calculations were based. At one time or another, he was a medical doctor, an astrologer, a mapmaker, an administrator of episcopal lands, a diplomat, a garrison commander in wartime, an economic theorist, an adviser to the Prussian diet, and a guardian to numerous nieces and nephews.

Life's Work

About 1507, Copernicus seems to have become persuaded that the Ptolemaic system (which asserted that the earth was the center of the universe) was incorrect. From that point on, he spent every spare moment trying to demonstrate the correctness of his insight that the sun was the center of the planetary movements (the solar system).

His first description of his theory, the *Commentariolus* (1514; English translation, 1939), circulated among his friends for many years. Eventually, it came to the ears of Cardinal Schönberg, who wrote a letter asking Copernicus to publish a fuller account. This letter was ultimately published in *De revolutionibus orbium coelestium* (1543; *On the Revolutions of the Celestial Spheres*, 1939) as a proof that high officials in the papal curia approved of scholars' discussing the existence of a solar sys-

tem. Copernicus made no answer. Instead, he asked his bishop to assign him light duties at some parish center where he could make his observations and concentrate on mathematical calculations. This request was difficult to grant, because Copernicus was known to be one of the more capable diocesan administrators.

For several years his work was interrupted by war. In 1520, the last grandmaster of the Teutonic Order, Albrecht of Brandenburg, made a final effort to reestablish his religious order as ruler of all Prussia. Copernicus led the defense of Allenstein (Olsztyn) and participated in the peace negotiations. In 1525, Albrecht, defeated at every turn, secularized the Teutonic Order in Prussia and became a Protestant vassal of the King of Poland. This brought about an immediate improvement of Albrecht's relationship to the rest of Prussia. Albrecht later called on Copernicus' services as physician, and, in 1551, he published a volume of Copernicus' astrological observations.

Copernicus labored for several years to restore order to the war-ravaged Ermland finances. He advised the Prussian diet to reform the monetary system, explaining that since everyone was hoarding good coins and paying taxes with debased coins, the income of the diet was being reduced significantly. Having expounded this early version of English financier Sir Thomas Gresham's law, he recommended that all coins be called in and new ones issued. The diet, aware that it did not have the bullion to mint a sufficient number of full-weight coins, took no action. There were other, more pressing problems: politics and religion.

The spread of Lutheran reforms through Poland was halted by royal action, but not before many cities and some prominent nobles had become Protestant. The ensuing era was filled with strident debate as fanatics on both sides denounced their opponents and demanded that all parties commit themselves to what they perceived as a struggle against ultimate evil. Copernicus sought to avoid this controversy but could not. When Ermland Bishop Johann Dantiscus sought to rid himself of all canons who gave any appearance of Protestant leanings, his eye fell on Copernicus, whose friends were corresponding with prominent Protestants and who, moreover, had as his housekeeper a young woman with children. Copernicus responded that his housekeeper was a widowed relative who could have no interest in a man as aged as he, but he argued in vain. He dismissed his housekeeper and watched as his friends went into exile. His health failing, Copernicus was indeed isolated from friends and family.

In 1539, a Lutheran mathematician at Wittenberg, Georg Joachim Rheticus, made a special journey to Frauenburg to visit Copernicus. Finding him ill and without prospect of publishing the manuscript he had completed at great labor, Rheticus extended his stay to three months so that he could personally copy the manuscript. He then arranged for the publication of *Narratio prima de libris revolutionum* (1540; *The First Account*, 1939) in Danzig and for the publication of the mathematical section in Nuremberg in 1542. Unable to supervise the printing of the theoretical section personally, Rheticus gave that task to another Protestant scholar, Andreas Osiander of Wittenberg.

Osiander was at a loss as to how to proceed. He saw that Copernicus had not been able to prove his case mathematically. Indeed, it would have been difficult for him to do so without inventing calculus (which was later created by Gottfreid Wilhelm Leibniz and Sir Isaac Newton independently of each other for the very purpose of calculating the elliptical orbits of the planets). Consequently, Copernicus had defended his ideas by demonstrating that Ptolemy's was not the only ancient theory describing the universe; indeed, there were ancient philosophers who believed that the sun was the center of a solar system. Moreover, he had argued that free inquiry into science was as necessary as freedom to write literature or produce fine art. In this respect, Copernicus was presenting his case to Renaissance Humanists, especially to the well-educated pope to whom he dedicated his book, as a test of free thought. Osiander, who perceived that the Catholic world was hostile to all innovations and was equally well aware of the debates raging in the Protestant world over biblical inerrancy, saw that Copernicus was treading on dangerous ground by suggesting an alternate view of the universe than the one presented in Scripture. Consequently, there was a real danger that the theory would be rejected entirely without having been read. To minimize that possibility, he wrote an unauthorized introduction which readers assumed was by Copernicus. This stated that the solar system was merely a hypothesis, a way of seeing the universe which avoided some of the problems of the Ptolemaic system. This led to much confusion and angered Copernicus considerably when he saw the page proofs. Copernicus, however, was too weak and ill to do anything about it. With a justice that is all too rare in this world, a copy of *On the Revolutions of the Celestial Spheres* arrived in time for him to know that his life's work was to survive.

Summary

Nicolaus Copernicus' theory was not immediately accepted, and not because of the controversies of the Reformation alone—although they made it dangerous for any scientist to suggest that the biblical descriptions of the heavens were incorrect. Copernicus' idealistic belief that God would create only perfectly circular planetary orbits made it impossible for him to prove his assertions mathematically. Nevertheless, Copernicus' theory was the only one to offer astronomers a way out of a Ptolemaic system of interlocking rings, which was becoming impossibly complex. His insights undermined the intellectual pretensions of astrology and set astronomy on a firm foundation of observation and mathematics.

Although Copernicus' defense of the freedom of inquiry was less important in the struggle against religious dogmatism than later demonstrations of the existence of the solar system, Copernicus became a symbol of the isolated and despised scientist who triumphs over all efforts by religious fundamentalists to silence him.

Bibliography

Armitage, Angus. *Sun, Stand Thou Still: The Life and Works of Copernicus, the Astronomer.* London: Sigma, and New York: Henry Schuman, 1947. The best-known of many biographies, its explanation of the conceptual problems facing Copernicus is easily followed by any sophisticated reader.

Beer, Arthur. *Copernicus Yesterday and Today.* Oxford and New York: Pergamon Press, 1975. A collection of useful essays which were delivered during the Copernicus celebration.

Copernicus, Nicolaus. *Three Copernican Treatises: The Commentariolus of Copernicus, The Letter Against Werner, The Narratio Prima of Rheticus.* Edited and translated by Edward Rosen. New York: Columbia University Press, 1939. This timeless translation of basic documents relating to Copernicus' achievement is accompanied by an extensive learned commentary. Rosen demonstrates that Copernicus put forward a "hypothesis" rather than a "theory" out of a fear of arousing opposition from religious fundamentalists rather than from any doubt that he was right.

Gingerich, Owen. *The Great Copernicus Chase and Other Adventures in Astronomical History.* Cambridge, Mass.: Sky Publishing, and Cambridge, England: Cambridge University Press, 1992. Harvard astronomer-historian Gingerich searches for all existing copies of Copernicus's monumental *De revolutionibus.* The title essay opens an engaging anthology of 36 episodes in astronomical history, including the origin of the zodiac, the first photograph of a nebula, and the discovery of the moons of Mars.

Kesten, Hermann. *Copernicus and His World.* New York: Roy Publishers, 1945. This literate biography deals with Copernicus' contemporaries as much as with the astronomer himself. Kesten presents Copernicus as a warrior in the contest between science and religion. He concludes with chapters on Bruno, Tycho Brahe, Kepler, and Galileo.

Rusinek, Michat. *The Land of Nicholas Copernicus.* Translated by A. T. Jordan. New York: Twayne, 1973. The text is relatively sparse, but the pictures and subtitles are unequaled in quality. The author traces the life of the astronomer through photographs of cities, castles, and personal possessions.

Stachiewicz, Wanda M. *Copernicus and the Changing World.* New York: Polish Institute, 1973. The four hundredth anniversary of Copernicus' birth brought forth a plethora of publications. This one is unique.

William Urban

FRANCISCO VÁSQUEZ DE CORONADO

Born: 1510; Salamanca, Spain
Died: September 22, 1554; Mexico City, Mexico
Areas of Achievement: Exploration and discovery
Contribution: As leader of the 1540-1542 expedition to the Seven Cities of Cíbola and Quivira, Coronado explored what became Arizona, Texas, New Mexico, Oklahoma, and Kansas and opened the Southwest to Spanish colonization and settlement.

Early Life

Francisco Vásquez de Coronado was born in 1510, in Salamanca, Spain, the second son of noble parents, Juan Vásquez de Coronado and Isabel de Luján (his proper family name was Vásquez, but Americans mistakenly call him Coronado). Only a few details abut his childhood are known. His father became governor (*corregidor*) of Burgos in 1512, an important royal appointment. In 1520, his father created an entailed estate, whereby the family property passed to Francisco's older brother Gonzalo. Although the other children received onetime settlements, with provision made for their education, they had to make their own way in life.

Coronado decided to seek his fortune in the New World. Handsome (perhaps fair complexioned, if a portrait of his brother Juan is any indication), generous, modest, and loyal, Coronado was a favorite at court and won the friendship and patronage of Antonio de Mendoza, the first viceroy of New Spain. Coronado sailed with Mendoza, arriving in Mexico City in November, 1535.

Mendoza's patronage was invaluable. In 1537, he chose Coronado to put down a rebellion of black miners. The following year, the viceroy named his young friend to a seat on the Mexico City council without even seeking royal approval for his appointment. Meanwhile, Coronado helped found the Brotherhood of the Blessed Sacrament for Charity, which provided alms for the needy and educated orphan girls. He was also married, to Beatriz de Estrada, whose father, Alonso de Estrada, had been New Spain's royal treasurer and was rumored to have been the illegitimate son of King Ferdinand. His wife's dowry included half of a large country estate. Coronado, the fortune seeker, had become a landed country gentleman. The marriage produced five children.

Again the viceroy called on Coronado. A serious Indian rebellion had convulsed the mining towns of New Galicia (northwestern Mexico), and Mendoza sent Coronado to suppress it and act as governor of the region. Coronado surmised that the Indians had risen because of horrible abuse and exploitation at the hands of the Spaniards.

Life's Work

News had begun to filter into Mexico about rich Indian cities lying far to the north. First had come Álvar Núñez Cabeza de Vaca, who had survived Panfilo de Narváez's disastrous expedition to Florida. He staggered into Mexico in 1536, with tantalizing but enigmatic stories about seven great and wealthy cities to the north. Mendoza sent Fray Marcos de Niza to verify Cabeza de Vaca's stories in early 1539. Coronado accompanied the friar on his way through New Galicia to the Seven Cities but then returned to his duties as governor. Fray Marcos returned in the fall, claiming to have actually visited Cíbola, the land of the Seven Cities. His report was more wondrous than Cabeza de Vaca's. Mendoza and Coronado began to plan an expedition to explore and conquer Cíbola. Speed was important. Charles V had commissioned Hernando de Soto, the new governor of Cuba and Florida, to explore north from Florida, and Hernán Cortés himself had returned from Spain, anxious to claim Cíbola as his own.

While men gathered in New Galicia for the expedition, Mendoza and Coronado dispatched another scouting party to Cíbola under Melchior Díaz, who was more knowledgeable about the northern frontier than any Spaniard. Before Díaz returned, a force of more than three hundred Spaniards was ready at Compostela, along with several priests, perhaps a thousand Indian allies, and about fifteen hundred horses and pack animals. Although subject to the viceregal government, the expedition was privately financed. Mendoza invested sixty thousand ducats in it, and Coronado, fifty thousand ducats from his wife's estate. Mendoza initially hoped to lead the foray himself but eventually named Coronado on January 6, 1540, to head it. Meanwhile, a small squadron under Hernando de Alarcón was to sail up the Gulf of California and support Coronado by sea, although Alarcón never did find Coronado.

The Coronado party set out from Compostela on February 23, 1540, without waiting for Díaz's report, but met the scout at Chiametla. He secretly

Coronado leads his expidition to find the mythological Seven Cities of Cibola

told Coronado that he had been to Cíbola and had found no gold, silver, or great cities. Rumors about the report upset the men, who were young adventurers and soldiers of fortune looking for gold, glory, and empire. Yet Fray Marcos reassured them that great riches awaited those with the courage to persevere.

After the force reached Culiacán, Coronado decided to push ahead quickly to Cíbola with a small party of eighty Spaniards, along with some Indian allies. The main group would follow later. During the long trek through Sonora and eastern Arizona, supplies dwindled and horses died. When Coronado reached Cíbola (Hawikuh) in July, 1540, his men were starving. Mendoza had ordered Coronado neither to abuse the Indians nor to make slaves of them. He thus tried to negotiate with the Zuni at Cíbola (there and elsewhere, most communication with the Indians was probably by sign language), but they ambushed his scouts and then attacked the whole party. Coronado besieged the fortified pueblo and was nearly killed. García López de Cárdenas, second in command, captured Cíbola but found none of the promised riches.

Recovered from his wounds, Coronado reassumed command. On July 15, 1540, he sent a small party under Pedro de Tovar to explore Tusayán to the northwest, home of the Hopi. It returned with reports of a great river and a land of giants somewhere beyond. In late August, Coronado dispatched López de Cárdenas with twenty-five horsemen to investigate: They discovered the Grand Canyon. For several days, three men tried to reach the Colorado River far below but managed to climb down only a third of the way. Disappointed but determined to press on, Coronado sent messengers, including a disgraced Fray Marcos, back to Mendoza.

Several Pueblo Indians arrived in Cíbola and invited the Spaniards to visit Cicúique (Pecos) and Tiguex, two hundred miles to the east near the headwaters of the Rio Grande. Coronado sent Hernando de Alvarado and twenty men to reconnoiter. They found pueblos of multistoried houses and friendly Indians but no riches. In late November of 1540, Coronado decided to move his force there for the winter, including the main expedition which had just arrived at Cíbola.

The Spaniards and Mexican Indians were not equipped for the harsh winter. Despite Coronado's attempts to treat the Indians humanely, the Spaniards forced one village of Indians to vacate their pueblo so that the intruders could live there. They took large amounts of food and winter clothing, and when a Spaniard molested an Indian woman and received no punishment, resentment smoldered.

Meanwhile, Alvarado found two Indian slaves, whom the Spaniards called Turk and Sopete. They told Alvarado about Quivira, a fabulously rich land farther to the east. Turk, whose fertile imagination concocted the type of reports the Spaniards wanted to hear, claimed that he had owned a gold bracelet from Quivira, which a Pueblo chieftain had stolen from him. This was the closest the expedition had come to gold, and Alvarado immediately imprisoned the chief.

Torture of the chief to locate the imaginary bracelet, together with the other abuses, transformed the previously friendly Indians into sullen and finally hostile hosts. The Tiguex War erupted. Coronado sent Cárdenas to deal with the rebellion, and he brutally suppressed it by March, 1541, mistakenly burning at the stake thirty or forty warriors who had surrendered during a truce at Arenal.

Coronado then decided to push on to Quivira, even though Sopete said that Turk's stories were lies. The expedition left for Quivira on April 23, 1541. The men found no gold, but their trek revealed huge buffalo herds and the plains Indians, including the Tejas tribe, which gave its name to Texas. With no topographical features to orient them on the flat plains, they piled buffalo chips to mark their trail. In the Texas panhandle, Coronado finally realized that Turk had deceived him. He placed Turk in chains, chose thirty-six men to continue on with Sopete as guide, and sent the remainder of the expedition back to Tiguex to wait. Sopete led them into central Kansas. There they found Quivira, land of the Wichita Indians, and final disappointment, for there was no gold or silver. In revenge, the Spaniards strangled Turk but left Sopete in his homeland as a reward for his service. Coronado then turned back toward Tiguex, arriving there in September.

A discouraged Coronado dispatched a report to the viceroy and spent the winter at Tiguex. On December 27, 1541, during a horse race, Coronado fell, and a horse stepped on his head, nearly killing him. Coronado never fully recovered. More somber and less vigorous, he consulted with his men and decided to return to Mexico. Three friars stayed to work among the Indians, however, and a few soldiers criticized him for not allowing them to remain and settle in the region. The expedition left Tiguex in April and straggled into Culiacán in June, 1542, where it disbanded.

Coronado's later years added nothing to the great explorer's fame. Despite Mendoza's disappointment over the expedition's failure, he sent Coronado back to New Galicia as governor. In 1543, Charles V ordered an inquiry into the conduct of the expedition, particularly its treatment of the Indians, and the following year, Coronado's performance as governor came under royal scrutiny. Absolved of the most serious charges, Coronado was nevertheless removed as governor by Mendoza, as much because of his poor health as for his misdeeds. Coronado thereafter lived in Mexico City, serving on the city council and administering his estates. He died on September 22, 1554.

Summary

As a leader, Coronado pales in comparison with someone such as Cortés. He owed his appointment to head the expedition to Mendoza; others, such as Melchior Díaz, were better qualified and more experienced. Perhaps his greatest weakness was his naïve acceptance of Fray Marcos' and Turk's lies. Still, Coronado endured the same hardships as his men, fought in the front ranks, and lost only about twenty men over the course of the entire expedition. Although a strict disciplinarian, he was not a tyrant but usually consulted with his men before making important decisions. Despite the Arenal atrocities, for which he was at least indirectly responsible, Coronado was remarkably humane in comparison with other Spaniards of his day.

Coronado's expedition was a major step in the exploration of North America. Although the Spaniards considered his mission a huge disappointment because it produced no gold, Coronado made important contributions by other standards. The trails he blazed, following the old Indian paths, served later Spanish parties as they moved north to settle and colonize the Southwest. He proved that the continent was much wider than previously thought and discovered the continental divide. His expedition brought back valuable information about the Indian tribes, wildlife, and geography of the region and added vast territories to the Spanish crown.

Bibliography

Aiton, Arthur S. *Antonio de Mendoza: First Viceroy of New Spain*. Durham, N.C.: Duke University Press, 1927. A scholarly biography of Coronado's patron. Discusses Coronado's expedition and provides valuable information on contemporary New Spain.

———. "The Later Career of Coronado." *American Historical Review* 30 (January, 1925): 298-304. By Mendoza's biographer, this article analyzes the period after the great expedition. Probably too critical of Coronado.

Bolton, Herbert Eugene. *Coronado on the Turquoise Trail: Knight of the Pueblos and Plains*. Albuquerque: University of New Mexico Press, 1949. A masterpiece based on a thorough use of archival records and the accounts left by its members. Bolton traveled the entire Coronado trail.

Day, A. Grove. *Coronado's Quest: The Discovery of the Southwestern States*. Berkeley: University of California Press, 1940. A readable, documented study of the expedition, written to commemorate its four hundredth anniversary. Contains several inaccuracies as to the location of Coronado's trail. Despite evidence to the contrary, Day argues that Fray Marcos never visited Cíbola.

Hammond, George Peter, and Agapito Rey, eds. *Narratives of the Coronado Expedition, 1540-1542*. Albuquerque: University of New Mexico Press, 1940. Extremely useful collection of English translations of reports, dispatches, and correspondence by Coronado, Mendoza, Alarcón, and others relating to Coronado's expedition and trail.

Hodge, Frederick W., ed. *Spanish Explorers in the Southern United States, 1528-1543*. New York: Scribner, 1907. Contains a translation of the account of Coronado's expedition written by Pedro de Castañeda, a participant, although he was not present at all the important events. Also contains a translation of Cabeza de Vaca's narrative.

Ortiz, Alfonso, ed. *Handbook of North American Indians*. Vol. 9. Washington, D.C.: Smithsonian Institution, 1979. Deals specifically with the Zuni, Pueblo, and Hopi Indians and contains historical, anthropological, and archaeological studies by experts in the various fields. Also contains an extensive bibliography.

Preston, Doug. "On the trail of Coronado and his Cities of Gold." *Smithsonian* vol. 20, no. 10 (January, 1990). Two "greenhorns" ride cross-country on the Spanish explorer's route of discovery in the Southwest.

Sauer, Carl O. *Sixteenth Century North America: The Land and the People as Seen by the Europeans*. Berkeley: University of California Press, 1971. The leading historical geographer of sixteenth century North America includes a chapter on the Coronado expedition, focusing on the environment rather than the man.

Winship, George Parker. *The Coronado Expedition, 1540-1542*. In *U.S. Bureau of American Ethnology, 1892-1893*, vol. 14, pt. 1, 329-613. Washington, D.C.: Government Printing Office, 1896. Contains a scholarly historical introduction to Coronado's expedition, Castañeda's narrative in both Spanish and English, translations of other relevant documents, a bibliography, maps, and illustrations.

Kendall W. Brown

CORREGGIO
Antonio Allegri

Born: c. 1489; Correggio, Duchy of Modena

Died: c. March 5, 1534; Correggio, Duchy of Modena

Area of Achievement: Art

Contribution: Correggio executed frescoes and paintings of religious and mythological subjects that demonstrate his skills as one of the greatest masters of the High Renaissance. Correggio's innovations in composition, expressiveness, and particularly in the illusionistic foreshortening of figures seen from below (*di sotto in su*) were to have a tremendous influence on later Baroque painters.

Early Life

Antonio Allegri was born in the town from which his name is taken, Correggio, Italy. The date of his birth to Pellegrino Allegri and Bernardina Ormani has been debated. The year was once thought to have been 1494 because artist-biographer Giorgio Vasari stated that Correggio died at the age of forty; however, most scholars now place his birth nearer to the year 1489. Correggio's uncle, Lorenzo Allegri, was a painter, under whom he may have studied. The apprenticeship is unclear, however, as are many details of his life because of the absence of documents. While the story that he was Bianchi Ferrari's pupil in Modena is plausible, Mantua is a more important place for Correggio's formative career. Some work there has recently been attributed to him, and the strong influence of both Andrea Mantegna and Lorenzo Costa on Correggio's work between 1510 and 1518 argues strongly for his presence in nearby Mantua around that time. Influences from Dosso Dossi in nearby Ferrara are also likely.

Yet by far the greatest formative influence on Correggio was Rome. The evidence is stylistic, based especially on paintings in the cupola of S. Giovanni Evangelista. There is a blend of antique classicism; Raphael's *Stanza della Segnatura* (1508-1511) and the Sistine Chapel ceiling by Michelangelo are evident. Generous borrowings from Leonardo da Vinci suggest that he may also have traveled to Milan.

While no known description of the artist exists, it has been proposed that the Saint Anthony of Padua in the *Madonna and Child with Saint Francis* in Dresden is a self-portrait. Half smiling, he appears there as having been graceful and decidedly shy or withdrawn, as Vasari described him.

Life's Work

With the varied impressions made upon Correggio, including Florentine cultural stimuli, one might assume Correggio to have been merely eclectic. Yet the opposite is true. His handling of figure, space, and color was accomplished with fluid, sensual harmony. Even the classical references are never dry or academic and appear with the graceful casualness that suggests intimate familiarity.

The earliest documentary evidence for a painting, the *Madonna of Saint Francis*, is the contract made on August 30, 1514. References to Leonardo da Vinci and Raphael may indicate that the Rome visit had already been made. Earlier than this, but firmly attributed to Correggio, are *Christ Taking Leave of His Mother* (1514-1517) and two pictures of the *Marriage of Saint Catherine* (1510-1514), which show the strong influence of Costa and Mantegna. Other works attributed to Correggio from the period prior to 1518 include *The Holy Family with the Infant Saint John the Baptist, Adoration of the Magi, Judith*, and *Nativity*. The atmospheric effects in landscape from the *Nativity* and the *Adoration of the Magi* suggest a Venetian origin by way of Ferrara; the latter also indicates familiarity with the protomannerism of Emilia such as is seen in the works of Dosso Dossi.

In 1518, Correggio was summoned to Parma to decorate the suite of Giovanna da Piacenza, abbess of the convent of S. Paolo. As no sightseers were admitted to the room for two centuries, the first detailed account of the work was not published until 1794. It is the artist's first major work in fresco. The largely decorative treatment of the vault, with a network of reeds carrying festoons of fruit pierced by ovals through which putti glance downward, is largely Mantegnesque. The bands of reeds terminate in illusionistic, monochromatic lunettes that reflect extensive familiarity with the antique. A figure of Diana moves across the great hood of the chimney, glowing with soft flesh tones. The total effect is rich, harmonious, and enchanting.

By 1520, Correggio was at work on the decoration of the church of S. Giovanni Evangelista in

Parma. The dome frescoes came first, then the half-dome of the apse, followed by frescoes on the underarches of the dome. He provided drawings for the nave frieze, executing a small portion of it which was finished by Francesco Mario Rondani and others. While he was in Parma, on November 3, 1522, Correggio signed a contract for the decoration of the choir and dome of the Cathedral of Parma. This year was the turning point in his career. Commissions for work began pouring in from various places. It is speculated that enough of the frescoes in S. Giovanni Evangelista were completed to have astonished Italy and created his fame.

The subject of the fresco in the dome of S. Giovanni Evangelista is the Vision of Saint John on Patmos, showing the risen Christ in the center surrounded by the glow of rich, luminous light. Cherubim surround this light, with the other apostles lining the base of the dome. There is a soaring effect, and illusionism, which was to impress later Baroque artists. It is evident that an audacious imagination was at work. The sculptural effect of the figures against the neutral background recall Raphael and Michelangelo. The atmospheric effect is the result of contact with Leonardo, the latest Venetians, and the swirling, last scenes by Michelangelo in the Sistine Chapel. The coloration and the sinuous soft form of Raphael's *Triumph of Galatea* (1511-1513) are present, but the overall effect is uniquely Correggio's, with his harmonious, fluid forms.

The ceiling painting in the Cathedral of Parma is a logical consequence of the preceding dome and can be seen as the culmination of Correggio's artistry and as his most imaginative and creative effort. The *Assumption of the Virgin* (1526-1530) is an exciting celestial vision with great illusionistic depth of space. It is filled with the fluid, energetic movements of frolicking angels on soft masses of clouds amid a golden, mysterious glow of light. Throughout there is a festive gladness and a sensual exaltation. The virtuosity of illusionism plus the intertwining and piling up of figures is a tour de force unequaled before the seventeenth century.

During the period of his work at Parma, Correggio executed many other single paintings, plus altarpieces and mythological scenes. He did two paintings for the private chapel of the Del Bono family around 1524. The new elements are to be present in the remainder of the artist's works. The two paintings, now in Parma's Galleria Nazionale, *The Deposition* and *The Martyrdom of Four Saints*, are both very emotional, exhibiting a bolder color, a stronger, more direct source of light, and the use of relative clarity to give attention to the focal points. In addition, there is a decided "mannerism," shown in the flattening of space, choice of color, and prominent use of hands for expression. Among the notable paintings executed during the early to mid-1520's are the *Madonna of Saint Jerome*, "La Notte," or *Adoration of the Shepherds*, with its brilliant illumination amid the darkness, and the *Holy Family with Saint Francis*.

Correggio executed several mythological and allegorical paintings for Federigo II Gonzaga, the Duke of Mantua, which are among the most delightful and popular of his works. These include the *School of Love* and its pendant, *Venus, Cupid, and Satyr*, both of which may have been executed in the 1520's. The four great *Loves of Jupiter* were done in the 1530's and a second series of *Loves of Jupiter* were under way when Correggio died. The *Danae, Leda, Io*, and *Ganymede* were given by Federigo to Holy Roman Emperor Charles V. All contain nudes executed with great subtlety and grace. The figures are monumental but softened by atmospheric shadows, sensual poses, and rich flesh tones.

Summary

The works attributed to Correggio constitute a prodigious oeuvre. Had he lived past his forty odd years, Correggio probably would have revolutionized art. As it is, his stature is only now coming to be appreciated. The illusionistic space of Correggio's domes, with its antecedents in Mantegna's ceiling in Mantua, masterfully anticipated the artists of Baroque decoration from the Carracci family and Guercino to Giovanni Lanfranco and Baciccia. The lessons of strength and drawing that Correggio learned from Raphael and Michelangelo were softened by the Venetian atmosphere and the shadows and smiles of Leonardo. In his own time, Parmigianino was profoundly influenced by Correggio when he worked by his side in Parma. Correggio in turn absorbed the lessons of the mannerists to a certain degree. The final outcome is a confusion about the exact position of Correggio's place in history. His art escapes easy labeling.

Correggio's abilities were to be greatly admired in the eighteenth century, the period of the discovery of his frescoes in San Paolo and the publication of documents by Girolamo Tiraboschi such as *Notizie de'pittori, scultori, incisori, e architetti natii degli stati del serenissimo duca di Modena*

(1786), as well as a history by Correggio's greatest admirer, Anton Raphael Mengs. Correggio's importance was eclipsed in the nineteenth century, and only recently have scholars seen his tremendous impact on artists from the later sixteenth and seventeenth centuries, from Baroccio, even Gian Lorenzo Bernini and the Carracci family, to a host of other lesser-known artists. Correggio evoked the true grandeur of Renaissance classicism but indicated a new direction that was profoundly to affect art for centuries.

Bibliography

The Age of Correggio and the Carracci: Emilian Painting of the Sixteenth and Seventeenth Centuries. Washington, D.C.: National Gallery of Art, 1986; Cambridge: Cambridge University Press, 1987. A beautifully produced catalog of more than two hundred Emilian paintings of the sixteenth and seventeenth centuries, organized and written by dozens of scholars for the exhibition appearing at the National Gallery of Art, Washington, the Metropolitan Museum of Art, New York, and the Pinacoteca Nazionale, Bologna. With beautiful illustrations, many in color, this is the most extensive treatment of the effects of Correggio on later sixteenth and seventeeth century art.

Ekserdjian, David. *Correggio*. New Haven, Conn.: Yale University Press, 1997. This book is the first full-scale chronological and critical account of the paintings and drawings of Correggio. Ekserdjian discusses Correggio's mythological, erotic, and religious paintings and looks closely at Correggio's drawings, which provide many interesting insights into the artist's creative process. The book's numerous color illustrations include recently cleaned frescoes in Parma and some previously unknown paintings and drawings that have re-emerged and are being published for the first time.

Corregio. *La 'opera completa del Correggio*. Edited by Augusta A. Quintavalle. Milan: Rizzoli Editore, 1970. With an introduction by Alberto Bevilacqua, this cursory study includes numerous illustrations and documentary material.

Gould, Cecil. *The Paintings of Correggio*. London: faber, and Ithaca, N.Y.: Cornell University Press, 1976. The most comprehensive, definitive, and up-to-date assessment of Correggio's paintings. It is well illustrated and includes documents and a helpful catalog of all surviving pictures including a discussion of attributions.

Longhi, Roberto. *Il Correggio e la Camera di San Paolo a Parma*. Genoa: Siglaeffe, 1956. Fundamental for the whole of Correggio's work as well as related matters of historiography.

Popham, Arthur E. *Correggio's Drawings*. London: Oxford University Press, 1957. A very valuable and well-illustrated treatment of the known drawings. Includes a discussion of drawings of questionable attribution.

Smyth, Carolyn. *Correggio's Frescoes in Parma Cathedral*. Princeton, N.J.: Princeton University Press, 1997. In the first book-length study in English of Correggio's depiction of the Virgin's assumption into heaven (painted in the cupola of the Duomo of Parma), Smyth counters negative criticism by taking into account the viewer's *in situ* experience of the frescoes. In so doing, she offers a new reading that explores the artist's deliberate use of figural perspective, the work's architectural and liturgical context, and the religious significance of its theme.

Vito Battaglia, Silvia de. *Correggio, Bibliografia*. Rome: Arti grafiche F. Lli Palombi, 1934. This standard work has collected all the documents and bibliographical references prior to 1934, and, while very reliable, it omits some references that are not art-historical.

Sharon Hill

HERNÁN CORTÉS

Born: 1485; Medellín, Extremadura, Spain

Died: December 2, 1547; Castilleja de la Cuesta, near Seville, Spain

Areas of Achievement: Exploration and the military

Contribution: Cortés skillfully led a small band of Spaniards and numerous Indian allies to the heart of the Aztec capital of Tenochtitlán (later Mexico City), and within two years he boldly conquered the powerful Aztec Empire. His most lasting contribution has been to western exploration and conquest of the New World.

Early Life

Hernán Cortés came from a Spanish region, Extremadura, where so many of the New World conquistadors originated. Although Cortés was born into a Spanish noble (Hidalgo) family, his parents—Martín Cortés de Monroy, an infantry captain, and Catalina Pizarro Altamirano—were of limited means. At the age of fourteen, Hernán was sent to school in Salamanca to prepare for a career in law. Cortés soon abandoned his studies and decided to follow in his father's footsteps and join the Spanish army, serving in Naples. In 1504, at the age of nineteen, hamstrung by what he perceived as limited possibilities in the Old World, the restless youth, like so many of his class, decided to board a ship bound for the Spanish Indies.

In many ways, the impressionable Cortés was a product of his times. Renaissance Spain was undergoing tremendous ferment during the last decades of the fifteenth century. For more than seven centuries, Spanish Catholics had fought an epic struggle against Islamic Moors called the *reconquista* (reconquest), and in 1492, under the recently unified leadership of Ferdinand of Aragon and Isabella of Castille, the Moors' final stronghold, Granada, fell. The *reconquista* markedly influenced succeeding generations of Iberians: It united Spain's divided kingdoms and regions into a strong nation-state with a powerful army; it rallied the country together under the banner of Catholicism—the young nation would embrace the faith with such religious fervor that it would take on the responsibility of defender of the Church throughout Europe and the New World; and it opened up economic possibilities for those Hidalgos who fought for the Crown and were rewarded for their efforts. Militarism, the rise of a Spanish national identity, the Catholic faith, and the seemingly unlimited potential for personal aggrandizement imbued succeeding generations of Hidalgos with a sense of commitment, purpose, and service to their Crown.

In the same year that Granada fell, Christopher Columbus discovered the New World, opening new military, religious, and economic possibilities for the expansion-minded Spanish state and for ambitious Hidalgos such as Cortés. Cortés secured a position as a notary on the island of Santo Domingo in the Caribbean and was given a small grant of Indians who provided labor and commodity tribute (*encomienda*). For six years, Cortés profited from his Indians, but once again he grew restless. In 1511, he joined Diego Velázquez's military conquest of Cuba, serving as a clerk to the treasurer. Rewarded by the conquistador Velázquez, who subsequently became governor of the island, Cortés was rewarded with another *encomienda* in Cuba and a government position. In Santiago de Baracoa, Cuba, Cortés attended to his bureaucratic duties, became a prominent local merchant, raised cattle, and had his *encomienda* Indians mine gold.

Life's Work

Just when it appeared that Cortés would settle down and tend to his thriving business concerns, reports began filtering back to Cuba from advance scouting expeditions of a fabulous Aztec Empire on the Caribbean mainland. In 1519, Governor Velázquez commissioned the thirty-four-year-old Cortés to lead an expedition to the Mexican mainland. As Cortés outfitted his expedition with men, ships, and provisions, Velázquez had second thoughts about Cortés' arrogant, pretentious manner. Fearing that he could not control his ambitious commander, Velázquez ordered the commission revoked. When Cortés learned that the governor planned to rescind his orders, he quickly set sail from Cuba on February 18, 1519, with 550 Spaniards, several Cuban Indians and black slaves, a few small cannons, sixteen horses, several mastiff dogs, and eleven small ships.

Cortés' two-year assault on the heavily populated Aztec Empire, against almost insurmountable odds, was one of the most formidable challenges of the age of exploration and conquest. Driven by the traits shared by all *reconquista* Hidalgos—religious zeal, dedication to the Crown, and a healthy lust for glory and gold—Cortés, both in his personal correspon-

The first view of the Mexican capitol of Tenochtitlan, now Mexico City, by Cortès and his son. Photo courtesy of the Institute of Texas Cultures

dence and in his riveting speeches to his men, evinced a single-minded obsession: to conquer the Aztecs or die trying. Chroniclers describe the conquistador as a man of average height, pale complexion, and a muscular frame. The standard that he carried into battle was particularly appropriate; fashioned of black velvet, embroidered with gold, with a red cross laced with blue-and-white flames, its motto was emblazoned in Latin: "Friends, let us follow the Cross; and under this sign, if we have faith, we shall conquer." From the moment the expedition landed off the coast of Yucatán until the final assault on the Aztec capital of Tenochtitlán in 1521, Cortés stayed true to that motto and never considered retreating or compromising.

Although the enemy enjoyed an overwhelming numerical superiority—the population of Tenochtitlán has been estimated at eighty thousand in 1519—Cortés was able to take advantage of a number of favorable factors. First, Cortés shrewdly perceived that many of the Indian subject provinces chafed under and bitterly resented Aztec rule. The Spanish invasion signified—to Indians such as the Tlaxcalans and later the Tarascans—a fortuitous opportunity to ally themselves with the foreign invaders, to overturn onerous Aztec tribute and to regain their independence. These subject populations not only provided Cortés with literally thousands of warriors but also complicated matters politically for the Aztec emperor Montezuma II. The emperor, who was coronated in 1503, had squelched serious rebellions throughout his reign. Yet, after more than a century of Aztec imperial rule, subject provinces who had provided commodity tribute and human sacrifice victims to the Aztecs on an unprecedented scale saw hope in an alliance with the Spaniards.

Cortés also benefited from the Aztecs' fatalistic religious vision. The Aztecs believed that the world had been destroyed and reborn by the gods on four separate occasions. Every fifty-two years, the cycle of destruction was at risk and the world might be destroyed. Cortés arrived in Mexico in the fateful fifty-second year (*ce atl*). Moreover, the Spanish at first were believed by the Indians to be gods, or at least, messengers of the gods. Native myth told of a light-skinned, bearded god, Quetzalcóatl, who believed in love, compassion, and mercy, and who forbade human sacrifice, practiced oral confession, baptism, and ascetic denial. This god, according to myth, had left the Valley of Mexico centuries before, vowing one day to return to reclaim his kingdom. The Christianity espoused by the Europeans almost surreally approximated the Quetzalcóatl cult. Montezuma, a devout philosophical and religious thinker in his own right, at times appeared almost mesmerized by the religious implications of the Spanish expedition.

Cortés did little to discourage the natives' religious uncertainties. The Spanish possessed the technological advantages of Spanish steel, muskets, crossbows, and armor. In addition, Cortés used psychological ploys to startle unsuspecting Aztec emissaries at propitious moments. From the deafening noise of the Spaniards' small cannons to the judicious use of the horses and menacing dogs—two animals which the Indians had never seen before—Cortés created an aura of invincibility around his troops that fortified his Indian allies, created indecision in the minds of the Aztec leadership, and bolstered the confidence of his soldiers.

Yet Cortés faced daunting odds. His expedition had lost its legal sanction from Velázquez, and he was perilously close to becoming an outlaw in the eyes of the Crown. Cortés, however, feigned ignorance of the revoked commission and founded a settlement on the coast of Mexico, La Villa Rica de la Vera Cruz (later Veracruz), claiming all the lands that he conquered for the King of Spain, Charles V. He shrewdly dispatched a ship to Spain with a letter to the king professing his loyalty to the Crown. Still, Cortés faced serious problems from Velázquez supporters in his midst.

Time and again on his climb up to Tenochtitlán, the Spanish commander demonstrated his uncanny ability to act decisively before the Aztecs and their allies could react. For example, at Cholula, the last major city on Cortés' route to the Aztec capital, the Spanish learned that they were about to be ambushed by an Aztec army. Cortés ordered a preemptive strike and massacred more than six thousand Indian warriors. (An Indian version of the conquest denies the ambush and characterizes Cortés' massacre as premeditated.) From that point on no serious attempts were made by the Aztecs to stop Cortés' advance on Tenochtitlán.

Another bold move was the decision to put Montezuma under house arrest while the Spanish stayed in the capital. As "guests" of the emperor Cortés and his troops could ensure that Montezuma was not organizing an uprising. The decision to rule through the emperor bought the Spanish valuable time.

When the Aztecs revolted on July 1, 1520 (called *la noche triste*—the sad night—by the Spanish), Cortés was forced to abandon Tenochtitlán. Bernal Díaz relates that 860 Spaniards died during the battle. Despite this overwhelming defeat, Cortés rallied his armed forces, convinced more than 100,000 native allies to join his cause, and launched a tactically brilliant land and naval invasion of Tenochtitlán less than a year later. Cortés' devotion to this cause was too much for the Indians, who by this time had been decimated by smallpox infection and were dying by the thousands in Tenochtitlán. On August 13, 1521, after fierce hand-to-hand combat in the capital, the last Aztec emperor, Cuauhtémoc, surrendered.

Cortés proved to be an able administrator of the colony, which he renamed New Spain. Charles V, facing troubles from nobles in Spain, was understandably reluctant to let conquistadors such as Cortés become too powerful. Royal officials replaced Cortés soon after the conquest, and Cortés returned to Spain to argue his case before the king. Although Cortés never became governor of New Spain, he was allowed to choose twenty-two towns of *encomienda* Indians (approximately twenty-three thousand Indians). Cortés chose the richest settlements in the colony. Moreover, he was named captain-general and awarded the title of Marqués del Valle de Oaxaca. While at the royal court, Cortés married the daughter of a count, further ingratiating himself with the Spanish aristocracy. He returned to New Spain in 1530 and lived there for ten years, where he introduced new European crops and products, looked for silver and gold mines, and encouraged exploration. Cortés' wealth and status made him a target of crown officials who distrusted his independent demeanor and feared his political contacts with the nobility in Spain. His last few years were spent in frustration in Spain. In 1547, he fell ill and died at his estate, Castilleja de la Cuesta, just outside Seville. According to his wishes his bones were moved to Mexico in 1556.

Summary

More than any other conquistador, Hernán Cortés embodied the characteristics of the group of fearless men who, imbued with the heady ideals of the *reconquista*, forged a massive Spanish Empire in the New World. Committed to service to the Crown, convinced that their cause was noble and just, comforted by the belief that they brought Christianity and civilization to barbarian peoples, and clearly motivated by material gain and glory, Cortés and his fellow conquistadors, at times ruthlessly and at times diplomatically, conquered the numerically superior Indians during the early sixteenth century. Unlike other conquistadors, however, Cortés had a strong commitment to the religious conversion of the natives. Moreover, he demonstrated himself to be an able and fair administrator in the first years after the conquest; again, a trait not shared by many conquerors. Although Cortés was denied the political post that he thought he deserved, he became one of the wealthiest men in the empire.

Interestingly, Cortés is today viewed unsympathetically in the land that he conquered. Ever since the Mexican Revolution (1911-1920), the pre-Columbian accomplishments of the Aztec, Maya, and Teotihuacán Indians have been lionized, while the "civilizing" efforts of Cortés and the Spanish have been lambasted by Mexican intellectuals. This view represents a complete turnabout for the historical legacy of the conquistadors, since prior to the revolution Spanish virtues were lauded while their defects were minimized. A black legend has been appropriated for Cortés as a symbol of all rapacious Spaniards. Postrevolutionary histories emphasize his ruthlessness, his defilement of Indian women, culture, and customs, and his single-minded obsession with the destruction of the Aztec Empire. Perhaps in the future a more balanced interpretation will prevail.

Bibliography

Almazan, Marco A. "Hernan Cortes: Virtu vs. Fortuna." *Journal of American Culture* 20 (summer 1997): 131. Almazan offers opinions on the mythical beliefs of the Mexicans concerning their culture, while focusing on the influence that Spanish conquistador Hernan Cortes had on the Mexicans. Information is provided on Cortes' background and on Mexican beliefs in general.

Cortés, Hernán. *Letters from Mexico*. Edited and translated by A. R. Pagden, with an introduction by J. H. Elliott. New York: Grossman, 1971; London: Oxford University Press, 1972. Self-serving letters written in the heat of battle by the conquistador, which detail conditions in Mexico during the conquest and give insight into the character of Cortés.

Díaz del Castillo, Bernal. *The True History of the Conquest of New Spain, 1517-1521*. Translated by Alfred Percival Maudslay, with an introduction by Irving Leonard. London: Haklugt, 1908; New York: Farrar Straus, 1966. A classic, riveting, first-person narrative of the conquest recollected by Díaz in his old age. Although Díaz believed that he was never given his just due—he was rewarded with a paltry *encomienda* in the hostile backlands of Guatemala—his account is relatively balanced. His descriptions of the Spanish entry to Tenochtitlán and the great Aztec market at Tlateloco are stunning.

Krauss, Clifford. "After 500 Years, Cortes' Girlfriend is Not Forgiven." *New York Times* 146 (March, 1997): A4. This article discusses La Malinche, the Indian mistress of Hernan Cortes, and the hostile feelings that still exist toward her in Mexico 500 years after her life. Krauss describes the house she lived in, the use of her name as an insult in Mexico, and her portrayal as the perpetrator of Mexico's "original sin."

León-Portilla, Miguel, ed. *The Broken Spears: The Aztec Account of the Conquest of Mexico*. Translated by Lysander Kemp. London: Constable, and Boston: Beacon Press, 1962. A compilation of Aztec and early missionary sources that offers a much-needed corrective to the Spanish versions of the conquest. Although these sympathetic "native" sources are as biased as the Spanish accounts they reject, this is an evocative portrayal of the Indian defeat. Some of the Aztec poetry included is powerful and moving and gives readers a sense of the psychological loss felt by the natives.

Padden, R. C. *The Hummingbird and the Hawk: Conquest and Sovereignty in the Valley of Mexico, 1503-1541*. Columbus: Ohio State University Press, 1967; London: Harper, 1970. A provocative account of the conquest that emphasizes Cortés' religious zeal and the fundamental importance of human sacrifice to the Aztec faith. Nowhere else in the literature are Cortés' religious motivations portrayed so prominently. Good bibliography of the secondary literature included.

Prescott, William H. *History of the Conquest of Mexico*. New York: Bantam Books, 1964; London: Dent, 1965. A standard mid-nineteenth century, secondary narrative of the conquest which relies heavily on Spanish chroniclers. Extraordinarily detailed account of the background, motivations, and battles of the conquest.

White, Jon M. *Cortés and the Downfall of the Aztec Empire: A Study in a Conflict of Cultures.* London: Hamilton, and New York: St. Martin's Press, 1971. A psychological and analytical portrait of Cortés and Montezuma that places both leaders in their religious and cultural milieu.

Allen Wells

MILES COVERDALE

Born: c. 1488; York, Yorkshire, England
Died: January 20, 1568; London, England
Area of Achievement: Religion
Contribution: The first translator of the complete and official Bible into English, Coverdale in the late Elizabethan era provided a link between the English Reformation and the first English Puritans.

Early Life

Miles Coverdale was born about 1488 in Yorkshire, England, probably in the city of York. Little is known about his family or about his early childhood years. He studied philosophy and theology at Cambridge, became a priest at Norwich in 1514 when he was twenty-six, and entered the convent of Augustinian friars at Cambridge. His friend John Bale said that he drank in good learning with a burning thirst.

No authentic portrait of Coverdale exists. One that has traditionally been accepted as a copy of an early sketch of Coverdale shows him as a grim-faced, austere, middle-aged Puritan with anxious brow and a sharply downturned mouth. His friends, however, described him as friendly and upright with a very gentle spirit. These friends were from all areas of society and opinion. Among them were a number of young men who met at the White Horse Inn in Cambridge to discuss the new Lutheran religious reform ideas. Many of England's earliest Protestants—Robert Barnes, Thomas Bilney, William Roy, George Joye, and John Frith—were in this group. Coverdale's friends also included Sir Thomas More, a reformer who later died as a martyr because he could not give up his allegiance to the Roman Catholic religion and Thomas Cromwell, a royal minister who became a powerful supporter of Coverdale.

In 1528, when Robert Barnes was arrested for preaching against the luxurious life-style of Cardinal Thomas Wolsey, the king's chief minister, Coverdale went to London to help Barnes prepare his defense. The charge was serious and Barnes was forced to recant his Protestant opinions in order to save his life. This experience affected Coverdale deeply. Shortly thereafter, he left the monastery to preach in the English countryside against the Mass, image worship, and confession to a priest. Forced to flee from England to avoid royal persecution, he joined William Tyndale in Hamburg in 1529 to help him translate the Old Testament. At the home of Margaret von Emersen, a well-to-do Lutheran widow, Coverdale and Tyndale spent six or seven months translating the first five books of the Bible. This edition of the Pentateuch was published in 1530 in Antwerp, where Coverdale, preparing for his life's work, then spent several years working as a proofreader for the printer Martin de Keyser.

Life's Work

In 1534, Coverdale published his first book, an English translation of a Latin paraphrase of the Psalms written by John van Kempen (Campensis). This book was followed in October, 1535, by Coverdale's English translation of the complete Bible—the first to appear anywhere. The merchant-printer Jacob van Meteren financed and printed this translation, which he had asked Coverdale to undertake.

The fate of this English Bible hung on political events of the time. As an orthodox Roman Catholic, King Henry VIII believed that ordinary people needed the help of the clergy to understand the Bible. By 1534, however, he had separated the English church from the Roman Catholic Church, divorced his first wife, Catherine of Aragon, and married Anne Boleyn, whose family was Protestant. Henry promised Anne to have the Bible translated into English and available in the churches. Because the English bishops declared Tyndale's and Coverdale's versions to be inaccurate and inadequate, the king asked Archbishop Thomas Cranmer to oversee a new translation.

Cranmer's first attempt to have the bishops translate the Bible themselves failed, and in 1538, Cromwell asked Coverdale to prepare a new official English Bible. Cromwell chose Coverdale as the most experienced translator of the time and the best scholar available. Coverdale used his own Bible published in Antwerp in 1535, Tyndale's New Testament and Pentateuch, and the new Matthew Bible translated by John Rogers as the basis for the new edition. He added a flattering dedication to King Henry VIII and omitted prologues and annotations. Cromwell ordered all bishops to have an English Bible conveniently located in each of their churches and to discourage no one from reading it.

King Henry licensed Coverdale and the printer Richard Grafton to provide this official Bible to be published in Paris, where better paper and type and

more skilled workmen were to be found. Henry asked and received for the project a Royal License from the French king. Even so, the printers in Paris were harassed, and in December, 1538, the French Inquisitor General halted the printing. Coverdale fled to England, and twenty-five completed Bibles were seized by French church officials. Coverdale and the English printers then exported the necessary type, printers, and paper to London, and in April, 1539, the Great Bible was finally distributed as the official edition to be used in all English churches.

Once again, English politics intervened. Anne Boleyn fell from favor, and Henry's Protestant wife Jane Seymour died in childbirth. The conservative bishops and Parliament issued the Six Articles in June, 1539, inaugurating a new wave of Protestant persecution. On July 28, 1540, Barnes was burned for his religious beliefs; on July 30, Cromwell himself was beheaded. Coverdale for the second time fled to Strasbourg in Germany with other English Protestants. Nevertheless, churches continued to be required to provide Bibles and by 1541, seven editions had been printed.

Shortly after leaving England, Coverdale married Elizabeth Macheson, whose sister had married Dr. Joannes Macchabaeus MacAlpinus, another religious exile, who was a cleric in the service of the King of Denmark and assisted with the translation of the Bible into Danish. In 1541 or 1542, Coverdale received his own doctor of divinity degree at Tübingen and, on the recommendation of Conrad Hubert, secretary of the great Protestant reformer Martin Bucer, he was named assistant minister and headmaster of the school at Bergzabern in the Rhineland. His assistance was a godsend to the head pastor, who wrote letters full of appreciation for Coverdale's piety, hard work, and scrupulous performance of his religious duties. Although Coverdale was shocked by the frivolous public dances of the townspeople and their irreverent behavior during divine services, he enjoyed his work. He begged money from friends to pay school fees for poor children and arranged for jobs in nearby churches and schools for fellow English exiles. Coverdale preferred exile with the people of God to living a life of compromise and hypocrisy in his native land. Meanwhile, in England in 1543, King Henry ordered all Bibles to be burned, and in 1546 Bishop Bonner burned Coverdale's books.

On March 26, 1548, several months after King Henry VIII had died and Edward VI had become king of England, Coverdale returned from exile. Edward's advisers revived Henry's early efforts toward reform and began to incorporate more of the ideas of Martin Luther and John Calvin. They recognized that Coverdale's goals were the same as theirs and named him to a post as royal chaplain. Serving also as almoner to the dowager queen, Catherine Parr, Henry's last wife, Coverdale wrote a dedication to a new English translation of Erasmus' Latin paraphrases of the Bible. When Queen Catherine died in September, 1548, Coverdale preached her funeral sermon.

In the early summer of 1549, Coverdale served as preacher to Lord John Russell on a military expedition to Devon and Cornwall to quell a rebellion against the new prayer book. When Russell had completed his task, Coverdale remained to pacify the people and return Protestant practice to the churches. Coverdale's loyalty and competence were rewarded by Northumberland in August, 1551, when Bishop John Veysey, whose sympathies were not with the Reformation, was ejected from office and Coverdale was appointed as the new bishop of Exeter. As bishop, Coverdale was charged with restoring property to Exeter, with enforcing Protestant practices in his churches, and with serving in the House of Lords. Coverdale and his wife were without question good and holy Christians, but Protestant supporters noted that the common people, still Roman Catholic at heart, would not accept him because he was a married man preaching the gospel. Despite this stubborn opposition, Coverdale continued to preach and carry out the duties of his office until Mary Tudor became queen in July, 1553, after Edward's death. Within a month after her accession to the throne, Coverdale was under house arrest, and in September, Veysey—now eighty-eight—was reinstated as Bishop of Exeter.

Mary Tudor, eldest daughter of Henry VIII and his first wife, Catherine of Aragon, did not make substantial changes in religion immediately. She did not ban the English Bible or order public burnings of it until 1556. Nevertheless, Coverdale had no doubts about her power or her intentions. Prepared to die for his faith, he was determined not to recant, go into exile again, or consent to do anything contrary to his beliefs in order to stay alive. He even added his name to a Protestant statement of belief written by twelve of his imprisoned brethren.

For more than a year, Coverdale remained under house arrest although not in the Tower. His wife's brother-in-law, the Reverend J. Macchabaeus MacAlpinus, enlisted the help of the King of Denmark, who wrote a series of letters to Queen Mary demanding Coverdale's release. Finally, in 1555, Mary issued Coverdale a passport. For the third time, Coverdale and his wife left England, this time for Denmark en route to the village of Bergzabern, where Coverdale spent the next two years teaching. His last years in exile were spent in Switzerland, first at Aarau and then in Geneva, where he stood as godfather to John Knox's son.

Queen Mary died in December, 1558, unable to restore her people's allegiance to the pope and unable to secure the throne with an heir. The following year, Coverdale, aged seventy-one, returned once again with his family to England.

In exile, Coverdale had become more puritanical in the practice of his religion. At the consecration of Archbishop Matthew Parker in 1559, when other returned Protestant clergy wore Anglican vestments, Coverdale insisted on wearing a plain black suit and hat. He refused to resume his place as Bishop of Exeter. It was not inability or timidity that kept him from the ministry, it was his age and his reluctance to participate in the rituals that were part of Queen Elizabeth's religious compromise. Finally in 1565, his friend the Bishop of London succeeded in getting him to accept a living at St. Magnus Church near London Bridge.

Coverdale preached at St. Magnus until Elizabeth ordered uniformity of practice among pastors—uniformity that included the dress they wore in the pulpit. Coverdale and several Puritan colleagues asked the queen to excuse them from wearing vestments. When the request was denied, Coverdale resigned his church. He continued to preach and to attract a following of Elizabethan Puritans who wanted less ritual and more Calvinism in their worship.

Coverdale died on January 20, 1568. His last sermon was preached in early January at the Church of the Holy Trinity in the Minories, a church which before the Reformation had been associated with the Augustinian friars—Coverdale's earliest religious home.

Summary

Miles Coverdale died protesting the royal religious policy, not violently but quietly, as he had lived most of his life. In contrast to other reformers of the period, Coverdale was moderate and accommodating. Because he was not shrill or dogmatic, he succeeded in getting royal approval for his Bible where Tyndale and others had failed. Coverdale's patient hard work, his modesty and overriding concern that all English people have immediate access to the Scriptures, disarmed even his most conservative critics. The omission of commentary, prologues, and annotations illustrates his faith in each person's ability to interpret the Bible.

Although Coverdale was less learned than Tyndale, he was more adept at writing smooth prose and poetry with an ear for the musical qualities of a sentence. Indeed, the Church of England had continued to use Coverdale's translations of the Psalms in the Psalter. Coverdale's English Bible was written for all people. Clear, graceful, free of Latinisms and learned jargon, it is a valuable heirloom of the English Reformation.

Bibliography

Bruce, F. F. *The English Bible: A History of Translations from the Earliest English Versions to the New English Bible*. London: Lutterworth Press, and New York: Oxford University Press, 1970. One of the most recent histories of Bible translations, it is easier to read than Westcott's study (see below) but less rich in stories and not as well documented. The focus is on literary comparison.

Clebsch, William A. *England's Earliest Protestants, 1520-1535.* New Haven, Conn.: Yale University Press, 1964. An excellent description of intellectual life in England as new Renaissance ideas about scholarship and religion seeped in before Henry VIII began to reform the church. Although Coverdale is seldom mentioned, this book is about people with whom he lived and worked.

Collinson, Patrick. *The Elizabethan Puritan Movement.* London: Cape, and Berkeley: University of California Press, 1967. Well-documented account of the radical Protestant Elizabethan church. Collinson includes interesting stories regarding acts of civil disobedience committed by sixteenth century Puritan clergy. Since Coverdale died just as the Puritans were beginning to voice their views, it is more valuable for the atmosphere of England at this time than for information about him.

Dickens, A. G. *The English Reformation.* 2d ed. London: Batsford, 1989; University Park: Pensylvania State University Press, 1991. A general survey of the English Reformation concentrating on its effect on ordinary men and women. Well written and documented, this work emphasizes religion, not politics.

———. *Thomas Cromwell and the English Reformation.* London: English Universities Press, and New York: Macmillan, 1959. One of several excellent short general works about the English Reformation and Cromwell's role in it. Discusses the relationship between Cromwell and Coverdale, and Cromwell's support for the Great Bible.

Mozley, James Frederick. *Coverdale and His Bibles.* London: Lutterworth Press, 1953. The standard biography. Although the focus is on Coverdale's writings, this book includes the most recent information about Coverdale's personal life. Presents Coverdale's best side.

———. *William Tyndale.* London: SPCK, and New York: Macmillan, 1937. An outdated and almost undocumented biography of the man who taught Coverdale his life's work. Tyndale's independence and dignity are compared to Coverdale's "overstrained humility," but this is a valuable corrective to Mozley's hagiography of Coverdale.

Westcott, Brooke Foss. *A General View of the History of the English Bible.* 3d ed. Revised by William Aldis Wright. London and New York: Macmillan, 1905. Although old, this well-documented and carefully annotated study is a valuable standard work. Based on letters and contemporary observations, it includes many stories about the early writers of the English Bible.

Loretta Turner Johnson

PÊRO DA COVILHÃ

Born: c. 1447; Covilhã, Beira, Portugal

Died: After 1526; Abyssinia (modern Ethiopia)

Areas of Achievement: Exploration, geography, and diplomacy

Contribution: Covilhã was the first Portuguese to visit India, one of the first Europeans to travel extensively in Arabia, the first to visit Sofala in southern Mozambique, and an unwilling resident of Abyssinia for at least thirty-three years. His report on his travels in India, Arabia, and along the coasts of India, Arabia, the Red Sea, and East Africa may have aided and influenced the course of Portuguese penetration of India and East Africa, and his residence in Abyssinia was critical in the opening of diplomatic relations between its emperor and Portugal.

Early Life

Pêro da Covilhã was born of humble parents in the town of Covilhã in Beira Baixa, about fifty miles from Coimbra and thirty from the Spanish border, around 1447. In his teens, Covilhã served the Duke of Medina-Sidonia in Spain, the head of the greatest of Castilian grandee families, the Guzmans. Their entourage was later to include both Christopher Columbus and Juan Ponce de León. While he was in Spain, Covilhã learned to fight and, more important, to rely on his wits; he also learned to speak both Spanish and Arabic fluently.

Covilhã returned to Portugal in 1474 and entered the service of Afonso V. In his years with Afonso, he gained distinction as a soldier in Afonso's campaign to enforce the claim of his wife, Juana, "La Beltraneja," daughter of Henry IV of Castile, to its throne against her aunt, Isabella the Catholic. Covilhã also visited France and Burgundy with the king in an unsuccessful attempt to gain aid from Louis XI and Charles the Bold.

When Afonso died in 1481, Covilhã continued in royal service under his successor, John II, holding the official position of squire of the royal guard. King John used Covilhã as a spy and diplomatic agent both in Spain, where there was a dangerous colony of rebellious Portuguese nobles living in exile, and in Morocco, where the Portuguese had captured Ceuta in 1415 and had been active ever since. On one of his trips to Morocco, Covilhã apparently used the purchase of horses as a cover for espionage and secret diplomacy.

Covilhã's proven resourcefulness, willingness to travel, courage, loyalty to the Crown, experience as a spy, and knowledge of Arabic were almost certainly the reasons why John and his successor, Manuel I, chose him for a mission that would take the rest of his life and secure for him a shadowy but significant place in the history of the Age of Exploration.

Life's Work

In May of 1487, John ordered Covilhã, about forty years old and recently married, and an Arabic-speaking Canarian, Afonso de Paiva, to carry out two exceedingly difficult missions: to gather information on India and the navigation and ports of the Indian Ocean, and to visit and establish contact with Prester John, the legendary Emperor of Abyssinia. Traveling by way of Valencia, Barcelona, Naples, and Rhodes, Covilhã and Paiva began their Eastern travels disguised as merchants buying honey in Alexandria to sell farther east. Since neither was ever challenged, it may be assumed that both Paiva and Covilhã had dark hair and complexions and spoke perfect Arabic. Both contracted fever in Alexandria and nearly died. The local authorities confiscated their cargo, anticipating their deaths, but indemnified them when they recovered, which allowed them to buy new trade goods. After this illness at the beginning of his travels, Covilhã was to remain healthy for the remainder of his life.

From Alexandria, they first went to Cairo and from there to Tor, on the Sinai Peninsula at the northern end of the Red Sea. From Tor they sailed down the Red Sea to Aden, where they parted company, agreeing to meet in Cairo in 1490. Paiva left for Abyssinia, but it is uncertain whether he ever reached the court of the emperor. The only fact known about his travels is that he died in Cairo, before Covilhã returned for their rendezvous.

Covilhã sailed from Aden to Cannanore on the west coast of India, disguised as an Arab merchant. From Cannanore, he went to Calicut, the major port for ships embarking westward with cinnamon, pepper, cloves, silk, pearls, gems, and other valuable Oriental products. From Calicut, he sailed, probably in early 1489, to Goa, then primarily a port for shipping horses. Impressed with the site, Covilhã apparently suggested it as a very promising center for Portuguese trade and occupation in his lost report to the Crown. Leaving India, he sailed to Hormuz, then the richest city on the Indian Ocean. From Hormuz, he continued his travels in the Indian Ocean, sailing down the west coast of Africa, arriving at Sofala in Mozambique at about the time that Bartolomeu Dias reached the Great Fish River on the east coast of South Africa. While on the African coast, Covilhã heard of the Isle of the Moon (Madagascar), which he also recommended as a potential Portuguese port of call or base. From Sofala, Covilhã returned to Cairo for his rendezvous with Paiva, stopping at Mozambique, Kilwa, Mombasa, and Malindi on the way.

In his travels, Covilhã had gathered priceless information, not only about trade, bases, and ports of call but also about the monsoons and their use by Arab and Chinese ships in the Indian Ocean. He had sailed from Aden to India on the summer monsoon of 1488 and had left for Hormuz and Arabia on the fall monsoon, shipping in both voyages as a passenger on merchant ships, which took advantage of the prevailing winds. This Arab practice of sailing with the monsoons was to become equally standard for Europeans sailing to India, starting with Vasco da Gama.

Arriving in Cairo in late 1490, Covilhã learned that Paiva had died and had left no account of his travels after they had parted company in Aden more than two years before. In Cairo, he met two Jewish agents sent by John II to find him, Rabbi Abraham of Beja and Joseph of Lamego, a shoemaker. They brought him new instructions from the Crown—that the mission to Abyssinia was essential and that Covilhã should finish it. Joseph of Lamego would take Covilhã's letters back to Portugal, but Covilhã and Rabbi Abraham would visit Hormuz; from Hormuz Covilhã would go to Abyssinia alone.

There is some doubt as to whether the Crown ever received the reports from Covilhã, which have never been found, although the majority of authorities believe that Lamego did return with them to Portugal and that copies were furnished to da Gama. Since many Portuguese records were destroyed in the Lisbon earthquake of 1755, it seems unlikely that they ever will be found. It is also possible that the reports carried by Lamego were lost in transit or even that Lamego never returned to Portugal. Even if the king never received any reports from Lamego, his successor, Manuel I, doubtless received some kind of oral report on Covilhã's eastern travels from Rabbi Abraham after his return from Hormuz.

Rabbi Abraham and Covilhã sailed together to Hormuz, where they parted company. Before he left for Abyssinia, Covilhã made a daring side trip; he visited Jidda, Mecca, and Medina. From Medina, he journeyed by caravan to Syria, hearing mass at the Convent of Saint Catherine on Mount Sinai. From Syria, he continued his travels, finally arriving at the court of the Emperor of Abyssinia in early 1494. There his travels ended.

Three successive neguses would not allow Covilhã to return to Portugal, although they sent an Abyssinian priest to Portugal as an envoy in 1510. Covilhã was granted lands and made an adviser and confidant of the royal family. He married an Abyssinian, by whom he had several children. He was not the only long-term honored captive. Other Europeans detained in Abyssinia included another Portuguese, two Catalans, a Basque, a German, a Greek, a Venetian, and eleven Genoese, mostly captives who had escaped from the Turks.

In 1520, Covilhã emerged from obscurity to play a crucial role in opening diplomatic relations between Portugal and Abyssinia. After many vicissitudes, a diplomatic expedition sent by the Portuguese from India led by Rodrigo de Lima arrived at the court of the reigning emperor, Lebna Dengel Dawit (David). Covilhã was able to assist the embassy through his knowledge of the language, country, and court. After a long stay in Abyssinia, the embassy was successful, finally returning to Portugal by way of Massawa and Goa in 1527. Covilhã did not return with the party but sent in his place a son, who died on the journey. Father Francisco Alvares, the chaplain of the embassy, published a memoir of the Lima mission, *Verdadeira informaúão das terras do Preste João das Indias* (1540; *The Prester John of the Indies: A True Relation of the Lands of the Prester John, Being the Narrative of the Portuguese Embassy to Ethiopia in 1520*, 1961), which is the principal source of both the mission and the career of Covilhã.

Nothing is known of the last years of Covilhã's life. He was still living when the Lima mission left Abyssinia in 1526, but he had died before the military expedition led by Estevão da Gama to assist the Abyssinians against an invasion by Islamic Somalis arrived in late 1541.

Summary

The effect of Pêro da Covilhã is extremely difficult to assess. No writings by him are known to exist, although the authenticity of his travels has never been questioned. If his accounts reached Lisbon in time to be of use to Vasco da Gama, then he is one of the most significant travelers in history; if not, then he is of secondary importance. His assistance to the Lima expedition is unquestionable, so it can safely be said that his place in history in helping to open diplomatic relations with the empire of Abyssinia is secure.

By any standard, Covilhã ranks with Marco Polo, Álvar Nuñez Cabeza de Vaca, and Sir Richard Burton as one of history's great wanderers. Traveling alone in hostile country—the Muslim world—he ran far greater risks than did Burton or Polo. Moreover, as a secret agent, Covilhã could anticipate only a pension and a title if he succeeded. These were ample rewards but hardly those which a successful sixteenth century conquistador or a nineteenth century explorer and travel writer might have received. Covilhã's travels seem an expression of a personal sense of duty to the Crown and of the spirit of adventure that was characteristic of the Renaissance.

Bibliography

Alvares, Francisco. *The Prester John of the Indies: A True Relation of the Lands of the Prester John, Being the Narrative of the Portuguese Embassy to Ethiopia in 1520.* Edited and revised by C. F. Beckingham and G. W. B. Huntingford. Translated by Lord Stanley of Alderley. Cambridge: Cambridge University Press, 1961. This is the fullest account of Covilhã and the source for most writings on him. Alvares, generally considered a very reliable source, came to know Covilhã well, and liked and admired him. Internal evidence indicates that the manuscript for *The Prester John of the Indies* was begun while Alvares was still in Abyssinia.

Diffie, Bailey W., and George D. Winius. *Foundations of the Portuguese Empire, 1415-1580.* Minneapolis: University of Minnesota Press, 1977. Diffie and Winius give an adequate description of Covilhã's travels, although they do not mention his trip to Mecca, Jidda, and Medina. They believe that news of Covilhã's travels did not reach Portugal before da Gama sailed, basing their judgment on errors that da Gama made in India, which a knowledge of Covilhã's travels would have prevented.

Hale, John R. *The Age of Exploration.* New York: Time, 1966. Like Diffie and Winius, Hale omits Covilhã's side trip to Mecca but believes that Covilhã's message to the king did arrive before da Gama left.

Landström, Björn. *The Quest for India.* London: Allen and Unwin, and New York: Doubleday, 1964. Translated by Michael Phillips and Hugh Stubbs. Contains one of the fullest accounts of Covilhã's Eastern travels but very little about his stay in Abyssinia and its significance.

Parry, J. H. *The Age of Reconnaissance.* London: Weidenfeld and Nicolson, and Cleveland: World Publishing, 1963. Parry gives a complete and sympathetic sketch of Covilhã's Asian travels but says virtually nothing about his stay in Abyssinia.

Penrose, Boies. *Travel and Discovery in the Renaissance, 1420-1620.* Cambridge, Mass.: Harvard University Press, 1955. Penrose writes an account much like Landstrom's—full on Covilhã's Asian travels, weaker on his Abyssinian years.

Prestage, Edgar. *The Portuguese Pioneers.* London: Black, and New York: Macmillan, 1933. Prestage's work is the fullest of all on Covilhã's African years and very good on his Asian travels. He also devotes more space to showing his significance than any other author except Beckingham.

Sanceau, Elaine. *The Land of Prester John: A Chronicle of Portuguese Exploration.* New York: Knopf, 1944. Sanceau provides what is both the fullest and most readable of all accounts of Covilhã's career. Writing for a popular audience, Sanceau says little on the significance of Covilhã's travels but compensates her readers with a very complete view of his life in Abyssinia.

John Gardner

LUCAS CRANACH, THE ELDER
Lucas Müller

Born: 1472; Kronach, Upper Franconia
Died: October 16, 1553; Weimar, Saxony
Area of Achievement: Art
Contribution: Cranach established an individual decorative style of paintings, drawings, and prints during his fifty-year career at the court of Wittenberg. A personal friend of Martin Luther, Cranach was one of the first German artists to incorporate elements of early Reformation theology into his pictures. His numerous examples of mythological subjects and portraits can be related to Humanist scholars at the University of Wittenberg and to erudite tastes of the Saxon court.

Early Life

Lucas Cranach, the Elder, probably received his first training as an artist from his father, Hans Müller, in Kronach. Cranach later changed his name to reflect the town of his birth. Older accounts of Lucas' life suggest that he might have accompanied Frederick III, Elector of Saxony, on a trip to the Holy Land in 1493. He is mentioned in Kronach documents between 1495 and 1498 and in Coburg in 1501.

Between this time and 1504, Cranach settled in Vienna, where he produced a series of distinctively dramatic paintings and woodcuts. The most notable of the Vienna paintings include the double betrothal portraits of the university rector Johannes Cuspinian and his wife, Anna (1502-1503), a *Saint Jerome in Penitence* (1502), and an asymmetrically composed *Crucifixion* (1503). Along with woodcuts, such as the *Agony in the Garden* (1502), these works show Cranach's flair for exaggerated gestures, emotive facial expressions, and bold draftsmanship. His interest in placing his figures in the ambient space of primordial Alpine landscape settings credits him with being an early founder of the "Danube style" of landscape painting. Some compositional elements in these early works show that Cranach was familiar with the art of his famous Nürnberg contemporary, Albrecht Dürer. Cranach's works up to 1504, however, show a conscious decision on his part to reject the studied geometry and classic proportions of Dürer's figures. Instead, Cranach's pictures seem more spontaneous and free, rendered in an almost nervous drawing style.

Life's Work

Cranach may have joined the court at Wittenberg as early as 1504, but he was definitely in Frederick's employ in April, 1505, at which time he was paid for making decorations at the elector's castle in Lochau. Cranach worked, uninterruptedly, for the court until his death in 1553, serving three successive heads of the Saxon court: Frederick III, John the Steadfast, and John Frederick the Magnanimous. In 1508, Frederick held him in high enough regard to grant him a coat of arms of a winged serpent, a device Cranach used to sign his pictures throughout his life.

In the same year, Frederick entrusted him with a diplomatic mission to the Lowlands. Cranach's biographer and friend, Christoph Scheurl, related the attention Cranach received from Netherlandish artists with his lifelike portrait of the youthful Charles V (which he supposedly painted on an Antwerp tavern wall). Cranach's familiarity with Netherlandish art is documented in his monumental *Holy Kinship Altarpiece* of 1509, which is clearly derived from Quenten Massys' triptych, now in Brussels.

After his return from the Lowlands, Lucas settled into a prominent and extremely comfortable life in Wittenberg. His wife, Barbara Brengbier, bore him two sons, Hans and Lucas the Younger, and three daughters. He was so successful in his business affairs that in 1528 he was listed as the second wealthiest burgher in Wittenberg. He owned an apothecary (which has functioned to modern times in the town), a winery, several houses, and a publishing house. He served on the city council between 1519 and 1549, and he was elected to three consecutive terms as burgomaster, 1537-1543.

Cranach's busy life and the vast number of pictures he produced have led most historians to believe that he was aided by a large and well-ordered shop of assistants. Certainly his two sons were central to his production. Little is known of Hans, but two dated paintings of 1534 and 1537 by him survive, along with an interesting sketchbook in Hannover; he died in Italy in 1537. It seems clear that Lucas the Younger was the inheritor of his father's workshop, and he no doubt played an increasingly important part in the workshop, especially in Lucas the Elder's later years. The role of the Cranach shop makes definite attributions of individual works to Cranach himself difficult to establish, even when they are signed and dated.

The terms of his court appointment were apparently never written down, but his position did entitle him to a yearly stipend and to a rather pampered life; moreover, there were seemingly no restrictions on commissions he could accept from outside the court. Court documents show that his clothing and that of his assistants, feed for his horse, kitchen provisions, and various household services were all provided to him on request. Except for the trip to the Lowlands in 1508 and local visits to the elector's castle in Lochau and his hunting lodge in Torgau to supervise decorations, Cranach rarely traveled. He was extremely reluctant late in his career to follow the court of John Frederick and consequently was dismissed from service temporarily between 1547 and 1550. He ultimately did obey John Frederick's request to move to Augsburg in 1550 and subsequently to Weimar in 1552, where he died the following year.

Between 1505 and 1510, Cranach's style manifests an interest in solid, three-dimensional figures, including a series of drawings on tinted paper, two-color chiaroscuro woodcuts, and large-scale altarpieces, particularly the Saint Anne Altar. By 1515, however, Cranach's style shifted to emphasize silhouetted shapes, strongly patterned compositions, and images with flatter, less insistent volume. Excellent examples of this stylistic change are two nearly life-size, full-length marriage portraits of Duke Henry the Pious and his wife, Duchess Catherine, of 1514. Accompanied by their pet dogs, the figures are spotlighted against plain dark backgrounds and dressed in rich, colorful costumes. The jaunty attitude of the two and the decorous surfaces of the panels communicate a statement of class rank that is unmistakably present in any number of other court portraits, including that of John Frederick of 1532-1535. The finery and aloofness of his court portraits contrast with another class of portraits of wealthy burghers of Wittenberg (such as *Dr. Johannes Scheyring*, 1529), in which Lucas presents a more straightforward and even plain characterization of his sitters.

There is a clear change in Cranach's art from his Vienna days. The boldness and expressiveness of his early works give way to works designed to cater to the effete tastes of a court hungry for decorative surfaces, erotic subjects, rich colors, and elaborately designed brocades. As a component of his "court style," Cranach developed a distinctive type

of female figure, more Gothic than Renaissance. In his early engravings of *The Judgment of Paris* of 1508 or his *Venus and Cupid* woodcut of 1509, his nudes followed the Vitruvian proportions of Jacopo de' Barbari and Dürer. Barbari had preceded Cranach at the Wittenberg court, and the two may have known each other. In these early works, Cranach's figures are full-bodied, with insistent three-dimensional modeling; they are faithful in spirit to the classical sources of Italian art. From the 1520's on, Cranach's nudes change dramatically from the geometric proportions and the volume influenced by Italian art. He preferred instead female nudes who are adolescentlike, with large abdomens, small buttocks, and tiny breasts. They are willowy and lithe but ungainly and self-conscious. They assume choreographed poses that conform totally to the decorative surface rhythms of his later pictures.

Among the many mythological subjects produced by his shop, three themes recur frequently: the judgment of Paris, the sleeping water nymph, and the Venus with Cupid. These subjects are preserved in a number of versions dating in the 1520's and 1530's. In the 1530 version of the *Judgment of Paris* in Karlsruhe, Cranach transforms the mythological narrative into a courtly event with Mercury and Paris dressed in contemporary armor. Similarly, Minerva, Venus, and Juno wear jewelry of the period and sport the latest coiffures. Their awkward poses and the coy expression of one of the graces, who brazenly looks out at the spectator, serve to heighten the eroticism of the scene.

Cranach's interest in mythological subjects was no doubt reinforced by Humanist scholars at the University of Wittenberg. Founded in 1502, the university had a distinguished faculty of Humanists teaching the classics and rhetoric, including Nikolaus Marschalk and Christoph Scheurl, among others. Such works as the *Reclining River Nymph at the Fountain* (1518) and *Venus with Cupid the Honey-Thief* (1530) were inspired by specific classical inscriptions. Cranach must have had help with these classical literary sources from his Humanist friends.

In 1508, Martin Luther was appointed professor of theology at the University of Wittenberg. Cranach knew him intimately. Cranach was a witness at Luther's wedding in 1525 and a godfather to his son Johannes. He also published some of Luther's writings and provided the designs for the title pages for two books by Luther published in 1518 and 1519. Cranach made several painted and printed portraits of Luther which serve to document Luther's life under the protection of Frederick III. Two of the most interesting of these are a painted panel and a woodcut, both of about 1521, which depict Luther in his disguise as Junker Georg after Luther's condemnation at the Diet of Worms.

The Lutheran message of direct redemption and the importance of faith alone in attaining salvation are themes that occur in several of Cranach's pictures and of those by Lucas the Younger. A late panel, often entitled the *Allegory of Redemption*, portrays the aging Cranach standing next to Luther beneath Christ on the Cross. Luther points to a passage in his translation of the Bible that promises direct salvation from Christ, while an arc of blood streams directly from the side of Christ onto Cranach's head. Begun by Cranach the Elder before his death, the work was completed by Cranach the Younger in 1555. A picture dating earlier in Cranach's career, the *Allegory of the Law and the Gospel* (1529), documents Luther's position that the Old Testament is incomplete without the New Testament. Such works by Cranach are clearly didactic, serving as a visual form to Luther's teachings.

Summary

Lucas Cranach, the Elder's lasting contribution to sixteenth century German art lies primarily in the quality of his works themselves. A prolific artist, no doubt aided by a well-supervised shop, Cranach produced a varied array of subjects in various media. They range in their scope from the naturalism of his portraits of real people to the impossible anatomy of his mythological nudes. Lacking the intellect of Albrecht Dürer's art or the sheer emotional power of Matthias Grünewald's paintings, Cranach's images seem more comfortable and less challenging. Yet Cranach was one of the first German artists to give visual form to early Reformation religious thought in his paintings, prints, and book illustrations. He developed conventions for illustrating classical mythology in an artistic tradition that had none. His art is a visual chronicle of the tastes and personalities of half a century of the Wittenberg court, a society that had a profound impact on the intellectual, religious, and political formation of sixteenth century Germany.

Bibliography

Bax, D. *Hieronymus Bosch and Lucas Cranach: Two Last Judgment Triptychs*. Translated by M. A. Bax-Botha. New York: North-Holland, 1983. A detailed discussion of the subject matter of a painting attributed to Hieronymus Bosch in Vienna and a work related to it ascribed to Cranach in East Berlin. A focused study, the book concludes that Cranach copied the front of a now lost altarpiece by Bosch.

Bruce, Donald. "Cranachs from Copenhagen." *Contemporary Review* 271 (July, 1997): 34. Analysis of three Lucas Cranach paintings that were lent to the London National Gallery during the refurbishment of Kunstnuseum in Copenhagen. Includes a description and history of "The Judgement of Paris," "Cupid the Honey-Thief," and a comparison of the Edinburgh and Copenhagen versions of "Melancholia."

Christensen, Carl C. *Art and the Reformation in Germany*. Athens: Ohio University Press, 1979. Discusses more than a dozen paintings by Cranach and his shop that demonstrate subjects directly influenced by Protestant thought. There is also an excellent summary of Luther's theology and its relation to sixteenth century German art.

Falk, Tilman, ed. *Sixteenth Century German Artists, Hans Burgkmair the Elder, Hans Schäufelein, Lu-*

cas Cranach the Elder. Vol. 11 in *The Illustrated Bartsch*, edited by Walter L. Strauss. New York: Abaris Books, 1980. Contains large illustrations of 155 engravings and woodcuts attributed to the artist. There is no commentary, but the illustrations provide an excellent resource of the prints by Cranach and his shop.

Friedländer, Max J., and Jakob Rosenberg. *The Paintings of Lucas Cranach*. Translated by Heinz Norden and Ronald Taylor. Ithaca, N.Y.: Cornell University Press, and London: Philip Wilson, 1978, The new English translation, along with the original German publication, is largely a detailed catalog of nearly four hundred works ascribed to Cranach and to his sons. Many details of the 1932 catalog have been updated with a new introduction by Rosenberg.

Grossmann, Maria. *Humanism in Wittenberg, 1485-1517*. Nieuwkoop: B. de Graaf, 1975. The author surveys the impact of German Humanism on the Reformation. Her chapter on the visual arts discusses Cranach's pictures in this context.

Hollstein, F. W. H. *Cranach-Drusse*. Vol. 6 in *German Engravings, Etchings, and Woodcuts, ca. 1400-1700*, edited by D. G. Boon and R. W. Scheller. Amsterdam: Menno Hertzberger, 1965. Provides lists of 140 prints and their locations by Cranach, the Elder, Cranach, the Younger, and impressions attributed to the Cranach workshop. Most entries are illustrated.

Merback, Mitchell B. "Torture and Teaching." *Art Journal* 57 (spring 1998): 14. Merback evaluates a set of woodcut sculptures depicting the martyrdom of the twelve apostles by the German artist Lucas Cranach, the Elder. The author discusses the use of martyrdom imagery to uphold the cause of Lutheran indoctrination during the Reformation era and the disciplinary dimension of Protestant education.

Schade, Werner. *Cranach: A Family of Master Painters*. Translated by Helen Sebba. New York: Putnam, 1980. The most comprehensive treatment of the subject to date. Schade's work discusses Cranach's life and art within the context of the contributions of his two sons. Profusely illustrated with many plates in color, the book also reprints in translation all documents relevant to the Cranach family with an extensive bibliography.

Snyder, James. *Northern Renaissance Art*. New York: Abrams, 1985. Intended as a general survey of Netherlandish, French, and German art, the book contains a separate chapter on Cranach. The author stresses Cranach's ties to Wittenberg Humanism and the Reformation aspects of his paintings.

Burton L. Dunbar III

THOMAS CRANMER

Born: July 2, 1489; Aslacton, Nottinghamshire, England

Died: March 21, 1556; Oxford, England

Area of Achievement: Religion

Contribution: Cranmer presided, along with Henry VIII and Thomas Cromwell, Henry's vicegerent in spiritual affairs, over the creation of the Anglican Church in England and separation from the Church of Rome. Cranmer was responsible for giving an English Bible to the English, drafting a new English service via the Book of Common Prayer (1549, 1552), and sealing England's commitment to a Protestant form of worship by his death under Henry's daughter Mary.

Early Life

Thomas Cranmer, the son of a country squire, was born at Aslacton, Nottinghamshire, on July 2, 1489. As a child he learned to hunt, shoot, and ride. He suffered under a cruel schoolmaster before going to Cambridge University, where he studied the classics, philosophy, logic, and Erasmus' works. He received the B.A. in 1511-1512, the M.A. in 1515. He held a fellowship from Jesus College but lost it upon marrying "Black Joan" of the Dolphin Inn. Both Joan and a child died within a year, and Cranmer returned as a Fellow at Jesus. He took Holy Orders as a priest prior to 1520 but did not take an oath of celibacy, since that was not required at the time. He received the B.D. degree in 1521 and the Doctor of Divinity in 1526, whereupon he became a public examiner in theology at Cambridge.

Cranmer's idea of enlisting European universities' opinions on the validity of Henry VIII's marriage to his first wife, Catherine of Aragon, brought him to Henry's attention in the summer of 1529. The marriage cause had been returned to Rome for final determination. At Henry's behest, Cranmer wrote a treatise on the subject and convinced learned men at Cambridge to side with the king. Eventually Oxford and the University of Paris took Henry's part, but no other universities did. Cranmer became chaplain to Anne Boleyn and a member of the household of her father, Thomas Boleyn, accompanying him on a mission in 1530 to Charles V, the Holy Roman Emperor. Two years later, Henry sent Cranmer as ambassador to Charles at Ratisborn and Nuremberg. While there, the forty-three-year-old Cranmer married Margaret, the twenty-year-old niece of Andreas Osiander, the Lutheran reformer. On the death of Thomas Warham, Archbishop of Canterbury, Henry determined to replace him with Cranmer and succeeded in securing Rome's approval of the appointment. Before returning to England, Cranmer secretly sent his wife there.

Reluctantly, Cranmer accepted the post as archbishop, being appointed March 30, 1533. Before taking his oath, however, he made a protest that the new oath did not bind him to do anything contrary to Henry's will. His first business was to pronounce in an ecclesiastical court on May 23 the invalidity of Henry's marriage to Catherine. Next, on May 28, he declared Henry's marriage of January 25 to Anne Boleyn lawful. On September 10, he became godfather to Henry and Anne's daughter Elizabeth, the future Elizabeth I, born on September 7.

Cranmer was a short man. The July, 1545, painting done by Fliccius shows him with a somewhat stern, forbidding countenance, but that may have been a pose for the painter, since Cranmer was gentle in his dealings with all. Clean-shaven in the portrait, with the suggestion of a fast-growing beard, he did grow a long beard during his imprisonment under Mary, Henry and Catherine's daughter, a devout Catholic.

Life's Work

As archbishop, Cranmer deferred to Henry, who was made Supreme Head of the Church by parliamentary statute in 1534, and to his friend Thomas Cromwell, who was appointed Vicar General in Spirituals in 1535. Cranmer saw that the pope's name was eliminated from all service books. Personally sympathetic to Thomas More, the former Lord Chancellor, and John Fisher, Bishop of Rochester, he saw them executed in 1535 for refusing to accept Henry's new succession to Anne's heirs and to Henry's new authority. The following year, in May, he visited Anne in the Tower, where she had been placed on charges of having had sexual relations with several men, including her brother Thomas. On May 17, Cranmer declared Anne's union with Henry as invalid from its inception, thus bastardizing Elizabeth, and gave Henry a dispensation to marry Jane Seymour, who, like Henry, was descended from Edward III. Anne was executed on May 19. Jane died twelve days after giving Henry a male heir, Edward, on October 12, 1537. Cranmer became Edward's godfather—evidence, again, of Henry's intimate affection.

Early in 1536, Cranmer had directed the religious convocation to approve the Ten Articles, the first formula of faith made by the Church of England. The Articles, as their revision the next year in the Bishop's Book reveals, had been set by Henry and edited by Cranmer. Collectively they denoted a drift toward reformation. Four of the seven Sacraments, matrimony, confirmation, religious orders, and extreme unction, were not mentioned; only baptism, the Lord's Supper, and penance were discussed.

Cranmer's longtime wish to make the English Bible available to the English people was successful when he secured, in August of 1537, Cromwell's permission to sell copies of Matthew's Bible, based on the work of the reformers William Tyndale and Miles Coverdale, to the public. This Bible, subsequently revised, became the Great Bible, known for its size, and was placed in each parish church from 1541 on. Parliament, however, in 1543 forbade the reading of the Bible at home by women and lesser folk. The Reformation in England had seen the abolition of holy days in 1536, including the celebration of St. Thomas à Becket's feast. Cranmer scandalized conservatives by eating meat on the feast's eve. Moreover, worship of images and veneration of relics were forbidden. Becket's shrine at Canterbury was destroyed. Nevertheless, Cranmer had little to do with the suppression of the monasteries which had led, in 1536-1537, to the uprising known as the Pilgrimage of Grace in the North of England. Even Henry had second thoughts about how far reform had gone and he introduced into Parliament the Six Articles of religious belief that reaffirmed transubstantiation in the Mass and clerical celibacy. Immediately Cranmer sent his wife to Germany. A common rumor was that she was carried from place to place in a large trunk, ventilated by air holes, to preserve the secrecy of his marriage.

Obediently, Cranmer married Henry to Anne of Cleves, then dissolved that marriage in 1540. Other council members asked Cranmer in the fall of 1541 to inform Henry of his fifth wife Catherine Howard's infidelity and loose morality. Like Anne, Catherine was executed. Even Cranmer did not escape the threat of the Tower. In 1543, the king's council secured Henry's consent to send Cranmer to the Tower, where he would be examined concerning his unorthodox religious views. Rather than let events take their course, Henry told Cranmer in advance and gave him his ring, by which he might appeal to the king for justice. Thus, the tables were turned on Cranmer's enemies, and no one said anything against him as long as Henry lived. That same year, Cranmer made known to Henry his secret marriage, and Margaret returned to England. At the king's request, during the following year he issued prayers in English and an English litany. Cranmer was with Henry the night he died, January 28, 1547.

The new king was Henry's nine-year-old son, Edward VI, who, along with Lord Protector Edward Seymour, Duke of Somerset, favored Protestantism. Thus it was possible for Cranmer in 1547 to prescribe new English homilies for preachers, the use of Erasmus' *Paraphrases of the New Testament* to assist in reading the English Bible, and in the following year to secure Communion in both kinds for the laity and the legality of clerical marriage. Furthermore, candles on Candlemas Day, ashes on Ash Wednesday, and palms on Palm Sunday were abolished. A new English catechism, based on a Lutheran one, was issued. In 1549 came the new order for the service in English in the Book of Common Prayer, mostly written by Cranmer. This occasioned revolt in the counties of Devon and Cornwall. Cranmer also invited distinguished European Protestants to England. He was unsuccessful in his attempts to secure a European synod of leading Protestants, and he was unable to secure a new revision of ecclesiastical law.

On Somerset's fall from power, Cranmer began to absent himself from the court of Somerset's successor, John Dudley, Duke of Northumberland. The Reformation proceeded nevertheless, and a revised prayer book was issued in 1552 and, in the following year, the Forty-two Articles of faith. On Edward's death, July 6, 1553, Cranmer reluctantly agreed to Northumberland's plan to make Lady Jane Grey (the grandaughter of Henry's favorite sister, Mary) queen. When this plan failed and Mary, Henry's daughter by Catherine of Aragon, became queen, Cranmer was sent to the Tower, deprived of his rank, and ultimately executed, on March 21, 1556, despite seven recantations of his Protestant views. In fairness to Mary, one must note that Cranmer was sent to the Tower for writing a tract against the Catholic Mass. Cranmer had fortuitously sent his wife to Germany in 1555. After his death, she married twice.

The spectacle of Cranmer's death at Oxford is one of the famous moments in Protestant history. Fear for his life brought him to recant. When he learned that Mary would not spare him, he courageously declared his true views. Before he was burnt at the stake, he spoke of his great regret at recanting his true faith and then almost ran to the place of burning. He bravely held the hand that had written the recantations in the flame and neither stirred nor cried out. He died quickly.

Summary

Henry VIII's need for a male heir and his decision to dissolve his union with Catherine of Aragon so that he could marry Anne Boleyn provided Thomas Cranmer with an opportunity to serve his king as Archbishop of Canterbury and his country as a facilitator of Reformation doctrines. As archbishop under Henry, Cranmer brought the English people the English Bible, the English Our Father and Creed, English prayers in the Litany of 1544, the abolition of holy days and images, and a subtle movement away from the Mass to a Communion service. Under Henry's son Edward, Cranmer's reformist tendencies flowered in the new English worship service as prescribed in the Book of Common Prayer, issued in 1549 and again, in altered form, in 1552. The Forty-two Articles of faith approved by Parliament in 1552 ultimately became the basis of the Thirty-nine Articles, the basic tenets of Anglicanism today. Though Cranmer's language was ambiguous, most scholars agree that he personally believed in a symbolic rather than a real presence in the Lord's Supper. By emphasizing Scripture as the determinant of religious belief and practice, Cranmer helped Bible-oriented Christians appropriate Scripture as a guide to life. By his own example he showed the world that clergy should marry. His stress on general confession (in which the whole congregation makes a general confession together) and his invitation to take Communion in both bread and wine were attempts to stimulate more frequent Communion by lay people. Finally, Cranmer's death for his faith became an important link in the building of the Anglican faith—that is, the faith of communicants in the Church of England—under his goddaughter, Elizabeth I, who chose to incorporate most of Cranmer's reforms in her religious settlement on succeeding her sister Mary as queen. Thus, Cranmer, along with Henry VIII, Edward VI, Elizabeth I, and Thomas Cromwell, became founders of the Church of England and the Anglican faith.

Bibliography

Bromiley, G. W. *Thomas Cranmer, Theologian.* London: Lutterworth Press, and New York: Oxford University Press, 1956. Assesses Cranmer's theological contributions, noting that he came only slowly to his views and that for the most part they were derivative, influenced in his view of the Eucharist by his friend Nicholas Ridley, Bishop of Rochester.

Cranmer, Thomas. *Cranmer's Selected Writings.* Edited by Carl S. Meyer. London: SPCK, 1961. Contains the Litany of 1544, assorted prayers and collects, the preface to the English Bible, sample homilies, and Cranmer's writings on baptism and the Lord's Supper. Gives the flavor of Cranmer's language and thought, as do the various editions of the Book of Common Prayer throughout history.

Dickens, A. G. *The English Reformation.* 2d ed. London: Batsford, 1989; University Park: Pennsylvania State University Press, 1991. Thoughtful, perceptive. Informed by vast learning. An intellectual challenge, but well worth reading and rereading. The best short explanation of Cranmer's view of the Eucharist.

Elton, G. R. *Reform and Reformation: England,*

1509-1558. London: Arnold, and Cambridge, Mass.: Harvard University Press, 1977. A detailed text for the period. Stresses the role of Thomas Cromwell rather than Cranmer in bringing the English Bible to the English people.

Hutchinson, F. E. *Cranmer and the English Reformation*. London: English Universities Press, and New York: Macmillan, 1951. A brilliant book and a good place to start one's search for an understanding of how the Reformation came to England and Cranmer's role in it.

MacCulloch, Diarmaid. *Thomas Cranmer: A Life*. New Haven, Conn.: Yale University Press, 1996. This prizewinning biography provides the definitive account of Thomas Cranmer. English Reformation scholar MacCulloch draws on new manuscript sources in Britain and elsewhere to create this vivid new study—the first on Cranmer in more than thirty years.

Maynard, Theodore. *The Life of Thomas Cranmer*. Chicago: Regnery, and London: Staples Press, 1956. Brief, readable account that stresses Cranmer's contributions to the Protestant tradition and emphasizes the drama of his life.

Ridley, Jasper. *Thomas Cranmer*. Oxford: Clarendon Press, 1962. Solid, scholarly, yet readable study of Cranmer and his times. Sets Cranmer in the context of the Protestant-Catholic historiographical debate in an introductory section. Puts Cranmer's Reformation contributions in the frame of his loyalty to the Crown. Definitive account.

Smith, Lacey Baldwin. *Henry VIII: The Mask of Royalty*. London: Cape, and Boston: Houghton Mifflin, 1971. Brilliant study of the aging Henry VIII at the time of the English Reformation.

M. J. Tucker

THOMAS CROMWELL

Born: 1485?; Putney, England
Died: July 28, 1540; London, England
Areas of Achievement: Politics and government
Contribution: During the 1530's, one of the most crucial and turbulent decades in English history, the chief minister of Henry VIII was Thomas Cromwell, who helped bring about the king's marriage to Anne Boleyn, the separation of the Church of England from Rome, the dissolution of the monasteries, and the establishment of Protestantism in England.

Early Life

Thomas Cromwell was born in Putney, probably in 1485, to Walter Cromwell, a blacksmith, brewer, armorer, and cloth merchant. Records of Thomas Cromwell's youth are scanty, based mostly on gossip or on Cromwell's own possibly unreliable accounts of his life. According to them, he fled from home in his teens and went to Italy, where he served as a soldier under the Italians and French. Leaving the army, he set himself up as a wool merchant in Florence and in the Netherlands. Some accounts say that while in Italy, he met Niccolò Machiavelli; what is certain is that he had read Machiavelli's work in manuscript and became a disciple of it. Largely self-educated, Cromwell became a book lover and taught himself Greek and Latin, Italian, and French.

By 1512 or 1513, he was back in England, where he married Elizabeth Wykys or Wykeys, a wealthy widow, and began to practice law, while continuing to operate as a wool merchant. Between 1514 and 1520, he made several trips to Rome. Around 1520, he began to perform legal and administrative jobs for Thomas Wolsey, Cardinal, Archbishop of York, and Lord Chancellor of England. In 1523, Cromwell became a member of the House of Commons, and the next year, a member of Gray's Inn.

Life's Work

Cromwell became increasingly useful to Cardinal Wolsey, who in 1525 employed him to dissolve several monasteries so that their confiscated wealth could be used to endow Wolsey's colleges at Oxford and Ipswich. Cromwell did this so satisfactorily that he became Wolsey's confidential secretary and thus the power behind the power behind the throne. No scruples deterred Cromwell from doing whatever was required to gain and keep power; in 1527, he advised Cardinal-to-be Reginal Pole to forget about ethics and practice the cynical power politics of Machiavelli's *Il principe* (1532; *The Prince*).

In 1527, Elizabeth Cromwell died, leaving her husband with a son and two daughters. He never remarried. Henry VIII, however, was eager to get rid of his wife, Catherine of Aragon, and to marry his mistress Anne Boleyn. When Wolsey failed to obtain for the king either an annulment or a divorce, Henry removed him from his offices and brought a bill of attainder against him. Despite his Machiavellian views, Cromwell defended Wolsey so ably that he earned the appreciation of the king, who took him into the service of the Crown and in 1531 made him Privy Councillor. The following April, he became Master of the King's Jewels and shortly thereafter Clerk of the Hanaper. In September, 1532, he became acting Secretary of State and in April, 1534, succeeded in ousting Secretary of State Stephen Gardiner and taking the post himself. A year earlier, he had already become Chancellor of the Exchequer. As Cromwell worked his way deeper into the king's confidence, he was rewarded by being made Master of the Rolls and in July, 1536, Lord Privy Seal and Lord Cromwell of Wimbledon.

To win the royal confidence and favor, Cromwell worked out a plan to obtain for Henry his divorce, his marriage to Anne Boleyn, supremacy over the Church in England, and the remaining wealth of the monasteries. To begin with, he proclaimed that all the nation's clergy had violated the Statute of Praemunire in recognizing the Legatine authority of Cardinal Wolsey, even though the king had sanctioned that authority. In consequence, the clergy had to pay an immense fine and acknowledge the king as the "Only Supreme Head" of the Church. In 1533, Cromwell wrote and forced through Parliament the Act in Restraint of Appeals, canceling appeals to the Papacy in marriage and testamentary cases. In January of 1533, Henry married the pregnant Anne Boleyn, and in May, the new Archbishop of Canterbury, Thomas Cranmer, pronounced Henry's first marriage invalid and his new one legitimate.

Continuing to gratify the king, Cromwell engineered through Parliament more legislation that led to the Act of Supremacy, which in defiance of Pope Clement V, who had declared in favor of Queen Catherine, made the king Supreme Head of the Church in England, effectively severing England from Rome and placing it in the Protestant camp.

Cromwell also had passed a new Act of Succession, in favor of Anne Boleyn and her children, and a new Treason Act making it treasonable to challenge either the king or the new queen. Thus, Cromwell forged an absolute despotism for King Henry and used it to execute any who obstructed his policies, chiefly Chancellor Thomas More and John Fisher, Bishop of Rochester. Cromwell harbored no hatred for his opponents; they were simply like chess pieces that must be removed.

When Henry became Supreme Head of the Church, he appointed Cromwell its Vicar-General. In that capacity, Cromwell ordered an investigation of the monasteries and between 1536 and 1540 dissolved the monastic houses and confiscated their wealth for the Crown. Cromwell's harsh attacks on the clergy and monasticism led to several Catholic rebellions, most notably the Pilgrimage of Grace in Yorkshire, which was brutally suppressed. In 1538, Cromwell claimed to have discovered a conspiracy in Salisbury and Exeter, and though the evidence was questionable at best, he had the Abbot of Glastonbury and other monastic leaders hanged and the king's cousin the Marquess of Exeter and the leaders of the Pole family executed as traitors. Systematically, Cromwell consolidated absolute power in the monarchy and enjoyed his share as the virtual ruler of England.

Meanwhile, Henry's matrimonial problems increased. When he wearied of Anne Boleyn, who had borne him a daughter, Elizabeth, rather than the son he craved for the royal succession, he wished to marry Jane Seymour, accused Anne of adultery and incest, and had Cromwell serve as prosecutor in the rigged trial that resulted in the execution of the queen and four of her alleged lovers, including her own brother, Lord Rochford. Jane Seymour bore Henry the male heir for which he so longed but died in childbirth. After a brief period of mourning, Henry began to look for a fourth wife.

Undertaking the role of marriage broker, Cromwell looked for a favorable foreign alliance. Though he had no strong religious principles and had engineered the break with Rome for reasons of expediency rather than belief, Cromwell had been maneuvering for an alliance with the German Lutherans to maintain a balance of power against a possible alliance between Spain and France in opposition to England. King Henry, who had earned the title "Defender of the Faith" by an early attack on Luther, still considered himself a Catholic of sorts, despite his break with Rome, and balked at such an alliance. Cromwell, however, was persuasive, and the king reluctantly allowed him to proceed. Accordingly, Cromwell negotiated a marriage with Anne, the niece of the Duke of Cleves. Henry had not met her but was persuaded of her charms by a flattering portrait of her by Hans Holbein. Yet when she arrived in England at the end of December, 1539, Henry was disenchanted, emphatically disliked her looks, and complained that Cromwell had deceived him. From that moment, Cromwell's days were numbered. The Duke of Norfolk introduced his attractive niece Catherine Howard to allure the king, who had already ordered Cromwell to extricate him from his latest marriage. Trying to keep the royal favor, Cromwell in April had Parliament confiscate the wealth of the Knights Hospitalers of St. John, and on April 17, the king named him Earl of Essex and on the next day made him Lord Great Chamberlain.

Cromwell, however, reached this height only to fall. Led by Norfolk, his enemies plotted against him and persuaded Henry that the man who had made the king the Supreme Head of the Church of England was in fact a heretic and hence a traitor. Cromwell's fate was that he had succeeded too well; he had done everything necessary to give the king absolute power, he had subdued the Church and seized its wealth, and he had killed off anyone who might be inclined to further rebellion. Only in foreign policy might he still be necessary, but it turned out that the French-Spanish alliance did not materialize and that the marriage to thwart it was a disaster. Not noted for gratitude, Henry attacked Cromwell with his own weapons and with no warning had him arrested on June 10, under a bill of attainder for treason. Imprisoned for a month and a half in the Tower of London, Cromwell was beheaded on July 28, at Tyburn.

Summary

As Henry VIII's chief minister during the 1530's, Cromwell brought about the separation of the Church of England from Roman Catholicism, and though he seems to have been utterly indifferent to religion himself, he was the person chiefly instrumental in making England officially Protestant. By making it possible for Henry to marry Anne Boleyn, Cromwell was in part responsible for her daughter Elizabeth's eventually becoming the legitimate heir and queen. Cromwell did more than anyone else to consolidate royal power and to create a national administration. A descendant of his

sister was Oliver Cromwell. He appears as a minor character in William Shakespeare's *Henry VIII* (1613; with John Fletcher) and is the title character in the apocryphal Shakespearean play *History of Thomas, Lord Cromwell* by "W. S." (1592). The latter play, written from a Protestant perspective shortly after the defeat of the Spanish Armada, makes Cromwell a martyr to the Protestant cause and portrays him as a paragon of Puritan virtues. Subsequent playwrights and novelists have all seen Cromwell as a cold, ruthless, unscrupulous person, the embodiment of Machiavellian ideology, who would not hesitate to dispose of any person or any institution that got in his way. He appears as a treacherous and self-serving antagonist in H.F.M. Prescott's novel *The Man on a Donkey* (1952), in Robert Bolt's play *A Man for All Seasons* (1954), in the film version of *Anne of the Thousand Days* (1969), and in the BBC television series *Henry VIII and His Six Wives* (1972). Historians are divided in their judgment of Cromwell, some seeing him as an efficient administrator, others deploring his ruthless methods. Yet he was loyal to Wolsey and to the king, and he changed the course of English history profoundly and irrevocably.

Bibliography

Beckingsale, B. W. *Thomas Cromwell, Tudor Minister*. London: Macmillan, and Totowa, N.J.: Rowman and Littlefield, 1978. Sees Cromwell as a dynamic visionary but also as a ruthless opportunist for whom the end justifies the means: "Amidst the sordid struggles of court politics he did retain a vision of a great monarchy, a prosperous commonwealth and a religion, purged of superstition."

Dickens, A. G. *Thomas Cromwell and the English Reformation*. London: English Universities Press, and New York: Macmillan, 1959. A brief study in the Teach Yourself History Library. Admires Cromwell's energy and abundance of new ideas; considers that "all the great constructive and destructive achievements of his [Henry VIII's] long reign were crowded into the eight brief years of Thomas Cromwell's ministry."

Elton, Geoffrey Rudolf. *Reform and Renewal, Thomas Cromwell and the Common Weal*. Cambridge: Cambridge University Press, 1973. One of the few studies that presents Cromwell approvingly. Sees Cromwell operating upon "firm principles of a spiritual renewal resting upon the truths of the past" and accordingly "less determinedly secular and less ruthlessly radical" than formerly portrayed.

Elton, Geoffrey. "How Corrupt Was Thomas Cromwell?" *Historical Journal* 36 (December, 1993): 623. Elton examines the corruption of Cromwell, including his rapaciousness and arrest in 1540.

Ferguson, Charles W. *Naked to Mine Enemies: The Life of Cardinal Wolsey*. London: Longman, and Boston: Little Brown, 1958. Examines Cromwell in his relationship to Wolsey, carrying out the cardinal's dissolution of monasteries, serving as his confidential secretary, and defending him against the royal bill of attainder.

Innes, Arthur D. *Ten Tudor Statesmen*. London: Nash, 1906; Port Washington, N.Y.: Kennikat Press, 1934. Devotes one chapter to Cromwell, stresses the influence of Machiavelli on him and considering him a relentless practitioner of political expediency. Sees Cromwell as the heartless forger of absolute despotism for Henry VIII.

Marius, Richard. *Thomas More, a Biography*. New York: Knopf, 1984; London: Dent, 1985. Examines Cromwell's role in the persecution of More for his refusal to approve the dissolution of the marriage between Henry VIII and Catherine of Aragon and Henry's marriage to Anne Boleyn. Shows Cromwell manipulating the law to cause More's downfall and death. Illustrated.

Mattingly, Garrett. *Catherine of Aragon*. Boston: Little Brown, 1941; London: Cape, 1942. The definitive biography of Catherine; presents Cromwell as an unscrupulous agent of the king, engineering the royal divorce and remarriage and the separation of the Church of England from Rome. Illustrated.

Maynard, Theodore. *The Crown and the Cross: A Biography of Thomas Cromwell*. New York: McGraw-Hill, 1950. The standard biography. Admires Cromwell's administrative, legal, financial, and diplomatic abilities but expresses disgust at his cold-blooded and sinister lack of compassion. Illustrated.

Scarisbrick, J. J. *Henry VIII*. London: Eyre and Spottiswoode, and Berkeley: University of California Press, 1968. The standard biography of Henry VIII, this volume considers Cromwell in his role of formulating and carrying out royal policy. Makes no judgment of Cromwell and sees him as a competent administrator who gave England "good governance." Illustrated.

Williams, Neville. *The Cardinal and the Secretary: Thomas Wolsey and Thomas Cromwell*. London: Weidenfeld and Nicolson, 1975; New York: Macmillan, 1976. Studies Cromwell as Wolsey's subordinate and successor. Sees Cromwell as a "real innovator, directing the complicated moves in the break with Rome to establish a national state." Considers Cromwell stronger in domestic concerns than in diplomacy.

Robert E. Morsberger

JOHN DAVIS

Born: c. 1550; Sandridge Barton, Devonshire, England

Died: December 29 or 30, 1605; near Singapore

Areas of Achievement: Exploration, navigation, and privateering

Contribution: The most diligent and successful of the English explorers who attempted to find a northwest passage to the Far East, Davis greatly enlarged knowledge of the islands, waters, and coastline of the northern edge of North America.

Early Life

John Davis was born around 1550 at Sandridge Barton, a farm in Devonshire, England. Little is known of his family background; his father was a yeoman farmer of some substance, enough that Davis was later able to describe himself as a "gentleman." He grew up not far from the family of Humphrey Gilbert, and in adult life the Gilbert family would help to sponsor his voyages. He went to sea while probably still an adolescent and became a privateer and shipmaster. On September 29, 1582, he married Faith Fulford, daughter of an important local landowner. By that time, he had become the close friend of Adrian Gilbert, younger brother of Humphrey; it was Gilbert who interested him in voyages to Canada in search of a new route to the Pacific.

Life's Work

After the early voyages of the Cabots, the English had been slow in developing their interest in exploring and colonizing outside Europe. When that interest became active in the late-sixteenth century, they found themselves closed off by the Spanish and Portuguese from the rich trade with China and South Asia, coveted by all European nations. Several Englishmen became convinced that they could gain access to Asia by sailing around the northern coast of Canada to the Pacific; they included Martin Frobisher (who made voyages to Greenland and Canada, with the aid of the Gilberts and others in 1576, 1577, and 1578) and John Dee, the resident philosopher, physician, and mathematician at the court of Elizabeth I, who argued that it was possible to get to Asia either by going west around Canada or north across the Pole. After the failure of Frobisher's third voyage, Davis and Adrian Gilbert met with Dee in 1579 to discuss possibilities for a new attempt. Another meeting in January, 1583, included the queen's secretary, Sir Francis Walsingham, and conferred the queen's approval of their undertaking.

In February, 1585, Gilbert and Davis received a patent from the queen to explore either to the north or northwest, giving them the right to create colonies and to hold trading monopolies with any regions they discovered. There was at that time no realistic possibility of exploring the North Pole—the technological and logistical difficulties would not be overcome before the twentieth century—but they found backers among London merchants for a northwestern voyage and within five months Davis was ready to set out, with two ships and forty-two men, including four musicians.

Davis left from Dartmouth on June 7, 1585, and crossed first to Greenland, which he called "Land of Desolation." He had his first encounter with native populations on the western coast of Greenland, near what is now Godthaab; in an effort to please the possibly hostile Eskimos, he had his orchestra play while he and the crew danced on a rocky island. The tactic worked, and he was able to trade with the Eskimos for sealskin clothes and boots. The first voyage explored the waters between Greenland and Baffin Island; he believed that he had found a northwest passage in Cumberland Sound, a large bay of Baffin Island. After sailing up the bay for 180 miles, he began to fear that he would be trapped by winter weather and returned to England, arriving near the end of August.

Davis was absolutely convinced that he had found the entrance to the northwest passage; he wrote to Sir Francis Walsingham that it "is a matter nothing doubtful, but at any time almost to be passed, the sea navigable, void of ice, the air tolerable, and the waters very deep." On the strength of his belief, he organized a new expedition the next year, funded by merchants of Exeter and Totnes as well as London. He took four vessels, plus a spare that had been dismantled and stored inside the largest ship. His plan was to test two possibilities simultaneously: He would take two ships back to Cumberland Sound while shipmaster Richard Pope would take the other two north to look for John Dee's polar route. Both efforts were fruitless. Davis substantially repeated his 1585 voyage, again skirting the coast of Greenland, where his men visited an Eskimo village and challenged the men to jumping and wrestling contests, then crossing to Baffin Island and Cumberland Sound. The weather, however, did not favor him; icebergs and contrary winds prevented him from exploring the sound, the Hudson Strait, which he passed after turning south, or Hamilton Inlet in Labrador, all of which he hoped would be the coveted passage to the Pacific. He returned to England in October after catching a good haul of codfish on the Newfoundland Banks. Meanwhile, his other two ships were inevitably thwarted by pack ice as they tried to sail north; they ended by following Davis to Greenland, where they had a football match with one village of natives and a fight with another in which three Eskimos were killed, and returned home. Davis remained optimistic; he believed that the entrance to the Northwest was one of four places he had found "or else not at all," and he was ready to sell his family estate, if necessary, for funds to try again.

The third voyage came closer to his goal. He took three small vessels from Dartmouth on May 19, 1587, a full month earlier than his previous tries, and proceeded much farther north up Davis Strait, now Baffin Bay. At the end of June, he reached a point he named Sanderson's Hope, after his principal London backer; if he had turned northwest he would have approached Lancaster Sound, the actual entrance to a northwest passage, but he was turned back by ice. A month later, he again passed the Hudson Strait, leading to Hudson Bay, but could not explore it and returned to England, stopping on the way in Labrador to fish—and to try deer hunting with some hounds he had brought. His haul of fish apparently paid for his voyage, but Davis never realized any personal wealth from his travels.

Davis remained convinced that a northwest passage would be found; he wrote after his return, "The passage is most probable, the execution easy." He was, however, diverted to other enterprises. He may have taken part in the fight against the Armada in 1588, and he later privateered in the Atlantic. When Thomas Cavendish attempted his second voyage around the world in 1591, Davis accompanied him to South America, trying three times to pass the Straits of Magellan in a lone ship, but was finally turned back by bad weather. He did become the discoverer of the Falkland Islands before he returned to England in 1593. In 1594 and 1595, during an enforced stay in England because of legal problems, he wrote two books, *Seaman's Secrets* (1594) and *World's Hydrographical Description* (1595); the former, a guide to practical navigation, became very widely used, with eight editions before 1660. His most ambitious voyage, across the Pacific to Southeast Asia, led to his death: He was killed in a fight with Japanese pirates on an island near Singapore at the end of 1605.

Summary

A careful navigator, a courageous and skilled captain, and a humane explorer, John Davis added much to knowledge of the waters and the land masses of the most inhospitable parts of North America, and he sailed farther to the north than any man before his time. Although he remained convinced that a practical northwest passage would be found, his voyages demonstrated that the route would be difficult and dangerous at best. Davis' later voyages in the South Atlantic helped to show that routes around Cape Horn could be used, and, meanwhile, English and Dutch seamen were able to reach the East by the long but less treacherous route around Africa. So interest in a northwest passage faded, and there was no successful navigation around the Canadian coast until modern times.

By the standards of the time, Davis was a considerate and even compassionate commander. He never sent his men where he would not go himself; he allowed a shipload of men who fell ill on the second voyage to return home; he maintained a careful eye on his supplies and did not allow his men to run short of food. He also treated North American natives with greater courtesy and respect than most European explorers, recognizing that in the long run the outcome of his voyages might depend on their goodwill. He gained less contemporary recognition than some of his more flamboyant peers and he never profited from his expeditions, but he was one of the most persevering and courageous of the North American explorers.

Bibliography

Dodge, Ernest S. *Northwest by Sea*. New York: Oxford University Press, 1961. The best overall narrative of efforts by English and Dutch explorers to establish a northwest passage. Davis receives careful and sympathetic attention.

Manhart, George B. *The English Search for a Northwest Passage in the Time of Queen Elizabeth.* Philadelphia: University of Pennsylvania Press, 1924. A meticulous scholarly work that traces the Davis voyages with greater detail than most readers will need. Originally a Ph.D. thesis, it is reliable but rather pedantic.

Markham, Sir Albert, ed. *The Voyages and Works of John Davis the Navigator.* London: Hakluyt Society, 1880; New York: Franklin, 1963. Difficult reading, but the most important source for Davis' life. It includes his two treatises on seamanship, otherwise unavailable to modern readers.

Markham, Sir Clements. *Life of John Davis.* London: Philip, and New York: Dodd, Mead, 1889. The closest approach to a full biography, now dated and limited in value. Full of admiration for the subject but lacking in historical analysis.

Morison, Samuel Eliot. *The Great Explorers.* Oxford and New York: Oxford University Press, 1978. A lively and readable narrative of European voyages to America from 1490 to 1600. Probably the most accessible and attractive introduction to the subject. Includes an excellent chapter on Davis.

Wright, Louis B. *West and by North: North America Seen Through the Eyes of Its Seafaring Discoverers.* New York: Delacorte Press, 1971. A compilation of selections from the accounts written by explorers and their contemporaries, skillfully arranged to present a coherent view of America as it was seen by sixteenth century Europeans.

Robert W. Kenny

BARTOLOMEU DIAS

Born: c. 1450; probably near Lisbon, Portugal
Died: May 23?, 1500; at sea off the coast of Brazil
Area of Achievement: Exploration
Contribution: Dias was the first to command a sea expedition around Africa's Cape of Good Hope, a feat that had been attempted for more than fifty years before his success and one that led to the opening of sea trade between Portugal and the Orient.

Early Life

Bartolomeu Dias, like many Portuguese explorers of his time, remains an enigma. Nothing is known about his life except for an incomplete account of his voyage around the Cape of Good Hope in 1488 and two other references regarding one previous and one subsequent voyage. He may have been related to Dinis Dias, another Portuguese captain, who also explored the African coast in search of a sea route to the Orient in 1445. Dias had at least one brother, Pedro, who accompanied him on the historic voyage around the cape. Dias was undoubtedly from a poor social class, since most seamen and explorers shared a similar humble upbringing, some of them even having criminal records.

The major reason for the lack of any solid information about Dias is that virtually all the early Portuguese explorations were conducted under strict secrecy. Portugal and Spain were in fierce competition at the time, both attempting to discover the most profitable trade route to the Orient. Since land routes from Europe through the Middle East to Asia were nearly impossible to traverse because of the Muslim Empire's hostile monopoly of the area, a sea route around the uncharted seas of Africa seemed to be the only alternative.

More than fifty years before Dias' historic voyage, the idea of sailing past Cape Bojador (the bulging cape) located off the coast of the Sahara Desert in southern Morocco, was unheard of. There was a great fear that just south of this barren cape was the end of the world, where the sea boiled and monsters thrived. The man most responsible for stimulating interest in exploring the African coast in the hope of finding a trade route to the Orient was Prince Henry, third son of King John I and Queen Philippa of Portugal, later to be known as Prince Henry the Navigator. Henry's motivation for so fervently supporting sea exploration around Africa to Asia stemmed from his fierce hatred of the Muslims. He was a devout Christian and grand master of the militant Order of Christ, who believed that if he could locate the whereabouts of a legendary African empire ruled by a powerful Christian king called Prester John, Portugal could join forces with this influential king and overpower the Muslims, thus liberating the Holy Land and opening trade with Asia. By sending ships along the African coast, Henry planned to seek Prester John while simultaneously seeking a sea route to the Orient.

In 1433, Henry sent his first captain, Gil Eanes, with the explicit order to sail past the desolate and feared Cape Bojador. This was at a time when no reliable maps existed of the African coast, navigational equipment was primitive, and sailing ships were experimental, still evolving from a traditional small Mediterranean sailing vessel to a larger and more rugged European caravel specifically designed for long voyages. Eanes failed to conquer Cape Bojador on his initial voyage, but the following year he tried again and this time sailed one hundred miles past the intimidating cape. What followed over the next five decades was a painfully gradual exploration of the African coast by dozens of Portuguese captains. Key outposts and fortresses were established along the coast and a lucrative though cruel slave trade began.

The earliest reference to Dias is connected with the establishment of a major new fortress along the Guinea coast near Mina in 1481, twenty-one years after the death of Henry. Dias was one of the captains who sailed with the chief engineer of the project and who helped construct this key outpost. The principal explorer of this time, however, was Diego Cão, who, in two long voyages, sailed as far south as Cape Cross, fifty miles north of Walvis Bay in Namibia. Along the way, and under direction of King John II, Cão erected huge seven-foot limestone markers called *padrões*, which he mounted on prominent points where they could be seen by passing ships. When Cão died during his final voyage back to Portugal in 1485, preparations were made for the most ambitious voyage yet attempted by Portugal.

Life's Work

In August, 1487, John commissioned Dias to command another voyage, one of major importance.

Dias taking leave from Queen Eleanor and King John before embarking on his explorations

Secrecy surrounding the expedition was so intense that no official report exists of the voyage. The most up-to-date maps and navigational instruments of the time, as well as the best-equipped and most carefully prepared ships, were used. For the first time, a cargo ship, stocked with food and provisions, accompanied the two sailing ships.

Dias' principal crew members were all distinguished sailors; Pedro de Alenquer, one of the best-known mariners of the period, was chief pilot of Dias' ship, the *São Cristovão*. John Infante, a knight, captained the second ship, the *São Pantaleão*. Dias' brother, Pedro, captained the supply ship with the pilot John de Santiago, who had sailed previously with Cão. Also on board, as a junior pilot, was Bartolomeo Columbus, younger brother of Christopher Columbus. Along with the sixty crew members of the ships were six African captives, who carried precious metals and spices and were to be put ashore at various places along the coast to trade with the natives and to try everything possible to locate the elusive Prester John. Dias also carried three *padrões* to mark his progress along the coast.

Dias sailed without serious problems to Mina, the port he had helped establish six years earlier. He restocked his ships and then sailed as far as Port Alexander in Southern Angola, where he landed two of the African captives. Farther south near Cape Cross, Dias anchored the supply ship, and the two remaining ships sailed on, passing Cão's southermost *padrõe* on December 1. One week later, the ships anchored in Walvis Bay, where they found protection from huge South Atlantic swells. Native villages could be seen nearby with the inhabitants herding cattle and sheep.

Two weeks later, they had sailed as far as Luderitz in southern Namibia, three hundred miles farther than any previous expedition. Because of continued foul weather, they anchored there for five days, while Dias put ashore another African emissary. When the winds became more favorable, they embarked again, only to encounter even more fierce weather. On January 6, 1488, Dias decided to sail into deeper waters, hoping to escape from the horrendous winds that had been battering them for a month. Dias and his crew had not been prepared for such harsh conditions, and they suffered horribly as the icy swells bashed their ships for thirteen days.

Finally, Dias gave the command to sail east in search of land. Yet no land was sighted on the eastern horizon. Dias swung from east to north in search of land, his crew becoming more and more frightened that they would never see land again. Finally, on February 3, land was sighted. Now, however, by their calculations, they were sailing east along the coast instead of south. Stunned and hardly believing the truth, Dias realized that during the thirteen days at sea fighting the storms, he and his crew had accomplished what so many before had attempted but failed to do. He had rounded the southernmost cape of Africa.

The weary mariners landed near Mossel Bay in South Africa and attempted to find provisions but were beaten back by hostile natives. They sailed to Algoa Bay and at last found refuge. Dias was elated with his achievement and erected his first *padrõe*. He was eager to continue on even farther and determined now to sail all the way to India. His crew, however, objected strongly. Many had died during the wicked storms and many more were sick. Provisions were nearly gone and the ships were tattered and badly leaking. Still, Dias wanted to continue, but the crew threatened to mutiny. Dias pleaded with his men, promising them great wealth if they would continue the great expedition. Second-in-command Infante, a knight with an aristocratic heritage and jealous of the low-born Dias, led the opposition, and in the end Dias was only able to persuade his men to proceed for three more days before turning back. To avoid dishonor, Dias made his officers and principal seamen sign a document which explained what had occurred. As the two ships turned back and passed the *padrõe* at Algoa Bay, Dias, according to a historian writing twenty years after the voyage, sadly bade farewell to the historic marker, "with as much pain and sentiment as if he were leaving a beloved son in eternal exile."

Six weeks later in April, they encountered the worst weather of the expedition and were forced to anchor for three weeks in South Africa's Cape Agulhas, where they overhauled their battered vessels. By the end of May, they were crawling once again along the coast. On June 6, they sighted the southernmost cape, the one they had passed in the terrible February storm. Because of the difficulties they had encountered in reaching this elusive location, Dias named it the Cape of Storms. Later, King John renamed it the Cape of Good Hope because of the promise it offered in the discovery of a sea route to India. Dias erected his second *padrõe* there and then retraced his course to Luderitz, where he placed the third and last *padrõe*.

After recovering and then burning his supply ship, Dias crawled up the African coast. He made several stops along the way and at one point rescued the shipwrecked crew of a previous Portuguese expedition. Finally, in December, 1488, after fifteen months and sixteen thousand miles, Dias and his crew sailed into Lisbon.

John was ecstatic. He was also determined to keep the success of the voyage a secret, however, and for the next eight years was able to suppress any information about the voyage as well as all other Portuguese voyages. One witness to Dias' historic return, the brother of one of the junior pilots, did make a notation in the margin of one of his books:

> Note: that in December of this year 1488, Bartolomeu Dias, commandant of three caravels which the King of Portugal had sent out to Guinea to seek out the land, landed in Lisbon. He reported that he had reached a promontory which he called Cape of Good Hope. . . . He had described his voyage and plotted it league by league on a marine chart in order to place it under the eyes of the said king. I was present in all of this.

The chronicler was Christopher Columbus, one of many who benefited from Dias' monumental achievement.

Summary

In addition to Columbus' note, only two other contemporary references to Bartolomeu Dias exist. First, he was influential in designing the ships that in July, 1487, carried Vasco da Gama around the Cape of Good Hope to India. Second, in March, 1500, less than a year after da Gama's historic return from India, Dias captained one of thirteen ships under the command of Pedro Álvars Cabral and sailed in search of an alternate route to the Orient. The result of this voyage was the exploration of the Brazilian coast of South America. Upon setting sail from Brazil to Africa, once again in search of the Cape of Good Hope and India, the expedition encountered a ghastly storm in late May, 1500. Four ships were lost with all crewmen. Dias was one of the casualties.

There is no understanding the importance of Dias' greatest triumph. He had boldly attained the goal set by Prince Henry the Navigator in the early 1430's, to prove that there was a route around Africa to India that could be used to skirt the land routes monopolized by the Muslims. During his voyage, he accumulated valuable data which were used by John to plan the voyage that would ultimately result in Vasco da Gama's reaching India. He not only paved the way to the Orient but also inspired Christopher Columbus and later Ferdinand Magellan to seek their own routes to the Indies.

Dias, however, never reached the Orient himself. Another chronicler, writing sixty years after Dias' death, summarized Dias' achievement: "It may be said that he saw the land of India, but, like Moses and the Promised Land, he did not enter in." Ultimately, it was Dias, more than anyone before him, who made it possible for Portugal to dominate the Indian Ocean and secure the vast treasures of the Orient.

Bibliography

Craig, Simon. "A Passage to India." *Geographical Magazine* 70 (July, 1997): 73. The article focuses on explorations that led to the discovery of Asia including Dias' passage along the Cape of Good Hope.

Hart, Henry H. *Sea Road to the Indies*. New York: Macmillan, 1950; London: Hodge, 1952. Although the majority of the book chronicles the life and achievement of Vasco da Gama, the first part of the book is a detailed account of the Portuguese explorers who preceded him. Chapter 5 is dedicated to Dias and quotes from early Portuguese historians who later pieced together the long-suppressed details of Dias' voyage. Extensive bibliography of both English and foreign references.

Humble, Richard. *The Explorers*. Alexandria, Va.: Time-Life Books, 1978. Good overview of the most influential early explorers: Dias, Columbus, da Gama, and Magellan, the latter three all inspired by and benefiting from Dias' achievement. Excellent early maps, plus illustrations and text on the development of the ships and navigational equipment used for all the major voyages. Dias' voyage is described in chapter 1, "The First Giant Stride on the Route to India." Profusely illustrated; contains a selected bibliography.

Parr, Charles McKew. *So Noble a Captain*. New York: Crowell, 1953; London: Hale, 1955. This biography on the life of Magellan contains a detailed description of Dias' voyage in chapter 1, plus information on Dias' influence on John and the building of the ships that da Gama used to sail to India. Extensive bibliography includes books on the history of Portuguese exploration, navigation, and sailing-ship construction.

Prestage, Edgar. *The Portuguese Pioneers*. London: Black, and New York: Macmillan, 1933.

Covers in detail the history of Portuguese exploration from the late fourteenth century to the major expeditions of Dias, da Gama, and Cabral through the early sixteenth century. Dias' voyage is detailed in "Progress Under John II—the Voyage of Diego Cão—the Search for Prester John—the Voyage of Bartholomew Dias."

James Kline

DONATELLO
Donato di Niccolò di Betto Bardi

Born: c. 1386; Florence
Died: December 13, 1466; Florence
Area of Achievement: Art
Contribution: One of the first great European artists to articulate fully the principles of perspective, Donatello has had an incalculable influence on his successors, who have derived their inspiration from his highly naturalistic and intense dramatizations of the human form.

Early Life

Donatello's complete name was Donato di Niccolò di Betto Bardi. He was the son of a wool carder. Very little is known about his life, except what can be surmised from contemporary records (such as payments to him for commissioned work) and from a biographical sketch in *Le vite de' più eccellenti architetti, pittori, et scultori italiani* (1550) by Giorgio Vasari, an Italian architect, writer, and painter. Vasari, however, is not entirely reliable on the subject of his predecessors. It is known that Donatello lost his father while still a young boy, and that he lived with his mother until his middle forties, when she died. He never married. According to Vasari, the artist was a poor but generous man.

Donatello's native city of Florence had been an Etruscan city, founded before Rome. Florence had a long tradition as a center of commerce and pleasure, where a young man such as Donatello could learn art and the practical skills of business. He was trained in the Stonemasons' Guild and was the master of many crafts, including goldsmithing, the making of inlays, engraving, carving, and the application of stucco ornaments to furniture.

The first record of Donatello as an artist (May, 1403) puts him in the shop of Lorenzo Ghiberti, a pioneer in the use of perspective, a technique that gives depth and three-dimensional quality to paintings and relief sculpture. By 1406, Donatello was at work on small marble figures of prophets for the Porta della Mandorla of the Duomo of Florence. On February 20, 1408, he received his first major commission, for a marble figure of David.

Life's Work

Donatello's first major work, the *David* in the Palazzo Vecchio, is a marble figure measuring six feet, three and one-half inches. At his feet rests the massive head of Goliath. Standing above the head, with his legs parted, is a lithe, almost delicate David, draped in a close-fitting cloak that emphasizes the youthful muscularity of his figure. His long right arm accentuates the power of the slingshot throw that brought Goliath to earth. The fingers of the right hand are bent in a grasping pose and were probably meant to hold a sling which has been lost. There is great vitality and strength in the sculpture, even though David is not depicted in action, because of the economy and the expressive precision of the details Donatello dramatizes, such as the way the index and middle fingers of his left hand press against his torso. Although David is a religious figure and embodies a myth, he is presented as an individual, a remarkable personality worthy of close inspection.

With the marble figure of *Saint John the Evangelist*, now in the southern aisle of the Duomo of Florence, Donatello made a larger than life-size statue that surpasses the *David* in the dynamic rendering of personality. Working with a somewhat shallow block of marble, the artist shaped the upper half of the body in high relief, thus leaving enough marble for the seated figure's thighs. By giving the figure no back, he foregrounded those aspects of Saint John's person he wished to highlight. It is the saint's human qualities, his piercing eyes and grave demeanor, that rivet the viewer. With book in hand, held meditatively, he appears as the very embodiment of the prayerful man.

Saint George and the Dragon, a marble relief on the outside of the Or San Michele in Florence, is noteworthy for Donatello's use of mountain and forest landscape. As in his previous work, there is a beautiful rendering of naturalistic elements, a grounding in the reality of human emotions and settings. The representation of such scenes in the Middle Ages was more formulaic, more centered on a static composition of all the elements of the myth. In Donatello, rearing horse, rider, and dragon collide, so that the meaning of the myth arises primarily out of the sense of movement. Donatello's sculpture is not so much allegory (a pictorial evocation of myth) as it is an action in itself, a story evolving out of the artist's powerful dramatic technique.

The Feast of Herod (also known as the *Dance of Salome*), when compared to Pietro Lorenzetti's

DONATELLO

earlier painting of the same name, confirms Donatello's deft handling of realistic human figures in dramatic settings. In Lorenzetti's work, each of the seven figures is carefully spaced and distinctly visible in the foreground and background. The scene is frozen, made static, so that the picture is complete, the story intact. In Donatello's bronze relief for the Siena Cathedral font, five figures in the foreground of the right side of the relief draw back in horror at the presented head of John the Baptist. One man partially covers his face with his hand, as though the full sight of the head is more than he can bear. The other four figures are drawn back, but a woman in profile—perhaps the dancing Salome—stares fixedly at the head. These five figures are bunched together, obscuring a full view of their faces. Indeed, one face cannot be seen at all—only a headdress is visible. The realism, drama, and human complexity of the reactions to this atrocity demonstrate how intensely Donatello wished to convey the very life of events and personalities and not merely their symbolism. His use of composition to render the psychology of his subjects is evident in the left side of the bronze relief, where five distinctly positioned figures complete the foregrounding of the work and relieve the congestion of the right side. There is an exquisite balance achieved in the framing of the scene, quite different from Lorenzetti's proportioning of space.

Between 1411 and 1427, Donatello received commissions to work on figures of *Saint John the Evangelist* and *Saint George and the Dragon*, the *Sacrifice of Isaac*, the tomb of Baldassare Cossa (Pope John XXIII), the *Head of a Prophet*, the *Head of a Sibyl*, and others for the Or San Michele, the Opera del Duomo, and the cathedral of Orvieto—all in Florence. In 1430, he went to Rome for three years and carved several tombs. By 1433, he had returned to Florence to design several stained-glass windows, marble tombs, and bronze heads.

One of Donatello's most notable works from this period and said to have been his favorite is the so-called *Zuccone* (pumpkinhead, or baldhead). Again, it is the strong personality of the figure that is so commendable to modern taste. The long angular face, accentuated by the tilt of the head downward, the long loosely flexed right arm, with the right hand casually thrust inside a belt, are all aspects of a highly individualized figure. This is a person with his own peculiar outlook on the world, not simply a study of human form, and a figure with a posture that bends with life.

The bronze *David*, the *Equestrian Monument of General Gattamelata*, and *Mary Magdalen* are representative examples of the power and variety of Donatello's final period of creativity. It seemed to the artist's contemporaries that *David* was cast from life, so natural and playful does this slight figure appear. There is a joy and a lightness in this work that is entirely different from the earlier *David* in marble. The bronze statue of General Gattamelata, which stands in front of the Church Sant' Antonio in Padua, where the artist lived for nearly ten years, is a ruggedly determined depiction of the commander in chief of the Venetian military forces who died at Padua on January 16, 1443. The tough, chiseled quality of the face, the tight, slight grimness in the lips bespeak a man girding himself for battle with the poised calm of a great leader. As Ludwig Goldscheider notes, the wood carving of Mary Magdalen is an especially vivid example of Donatello's final naturalistic phase. The roughly hewn wood exaggerates the worn, beaten-looking, bony face, with its broken-toothed, grotesque mouth, while the strong hands, with fingers not quite touching one another in the sign of prayer, suggest the spirituality that inheres in this crude body.

Summary

Donatello is regarded as one of the great innovators of Renaissance art. The bronze *David*, for example, is one of the first nude freestanding Renaissance statues. His great contributions were recognized in his time, especially at Padua, where he was the head of an enormous workshop. In his last years, he created an extraordinary set of reliefs for the pulpits of San Lorenzo. Most of his work remains in Florence, although an unfinished *David* is exhibited at the National Gallery of Art in Washington, and a *Madonna* is in the Boston Museum.

The portrayal of human bodies is certainly one of Donatello's greatest achievements. The personality seems to express itself from within his dynamic figures, and there is never the sense that the faces he gives his figures are simply imposed upon them. In the perfect disposition of each physical feature, of every detail of clothing and setting, the artist perfects both the objective and psychological points of view. His figures are real people in a real world, observed with sharp accuracy.

Donatello can rightly be regarded as one of the precursors of modern art because his sculpture is autonomous, a thing in itself that is never simply illustrative of the subjects he carved and casted.

Like his contemporary Fra Angelico, Donatello excels in the dramatization of whole scenes, relying not only on his deft manipulation of human figures but also on his profound understanding of architecture and of the spaces his figures and objects occupy. Where he differs from Fra Angelico is in the heroic quality of so many of his human figures. It is, in the last analysis, his ability to portray depth powerfully—in his human subjects and in his settings—that continues to make his work worthy of the most serious study.

Bibliography

Avery, Charles. *Donatello: An Introduction*. New York: Icon Editions, 1994. A concise, illustrated survey of the life and work of Donatello, this book provides balanced coverage of Donatello's sculpture in different media and in different cities of Italy, and discusses his importance and influence. An ideal introduction for general readers, tourists, or students, Avery's book shows how Donatello's influence helped to create a new humanism that was a hallmark of the Renaissance.

———. "Donatello: Rough and Simple in Everything But His Sculpture." *Sculpture Review* vol. 46, no. 3 (1998). Charles Avery gives a vivid account of the character of Donatello, who was remarkably productive in his career but had a history of having strained relations with patrons.

Balcarres, Lord. *Donatello*. London: Duckworth, 1903. This study is still worth consulting for its detailed account of Donatello's career and its informative account of art history. Contains a large number of plates and an appendix of work lost or not executed. Out-of-date bibliography.

Goldscheider, Ludwig. *Donatello*. London: Allen and Unwin, and New York: Oxford University Press, 1941. Excellent reproductions of the artist's major sculptures with many plates focusing on interesting details. A well-written introduction to the significance of Donatello's work, a detailed catalog of major and minor sculpture, and an index of museums, collections, and places where Donatello's work appears make this an indispensable volume.

Janson, Horst Woldemar. *The Sculpture of Donatello*. 2 vols. Princeton, N.J.: Princeton University Press, 1957. Volume 1 is devoted to large black-and-white plates of the artist's work. Volume 2 contains a critical catalog that establishes accurate dating and documentation of Donatello's work. Extensive references to previous scholarship make this a dialogue between art historians as much as a discussion of Donatello's sculpture. Includes a very detailed and useful index.

Lightbown, R. W. *Donatello and Michelozzo: An Artistic Partnership and Its Patrons in the Early Renaissance*. 2 vols. London: Harvey Miller, and Philadelphia: Heyden, 1980. Although there is scant discussion of Donatello's individual works, this study provides excellent background for an understanding of the world in which Donatello worked. Should also be consulted for its glossary, a table showing popes in the fourteenth and fifteenth centuries, a chronology of Donatello, and beautiful plates with close-ups of the artist's greatest work.

Meyer, Alfred Gotthold. *Donatello*. London: Grevel, 1904. Contains 140 black-and-white illustrations from pictures, etchings, and drawings, as well as detailed accounts of Donatello's art. The style is sometimes exaggerated. Scholarship superseded by more recent studies. Includes an index of artists.

Carl Rollyson and Lisa Paddock

SIR FRANCIS DRAKE

Born: c. 1540; Crowndale, Devonshire, England
Died: January 28, 1596; at sea off Porto Bello, Panama
Areas of Achievement: Exploration and navigation
Contribution: A flair for leadership, combined with fearlessness and a powerful spirit of adventure, afforded Drake the most prominent place among those Elizabethan explorers and naval commanders who pioneered England's overseas expansion.

Early Life

Francis Drake was born around 1540 in Crowndale, a village near Tavistock, in Devonshire, England. Nothing is known of his mother. His father, Robert Drake, was the third son of John Drake of Otterton. Unsuccessful in business and committed to advancing the reformed religion, the father bore responsibility for his family living in humble circumstances. Many of Francis Drake's twelve siblings reputedly were born in the hull of a ship moored in the Thames in Kent, where the family had been forced to relocate as a result of the father's vocal Protestantism. There is a certain fitness in this connection with the sea, where most of the Drake offspring made their marks and ultimately died.

As a boy, Francis Drake was apprenticed to the master of a coasting vessel and acquired both a love for the sea and the skills that served him well during his career. Upon the death of the master, Drake assumed command of his ship and continued trading for a brief period. His spirit of adventure and his ambition proved, however, to be too strong, and by 1565 he joined expeditions that were mounted first to Africa and then to the Spanish Main. These voyages whetted his appetite for exploration and further stirred his ambition, so in 1567 he decided to join the third expedition organized by his cousin, John Hawkins, to capture black slaves in Africa and sell them to the Spanish colonists in the New World. Drake's decision to join Hawkins' third slaving voyage proved to be the turning point in his career, for Hawkins' fleet, including the ship *Judith*, commanded by Francis Drake, was attacked at San Juan de Ulúa, a small island off Veracruz, by a powerful Spanish force commanded by the Viceroy of New Spain. In the ensuing battle, only two of Hawkins' ships, the *Jesus of Lubeck*, commanded by Hawkins, and the *Judith*, captained by Drake, escaped and made their way back to England. Both Hawkins and Drake vowed to be avenged for what they viewed as the "treachery" of the Spaniards, and while both men made good on their vow, Francis Drake not only struck numerous and devastating blows against King Philip II of Spain, but also laid the foundation for the maritime traditions that spread England's power and influence around in the world in subsequent centuries.

Life's Work

In the years following the attack in Mexico, Drake embarked on a series of maritime adventures that established his reputation as the quintessentially daring English sea captain. Determined to strike a blow at Spain, Drake used his knowledge of the flow of Spanish treasure from America to Europe with dramatic effect. First, in 1570 and 1571, he mounted small reconnoitering voyages to the Gulf of Mexico to collect detailed information. Then, in 1572, he executed his masterstroke by sailing from

Plymouth to attack the Spanish at their most vulnerable point, the area of the production of precious metals in the New World. Knowing that the produce of the silver mines of Peru was transported by mule train overland through Panama, Drake determined to attack the unescorted treasure trains and seize their booty. Upon landing in Panama, Drake made contact with the Cimaroons and developed a plan to waylay the Spanish treasure train that regularly crossed the Isthmus of Panama. Providentially, Drake was taken by his guides to a high point in Panama where he could see both the Gulf of Mexico and the Pacific Ocean, which made him the first Englishman to see the Pacific. Vowing someday to sail an English ship on the Pacific, Drake and his force pressed on and soon enjoyed spectacular success by capturing an entire treasure train that yielded so much silver that they took what they could carry back to their ships and buried the rest. Drake arrived back in England on August 9, 1573. His expedition made him a wealthy man, endowed him with a reputation for courage and daring, and gave him what proved to be a brilliant idea for his next enterprise against the Spanish.

Knowing that the Spanish treasure route was from Peru to Panama by ship, then across the Isthmus by mule train, and finally on to Spain by ship, Drake plotted to lead a fleet to the western coast of South America. Once there, he intended to attack the unprotected Spanish ships that carried the bullion to Panama, take as much treasure as his ships could carry, and return to England. From the seed of this plan, Drake became the first man to circumnavigate the globe. Leaving Plymouth on December 13, 1577, Drake and his fleet sailed southward. By the time he entered the Pacific through the Strait of Magellan, only his ship the *Golden Hind* remained of the fleet that had left Plymouth. From the autumn of 1578 through the spring of 1579, Drake sailed northward, capturing treasure all along the way. He continued on a northerly course until he reached the area that is now San Francisco, then turned westward, crossing the Pacific and Indian oceans, rounding the Cape of Good Hope, and proceeding northward along the African coast to England. Drake arrived home on September 26, 1580, after nearly three years at sea. A few months later, he was knighted and assumed the premier position among English mariners of his era.

As Anglo-Spanish relations deteriorated during the 1580's, Drake was called upon by the Crown to lead the English naval forces against the Spanish. In 1585, Drake led a fleet against Spanish possessions in the New World, where the colonial cities of San Domingo and Cartagena were captured. Shortly after his return home in July, 1586, Drake was placed in command of an English fleet at Plymouth, and in the spring of 1587 he led an expedition against Spain to disrupt the formation of an armada then assembling to invade England. By attacking the Spanish fleet in Cadiz and destroying more than thirty ships and tons of supplies, Drake delayed the formation of Philip's armada for more than a year and also ensured that when it sailed it would be critically weakened. The effect of Drake's assault in 1587 was demonstrated in July, 1588, when the Spanish Armada approached England. Drake was the first English commander to intercept the Spanish, and throughout the course of the subsequent battle his ship the *Revenge* was always in the forefront of the action. His leadership was largely responsible for the English victory over the Armada, and the triumph provided the capstone for his reputation. Ironically, his unbroken success against the Spanish indirectly led to his death, for in 1595 Queen Elizabeth appointed Drake and Sir John Hawkins cocommanders of a fleet directed to attack Spanish possessions in the New World. During the campaign, both Hawkins and Drake contracted diseases that led to their deaths. A victim of dysentery, Sir Francis Drake died aboard his flagship the *Defiance* off Porto Bello, Panama, on January 28, 1596, and appropriately was buried at sea.

Summary

At first glance, Sir Francis Drake's career appears to have been characterized primarily by military exploits at sea. Virtually every action that he took, including even the magnificent feat of exploration and seamanship of the circumnavigation, was warlike, directed against the Spanish Empire, and had significant overtones of greed and personal ambition. Yet Drake was far more than one of a long line of successful English warriors, for he personified the spirit of adventure and expressed the indomitable courage and insatiable curiosity that typified the Elizabethan era. Because of Drake and those he inspired, England's knowledge of the world was vastly expanded, the nation's economy was stimulated, a national confidence in the ability to overcome the most daunting obstacles was inspired, and a sense of England's place among the leading powers of Europe was firmly established. Yet the most important of Drake's accomplishments came in the area of maritime affairs, for he demonstrated to his countrymen that their destiny lay on the oceans of the world, regardless of whether they defended their island against foreign invaders or sought to explore the unknown lands of the Pacific. The ultimate English adventurer, Francis Drake was more responsible than any of his contemporaries for establishing an international presence for England that endures to the present day.

Bibliography

Bell, Douglas. *Drake*. London: Duckworth, 1935. A readable, short biography of Drake that covers the main events of his career. While this study lacks depth of analysis, it nevertheless provides a good summary of Drake's life and includes a bibliography that admirably summarizes important works up to 1935.

Bradford, Ernle Dusgate Selby. *The Wind Commands Me: A Life of Sir Francis Drake*. New York: Harcourt Brace, 1965. This work tries to portray Drake as a whole person rather than a naval legend, and manages to delineate his compassion as well as his courage. Altogether a respectable biography.

Corbett, Sir Julian. *Drake and the Tudor Navy.* London and New York: Longman, 1898. Despite its overwhelmingly favorable view of Drake, this work remains the standard biographical account. A meticulously scholarly work that includes material gleaned from both English and Spanish manuscript sources, this study also details the rise of England as a maritime power while it relates Drake's career to that development.

Hampden, John, ed. *Francis Drake: Privateer.* London: Methuen, and University: University of Alabama Press, 1972. A collection of documents relevant to Drake's exploits that provides a unique view of the range and significance of his achievements. The glossary is particularly helpful.

Kelleher, Brian T. *Drake's Bay: Unraveling California's Great Maritime Mystery.* Cupertino, Calif.: Kelleher and Associates, 1997. Kelleher has directed state archaeologists to the shores of a small cove forty miles north of San Francisco, California, where he contends that Sir Francis Drake grounded the legendary Golden Hind, and, with his company of fifty men and a young woman, constructed British-Colonial America's first fort. Includes 176 illustrations, 39 maps, extensive footnotes, and a comprehensive bibliography.

Roche, T.W.E. *The Golden Hind.* London: Berker, and New York: Praeger, 1973. A fascinating study that concentrates on Drake's ship used in the circumnavigation, life at sea in the sixteenth century, and the role of Sir Christopher Hatton in sponsoring the expedition. The photographs and maps are especially well done.

Ruhge, Justin M. *Drake in Central California, 1579: Unraveling One of California's Great Historical Mysteries.* Goleta, Calif.: Quantum Imaging Associates, 1990. Sir Francis Drake's reputation as a seaman, explorer, and raider of the Spanish Main has always been of great interest to students of history. Part of this interest concerns where Drake spent thirty days on the coast of California in 1579, during which he repaired his ship, the Golden Hind, and reported on the natives and their culture. This study takes a completely new approach to defining the location on the central California coast based on data from the Portola expedition in 1769 and a reevaluation of maps and other geographic data.

Williamson, James A. *The Age of Drake.* London: Black, 1938; New York: World Publishing, 1965. Although somewhat dated, this study weaves the details of Drake's life and the specifics of England's overseas expansion into something that is both a biography and a thoughtful sketch of a critical period in the evolution of the island kingdom.

Ronald L. Pollitt

JOHN DUNSTABLE

Born: c. 1390; England

Died: December 24, 1453; probably London, England

Area of Achievement: Music

Contribution: Through a strategic use of dissonance and harmonic structure, Dunstable became one of the most influential composers of the fifteenth century, laying the foundation for music in the Renaissance.

Early Life

Though he is unquestionably the first great English composer in the history of music and an important link between the medieval and Renaissance styles, little is known about the life and career of John Dunstable. This uncertainty is not surprising when one considers the status of musicians and composers in the medieval period—a status on a level with those anonymous craftsmen and artisans who designed and built the great cathedrals of the era or who worked diligently for their masters or in the service of the Church, the great stabilizing institution of the period.

Still, there is much circumstantial evidence that teases the imagination. A Latin inscription on the cover of an astronomy book states that the volume belonged to a John Dunstable, musician in the service of the Duke of Bedford. The duke was the brother of Henry V, King of England from 1413 to 1422, and served as regent to the King's nephew, Henry VI, in "occupied" France from 1422 until his own death in 1435. If, as seems likely, Dunstable, as court musician, accompanied Bedford to France, this period would be the earliest record of Dunstable's career, however speculative. It was during this period, interestingly, that Joan of Arc was captured by the English forces under Bedford and burned at the stake in 1431.

What Dunstable's formative years were and what training he received are unknown, but his connection with astronomy suggests that he was a learned man, probably versed in the other medieval academic disciplines of mathematics, arithmetic, and certainly music. The breadth of his learning is supported by one of several epitaphs written in Latin which commemorates Dunstable as "an astrologian, a mathematician, a musician and what not."

Just when he began to compose is also problematic, but scholars have compared his work with some of the most important sources of the period, particularly the Old Hall manuscript, containing pieces by English composers, and the evidence is strong that his first work began to appear about 1415.

Ironically, the only fact about Dunstable's life that is certain is the date of his death. Once again, an epitaph provides the information. Taken from the church in which Dunstable was buried, the Latin inscription declares him to be the glory of music, who passed among the constellation of the stars, "on the day before Christ's birthday," 1453.

Life's Work

The extent of Dunstable's influence on the development of Western music may be gauged by, among other things, the famous assessment of Johannes de Tinctoris, a Renaissance musicologist and the editor of one of the first musical dictionaries. He affirmed Dunstable to be the founder of "the English style" of music, which spread to the Continent and which became the standard of artistic achievement. Tinctoris had even let his enthusiasm for Dunstable's work lead him to declare that nothing in music was worth hearing before Dunstable's time. As overripe as Tinctoris' esteem might appear, however, the existence of manuscripts of Dunstable's works on the Continent, particularly in Italy, attests his influence and importance as a transmitter of this new style.

Both the variety and the number of his compositions are impressive. His works total about seventy-five pieces. All of them are for voices alone (*a cappella*), mostly for two or three parts, and the majority are religious works intended for church use, though not necessarily for any specific liturgical event. As with most music before 1500 or so, the human voice was the primary medium of expression, and though there was a significant production in secular music as early as the fourteenth century, vocal music centering on the church service was the primary focus of most serious composers.

The Latin church music of Dunstable shows a mastery of the polyphonic vocal technique then reaching its flowering. Originating sometime around the eleventh century, polyphony is the simultaneous singing of two or more independent melodies. By the fourteenth century, the texture of much polyphonic writing had become rigid, complex, and technically dense. Working within his English musical traditions, Dunstable produced compositions which were freer, less obtuse, and structurally clearer than much of the work of other composers. The key to this clarity was his control of dissonance.

To the modern ear, much medieval music sounds somehow unresolved. In that period before a major and minor tonal system (a development of the Baroque period, beginning about 1600), the melodic progression of a musical composition often depended on the main melody, called the *cantus firmus*, which was supported by a second, third, or fourth voice. These voices, or parts, often embroidered the *cantus firmus* so heavily that the work resulted in a rhythmic density, technically brilliant but hard to follow. Such a density is typical, for example, of the French polyphonic tradition of the fourteenth century, called *Ars nova.*

Dunstable freed polyphonic writing from this density. By taking control of the dissonance inherent in such embroidery, he simplified the melodic progression and created work of unmatched sonority. His hymn *Ave maris stella* is an excellent example of controlled dissonance, an innovation that looked ahead to the harmonic principles of a later generation.

Several types of compositions distinguish the work of Dunstable. The largest group can be classified as *ballades*, a sort of free-style composition whose origins are in the secular music of the previous century. Dunstable's *ballades* are characterized by a clear melody carried by one or more voices and are largely songs of praise to the Virgin. Such works as *Sancta Maria, non est*, *Salve Mater*, and *Salve Regina* are obvious examples of Dunstable's skillful adaptation of secular models for sacred purposes. Like his other works in general, these are marked at once by their seeming spontaneity, their sonority, their melodic charm.

Dunstable's most complex works are the isorhythmic motets. One of the most important medieval and Renaissance forms, the motet is a polyphonic composition using a biblical text. Sometimes a different, though complementary, text was assigned to each voice. Dunstable wrote more than a dozen motets in what is called "isorhythmic" structures, a precisely mathematical form in which the main melody is repeated several times, along with the rhythmic pattern, though the time values of the notes are proportionately reduced as the music progresses, the voices now coming together, now separating. Highly sophisticated, such works as *Veni Sancti Spiritus* (1431?) established Dunstable as one of the century's leading composers. The arithmetical precision of these motets strengthens the validity of those epitaphs which praise him as a mathematician.

For all the complexity of such isorhythmic motets, Dunstable also produced, probably between 1420 and 1435, a number of "declamatory" motets which scholars praise as his most original contribution to the form. His most famous of this type is *Quam pulcra es*. In this motet, the rhythm is allowed to take the pattern demanded by the text, following the natural inflections and accents of the voice. Melody is thus subordinated to the sense and rhythm of the words, and the result is an expressiveness unmatched in the period. There is a quality of improvisation in these works, an easy freedom that anticipates much of the music of the Renaissance.

Finally, Dunstable seems to have been among the earliest composers to attempt a musical unification of the Mass. Previous to him, the sung parts of the Mass—such as the Kyrie, the Gloria, and the Credo—were conceived as independent, unrelated musical structures. Though the French composer Guillaume Machaut (1300-1377) is generally credited with producing the first polyphonic setting of the complete Mass in 1364, the thematic unity of the work is questioned by some scholars, and the piece is, in any case, virtually unique amid the composer's vast body of secular compositions.

Dunstable's work, however, shows a clear attempt at thematic unification of the various parts of the Mass. His *Rex seculorum* Mass unites the five sections—Kyrie, Gloria, Credo, Sanctus, and Agnus Dei—through the use of a single common melody. The music is clear, expressive, and remarkably sonorous.

Little evidence suggests that Dunstable composed after the death of Bedford in 1435. Some scholars speculate that he "retired" to London to pursue his astronomical studies, especially in the light of a book of astronomical treatises to which he contributed about 1440. Certainly he was well known on the Continent by that date and was already being praised as a musical genius. By the time of his death, in 1453, the Renaissance was in full flower.

Summary

John Dunstable was the acknowledged leader of a group of English composers at the end of the Middle Ages who were writing polyphonic compositions indigenous to their own musical tradition. In style and technique, the music was basically conservative, but there was an emphasis on the use of certain chords and harmonic structures that came closer to modern musical techniques than to any other music produced at that time.

The particular distinction of this English school was its development of what is called a "pan-consonant" style—music characterized by a freer melodic line, a more impromptu and spontaneous use of rhythm, a greater flexibility in the arrangement and grouping of the voices, and, especially in the case of Dunstable, a control of dissonance—what to a modern ear are those harsh and unresolved notes that do not seem to harmonize with the basic melody.

Like Johann Sebastian Bach, composing some three hundred years after him, Dunstable was not so much an innovator as a great synthesizer. He built his music on an older tradition, fusing it with newer elements from the French and Italian schools, and produced something fresh and original, works of unusual sweetness and euphony.

Dunstable's musical strategy was toward clarity and simplicity. If much of the polyphonic music of the era can be compared to massive cathedrals of sound, aesthetically analogous to those stone-hewn monuments of prayer that are the glories of medieval architecture, then Dunstable's music can be viewed as a magnificent church, lighter, less stupefying, but more personal, more intimate, and still wonderfully crafted.

Coming at the end of the Middle Ages, Dunstable's music is a summation of much that went before and an affirmation of what was to come: a perfect transition between the medieval and Renaissance styles. Ironically, after his own time, little of his music was known until the end of the nineteenth century, and the complete edition of Dunstable's works was not published until 1953, some four hundred years after his death.

Bibliography

Bent, Margaret. *Dunstaple*. London and New York: Oxford University Press, 1981. A brief, close study of the technical aspects of Dunstable's work, intended largely for the student of music rather than the casual, curious lay reader. An accurate, clinically objective account.

Davey, Henry. *History of English Music*. London: Curwen, 1895; New York: DaCapo, 1969. This is the most enthusiastic account of the composer and his music. Davey suggests that Dunstable is the leader of the school that "invented the art of musical composition," an excessive claim. Written with a neo-Victorian chattiness that tends to lessen the scholar's objectivity, it is fun to read.

Harrison, Frank L. *Music in Medieval Britain*. London: Routledge, 1958; New York: Praeger, 1959. An exhaustive treatment of English choral and vocal music from the Norman Conquest to about 1550. A pioneering study, the work is an important source for placing Dunstable and his music in a meaningful position within a long, native tradition.

Reese, Gustave. *Music in the Middle Ages*. New York: Norton, 1940; London: Dent, 1941. An excellent, thorough study of the range of Western music up to the Renaissance. The final chapters deal with polyphony in England to the death of Dunstable and suggest a creative cross-pollination between Continental and English composers.

Walker, Ernest. *A History of Music in England*. 3d ed. Oxford: Clarendon Press, 1952; New York: DaCapo Press, 1978. Contains an early chapter on Dunstable and the period. Brief, pithy, and readable.

Edward Fiorelli

ALBRECHT DÜRER

Born: May 21, 1471; Nuremberg, Bavaria
Died: April 6, 1528; Nuremberg, Bavaria
Area of Achievement: Art
Contribution: Dürer has often been called the "Leonardo of the North" because of his diverse talents. Painter, graphic artist, and theorist, he moved in elite intellectual circles that included some of the most famous men of his time. As a graphic artist, Dürer has never been surpassed. He helped bring Italian Renaissance ideas to the art of northern Europe.

Early Life

Albrecht Dürer was born in Nuremberg at a time when that city was moving from its Gothic past to a more progressive style of Renaissance Humanism, exemplified by Vienna and Basel in northern Europe. His father, a goldsmith, had come from Hungary to Nuremberg, where he met and married Dürer's mother. The third of eighteen children, Dürer showed unusual artistic inclinations at an early age. After working with his father during his younger years, Dürer, at age fifteen, was apprenticed to Michel Wohlgemuth, head of a large local workshop that produced woodcuts for printers as well as painted altarpieces.

It was the custom for apprentices to complete their training period with a *Wanderjahre* or wandering journey, in order to seek new ideas from outside sources before submitting their own *Meisterstück* or masterpiece, to the guild so as to obtain a license as an artist within the city. Dürer, after completing three years with Wohlgemuth and becoming familiar with both painting and graphic technique, began his own journey. Little is known about the first year or so, but it is known that the young artist traveled to Colmar with the intention of working with the famed engraver and printer Martin Schongauer. Unfortunately, the older artist had already died before Dürer's arrival, so he journeyed to Basel to work with Schongauer's brother, Georg.

Dürer's intellectual curiosity and winning personality, affirmed by references in letters by his contemporaries, soon won for him valuable contacts in Basel. Designs in many of the illustrated books published there have been attributed to him, including those in the 1494 edition of Sebastian Brant's famous *Das Narrenschiff* (*This Present Boke Named Shyp of Folys of the Worlde*, 1509). Scholars agree that he did the frontispiece, *Saint Jerome Curing the Lion*, for *Epistolare beati Hieronymi* (letters of Saint Jerome), published in 1492 by Nikolaus Kessler.

In July of 1494, after a brief stay in Strasbourg, Dürer returned to Nuremberg to marry Agnes Frey, the daughter of a wealthy local burgher. Even considering that the marriage was an arranged one, as was the custom, the young couple seem to have been totally unsuited for each other. They had no children, and a few months after his wedding day Dürer went with friends to Italy, where he stayed for about a year.

Through his friendship with the Nuremberg Humanist Willibald Pirkheimer, a confirmed lover of classical objects, and through his own copying of prints by Italian masters, Dürer took full advantage of his stay in Italy. Drawings and watercolors of Venice, sketches of nudes and statuary, and especially his outdoor paintings of the Alps of the southern Tirol attest Dürer's fascination with the South and its artistic climate. A self-portrait done in 1498 shows the artist's conception of himself as a well-dressed, confident, and dignified young gentleman. Dürer early enjoyed an enviable reputation as a gifted artist and knowledgeable companion, and upon returning to Nuremberg he moved easily in the upper social and intellectual circles of that city. He was a good businessman and took advantage of the psychological impact of the projected year 1500, when the Last Judgment was supposed to occur, by completing German and Latin editions of the illustrated *Apocalypse* in 1498.

Life's Work

The awakening Renaissance and Humanistic tendencies in the previously Gothic North, along with the popularity of illustrated printed books, created a growing need for graphic artists. Dürer's graphic talents continued to deepen and become more refined. His mature works display a greater luminosity as well as a wider range of dark, light, and middle tonalities. By financing, illustrating, and printing *Apocalypse*, Dürer further enhanced his reputation as a master artist. An unusual *Self-Portrait* of 1500 reveals his mature self-esteem, as he shows himself remarkably like images of Christ. On the question of the role of artists—as craftsman or as creative genius—Dürer clearly assumed the latter designation.

Dürer took a second trip to Italy in the fall of 1505. By then, his reputation was widely established. *The Feast of the Rose Garlands*, made for the altar of the fraternity of German merchants in the Fondaco dei Tedeschi in 1506, is a large panel celebrating Christian brotherhood in the Feast of the Rosary. Perhaps this painting is an attempt to demonstrate the supremacy of Northern art. During his time in Italy, Dürer was especially fascinated by Italian theories of perspective and by studies of human proportions.

Two engravings by Dürer, *Adam and Eve* (1504) and *Melencolia I* (1514), illustrate the artist's complex personality and goals. Done very shortly before his second trip to Italy, *Adam and Eve* relied on Italian artists such as Andrea Mantegna and Antonio Pollaiuolo for a canon of the body's ideal beauty. Familiar with the writings of the classical writer Vitruvius on human proportions, Dürer chose two popular statues of antiquity, the Apollo Belvedere and the Medici Venus, as his models. Thus, the models of Italian classicism, only slightly altered in form, find themselves in Dürer's engraving, in a dark, Gothic northern forest. The Tree of Life with the parrot holds a plaque with the Latin inscription "Albertus Dürer Noricus faciebat 1504," demonstrating the artist's pride in his home city of Nuremberg. Dürer's usual signature is inconspicuously added. Eve receives the forbidden fruit from the center Tree of Knowledge. The Fall of Man results in the characters' loss of ideal form as well as loss of paradisiacal innocence; the animals at the first couple's feet symbolize the various human temperaments. The inevitable control these temperaments held on mankind after the Fall displays pessimism regarding the human condition as well as the northern taste for disguised symbolism. An uneasy tension exists between the Italianate classical figures and their northern environment.

Melencolia I was done seven years after Dürer's return from his second Italian trip. He was fully aware of the Italian Renaissance notion of the artist as a divinely inspired creature, but here Dürer shows in the large winged figure the personification of melancholic despair. The objects at her feet are tools for creating art, especially architecture, but they are useless in this context, as the seated figure suffers from the debilitating inactivity caused by the divine frenzy, or *furor melancholicus*. The idea is intensified by the bat, a symbol of the diabolical temperament, which carries the title banner across the sky. Thus, the message is clear that the artist, "born under Saturn" and endowed with potentially special gifts, is frustrated and unproductive in the search for an absolute beauty that only God knows. Both the *Adam and Eve* and *Melencolia I* engravings demonstrate Dürer's astonishing mastery of the medium in their complexity and luminosity.

Dürer's equal expertise with the woodcut medium is shown in *The Four Horsemen of the Apocalypse* (c. 1497-1498) from the *Apocalypse* series, which illustrates scenes from Revelation in the Bible. Dürer's rapid development of technique can be traced by comparing one of his earliest engravings, *Holy Family with the Butterfly* of about 1495, with a late work, the *Erasmus of Rotterdam* of 1526. In the former, some hesitancy can be seen in the cross-hatching of drapery folds and unconvincing variations of light and shade. In the mature work, one finds precise and sensitive modeling of forms, a broad range of light-and-shade tonalities, and a luminosity that bathes the figures in reflected light.

Among Dürer's many important patrons was Frederick the Wise, who commissioned a portrait and also asked Dürer to paint the altarpieces *Madonna and Child* (c. 1497) and *The Adoration of the Magi* (1504). In these paintings, Dürer demonstrates that he is primarily a graphic artist, as the paintings are more dependent on linear design than on color. Two paintings of Adam and Eve, done after Dürer's return to Nuremberg in 1507, indicate that he was influenced by premannerist tendencies found in Italian and German art of the early 1500's. The influence of Italian theory is also evident in his four-book study on human proportions, published shortly after his death. In 1511, Dürer published three picture books, *The Life of the Virgin*, *Great Passion*, and *Small Passion*. Some of the prints were issued as independent woodcuts.

During 1513 and 1514, Dürer issued three famous prints: *Knight, Death, and Devil*, *Saint Jerome in His Study*, and the *Melencolia I*. Had these been his only works, his fame would have been assured. In 1512, he was appointed court artist for Emperor Maximilian I, for whom he did a series of large woodcuts. In 1520, Dürer journeyed to western Germany and the Netherlands, and at this time did a portrait of King Christian II of Denmark, who was traveling through Antwerp.

Dürer's last major painting, *Four Apostles* (1526), is in many ways a memorial to the Reformation. He gave it to the city of Nuremberg, which had recently adopted Lutheranism as the official

creed. The text below the figures issues a warning to the city to heed the words of the figures depicted—Peter, John, Paul, and Mark.

Summary

Albrecht Dürer was a man and an artist of exceptional talents who lived through a particularly crucial time in Germany, the age of the Reformation. Dürer was very much a man of his own time. A scholar and theorist as well as a gifted artist, he was cognizant of and contributed to the great accomplishments and ideas in art in the period between the late fifteenth and early sixteenth centuries in Europe. A careful scrutiny of his self-portraits alone suggests his growing self-awareness of the artist as no longer a mere anonymous craftsman but as an individual of extraordinary ability and special importance. Like one with whom he has often been compared, Leonardo da Vinci, Dürer approached art (that is, painting and the graphic arts) as one of the seven liberal arts rather than as a purely mechanical exercise. With his keen interest in Italian ideas of proportion of the human figure and of perspective, Dürer could be said to have almost single-handedly wedded Italian Renaissance to northern Gothic art.

Dürer was famous in his own time. On his late journeys to Antwerp and elsewhere, he was sought by the highest social and intellectual groups of the area. His diary and his theoretical writings show him to have been a person of broad knowledge and diverse interests. His treatise on proportions, together with that of Leonardo, constitutes a most important contribution to Renaissance art theory. Unlike Leonardo's works, Dürer's contributions became accessible to a large public through printed publication. Through his own use of Italianate classical models, Dürer increased public appreciation for classical art. In turn, Dürer influenced later Italian artists by his integrated style.

Dürer's late works, although fewer in number than his earlier output, do not diminish in power or originality. His great talents are particularly remarkable in the engravings and woodcuts, which he favored since they, unlike commissioned paintings, allowed him independence from patrons and served as a source of income through the popular prints. Dürer is one of the central figures of European art.

Bibliography

Anzelewsky, Fedja. *Dürer: His Art and Life*. London: Chartwell, and New York: Konecky, 1980. A straightforward account of Dürer's life within the context of Renaissance and Reformation Europe. Special attention is paid to Dürer's writings, especially the treatises on art theory. Emphasizes Dürer's religious and humanistic beliefs. Good reproductions, many in full color. Useful bibliography.

Dürer, Albrecht. *The Intaglio Prints of Albrecht Dürer: Engravings, Etchings, and Drypaints*. Edited by Walter L. Strauss. New York: Kennedy Galleries, 1977; London: Orbis, 1979. The most complete catalog of the intaglio prints in English. Illustrations after each catalog entry. Includes introduction, full catalog entries to all previous literature, and an annotated bibliography. Especially useful in that prints are reproduced in actual size. Important to an understanding of Dürer's graphics. Recommended for the general Dürer reader.

Hutchison, Jane Campbell. *Albrecht Dürer: A Biography*. Princeton, N.J.: Princeton University Press, 1990. Dürer is thought by many to be one of the world's great artistic geniuses, unique in his ability to translate the basic principles of the Italian Renaissance into the northern European style to which he was born. This major biography links Dürer's artistic development to his personal life and to the turbulent history of pre-Reformation Europe.

Koerner, Joseph Leo. *The Moment of Self-Portraiture in German Renaissance Art*. Chicago: University of Chicago Press, 1993. In this study, Joseph Koerner discusses the character of Renaissance art in Germany by examining how the works of artists such as Dürer and Hans Baldung Grien reflected the changing status of the individual in sixteenth century Germany.

Panofsky, Erwin. *The Life and Art of Albrecht Dürer*. Princeton, N.J.: Princeton University Press, 1955. A paperback reprint of a classic, unmatched for sensitivity to and comprehensive analysis of Dürer's life and work. Omits now-outdated list of Dürer's works but retains excellent interpretive essays. Good illustrations. Very useful for student and general reader.

Rowlands, John. *The Age of Dürer and Holbein*. Cambridge and New York: Cambridge University Press, 1988. This book contains high-quality reproductions of Dürer prints and drawings as well as several watercolor studies. Surveys, through works in the British Museum and private and public British collections, art development from late Gothic style to Northern Renaissance naturalism. In addition to Dürer and Holbein, offers valuable coverage of their predecessors and contemporaries.

Russell, Francis. *The World of Dürer, 1471-1528*. New York: Time Books, 1967. An excellent text, introductory level, with many good reproductions, some full page and full color, as well as explanatory maps and graphics. Traces Dürer's development and life within the social, religious, and political context of his time. Chronology chart shows artists of Dürer's era. Limited but useful bibliography.

Scheller, Robert W., and Karel G. Boon, comps. *The Graphic Art of Albrecht Dürer, Hans Dürer, and the Dürer School*. Amsterdam: Van Gendt, 1971. This catalog is based on Joseph Meder's classic *Dürer—Katalog* (Vienna, 1932) and is notable for making available in English the pioneering Dürer works by Meder and Hollstein. Excellent introductory section on Dürer as a graphic artist. Many prints, some of uneven quality. Valuable book for all levels.

Snyder, James. *Northern Renaissance Art: Painting, Sculpture, the Graphic Arts from 1350 to 1575*. New York: Abrams, 1985. Full coverage of the Northern Renaissance, with an excellent chapter entitled "Albrecht Dürer and the Renaissance in Germany." Discusses in detail, with good reproductions, many examples of Dürer's graphic works and paintings. Text includes recent interpretations and theories. Includes a timetable of the arts, history, and science from 1300 to 1575. Valuable for the general reader.

Mary Sweeney Ellett

EDWARD IV

Born: April 28, 1442; Rouen, Normandy, France
Died: April 9, 1483; Westminster Palace, England
Area of Achievement: Government
Contribution: Utilizing instruments of government inherited from the Lancastrian kings, as well as molding pragmatic methods which anticipated those of the Tudors, Edward of York restored both the authority and prestige of the English monarchy following the dangers and drift of the reigns of the Lancastrian kings. He was aided in this success by the end of the Hundred Years' War (1453), which had become both a distraction and a financial and military disaster for the English monarchy.

Early Life

Nothing is known of the childhood of Edward IV; he was the son of Richard, Duke of York, and of Cecily Neville, daughter of Ralph, Earl of Westmoreland. Edward was not born to kingship; he won it at the battles of Mortimer's Cross and Towton Field (both fought in 1461); although he was proclaimed king between the fighting of the two battles, domestic conflict with the deposed Henry VI and his supporters, foreign complications with France and Burgundy, and the whirling allegiance of Richard Neville, Earl of Warwick (the "Kingmaker") prevented the full and unchallenged exercise of Edward's royal power until 1471, by which time Henry VI and his son, and Warwick, lay dead. England, exhausted by 116 years of intermittent and ultimately unsuccessful war in France, and by the Wars of the Roses, which kept parts of England in turmoil from 1455 until 1471, was ready for a period of tranquillity guaranteed by abundant governance and wise foreign policy. Edward IV provided both.

The young king was handsome, magnificently dressed and groomed, affable, open in his relations with all but those who posed a threat to his rule (such as his brother George, Duke of Clarence, who was executed in 1478, allegedly drowned in a barrel of that sweet Mediterranean wine now known as Madeira). Sir Thomas More in his *The History of King Richard the Third* (1543) described Edward as

> a goodly parsonage, and very Princely to behold, of hearte couragious, politique in counsaille, in aduersitie nothynge abashed, in prosperitie, rather ioyfulle than prowde, in peace iuste and mercifull, in warre, sharpe and fyerce, in the fields, bolde and hardye, and natheless no farther than wysedom woulde, aduenturous.

More also noted Edward's inclination to "fleshlye wantonnesse" and to overindulgence in the pleasures of the table, which led to corpulence in his early middle age.

Life's Work

Edward's rule did not really begin until after the bootless attempt by Warwick to restore Henry VI to his lost crown ended at the Battle of Barnet in 1471; Warwick died in the battle, and the captured Henry VI died shortly thereafter—Edward IV could hardly tolerate the continued existence of his predecessor. The last Lancastrian king could not be permitted to live; he, alive, would have been a threat to the rule of Edward IV, a focus for the loyalties of those elements of the polity who opposed the policies and rule of the first Yorkist king. Thus, Henry paid the ultimate price for royal failure in fifteenth century

England in 1472. Barnet marked the last attempt of overmighty nobles to control or to replace the king; the Wars of the Roses were now over.

From 1471 to 1483, Edward ruled England with vigor and efficiency, providing the businesslike government usually associated with the rule of the Tudors. This period of his reign was facilitated not only by the death of old rivals, but by the eclipse of the Nevilles and of the Woodvilles, the family of his queen, and also by the settlement of the lingering diplomatic problems with France in 1475. As of 1471, then, Edward was unencumbered by extraneous considerations: Domestic conflict was ended and foreign peace achieved, Parliament and council no longer enjoyed public approbation, and attainder (often more important as a threat than as actuality) had undermined the position of the greater nobility. For the first time since the death of Edward III in 1377, the king could concentrate on being king.

Edward IV relied heavily upon his administrative officials in the conduct of his government, since council and Parliament had declined in public esteem, although the precedent for the council acting as the Tudor Court of Star Chamber falls to this reign. The Lancastrian parliaments had not inspired general confidence; owing to the lack of effective rule by kings who were successively moribund, absent, or sickly, parliaments had fallen under the control of magnates and their affinities; lacking any real counterbalance to his authority, Edward governed his country with little need to regard institutional opposition as a reality. Like the Tudors who were to succeed his brother Richard III in 1485, Edward was astute in favoring, and in winning the support of, the middle classes. This is why monarchy is regarded as a progressive force in the English Middle Ages; the first Yorkist king allied himself and his policies with the new class rising to a political influence which, under the Tudors, was to be commensurate with their economic importance. Edward and his immediate successors knew where money was to be found, and he cultivated the people who had it. The commons were worth cultivating: they were the source of funds, and of attainders against those viewed by the king as dangerous. Yet there were few parliaments convened in Edward's reign, a reflection of the fact that his own personal financial resources were sufficient to maintain a large portion of his needs, and of the ending of the French wars. Parliament was not an independent body in the fifteenth century; it was controlled by either the king or the magnates, and so it was to remain until the turbulent seventeenth century. As well, Edward utilized fiscal means derived from sources not granted from Parliament, especially the "benevolences," which were a form of compulsory loan. Edward was not the first English king to find extraparliamentary sources of funding the expenses of government; the precedents go at least as far back as the reign of King Edward I (1272-1307).

Edward was a king who pursued pragmatic policies; there is evidence neither of system nor of theory in his rule. He did much to tidy up the disorder of the Lancastrian period (1399-1461), both in foreign and in domestic policies: The Continental involvements of England were ended, and the internal disruption so characteristic of the earlier fifteenth century—livery and maintenance, private war, brigandage beyond the power of the government to control—was effectively stifled by the end of Edward IV's reign. Edward's tools of suppression were what were later to be known as courts of high commission (in this reign, the precursor of the Court of Star Chamber) and special judicial commissions sent out into the shires to hear and determine(*oyer* and *terminer*) cases of criminal conduct. In addition, the reign of Edward IV witnessed yet another innovation usually attributed to the Tudors: Although not yet so called, the Council of Wales and that of the North were in being before the end of Edward's custody of his office. These local councils acted with the king's power in areas distant from London, where endemic local strife made prompt official response necessary.

The cause of Edward's death is not precisely known; whatever the precise etiology, it is likely that he died of some complication—probably left undefined lest the delicate be offended—of what More, quoted above, called an excess of "fleshly wantonness."

Summary

While to place kings and reigns into semantic boxes is poor history, Edward IV may be described both as the last medieval and the first modern King of England. He did much to centralize royal authority, to place his rule on a sound financial basis, and to restore its standing both in domestic and in foreign eyes. By the end of his reign, there was no effective domestic challenge remaining to his rule in England. He also brought the culture of his court into conformity with contemporaneous developments in the courts of the Continent, patronizing humanists, and William Caxton.

Bibliography

Acheson, Eric. *A Gentry Community: Leicestershire in the Fifteenth Century, c. 1422-c. 1485.* Cambridge and New York: Cambridge University Press, 1992. This book examines the fifteenth century Leicestershire gentry under five broad headings: as landholders; as members of a social community based on the county; as participants in and leaders of the government of the shire; as members of the wider family unit; and, finally, as individuals. They are shown to be a socially cohesive group with a strong sense of individualism, and, while not removed from the economic problems of their time, they proved opportunistic enough to survive.

Chrimes, S. B. *Lancastrians, Yorkists, and Henry VII.* 2d ed. London: Macmillan, and New York: St. Martin's Press, 1967. A standard history of the late fifteenth century England, stressing dynastic politics.

———. "The Reign of Edward IV." In *Fifteenth-Century England, 1399-1509: Studies in Politics and Society*, edited by S. B. Chrimes, C. D. Ross, and R. A. Griffiths. Manchester: Manchester University Press, and New York: Barnes and Noble, 1972. An excellent brief introduction to the reign.

Clive, Mary. *This Sun of York: A Biography of Edward IV.* London: Macmillan, 1973. This and the book immediately following are popular history at its best.

Falkus, Gila. *The Life and Times of Edward IV.* London: Weidenfeld and Nicholson, 1981. Very well illustrated.

Hicks, M. A. *False, Fleeting, Perjur'd Clarence: George, Duke of Clarence, 1449-78.* Gloucester: Sutton, and Atlantic Highlands, N.J.: Humanities Press, 1980. Despite the awkward title (Shakespeare, its source, never titled a play in so wordy a fashion), an excellent biography of Edward IV's younger brother.

Jacob, E. F. *The Fifteenth Century, 1399-1485.* Oxford: Clarendon Press, 1961; New York: Oxford University Press, 1978. Although now somewhat old-fashioned in its approach, this remains the standard history of fifteenth century England. Excellent bibliography.

Kendall, Paul Murray. *Warwick the Kingmaker.* London: Allen and Unwin, and New York: Norton, 1957. The best biography of Richard Neville, who dominated both the person and the policy of Edward IV in the first nine years of his reign.

Lander, J. R. *Crown and Nobility, 1450-1509.* London: Arnold, and Montreal: McGill-Queen's University Press, 1976. This book, with the immediately following one, constitutes the best narrative and analytical portrayal of English politics and society in the Yorkist period.

———. *Government and Community: England, 1450-1509.* London: Arnold, and Cambridge, Mass.: Harvard University Press, 1980.

Ross, Charles. *Edward IV.* Rev. ed. New Haven, Conn.: Yale University Press, 1997. This classic study places the reign of Edward IV solidly in the context of Renaissance power politics. Ross analyzes the methods by which Edward sought to retain his throne while reasserting the power of the monarchy, which had been seriously weakened by the rule of Henry VI. Edward's relations with the politically active classes, merchants, gentry, and nobility form a major theme, and against this background Ross evaluates the many innovations in government on which the king's achievement rests.

Scofield, Cora. *The Life and Reign of Edward the Fourth.* 2 vols. London and New York: Longman, 1923. Numbingly thorough, this work remains a standard narrative history of the reign of King Edward IV.

Storey, R. L. *The End of the House of Lancaster.* London: Barrie and Rockliffe, 1966; New York: Stein and Day, 1967. Dynastic politics of the fifteenth century presented in a social context.

James W. Alexander

EDWARD VI

Born: October 12, 1537; Hampton Court Palace, London, England

Died: July 6, 1553; London, England

Area of Achievement: Government

Contribution: Edward's reign definitively established the strong Tudor monarchy and English Protestantism. Despite his youth, the king played a significant role in both.

Early Life

Edward VI's birth to Henry VIII and his wife, Jane Seymour, secured the Tudor male succession. To this end, Henry had in the past decade discarded two wives and separated the English church from the Papacy. With both of Henry's previous wives now dead, illegitimacy did not shadow Edward as it did his two sisters, Mary and Elizabeth. Jane Seymour died twelve days after Edward's birth; within the next six years, his father took three more wives, but he had no more children. The last marriage, to Catherine Parr in 1543, provided Edward with a stepmother who brought the king's children together in a harmonious household and made the court a center of the New Learning (Protestantism).

Henry VIII was already forty-six at Edward's birth and, though a fond parent, had little association with his son; the boy patterned himself on his tutors and grew up serious and scholarly. He found in the classroom liberation from the society of women, among whom he had spent his first six years. His first tutors, Richard Cox and John Cheke, were Cambridge scholars and staunch Protestants, friends of Archbishop Thomas Cranmer. For schoolmates, they selected sons of noblemen; one of them, Barnaby Fitzpatrick, Edward's whipping boy, remained a lifelong friend. In the Renaissance style, the boys learned classical and modern languages as well as music, astronomy, and athletics. Tutors of Princess Elizabeth, four years older, came from the same background; she and Edward wrote letters to each other as school exercises. Princess Mary, twenty-one years older than her brother and a devoted Roman Catholic, had completed her education, but with Queen Catherine's encouragement, she translated from Desiderius Erasmus' Latin.

Edward's education continued for three years after he became king; he turned from analyzing classical texts to writing position papers on a variety of subjects which he presented to his council. Similarly, the chronicle which he wrote in 1552 about his life and times (published as his *Journal* in 1857, and republished, with his political papers, in 1966) developed from early concentration on battles and tournaments to concern about various problems of government. From vicious political struggles in the Council, Edward early learned discretion; he took boyish delight in having his own locked desk. Being his father's son, he showed interest in his own marriage; the characteristic restraint of the *Journal* gives way when he writes about his engagement to Princess Elizabeth, daughter of Henry II of France. Once, he jokingly suggested that he might marry Anne of Cleves, his father's divorced fifth wife.

Portraits of Edward by Hans Holbein, William Strates, and others show the young king as a fat baby growing into fragile adolescence: thin, shorter than average, with gray eyes, reddish hair, and a pale complexion. Girolamo Cardano, the famous Milanese physician, praised Edward's intellectual attainments in the last year of his life, but he also told of what portraits do not show: one shoulder blade higher than the other, nearsightedness, and slight deafness.

Life's Work

Foreign diplomats remarked on the reverence shown to a mere boy and on his participation in government. Yet, though crowned King of England, Ireland, and France, at first he served as little more than a pawn, and he never stood against whatever faction controlled the Council. His reign began, as it ended, with a challenge to the will of Henry VIII, which had prescribed government by a council made up of his executors. Instead, Edward's uncle, Edward Seymour, Earl of Hertford (soon to be the Duke of Somerset), influenced the Council to turn authority over to him as governor of the king's person and protector of the kingdom. Almost immediately, a contest for control developed between Somerset and his brother, Thomas Seymour, Lord Sudley, Lord Admiral, who shared booty with pirates he was supposed to pursue. Sudley supplied the young king with money and married Dowager Queen Catherine. More ominously, he flirted with Princess Elizabeth, who lived with Catherine, and paid her suit after Catherine's death. Against Somerset's plans, he intrigued for Edward's marriage to Lady Jane Grey, granddaughter of Henry VIII's sister. Arrested and condemned to death, Sudley wrote secretly urging Mary and Elizabeth to conspire against Somerset, charging him with profiteering.

Historians have championed one or another of the politicians around Edward as comparatively high-minded or as victims of circumstances, but all struggled for power in order to despoil the Church in the name of their Protestantism. The exclusion of Catholics, such as Stephen Gardiner, Bishop of Winchester, from the Council, and Edward's youth gave them a free hand. By the time Sudley died, John Dudley, Earl of Warwick (later the Duke of Northumberland), was challenging Somerset's control. Archbishop Cranmer, who shepherded the establishment of English Protestantism, remained financially disinterested. He had already shown himself a trimmer, however, and his basic Erastianism remained suspect from a strictly Protestant viewpoint. Parliament enacted religious changes, and the courts enforced them, in the king's name, emphasizing the question of loyalty rather than theology.

At first, religious changes from Henry VIII's church attracted limited resistance. Few complained about the repeal of heresy laws, and chantries disappeared gradually. A crisis came with the implementation of the Act of Uniformity on Whitsunday, 1549, requiring a new order of worship, Cranmer's Prayer Book, with the obvious change from Latin to English. The rising in Cornwall and Devon (the Western Rebellion) represented a protest in favor of a return to the "old" ways of Henry VIII. A contemporaneous rising in Norfolk (Robert Kett's Rebellion) came mainly from secular problems. Somerset had already attacked enclosure of common lands by the gentry as causing the dislocation of peasants and vagabondage, whose hardship was aggravated by bad harvests and debasement of the coinage. Causes for rebellion varied greatly, however, within the larger pattern.

Somerset's failure to control the risings brought his fall from power. Northumberland took control, ended the Protectorate, and imprisoned him. The Council's new leaders put down the rebellions ruthlessly, using German and Italian troops brought over the channel to fight in Scotland. Somerset had proved as inept in foreign affairs as at home. He went to war in 1547 with the intention of aiding Scottish Protestants and undermining French influence by a marriage, discussed almost from Edward's birth, with the child Queen Mary Stuart. His armies harried the country and thus drove the Scots into a firm alliance with France, including the queen's marriage to the dauphin. War between England and France followed in 1549.

Even more than Somerset, Northumberland controlled through Edward. From fall, 1551, the young king presided over the Council and signed official documents without a countersignature. He did nothing to save his uncle from execution in January, 1552; Somerset, released from prison, had tried to rally support against Northumberland. Before 1552, Edward had lived close to London; his progress from July to September of that year, taking him as far as Salisbury, showed growing maturity. Without Edward's strong backing, Cranmer would not have pushed further the church reform called for by Bishops Hugh Latimer and Nicholas Ridley. A second Prayer Book and Act of Uniformity (1552) mandated attendance at the reformed service, and the Forty-two Articles defined Englishmen's creed. Northumberland's regime remains controversial. The loss of religious freedom and the destruction of Catholic books and artifacts were balanced by ideals of a Puritan Commonwealth. Northumberland sacrificed Boulogne to gain peace with France, but Somerset had begun that war. If that peace, including Edward's engagement to the princess, endangered relations with the Empire, Charles V had threatened to intervene in England in Princess Mary's interest.

Northumberland's partnership with the king became very clear from the late winter of 1553. Edward's health, deteriorating rapidly from tuberculosis, caused both to feel concern about the provision in Henry VIII's will for Mary's succession. Northumberland bolstered his own position for any eventuality by arranging marriages between his son Guildford Dudley and Lady Jane Grey and their siblings with sons of other counselors, the Earls of Pembroke and Huntingdon. Edward, characteristically, had written up a plan for his succession: Before he died, he turned it into a will leaving the throne to Lady Jane. As Edward lay dying, the Council summoned Mary to London, but she retreated to Norfolk, and, after Edward's death, on July 6, she proclaimed her succession. In London, the Northumberland faction proclaimed Lady Jane's succession. Few resisted Mary's triumphant progress to London. Men deserted from the army Northumberland led against her, and the Council did not send reinforcements. When London's populace boisterously welcomed Mary on July 19, the Council proclaimed her queen and ordered Northumberland to disband his army.

Edward was buried in Westminster Abbey on August 8 with little ceremony; no marker was ever raised to his memory. After a futile effort to appease Mary by converting to Catholicism, Northumberland died for his treason against her. Lady Jane and her husband survived until the Thomas Wyatt rebellion in 1559 proved them dangerous. Many Edwardian church reformers died as Marian martyrs.

Summary

Mary's triumph came neither from lack of parliamentary ratification of Edward VI's will nor from a reaction against his religious reforms. It did not even depend on Northumberland's unpopularity. She triumphed as the generally recognized embodiment of the hereditary English national monarchy. Confirmation and continuation of that tradition proved Edward's principal achievement. His youth, like Mary's womanhood, emphasized the monarchical principle, in clear contrast to the situation of Edward V sixty-five years before.

For a brief moment, European attention focused on Edward's England in a new way. Cranmer failed in his effort to organize a general Protestant equivalent of the Council of Trent, but Edward's church became the great experiment in national Protestantism. Though refugees such as Martin Bucer and Pietro Martire Vermigli (Peter Martyr) contributed to it, it remained a clearly English phenomenon which found its great spokesman in the Elizabethan Richard Hooker. In other ways, too, Edwardian beginnings found Elizabethan fulfillment. This shows in the careers of men such as William Cecil, Henry Sidney, and Thomas Gresham. Despite upheavals in the Council, government and business continued to cooperate in commercial exploration overseas. A government pension tempted Sebastian Cabot to return from Spain, forging a link between the first exploratory voyages under King Henry VII and the great trading companies of the seventeenth century.

Bibliography

Acheson, Eric. *A Gentry Community: Leicestershire in the Fifteenth Century, c. 1422-c. 1485.* Cambridge and New York: Cambridge University Press, 1992. This book examines the fifteenth century Leicestershire gentry under five broad headings: as landholders; as members of a social community based on the county; as participants in and leaders of the government of the shire; as members of the wider family unit; and, finally, as individuals. They are shown to be socially cohesive group with a strong sense of individualism, and, while not removed from the economic problems of their time, they proved opportunistic enough to survive.

Aston, Margaret. *The King's Bedpost: Reformation and Iconography in a Tudor Group Portrait.* Cambridge and New York: Cambridge University Press, 1993. This book is a fascinating and lavishly illustrated story about the important allegorical painting "Edward VI and the Pope," which the author has redated through the discovery of its Dutch sources. The anatomy of the picture and the imagery to which it is related open a broad discussion that contributes to the iconography, history, and religious developments of the period. A large and varied cast of characters joins the Tudor monarchs as the tale unfolds.

Beer, Barrett Lynn. *Northumberland: The Political Career of John Dudley, Earl of Warwick and Duke of Northumberland.* Kent, Ohio: Kent

State University Press, 1973. Frankly revisionist, this biography searches beyond Jordan's monumental history of the reign. It sees Northumberland in context, not worse than other members of the Council.

———. *Rebellion and Riot: Popular Disorder in England in the Reign of Edward VI.* Kent, Ohio: Kent State University Press, 1982. A useful, scholarly effort to focus away from court politics. Evident are imperfectly developed classifications and methodology, inevitable in a pioneering work.

Bush, Michael Laccohee. *The Government Policy of Protector Somerset.* London: Arnold, and Montreal: McGill-Queen's University Press, 1975. Like Beer, Bush demythologizes his subject. Somerset was an ordinary man, a pragmatist governed by consequences of his Scottish war.

Edward VI. *The Chronicle and Political Papers of King Edward VI.* Edited by Wilbur Kitchener Jordan. London: Allen and Unwin, and Ithaca, N.Y.: Cornell University Press, 1966. The indispensable journal kept by Edward between the ages of ten and fifteen. Careful editing and copious notes make this the best edition.

Hoak, Dale Eugene. *The King's Council in the Reign of Edward VI.* Cambridge and New York: Cambridge University Press, 1976. Traditional constitutional history and interpretation, blaming Somerset and Northumberland as opportunists. A study of the working of the Council, which Somerset tended to ignore, Northumberland to dominate.

Jordan, Wilbur Kitchener. *Edward VI: The Young King, the Protectorship of the Duke of Somerset.* London: Allen and Unwin, and Cambridge, Mass.: Harvard University Press, 1968.

———. *Edward VI: The Threshold of Power, the Dominance of the Duke of Northumberland.* London: Allen and Unwin, and Cambridge, Mass.: Harvard University Press, 1970. The long-needed, exhaustively scholarly study of this reign. Carefully revisionist, sees Somerset as a man beyond his depths, and the usurpation of Lady Jane Grey as Edward's scheme more than that of Northumberland.

McConica, James Kelsey. *English Humanists and Reformation Politics Under Henry VIII and Edward VI.* Oxford; Clarendon Press, and New York: Oxford University Press, 1965. Continuity of the Henrician Renaissance beyond the death of Thomas More, misses its Edwardian Protestant culmination.

Paul Stewart

ELIZABETH I

Born: September 7, 1533; Greenwich, England
Died: March 24, 1603; Richmond, England
Areas of Achievement: Politics and government
Contribution: The last of the five Tudor monarchs, Queen Elizabeth I earned the respect of her associates and the love of her subjects while ruling her people longer and more capably than most kings of her time.

Early Life

The second child of King Henry VIII, Elizabeth, was born on September 7, 1533, at Greenwich Palace. Before she was three years old, her father nullified his marriage to her mother, Anne Boleyn, whom he then had tried for adultery and conspiracy, convicted, and beheaded. Like her older half sister, Mary, before her, Elizabeth was declared to be illegitimate, and Henry immediately took another wife, Jane Seymour. A statute of 1544, while not reversing the earlier decree, nevertheless placed Elizabeth third in line to the throne after Edward, born to Henry and Jane in 1537, and Mary, daughter of Henry's first wife, Catherine of Aragon.

Elizabeth's education commenced under several eminent Cambridge scholars, one of whom, Roger Ascham, wrote a distinguished educational treatise called *The Schoolmaster* (1570). She proved an apt student, studying Greek and Latin and attaining fluency in French and Italian. Languages were the key to familiarity not only with literature but also with the New Testament and the scholarship of Europe. Because of her linguistic aptitude, Elizabeth would not later have to rely on translators, as did many sovereigns, when dealing with foreign ambassadors.

Elizabeth learned other practical lessons during the years from 1547, when her father died, until 1558, when she succeeded. While she lived with Catherine Parr, Henry's last wife and the closest approach to a mother she would ever know, Catherine's marriage to the promiscuous Thomas Seymour taught her the importance of being on her guard, for Seymour made advances to the now attractive teenager. Her subsequent determination not to allow men to manipulate her became an important factor in her forty-five-year reign. Political events tested her mettle early. Seymour fell under suspicion of treason against his brother Edward, Lord Protector of Edward, the boy king, and Elizabeth was sharply questioned about possible complicity. The fifteen-year-old princess responded shrewdly and prudently, and though Seymour was executed, she was permitted to live quietly until Edward's death in 1553.

Those who saw Elizabeth take part in her sister's coronation ceremony saw a young woman somewhat taller than average, with reddish-gold hair and light skin. Although her portrait was often painted, the stylized likenesses of Renaissance royalty often prove unreliable, and even eyewitnesses disagreed considerably about the details of her physical appearance, but everyone credited her with beautiful hands. While not a particularly religious person, Elizabeth deplored Mary's Roman Catholicism and, like many English patriots, was apprehensive about Mary's decision to marry the Catholic Prince Philip of Spain. Again, in Mary's reign, Elizabeth was suspected of treason, this time in connection with Sir Thomas Wyatt the Younger's plan to depose Mary in favor of her, for presumably Elizabeth would marry an Englishman and a Protestant and thus avert the danger of the crown passing to an offspring of Philip and Mary. Though imprisoned in the Tower of London for a time, Elizabeth again dodged the extreme penalty; she emerged understanding thoroughly, however, the danger of even the appearance of treason.

Eventually, Philip, seeing his wife childless and ill and viewing Elizabeth as preferable to such a claimant as Mary Stuart, wife of French Dauphin, became the protector of the future queen. This precarious period in the princess' life ended on November 17, 1558, when the unpopular Mary died and Elizabeth, at the age of twenty-five, became the third of Henry VIII's children to wear the English crown.

Life's Work

Elizabeth understood the presumably modern art of public relations, and from her coronation onward she worked to gain the admiration of her subjects. She also surrounded herself with able advisers, the most faithful of whom was William Cecil (from 1571, Lord Burghley), and he served her well for forty years. The domestic question—whom would she marry?—early became a question of foreign relations also, for the most ambitious bachelors of Western Europe recognized her as the greatest available prize. The Archduke Charles of Austria offered a politically advantageous match, but both Elizabeth and her subjects shied away from his Ro-

man Catholicism. Elizabeth appeared to prefer one of her own subjects, Robert Dudley, Earl of Leicester, eligible in 1560 after the death of his wife Amy Robsart, but the mystery surrounding her fatal fall down a flight of stairs cast a shadow over his name. There was no lack of other suitors, and all England expected Elizabeth to avert the disorder likely at the death of an unmarried and childless queen, but the strong-willed sovereign did not intend to yield an iota of her sovereignty to any man, and the sort of man who would content himself with being a mere consort probably appealed little to her imagination. Throughout the early years of her reign, she kept everyone guessing about her marriage plans, but she made no commitments.

Mary, Queen of Scots, whose grandmother—Henry VIII's sister—had married the Scottish King James IV, posed one threat to England's security, particularly after her first husband became King Francis II of France in 1559, for France was England's traditional enemy. To neutralize the French threat, Elizabeth encouraged Scottish fears of foreign authority, even suggesting the possibility of her own marriage to the Earl of Arran, whose family ranked high in the Scottish succession. When Francis died in 1560, however, Mary's influence declined, and her subsequent marriage to her kinsman, the unstable Lord Darnley, led to her undoing. Eventually, she was deposed, Darnley died, and for many years Mary languished, a virtual prisoner of Elizabeth in England. For nearly two decades, Elizabeth allowed no harm to come to her Scottish cousin, but neither did she intend to allow conspirators to build upon Mary's claim to the English throne.

For the first decade of her reign, with much of the European continent in turmoil, Elizabeth kept England at peace, but in 1569 she was forced to put down a rebellion in the North fomented by Thomas Howard, Duke of Norfolk, whose ambitions spurred him to seek marriage to the deposed Queen of Scots. The rebellion was speedily checked, and Elizabeth merely placed Norfolk under house arrest until she learned that he was plotting with foreign agents to overthrow her directly. Meanwhile, Pope Pius V excommunicated Elizabeth, who had never considered herself a Roman Catholic anyway, but this action, focusing Catholic enmity on her, created a dangerous atmosphere at a time when English cordiality toward Catholic Spain was steadily lessening. Therefore, Elizabeth, while continuing to spare Mary, allowed Norfolk, the only duke in her kingdom, to be tried, convicted, and executed early in 1572.

At this time, another problem was developing in the Netherlands in the form of a provincial rebellion against Spanish authority. An increased Spanish presence just across the English Channel or the possible alternative of a French buildup in response to Dutch pleas for assistance could spell trouble for England. Remaining officially neutral, Elizabeth encouraged support by volunteers and through private subscriptions; eventually, she made large loans to the rebels out of her treasury, though not in amounts sufficient to turn the tide against Spain decisively. She hoped that the Netherlands could unite under the Protestant William of Orange, but in vain. When, finally, in 1585 she committed troops to the struggle, she chose her old favorite Leicester as commander. He also shared political authority with a provincial council, but his blunders led to serious divisions among the provinces on the eve of the Spanish Armada's attack on England, a crisis brought on in large measure by Sir Francis Drake's harassment of Spain's American colonies.

While England's lighter, more maneuverable fleet took advantage of westerly winds which helped drive the Armada away from England's southern coast toward France, Elizabeth visited her army at Tilbury near the mouth of the Thames and showered encouragement and eloquence upon her soldiers. Skillfully, she braced them for the land battle which fortunately never erupted. Instead, what was left of the badly battered Spanish fleet limped back to Spain, and the greatest external threat of her reign ended in increased prestige for the nautical and military skill of England.

During the earlier years of the Netherlands venture, Elizabeth still gave the appearance of considering marriage offers. As late as 1581, Francis of Valois, Duke of Alençon, was pursuing her, but Elizabeth, while willing to use him to preserve a truce with the French ruler, Henry III, firmly rejected his offer. By this time, it appeared that the queen, now in her late forties, would probably never marry and almost certainly never bear children, but events of the next few years clarified the succession. James VI, son of the deposed Mary, was demonstrating ability on the Scottish throne, and though he flirted with Roman Catholicism as Elizabeth did with her suitors—for diplomatic leverage—his religious views and sense of the place of religion did not differ greatly from Elizabeth's own. She drew closer to James, and when yet another conspiracy, led by one Anthony Babington, implicated James's mother and caused Elizabeth to execute her in 1587, James merely protested formally. Not until she lay on her deathbed did the cautious Elizabeth confirm the fact, but England now understood that the crown would pass peacefully to James.

The foreign operations had imposed a heavy financial burden on Elizabeth. Meanwhile, poor harvests and adverse trade conditions impoverished the realm, and the surge of euphoria occasioned by the repulsion of the Spanish naval threat faded as the century waned. By the final years of Elizabeth's long rule, many agreed with Hamlet: "the time is out of joint." Another of the queen's onetime favorites, Robert Devereux, Earl of Essex, mounted a rebellion in 1601, and again she felt obliged to respond with the death penalty. Until her seventieth year, Elizabeth enjoyed robust health; only at the beginning of 1603 did she succumb to what may have been a severe bronchial illness. She continued her duties until her worried councillors persuaded her to take to her bed on March 21. Early in the morning of the third day following, she died quietly.

Summary

Many students of Queen Elizabeth I's reign have found her to have been shrewd and resourceful, able to keep opponents guessing and off balance while she guided her ship of state through perilous seas. To others, she has seemed procrastinating and indecisive, unable to carry out her policies efficiently. Her subjects expected her to rule firmly and to provide for her successor, but in the case of a queen, one of these goals would easily preclude the other. If she married to produce an heir or designated a successor, her authority would diminish. If she named an ambitious person without the patience to await her death, she might well endanger both her life and domestic tranquillity. She did well to allow James to emerge gradually as her candidate without officially nominating him. By playing off her suitors against one another, she kept England free from the very real possibility of foreign political and religious domination. Throughout her reign, she bargained adroitly with foreign powers without committing herself to unmanageable situations.

No doubt, Elizabeth sometimes relied too heavily on her favorite strategies, but most often they were well adapted to the needs of the relatively small and poor nation she ruled. Her prudent management kept the cost of government within the capacities and tolerance of her subjects. Under her, England became what it would remain for centuries: a recognized naval power. At a time of serious religious conflict, she pursued a policy remarkably tolerant and unprovocative. A nation which had endured the last unreasoning years of Henry VIII, internecine power struggles under the Edwardian regency, and a few bloody years under the erratic Mary and her Spanish husband gained confidence and security.

While not generally extravagant, Elizabeth understood the social and psychological value of magnificent progresses and dignified receptions. She captured the imagination of poets such as Edmund Spenser and Sir Walter Raleigh, who helped spread her fame beyond the range of those who actually saw her. She was Spenser's Faerie Queene in one of that character's guises, the Gloriana who summed up the glory of England. Indeed, Elizabeth appreciated poetry and the arts generally and wrote competent poetry herself. During the second half of her reign, English literature reached an unprecedented peak. Her subjects responded enthusiastically to her preference for the arts—including the art of peace—and to her genuine love for them. The affection of the English for their monarch still alive in the time of the second Elizabeth owes much to the precedent of the first. She was the first of only two English queens to give her name to a considerable wedge of history, but whereas Victoria merely symbolized an age created by others, Elizabeth stands as both symbol and substance of hers. The policies of England in the latter half of the sixteenth century, when the nation rose to prominence in Europe, were her policies. The wisdom of most of those policies was her wisdom and that of councillors she appointed. Altogether she is one of history's most remarkable women.

Bibliography

Camden, William. *The Historie of the Most Renowned and Victorious Princesse Elizabeth Late Queene of England*. Chicago: University of Chicago Press, 1970. These selections from the annals of a scholar from Elizabethan times represent the earliest authoritative study of her reign. Camden wrote in Latin; this version, the work of an anonymous seventeenth century translator, conveys Camden's commitment to a plain, factual record. Though lacking in color and narrative skill, Camden gives the modern reader a sense of the way Elizabeth's reign looked to a learned contemporary.

Erickson, Carolly. *The First Elizabeth*. London: Macmillan, and New York: Summit Books, 1983. One of Erickson's purposes is to counter the traditional emphasis on the "Virgin Queen" by stressing her use of her sexual power to attain her ends. Like Jenkins' book, this biography represents a woman's viewpoint but one sharply different in its heavily psychological interpretation of its subject.

Frye, Susan. *Elizabeth I: The Competition for Representation*. New York: Oxford University Press, 1993. Elizabeth I was perhaps the most visible woman of early modern Europe, yet little attention has been paid to the difficulties of a woman reigning in a patriarchal society. This study examines her struggle for authority. Based on a variety of extant historical and literary materials, Frye's interpretation focuses on three representational crises spaced fifteen years apart: the London coronation of 1559; the Kenilworth entertainments of 1575; and the publication of *The Faerie Queene* in 1590.

Guy, John, ed. *The Reign of Elizabeth I: Court and Culture in the Last Decade*. Cambridge and New York: Cambridge University Press, 1995. This book is about the politics and political culture of the last decade of the reign of Elizabeth I (1585 to 1603). Many teachers and their students have failed to consider the last decade in its own right, having begun their accounts in 1558 and struggled on to the defeat of the Armada in 1588. Only two major political surveys have been attempted since 1926.

Jenkins, Elizabeth. *Elizabeth the Great*. London: Gollancz, and New York: Coward-McCann, 1959. Relying on previously published sources, this biography attained popular and critical success upon publication and continues to deserve praise as a perceptive and readable interpretation of Elizabeth's character. As her title suggests, Jenkins emphasizes the positive elements contributing to Elizabeth's eminence.

Johnson, Paul. *Elizabeth I*. London: Weidenfeld and Nicolson, and New York: Holt Rinehart, 1974. Johnson depicts court life clearly but is less convincing on some aspects of the background of the age, particularly Puritanism. The informing theme of his study is the relationship between Elizabeth's exercise of her secular power and the political implications of the religious authority that she inherited from her predecessors.

MacCaffrey, Wallace T. *The Shaping of the Elizabethan Regime*. Princeton, N.J.: Princeton University Press, 1968; London: Cape, 1969. This specialized study should interest anyone seeking a detailed understanding of the first fifteen years of Elizabeth's rule, or what the author calls its "testing time." This work makes extensive use of state papers and documents from the Public Record Office in London.

Neale, J.E. *Queen Elizabeth I: A Biography*. London: Cape, and New York: Harcourt Brace, 1934. The great pioneer among modern biographers of Elizabeth, Neale is a master of unpretentious narrative history. Though undocumented, this classic biography has earned the respect of all Elizabethan researchers. Age has not dimmed its appeal.

Read, Conyers. *Lord Burghley and Queen Elizabeth*. London: Cape, and New York: Knopf, 1960. More specifically the second volume of a life of Elizabeth's ablest adviser, this book, covering the years 1570 to 1598, explores in meticulous detail the working relationship between the two. Read is one of the greatest of modern Elizabethan scholars.

Williams, Neville. *Elizabeth the First: Queen of England*. New York: Dutton, 1968. A senior official of the Public Record Office, Williams predictably draws extensively on the documents thereof. He presents a particularly good picture of Elizabeth's domestic life. An objective, competently written, but sometimes stodgy biography.

Robert P. Ellis

DESIDERIUS ERASMUS

Born: October 27, 1466?; Rotterdam or Gouda, the Netherlands

Died: July 12, 1536; Basel, Switzerland

Areas of Achievement: Education, religion, and literature

Contribution: Of the intellectuals who transmitted and adapted the Renaissance spirit to northern Europe, Erasmus was the greatest. Taken together, his writings reflect a rare combination of practical Christian piety, biblical and patristic scholarship, and broad humanistic learning.

Early Life

Erasmus was born in Rotterdam, or possibly in the Dutch village of Gouda, on October 27 in the late 1460's (the exact year is disputed) to Margaret, a physician's daughter, and a priest probably named Gerard, for whom she served as housekeeper. As one of two illegitimate sons born to this couple, the sensitive Erasmus (he took the additional name Desiderius later in life) would endure shame and legal problems, but his parents lived together for many years and appear to have been devoted parents. Erasmus' childhood coincided with the ongoing war between the Duchy of Burgundy, which controlled Holland, and France. He grew to despise the Burgundian knights, whose cruelty belied the chivalric ideal expressed by Charles the Bold. He also developed an aversion to the provinciality and social rigidity of his homeland.

Around 1478, Erasmus' mother enrolled the two boys at a school in Deventer, about seventy-five miles inland, conducted by the Brethren of the Common Life, a lay society dedicated to the imitation of primitive Christianity. Although Erasmus later expressed contempt for the Brethren's teaching methods, both their piety and a humanistic strain which entered the school at this time helped shape the young student. His schooling at Deventer ended in 1483 or 1484, when the plague claimed the lives of both his parents. Three guardians appointed by his father sent Erasmus to another more conservative and even less congenial of the Brethren's schools for three additional years.

He entered the Augustinian priory at Steyn about 1487. There, the critical young man learned to dislike the ascetic routine and prevailing mysticism, but he enlarged his grasp of classical literature and wrote the first two of his many books, a conventional treatise on monastic life and a book of Latin verse. His years at Steyn climaxed with his ordination as priest on April 25, 1492.

Life's Work

About a year after his ordination, Erasmus accepted a post as Latin secretary to the ambitious Henri, Bishop of Cambray. While in his service, Erasmus wrote, in the form of a Platonic dialogue, an attack on Scholasticism, the dominant philosophy of the Church, although the book remained unpublished for nearly thirty years. In 1495, Bishop Henri assisted Erasmus in gaining entrance to the University of Paris, a hotbed of Scholasticism, presumably to study for his doctorate in theology. At the College of Montaigu in Paris, he made Humanist friends, including an elderly man named Robert Gaguin, who had been a pupil of the noted Florentine Platonist Marsilio Ficino, and who now encouraged Erasmus to study the Neoplatonists. Constantly seeking the independence that would enable him to spend his life studying in reasonable comfort, he accepted in 1499 the patronage of the Englishman William Blount, Lord Mountjoy, and thus visited England for the first time. There he established friendships with leading scholars such as William Grocyn, Thomas Linacre, John Colet, and—preeminently—Sir Thomas More.

Already the wandering pattern of the man who later called himself a citizen of the world was being established. He returned to France the next year and began a routine of scholarly activity that included the study of Greek, the compilation of a book of proverbial wisdom, *Adagia* (1500; *Proverbs or Adages*, 1622), and a manual of Christianity written for the laity from the point of view of a monk who, at this point, was living in the manner of a principled Christian layman. *Enchiridion Militis Christiani* (1503; *The Manual of the Christian Knight*, 1533) became the best-known of his works in this genre. His study of Lorenzo Valla's exegesis of the New Testament, a work which he edited and published in 1506, quickened his determination to master the original Greek. After another sojourn in England with his Humanist friends there, he accepted a tutoring appointment which took him to Italy.

His work took him on a tour which included Turin, at whose university he received a doctorate in divinity in 1506, and Florence, Bologna, and Venice, where he met the distinguished printer Aldus Manutius, with whom he worked to produce a handsome revision of *Proverbs or Adages*. In Rome, he witnessed the growing corruption of the papal court, after which Mountjoy persuaded him to return to England. It has been argued that had the now influential Erasmus remained in Rome during the next crucial decade, he might have furthered the cause of reform, prevented the excommunication of Martin Luther, with whom he corresponded, and thus changed the course of religious history.

Upon his arrival in London, while awaiting the arrival of his books, he lived in Thomas More's house and wrote there a book, which he certainly did not consider among his most important but which, more than any other, has immortalized him: *Moriae Encomium* (1511; *The Praise of Folly*, 1549). By a species of pun congenial to him and to his host, the title also signifies "the praise of More," though without any suggestion that More was foolish. While the book is, like Sebastian Brant's *Narrenschiff* (1494; *Ship of Fools*, 1509), a satire on human folly, Erasmus' characterization of Folly is a rich and original conception depicting not only gradations of conventional foolishness but also ultimately figuring the Christian fool, whose folly is in reality wisdom.

Later, he became the first man to teach Greek at Cambridge. During his two and a half years on the faculty of the English university, he wrote *De Duplici Copia Verborum ac Rerum* (1512; *On the Twofold Abundance of Words and Things*, 1978, better known as *De Copia*), which would hold its place as a standard textbook on literary style for two centuries. Nevertheless, Erasmus was not happy at Cambridge, blaming the cold, damp climate for undermining his always frail health and finding Cambridge intellectually mediocre and provincial. His more enlightened Humanist English friends resided, for the most part, in London.

He was even less pleased with the prospect of returning to monastic life at Steyn, to which he was recalled in 1514, more than two decades after gaining permission to leave: Erasmus relayed his firm intention to return; it required, however, dispensation from Pope Leo X, which took him three years to acquire, to free himself from all possibility of further obligation to his order. While this appeal was pending, he completed his own Latin version of the New Testament, based on Greek manuscripts and more accurate in many (though not all) details than the standard Latin Vulgate. His translation reflected his conviction that Christ's teachings are easily understandable and not meant to be encrusted by the commentary of theologians. Strategically, he dedicated his work to Leo and also recommended that the Bible be translated into the vernacular tongues so that it might be accessible to the less educated.

Among his other works in this busy period were a nine-volume edition of the works of Saint Jerome and a manual, *Institutio Principis Christiani* (1516; *The Education of a Christian Prince*, 1936). Sharply contrasting with Niccolò Machiavelli's *Il principe* (wr. 1513; *The Prince*, 1640), Erasmus' advice to the prince included pleas for restraint in taxation and in the waging of war. Unlike Machiavelli, Erasmus regarded politics as a branch of ethics in the classical manner. Unenthusiastic about the tyranny of princes, Erasmus could see no other acceptable alternative to anarchy. In this work and in two other treatises of this period, Erasmus' thought tended toward pacifism, a shocking philosophy in an age that looked on the willingness to wage war as a certification of one's conviction.

During a stay at Antwerp in 1516-1517, Erasmus was painted by Quentin Massys, the first of three famous artists for whom he sat. In this portrait, Erasmus, then middle-aged, is at his writing desk, intently serious. Portraits by Albrecht Dürer and Hans Holbein the Younger a few years later interpret the Dutch scholar quite differently, but all three artists agree that Erasmus had a very long, somewhat aquiline nose, a wide mouth with thin lips, and a strong chin. Both Dürer and Holbein (in a late portrait of about 1532) endow the writer with a faint, enigmatic smile, which many viewers have seen as mocking human weakness as does his character Folly. All of these portraits show Erasmus wearing a flat cap.

From 1517 to 1521, Erasmus lived at Louvain. He published one of his most enduring works, *Colloquia Familiaria* (1518; *The Colloquies of Erasmus*, 1671), and also continued his task of editing the early fathers of the Church, spending all day and much of the night at his writing desk and turning out a stupendous volume of work for publication and hundreds—probably thousands—of gracefully written letters to correspondents all over Europe. Having made a number of severe criticisms of the Church, Erasmus received overtures from his fellow Augustinian Martin Luther, but while refusing for years to denounce Luther—many of whose famous ninety-five theses he anticipated—he did not support him either. In the interests of Christian unity, more important to Erasmus than most of the theological points on which Luther challenged the Church, he attempted to mediate the quarrel, but observing the intransigence of both Church and reformers, he refused an invitation to the Diet of Worms, where, in 1521, Luther's doctrines were condemned. Solicited by both sides but widely viewed as cowardly for his unwillingness to back either unequivocally, Erasmus made many enemies. Although he had little reason to fear the Protestant majority in Basel, where he lived during most of the 1520's, he refused to endorse even tacitly the city's denial of religious liberty to Catholic citizens and left for Freiburg in 1529.

He unsuccessfully urged the warring Christians to compromise and focus on the Turkish threat in the Balkans and continued to prepare editions of early Christian thinkers. In 1535, his own health failing, he learned of King Henry VIII's execution of his good friends More and Bishop John Fisher. In the final months of his life, he returned to Basel, dying there on July 12, 1536. In 1540, a wooden statue of Erasmus was erected in Rotterdam, the city he claimed as his birthplace, and Johann Froben published an edition of his collected works in Basel. The statue did not survive the Spanish occupation of the Netherlands and many of his books were burned, but the centuries that followed have proved Erasmus ineradicable.

Summary

Before the heyday of the Protestant Reformers, Desiderius Erasmus articulated his dismay at the excesses of an increasingly worldly and corrupt Church and urged a return to Christian essentials. His numerous editions of early Christian theologians and his Latin version of the New Testament signaled his contempt for the decadent but still-prevailing Scholasticism, while his manuals of practical piety reflected his conviction that what he called "the philosophy of Christ" was a simple and achievable attainment.

Erasmus' tolerance and pacifism, which owed something to his physical timidity but more to his capacity for rational analysis and insight into the futility of religious confrontation, turned both the Catholics and Protestants against him. In an ecumenically minded world, however, what appeared to his contemporaries as cowardice or indecisiveness looks more like wisdom.

As the greatest of the northern Humanists, he communicated not only the learning of the ancients but also their spirit of inquiry and independence to educated people of his time. He saw harmony in the best of classical and Christian thought. He also understood the potentialities of mass-produced books—a new development in his lifetime—and thus devoted his life to incessant writing. A bibliographical analysis by an Erasmian scholar in 1927 produced an estimate that two million copies of his books had been printed, one million of them textbooks. Erasmus never understood, however, why more people did not submit to the logic of his arguments. Paradoxically, his books enjoyed more popularity in the later sixteenth and seventeenth centuries, when his personal reputation was ebbing; today a torrent of scholarly works interpret his character much more favorably, but he is much less read. Only *The Praise of Folly* is still widely admired for its wit, subtlety, and the universality of its analysis of human folly. Readers who find their way to *The Colloquies of Erasmus*, however, discover that no writer since Plato has used dialogue so well to express his thought in a persuasive and readable form.

Taken as a whole, Erasmus' writings cast more light on the great European movements of his time—the Renaissance and the Reformation—than does the work of any other eyewitness. This wandering Augustinian monk was an intellectual seismograph who registered the brightest hopes and most profound disappointments of Western civilization in the stormy period of his life.

Bibliography

Bainton, Roland H. *Erasmus of Christendom*. New York: Scribner, 1969; London: Collins, 1970. Probably the closest thing to a standard biography, Bainton's study has relatively little to say about Erasmus' more imaginative works but is particularly good on his less well-known ones. Scholarly, thoroughly documented, yet never ponderous, this book ably interprets Erasmus' complex relationships with Luther and other reformers.

Faludy, George. *Erasmus of Rotterdam*. London: Eyre and Spottiswoode, 1970. An excellent general reader's biography. Faludy explains the historical and intellectual contexts of Erasmus' work clearly and tactfully. He uses few footnotes but displays a thorough grasp of Erasmian scholarship.

Huizinga, Johan. *Erasmus and the Age of Reformation*. Translated by F. Hopman. New York: Harper, 1957. Originally published as *Erasmus of Rotterdam* in 1924, Huizinga's biography has worn well. Not only was this Dutch scholar a recognized expert on Erasmus' era, but also he grasped the psychology of his subject as few other biographers have.

Mangan, John Joseph. *Life, Character, and Influence on Desiderius Erasmus of Rotterdam*. 2 vols. London: Burns and Oates, and New York: Macmillan, 1927. Though dated in some of its interpretations, this lengthy biography prints translations of large chunks of Erasmus' writings, especially letters. Its last chapter contains extensive information on Erasmus' later influence as measured by editions and translations of his many works.

Phillips, Margaret Mann. *Erasmus and the Northern Renaissance*. London: English Universities Press, 1949; New York: Macmillan, 1950. A somewhat elementary introduction to Erasmus and his age. Contains two chapters that can be especially recommended: "Portrait" and "The World Through Erasmus's Eye." Useful for beginning students of the Renaissance.

Smith, Preserved. *Erasmus: A Study of His Life, Ideals, and Place in History*. London and New York: Harper, 1923. This reprint of a study published in 1923 views Erasmus as champion of "undogmatic Christianity" and thus emphasizes his subjects' relations with, and differences from, the Protestant Reformers. Less useful on the Humanist aspect. A patient, scholarly life with an extensive bibliography of nineteenth and earlier twentieth century studies, chiefly by European scholars.

Wengert, Timothy J. *Human freedom, Christian Righteousness: Philip Melanchthon's Exegetical Dispute with Erasmus of Rotterdam*. New York: Oxford University Press, 1998. This book argues that Philip Melanchthon was, at least theologically, not Erasmian at all, but in fact sharply anti-Erasmus; this runs contrary to conventional thought, which places him as caught between Erasmus and Luther. Wengert draws largely on Melanchthon's *Scholia* on the Epistle of Paul to the Colossians as well as on a range of other contemporary sources. He addresses a number of important questions, including the complicated relationship between humanism and the Reformation, and the issues of proper biblical interpretation of free will, of divine and human righteousness, and of political order.

Zweig, Stefan. *Erasmus of Rotterdam*. Translated by Eden Paul and Cedar Paul. London: Cassell, and New York: Viking Press, 1934. A lively popular life by a master of general readers' biographies. Although not always accurate in details or judicious interpretations, Zweig's life may well stimulate the beginning student of Erasmus to delve into more detailed and critical accounts of his life and achievements.

Robert P. Ellis

JAN VAN EYCK and HUBERT VAN EYCK

Jan van Eyck

Born: c. 1390; possibly Maastricht, Flanders
Died: July 9, 1441; Bruges, Flanders

Hubert van Eyck

Born: Before 1390; possibly Maastricht, Flanders
Died: Probably September 18, 1426; Ghent, Flanders
Area of Achievement: Art
Contribution: In paintings of unprecedented accuracy of observation and coherence of form, the van Eycks achieved a fusion of Christian religious content with a passionate devotion to visual fact.

Early Lives

The commonplace facts of the lives of Jan and Hubert van Eyck are almost entirely absent from the historical record. Jan's estimated year of birth, 1390, seems reasonable in view of the established details of his early career, as well as his date of death, 1441. Of Hubert, whose very existence has occasionally been called into question by scholars, evidence suggests that he was an elder brother; a taxation document from 1426 establishes that he died at about that time.

Both Hubert and Jan may have worked in The Hague from about 1415 to 1417, and it is certain that Jan was employed in that city from 1422 to 1424 by John of Bavaria, who as Count of Holland maintained his court there. A document indicates that Jan was accompanied in his work there by at least two assistants. In early 1425, civil war broke out in Holland, and Jan sought refuge in Flanders, where Hubert had already gone. On May 19, Jan van Eyck entered the service of Philip III, Duke of Burgundy. Philip the Good, as he was known, had a high regard both for Jan's artistic abilities and for his skills as a negotiator, since over the next several years Jan was engaged in various missions on Philip's behalf, including a journey in 1428 to negotiate Philip's marriage to Isabella, daughter of King John I of Portugal. Jan's role, at minimum, was to paint portraits of Isabella to help Philip come to a decision about the match. For the sake of security, two pictures were returned to Bruges, one by sea and the other by land.

Of the circumstances of Hubert's death, and of its effect upon the work in which he and Jan may have been jointly engaged, there is no documentation; their artistic and professional relationship can only be inferred from the paintings that have been attributed to them. A third brother, Lambert, who survived Jan, seems not to have been an artist.

Around 1432, Jan van Eyck bought a house in Bruges. By 1434 he had married, and in that year his son was born; a daughter was born several years later. Only the first name of Jan's wife, Margaretha, is known; of her social origins there is no record, but it may be assumed that a renowned artist of van Eyck's stature would seek a favorable marriage. Jan's portrait of her when she was thirty-three, painted in 1439, shows a woman of great intelligence, if not beauty. If Jan's painting of 1433, known as *The Man with the Red Turban*, is, as seems likely, a self-portrait, the modern viewer has a visual document of a prosperous fifteenth century husband and wife.

Life's Work

The dominant form of painting in northern Europe during the youth of Jan and Hubert van Eyck was manuscript illumination, a form that dominated the art of the Middle Ages and that was a particularly vital element of what came to be known as Gothic art. The small scale of manuscript illumination required extremely precise technique; that, and the need to include decorative elements and writing within the page, tended to favor qualities of abstract form and color rather than observation of nature. Around 1400, however, a trend toward naturalism in manuscript painting gained momentum in many northern European centers, including the region of Limbourg, near the van Eycks' birthplace. The origins of this new attention to natural appearances are varied, but the influence of Giotto di Bondone and his successors is certain. These fourteenth century Italian masters irreversibly influenced the depiction of the human figure, presenting it as a three-dimensional mass in an illusionistic space. The representation of natural light and the convincing portrayal of action and emotion were other progressive elements of Italian art which spread to major centers of artistic production in fifteenth century Europe.

In the earlier parts of their careers, the van Eycks were almost certainly occupied with manuscript painting. Probably the earliest works which could be attributed to Jan or Hubert are the *Heures de*

Turin (the Turin hours), several paintings which were once part of a book of miniatures, *Très Belles Heures de Notre Dame*. This volume was the effort of many artists working over an extended period of time whose identities are elusive, but in the case of the *Heures de Turin*, the modernity of the use of space in landscape and the subtle modulation of tones suggest the involvement of artists of very progressive tendencies. No more likely candidates than the van Eycks have been proposed, but opinion has always been divided about which particular characteristics in the works can be attributed to Hubert and which to Jan, or in fact whether the works represent a collaborative effort at all. All that can be said with assurance is that the *Heures de Turin* represent the vital trends that reach fulfillment in later works of the van Eycks.

Generally accepted as a work of Hubert is *The Three Marys at the Sepulcher*, a painting on a wooden panel that is substantially larger than a typical manuscript illumination. Although undated, it is considered a work of Hubert's mature years and exhibits many qualities thought to be uniquely his own, such as a sharply inclined ground plane, awkward perspective, and slender, small-headed figures. There is an intensity of narrative interest in the figures which is thought to be atypical of the work of Jan. Its great significance, however, is that, in it, the vigor and monumentality of the style of the *Heures de Turin* are rendered on a larger scale.

The scholarly problem of distinguishing between the work of Jan and Hubert van Eyck recurs in connection with the great polyptych, *The Ghent Altarpiece*, but here a consensus has emerged from decades of study. An inscription on the painting, placed there by order of the patron who commissioned it, states "Hubert van Eyck, the greatest painter who ever lived, began the work, which his brother Jan, the second in art, finished at the instigation of Jodocus Vijdt. With this verse, on 6 May [1432] he invites you to look at this work." Given such a documentary starting point, if the altarpiece were less complex, attribution of its design and execution would not be problematic. The altarpiece is, however, composed of twenty panels of differing shapes, dimensions, and representational scales. When closed, the work's eight exterior panels comprise an area 218 centimeters wide and 314 centimeters high; opened, its twelve panels together measure 455 centimeters in width. Within this impressive format, a multitude of figures is presented in an upper and lower register; centrally placed in the upper register is the seated figure of God, representing the Trinity. This figure, larger than life-size, is clothed in resplendent garments painted with an almost miraculous precision and vibrancy of color. To the left is the Virgin, and to the right is Saint John the Baptist. On either side of this central group are panels depicting angel musicians, and at the sides of this upper portion are the figures of Adam, on the left, and Eve, on the right.

Hubert van Eyck

The lower register consists of five panels which together form a continuous landscape. The large central panel, which is the width of the four flanking panels combined, is a scene of the Adoration of the Lamb representing Revelation 7:2-10: "After this I beheld, and, lo, a great multitude, which no man could number, of all nations, and kindreds, and people, and tongues, stood before the throne, and before the Lamb, clothed with white robes, and palms in their hands. . . . " The outer panels show the Just Judges, the Warriors of Christ, the Holy Hermits, and the Holy Pilgrims. In its entirety, the Adoration panels may be considered as the evocation of either an Earthly Paradise or the New Jerusalem. There is everywhere a profusion of grass, flowers, trees, and fruit, enveloped by a radiant, unifying light.

The consensus of scholars, which seems unlikely to be changed by further study, is that Hubert was largely responsible for the design of the altarpiece and for much of its execution, while Jan was the designer and painter of the figures of Adam and Eve and of parts of the rest, including the orange trees, palms, and cypresses of the Adoration of the Lamb. The question has been raised whether *The Ghent Altarpiece* was actually envisioned from the start in its present form by either Hubert or Jan, calling into question the unity of the overall structure. Yet few believe that the difference in scale, for example, of the figures in the upper and lower parts is anything but intentional; the contrast in scale seems visually and emotionally effective, and it is theologically sound.

With *The Ghent Altarpiece*, the technique of painting reached a degree of perfection that was the envy of painters in succeeding generations. The impression was given by the Italian artist Giorgio Vasari, writing in 1550, that Jan van Eyck had invented the technique of painting with oil. Oil had been used in the Low Countries as a medium before the van Eycks, but it is clear that the reputation for brilliance and subtlety gained by their works was in some measure the result of new methods in the preparation of paint, probably involving the use of a superior oil and more painstaking grinding of the pigment. The effects of their improvements were both aesthetic—a gain in the ease and flexibility with which paint could be applied—and physical, in that the paintings proved remarkably durable.

While working on *The Ghent Altarpiece*, Jan van Eyck accepted other commissions, but his next major works appeared after its completion in 1432. *The Arnolfini Wedding*, perhaps his best-known painting, was finished in 1434. It represents the wedding of Giovanni Arnolfini and Giovanna Cenami, natives of Lucca who resided in Bruges. It has been shown that each detail of the work has symbolic meaning and that the painting is in a sense almost a legal documentation of a wedding, with the two witnesses (the painter himself, and his wife—a priest was not strictly necessary) shown reflected in a convex mirror at the back of a small room in which the ceremony takes place.

The years which remained to Jan van Eyck were as productive as those preceding *The Arnolfini Wedding*. In addition to portraits of Arnolfini, Margaretha van Eyck, and others, he completed several panels in which the donor is represented appearing before the infant Christ and the Madonna in a contemporary setting. Of these, the finest is perhaps *Madonna with Chancellor Rolin*, which places the subjects in a beautifully rendered Romanesque palace, with a view of a city on a river receding to a distant mountain landscape.

Summary

Jan and Hubert van Eyck began their careers in a milieu where artistic endeavor tended to be anonymous and guilds controlled the standards and methods of production in the arts. Jan's career—there is no direct evidence of a "career" for Hubert, in this respect—demonstrated that an artist could achieve individual distinction and be recognized not merely by fellow artists but by citizens generally. Artists began to gain status beyond that of mere specialized craftsmen. Jan van Eyck's missions on behalf of his patron Philip the Good show that he was a trusted representative in political and personal matters, and one can infer that he was a man of substantial intellect.

Regardless of the credit due individually to Hubert or Jan in their works, each possessed a receptiveness to new ways of seeing the world, with the skill and sense of organization to complete projects of major physical and spiritual scope. On the slender evidence of Hubert's attributed works, one might say that he was the more passionate and Jan the more analytical personality. Both, however, presented the world as suffused with a unifying light and color which incarnate spiritual unity. The diversity of the natural world is seen with a fresh eye, but not as purely optical phenomena.

The paintings of the van Eycks belong to the first flowering of the Renaissance in the art of northern Europe. Their conquest of natural appearances, even though it was pursued in the realm of religious art, contributed to a process of secularization that affected all facets of life.

Bibliography

Baldass, Ludwig. *Jan van Eyck*. London and New York: Phaidon Press, 1952. This major monograph on Jan van Eyck is exceptionally detailed both in text and illustrations. It gives a good account of the historical context of the van Eycks' work and has thorough appendices. The high-quality black-and-white reproductions are somehow more sympathetic to the works than those in most later publications.

Brockwell, Maurice W. *The van Eyck Problem.* London: Chatto and Windus, 1954; Westport, Conn.: Greenwood Press, 1971. Brockwell's long essay is a sort of case study of art historical inference, supposition, wishful thinking, and fashion, using *The Ghent Altarpiece* and the cloudy identity of Hubert van Eyck as the source material. The black-and-white illustrations are mediocre, and documentary material from several languages is not translated.

Faggin, Giorgio T. *The Complete Paintings of the van Eycks.* London: Weidenfeld and Nicolson, and New York: Abrams, 1970. This volume, originally published in Italian in 1968 and subsequently updated, presents all the known paintings of the van Eycks. Major works are reproduced in color, many of them accompanied by enlarged details. The remainder of the reproductions are found in a separate section at the back of the book, which also contains extensive notes ranging from anecdotes to scholarly information. An introduction by Robert Hughes, though interesting, is not coordinated with the illustrations or the notes. A selection of comments on the van Eycks by writers through the centuries, a chronology, and appendices make this book useful and engrossing.

Harbison, Craig. *Jan van Eyck: The Play of Realism.* London: Reaktion Books, and Seattle: University of Washington Press, 1991. Interpretation of the elements of realism in the art of Jan van Eyck.

Panofsky, Erwin. "Jan van Eyck's Arnolfini Portrait." In *Renaissance Art*, edited by Gilbert Creighton. New York: Harper, 1970. This classic essay was first published in *The Burlington Magazine* in 1934, introducing the theory of "disguised symbolism," which became a standard tool of art history. Panofsky was one of the great scholars of art history, and he remains one of the most readable.

Pächt, Otto. *Van Eyck: And the Founders of Early Netherlandish Painting.* Foreword by Arthur Rosenauer; edited by Maria Schmidt-Dengler; translated by David Britt. London: Miller, 1994. Criticism and interpretation of the works of Hubert and Jan van Eyck.

Van Puyvelde, Leo. *Flemish Painting from the Van Eycks to Metsys.* London: Weidenfeld and Nicolson, and New York: McGraw-Hill, 1970. Readable but by no means authoritative, this book devotes about one-fifth of its pages to the van Eycks. Reproductions vary in quality from good to very good.

C. S. McConnell

ALESSANDRO FARNESE

Born: August 27, 1545; Rome
Died: December 2-3, 1592; Arras, France
Area of Achievement: The military
Contribution: Combining prodigious military ability and political talent, Farnese came close to retaking all of the Netherlands for Spain before imperial distractions and drains on Philip's finances elsewhere combined to undermine his achievements.

Early Life

Alessandro Farnese had illustrious ancestry. His great-grandfather on his father's side, for whom he was named, was Pope Paul III. His mother, Margaret of Austria, was the natural daughter of the Emperor Charles V. Two years after his birth, his father, Ottavio Farnese, inherited the Duchy of Parma. Alessandro and his twin, Carlo (named for his maternal grandfather), were the only children of his parents' marriage. Carlo died within a few months of birth, making Alessandro the only legitimate heir to Ottavio and a treasured only child to Margaret.

In 1556, to cement the alliance between his father and Philip, the regent of Spain, Alessandro was sent to Brussels to reside at the Spanish court. For the next nine years, until his marriage and subsequent return to Parma, Alessandro would serve as a hostage to his family's good faith and would complete his education in the Low Countries and Spain. He studied for a time in the great university town of Alcalá de Henares, where his course of study, shared with his contemporaries the Crown Prince Don Carlos and his uncle Don Juan of Austria, was designed by his uncle Philip II. Although Alessandro and Don Carlos found a common interest in military science, it was his young uncle Don Juan who became his closest friend. The young Italian nobleman was well received at the Spanish court in Madrid and admired for his manners, linguistic ability, and skill in the military arts.

After the number of plans to ally the house of Farnese with other prominent families fell through, at length a suitable match was approved by his father and Philip II. In November, 1565, Alessandro married Princess Maria of Portugal. The bride was considerably older than the groom, and she was considerably more enamored of him than he was of her, but it proved a fruitful marriage, producing two sons and a daughter before Maria died. After the marriage, the young couple settled in Parma, where Alessandro found that the combination of matrimony and the quiet life made him restless. After much pleading and many frustrations, he received the opportunity to join in the Crusade against the Turks in 1571, serving under Don Juan.

Life's Work

The campaign against the Turks gave Farnese a chance to demonstrate his military prowess and personal courage. He joined the expedition with three hundred soldiers and eighty-two knights from the Duchies of Parma and Piacenza. Don Juan gave him charge of several Genoese galleys in the international fleet. Farnese acquitted himself well at the Battle of Lepanto, personally leading the boarding party which captured the treasure ship of the Turkish fleet. After this great victory, which made Don Juan a national hero, life quieted down again for Farnese until 1577, when he was given command of the relief forces sent to assist Don Juan, now governor of the rebellious Low Countries. In the Netherlands campaigns of the next fifteen years, Farnese would establish a reputation for military genius and political astuteness which would outstrip that of his illustrious uncle. Farnese's army reached the scene of the fighting in time to tip the balance in the Battle of Gembloux in December, 1577. Using a brilliantly conceived strategy, Farnese surprised the rebel army and triggered a rout which completely destroyed it. Farnese quickly became Don Juan's best and most trusted commander, and when this revered leader lay dying in October, 1578, he appointed Farnese as his interim successor. Philip II made the appointment as governor of the Low Countries permanent.

Now in his early thirties, Farnese was described as having

> black, closely-shorn hair . . . erect and bristling. The forehead was lofty and narrow. The features were handsome, the nose regularly aquiline, the eyes well opened, dark, piercing . . . he was of middle stature, well formed, and graceful in person, princely in demeanor, sumptuous and stately in apparel.

He was revered by his men and respected by his enemies for his intelligence, personal bravery, and skill.

As governor of the Low Countries, Farnese combined military genius with an effective diplomacy. Through organizational skill and the sheer force of his personality, he molded an army of disparate elements into an efficient fighting machine which struck fear into the hearts of the enemy. In particular, he was effective in his utilization of mercenary troops. As a negotiator, he utilized the knowledge of the tensions and jealousies within the Netherlands nobility, gained both from his youthful experiences there and from intelligence from an extensive network of spies. He won defections to the Spanish side using a combination of persuasion and bribery, offered with the utmost delicacy and graciousness. That not only conserved men and money but also allowed Farnese to concentrate his forces on those towns still resisting. By these methods, Farnese became the most successful of Philip's governors of the Spanish Netherlands.

Between 1579 and 1585, Farnese systematically reconquered most of the southern provinces, earning a place in history as the creator of modern Belgium. He reached the high point of his military success in the summer of 1585, with the successful culmination of the Seige of Antwerp. He seemed poised to complete his task of subjugating all the rebellious provinces until international politics, in the form of English aid, intervened in 1586. This aid stiffened Dutch resistance and turned Philip's attention toward invading England, which he believed would secure England for Catholicism, perhaps gain for him the throne, and solve the thorny problem of the Netherlands once and for all. Farnese played a major role in the preparation of the Invincible Armada. Philip requested plans for an invasion of England from his greatest sailor, the Marquis of Santa Cruz, and his greatest soldier, Alessandro Farnese. Farnese's original plan was for a secret operation ferrying some thirty thousand crack troops across the Channel in barges to link with an uprising of English Catholics. The Marquis of Santa Cruz recommended a large fleet of five hundred vessels carrying sixty thousand soldiers, capable of defeating the English fleet. Philip's plan combined parts of both. Spain would assemble a large fleet with Spanish infantry on board to escort an invasion force from the Netherlands to England.

Farnese recommended October, 1586, for the invasion, but delays in the assembly of the fleet in Lisbon made this impossible. By the time the Armada sailed in the summer of 1588, Farnese's reinforcements were greatly depleted by illness and desertion after months of inactivity. Logistical problems and communication breakdowns between Farnese and the Duke of Medina Sedonia, the Armada commander, doomed the invasion even before the defeat of the Armada at Gravelines and its destruction by storms as it attempted the circuitous voyage home.

After the Armada disaster in 1588, Farnese's position in the Netherlands became progressively weaker. Spanish finances, stretched to pay for the Armada, were chronically inadequate to meet Farnese's needs. His unpaid troops began to be hard to control. Worse, perhaps, Dutch resistance was bolstered by this clear sign that the Spanish were not invincible. Events in France, also triggered partly by the Armada, distracted Philip, with consequences harmful to the Spanish Netherlands.

The civil war in France had worsened, and with the assassinations of the Duke of Guise and the Cardinal of Lorraine at the hands of Henry III, and Henry's subsequent assassination in August, 1589, Philip saw not only a chance to defeat the Protestant forces of Henry of Navarre but also an opportunity to put himself or his heirs on the throne of France. To these ends, he put the Netherlands on the back burner and ordered Farnese to take an army into France in 1590 to relieve the Siege of Paris by Henry and the Protestants.

Farnese relieved Paris, but at the cost of a serious deterioration in his position in the Netherlands. While still struggling to regain control of the situation in the Low Countries, Farnese was again ordered into France in 1591, over his strenuous objections, to help the forces of the Catholic League. He succeeded in that, but the campaign cost him dearly, both personally and as a commander. He returned to Flanders in 1592 a sick man. He was ordered back to France in 1592 and died at Arras in December. At his death, he was unaware that Philip had sent an envoy with orders to replace Farnese and send him back to Madrid to face charges of defrauding Philip of the money sent to finance military operations in the Low Countries.

Summary

In spite of Philip's ultimate distrust and rejection of him, Alessandro Farnese served his monarch well, often at personal sacrifice. The demands of his governorship separated him from his home and family. He was unable to return to Italy when his wife died in 1577 or when his only daughter married. He became Duke of Parma and Piacenza at his father's death in 1586, but, unable to leave his post in the Netherlands, had to appoint his seventeen-year-old heir, Ranuccio, to serve in his place.

An extensive correspondence between father and son indicates a high degree of interest in the affairs of Parma despite Farnese's major responsibilities in the Low Countries. Despite a growing weariness with the incessant war in the Netherlands, Farnese would not live to retire in peace to rule his inheritance. He died while obediently making one more march into France at the order of his monarch.

Bibliography

Lynch, John. *Spain Under the Hapsburgs*. 2d ed. Oxford and Cambridge, Mass.: Blackwell, 1992. Volume 1 addresses Farnese's career in the service of Spain. Lynch takes a very positive view of Farnese's character and abilities and is sympathetic to the constraints and frustrations under which he had to operate in dealing with Philip II. Extensive notes provide citations of mostly foreign-language sources.

Mattingly, Garrett. *The Armada*. Boston: Houghton Mifflin, 1959. The most readable account of the invincible Armada. Mattingly highlights Farnese's important role in the planning and implementation of the attempted invasion of England. Defends Farnese's actions in preparing his army to invade England, seeing his lack of preparedness to embark his men in August, 1588, as a sign of his military acumen.

Merriman, Roger Bigelow. *The Rise of the Spanish Empire in the Old World and in the New*. Vol. 4, *Philip the Prudent*. New York: Macmillan, 1936. Addresses the reign of Philip. Contains a significant amount of material about Farnese in all aspects of his service to the Crown. Merriman's coverage of Farnese is less extensive and his writing is less colorful than that of John Motley, but his treatment of Spain and Farnese is far more objective.

Motley, John Lathrop. *The Rise of the Dutch Republic: A History*. 3 vols. New York: Harper, 1852; London: Harper, 1883. Volume 3 contains extensive references to Farnese during his involvement in the Netherlands campaigns from 1577 to 1584. Motley has a strong anti-Spanish bias, but the work is useful because it is based on published narratives and documents from the period. Motley admires Farnese's military and political genius, even though it worked against what Motley considers to be the forces of modernism and progress.

———. *The United Netherlands: A History from the Death of William the Silent to the Twelve Years' Truce, 1609*. 4 vols. London: Murray, 1904. A continuation of the history of the Netherlands, picking up in 1584 where *The Rise of the Dutch Republic* ends. Volumes 1, 2, and 3 contain extensive discussions of Farnese's service as governor of the Low Countries from 1584 to his death in 1592. This work has the same drawbacks and strengths as Motley's other volumes.

Parker, Geoffrey. *The Dutch Revolt*. London: Allen Lane, and Ithaca, N.Y.: Cornell University Press, 1977. A good summary of Farnese's successes and failures in the Netherlands campaigns, based heavily on archival sources. Parker admires Farnese and ascribes much of the blame for his failures to lack of consistent financial support and leadership from Philip.

Robertson, Clare. *Il Gran Cardinale: Alessandro Farnese, Patron of the Arts*. New Haven, Conn.: Yale University Press, 1992. Highlights Farnese's life as a patron of the arts during the Renaissance.

Victoria Hennessey Cummins

GUY FAWKES

Born: April 13, 1570; York, England
Died: January 31, 1606; Westminster, England
Areas of Achievement: Government and politics
Contribution: Guy Fawkes was a key conspirator in the Gunpowder Plot, a secret attempt to destroy the English king and Parliament. Discovery of the plot intensified Protestant suspicions of Catholics and led to a period of reduced tolerance of Catholicism in England.

Early Life

Guy Fawkes's parents, Edward Fawkes and the former Edith Jackson, came from different religious backgrounds. The Fawkeses were conventional Protestants, many of whom held public-service positions. The Jacksons, however, were classified as recusants, or Catholics who refused to join the Church of England. During the reign of Elizabeth I, recusancy was a punishable crime. During Guy's early childhood, the Fawkeses were not openly Catholic. After the death of his father, when Guy was eight, his mother married Dennis Bainbridge, who was also a recusant.

Guy was soon sent to St. Peters Catholic School in York, an experience that reinforced the Catholic influence he now received at home. His friends at school included John and Christopher Wright, who were also destined to become involved in the Gunpowder Plot. These friends, other classmates, and teachers undoubtedly influenced the boy throughout his years at school, and he eventually became a devout Catholic and highly critical of the government persecution of Catholics. For a mere youth such as Fawkes to renounce the official Protestantism of England required considerably moral and physical courage, qualities that he displayed throughout his life.

After he left school, Fawkes assisted his stepfather for several years with the management of his estate in the Yorkshire countryside. There, Fawkes probably first met Thomas Percy, the future instigator of the Gunpowder Plot. During the 1590's, Fawkes embarked on a military career. He became a soldier of fortune in the Spanish army of the Netherlands, not an uncommon practice for English Catholics of the period. By all accounts he was an exemplary soldier, displaying not only courage and loyalty but also great piety. These qualities, in addition to his experience with explosives, led to Fawkes's involvement in the conspiracy. During several military campaigns, Fawkes had become acquainted with the use of gunpowder and its effectiveness for destroying defensive walls and buildings. The leaders of the Gunpowder Plot knew that the participation of someone with this practical knowledge was crucial if the plot was to be successful.

While abroad, Fawkes grew more and more discontented with the English persecution of Catholics, a view that was fostered by many of his military comrades and leaders. By early 1600, Fawkes left his regiment to work as a steward for Sir William Stanley, a former regiment commander who shared Fawkes's hatred of Elizabethan attitudes toward Catholics. Stanley worked hard to improve conditions for the Catholics and sent Fawkes to Spain in 1601 and again in 1603 to seek miliary aid from King Phillip II. These missions proved to be unsuccessful, leaving only civil anarchy as a means to redress the grievances of the disheartened English Catholics.

Life's Work

Guy Fawkes is best remembered for his role in the Gunpowder Plot, a conspiracy by a small group of English Roman Catholics who were discontent with the polices of King James I. Their plan was to blow up the king, his ministers and family, and the entire executive government during the opening of Parliament on November 5, 1605. After the destruction of the monarchy and the government, the conspirators hoped, an uprising by English Catholics would follow and enable them to take over the country.

Under Elizabeth I, persecution of Catholics was widespread. Executions and imprisonments were not uncommon in extreme cases. The introduction of recusancy laws, which fined people for failure to attend Anglican church services, was also extremely unpopular among English Catholics. Some individuals were forced to pay thousands of pounds in recusancy fines over the years. The accession of James I to the throne in 1603 brought hopes of greater tolerance for Catholics. Two years earlier, Thomas Percy, who was to become one of the plot's leaders, had even persuaded James, then king of Scotland, to put in writing his intentions to relax Elizabeth's persecution of the Catholics. Once seated on the English throne, however, James broke his promise, to the disappointment and anger of most Catholics.

Fawkes preventing Sir William Radcliffe from joining in the Gunpowder Plot conspiracy

The broken promise and a general dislike of the accession of the Scottish king to the English throne were important reasons that the Gunpowder Plot conspiracy was initiated. The leader of the plot was Robert Catesby, who, having seen his family persecuted under Elizabeth, was quite willing to seek violent revenge on the Protestant government. In March, 1604, Thomas Percy and Thomas Winter were told of the plot to blow up Parliament. At first, they were shocked by the plan; eventually, though, they came to the conclusion that violence was the only way to bring about government concessions for Catholics.

Returning to England from the Netherlands in May, Winter brought with him Fawkes, who he believed would be an asset to the plans because of his military experience. Later that month, the conspirators rented rooms near Parliament House. The conspiracy had grown to include John and Christopher Wright, Robert Winter, and John Grant; in the following year, Ambrose Rokewood, Francis Tresham, and Sir Everard Digby were added to help finance the operation.

The conspirators' plan—to dig a tunnel to the House of Lords and place a large quantity of gunpowder near the government's meeting site, where it could be detonated when Parliament was in session—was fraught with problems from the start. With the exception of Fawkes, who had some experience in mining operations, the conspirators were members of the gentry with no experience of digging. Consequently, they found their task to be very physically challenging. Money was also a problem; the addition of Rokewood, Digby, and Tresham improved the conspiracy's finances, but the full details of the plot were not revealed to all of them.

Although the opening of Parliament was delayed many times, the workers began to despair of the tunnel. In February, 1605, however, they learned of a cellar for rent under the House of Lords. They abandoned the tunnel and rented the cellar, supposedly for the storage of coal and wood. By April, they had succeeded in storing some twenty barrels of gunpowder in the cellar. The conspirators disbanded and arranged to meet later in the year to discuss the final steps of the plot.

While the conspirators waited for Parliament to commence, several began to have second thoughts. Catesby, however, managed to convince most of the conspirators to continue with the plot as planned. He also acquired horses and weapons, which he stationed in small groups throughout the West Midlands. These were to be used in the uprising he believed would follow once the plot had been executed.

When Tresham learned the full implications of the plot and discovered that his brother-in-law, Lord Monteagle, would be a victim of the explosion, he was shocked. Unable to convince Catesby to seek a less violent means of achieving their political goals, Tresham decided to reveal the plot by warning his brother-in-law not to attend the opening of Parliament. On October 26, Monteagle held a dinner party at his home. During the evening, a messenger delivered an anonymous letter to him, which he instructed to be read allowed. The letter warned of a plot to blow up Parliament, although no names of conspirators were mentioned.

It has been suggested that both Tresham and Monteagle conceived the idea of the "anonymous" letter and believed that by having it read in public, it would alert the government to the plot without involving Tresham as a conspirator. It was Tresham's hope that once alerted to the plot, the government would intercede and prevent the tragedy from occurring. In addition, Tresham believed, news that the plot had been discovered would reach his fellow conspirators, and they would abandon their plans and have time to flee to safety abroad.

Between October 26 and November 4, little action was taken by the authorities. It was only during the few days prior to November 5 that most of the conspirators decided to abandon the plot and flee. When the authorities eventually searched the cellar containing the concealed gunpowder, they met a man named Johnson, who claimed to be Thomas Percy's servant. According to Johnson, his master was using the area for coal storage. Moments before midnight on November 4, the cellar was visited again by authorities. This time, the concealed gunpowder casks were discovered, and Johnson was arrested. Johnson was interrogated over several days. He was subjected to torture, and he eventually revealed his true name: Guy Fawkes.

Shortly after Fawkes was discovered, the king appointed a commission to investigate the Gunpowder Plot. The commission was composed of the attorney general, Sir Edward Coke, and seven privy councillors. Over a period of about two weeks, Fawkes eventually provided most of the details of the plot, including the names of the conspirators. By this time, many days of torture had reduced the strong and willful Fawkes both physically and emotionally. Even without Fawkes's early cooperation, the identity of many of the conspirators was probably suspected. Many of them, including Catesby, Percy, Grant, Thomas Winter, and Christopher Wright, were well-known as Catholic sympathizers, and warrants were issued for their arrest.

Around the time of Fawkes's arrest, the remaining conspirators had participated in what they hoped would be the outbreak of rebellion in other parts of the country. The fighting was short-lived, however, and many of the conspirators were killed, including Catesby, Percy, and both the Wrights. Thomas Winter was wounded and arrested with the others shortly thereafter. Those who survived, including Fawkes, were tried, convicted, sentenced to death, and executed at the end of January, 1606.

Summary

Studies of the Gunpowder Plot have been hindered by a 1619 fire that destroyed many of the privy council's records. It has been suggested that the plot was instigated by members of the government in an attempt to discredit the Catholics and that Fawkes may have been simply a "fall guy" for the government. While the existence of a real plot is generally not disputed, the extent of government involvement has long been debated. Doubt has also been cast on the reliability of Fawkes's testimony under torture. Historically, tortured prisoners have often confessed guilt even for crimes of which they have been innocent. Despite such doubts, the Gunpowder Plot's revelation caused English Protestants to become yet more suspicious of Catholics and reinforced resentment toward them. The unpopular recusancy law was also enforced more rigorously. Since 1606, November 5 has been a day of public thanksgiving in Great Britain; commonly known as Guy Fawkes Day, it is celebrated with fireworks and bonfires.

Bibliography

Edwards, Frances. *Guy Fawkes: The Real Story of the Gunpowder Plot?* London: Rupert Hart-Davis, 1969. An easy-to-read account of the plot, with emphasis on the role played by Fawkes.

Fraser, Antonia. *Faith and Treason: The Story of the Gunpowder Plot*. New York: Doubleday, 1996. Draws a parallel between the Gunpowder Plot and instances of twentieth century terrorism.

Gardiner, Samuel R. *What Gunpowder Plot Was*. New York: AMS Press, 1969. Examines the historical evidence for the plot and discounts the possibility of high-level government involvement.

Garnett, Henry. *Portrait of Guy Fawkes*. London: Robert Hale, 1962. Deals with Fawkes's life before, during, and after the plot. Contains an interesting collection of reproduced historical documents related to the incident.

Nicholls, Mark. *Investigating Gunpowder Plot*. New York: St. Martin's Press, 1991. Examines how King James and his privy council approached the investigation of the plot. Contains a useful bibliography.

Toyne, S. M. *Guy Fawkes and the Powder Plot. History Today* 1 (1951): 16-24. A delightful summary of the events leading to the plot and the reasons behind the conspiracy.

Wormald, Jenny. *Gunpowder, Treason, and Scots. Journal of British Studies* 24 (1985): 141-168. Attempts to explain why the conspirators resorted to violence to address their grievances.

Nicholas C. Thomas

FERDINAND II and ISABELLA I

Ferdinand II

Born: March 10, 1452; Sos, Spain

Died: January 23, 1516; Madrigalejo, Spain

Isabella I

Born: April 22, 1451; Madrigal, Spain

Died: November 26, 1504; Medina del Campo, Spain

Areas of Achievement: Monarchy, the military, politics, and government

Contribution: The Catholic monarchs directed Spain's transition from medieval diversity to national unity. They achieved governmental and ecclesiastical reform, and established a continuing Spanish presence in Italy, America, and northern Africa.

Early Lives

Ferdinand and Isabella were each born to the second, much younger wives of kings. A much older half brother stood between each of them and the throne; their siblings died with considerable suspicion of poisoning. Thus the young prince and princess grew up the focus of intrigue. Their marriage represented an alliance between Ferdinand's father, John II of Navarre (from 1458 of Aragon), and a faction of Castilian nobles, including his mother's kinsmen, the Enríquez family, and Isabella's protector, Archbishop of Toledo, Alfonso Carrillo.

John II of Castile, Isabella's father, died when she was three and her brother Alfonso less than a year old. Their mother, Isabella of Portugal, withdrew to her cities of Arevalo and Madrigal to maitain her independence. This dowager queen, a woman of exemplary piety, became increasingly unstable, and King Henry IV, Isabella's half brother, brought the children to his court in 1461. In 1462, young Isabella stood sponsor at the baptism of the king's daughter Juana. Henry had married Juana of Portugal, mother of Princess Juana, within a year after his divorce from his first, childless wife, Blanche of Navarre, on the grounds of his own impotence. Princess Isabella and her brother Alfonso, who died in 1465, became involved in several plots that included challenging the legitimacy of Princess Juana, deposition of Henry, and various plans for Isabella's marriage, which led to her union with Ferdinand of Aragon in 1469.

Her isolated childhood and her preferred semi-isolation at Henry's gay court caused Isabella to grow up pious and rather bookish. Gonzalo Chacón, chosen by their mother to supervise Isabella and Alfonso, proved a guiding influence in her early life and later. This man had been a confidant of Álvaro de Luna, John II's great Constable of Castile. A description of the princess at the time of her marriage tells of golden red hair, gray eyes with long lashes and arched brows, and a red-and-white complexion. A long neck and slim, erect posture set off her face and gave an effect of dignity and majesty.

Ferdinand early became the focus of a quarrel between his father and his own half brother, Prince Charles of Viana, who was supported by the city of Barcelona. Almost from birth, the boy participated in Barcelona's elaborate ceremonies, and at the age of ten he and his mother, Queen Juana Enríquez, were besieged in Gerona by the Barcelona army and rescued by his father. Though Ferdinand had tutors and attendants to teach him to read and ride, his father was his great teacher. John II of Aragon involved his son in war and government as much as the boy's years allowed. Aragonese politics involved the same kind of intrigue as Castile's but were complicated by the complex nature of the Crown, which included Aragon, Catalonia, Valencia, Mallorca, Sardinia, and Sicily. In 1468, John II entitled Ferdinand King of Sicily, a position that gave him superior rank to his bride and that gave them both status in their struggle against Princess Juana and her uncle-fiancé, King Afonso V of Portugal, to win Castile.

Ferdinand's portraits show a red-and-white complexion with dark eyes and a full mouth. He wore his dark brown hair rather long, in the style of the day; his hairline began early to recede noticeably. In riding, warfare, athletics, and dancing, he performed with perfect skill and ease.

Life's Work

During the first decade of their marriage, Ferdinand and Isabella struggled to establish themselves in Castile, first to gain the good graces of Henry IV and, after his death, to dominate the barons. Men like Carrillo changed sides as it suited their interests; having supported Isabella, Carrillo turned to Princess Juana when it became clear that the newlyweds would not take direction from him. An incident in the early stages of the war against

King Ferdinand and Queen Isabella receiving Columbus after his first trip to America

Portugal limns the characters of the young couple. When cautious, shrewd, self-confident Ferdinand withdrew, avoiding a confrontation at Toro in July, 1475, rather than risk defeat, his insecure, impetuous, chivalric wife gave him a very chilly homecoming. His victory on March 1, 1476, near Toro (at Peleagonzalo) was more a victory of maneuver than a battle, and historians dispute the question of who actually won. In this period, Isabella played a role of great importance. For example, when the Master of the Crusading Order of Santiago died in 1475, she pressured its members into accepting her husband as their leader. That same year, the monarchs put under royal control the militia and treasury of the Holy Brotherhood, the medieval alliance of Castilian cities. With these forces and loyal barons, they subdued the others. Nobles who would not accept royal authority had their castles destroyed. By 1481, Ferdinand and Isabella stood masters of Castile. The longevity of Ferdinand's father, who died in 1479, preserved control in Aragon, while Ferdinand and Isabella won Castile.

The next decade brought the glorious conquest of the Kingdom of Granada. In the medieval tradition, King Abu-l-Hassán had adopted an aggressive attitude during the Castilian disorders; now his son Muhammad XI (or Boabdil to the Spanish) faced a united Aragon and Castile. In the period 1482-1492, the "Catholic Monarchs," as Pope Alexander VI called Ferdinand and Isabella, waged continuing warfare against the Muslims. Ferdinand headed Castilian forces in this great adventure and so consolidated his personal leadership. Isabella's role in providing funds, men, and supplies confirmed the essential importance of their partnership. Muhammad's surrender ended the 780-year Christian reconquest of Iberia and brought Spain's middle ages to an end; that same year, sponsorship of the first Christopher Columbus voyage and a decree expelling Jews from Castile signaled the beginning of Spain's modern age.

The years from the victory in Granada to Isabella's death brought signal triumph and personal disappointment. In 1495, Ferdinand and Isabella launched a war commanded by a Castilian nobleman, Gonzalo Fernández de Córdoba, against Aragon's traditional enemy, France, for control of the Kingdom of Naples. Continued by their successors, this struggle brought Spain's domination of Italy. A series of marriage alliances further strengthened them against France. The Portuguese alliance always remained paramount. Their eldest daughter, Isabella, married, first Prince John, son of John II of Portugal, and, after his death, King Manuel I. When this Isabella died, Manuel married her sister Maria. Typical of the new era of peaceful relations with Portugal, the 1494 Treaty of Tordesillas amicably adjusted the 1493 Papal Line of Demarcation which, consequent to the Columbus voyage, had divided the non-European world into Spanish and Portuguese hemispheres. Ferdinand and Isabella's only son, John (who died in 1497), married a Habsburg and their second daughter, Joan, married Philip of Burgundy, who was also a Habsburg. Ferdinand and Isabella's daughter Catherine (of Aragon) embarked on a tragic career in Tudor England as wife of Prince Arthur and later of King Henry VIII.

After Isabella's death, her husband continued their life's work, his course shaped by a series of accidents. Castile passed to the control of Joan and her Habsburg husband, and Ferdinand married a second wife, Germaine de Foix. Ferdinand and Germaine's son died soon after his birth. Joan's mental instability and her husband's death in 1506 restored Ferdinand's position as regent, now for Joan's son Charles (later King Charles I of Spain and Emperor Charles V). Yet only Ferdinand's military defeat of the Andalusian nobles made the regency effective. A series of ventures in North Africa culminated in the 1509 conquest of Oran, financed by Archbishop of Toledo Francisco Jiménez de Cisneros. A final triumph came in the conquest of Spanish Navarre in 1512, realizing the claim of Queen Germaine to that region. This conquest rounded out Spain's national boundaries; for the rest of his life, Ferdinand devoted himself to aligning Spanish policy with that of the Habsburgs.

Summary

In many ways, Ferdinand II and Isabella I superintended a transition to the national and cultural unity that provided the base for Spain's modern world influence. Though they left local affairs largely in the hands of barons and city oligarchies, the Royal Council provided a protobureaucratic center. This council took charge of the Holy Brotherhood, and one of its members became president of the *Mesta*, Castile's great sheepherders' guild. Through meetings of the Cortes and the junta of the Holy Brotherhood, the monarchs maintained contact with representatives of the cities, and *corregidores* acted as their agents in the cities. If Spain's laws remained as diverse as the multiplicity of its political units, Ferdinand and Isabella ordered compilations of Castile's medieval laws and their own proclamations as a guiding framework. They themselves traveled constantly through their kingdoms, providing personal justice.

Their strengthening of the Catholic culture and fostering of a Spanish national type made Spain a leader in the Catholic Reformation in Europe and the world. A papal decree in 1478 established the Spanish Inquisition under royal control to ferret out crypto-Jews. Combined with edicts in 1492 and 1502 obliging Jews and Muslims respectively either to convert or to leave Castile, the Inquisition largely established a Christian norm in place of medieval cultural diversity. Later it repressed Protestantism in Spain. In Aragon, Ferdinand reactivated the older Papal Inquisition, but the appointment of Tomás de Torquemada as High Inquisitor for both kingdoms and the establishment of a Council of the Inquisition made it a national institution. Appointment in 1495 of Isabella's confessor, the ascetic, selfless Jiménez de Cisneros as Archbishop of Toledo, in contrast to the lusty and ambitious Carrillo, acted to reform and control the Church. (Jiménez became High Inquisitor in 1507.) Jiménez de Cisneros' reform of the Spanish Franciscans and his founding of the University of Alcalá de Henares show a more positive dimension. The university adopted the Erasmian approach of using Renaissance scholarship for religious purposes.

Certainly no act of the reign had greater long-range impact than sponsorship of Columbus. Though Castile had engaged in conquest of the Canary Islands since 1479, the American voyages looked beyond Africa to world empire. Hampered by very limited revenues, Ferdinand and Isabella continued their sponsorship of this enterprise when significant monetary returns seemed problematical. The new American empire posed unprecedented problems of distance and dimension involving treatment of the Indians and control of Columbus' enormous claims as discoverer. Their development of viceregal authority went beyond anything in the tradition of Aragon, the conquest of the Canaries, or the feudalism of the Reconquest.

Bibliography

Hillgarth, J. N. *The Spanish Kingdoms, 1250-1516*. Vol. 2, *1410-1516, Castilian Hegemony.* Oxford: Clarendon Press, 1976. A work of solid scholarship, following recent Spanish interpretations with special emphasis on the reign of Ferdinand and Isabella. The great advantage of the book lies in its consideration of events in Aragon and the other Spanish kingdoms.

Kamen, Henry. *Spain, 1469-1714: A Society in Conflict*. 2d ed. London and New York: Longman, 1991. This book reviews material covered in J. H. Elliott's 1963 book, *Imperial Spain*. Provides an up-to-date view of Spain's Golden Age. Both utilize recent Spanish scholarship and considerably revise older interpretations. Kamen, also author of a book on the Spanish Inquisition, here pays attention to the needs of students, providing both an introduction and a reference tool.

Liss, Peggy K. *Isabel the Queen: Life and Times*. New York: Oxford University Press, 1992. Biography of Isabella I.

Lunenfeld, Marvin. *Keepers of the City: The Corregidores of Isabella I of Castile*. Cambridge and New York: Cambridge University Press, 1987. Based on archival research, this book is the sort of institutional history that has made possible the new interpretations of the subject. Lunenfeld has also written a similar book on the Council of the Holy Brotherhood.

Merriman, R. B. *The Rise of the Spanish Empire in the Old World and the New*. Vol. 2, *The Catholic Kings*. New York: Macmillan, 1918. A monumental work with narrative detail not found elsewhere in English, but for this reign the book is otherwise superseded by the books of Hillgarth and the others cited above. Its interpretations are outmoded, and its facts not always reliable. Its long reign as the standard English work on Ferdinand and Isabella partly explains the even longer reign of William Prescott's biography.

Miller, Townsend. *The Castles and the Crown: Spain, 1451-1555*. London: Gollancz, and New York: Coward-McCann, 1963. Although written with a lively style and based on chronicles, this book does not take account of recent scholarship. Its interpretations are of the Prescott school.

Nader, Helen. *The Mendoza Family in the Spanish Renaissance, 1350-1550*. New Brunswick, N.J.: Rutgers University Press, 1979. A work of solid scholarship with a very important focus on a great baronial family. The Mendozas and their ilk were as important in this reign as the kingdoms of Castile and Aragon.

Prescott, William H. *History of the Reign of Ferdinand and Isabella, the Catholic*. 3d rev. ed. 3 vols. New York: Hooper Clark, 1841. The pioneering work in English that is also the longest. Many of Prescott's interpretations and his scholarship are inevitably and completely outdated. The book, for example, overemphasizes Isabella's importance by denigrating Ferdinand. Like Miller's books, it can still be read for pleasure.

Saunders, Steven. *Cross, Sword, and Lyre: Sacred Music at the Imperial Court of Ferdinand II of Habsburg (1619-1637)*. Oxford: Clarendon Press, and New York: Oxford University Press, 1995. This book introduces a nearly lost music culture: the Vienna court of Emperor Ferdinand II. Saunders looks at the music in its cultural context, showing how the composers, institutions, and ideas of the period shaped sacred music at this pivotal center.

Walsh, William Thomas. *Isabella of Spain, the Last Crusader*. New York: McBride, 1930; London: Sheed and Ward, 1931. Deserves attention as a long, detailed work that is a biography of the queen, not a history of the reign or a study of Spain in her times.

Paul Stewart

SAINT JOHN FISHER

Born: 1469; Beverley, Yorkshire, England
Died: June 22, 1535; London, England
Areas of Achievement: Education and religion
Contribution: Fisher strongly contested the views of Martin Luther through his writings, supporting the Catholic faith, the Catholic Church, and the idea of the real presence in the Eucharist. He was canonized as a saint by the Roman Catholic Church in May, 1535.

Early Life

John Fisher, the eldest son of Robert and Agnes Fisher, was born at Beverley, Yorkshire, in 1469. His father was a well-to-do mercer who died when Fisher was seven or eight. Fisher was educated at the cathedral school attached to Rochester Cathedral, then went to Michaelhouse, Cambridge. He took his B.A. in 1487 and his M.A. in 1491. He became Fellow, then proctor, and finally Master of the college in 1497. As a proctor, he went to the royal court on college business and met Margaret Beaufort, Henry VII's mother. In 1497, she made him her confessor. Later, she founded a chair of divinity at Cambridge and appointed him its first incumbent in 1503. Fisher also helped her found Christ's College there in 1505. Before, in 1504, he had been elected chancellor of all Cambridge University, a post to which he was reelected at ten-year intervals and then for life. In the same year he became Bishop of Rochester, a post that he held until deprived shortly before death, declining to accept other, richer bishoprics. He preached the funeral sermons of both Henry VII, who died on April 21, 1509, and of Margaret Beaufort, who died three months later, and he brought Lady Margaret's works of charity and ascetic practices to the attention of the world.

Fisher was six feet tall, unusually tall for the times and only two or three inches shorter than his sovereign, Henry VIII. Hans Holbein, Henry's court painter, painted Fisher, probably in 1527; the portrait depicts an ascetic face, high cheekbones, and sharp eyes. He was fifty-eight at the time and not well. In fact, ill health plagued him the last years of his life.

Life's Work

With the death of his patroness, Lady Margaret, Fisher was comfortably ensconced in his posts as chancellor of Cambridge University and Bishop of Rochester. Like his contemporaries Thomas More, John Colet, and Erasmus, he favored the new learning and also a reforming within the Church of lax Christian practice. He demonstrated his commitment to the new education by carrying out Lady Margaret's bequest to found St. John's College at Cambridge (1511). He also facilitated Erasmus' teaching Greek at Cambridge (1511) and set up lectureships at St. John's in Greek and Hebrew. He himself started learning Greek in his forties. He came afoul of Cardinal Thomas Wolsey, Henry's chancellor, in 1517, when he preached at Westminster against clerical high living and greed. Moreover, in 1523 in the religious convocation, he resisted Wolsey's demand for money to wage a war with Flanders.

Fisher hated Luther and his doctrine. On May 12, 1521, at Paul's Cross, London, he preached against Luther's writings. After the sermon, Luther's books were burned. Fisher wrote several tracts against Luther: *Assertionis Lutheranae confutatio* (1523), *Sacri sacerdotii defensio* (1525), *Defensio Regie assertionis contra Babylonicam captiuitatem* (1525), a defense of the work that had earned for Henry the papal title Defender of the Faith. Fisher became more conservative as he aged. At the opening of the Reformation Parliament in the fall of 1529, he spoke out against Henry's plan of church reform. To Henry's demand in the same Parliament in 1531 for a submission of the clergy, Fisher convinced the assembly to add the clause "as far as the law of God allows" to give the clergy room to save their individual consciences and to attest their primary allegiance to God.

The Reformation Parliament had been called as a consequence of the king's "Great Matter," Henry's desire to nullify his marriage to Catherine of Aragon in order to marry Anne Boleyn. Before Parliament had been called, a special legatine court had been convened in May, 1529, under the direction of Cardinals Wolsey and Campeggio, specially sent from Rome to hear the case. In June, Fisher stoutly defended the legality of Henry's marriage to Catherine, thus incurring Henry's deep hatred. The marriage case was revoked to Rome in July, 1529, and it was not until May, 1533, that a court convened by the new Archbishop of Canterbury, Thomas Cranmer, found for Henry, formally declaring null his first marriage and attesting the legality of his second secret marriage of January, 1533, to

Anne Boleyn. Events now moved quickly as Henry pushed Parliament to legalize his heirs by Anne and disinherit his daughter Mary by Catherine via the Act of Succession of March, 1534. Henry continued his attack on the Church by the Act of Supremacy of November, 1534, by which he became Supreme Head of the Church, denying papal power over the English church. Fisher had been in trouble before the passage of these acts as a consequence of his defiance of Wolsey and Henry and also for his support of Elizabeth Barton, the Nun of Kent, who prophesied against Henry's marriage to Anne. The nun was executed. Fisher was implicated in the proceedings against her, but eventually was let off with a fine of three hundred pounds. After refusing to take the oath required by the Act of Succession, Fisher was sent to the Tower of London on April 16, 1534. On the passage of the Act of Supremacy, he was deprived of his bishopric. His refusal in May, 1535, to swear to Henry being Supreme Head of the Church and Pope Paul III's decision to make Fisher a cardinal sealed his fate. He was tried on June 17, found guilty, and sentenced to death by hanging, drawing, and quartering, which later was commuted to beheading on Tower Green. Fisher was executed on June 22, 1535; he met his death with calmness and dignity. His head was impaled on a pike on London Bridge and did not decay, demonstrating to the superstitious Fisher's sanctity. His body, at first sent to the Church of Allhallows Barking, was later taken to the Church of St. Peter ad Vincula in the Tower, where it lies near that of More, who had been executed two weeks after Fisher.

Summary

Saint John Fisher was a man of his age and in some ways a man for all ages. While he looked forward to the new humanistic biblical scholarship and fostered the study of Greek and Hebrew, even learning Greek in his forties, he looked backward to the glories of the Roman Catholic Church and defended them with his life. As a scholar and university statesman, Fisher helped Lady Margaret found Christ's and St. John's colleges at Cambridge. At St. John's, he founded lectureships in Greek and Hebrew. He also sponsored the celebrated humanist Erasmus and his teaching at Cambridge. Moreover, Fisher held the office of chancellor of Cambridge University for life.

In his writings, Fisher defended church doctrine and tradition against Luther and other reformers. When the time came to defend the sanctity of Catherine's marriage to Henry, he alone of the bishops spoke for her with vigor and conviction. He wrote books as well defending her right, nor did he ever desert the woman for whom he served as confessor. Fisher also showed courage in suggesting the saving clause to the clergy's submission in 1531, when he suggested that they protect their consciences by swearing "as far as the law of God allows." When he could not accept the Act of Succession, which denied Catherine's marital right and her daughter Mary's right to inherit, Fisher was sent to the Tower. He could neither swear to the oath required by the Act of Succession nor the further oath required by the Act of Supremacy saying that Henry was Supreme Head of the Church. By supporting Catherine even to the point of writing to the Emperor Charles V asking him to invade England and save English Catholicism, Fisher was unquestionably guilty of treason. The evidence that convicted him was his confidential conversation with Richard Rich, Solicitor General, when Fisher had denied Henry's supremacy. As Fisher faced the crowd that had come to see him die, he proclaimed to them: "Christian people, I come hither to die for the faith of Christ's holy Catholic Church." Fisher's death shocked Europe; Henry's decision to have his way with the Church had become clear to all. Soon, More joined Fisher, being executed July 6, 1535. Both men were canonized as saints by the Roman Catholic Church in May, 1935, as Adolf Hitler was building his war machine in Germany. In a way, both men, Fisher and More, demonstrated that there is a higher law, an authority superior to that of the prince and the state. They died for that principle and became examples to others who have meditated on what is worth living for and what is worth dying for.

Bibliography

Bradshaw, Brendan, and Eamon Duffy, eds. *Humanism, Reform and the Reformation: The Career of Bishop John Fisher.* Cambridge and New York: Cambridge University Press, 1989. Discussion papers from a 1985 symposium sponsored by Cambridge University and held at Queens' College.

Dickens, A. G. *The English Reformation.* 2d ed. London: Batsford, 1989; University Park: Pennsylvania University Press, 1991. A bit of an intellectual challenge, but still the best one-volume survey of the English Reformation. Puts Fisher in his context.

Elton, G. R. *Reform and Reformation: England, 1509-1558.* London: Arnold, and Cambridge, Mass.: Harvard University Press, 1977. Massively detailed account of the coming of the Reformation to England. Stresses the constitutional and legal ramifications. Utilizes much unpublished doctoral work. Good explanation of the process of oath taking that put Fisher on the spot.

Erickson, Carolly. *Great Harry: The Extravagant Life of Henry VIII.* London: Dent, and New York: Summit Books, 1980. Interesting insights into Fisher, especially at death, and a wonderful reading experience. Erickson has the knack of recreating people from the past by making one see life through their eyes.

Macklem, Michael. *God Have Mercy: The Life of John Fisher of Rochester.* Ottawa, Canada: Oberon Press, 1967. A good place to start reading about Fisher. Readable, sympathetic. Based on the sources.

Parker, T. M. *The English Reformation to 1558.* 2d ed. London and New York: Oxford University Press, 1966. Short, crisp account of the Henrician religious reformation that carries it through changes under his son Edward and reaction under his daughter Mary. Easy reading.

Rex, Richard. *The Theology of John Fisher: A Study in the Intellectual Origins of the Counter-Reformation.* Cambridge and New York: Cambridge University Press, 1991. This book investigates the intellectual career of Fisher.

Reynolds, E. E. *Saint John Fisher.* Rev. ed. Wheathampstead: Anthony Clarke, 1972. Detailed, absorbing, reverent treatment of Fisher's life.

Smith, Lacey Baldwin. *Henry VIII: The Mask of Royalty.* London: Cape, and Boston: Houghton Mifflin, 1971. Wonderful insights into the aging Henry as he pushed through his second marriage at the cost of Fisher and More's lives.

Surtz, Edward. *The Works and Days of John Fisher: An Introduction to the Position of Saint John Fisher, 1469-1535, Bishop of Rochester, in the English Renaissance and Reformation.* Cambridge, Mass.: Harvard University Press, 1967. For the more ambitious student. Defines Fisher's intellectual and theological positions on sixteenth-century issues of education, faith, and politics.

M. J. Tucker

SIR JOHN FORTESCUE

Born: c. 1385; Norris, Somerset, England

Died: c. 1479; Ebrington, Gloucestershire, England

Areas of Achievement: Political theory and law

Contribution: The first English thinker to recognize that Parliament's power over legislation and taxation had made England a limited rather than an absolute monarchy, Fortescue played a major role in shaping English constitutional concepts.

Early Life

Lamentably little is known of Sir John Fortescue's early life. He was born at Norris in Somerset. His father, a knight, had much land in Devon, providing for his son's lengthy legal education at the Inns of Court. No man, John Fortescue later asserted, could become a sergeant-at-law—as he did in 1430—without having studied the law for sixteen years. Becoming a sergeant not only marked the culmination of Fortescue's study of and apprenticeship in England's common law but also admitted him to the lucrative practice of law before the Court of Common Pleas. After this, the records indicate, he began to acquire wealth and responsibilities, both from the flourishing of his legal career and from his marriage to an heiress in 1435 or 1436. In 1442, he was appointed chief justice of the Court of King's Bench and was made a knight a few months later.

Fortescue left no private letters or memoirs, and no contemporary penned a description which would permit one to gain personal knowledge of the man himself. Virtually all that can be grasped of his character and personality must be deduced from his books and from the scant facts about his life which have survived. Even a glance at his writings, though, shows us an agile and energetic mind. While other thinkers of his time based their conclusions on the ideal of what should be or on the received wisdom of the past, Fortescue had the strikingly modern habit of observing and analyzing the way things really worked. He would then take this knowledge, gained from long experience in wrestling with problems of law and politics, and use it to suggest changes which could make institutions work better. He had a buoyant, optimistic faith that truth and justice would ultimately prevail, which stands out vividly against the grim fabric of his age. An underlying human decency is also revealed in the abhorrence with which he regarded torture and in the satisfaction he derived from the fact that in England even the peasants lived reasonably well, not crushed by taxes and the exactions of the nobles, as in France.

Life's Work

Fortescue served as chief justice of the Court of King's Bench for nearly two decades, absorbed in his judicial duties and his growing political role as a firm supporter of the ruling Lancastrian dynasty. Meanwhile, the restlessness of a number of powerful barons, led by the Duke of York, was creating an increasingly turbulent political situation in England. In 1455, the Wars of the Roses began as these aristocratic opponents of Henry VI, the feckless Lancastrian monarch, turned to violence. By 1461, the Yorkists had triumphed; their leader sat upon the throne of England as King Edward IV. Fortescue fled into exile with Henry VI and his family. For the next decade, he would share their troubles; his intelligence, experience, and energy making him one of the most prominent figures in their train. Year after weary year, in Scotland, Bur-

gundy, and France, he participated in an endless round of negotiations and intrigues designed to restore Henry VI to the throne. In 1470, he helped secure French help and an alliance with England's powerful Duke of Warwick. This shaky combination was able to force the Yorkists to flee, and for a few heady months Henry VI was once again England's king. Edward IV quickly rallied his supporters, though, and on April 14, 1471, he overthrew Henry once again.

Fortescue had landed in England full of hope that very day, ending his long exile. The bitter news of Henry's defeat was followed a few weeks later by the final crushing of the Lancastrian forces at the Battle of Tewkesbury. The Yorkists permitted neither Henry VI nor his son to live to threaten their power again. With the Lancastrian cause thus irretrievably shattered by their deaths, Fortescue, who had been captured at Tewkesbury, soon made his peace with the triumphant Yorkists. His reputation for wisdom and honor made his support valuable to them. He recognized reality and let himself be persuaded to write a defense of the legitimacy of Edward IV's title to the throne, disavowing his earlier works to the contrary. In return, he was pardoned and his estates were restored to him. He retired to private life and to a death, in Ebrington, Gloucestershire, as obscure as his birth. The last documentary evidence of Fortescue being alive dates from May, 1479.

Fortescue's life spanned some of the most violent decades in English history. He saw ruthless and powerful men subvert the laws, intimidate and corrupt officials, and reduce the royal government to impotence. The bloodshed and disorder of his age had a powerful effect on him, shaping the ideas about royal government which he put into his last important book, apparently written in the years just before his death, *The Governance of England: Otherwise Called the Difference Between an Absolute and a Limited Monarchy* (1885). With a keen awareness of the close relationship between wealth and political power, he strongly recommends that the Crown recover its lost riches and keep this wealth under its own control. The king, he argues, should have at least double the disposable income of any of his people, lest an overmighty subject become strong enough to challenge him. Fortescue also advises that a wise king will lessen the power of the nobles and decrease his own dependence on them by choosing men of proven integrity and talent to advise him, rather than let the great barons dominate his council. The king should also regain control of patronage, directly giving offices and commissions to men chosen by and loyal to himself, instead of allowing the barons to distribute these plums. Many of the policies followed by Edward IV and Henry VII, as they rebuilt the crumbling edifice of English monarchy at the end of the fifteenth century, are strikingly in tune with Fortescue's advice, though it is doubtful whether they were consciously using his work as a model.

For all of his recognition of the need for a strong king to keep order and secure the property and tranquillity of his subjects, Fortescue was far from recommending absolute monarchy. Indeed, his chief importance in the history of English political thought comes from his insistence on the limited nature of royal authority. His constitutional ideas were spelled out most completely in two Latin tracts: *De natura legis naturæ* (1864; on the nature of natural law), written between 1461 and 1463, and the better-known *De laudibus legum Angliæ* (1537; in praise of the laws of England), written about 1470. In these works, Fortescue divides monarchies into two types. One, for which France is his model, is characterized as *dominium regale* (absolute monarchy). Here, what pleases the king has the force of law; the bodies and possessions of his subjects are completely at his disposal. England, he states with pride, is not under the heavy hand of such an unlimited ruler. It is an example of the second type of monarchy: *dominium politicum et regale* (limited monarchy). England's kings, he insists, were bound to observe the laws and customs of their kingdom. Indeed, he points out that English judges had to swear not to give judgments which went against existing laws, even if the king himself commanded them to do so. In addition, English kings could neither make laws nor tax their people on their own authority. The consent of Parliament, Fortescue maintains, was necessary for laws or taxes to have validity.

Summary

Sir John Fortescue occupies a significant place in the transition from medieval to Renaissance England. His concern for wrokable solutions to actual problems and his ability to draw on his own direct experience of the institutions and the practices of his day are modern characteristics not often seen in the minds of fifteenth century men. He is the author of the first substantial discussion of the English government and its legal foundations to be written in the English language. Most important, his demonstration that the kings of England were limited not only by law but by the decisions of Parliament as well is regarded as a milestone in English constitutional thought. His *De laudibus legum Angliæ* was translated into English and published no fewer than seven times in the sixteenth century, with three more editions appearing in the seventeenth. Particularly during the crucial constitutional struggles of the seventeenth century, the opponents of the Stuart kings frequently referred to Fortescue in developing their arguments in favor of the prerogatives of Parliament. He stands as one of the fathers of the English concepts of limited monarchy and parliamentary power.

Bibliography

Burns, J.H. "Fortescue and the Political Theory of Dominium." *The Historical Journal* 28 (1985): 777-797. A rather complex discussion of the way in which Fortescue used the Latin term *dominium* and its significance in his thought. Some familiarity with Latin is necessary to understand this article.

Chrimes, S. B. *Lancastrians, Yorkists, and Henry VII*. 2d ed. London: Macmillan, and New York: St. Martin's Press, 1967. A good, brief introduction to fifteenth century England by a master scholar, particularly strong on government.

Fortescue, John. *De laudibus legum Angliæ*. Edited by S.B. Chrimes. Cambridge: Cambridge University Press, 1942; Birmingham, Ala: Legal Classics Library, 1984. This modern edition of Fortescue's most important work has both the Latin text and a scholarly English translation. Chrimes's lengthy introduction is extremely helpful on Fortescue's life and works, including *De natura legis naturæ*, for which as yet no adequate English translation has been published. This book also contains a splendid preface by Harold D. Hazeltine on Fortescue's place in the history of English jurisprudence.

———. *The Governance of England: Otherwise Called the Difference Between an Absolute and a Limited Monarchy*. Edited by Charles Plummer. Oxford: Clarendon Press, 1885; Westport, Conn.: Hyperion Press, 1979. This is the only acceptable modern edition of the work by Fortescue. Unfortunately, the text has been kept in Middle English rather than modernized, so most readers will find it slow going. Plummer's introduction, though, contains a very fine biographical sketch of Fortescue and a clear discussion of his ideas.

———. *Sir John Fortescue: On the Laws and Governance of England*. Edited by Shelley Lockwood. Cambridge and New York: Cambridge University Press, 1997. This convenient volume brings together for the first time new editions of Fortescue's two major works—*In Praise of the Laws of England* and *The Governance of England*—with references and suggestions for further reading. These works, arguably the earliest in English political thought, form a coherent argument for justice against tyranny and afford unique insights into the law and governance of fifteenth century England.

Hinton R. W.K. "English Constitutional Theories from Sir John Fortescue to Sir John Eliot." *English Historical Review* 75 (1960): 410-425. Presents Fortescue's ideas in the context of the development of English constitutional thought.

Lander, J.R. *Government and Community: England, 1450-1509*. London: Arnold, and Cambridge, Mass.: Harvard University Press, 1980. Excellent background on the England of Fortescue and its problems. More detailed than the work by Chrimes cited above, particularly strong on social and cultural history.

Shephard, Max Adams. "The Political and Constitutional Theory of Sir John Fortesque." In *Essays in History and Political Theory in Honor of Charles H. McIlwain*, edited by Carl Wittke. Cambridge, Mass.: Harvard University Press, 1936. Once past the nonsense about Fortescue having been a representative of the rising middle class and its socioeconomic interests, the reader will find a clear and coherent discussion of Fortescue's basic ideas.

Skeel, Caroline A.J. "The Influence of the Writings of Sir John Fortescue." *Transactions of the Royal Historical Society* 10 (1916): 77-114. Though dated, this article has the most thorough discussion available of the ways in which Fortescue's successors used his concepts. Particularly good for the seventeenth century.

Wilkinson, Bertie. *Constitutional History of England in the Fifteenth Century (1399-1485)*. London: Longman, and New York: Barnes and Noble, 1964. An extremely detailed discussion of the political institutions of fifteenth century England, how they worked, and the theories behind them.

Garrett L. McAinsh

GIROLAMO FRACASTORO

Born: c. 1478; Verona, Venetian Republic
Died: August 6, 1553; Incaffi, Venetian Republic
Areas of Achievement: Medicine, philosophy, astronomy, and literature
Contribution: Fracastoro clearly described contagious diseases, and his prophetic hypotheses on their causes foreshadowed by centuries the modern understanding of microbial infections.

Early Life

Girolamo Fracastoro was born into an old and distinguished Veronese family. His grandfather had been a physician to the reigning Scala family of Verona. After training at home, he was sent to the University of Padua, where he was entrusted to an old family friend, Girolamo della Torre, who taught and practiced medicine there. Before his medical studies began, Fracastoro, following a well-established practice, pursued the liberal arts, which also included mathematics and astronomy, under Nicolo Leonico Tomeo and philosophy under Pietro Pomponazzi. Among his teachers of medicine was Alessandro Benedetti, through whom he could come in contact with the Ferrarese humanistic medics, as well as with Girolamo della Torre and his son Marcus Antonio della Torre. Among his fellow students were the future cardinals Ercole Gonzaga, Gasparo Contarini, and Pietro Bembo, through whom he might have met members of the Aldine circle at Venice. He also befriended Giovanni Battista Ramusio, who gained fame in later life as a geographer.

Barely finished with his studies at Padua, Fracastoro was there appointed lecturer in logic in 1501 and the next year became an anatomical councillor, thus starting a traditional academic career in medicine. By 1508, wars interrupted his academic career and the remainder of his life was spent at Verona, practicing medicine or managing his private landed estate at Incaffi. From 1505, when he had been elected to the College of Physicians at Verona, he remained its faithful member. His hour of glory arrived in 1545, when the pope made him physician of the Council of Trent.

Life's Work

Venice had always maintained close ties with Constantinople, and when Padua came into its hands in 1404, Greek influence became dominant there as well. While in other parts of Italy Humanists strove to revive Roman glories, Venice was more interested in resurrecting the achievements of the Greeks. At the University of Padua the prevailing form of Aristotelianism, originally developed by the Parisian Averroists, was one in which Aristotle was not perceived as the ultimate "master of those who know," and his theories and methodologies were constructively criticized. Philosophical considerations were subordinated to his scientific work. Theology and metaphysics in general were gradually replaced by a closer study of nature. It was at the University of Padua that Fracastoro's scientific outlook was formed.

The work that brought most fame to Fracastoro was a lengthy narrative poem *Syphilis sive morbus Gallicus* (1530; *Syphilis: Or, A Poetical History of the French Disease*, 1686), written in verses similar to Vergil's *Georgics* (c. 37-29 B.C.). Fracastoro started working on this poem as early as 1510, but it was not until 1525 that it was presented in two books to Pietro Bembo, who at the time was considered to be the premier stylist. When it finally appeared in print in 1530 at Verona, it consisted of three books of some thirteen hundred hexameters.

In the first book, Fracastoro describes the horrors of the disease that had recently appeared in Europe and in a few years after 1495 spread across the whole continent. The disease was supposedly controlled by the sublime influence of the planets, which could be interpreted as the council of gods. The epidemic of syphilis was reminiscent of previous plagues and gave Fracastoro an opportunity to make allusions to pagan science, where the cosmic change is transmitted by the Lucretian seeds (*semina*) through the air.

The second book is devoted to cures. Fracastoro opens by describing his times, an age when disasters have been compensated for by the voyages of discovery. By judicious selection, he lists various cures and preventatives for the disease, setting the whole in a bucolic mood. He concludes the book with the myth of Ilceo, a shepherd in Syria, who, like Adonis, kills a stag sacred to Diana. As a punishment, he is stricken with a dreadful malady of the skin for which there is no remedy. Ilceo, through a dream, is directed to the underworld, where he is met by the nymph Lipare, who instructs him to wash himself in the river of flowing silver (mercury), which allows him to shed his skin like a snake and in this way rid himself of the disease. The whole is permeated with the influence of Vergil.

Book 3 contains another extended myth forming a short epos, on Christopher Columbus' voyage to the West Indies and the discovery of the Holy Tree, the guaiacum, which is a specific remedy against syphilis, which was endemic among the natives. The origin of this disease is explained by two stories. In the first, the natives are represented as survivors of Atlantis, which was destroyed by earthquakes and floods for its wickedness and afflicted by this dreaded disease. In the second story, Syphilis, another shepherd, blasphemed against Apollo the sun god and encouraged his king, Alcithous, to assume the prerogatives of a god. As a punishment, he was stricken by Apollo with this pestilence. After proper expiatory sacrifices were performed, Juno and later Apollo relented, the healing tree was provided by the gods, and Syphilis was cured.

It has been suggested that the subjects treated in this poem are but a pretext for positing the much deeper problem of the mutations that take place in nature. Nature constantly creates and destroys, distributing misery and happiness, without being influenced in any way by man's prayers and supplications. It is only through science that man can hope to tame nature and make it work for his benefit.

In 1538, Fracastoro published a work on astronomy, *Homocentricorum sive de stellis* (homocentricity on the stars), which he dedicated to Pope Paul III. He tried to represent the motions of the planets without having recourse to the epicycles or eccentrics and relying solely on circular motions about a single center (homocentric spheres). In this work, he was following the notions of two students of Plato, Eudoxus and Callippus, rather than ideas presented by Aristotle and developed by Ptolemy. Fracastoro's theory represents one of the last attempts to solve the planetary riddle before Nicolaus Copernicus.

This same book also contained his tract, this time of medical interest, *De causis criticorum dierum libellus* (1538), in which Fracastoro rejected the astrological explanation of the critical days as being dependent on the quarters of the moon, a notion which had been accepted by Galen. Fracastoro postulated his theory on two grounds: that ascription of critical days to the virtue of number was false, because neither number nor quantity can be the principle of action, and that the days of a disease seldom coincided with the phases of the moon. Fracastoro did not reject critical days as such, but he believed

the causes underlying them have to be sought in the nature of the disease itself, that is, qualitative and quantitative alterations of the humors.

Many scholars have praised Fracastoro as a forerunner of the germ theory of infectious diseases, ascribing to him prophetic intuition. Most of his thinking on this subject is found in his *De contagionibus et contagiosis morbis et eorum curatione libri tres* (1546; *De contagione et contagiosis morbis et eorum curatione*, 1930), but one should remember that this tract is preceded in the same volume by his *De sympathia et antipathia rerum* (1546; on the attraction and repulsion of things), in which he stated that without understanding sympathy and antipathy one cannot deal with contagion. It is based on ancient theories of the continuity of nature and avoidance of a vacuum as well as the tendency of the elements toward their own natural places and the attraction of like for like. All of it is expounded in terms of Aristotelian philosophy, without any trace of experimental method. As far as contagion is concerned, Fracastoro postulated three means by which disease can be spread: by simple contact, as in the case of scabies or leprosy, by *fomites*, such as clothing or bedsheets, or at a distance, through the propagation of *seminaria morbi* (seeds of contagion), which propagate either by joining humors that have the greatest affinity or by attraction, penetrating through vessels. These *seminaria* proliferate rapidly in the human body and cause the humor to which they have closest affinity to putrify. He believed, however, that these seeds of contagion perish in a dead body. As far as his explanations are concerned, Fracastoro remains a product of his time, but, when he concerned himself with observed clinical phenomena, he demonstrated an acute ability in differential diagnosis.

Among his philosophical works, one must count three dialogues dealing with poetics, the intellect, and the soul: *Naugerius sive de poetica dialogus* (1549; English translation, 1924), and "Turrius sive de intellectione dialogus" and "Fracastorius sive de anima dialogus," which were published posthumously. The first of these is a panegyric of poetry as the most complete of the arts and the most useful. The second discusses such psychological problems as cognition, mind-object relationships, and the location of memory. It is interesting to note that Fracastoro perceived man as a microcosm. The last dialogue was claimed to have been written to denounce the teachings of his professor at Padua, Pomponazzi, who promoted the idea that the human soul is perishable; yet not one harsh word can be found against him in this work. Basically, it is an attempt to reconcile Aristotle with Christianity, relying not on dogmatic assertions but on experimental procedure and critical reasoning, which he was forced to abandon when he realized to which conclusions it was leading. In the end, Fracastoro himself was forced to assume a theological position.

Fracastoro produced various other shorter works of literary as well as scientific interest, some of which were printed centuries after his death, on August 6, 1553. He remains an exemplar of Italian Humanism, who, contrary to accepted wisdom, began to show interest in natural sciences.

Summary

Girolamo Fracastoro better than anyone else demonstrated the aspirations as well as the limitations of premodern science. To him poetry was the preferred vehicle to transmit information, and he was more concerned with demonstrating to his readers his classical erudition than his medical acumen. He can easily stand for the typical post-Renaissance man, who is clearly exhibiting his intellectual roots. He is almost an exact replica of Dante, though more than two centuries separate them and no one reading Vesalius would realize that he and Fracastoro were contemporaries. Yet most people tend to accept the great anatomist as a typical representative of the medical mentality of his age and try to make Fracastoro fit that mold. The fundamental difference between Fracastoro and Dante was their attitudes toward authority. Dante lived in a world of tamed Aristotelianism, where natural philosophy was still the preserve of the theologians, whereas Fracastoro was educated by physicians who believed in the separation of the two realms of theology and science; it was this new attitude that made the scientific revolution possible.

Bibliography

Fracastoro, Girolamo. *Fracastoro's Syphilis*. Translated with introduction, text, and notes by Geoffrey Eatough. Liverpool: Francis Cairns, 1984. Written mainly from the point of view of a literary scholar who stresses Fracastoro's poetic achievements. Contains a detailed analysis of the poem *Syphilis*. Includes a computer-generated word index.

Greswell, W. Parr, trans. *Memoirs of Angelus Politianus, Joannes Picus of Mirandula, Actius Sincerus Sannazarius, Petrus Bembus, Hieronymus Fracastorius, Marcus Antonius Flaminius, and the Amalthei*. London: Cadell and Davies, 1805. An early biography of Fracastoro, based primarily on an even earlier life by F. O. Mencken. It is concerned primarily with Fracastoro as a literary figure. Especially good on reporting on his contemporaries' opinions about him. Contains notes and observations by Greswell.

Pearce, Spencer. "Nature and Supernature in the Dialogues of Girolamo Fracastoro." *Sixteenth Century Journal* 27 (spring 1996): 111. Pearce analyzes the supernatural in the dialogues of Fracastoro.

Rosebury, Theodor. *Microbes and Morals: The Strange Story of Venereal Disease*. New York: Viking Press, 1971; London: Secker and Warburg, 1972. Two chapters are devoted to Fracastoro, dealing specifically with syphilis as a medical problem. This book presents the best semipopular treatment of the origins of syphilis and whether it was brought from the Americas by the sailors of Columbus.

Thorndike, Lynn. "Fracastoro (1478-1553)." In *A History of Magic and Experimental Science*, vol. 5. New York: Columbia University Press, 1941. A short critical treatment of Fracastoro's scientific contributions. Thorndike was one of the first to realize that the Middle Ages were not quite as dark or the Renaissance quite as brilliant as was commonly accepted. In making this point, Thorndike uses evidence skillfully.

Truffi, Mario. "Fracastor's Life." In *Syphilis*, by Hieronymus Fracastor, revised by Mario Truffi. St. Louis: Urologic and Cutaneus Press, 1931. A rather laudatory treatment of Fracastoro, written by a physician and therefore slanted more toward medical aspects of his life. A good counterbalance for the previous entry.

Leonardas V. Gerulaitis

FRANCIS I

Born: September 12, 1494; Cognac, France
Died: March 31, 1547; Rambouillet, France
Areas of Achievement: Monarchy and patronage of the arts
Contribution: Francis I, France's Renaissance monarch, increased the power of the Crown within France, led his country in a series of wars against the Habsburgs, created a glittering court, and helped to introduce the Italian Renaissance into France.

Early Life

When Francis was born to Charles d'Angoulême and his young wife, Louise of Savoy, he was not expected to become King of France. Only after Charles VIII died childless three years later, making Francis' cousin King Louis XII, did he become next in line to the throne. Indeed, not until Louis died in 1515 without having fathered a son was it absolutely certain that the twenty-year-old Francis would take the throne. After the somber last years of his aged, weary predecessor, Francis on his accession represented youth, vigor, and enthusiasm to his subjects. He had developed into a tall, athletic man with a lively and expressive, rather than handsome, face. His education in academics and statecraft had been haphazard at best, and his great passions were for the chase and for seduction, rather than for the sedentary arts of statesmanship. Throughout his reign, Francis maintained a court notorious for its elegance, gaiety, and erotic exuberance. Notwithstanding his sensual self-indulgence, this cheerful, gracious, and dashing young man would become one of France's most respected sovereigns.

Life's Work

The land to which Francis fell heir in 1515 was growing steadily in prosperity, population, and power. The ravages of the Hundred Years' War were a rapidly fading memory, and the feudal dynasties which had checked the power of France's kings for so long had mostly disappeared. The nobles were clamoring for the adventure, glory, and profits of conquest, and their young king was eager to oblige them. In July, 1515, Francis led an army into northern Italy, continuing Louis XII's policy of seeking to control the wealthy Duchy of Milan. In September, he won the greatest victory of his reign at the Battle of Marignano. Charging joyously at the head of his cavalry, Francis shattered the dreaded Swiss pikemen. This left him the master of Milan and the dominant power in northern Italy, a happy situation which would not last long. The deaths of Ferdinand of Aragon in 1516 and of the Emperor Maximilian in 1519 made their grandson, Charles V of the house of Habsburg, ruler of Spain and its possessions in the New World, of Austria, of the Burgundian lands, and of much of Italy as well. When Charles was elected Holy Roman Emperor in 1519, France was virtually encircled by his power.

Francis spent much of the rest of his reign fighting with Charles, trying to maintain his own power in Italy and to prevent Charles from dominating all of Europe. In 1525, Charles's armies routed the French at the Battle of Pavia, and Francis learned the folly of a king trying to lead his troops in the field: He was captured, and Charles replaced him as the dominant power in Italy. Francis was forced to spend the next year as Charles's prisoner in Spain, gaining his release only by agreeing to a humiliating treaty. Once free, Francis swiftly repudiated the treaty and resumed hostilities. In a series of punishing wars over the following two decades, joined at various times by Venice, England, the Papacy, Protestant German princes, and even—to the horror of all Christendom—the Turks, Francis struggled unsuccessfully to regain Milan and to break the Habsburg hold on Italy. This great contest, the rivalry between the house of Habsburg and the French Crown, would continue to dominate European power politics until the eighteenth century.

Francis was able to mobilize his kingdom's human and material resources in the service of his Italian ambitions to an extent which would have dazzled his predecessors. Many scholars, impressed by the obedience and support which he commanded, have regarded him as a key figure in the development of France's absolute monarchy. There are strong arguments in favor of this view. Public opinion and the most important French political theorists of the time, reacting against the civil wars and vulnerability to invasion which had bedeviled France in earlier centuries when the Crown was weak, were inclined to stress the absolute nature of the royal prerogative. Tracts such as Guillaume Budé's *De l'institution du prince* (1547, wr. 1518) argued that the king's power was limitless and that he was not bound to respect any rights of his subjects.

Without question, Francis himself subscribed wholly to Budé's views. Throughout his reign he showed little inclination to let any considerations of customs or rights, no matter how venerable, interfere with the accomplishment of his desires. As he was energetic, charming, intelligent, and determined enough to win the respect and support of most of the politically active population of his kingdom, Francis was generally successful. He was able to absorb into the royal domain the vast holdings of Charles, Duke of Bourbon, after Bourbon betrayed him in 1523. Francis also reformed and centralized the fiscal administration of the Crown, and he significantly increased the control of the central government over its provincial officials. He was able repeatedly to bulldoze his way past objections to his policies and edicts voiced by the Parlement de Paris, ignoring its traditional function as a check on the legal absolutism of French kings.

Francis' most important struggles with the Parlement concerned religion. In 1516, fresh from his great victory at Marignano, he negotiated the Concordat of Bologna with the pope. This agreement restored the Papacy's right to tax the French church, in exchange for confirming and extending Francis' power over appointments to high church offices in France. The Parlement's genuine outrage over this double blow to the independence of the French church was contemptuously rejected by Francis, who forced the body to register the Concordat in 1518. The Parlement was equally distressed by Francis' reluctance to persecute religious dissidents, particularly the adherents of the new Protestant ideas which began seeping into France as early as 1519. Again, however, their remonstrances went unheeded by the king. Not until the mid-1530's, when Francis himself became concerned about the increasing radicalism of the reformers, did he inaugurate systematic persecution. By this time, though, the new ideas had become too strong to be dislodged without a protracted, agonizing struggle.

Francis was obviously a far stronger king, more securely in control of his government and his kingdom, than any of his predecessors. That does not, however, mean that his power was absolute. Francis' subjects, particularly the nobles and the wealthy bourgeoisie, continued to possess independent military and political strength which Francis was forced to respect. That can be seen most clearly in the field of finance. Even though Francis' extravagance and his endless wars left him chronically in need of funds, he did not dare to raise taxes enough to meet his needs. He knew too well that his subjects could still rebel against him if he pushed his prerogative too far, infringing on what they considered to be their own traditional rights. That was shown in 1542, when an attempt to impose new taxes in the southwest of France provoked a serious armed rebellion.

For the most part, therefore, Francis had no choice but to raise the money he needed by a series of expedients which inevitably undermined royal power in the long run. He sold public offices and titles of nobility, he sold royal lands, and he borrowed. Thus, he bequeathed to his son and heir, Henry II, a number of officials who could neither be fired nor relied upon, shrunken revenues from the royal domain, and a discouraging mound of debts. Clearly Francis' absolutism did not include unlimited power to tap the wealth of his subjects. In addition, though the Parlement and other institutions had been cowed into obedience by Francis, once his strong hand was removed from the scene they lost little time in reasserting themselves under his successors. Francis as an individual was popular and respected enough to get most of what he wanted done, but his reign does not appear to have left the monarchy as an ongoing institution significantly stronger than it had been before.

Francis is more admired today for his role as a generous and discriminating patron of culture than for his political or military policies. Throughout his life, Francis maintained a lively interest in intellectual and artistic pursuits, particularly after his early campaigns in Italy exposed him to the Humanism of the Renaissance there. Back in France he established lectureships in classical Latin and Greek, in Hebrew, and in mathematics, which would ultimately evolve into the Collège de France. He was an avid amasser of both books and manuscripts, and his collections would form the nucleus of the Bibliothèque Nationale, the French national library.

Francis' generosity toward artists attracted Leonardo da Vinci, Benvenuto Cellini, Andrea del Sarto, and other Italian masters to France, helping to establish the Renaissance style there. Many of their works, including Leonardo's *Mona Lisa*, have remained among the treasures of France ever since Francis' reign; indeed, Francis' extensive collection of paintings and other artworks have become the nucleus of the collection of the Louvre. Francis' interest in the arts can also be seen today in the numerous châteaus which he built or modified, again spreading Renaissance styles into France. Among the most notable are those of Chambord, Blois, and Fontainebleau. At these and similar pal-

aces, Francis did much to introduce a still-coarse and turbulent French nobility to a more elegant, sophisticated, and graceful way of life. His reign significantly improved the manners, if not the morals, of the French elite.

Summary

As a man Francis I is best remembered for his charm, the refinement and elegance which he brought to the French court, and for his numerous love affairs and gallant dalliances. As a king he was popular and successful, though not a reformer or innovator of great significance. While it is an exaggeration to regard him as an absolute monarch or even as a major architect of the absolute monarchy of the late seventeenth century, he made the power of the Crown felt in France to an unprecedented extent during his reign. As a statesman his wars against Charles V, even though unsuccessful, did keep France independent and established it even more firmly as one of the great powers of Europe. As a patron of culture he is largely responsible for spreading the styles and standards of the Italian Renaissance into France, raising the level of civilization there and endowing his kingdom with many lasting treasures.

Bibliography

Hackett, Francis. *Francis the First.* London: Heinemann, 1934; New York: Doubleday, 1935. A highly readable, romantic popular biography, but dated and not always judicious in its conclusions. Hackett's enthusiasm for psychoanalyzing Francis and other figures unfortunately entailed the construction of great edifices of interpretation on flimsy foundations of fact. No notes or bibliography.

Knecht, Robert Jean. *Renaissance Warrior and Patron: The Reign of Francis I.* Rev. ed. Cambridge and New York: Cambridge University Press, 1994. This is a completely revised edition of Knecht's earlier study of the king, first published in 1982 and for many years the standard work on the subject. That edition is now superseded by this substantially larger work, in which much new written and illustrative material has been included.

———. *Francis I and Absolute Monarchy.* London: Historical Association, 1969. This brief pamphlet argues cogently in favor of regarding Francis as an absolute monarch. It is basically a response to the work of Major, cited below.

McNeil, David O. *Guillaume Budé and Humanism in the Reign of Francis I.* Geneva: Librairie Droz, 1975. Concentrates on religious and intellectual developments during Francis' reign, centering on the life and works of Budé. McNeil also discusses Budé's significant role in the politics of the times. Contains a comprehensive bibliography on the subject.

Major, J. Russell. *Representative Institutions in Renaissance France, 1421-1559.* Madison: University of Wisconsin Press, 1960. This controversial, seminal volume by a great scholar argues that the absolutism of Francis and other sixteenth century French kings has been much exaggerated. Should be read in conjunction with the works by Knecht cited above.

Salmon, J. H. M. *Society in Crisis: France in the Sixteenth Century.* London: Benn, and New York: St. Martin's Press, 1975. Though the bulk of this book deals with the religious conflicts of the second half of the century, the opening chapters contain a serious analysis of all aspects of the France of Francis I. Economic and social structures, the institutions of government, and cultural developments, rather than narrative political history, are emphasized. A detailed index, an extensive bibliography, genealogical charts, and a glossary of French terms help make this work an excellent reference.

Seward, Desmond. *Prince of the Renaissance: The Golden Life of François I.* London: Constable, and New York: Macmillan, 1973. A beautifully illustrated and lively, though brief and rather superficial, popular biography. Very thorough on Francis' patronage of the arts but tends to exaggerate his role in shaping French culture. The work must also be used with caution on diplomacy and government, as Seward tends to let his flair for the colorful and the dramatic get the best of his judgment. Skimpy bibliography and few notes.

Garrett L. McAinsh

SIR MARTIN FROBISHER

Born: c. 1535; Pontefract, Yorkshire, England

Died: November 22, 1594; Plymouth, Devon, England

Area of Achievement: Exploration

Contribution: Frobisher's search for the Northwest Passage failed, but he and his English contemporaries helped establish an English presence in the Atlantic.

Early Life

Although Martin Frobisher was born into the country gentry of England, where record keeping usually was more precise than for the lower classes, researchers still do not know the exact date of his birth or even the exact year, although most historians have guessed at about 1535. What is known is that Frobisher was brought up in Yorkshire until the early death of his father in 1549, when Frobisher had barely reached adolescence. Thereupon, his mother dispatched him to London to be raised by her brother, Sir John York. He early on showed far more promise as a mariner than he did as a student. Frobisher's personality and talents, indeed, were not typical of his social class, and he was in temperament far more like the common mariner he commanded in later life than he was like the captains who were to be his colleagues.

Frobisher was at sea by the time he entered his teenage years. His first recorded expedition took place at the age of fifteen, on a disastrous pirate voyage to West Africa commanded by Thomas Wyndham, from which he was one of the few to return alive. Frobisher's career could not have prospered, though, without the help Frobisher was given by the powerful Lok family of mariners. John Lok was a merchant whose activities basically amounted to piracy; he spent much of his time at sea while the business affairs were handled by his brother Michael. His approach of aggressive, financially motivated expansionism became Frobisher's own.

In 1562, Frobisher returned to Africa with Lok. Frobisher was taken hostage by the Portuguese and imprisoned for four months. Upon his release, he became even more dedicated to carrying on the fight against England's enemies.

Life's Work

Frobisher fought for England in Ireland, where the Catholic population was restive under the control of their newly Protestant overlords. His heart remained with the sea, however, and he participated in raids on the Spanish, Portuguese, and French fleets. As successful as the English were against their opponents in individual raids, Spain and Portugal continued to control the lucrative trade route to Asia. The only alternative was to try to discover the theoretical Northwest Passage to Asia, going to the north of North America in what is now called the Arctic Ocean. Frobisher's relative youth (he was in his early forties in 1576), as well as his energy and experience, led to his appointment to lead the first English expedition in search of the Northwest Passage.

Frobisher embarked on June 7, 1576, with three ships, financed by the Lok brothers and a group of wealthy backers. The ships were stocked with the latest scientific equipment and navigational guides. By July, they had arrived at Greenland. Sailing around the southern tip of that island, they eventually came to Baffin Island in present-day Canada. Here, on August 19, Frobisher and his fleet had their first encounter with the Inuit people of the region. Frobisher was the first English-speaker to encounter the Inuit, many of whom would, centuries later, be subject to the British crown. Though at first Frobisher's relations with the Inuit were friendly, relations deteriorated after the Inuit kidnapped several men of Frobisher's fleet. Soon, Frobisher decided to return home, in the deluded hope that he had found the way to Asia when in fact all he had done is probe deeper into the Arctic ice. His fleet had, however, found some lumps of ore that they determined to be gold, and they brought it home to England. Frobisher became a national hero and was able to marry Isabel Riggatt, a wealthy widow whose money helped finance subsequent voyages.

The gold was in fact not gold at all, and even Michael Lok, who stood to profit substantially if it were gold, did not think it was. Nonetheless, the hunger for gold, more than a pure interest in exploration, allowed for the speedy financing of a second voyage by Frobisher in search of the Northwest Passage and more "gold." This time, Queen Elizabeth I of England contributed to the cost and lent her personal support to the voyage. The expedition was better manned, having more navigational experts and scientists among the crew. It was also better equipped, with the addition of the tall ship *Aid* to the two large ships of the first voyage, the *Gabriel* and *Michael*.

Frobisher was generally a popular leader among his men. Expectations were high that the second voyage would confirm the perceived success of the first. They returned to the inlet of Baffin Island that is now known as Frobisher Bay in commemoration of its first European explorer. It is difficult for contemporary readers to realize how distant in terms of perception the icy, barren landscapes of Baffin Island were from the sailors' home. There was a sense of near-total isolation and remoteness that can only be compared to the feelings of astronauts who explored the Moon, except that the astronauts were in constant communication with Earth. Frobisher and his men not only had no communication with home but also, due to the limitations of the maps and navigational tools available to them, had no sure idea of where they were. Frobisher still believed that Baffin Island was Asia. He laid a cross upon a nearby hill, thinking that he was taking possession of Asia in the name of the Queen. He thought that the Inuit were some manner of coastal Asian people.

Given the kidnapping on the previous voyage, relations with the Inuit were hostile from the start. Frobisher had to wage a series of skirmishes against them. Defeating the Inuit, he took some more ore as well as two live captives, the first to be taken by the English. Although the captives died a short time after their return to England, they were the subject of a great frenzy in England and, combined with the supposed gold, led easily to the manning of a third Frobisher expedition.

Frobisher's final voyage to the Arctic left at the end of May, 1578. Again, the ship approached Greenland, this time landing on the island itself. The voyage then proceeded back to the now-familiar area of Frobisher Bay. In search of the Northwest Passage, the ships plunged into Hudson Strait, which if explored until the end would have led to the waterways they were seeking, although they were far more icebound and impassable than the Europeans imagined at the time. Once more mining for ore, Frobisher wanted to leave a hundred men on Baffin Island to winter there and set up a permanent gold-mining base. However, fearing the harshness of the winter, the crew was not enthusiastic, and Frobisher was persuaded to return to England, losing one of his ships in the process but returning with most of his crew and bounty intact.

Unfortunately, euphoria about this voyage was short-lived, as it was soon proved conclusively that the ore was not gold. From the outset, the English had wanted so badly to believe it was gold that they would not accept the evidence before their own eyes. It was only when all hope had vanished that the reality of its worthlessness was admitted. Frobisher's popularity faded rapidly, even though he was not suspected of using the supposed gold for personal financial gain. Many of the people who had invested in his voyages were financially ruined (as was Frobisher himself) or were furious because they thought they had been defrauded. Adding to his troubles, Frobisher's wife Isabel became disillusioned with him due to his loss of their wealth; she then died not a year after the return of the third voyage.

This financial disaster meant that Frobisher had to return to piracy. As a pirate, he became successful enough to be offered a position of command under Sir Francis Drake. Thereafter, his career would be a more traditionally military one. He would serve under the command of the government rather than as the representative of a privately controlled, mercantile concern. Frobisher redeemed himself by fighting for the English cause in Ireland in 1580. In 1585, he became the major lieutenant to Drake in the West Indies, where his experienced seamanship and empathy with the common sailor proved crucial to Drake's victories in battle after battle against Spain and in the sacking of Cartagena in present-day Colombia. In 1588, the Spanish Armada prepared to invade England itself. Successfully commanding the Channel fleet and then the ship *Triumph*, Frobisher was knighted after the defeat of the Spanish. His personal relations with Drake, though, were not as positive, as he chafed under the command of the other great captain, whom he suspected of wanting to take all the fleet's profits for himself.

Frobisher, who by this time had married Lady Dorothy Widmerpole, spent his final years in expeditions against the Portuguese-controlled Azores and the French coast. In one of his assaults upon the latter, at Brest, he received a wound in his leg which became infected and led to his death at Plymouth in late 1594.

Summary

Martin Frobisher's lack of learning and the fact that his goals seemed more mercantile than scientific have contributed to his not being one of the more famous European explorers. Still, he deserves fame, not only for being one of the first Englishmen to explore the territory that eventually became Canada but also because his deeds and explorations changed the course of European and North American history. Without his enthusiasm, popularity, and leadership qualities, the three voyages to the Arctic in the late 1570's would never have occurred. Until Frobisher's era, the sea and all world exploration were largely controlled by the Spanish and Portuguese. Frobisher and his English contemporaries helped establish an English presence in the Atlantic. This achievement proved to be a far more enduring one than the search for the Northwest Passage. The Northwest Passage continued to be hunted for another three centuries, by which time it had become of far more scientific than practical interest.

Bibliography

Asimov, Isaac. *The Ends of the Earth: The Polar Regions of the World*. New York: Weybright and Talley, 1975. Skillfully and clearly written history of polar exploration, emphasizing the scientific side of the effort. Also provides some historical background. A good source for students beginning their study of polar discoveries.

Fitzhugh, William, and Jacqueline S. Olin, eds. *Archeology of the Frobisher Voyages*. Washington, D.C.: Smithsonian Institution Press, 1993. Examines the material remains of Frobisher's three voyages to what is now Canada in search of the Northwest Passage. For supplementary historical or biographical use.

Keating, Bern. *The Northwest Passage: From the Mathew to the Manhattan, 1497 to 1969*. Chicago: Rand McNally, 1970. A convenient source that is indispensable on the geography of Frobisher's voyages. Contains many colorful and detailed maps.

McFee, William. *The Life of Sir Martin Frobisher.* New York: Harper, 1928. Written by a seaman himself, this is the only biography of Frobisher that is at all reliable in scholarly terms. Out of date and hard to find, it contains much information crucial to the student. It is necessarily sketchy on the early life but provides details on the West Indian years that are not otherwise easily accessible, given that most sources concentrate on the North Atlantic voyages.

Morison, Samuel Eliot. *The European Discovery of America: The Northern Voyages*. New York: Oxford University Press, 1971. The most available and most valuable source on Frobisher. Thorough, insightful, written with wit and flair, and concerned to defend Frobisher against his detractors, particularly those who accuse him of being greedy or unscientific. Also provides an excellent survey of the process of discovery and exploration in the North Atlantic in which Frobisher played such a pivotal role.

Quinn, David Beers. *England and the Discovery of America, 1481-1620*. New York: Knopf, 1974. The best single-volume history of English exploration in the Atlantic, with an excellent bibliography. Occasionally stuffy, pedantic, and self-indulgent, this book nonetheless provides a good overview of Frobisher's maritime era.

Nicholas Birns

ANDREA GABRIELI

Born: c. 1520; in or near Venice
Died: 1586; Venice
Area of Achievement: Music
Contribution: Gabrieli was one of the most versatile musicians of his generation. His compositional output includes sacred vocal music, secular vocal music, instrumental ensemble music, and organ music.

Early Life

Very little is known about Andrea Gabrieli's early life. He was probably born in the northern (or Canareggio) section of Venice. Although most biographers have stated that he was born around 1510, the lack of available information on Gabrieli until the 1550's suggests a birth date of around 1520. It is possible that he may have received some early training from the organist at San Geremia in Canareggio (Baldassare da Imola), and that he may have been a singer at St. Mark's Cathedral in Venice in 1536, although there is no documentation to prove either of these assumptions. Nor is there evidence to suggest that he was a pupil of Adrian Willaert, the chapel master of St. Mark's at that time.

Since Gabrieli's first published composition appears in a 1554 collection of madrigals by Vincenzo Ruffo, it is possible that he may have been a musician at the Verona cathedral, where Ruffo worked during the 1550's. The first indication of Gabrieli's activities as a church organist dates from 1557-1558, when he was organist at San Geremia. Although he competed unsuccessfully for the position of second organist at St. Mark's Cathedral in 1557, he must have already been an accomplished organist, for he was a member of the Accademia della Fama in Venice by 1558.

Perhaps the most significant event in Gabrieli's musical training is his connection with the court of Munich during the early 1560's. As court organist to Duke Albrecht V of Bavaria in 1562, he accompanied the duke on several journeys and became friends with the duke's music director, Orlandus Lassus. Before his period at the court of Munich, Gabrieli had published only four compositions, all madrigals that suggest the influence of Cipriano de Rore. This contact with Lassus heavily influenced Gabrieli's many subsequent publications of both sacred and secular compositions and assured his future position as one of the most important musicians in Venice.

Life's Work

Gabrieli became second organist at St. Mark's in 1564. His growing popularity in Venetian musical life is attested to by the fact that he composed ceremonial music for various state occasions—the visit of Archduke Karl of Graz (1569), the festivities after the Venetian republic's victory against the Turks (1571), and the visit of King Henry III of France (1574). During these mature years, he also attracted a number of talented students, including Hans Leo Hassler, Ludovico Zacconi, and his nephew Giovanni Gabrieli. He became first organist at St. Mark's in 1584, a position which he retained until his death late in 1586.

Unfortunately, much of Gabrieli's music was published late or posthumously, making it difficult to trace the development of his musical style. For this reason, his life's work is best discussed by types of compositions, divided into the following categories: madrigals, villanelle, sacred vocal music, ceremonial music, instrumental ensemble music, and keyboard music. Gabrieli's seven books of mature madrigals were published between 1566 and 1589. With these collections, he established himself as a master of the lighter type of madrigal that became a fashionable reaction to the serious, avant-garde madrigals of many late sixteenth century composers. Petrarch's texts are set in a less serious style, and many madrigals use the lighter pastoral verses of such poets as Battista Guarini and Torquato Tasso. Gabrieli achieves a less contrapuntal, more appealing style in these madrigals through the use of closely spaced imitative entries and through a greater tendency toward homophonic writing with various combinations of voices. Some phrases have two melodic voices and a harmonic bass, a tendency that anticipates the texture of Baroque music. The harmonic style shows a preference for major triads and a feeling for tonal clarity resulting from the use of few altered notes. In these madrigals, Gabrieli is still attentive to the words but avoids the manneristic tendency to disturb the musical flow of a composition by his lighter treatment of the texts.

Gabrieli also contributed to the development of the villanella, a light type of secular vocal composition that was a reaction to the more serious sixteenth century madrigal. He composed two types of local Venetian villanelle, greghesche and giustiniane, both influenced by the villanelle of Lassus.

Greghesche have verses that characterize *commedia dell'arte* figures and are written in a mixture of Venetian and Greek. Giustiniane have texts that repeat certain syllables to portray the stuttering of a Venetian patrician. In most cases, both types of pieces have three voice parts that move in a simple, homophonic style.

Gabrieli's sacred music also shows the influence of Lassus and suggests that he may have been attentive to the requirements of the Council of Trent. The words are easily understood because of the tendency toward homophonic writing, the syllabic text setting, and the clear-cut phrases. These masses and motets are generally diatonic with a harmonically oriented bass. Like Lassus, Gabrieli was interested in setting the penitential psalms to music. His *Psalmi Davidici* (1583; psalms of David) reflect the Council of Trent's goals by taking a greater interest in sonority, simplifying the texture, and avoiding obvious word painting.

Gabrieli's ceremonial music includes compositions set to both sacred and secular texts. His eight-voiced madrigal "Felici d'Adria" was composed in 1567 for the visit of Archduke Charles of Carinthia to Venice. In the *Concerti*, published posthumously by his nephew Giovanni in 1587, motets for eight or more voices are found that have texts dealing with major festivals of the Venetian year. Some ceremonial works by Gabrieli have separate choirs that alternate unpredictably in phrases of different lengths. At other times, he creates variety by constantly changing the grouping of the voices and by mixing homophonic with contrapuntal writing. His last occasional music may have been written for the opening of the Teatro Olimpico in Vicenza, for which he composed sixty-four choruses to a translated version of Sophocles' *Oidipous Tyrannos* (c. 429 B.C.; *Oedipus Tyrannus*).

Gabrieli's contributions to the development of instrumental music have never been fully appreciated. For four-part instrumental ensembles, Gabrieli composed a number of ricercars that are suitable for many combinations of early string or wind instruments. His interest in thematic unity is clearly seen in these ricercars, which are usually based on one or two melodic ideas that are repeated extensively in all four instrumental parts. He achieves variety by writing duet passages, by alternating overlapping imitative entries with entrances of the thematic material that do not overlap, and by developing one thematic idea sometimes and juxtaposing two thematic ideas at other times.

Gabrieli composed several types of pieces for keyboard instruments: intonazioni, toccate, canzone, and ricercar. His intonazioni and toccate reflect the spirit of sixteenth century improvisation and could have served as preludes to other compositions. Gabrieli composed two types of keyboard canzone, those that are not based on vocal compositions and those that are based on secular chansons of well-known composers. The canzone that are not derived from vocal works are characterized by the imitation of a number of successive thematic ideas and have sections in contrasting meters and tempos. Those that are based on chansons follow their vocal models but add extensive ornamentation.

Some of Gabrieli's keyboard ricercars are freely composed, while others are based on vocal compositions. Those belonging to the latter category do not follow the vocal model as closely as Gabrieli does in his canzone. In these ricercars, each melodic motive is treated at greater length than in the vocal model itself. Thus, instead of imitating each motive once in each of the four polyphonic parts, they show their clearly instrumental character by normally having five to ten imitative entries for a melodic motive. The freely composed ricercars can be divided into three categories: those that have one thematic idea prevailing throughout, those that employ two complementary thematic ideas, and those that have a number of thematic ideas that are derived from the opening idea. Some of the imitative entries over these thematic ideas overlap in typical Renaissance fashion. At other times, the imitative entries anticipate Baroque fugal procedure by not overlapping. Some ricercars demonstrate Gabrieli's contrapuntal skill by lengthening the thematic idea to two or four times the length of the original note values (augmentation), or by inverting the melodic intervals of the thematic idea. Whatever the special devices, the opening thematic idea or one of the other main thematic ideas is present most of the time.

Summary

During his lifetime, Andrea Gabrieli made significant contributions to many of the genres current in his day—secular vocal music, sacred vocal music, ceremonial music, and keyboard music. His villanelle and madrigals are important to the development of secular vocal music, for they represent a lighter alternative to the more serious, highly expressive avant-garde madrigals that many other composers were writing. Because of their humorous texts, his villanelle are important predecessors of the early seventeenth century madrigal comedies by Adriano Banchieri and Orazio Vecchi. His sacred vocal music reflects the needs of the Council of Trent; the simpler textures and diatonic style of writing served as a model for other composers wishing to compose in a style acceptable to the Catholic Church. His ceremonial music influenced other composers, particularly because of the changing textures or the alternation of separate choirs. Although the origins of Baroque style lie primarily in the works by those composers who believed in more serious text expression, Gabrieli's vocal works do anticipate certain Baroque traits in their tendency toward homophonic writing, clear-cut phrases, a simpler harmonic style, and an increased vertical orientation.

Gabrieli's greatest impact, however, was in the realm of keyboard music. His intonazioni and toccate reveal much about sixteenth century improvisation. His sectional canzone anticipate the early Baroque canzona and sonata, while his chanson-based canzone are excellent examples of Renaissance ornamentation practices. Gabrieli's ricercars, because of their tendency toward thematic unity, the persistent use of imitation, and the use of special contrapuntal devices, foreshadow the fugal procedures of the seventeenth century. Although the works of Gabrieli are not as well known as those of his nephew Giovanni, Andrea is far more significant, for he contributed to a wider variety of vocal and instrumental genres than did his nephew and had a greater influence on more composers. He helped to make Venice one of the most important centers of musical activity in Europe.

Bibliography

Apel, Willi. *The History of Keyboard Music Before 1700*. Translated by Hans Tischler. Bloomington: Indiana University Press, 1972. The most thorough description of Gabrieli's keyboard music. Stresses the importance of Gabrieli's ricercars as predecessors of the Baroque fugue and describes his canzone, intonazione, toccate, and organ masses.

Arnold, Denis. "Ceremonial Music in Venice at the Time of the Gabrielis." *Proceedings of the Musical Association* 82 (1955/1956): 47-59. States that music for separated choirs fulfilled the need for ceremonial music on important festive occasions in Venice. Discusses Gabrieli's role in the history of Venetian ceremonial music and describes the major influences on his music for separated choirs.

———. *Giovanni Gabrieli and the Music of the Venetian High Renaissance*. Oxford and New York: Oxford University Press, 1979. Although primarily about Andrea Gabrieli's nephew, this book contains some useful biographical information and general discussions of Gabrieli's motets, masses, instrumental ensemble music, and keyboard music. Emphasizes the influence of Gabrieli upon his nephew but clearly distinguishes their musical styles.

Einstein, Alfred. *The Italian Madrigal*. Translated by Alexander H. Krappe, Roger H. Sessions, and Oliver Stunk. Princeton, N.J.: Princeton University Press, 1949. A dated but useful discussion of Gabrieli's villanelle and madrigals. Emphasizes Gabrieli's role in the development of the madrigal and suggests that his light madrigals reflect sixteenth century Venetian life. The musical style of several madrigals is described in detail.

Gabrieli, Andrea. *Andrea Gabrieli: Complete Madrigals*. Vols. 41-52. Edited by A. Tillman Merritt. Madison, Wis.: A-R Editions, 1981-1984. The introduction contains information about Gabrieli's life and musical style. It also lists the major sources of his vocal and instrumental works. All the volumes have detailed discussions of the texts and music edited in each volume.

John O. Robison

GIOVANNI GABRIELI

Born: c. 1556; Venice
Died: August 12, 1612; Venice
Area of Achievement: Music
Contribution: Gabrieli was one of the most gifted of the Venetian school of composers of the Renaissance and Baroque eras. Through his teaching of northern European students, particularly Heinrich Schütz, and the wide circulation of his published music north of the Alps, Gabrieli is considered an important influence on the development of German music during the Baroque period.

Early Life

Very little is known of Giovanni Gabrieli's early life, as is typical for composers of the Italian Renaissance. Unlike the greatest artists, musicians were usually regarded as servants, not celebrities. Even the year of his birth is unknown, since the notice of his death in the records of his parish church lists his age at death as fifty-six, while the Venetian public health records give it as fifty-eight. His parents were Pietro de Fais, a weaver, and Paola, the sister of Andrea Gabrieli (c. 1520-1586), a noted composer. Sadly, many documents relating to his life may have been destroyed by Napoleon I's armies in 1797, and others at the end of World War II in 1945.

Giovanni's first teacher was his uncle, with whom he went to Munich, probably in 1575, as a musician at the court of the Duke of Bavaria, Albrecht V. In Munich, Giovanni was associated with a number of other noted composers besides his uncle, notably Orlando de Lassus. Two other gifted composers he came to know in his formative years became lifelong friends, Giuseppe Guami, another musician at the Bavarian court, and Hans Leo Hassler, a student of Andrea. Giovanni's adoption of his uncle's surname and his painstaking editing of his uncle's works after Andrea's death indicate his closeness to his relative and teacher. Giovanni's own pupil Schütz was to be another close friend.

It is clear that Gabrieli made friends easily and that many of his friends throughout his life were other musicians, including several Germans. It is quite possible that at least some of Gabrieli's recognized influence on the development of German early Baroque music came about through his friendships as well as his gifts. That would not be unique in musical history. Some of the influence of the Netherlands school may have been as a result of the attractive personalities of its members, particularly Johannes Ockeghem and Lassus. During the classical period, Franz Joseph Haydn's good nature may have contributed to his success. Unfortunately, much more is known about the lives and personalities of Ockeghem, Lassus, and Haydn than is known about the life and personality of Gabrieli.

Life's Work

Gabrieli was already a respected composer when he returned to Venice, sometime between 1579 and 1584. In 1584, he was hired as a temporary organist at St. Mark's Basilica and won the permanent post of second organist the following year. He was to hold it for life. St. Mark's had two organs in lofts at the north and south ends of the building, so there were always two organists. During Gabrieli's tenure, a third (chamber) organ was added. Normally the organists used only one and played on alternate Sundays, but on great feast days all three organs would be used. There was no difference in salary and responsibilities between the first and second organists. When Giovanni was hired, his uncle was the first organist. From 1588 to 1591, the first organist was Giovanni's friend Guami, while for the remainder of Giovanni's life, the other organist was Paolo Giusto. In 1585, Giovanni became organist for a lay religious society, the Scuola Grande di San Rocco. Both posts required the organist to compose as well as to play, which was a general requirement for salaried organists and music directors (*Kappelmeisters*) until about the beginning of the nineteenth century.

At St. Mark's, Gabrieli had the use of one of the largest and best-trained musical establishments in Europe, partly built by his uncle during the twenty years (1566-1586) Andrea was an organist at the basilica. The paid permanent ensemble included thirty or more singers and four instrumentalists (two cornets and two trombones). Moreover, Gabrieli could draw on far larger resources on special occasions, such as great feasts of the Church and public festivals. Since many of his instrumental pieces called for strings, woodwinds, and additional brasses, it is clear that Gabrieli regularly hired additional musicians. These could have come from many sources and may have included women as well as men.

Venetian *ospedales* (foundling homes and orphanages) included such excellent music instruction that, a century later, Antonio Vivaldi's girls at the Pietà are thought to have been the best ensemble in Europe, providing the orchestra for all of his works and the soloists for all of his concertos, except those for violin. Other resources that could be drawn on included church choirs, the professional trumpeters who accompanied the Doge, and the musicians of the several religious confraternities, among them Gabrieli's own Scuola Grande di San Rocco. Very few other cities had such numerous, varied, and talented bodies of musicians available, and Venetian composers from Adrian Willaert to Vivaldi made full use of them. It was this unmatched abundance of players and singers that helped attract talented composers to Venice and that helped to make the Venetian school distinct from the musicians of other Italian regions. Venetian music, like Venetian painting, imparts a feeling of opulence. Some of Gabrieli's best works drew on all of these resources, stretched them further than had earlier Venetian composers, and achieved a kind of massive grandeur which was opulent even by Venetian standards and entirely appropriate to the richness of St. Mark's.

Associated as he was with St. Mark's and other religious bodies, a great part of Gabrieli's output was of sacred music. He wrote madrigals while in Bavaria, but, apparently, very few after he returned to Venice. There is no evidence of his ever having written dance music. Instead, he devoted himself to the composition of religious works, primarily for St. Mark's, and ceremonial music for both St. Mark's and the religious processions of the Scuola Grande di San Rocco.

Venetian composers, starting with Willaert, who introduced Venice to the advanced ideas of the Netherlands school to which he belonged, had made use of the large size, multiple organs and choir lofts, and long echoes of St. Mark's by separating their choirs and placing choirs or sections in different parts of the cathedral, often with instrumentalists, chiefly trombones, trumpets, and bassoons. They might play and sing together or antiphonally—choirs answering one another. Called *cori spezzati*, they made the listener seem to hear the music as coming from different directions, and, if all musicians were playing and singing, from all directions. Ideally suited to St. Mark's, this practice lasted longer in Venice than anywhere else in Italy. Gabrieli was the last major Italian composer to use *cori spezzati* in his church pieces, and he also introduced the practice into his many canzonas, short works for instruments, usually brass and organ. The effects were rich and majestic, even by Venetian standards.

Cori spezzati composition and performance endured much longer in Germany than in Italy, for a variety of reasons. The Germans, on the whole, were more religious than the Italians. Gabrieli's successors at St. Mark's, Claudio Monteverdi and Giacomo Carissimi, were the last significant Italian religious composers before Vivaldi. Even Monteverdi's operas and madrigals are at least as well known as his sacred music. Secular music, not sacred, was what the Italian public wanted. In Germany, on the other hand, the chapel, not the opera house, was where the audience went to hear music. German and Austrian composers continued to write large quantities of church music, Catholic and Protestant, throughout the seventeenth and eighteenth centuries. Many German cathedrals were as suited to separated choirs as St. Mark's. Indeed, many composers who worked in Germany, including Andrea Gabrieli and Lassus, composed for *cori spezzati*. Another reason for its survival in Germany was that Venetian works were common and appreciated north of the Alps. Many German musicians had studied in Venice because of the excellence of its resources and teaching. Moreover, Venice was then the most important center for music publication. The publication of Gabrieli's own works, begun during his lifetime with madrigals composed while he was in Bavaria, continued with *Sacrae symphoniae* (1597) and the posthumous *Canzoni e sonate* (1615). Many works still remained in manuscript at that time. In 1956, Denis Arnold began publishing Gabrieli's complete works, but some lost ones have been discovered during the 1980's.

As little is known of Gabrieli's later years as is known of his early life. It is probable that he married and had a large family, and it is certain that he spent a good part of his spare time in the German community, where he had many friends. Aside from this, it is known only that he died from kidney stones after a long illness in 1612.

Summary

Giovanni Gabrieli's place in history seems secure. Unlike the works of most early Baroque and Renaissance composers, his choral works, in particular, sometimes were performed during the nineteenth and early twentieth centuries. His popularity resulted from one of the earliest important musicological studies, Carl von Winterfeld's *Johannes Gabrieli und sein Zeitalter* (1834), which reintroduced his work at a time when practically no Renaissance and early Baroque music was played or sung, except for that of Giovanni Pierluigi da Palestrina. While Winterfeld's work contained a number of exaggerated claims for Gabrieli that later scholars have rejected, the work did influence continuing research on and performance of the Venetian master. Winterfeld was particularly interested in Gabrieli's choral works, while later studies have concentrated more upon his instrumental pieces.

Gabrieli and his younger Roman contemporary, Girolamo Frescobaldi, are usually considered the most important Italian organ composers. In Gabrieli's case, his fame rests on a number of pieces ranging from ricercars, toccatas, and fugues, all exercises in theme and variation, to intonations, short pieces of a few bars which introduce longer works, usually for choir, organ, and instruments. Gabrieli's compositions for instrumental ensembles have especially interested modern musicologists and performers, particularly brass players. Musicologists see them as leading directly to the sonata and concerto. While some are for strings and organ and others for strings, organ, and winds, many are for brass or brass and organ. Since the brass repertory is rather limited, Gabrieli is a favorite of most brass ensembles. In composing some of his instrumental music, Gabrieli was one of the first composers to specify whether music should be played loudly or softly.

The vocal music of Gabrieli and his German admirers, such as Schütz and Michael Praetorius, has frequently been recorded. Massive works requiring multiple choirs, vocal soloists, organs, and brasses placed in different positions in echoing cathedrals are a perfect subject for stereophonic and quadrophonic recording. A few contemporary musical groups and composers have composed and performed works for *cori spezzati.*

Bibliography

Arnold, Denis. *Giovanni Gabrieli and the Music of the Venetian High Renaissance*. Oxford and New York: Oxford University Press, 1979. This is the fullest and most readable biography of Gabrieli in English. Arnold sees Gabrieli as a brilliant conservative, a late sixteenth century Bach.

Charteris, Richard. *Giovanni Gabrieli (ca. 1555-1612): A Thematic Catalogue of His Music with a Guide to the Source Materials and Translations of His Vocal Texts*. Stuyvesant, N.Y.: Pendragon Press, 1996. Since the time when Charteris was invited by the American Institute of Musicology to edit Gabrieli's complete works in twelve volumes for the series *Corpus mensurabitis musicae*, he has uncovered a considerable number of previously unknown works by this composer. He has also discovered a vast quantity of hitherto unknown sources of Gabrieli's music. This thematic catalogue presents data about these and other discoveries, and collates an enormous amount of widely scattered information.

Grout, Donald Jay. *A History of Western Music*. Rev. ed. New York: Norton, 1973. This fine general work is useful in placing Gabrieli and other composers in perspective.

Kenton, Egon. *Life and Works of Giovanni Gabrieli*. Rome: American Institute of Musicology, 1967. A highly technical work for the professional musician, musicologist, or music historian. Kenton's work is of value to the amateur student chiefly as a second opinion to balance that of Arnold.

Robertson, Alec, and Denis Stevens, eds. *A History of Music*. Vol. 2, *Renaissance and Baroque*. London: Penguin, 1963; New York: Barnes and Noble, 1965. Like that of Grout, this is a general work. Its particular value for the student is in putting Gabrieli and other Renaissance and Baroque composers in perspective in the European musical scenes of their times.

Selfridge-Field, Eleanor. *Venetian Instrumental Music from Gabrieli to Vivaldi*. 3d ed. New York: Dover, 1994. In chapter 4, which is devoted to Gabrieli, Selfridge-Field portrays him as playing a crucial role in the creation of the Baroque era and in anticipating the concerto and the sonata.

John Gardner

VASCO DA GAMA

Born: c. 1460; Sines, Portugal
Died: December 24, 1524; Cochin, India
Areas of Achievement: Exploration and the military
Contribution: Da Gama was the first European during the Age of Discovery to reach India by sailing around Africa. His voyage culminated decades of Portuguese efforts at exploration and began Portugal's era as a spice empire.

Early Life

Vasco da Gama was born about 1460 (although possibly as late as 1469) at the small coastal town of Sines in southern Portugal. His parents, Estevano da Gama and Isabel de Sodre, were members of ancient but poor families of the lesser nobility. Their marriage produced four children, of whom Vasco was the third son. His two elder brothers were Paulo and Estevano (or Ayres), and there was a sister named Theresa. When he reached the proper age, Vasco was sent to school at the inland town of Evora. What he studied, however, is not known, and little other information survives concerning his early life.

All da Gama men had a reputation for bravery. That reputation was supplemented by a certain notoriety for being quarrelsome and unruly people. According to tradition, Vasco da Gama repelled by sheer force of personality the alcalde and night watch of Setubal during a nocturnal confrontation. His first documentable historical appearance occurred in 1492, during a diplomatic crisis between King John II of Portugal and Charles VIII, the King of France. As part of the effort to prepare Portugal for the possibility of a war, the king sent da Gama to Setubal to take care of affairs in the Algarve. The Portuguese king's choice for this important assignment reflected his great confidence in da Gama, which was based on the young man's successful but unspecified service in the fleet, probably against pirates. Some historians also speculate that various undocumented and secret Portuguese voyages of exploration in the southern Atlantic and along the East African coast took place during the last years of the 1480's and the first years of the 1490's. It is also thought that, if so, da Gama may have commanded one or more of these expeditions.

Life's Work

King John II had long planned a follow-up expedition to Bartolomeu Dias' discovery of the Cape of Good Hope in 1488, but various circumstances had delayed it. Originally the king wanted to appoint Estevano da Gama as commander of the expedition, and when he died the post devolved on his son Vasco by at least December, 1495. It may even have been first offered to da Gama's elder brother Paulo, who declined because of ill health.

Da Gama's expedition consisted of four ships, which departed from Portugal on July 8, 1497. His objectives were to find a sea route to India, to engage in the Eastern spice trade, and to make contact and treaties with local Christian rulers. The expedition was primarily one of exploration and not trade. Arriving at Santiago in the Cape Verde Islands on July 27, the expedition rested and then took to the high seas on August 3, steering a southwesterly course and ignoring the coastal route used by Diogo Cão and Dias.

The Portuguese were attempting to take advantage of favorable wind patterns which, on this occasion, turned out to be abnormally weak. Turning eastward after a long passage, they did not sight land until November 4, at about the region of Santa Helena Bay. It was an impressive navigational accomplishment for that age. Next, da Gama's fleet rounded the Cape of Good Hope on November 22, after which they broke up their supply ship and distributed its contents. As they sailed up the eastern coast of Africa, scurvy began to appear in the crew, but they soon contacted Arab traders and obtained supplies of fresh fruit. On March 29, 1498, they arrived at the hospitable city of Malindi, where they took on a skillful pilot, probably the famous Ahmed ibn Madgid. With his aid, they proceeded northward and caught the monsoon, which quickly transported the expedition to the Malabar coast of India on May 18. They arrived at the town of Capocate on May 20 and on May 21 went ashore, where they met two Spanish-speaking Tunisian merchants, who exclaimed, "May the Devil take you! What brought you here?" The Portuguese replied, "Christians and spices." That exchange foreshadowed the type of reception that they would continue to receive in India during their visit.

It was not until May 30, 1498, that da Gama managed to get an audience with the Samorin of Calicut, the most powerful local ruler and controller of the spice trade. By that time, the Portuguese had discovered that their trade goods were better suited for the primitive Hottentots of southern Africa, while the sophisticated Hindus held the scruffy Portuguese

and their goods in contempt. At the same time, da Gama remained hopeful because of his mistaken belief that the Hindus were Christians of some sort. Mutual suspicions grew, however, and the Portuguese only managed with the greatest of difficulty to trade their shoddy cargo for some spices and precious stones. About August 12, they approached the samorin for permission to depart; he refused and instead took some hostages. The Portuguese retaliated by taking some Indian hostages on August 19. An exchange was negotiated and then made on August 29. Da Gama sailed the next day, although he had to fight a short battle with some of the samorin's navy. Steering north, the expedition stopped at Angediva Island for a rest.

Da Gama and his fleet left Angediva Island on October 5. Unfortunately on this passage they encountered very unfavorable winds as the monsoons had not yet shifted, and so little progress was made. Scurvy broke out with great intensity, and eventually thirty men died. After the monsoons arrived, the Portuguese finally sighted Africa on January 2, 1499. Losses among the crew forced them to abandon one vessel at Malindi before they went on to Portugal. Da Gama split the expedition at the Cape Verde Islands and rushed his ailing brother Paulo to the Azores in the vain hope of saving his life. Meanwhile, another captain, Nicolau Coelho, sailed for Portugal and arrived on July 10. It was not until late August or early September, 1499, that da Gama reached Lisbon, where he received an enthusiastic reception.

King Manuel rewarded da Gama with the title of Admiral of the Sea of the Indies and made him proprietary owner of his birthplace, Sines. Sometime between 1499 and 1502, da Gama married Catarina d'Atayde. He also prepared detailed sailing instructions for the expedition of his successor, Pedro Cabral, in 1500. That expedition resulted in even greater hostilities between the Portuguese and the Muslim merchants of Calicut. Apparently dissatisfied with Cabral's performance, Manuel named da Gama commander of the next expedition to India. This expedition's purpose was conquest, not trade, and was the most powerful fleet yet sent to the Indian Ocean. It consisted of fifteen ships under the command of da Gama and another five ships under his brother Estevano. They sailed for India in February and March, respectively. Arriving off the Malabar coast, da Gama intercepted a Muslim ship full of pilgrims returning from Mecca; he massacred the passengers and burned the ship. He proceeded to Calicut on October 30, where he demanded the expulsion of the hostile Muslim merchant community. When the samorin refused, the Portuguese shelled the city. Next, they visited the friendly cities of Cochin and Cananore and picked up a cargo of spices. They then returned to Portugal and arrived home on September 1, 1503. Da Gama left five ships behind under the command of Vincente Sodre to protect Cochin and the Portuguese factory there. These expeditions of Cabral and da Gama forced the Portuguese into a policy of conquest, as the Muslim merchants persuaded the Mamluks of Egypt and the Gujaratis to form an alliance to drive the intruding Portuguese from the Indian Ocean.

After the expedition of 1502-1503, da Gama returned to private life. His resentment over what he considered inadequate rewards for his great achievements simmered. In 1518, Manuel managed to placate him somewhat by appointing him Count of Vidigueira. Meanwhile, the Portuguese empire in the East, which had been established by his great successors Francisco de Almeida and Afonso de Albuquerque, began to flounder under a series of incompetent and corrupt governors. In 1524, King John III appointed da Gama Viceroy of India. Da Gama left for India on April 9, 1524, and, immediately upon his arrival at Goa, began restoring discipline and harassing Portugal's enemies. Traveling to Cochin, he arrested the departing Governor Duarte de Menezes, but overexertion and the tropical climate worked their ill effects on the now elderly da Gama. He died on December 24, having barely begun the much-needed reformation of the Portuguese spice empire.

Summary

The years 1498-1945 have been dubbed the "Vasco da Gama Epoch" in Asian history. That era basically consisted of Europe's navies' dominating Asian coastlines, which further resulted in European control of the Asian economy and politics; da Gama had begun this domination. The goods he brought to Calicut may have been inferior; he and his men may have been almost intolerably dirty and rude by Hindu standards. Yet they possessed decisive superiority in one crucial area: Their ships were more seaworthy and far more heavily armed with cannons than any Asian ships. As a result, da Gama and his successors were able to create a vast spice empire in spite of vigorous Muslim and Hindu resistance. Only a similarly and even more heavily armed European rival, the Dutch, was able to dislodge the Portuguese from their monopoly of the spice trade.

Da Gama served the Portuguese crown as well as any man, exhibiting bravery, cunning, and authority. Yet he was not an indispensable man; Portugal possessed many men like da Gama. It was da Gama's good fortune to be at the right place to obtain the assignment that would make his name live forever. In fact, if he held the same opinions as his descendants, the immediate material rewards of his voyages mattered far more to him than a permanent and respected place in history based on his achievements in Asia.

Bibliography

Cortesão, Armando. *The Mystery of Vasco da Gama*. Coimbra, Portugal: Junta de Investigacoes do Ultramar, 1973. The "mystery" is whether any Portuguese voyages of exploration took place between Dias' discovery of the Cape of Good Hope in 1487 and da Gama's voyage to India in 1497. Cortesão contends that such voyages did take place and that da Gama actually commanded at least one of them.

Diffie, Bailey W., and George D. Winius. *Foundations of the Portuguese Empire, 1415-1580*. Minneapolis: University of Minnesota Press, 1977. This detailed and authoritative survey of the early phase of Portuguese trading and colonial enterprise is excellent for obtaining a reasonably detailed introduction to da Gama's career, along with placing it firmly in its historical context. Particularly useful for debunking various misconceptions and myths associated with the Age of Discovery.

Hart, Henry H. *Sea Road to the Indies: An Account of the Voyages and Exploits of the Portuguese Navigators, Together with the Life and Times of Dom Vasco da Gama, Capitão-Mor, Viceroy of India, and Count of Vidigueira*. New York: Macmillan, 1950; London: Hodge, 1952. Covers both the background to and the substance of da Gama's explorations and the conquests in the Indian Ocean. Detailed and contains many interesting anecdotes. Unfortunately, the author takes an uncritical approach to the sources and should be read with caution.

Jayne, Kingsley Garland. *Vasco da Gama and His Successors, 1460-1580*. London: Methuen, 1910; New York: Barnes and Noble, 1970. This well-written study is still worth consulting. The account of da Gama's first voyage is quite detailed. Furthermore, unlike most books dealing with the founding of the Portuguese spice empire, Jayne's narrative supplies information about da Gama's years of retirement between his second voyage to India in 1502-1503 and his viceroyalty in 1524.

Nowell, Charles E. "Vasco da Gama—First Count of Vidigueira." *Hispanic American Historical Review* 20 (August, 1940): 342-358. This useful article discusses the reasons for da Gama's being neglected by biographers and blames the situation on the lack of information about his youth and personality. Existing printed primary sources are then described and evaluated. Da Gama is assessed as a product of his time.

Pearson, M. N. *The Portuguese in India*. Cambridge and New York: Cambridge University Press, 1987. Largely dealing with the late fifteenth through the mid-seventeenth centuries, this authoritative volume is the most recent study of Portuguese activity in India. Supplies the Asian context for da Gama's voyages along with an up-to-date bibliography for further reading on the topic.

Sanceau, Elaine. *Good Hope: The Voyage of Vasco da Gama.* Lisbon: Academia Internacional da Cultura Portuguesa, 1967. This well-written book basically is a detailed narrative of da Gama's first heroic voyage to India. Its author has written extensively on the history of Portuguese exploration. Unfortunately, the scholarly level of her historical methods is sometimes not high enough to satisfy many academic historians.

Subrahmanyam, Sanjay. *The Career and Legend of Vasco da Gama.* Cambridge and New York: Cambridge University Press, 1997. Little is known about the context within which Vasco da Gama 'discovered' the all-sea route to India in 1497-99. This book places da Gama in the social and political context of Portugal and argues that politically he was an unlikely candidate for a nationalist hero.

Ronald H. Fritze

STEPHEN GARDINER

Born: c. 1497; Bury St. Edmunds, Suffolk, England

Died: November 12, 1555; Whitehall Palace, London, England

Areas of Achievement: Religion, politics, and diplomacy

Contribution: As one of the most talented of the defenders of religious conservatism and traditional doctrine in early Tudor England, Gardiner fought the advance of Protestantism in church and state. Although his personal efforts were largely successful, ultimately his cause suffered defeat.

Early Life

Stephen Gardiner was born about 1497 at Bury St. Edmunds, England. His parents were the well-to-do clothmaker John Gardiner and his wife, Agnes. Stephen appears to have been the youngest of three sons and as early as 1507 was destined for university study and a clerical career. He duly entered Trinity Hall at Cambridge University in 1511, a college founded to promote the study of civil and canon law. Although he possessed a working knowledge of humanistic subjects and Greek, his formal degree study was in the law. In 1518, he earned the degree of bachelor of civil law, followed by the degrees of doctor of civil law in 1521 and doctor of canon law in 1522. Meanwhile, about 1521, he was ordained as a priest. From 1521 to 1524, he lectured on civil and canon law at Cambridge University and attained sufficient respect to be elected master of Trinity Hall in 1525. His old college still possesses two portraits of him that show a solidly built, clean-shaven man with penetrating eyes and a large straight nose.

During these years, Gardiner also made his initial contacts with the world of the court and government of Henry VIII. His first important post was as a tutor for a son of Thomas Howard, the influential third Duke of Norfolk. Possibly through this position or through work representing Cambridge University, Cardinal Thomas Wolsey, the lord chancellor and the king's chief minister, noticed Gardiner's talents and made him his secretary in late 1524. This appointment marked the beginning of Gardiner's career as a clerical statesman.

Life's Work

Gardiner's first two years in Wolsey's service were quiet and unremarkable, but in 1527 that changed. From that point onward, Wolsey began using Gardiner as a diplomat on three lengthy missions during 1527, 1528, and 1529 to secure Henry VIII's wish for an annulment of his marriage. When the king's disputed marriage finally came to trial during June and July of 1529, Gardiner served as legal counsel to the king. He performed ably in that capacity and even though the trial ended in failure, a grateful Henry VIII appointed him as his principal secretary on July 28, 1529. This appointment allowed Gardiner to miss the final wreck of his former master Cardinal Wolsey's fortunes in October, 1529.

Initially, Henry VIII's divorce appeared to be a traditional problem in which manipulating the canon law and securing a papal dispensation would secure the desired end. It was a task seemingly well suited to Gardiner's legal training and political skills. As a result, Henry VIII again rewarded his good work in 1531 by making him Bishop of Winchester, the second-richest diocese in England. Unfortunately, the diplomatic obstacles that had prevented an annulment persisted. This continuing

stalemate left Gardiner powerless to aid the king, since he could envision no solution outside the existing legal and constitutional structures. By the spring of 1532, Gardiner was favoring the abandonment of the quest for an annulment of the royal marriage.

Leadership slipped from Gardiner's hands during 1532 as an activist faction lead by Thomas Cromwell came forward. They offered Henry VIII a way out of his marital difficulties by replacing papal control with royal control over the English church. This approach was completely uncongenial to Gardiner, since it involved the reduction of clerical privilege and possessed strong associations with the growing Protestant movement. He defended the clergy's position so vigorously against the Common's *Supplication Against the Ordinaries* in April, 1532, that Henry VIII was alienated. It was an ill-timed move. Gardiner, previously thought to be next in line for the archbishopric of Canterbury, was passed over. Instead, the vacant office went in 1533 to Thomas Cranmer, a Protestant. Later, in April, 1534, Gardiner lost his principal secretaryship to his archrival Cromwell, also a Protestant.

Gardiner quickly became one of the leaders of the conservative opposition to Protestantism in Henry VIII's court and government. In 1535, he rehabilitated himself with the king by publishing *Episcopi de vera obedientia oratio* (1535; Bishop's speech on true obedience), which provided the most convincing intellectual defense of the royal supremacy over the Church of England. Henry VIII rewarded the achievement by making him resident ambassador to France, where he stayed from October, 1535, until September, 1538. It was not a particularly satisfying reward, as Gardiner disliked ambassadorial work, and by 1538, Henry VIII and Cromwell were so dissatisfied with his performance that they recalled him.

Returning to England, Gardiner retired to his diocese, where he opposed Cromwell's policies at the local level and his publishing of the Great Bible in English in 1539. Fortunately for him, Henry VIII's basic doctrinal conservatism began to recoil from the increasing Protestant influences over the English church. As a result, Gardiner and the conservatives seized the initiative in Parliament from Cromwell and secured the passage of the doctrinally conservative Act of Six Articles in June. It is highly probable that Gardiner was actually even its author. The conservative offensive continued in the spring of 1540, although at first it appeared that Cromwell might still survive. Yet the incessant and effective sniping of Gardiner and the Duke of Norfolk combined with the fiasco of the king's marriage with Anne of Cleves to bring about Cromwell's fall in June, 1540.

Cromwell's fall brought Gardiner little profit except that he replaced his old rival as the chancellor of Cambridge University. Henry VIII quickly sent him off on an embassy to Emperor Charles V at Regensburg from November, 1540, through September, 1541. For the remainder of the reign, Gardiner served the king on various foreign embassies, helped procure supply for the wars against France and Scotland, and aided in the preparation of the conservative doctrinal statement known as the *King's Book* in 1543. During the spring of 1542, Henry VIII even named him as his chief minister, although he never allowed him to exercise the same authority as Wolsey or Cromwell. It was Gardiner's misfortune that Henry VIII found him to be talented but overly aggressive and therefore contrived to keep him out of the center of power for the remainder of his reign and afterward.

Henry VIII's will barred Gardiner from the regency council of Edward VI. Instead, power rested with Edward Seymour, the young king's uncle and the soon-to-be Duke of Somerset. Protestants now controlled the government although Gardiner doggedly resisted their reforms of the Church of England. The problems began when Archbishop Thomas Cranmer issued a set of reformed injunctions for the Church and his *Book of Homilies* in August, 1547. Gardiner protested and quickly found himself either imprisoned in Fleet Prison or under house arrest from September, 1547, through February, 1548. The reformers released him from house arrest for several months in the spring of 1548 when they thought they had converted him to their cause. Yet they did not know their man. Gardiner publicly proclaimed his adherence to traditional Catholic doctrines during a sermon he delivered at Paul's Cross in London on June 29, 1548. The next day, he was placed under close confinement in the Tower of London, a sentence which lasted until August, 1553, after Edward VI's death.

The Edwardian Protestants had decided to try the stubborn Gardiner in December, 1550, since his continued imprisonment without trial was highly illegal. Although he escaped condemnation for treason, the trial deprived him of the bishopric of Winchester and continued his imprisonment. Sometime earlier he had also lost the mastership of his beloved Trinity Hall. Throughout this ordeal, he retained a sense of optimism, which was repaid when the the sickly Edward VI died on July 6, 1553.

With Queen Mary Tudor on the throne, Gardiner soon returned to the center of power. Released from the Tower in August, 1553, he reclaimed his diocese of Winchester, the mastership of Trinity Hall, and the chancellorship of Cambridge University. Furthermore, Mary appointed him as lord chancellor on August 23, 1553. During the first Parliament of Mary's reign, Gardiner helped to secure the repeal of the Edwardian Protestant statutes but failed to obtain a revival of the medieval heresy laws. More successfully, he began recruiting the faithful bench of Catholic bishops for the Marian church that proved so effective and later fiercely resisted the Elizabethan regime in a way unheard of from their Henrician predecessors.

Gardiner quickly discovered the limits of his new authority. Queen Mary decided to marry Philip II of Spain although her lord chancellor and subjects favored a native English aristocrat. Still, Gardiner swallowed his pride and married the couple at Winchester Cathedral during November, 1554. The next month Parliament reenacted the old heresy laws, making a systematic persecution of Protestants possible. Gardiner had already vengefully begun arresting available Protestant leaders such as Cranmer, Hugh Latimer, and Nicholas Ridley for treason that autumn. Then, in January, 1555, he tried and condemned to burning five prisoners in the Tower. His hope was that the example of a few burnings would break the Protestants' will to resist. That expectation quickly ended when he discovered that the burnings were instead creating revered martyrs. With that realization, he tried unsuccessfully to persuade Queen Mary and the new Archbishop of Canterbury, Reginald Pole, to abandon persecution. Yet time was running out for Gardiner. Overexertion brought on attacks of edema and jaundice in September. Instead of seeking rest, the Chancellor continued to labor for his queen. As a result, his condition continued to worsen, and he died on November 12, 1555, at Whitehall Palace in London.

Summary

Stephen Gardiner was the last of a dying breed of English clerical statesmen. He stood as a defender of clerical privilege and attempted to preserve traditional Roman Catholic doctrine just when the course of events was moving the English church into the Protestant camp. Within a mere three years of his passing, the death of Queen Mary would completely undo the restoration of England's obedience to the Papacy that he had helped to bring about. In spite of his great gifts as a scholar, a churchman, an administrator, and a leader of men, he left little legacy except for a somewhat overblown reputation as a reactionary and persecuting Catholic prelate. Few English churchmen would ever again achieve the power and authority in the state that Gardiner exercised.

Bibliography

Dickens, A. G. *The English Reformation.* 2d ed. London: Batsford, 1989; University Park: Pennsylvania University Press, 1991. The best one-volume survey of the subject, Dickens' work covers the period from late medieval England through the beginning of Elizabeth I's reign and places Gardiner in the context of the religious struggle taking place around him.

Elton, G. R. *Reform and Reformation: England, 1509-1558.* London: Arnold, and Cambridge, Mass.: Harvard University Press, 1977. The up-to-date research of this excellent survey places Gardiner firmly in the context of his own times. Interprets events in the light of the author's "Tudor Revolution" thesis, which emphasizes the ideological and religious antagonisms between Gardiner and Cromwell. The author is somewhat hostile to Gardiner.

Gardiner, Stephen. *The Letters of Stephen Gardiner.* Edited by James A. Muller. New York: Macmillan, and Cambridge: Cambridge University Press, 1933. Reprints 175 letters with annotations and headnotes. An excellent source that includes a biographical sketch, a chronological outline, and a bibliographical essay on the state of Gardiner studies at that time.

———. *A Machiavellian Treatise.* Edited by Peter Samuel Donaldson. Cambridge and New York: Cambridge University Press, 1975. An edition of Gardiner's previously unprinted and unstudied last known political treatise. It was his advice to Philip of Spain on the proper way to rule England. Donaldson asserts that Gardiner's opposition to the Spanish match was a negotiating strategy, not a manifestation of a rigid and myopic nationalism. The authenticity and significance of this work remains somewhat controversial.

———. *Obedience in Church and State: Three Political Tracts by Stephen Gardiner.* Edited by Pierre Janelle. Cambridge: Cambridge University Press, 1930; New York: Greenwood Press, 1968. A scholarly edition and translation with a lengthy introduction of Gardiner's *Episcopi de vera obedientia oratio* and two unpublished tracts concerning the execution of bishop John Fisher and a view of obedience to the law in contrast to the views of Martin Bucer. Shows Gardiner's development as a supporter of Henry VIII's royal supremacy over the English church but tempered by an increasing firm support of traditional doctrine.

Loades, D. M. *The Reign of Mary Tudor: Politics, Governments, and Religion in England, 1553-1558.* 2d ed. London and New York: Longman, 1991. A contemporary study of this troubled period in English history by a leading expert. Loades places Gardiner in his period of greatest triumph and death.

MacCulloch, Dairmaid. "Two Dons in Politics: Thomas Cranmer and Stephen Gardiner, 1503-1533." *Historical Journal* 37 (March, 1994): 1. The article contrasts the early careers of Gardiner and Thomas Cranmer, two "dons" of Cambridge University who eventually entered politics in the late 1520s. The two men are compared with respect to conventionalism, humanism, and the religious changes of the period.

Muller, James A. *Stephen Gardiner and the Tudor Reaction.* London: SPCK, and New York: Macmillan, 1926. Dated but still useful biography. It is sympathetic to Gardiner and should always be compared to the relevant account of events presented in Dickens, Elton, or Loades.

Ronald H. Fritze

ALBERICO GENTILI

Born: January 14, 1552; Castello di San Ginesio, Ancona, Papal States
Died: June 19, 1608; London, England
Area of Achievement: Law
Contribution: Gentili, a precursor of Hugo Grotius, brought the study of international law into modern times by recognizing that all the states of Europe belonged to one community of law, by applying the principles of morality to international law and particularly to war, and by separating international law from its religious basis (though not from morality) and placing it instead upon a basis of practicality.

Early Life

Known also by the Latin name of Albericus Gentilis, Alberico Gentili was born in the ancient town of Castello di San Ginesio in the march of Ancona in the Apennines facing the Adriatic Sea. One of seven children born to Matteo, a physician, and Lucretia, Alberico was educated in law at the University of Perugia, where one of the most celebrated teachers was Rinaldo Rodolfini. Shortly after being graduated on September 22, 1572, with a doctor's degree in civil law, Alberico was elected a judge at Ascoli and then in 1575 elected to the office of advocate in San Ginesio.

In 1579, the family was broken up by Matteo's and Alberico's religious tendencies toward Protestantism and their flight in order to escape the Inquisition, with the youngest son, Scipio, to Laibach in Carniola, Austria, where Protestantism was still tolerated. Unwilling to leave, Lucretia stayed behind with the remainder of her children. Thereafter, an additional split in the family occurred when Matteo, remaining for a time in Laibach, sent Alberico to England and Scipio to universities in Germany and the Low Countries. Not long afterward, finding that Austrian policy toward Protestantism was changing, Matteo followed his son to England and died there in 1602. Scipio eventually found fame as a scholar, poet, jurist, and professor of law at Altdorf, where he died in 1616.

Life's Work

Reaching England in August of 1580, after brief stays in Tübingen and Heidelberg, Gentili met, through the small congregation of Italian Protestants in London, a number of distinguished people, including Robert Dudley, Earl of Leicester, who had been chancellor of the University of Oxford since 1564. From Dudley, Gentili obtained a letter of recommendation to the authorities of the university describing Gentili as one who, "being forced to leave his country for religion, is desirous to be incorporated into your University, and to bestow some time in reading and other exercise of his profession there." Granted small amounts of money for his support, he took up residence in Oxford, receiving his degree on March 6, 1581, and thereupon devoted himself to teaching and writing. His activities in writing were so extensive as to produce until the end of his life at least one book each year, beginning with *De iuris interpretibus dialogi sex* (1582; six dialogs), which was dedicated to the Earl of Leicester.

When the Spanish ambassador to England was found plotting against Queen Elizabeth I in 1584, Gentili and John Hotoman were consulted by the Crown as to the course of action to be followed by the English government. Largely on their advice, the ambassador was treated with civility and permitted to leave the country unharmed. Gentili's research into the field of foreign ministries led to the publication of his *De legationibus libri tres* (1585; *Three Books on Embassies*, 1924).

In the autumn of 1586, through the influence of the queen's close adviser Sir Francis Walsingham, Gentili accompanied Horatio Pallavicino as ambassador to the elector of Saxony in Wittenberg, but returned to England in 1587 to be appointed regius professor at Oxford, on June 8, 1587. The experience in Germany elevated further his interest in international law and led to the publication of his major work: *De iure belli libri tres* (1588-1589; *The Three Books on the Law of War*, 1931), a work in three volumes that appeared again in a thorough revision in 1599. In 1589, he married Hester de Peigni, and the couple eventually had five children.

In the meantime, Gentili's knowledge was being called more and more into service for actual trial work before the courts in London, where he came to reside. He was admitted in 1600 to Gray's Inn (one of England's Inns of Court), leaving his duties at the University of Oxford more frequently to a deputy. In 1605, Gentili was nominated by the Spanish ambassador to England, Don Petrus de Zunica, with permission of King James I, to be advocate to the Spanish embassy of Philip III of Spain and his successors. England was neutral in the struggle then occurring in the Spanish effort to quell the Dutch Protestant revolt, with the result that many cases involving the British merchant marine came before the English Court of Admiralty. Gentili's notes on these cases were collected and published by his brother Scipio in 1613, five years after Gentili's death, under the title *Hispanicae advocationis libri duo* (*The Two Books of the Pleas of a Spanish Advocate*, 1921).

Gentili suffered obscurity in the light of Hugo Grotius' work until Gentili's achievement was largely uncovered by Thomas E. Holland of the University of Oxford in 1874; much of what is known of Gentili is the result of Holland's original research. Holland encountered two forces in opposition to the resurrection of Gentili's reputation: the first originating in the Roman Catholic Church, which had centuries before placed Gentili's name in the Index of heretics whose writings were not to be read, and the second, among the Dutch, who carefully guarded any diminution in the reputation of their compatriot Hugo Grotius. Not until 1877 was a monument to Gentili placed in St. Helen's Church, Bishopsgate, where he was buried, and a new edition of *The Three Books on the Law of War* was published. In 1908, a statue of Gentili was unveiled in his native town.

Of the many books that Gentili wrote, he is best known for *Three Books on Embassies, The Three Books on the Law of War*, and *The Two Books of the Pleas of a Spanish Advocate*. Although he dealt with the practicalities of modern life, divorcing his ideas from the mere dogmas of any specific religion, as the basis for his thought, he infused morality into the foundation of international behavior. In this respect, he departed from the concepts of Niccolò Machiavelli's *Il principe* (wr. 1513, pb. 1532; *The Prince*, 1640) in that he viewed good faith, proper behavior among nations, honesty, and respect as the truly effective qualities, whether in war or peace, among the community of nations. Drawing upon his scholarship and experience, Gentili, in the first book of *Three Books on Embassies*, gives his definition of legations and their history. The second book discusses the rights and immunities of ambassadors in foreign lands, and the third book discusses the behavior and conduct of ambassadors and ministers to foreign countries.

In Gentili's opinion, war is *publicorum armorum justa contentio* (the community clothed in arms for a just cause). As to the definition of the term "just," Gentili said that justice expresses not only law but also what is from all perspectives righteous, as exemplified by self-defense, the defense of others, necessity, and the vindication of natural and legal rights. He believed in honest diplomacy, even among warring enemies, and eschewed verbal trickery. He approved strategy but not perfidy, for example. He also analyzed the treatment of prisoners of war, the taking of hostages, the burial of the dead after battle, behavior toward noncombatants, and the rights of noncombatants. In *The Two Books of the Pleas of a Spanish Advocate*, Gentili displays his concern for the neutral rights of nonbelligerents. Acting as counsel for Catholic Spain against the Protestant Netherlands, in determining the claimed right of the Netherlands to capture Spanish prizes in English waters, Gentili presented a strong statement of territorial sovereignty, jurisdiction of sovereignties over adjacent seas, and the rights of both belligerents and neutrals.

In his last will, made in London, Gentili expressed the desire that he be buried as closely as possible to his father and that all of his unpublished manuscripts, except those referring to the Spanish advocacy, be destroyed, as he considered the remainder of his manuscripts too unfinished to be preserved. The first request was carried out, and he was buried beside his father in the churchyard of St. Helen's, Bishopsgate. The destruction of the manuscripts apparently did not take place, because twenty-eight volumes came into the possession of a book collector in Amsterdam and were thereafter purchased from his successors in 1804 for the Bodleian Library in Oxford, where they remain.

Summary

Alberico Gentili has been heralded as the first knowledgeable author of modern international law and the first clearly to define its subject matter. Francis Bacon insisted on an empirical or inductive method of achieving a true science, as distinct from the deductive, a method that Gentili maintained is the true method of determining international law: that is, to examine the behavior and situation of states, and the changes of society, and, by a process of induction, to modify, cancel, and adjust international law to suit the specific circumstances as newly discovered facts and situations become available. He conceived of nations as a community of states; he believed in freedom of the seas and in the freedom of intercourse among nations; he insisted that the monarch or leader of a nation exists for the state, not the state for the monarch; and he opposed war generally but recognized that, if war must take place, it must be conducted with honor insofar as war and honor can coexist. In addition to international law, Gentili gave attention in his writings to other controversies of his time, including the limits of sovereign power, the problem of remarriage, the union of England and Scotland, the respective jurisdictions of canon and civil law, and the use of stage plays for the airing of legal and moral questions.

Bibliography

Gentili, Alberico. *De iure belli libri tres.* 2 vols. Oxford: Clarendon Press, 1933; New York: Oceana, 1964. In the Classics of International Law series. The first volume is a photocopy of the original edition in Latin; the second volume contains the English translation by John C. Rolfe and a superb introduction by Coleman Phillipson. This introduction deals with the precursors of Gentili, the place, life, and works of Gentili, his position in law, and his method and conception of law.

———. *De legationibus libri tres.* 2 vols. New York: Oxford University Press, 1924; London: Wiley, 1964. This is also in the Classics of International Law series. The first volume is a photocopy of the Latin edition of 1594; the second volume contains the translation by Gordon J. Laing, with an introduction by Ernest Nys dealing with a good concise presentation of the life of Gentili.

Holland, Thomas Erskine. *Studies in International Law.* Oxford: Clarendon Press, 1898; Buffalo, N.Y.: Hern, 1984. The article on Gentili was delivered at All Souls College, November 7, 1874, and, after some additions by Holland, was translated into Italian by Count Aurelio Saffi, thereby reviving both an interest in and a knowledge of Gentili. The first part of the article gives a substantial chronology of Gentili's life; the second part gives an assessment of his work in international law. Includes an appendix with information on the background of the Gentili family, the controversy over the dates of Gentili's birth and death, his will, his published and unpublished writings, and the revived interest in the subject as a result of the lecture.

Phillipson, Coleman. "Albericus Gentilis." In *Great Jurists of the World*, edited by Sir John MacDonell, vol. 2. London: Murray, 1913; Boston: Little Brown, 1914. Part of the Continental Legal History series. A brief summary of the facts of Gentili's life, with extensive analysis of his three main works.

Simmonds, K. R. "Some English Precursors of Hugo Grotius." *Transactions of the Grotius Society* 43 (1962): 143-157. This is a paper originally read before the Grotius Society on May 1, 1957, dealing with the English precursors of Hugo Grotius in international law, including Gentili. Contains only a brief presentation of Gentili's life and place in the field of international law.

Walker, Thomas Alfred. *A History of the Law of Nations: From the Earliest Times to the Peace of Westphalia, 1648.* Vol. 1. Cambridge: Cambridge University Press, 1899. Presents a few facts of Gentili's life but is largely concerned with the content of *The Three Books on the Law of War.*

Robert M. Spector

CONRAD GESNER

Born: March 26, 1516; Zurich, Swiss Confederation
Died: December 13, 1565; Zurich, Swiss Confederation
Areas of Achievement: Philology, medicine, and natural history
Contribution: Gesner was a Renaissance man, who collected, studied, and published the works of earlier literary, medical, and natural history authorities; he also compiled encyclopedic surveys of earlier scholarship in these fields. Equally as important, however, was Gesner's extension of knowledge, particularly in the fields of philology and natural history.

Early Life

Conrad Gesner was one of many children of Ursus Gesner, a Zurich furrier, and Agathe Frick. His family formed an undistinguished branch of a Swiss family that would become famous for having produced several acclaimed scholars, physicians, and scientists in the sixteenth through eighteenth centuries. Conrad was the godson and protegé of the Swiss Protestant reformer Huldrych Zwingli, and during his early school years he lived with an uncle, a minister, who engendered in him an interest in theology and botany. First Gesner attended the Carolinum, then he entered the Fraümunster seminary, in Zurich. There, in the Humanist tradition, he studied the Latin classics. After the death of both Zwingli and Gesner's father on the battlefield at Kappel in defense of Zwingli's reformed religion in 1531, Gesner left Zurich for Strasbourg. There he expanded his study of the ancient languages by studying Hebrew with Wolfgang Capito at the Strasbourg Academy.

After his interest in theological studies waned, Gesner began to study medicine alongside his studies of ancient languages. Gesner traveled to Bourges and then to Paris for medical studies. In 1535, he returned to Strasbourg, then to Zurich. In Zurich, Gesner married a young girl from a poor family, whose later ill health placed great strain on his meager financial resources. They lived for some time in Basel, before moving to Lausanne.

Life's Work

From 1537 until 1540, Gesner held the first chair of Greek at the Lausanne Academy, after which he resigned his position in Lausanne and moved to Montpellier to continue medical and botanical studies. He received a doctorate in medicine at Basel in 1541. Later that year, Gesner settled in Zurich, where he became the city's chief physician. In Zurich, Gesner also held the chair of philosophy. In 1552, a serious illness sapped his strength. Gesner lived on the edge of poverty, but about this time he was awarded the position of *canonicus* in an attempt to improve his financial situation. Although Gesner's health suffered during the last ten years of his life, in 1555 the Zurich city magistrates appointed Gesner professor of natural history. He held this professorship until his death during an epidemic of the plague in Zurich in 1565. Gesner's scholarship centered on philology, medicine, and natural history. His work in natural history, which interested him most, was in the fields of botany, zoology, paleontology, and crystallography.

Proficient in many languages, Gesner undertook numerous philological and linguistic studies. His most significant contribution in philology is his four-volume *Bibliotheca universalis* (1545-1555), a biobibliography of all Greek, Latin, and Hebrew writers, ancient to contemporary, known in Gesner's day. Considered the first great annotated bibliography of printed books, it established Gesner's reputation as a philologist and put him in contact with many contemporary scholars. Gesner also published translations and editions of many classical texts. In linguistics, he produced a Greek-Latin dictionary, one of the first studies ever attempted in comparative grammar, in which he cataloged around 130 ancient to contemporary languages and dialects. Gesner also prepared editions and compilations of classical medical texts, as well as publishing original treatises on medical and pharmaceutical topics.

Gesner's observation of plants, a result of his philological work, led to his interest in their medical uses. He collected and read widely in classical botanical works, from which he extracted information for encyclopedic publications such as his *Historia plantarum et vires ex Dioscoride, Paulo Aegineta, Theophrasto, Plinio, et recētioribus Graecis* (1541; the history of plants and their powers from Dioscorides, Paulo Aegineta, Theophrastus, Pliny, and the more recent Greek authors).

Gesner also developed an interest in plants and animals, and, like most sixteenth century botanists, he focused upon collecting, describing, and classifying both known and newly discovered plants. Along with other northern botanists, Gesner increased the number and accuracy of available empirical descriptions of plants in several ways. He recorded many original empirical observations, and he provided numerous descriptions of new and little-known plants. For example, his treatise *De tulipa Turcarum* (1561; on the Turkish tulip) was the first descriptive monograph on that plant. One of the leaders of the trend toward realistic illustrations, this botanist himself drew more than fifteen hundred plates for his *Opera botanica* (1751-1771; botanical works), which contained the bulk of his botanical writings. Gesner also encouraged observation of plants by founding a botanical garden and a natural history collection in Zurich.

Gesner is especially noteworthy in this period for the system of botanical classification he developed. Gesner grouped plants according to whether they were flowering or nonflowering and vascular or nonvascular, among other things. Upon the suggestion of Valerius Cordus, Gesner also chose a plant's organs of generation, the flower and fruit, as the key characteristics by which to classify it. In addition, Gesner first advanced the idea of natural families, and in so doing he moved biological classification toward natural systems. He distinguished different species of a genus and was the first botanist to utilize seeds to establish kinship between otherwise dissimilar plants.

Among Gesner's contributions to zoology can be listed editions of earlier zoological treatises, but his most important accomplishment in this field was the publication of his monumental, five-volume *Historiae animalium* (1551-1587; history of animals). In *Historiae animalium*, Gesner included all animals described by earlier authorities, generally without questioning the real existence of the animal or the validity of the description. He classified members of the animal kingdom according to the Aristotelian scheme, and within each group he arranged individual animals alphabetically by name. For each animal included, Gesner listed all known names, as well as the animal's range and habitat, habits, diet, morphology and anatomy, diseases, usefulness (including medical uses), and role in literature and history. The work is heavily illustrated, containing a woodcut for every animal. Many of the illustrations, drawn by the author himself, are quite novel and show evidence of careful empirical observation.

In Gesner's only publication in the field of paleontology, *De rerum fossilium, lapidum, et gemmarum maximè, figuris et similitudinibus liber* (1565; on the shapes and resemblances of fossils, stones, and gems), Gesner used the term "fossil" to refer to any object dug from the earth. He included extinct vegetable and animal forms, now rightly called fossils, in this group, but he also included minerals, ores, shells, stone axes, pencils, and other debris in the same category. Although Gesner did regard some exceptional fossils as petrified animals, for the most part he accepted the traditional theory that they were figures formed in stone by astral influences, by subterranean vapors, or by internal vegetative forces during the growth of the surrounding stone. In his classification of these objects, Gesner abandoned the medieval alphabetical system. Instead, Gesner divided his fossils into fifteen categories, using the criteria of their geometric shapes or resemblance to a variety of inanimate and living things. Gesner placed crystals in his first category (fossils whose forms are based upon geometric concepts) and described them according to the angles they exhibited. His *De rerum fossilium* was the first work on fossils to contain a significant number of illustrations, as well as one of the earliest works to include illustrations of crystals.

Summary

As a Renaissance Humanist, Conrad Gesner placed great value on studying previous scholarly works; in so doing, he accumulated an encyclopedic knowledge of the arts, the sciences, and medicine. Gesner also collected, edited, and published the works of selected literary, medical, and natural history writers, from the Greek and Latin classics to his own day. He is credited with collecting and surveying a vast amount of previous knowledge in encyclopedic publications in philology and natural history. He was one of the earliest and best postmedieval encyclopedists. In philology, his work initiated modern bibliographical studies and earned for him the title "father of bibliography." Writing just before European biologists were swamped by the deluge of new plant and animal forms from the New World and the microscopic realm, Gesner sought to collect previous knowledge about the living world, and his massive histories of plants and animals are testaments to his industry. Of the few zoological encyclopedias produced in the sixteenth century, Gesner's *Historiae animalium* ranks as the best, and it immediately earned for him an international reputation. Moreover, Gesner made original contributions to the fields of philology, medicine, botany, zoology, and geology. In philology, his research in comparative linguistics was unprecedented.

In extending knowledge, however, Gesner's most important contribution was to natural history. He was among the first early modern authors to question earlier biological accounts and to present firsthand descriptions and illustrations based on his own observation of nature. In botany, Gesner offered improved illustrations and innovative classification schemes. In presenting a scheme of classification according to structure, particularly according to the reproductive organs, Gesner advanced an idea that would later transform the study of botany. Although Gesner exerted little influence upon contemporary natural historians, in the eighteenth century the biologist Linnaeus acknowledged his debt to Gesner's focus on floral structures and the nature of seeds in botanical classification. Today the plant family *Gesneriaceae*, composed of about fifteen hundred species of plants, is named in Gesner's honor.

Gesner also contributed to the sweeping changes under way in the fields of zoology and geology in the sixteenth and seventeenth centuries. His *Historiae animalium*, a landmark in the history of zoology, occasionally displays a critical attitude when presenting collected knowledge. The studies of animal physiology and pathology presented there have led some historians to consider Gesner the founder of veterinary science. The *Historiae animalium* is also significant in the history of zoology because it introduced new and accurate descriptions and illustrations of the animal world. So innovative was that zoological work that Georges Cuvier considered it to be the founding work of modern zoology. Finally, even in his last treatise on fossils, Gesner broke ancient and medieval bonds. His classification and illustrations of fossils set the stage for the development of modern paleontology and crystallography.

Bibliography

Adams, Frank Dawson. *The Birth and Development of the Geological Sciences*. London: Bailliere, and Baltimore: William and Wilkins, 1938. Adams' excellent history of geology includes the best account in English of Gesner's system of fossil classification, two pages of reprinted illustrations of fossils from *De rerum fossilium*, as well as a brief biography.

Bay, J. Christian. "Conrad Gesner (1516-1565): The Father of Bibliography." *Papers of the Bibliographical Society of America* 10, no. 2 (1916): 53-86. The best existing biography of Gesner in English. Focuses on Gesner's contribution to bibliographic studies and places it within the context of the humanistic studies of the Reformation. Contains a helpful bibliography of the early editions of Gesner's *Bibliotheca universalis, Historiae animalium*, and supplements to them where applicable.

Crombie, A. C. *Medieval and Early Modern Science*. Vol. 2, *Science in the Later Middle Ages and Early Modern Times, XIII-XVII Centuries*. New York: Doubleday, 1959. Offers a general description of Gesner's work in botany, zoology, and paleontology. Gesner is placed within the broader history of these sciences.

Debus, Allen G. *Man and Nature in the Renaissance*. Cambridge and New York: Cambridge University Press, 1978. Debus presents a very good, brief, and somewhat detailed account of Gesner's *Historiae animalium*. Chapter 3, "The Study of Nature in a Changing World," is especially recommended for placing Gesner's scholarship in natural history within the context of Renaissance science.

Reed, Karen M. "Renaissance Humanism and Botany." *Annals of Science* 33 (1976): 519-542. This excellent article describes the translating, collecting, and other work of the Renaissance Humanists in botany in the late fifteenth and sixteenth centuries. Reed gives an account of the milieu in which Gesner's work took place.

Topsell, Edward. *The Historie of Foure-Footed Beastes*. New York: Da Capo Press, 1973.

———. *The Historie of Serpents*. New York: Da Capo Press, 1973. Both of these works are based heavily upon Gesner's work. They are recommended reading as primary documents illustrating Gesner's zoological work.

Martha Ellen Webb

LORENZO GHIBERTI

Born: c. 1378; Pelago, near Florence
Died: December 1, 1455; Florence
Area of Achievement: Art
Contribution: Ghiberti's sculpture for the baptistery in Florence is often considered the first example of Renaissance art in Italy.

Early Life

Lorenzo Ghiberti was born in Pelago, near Florence, into a family connected to the arts. His father was a goldsmith, and Ghiberti was educated in that craft, which went beyond the obvious training in mechanical skill to an understanding of the problems of design and a general theoretical knowledge of art. Ghiberti began his career as a fresco painter, and he painted a very good fresco in the palace of Sigismondo Malatesta, the ruler of Rimini. He had probably gone there first to avoid the plague which had infested Florence, but in 1401 he was urged to return to Florence in order to enter a competition for a commission to produce a set of doors for the baptistery there, a building of considerable age and reputation to which the Pisan sculptor Andrea Pisano had added a much-admired set of decorated bronze doors in the 1330's.

The competition for this major project was formidable and included Filippo Brunelleschi, who had a considerable reputation. Ghiberti was still relatively unknown, and his credentials rested on his skills not as a sculptor but as a goldsmith and fresco painter. According to one report of the contest, the list of candidates was eventually reduced to Brunelleschi and Ghiberti, and the suggestion was made that the two men collaborate. Brunelleschi may have withdrawn because of a reluctance to work in tandem or because of friendship with Ghiberti. Whatever the case, Ghiberti was awarded the commission, and the rest of his artistic life was spent, in the main, on his work on the doors, since the first set (begun in 1403) led his sponsors to order a second set in 1425.

Life's Work

The baptistery of the cathedral at Florence is separated from the main building, standing a street's width to the west of the entrance to the church. It is a very old building, built on the site of a Roman ruin, and may have been begun as early as the fifth century. Dressed in green-and-white marble, it is a work of art in its own right. In the early 1300's, however, the Guild of Cloth Importers, which had assumed the responsibility for decorating the building, had Pisano, a Pisan sculptor, add a double-leaf door to the south side of the building. It was the first major use of bronze in Florence and proved a great artistic success, clearly indicating in its fundamentally Gothic elements the influence of classical design. This development was a precursor to the change in artistic sensibility which led to the beginnings of Renaissance sculpture.

If Pisano's door suggested that the Gothic world was passing, it has been said that Ghiberti's execution of the second set of doors marks the beginning of the Renaissance in Florence—and the beginning of the grandest period in the use of bronze sculpture in the city. It would be unfair to patronize Pisano and his work on the baptistery; Ghiberti, while generally thought to be the finer artist, had the advantage of Pisano's example, both technically and artistically. Bronze sculpture was a lost art in the Middle Ages, and Pisano had been obliged to bring a bell maker in from Venice to cast his doors. Ghiberti spent years training his crew in the art of bronze casting, and in the process he added to the sophistication and subtlety of the very difficult technique of that art. More important, perhaps, was the way in which Ghiberti took the design of the doors forward into the wider, freer, more dramatic world of Renaissance art.

The simplest, crudest definition of the birth of the Renaissance is that sensibility (social, religious, aesthetic—indeed, psychological) of Italy turned from Heaven to the world, from God to man, to an appreciation of the fact that life need not simply be a preparation for the afterlife but was an exciting, potentially wide-ranging celebration of existence, however fragile that existence might be. In Greek and Roman sculptures, the artists found their models for such expressions of exultation and confidence in man at his best. The body became the outward, aesthetic sign not only of the beautiful soul (in Neoplatonic terms) but also of the beautiful life, the boundless possibilities for the individual and for the state. That beautiful body shows up stunningly in Ghiberti's work on the doors. Indeed, Ghiberti's competition piece, which was set for all the competitors, probably shows this shift most clearly—how the Gothic inclination toward flatness and rejection of realism and drama had (with Pisano's help) been overcome. Isaac, on his knees, his glowingly muscled torso turned in *contrapposto*, his head skewed to expose his neck to Abraham's knife, is a gorgeous young man, sculpted tenderly, with an appreciation for the human body.

The Ghiberti doors did not, however, stop at graceful celebrations of human comeliness. Ghiberti's subjects were quite properly religious, and in his accommodation of the human figure to the stories from the Bible, he also added a realistic sense of place and a sense of psychological moment. The north door was his first commission; it took twenty-one years (from 1403 to 1424) to complete it. (Donatello, who was to become a far greater sculptor than his master, was a member of Ghiberti's young crew.) The subjects of the twenty-eight panels included figures from the New Testament, Evangelists, and the Fathers of the Church.

Yet such seemingly austere subjects did not deter Ghiberti from putting into play a much more dramatically exciting conception of how the panels could be used. There is something flatly stagy about the Pisano work; it is splendidly worked technically, but it is somewhat stiff. Ghiberti, however, takes to the contours of the Gothic borders of the panels (a holdover from the Pisano design) with ease and makes use of the space much more gracefully. Pisano's work is clearly rectangular, set tightly inside the flow of the margins; Ghiberti worked his design into the concave spaces, achieving a sense of space, of depth into the panels. He also possessed a deeper understanding of how to make the figures tell a story that would appeal to the emotions.

Ghiberti's determination to make his art real, to give it depth, was his greatest gift. His second set of doors, which took up the last half of his career, were begun in the mid-1420's and not completed until 1452. They are considered his masterpiece, and they allowed him to extend himself in ways which were severely limited in the earlier work. He was able to break away from the small panels into ten larger, rectangular spaces, which gave him not only more room but also a shape he really understood. As John Pope-Hennessy, one of his best critics, said, it is important to remember that he was a painter and that he knew how to put more than one thing into a seemingly flat, extended area.

With the second set, Ghiberti continued his biblical tales, often working a series of incidents into the bronze in ways which led to the culminating moment with considerable dramatic skill. He knew how to tell a story, and he knew how to divide his space horizontally, vertically, or diagonally in order to

make the divisions support the narrative sequence of the various scenes. Also, he was much better at creating a sense of internal space within the panels.

Although Ghiberti's international reputation rested heavily on his work on the doors, he was not confined to working on them exclusively. He was equally adept at two-dimensional design, and his windows for the cathedral, if less well known, are also masterpieces. His window depicting the Assumption of the Virgin is strongly realistic not only in its portrayal of the Virgin's clothing but also in its depiction of her as a poignant young human being. Enthroned in a triumphant circle of swirling angels, she is proportionally sized to give a sense of depth.

There are also a handful of freestanding statues by Ghiberti in Florence. The first of these, a figure of Saint John the Baptist (1412-1416), is important for being bronze (Florentine sculptors normally worked in marble), but it is also significant because it strongly reveals an aspect of his work which can sometimes be missed in the enthusiasm for the revolutionary aspects of his bronze sculpture. This piece is clearly of an earlier time, an example of what is called the International Gothic style, and underlines the point that Ghiberti never entirely broke free from late Gothic tendencies, which can be seen closely entwined with the classical elements in all of his work, particularly in the graceful, sweeping postures which his figures often affect.

As is often the case at the beginning of a change in the artistic sensibility, Ghiberti was soon overshadowed by younger men, such as Donatello and Nanni di Banco, who were less encumbered by the last vestiges of the Gothic and whose work is less stylized, less elegantly mannered, and just slightly further down the line toward the new Humanism in their more realistic vivacity. Still, Ghiberti's work on the baptistery, particularly in the later door, called the "Porta del Paradiso," shows that he broke with tradition more as he grew older. At the National Gallery in Washington, D.C., there is a terra-cotta sculpture of the Madonna and Child—intimate, natural, and lyrically serious—which is attributed to Ghiberti; if it was indeed executed by him, it is clear that there were moments when Ghiberti was as much a Renaissance artist as Donatello.

In his later years, he kept a journal of his ideas as a practicing artist, *I commentarii* (c. 1447; commentaries), in which he discussed not only the technical aspects of his craft but also the relation of art to society, morals, and religion. That modest pride can be seen again on the Paradise door; in one of the ornamental roundels that decorate the frame, Ghiberti's bald, round head, his arched eyebrows, and his slightly pawky look suggest that he was a man well satisfied with what he had wrought.

Summary

If Pisano was the man responsible for bringing bronze to Florence, then Lorenzo Ghiberti was the artist who established its use as a medium for expressing the glorious aspirations of the Renaissance. Taking the example left by Pisano almost seventy years previous, he brought it into the mainstream of intellectual and aesthetic expression. Clearly a lesser artist than Donatello, Ghiberti was no less a major contributor to the aesthetic perfection of Florence, and his doors on the baptistery in Florence well deserve the attention they have always received. Indeed, a walk around the outside of the baptistery is a journey not only through time but also through the process whereby a civilization moves forward, in this case from modest intimations of things to come in the Pisano door through the surprising leap forward in Ghiberti's first door to the aesthetic triumph of the second door.

Bibliography

Avery, Charles. *Florentine Renaissance Sculpture.* New York: Harper, and London: Murray, 1970. This handsome, modest paperback is well illustrated. Its first three chapters lead the reader into the late Gothic and on to the Renaissance, putting Ghiberti firmly between his predecessor, Pisano, and his successor, Donatello.

Borsook, Eve. *The Companion Guide to Florence.* 6th ed. Woodbridge, Suffolk, and Rochester, N.Y.: Companion Guides, 1997. A guidebook to the city, this volume will help place Florence's artists in context.

Godfrey, F. M. *Italian Sculpture: 1250-1700.* New York: Taplinger, 1967; London: Tiranti, 1968. A well illustrated, step-by-step historical survey beginning with the Romanesque period and ending with the Baroque. With very clear, helpful comments on Ghiberti.

Krautheimer, Richard. *Lorenzo Ghiberti.* Princeton, N.J.: Princeton University Press, 1956. This work may be somewhat daunting to the lay reader, but it is worth the effort.

Paolucci, Antonio. *The Origins of Renaissance Art: The Baptistery Doors, Florence.* Translated by Françoise Pouncey Chiarini. New York: Braziller, 1996. Discussions of Renaissance sculpture. Criticism and interpretation of works by Ghiberti, Andrea Pisano, and Battistero di San Giovanni.

Pope-Hennessy, John. *The Study and Criticism of Italian Sculpture.* Princeton, N.J.: Princeton University Press, 1980. Includes a detailed essay on Ghiberti by an expert on the subject. Excellent illustrations.

Sanders, Mary Lois. "Contest for the Doors of the Baptistery." *Calliope* 4 (May/June, 1994): 10. Sanders looks back at the contest held by the city of Florence, Italy, in 1402 in which Ghiberti and Filippo Brunelleschi competed for the honor of producing the decorations on the bronze doors of the Baptistery. The influence of the competition on the development of Renaissance art and architecture are explored.

Seymour, Charles. *Sculpture in Italy: 1400 to 1500.* London and Baltimore: Penguin, 1966. Particularly good on the detail of the bronze doors. Contains a chapter on the competition which resulted in Ghiberti's winning the commission.

Charles Pullen

GIORGIONE

Born: c. 1477; Castelfranco, Republic of Venice
Died: c. 1510; Venice
Area of Achievement: Art
Contribution: The Renaissance celebration of the ordinary human being enjoying the pleasures of the natural life not in the great public paintings, but in the intimacy of the small canvas, suitable for displaying in the simple living room, found its painter in Giorgione, the master of the private moment.

Early Life

Giorgione is one of the great mysteries of art history. Little is known of his life, early or middle, and there is no late since he died so young. Of that death, there is some certainty, since comment is made upon it in a letter. He was probably born in the Veneto in the small town of Castelfranco, probably of humble parents. He was probably known originally in Venice as Giorgio da Castelfranco, although Giorgio seems to have given way to the Venetian version of the same name, Zorzo.

Given the extent of his career in Venice, it is likely that Giorgione came into the city sometime around 1500, and joined the workshop of Giovanni Bellini. He seems to have established a reputation for himself quickly, and in the decade left to him he established himself not only as a painter but also as a fresco artist, and several fresco faúades on buildings throughout the city are supposed to have been painted by him, none of which is extant. The source for any knowledge of him lies mainly with the painter-historian Giorgio Vasari, who presents a romantic picture of a handsome, diminutive, gregarious man, socially popular and eagerly sought after for his art. Yet Vasari wrote some thirty years or more after Giorgione's death, and there was a tendency in biography at that time to romanticize subjects. Still in existence, however, is a 1507 document in which Giorgione is commissioned to do a painting for the Doge's palace; evidence of a quarrel over a fee for a fresco, which was settled by a panel of adjudicators, including Giovanni Bellini, in Giorgione's favor; and a letter announcing his death.

It is likely that Bellini was Giorgione's teacher as well as employer, since much of what would be seen as Giorgione's style can be traced to certain aspects of Bellini's own work. Whatever the facts, Giorgione was busily at work in the middle of the first decade of the sixteenth century. His was a short career, but he was to be mentioned as one of the great painters by Baldassare Castiglione in *Il libro del Cortegiano* (1528), and Marcantonio Michiel, in *Notizia d'opere di disegno* (wr. 1525-1543, pb. 1800), lists sixteen paintings by Giorgione in Venetian collections and numerous fresco commissions. Hardly a handful of these paintings is extant.

Life's Work

Vasari speaks confidently of Giorgione as one of the best painters in the "modern style," linking him with Leonardo da Vinci, Raphael, Michelangelo, and Correggio. His modernity, however, is somewhat peculiar to himself, and he is best understood as being at once one of the innovators of the early Renaissance style in painting and an individual stylist of peculiar felicities, which made him so popular with Venetian collectors of paintings. His best work is not public; rather, it is private.

Painting during the Middle Ages was, in general, at the service of the church and state, recording high moments in the histories of those two mainstays of medieval society. In the fifteenth century, particularly in the later years, there was an inclination in the social and religious sensibility to put some emphasis upon the life of the individual, to see life as not simply a vale of tears leading to eternal salvation or damnation but as a place of some pleasure in and of itself. This vague tendency to think about life as worth living began tentatively to reveal itself in the arts thematically, tonally, and technically. Bellini, for example, continued to paint Madonnas, but in his later work the modeling of the figures became less dry and stiff, and tended to dwell on the physical beauty of the human subjects with considerable tenderness. Occasionally, Bellini would go even further in his exploration of the beauty of the human form. His *Toilet of Venus* (1515) is a quite magnificent painting per se; it is a painting clearly in the full flow of Renaissance enthusiasm for the human body and the richness of life at its best. Two other aspects of Bellini's work had influence on Giorgione. Tonally, Bellini brought to his Madonnas and to his altarpieces a kind of dreamy hush, a low-keyed softness that is perhaps best exemplified in what are called his *sacra conversazione* paintings, in which the Madonna and Child are adored quietly by a combination of contemplative saints and angels playing musical instruments. This "tonality" was taken out of the sacred realm with great success by Giorgione. Giorgione was also indebted to Bellini in part for his landscapes. Bellini used landscapes in the common tradition of the time as backgrounds for his enthroned Madonnas. These works tend to be somewhat stiffly idealized versions of the local landscapes, but they also tend to become softer and more natural as Bellini's career progressed. Giorgione noticed Bellini's idea of the softened natural scene and created his own version of it.

What is immediately apparent in Giorgione's work is how felicitously he adopted the then new ideas of allowing human feeling and pleasures onto the face of the work of art and how the use of oils and canvas, both relatively new elements in painting at the time, allowed Giorgione much greater ease in expressing himself. Bellini worked mainly in tempera on wood, and he stayed with the wood in his early oils. Yet younger artists such as Giorgione made the double jump to oils and to canvas, which allowed them to escape the dryness of tempera and the stiffness of modeling, and to achieve great subtlety in the use of color.

Giorgione proved to be the master of the new mode of wedding canvas and oil, and he developed the reputation for modeling through color rather than through line, a technique which was to become the touchstone of Venetian art. In a sense, modern art began with Giorgione. The idea that art could be used for the simple purpose of enriching life by its very presence without necessarily illustrating some historical or religious act of importance and that the artist might make a living providing canvases of modest size, illustrating modest moments of common life, is an obvious aspect of Giorgione's career. He seems only occasionally to have done public commissions, and his patrons, so far as is known, were not the most important members of Venetian society. His patrons tended to be people of property but not of particularly imposing reputation or power, as had usually been the case of patrons prior to this time and would continue to be the case in the career of painters such as Titian.

What might have happened had Giorgione lived is another matter. Titian might have begun as Giorgione's pupil, or both painters might have been with Bellini. What is known is that in the early years of his career, Titian, who was slightly younger than Giorgione, was closely associated with him. They often worked together, and, after Giorgione's death, Titian finished some of Giorgione's work. Indeed, they were so similar stylistically that

some paintings, including the famous *Concert Champêtre*, are sometimes credited to Giorgione and sometimes to Titian. Whatever the case, Titian went on to an international career, and it is presumable that, given his early reputation, Giorgione might have taken a similar road to wider reputation had he lived.

Giorgione left, however, a group of quite enchanting paintings, almost all of which have a worldwide reputation and at least two of which, the *Concert Champêtre* (if it is his, or partly his) and *The Tempest* (c. 1505), are among the best-known paintings in the world. These paintings seem to say something about life, which, like poetry, is virtually untranslatable into rational concepts. The tender, soft sweetness of the painting, the colors, the posture of the participants, the opulent dreaminess, the hints of symbolism not quite fully formed, and the elegiac pastoral melancholy come together in surprisingly uncluttered masterpieces of very modest size. These qualities are the signature of Giorgione and can be seen to a slightly lesser extent in his altarpiece at Castelfranco and in *The Three Philoso-*

phers (c. 1510) in Vienna. The paintings seem to say something beyond their content, while drawing the viewer to a kind of hypnotic conclusion that whatever the meaning may be matters little in the face of such glorious modeling, rich coloring, and consummate rendering, particularly of the human body. Giorgione did not live long enough to paint anything of a lesser order.

Summary

What Giorgione did was to free painting from the institutions that had fostered and dominated it through the Middle Ages. That dominance did not diminish immediately, but painters, and to a lesser extent sculptors, were to discover a new market for their work, a market which was to allow them the opportunity to experiment with new themes. Giorgione also helped to educate the public that art was not only a reminder of social, political, and religious responsibilities but also a medium of pure pleasure.

The fact of Giorgione's popularity is an indication of the developing Renaissance sensibility. It was one thing for Giorgione to make paintings of simple, intimate moments of innocent encounter; it is the mark of the great artist to meet instinctively that inchoate appetite of society, vaguely struggling to understand its desire to celebrate and enjoy life rather than simply bear it with religious stoicism. A Giorgione painting, small enough to be hung in a living room, had nothing to do with religion, or history, or politics, or worldly success; it had to do with the beauty of nature and of human beings, and with the sympathetic connections of humanity with landscape. His paintings provided the example of a metaphysical tenderness, which was later pursued by painters such as Antoine Watteau, Jean-Baptiste-Siméon Chardin, and Paul Cézanne. After Giorgione, paintings no longer had to stand for something but could be something, a center for contemplative pleasure by the individual. It was more than the discovery of the innocent subject that made Giorgione important. He was one of the first and also one of the finest practitioners of oil on canvas, immediately capable of understanding how that combination made painting more lushly bright and how paint, used tonally, could be used as a medium for supple draftsmanship, which would be one of the distinguishing marks of Venetian painting. Art became part of ordinary life, not simply a record of its more glorious moments. With the intimate Giorgione, art entered the home and made way for the modern idea of the artist as the glory of humanity. The artist was to become as important as the art.

Bibliography

Beck, James. *Italian Renaissance Painting*. New York: Harper, 1981. Giorgione's contribution can be best understood in the light of the whole movement of art as it works its way out of the medieval period into the early stages of the Renaissance. This sensible survey is easily understood.

Berenson, Bernhard. *The Italian Painters of the Renaissance*. London: Phaidon Press, and New York: Meridian, 1957. Berenson, one of the great critics of Italian art, puts Giorgione in the context of Venetian painting and Venetian social history.

Knoenagel, Alex. "The History of Art and the Art of History: Hugh Hood's Five New Facts About Giorgione." *Mozaic* vol. 27 (March, 1994). Hugh Hood's novella raises questions about art history that correspond to the current debate about the nature of historiography. Knoenagel's essay focuses especially on the ethics of revising history and the way in which Hood plays upon the reader's lack of specialized knowledge about Venetian Renaissance painting.

Phillips, Duncan. *The Leadership of Giorgione*. Washington, D.C.: American Federation of Arts, 1937. A charming book, somewhat heavy on speculation, but wide-ranging in the associations it brings to the contemplation of the mystery of Giorgione's career.

Pignatti, Terisio. *Giorgione*. Translated by Clovis Whitfield. London and New York: Phaidon Press, 1971. A scholars' text, dealing briskly, but with confident economy, with the problem of the life and the canon.

Settis, Salvatore. *Giorgione's Tempest: Interpreting the Hidden Subject*. Translated by Ellen Bianchini. Cambridge: Polity Press, and Chicago: University of Chicago Press, 1990. Criticism and interpretation of Giorgione's *Tempesta*.

Vasari, Giorgio. *Lives of the Artists*. Translated by George Bull. London and Baltimore: Penguin Books, 1965. An inexpensive paperback in which the facts (if they are that) of Giorgione's life and art are presented by a near contemporary. Other artists of the time are also represented and form a valuable frame for considering Giorgione.

Charles Pullen

BORIS FYODOROVICH GODUNOV

Born: c. 1551; place unknown
Died: April 23, 1605; Moscow, Russia
Areas of Achievement: Government and politics
Contribution: Godunov provided a brief period of stability between the harsh rule of Ivan the Terrible and the unsettled period of the Time of Troubles.

Early Life

Boris Fyodorovich Godunov was born about 1551. His father, Fedor Ivanovich, was a moderate landowner in Kostroma on the Volga River. Most sources claim that the Godunovs were Tartar in origin and could trace their Muscovite service to approximately 1330. At best, Godunov's education was limited. He was superstitious, which was not unusual for his time. Following his father's death, Godunov became connected with his uncle, Dmitri Ivanovich Godunov. Through the association, the younger Godunov became a member of the *Oprichnina*, which was orgasnized by Ivan the Terrible to restructure Muscovy (modern Moscow) and provide a secret police.

Godunov's career began to advance rapidly in 1570, when he married Maria, the daughter of Grigori Malyuta, a trusted and loyal supporter of Ivan. Thus entrenched at court, Godunov became a constant companion to the czar's sons and a member of Ivan's personal entourage. Ivan selected Godunov's sister, Irina, to be the wife of Fyodor, his second son. This relationship proved beneficial for Godunov when Ivan's death in 1584 brought the feebleminded Fyodor to the throne. Ivan had previously killed the eldest son in a fit of rage.

There was a drastic difference between the court of Ivan the Terrible and the one ruled by Fyodor and Godunov. Ivan's years had been full of violence and death. The court of Fyodor and Godunov was peaceful and quiet. Ever careful to govern jointly in their names, Godunov was the actual ruler. While many of the princely boyars resented the rise of Godunov to power, the English actually called him "Lord Protector" of Muscovy.

Life's Work

To many, Godunov was a handsome and striking figure. He was average in height. He was outwardly kind and possessed a captivating charm. To those who were of princely origin, he displayed an appropriate degree of subservience. Many contemporaries commented on his concern for the poor and observed that Godunov did not like to see human suffering.

One of Godunov's major achievements was the establishment of the Moscow Patriarchate. Muscovites considered themselves the "Third Rome." To enhance this claim, they demanded that their church be raised to the position of a patriarchate. This dream became possible when Jeremiah II, the Patriarch of Constantinople, came to Muscovy in 1589 to collect alms for the church. Godunov prevailed upon him to approve the establishment of a patriarchate for Muscovy. After much consideration, Jeremiah agreed, even allowing the Russian metropolitan Iov to fill the position. The Council of Eastern Churches officially recognized the decision in the spring of 1590.

Perhaps the most significant event in Godunov's career, however, was the death in May, 1591, of the young Dmitry, the son of Ivan by his seventh wife, Maria Nagoi. While the boy's possible claim to the throne was weak since his mother's marriage was uncanonical, he would have been a serious claimant to the throne when Fyodor died without heirs. Godunov immediately appointed a special commission of inquiry to determine what had happened to Dmitry. The official story that emerged was that, while playing a game with friends, the nine-year-old boy suffered an epileptic fit and killed himself with a knife. Some doubted that story.

Another major crisis began to emerge in the late 1590's because of a decline in population in certain areas of Muscovy. In an attempt to keep people on the lands, Godunov issued in 1597 a decree that ordered all peasants who had deserted the lands since 1592 to be returned to their landlords. This limiting of peasant movement greatly aided the establishment of serfdom.

On January 7, 1598, Fyodor died without heirs, which caused much fear in Muscovy. To Muscovites, the end of a dynasty was similar to the end of the world. The czar was considered a Godhead, closer to God than even the patriarch. With the end of the dynasty, many believed that God's favor had been withdrawn.

According to church sources, Fyodor appointed his wife, Irina, to be the ruler. She refused the position, desiring to enter the church instead. Some supporters urged her to reign but to allow Godunov to rule as he had done under Fyodor. She refused.

Meanwhile, Godunov had retired to a monk's cell to await the outcome. Undoubtedly, Godunov planned his election. He realized that he had to be careful as there were several other possible claimants to the throne. His most serious opponent was Fyodor Nikitich Romanov from the powerful Romanov family.

The Patriarch Iov and his party came to Godunov and pleaded with him to take the throne. Godunov knew the boyars would accept him only if they could limit the czar's authority. Since he refused any conditions, he told Iov that he would accept the throne if a *zemsky sobor* (assembly of the land) asked him to do so. Iov immediately called an assembly that, according to custom, contained clergy, boyars, gentry, and merchants to meet in February, 1598. The assembly offered the crown to Godunov, who accepted. The boyar-dominated duma, however, did not like the election.

Godunov had many plans for his reign. To solidify his dynasty, he tried to arrange a European marriage for his daughter, Kseniya. His first attempt was with the exiled Gustavus of Sweden, but this failed. He then attempted to arrange a marriage with Duke Johann, the brother of Christian IV of Denmark. Johann died, however, before a marriage could take place. Realizing that Muscovy needed Western technology, Godunov hired many European doctors, engineers, and military men. Though not formally educated himself, he wanted to establish a university in Moscow. When this idea failed, he sent eighteen students to study in Europe, but none ever returned.

Heavy rains began to fall during the spring of 1601 and continued for ten weeks; the grain could not ripen. In mid-August, severe frosts killed what few crops that grew in the fields. Grain stocks were soon exhausted, and by the winter the people were starving. Muscovy had entered the period known as the Time of Troubles. Nothing Godunov did seemed to help. He opened many granaries in Muscovy and distributed their contents to the people, and he launched a massive building program to increase employment. Yet people still died. To Muscovites, a famine signified a visitation of God's displeasure, and they worried.

Godunov became paranoid. He was convinced that plots were being hatched against him. He counteracted with an elaborate system of spies, who performed effectively. Indeed, they discovered a serious plot concerning the young Dmitry, who had supposedly died in 1591. The false Dmitry, as he is portrayed, appeared in Poland claiming to be the real Czar of Moscow. While King Sigismund III of Poland refused to grant the pretender any official support, the monarch allowed the false Dmitry to raise money and men. With this and strong support from the Catholic Church, the false Dmitry invaded Muscovy to claim the throne. Godunov asserted that the false Dmitry was really the monk Grigorii Otrepev, who had at one time been in the employ of the powerful Romanov family, Godunov's major continuing opposition.

Godunov continued to fight the invasion, but on April 23, 1605, he died unexpectedly. His sixteen-year-old son, Fyodor, succeeded him, but the false Dmitry seized control of the throne within six weeks. A popular theory concerning Godunov's death is that he had been poisoned at the dinner table. The more likely story is that he died of heart disease, as he had experienced severe troubles with his heart since suffering a stroke in 1604.

Summary

Boris Fyodorovich Godunov stands as a significant figure in the history of Muscovy. Following the rule of the powerful Ivan, who literally reshaped the state in a brutal fashion, Godunov provided a brief period of peace and governmental reorganization. Fyodor was not able to rule effectively; therefore, Godunov was forced to do so. He reestablished respectable relationships with the West, advocating trade and closer contacts. He wanted European technology and European educational standards for his people. One of his most notable accomplishments was the establishment of the patriarchate. Godunov loved power and proved effective at using it.

Despite his accomplishments, Godunov remains a puzzle to contemporary historians. When the Orthodox Church accepted the false Dmitry as the legitimate czar, Godunov became the recinarnation of evil, an attempted murderer. Seventeenth and eighteenth century Russian historians apparently accepted the premise that Godunov attempted to have the young boy killed and thus greatly condemned him. The official Russian version was established by a noted Russian historian, N. M. Karamzin, who painted Boris as nothing more than a power-hungry despot who deserved what happened to him. In the West, Godunov is primarily known through a drama written by Alexander Pushkin, who took his position from Karamzin. Another vehicle of knowledge about Godunov comes from the opera composed by Modest Mussorgsky, who was influenced by Pushkin. In all probability, a historical consensus on Godunov is unlikely.

Bibliography

Emerson, Caryl. *Boris Godunov: Transpositions of a Russian Theme*. Bloomington: Indiana University Press, 1986. The author attempts to examine Godunov as he has appeared in the different periods of literature. He explains how Godunov has evolved in literature and how various writers treat him. The notes are valuable in gathering bibliographical information.

Graham, Stephen. *Boris Godunof.* London: Benn, and New Haven, Conn.: Yale University Press, 1933. Graham does not like Godunov. He attempts to present the good points of Godunov, but it is very obvious that this is a major effort. Contains a short bibliography.

Grey, Ian. *Boris Godunov: The Tragic Tsar.* London: Hodder and Stoughton, and New York: Scribner, 1973. This book tends to be one of the most apologetic books in English on the subject. Grey depicts Godunov as an able, honest, and even humane ruler. Furthermore, Grey sees him as a person whom historians have slandered. In his attempt to explain Godunov in a good light, Grey often loses sight of his subject. Makes good use of most published biographies. Easy to read and has an adequate bibliography.

Platonov, S. F. *Boris Godunov: Tsar of Russia.* Translated by L. Rex Pyles. Gulf Breeze, Fla.: Academic International Press, 1973. Platonov presents a rather colorful account of his subject's life with the aim of restoring Godunov to his proper place in historical scholarship. Provides a satisfactory overview of the subject. Contains a short bibliography from the translation and one from the author which is in Russian.

———. *The Time of Troubles: A Historical Study of the Internal Crisis and Social Struggle in Sixteenth and Seventeenth Century Moscow.* Translated by John Alexander. Lawrence: University Press of Kansas, 1970. Platonov offers a picture of the entire period of Russian history known as the Time of Troubles. The work has approximately thirty-seven pages on Godunov and is a good, brief account.

Skrynnikov, Ruslan G. *Boris Godunov.* Edited and translated by Hugh F. Graham. Gulf Breeze, Fla.: Academic International Press, 1982. Skrynnikov published several articles on Godunov during the 1970's. He is generally favorable toward Godunov. He disputes the prevailing view that Godunov's family was descended from Tartar nobility and claims that the story was created to make Godunov appear more in the line of royalty. A straightforward account. The bibliography is short and entirely in Russian, as are most of the notes.

Vernadsky, George. *A History of Russia.* Vol. 5, *The Tsardom of Moscow, 1547-1682.* New Haven, Conn.: Yale University Press, 1969. Vernadsky is a Russian émigré who has written many books on Russian history, including the multivolume *A History of Russia.* Generally, he presents a balanced but brief view of Godunov. He has a large bibliography for the entire period.

Eric L. Wake

EL GRECO
Doménikos Theotokópoulos

Born: 1541; Candia, Crete
Died: April 7, 1614; Toledo, Spain
Area of Achievement: Art
Contribution: Adapting principles he learned in Venice and Rome, El Greco achieved a unique artistic style and became Spain's greatest religious artist and one of the world's foremost portrait painters.

Early Life

El Greco (Doménikos Theotokópoulos) was born in Candia, Crete, in 1541. Of his family, little is known, except that his father's name was Jorghi and one brother was named Manoussos. Since his knowledge of languages and his wide intellectual interests suggest a good education, El Greco's biographers have assumed that his Greek family belonged to the middle class. During his boyhood, Crete was a center of Byzantine culture and Greek Orthodox religion. Art on the island was primarily church related, depicting saints in the somber manner of orthodox iconography. Intended to inspire devotion, it often features stereotypical human forms against a dark and undeveloped background. From a surviving document, it is known that by age twenty-five El Greco was a practicing artist.

For unknown reasons, El Greco left Crete, probably in 1567, for Venice, where he continued his study of painting. There he encountered the warm, rich coloration and carefully balanced perspective of the Venetian school. Biographers have surmised that he became a member of Titian's workshop. In Venice, he adopted the nickname "Il Greco" (the Greek), later changing the article to the Spanish *El.*

In 1570, El Greco left Venice for Rome, where he came under the influence of the Florentine-Roman school, dominated by the rich artistic legacy of Raphael and Michelangelo. The mannerist influence of Roman painting, which featured elongated human forms, unusual gestures, convoluted and contorted body positions, foreshortening, and half figures, left a lasting impression on El Greco's work. In 1572, he was admitted to the Roman Academy of St. Luke, the painters' guild, a membership that entitled him to artistic patronage and contracts. Among the paintings that remain from his Roman experience are one extraordinary portrait, that of his patron Giulio Clovio, *Christ Healing the Blind* (1577-1578), and *Purification of the Temple* (c. 1570-1575), an early work that includes a large group of figures. According to anecdote, El Greco did not thrive in Rome because he made disparaging remarks about Michelangelo, and, while that cannot be confirmed, his later written comments reveal that he thought Michelangelo's work defective in coloration. Among his circle of acquaintances in Rome were two Spanish theologians who later became his patrons, Luis de Castilla and Pedro Chacón, both from Toledo. Sometime during the middle 1570's, he left Rome for Spain, where he hoped to secure patronage and to establish his reputation.

Life's Work

In 1577, the year of El Greco's arrival, Toledo reflected the culture of Spain following the Council of Trent, an event which inaugurated the Catholic Counter-Reformation. In art, its canons called for religious themes and events to be related closely to human experience and to embody strong and immediate sensory appeal. The Spanish monarch Philip II was intent on preserving Spanish power, prestige, and grandeur, and commissions for artists were readily available. Among El Greco's early Spanish paintings, *The Martyrdom of Saint Maurice* (c. 1580) was commissioned by the king for his palace, El Escorial. The painting did not please the royal patron, for he did not regard it as adequately devotional; thereafter, El Greco acquired most of his patronage from Toledo. Shortly after his arrival in the city, El Greco settled into domestic life. His Spanish mistress, Doña Jerónima de las Cuevas, bore in 1578 his son Jorge Manuel Theotokópoulos, whom he trained as an artist and collaborator. In the Villena Palace, he acquired spacious apartments (twenty-four rooms) and established a workshop employing several assistants. There is some indication that he lived an affluent if not lavish life-style. He accumulated a substantial library, largely of classics and Italian literature, and hired musicians to perform during his dinner. His personality was somewhat haughty and contentious, and he often found himself involved in conflicts over the remuneration for his work, which at times resulted in lawsuits.

The workshop approach and collaborators were necessitated by the exigencies of contracts available at the time. The most profitable were for altarpieces, groups of five or six large paintings arranged above and beside the altars of churches and chapels. These paintings required elaborately sculpted bases and frames, and the artist who was prepared to undertake an entire project held an advantage. Contracts were usually specific as to subject, size, and arrangement. Many of El Greco's best-known paintings resulted from such contracts; for example, his masterpiece *The Burial of the Count of Orgaz* (1586), a painting that measures ten by sixteen feet, has never been removed from the Church of Santo Tomé, Toledo.

El Greco's total output is estimated at 285 paintings, although the number attributed to him has ranged upward to 850. A firm figure is not easily ascertained for several reasons. First, he often produced several versions of the same subject, and these can easily be classified as copies or imitations. Second, his workshop produced smaller-scale copies of his better-known works for sale to clients, and these can easily be mistaken for originals. Third, paintings by an obscure contemporary, named Doménikos, have been confused with those of El Greco. Finally, after his death, his associates continued to paint in his style, and some of their paintings have been attributed to him.

A number of paintings represent portraits of his contemporaries, usually Spanish clergy, gentry, and nobility. El Greco, however, was primarily a religious painter. His normal subjects are Christ and the Holy Family, New Testament scenes, miracles from the New Testament and from the early Christian era, saints, and significant rites. While some are epic in scale, presenting views of heaven, earth, and hell, and including divine, angelic, and human figures, others include single saints or clergymen.

El Greco considered himself a learned painter as opposed to an artisan; thus, he sought to formulate a theory of painting and to apply it. Francisco Pacheco, a lesser Spanish artist, mentions his writings on painting, sculpture, and architecture, though none exists today. Yet some evidence of El Greco's aesthetic judgment may be gleaned from extant marginalia in books he owned. In practice, he consciously attempted to combine the rich coloration of the Venetian school and the mannerist style of the Florentine-Roman school. These two cultural influences, combined with the canons of religious art of the Counter-Reformation and his iconographic background, represent the dominant influences on his artistic production. Although nothing in El Greco's art is entirely original, the combination of disparate influences creates a strong impression of originality and even of eccentricity.

In exploring the prominent features of his work, one may consider composition, color, and illumination. Except for the early paintings, incorporating architectural forms and the views of Toledo, the paintings usually have a shallow background. Distant perspective is interrupted by a wall or draperies, or by the darkened, cloudy sky so prevalent in his work. In general, dimensions are handled aesthetically, not naturalistically, creating within a single painting a combination of flatness and depth. The focus of most paintings is the human form, whether in portraits or in the epic paintings featuring numerous individuals. The body is often elongated, perhaps the most characteristic feature of El Greco's composition, as if to intimate that the character has striven to surpass human limitations. Often, the heads, with gaunt and angular faces, appear too small for the long bodies. Following the mannerist tradition, El Greco often foreshortens some figures, includes half figures that are cut by the edges, and places human forms in curved positions, contributing to a geometric pattern in the painting as a whole. In addition, arms and legs are sometimes positioned at unusual angles, creating the effects of imbalance and distortion.

Viewing El Greco's human forms, one is drawn to their faces and hands, their most expressive elements. The hands are sometimes pointing, sometimes clasped, sometimes at rest, but always refined, graceful, and expressive. The faces—usually angular, unlined, and elongated—reveal a limited range of human expression. El Greco's gaunt faces carry a serious cast, accompanied by the appropriate religious emotions. His subjects are grave, restrained, reserved, devout, and penitent. In some paintings, the eyes peer upward toward heaven with a facial expression mingling devotion, fear, and hope. In others, they look directly at the viewer, but somehow past him, as if to perceive a spiritual world that remains invisible to others. It may be that the contrast between the extravagant gestures in the paintings and the taut control of the faces represents El Greco's most compelling technique of composition. The restraint and self-control evident in the faces suggest that the individual will has been conquered, and the gestures denote a spiritual significance that transcends time.

A painter whose early experience was with the dark tones of Orthodox iconography must have found the bright colors of the Venetian school highly pleasing. El Greco sought to use a range of colors to enliven religious art, though the bright reds and blues of his early paintings darken during the course of his career. His preferred colors are blue, red, yellow, yellowgreen, and slate gray, though his use of neutral tones appears to increase with time. Illumination, as critics have observed, is aesthetic rather than naturalistic. Typically, light from an undetermined source is directed toward the most significant portions of a painting. In *The Trinity*, (1577-1579), for example, God the Father embraces the crucified Christ. Christ's body is illuminated from a source to the left and behind the viewer, while, at the same time, light radiates outward from heaven behind the Father's head. At times El Greco's illumination has the yellowish-green cast of early morning or of light breaking through a darkened, cloudy, windswept sky, creating heightened tones not of the familiar world.

Despite his success as a painter and his many large commissions, El Greco did not attain wealth, though numerous contemporaries praised his genius. He died in Toledo on April 7, 1614, and was interred in the Church of Santo Domingo el Antiguo, which he had decorated.

Summary

El Greco's mannered style, his unusual handling of illumination, and his intensely religious subjects proved difficult for succeeding ages to appreciate. Because his paintings were not seen outside Spain and because Spain possessed no critical tradition in art, he became a forgotten artist in the rest of Europe. Although El Greco was capable of finely detailed drawing, he was inclined to leave large portions of his paintings indistinct, producing a blurred effect. This tendency is pervasive in the later paintings, especially those dealing with miracles and mystical events. During the late nineteenth century, he was discovered by the French Impressionist Édouard Manet, who saw in El Greco an earlier practitioner of Impressionist aesthetics. Like them and like the expressionists, he freely altered reality in order to enhance aesthetic effect.

Once his artistic power became recognized and widely acclaimed, art critics sought to account for him through a number of highly speculative theories: that he was a mystic, that he elongated figures because of astigmatism, or that he was quintessentially Spanish. More systematic and careful scholarship has demonstrated that El Greco derived from his study and experience, largely of Italian painting, the characteristic elements of his art. To be sure, he combined the influences of Italy in an unusual and highly original way and adapted his painting to the Spanish Counter-Reformation. He is recognized as among some half dozen of the world's greatest portrait painters and as Spain's greatest religious artist.

Bibliography

Brown, Jonathan, ed. *Figures of Thought: El Greco as Interpreter of History, Tradition, and Ideas.* Washington, D.C.: National Gallery of Art, 1982. An illustrated collection of six essays by El Greco scholars. Centers on individual paintings and portraits. The final essay explores the artist's legal entanglements over the remuneration for his works.

Greco. *El Greco of Toledo.* Boston: Little Brown, 1982. A catalog of the 1982-1983 international El Greco exhibit. Includes numerous color and black-and-white reproductions and three valuable scholarly essays concerning the history of Toledo, El Greco's career and life, and the altarpieces that he completed.

Guinard, Paul. *El Greco.* Translated by James Emmons. Lausanne, Switzerland: Skira, 1956. In this small book with fifty-three high-quality color reproductions, Guinard presents a biographical and critical study attempting to correlate the painter with his milieu. Back matter includes commentary on the artist by six contemporaries, biographical sketches of twenty-five contemporaries, and an annotated bibliography.

Itzhaki, Jane. "El Greco Had Style Not Astigmatism." *New Scientist* 147 (September, 1995): 12. Itzhaki denounces the widely accepted belief that the stretched images in El Greco's paintings were due to astigmatism. Includes a description of an experiment carried out by Stuart Anstis, a psychologist at the University of California, San Diego.

Theotocopuli, Domenico, called El Greco. *El Greco.* Edited by Léo Bronstein. New York: Oxford University Press, 1938. This work offers reproductions in color of approximately forty of El Greco's better-known paintings, with evaluation and analysis. The comments, written for the nonspecialist, emphasize technique and appreciation.

———. *El Greco*. Edited by Maurice Legendre. New York: Hyperion Press, 1947. Primarily a volume of reproductions, most in black and white. Offers a brief, interesting, and highly conjectural assessment of the artist's life, work, and philosophy, plus an extended unannotated bibliography.

Wethey, Harold E. *El Greco and His School*. 2 vols. Princeton, N.J.: Princeton University Press, 1962. Applying sound scholarly research, Wethey explores questions of authenticity in an effort to establish El Greco's canon. He describes each painting and provides a complex classification according to subject matter. His biographical account of El Greco places heavy emphasis on the Venetian period. The work is comprehensive, reliable, and highly detailed—indispensable for serious students.

Stanley Archer

SIR RICHARD GRENVILLE

Born: c. June 15, 1542; Buckland Abbey?, Devonshire, England

Died: c. September 3, 1591; at sea, off Flores, the Azores

Area of Achievement: The military

Contribution: Grenville's heroic death in battle against an overwhelming fleet was an inspiration to Elizabethan Englishmen in their war against a powerful Spanish Empire.

Early Life

Sir Richard Grenville was born about June 15, 1542, into an old Cornish family of some distinction. The first record of Grenvilles in the west country can be dated to 1145. Grenville's grandfather was a soldier and trusted official under Henry VIII and became one of the richest men in Cornwall. His father, Sir Roger Grenville, commanded the royal ship *Mary Rose* and was tragically drowned when it sank at Portsmouth in July, 1545. His mother, Thomasina Cole, remarried Thomas Arundell of Leigh. On the death of his grandfather in 1550, Grenville inherited his substantial property.

Of Grenville's early life and education little is known, but in 1559 he attended the Inner Temple, one of the Inns of Court, rather than going to one of the universities. Late in 1562, he was involved in a brawl in which he killed a man and had to be pardoned by the queen. Despite the misadventure, it is possible that he was the same Grenville who was elected to Parliament in 1563 for a Cornish borough. By early 1565, after coming into control of his inheritance, he married Mary St. Leger. Their first son, Roger, died at the end of that year, but in 1567 they had a second son, Bernard, who survived to succeed his father.

Both as a result of his temperament and because of the military tradition in which he had been reared, it was inevitable that, after reaching manhood, Grenville would join the military. In the summer of 1566, leaving his pregnant wife behind, he went off with some of his cousins to Hungary, where he served for a time in the army of Emperor Maximilian II fighting the Turks. By 1568, after a temporary peace had been negotiated, Grenville returned unscathed to England.

In 1569, still restless, Grenville took his family to Ireland where, working with Warham St. Leger, the cousin of his father-in-law, he hoped to advance his fortunes. At the time, Ireland was regarded as frontier country, wild and savage as the distant New World and ripe for exploitation and colonization. Grenville found himself involved at once in suppressing a serious revolt by the native Irish. By 1570, disappointed in his hopes, Grenville returned to England.

In 1571, and again in 1572, Grenville was elected to Parliament for Cornwall. Up until that point, there was little remarkable about Grenville's life and career. He had done nothing that might not have been expected from any other wealthy gentleman of the age with a restless temperament and a taste for adventure.

Life's Work

Although in the 1570's Grenville settled into the prescribed pattern for a leading member of the country gentry—serving in Parliament and taking his place as an important figure in the local government of Cornwall as a justice of the peace and deputy lieutenant and, in 1577, sheriff of Cornwall—his great energies found another outlet. The west country, thrusting out into the Atlantic like a long wedge, was the nursery of many of England's boldest seamen, merchants in foreign trade and explorers. From the area came a stream of brave adventurous captains such as Sir John Hawkins and Sir Francis Drake, ready to take risky voyages for profit anywhere in a widening world. For men of greater wealth and social standing—men such as Grenville and his cousins Sir Humphrey Gilbert and Sir Walter Raleigh—there was a larger role to be played: organizing and securing funds for voyages whose exploration of uncharted waters would add to England's territory as well as enrich its projectors. One great hope was that a passage could be discovered around the New World, a route to the wealth of Asia, one not dominated by a rival power. In the 1570's, Gilbert was promoting a search for a northwest passage. Alternatively, Grenville was trying to drum up interest in a southwesterly route around South America. Going by the southwestern route, Englishmen would be trespassing on Spanish claims, but relations with that great empire were already deteriorating. Eventually, Grenville's own plan for a Pacific expedition came to nothing, and it was Drake who first made the striking voyage of circumnavigation for England on the southerly route from 1577 to 1580, raiding the wealth of the virtually undefended Pacific coast of

Spanish South America, coming home ballasted with silver.

After Gilbert died in 1583, Raleigh inherited his role as the leading projector of English schemes to explore, settle, and develop the New World. A colony established there offered the prospect both of cheap land and of a base for privateers to raid Spanish commerce. In this effort, Grenville became one of Raleigh's principal supporters and led the first expedition sent out in 1585 to settle Virginia (the same expedition that established the ill-fated Roanoke settlement). It was his first naval command. Having left a party behind to establish a permanent English settlement in North America, Grenville and his small fleet returned home, capturing a rich Spanish merchant en route.

At that point, after a decade and a half of steadily worsening relations, England finally became involved in a full-scale war with Spain. Spanish attempts to close its empire to trade with outsiders and to regard interlopers as pirates, had long antagonized English commercial interests and led to an undeclared private war, although neither side was eager for an open conflict. The endless flow of gold and silver from a vast empire, however, transformed Spain into the most powerful state in the Western world. Spain had thus replaced France as the principal threat to English security. In Europe, Spain was committed to the suppression of Protestant heresy. In the nearby Netherlands, Spain had been trying since 1568 to put down a rebellion by its own Protestant subjects. Many in England feared that if Spain succeeded there, England would be next. Queen Elizabeth, although she detested rebellion, agreed and provided aid to the Dutch.

Once war was declared, England had to be prepared to resist a mighty Spanish invasion fleet. Grenville, returning home from his second Virginia voyage, profitably raided the Spanish Azores on the way home. Then, as an experienced soldier, he was busy organizing the land and sea defenses of the west country, the first line of battle if the country were to be invaded by Spain. When the armada finally came, it was decisively defeated, though the danger was far from over. Grenville's part in the victory was modest. His own fleet of ships, being outfitted for the resupply of Virginia, had been commandeered to support Drake.

With the most pressing fear of invasion over, the war settled in to a stalemate. Long-standing English naval strategy was to recognize the unequal strength of the two sides. It was impossible for England to defeat preponderant Spanish power directly. Spain could only be induced to make peace on favorable terms if the war could be made too costly for them by cutting the supply of gold and silver from the Americas. The most effective way to carry on such a campaign would be to have a naval base on or close to Spain's gold lifeline, either on the Iberian coast or in the Azores, the principal base from which the Spaniards convoyed the incoming treasure fleets to safety.

Furthering this strategy, in 1591, Lord Thomas Howard commanded a small fleet of some sixteen ships to the Azores. Grenville went out in command of the *Revenge*. At the end of August, the English fleet, after many months cruising off the Azores, was caught by surprise by a large Spanish squadron of fifty-three ships. Howard managed to extricate his ships from the action, but Grenville declined to run. The *Revenge*, alone, stood up to the overwhelming power of the Spanish fleet for some fifteen hours while the ship was pounded to pieces. At last, awash with the blood of her crew, and with Grenville himself mortally wounded, the *Revenge* was forced to strike her colors. The dying

Grenville was taken aboard the Spanish flagship, where he died within a few days. Of his crew of 150, only twenty survived. Though the destruction of the *Revenge* was the result of Grenville's foolhardy stubbornness, the episode was quickly taken up by the ballad singers and mythmakers. Grenville's heroism in the face of impossible odds became a watchword for Englishmen, and even the Spaniards acknowledged the raw courage and devotion to honor in a gallant, if useless, death.

Summary

In the main lines of his career, Sir Richard Grenville was a typical important country gentleman, a Member of Parliament and participant in local government. What distinguished him from his fellows and put him in the company of the other gentlemen of late Elizabethan England whose lives acquired legendary stature—Raleigh, Drake, and Hawkins—was that he was one of a small number of bold spirits who were prepared to risk life and fortune for the Virginia project. Though the first Virginia effort, in which he played so large a part, failed, the path had been blazed, and in the next generation the enduring settlement of British North America began in Virginia. If Grenville's role in the Virginia project entitles him to some special attention, his other claim to fame, and the major reason he is remembered after nearly four hundred years, is one bloody day's fighting at sea. For late sixteenth century Englishmen, the defeat of the *Revenge* was like Thermopylae, a moral tale about stout courage and fidelity to duty, the willingness to sacrifice all for the love of queen and country. In the exuberant patriotism of Elizabethan England, this was an episode to be cherished, and so it remained for many centuries, the subject of poems and admiring legend. In a more skeptical age, it might be more readily said of Grenville's death, as of another famous episode, that it was magnificent, but it was not war.

Bibliography

Andrews, Kenneth R. *Elizabethan Privateering, 1583-1603.* Cambridge: Cambridge University Press, 1964. An authoritative work on privateering in England during the war with Spain of 1585-1603. Provides background on Grenville's activities, with some specific references to him and to his west country associates. A useful bibliography.

———. *Trade, Plunder, and Settlement: Maritime Enterprise and the Genesis of the British Empire, 1480-1630.* Cambridge and New York: Cambridge University Press, 1984. Provides a careful summary of what is known about all the British voyages of exploration and settlement.

Black, J. B. *The Reign of Elizabeth, 1558-1603.* 2d ed. London: Oxford University Press, 1959. A volume in the standard *Oxford History of England,* Black's work is still the best general textbook covering the entire Elizabethan period.

Cheyney, Edward P. *History of England from the Defeat of the Armada to the Death of Elizabeth.* 2 vols. London: Longman, and New York: Smith, 1914-1926. Despite its age, Cheyney's is still the best detailed history of the period 1588-1603 and is very helpful on the general context after the defeat of the armada.

Read, Conyers. *Lord Burghley and Queen Elizabeth.* London: Cape, and New York: Knopf, 1960. The second volume of a two-volume work. A detailed study of the queen's principal adviser on domestic and foreign issues and therefore a close account of the policy background for Grenville's public career after 1570.

Rowse, A. L. *Sir Richard Grenville of the Revenge.* London: Cape, and Boston: Houghton Mifflin, 1937. The only modern life. Rowse provides much critical comment and analysis of the sources as well as a thorough background on the west country itself.

Wernham, R. B. *The Making of Elizabethan Foreign Policy, 1558-1603.* Berkeley: University of California Press, 1980. A brief overview, by a leading scholar, of the foreign policy background for Elizabeth's reign. The best concise introduction, with helpful suggestions for additional reading.

Williamson, J. A. *The Age of Drake.* London: Black, 1938; New York: World Publishing, 1965. A study by one of the principal researchers in the field of British maritime history during its great age; a classic in that field. Much else that Williamson has written is helpful as background.

S. J. Stearns

LADY JANE GREY

Born: October, 1537; Leicestershire, England
Died: February 12, 1554; London, England
Area of Achievement: Monarchy
Contribution: Had her reign as queen of England been fully legal and more lengthy, Jane Grey would have been England's first ruling queen and likely a successful monarch.

Early Life

Lady Jane Grey was born in October, 1537, to Henry Grey and Frances Brandon, the duke and duchess of Suffolk. Jane's mother was also a distant heir to the throne as the daughter of Henry VIII's sister Mary. Her parents, being Protestant, saw to it that Jane, the eldest of three daughters, had a proper education in the "new religion," as the Protestant faith was called. Jane was an intelligent, learned, clever, and scholarly girl; by the time of her death, she could read six languages, including Greek and Hebrew. She was well versed in the Greek and Roman classics, philosophy, and contemporary religious doctrine, and she early on developed a reputation as a precocious child nearly obsessed with her studies.

Jane's parents, while not particularly well-schooled nor overwhelmingly enthusiastic about their eldest daughter's dedication to learning, did not mind sending Jane off to court to study with her cousins, the Princess Elizabeth and the future King Edward. Such connections could potentially benefit Jane's parents, for as provincial nobility, they were constantly struggling for political and social influence. These potential political connections could also benefit them in pursuit of a suitable husband for their daughter.

Life's Work

Jane's availability and attractiveness as a marriage prospect, along with her religion, made her a pawn in the political power plays of the day. Henry VIII died in early 1547, and the throne passed to his nine-year-old son, Edward VI. The boy's uncle, Thomas Seymour, duke of Somerset, became the "protector" of the realm and regent to the young king. Somerset suggested several times to Jane's parents that a marriage between Edward and Jane would benefit all involved. There was also talk of Jane marrying Somerset's son. Somerset, though, fell from power, primarily due to political maneuvering by John Dudley, duke of Northumberland, and thereafter the Seymours had little to offer.

The issue of religion was one that plagued all of the Tudor family monarchs. Henry VIII had split from the Catholic Church in order to divorce his first wife, unwittingly laying the groundwork for the Church of England. Many of his top advisers during his last years were moderate Protestants, as were virtually all of Edward's counselors. As the succession stood, should Edward die before having children, the throne of England would pass to Henry's eldest daughter, Mary. This possibility raised the religious issue again, for Mary was Catholic, and many of Edward's advisers, especially Northumberland, were concerned that Mary's accession would result in England's return to Catholicism. The religious differences between Edward's advisers and Mary also virtually guaranteed for the counselors at best the loss of prestige, at worst perhaps torture or death for their heretical beliefs.

The ill health of the king also became a major concern. Despite his love of outdoor activities, Edward had never been particularly healthy, and his health worsened as he aged. There was growing alarm that Edward's sicknesses could become life threatening, and Northumberland knew his power rested solely with Edward. In 1553, when the young king was fifteen, a cold developed into a more serious lung ailment. Repeated treatments by doctors proved fruitless, and Edward slowly worsened. It was obvious that the boy-king's days were numbered.

Northumberland, understandably worried about his position should Mary succeed her half-brother Edward, and perhaps also concerned about the likely return to Catholicism, agonized over possible courses of action. Edward was getting sicker and sicker, and Northumberland decided that Mary had to be somehow excluded from the succession. According to Henry's will, the next successor after Mary was Elizabeth, his daughter with Anne Boleyn. Elizabeth was a Protestant, but Northumberland had little influence over her. Following Elizabeth was Frances Brandon, followed by Lady Jane. If Northumberland could alter the succession to elevate Frances or Jane to the throne, he could continue to exert his considerable influence over the government.

Lady Jane's dedicated Protestantism and her place in the succession made her an attractive pawn. Jane had engaged in theological debates with numerous religious scholars and had even confronted her cous-

Lady Jane signs her death warrant for treason

in Mary regarding the sanctity of the Catholic "host." The details of Jane's accession to the throne, however, are fairly complex.

Northumberland had Edward draft a will of his own that precluded his two sisters, Mary and Elizabeth. (Elizabeth was excluded on the pretext that she might marry a foreigner, which the English did not want.) This left Frances as the heir, but Northumberland had her sign away her claim, essentially "abdicating" in favor of her daughter. Lady Jane was thus left as the primary heir. Yet this new succession was far from secure. While it was entirely a monarch's prerogative to change his or her will, and the duty of the kingdom to follow the will's provisions, any change in the succession had also to be approved by Parliament. Thus, despite the fact that Edward's will was a binding legal document and that anyone who refused to carry out its provisions was guilty of treason, the entire will was not legal until approved by Parliament. Anyone who did follow the will, then, was breaking the law. There is also some uncertainty as to whether Edward himself wrote the new will or whether Northumberland wrote it and simply had the sick king sign it.

Meanwhile, Northumberland had proposed a marriage between his youngest son, Guildford, and Jane. Such a match was an advantageous one for the Greys, and they approved. Jane protested violently; though noble children rarely had any say in their marriages, she pleaded to not be married. Regardless, Jane and Guildford were hastily married on May 25, 1553. Noble weddings tended to be large affairs, but this ceremony was a small and hasty event, with few guests and little joy. At first, the two newlyweds were allowed to stay with their families rather than to live with each other, but Jane's parents later insisted that they stay together, presumably so that Jane could conceive an heir to the throne. With the potential royal couple waiting in the wings, Edward in June formally changed his will; he also declared his two half-sisters illegitimate, which effectively removed them from the succession regardless of the will.

Northumberland took the king's will and had Edward's advisers sign it to acknowledge their support for the plan, though few were eager to do so. Since Parliament was not in session, however, Parliament's approval was not likely to come before Edward's death. In place of a legitimate parliamentary approval, Northumberland had as many Parliamentarians as he could locate sign the document, thus providing some semblance of legality. Had it been in session, Parliament as a whole would most likely have debated the new will fiercely, since it skipped the two most rightful heirs. Edward VI died on July 6, 1553, and Northumberland quickly pressured remaining advisers to support his plot. On July 9, at Syon House, north of London, Jane was told that she had been declared queen. She was shocked, and at first she refused the crown. It became clear to her, belatedly, that she was simply a pawn.

News spread of Edward's death, and Jane's accession was announced on July 10, but few greeted either announcement with any enthusiasm. Despite the Catholicism of Mary, she was the rightful ruler, and most preferred a legal Catholic queen over an illegal Protestant one. Most of Edward's counselors fled, many going to Mary personally and begging her forgiveness for their parts in the plotting. For her part, Mary remained in hiding for most of Jane's nine-day reign.

While it is not clear whether Jane might have shed the influence of Northumberland and her parents easily had she remained queen, it seems likely that she would have been a successful ruler. She displayed a fiery spirit and courage, and after ascending the throne, she refused to crown Guildford king, instead making him a duke. As an educated and strong-willed woman, she might have had a long successful life and reign similar to that enjoyed later by Elizabeth. During her brief occupation of the throne, Jane overruled Northumberland on who would lead troops to capture Mary; Dudley wanted Henry Grey to go, but Jane instead ordered her father-in-law to assume command. What little support Jane enjoyed quickly evaporated, however, and exactly nine days after being crowned, she was placed under house arrest as Mary approached London.

Northumberland and Henry Grey were arrested along with Guildford and Northumberland's other sons. Frances Grey begged Mary for forgiveness for her husband, but it appears that no one pleaded for Jane. Instead, Jane wrote a letter to her cousin asking forgiveness and saying that she had been foolish to have even accepted the crown, since she had never wanted to be queen anyway. Mary, who initially showed great compassion, forgave both, though Jane and Guildford were convicted of treason and confined in the Tower of London. Mary even took Jane's two younger sisters into her employ as attendants. Northumberland, despite a last-minute conversion to Catholicism, was beheaded.

Jane may have lived out a long but lonely life in prison had it not been for a rebellion that started in January, 1554, in southern England. Wyatt's Rebellion was essentially an uprising opposed to Mary's planned marriage to Philip of Spain, but some of the rebels called for Jane to be restored to the throne. Foolishly, Henry Grey also participated in the uprising, which failed when the rebels were prevented from entering London. While Jane was certainly not involved in the rebellion, it was clear that as long as she lived, she could be a catalyst for further unrest. The Spanish ambassadors who were in England making marriage arrangements pressured Mary to rid herself of Guildford and Jane, insinuating that Philip would never marry her if they lived. Much like Jane, then, Mary was a victim of circumstance, and she ordered the execution of Jane and her husband in early February, 1554.

Jane had been unaware of the rebellion and its aftermath, but she was told of her father's involvement and of her impending execution. Mary sent her priest, Doctor Feckenham, to try to reconvert Jane, and though the two engaged in the religious debate that was so characteristic of the young former queen, she remained dedicated to her Protestant faith.

Guildford was executed outside the Tower on February 12; as his body was brought back into the complex, Jane apparently passed the cart on the way to her own death inside the Tower grounds. On the scaffold, Jane delivered a short speech expressing her faith and asking God to forgive her. After tying a scarf around her eyes, kneeling in the straw, and placing her head on the block, Jane was beheaded.

Summary

Jane's impact on English history is limited. While potentially an excellent ruler, she did not rule with enough support or long enough to make any lasting contribution. Although Jane displayed the characteristics that made the Tudor family popular, such as courage, a dedication to ideals, and a noble bearing, her story remains primarily a romantic but unfortunate addendum to the Tudor-Stuart period.

Bibliography

Foxe, John. *Foxe's Book of Martyrs*. Edited by Marie Gentert King. Old Tappan, N.J.: Spire Books, 1987. An account of Protestant martyrs written in the late 1500's. Favorably inclined toward Jane and Edward, but a primary source not to be missed.

Geary, Douglas, ed. *The Letters of Lady Jane Grey*. Ilfracombe, England: Arthur Stockwell, 1951. This work includes virtually all the literary remains of Jane, including letters, notes, and the text of her speech on the scaffold. Invaluable primary material.

Luke, Mary. *The Nine Days Queen*. New York: William Morrow, 1986. A well-written, factually sound account of Jane's life and brief rule. Few footnotes, but the most accessible and accurate modern account.

Mathew, David. *Lady Jane Grey: The Setting of the Reign*. London: Eyre Methuen, 1972. Provides a respectable background to the reign of Jane, though it says little of Jane herself.

Plowden, Alison. *Lady Jane Grey and the House of Suffolk*. New York: Franklin Watts, 1986. Delves into the political workings of Jane's family and Northumberland, and is useful in conjunction with other overall texts on Jane.

Wayne Ackerson

MATTHIAS GRÜNEWALD
Matthias Gothardt

Born: c. 1475; Würzburg
Died: August, 1528; Halle, Magdeburg
Area of Achievement: Art
Contribution: Grünewald was the culmination of the Gothic tradition in German painting while giving evidence of the primacy of individual artistic expression within the tradition of the Italian Renaissance. He employed Gothic principles of expressiveness and Renaissance pictorial conventions, creating a unique style which transcended the limitations of the traditions out of which he worked.

Early Life

Matthias Grünewald, a figure of great stature in his own time, appears to have been quickly forgotten after his death. This neglect may be attributed in part to his preference for Gothic expressiveness in a period given over to the aesthetic concerns of the Italian Renaissance. Grünewald's preoccupation with mystical interpretations and paintings which were largely religious was out of place in an increasingly worldly age for which strong, stark religious themes had less and less impact and significance. Direct knowledge of Grünewald is scant. Besides his extant works, little was left behind by the artist himself which would give a clear picture. Instead one must rely on secondary sources and documents and letters of the time. Early knowledge of Grünewald arose from the efforts of Joachim von Sandrart, a seventeenth century German artist and historian. Even Sandrart had difficulty in finding information on Grünewald. In the early twentieth century, another German scholar, Heinrich Schmidt, uncovered some of the facts of Grünewald's life. In the 1920's yet another German scholar, W. K. Zulch, wrote the basic modern work on Grünewald, discovering Grünewald's actual surname in the process. There exists no unchallenged portrait of Grünewald, although the painting of Saint Sebastian in Grünewald's Isenheim altarpiece is thought to be a self-portrait. Grünewald is thought to have been born near Würzburg around 1475. Of his early life little is known. The exact place and source of his training is not known, although it is generally believed that Grünewald's general style and coloring reflect the predisposition of artists who worked in the Franconian region along the Main and Rhine Rivers.

Life's Work

Grünewald's first known work is the Lindenhart altarpiece, dating from 1503. Between 1504 and 1519, he was a resident in Seligenstadt, outside Würzburg. There he is listed as a master with apprentices; he executed paintings, the Basel *Crucifixion* for one, and was court painter to Archbishop Uriel von Gemmingen from 1508 to 1514. During this same period, Grünewald supervised design and repair of various buildings, notably Schloss Aschaffenburg. In 1514, during the difficult time of the Thirty Years' War between Protestant and Catholic factions in Germany, Grünewald became the court painter for Albrecht von Brandenburg. In 1519, Grünewald is believed to have married, although the marriage may not have been a happy one. His wife brought with her a son, Andreas, whom Grünewald adopted. He apparently used his wife's surname, Niethart, occasionally. In 1525, Grünewald left the service of the archbishop under accusations related to his sympathies with the Peasants' War. He was acquitted by the archbishop but did not return to his service. Books he left behind at his death testify to his Protestant/Lutheran sympathies. These included a New Testament, a number of sermons, and pamphlets, all by Martin Luther. In 1526, Grünewald apprenticed his adopted son, Andreas Niethart, to Arnold Rucker, an organ builder, sculptor, and table maker. Grünewald died in August of 1528, while working on a commission for the cities of Magdeburg and Halle in Saxony.

Grünewald treated exclusively religious subjects when he painted. Only a small number of Grünewald's works have survived, but his total output was probably not extensive. Only two of his works bear autograph dates, and these form the basis for a chronology of all of his work. These works include the Bindlach altarpiece (1503) and his greatest work, the Isenheim altarpiece (1515). Two other works are dated on the frames, *The Mocking of Christ* (1503) and the Maria Schell altarpiece (1515). All other dates are conjecture, based on historical clues and stylistic evidence. As did his contemporaries Albrecht Dürer, Hans Burgkmair, and Lucas Cranach, the Elder, Grünewald did not conform to the fashions of the time or concede to the ideals of the Italian Renaissance which dominated in matters of taste and style. In his gruesome realism and complex iconography, Grünewald remained German and Gothic in his treatment of his subjects. He restricted himself to illustrating the fundamental themes of Christian faith, rendered with a sense of the mystical and the ecstatic.

Grünewald painted the Madonna and saints, but either by conscious intent or out of religious fervor and fascination with the subject—or both—he specialized in painting the Passion of Christ. From the beginning to the end of his career, Grünewald returned time after time to the subject of the Crucifixion, of which four versions are still preserved in galleries in Switzerland, the Netherlands, and West Germany.

Grünewald's work is subjective, the intuitive product of a personal artist who feels his work deeply. Grünewald's work substitutes force and sincerity in place of the Italian Renaissance preference for beauty and elegance. Instead of the concrete depiction of form through the use of descriptive line and chiaroscuro, Grünewald emphasizes the mystical through expressive line and color. While he understood and made use of the Italian Renaissance conventions of perspective and correct proportion, Grünewald saw them as being of lesser value than the spiritual qualities of his work. For the artists of the Italian Renaissance, the new conventions were at least as important as the old values which arguably might be said to have become means to using the new conventions as much as anything else. All the qualities the Italian Renaissance considered important—dignity, repose, symmetry, balance, serenity, perfection—were for Grünewald merely ornamentation, elements not pertinent to his interest and interpretation of his subject.

Yet Grünewald's work was not merely emotional display. For one thing, he did not portray superficial emotions. The emotive character of his work came from his use of strong dichotomies—real, temporal, and secular versus ideal, eternal, and spiritual—in his interpretation of his subject. The conditions of his figures are symbolic, with emphasis placed on their devotional and spiritual aspects rather than their merely being descriptive and narrative. His subjects were traditional, but his treatment of them is unique, often overwhelming. An excellent example is Grünewald's interpretation of the risen Christ in the Isenheim altarpiece, which makes use of all the above-mentioned dichotomies.

One is prepared by one's initial encounter with the excruciating, visceral vision of the painfully crucified Christ on the outside panel of the altarpiece. Then to behold the risen Christ on the inside is to be moved ecstatically. Grünewald, moved as he had to have been by his desire to express the spirituality of his subject, transcended the limitations of the medium and conventions he employed. One's admiration is inspired not by the artist's mastery of technique, though clearly Grünewald was a superb craftsman, but by the spiritual impact of his work, which is as real and felt today as it surely had to have been when it was first viewed in the sixteenth century. His figures appear forced and affected in pose and manner, because they are meant to be larger than life—more than mere representations of a historical event. While understanding line and form in realistic representation, Grünewald gives primacy to expression of qualities rather than to accurate depiction of appearances. He did this through his extreme treatments of the human figure, creating the expressiveness of a psychic condition and presenting a spiritual reality as much as a visual image.

Summary

Matthias Grünewald was a Gothic artist with the sensibility of the spirituality of the Middle Ages. To compare Grünewald's work and style with the standards of the Italian Renaissance would be a misplaced attempt to understand and appreciate his work. Judged in terms of the Italian Renaissance, Grünewald's work appears repellent, disdainful of form, contemptuous of moderation, and lacking in grace. Judged in terms of an individual's ability to give form and expression to those images central to Western Christian spirituality, Grünewald's work appears poignant, penetrating, and transcendent. Grünewald was not so much a Gothic artist as he was an artist who recognized that the Gothic era gave best and fullest expression to spirituality. Grünewald did not imitate the Gothic style, but he adopted fully the principles of the Gothic, realizing their timeless nature. Nor did Grünewald refute the ideals of the Italian Renaissance as much as he ignored them, choosing only to use those formal elements useful to his artistic purpose.

Bibliography

Benesch, Otto. *German Painting from Dürer to Holbein*. Translated by H. S. B. Harrison. Geneva: Éditions d'Art Albert Skira, 1966. Based on a series of lectures given by Benesch in 1959 and 1960 at the University of Vienna. Benesch, an eminent scholar, emphasized the Germanic and Gothic aspects of his subjects' work.

Burkhard, Arthur. *Matthias Grünewald: Personality and Accomplishment*. Cambridge, Mass.: Harvard University Press, 1936. The first comprehensive treatment in English of the life and work of Matthias Grünewald. The author's intent is to suggest the aesthetic and personal underpinnings of Grünewald while connecting him closely with his German Gothic heritage. The extensive bibliography cites only German sources.

Cuttler, Charles D. *Northern Painting from Pucelle to Brueghel: Fourteenth, Fifteenth, and Sixteenth Centuries*. New York: Holt Rinehart, 1968. A later study of painting of Northern European artists, attempting not only to place them in context with the Italian Renaissance but also to show their own peculiar characteristics and styles. Suggests the social, philosophical, and aesthetic influences of the time.

Mellinkoff, Ruth. *The Devil at Isenheim: Reflections of Popular Belief in Grünewald's Altarpiece*. Berkeley: University of California Press, 1988. A lavishly illustrated iconographic study of the Isenheim altarpiece. Mellinkoff focuses on the panel depicting the Madonna and Child being honored by a concert of angels; in an original and persuasive interpretation, Mellinkoff argues that among the angels is Lucifer himself, shown in the moment of awareness of the folly of his rebellion.

Monick, Eugene. *Evil, Sexuality, and Disease in Grünewald's Body of Christ*. Foreword by David L. Miller. Dallas, Tex.: Spring Publications, 1993. Criticism and interpretation of Grünewald's work from a religious psychology perspective.

Richter, Gottfried. *The Isenheim Altar: Suffering and Salvation in the Art of Grünewald*. Edinburgh: Floris Books, 1998. Discussion of the Isenheim altarpiece—its symbolism and place in Gothic Christian art.

Scheja, Georg. *The Isenheim Altarpiece*. Translated by Robert Erich Wolf. New York: Abrams, 1969. An extensive, authoritative discussion of Grünewald's best-known work. The author cites possible visual and literary sources for the work. The extensive footnotes are an excellent second source of information.

Donald R. Kelm

FRANCESCO GUICCIARDINI

Born: March 6, 1483; Florence
Died: May 22, 1540; S. Margherita ia Montici, Florence
Area of Achievement: Historiography
Contribution: Guicciardini helped revolutionize history writing by breaking with Humanist conventions. He was one of the first historians to present history as a series of interrelated causes and effects and to treat the history of Italy in the larger context of European affairs.

Early Life

The Guicciardini family was one of the aristocratic supports of the early (circa 1430) Medici regime in Florence. Francesco Guicciardini's father had close ties to Lorenzo de' Medici, evidenced by the many positions offered him by Lorenzo and by the fact that Marsilio Ficino, Lorenzo's colleague in the Platonic Academy and a member of the Medici household, was godfather to young Francesco. At his father's urging, Guicciardini pursued a career in law. He studied at the Universities of Pisa, Ferrara, and Padua. Upon his return to Florence, he established himself as a lawyer and professor of law and in 1508 married Maria Salviati, whose family was active in the affairs of republican Florence. His earliest writings belong to this period and include his family memoirs and the Storie fiorentine (1509; The History of Florence, 1970), which covered the years 1378 to 1509. The latter is an important source for historians interested in the Florentine Republic.

Life's Work

In 1511, the year of Pope Julius II's formation of a Holy League against France—consisting of the Papal States, Venice, Aragon, and the Holy Roman Empire—Guicciardini was elected to his first public post, as ambassador to the court of Ferdinand II of Aragon. When he returned to Florence three years later, he found the Medici family restored to power and Florence a member of the league. He returned to his legal profession, and, though no friend to the younger generation of Medici, he served the new rulers first as a member of the *Balia*, or body of eight, in charge of internal security and in 1515 in the *Signoria*, the governing council of the city.

Guicciardini's career took a new course in 1516, when he was appointed by Pope Leo X to a series of posts. He would serve the Papacy almost continuously until 1534. Until 1521, he was Governor of Modena and Reggio and general of papal armies. Temporarily removed from these posts upon the death of Leo X, Guicciardini was reappointed by Pope Adrian VI. Under his harsh but efficient rule, these provinces were brought under control. The war in Italy between the Valois French and the Habsburg, Charles V, Holy Roman Emperor and King of Spain, turned Reggio into a military outpost of the Papal States. Guicciardini's major military success was the defense of Parma against the French in December, 1521. He also successfully preserved Modena from the Duke of Ferrara, though Reggio capitulated.

Guicciardini's literary output during this time consists of numerous letters and memorandums that manifest his tireless energy in the performance of his duties. From 1521 to 1526, he wrote *Dialogo del reggimento di Firenze* (dialogue on the government of Florence). From a historical case study illustrating the defects of one-man rule and of democracy, Guicciardini deduced his ideal Florentine government: a republic in which the aristocratic element has a leading role. In 1521, too, began Guicciardini's correspondence with Niccolò Machiavelli. From 1501 until the restoration of the Medici in 1512, Machiavelli had been a leading actor in Florentine affairs under Piero Soderini, the ensign-bearer of the republic. The Guicciardini and Salviati families had been aristocratic opponents of that regime, and Guicciardini had called Machiavelli the "tool of Soderini." The two found a common bond in their distaste for Medici rule after 1512. Though younger by fourteen years, Guicciardini played the aristocratic patron to Machiavelli the commoner. About 1530, he began *Considerazioni sui "Discorsi" de Machiavelli* (*Considerations on the "Discourses" of Machiavelli*, 1965), which he never finished. He criticized Machiavelli's theories and his interpretation of Roman history as a guide to contemporary political thought.

Guicciardini's star continued to ascend under Pope Clement VII, a Medici family member with whom he was friends. In 1524, he was made president of the Romagna region, and he became a trusted adviser to the pope. The victory of Charles V over Francis I of France at Pavia in 1525 proved a turning point in the life and the historical consciousness of Guicciardini. He was catapulted into the highest echelons of European politics. From then on, he was both enabled and required to comprehend events in Italy as intricately bound up in the larger schemes of the great powers. In 1526, Guicciardini was in Rome as a papal adviser. His advice was important in the formation of the League of Cognac, the alliance of the Papacy with France and Venice against the Habsburgs; Machiavelli also supported this alliance. Guicciardini became the lieutenant-general of the league's forces. This action by the Medici pope placed Florence in danger of Habsburg reprisal and resulted in another overthrow of Medici rule in 1527, ten days after the sack of Rome by Habsburg troops under the Duke of Bourbon. Guicciardini thus found himself out of favor with the pope and unwelcome in Florence, because of his Medici associations. He later commented that he had suddenly been thrown from the height of honor and esteem to the other extreme. He began to comprehend the power of fortune in historical events, a notion which would attain increasing prominence in his thought.

Guicciardini retired to his villa at Finocchietto, where he worked on *Cose fiorentine* (Florentine affairs), *Ricordi* (partially translated as *The Maxims of Francesco Guicciardini*, 1845), and three personal pieces—*Consolatoria, Accusatoria*, and the unfinished *Defensoria*. These three personal pieces are written as speeches against himself; they contain indictments of actions which had long bothered him, including his formation of the league, the sack of Rome, and the pope's imprisonment. A major charge by his imaginary accuser was that he had used high position for personal gain. The *Ricordi* is a collection of political maxims culled from his various papers and treatises. Their tone is uniformly cynical, more so, even, than Machiavelli's writings; for example, Guicciardini suggests that one should gain a reputation for sincerity in order to be able to lie successfully on an important matter. In *Cose fiorentine*, a second history of Florence covering 1375 to 1494, Guicciardini returned to the classical Humanist style of history, but he surpassed the typical Humanist histories by using many sources, including documents. In this and in his conviction that to understand the history of Florence one must also understand events throughout all Italy, Guicciardini was taking the first steps in modern historiography. He never finished his Florentine history; in 1529, the Treaty of Cambria dictated the return of the Medici to power in Florence, and Guicciardini returned to eminence under Alessandro de' Medici's rule.

Personally opposed to Medici rule, Guicciardini still aspired to a leadership role in Florence, but his political career lacked luster during his later years. Pope Clement appointed him Governor of Bologna in 1531; Pope Paul III removed him in 1534. In Florence, Guicciardini was legal adviser to Alessandro until his assassination in 1537. Duke Cosimo de' Medici allowed Guicciardini to remain in office but with an ever-diminishing influence over affairs.

In 1536 Guicciardini began *Storia d'Italia* (1561-1564; *The History of Italy*, 1579), the only book he wrote not for himself but for public consumption. Retiring in 1537 to his villa, he took with him the entire foreign correspondence of the Florentine Republic. *The History of Italy* was written, revised, and polished many times during the last three years of Guicciardini's life. Aside from its value as a source for the years 1494-1532, it is a great milestone in historiography. Guicciardini had come to believe that traditional Humanist history was artificial and prevented history from being useful. He thought that the Humanist view that the moral failures of individual Italian princes were responsible for conflict was inadequate; he believed that not man but uncontrollable fortune governed events. Most important, he realized that the wars of foreign powers in Italy had causes from beyond the Alps. Guicciardini viewed *The History of Italy* as a tragedy brought on Italians by themselves. Because of their rivalries, Italian rulers invited foreign powers onto Italian soil. Guicciardini frequently reiterates that all men act only from self-interest, and the interests of the foreign powers caused the Italian rulers to be initiators of events no longer, so that even their best efforts could not relieve the situation. It was Guicciardini's gift to show how human illusions are an integral part of history and how events, or fortune, and human intentions constantly act and react upon one another. Is history still useful if it teaches nothing but the arbitrariness of fortune? Guicciardini believed that the value of history was as a reminder to men to consider the effect of their every action upon their names and dignity. He died while still polishing his book on May 22, 1540.

Summary

Francesco Guicciardini's achievement was to set the writing of history on a new and intellectually sound path. Before his generation, Humanist historians had slavishly imitated the historians of classical antiquity. If the main subject was a war, then

Sallust was to be imitated and attention devoted to the generals' speeches before a battle and to the battle itself. If the focus was the history of a particular city, then Livy was the preferred model. History was regarded as a branch of rhetoric whose purpose was to provide moral instruction by examples. Thus, history did not require completeness but merely those episodes which demonstrated a certain virtue or vice.

Guicciardini accepted the didactic purpose of history (he quoted Cicero's prescription for writing history), but he saw it as teaching the concrete effects of various types of government rather than the general rules of ethics. In the end, he concluded that men always act from personal interest and that fortune plays its fickle part more frequently than one might think. Throughout a lifetime as an actor at the edge of events, he came to perceive the complex networks of causation between events, so that episodic history was no longer plausible to him. Another contribution was his heightened standard of factual accuracy, possible only by comparing literary sources and documents.

Guicciardini's the *Ricordi* and *The History of Italy* were published soon after his death. His other writings, ten volumes of *Opere Inedite* (unedited works), did not see print until 1857-1867.

Bibliography

Cavallar, Osvaldo. "Francesco Guicciardini and the 'Pisan Crisis': Logic and Discourses." *Journal of Modern History* 65 (June, 1993): 245. Cavallar considers some of the ideological strategies employed by Florentine lawyers to address the mass of legal cases created by the 'Pisan Crisis.' Includes the Florentine ruling class's conceptions of their empire and the nature of the Florentine territorial state, and delves into Guicciardini as lawyer, historian, and political thinker.

De Sanctis, Francesco. *History of Italian Literature*. Translated by Joan Redfern. 2 vols. London: Oxford University Press, 1930; New York: Harcourt Brace, 1931. Chapter 15 compares Machiavelli and Guicciardini. Gives an unfavorable view of the career and mind of Guicciardini as advocating self-interest as the motive force of history.

Gilbert, Felix. *Machiavelli and Guicciardini: Politics and History in Sixteenth Century Florence*. Princeton, N.J.: Princeton University Press, 1965; London: Norton, 1984. A survey of Guicciardini's career and literary output seen against the tradition of Renaissance historiography prevalent in his day. Contains an excellent annotated bibliography.

Guicciardini, Francesco. *The History of Florence*. Translated by Mario Domandi. New York: Harper, 1970. The complete text in English with an excellent and detailed introductory biography.

———. *The History of Italy*. Translated by Sidney Alexander. New York: Macmillan, 1969. Contains extensive and well-chosen excerpts in English from his twenty-volume history.

———. *Maxims and Reflections of a Renaissance Statesman*. Translated by Mario Domandi. New York: Harper, 1965. An English translation of the *Ricordi*.

———. *Selected Writings*. Edited by Cecil Grayson. Translated by Margaret Grayson. London and New York: Oxford University Press, 1965. A good sampling of Guicciardini's various writings in English translation.

Luciani, Vincent. *Francesco Guicciardini and His European Reputation*. New York: Otto, 1936. Contains copious scholarly material on Guicciardini; lists editions and translations of his works up to 1936. Discusses *The History of Italy* as a historical source and summarizes the views of it held by Italian, French, Spanish, Catholic, Protestant, and nineteenth century historians.

Ridolfi, Roberto. *The Life of Francesco Guicciardini*. Translated by Cecil Grayson. London: Routledge, 1967; New York: Knopf, 1968. An intimate, thoroughly footnoted, highly favorable biography by a major Guicciardini scholar.

Daniel C. Scavone

JOHANN GUTENBERG
Johannes Gensfleisch zur Laden

Born: 1394-1399; Mainz, Germany
Died: Probably February 3, 1468; Mainz, Germany
Areas of Achievement: Invention and technology
Contribution: Gutenberg invented printing with movable metal type.

Early Life

Johann Gutenberg was born in Mainz, an important German city on the Rhine River which was the seat of an archbishop. In the absence of a documented record, his birth date is placed between 1394 and 1399. His family, known as Gensfleisch zur Laden, was of the patrician class, but they were generally called Gutenberg, after their place of residence. Most members of his father's family were skilled metal craftsmen for the archbishop's mint in Mainz. Although there is no firm evidence about Gutenberg's education, he presumably continued his family's association with metalworking by being trained in this craft.

During his youth, Mainz was experiencing political turmoil because of conflicts between patrician and working classes. This civil strife led Gutenberg's father, Friele zum Gutenberg, to go into exile from the city in 1411. After similar disruptions in 1428, during which the Mainz guilds revoked civic privileges from the patricians, Gutenberg, who was probably around thirty years old at that time, settled in Strasbourg, a German city on the Rhine.

Life's Work

Gutenberg's activities during his mature life are of primary interest because of the evidence they contribute to knowledge about the invention of printing with movable type in Western Europe. His life and work can be divided into two chronological periods. During the first period, between 1428 and 1448, when he was living in Strasbourg, he probably began developing the printing process. In the last twenty years of his life, from 1448 to 1468, he returned to Mainz, where he brought his invention of printing with movable metal type to fruition in a Bible (now known as the Gutenberg Bible, the first complete book printed with movable metal type in Europe) and other printed books.

Information about Gutenberg's life in Strasbourg comes mainly from court records of lawsuits in which he was involved. Except for one case in 1436, when he was sued for breach of promise regarding marriage, these records are important because they show that he both practiced metalworking and was developing printing technology. One lawsuit in 1439 provides useful insights into Gutenberg's involvement with printing. The suit arose because, in 1438, Gutenberg had formed a partnership with several Strasbourg citizens to produce mirrors to be sold to pilgrims on a forthcoming pilgrimage to Aachen. Upon learning that the pilgrimage was to take place a year later than they had anticipated, the partners entered into a new contract with Gutenberg so that he would instruct them in other arts that he knew. One clause stipulated that if a partner died, his heirs would receive monetary compensation instead of being taken into the partnership. Soon after the contract was negotiated, one of the partners, Andreas Dritzehn, died, and his two brothers sued to become partners. The court determined that the contract was valid, and Gutenberg won the case.

Testimony of witnesses for this lawsuit has been interpreted as showing that Gutenberg was experimenting with printing using movable metal type. A goldsmith testified that Gutenberg paid him for "materials pertaining to printing." One witness mentioned purchases of metal, a press, and *Formen* (which became the German word for type). Another described how Gutenberg instructed him to dismantle and place on the press an object consisting of four pieces held together with screws which had been reconstructed as a typecasting mold. These combined references indicate that Gutenberg was working out the printing process, but no tangible evidence of his work with printing from this Strasbourg period has survived.

By 1448, Gutenberg had returned to Mainz. One document—a record of an oath made by Johann Fust on November 6, 1455, during a lawsuit that Fust, a Mainz businessman, had brought against Gutenberg—helps to reconstruct Gutenberg's work in Mainz from around 1448 to 1455. The document, known as the Helmasperger Instrument from the name of the notary who drew it up, also has been used to connect this activity with the production of the Gutenberg Bible.

Fust was suing to recover loans that he had made to Gutenberg. The first loan of eight hundred guil-

GUTENBERG
GUTENBERG

ders at six percent interest was made in 1450 and the second, also for eight hundred guilders with interest, in 1452. The loans were intended to provide for expenses in making equipment, paying workers' wages, and purchasing paper, parchment, and ink. In the second loan, Fust and Gutenberg became partners for "the work of the books." Testimony also establishes that Gutenberg had several workers and assistants. Peter Schoeffer, who had earlier been a scribe, was a witness for Fust, and soon thereafter Fust and Schoeffer established a flourishing printing business in Mainz. Gutenberg's two witnesses, Berthold Ruppel and Heinrich Kefer, who were his servants or workmen, also later became independent printers. Fust won the suit, since the court decided that Gutenberg should repay the original loan with interest. This document indicates that Gutenberg, using capital loaned to him by Fust, was operating a workshop with assistants for the purpose of producing books, probably by printing.

Bibliographical study of the Gutenberg Bible adds evidence to support the theory that Gutenberg's primary "work of the books" was printing the Gutenberg Bible. Notation in a copy of this Bible at the Bibliothèque Nationale in Paris indicates that Heinrich Cremer, vicar of the church of St. Stephen at Mainz, completed its rubrication and binding in two volumes in August, 1456. Study of paper, ink, and typography of the Gutenberg Bible suggests that it was in production between 1452 and 1454. This analysis also demonstrates that several presses were printing this Bible simultaneously. Thus, evidence from examination of surviving copies of the Gutenberg Bible correlates with information from Fust's lawsuit to show that the Bible was at or near completion at the time of the 1455 suit. Also, the substantial amount of money loaned and the types of expenses for equipment, supplies, and wages for several workmen are consistent with the production scale using several presses. Scholars have thus concluded that soon after Gutenberg returned to Mainz, he was responsible for producing the first complete printed book in Western Europe, the Gutenberg Bible.

A major question about Gutenberg's later life concerns his continued production of printed books after Fust's lawsuit in 1455. Again, documented evidence about this period is meager. He seems to have received some patronage and support from Konrad Humery, a Mainz canonist, who, after Gutenberg's death in early February, 1468, attested that he owned Gutenberg's printing equipment and materials. In addition, in 1465, the Archbishop of Mainz had accorded Gutenberg a civil pension whose privileges included an annual allowance for a suit of clothes, allotments of corn and wine, and exemption from taxes.

Determining Gutenberg's production of printed matter besides the Gutenberg Bible therefore depends on interpretation of these documents, including the financial ramifications of the 1455 lawsuit, and especially bibliographical analysis of early examples of printing. One group of these printed materials is called the "B36" group. The name comes from a Gothic type similar to but somewhat larger and less refined than the type used for the forty-two-line Gutenberg Bible. Works associated with this group include some broadsides, traditional grammar texts by the Roman author Donatus, and a thirty-six-line Bible printed in Bamberg, dated 1458-1459. Another group comes from the press that printed the *Catholicon*, a Latin dictionary put together in a smaller Gothic type by Johannes Balbus in Mainz in 1460. At least two other books and broadsides are connected with this press.

According to some sources, Gutenberg had to give up his printing materials to satisfy repayment to Fust. This financial disaster, combined with the somewhat inferior quality of printing using variants of the thirty-six-line Bible type, suggests that few, if any, other surviving early printed works can be attributed to Gutenberg. Another interpretation holds that the settlement with Fust did not deplete Gutenberg's financial or material resources to which Humery's support added. The comparative irregularities in the B36 type show that it was being developed earlier than the perfected Gutenberg Bible font, and this evidence suggests that Gutenberg was printing other works concurrently with and subsequently to the Gutenberg Bible using this more experimental type. Technical innovations in the type and setting of the *Catholicon*, along with its colophon extolling the new printing process, make Gutenberg, the inventor of printing, the person most likely to have executed the printing from the *Catholicon* press. Thus, it makes sense that Gutenberg probably printed various items comprising the B36 and *Catholicon* press groups throughout his career based in Mainz.

Summary

While further research in many areas will continue to add greater precision to identifying the corpus of Johann Gutenberg's printed works, his most significant achievement is the invention of printing with movable metal type. From the 1430's to the completion of the Gutenberg Bible around 1455, Gutenberg utilized his metalworking skills to develop a process of casting individual letters that could be arranged repeatedly into any alphabetic text. When combined with paper, his new oil-based typographic ink, and a printing press, Gutenberg's process succeeded in merging several distinct technologies, making possible the production of multiple identical copies of a text. Although the changes that printing brought developed gradually during the succeeding centuries, the use of printing has had major effects on almost every aspect of human endeavor—including communications and literacy, economic patterns of investment, production, and marketing, and a wide range of intellectual ideas.

The Gutenberg Bible is an outstanding symbol of his invention. The copies that are still extant (forty-eight out of an original printing of about 180) demonstrate the high level of technical and aesthetic perfection that this 1,282-page book attained. The regularity of the lines, the justification of the margins, the quality of the ink, and especially the beautiful design of the type show how Gutenberg raised the printing process beyond a technological invention to an art.

Bibliography

Febvre, Lucien, and Henri-Jean Martin. Translated by David Gerard. *The Coming of the Book: The Impact of Printing, 1450-1800*. London: NLB, 1976. Discusses Gutenberg's role in the invention of printing in the context of the transition from manuscripts to printed books. Also examines the impact of printing on varied aspects of book production and the book trade in early modern Europe.

Fuhrmann, Otto W. *Gutenberg and the Strasbourg Documents of 1439: An Interpretation*. New York: Press of the Woolly Whale, 1940. Gives a transcription of the original German text of the lawsuit against Gutenberg in Strasbourg in 1439 that is important for reconstructing Gutenberg's early printing efforts. The book provides translations in modern English, German, and French, as well as a discussion of the meaning of the Strasbourg suit.

Goff, Frederick R. *The Permanence of Johann Gutenberg*. Austin: University of Texas at Austin, Humanities Research Center, 1969. Includes an essay on Gutenberg's invention and evidence for what he printed. Also discusses the significance of Gutenberg's invention.

Ing, Janet. "Searching for Gutenberg in the 1980s." *Fine Print* 12 (1986): 212-215. This article summarizes the technical bibliographical studies concerning Gutenberg's printing during the twentieth century. Its focus is on scientific methods of analysis of paper and ink and typographical studies done in the 1970's and 1980's. References are included.

Kapr, Albert. *Johann Gutenberg: The Man and His Invention*. Aldershot and Brookfield, Vt.: Scolar Press, 1996. Kapr has written a scholarly biography, bringing together widely dispersed literature to produce a revealing account of Gutenberg the individual. Acting as historical detective, Kapr has based his portrait on original documents and references, the majority of which are reproduced. He considers the different aspects of Gutenberg's life, personality, and achievements within a wide cultural and historical context.

Karwatka, Dennis. "Johann Gutenberg." *Tech Directions* 57 (September, 1997): 14. This article includes a brief history of Gutenberg and a review of the technological methods he used.

Lehmann-Haupt, Helmut. *Gutenberg and the Master of the Playing Cards*. New Haven, Conn.: Yale University Press, 1966. This book suggests that Gutenberg may have been involved with developing techniques for printed reproduction of designs for book decoration and illustration necessary to produce, in printed form, the effect of finely illuminated manuscripts.

McMurtrie, Douglas C. *The Gutenberg Documents*. New York: Oxford University Press, 1941. Contains all the known documents associated with Gutenberg in English translation. Includes notes.

Needham, Paul. "Johann Gutenberg and the Catholicon Press." *Papers of the Bibliographical Society of America* 76 (1982): 395-456. Discusses bibliographical problems relating particularly to evidence from paper and typography in works from the *Catholicon* press. Needham's conclusions summarize arguments for Gutenberg's role in printing material in the *Catholicon* press group.

Painter, George D. "Gutenberg and the B36 Group: A Re-Consideration." In *Essays in Honor of Victor Scholderer*, edited by Dennis F. Rhodes. Mainz: Karl Pressler, 1970. This article discusses the examples of printing in the B36 group and argues that Gutenberg printed these pieces.

Scholderer, Victor. *Johann Gutenberg: The Inventor of Printing*. 2d ed. London: Trustees of the British Museum, 1970. The most complete biography of Gutenberg in English. It covers the various types of evidence for documenting Gutenberg's life and activity as the inventor of printing. Contains bibliographical references and good illustrations.

Karen Gould

HENRY IV

Born: December 14, 1553; castle of Pau, Basses Pyrenees

Died: May 14, 1610; Paris, France

Areas of Achievement: Monarchy, government, and politics

Contribution: Henry IV brought peace and national prestige to France within the structure of powerful monarchy after protracted strife, which had included eight civil wars. He settled the long-standing Catholic-Protestant conflict by embracing Catholicism while granting broad toleration to the French Reformed church. He is the most noteworthy of early modern rulers who made religious liberty the law of the state.

Early Life

Henry of Navarre, first of the Bourbon line, was born in the castle of Pau in the Pyrenees Mountains to Antoine de Bourbon, Duke of Vendôme, and Jeanne d'Albret, Queen of Navarre. He was a direct descendant of Louis IX, one of France's most illustrious rules. Although he was baptized a Catholic, Henry received instruction in the Calvinist (Reformed) faith at his mother's direction, and he eventually joined the French Protestants, then known as Huguenots. In 1568, his mother placed Henry in the service of Admiral Gaspard de Coligny, the leader of the Protestant cause. As a soldier in the Huguenot army, he fought bravely and acquired a reputation as a skillful military leader. When Jeanne d'Albret died in 1572, Henry succeeded her as monarch of Navarre. That same year, he married Margaret of Valois, sister of King Charles IX of France.

Life's Work

By the time Henry joined Coligny in 1568, France had been wracked by civil war for more than eight years. The death of Henry II in 1559 initiated a power struggle in which political and religious considerations were intertwined. Francis II and Henry II had tried to crush the Protestants, but the Reformed faith had made impressive gains nevertheless, especially among the bourgeoisie and the aristocracy. Calvinism gained adherents who could exert far greater influence than their numbers would seem to indicate.

Because the sons of Henry II were feeble rulers, nobles asserted their authority and rival factions competed for power. Antoine de Bourbon and Louis I de Condé, both princes of the blood, allied with Coligny to promote the Protestant cause. The family of Guise, with Duke Francis at the head, led the Catholic faction. When Francis II succeeded to the throne as a minor in 1559, the Guises obtained control of the government. After they executed some of their opponents, Protestants responded with militant resistance. Francis II died after one year on the throne, and Charles IX became king with his mother, Catherine de Médicis, as regent. She then became the pivotal figure in French politics for the next quarter century. Catherine had no deep religious convictions, so she tried to manipulate both sides and to create a moderate party loyal to the Crown. In 1562, however, the Guises seized power and forced the regent to resume persecuting the Protestants. France became the scene of all-out civil war.

The marriage of Henry of Navarre to Margaret of Valois occurred in 1572, as Catherine de Médicis tried to placate the Huguenots by marrying her daughter to one of their most popular leaders. The nuptial festivities, however, became the occasion for the Saint Bartholomew's Eve Massacre, in which Coligny and some other Protestants were murdered. Although the assassins may have intended to kill only a few Huguenot leaders, word of the slayings soon led to the slaughter of thousands of Protestants across France. The civil war resumed with renewed fury.

The sickly Henry III became king in 1574, and soon a militant Catholic faction, now led by Duke Henry of Guise, organized the Catholic League without royal approval. The civil strife then became the War of Three Henrys, as Henry III, Henry of Guise, and Henry of Navarre fought for control of the kingdom. The eventual assassination of the king and the duke left the Protestant Henry of Navarre the legal heir to the throne. He declared himself King of France in 1589. Civil war continued, however, until the last remnants of the Catholic League abandoned resistance in 1596. The concurrent war with Spain did not end until 1598.

Although Henry IV had become king legally, he knew that his throne would never be secure so long as he remained a Protestant. His Huguenot supporters, only 10 percent of the population, were unable to cement their leader's authority. Moderate Catholics urged the king to convert, but Henry delayed because he wanted his enemies to recognize his kingship first. When he became convinced that that would not happen, he announced his decision to become a Catholic. An old but probably apocryphal account relates that he justified changing religions with the remark "Paris is well worth a Mass." Henry's embrace of Catholicism shows clearly that this king was a *politique*, that is, one without strong religious beliefs who follows the course of action he deems politically advantageous. He had done this before, when he had joined the Catholic Church to marry Margaret of Valois, only to return to the Reformed faith in 1576.

In order to obtain papal approval for his succession, Henry had to seek absolution for his Protestant heresies, something the Vatican was in no hurry to grant. Pope Sixtus V had tried to block his path to the French throne and had declared him deposed as King of Navarre. The reigning pontiff, Clement VIII, chose to defer action on the royal request, even though French prelates had hailed the king's return to the Church.

Henry chose Jacques Davy Duperron as his emissary to Rome. Duperron, who had once been a Huguenot and had adopted Catholicism after reading Thomas Aquinas' *Summa theologica* (1266-1273), supervised the religious instruction of the royal convert. Since Duperron was a learned apologist for Catholicism, he was an effective representative to the pope. As a reward for his services, the king made Duperron a royal chaplain and a councillor of state, and, in 1596, Bishop of Evreux. In order to convince the pope of his sincerity, Henry promised to rebuild monasteries destroyed in the civil wars, and he agreed to support the decrees of the Council of Trent (1563), the Counter-Reformation program to combat Protestantism. At the least, this meant that the king would maintain the Catholic religion in all areas of France that had supported the Catholic League. He promised similarly to prohibit Protestant worship in Paris, Lyons, Rouen, and other cities.

Moderate Protestants accepted Henry's conversion and his concessions to Rome as necessary for the peace and security of France. Militant Huguenots, however, protested. The king had to deal with them cautiously to prevent them from deserting him. It is a tribute to Henry's diplomacy that he was able to pay the price demanded by the pope without alienating his Protestant supporters completely. By 1598, Henry was convinced that his rule was secure, so he took a bold step to reassure the Huguenots of his goodwill. The king proclaimed the Edict of Nantes, a landmark enactment in the history of religious freedom.

The Edict of Nantes expressed the king's wish for the eventual reunion of all Christians, but its provisions show that Henry knew that that would not occur. This law ratified concessions granted to Protestants earlier, and it recognized full freedom of belief and the right to public worship in two hundred towns and in many castles of Protestant lords. Calvinists could worship in private elsewhere, and they would be eligible for most public offices. The king also granted subsidies for a number of Protestant schools and colleges, and the edict created special sections of the *parlements* (royal courts) to try cases in which Protestant interests were involved. The king allowed the Huguenots to fortify about two hundred towns under their control. The policy of toleration satisfied the Protestants, and it contributed immediately to the achievement of national union. Its provisions, however, created almost a state-within-the-state, a condition which was to cause disruption at a later time, when subsequent monarchs tried to impose their authority upon those towns.

Catholic reaction to the Edict of Nantes was predictably hostile. Pope Clement VIII denounced it, and some *parlements* tried to obstruct publication of the royal decree. Militant opponents of toleration tried to reactivate the Catholic League, and the government discovered several plots to assassinate the king. Most Frenchmen, nevertheless, were too weary of strife to support another civil war, and news about the plots against the king caused an upsurge of support for his policy. His opponents could not find a single magnetic leader. Under royal pressure the Parlement of Paris registered the edict, and the other courts followed suit. Extensive, though not complete, religious freedom became the policy of Western Europe's largest state.

Whatever satisfaction Henry derived from the success of his policy toward religion, it could not obscure the serious problems which confronted him as king. Foreign and domestic wars had brought France to a state of impoverishment approaching bankruptcy. The kingdom was almost impotent in foreign affairs. Henry faced the mammoth task of rebuilding with determination. Although he was an intelligent and energetic ruler, Henry was not a skilled administrator. He entrusted that responsibility to the Duke of Sully, a Protestant and a longtime friend. Under Sully's competent direction, the government eliminated much corruption and inefficiency, reformed taxation, and gained solvency. Financial success made it possible to improve the army and to initiate public works for building canals, roads, and harbors to promote economic growth. The government sponsored the expansion of arable lands by draining swamps, and it developed new industries, including the production of silk. Henry founded the French colonial empire by sending the first French explorers and settlers to Canada.

In foreign affairs, Henry sought to protect France from the encircling power of the Habsburgs of Austria and Spain. Because he knew that France was vulnerable to Habsburg attack, he allied with Protestant states in Germany and with the Netherlands. Just when he was ready to strike at his enemies, however, an assassin struck him. He died on May 14, 1610, at the hand of François Ravaillac. The assailant seems to have acted on his own to slay a Catholic monarch who had decided to war against the Catholic Habsburgs, which would have aided the Protestant cause internationally. Although his enemies rejoiced at the death of Henry, the French people mourned the passing of a great, humane king.

Summary

Henry IV was a popular ruler because he truly cared for the welfare of his subjects. Most Frenchmen accepted his absolutism as the only alternative to the anarchy which had prevailed for so long. His pragmatic policies brought peace and prosperity with order.

Although Henry was a hero to the Huguenots, despite his defection to Catholicism his private life must have offended their stern Calvinist moral sensibilities. In 1599, he obtained papal dissolution of his marriage to Margaret of Valois and quickly took Marie de Médicis as his next wife. He was not faithful to either wife but had several mistresses and illegitimate children. He was not above practicing ecclesiastical corruption, as when he made one of his bastards Bishop of Metz at age six. Henry often coerced *parlements* and subjected provincial and local officials to forceful supervision. He controlled the nobles effectively and left his son Louis XIII a kingdom at peace, one where royal authority was supreme and prosperity was in progress.

Bibliography

Daumgartner, Frederic. "The Catholic Opposition to the Edict of Nantes." *Bibliothèque d'Humanisme et Renaissance* 40 (1970): 525-537. This valuable study relates how Henry shrewdly overcame the criticisms of his opponents. A work of thorough research that propounds a convincing argument. The notes are rich in research data.

Dickerman, Edmund H. "The Conversion of Henry IV." *The Catholic Historical Review* 68 (1977): 1-13. While others have concluded on the basis of appearances and superficial research that the king was a *politique*, Dickerman has made a penetrating examination of the sources to show how and why Henry regarded religion pragmatically.

Gray, Janet Glenn. *The French Huguenots: The Anatomy of Courage*. Grand Rapids, Mich.: Baker Book House, 1981. This decidedly partisan survey of the religious and political climate in France is vivid in descriptions and contains many perceptive interpretations. Places Henry's career in the context of the French and European struggles for religious liberty.

Grummitt, David. "The Financial Administration of Calais During the Reign of Henry IV, 1399-1413." *English Historical Review* 113 (April, 1998): 277. The author presents the major features of government policy regarding the English government's financing of Calais, France, in the reign of Henry IV. Grummitt details the way in which effective financing was accomplished and developed during the reign of Richard II.

Leathes, Stanley. "Henry IV of France." In *The Cambridge Modern History*, edited by A. W. Ward et al., vol. 3. Cambridge: Cambridge University Press, and New York: Macmillan, 1904. This substantial essay, despite its age, is indispensable to any serious study of the subject. An excellent source with which to begin one's inquiry.

Russell, Lord of Liverpool. *Henry of Navarre*. London: Hale, 1969; New York: Praeger, 1970. For the average reader, this is probably the most enjoyable biography of the subject. Portrays the king as a humane ruler, licentious in life and a *politique* in religion. The author is an exceptionally talented writer.

Sutherland, N. M. *The Huguenot Struggle for Recognition*. New Haven, Conn.: Yale University Press, 1980. This thorough study of the Huguenot movement and the issues which it raised for church and state in France is a model of research and writing by a truly erudite scholar. Not for beginners.

Walker, Anita M. "Mind of an Assassin: Ravaillac and the Murder of Henry IV of France." *Canadian Journal of History* 30 (August, 1995): 201. The article examines the motives behind Francois Ravaillac's murder of Henry IV. Walker includes details of the murder and Ravaillac's interrogation, a psychological profile of the assassin, and views on Henry IV and the period's religious environment.

Willert, P. F. *Henry of Navarre and the Huguenots in France*. New York: Putnam, 1893; London: Putnam, 1924. Although more recent treatments have superseded this one and brought some of the author's judgments into question, this work remains a useful and rather full account which features lucid style and interesting coverage.

James Edward McGoldrick

HENRY V

Born: September 16, 1387; Monmouth Castle, England
Died: August 31, 1422; Bois de Vincennes, France
Area of Achievement: Government
Contribution: Henry V gave England justice and stability at home, while his military and political genius enabled him to proceed in the conquest of France and claim to its crown. He left England a strong power in European affairs.

Early Life

The man who would become Henry V, King of England and Regent of France, was born on September 16, 1387, at Monmouth Castle in western England (this date of birth is sometimes given as August 9). He is familiar to modern readers and audiences as the Prince Hal of William Shakespeare's plays, but his contemporaries knew him in his youth as Henry of Monmouth. His father, Henry, Duke of Lancaster, was similarly known from his birthplace as Henry Bolingbroke and was the cousin of the reigning monarch, Richard II.

Henry was well educated; the records for the Duchy of Lancaster show early payments for his books, a harp, and a sword. Unverified tradition says that he was educated at Oxford. Whatever his background, during his reign he showed considerable ability in a variety of fields, from the military (he was an outstanding general) to the musical (he composed several pieces of church music).

In 1389, Richard II exiled Henry Bolingbroke, whose sons were taken into the court, partly as kinsmen, partly as hostages. Richard displayed real affection for the younger Henry, taking him in May, 1399, on an expedition to Ireland, where the king himself knighted the youth. In August of that year, however, Bolingbroke returned to England in revolt; Richard rebuked his young relative, but Henry seems to have had no forewarning of his father's actions.

Bolingbroke was quickly able to depose Richard, largely because the king's erratic and willful actions had seriously undermined his support among the nobility. In October, Henry IV was crowned in London; his son participated in the ceremony and two days later was created Earl of Chester, Duke of Cornwall, and Prince of Wales. He was soon after given the title of Duke of Aquitaine, the English possession on the Continent, and Duke of Lancaster, his father's former title.

From 1400 until 1408, Henry was occupied in subduing rebellion in his princedom of Wales. First, as figurehead of a council of nobles, and later on his own, he planned and led raids and skirmishes against the Welsh. In 1403, this struggle was interrupted by the conspiracy of the powerful Percy family of northern England. Henry IV and his son combined their forces to defeat the Percys at the Battle of Berwick (July 21, 1403), during which the prince was wounded in the face but continued in the fight.

By 1408 the Welsh had been hammered into submission, and Henry was more active in London and in the king's council. In 1409, he was made Warden of the Cinque Ports and Constable of Dover, both important military posts. He was also taking a larger part in the government, partly because of Henry IV's steadily weakening condition, caused by an unknown but disfiguring disease. It is likely that by 1410 the prince was ruling in his father's name, aided by his relative Thomas Beaufort, the new chancellor. The Beauforts were to be valuable servants during Henry V's reign. In 1410, Henry was also given the vital post of Captain of Calais, England's stronghold in France.

An attempt to have the king abdicate in favor of his son led to the removal of Beaufort as chancellor and the temporary withdrawal of Henry from the court and council, but on March 20, 1413, Henry IV died and his son, at age twenty-six, became King of England.

There are several contemporary descriptions and portraits of Henry V, and they generally agree that he struck an appropriately kingly figure. He was above medium height, with a slender, athletic body, and was known as an exceptionally swift runner. His hair was smooth, brown, and thick; he had a cleft chin and small ears. The feature most noted by Henry's subjects was his eyes, which were said to be those of a dove in peace but a lion's when he was angered.

Life's Work

Henry V was crowned on April 9, 1413 (Passion Sunday), in an unusual spring snowstorm. Equally unusual, and commented upon by his contemporaries, was the marked change in his character, which immediately became more somber and regal. The total reversal is heightened, however, in Shakespeare's *Henry V* (1598-1599), for dramatic empha-

sis; Henry's youth had been spent largely in camp and council, rather than in taverns and the streets.

One of the complaints voiced in Henry's first parliament, in 1413, was the weakness of royal power during his father's last years. The son moved decisively to counter this and appointed such skilled and experienced officers as his kinsman and new chancellor, Henry Beaufort. Throughout his reign, Henry was well served by his officers and officials.

In December, 1413, Henry had the remains of Richard II, the monarch deposed and perhaps ordered killed by his father, reburied with royal pomp at Westminster. This action was an indication both of Henry's affections for the man and of his allegiance to the ideal of kingship as a station partially sacramental in nature.

Henry was noted for his orthodoxy and concern for the unity of the Church, and he was greatly concerned with the growing Lollard movement in England, which threatened both ecclesiastical and social stability. The Lollards, a form of early protestants, were led by Sir John Oldcastle, who was arrested in September, 1413, and interrogated by numerous officials, including the king himself. Oldcastle escaped and early the next year devised a plot to seize the king and his brothers. Acting with his customary decisiveness, Henry surprised the rebels as they gathered at St. Giles' Field outside London, and crushed the revolt. Sir John escaped again but was later captured and executed in 1418 while Henry was campaigning in France.

France was the dominant theme of Henry's reign. English kings had held territory in France, and Henry was determined to reconquer that which had been lost; he also sought the crown of France itself. In the Parliament of 1414, Henry's claims were asserted, and support was given for a military expedition.

The English asserted title to the provinces of Normandy, Touraine, Anjou, Maine, and Ponthieu, as well as border territories ceded to them by previous treaties. Henry also desired a marriage with Catherine, daughter of the French King Charles VI, and a large dowry for the bride. The demands were considerable, but they were made at an appropriate moment.

Charles VI was a weak monarch, frequently insane, and control of France was split between the Dauphin and his supporters, the Armagnacs, and John, Duke of Burgundy. Although powerful, France was largely incapable of using that power. By contrast, Henry V brought to the struggle both unshakable personal conviction and national unity.

The first of Henry's three expeditions to France began on August 11, 1415, when he sailed with twenty-five hundred men-at-arms and eight thousand archers from Portsmouth. After a two-month siege, the port of Harfleur capitulated. Rather than return by sea to England, Henry marched overland toward Calais in a striking demonstration of claim to the disputed territory. The march also put his small army in great danger.

On October 25, 1415, near the castle of Agincourt, and only two days' march from the safety of Calais, Henry and his now seven thousand men found their way blocked by at least fifty thousand French troops. The English line drew up between two forests, with their front protected by pointed stakes driven into the ground. When the heavily armored French knights attacked across a muddy field, the English longbowmen devastated their ranks. Continued French assaults only increased the disaster, and an English counterattack finished the French. Henry arrived in England with more than two thousand prisoners from the French nobility, and the battle won on St. Crispan's Day became the centerpiece of Shakespeare's *Henry V* and an enduring part of England's national mythology.

The new importance of Henry and England was signaled in 1416 by the visit of Sigismund, the Holy Roman Emperor. The emperor and Henry concluded a treaty which ended the schism in the Church between rival popes by the election of a new pontiff, Martin V, and promised a joint crusade in the future. Henry's long-range goal was to lead a united Europe in reconquest of the Holy Land.

As part of that plan he pressed his claim to the French Crown. In the fall of 1416, he carefully prepared for his second expedition, and his extensive shipbuilding efforts can justly qualify him as the founder of the Royal Navy.

In July, 1417, Henry sailed with fifty thousand troops. He landed in Normandy, cut off the province's communications with the rest of France, and secured a base of operations. This was done through a series of sieges conducted by Henry and his lieutenants. By the end of July, Henry had invested the strategic town of Rouen, which held out until January of 1419 but which was forced to surrender because of famine and lack of support. Significantly, the French, split between Armagnac and Burgundian factions, were unable to relieve the town.

Henry skillfully exploited this internecine feud in his negotiations, which brought success in May, 1420, with the Treaty of Troyes. This agreement between Henry, Philip of Burgundy (his father, John, having been killed), and Charles VI excluded the Dauphin from succession, recognized Henry as the heir to the Crown after Charles's death, and made him regent during the king's life. It also confirmed Burgundy in alliance against the dauphin and granted Catherine to Henry in marriage. The marriage was celebrated on June 2, 1420 (Trinity Sunday); a son, Henry, was born on December 6, 1421.

After the treaty, Henry entered Paris and established his officers there. By the end of the year, the royal couple had sailed to England, where Catherine was crowned at Westminster on February 24, 1421. A triumphal royal progress through England was cut short in April with the news of the defeat and death of Henry's brother, the Duke of Clarence, in France. On June 10, Henry left England on his third, and final, expedition.

Once in France, Henry quickly reversed the military situation in favor of the English. On October 6, he invested the town of Meaux; the siege lasted until May, 1422, and during the long winter months, in the crowded, unsanitary conditions of the camp, Henry contracted the dysentery that would kill him.

During the spring and summer, Henry grew steadily weaker, and in August he was carried to Vincennes, his health rapidly failing. Realizing his state, he made arrangements for the education of his son, for the government of England and France, and for the continuation of his policies. He died early in the morning of August 31, 1422, at the age of thirty-five. There was an elaborate funeral procession which culminated on November 11 with his burial at the Chapel of Edward the Confessor at Westminster Abbey. On his splendid tomb his effigy lay, carved in oak with a cover of silver gilt and a head of solid silver. The head was stolen in 1545 but replaced by a bronze one in 1972. After many centuries, Henry V remains one of England's most favored kings.

Summary

Henry V was judged by his contemporaries to be an outstanding, even exemplary, monarch. According to the standards of the time, he indeed was, since he brought his realm peace and justice at home and legitimate martial glory abroad.

Within England, Henry V's reign was marked by tranquillity and order. Failure to ensure such order was probably the worst fault attributable to a late medieval monarch. Such failure had led to the fall of Richard II and had darkened the last years of Henry's father. Largely because of his personal example and wise selection of deputies, Henry V provided his kingdom with the peace it desired.

Henry was noted for his sense of justice, which at times seemed to border on the inflexible. In this, however, as in his steadfast devotion to the Catholic Church, Henry was motivated by the ideal standards which he believed should guide a monarch. In any event, his consistent adherence to these standards helped assure a quiet realm in England, even though he was on campaign for almost half of his nine-year reign.

Henry's campaigns in France form the keystone to Henry V's fame during his life and his enduring memory after his death. His wars were supported by his countrymen for many reasons, but chief among them were Henry's careful presentation of his efforts as a legitimate response to French provocations and his continued victories. Judged as a military monarch, Henry was outstanding, not only for the famous victory at Agincourt but particularly for his careful and thorough planning of his expeditions and his acute sense of posibilities and appropriate, effective strategy. He shared the hardships of campaigns with his troops, and his combination of talent and leadership made him the outstanding warrior of his day.

That day was short, but while he lived, Henry accomplished two of his goals. He had gained, although not consolidated, his claims to French territory and was assured the French Crown at the death of Charles VI. By an irony of history, the victorious, younger king died before the insane, older one, and Henry V never had the opportunity to rule both England and France, or to lead Europe on a new crusade. Still, while what might have been remains unknown, it is clear that the young King Henry V left England a stronger nation for his reign, and a name that yet lives.

Bibliography

Hutchison, Harold. *Henry V: A Biography.* London: Eyre and Spottiswoode, and New York: John Day, 1967. A leisurely, discursive biography of Henry V and his times, with admirable treatment of the background and milieu of the early fifteenth century. A good introduction to readers unfamiliar with the characters or characteristics of the late Middle Ages.

Jacob, E. F. *Henry V and the Invasion of France.* London: English Universities Press, 1947; New York: Macmillan, 1950. A thorough, yet readable, study of Henry's campaigns. Since his conquest of France is the most important aspect of his kingship, this comprehensive overview is extremely valuable for understanding Henry's accomplishments.

Keegan, John. *The Face of Battle.* London: Cape, and New York: Viking Press, 1976. This is a remarkable book which explores and explains the nature of warfare from the participant's point of view. The section on Agincourt is a stunning recreation of medieval combat and gives the reader a real understanding of what must have happened and why. Highly recommended.

Labarge, Margaret Wade. *Henry V: The Cautious Conqueror.* London: Secker and Warburg, and New York: Stein and Day, 1975. A brisk, quickly moving account of the life and actions of the king; introductory students of the period may find that the book assumes at least some familiarity with the actors of the time.

McFarlane, Kenneth B. *Lancastrian Kings and Lollard Knights.* Oxford: Clarendon Press, 1972. Divided into two sections, the first primarily about Henry IV, the second about the Lollard movement in fourteenth century England. There is, however, a good general essay titled "Henry V: A Personal Portrait," which is an excellent place for the beginning student to start. McFarlane has high praise for Henry V: "Take him all around and he was, I think, the greatest man that ever ruled England."

Powell, Edward. *Kingship, Law and Society: Criminal Justice in the Reign of Henry V.* Oxford: Clarendon Press, and New York: Oxford University Press, 1989. This work includes a constitutional history of fourteenth and fifteenth century England and outlines the relevant concepts of law, justice, and kingship. The structure of the legal system is discussed, including the workings of the courts, settlement of disputes, and enforcement of criminal justice.

Wylie, James H. *The Reign of Henry the Fifth.* 3 vols. Cambridge: Cambridge University Press, 1914-1929; New York: Greenwood Press, 1968. Still the definitive study of Henry V's kingship, this work goes into great detail on every aspect of the reign; invaluable for students who want to concentrate on specific moments of Henry's career.

Michael Witkoski

HENRY VI

Born: December 6, 1421; Windsor, Berkshire, England

Died: May 21, 1471; London, England

Areas of Achievement: Government and politics

Contribution: As the realm recoiled from the confusion of a Continental conflict and a civil war, Henry VI, the third and last Lancastrian king of England, abrogated his role as an effective monarch and became a pawn of his relatives and great nobles.

Early Life

Born on December 6, 1421, at Windsor, and the only child of England's Henry V and Catherine of France, Henry of Windsor found himself to be a fated figure in the events of the Hundred Years' War between England and France and the subsequent Wars of the Roses, which pitted England's rival noble factions, the Lancastrians and Yorkists, against each other. After the death of Henry V on August 31, 1422, he ascended the throne as Henry VI, the third Lancastrian monarch of England. When his maternal grandfather, Charles VI, died a few weeks later, Henry was also acclaimed King of France. Henry's lifelong naïveté colored his almost forty-year rule, and his reign marked the pinnacle of royal impotence, giving credence to the well-known text from Ecclesiastes, "Woe to thee, O land, when the king is a child."

Head of a dual monarchy before his first birthday, Henry VI ruled for sixteen years under the regency of his father's brothers. John, Duke of Bedford, an efficient administrator and capable soldier, oversaw France; the less competent Humphrey, Duke of Gloucester, served as regent in England. A fierce rivalry erupted between Gloucester and the chancellor, Henry Beaufort, Bishop of Winchester and the king's great-uncle. The two intrigued against each other, and their bickering disrupted the machinery of government and weakened the war effort abroad. Despite their differences, the uncles maintained the fiction of personal government, but the influence of an infant sovereign was negligible. At the age of two, Henry gave permission for his own chastisement, assuring his staff he would bear no grudges. The king's boyhood appearances, however, remained few and were confined to ceremonial acts, such as the opening of Parliament, his coronation at Westminster Abbey in 1429, and the French crowning in 1431. For the most part, he lived in comparative seclusion in the Thames Valley.

Although he hunted with falcon and hawk and had his own suits of armor, the bilingual young king preferred to spend his time reading religious tomes and the historical writings of English priests. A meek and devout boy whose piety bordered upon smugness, Henry grew into a well-meaning but incapable recluse, better suited for the monastery than for the monarchy. His greatest oaths consisted of "forsooth and forsooth" and an occasional "St. Jehan grant mercis," and nothing, not even stampeding horses and collapsed tents, roused him to profanity. Benevolent to the point of lunacy and oblivious to the sway of politics about him, the tall, studious Henry VI remained throughout his life the perfect pawn in the hands of his relatives and great nobles.

Life's Work

In the autumn of 1437, just before his sixteenth birthday, Henry VI ended his minority and began to issue warrants under his own seal. He traveled about the kingdom and involved himself in endowing a grammar school at Eton, establishing King's College at Cambridge, and authorizing a library for Salisbury Cathedral. The demands of the royal office rankled, and he soon allowed the nobles to resume the direction of affairs of state. As the power of the English monarchy declined, the prosecution of the war against France became a pivotal issue in politics. Beaufort, as well as his nephew Edmund Beaufort, Duke of Somerset, and their ally William de la Pole, Earl (later Duke) of Suffolk, favored peace. Though Bedford had died in 1435, Gloucester and Richard, Duke of York, next in line for the throne, wished to continue the war.

Ignoring Gloucester, Henry VI chose to end the conflict, which had gone badly after the 1429 French victory at Orléans, led by Joan of Arc. Since Beaufort was old and Somerset incompetent, Henry depended upon Suffolk, whom he showered with offices and lands. Suffolk governed the court and in 1445 won a two-year truce in the war by arranging the marriage of Henry VI to Charles VII's niece, Margaret of Anjou. An assertive, capable beauty, the new queen assumed the necessary role of authority and persuaded her gentle husband to surrender Maine to the French and to reduce the English garrisons in Normandy. Gloucester and Beaufort both died in 1447, leaving Suffolk and

Margaret in power and the Duke of York biding his time. Losses in Normandy in 1449 and 1450 soon made Suffolk unpopular, and the House of Commons sought his impeachment. Six months later, Jack Cade led a force of thirty thousand discontented Kentsmen to London, yet their rout did not end the country's unrest.

Royal authority continued to decline throughout the 1450's. The year 1453 proved particularly traumatic. In July, England experienced her final military humiliation in the Hundred Years' War with the loss of all Continental territory except the city of Calais; in August, Henry suffered a total mental and physical collapse. In the face of disaster, Parliament named the Duke of York Lord Protector, but Yorkist control lasted only as long as the king's madness. When Henry regained his senses in December, 1454, Margaret, who had given birth to a son two months earlier, and her Lancastrian associates recovered their influence over royal administration. Confronted with an heir to the throne and a forceful queen, York, aided by his cousin Richard Neville, Earl of Warwick, took action and the struggle for power erupted onto the battlefield.

At St. Albans in May, 1455, a Yorkist army defeated the Lancastrians in a battle that traditionally marks the beginning of the Wars of the Roses. Somerset died in the conflict, the king was wounded by an arrow in the neck, and York seized the opportunity to retake the protectorship as Henry suffered a second mental collapse. York did not hold power long, for the king regained a semblance of sanity in 1456 and the queen regained control at court. The next four years marked a period of Royalist reaction. Because of political tension in the countryside and growing tumult in London, the royal court resided primarily in the Midlands. Henry now became a pathetic shadow of a king, but he did strive intermittently for reconciliation with his opponents, offering them pardons. Morbidly preoccupied with death, Henry spent several months planning his vault and having workmen mark his exact measurements on the floor of Westminster Abbey. The direction of the affairs of state lay with the masterful Margaret, who prepared for war with the Yorkists.

In 1460, York, disgusted by the puppet king, claimed the throne as his birthright—he was descended from Edward III's third son, while Henry's claim came from kinship with the fourth son. The civil conflict now began in earnest, with the fortunes of war fluctuating wildly. The Yorkists triumphed over the Lancastrians in July; Henry was taken prisoner and forced to acknowledge Richard to the exclusion of his young son. In December, the Lancastrians succeeded in a battle in which York met his death. In February, 1461, the Lancastrians won again, gaining for Henry his freedom, but in March, Warwick and the new Duke of York, Edward, decisively defeated the Lancastrians in a savage seven-hour battle during a blinding snowstorm. The Lancastrians never recovered from this defeat, and Warwick the "Kingmaker" successfully placed the Duke of York on the throne as Edward IV. Henry VI spent the next three years in exile in Scotland; his movements during this period hardly reveal him to be a sane individual. He returned to take part in an abortive rising in 1464 but a year later was captured and taken as a prisoner to the Tower of London, where he remained until 1470.

As the Lancastrian menace lessened and peace seemed permanent, the friendship between Edward and Warwick paled. When Edward chose his own bride, ignoring his chief adviser's plans for a French marriage, Warwick joined the Lancastrian cause and aided Margaret in an attack upon his former ally.

Edward fled to the Continent. On October 3, 1470, Henry VI, a shuffling imbecile, left the Tower to be proclaimed monarch again by the Kingmaker. Recaptured by Edward in April, 1471, Henry accompanied his Yorkist foe to Barnet, where the Lancastrians again tasted defeat and Warwick died. Another failure at Tewkesbury brought about the death of the Prince of Wales, the capture of the queen, and the end of the Lancastrian cause. Henry VI died in the Tower, probably at the hands of an assassin, on May 21, 1471. His body was placed in an obscure grave in Chertsey Abbey and then reinterred at St. George Chapel, Windsor, in 1484.

Summary

The reign of Henry VI, England's last Lancastrian monarch, has a number of dramatic ironies. Henry VI has the distinction of being the youngest ruler to ascend the English throne. He was also the only English ruler to be acknowledged by the French as the legitimate King of France and to receive coronation at Notre Dame Cathedral in Paris. Because he was less than a year old at the time of his succession to two thrones, there was no time in Henry's memory when he was not a monarch, and he knew no effective role models for the task of governing. He also assumed his majority earlier than any of his predecessors and successors, and his thirty-nine-year reign provided ample opportunity for flaws to magnify themselves. Furthermore, Henry's rule coincided with, and contributed to, a debilitating civil war which cost him his throne. In the dynastic revolution which followed, he was briefly restored, thereby becoming the only British king to have two separate reigns.

Henry was a well-intentioned man with some laudable aspirations for improving relations with France, fostering educational advantages, and rewarding friends and servants. As intelligent and as thoroughly schooled as his contemporaries, he never lost his youthful reliance upon others to make decisions for him. He was also far too compassionate toward lawbreakers and lacked the ability to sense the implications of their activities. Henry VI's mental breakdown in 1453-1454, followed by his recovery and a subsequent relapse in 1455, vitiated any further possibility of effective leadership. An almost total dependence upon others marked the last fifteen years of his life. Henry VI died a demented, pathetic figure who was denied even his fondest dream, burial at Westminster Abbey. Later efforts to canonize him provided posthumous praise. In death, Henry VI realized the potential he never achieved in life.

Bibliography

Bagley, John J. *Margaret of Anjou, Queen of England.* London: Herbert Jenkins, 1948. Dated, biased biography, but still the only reasonable account of the formidable queen who shed her French prejudices and became a purposeful Lancastrian determined to preserve the English crown for her son.

Chrimes, Stanley Bertram. *Lancastrians, Yorkists, and Henry VII.* London: Macmillan, and New York: St. Martin's Press, 1964. General survey of the political and dynastic history of fifteenth century England with emphasis upon constitutional issues. Denies that there was true "war" in the Wars of the Roses and insists that the conflict was a struggle for power based upon dynastic rivalries. Makes an excellent supplement to William Shakespeare's historical plays.

Gillingham, John. *The Wars of the Roses: Peace and Conflict in Fifteenth Century England.* London: Weidenfeld and Nicolson, and Baton Rouge: Louisiana State University Press, 1981. Maintains that the Wars of the Roses were, in reality, three separate wars and that the first one (which the author dates from the 1450's to 1464) was caused by Henry VI's shortcomings and his inability to hold France or govern England. Suggests that Henry's mental collapses may have been a case of catatonic schizophrenia.

Griffiths, Ralph A. *The Reign of King Henry VI: The Exercise of Royal Authority, 1421-1461.* London: Benn, and Berkeley: University of California Press, 1981. The definitive study of Henry VI and the entire spectrum of political life during his reign. Discusses relations among political groups, financial concerns, administration of justice, and foreign affairs. Portrays the last Lancastrian king as a well-meaning incompetent, and questions if, after the mental collapse of 1454-1455, Henry VI ever again had the capacity to carry out his official responsibilities. A major contribution to fifteenth century English historiography.

Gross, Anthony. "Lancastrians Abroad, 1461-71." *History Today* 42 (August, 1992): 31. Gross traces the efforts of Henry VI's partisans to regain the throne from the House of York and examines this strange alliance that nearly paid off. The article details the shifting fortunes of Henry and his family while exiled, the motives for Lancastrian loyalty, and the dynasty's renewed political importance.

Jacob, Ernest Fraser. *The Fifteenth Century, 1399-1485.* Oxford: Clarendon Press, and New York: Oxford University Press, 1961. Comprehensive and authoritative account of the fifteenth century in all its complexities and paradoxes. Provides more information than stimulus and has a detailed but dated bibliography. Contains no analysis of the character of Henry VI.

Kendall, Paul Murray. *Warwick the Kingmaker.* London: Allen and Unwin, and New York: Norton, 1957. Excellent and well-documented account of Warwick as a public figure. In a colorful format, follows the tangled relations between factions in fifteenth century England. Glimpses of Henry VI reveal an insane king who existed in an animal-like stupor. Presupposes extensive background knowledge.

Lander, Jack Robert. *Crown and Nobility, 1450-1509.* London: Arnold, and Montreal: McGill-Queen's University Press, 1986. Traces struggle for supremacy between the Crown and the nobility in the latter half of the fifteenth century and contains a historiographical essay on period studies. Questions the stories of Henry VI's 1455 mental breakdown as the reason for the Duke of York's second protectorate and sees events in the light of York's possibly treasonable desire to have the throne.

Smith, Lacey Baldwin. *This Realm of England, 1399 to 1688.* 7th ed. Lexington, Mass.: Heath, 1996. A very readable, general account of English history from the fifteenth through the seventeenth centuries. Includes a basic narrative of the fifteenth century "curse of disputed succession" and identifies Henry VI as a cipher more qualified for the Church than the Crown.

Storey, Robin Lindsay. *The End of the House of Lancaster.* London: Barrie and Rockliffe, 1966; New York: Stein and Day, 1967. Finds the causes of the Wars of the Roses to be far more than conflicting hereditary claims to the throne. Places emphasis upon the role of the nobility, who were concerned with getting and keeping real estate, not realms. Indicates that Henry VI had small capacity for kingship before his mental breakdown in 1454 and certainly none after that date.

Watts, J. L. "The Counsels of King Henry VI, c. 1435-1445." *English Historical Review* 106 (April, 1991): 279. This article shows the inappropriateness of the 'Royal Council' model using evidence drawn primarily from the middle years of Henry VI's reign, when ideas of counsel were brought to the fore by a combination of the king's public assumption of power and his personal inadequacy. The author covers attitudes, how counsel created a better government, and the various means of authentication used under Henry VI.

———. *Henry VI and the Politics of Kingship.* New York: Cambridge University Press, 1996. Watts looks at the nature of Henry VI's inadequacy, and the reasons why it had such ambivalent and complicated results. This book looks intensely at the political system itself, rather than at individuals' personalities and patronage networks, and thus offers the first truly structured narrative of the reign.

Carol Crowe-Carraco

HENRY VII

Born: January 28, 1457; Pembroke Castle, Pembrokeshire, Wales

Died: April 21, 1509; Richmond, Surrey, England

Area of Achievement: Government

Contribution: Henry's sense of caution, his flair for public relations, and his knowledge of the importance of timing allowed him to end the Wars of the Roses and lay the foundations of England's Tudor dynasty.

Early Life

Henry Tudor spent his childhood and young adulthood in exile. The child who would one day found one of England's most illustrious dynasties became, at an early age, a pawn in that long, bitterly fought family squabble known as the Wars of the Roses. As the grandson of Catherine of France, King Henry V's widow, and Owen Tudor, a Welsh squire and courtier, young Henry was a relatively obscure Lancastrian claimant to the throne. On his mother's side, his blood was more legitimately royal and his claim to the throne was stronger. His mother, Margaret Beaufort, was the great-great-granddaughter of King Edward III and therefore an undisputed Lancastrian princess. Henry's father, Edmund Tudor, Earl of Richmond, died in 1456, only a few months before young Henry's birth, and the child was then adopted by his uncle Jasper Tudor, Duke of Bedford, a diehard Lancastrian who was to defend the boy from Yorkist intrigue and advance his claim to the throne in the ensuing turbulent years.

The Lancastrian cause suffered a crushing blow at the Battle of Mortimer's Cross in 1461, and with it fell the fortunes of the Tudor family. Henry's grandfather, Owen Tudor, was captured by the Yorkists and publicly beheaded, while Jasper Tudor managed to escape and go underground. Young Henry fell into the hands of the Yorkists when they overtook Pembroke Castle in Wales, Jasper Tudor's stronghold. Taken from his mother, he was given over to the custody of Lord Herbert of Raglan, and he spent the next nine years of his life undergoing careful, but ultimately futile, Yorkist indoctrination. With King Henry VI imprisoned in the Tower of London and the Yorkist King Edward IV on the throne, the Lancastrian cause seemed lost forever. The unexpected restoration of Henry VI in 1470, however, brought the Lancastrians back to power and the Tudors back to royal favor. Now fourteen, Henry Tudor was taken from the Herberts by his uncle Jasper and presented at King Henry's court. Yet another Yorkist uprising toppled Henry VI a mere six months after his restoration, however, and Edward IV reclaimed the throne. Jasper and Henry Tudor managed to escape the ensuing bloodbath and took refuge in Brittany, where they remained in relative seclusion for the next twelve years.

With the death of Edward IV in 1483, England again fell into political turmoil. Richard, Duke of Gloucester (later King Richard III), the brother of the late king, installed the king's two young sons in the Tower, where they apparently died or were murdered by the ambitious Richard (though the facts in this case are still disputed). Meanwhile, however, Richard had declared them illegitimate and their claim to the throne invalid. In June of 1483, he seized power and claimed the throne. His reign, however, was to be relatively short-lived, for a Tudor conspiracy was brewing both in Brittany and among the dispossessed Lancastrian factions of England. Henry Tudor's mother, Margaret Beaufort, now married to the Yorkist Thomas, Lord Stanley, had apparently never given up hope of placing her son on the throne, and she was able to enlist the help of Queen Elizabeth Woodville, Edward IV's widow, as well as that of the powerful Duke of Buckingham and, to a lesser extent, that of the seigneurial Stanley family. In August, 1485, a rebel army led by Jasper and Henry Tudor defeated the much larger but evidently less faithful army of Richard III at the Battle of Bosworth Field. Legend has it that the crown worn by the slain Richard III fell into a thorn bush, from which it was retrieved by the man who then placed it on his head and proclaimed himself King Henry VII.

Life's Work

Almost at once, Henry VII began to exhibit the sure sense of public relations that would characterize his reign, that of his son, Henry VIII, and that of his granddaughter, Elizabeth I. His coronation, which took place on October 30, 1485, in Westminster Abbey, was a grand affair, full of the splendor, pomp, and pageantry that the English people expected from the monarchy. His marriage, on January 16, 1486, to Elizabeth of York, the daughter of Edward IV, was also a great and glamorous state ceremony, as was the christening of their first son, Prince Arthur, in September, 1486. Yet none of

these showy and expensive public celebrations betrayed a mere love of luxury on the king's part; on the contrary, each of them bespoke Henry's characteristic political shrewdness. The new king realized that his claim to the throne was more one of conquest than of birth, and that the greater the measures he took to make his reign appear legitimate, the better. Though his marriage is generally considered to have been a happy one, it was purely politically motivated: Elizabeth was the principal female heir of the House of York, and Henry's marriage to her went far toward healing the factious wounds inflicted by the seemingly endless Wars of the Roses. Even the infant Prince Arthur served his father's political purposes, since a new dynasty required a male heir to ensure a smooth succession. Arthur's birth was followed by those of Princess Margaret, Prince Henry (later King Henry VIII), Princess Elizabeth, Princess Mary, and Prince Edmund.

Despite Henry's surprisingly successful attempts to consolidate his power, however, Yorkist intrigue persisted, and at least two Yorkist plots seriously threatened to undermine his hold on the throne. In 1487, a man claiming to be the Earl of Warwick, Edward IV's nephew and the principal Yorkist pretender to the throne, surfaced in Ireland and was given support by the Irish nobility and by the Duchess of Burgundy, Edward IV's sister. Though it was obvious to Henry that the man was an impostor (the real Warwick had been imprisoned in the Tower since the Battle of Bosworth Field), he was no less a threat, especially after the Irish "crowned" him Edward VI in Dublin. Henry was able to thwart this plot, but only after a narrowly won battle at Stoke in the summer of 1487. The "Earl of Warwick," in reality a commoner named Lambert Simnel, proved to be no more than a puppet of the Duchess of Burgundy, and Henry, rather than executing him, put him to work in the royal kitchens. In 1491, yet another "Warwick" appeared in Ireland, this time in the person of one Perkin Warbeck; once again, the treacherous Margaret of Burgundy seems to have been responsible. Warbeck presented a greater threat to Henry's reign than had Simnel, for he was later recognized not as Warwick but as the Duke of York, one of the presumably slain sons of Edward IV, by no less a personage than King Charles VIII of France. The Warbeck affair continued to trouble Henry for some time, and before it was over, Henry had discovered that one of its sponsors was Sir William Stanley, his mother's brother-in-law, whom he then executed for treason in 1495. Warbeck was later supported by King James IV of Scotland, but by 1497, popular support for the scheme had dwindled, and Warbeck was executed, along with the true Earl of Warwick, in 1499.

When he was not occupied with putting down Yorkist plots against his reign, Henry sought to strengthen his international prestige through a series of matrimonial alliances, and in this area he was equally adept. In 1496, he successfully negotiated the betrothal of Prince Arthur to Princess Catherine of Aragon, daughter of Ferdinand and Isabella of Spain, and the two were married in 1501 (Arthur died in 1502, and Catherine later married his brother, Henry, and became Queen Catherine, the first of the six wives of Henry VIII). In 1503, Henry married his eldest daughter, Margaret, to King James IV of Scotland. Several other attempts at matrimonial diplomacy met with less success, including, after Queen Elizabeth's death in 1503, Henry's own marriage to Princess Margaret von Habsburg, daughter of Emperor Maximilian I of the Holy Roman Empire and, later, to

Queen Juana of Castile, another daughter of Ferdinand and Isabella. On the complicated political scene of medieval Europe, marriage was the preferred method of diplomacy, and Henry's matrimonial negotiations ensured a measure of peace between his island kingdom and the eternally warmongering Scottish to the north and a certain amount of strength through his association with the all-powerful Spanish and Austrians.

Henry's domestic policies were less daring, but equally as shrewd as his foreign policies. Justified or not, his reputation has often been that of a skinflint who kept the peace only because war was expensive, but his concern for financial stability is surely understandable in the light of the turmoil by which he came to power and of the comparative poverty in which he spent his youth. Through an aggressive trade policy and through vigorous taxation, he enriched a treasury that he had found sadly depleted. He showed considerable foresight in backing the explorer John Cabot, whose voyages cleared the way for the empire that would reach its height under Henry's granddaughter, Elizabeth I. Never a true innovator in the ways of government, Henry nevertheless valorized the virtues of caution and frugality by leaving an impressive budget surplus to his son, Henry VIII.

Summary

When he died on April 21, 1509, Henry VII left behind an England much more powerful and prosperous than it had been when he had seized power nearly twenty-four years earlier, and it is by his effect on his country that he must be judged, especially in the light of the paucity of information about his private life and personality. Clearly, he was ruthless when his crown was at stake, as is evidenced by his execution of the innocent Earl of Warwick in 1499. Yet though he was merciless to those who threatened or appeared to threaten his dynasty, he was unfailingly generous to those who helped him establish it, and he never forgot a favor. In no way an intellectual, Henry contented himself with being crafty, and his ability to focus his attention on purely practical matters made possible the unparalleled patronage of the arts practiced by Henry VIII and Elizabeth I. Though he had little of the personal charisma enjoyed by his son and granddaughter, the great majority of his people revered him, but even here he was not overconfident and supplied them with lavish shows of royal pomp and ceremony whenever possible.

Modern interpretations of this first Tudor monarch differ vastly. To some historians, he was the ruthless and penurious king who overtaxed his subjects and used his marriageable children as mere instruments of statecraft, while to others, he was an innately kindly man who was ambitious and vengeful only because circumstances forced him to be. Perhaps Henry Tudor is best judged in the light of Niccolò Machiavelli's *The Prince* (1517), published a decade after Henry's death. Though Machiavelli had in mind the Borgia family of Italy while writing this masterpiece of political philosophy, his description of the pragmatic ruler whose morals must adapt themselves to the shifting political climate lends itself particularly well to this tough-minded Welshman who became King of England through sheer force of will.

Bibliography

Alexander, Michael Van Cleave. *The First of the Tudors: A Study of Henry VII and His Reign*. London: Croom Helm, and Totowa, N.J.: Rowman and Littlefield, 1980. This highly readable work, intended primarily for the general reader rather than the historian, seeks to supplement the rather scanty information about Henry's personality and to suggest how the political influenced the personal, and vice versa, in Henry's life. Alexander succeeds admirably in dispelling the myth of the dull and parsimonious king.

Chrimes, S. B. *Henry VII*. London: Methuen, and Berkeley: University of California Press, 1972. This book is probably the best available source of information about the changes in governmental policy brought about by Henry Tudor. Chrimes has drawn on rarely consulted government documents to create a comprehensive interpretation of Henry's relations with Parliament and with the European community. The result is solid and reliable, but the general reader may find it dry.

Currin, John M. "Henry VII and the Treaty of Redon (1489): Plantagenet Ambitions and Early Tudor Foreign Policy." *History* 81 (July, 1996): 343. Currin discusses Tudor foreign policy during the reign of Henry VII; the transition from the policy pursued by the Plantagenets of acquiring and holding territories in France; revival of the treaty of Redon in the alliance; and mediation between the king of France and the Duke of Brittany.

Elton, Geoffrey R. *England Under the Tudors*. 2d ed. London: Methuen, 1974; New York: Routledge, 1991. Elton's study also focuses on the political and governmental but places Henry's reign in the larger context of the sixteenth century—what Elton calls "the Tudor century." Thus, his discussion of Henry VII is skillfully connected to those of Henry's successors. A good, if overdetailed, one-volume introduction to the Tudor dynasty.

Gunn, Steven. "Henry VII and Charles the Bold." *History Today* 46 (April, 1996): 26. The author discusses the similarities in the styles of governance employed by Henry VII of England and Charles the Bold of Burgundy, including the attitudes of both rulers toward wars and their policies on taxation.

Mackie, John D. *The Earlier Tudors, 1485-1558.* Oxford: Oxford University Press, 1952. A heavily interpretive and consistently interesting account of nearly every conceivable facet of Henry's reign, and indeed of the reigns of all the Tudor rulers up to Elizabeth. This study also serves as a concise overview of European politics during the Tudor years. A lavishly detailed table of contents will aid the reader in finding what he or she seeks in this comprehensive account.

Simons, Eric N. *Henry VII: The First Tudor King*. London: Muller, and New York: Barnes and Noble, 1968. Breezy and clearly written, this book often sacrifices rigor to romanticism, but the nonspecialist reader will find it an entertaining introduction to Henry's reign.

J. D. Daubs

HENRY VIII

Born: June 28, 1491; Greenwich, England
Died: January 28, 1547; London, England
Areas of Achievement: Government and religion
Contribution: Through administrative changes and his break with the Roman Catholic Church, and the subsequent establishment of the Church of England, Henry VIII strengthened the position of the monarch in English society.

Early Life

Henry VIII was born on June 28, 1491, in Greenwich, England. He was the second son of the first Tudor king and the Lancastrian claimant to the throne, Henry VII, and Elizabeth, the daughter of the Yorkist Edward IV. Henry VII gained the Crown by defeating Richard III at Bosworth Field in 1485; Richard III was killed in the battle, and Henry Tudor, a Welshman, immediately assumed the throne. During his early years, Prince Henry was overshadowed by his older brother, Arthur, who was his father's heir. Little is known of Henry's education except that the poet John Skelton was involved; Skelton wrote *Speculum Principis* in 1501 as a guidebook for Henry. It is also believed that Lady Margaret Beaufort, Henry VII's mother, was involved with her grandson's education. Whatever the nature and source of his education, Henry later demonstrated that he had a firm grasp of the classics, a limited knowledge of music, and fluency in three languages. Young Henry was interested in most forms of contemporary sport and was recognized for his athletic abilities.

Henry remained a secondary figure as long as his brother was alive. His father never assigned him any responsibility or seriously pursued any marriage arrangement for Henry. Henry VII did express some tentative interest in a marriage between Prince Henry and Eleanor, daughter of Philip, the Duke of Burgundy, but it was not seriously considered. In April, 1502, Prince Arthur, recently married to Catherine of Aragon, died in Wales from tuberculosis at the age of fifteen. Suddenly, the overlooked second son became the heir to the Crown and the focus of great attention and interest. Henry VII became very protective of his only surviving son. Negotiations with Madrid were conducted in 1503, and on June 23 of that year a treaty was signed which provided for the marriage of Henry to the widow, Catherine of Aragon, upon Henry's attainment of the age of fifteen. One obstacle which had to be overcome was acquiring a dispensation from Rome to permit the marriage. The need for the dispensation was based on a scriptural directive that prohibited one from marrying the widow of one's brother. Catherine argued that only a dispensation on the basis of the impediment of public honesty was required because the marriage had never been consummated. Both English and Spanish officials agreed, however, that a dispensation on the basis of the impediment of affinity in the first degree collateral should be obtained. Problems (financial, political, personal, and with the Church) continued to plague the marriage treaty. On April 22, 1509, Henry VII died at Richmond Palace; six weeks later, on June 11, 1509, Henry VIII married Catherine of Aragon.

Life's Work

The thirty-six-year reign of one of the greatest monarchs in English history began with great expectations for a bright and progressive era in English affairs. Henry VIII, the eighteen-year-old king, was an exceptionally handsome man who stood slightly over six feet in height. He was clearly different from his father: Whereas Henry VII was reserved and secretive, Henry VIII was open and frequently discussed matters of state freely. Henry VIII set out to create a public image of himself as a Renaissance prince in the tradition of Desiderius Erasmus and other notables of the Northern Renaissance. In fact, while he was familiar with the general scope of the literature, Henry VIII did not understand the ideals which motivated the writings of Erasmus, John Colet, and Sir Thomas More. On the second day of his reign, Henry ordered the arrest of two of his father's principal advisers and administrators, Richard Empson and Edmund Dudley, on charges of extortion. They were executed sixteen months later.

During the early years of his reign, Henry was content to pursue sports and court games. In 1512, in an effort to demonstrate that he was a warrior king, Henry entered into an alliance with Spain against France. While nothing of military substance emerged from the war, Henry gained popularity through the capture of Tournai. The most significant development of the war was Henry's recognition of the abilities of Thomas Wolsey. From 1515 to 1529, Wolsey served Henry as Lord Chan-

cellor of England and as Archbishop of York; Wolsey also became a cardinal of the Roman Catholic Church and entertained the ambition of becoming pope. In 1517, another able administrator, More, was named as a councillor to the king. More, who was considered one of the superior intellects of the age and who was the author of *Utopia* (1516), observed that Henry compartmentalized his thoughts and discussions. Philosophic consideration of ideals had no impact on pragmatic situations; Henry did not allow these two separate concerns to intersect, for the result would be unpredictability, and with that, danger.

As Lutheranism developed on the Continent, Henry stood firm in his support of Rome. In 1520, Martin Luther wrote several pamphlets in which he denied or challenged several major tenets of Catholic theology. One of the most serious of Luther's assertions concerned sacramental theology; in response, Henry, in 1521, wrote *Assertio septem sacramentorum adversus Martinum Lutherum*, which denounced Luther's views and reaffirmed the traditional Catholic teaching on the Sacraments.

As the 1520's progressed, Henry's reign entered a period which became increasingly unsettled; this situation was a result of a number of factors. The public enthusiasm for the king which had greeted the new monarch and carried him through the early years of the reign was diminished significantly. Further, Henry, as well as the other monarchs of Europe, ruled in the shadow of Charles V, the Holy Roman Emperor, and unquestionably the most powerful individual in Europe during the first half of the sixteenth century. Finally, and most important for Henry, his marriage with Catherine had produced only one surviving child, Mary, and no male heir.

In 1527, Henry directed Wolsey to obtain an annulment of his marriage to Catherine so that he could be free to marry Anne Boleyn. Negotiations with Rome dragged on for years as Charles V, at the urging of his aunt, Catherine of Aragon, pressured Pope Clement VI not to grant the annulment. Henry's increasing frustration led to the fall of Wolsey in 1529 and the subsequent rise of Thomas Cromwell and Thomas Cranmer as the principal advisers to the king on state and religious matters. The influence of Protestants at the court became evident during the early 1530's. In 1533, a group of English bishops granted the king his annulment; Henry married Boleyn, who soon gave birth to Princess Elizabeth. In 1534, Henry and Cromwell pushed the Acts of Supremacy and Uniformity from the Reformation Parliament, and the break with Rome was complete. In 1535-1536, the Henrician government suppressed opposition to these policies through the Pilgrimage of Grace in the northern counties. In 1536, the dissolution of the monasteries took place and the Ten Articles of Faith, which were sympathetic to the Protestants, appeared. In 1539, when it was perceived that the public did not support the recent changes, the Six Articles of Faith, which were Catholic in tenor, were pronounced. During the 1530's, Henry and Cromwell reorganized the administration of the government; the result was a primitive but effective bureaucracy. In 1540, Cromwell was executed on the charge of treason.

In 1536, Boleyn was executed on the charge of adultery. Henry's next wife, Jane Seymour, provided him with a son, Edward, in 1537 and then died of natural causes associated with the birth. Marriages to Anne of Cleves, Catherine Howard, and Catherine Parr followed. Only Parr survived Henry.

During the 1540's, Henry's health declined steadily, but he retained his mental acumen. Before his death, he wrote a will which provided for a regency to rule the country during his son's minority. If Edward died without heirs, the Crown would pass to Mary, and similarly, on to Elizabeth. Henry died on January 28, 1547.

Summary

The impact of Henry VIII on the development of the English nation and constitution is extensive. Through the manipulation of Wolsey and Cromwell, Henry managed to expand his powers over church and state. Yet he appeared to do so in full cooperation with Parliament. From his personal perspective, the reign was a triumph because he succeeded in transferring the Crown to his son, Edward Tudor, and, in so doing, maintained the Tudor dynasty. His chaotic and violent marital history revealed a side of Henry's character which is ambiguous and has led many scholars into the realm of psychological speculation.

Bishop William Stubbs, a leading English historian of the late nineteenth century, once remarked that Henry was such a complex and immense historical figure that no biographer or historian should undertake to master all aspects of his turbulent life. Stubbs's caution has been accepted by some, rejected by others, but most historians credit Stubbs with making an astute observation.

Bibliography

Bernard, G. W. "The Making of Religious Policy, 1533-1546: Henry VIII and the Search for the Middle Way." *Historical Journal* 41 (June, 1998): 321. The author presents his opinions on religious policy in England, referring to the role that Henry VIII played in its implementation and providing information on the abolition of papal authority.

Byrne, Muriel St. Clare, and Bridget Boland, eds. *The Lisle Letters: An Abridgement.* Chicago: University of Chicago Press, 1981. In this collection of the letters of Lord Lisle (Arthur Plantagenet) and other members of his family between 1533 and 1540, when Lisle served as Deputy of Calais, Henry is presented as an individual who was motivated by his determination to secure the continuance of the Tudor dynasty and by his policy to establish an effective, centralized government.

Dickens, Arthur G. *The English Reformation.* 2d ed. London: Batsford, 1989; University Park: Pennsylvania University Press, 1991. Dickens' analysis of Henry's performance in the development of the English Reformation is generally sympathetic. By the late 1520's, Henry was viewed as sympathetic to many of Luther's concepts; the Henrician Reformation was part of a larger movement on the Continent.

Elton, Geoffrey R. *The Tudor Constitution, Documents, and Commentary.* 2d ed. Cambridge and New York: Cambridge University Press, 1982. Elton stresses the impact of Cromwell on administrative changes. Through the use of primary documents relating to the Crown's approach to the Reformation, the council, finances, and the courts, the Henrician administration of the 1530's is interpreted as the work of a master political architect, Cromwell.

———. *The Tudor Revolution in Government, Administrative Changes in the Reign of Henry VIII.* Cambridge: Cambridge University Press, 1953. In this classic study the author argued that the policies and achievements of Cromwell during the 1530's constituted a revolution in the management of the English state. The beginnings of the modern bureaucratic English government can be traced to Cromwell.

Jensen, De Lamar. *Reformation Europe: Age of Reform and Revolution.* 2d ed. Lexington, Mass.: Health, 1992. In this general survey of the Reformation, Henry is presented as a brilliant politician, a man clear in his purposes, who manipulated his ministers as well as situations in order to pursue his goals.

Lockyer, Roger. *Tudor and Stuart Britain, 1471-1714.* London: Longman, and New York: St. Martin's Press, 1964. From the late 1520's to his death, Henry became more involved with governmental matters. While he allowed Wolsey and Cromwell considerable latitude, their actions had to conform to his determined policies, and he was vigilant of his ministers to assure compliance with his will.

Newcombe, D.G. *Henry VIII and the English Reformation.* London and New York: Routledge, 1995. The English Reformation in the sixteenth century was quite different in its methods, motivations, and results than that taking place on the continent. This book examines the influences of continental reform on England; describes the divorce of Henry VIII and the break with Rome; discusses the political and religious consequences of the break; assesses the success of the Reformation up to 1547; and provides a clear guide to the main strands of historical thought on the topic.

Scarisbrick, J. J. *Henry VIII.* London: Eyre and Spottiswoode, and Berkeley: University of California Press, 1968. In this definitive study of Henry, the king emerges as the man in control of the regime, a bright and clever politician, and a dedicated reformer in religion. The Scarisbrick thesis has become the standard interpretation of Henry VIII and has superseded the thesis advanced by A. F. Pollard in *Henry VIII* (1902), in which the king was viewed as a reluctant reformer who was loyal to Catholic doctrines.

Slavin, Arthur Joseph. *The Precarious Balance: English Government and Society.* New York: Knopf, 1973. Henry effected changes in procedures which transformed the internal balance of power in favor of the central government. Evasion of taxes by the nobility was rendered more difficult by the legal and administrative devices established by the Henrician regime.

Smith, Lacey Baldwin. *Henry VIII: The Mask of Royalty.* London: Cape, and Boston: Houghton Mifflin, 1971. Henry is portrayed in this biography as an observant and effective administrator who was eccentric in his work habits. The eccentricity frequently led contemporaries to conclude that Henry was not interested in the administration of the realm.

Starkey, David. "After the 'Revolution.' " In *Revolution Reassessed: Revisions in the History of Tudor Government and Administration*, edited by Christopher Coleman and David Starkey. Oxford: Clarendon Press, and New York: Oxford University Press, 1986. In this article, the author summarizes the attacks which have dismantled the principal points of the Elton thesis.

William T. Walker

PRINCE HENRY THE NAVIGATOR

Born: March 4, 1394; Porto, Portugal
Died: November 13, 1460; Sagres, Portugal
Areas of Achievement: Exploration and warfare
Contribution: Although Prince Henry considered crusading against the North African Muslims to be his primary task, it was his African explorations that later put Portugal at the forefront of the European age of discovery.

Early Life

On February 14, 1387, King John I of Portugal married Philippa, the eldest daughter of Prince John of Gaunt of England. The union proved quite fertile, and the queen gave birth to a succession of children: Duarte in 1391, Pedro in 1392, and her best-known child, Henry (or Enrique) on March 4, Ash Wednesday, 1394. These children were followed by a daughter, Isabel, and two more sons, John and Fernando. Little is known about Prince Henry's youth, although it appears that he grew up in close association with his two elder brothers. They received the usual upbringing of noble youths, learning horsemanship, hunting, and the skills and values associated with late medieval chivalry.

Chivalric values were new to late fourteenth century Portugal, with its isolated location on Western Europe's periphery. It appears that these values arrived with the chaste Queen Philippa from England, and King John I quite readily adopted chivalric ideals for his court and family. Chivalry imposed restraint and sophistication on the rough-and-ready crusading spirit that had long been indigenous to the Iberian peninsula. These twin value systems of chivalry and crusade against infidels would be the predominant influences on Prince Henry's actions through his entire life.

In 1411, King John I made peace with Castile and declared that he would celebrate the occasion with a joust during which his three oldest sons would be knighted. His sons objected, however, and asked that they be given a chance to earn their knighthood in actual combat according to the best chivalric practices. Since Portugal had just reached a peace treaty with neighboring Castile, the warlike energies of John I's sons needed to be directed farther afield. The Moorish city of Ceuta, located strategically opposite Gibraltar, became their objective. It would be the first major Portuguese move against Islamic territory since about 1250. The expedition was quite large, consisting of 240 ships, thirty thousand sailors, and twenty thousand soldiers, and took two years to prepare. Sailing from the Tagus River on July 23, 1415, the expedition landed at Ceuta on August 21 and immediately assaulted the city. An easy and overwhelming victory resulted for the Crusaders. John's three sons all fought bravely and earned their knighthoods. Furthermore, Pedro obtained the additional reward of the dukedom of Coimbra, while Henry received the dukedom of Viseu. Returning to Portugal, the young Prince Henry took up frontier guard duty at Viseu for the next several years.

Life's Work

The capture of Ceuta proved quickly to be an expensive disappointment for the Portuguese. Its thriving caravan trade was soon diverted to other coastal cities, while the surrounding Muslim states maintained an attitude of implacable hostility. One party of Portuguese had opposed the expedition to Ceuta from the beginning, and after the conquest they advocated immediate evacuation. Another party, which included Prince Henry, called for the retention of Ceuta and further expansion against the Muslim powers. Their ultimate goal was the winning of North Africa for Christendom. To achieve their objective, Prince Henry advanced a policy of attacking the Muslims head-on in the region of Ceuta, while at the same time trying to approach them from behind by a flanking movement down the west coast of Africa.

In 1416, King John I appointed Prince Henry as governor of Ceuta, although the young man continued to reside at Viseu. A Muslim threat against Ceuta in 1418 prompted Portugal to organize a relief expedition under Henry's command. By this time, the character of the young prince was formed, and he was at the height of his physical powers. According to his chronicler, Gomes Eannes de Zurara, Prince Henry was tall and dark, with a large build and thick, shaggy black hair. His face wore a grave expression that aroused a sense of fear in those around him. Unlike many profligate noblemen of the late Middle Ages, he ascetically shunned both wine and women. In fact, he never married and was reputed to have died a virgin. Instead, Prince Henry directed his abundant energies into crusading and exploring.

Crusading and exploration were expensive enterprises, and throughout his life Prince Henry, who enjoyed living in a princely style, was chronically short of money. He drew revenues from his dukedom of Viseu, to which were added the governorship of Algarve in 1419 and the headship of the Military Order of Christ in 1420. Still, these were not enough, and Henry continually had to seek further sources of revenue. It is this constant quest for money that explains his role in the settlement of Madeira and the Azores Islands and in the Castilian-Portuguese rivalry over the Canary Islands.

It is possible that Europeans discovered the Madeiras as early as 1339, but it is definite that they knew about the islands by 1417, when a strong Castilian expedition visited Porto Santo. Portugal reacted by quickly occupying the islands during 1419 and 1420 with settlers from Prince Henry's province of Algarve. In 1433, King Duarte granted the islands to Henry as a fief, and he drew income from their production of dye-stuffs and grain. The same situation applied to the Azores, which the Portuguese Diogo de Senill discovered in 1427. Domestic animals were dropped off on the islands during the early 1430's in preparation for human settlement. It was not until 1439 that the regent Dom Pedro gave his brother Prince Henry a charter to settle the islands; colonization was begun in the early 1440's. Once again, the production of dyestuffs and grain provided the profits which helped to fuel Prince Henry's explorations and crusades.

Meanwhile, the exploration of the African coast was delayed by the navigational and psychological barrier of Cape Bojador. This barren promontory extended twenty-five miles out into the Atlantic, where great waves crashed and adverse winds and currents made sailing treacherous. Beyond lay the "Green Sea of Darkness" from which no one ever returned. Between 1424 and 1434, Prince Henry sent out fifteen expeditions with orders to round it. Finally, in 1434, a squire of Prince Henry's household, Gil Eannes, sailed past the dreaded cape on his second attempt. His success removed a formidable psychological barrier to exploration, although the cape still remained a serious navigational menace. The conquest of Cape Bojador was probably Prince Henry's most important contribution to European exploration.

After the passage of Cape Bojador, exploration of the African coast made greater progress. In 1436, the explorer Afonso Gonzalves Baldia reached the bay that he mistakenly called the Rio de Ouro. After that, however, exploration stopped temporarily while Prince Henry concentrated on his true love, a crusade against the Muslims in what became the disastrous Tangier expedition of 1437. From 1438 to 1441, the tumultuous early years of the minority of Afonso V intervened to occupy Portuguese energies, until Henry's brother Pedro defeated the Queen-Mother Lenora for the regency.

A return of stability brought a resumption of exploration. In 1441, Antao Gonzalves brought back the first black slaves from Africa, beginning a profitable but inhumane trade, while Nuno Tristano discovered Cape Blanc. The next year, 1442, saw the first African gold brought back to Portugal, an achievement which allowed them to bypass the Muslim caravan trade. At that point, Prince Henry obtained a royal monopoly of all trading south of Cape Bojador and proceeded for a fee to issue trading licenses to eager merchants.

By 1446, trading expeditions far outnumbered voyages of further discovery. Still, exploration also progressed rapidly with the encouragement of both Prince Henry and his brother Dom Pedro, whose role in early Portuguese exploration has been unfairly ignored. With their encouragement, Dinis Dias discovered Cape Verde in 1444, while Alvaro Fernandes reached the Gambia River the following year. After Pedro fell into disgrace in 1448, however, and was killed at the Battle of Alfarrobeira on May 20, 1449, much of the drive for new discoveries appears to have ended. It revived somewhat during 1454, when the Venetian merchant Alvise da Cadamosto joined the service of Prince Henry. He reached Portuguese Guinea in 1455 and proceeded even farther south the following year, accidentally discovering the Cape Verde Islands and the Bissagos Islands. Cadamosto's primary interest was trading, and it was between 1455 and 1461 that Prince Henry established the fortress-trading post on Arguim Island, near Cape Blanc.

Meanwhile, back in Portugal, the siren call of a crusade against the Muslims tempted the aging Prince Henry once again. During 1456 and 1457, Portugal prepared for a papal crusade against the Ottoman Turks in response to their capture of Constantinople in 1453. When the general crusade failed to materialize, the Portuguese simply redirected their efforts against the Muslims of North Africa. Their fleet, including King Afonso and Prince Henry, sailed on October 17, 1458, and arrived off the Muslim city of Alcacer-Seguer on October 22, capturing it two days later. It was to be Prince Henry's last crusade.

Exploration of the African coast also slowed during Henry's last years, although a brisk trade continued. Pedro de Sintra may have reached Sierra Leone in 1460, but as the farthest point of Portuguese discovery achieved in Prince Henry's lifetime, it was not a particularly impressive addition to the achievements of Cadamosto in 1456. Back in Portugal, the old Prince Henry fell ill at his residence of Sagres and died on November 13, 1460.

Summary

Prince Henry the Navigator is one of the romantic historical figures of whom stories are told to all schoolchildren in the Western world. Modern society finds this Henry attractive, since he was supposedly a lone giant pushing back the darkness of geographic ignorance. It is claimed that he was a navigational innovator, the founder of a school and an observatory for geographic studies at Sagres, and a systematic promoter of exploration, with a view to reaching India by sea. In fact, he was none of these things. Recent scholarship finds no evidence for any technical innovations, any school, or any systematic plan of exploration, especially anything including India as its ultimate goal. Present-day Portuguese do not even recognize him as "the Navigator"; that title was bestowed on him by his English biographer Richard Henry Major in 1868.

The fact is that Prince Henry was a man of the late Middle Ages; chivalric and crusading values motivated him to attack the Muslims and to explore Africa. In addition, as his chronicler Zurara pointed out, his actions befitted the stars under which he was born. Prince Henry's horoscope showed that he "should toil at high and mighty conquests, especially in seeking out things that were hidden from other men and secret." People in medieval times took these predictions seriously, and it was as a medieval Crusader that Prince Henry uncovered places that were hidden and secret and inadvertently helped to open up the great age of discovery in the late fifteenth and sixteenth centuries.

Bibliography

Beazley, Charles Raymond. *Prince Henry the Navigator: The Hero of Portugal and of Modern Discovery, 1394-1400 A.D.* New York: Putnam, 1894; London: Putnam, 1923. Beazley follows Major (see below) in viewing Prince Henry as a man of science living before his true time and as a great precursor of the age of exploration. Almost half the book deals with geographical, scientific, and political developments leading up to the time of Prince Henry.

Diffie, Bailey W., and George D. Winius. *Foundations of the Portuguese Empire, 1415-1580.* Minneapolis: University of Minnesota Press, 1977. Although part of a general history of the Portuguese Empire, the first quarter of the volume provides information and interpretation of Prince Henry's career. It is a well-written study and is solidly based on primary and secondary sources. Prince Henry clearly appears as a medieval Crusader.

Major, Richard Henry. *The Life of Prince Henry of Portugal Surnamed the Navigator and Its Results*. London: Asher, 1868. Major is responsible for Prince Henry being popularly known throughout the English-speaking world as "the Navigator." This biography remains useful, even though it is quite dated in its attribution to Henry of a scientific spirit and of the sole motivating force behind Portuguese exploration.

Sanceau, Elaine. *Henry the Navigator: The Story of a Great Prince and His Times*. New York: Norton,

1947. As the author of several biographies of great figures from the age of Portuguese expansion, Sanceau possesses consid-erable skill in artfully blending documentary evidence into an exciting narrative. Unfortunately, she follows the romantic school of interpretation regarding Prince Henry. Her biography should be preferred, however, to the more recent one by John Ure.

Ure, John. *Prince Henry the Navigator.* London: Constable, 1977. Written by an English diplomat who served in Portugal, this full-scale biography does a good job of emphasizing Henry's medieval crusading mentality. It unfortunately also continues to view him as possessing a modern spirit of inquiry and so is largely a mild updating of the earlier romantic interpretations of Prince Henry as the indispensable man of the age of discovery.

Zurara, Gomes Eannes de. *The Chronicle of the Discovery and Conquest of Guinea.* 2 vols. Edited and translated by Charles Raymond Beazley and Edgar Prestage. London: Hakluyt Society, 1896-1899; New York: Franklin, 1963. These contemporary chronicles are the most extensive source for an account of the early Portuguese discoveries and are the only source for some incidents. Unfortunately, they end with the year 1448. The values of chivalry and crusading definitely influenced Zurara, a member of the Order of Christ and the official historian of Prince Henry's career.

Ronald H. Fritze

HANS HOLBEIN, THE YOUNGER

Born: 1497 or 1498; Augsburg
Died: 1543; London, England
Area of Achievement: Art
Contribution: A master of portraits and an excellent draftsman, Holbein was an important transitional figure in European art. Holbein's portraits offer a revealing look at the personalities of his time.

Early Life

Hans Holbein, the Younger, was born in either 1497 or 1498 in the city of Augsburg, at that time an important commercial center of the Holy Roman Empire. The Holbein family was an artistic one: Hans Holbein, the Elder, was a widely known painter, much sought after for his skill in portraits, while his brother Sigmund was also an artist. The younger Holbein and his brother, Ambrosius, spent their early years learning the craft of painting from their father.

In 1515, Holbein moved to Basel, Switzerland, where he came to the attention of the noted printer and publisher Johann Froben, also known as Frobenius. Holbein was soon actively designing book illustrations and title-page borders for Froben and other printers in Basel. Since Froben was the publisher of Desiderius Erasmus, a noted Humanist scholar, Holbein came to know that internationally famous writer. Through Erasmus, Holbein was introduced to the circle of Humanist thinkers and leaders of the time. Holbein made other important contacts, including a 1516 commission to paint the portrait of Jacob Mayer, Burgomaster of Basel, and his wife; this work is an early indication of Holbein's mastery of the portrait genre. During this time, he also produced several conventional religious paintings, a form of art popular at the time.

From 1517 to 1519, Holbein was away from Basel, perhaps traveling with his father on commissions in Switzerland, perhaps on a brief visit to northern Italy. By the fall of 1519, he had returned to Basel, for on September 25 of that year he was admitted as a master in the Painters' Guild. The next year, Holbein became a citizen of the town and married Elsbeth Schmid, the widow of a tanner; the couple had four children.

Holbein received a considerable amount of work in Basel, primarily designs and illustrations for printers, but also a series of religious paintings influenced by his contemporary Albrecht Dürer; mural decorations for the Basel Town Hall; and more portraits, including his 1519 portrayal of the lawyer and scholar Bonifacius Amerbach. This portrait is the first showing Holbein's true genius in portraiture; fittingly, Amerbach later became the earliest collector of Holbein and preserved much of his work. In 1523, Holbein produced his first portrait of Erasmus; a second soon followed, which Erasmus sent to his friend Sir Thomas More in England. The English connection, so important in Holbein's life and career, was soon to be established.

A number of Holbein self-portraits have survived. They show him with a square, rather full face, a short, neatly trimmed beard but no mustache, and hair that was dark and worn moderately long. The most notable features are his mouth, firmly and tightly closed, and his eyes, which have a careful, wary expression. It is not the face of a man who revealed himself lightly or freely.

Life's Work

During the mid-1520's, the Protestant Reformation swept through Basel and the climate for the visual arts became much less favorable than before. In 1524, Holbein found it convenient to depart on an extended visit to France, where he was exposed to the influence of Italian painting, including the work of Leonardo da Vinci. In August of 1526, he left Basel again, this time for England. He carried with him a letter of introduction from Erasmus; once in England, he was welcomed into the household of Erasmus' good friend Sir Thomas More.

Through More, Holbein had an entry into the court of Henry VIII, then approaching the apogee of its brilliance. While Holbein did execute some decorations for court pageants, his initial relationship with the monarch was not as close as it would later become. Instead, he concentrated on portraits of prominent individuals and groups. One of his most striking works from this time, a group portrait of the More family (most likely painted in 1528) has been lost, but the preparatory drawings remain. As always, Holbein captures the character of his sitters with deft precision; equally important, this group portrait is the first known example in northern European art where the figures are shown sitting or standing in natural positions, rather than kneeling, a definite break with the religiously oriented art of the Middle Ages.

In 1528, Holbein returned to Basel, probably because of a previous agreement with the town council, since he promptly resumed his work of public commissions, devoting much time and energy to them over the next two years. The financial rewards seem to have been considerable, since he was able to purchase a new house and, in 1531, to buy the adjoining property as well. The same year as his return, Holbein was admitted into the Lutheran faith. Within two years, and certainly by late 1520, however, Holbein seems to have ceased all work in the area of religious painting, once a staple of any artist's career. Perhaps that reflected the preferences of the Reformation; it certainly allowed Holbein's talents to flow into paintings and portraits which favored his realistic and psychological technique.

Holbein's ability in portraiture reached its most profound and personal depths in his *Portrait of His Wife and Two Elder Children* (1528). In this searching, almost painful work, Holbein presents part of the family from which he was so long and so often absent. The painter's wife, Elsbeth, seems weary, perhaps sad; has this been caused by the absence of the artist who still records her features so faithfully? That is impossible to determine, but the technical mastery of the work is undoubted, as is its debt to Holbein's study of the works of Leonardo.

Leaving his wife and children in Basel, Holbein returned to England in 1532; he would remain there for the remainder of his life. His friend More had fallen from the king's favor over the matter of divorcing Queen Catherine and the marriage to Anne Boleyn, so Holbein first concentrated on a series of portraits of German merchants living in London. Called the "Steelyard portraits," after the section of town where the sitters lived, these works marked a new development in Holbein's art. His acute perceptions of character increased, his draftsmanship acquired new and fluid power, and attention was focused upon the person, because backgrounds and surroundings were greatly simplified.

Holbein also began to paint portraits of members of the court, including Thomas Cromwell, More's successor as Lord Chancellor; eventually, Holbein came to the attention of Henry himself. In 1537, Holbein executed a fresco for the royal palace of Whitehall, which brought him considerable fame (the work was destroyed in a 1698 fire). In 1538 came the first entry in the royal accounts of a salary paid to Holbein, indicating that he had officially entered the service of the king. Over the next five years, he would complete more than 150 portraits, in oils, chalk, and silverpoint, capturing some of the most influential and memorable figures from one of England's most turbulent periods. Holbein also remained active in preparing illustrations for printers, including the woodcut borders for the important English Bible of 1535, and he designed costumes, jewelry, cups, and other art objects for the court.

Holbein's portraits remain his most important and enduring work. Among his sitters were Henry VIII himself and most of the major figures of his court, including several of Henry's wives. Most of these works have survived in chalk, or pen-and-ink studies, rather than completed oils, yet all of them retain the vitality and insight which Holbein brought to his work. Some of them, such as the stunning full-length portrait *Christiana of Denmark, Duchess of Milan* (1538), rank among Holbein's supreme achievements.

The portrait of Christiana was painted for one of the frequent marriage negotiations engaged in by Henry; he often assigned Holbein to capture the likeness of a prospective bride. One of these, Holbein's study of Anne of Cleves (1539), seems to have been his downfall. Pleased by the portrait, Henry agreed to the marriage, but within six months he divorced the woman he called "the Flanders mare." After this, there were no more important royal commissions for Holbein.

Holbein continued to live in London, securing work from other patrons. His last portrait of Henry, for example, is that of the king granting a charter to the Barber-Surgeon's Company. The work was painted for that guild and was commissioned in 1541. Significantly, Holbein did not paint Henry from life but rather copied him from earlier works. Holbein did not live to complete the painting, for he died during an outbreak of the plague in London in 1543. His wife and children in Basel were attended to by his estate there and by a pension negotiated with the town council. In his last will in England, Holbein left funds for the keeping of two young children there. He was forty-six years old when he died.

Summary

Hans Holbein, the Younger, marks a turning point in the development of European art. His portraits show a decisive change from the older, religious orientation to the newer, more secular and worldly temper of the Renaissance and modern times. A number of critics have remarked on a lack of spiritual involvement by Holbein with his work, and perhaps Holbein did concentrate upon the actual, the physical, and the immediate. That was appropriate, however, for his sitters were men and women of intense individuality, and often of supreme ambition; their concerns were often not spiritual but temporal. Holbein's portraits may lack piety, but they have psychological insight, an insight that he captured not by hands clasped in prayer or holding a Bible but by hands fingering a jewel given by Henry VIII or the look of shrewd eyes calculating the latest events in the king's court. With Holbein, medieval painting departs and the art of the modern world begins.

Even in his religious paintings, Holbein took a new and sometimes disturbing stance. One of his most famous works, *The Body of the Dead Christ in the Tomb* (1521-1522), has intrigued and unsettled viewers since its creation. Some have complained that the painting dwells too closely on the material nature of Christ, slighting the spiritual side. While other religious paintings of the time used Christ's physical sufferings as an aid to devotion and meditation, Holbein's work is different and evokes different responses, because of the intense, unflinching realism in which it is rendered. There is no softening or evading the facts of brutal bodily injury and certain death.

Occupying a pivotal point in European artistic development, Holbein was not entirely a modern painter. The influence of older forms is seen most clearly in his woodcuts and illustrations, in particular the Dance of Death series, designed from 1522 through 1524, and executed by the brilliant woodblock carver Hans Lützelburger. Although not published until 1538, this series is one of the most famous variants on the "Dance macabre" theme so popular in the Middle Ages.

It is Holbein's portraits, however, which are the key to his work. His technical mastery is unmatched, and his ceaseless efforts at perfection allowed him to produce a series of masterpieces of psychological interpretation. Most famous are the portraits Holbein produced at the court of Henry VIII, which have left for later generations a true sense of the important and intriguing figures of the time, from the king himself to his friend and victim, Sir Thomas More. In these, and other drawings, portraits, and paintings, Holbein captured the essence of the northern Renaissance and the men and women who created it. Through the works of Holbein, that world comes to life in all its vibrant energy.

Bibliography

Holbein, Hans, the Younger. *Holbein*. Introduction by Roy Strong. New York: Rizzoli, 1980. This slender volume is one of the Every Painting series. Gives a rapid visual overview of Holbein's career. Especially useful in conjunction with any of the other volumes mentioned here.

Hueffer, Ford Madox. *Hans Holbein the Younger: A Critical Monograph*. London: Duckworth, and New York: Dutton, 1905. A perceptive, if sometimes highly individual study of Holbein's work by the famous English novelist, better known as Ford Madox Ford. The book does well in placing Holbein within the atmosphere of the Renaissance and provides a good, if idiosyncratic, overview of his achievement.

Michael, Erika. *Hans Holbein the Younger: A Guide to Research*. New York: Garland, 1997. The first part of the book, "Some Notes on Reception," contains overviews of texts about specific works such as *The Dead Christ*, *The Solothurn Madonna*, and *The Meyer Madonna*. Other themes addressed include the perception of Holbein's character and his place among other Renaissance masters, his work as a portraitist, his use of illusion, authenticity controversies, and a brief chronicle of Holbein collectors. The second part of the book is a comprehensive listing of more than 2,500 bibliographic citations for works dealing with Holbein and his oeuvre, each accompanied by an annotation outlining the authors' principal contributions. The range of material covered includes not only books and scholarly journals, but also newspapers and other popular publications.

Roberts, Jane. *Holbein*. London: Oresko Books, 1979; New York: Jupiter, 1981. A good study of Holbein's art, with particular emphasis on the drawings and portraits of his two English sojourns. There is a brief, but generally informative biography.

Rowlands, John. *Holbein: The Paintings of Hans Holbein the Younger*. Oxford: Phaidon Press, and Boston: Godine, 1985. Essentially a study of Holbein's works in oil, this book contains an excellent introductory biography. Very helpful in providing accessible critical commentary on the artist's work.

Strong, Roy. *Holbein and Henry VIII*. London: Routledge, and New York: Pantheon, 1967. A volume in the Studies in British Art series, this work provides an extensive review of Holbein's relationship with the Tudor court. In addition to the paintings and drawings, Holbein was productive in all aspects of decorations and embellishments.

Michael Witkoski

FRANÇOIS HOTMAN

Born: August 23, 1524; Paris, France

Died: February 12, 1590; Basel, Swiss Confederation

Areas of Achievement: Law and political science

Contribution: Hotman, a brilliant French legal scholar and teacher, used his considerable knowledge and writing ability for the Huguenot cause of freedom of conscience, and, in the process, developed a philosophy of limited constitutional monarchy and became one of the first modern revolutionaries.

Early Life

François Hotman was born on August 23, 1524, in Paris, France. His father, Pierre Hotman, was a successful lawyer and landowner who, in 1524, had just entered the king's service. He was to be rewarded after twenty years for his loyalty to the Crown with an appointment as Conseiller in the Parlement de Paris, which made him an important member of the feudal office-holding nobility. Little is known of François' mother, Paule, née de Marle, or of his early childhood, except that, as the eldest son who would inherit his father's fief and office, he grew up being prepared for a legal career.

In 1536, Hotman entered the University of Paris, where he was exposed to the new Humanistic learning and developed considerable enthusiasm for classical literature and languages. At fourteen, considered something of a prodigy, Hotman enrolled in the school of law at the University of Orléans. Although the teaching of law was dominated by the Scholastic method, Hotman was also exposed again to the new Humanist approach and learned the methodology of subjecting civil law to historical criticism. The curriculum was rigorous, but Hotman worked hard and received his license in civil law in only two years. Returning to Paris to begin his career, he soon made friends with several leading Humanist scholars, who increased his devotion to the historical school of interpreting the law. Within one year, he had published the first of his many books on law, and, in August of 1546, he assumed his first teaching position at the University of Bourges.

The Reformation, which in time would shake Western civilization to its foundations and profoundly affect Hotman, had begun in earnest only seven years before he was born. In 1536, the Reformation entered a new and more troubled phase with the publication of John Calvin's *Christianae religionis institutio* (*Institutes of the Christian Religion*, 1561). Little is known of when Hotman first came into contact with Reformation ideas. His conversion to Calvinism seems to have begun slowly during his years at the Universities of Paris and Orléans, quickened after his return to Paris, and culminated during his first visit to Switzerland in 1547.

Hotman returned from the University of Orléans to live at home with his parents for some months, but his father's work on a special tribunal of the Parlement de Paris, which was hearing the cases of Lutheran and Calvinist "heretics," apparently became more than he could tolerate. He fled in the spring of 1548, constantly afraid of pursuit by his father. He ended up in Geneva, where, for a short time, he was secretary to John Calvin, the man he now considered his spiritual father. Hotman's break with home and parents was complete and painful. His father disinherited him and the French government and French Catholic Church began to consider him dangerous because of his writings in support of the Huguenot cause. Hotman was never again either financially secure or able to return to France and Paris for any length of time. Geneva had become and remained the spiritual, intellectual, and often physical focus of Hotman's life.

Hotman was a moderately attractive man but otherwise had no outstanding or remarkable physical characteristics. His portrait shows penetrating, wide-set eyes and a high forehead and receding hairline that left him mostly bald by middle age. In the fashion of most Huguenots, he wore a beard and mustache but kept them relatively short, unlike many of his long-bearded colleagues. Within a year of arriving in Geneva, he married Claude Aubelin, the daughter of Sieur de la Rivière, formerly of Orléans, but who now was a fellow exile in Geneva for the Huguenot faith. Eleven children were born to them, eight of whom reached adulthood. Despite the frequent moves of the household, the uncertainty, and, occasionally, the fear of French reprisals, the marriage seems to have been a happy one.

Life's Work

Calvin took a deep interest in his followers. Now that Hotman was married, he needed a position with a larger income. Calvin found it for him at the

Academy of Lausanne, where Hotman was to teach dialectic and Greek and Latin literature. The Lausanne Academy was the oldest Reformed (non-Catholic) school in a French-speaking area, and Hotman's salary was adequate. During these early years, he published a series of translations and commentaries on great Greek and Latin classical works. He also produced books and tracts on law, but only one of these won for him any particular recognition. In 1551, Hotman published his *De statu primitivae ecclesiae* (1553; state of the primitive church), a Calvinist tract that attacked the Catholic Church for its deviations from original Christianity. His particular achievement with this work was to take standard Calvinist doctrine and support it with a wide selection of legal and historical authorities and precedents, a style he would perfect in the years to come.

In time, Hotman grew restless in Lausanne. In 1554, he returned to Geneva, which had granted him citizenship, and was soon involved in promoting the Huguenot cause. He did not stay long, however, moving to Strasbourg in October of 1555, where he remained eight years teaching at the academy there. Although not the oldest, it was the most famous and successful of all the Protestant schools and an important adjunct to the Calvinist church in Geneva. The new position had special significance for Hotman because he was taking the place of a rival legal scholar who had fallen out with Calvin, partly because of Hotman. In Strasbourg, Hotman was able to concentrate on teaching and studying civil law, especially the examination of Roman law from a historical point of view. His study of Justinian's *Corpus juris civilis* led to a number of publications over the next five years and laid the foundations of his fame as a distinguished legal scholar of the Humanist school. These works also earned for him the doctoral degree from the University of Basel in 1558.

During this time, Hotman's vital interests in Calvinism and in legal scholarship combined, as his consciousness of politics awakened, into a career as a revolutionary propagandist. His central theme became the need to limit constitutionally the power of the French government, especially in religious matters. To this end, he built a case, based on legal and historical precedent, that it was legitimate to resist the exercise of unjustified authority by the French monarchy. Hotman discussed these matters with anyone who was interested and acquired a network of contacts with Protestant leaders all over

Europe. He exchanged a large volume of letters with them over the years. He particularly admired the English and regarded Elizabeth I as one of the great hopes of the Protestant cause. He sent Jean, his eldest son, to study at the University of Oxford.

His first major propaganda pamphlet was published in 1560. It was a vigorous denunciation of the noble house of Guise, especially Charles, Cardinal of Lorraine, who led the ultra-Catholic party in France. The cardinal and the Guise family had pressured King Henry II and his successors to increase the repression of Protestantism in France to counteract the increasing popularity of Calvinism, particularly among the French nobility and burgher classes. Following Hotman's lead, and in some cases undoubtedly with additional contributions written but not publicly acknowledged by him, a large number of Huguenot propaganda pamphlets were published attacking the Cardinal of Lorraine and his faction, and presenting the Huguenot case. The Guises countered with claims that the Huguenots had attempted to murder the Catholic party's leaders and the king, and were also guilty of heresy and sedition. These were the opening salvos of what became a series of eight religious civil wars in France. Hotman had become the leading ideologist of the Huguenot cause for liberty of conscience, one of the trusted diplomatic agents and advisers of the Huguenot leadership, and a revolutionary.

By August of 1572, Hotman's reputation as a scholar and his list of texts and essays on legal subjects had grown considerably. His work for the Huguenots had brought him many friends and admirers among the Protestant leadership. His connections with important French nobles had made possible a return to France and a position at the University of Bourges. The Saint Bartholomew's Day Massacre, however, caused him to leave again. In Paris on August 23, 1572, Hotman's forty-eighth birthday, the ultra-Catholics began slaughtering Huguenots. The king and the queen mother were parties to this butchery, which spread from Paris throughout France wherever there were concentrations of Huguenots. Suspicious of what could happen, Hotman walked out of town in disguise and without any of his possessions the instant he learned of the events in Paris. He and his family lost everything, although Hotman was later able to recover a few of his more important manuscripts. Once again, now in midlife, he sought asylum in Geneva, where after a few months he accepted a faculty position at the Geneva Academy.

The Saint Bartholomew's Day Massacre resulted in the fourth of the French religious civil wars and in making Hotman an overtly declared revolutionary. In the propaganda tracts that were pouring from his pen, he no longer blamed the political tyranny and persecution of the Huguenots on the ultra-Catholic party but took aim directly at the king. Hotman spent much of the rest of his life developing his ideas on limited constitutional monarchy and freedom of religion and conscience.

Hotman's masterwork on these themes was *Franco-Gallia*. Although he had been working on this project for at least six years, its publication in 1573 was especially timely. Hotman's fundamental proposition, supported with a wide variety of evidence, was that the ancient and medieval Gauls and Franks had a constitution that limited the monarch's authority by requiring that the making of law be shared with a national council called the Estates-General. This council also elected the king. In Hotman's description, the powers of the Estates-General were remarkably similar to those of a twentieth century legislature and not a medieval assembly. Hotman argued that the king did not rule by hereditary right but by the authority of the people as expressed in the Estates-General. After equating royal absolutism with tyranny, Hotman suggested that the people have the right to depose a tyrant king. That was probably his most radical proposition. In an obvious reference to the Guise family of Lorraine, which was not considered an integral part of France at the time, Hotman also included the use of foreign mercenaries as typical of tyrants.

In *Franco-Gallia*, Hotman was clearly attempting to prove that ancient and medieval France had known a considerable degree of political and religious freedom that more recent national leaders, specifically the Queen Mother Catherine, her sons, and the Guise family, had distorted and corrupted for their own personal gain and at the people's expense. It was an enormously popular work among Protestants—infamous among the ultra-Catholics—and was translated into several other languages and went through several editions in Hotman's lifetime. It was a propaganda work and not entirely accurate historically but so impressive in its demonstrated learning and so brilliantly done that the Calvinist king, Henry of Navarre, who in time would end the French religious civil wars and become King Henry IV of France, enlisted Hotman's aid on numerous occasions. On the other hand, the Catholic party felt obliged to put their best talent to work in trying to refute Hotman.

Hotman's remaining years were not spent in comfort. When a temporary peace came in the French religious wars in 1576 and various offers came to return to France, Hotman was too fearful of another massacre of Huguenots and rejected all offers. His financial situation in Geneva was grim, and his health was deteriorating. To make matters worse, Geneva, which had been threatened by the Duchy of Savoy periodically for years, entered a prolonged period of heightened anxiety over the possibility of being attacked and invaded. When the constant state of fear became more than he could bear, Hotman once again moved his family in August of 1578. He had had numerous offers but decided to accept a teaching position at the University of Basel, where he thought he could live and work in peace. While that proved to be true, his financial condition did not significantly improve and he found that his faith was tolerated but increasingly unpopular. Hotman's physical retreat to Basel, however, was only a semiretirement, not a full retreat from the Huguenot cause. He continued to be actively involved in the plots and schemes of his party, and in writing tracts and pamphlets. As something of a celebrity whose list of frequent correspondents contained the greatest minds of Protestant Europe, he also had many visitors, including the famous essayist Michel de Montaigne.

Basel was not immune to the ravages of the plague, which, in February of 1583, swept through the region. Hotman's wife, who had always taken extraordinary measures to get herself and her family away whenever the plague broke out, caught the disease this time and died soon afterward. Hotman was further deeply disturbed when Daniel, one of his sons, converted to Catholicism. As he had done so often before when distressed, he moved, this time back to Geneva, in late September, 1584, where he knew that a position at the academy was still available to him.

Besides the troubles in his personal life, the urging of his coreligionist Henry of Navarre to write in support of his claim to the French throne may also have influenced Hotman to return to Geneva. After Charles IX died in 1574, his brother became King Henry III. Henry III's only heir, however, had died in 1584 and the succession was between Henry of Navarre, now the most legitimate heir, and his uncle, the Cardinal of Bourbon, who had the support of the ultra-Catholics. Hotman wrote and published several works on the question, basing the case for Henry of Navarre on fundamental constitutional law. The Guises were sufficiently disturbed by Hotman's work to set several of their best writers to work answering him. Henry of Navarre was sufficiently impressed and made Hotman a councillor and member of his privy council in 1585, a position Hotman held until his death. In that same year, the ultra-Catholics virtually forced Henry III to provoke a war with Henry of Navarre and the Huguenots. This was the War of the Three Henrys, the eighth and final religious civil war in France. Apparently, the Guises hoped that the war would eliminate Henry of Navarre as a possible heir to the throne. The war, although not decisive, went more in favor of the Catholics than the Huguenots until 1589. In that year, Duke Henry of Guise seemed to be positioning himself to seize the throne and Henry III had him assassinated. The ultra-Catholics rose in rebellion, and Henry III was forced to flee. On his way to Henry of Navarre for sanctuary, he was murdered by a Catholic monk. Meanwhile, the situation in Geneva was bleak. Savoy was once again threatening and the city was in a virtual state of siege. In September of 1589, Hotman and his remaining three unmarried daughters escaped Geneva by water on Lake Lausanne to Basel. His health had been declining for some time and severe edema was added to his other health problems. On February 12, 1590, he died. In his will, he disinherited his son Daniel. To the end, his cause was the most important aspect of his life.

Summary

François Hotman was an uncompromising idealist and would have had mixed reactions to the immediate outcome of his cause. He would have been overjoyed when Henry of Navarre finally prevailed in the field of battle over the ultra-Catholics and became King Henry IV of France in 1594. He also would have applauded Henry IV's Edict of Nantes in 1598, which gave the Huguenots political and religious rights. He would have been appalled, however, by the high cost: the conversion of Henry IV to Catholicism. He would also have been disturbed by the failure of the Estates-General to develop into an institution capable of limiting and controlling royal authority. In the next century, Catholicism regained much of the ground lost to the Huguenots, sometimes by force, as in Louis XIV's Revocation of the Edict of Nantes in 1685. In 1789, during the reign of Louis XVI, the Estates-General would emerge as a limiting force, but with such suddenness and violence as to create a great revolution.

Hotman, who wanted to restore religion and law to an idealized primitive perfection and thereby establish popular sovereignty and liberty of conscience, did not succeed in his own time. He did succeed, however, in raising issues and laying foundations upon which later theorists of the seventeenth and eighteenth centuries would build a new vision of the state, which included not only concepts of popular sovereignty and religious freedom but also of social contract, individual freedom, and the rule of law.

Bibliography

Bainton, Roland H. *The Reformation of the Sixteenth Century.* Boston: Beacon Press, 1952; London: Hodder and Stoughton, 1953. For those interested in the religious issues of Hotman's era, this older but still quite useful work explains the development of Protestant thought and doctrine with sympathy and precision.

Dunn, Richard S. *The Age of Religious War, 1559-1715.* 2d ed. New York: Norton, 1979. An excellent, readable, yet scholarly general history of Europe which includes the era of the wars between Protestants and Catholics that began in the latter half of the sixteenth century and lasted until the mid-seventeenth century. The Catholic-Huguenot wars of France and how they fit into the overall pattern of European history are well presented.

Kelley, Donald R. *François Hotman: A Revolutionary's Ordeal*. Princeton, N.J.: Princeton University Press, 1973. The only full-length biography of Hotman in English. A sympathetic treatment of Hotman's life, but it does not ignore his faults. Sometimes omits background that increases understanding of the significance of Hotman's work.

Myers, A. R. *Parliaments and Estates in Europe to 1789*. London: Thames and Hudson, and New York: Harcourt Brace, 1975. A good general discussion of the origins and evolution of representative political assemblies and legislatures in Europe from their medieval origins to the French Revolution. Mentions Hotman in the discussion of the French Estates-General and the impact of the religious wars.

Neale, J. E. *The Age of Catherine de Medici*. London: Cape, 1943; New York: Barnes and Noble, 1959. An excellent history of France during the latter half of the sixteenth century. Concentrates on political and legal issues, the collapse of the Valois dynasty, and assumption of the French throne by Henry of Navarre.

Reynolds, Beatrice. *Proponents of Limited Monarchy in Sixteenth Century France: François Hotman and Jean Bodin*. New York: Columbia University Press, and London: King, 1931. An older but still interesting, in-depth treatment of Hotman's ideas of constitutional monarchy. Not as clear as it could be on the relationship of Hotman's political ideas to his religious beliefs.

Skinner, Quentin. *The Foundations of Modern Political Thought*. 2 vols. Cambridge and New York: Cambridge University Press, 1978. Perhaps the best scholarly study of the political philosophy of the Renaissance and Reformation. Volume 2 has numerous references to Hotman and the Huguenot cause. Particularly valuable in explaining the connections between religious doctrine and political philosophy.

Richard L. Hillard

CATHERINE HOWARD

Born: c. 1521; probably at Horsham or Lambeth, England
Died: February 13, 1542; London, England
Area of Achievement: Monarchy
Contribution: As fifth wife to King Henry VIII, Catherine Howard briefly reigned as queen of England until revelations about her personal life brought about her sudden downfall and execution.

Early Life

Catherine Howard was born into the English aristocracy, her father being Lord Edmund Howard, a younger son of Thomas Howard, second duke of Norfolk. Through her Howard connections, Catherine was ironically a first cousin to Anne Boleyn, Henry VIII's second queen. Little is known about the future queen's childhood. She grew up in a large family of ten children and received little formal education. Her mother, Joyce Culpeper, died when Catherine was quite young. Her father, Lord Edmund Howard, subsequently married two more times, but he saw little of his daughter. Being a younger son, Lord Edmund did not inherit the considerable family estates, and he experienced continual financial difficulties, even after his appointment as controller of Calais in 1534. Never a major influence on his daughter's life, he died in 1539, a year before Catherine's dramatic rise to power.

The most significant development of Catherine's childhood occurred when her father sent her to live with his stepmother Agnes, the dowager duchess of Norfolk. One of the wealthiest and most influential women of her day, the duchess maintained a grand household at her country estate at Horsham in Sussex and her town house at Lambeth, across the River Thames from London. The duchess exercised only a loose supervision over her numerous charges; at Horsham, young Catherine soon engaged in a serious flirtation with Henry Manox, a musician hired to teach her to play the lute and virginal. Although the relationship did not become an actual affair, Manox followed Catherine to Lambeth and openly bragged to numerous people in the household of the liberties he had enjoyed with the duchess' charge.

While at Lambeth, probably in 1538, Catherine became sexually active with her next serious suitor, Francis Dereham, a distant kinsman of Duchess Agnes and a pensioner in her household. The two lovers openly exchanged gifts and were heard to call each other "husband" and "wife." Their clandestine nighttime meetings became something of a scandal and provoked the jealousy of Manox, who sent an anonymous note to the duchess informing her of the relationship. Discovering the two in an ardent embrace, she angrily struck both of them. Dereham soon left to seek his fortune in Ireland, leaving his life savings with his paramour. Catherine's passion for Dereham quickly cooled, because in 1540 her uncle Norfolk used his influence to secure her a position at court, an event that drastically transformed the fortunes of this previously obscure young woman.

Life's Work

The Howard family used Catherine as a pawn in the dangerous political game for dominance at the court of the aging Henry VIII. The duke stood as the representative of the conservative faction of old nobility who opposed the pro-Protestant policies of Thomas Cromwell, Henry's lord chancellor and the guiding genius behind the English Reforma-

tion. To cement an alliance with the German Protestants, Cromwell had just engineered the king's marriage to Anne of Cleves. From their first meeting in January, 1540, Henry had openly expressed his displeasure with his new foreign bride. Sensing Cromwell's vulnerability, the Norfolk faction brought Catherine to court and coached her on ways to attract the monarch's attention.

Henry evidently met Catherine at a banquet hosted by Norfolk's ally, Stephen Gardiner, bishop of Winchester; by April, the king was obviously smitten. On April 24, he granted her the lands of a convicted felon, and even more lavish gifts followed the next month. Queen Anne's last public appearance with Henry occurred at the May Day festivities; soon thereafter, he sent her to the country so that he could court Catherine openly. On many spring nights, the royal barge crossed the Thames to visit Duchess Agnes' Lambeth residence so that Henry could enjoy Catherine's company.

Catherine's triumph came swiftly. On June 10, Henry ordered Cromwell's arrest on charges of heresy and treason. Facing death, the former chancellor agreed to supply information to enable Henry to divorce his German consort. Anne did not oppose Henry's schemes, and the grateful monarch offered her a generous settlement. Their divorce became final on July 9. Nineteen days later, ironically on the day Cromwell was beheaded, Henry summoned the bishop of London to the royal palace at Oatlands, where he secretly married Catherine. He publicly acknowledged her as his new queen at Hampton Court on August 8.

The aging, increasingly bloated monarch initially seemed besotted by his lively teenage bride. Catherine's youthful vigor, coupled with her submissiveness and outward virtue, rejuvenated her husband, who showered her with public caresses and worldly goods. He soon bestowed on her all the lordships and manors that had belonged to his beloved Queen Jane Seymour, as well as some of Cromwell's former properties. The new queen chose "No other wish but his" as the motto above her new coat of arms.

Although Catherine's Howard relatives again found themselves in a position of preeminence at court, the new queen was far more naïve about court politics and factions than her two English predecessors, Anne Boleyn and Jane Seymour. Also unlike some of Henry's previous spouses, Catherine evidently made no real attempt to preoccupy herself with politics or interfere with state affairs, except for a handful of intercessions on behalf of prominent prisoners in the Tower. Throughout her brief reign, her main preoccupation seemed to be clothes and dancing, not political intrigue. The king appeared delighted with his young bride; the two remained constantly in each other's company until February, 1541.

Sometime in the spring of 1541, though, Catherine embarked upon more dangerous behavior, which culminated in an affair with a distant cousin, Thomas Culpeper, an attractive young courtier who was several decades younger than her husband. The only surviving letter in Catherine's hand, written in April, 1541, is a love letter to Culpeper in which she recklessly pronounced herself "Yours as long as life endures."

Their affair evidently continued throughout the summer and autumn while Henry took his bride on a tour of northern England. Lavish ceremonies awaited the royal couple as they visited numerous towns. At Pontefract in Yorkshire, Francis Dereham reappeared in Catherine's life and demanded a post at court. On August 27, she unwisely appointed him her private secretary, perhaps to buy his silence about their previous relationship.

The royal entourage returned to Hampton Court on October 30, and Henry gave orders for a special thanksgiving service to be held celebrating his marriage. However, a sudden turn of events brought an end to the marriage and death to the young queen. Shortly before their return, Archbishop Thomas Cranmer had received disturbing reports about Catherine's clandestine life before her marriage. The initial source of this news was John Lascelles, whose sister, Mary Hall, had been in the dowager duchess of Norfolk's service while Catherine lived with her. A zealous Protestant, Lascelles was not a personal enemy of the queen, but he did despise what she represented—the triumph of the Howard faction at court. After consultations with other leading men at court, Cranmer handed the king a note with the damning information while Henry was hearing a mass for the dead.

Initially astonished and unwilling to believe the charges, Henry nevertheless ordered the archbishop to conduct a thorough investigation and to confine the queen to her apartments pending its outcome. He never saw her again, as interrogation of numerous witnesses confirmed his worst fears. Upon being informed by his council that the allegations against Catherine had a sound basis, the king openly broke down and cried. Subsequently, increasingly outraged at being cuckolded, he furiously called for a sword so that he could execute his adulterous spouse personally.

Whereas Anne Boleyn had immediately been sent to the Tower after allegations of her infidelity, Catherine was instead placed under house arrest at the Abbey of Syon in Middlesex. The king allowed her to have four attendants and access to three chambers during this initial stage of her confinement. He also let Cranmer hold out some hope of royal mercy to Catherine if she would fully confess.

After initially denying the charges against her and changing her story several times, the queen eventually confessed her guilt to Cranmer. As evidence accumulated, it became obvious that Catherine had been not only indiscreet before her marriage to Henry, but also unfaithful to him afterward. On November 22, a royal proclamation announced that she had forfeited her rights as queen; two days later, she was formally indicted both for having concealed her relationship with Dereham before her marriage and for having committed adultery with Culpeper after becoming Henry's wife.

Culpeper and Dereham paid for their folly by being executed on December 1. The king decided against a public trial for his unfaithful wife. Instead, she was condemned by a special act of attainder passed by Parliament and approved by the king in early February. On two occasions, members of the council invited Catherine to come before Parliament to defend herself, but she refused, admitting her guilt and hoping for the king's mercy.

On February 10, Catherine was removed to the Tower, and on the evening of February 12, she was told she would die the following morning. She requested that the block on which she was to be executed be brought into her room in the Tower so that she could practice how to place herself. Early on February 13, guards escorted the prisoner to a spot within the Tower grounds, the same location where her cousin had been beheaded nearly six years earlier. Catherine made a brief speech admitting her sins to both God and king, after which the executioner severed her head with a single stroke from his axe. Like Anne Boleyn's before her, her body was interred in the chapel of St. Peter ad Vinicula within the Tower.

Summary

Catherine Howard reigned only some eighteen months as Henry VIII's fifth queen, and fewer details about her brief life exist than for any of his other consorts. Except for a possible depiction in a stained-glass window in King's College Chapel, Cambridge, no contemporary portrait of her survived. Nor did Catherine play a significant role in determining policy during the tempestuous final years of Henry's reign. Rather, her powerful Howard relations used her as a pawn to forward their own ambitions at the volatile court of the second Tudor king.

Catherine became Henry VIII's final passion. His immediately preceding marriage with Anne of Cleves had been arranged, but Henry deliberately chose the young and seemingly innocent Catherine, some three decades his junior. For a few months, she succeeded in reinvigorating her prematurely aging husband. Her fall left him an increasingly embittered and dangerous sovereign and resulted in the temporary disgrace of her family. Her uncle Norfolk managed to save his life by abandoning Catherine and joining in her condemnation, as he had done with his other royal niece, Anne Boleyn; but Howard influence at Henry's court ended as the result of the scandal. An odd sequence of events had briefly turned this obscure young woman into the most prominent lady in the realm. Her indiscretions both before and after her marriage brought a tragically early end to her life.

Bibliography

Fraser, Antonia. *The Wives of Henry VIII.* New York: Knopf, 1992. Part 4 of this well-written and researched collective biography by one of Britain's most popular writers provides a colorful portrait of Catherine and her contemporaries.

Lindsey, Karen. *Divorced, Beheaded, Survived: A Feminist Reinterpretation of the Wives of Henry VIII.* New York: Addison-Wesley, 1995. This lively collective biography examines the position of Catherine and Henry's other wives based upon recent feminist interpretations of the role of women in Tudor society.

Loades, David. *Henry VIII and His Queens.* Gloucestershire, England: Phoenix Mill, 1994. This short and highly readable work by a respected British historian provides a useful introduction to the topic.

Smith, Lacey Baldwin. *A Tudor Tragedy: The Life and Times of Catherine Howard.* London: Clay, 1961. This sympathetic study by a leading Tudor-Stuart historian remains the standard biography.

Weir, Alison. *The Six Wives of Henry VIII*. New York: Grove Press, 1991. Chapters 13 to 15 of this collective biography complement the work of Fraser. Weir asserts that Catherine was born circa 1525, making her younger than other scholars assume.

Tom L. Auffenberg

HUÁSCAR

Born: c. 1495; Cuzco, Peru
Died: 1532; Andamarca, Peru
Areas of Achievement: Monarchy and military
Contribution: Huáscar, the last ruler of the Incas, has the unenviable renown of losing the mightiest empire in pre-Columbian America.

Early Life

Few details of the birth, childhood, and youth of Tupac Cusi Huallpa, known as Huáscar, survive. His father, Huayna Capac, was "the Inca," eleventh in his line. From 1493 to 1525, he ruled Tahuantinsuyu ("four quarters"), the empire that stretched from northern Chile to Ecuador's border with Colombia. Huáscar's mother, Ragua Ocllo, was Huayna Capac's sister, as custom required for a queen, or *qoya*. Huáscar was born in the capital, Cuzco, on the eastern slopes of the Andes Mountains in southern Peru about 1495.

Huayna Capac celebrated Huáscar's weaning-and-hair-cutting ceremony, an initiation rite, by ordering craftsmen to fashion an immense golden chain. According to one account, the chain—*huasca* in the Incan language—was seven hundred feet long and so heavy that two hundred men could not lift it. This extravagant gift is supposed to have inspired the name by which Huáscar is best known.

As a teenager, Huáscar remained behind in Cuzco when Huayna Capac left on extensive military campaigns, taking with him Huáscar's two elder half-brothers, Ninan Cuyochi and Atahualpa. Huayna Capac was especially fond of the latter and spent the last twelve years of his reign with Atahualpa in Quito (now the capital of Ecuador).

Life's Work

Who was to succeed Huayna Capac appears to have been unsettled, as if the Inca could not make up his mind. Historical sources speak of Huáscar as if he were the heir, but his mother was Huayna Capac's second oldest sister, and Ninan Cuyochi, the son of the Inca's oldest sister, had the better claim. Furthermore, Atahualpa stood highest in his father's affection and had been groomed by the Inca to be a leader, although he could not hold supreme power because his mother was not of royal blood.

When Huayna Capac fell ill from smallpox in 1525, he had a premonition of death. He dispatched advisers to prepare Ninan Cuyochi to assume power, but the eldest son himself was already dead of smallpox. Huayna Capac then named Huáscar the heir, although with an important provision. He made Huáscar promise to treat the region around Quito as a semiautonomous province to be ruled by Atahualpa as a viceroy. Huáscar readily agreed. When Huayna Capac died, Huáscar received the *borla* in the official coronation ceremony in Cuzco. The *borla*, the insignia of the Inca, was a headband with a fringe in front that hung down to the wearer's eyebrows. With the assumption of power, Huáscar became a god in Incan religion, to be obeyed unquestioningly, upon pain of death.

God or not, he was still subject to the intricate politics of the Cuzco court. Huayna Capac had left Huáscar with many half-brothers, some loyal and some ambitious on their own behalf. The situation was ripe for intrigue, especially since Atahualpa commanded one-fifth of the realm from Quito, where the most experienced military officers lived and supported him. Moreover, an ancient division of Cuzco into Hanan and Hurin moieties had evolved into politically opposed factions; Huáscar was Hurin, while his mother and Atahualpa were Hanan. Huáscar could count on the loyalty of neither his capital nor his close kin.

Huáscar was aware of the dangers to his reign. He was far from stupid, but having been raised a royal heir in the narrow, elitist atmosphere of the Cuzco court, he was haughty, impulsive, and tactless. He may also have suffered from neuroses: Some contemporary sources call him "half mad" and argue that the ugliness of his short, swarthy physique proved that he was unfit to rule. Inexperience and willfulness, probably manipulated by the self-interested counsel of courtiers, soon made him disliked in the capital as arrogant and irresponsible. In any case, he quickly committed a series of major blunders.

The first occurred when he summoned Atahualpa to Cuzco. Atahualpa, Ragua Ocllo, and others of the royal court were to accompany the corpse of Huayna Capac to the capital for interment. While there, Atahualpa was to pledge his loyalty to the new Inca, as the law required. Atahualpa accompanied the group for awhile but then turned back, sending a trusted friend of his father to assure Huáscar of his loyalty. When the dead Inca's entourage was near Cuzco, Huáscar learned that his half-brother was still in Quito; he became enraged, interpreting Atahualpa's absence as disrespect. Deeply suspicious, he overreacted. He arrested the whole group, confined his mother, and tortured and executed Atahualpa's emissary.

If Atahualpa suspected that he was not safe in Huáscar's hands, as seems likely, he now had clear reason for his distrust. Worse for Huáscar, he had turned his mother into a political opponent. When he sought to take his eldest sister as his *qoya*, he needed Ragua Ocllo's formal permission. She refused it until he threatened her, hardening her enmity toward him.

Atahualpa sent another group of five noblemen to convey his loyalty to Huáscar. Before going to the Inca, however, the principal emissary visited Ragua Ocllo, who received him warmly. That meeting further inflamed Huáscar's suspicions. He executed four of the group and sent the last back to Atahualpa with a preemptory summons.

Atahualpa had no intention of delivering himself into Huáscar's power. With the support of his advisers, he gathered military forces, whereupon Huáscar declared Atahualpa to be a traitor. This was another blunder. Instead of coming to terms with his brother, Huáscar forced him into outright civil war.

Huáscar could not afford a civil war, politically or financially. Economics especially were a problem. Incan law devoted the income from areas conquered by previous rulers to supporting their households and the religious cults devoted to them. Each equal in size to Huáscar's court, the courts of the dead Incas drained off most state revenues. To support himself, Huáscar had to conquer new territory of his own. His attempts to do so in the south met with little success. The richest prizes lay to the north, in Colombia, but Atahualpa blocked the way. Huáscar tried to remedy the problem with reform: He moved to disband the cults of the dead Inca. Fierce opposition from the Incan priesthood stymied him, and all he achieved was to make the priests into political opponents.

Huáscar dispatched an army, commanded by a loyal half-brother, to destroy Atahualpa in Quito. Although Atahualpa had far fewer resources to support a war, he had better troops and officers. In fact, his two top generals, Quizquiz and Chalicuchima, are thought to have been the ablest military leaders produced by the Inca Empire. The rebel army that met the Incan forces in southern Ecuador was seasoned from many campaigns under Huayna Capac. Atahualpa's generals won battle after battle, turned back the Incan army, and pushed it relentlessly toward Cuzco. Atahualpa followed well behind the main army, meeting with tribal leaders along the way and requiring them to swear allegiance to him. He ordered his troops to devastate the villages of those who refused.

Although Huáscar reinforced his army and changed commanders, Atahualpa's troops pressed on until they stood near Cuzco itself. At this point, Huáscar took personal command. He succeeded in punishing the enemy during a protracted battle, but his military inexperience showed. He was lured into an ambush and captured by Chalicuchima. Huáscar's army fell apart when it learned that he had been captured; soon afterward, Cuzco fell to Quizquiz with little resistance, almost certainly because the Hanan faction was happy to see Huáscar defeated.

On orders from Atahualpa, still well behind the army, Quizquiz massacred Huáscar's family and followers before his eyes, and he was publicly humiliated. Atahualpa donned the *borla* and deported himself as the new Inca, but he could not truly be the Inca until he was officially crowned in Cuzco.

On his way there, he heard news that a band of bearded strangers were advancing into the Andes from the coast. The new arrivals were Francisco Pizarro and an army of fewer than two hundred Spaniards. Curious, Atahualpa turned aside to meet them in Cajamarca. He had heard of the Spaniards and, with tens of thousands of warriors around him, he intended to capture them. Pizarro tricked Atahualpa and captured him first. Still vastly outnumbered, the Spaniards held on to Atahualpa and bargained for a ransom. Fearing that Pizarro might use Huáscar to further weaken his bargaining power, Atahualpa secretly ordered Huáscar killed. The twelfth and last anointed Inca was put to death in Andamarca, not far from Cajamarca, where Atahualpa was held prisoner. Pizarro killed him a few months later.

Summary

With the last Inca, Huáscar, dead, as well as his rival, Atahualpa, the Inca armies fell into disarray, and the Spanish were able to conquer the Inca Empire, even though it was vastly superior in numbers of fighters and resources. Pizarro's astonishing success reveals several weaknesses in the Inca state.

First, succession of power from one Inca to the next was unfixed. The dying Inca, in fact, was responsible for naming his heir, who could be any of his pure-blood sons. Huayna Capac almost guaranteed trouble when he was indecisive about an heir and then apportioned part of his realm to a favorite not in line to succeed, Atahualpa.

Second, the Inca state relied precariously on one man, the Inca. Tahuantinsuyu had been blessed with a series of talented military leaders and administrators who held power firmly and expanded the empire's territories, but the state did not fare well without a dynamic Inca. The Inca Empire was vulnerable to the political intrigue among ambitious lieutenants that arises around a leader's incompetence.

Third, the Incas' own mythology worked against them. Although Huayna Capac, Atahualpa, and Huáscar knew about the invasion of South and Central America by white strangers, they thought it possible that these strangers were gods whose arrival had been prophesied. This uncertainty may have kept Huayna Capac from ensuring that the Spaniards could not threaten him.

Because they brought with them new diseases that were lethal to the Incas, the Spaniards may well have triumphed anyway. Smallpox, which was particularly virulent, reached the Incas even before Pizarro did, and it decimated the nobility and army. The civil war between Huáscar and Atahualpa, which by some estimates killed up to a hundred thousand warriors, further crippled the Incas and prepared the way for the Spanish victory.

Bibliography

Betanzos, Juan de. *Narrative of the Incas*. Translated by Ronald Hamilton and Dana Buchanan. Austin: University of Texas Press, 1996. An example of the kind of contemporary source upon which historians depend. Married to a royal Inca, Betanzos finished this somewhat slanted history in 1557.

Brundage, Burr Cartwright. *Empire of the Inca*. Norman: University of Oklahoma Press, 1963. Brundage relates, in a convoluted prose style, the rise of the Inca state, the careers of its twelve emperors, its social and religious organization, and its conquest by the Spanish.

Davies, Nigel. *The Incas*. Niwot: University Press of Colorado, 1995. A close analysis of the Spanish sources of Incan history, the archaeological evidence, and scholars' interpretations of both. Davies argues that little is known with certainty about the Inca rulers.

Hemmings, John. *The Conquest of the Incas*. New York: Harcourt Brace, 1970. This captivating, richly detailed book chronicles the conquest of the Inca empire by Spaniards. The opening chapters describe Pizarro's encounter with Atahualpa and the fate of Huáscar.

Hyams, Edward, and George Ordish. *The Last of the Incas*. New York: Simon and Schuster, 1963. A provocative review of the rise and fall of the Incas that insists the empire was socialistic and the Incan skill for government was inherited. Hyams and Ordish find the Incas more benevolent than do other historians.

McIntyre, Loren. *The Incredible Incas and Their Timeless Land*. Washington, D.C.: National Geographic Society, 1975. Relates basic Incan history vividly and describes the society and its physical environment. Many lovely color drawings and photographs complement the text.

Malpass, Michael A. *Daily Life in the Inca Empire*. Westport, Conn.: Greenwood Press, 1996. Written for complete newcomers to pre-Columbian history, the text carefully defines Inca terms and anthropological concepts as it describes Inca culture and history. With illustrations and a handy glossary.

Roger Smith

JÁNOS HUNYADI

Born: c. 1407; place unknown
Died: August 11, 1456; Zimony (Zemun)
Areas of Achievement: Warfare and government
Contribution: By organizing, financing, and leading the Hungarian and Central European military forces, Hunyadi halted the Ottoman Empire's advance at the Balkan Mountains, postponing for some seventy years the Turkish conquest of central Hungary.

Early Life

Popularly believed to be the son of Sigismund, King of Hungary and Holy Roman Emperor, János Hunyadi was in fact the eldest child of Vojk, a lesser noble of Walachian origin who had moved to Hungary around 1395 and then had married into a Hungarian noble family. Besides János, the marriage produced two sons, as well as at least one daughter. János' father became a royal soldier and counselor, and in 1409 he received for his services an estate in Transylvania—called Vajdahunyad—from which the family took its name.

Little is known of Hunyadi's youth, since few extant records of the period mention him. Nevertheless, since he was for the most part a resident at the court of Sigismund, he presumably received early military training. This is all the more likely since soldierly prowess was generously rewarded with sizable grants of land, which in turn meant wealth and power.

Said to have been a born soldier, Hunyadi cut an impressive figure. He was of medium height and had a thick neck, long chestnut-brown hair, large, penetrating eyes, and a well-proportioned body. He began his military career in the 1420's under Pipo of Ozora. Around 1428 he married Erzsébet Szilágyi, herself a daughter of a noble family. Their marriage produced two sons, László and Mátyás, the latter destined to become perhaps Hungary's most illustrious king as Matthias Corvinus.

In 1430, Hunyadi entered the service of the king, accompanying Sigismund to Italy. There the young soldier served Fillippo Maria Visconti, Duke of Milan, for a time. In 1433, Hunyadi was reunited with Sigismund and accompanied him on many trips, including one to Bohemia in 1437. By then expertly trained in mercenary warfare, well acquainted with the most up-to-date Italian and Hussite military tactics and procedures, and experienced in the methods of the Turkish armies, Hunyadi dedicated himself to the struggle against the Ottomans.

Life's Work

In the fifteenth century, the Ottoman Empire was still dedicated to expansion and military conquest. This awesome momentum, created by economic need and religious fervor, had by Sigismund's time already carried the Turks deep into the Balkan Peninsula. The Ottoman wave would soon sweep over Hungary, whose own southern frontier reached into the Balkans.

Unfortunately, the Hungarian distribution of land and wealth, favoring the aristocrats at the expense of the Crown, did not seem a likely source for the centralized, unified effort that would be required to hold the great Turkish empire in check. Nevertheless, the single most powerful aristocrat in the country was a man both eminently qualified and highly motivated to stem the Ottoman advance: János Hunyadi.

According to the chronicler Thuróczy, Hunyadi's military virtues were great; the account cites his strength and courage as a soldier as well as his strategical and tactical acumen. Though an accurate portrayal of him, Thuróczy's account fails nevertheless to consider certain other necessary aspects of Hunyadi's character. He was also a crafty politician who, though disliked by his fellow aristocrats, managed to create important if short-lived alliances with his peers. Moreover, able to count on neither the king, whose own landholdings had seriously dwindled, nor the barons, who were reluctant to dip into their vast resources, Hunyadi organized and financed his armies himself, drawing on the revenue of his approximately six million acres of property.

Under Albert II of Habsburg (reigned 1437-1439), Sigismund's son-in-law and successor, Hunyadi and his brother served as joint military governors of Szörény (Severin). Hunyadi continued as Bán of Severin until 1446, protecting that area from the Ottoman menace. It was, from all accounts, these experiences which hastened his assimilation. To Hunyadi, himself an immigrant without a Magyar pedigree, the *patria* encompassed not merely the nobility but the people as a whole.

In 1440, a few months after Albert's death, the Polish king Władisław III was elected King of Hungary by the Diet. Władisław, who saw Hunyadi as the real leader against the Turks, put him in charge of the key fortress in Belgrade and of the southern border region as a whole. In 1441, he appointed Hunyadi both Voivode of Transylvania and Ispán of Temesvár (Timişoara), offices he would hold until 1446. Hunyadi organized and equipped an army composed mainly of Bohemian Hussite mercenaries, but he rounded it out with his own adherents, relatives, noble vassals, and even peasants. He enjoyed his first victory over the Ottomans in 1442, driving the invading army out of Transylvania. This was the first such defeat ever suffered by the Ottomans in Europe, and news of it quickly spread, reviving hopes that the Balkans would indeed be liberated from the Turkish yoke.

Doubting that a passive defense would be adequate to deal with the Turkish menace, Hunyadi decided to take the offensive. Pressing toward the heart of the Ottoman Empire, he led his forces to one victory after another, occupying as he went the towns of Nish and Sofia. Though his long march was stalled not long after, his victories persuaded Sultan Murad II to negotiate for peace. Unfortunately, the treaty had no sooner been signed with the sultan's emissaries in Szeged than, at the behest of the papal legate, Władisław broke his word and launched a new attack. The foreign support which had been promised failed to materialize, and Hunyadi's forces were routed at Varna in 1444. The king fell in battle, while Hunyadi managed a narrow escape.

Although the Diet of 1445 recognized the succession of Albert's son László, Emperor Frederick III, who had custody of the young Habsburg, refused to surrender him. The problem of the succession was given a temporary but happy solution the following year: Hunyadi was acclaimed the Hungarian regent, a result largely of the vigorous campaign of János Vitéz, Bishop of Várad (Oradea).

It was not until 1448 that Hunyadi built up sufficient strength for a new offensive. Leading his army deep into the Balkans, he engaged the Turkish army at Kosovo. Betrayed, however, by the Serbian despot George Brankovich, Hunyadi was not only defeated but taken temporarily captive as well. In 1450, Hunyadi concluded an agreement with Frederick III that recognized the legitimacy of László. In 1453, the once-vacant throne now occupied, Hunyadi dutifully resigned as regent but was appointed by László his commander in chief and royal treasurer.

Unfortunately, the king fell under the influence of Ulrich von Cilli, a longtime rival of Hunyadi.

Monument to Hunyadi in Hungary

Cilli now became allied with several aristocrats against Hunyadi. In addition, Hunyadi's old friend and ally János Vitéz, always a staunch foe of baronial power, put forward a plan for centralization which would have seriously weakened Hunyadi's position. When the Hungarians learned that Constantinople had fallen (in 1453) and that Sultan Mehmed II was gathering his forces to attack Hungary, Vitéz's plan was prudently withdrawn from consideration.

In 1456, the Ottomans besieged Belgrade, sending forth an army one hundred thousand strong. Neither the king, who fled the country, nor the barons came to the aid of Hunyadi's hopelessly outnumbered army. Eventually, however, help came. Franciscan friar John of Capistrano, sent by the pope to organize a Crusade, managed to recruit into Hunyadi's army some twenty thousand soldiers. On July 21, the city's walls already penetrated, the Turks launched an all-out attack but were defeated and withdrew en masse.

Not for another seventy years would a major battle be fought between Hungarian and Ottoman forces. Hunyadi, who had saved Hungary from Turkish conquest, died of the plague not long thereafter.

Summary

Hungary in the fifteenth century was poised between the Middle Ages and the Renaissance. It was also the meeting place of Western and Eastern Europe. Themselves the scourge of the West some five centuries earlier, the Hungarians, now Christian and in possession of one of the most powerful states in Europe, hoped to bar the way of the new terror of Europe, the Ottoman Turks. It was mainly through Hunyadi's efforts that Hungary survived and Western Europe was spared the Turkish scourge. Yet—and this cast a dark shadow over Hungary—virtually all the border fortresses had fallen to the Turks.

When Hunyadi died, his first son, László, was killed by anti-Hunyadi conspirators, while his other son, Mátyás, was imprisoned. Upon King László's unexpected death in 1457, however, the Diet elected Mátyás king. Exploiting the peace created by his father, Mátyás, called Matthias Corvinus, inaugurated a glorious era for Hungary. Not only did it grow stronger both militarily and economically, but it became the center of Renaissance culture in East Central Europe as well. That this era would not last, indeed would pass into a century-and-a-half-long nightmare beginning with the Battle of Mohács in 1526, was the result at least in part of Mátyás' almost total neglect of the slumbering, but by no means extinct, Ottoman threat.

Bibliography

Held, Joseph. *Hunyadi: Legend and Reality.* New York: Columbia University Press, 1985. The most up-to-date and detailed work on Hunyadi that exists in English. Includes an index, a list of place names, maps, illustrations, and a brief note on primary sources.

Macartney, C. A. *Hungary: A Short History.* Chicago: Aldine, 1962. An excellent overview of Hungarian history by an eminent British historian. Though it gives only a brief account of Hunyadi, it is stylishly written and includes an index, maps, photographs, tables, a comparative chronology, biographies, and a bibliography.

Sinor, Denis. *History of Hungary.* London: Allen and Unwin, and New York: Praeger, 1959. A crossover effort, this entertaining treatment of Hungarian history was written by an Inner-Asian specialist and it includes an account of Hunyadi. Includes both an index and a chronology of events.

Vambéry, Arminius. *Hungary in Ancient, Medieval, and Modern Times.* 2d ed. London: Unwin, and New York: Putnam, 1887. In this readable but dated survey, a full chapter is devoted to the career of Hunyadi. Includes an index and illustrations.

Zarek, Otto. *History of Hungary.* London: Selwyn and Blount, 1939. Translated by H.S.H. Prince Peter P. Wolkowsky. The sixth chapter of this work is mainly devoted to Hunyadi. Features an index, a map, and an aid to pronunciation.

Gregory Nehler

ITZCÓATL

Born: c. 1382; place unknown

Died: 1440; probably Tenochtitlán (modern Mexico City)

Area of Achievement: Government

Contribution: As the founder of the Mexican state, Itzcóatl was largely responsible both for the strengths which enabled it to survive until the Spanish conquest and for the weaknesses which contributed to its destruction.

Early Life

Itzcóatl (obsidian serpent) was the illegitimate son of Acamapichtli, the first king of the Mexica, the Aztec tribe that founded Tenochtitlán and came in time to dominate central Mexico. His mother was a seller of herbs or vegetables and apparently a slave, but Itzcóatl distinguished himself as a military commander and statesman before he himself became king of the Mexica about 1427. Except for the remarkable fact of his parentage, nothing is known of his personal life, and his public life can only be understood in relation to the political development of Mexico in his lifetime.

The early struggle of the Mexica to establish themselves in the Valley of Mexico and to achieve hegemony over its various tribes must not be understood as a war among nations but as a conflict of city-states which fought each other in loose alliances. The arena of this struggle was a relatively small area in the vicinity of modern Mexico City, the heart of which is the site of Tenochtitlán.

The various chronicles of early Mexican history, all written from memory after the Spanish conquest, do not agree as to dates. The Mexica entered the Valley of Mexico from the north in the latter half of the thirteenth century, the last Náhuatl-speaking tribe to make this migration. They were in their beginnings a poor tribe of nomads, without the complex social and political structure or the elaborate system of religious ritual which they developed later. When they arrived, the valley was dominated by Azcapotzalco, the premier Tepenecan city on the west shore of Lake Texcoco; Tlacopán, on the mainland due west of Tenochtitlán; Coyoacán, on the southwest shore; Xochimilco and Chalco, in the south; and Texcoco, the intellectual center of the valley and the dominant power east of the lake. The Mexica, possessing no lands, indeed no resources but the prowess of their warriors, enlisted as mercenaries in the employ of other cities. In the early fourteenth century, one faction of the Mexica, defeated by the enemies of their employers, fled to a swampy area in the lake and began the slow process of building up the land upon which they established the town of Tlatilulco. Later—in 1369, according to one account—another faction, also forced to flee from their mainland enemies, established a second town nearby: Tenochtitlán.

In their wanderings and their early years in central Mexico, the basic organs of civil and military management of the Mexica were the clans, each of which was governed by its own council of elders, a headman, and a "speaker" who represented it in the council of the Mexica. After the founding of Tenochtitlán, however, a steady process of centralization began, and by 1375, when Acamapichtli was chosen the first king of Tenochtitlán, this process was virtually complete, so that a great gulf had opened between the council and the commoners, with real power concentrated in the hands of an oligarchy composed of a few great families who dominated the council and monopolized all administrative and religious power.

Acamapichtli's successor was his son, Huitzilhuitl, who became king in 1404, married the daughter of Tezozómoc, the king of Azcapotzalco, and was succeeded in 1416 by his ten-year-old son Chimalpopoca, during whose reign the inevitable conflict with Azcapotzalco came to a head.

Life's Work

Itzcóatl may have been speaker under Huitzilhuitl, and he certainly filled this post during the reign of Chimalpopoca. In that role, he astutely and cautiously extended the trade and influence of the Mexica to the shore towns while avoiding an open clash with Azcapotzalco. In 1426, Tezozómoc of Azcapotzalco died and was succeeded by his son Maxtla, who was determined to end the rivalry of the upstart Mexica and, according to one account, arranged the murder of Chimalpopoca in 1427.

Another account, however, suggests that Chimalpopoca was murdered by the war faction in the Mexican council. According to this story, the Mexica demanded materials from Tezozómoc for building a causeway to bring water from Chapultepec, on the west shore of the lake. The allies of Azcapotzalco, realizing that such a causeway would strengthen Tenochtitlán, resisted this demand and determined to destroy the Mexica. They cut off all trade and other contact with Tenochtitlán, and when Tezozómoc died, Chimalpopoca, no longer able to count upon his grandfather's protection, was murdered. In any case, the council of the Mexica elected Itzcóatl as his successor. Itzcóatl was recognized for both his bravery and his prudence; in fact, one source gives credit to him as a military leader and an important administrator as early as 1407. Another says that he had commanded armies for three decades. These achievements probably account for his election in spite of his illegitimacy. He was at that time about forty-five years old.

Itzcóatl's situation when he became king was precarious because of the forces arrayed against the Mexica, but he had strong allies in Tlacopán and in the king of Texcoco, his nephew Nezahualcóyotl, who was putting together an alliance of all the cities east of the lake. It was also at this time that Itzcóatl succeeded, perhaps by marriage to a princess of the other Mexican city in the lake, Tlatilulco, in achieving an alliance which led eventually to the merger of the two cities. Itzcóatl's further achievement of a triple alliance of Tenochtitlán-Tlatilulco with Texcoco and Tlacopán was perhaps his greatest political achievement, and it survived, with Tenochtitlán the dominant force in the alliance, until the Spanish conquest.

In 1428, Itzcóatl gathered the council in Tenochtitlán and demanded war against Azcapotzalco and its west-shore allies. Strong arguments were made in the council for peace, but the military party had everything to gain from a war. The power of the state, in the hands of the oligarchy, had been partially thwarted by certain elements in Tenochtitlán society which would be rendered powerless by a major victory against the city's enemies. In fact, the accounts which blame the Tepanecs for the death of Chimalpopoca may have been written to justify the war with them. In any case, Itzcóatl, encouraged by his nephew Tlacaelel, who shared his sense of the destiny of the Mexica to rule all the Valley of Mexico, prevailed in the council. A peace proposal was sent to Azcapotzalco, combined with a threat of war if it were not accepted. Its rejection was followed by a Tepanecan attack across the causeway from the mainland. Nezahualcóyotl had brought his Texcoco warriors to Tenochtitlán, and the Mexica of Tenochtitlán and Tlatilulco were united. As a result, the Tepanecs, completely routed, fled to Azcapotzalco, which fell to the allies after a siege of four months. It was completely destroyed, and the few of its population who did not escape were exterminated or enslaved.

In 1429-1430, the Mexica repaid Nezahualcóyotl for his support by helping him recover control of those cities east of the lake which had rebelled with the encouragement of Azcapotzalco. In 1430, Tenochtitlán asked—or demanded—that Xochimilco provide stone and logs for the expansion of the temple of Huitzilopochtli. When these materials were denied, Xochimilco was blockaded and eventually conquered. Its lands were distributed among Itzcóatl's closest supporters, and Xochimilco agreed to provide the materials and the slave labor to build a great causeway to join Tenochtitlán to the mainland from the south. A year later, Coyoacán broke off trading relations with Tenochtitlán, in effect declaring war, and was subsequently conquered. In all, according to one account (the Codex Mendoza), Itzcóatl is credited with the conquest of twenty-four towns.

In 1431, Nezahualcóyotl was crowned emperor of the three-city league, but events had already set in motion the process by which Tenochtitlán and its kings would be the dominant power in Mexico.

For a period of five or six years after the war, the slave laborers and the tribute won in the war were used to erect palaces, expand Tenochtitlán-Tlatilulco, build canals within the city, and erect greater shrines to the gods. In the center of Tenochtitlán was built the monumental shrine to the god of war, Huitzilopochtli.

The primary result of the war was the total reorganization of Mexican society. Itzcóatl created twenty-one titles for the greatest families and established a system of succession that endured until the Spanish conquest: When a king was chosen, four brothers or other close relatives were elevated to special titles, and one of them was named to be his successor. The conquered agricultural lands were distributed to a relatively small number of Mexican leaders, thus magnifying the power of the oligarchy; political power was concentrated in the hands of the king, the speaker, and the council; and the power of the military class was considerably enhanced. Above all, the cult of Huitzilopochtli, the god of war whose demands for sacrificial victims, as interpreted by the priests, were virtually insatiable, was greatly augmented. The result, in other words, was profoundly ideological—the dictatorship of the oligarchy supported by the warrior elite was justified by a constant state of war, and warfare was required by the constant need for sacrificial victims. Political, military, and religious concerns were supportive of one another.

Several accounts maintain that before the attack on Azcapotzalco the commoners were fearful of the consequences of a possible defeat. According to one account, Itzcóatl is supposed to have offered a wager to them: If the warriors failed, the king and his council would permit themselves to be killed and eaten. The commoners, in turn, agreed that if the warriors were victorious, they would accept a state of virtual slavery. This strange wager would seem, however, to be pure propaganda written after the event. In fact, most accounts agree that after the Mexica had won the Tepanec War, Itzcóatl ordered the destruction of existing accounts of the Mexican past and their rewriting to emphasize the grandeur and the justice of Tenochtitlán's rise to power. Apparently, the reforms also included a manipulation of education and of art and literature in the service of the state: Itzcóatl was the first king of Tenochtitlán to have his likeness carved in stone. Clearly, the most appalling aspect of the ideological reforms of Itzcóatl's reign was the sharp increase in the magnitude of human sacrifice.

Most accounts agree that Itzcóatl died in 1440 and was succeeded by Montezuma I, who expanded the Aztec Empire by using the methods and the ideology that his predecessor had developed.

Summary

Itzcóatl must be credited with the foundation of the Mexican monarchy, which became the dominant power in central Mexico under the rule of his successors, and he established the political and military institutions, including the political alliance with Texcoco and Tlacopán, that made possible the Aztec Empire, which endured until the arrival of the Spanish in 1519. The human cost of this achievement, however, was outrageously high.

The state which Itzcóatl was primarily responsible for creating existed for its own glorification. Even European monarchies of the time were less powerful in their control of their people—if only because they were subject to the disapproval of the Church—than was the oligarchy to which Itzcóatl gave power. Indeed, Itzcóatl, with the aid of like-minded individuals, created the kind of absolute totalitarian state which Europe did not suffer until the twentieth century. The oligarchy controlled the education of young nobles, who were taught to serve the state, and literary and artistic culture was dedicated to the glorification of the state. Furthermore, the destruction of historical chronicles and rewriting of history to make the state and its keepers the absolute political reality was something unknown in Europe until modern times.

Itzcóatl's use of the cult of Huitzilopochtli for political ends, considering that it was a cult that demanded human sacrifice, is the most extraordinary aspect of the totalitarian system he created. Admittedly, the numbers of sacrificial victims were inflated by Spanish chroniclers, but even when those numbers are reduced, the hard kernel of historical fact still horrifies. This religion of blood was put to the service of the state, and the state engaged in warfare to serve the religion. This inevitably vicious circle produced slaughter too appalling to condone, whatever the numbers. Certainly, Itzcóatl, though he had the encouragement of his colleagues, must receive the largest share of the blame. After the conquest of Azcapotzalco, he issued an edict proclaiming Huitzilopochtli the supreme god of the Mexica, and after the conquest of Coyoacán, he issued another which defined the divine mission of the Mexica as bringing all the nations of the world to the worship of that god by force of arms. The "flower wars" that provided victims for the priest-executioners of Tenochtitlán during the eighty years after Itzcóatl's death were the terrible legacy of his reign, and they contributed more than anything else to the destruction of the state which he created, for the Spanish were welcomed by the enemies those wars produced.

Considering all this, it is an error to condemn Hernán Cortés and the Spanish conquest without taking account of the fact that, in spite of the excesses of that conquest, it did not introduce to the Mexican people any violence, exploitation, or infringement of liberty that was new to them. If the priests who accompanied Cortés burned Aztec libraries, Itzcóatl had done the same before them; if they enslaved the Aztecs, the enemies of the Aztecs also had been enslaved; if they enforced conversion to christianity, the Aztecs had sought the same ends on behalf of Huitzilopochtli, whose demands upon the common people of Mexico were infinitely bloodier.

Bibliography

Brundage, Burr Cartwright. *A Rain of Darts: The Mexica Aztecs*. Austin: University of Texas Press, 1972. The most thorough one-volume history of the Aztecs, from their obscure origins to the destruction of Tenochtitlán in 1521. Brundage has carefully weighed all the evidence of the codices, and his book provides the most likely dates for the events of Aztec history.

Conrad, Geoffrey W., and Arthur A. Demarest. *Religion and Empire: The Dynamics of Aztec and Inca Expansionism*. Cambridge and New York: Cambridge University Press, 1984. A comparative study, as the subtitle indicates, which thoroughly examines the political and social factors which led to Aztec expansion and evaluates the theories which modern scholars have proposed to account for it.

Duran, Diego. *The Aztecs: The History of the Indies of New Spain*. Translated by Doris Heyden and Fernando Horcasitas. London: Cassell, and New York: Orion Press, 1964. Duran was a Dominican friar who came to Mexico only twenty years after the conquest and based his account on the codices and the memory of informants. It was written to help Christian missionaries understand Aztec paganism, but it reveals considerable sympathy for the Indians.

Gillmor, Frances. *The King Danced in the Marketplace*. Tucson: University of Arizona Press, 1964. The king of the title is Montezuma I, but this book deals also with the events of Itzcóatl's reign. Based on solid research and thoroughly documented, but written in a novelistic style which makes the actual historical events sometimes difficult to follow.

Padden, R. C. *The Hummingbird and the Hawk: Conquest and Sovereignty in the Valley of Mexico, 1503-1541*. Columbus: Ohio State University Press, 1908; London: Harper, 1970. A thoroughly researched study of the conflict of Aztec and Spanish religious beliefs during the reign of Montezuma II, the conquest, and its aftermath, this account offers many insights into the rise of the Mexica during the reign of Itzcóatl.

Radin, Paul. "The Sources and Authenticity of the History of the Ancient Mexicans." *University of California Publications in American Archaeology and Ethnology* 17 (1920-1926): 1-150. Useful because it provides translations of various Aztec codices, including the lengthy Codex Ramírez, which deals more fully than most of the primary documents with the events of the reigns of Itzcóatl and his predecessors.

Robert L. Berner

IVAN THE GREAT

Born: January 22, 1440; Moscow, Russia
Died: October 27, 1505; Moscow, Russia
Areas of Achievement: Government and politics
Contribution: Ivan the Great laid the foundation for the political centralization and territorial unification of the Russian national state and the consolidation and growth of imperial autocracy. Known in the history of Russia as "the gatherer of the Russian lands," he united all the Slavic independent and semi-independent principalities and cities under the aegis of the Muscovite rulers and began the long struggle with Poland-Lithuania and Sweden for recovering Russia's "historical" lands of the Ukraine, White Russia, and the Baltic States. Ivan was also the Grand Prince of Muscovy who ended Russia's 240 years of Mongol or Tatar rule and proclaimed the independence of his country.

Early Life

Ivan III Vasilyevich, better known as Ivan the Great, Grand Prince of Muscovy, was born in Moscow on January 22, 1440. He was the son of Grand Prince Vasily II and Maria Yaroslavna. Vasily's reign was beset from the beginning by a series of savage civil wars with his rebellious uncles and cousins, who contested the throne of Muscovy. One of Vasily's uncles, Prince Yury, defeated him in 1433 and assumed the title of grand prince. When Yury died in 1434, one of his sons, Dmitri Shemyaka, claimed the throne, arrested Vasily, blinded him, and sent him into exile. The young Ivan, only six years old, was also seized by agents of Shemyaka and jailed with his father. Vasily, however, recovered his throne in 1447 and, despite being blind, ruled for another fifteen years.

Throughout the remainder of Vasily's reign, Ivan was closely associated with his father's administration. The blind Vasily assigned to him many of the daily duties and tasks of his government, providing him with valuable experience and political training in the affairs of the state. At the age of nine, Ivan was proclaimed grand prince and coruler in order to eliminate any question as to the succession to the throne. When Ivan was twelve years old, his father arranged, perhaps for political considerations, the marriage of his son to Maria, the daughter of the Grand Prince of Tver. In 1452, Ivan was at the head of an army that defeated his father's enemy, Shemyaka. In 1458, Ivan was in charge of a successful military campaign against the Tatars to the south. Upon the death of his father on March 27, 1462, Ivan ascended the throne as Grand Prince and Sovereign of Moscow at age twenty-two.

Life's Work

Ivan's reign was characterized by a series of foreign and domestic threats, all of which he was able to overcome. He proved to be a remarkable ruler of Russia, a man of unusual political foresight and bold accomplishments. Ivan was endowed with extraordinary energy and native intelligence. He was persistent, calculating, and, at the same time, excessively cautious, secretive, and cunning to the extreme. He often avoided taking chances and was hesitant of drastic measures. Instead, he preferred to achieve his goal within the limits of his own power and resources. He employed discretion, calmly tolerated delays—often breaking his word—and used sinuous diplomacy, of which he proved to be a Machiavellian master. These attributes made him secure of himself and brought him many victories, for which he earned the appellation "the Great."

Ivan's major objective was to transform the small and often contested role of the principality of Moscow into the political center of a unified Russian state. He achieved this task through conquest, diplomacy, the purchasing of land, annexation, and voluntary surrender of independent and semi-independent Russian principalities and free cities. He replaced the regional political fragmentation with a strong centralized administrative state. By the end of Ivan's reign, he had gathered all the Russian territories under the rule of the Muscovite grand prince and had incorporated them into the Muscovite state, increasing its territory from 150,000 square miles to nearly 400,000 square miles at the beginning of the sixteenth century.

At the time of Ivan's accession to the throne, there were four major principalities independent of Moscow—Yaroslavl, Rostov, Tver, and Ryazan—and three city-states—the republic of Novgorod the Great, Vyatka, and Pskov. The principalities of Yaroslavl and Rostov were among the least independent Russian lands. By the treaties of 1463 and 1474, they were both formally annexed to Moscow.

Ivan's most important acquisition was the ancient city-republic of Novgorod the Great and its extensive colonies to the northeast. The republic of Novgorod preserved its independence for many centuries from both the Mongols and the Teutonic knights. Since the fifteenth century, however, Novgorod vacillated between Moscow and Poland-Lithuania. The Princes of Moscow viewed Novgorod's relations with these Catholic states with suspicion and distrust. When a pro-Lithuanian party turned to Casimir IV, King of Poland and Grand Prince of Lithuania, seeking to select as their prince a Lithuanian, Ivan III turned against the Novgorodians, accused them of apostasy, invaded the city in the spring of 1471, and imposed upon them a treaty that bound the city closer to Moscow. Within a few years, however, the Novgorodians broke the terms of the treaty and a pro-Polish party turned again to Poland-Lithuania. This new development forced Ivan to attack the city in 1478 for a second time, and to order the annexation of its territory to Moscow, the confiscation of church lands, and finally the deportation and exile of hundreds of prominent noble families, confiscation of their estates, and parceling out of these lands to individuals of lower classes conditional on military service. Ivan's acts signaled the end of Novgorod's independence.

The principality of Tver was the second most important of Ivan's acquisitions. For centuries, Tver had been Moscow's chief contender for control of Russia. When the Grand Prince of Tver, Mikhail, concluded a political alliance with Lithuania in 1483, Ivan used this act as an excuse to invade Tver and officially annex it. The city of Vyatka, a former colony of Novgorod, was annexed in 1489. Finally, the principalities of Ryazan and Pskov came under Moscow's control, but they were annexed by Ivan's son and successor, Vasily III, in 1521.

In the area of foreign affairs, Ivan was successful against both the Tatars to the east and the Poles and Lithuanians to the west. The Tatars, who established the Golden Horde in the southeastern part of Russia, remained potentially the most dangerous adversaries since the thirteenth century. Yet in the second half of the fifteenth century, the Golden Horde broke up into the independent khanates of Kazan, Astrakhan, and the Crimea. Ivan's goal was not only to terminate Moscow's nominal subservience to the Khan of the Golden Horde but also to secure the southeastern boundaries of his realm from further attacks and incursions by the Tatar forces, and to allow him to focus his attention on his principal task: the recovery of the Russian historical lands from Poland-Lithuania.

The friction between Moscow and the Golden Horde came to a head in 1480, when Khan Akhmed concluded an alliance with Poland-Lithuania and staged an attack on Moscow on the grounds that Ivan refused to pay him the customary annual tribute. The Russian and Tatar armies met on the opposite banks of the Ugra River in the fall of 1480. For more than two months, neither Akhmed nor the Russians attempted to attack each other. After waiting for the arrival of the Lithuanian and the Polish armies (who failed to appear), Akhmed suddenly withdrew his troops without giving a battle. In this rather unheroic manner, Ivan terminated Moscow's 240 years of Mongol domination. Ivan also organized military campaigns against the Tatar khanate of Kazan to the southeast of Moscow. In 1487, Ivan captured the khanate and placed on its throne a Tatar vassal ruler, further stabilizing the southeastern boundaries of his realm for some time to come, until it was finally annexed by Ivan IV in the 1550's. Ivan maintained friendly relations with the Tatar khan of Crimea and the Ottoman sultan. In 1480, he signed a treaty with the Crimean leader, Mengli Giray, against the Golden Horde and Poland. Though the Crimean Tatars remained unreliable allies, their hostility toward Lithuania and Poland helped Ivan in his plan to recover the ancient territory of Kievan Russia. In 1494, Ivan seized the town of Vyazma and annexed it to Moscow. A year later, he concluded a truce and entered into dynastic relations with the Grand Prince Alexander of Lithuania by offering his daughter in marriage. This arrangement, however, did not prevent Ivan from going to war with his son-in-law in 1500, on the grounds that his Orthodox subjects had allegedly been persecuted by the Catholic Church. When the war ended in 1503, Ivan captured much of the western Russian lands, except the cities of Kiev and Smolensk.

Finally, Ivan faced the growing power of Sweden, a perennial adversary of the Russians since the thirteenth century. In 1493, Ivan and the King of Denmark signed an alliance against Sweden. The same year, Ivan went to war against Sweden, trying to gain control of Finland and the Baltic States. The Swedes, however, retaliated and attacked northern Russia, forcing Ivan to sign a truce in 1497. It was left to Peter the Great to break the power of Sweden in the eighteenth century.

Ivan's successes to the east against the Tatar khanates made Moscow the most powerful state on the Eurasia steppes by replacing the Golden Horde.

His victories over Lithuania brought him into direct contact with Europe, and its sovereigns began to view him as a powerful and independent ruler. At the same time, Moscow gradually increased its economic and cultural ties with the West. In 1472, after the death of his first wife, Ivan married Zoë Palaeologus, better known by her Orthodox name of Sophia, the niece of the last Byzantine emperor. The marriage of Sophia to Ivan was arranged, strangely enough, by Pope Paul II, who hoped to bring the Russian Orthodox church under the orbit of the Roman Catholic Church. Ivan remained faithful to his orthodoxy, however, and used the marriage to the Byzantine princess to buttress the prestige and power of the Muscovite ruler. To underscore the importance of his new position, he adopted the double-headed black eagle of Byzantium to his family coat of arms, called himself autocrat, or *samoderzhets*—an imitation of the Byzantine emperors—and added the complex Byzantine court ceremonies to his own. Ivan was also the first Russian ruler to use the title of "czar" (Latin caesar) and "sovereign of all Russia." Moscow would henceforth claim to be the "Third Rome" after the fall of Constantinople in 1453, and the imperial idea became part of Russia's messianic tradition to modern times.

In his internal policy, Ivan was largely responsible for the administrative system he introduced, which lasted until the seventeenth century. He reformed the local government by introducing the system known as *kormlenie*, or "feeding" system. This administrative innovation called for the appointment of district and provincial governors, who were charged with collecting taxes and custom duties for the grand prince, running the army and local militia, and administering justice. The governors were practically supported by taxes they extracted from the local population, thus the meaning of the term "feeding."

Ivan further suppressed and weakened the power of appanage princes, eliminated their separatist tendencies, and confiscated their landholdings. He replaced the hereditary aristocracy and created a new service system, known as *pomestie*. Under this system the officials of the grand prince were granted land in return for military service. This new development led, in turn, to the formation of a new social class, the service gentry, or *dvorianstvo*. This service class became the core of Russia's military power and the staunch supporter of autocracy. Ivan reformed the executive organs of the central government. At the end of the fifteenth century, the first bureaus, known as *prikazy*, were established and were in charge of the various departments of the grand prince's government and run by secretaries. Ivan also improved the system of justice. In 1497, he issued the first code of law, called *Sudebnik*. The code provided a uniform legal system and court procedure for the entire territory of the Muscovite realm. The law also outlined the rules and obligations of the peasants to their landlords, placing the first restrictions on their freedom to move about the land, as the gentry class demanded more peasant labor to till their land. These restrictions foreshadowed the beginning of serfdom in Russia.

During the last years of Ivan's reign, the Russian Orthodox church underwent a serious inner crisis. There was growing opposition to the vast accumulation of wealth and land by the Church and by monasteries. A group, called *strigolniki*, a religious sect known as Judaizers, and a minority of churchmen called the Trans-Volga Elders or "Non-Possessors," led by Nil Sorsky, criticized high prelates, monastic life, rituals, liturgy, icon worship, moral corruption, and simony within the Church. The majority of the conservative hierarchy of the Church, led by Joseph Sanin, defended the Church and monastic lands, condemned the reformers, supported the divine right of autocracy, and asked Ivan to suppress and persecute the reformers as heretics. Ivan pondered for some time upon the growing power of the Church that appeared a rival of the state and would have sided with the Trans-Volga Elders and secularized the Church lands, but, at the Church Council of 1503, he yielded to the demands of the Josephites and condemned the critics as heretics. At that point, Ivan was greatly concerned with family rivalry over the question of succession to the throne. He yielded to his wife, Sophia, and bestowed upon his son Vasily the title grand prince and asked the boyars to swear allegiance to him. In the meantime, the khanate of Kazan broke away from Moscow's subservience, and the Lithuanian War ended in 1503 rather inconclusively, as Ivan failed to recover all the Russian historical lands in the West. Two years later, on October 27, 1505, Ivan died at the age of sixty-five, unlamented and apparently unloved by his own people. He was succeeded by his son Vasily.

Summary

Ivan the Great was an outstanding ruler. His reign marked a turning point in the history of Russia from the medieval to the modern age. He built up and created modern Russia. By gathering the Russian lands around the principality of Moscow, Ivan strengthened the power of the central government and increased the role and prestige of the Muscovite state and its ruler, both at home and abroad. Indeed, Ivan's diplomatic, political, military, and administrative achievements were comparable to those of his contemporaries Louis IX of France, Henry VII of England, and Ferdinand II and Isabella I of Spain. Ivan was the first to encourage economic and cultural relations with the West and invited foreign craftsmen and artisans to Moscow, among them the noted Italian architect Aristotle Fioravanti, who built the famous Assumption (Uspenski) Cathedral in the Kremlin and other Italian-style palaces. Contacts with the Europeans convinced Ivan that Russia could learn from the West and that Russia could borrow its technical knowledge in order to strengthen its new position and compete successfully with other states. At the same time, Ivan protected and defended the Orthodox faith from Roman Catholicism and made the institution of the Church the loyal supporter and advocate of Russian autocracy. In more than one way, Ivan's accomplishments determined the course that Russia was to follow. He was the first to forge the great beginnings of Russia, which was destined to become a great European power. His appellation of "the Great" is deserved.

Bibliography

Fennell, J. L. I. "The Attitude of the Josephians and the Trans-Volga Elders to the Heresy of the Judaisers." *Slavonic and East European Review* 29 (June, 1951): 486-509. An inquiry into the different views of supporters of Sanin and the reformers of Sorsky toward the religious sect of the Judaizers.

———. *Ivan the Great of Moscow.* London: Macmillan, New York: St. Martin's Press, 1962. The most complete and detailed study of all aspects of Ivan's reign in any language. The author emphasizes Ivan's foreign policy, diplomatic methods, and military campaigns in the Russo-Lithuanian War. Contains an extensive and valuable bibliography.

Grey, Ian. *Ivan III and the Unification of Russia.* London: English Universities Press, 1964; New York: Collier, 1972. This is a well-written, detailed biography by a writer and biographer whose other work includes an account of Ivan the Terrible. Discusses the process of the unification of the Russian lands under the Muscovite princes, the wars and military campaigns against domestic and foreign enemies, and the emergence of the Grand Prince of Moscow as the leader of a strong and unified Russian state. Contains an index and brief bibliography.

Solovev, Sergei M. *History of Russia: The Reign of Ivan III the Great.* Edited and translated by John D. Windhausen. Gulf Breeze, Fla.: Academic International Press, 1979. A very important study of Ivan's reign by a great, "classic" Russian historian. Solovev discusses Ivan's campaigns against Novgorod the Great, the acquisition of the various Russian principalities, his wars with the Eastern khanates, and Sophia and her influence in Russia.

———. *History of Russia: Russian Society in the Age of Ivan III.* Translated and edited by John D. Windhausen. Gulf Breeze, Fla.: Academic International Press, 1979. A continuation of the previous work. Includes chapters on Ivan's wars with Lithuania and Livonia and a discussion of Russian society under Ivan.

Vernadsky, George. *Russia at the Dawn of the Modern Age.* New Haven, Conn.: Yale University Press, 1959. The most complete account and interpretation of Ivan's reign by an expert on the history of Russia. Vernadsky argues that Sophia had little influence in the court or upon Ivan. Contains an extensive bibliography of Russian works.

James J. Farsolas

IVAN THE TERRIBLE

Born: August 25, 1530; Moscow, Russia
Died: March 18, 1584; Moscow, Russia
Areas of Achievement: Politics and government
Contribution: Of all the Russian czars, Ivan contributed the most in giving shape to Russian autocracy as it would exist until the end of serfdom in 1861. He also conquered Kazan and Astrakhan, significantly reducing the Tatar threat and securing the important trade routes in the Volga region, and took the first steps toward the incorporation of Siberia.

Early Life

Ivan the Terrible was born in the Kremlin Palace in Moscow on August 25, 1530. His father, Vasily III, had married Ivan's mother, Princess Elena Glinskaya, when his first wife failed to provide him an heir. Vasily died in 1533, leaving the three-year-old Ivan to be reared in the world of Kremlin politics marked by violence, intrigues, and unashamed struggles for power among the hereditary nobles (boyar) and princely families. In order to forestall any threat to Ivan's succession, especially from his two uncles, Ivan was immediately declared as the next ruler. Under Muscovite law and custom, it was his mother who now exercised power as the regent. Although the next five years, until Elena's death in 1538, were normal years for Ivan, the Kremlin politics were far from normal. Elena faced threats from her husband's two brothers, forcing her to order their arrest and imprisonment. Even her own uncle, Mikhail Glinsky, on whom she had relied in the beginning, appeared too ambitious; he suffered the same fate as the others.

Elena's death in 1538 opened a new chapter in young Ivan's life. Within a week of his mother's death, his nanny, Agrafena Chelyadina, who had provided him with loving care and affection, was taken away. The Kremlin now reverberated with the intrigues and counterintrigues, especially of two princely families, the Shuiskys and the Belskys. Power changed hands more than once. The first round went to the Shuiskys. Of the two brothers, Vasily and Ivan Shuisky, who exercised power through the boyar Duma in succession, the latter made a special point of neglecting and insulting Ivan and his brother. Ivan later recalled that Ivan Shuisky once "sat on a bench, leaning with his elbows on our father's bed and with his legs upon a chair, and he did not even incline his head towards us . . . nor was there any element of deference to be found in his attitude toward us." Then, when power had passed to the Belskys and Ivan Shuisky was trying to regain it, Ivan had the horrifying experience of Shuisky's men breaking into his bedchamber in the night in search of the metropolitan. Ivan thus developed deep hatred for the boyars, especially for the Shuiskys, who now once again controlled power. Andrey Shuisky, who became the leader of this group after Ivan Shuisky's illness, imposed a reign of increased corruption and terror. Ivan, in a bold move in 1543, when he was only thirteen years old, ordered Prince Andrey to be arrested and brutally killed.

During these early years, Ivan not only witnessed cruel acts perpetrated around him that implanted fear and suspicion of boyars in his young heart but also engaged in such acts himself for fun and pleasure. Torturing all kinds of animals, riding through the Moscow streets knocking down the young and the old, including women and children, and engaging in orgies became his pastime.

Ivan, especially under the guidance of Metropolitan Makary, also read the Scriptures and became the first really literate Russian ruler. Some scholars have cast doubt on this, challenging the authenticity of his correspondence with Prince Andrey Kurbsky after the defection of his once-trusted adviser to Lithuania, but most evidence suggests that Ivan became a well-read person. In Makary, Ivan also found support for his belief in his role as an absolute ruler whose power was derived from God.

Toward the end of 1546, when he was still sixteen, Ivan decided to have himself crowned as czar. He also decided to search for a bride from his own realm. Although his grandfather, Ivan III, had used the title of the czar, Ivan IV was the first to be so crowned in a glittering ceremony in Moscow on January 16, 1547. On February 3, he was married to Anastasia Romanovna Zakharina, of a boyar family. She was to provide him fourteen years of happy married life and to serve as a calming influence on his impulsive personality.

Life's Work

The first part of Ivan's rule as Russia's czar was marked by several important reforms. He hated the boyars but did not try to dismantle the boyar Duma at this time; instead, he created a chosen council consisting of some of his close advisers that in-

cluded Metropolitan Makary, Archpriest Silvester, and Aleksey Adashev, a member of the service-gentry class. He also called the *zemskii sobor* (assembly of the land), representing the boyars and the service gentry as well as the townspeople, the clergy, and some state peasants.

A major drawback that adversely affected the fighting capacity of the Russian army was the system known as *mestnichestvo*, by which the appointments to top positions were based on the birth and rank of various boyars, not on their ability to command and fight. As he had done with the boyar Duma, Ivan did not end the system but provided for exceptions in case of special military campaigns. He also created regular infantry detachments known as the *streltsy*, to be paid by the state and to serve directly under the czar, and he regularized the terms and conditions under which a nobleman was expected to serve in the army. These steps greatly enhanced the army's fighting ability.

Some reforms in the system of local self-government were also undertaken in order to make it more efficient, especially for the purpose of tax collection. A collection and codification of laws resulted in the law code of 1550. A church council, the Hundred Chapters Council (for the hundred questions submitted to it), seriously undertook the question of reform in the Russian Orthodox church. Ivan, though not successful in secularizing church lands, was able to limit the church's power to acquire new lands which, in the future, could be done only with the czar's consent.

This early period of reform also saw the establishment of important trade links between Russia and England. In search of a northeastern passage to China, the English explorer Richard Chancellor found himself in the White Sea. Ivan warmly received him in Moscow and granted the English important trading privileges, hoping to acquire arms and support from the English against Ivan's European adversaries in his drive to find a foothold on the Baltic coast.

This earlier period of reforms was also marked by important successes in foreign policy. Although the long Mongolian domination over Russia had come to an end during the reign of Ivan's grandfather, Ivan III, the Mongolian khanates in the East and South still created problems. Their rulers undertook occasional raids against Moscow and the Muscovite territories. Ivan finally decided to undertake a military campaign to conquer the Kazan khanate in the upper Volga region. After some initial setbacks, he succeeded in capturing and annexing the whole khanate in 1557. While the Mongolian rule in Ivan III's time had ended without a major fight, the bloody battle at Kazan, with heavy casualties on both sides, came as a sweet revenge for the Russians. Ivan followed this by conquering Astrakhan in the south, thus acquiring the whole Volga region that now provided access to the Caspian Sea.

At this midpoint in his reign, Ivan experienced some unusual developments that reinforced his suspicion and hatred for the boyars. The result was the start of one of the bloodiest chapters in Russian history, during which thousands of people were tortured and executed. During his brief but serious illness in 1553, Ivan had asked various princes and boyars to take an oath of loyalty to his infant son, Dmitry. To his surprise and horror, he found that not everyone was ready to do so, including some of his closest advisers such as Silvester. Then, the dispute arose over Ivan's desire to engage in a war in the north to acquire territories on the Baltic coast from the Livonian Order of the German Knights. While Ivan decided to embark on the Livonian campaign in 1558, achieving some initial successes, the war was opposed by several members of the chosen council who noted the difficulties of fighting a two-front war. Finally, his beloved wife, Anastasia, died in 1560, removing a calming and restraining influence from his life.

Apparently deciding to destroy the power of the boyars, the hereditary aristocracy in Russia, Ivan undertook a reign of terror. Some, like Adashev, were thrown in prison, where they died of torture and hunger. Others, like Prince Kurbsky, fled the country and joined Ivan's enemies, further intensifying the czar's suspicions about their loyalty. Ivan, in a well-planned move in December, 1564, suddenly decided to leave Moscow in full daylight with his belongings and settled at nearby Alexandrovskaia Sloboda. In his message to the people of Moscow, he charged the boyars with disloyalty and treason but expressed faith in the ordinary people. As he had calculated, in asking him to return to Moscow, the people agreed to his condition that he should be allowed a free hand in punishing the boyars as well as in creating a separate state for himself that would be outside the jurisdiction of regular laws; this was to be known as *Oprichnina*. Ivan took immediate steps to assign vast tracts of land in the Moscow region and other parts of Russia to this autonomous state. As he did this, his objective seemed somewhat clearer. Much of the land belonged to the boyar families who were now forced to flee and seek land elsewhere. Ivan also selected a band of loyal guards, known as the *oprichniki*, whose number eventually rose to six thousand. They were assigned some of the newly vacated lands with the understanding that they would have the obligation to serve the czar. Thus, they became a part of the expanding service-gentry class.

While the aims of the *Oprichnina* seemed quite rational, what appeared incomprehensible was the excessive use of torture and murder by Ivan and his *oprichniki*. The job of the *oprichniki* was to clear the land of all possible traitors, but they themselves became a scourge of the land, killing and robbing innocent people. Anyone who criticized or opposed Ivan became his victim. Metropolitan Philip, who courageously castigated the czar for loosing these death squads on the Russian people, was thrown into a monastery and later strangled by one of Ivan's men. Ivan's cruelty, which bordered on insanity, was evident in the killings of thousands of innocent people that he personally undertook in Novgorod in 1570 on the suspicion that the territory was planning to defect to Lithuania.

In 1571, when the Crimean Tatars raided Moscow, the *oprichniki* failed to protect it. Instead, Moscow was saved when, in 1572, Russia's regular forces inflicted a crushing defeat on the Tatar army. Ivan then decided to disband *Oprichnina*. The Livonian War, however, did not go well for Ivan. After twenty-five years of fighting, Russia appeared exhausted. When the war ended in 1583, the country had lost all the gains it had made in the initial stages of the war. Indeed, Ivan had stretched himself too far. The end of the Livonian War also marked the end of his reign, as he died in 1584.

Summary

Ivan the Terrible's reign remains one of the most controversial eras in Russian history. There is no doubt that his achievements were many. The victory over Kazan, which Ivan memorialized in the construction of the magnificent St. Basil's Cathedral in Moscow, and the conquest of Astrakhan made available the whole Volga region for Russian trade and because of the exploits of the Cossack leader Yermak Timofey, started Russia on its march into Siberia. Ivan's reforms, undertaken painstakingly and thoughtfully in the earlier period of his reign, provided for a more efficient civil administration and a better fighting force. Without these reforms, his victory over Kazan would not have been possible.

Even his struggle against the hereditary boyars and the resulting expansion of the service-gentry class, essential elements in the strengthening of Russian autocracy, constituted a continuation of the process that had already existed. What makes this period so puzzling is the excessive amount of force, including the use of inhumane torture, freely used by Ivan in order to weaken the power of the boyars. Providing a pathological interpretation, some historians find Ivan a paranoid and his *Oprichnina* the work of a madman. Others, although acknowledging his excessive cruelty, see him not as a madman but as one who had lost his peace of mind and was haunted by an intense feeling of insecurity for himself and his family. Still others point to the fact that if Ivan used excessive force, it was not uncommon in a Europe dominated by the ideas of Niccolò Machiavelli. For them, Ivan, like some of his contemporaries, was a Renaissance prince. Whatever the final judgment may be, Ivan significantly expanded Russian frontiers and gave shape to a Russian autocracy that, in its essential contours, remained unchanged until the Great Reforms undertaken by Alexander II during the 1860's.

Bibliography

Beech, Hannah. "Annals of Repression." *US News and World Report* 119 (August, 1995): 36. Beech considers the constancy of the secret police in Russian politics, citing leaders from Ivan the Terrible in 1565 to Boris Yeltsin in 1995, and outlines their relationships with security forces.

Cherniavsky, M. "Ivan the Terrible as Renaissance Prince." *Slavic Review* 27 (March, 1968): 195-211. This article argues that Ivan was no exception in using excessive force against his enemies in a Renaissance Europe dominated by Machiavellian ideas.

Grey, Ian. *Ivan the Terrible*. London: Hodder and Stoughton, and Philadelphia: Lippincott, 1964. A popular biography that presents an uncritical portrait of Ivan the Terrible. Blame for much of Ivan's cruelty is placed on his opponents. Contains a limited bibliography.

Keenan, Edward. *The Kurbskii-Groznyi Apocrypha*. Cambridge, Mass.: Harvard University Press, 1971. This book challenges the authenticity of Ivan's correspondence with Prince Kurbsky. Keenan's view remains controversial.

Kurbskii, A. M. *The Correspondence Between Prince A. M. Kurbsky and Tsar Ivan IV of Russia, 1564-1579*. Edited and translated by J. L. I. Fennell. Cambridge: Cambridge University Press, 1955. An excellent translation of a valuable but controversial historical source.

———. *Prince A. M. Kurbsky's History of Ivan IV*. Edited and translated by J. L. I. Fennell. Cambridge: Cambridge University Press, 1965. Written by Prince Kurbsky after his defection, the book describes the events from 1533 to the early 1570's in a most critical manner. Though a valuable historical source, it is a highly partisan study of Ivan's reign.

Platonov, S. F. *Ivan the Terrible*. Edited and translated by Joseph L. Wieczynski. Gulf Breeze, Fla.: Academic International Press, 1974. An excellent translation of a work by a famous Russian historian of the old St. Petersburg school of Russian historiography, which emphasized facts in making historical interpretations. While Platonov does not accept the view of Ivan as paranoid, the book has an introductory part, "In Search of Ivan the Terrible," by Richard Hellie, that does.

Skrynnikov, Ruslan G. *Ivan the Terrible*. Edited and translated by Hugh F. Graham. Gulf Breeze, Fla.: Academic International Press, 1981. A serious and balanced study by a Soviet historian that presents Ivan and his *Oprichnina* in a nonideological framework. Contains a short bibliography of Russian-language books and articles.

Surendra K. Gupta

JACOPO DELLA QUERCIA

Born: c. 1374; probably Siena
Died: October 20, 1438; Siena
Area of Achievement: Art
Contribution: Heir to the late Gothic sculptural style of fourteenth century Italy and influenced by the spatial massing of form found in ancient classical art, Jacopo forged an independent, monumental style of great expressive power. Along with Lorenzo Ghiberti, Donatello, and Nanni di Banco, he is considered one of the most significant sculptors working in the early decades of the Italian Renaissance.

Early Life

While the sculptural commissions executed during Jacopo della Quercia's mature career are amply documented, very little is known about his early life. His father, Piero di Angelo, was a Sienese goldsmith and wood-carver who was married in 1370. Giorgio Vasari, a sixteenth century art historian, has left two versions of Jacopo's life. In the first version, written in 1550, he attributes to Jacopo an equestrian statue of the condotierre (mercenary military leader) Giovanni d'Arco that is now lost but was executed in 1391. To receive such a commission, Jacopo would have to have been at least nineteen years of age, placing his birth date around 1371. Vasari's second version, written in 1568, claims that Jacopo was sixty-four years of age when he died in 1438, which calculates to a slightly later birthdate. What is known for certain is that by 1401, when Jacopo entered the famous competition for the Florentine baptistery doors commission, he must have been a master sculptor of some renown.

The meaning and origins of the name "della Quercia" is a mystery. He was identified by this name as early as the mid-fifteenth century, but early documents refer to him as "Jacopo di Maestro Piero," after his father, and even later he is occasionally called "Jacopo delle Fonte" in reference to his work on the Fonte Gaia in Siena. It is possible he either inherited the "della Quercia" from his grandfather, or that it refers to a district of Siena where he was born or lived. It is extremely doubtful that it indicates a birthplace outside Siena.

Jacopo's early career is the subject of scholarly conjecture. It is safe to assume that, in the tradition of the time, he received his initial training from his father, who worked as a wood-carver. Piero di Angelo did not carve in stone, however, nor was there much activity in that medium in Siena during the last years of the fourteenth century. It is generally accepted that during the 1490's Jacopo probably traveled to one of the Italian cities where major stone or marble sculptural programs were in progress. The possibilities include Bologna, Milan, or Venice, but theories concerning his activities in any of these cities are purely tentative.

The first firmly documented event in his life is his participation in the competition for the commission to create a set of bronze doors for the baptistery of the cathedral in Florence. Lorenzo Ghiberti won the competition, and Jacopo's bronze relief competition panel has not survived.

In 1403, Jacopo was in Ferrara, where he began an altar for the Silvestri family, completion of which occurred in 1408. A marble Madonna and Child created for this altar is the earliest extant work universally accepted by scholars as being an example of his style. (Earlier works have been attributed to him, but the attributions are controversial.) During these same years, he also traveled to Lucca to execute the sepulchral monument to Ilaria del Carretto-Guinigi, who died in 1405.

These two youthful works demonstrate a flexibility of expression which would mark his entire career. The *Silvestri Madonna* is boldly carved, forthright, and monumental. The Ilaria sepulcher, with its graceful effigy and sarcophagus base, presents a quieter, more romantic expression fitting to its subject. In both works one finds a classical, spatial massing of form coexisting with a rhythmic, elegant line derived from Gothic antecedents.

Life's Work

In 1408, Jacopo received a commission which would occupy him, on and off, until 1419. That was for the Fonte Gaia in Siena, a large fountain in the center of town, which would serve as a civic focal piece. Contemporary documents indicate that physical work on the fountain did not begin until 1414. The plan of the fountain ultimately included numerous figural and decorative reliefs and statues. The overall scheme, as well as the handling of the human figures and decorative motifs, were heavily influenced by antique classicism. In particular, the high reliefs depicting scenes from Genesis display, despite their badly weathered condition, an unusually well-developed sense of classically inspired physicality and of the potential for form to create emotional expression.

Concurrent with the Sienese project, Jacopo was executing commissions in Lucca. In 1412, Lorenzo Trenta, a wealthy Lucchese merchant, began building a family burial chapel in the Church of San Frediano. Jacopo was put in charge of the project, which was not totally finished until 1422. The archaic gothicisms which flavor the chapel's tomb markers and altar, especially surprising in the light of the contemporary Fonte Gaia, reflect Jacopo's willingness and ability to alter his style in the interests of harmonizing his work to the taste and style of its surroundings.

It is clear from the documentary sources that Jacopo was an ambitious sculptor who rarely refused an important commission. The result was delay and procrastination, as he attempted to juggle his various commitments. For example, while under contract for both the Fonte Gaia and the Trenta chapel, he accepted yet another assignment. In 1417, he was commissioned to make two bronze reliefs for the Siena baptistery font. By 1425, he still had not delivered the reliefs and the Opera del Duomo (cathedral works committee), which had already reassigned one panel to the Florentine sculptor Donatello, sued Jacopo for return of the money advanced. Not until 1430 would Jacopo be paid for completing his relief depicting the Annunciation to Zachariah. Despite his procrastination, in 1427 he was placed in charge of the entire baptistery font program, perhaps in a bid to secure his attention.

In 1425, Jacopo began work on his most famous sculptural program, the main portal (porta magna) of the Church of San Petronio in Bologna. From then until his death in 1438, he would maintain two workshops, one in Bologna and one in Siena. The Sienese would try to keep him at home with commissions (the Vari-Bentivoglio monument and the Casini altar), fines, and finally, in 1435, an appointment as architect-in-chief of the cathedral works. Despite these demands, Jacopo would make one of his greatest artistic statements in the San Petronio sculpture, where the low relief Old Testament scenes display simplified, monumental compositions and classically rendered human nudes. The *Madonna and Child* for the project is admired for its handling of spatial massing, and all the sculpture is marked by a rippling, mobile line.

A fairly complete picture of Jacopo the sculptor emerges from the historical and physical evidence of his professional career. He personally traveled to marble quarries to choose the raw material for his projects but had little compunction about leaving major programs in the hands of assistants when other commitments required his absence. The work secured to his hand displays an ability to infuse classical forms with a high level of emotion. His compositions are marked by rhythms of line and form which imbue them with an unmistakable sense of movement. Rarely in sculpture does one find works in which line and mass coexist on such equal footing.

Jacopo is considered an independent artist, partly because his career took place outside of Florence, the major Italian center for sculpture in the early fifteenth century. He was well aware of the achievements of the Florentine artists, but forged a different, almost idiosyncratic, style connected to theirs but, at the same time, separate. The Florentine achievements in pictorial space, for example, never really concerned Jacopo. His emphasis was always on the heroically scaled foreground figures. Backgrounds and details were reduced to a minimum. His insistent, rippling line, at times poetic and at other times nervous and expressive, defined outlines and contours and had no equivalent among his major contemporaries.

The picture of Jacopo the man is less complete. Little is known about his private life. An impending marriage is recorded in 1424, but there is no evidence that it took place and neither a wife nor children were mentioned in his will. In 1413, he was involved in an affair with the wife of a wealthy Lucchese merchant, and that year he and one of his assistants were accused of theft, rape, and sodomy. The assistant spent several years in prison, but Jacopo escaped Lucca, only returning upon receipt of safe conduct in 1416. This event did not seem to affect either his professional or social position. In 1418 and 1435, he was elected to the Sienese City Council, and in 1420, he was chosen to serve as the prior of his district in Siena. His inimitable style seems to have secured for him a fair degree of wealth, position, and protection. It certainly secured for him a prominent place in the history of art.

Summary

Although Jacopo della Quercia exerted some stylistic influence during his career and immediately after his death, full appreciation of his legacy did not develop until one hundred years later. In the late fifteenth century, another sculptor, also an independent and also fascinated by the expressive possibilities of form and heroic physicality, would be greatly impressed by exposure to Jacopo's work. That sculptor was Michelangelo. That Michelangelo studied Jacopo's sculpture is proved not only by historical documentation but also by the frequent quotations of Jacopo's San Petronio reliefs in Michelangelo's Sistine Chapel paintings. In Jacopo, Michelangelo found a stylistic ancestor. In Michelangelo, Jacopo's experiments in heroic form found their fulfillment.

A study of Jacopo's sculpture forces the viewer to confront the complexities of artistic style at the dawn of the Italian Renaissance. The Gothic style had not disappeared overnight. The forms and techniques of ancient classical art were not revived indiscriminately. The two traditions had been influencing Italian sculptors since the mid-thirteenth century, and they continued to coexist in Jacopo's work. Jacopo's responses to these traditions, however, were personal and independent. Gothic line and classical form were reinterpreted to ends that were expressive without being expressionistic and were classical without being revivalistic.

Bibliography

Hanson, Anne Coffin. *Jacopo della Quercia's Fonte Gaia*. Oxford: Clarendon Press, 1965. A monograph on one of Jacopo's most important commissions, giving special emphasis to the fountain's iconographic program and its joint civic and religious function.

Pope-Hennessy, John. *Italian Gothic Sculpture*. 4th ed. London: Phaidon Press, 1996. The chapter on Jacopo places him at the end of the development of late Gothic Italian sculpture. Comparative photographs support the often-neglected stylistic ties of Jacopo to this older tradition. Includes critical analysis, biographical and bibliographical summaries, an index, and photographs of major works with accompanying catalog entries.

Seymour, Charles. *Jacopo della Quercia: Sculptor*. New Haven, Conn.: Yale University Press, 1973. The standard monograph in English. Discusses the documentary evidence of the major works and includes insightful critical commentary. Ample photographic reproductions including many details. Includes a chronological compendium of the documents, as well as the actual text of major contracts (not translated). Includes an index and a selected bibliography.

———. *Sculpture in Italy, 1400-1500*. London and Baltimore: Penguin, 1966. The chapter on Jacopo provides an excellent summary of the artist's career and places him within the context of the early Italian Renaissance. Includes photographs, an index, a biographical summary, and a brief bibliography.

Vasari, Giorgio. *Lives of the Most Eminent Painters, Sculptors, and Architects*. Translated by Gaston du C. de Vere. Vol. 3. London and New York: Macmillan, 1912-1914. A translation of the 1568 edition of Vasari's biographies. An expanded biography of Jacopo, based most likely upon oral tradition.

Madeline Cirillo Archer

FRANCISCO JIMÉNEZ DE CISNEROS

Born: 1436; Torrelaguna, Province of Madrid, Spain

Died: November 8, 1517; Roa, Spain

Areas of Achievement: Government, politics, religion, and education

Contribution: Jiménez worked to maintain a united Spain at the beginning of the sixteenth century. He founded the University of Alcalá de Henares and sponsored the famous Polyglot Bible.

Early Life

Gonzalo Jiménez de Cisneros, the baptismal name of the future Regent of Spain, was the first son of a family of esteemed lineage and humble means. His father, Alonso Jiménez de Cisneros, was trained in the law and made a modest living as collector and administrator of the papal tithe in the town of Torrelaguna. Young Gonzalo received his earliest training in Latin and reading at the household of an uncle, Alvaro, a priest in Roa. He then traveled to Alcalá and continued his studies of Latin and humanities in a school operated by the Franciscan Order. He entered Spain's prestigious University of Salamanca in 1450 and remained there until he completed a degree in canon and civil law. He also became well versed in the philosophical currents of the day, showing particular affinity for biblical scholarship. Jiménez then traveled to Rome in search of more promising opportunities. In Italy, Jiménez made a living as a lawyer, representing cases before consistorial courts. He left Rome in 1465 and returned to his birthplace to care for his recently widowed mother.

Life's Work

Aside from his ordination and legal experience, Jiménez's most promising professional prospect upon his return was the hope of fulfilling the terms of a *letrae expectativae*, a promissory papal letter appointing its possessor to any expected vacancy in a particular diocese. Jiménez had to wait years for a suitable opportunity. He lived in Torrelaguna until he received news of a vacancy in Úceda, in the diocese of Toledo. The Archpriest of Úceda had recently died, and Jiménez made a claim to that benefice in 1473. His ambitions were frustrated, however, when the powerful Archbishop of Toledo Alfonso Carrillo blocked his candidacy. Jiménez's stubborn refusal to relinquish his right to Úceda so enraged Carrillo that he had Jiménez imprisoned. Jiménez was jailed for six years and was released in 1479, when influential relatives pleaded on his behalf. Once out of prison, Jiménez took possession of the Úceda post.

By now in his forties, Jiménez would soon enter the most productive and important stage of his career. He had the good fortune to come under the protection of the Archbishop of Seville Cardinal Pedro de Mendoza, and under his tutelage Jiménez moved to the chaplaincy of the Cathedral of Sigüenza in the archdiocese of Seville. Mendoza, an enemy and rival of Carrillo, was the scion of one of Spain's most influential and accomplished families and a political ally and confidant of Queen Isabella I of Castile. Jiménez's advancement was now assured.

Mendoza promoted Jiménez once again, to the post of General Vicar of Sigüenza, and even greater opportunities opened up when Mendoza succeeded Carrillo to the see of Toledo in 1483. Jiménez, however, opted for a different path. After his mother's death in 1486, he decided to set aside secular concerns and enter the Franciscan Order. He took vows in 1486, changed his name from Gonzalo to Francisco—in honor of the order's founder—and began a new life devoted to prayer, fasting, and contemplation. The physical descriptions and portraits of Jiménez that have survived depict his slight build, weather-beaten skin, sharp profile, and thin body, features believed to have resulted from his rigid adherence to the physical rigors of monastic life.

Jiménez played a central role in the events that shaped the last quarter of the fifteenth century. His belated and somewhat surprising rise as a public figure began when, at the recommendation of Mendoza, he was invited to the royal court to serve as Isabella's confessor. Isabella became devoted to her confessor. In the fall of 1495, in a bold move, she selected Jiménez to the archbishopric of Toledo. Mendoza had died earlier that year, and Isabella secured papal approval to appoint Jiménez to preside over Spain's wealthiest and most important ecclesiastical see. She had to defend and impose her will over her husband, who wanted the prestigious post reserved for his illegitimate son. Jiménez accepted this great honor without hesitation and proceeded to reorganize the archiepiscopal see to reflect his religious convictions, tastes, and predilections.

A story associated with this period of Jiménez's career merits repetition. When Jiménez moved into his new quarters at the archiepiscopal palace in Toledo, the story goes, he ordered his staff to live, dress, and eat with the simplicity and austerity of Franciscan monks. Believing that such external signs of humility would undermine the prestige of the see, members of his staff appealed to the pope, asking him to help persuade Jiménez to reconsider. It seems that Jiménez heeded papal advice rather well. The Toledean ecclesiastical palace became once again the model of elegance and splendor it had always been. Jiménez undertook a series of building projects such as the reconstruction of the main altar of the cathedral, contracting for that purpose the most accomplished architects, sculptors, and artists of the period. He also commissioned plans for the construction of his proudest achievement, the new University at Alcalá de Henares, which he foresaw as a center for humanistic learning. He entrusted the project to Pedro Gumiel, after receiving approval in a papal bull issued in April, 1499. The plans would come to fruition when several of the university's many colleges opened in 1508.

A related project was Jiménez's wish to prepare the world's first edition of a Polyglot Bible, intended to contain parallel, annotated Hebrew, Aramaic, Greek, and Latin versions of the Old Testament, and a Greek and Latin version of the New Testament. Jiménez gathered lexicographers and biblical scholars at Alcalá and purchased and borrowed an impressive number of biblical manuscripts from libraries throughout Europe for his scholars to consult and compare. The resulting six-volume work, known as the Alcalá or Complutensian Polyglot Bible, was printed in 1517 and distributed for the first time three years later.

Jiménez's interest in learning, evident during his years at Salamanca and in his sponsorship of the university and important works of scholarship, contrasts with his harsh treatment of the Muslim population of Granada. According to the terms of surrender of 1492, Spain's new subjects were assured freedom of religion. Ferdinand II and Isabella I hoped, however, that all Spanish Muslims would eventually renounce their faith and adopt Christianity. Isabella had appointed her own confessor Hernando de Talavera to oversee this transition. In 1499, impatient with the pace of Talavera's methods, Jiménez traveled to Granada to inject fervor and zeal into the process. When the Muslim majority protested his intrusion, Jiménez retaliated by ordering all Arabic books, sacred and secular, burned in public squares. He spared three hundred medical works, a collection destined for the bookshelves at Alcalá de Henares.

Jiménez's harsh methods backfired and caused a number of serious and violent uprisings. He is held responsible for the unnecessary chaos, bloodshed, and distrust that ensued and for the wanton destruction of precious and irreplaceable Muslim books and manuscripts. This entire episode served to tarnish his image as a Humanist and lover of learning, although it did not affect his relationship with his patron, Isabella. He remained her trusted and respected adviser until her death in 1504.

Isabella's death produced a political crisis in Spain by jeopardizing the partnership of the two crowns, Castile and Aragon, that comprised the nation. The union between the two had come about through marriage and personal agreement, and the death of one of the partners threatened this fragile arrangement. The question of inheritance was, then, crucial.

Isabella's choice of heir for the crown of Castile was her third daughter, Joan, who in 1496 had married Philip of Habsburg—Archduke of Austria and son of Emperor Maximilian of the Holy Roman Empire. The couple lived in Flanders. Isabella, recognizing her daughter's incapacity to rule—Joan was emotionally unstable and is known as "the Mad"—intended for the couple to rule jointly and to be succeeded by their first son, Charles. Isabella had also appointed her husband Ferdinand regent; he was expected to govern the country until Joan and Philip made their way to Spain. Rivalry between Philip and Ferdinand soon developed, however, and each side tried to recruit supporters from the always quarrelsome Castilian nobility.

Joan and Philip arrived in Castile in 1505, but their rule was a brief one; Philip died mysteriously in the fall of 1506, and Joan's mental state took a turn for the worse. Jiménez, in the absence of Ferdinand, who had removed himself to Aragon and then to Italy, assumed the regency until Ferdinand's return in 1507. As regent, he acted to protect the interests of Castile, while keeping in check the ambitions of a number of restless courtiers. That same year, Jiménez was elevated to cardinal by the Holy See, and Ferdinand conferred on him the title of Inquisitor General of Castile.

Jiménez the statesman and clergyman was also, for a brief time, a soldier. Using the rich rents of his archbishopric of Toledo, he persuaded Ferdinand to order a military campaign against the North African port of Oran, a favorite refuge of pi-

rates who raided Spanish ships and ports. Jiménez planned and executed the military campaign that captured the city in 1509. Oran was to remain in Spanish hands until the eighteenth century.

After his military triumph, Jiménez returned to Alcalá de Henares to oversee the opening of the university and to attempt to recoup funds spent on the campaign. He remained in close contact with Ferdinand and might have been instrumental in persuading the king to cede the crowns of Aragon and Navarre (annexed by Ferdinand in 1512) to his grandchild Charles, as Isabella had done with Castile. Ferdinand's original choice had been his second grandchild and namesake who, unlike Charles, had been reared in Spain.

When Ferdinand died in 1516, Jiménez assumed the regency of Castile for a second time, in anticipation of the arrival and majority of Charles, who had remained in Flanders after his parents' return to Spain. Charles arrived on September 19, 1517, and was poised to claim the throne of a strong and united state composed of Castile, Aragon, and Navarre. The young king had intended to dismiss Jiménez, but Jiménez died on November 8, 1517, before receiving official notification of his dismissal. He was buried in the College of Saint Ildefonso at the University of Alcalá de Henares, and a magnificent marble monument was built over his grave two years later. The college fell into ill repair after the university moved to Madrid in 1836, and in 1857, the cardinal's remains were transferred to the Church of San Justo y Pastor in the city of Alcalá.

Summary

Francisco Jiménez de Cisneros was, in many ways, the quintessential Spaniard of the Renaissance, embodying all the conflicts and contradictions of the period. Personally and intellectually devoted to rigid Christian observance, he nevertheless displayed great interest in scholarship and learning. He at once persecuted Muslims and collected their medical works. As inquisitor general, he investigated and intimidated some Jewish converts to Christianity, while employing others in his biblical project. A Franciscan by choice and training, he was committed to a life of austerity; yet his personal disregard for material comforts did not interfere with his sense of duty and the demands of the high office he occupied. As Archbishop of Toledo, he was known to wear the coarse Franciscan hair shirt under the splendid robes of the office. Eager to devote himself to a life of contemplation, he led armies into battle more effectively than he led his own Franciscan monks to accept reform.

Jiménez's greatest achievement, however, might very well be his years of loyal service to Isabella and, after her death, to Ferdinand and the couple's heirs. As a statesman, he was dutiful and loyal, placing the interests of his patrons above his own and leading a life above reproach. While he did not introduce any significant new policies, through his patient and devoted service he made possible the continued union of Castile and Aragon, which made Charles the most powerful king of his age.

Bibliography

Lyell, James P. R. *Cardinal Ximenes*. London: Grafton, 1917. A brief account of the cardinal's career, which attributes to Jiménez a greater degree of cunning and deception than most of his other biographers.

Lynch, John. *Spain Under the Habsburgs*. Vol. 1, *Empire and Absolutism, 1516-1598*. 2d ed. Oxford: Blackwell, and New York: New York University Press, 1981. A serious and academic treatment of the first century of rule by the house of Austria; an excellent survey of all aspects of Spanish society during the 1500's.

Mariéjol, Jean-Hippolyte. *The Spain of Ferdinand and Isabella*. Edited and translated by Benjamin Keen. New Brunswick, N.J.: Rutgers University Press, 1961. A favorable account of the role of Jiménez in the reign of the Catholic monarchs. The author praises Jiménez for undertaking the publication of the Polyglot Bible yet criticizes him for not requiring a more critical approach toward the material on the part of those who participated in the project.

Merton, Reginald. *Cardinal Ximenes and the Making of Spain*. London: Kegan Paul, 1934. A fairly detailed biography of Jiménez. Merton believes that King Ferdinand and Jiménez were essentially rivals. In this account, Jiménez emerges as a paragon of virtue and statesmanship.

Prescott, William H. *History of the Reign of Ferdinand and Isabella, the Catholic*. 3 vols. 15th ed. London: Routledge, and Boston: Phillips Sampson, 1859. The third and last volume of this classic work is devoted to a detailed narrative account of the final period of the reign of the Catholic monarchs. Prescott, a liberal thinker, is critical of Jiménez's dogmatism and of his religious bigotry, assigning part of the blame to the society and period in which Jiménez lived.

Starkie, Walter. *Grand Inquisitor*. London: Hodder and Stoughton, 1940. The author, whose interest in Spain is wide-ranging, approaches Jiménez as a cultural figure who embodies certain qualities associated with the national character, such as faith and the tragic sense of life.

Clara Estow

JOAN OF ARC

Born: c. 1412; Domremy, France

Died: May 30, 1431; Rouen, France

Areas of Achievement: Government, politics, and religion

Contribution: Joan's victories initiated the withdrawal of English troops from France to end the Hundred Years' War, and she made possible the coronation of Charles VII at Reims. As a martyr to her vision and mission, she had as much influence after her death as in her lifetime.

Early Life

Usually identified with the province of Lorraine, Joan of Arc grew up a daughter of France in Domremy, a village divided between the king's territory and that of the Dukes of Bar and Lorraine. Bells from the church next to her home sounded the events of her youth. Her father, Jacques, was a peasant farmer and respected citizen. Joan learned piety from her mother, Isabelle Romée, as part of a large family. She took special pride in spinning and sewing; she never learned to read or write. By custom, she would have assumed her mother's surname, but in her public career she was called the Maid of Orléans, or Joan the Maid (with the double sense of virgin and servant).

Joan was born into the violence of both the Hundred Years' War and the French Civil War. Henry V, King of England, had gained control of most of northern France and, with the aid of the French Duke of Burgundy, claimed the crown from the insane Charles VI. The heir to the throne, Charles VII—or the Dauphin, as he was called—was young and apparently believed that his cause was hopeless. Five years after his father's death, he was still uncrowned, and Reims, the traditional coronation site, was deep in English territory. Domremy, on the frontier, was exposed to all the depredations of the war and was pillaged on at least one occasion during Joan's childhood.

Joan began to hear voices and to be visited by the patron saints of France, Saint Michael, Saint Catherine, and Saint Margaret, when she was thirteen or fourteen years old. She claimed that she heard and saw the saints, who became her companions and directed her every step. Initially, she took the voices as calling her to a holy life, and she pledged her virginity and piety. Later she came to believe that it was her mission to deliver France from the English.

Paintings and medals were made of Joan, but no genuine portrait has been identified; a contemporary sketch survives by a man who never saw her. Three carved limestone heads in helmets (now in Boston, Loudun, and Orléans) may represent near-contemporary portraits. They show a generous nose and mouth and heavy-lidded eyes. She had a ruddy complexion; black hair in a documentary seal (now lost) indicates her coloring. Sturdy enough to wear armor and live a soldier's life, she had a gentle voice. She wore a red frieze dress when she left Domremy; when she approached the Dauphin at Chinon, she wore men's clothing: black woolen doublet and laced leggings, cap, cape, and boots. She wore her hair short like a man's, or a nun's, cut above the ears in the "pudding basin" style which facilitated wearing a helmet and discouraged lustful thoughts. Later, the Dauphin provided her with armor and money for fashionable clothing. The gold-embroidered red costume in which she was finally captured may have been made from cloth sent to her by the captive Duke of Orléans.

Life's Work

In 1428, Joan attempted to gain support from Robert de Baudricourt, the royal governor of Vaucouleurs. (The pregnancy of a kinswoman living two miles from Vaucouleurs provided Joan with a pretext to leave home.) Baudricourt, after rejecting her twice—as the voice had predicted—became caught up in Joan's mission. The English had besieged Orléans, as she had told him they would, and he, similarly besieged, had to agree to surrender his castle unless the Dauphin came to his aid by a specified date. Before sending Joan to the Dauphin, he had her examined and exorcised.

Charles agreed to the interview with Joan in desperation. Orléans, besieged since October of 1428, had great strategic importance; its fall would shake the loyalty of his remaining supporters and the readiness of his cities to provide money. Joan's appearance at court on February 25, 1429, after traveling through enemy territory for eleven days, brought fresh hope. She identified the Dauphin at once in the crowded room, and she gave him some sign, "the King's Secret," which confirmed her mission but whose nature is still debated. A second exhaustive investigation of Joan occurred at Poitiers, where her piety and simplicity impressed everyone. Charles established a household for her.

She had a standard made and adopted an ancient sword, discovered, through her directions, buried in the church of Sainte-Catherine-de-Fierbois.

On April 28, 1429, Joan and an expedition, believing they were on a supply mission, entered Orléans. Joan addressed the English commander, calling on him to retreat. She turned rough French soldiers into crusaders, conducting daily assemblies for prayer and insisting that they rid themselves of camp followers and go to confession. When a party bringing supplies to the city on the opposite bank found the wind blowing against them, she predicted the sudden change of wind that permitted the boats to cross. Nonplussed Englishmen allowed another shipment led by priests to pass without firing on it; they explained their lack of action as the result of bewitchment. Within the city, Joan's inspired leadership encouraged the troops to follow her famous standard and her ringing cry, "In God's name, charge boldly!" On May 7, though seriously wounded as she had predicted, she rallied the troops to victory at the Tourelles fortification, after the French captains had given up hope. The next day, the English withdrew from Orléans.

In little more than a week, with much plunder and killing of prisoners, the French drove their enemies from the remaining Loire strongholds of Jargeau, Meung, and Beaugency. Though Joan took part in these actions, her principal influence remained her extraordinary attraction and rallying of forces; she later said that she had killed no one. The troops of Arthur de Richemont, brother of the Duke of Brittany, who now joined the Dauphin, counted decisively in another victory at Patay on June 17.

Charles's coronation on July 17 at Reims, deep in enemy territory, clearly shows Joan's influence. Counselors and captains advised Charles to take advantage of his victories and move against Normandy. Joan persuaded him instead to travel to Reims, and city after city yielded to siege or simply opened its gates to the Dauphin: Auxerre, Troyes, Châlons, and Reims itself. The stunned English regent, the Duke of Bedford, offered no resistance.

After the coronation, Joan's single-minded drive to take Paris and gain the release of the Duke of Orléans conflicted with a royal policy of caution and diplomacy based on the expectation that Burgundy, too, would rally peacefully to Charles. Charles ennobled Joan and her family and provided her with attendants and money, but she was too popular to permit her return to Domremy. Her voices warned that she had little time. By September 8, when the assault on Paris finally began, the English had regained their aplomb. Joan, again wounded, unsuccessfully urged an evening attack. Charles's orders the next day forbade an attack, though the Baron of Montmorency and his men came out of the city to join the royal army, and on September 13, Charles withdrew his troops.

Joan now joined in a holding action to prevent the English forces from using the extended truce to retake their lost positions. Her men took Saint-Pierre-le-Moûtier, but lack of supplies forced her to abandon La Charité. In the spring of 1430, she led volunteers to stiffen the resistance of Compiègne against the Burgundians, contrary to the royal policy of pacification. That helps to explain Charles's failure to negotiate her release after her capture at Compiègne on May 23—an event also predicted by her voices. The Burgundians sold her to the English authorities.

Joan's trial, which ran from January 9 through May 30, 1431, tested her faith and gave her a final opportunity to uphold the French cause. Her death was a foregone conclusion; the English reserved their right to retry her if the Church exonerated her. Bishop Pierre Cauchon of Beauvais took the lead, realizing that a church trial, by proving her a witch, would turn her victories to Anglo-Burgundian advantage. Indeed, her captors may have believed her a camp trollop and sorceress until a physical examination by the Duchess of Bedford, the sister of Philip of Burgundy, proved Joan's virginity. That made it clear that she had not had carnal relations with Satan, a sure sign of sorcery.

After twice attempting to escape (for which her voices blamed her), she stood trial in Rouen. The two earlier investigations and Joan's impeccable behavior obliged Cauchon to falsify evidence and maneuver her into self-incrimination. She showed great perspicacity—her voices told her to answer boldly. Cauchon finally reduced the seventy-two points on which she had been examined to twelve edited points, on which her judges and the faculty of the University of Paris condemned her.

Seriously ill and threatened by her examiners, Joan apparently signed a recantation which temporarily spared her life. Cauchon claimed that she had renounced her voices; some historians claim forgery, admission to lesser charges, or some code by which she indicated denial. In any case, she returned to woman's clothing as ordered and to her cell. She was later found wearing men's clothing (perhaps partly to protect herself from her guards).

When questioned, Joan replied that her voices had rebuked her for her change of heart. On May 29, the judges agreed unanimously to give Joan over to the English authorities. She received Communion on the morning of May 30 and was burned as a heretic.

Summary

Mystics with political messages abounded in Joan's world, but none had Joan's impact on politics. Widespread celebration in 1436 of Claude des Armoises, claiming to be Joan escaped from the flames, demonstrated her continuing popularity. Orléans preserved Joan's cult, and Domremy became a national shrine. A surge of interest beginning in the nineteenth century with Napoleon has made Joan one of the most written-about persons in history, but efforts to analyze her in secular terms reaffirm the continuing mystery of her inspiration.

Many people in the huge crowd that witnessed Joan's death believed in her martyrdom and reported miracles. English insistence on complete destruction of her body, with her ashes thrown into the Seine, underscored the point. When he took Rouen and the trial records in 1450, Charles VII ordered her case reopened, but only briefly. Too many influential living persons were implicated in Joan's condemnation, and a reversal of the verdict would also support papal claims to jurisdiction in France. A papal legate, Guillaume d'Estouteville, later encouraged Joan's aged mother to appeal to the pope, which brought about rehabilitation proceedings and the declaration of her innocence in 1456. Even then, the revised verdict merely revoked the earlier decision on procedural grounds without endorsing Joan's mission or condemning her judges. Joan was canonized by Pope Benedict XV on May 16, 1920, and France honors her with a festival day on the second Sunday of May.

Bibliography

Duby, Georges. *France in the Middle Ages, 987-1460: From Hugh Capet to Joan of Arc.* Oxford and Cambridge, Mass.: Blackwell, 1991. Duby has changed the concept of the operation of feudal society. In this book, he examines the history of France from the rise of the Capetians in the mid-tenth century to the execution of Joan of Arc in the mid-fifteenth. He takes the evolution of power and the emergence of the French state as his central themes, and guides the reader through complex terrain.

Fabre, Lucien. *Joan of Arc.* Translated by Gerard Hopkins. London: Odhams, and New York: McGraw-Hill, 1954. Fabre's account reflects the French and Catholic position. He calls the English "Godons," as Joan did (from their characteristic oath), and makes Cauchon a monster. He bases conclusions about the various puzzles on documents and provides a guide to the vast literature.

Guillemin, Henri. *The True History of Joan "of Arc."* Translated by William Oxferry. London: Allen and Unwin, 1972. An example of the tradition that Joan did not die in 1431. One of the many variations in this tradition makes her the sister of Charles VII. Historians have never given much credence to books of this genre.

Lightbody, Charles Wayland. *The Judgments of Joan: Joan of Arc, a Study in Cultural History.* London: Allen and Unwin, and Cambridge, Mass.: Harvard University Press, 1961. A 171-page book on a very large topic. Lightbody treats the literature on Joan through the trial for rehabilitation; by way of apology, he promises a fuller treatment, which never appeared. Worth reading, but any author who treats George Bernard Shaw's play as revelatory about Joan and her times must be held suspect.

Lucie-Smith, Edward. *Joan of Arc.* London: Allen Lane, 1976; New York: Norton, 1977. The necessary counterbalance to Fabre's biography. An objective and scholarly accounting, but in treating Joan's voices as hallucinations the author loses touch with Joan and her times. Lucie-Smith suggests a sympathetic approach to Joan's judges.

Pernoud, Régine. *Joan of Arc by Herself and Her Witnesses.* Translated by Edward Hyams. London: Macdonald, 1964; New York: Stein and Day, 1966. A work of great integrity and judgment by the director of the Centre Jeanne d'Arc in Orléans. She has culled documents of Joan's own times for an extremely useful book.

———. *The Retrial of Joan of Arc: The Evidence of the Trial for Her Rehabilitation, 1450-1456.* Translated by J. M. Cohen. Foreword by Katherine Anne Porter. London: Methuen, and New York: Harcourt Brace, 1955. Though incomplete, this includes the essential 1455-1456 testimony by 144 persons who knew Joan at various stages of her life, making her one of the best-documented personalities of her century. Intended to counteract the earlier trial, it proves something of a whitewash, but it also gives a valid picture of what Joan meant to the French people.

Vale, Malcom G. A. *Charles VII.* London: Methuen, and Berkeley: University of California Press, 1974. A biography of sound scholarship which provides a better guide to the political world than do Joan's biographies. Vale, an Englishman, plays down Joan's own importance.

Warner, Marina. *Joan of Arc: The Image of Female Heroism.* London: Weidenfeld and Nicolson, and New York: Knopf, 1981. Warner finishes what Lightbody began, ranging through the centuries. She is notably good in utilizing recent scholarship, providing, for example, a hard look at how little is really known about Joan's appearance. Warner's feminist interpretation, however, imposes modern notions on fifteenth century experience. She plays down Joan's voices and treats her fasting as possible anorexia and her adoption of men's clothing as psychologically significant.

Wood, Charles T. *Joan of Arc and Richard III: Sex, Saints, and Government in the Middle Ages.* New York: Oxford University Press, 1998. Wood's study of French and English history seeks to push readers into reconsidering their notions on a variety of typically controversial subjects.

Paul Stewart

SAINT JOHN OF THE CROSS
Juan de Yepes y Álvarez

Born: June 24, 1542; Fontiveros, Spain
Died: December 14, 1591; Úbeda, Spain
Areas of Achievement: Church reform and religion
Contribution: Saint John of the Cross contributed to the renewal of monastic life and to the development of mystical theology during the golden age of the Catholic Reformation. His most lasting contribution has been to Western mysticism.

Early Life

Juan de Yepes y Álvarez (Saint John of the Cross) was born on June 24, 1542, in Fontiveros, Spain, a town of five thousand inhabitants situated on the Castilian tableland. His father, Gonzalo de Yepes, was the son of a prosperous local silk merchant. Gonzalo was disinherited for marrying Catalina Álvarez, an impoverished and orphaned Toledan, apprenticed to a weaver in Fontiveros. John was the third son born to this union. The death of his father following a prolonged illness when John was only two left John, his mother, and his siblings in dire poverty. Seeking help, Catalina left Fontiveros, going initially to the province of Toledo but later settling in Medina del Campo, a city of thirty thousand. In Medina, there was a doctrine, or catechism, school. As much an orphanage as an educational institution for the poor, this school received John as a student. Children were fed, clothed, catechized, and given a rudimentary education. Apprenticeship in various trades was also part of the program of the doctrine school. Little is known of the four trades that John tried, except that his efforts were unsuccessful. Since in later life John was fond of painting and carving, his failure, perhaps, was one of premature exposure rather than of aptitude. John was next attached to the Hospital de la Concepción, where he worked as a male nurse, begged alms for the poor, and continued his studies. Academic success caused him to be enrolled at the Jesuit College, situated barely two hundred yards from the hospital. Founded in 1551, this school enrolled forty students at the time John was in attendance, probably from 1559 to 1563. John's teachers recalled his passionate enthusiasm for books. With a good education in the humanities, John in 1563 found his life's vocation, taking the dark brown habit and white cloak of the Carmelites.

Life's Work

At the age of twenty-one, John entered the small community of the Carmelite brothers in Medina, then a fellowship of perhaps six members. The Order of Our Lady of Mount Carmel had been founded four centuries earlier, in 1156, in Palestine by Saint Berthold as one of extreme asceticism and of great devotion to Mary. By the sixteenth century, it admitted female as well as male members. The so-called Original or Primitive Rule of 1209 had been relaxed, the order following a Mitigated Observance. Why John selected this order is not known. Perhaps it was his love of contemplation, his devotion to the Virgin, or his practice of extreme asceticism that attracted him to the Carmelites. John of Yepes now took the name Fray Juan de Santo Matia (Brother John of Saint Mathias), though, five years later, when, on November 28, 1568, he professed the Carmelite Primitive Rule, he would change his name to Fray Juan de la Cruz (Brother John of the Cross). As a monastic reformer, John was to make a lasting contribution to Christianity.

Following his profession as a Carmelite, John continued his education at the College of San Andres, a school for sixteen years attached to the famed University of Salamanca. A good Latinist and an excellent grammarian, John took classes in the college of arts at Salamanca from 1564 to 1567. Perhaps seven thousand students were matriculated at the University of Salamanca at that time. Taught by a faculty known throughout Spain and the Habsburg lands, the young monk next turned his attention to theology, attending lectures in divinity in 1567-1568. At Salamanca, John was taught a clear-cut Thomism and was deeply immersed in the philosophy of Aristotle and the theology of Saint Thomas Aquinas. Concurrently, John was a master of students at San Andres.

Following his ordination as a priest in 1567, John met Saint Teresa de Jesús of Ávila. Daughter of a noble Spanish family, Teresa had entered the Carmelite Convent of the Incarnation (Mitigated Observance) at Ávila in 1535. Teresa had become persuaded that discipline was too relaxed and that there ought to be a return to the Primitive Rule of the Carmelites. Her followers were called Discalced Carmelites, in opposition to the Calced Carmelites, who continued to follow the Mitigated rather than the

Primitive Rule. Within a year of his meeting with the remarkable Mother Teresa, John was committed to the so-called Teresian Reforms of the Carmelite Order. For that reason, in November, 1568, John was made professor of the Primitive Rule of the Carmelites at Duruelo. Resolving "to separate himself from the world and hide himself in God," John sought a strictly contemplative life. That wish was never granted, for John was often sought as a counselor and confessor (for the laity and the religious) and as a popular and persuasive preacher.

Soon John became subprior, then novice master, and finally rector of a new house of studies founded at Alcalá. This was a creative time for John, who was able to integrate the intellectual and the spiritual life and who could combine contemplation with active service, including becoming Teresa's confessor after 1571. John found "the delights which God lets souls taste in contemplation," but he was advised by Teresa that "a great storm of trials" was on the horizon.

Disputes between the Carmelites who followed the Primitive Rule and those who held to the Mitigated Observance caused John to become a focus of attention. Following an initial imprisonment in 1576, John was seized on December 2, 1577, by some of the Calced Carmelites and taken to Toledo, where he was commanded by superiors to repent of his reforms. This was yet another step in the antireformist policies that had prevailed in the Carmelite Order since a general chapter meeting in 1575. Because John refused to renounce the reforms, he was imprisoned for some nine months in a small cell. There was only one small opening for light and air. John's jailers were motivated by "vindictiveness . . . mingled with religious zeal," for they believed that his reforms of the order were a very great crime and revealed a stubborn pride and insubordination. John accepted his imprisonment, with its insults, slanders, calumnies, physical sufferings, and agonies of soul as a further labor by God to purify and refine his faith.

In August, 1578, John escaped from his captors and fled to southern Spain. The separation of the two branches of the Carmelite Order, the Calced and the Discalced, occurred in 1579-1580. John became the rector of a Discalced Carmelite college in Baeza in Andalusia, serving also as an administrator in the Reformed Carmelite Order, being Prior of Granada in 1582 and of Segovia in 1588. Vicar provincial of his order's southern region, by 1588 John was major definitor and was a member of the governing body of the society.

John's contemporary, Eliseo de los Martires, described him as "a man in body of medium size" and one of "grave and venerable countenance." His complexion was "wheaty," or "somewhat swarthy," and his face was filled with "good features." Normally John wore a mustache and was often fully bearded. Dressed in "an old, narrow, short, rough habit," one so rough it was said that "the cloak seemed to be made of goat-hair," John reminded many of a latter-day John the Baptist. John impressed those he met with his purity of character, his intensity of spirit, his austerity of life, his profound humility, his fondness for simplicity, and his honesty and directness in speech. Contemporary biographers also recalled his sense of humor, noting that he delighted in making his friars laugh, often sprinkling his spiritual conversation with amusing stories.

Perhaps John's greatest legacy to the world community is his writing about the interior life. During his trials, tribulations, and travels, John wrote of his encounters with God. These extensive treatises on the mystical life are a unique combination of his poems and his commentaries on those poems. *Cántico espiritual* (1581; *A Spiritual Canticle of the Soul*, 1862), part of which was said to have been composed while John was on his knees in prayer, is such a synthesis of poetry and commentary. That poetry is both didactic and symbolic, practical and devotional. The ancient threefold route of the soul to God is described in *A Spiritual Canticle of the Soul*. One moves from purgation (or confession of sin, the emptying of the self) to illumination (or instruction, revelation of God, filling with the divine) and then to union or perfection (going beyond a sense of separation to one of complete integration with God). This ongoing colloquy of Christ and the soul draws on the rich imagery of courtship and love, starting with the soul's search for the Beloved, continuing to an initial meeting, then describing the perfect union, and concluding with a discussion of the poignant desire for an everlasting intimacy with the Eternal, a longing that can only be fulfilled in eternity. *La subida del Monte Carmelo* (1578; *The Ascent of Mount Carmel*, 1862) is also a discussion of how the soul can attain mystical union with God. The journey to God contains a "Dark Night" because the spirit must quite literally mortify, or put to death, sensory experience and sensible knowledge and then maintain itself by pure faith. Following such purgations, as well as those that come from the faith experience itself, the soul enters into a transforming union with God. This is truly a passion, for it combines both intense suffering and ecstatic pleasure, the two components of overwhelming love. In *Llama de amor viva* (1581; *Living Flame of Love*, 1862), the spiritual marriage, or divine union, is further described.

Though he longed only for contemplation, John once more was caught up in controversy. In 1591, he found himself banished to Andalusia. After some time in solitary life, John became extremely ill, going to Úbeda for medical attention. Following extreme pain, John died at Úbeda on December 14, 1591. In his dying moments, John requested the reading of the "Canticle of Canticles," the moving love poem of the Old Testament. Interpreting it as an allegory of the soul's romance of God, John commented, "What precious pearls."

Summary

While controversial during his lifetime, Saint John of the Cross was commended by the Catholic Church, following his death, as both a saint and teacher. Beatified by Pope Clement X in 1675, John was canonized in 1726 by Benedict XIII. In 1926, Pius XI declared him a doctor of the Church, one of perhaps thirty Catholics deemed a theologian of both outstanding intellectual merit and personal sanctity and to be received universally with appreciation.

John surely was a mighty doctor of the Church, embodying the profound spirituality of the Catholic Reformation in Spain, drawing on the same religious energies that inspired Teresa, Ignatius of Loyola, the founder of the Society of Jesus, and Francis Xavier, a missionary-evangelist of Asia. He will forever be one of the treasures of the Roman Catholic tradition.

As reformer, master, saint, doctor, poet, and seer, John transcended the limits of either one country or creed. His significance is greater even than that of enriching the piety of Roman Catholicism and of enhancing the literature of his native Spain. John's profound mysticism causes him to be ranked alongside the great religious seekers of all human history—with the saints of Hinduism, the sages of Buddhism, the Sufis of Islam, the seekers of Taoism, the teachers of Confucianism, the visionaries of Protestantism, and the holy men and women of Orthodoxy and Oriental Christianity. As such, John of the Cross is one of the major figures of world religion, combining intellectual rigor with a vigorous work ethic, wrapping both in a profound and appealing spirituality.

Bibliography

Bruno de Jesus-Marie. *St. John of the Cross*. Edited by Benedict Zimmerman, with an introduction by Jacques Maritain. London and New York: Sheed and Ward, 1936. This extensively documented 495-page study by a Roman Catholic priest attempts to do justice to John as a reformer, theologian, and mystic, drawing on the insights of philosophy, history, and biography. The central thesis is that John was not simply a "Quietistic Mystic" who had mastered the interior life, but that he was also an "Activistic Churchman" who had a powerful impact on the external world of sixteenth century Catholicism.

Crisógono de Jesús. *The Life of St. John of the Cross*. Translated by Kathleen Pond. London: Longman, and New York: Harper, 1958. A thoroughly documented biography of John both as a person and as a monk. Illustrations, charts, notes, and references make this a useful starting point for further research.

Cugno, Alain. *Saint John of the Cross: Reflections on Mystical Experience*. Translated by Barbara Wall. London: Burns and Oates, and New York: Seabury Press, 1982. This concise study in 153 pages contends that John was perhaps the greatest mystic produced by Christianity. Originally written for the University of Tours, this text attempts to understand John from a philosophical rather than a theological or mystical viewpoint. In six succinct and tightly written chapters, it explores such major themes in the philosophy of religion as the absence of God, the meaning of mysticism, the role of desire in religion, and the doctrine of the Kingdom of God.

Frost, Bede. *Saint John of the Cross, 1542-1591, Doctor of Divine Love: An Introduction to His Philosophy, Theology, and Spirituality.* London: Hodder and Stoughton, and New York: Harper, 1937. This classic study of John's thought attempts to do justice to the complexity and variety of the saint's writings. The author admits the inherent twofold difficulty of exploring John's thinking: mystical experiences in and of themselves are incommunicable and language proves inadequate to the description of such experiences, without the compounded problem of translation from Spanish to English.

John of the Cross, Saint. *The Ascent of Mount Carmel.* Translated by David Lewis, with a preface by Benedict Zimmerman. New York: Benziger, 1906; London: Baker, 1928. This indexed edition of John's major mystical work is useful as an introduction to a primary source for his thought. Indexed both by topic and by Scriptural references, the volume facilitates both the study of selected topics in John's piety and the identification of biblical sources for his themes.

John of the Cross, Saint. *St. John of the Cross (San Juan de la Cruz): Alchemist of the Soul.* Edited and translated by Antonio T. de Nicolas. New York: Paragon House, 1989. This work has three parts—"The Life," "The Poetry" (bilingual), and "The Prose" (excerpts and commentary)—that describe St. John's mystic journey as he sought the source of the prophetic voice. There is an excellent chronology of his life and an ample bibliography.

Maio, Eugene A. *St. John of the Cross: The Imagery of Eros*. Madrid: Playor, 1973. In brief compass, the author introduces the reader to the mystical tradition of love, a theme central to John's life and thought. Chapters relate John to the poetic and mystical traditions of Spain, examine the role of Neoplatonism in Christian thought, and then explore the dynamics of John's spirituality. Contains an extensive bibliography.

Sencourt, Robert. *Carmelite and Poet: A Framed Portrait of St. John of the Cross, with His Poems in Spanish*. London: Hollis and Carter, 1943; New York: Macmillan, 1944. This illustrated biography in 253 pages, with an appended anthology of John's verse in Spanish, examines the man from the standpoint of literature, providing the reader with "both the soul of poetry and the poetry of the soul." Extensive annotations compensate for the lack of a bibliography.

C. George Fry

JULIUS II
Giuliano della Rovere

Born: December 5, 1443; Albisola, Republic of Genoa

Died: February 21, 1513; Rome

Areas of Achievement: Religion, the military, and patronage of the arts

Contribution: Julius II, the Warrior Pope, was the first and only pontiff personally to command and lead a papal army into battle. His military exploits regained large amounts of territory lost to the Papal States in wars with France and small Italian republics. Besides his attempts to strengthen church administration and reduce nepotism, he was also a patron to Michelangelo, Raphael, and Donato Bramante.

Early Life

Giuliano della Rovere was born in the small town of Albisola, Italy, in 1443. When his father's brother, Francesco della Rovere, became head of the Franciscan Order, Giuliano was educated under the direction of the Franciscans; soon after his studies were completed, he was ordained a priest. When his uncle became pope and took the name Sixtus IV in 1471, Giuliano was made a cardinal in the same year. Over the next few years, Cardinal della Rovere held eight bishoprics, controlled many more abbeys and benefices, and assumed the title of Archbishop of Avignon.

From 1480 to 1482, della Rovere served as legate to France. In this capacity, he showed great diplomatic skill in reconciling the differences between Louis XI of France and Maximilian of Austria. He returned to Rome when Sixtus IV died in 1484 and bribed many cardinals into electing Batista Cibo as Pope Innocent VIII. Innocent was controlled rather easily; indeed, his policies were to a large extent determined and implemented by della Rovere.

Because of his strong influence over Innocent, della Rovere was opposed by Cardinal Rodrigo Borgia; in a short time, the two men became bitter rivals. Their disagreements escalated to such an extent that, when Innocent died in 1492 and Cardinal Borgia was elected Pope Alexander VI, della Rovere was forced to flee to France in order to save his life.

Della Rovere tried to convince King Charles VIII of France that church reforms in Italy could only be achieved with his personal support. In fact, della Rovere was seeking help in removing Alexander from the Papacy. When Charles VIII decided to invade Italy, della Rovere accompanied him and attempted to win his backing for the convocation of a council to depose the pope on the grounds of his having won the election of 1492 through bribery. Unfortunately for della Rovere, Charles negotiated and signed a conciliatory treaty with Alexander in 1495—all della Rovere's efforts to get rid of his enemy were frustrated.

In 1498, della Rovere was reconciled with Alexander when his diplomatic skills helped to arrange the marriage of Charlotte d'Albret, sister of the King of Navarre, to Cesare Borgia, a relative of the pope. When Borgia attacked the dukedom of Urbino, however, where della Rovere's nephew stood next in line to succeed the duke, the peace was over. Once again, della Rovere had to flee far from Rome. Only the death of Alexander in August of 1503 made it possible for the cardinal to return to Rome.

Believing that the way was now clear for him to become pope, della Rovere did everything in his power to assure the outcome of the election. Yet the Italian cardinals were divided as to which candidate to support and della Rovere, although he received a majority of the votes, fell two short of the required two-thirds. Realizing that he was not going to be elected to the Papacy, he threw his support to the Cardinal of Siena, Francesco Piccolomini, who took the name Pius III. Yet della Rovere knew that the new pope's age and ill health meant a short tenure in office. When Pius died after only twenty-six days, della Rovere prepared for one last chance to wear the tiara.

Life's Work

By extensive promises to his opponents, and by resorting to bribery when necessary, della Rovere was unanimously elected pope on November 1, 1503, in the shortest conclave ever recorded, less than twenty-four hours. A proud and egotistical man, he changed two syllables of his given name, Giuliano, to come up with his papal name, Julius II. Extremely confident, impetuous, hot-tempered, and impatient, Julius soon gained the reputation of an activist pope, unable to listen to advice. He insisted on doing everything himself and was almost

impossible to consult; when faced with a contrary opinion, he would stop the speaker with a little bell kept near him at all times. Although he was sixty years old at the time of his election to the Papacy and suffering from gout and kidney ailments, his spirit was indefatigable. He was a large man with a tight mouth and dark eyes; the word most often used by Italians in describing him was *terribilitá*, or "awesomeness."

Julius immediately began to repair the damage wrought on the Church by Alexander VI. He reorganized papal administration, planned to achieve financial solvency for the Church, promised to eliminate simony, and began to reduce nepotism. He established order in Rome by implementing harsh measures against bandits and hired assassins who had run rampant under Alexander; to serve as a bulwark against any foreign or domestic threat to himself, he hired mercenary Swiss guards as protectors of the Vatican.

Believing that the authority of the Papacy could be enhanced by the exercise of temporal power, Julius implemented a strategy of territorial conquest, expedient diplomacy, and the show of external pomp and glory. Accordingly, his first major decision as supreme pontiff was to recover the territories lost to the Papal States under the administration of and following the death of Alexander.

In the first year of his pontificate, Julius set out to regain the cities that Venice had seized from the Holy See and later occupied. Initially, he used diplomatic measures to isolate and pressure the Venetian republic to release its holdings. Venice did give back some of the land but continued to hold the cities of Rimini and Faenza. Frustrated by Venice's intransigence, the pope turned his attention to the recovery of Bologna and Perugia, two of the most important cities within the Papal States whose leaders ignored the authority of Rome. Impatient and reckless in his desire to recapture the land, Julius ignored the objections of many cardinals and shocked all of Europe when he personally rode at the head of his army to conquer the cities in 1506. Shortly afterward, when the papal fief Ferrara turned against him, the white-bearded pope donned helmet, mail, and sword, and led his troops in an attack through a breach in the fortress wall. During these years of violent disputes, Julius was continually on horseback, encouraging his soldiers, directing their deployment, and making certain that they used the armaments of modern warfare correctly.

Still unable to subdue Venice, Julius sought the help of the Holy Roman Emperor Maximilian and Louis XII of France. Julius convinced the two men to declare war on the republic and, with the added participation of Spain and Swiss mercenaries, formed the League of Cambrai to execute his plan. Julius also issued a bull of excommunication and interdict for the entire population of the city. When the Venetians were finally defeated at the Battle of Agnadello in May of 1509, one of the bloodiest conflicts in the history of warfare, the pope's troops reclaimed Rimini, Faenza, and other territories previously held by the republic.

Only one year later, Julius received a formal confirmation of ecclesiastical rights and authority in the Venetian territory; with this reconciliation, he lifted the ban of excommunication. Yet neither Louis XII nor Maximilian was ready to make peace and leave Italy; the expansion of their empires now dominated their strategy. Julius quickly recognized that there could be no consolidation of the Papal States as long as the French and the emperor remained in Italy. Convinced of the growing danger that foreign troops in Italy now posed, Julius made a complete about-face and formed an alliance in 1510 with Venice and Spain, along with Swiss mercenaries, against France. This new combination was called the Holy League, and Julius' new battle cry was, "Out with the barbarians!"

King Louis XII's resentment and animosity ran so deep as to label the war against himself illegal and convene, with the support of Emperor Maximilian and prominent French cardinals, a synod at Tours intended to depose Julius from the Papacy; in 1511, at the instigation of the French king, the rebel cardinals established their own antipapal council at Pisa. At the time, Julius was again waging war in person, on this occasion against the Duke of Ferrara, who supported the French. When he received news of the attempts to remove him from office, however, the pope reacted swiftly: He excommunicated Louis and the rebellious cardinals, convinced England to join the Holy League, and convened the Fifth Lateran Council in 1512 to oppose the schismatic meeting at Pisa and reassert his own papal authority.

After a number of setbacks, Julius and the Holy League finally defeated the French at the Battle of Ravenna and drove them across the Alps. With a few concessions to Maximilian, the pope's campaign to oust foreign troops from Italy came to a successful conclusion. Yet, even though Julius had regained large tracts of land for the Papal States, the nature of Italian politics and diplomacy frustrated him in providing definite and long-lasting resolutions to many territorial problems.

Weary with war and in ill health, Julius turned his attention to the Lateran Council and church reform. Initially, the council was preoccupied with problems surrounding the French presence in Italy and with the illegitimate council at Pisa. With the defeat of the French and the dissolution of the assembly at Pisa, Julius pushed for needed reforms and the Lateran council responded. One of the most important of Julius' papal bulls confirmed by the council voided any papal election tainted with simony; any offender would suffer the loss of his office and endure large financial penalties. The council also confirmed Julius' renewal of a bull by Pius II which prohibited switching an ecclesiastical appeal from a pope to a council.

One of Julius' last acts as pope, and one of the most far-reaching, was to grant a dispensation to Prince Henry of England, later King Henry VIII, enabling him to marry Catherine of Aragon. Julius II died on February 21, 1513, in Rome, but the Fifth Lateran Council he had convened remained in session for another four years.

Summary

The goal of consolidating the Papal States, Julius II believed, could only be attained by keeping France and the Holy Roman Empire out of Italy. This strategy was achieved in three stages: the regaining of lost territories, the expelling of all so-called foreigners from the Italian peninsula, and the assuring of papal authority in Rome and throughout the Papal States. For these reasons, Julius is regarded by many historians as one of the earliest and most important proponents of Italian unification.

Yet since the great powers returned to plague Italian politics after the pope's death, it is arguable that Julius' more significant and lasting contribution to the Papacy involved his patronage of the arts. He beautified Rome and initiated a large amount of new construction, including new and rebuilt churches, such as Santa Maria del Popolo and Santa Maria della Pace, and he helped establish the Vatican Library. He commissioned Raphael to paint new frescoes for the papal apartments. Michelangelo, against his will, was browbeaten by the pope into painting the ceiling for the Sistine Chapel; working alone on a scaffold for almost four years, Michelangelo allowed no one but Julius to view his work.

Bramante was one of the pope's favorite artists; Julius assigned Bramante the task of designing and building the courts of the Belvedere, where he started a collection of ancient sculpture. The monument to Julius' papacy was also given to Bramante to execute—the demolition of the old Basilica of St. Peter's and the construction of a new one. The cost of replacing the older building with a grander edifice significantly exceeded existing papal revenues and led Julius to implement a practice of dire consequence, the public sale of indulgences in Papal States. When the next pope extended the practice to Germany, it precipitated a revolt by a disillusioned and angry young cleric named Martin Luther.

Bibliography

Chambers, D. S. *Cardinal Bainbridge in the Court of Rome, 1509 to 1514*. London: Oxford University Press, 1965. An account of one cardinal's tenure in Rome and his eyewitness observations of the persons and events surrounding the Papacy during Julius' reign. Particularly good in relating the machinations involved in ecclesiastical politics.

Erasmus, Desiderius. *Julius Exclusus*. Translated by Paul Pascal. Bloomington: Indiana University Press, 1968. This work was completed after the pope's death. Julius is characterized as the embodiment of war and all its accompanying evils. An extremely hostile polemic against Julius. Not until the twentieth century was Erasmus' authorship verified.

Gilbert, Felix. *The Pope, His Banker, and Venice*. Cambridge, Mass.: Harvard University Press, 1980; London: Harvard University Press, 1991. A detailed examination of Julius' involvement in the League of Cambrai and his war against the republic of Venice. Stresses the financial arrangements made by both the pope and the Venetian republic to carry out the extended conflict. An excellent insight into the diplomatic and financial policies at work in the Papacy. Notes at the end of the book shed light on some of the more elusive historical problems during Julius' pontificate.

O'Malley, John W. "Fulfillment of the Christian Golden Age Under Pope Julius II: Text of a Discourse of Giles of Veterbo, 1507." *Traditio* 25 (1969): 265-338. A contemporary interpretation of Julius' policy that temporal power gives authority and prestige to the Church. Focuses on the interaction between secular and spiritual pursuits in war, diplomacy, and art.

Shaw, Christine. *Julius II: The Warrior Pope*. Oxford and Cambridge, Mass.: Blackwell, 1997. This book is the first biography of Julius II to be based on an extensive use of archival sources. Shaw's account includes new material about Julius' career as a cardinal, providing fresh perspectives on his policies as pope. The reports of those who negotiated with him, observed him, spied on him, ridiculed him, and admired him, are used to depict his vivid, powerful, and humorous personality and the impact he had on his times.

Tuchman, Barbara. *The March of Folly: From Troy to Vietnam*. New York: Knopf, and London: Joseph, 1984. A general overview of how the late Renaissance popes set the stage for Martin Luther's Reformation movement. More specifically, a character study of Julius II that raises questions about the propriety of his decision to lead an army into battle.

Thomas Derdak

JOHN KNOX

Born: c. 1514; Giffordgate, near Haddington, East Lothian, Scotland

Died: November 24, 1572; Edinburgh, Scotland

Area of Achievement: Religion

Contribution: The leading reformer and historian of the Protestant Reformation in Scotland, John Knox gave to Calvinism its Presbyterian expression in both England and Scotland and found in covenant theology the rationale for political militancy.

Early Life

Although the exact date of his birth is still in dispute, John Knox was probably born about 1514 at Giffordgate, near Haddington, a small town located eighteen miles east of Edinburgh in the coastal district of East Lothian. His father, William Knox, was a modest tradesman, and his mother's maiden name was Sinclair, but not much else is known about his family. He had a brother, William, who became a merchant at Prestonpans and traded goods between England and Scotland, but no other siblings are known. Like most bright young men of humble birth, Knox was educated for the Church. He attended Latin school at Haddington, but his college training is far from certain. Historians once thought that he went to the University of Glasgow, but the judgment now is that he attended St. Andrews University in the late 1520's and early 1530's and studied under John Major, one of the leading Scholastic thinkers of the day. While his style of argumentation owed much to Scholasticism, Knox was not taken by the Aristotelian teachings of Major. Years later, he claimed to have been quite moved by church fathers such as Augustine, John Chrysostom, and Athanasius. He also studied law. Thanks to a special dispensation, he was ordained into the priesthood before the canonical age of twenty-four. There were, however, many more priests than decent livings in the parishes of early sixteenth century Scotland, and Knox found employment as an apostolic notary, working in effect as a small country lawyer.

Except for his signature on several legal papers, almost nothing is known about Knox during the 1530's. Those documents, however, make clear that he dealt regularly not only with the common people but also with the lesser lairds and nobility. He must have been aware of the inroads being made by Protestant ideas and the ridicule being heaped upon the Church for its wealth and for its many ignorant, venal, and immoral clergymen. By 1544, Knox was working as a tutor, instructing the sons of several Lothian lairds friendly toward George Wishart, a Lutheran preacher fleeing from James Beaton, Cardinal and Archbishop of St. Andrews. Much influenced by the charismatic Wishart, Knox traveled with him as he preached throughout East Lothian, reportedly brandishing a sword to protect Wishart. In January, 1546, however, Wishart was captured; quickly tried and convicted of heresy, he was burned at the stake the following March. In retaliation, Wishart's supporters murdered Cardinal Beaton in May, seized St. Andrews Castle, and sought the help of Scotland's ancient enemy, England, then undergoing religious reformation under Henry VIII.

Other Scottish Protestants took refuge in the castle of St. Andrews, including John Knox and his pupils. After hearing the fiery Knox preach, the people gathered at the castle called him to be their minister. For more than a year he served the congregation at St. Andrews, vigorously attacking the Papacy, the doctrine of purgatory, and the Mass. On July 31, 1547, the St. Andrews Protestants capitulated to a combined force of Scottish troops loyal to the Queen Regent and a fleet of French galleys. According to the terms of surrender, the prisoners, including Knox, were to be taken to France and there freed or transported to a country of their choice. Instead, they were either imprisoned in France or forced to labor as galley slaves. Knox remained in the galleys, probably chained much of the time to his oar, with little likelihood of ever being freed. The hardships deepened his commitment to Protestantism. After serving as a galley slave for nineteen months, Knox, along with several other prisoners, was freed, apparently through the diplomatic efforts of young Edward VI.

Life's Work

Making his way to England in early 1549, Knox was warmly received by the king's privy council, awarded a modest gratuity, and commissioned to preach in Berwick-upon-Tweed, located near the Scottish border. In late 1550, he removed to Newcastle, where he preached in the Church of St. Nicholas. The next year, he was among the six chosen as royal chaplains, thanks no doubt to his chief patron, the Duke of Northumberland, a leading Protestant nobleman. Always vehement in his denunciations of the Roman Catholic church, Knox

believed that the Church of England remained tainted by Catholic doctrine and ritual. He was among those who revised the Book of Common Prayer in 1552, contributing specifically the "black rubric" which denied that kneeling before the table implied adoration of the bread and wine. His inflexibility probably cost Knox the bishopric of Rochester, and even Northumberland grew weary of the opinionated preacher, though he never doubted Knox's utility and protected him from the mayor of Newcastle, who despised the irascible Scot. In June, 1553, Knox was sent to preach in Buckinghamshire. Mary Tudor, a Roman Catholic, became queen in May, 1553, however, and English Protestants shortly found themselves facing persecution. Near the end of that year, Knox fled to France, joining a growing number of English Protestants known as the Marian exiles.

Accompanying him to France was his wife, Marjory, daughter of Elizabeth and Richard Bowes of Streatlam Castle, Durham. While preaching at Berwick, Knox had become good friends with Elizabeth Bowes. She encouraged Knox to marry her fifth daughter, though Knox was as old as Mrs. Bowes herself. Her husband, Richard Bowes, did not approve of the match, and Mrs. Bowes would later leave her husband and join Knox and her daughter in Geneva, where John Calvin provided refuge for the Marian exiles. At Calvin's urging, the Scotsman became the preacher to the English congregation at Frankfurt am Main, but was forced to resign after a few months because the Anglican majority there objected to his strict Calvinism in church polity and liturgy. He was then called as pastor to the English congregation in Geneva. Thriving on controversy, he increasingly saw himself as a prophet of the Lord, calling both England and Scotland to repentance and right worship.

Knox returned to Scotland in late 1555. He felt secure enough to do so because Mary of Guise, the Queen Mother and regent for the young Mary, Queen of Scots, had found it expedient to tolerate Protestantism while she cultivated support for the marriage of her daughter to the Dauphin of France. For almost nine months, Knox preached throughout the Lowlands, encouraging Protestant lords and the growing congregations of the faithful. He welcomed the support of John Erskine, Lord of Dun, and Lord Lorne, later the fifth Earl of Argyll. He was also heartened that Protestantism could claim the prior of St. Andrews, Lord James Stewart, who later would become the regent, Lord Murray. Knox was well aware, however, that the nobility was largely self-serving and unreliable. His strongest support came from the lesser lairds and the merchants and tradesmen of the towns and cities, where Protestantism was burgeoning. Around Easter, 1556, Knox and his followers, nobles and commoners alike, pledged themselves to advance "the true preaching" of the Gospel. This was the first of several "covenants" inspired by Knox, who was already looking to Calvin's federal theology to justify political resistance.

Protected by armed noblemen, Knox preached freely and dared to debate Catholic bishops. He was even bold enough to call upon the Queen Regent herself to reform the Scottish Kirk. After he returned to his congregation in Geneva in the fall of 1556, however, the Scottish bishops condemned him *in absentia* and burned his effigy, and the Queen Regent ridiculed his plea that she embrace Protestantism. The Protestant party in Scotland needed time to grow stronger, and Knox himself needed to refine his own thinking. Over the next three years, Knox learned much from and became close friends with John Calvin. He found Geneva under Calvin's rule "the greatest school of Christ" since the days of the Apostles. He longed for the triumph of Calvinism in both England and Scotland and prayed that both might be delivered from the Catholic women who ruled them. In fact, much to the chagrin of Calvin himself, Knox was hard at work developing a political theory justifying the revolution of godly subjects against ungodly rulers.

In a series of pamphlets published in 1558, Knox set forth his radical political ideas. He began by denouncing women rulers as monstrous and against the laws of God and nature. He then called upon the Scottish nobility and the covenanted commoners to take up the sword and defend the faith against their Catholic rulers. Knox himself returned to Scotland in 1559 and became the central figure in its reformation. He wielded terrific political and religious influence, founding Presbyterianism and lecturing Mary, Queen of Scots, on the virtues of the good ruler. His first wife having died, Knox married for a second time in 1564. His bride was thirty-three years his junior and daughter to a laird of the powerful Stewart clan. Knox died in 1572, only two years before the disestablishment of the Catholic church in Scotland. His famous *The History of the Reformation of Religion Within the Realm of Scotland* was published posthumously in 1587.

Summary

John Knox was a popular preacher who contributed significantly to the Protestant triumph in both England and Scotland. The Presbyterian church of Scotland did not completely triumph until a few years after his death. Nevertheless, its congregational Calvinism clearly reflected Knox's views on church polity and would serve as a source of inspiration for the English Puritans, who grew increasingly restless with Anglicanism during the long reign of Elizabeth II. Knox's Calvinism made him an internationalist in the faith, but he was first and last a Scotsman and infused Calvinism into Scottish nationalism. His writings did much to popularize the Scottish language. *The History of the Reformation of Religion Within the Realm of Scotland,* though extremely biased, is the fullest contemporary account of that upheaval. Inspired by Calvin's Geneva, Knox had plans for transforming his homeland into the City of God he detailed in *The First Book of Discipline* (1560), which the nobility refused to endorse. Those plans included a national system of poor relief and public education, both supervised by the Reformed Kirk. The subsequent success of Scottish Calvinists in education owes no small debt to Knox's nationalistic vision.

As a political thinker, Knox is acknowledged as the best-known sixteenth century misogynist. In fact, *The First Blast of the Trumpet Against the Monstrous Regiment of Women* (1558) was a thoroughly uncompromising complaint against women rulers generally, though it was specifically directed against "Bloody Mary" Tudor of England. Knox was also thinking about Mary of Guise and her daughter, Mary, Queen of Scots. Ironically, shortly after the publication of his complaint, Bloody Mary died, and Protestant Elizabeth I came to the throne. Elizabeth never forgave Knox for what he had written about the illegality of women rulers, and Knox, though he tried to flatter and encourage Elizabeth as the long-sought-after Protestant deliverer, never repudiated his views about women in politics. Knox's primary concern, however, was justifying the taking of power from Catholic rulers and giving it to Protestant leaders. He thought he had found ample justification in Calvin's covenant theology.

Not individuals, but the godly congregation covenanted together was the final authority for church polity. Should not the godly so covenanted resist an evil ruler? Passive resistance was as far as Calvin would ever go, fearing the political anarchy associated with Protestantism during the early years of the Reformation. By 1558, Knox was prepared to go much further. His attack on women rulers was less radical than what he had to say about the responsibility of godly nobility and even the commonalty to resist godless rulers. Shortly after *The First Blast of the Trumpet Against the Monstrous Regiment of Women,* in 1558, Knox published *The Appellation of John Knox . . . to the Nobility, Estates, and Commonalty* (of Scotland), in which he renounced the doctrine of Christian obedience to civil authority if the people in authority were ungodly. He told the nobility that it was their Christian duty to resist the ungodly Queen Regent. That was bold enough, but Knox had little confidence in the nobility. His most reliable support came from the commonalty, those sturdy farmers, merchants, and tradesmen of the congregations.

Appended to Knox's appeal was his *Letter to the Commonalty of Scotland*<, in which Knox clearly stated that it was the duty of the common people to protect the true preaching of the Word. The congregations were to follow the nobility, if the lords would take the initiative and fight for reformation of church and state. If the nobility would not, the congregations must take matters into their own hands. It was their duty, as God's people, and to do less was to risk God's punishment on earth and eternal damnation. It is important to note that, in speaking of the power of the people, Knox was referring to the people of God, under the discipline of the congregation, not to the people generally. Indeed, Knox believed that the godliness of the people justified their assumption of power, when all else failed.

Although surely no democrat in the modern sense of the word, Knox contributed mightily to the notion that the people who made the rules for the church could also rule the state. His thinking was widely endorsed by the English Puritans of the next century, who overthrew Charles I and who founded New England in North America. Indeed, John Knox's legacy to both religion and politics has been a lasting one.

Bibliography

Greaves, Richard. *Theology and Revolution in the Scottish Reformation: Studies in the Thought of John Knox.* Grand Rapids, Mich.: Christian University Press, 1980. This is a fine analysis of Knox's theological and political thought by a leading scholar of the Reformation. It places Knox's ideas in historical perspective.

MacGregor, Geddes. *The Thundering Scot: A Portrait of John Knox.* Phikadelphia: Westminster Press, 1954; London: Macmillan, 1958. A sympathetic portrayal of Knox, this popular biography reads like a novel and captures the hardships and triumphs of the Scottish reformer. It embellishes the facts somewhat but remains close to the secondary sources.

Reid, W. Stanford. *Trumpeter of God: A Biography of John Knox.* New York: Scribner, 1974. A scholarly study, this work examines the historiography on Knox, carefully separates the man from the stereotype, and goes into some detail about the political and religious forces and the personalities that shaped the Scottish Reformation and its leading preacher

Ridley, Jasper. *John Knox.* Oxford: Clarendon Press, and New York: Oxford University Press, 1968. The most extensive biography of Knox to date, this study is drawn largely from the primary sources, especially Knox's own writings. It is especially strong on politics and Knox's political thought, but it does not neglect the theological or the personal faith of the reformer.

Walzer, Michael. *The Revolution of the Saints: A Study in the Origins of Radical Politics.* Cambridge, Mass.: Harvard University Press, 1965; London: Weidenfeld and Nicolson, 1966. This is a remarkable study which demonstrates how Calvinism provided the basis for a political ideology that sanctioned revolution as a positive duty. Walzer sees Knox as an early personification of that radical perspective that contributed much to the concept of popular sovereignty in the Western world.

Watt, Hugh. *John Knox in Controversy.* London and New York: Nelson, 1950. An early scholarly study that challenged the traditional view of Knox as simply an obnoxious bigot. Watt explains the provocation for Knox's polemics and emphasizes his contribution to building the Scottish Kirk.

Ronald William Howard

BARTOLOMÉ DE LAS CASAS

Born: August, 1474; Seville, Spain
Died: July 31, 1566; Madrid, Spain
Areas of Achievement: Religion, colonial administration, and social reform
Contribution: Las Casas wrote a history of the early Spanish conquests in the New World and participated in the Spanish conquest of the Caribbean. Concerned with the plight of the Indians, he spent more than fifty years attempting to free the Indians from the oppression of their European conquerors, working to destroy the *encomienda* system and finding new ways of converting the Indians to Christianity.

Early Life

Bartolomé de Las Casas was born in Seville in 1474 into the family of a not very successful merchant, Pedro de Las Casas, who sailed with Christopher Columbus on his second voyage to the New World. Las Casas had witnessed the triumph of Columbus' return to Seville from his first voyage (March, 1493). He saw service in the militia against Moors in the Granada Rebellion (1497), studied Latin and theology at the cathedral academy in Seville, and became a lay teacher of Christian doctrine.

He accompanied Nicolás de Ovando, the designated governor, to Española (1502). There, he participated in putting down Indian uprisings, for which he was rewarded with a royal grant of lands and Indians (*encomienda*). He was successful as a planter, and he began to evangelize the Indians in his role as lay catechist. In 1506, he gave up his lands, going to Rome, where he took vows in the Order of Preachers (Dominicans). On his return to Española, in 1512, he was ordained a priest—probably the first in America to receive Holy Orders. He was made chaplain with the forces that were engaged in the conquest of Cuba (begun in 1511 by Diego Velázquez de Cuéllar, although Las Casas was there only in the last year, 1513), for which he again received a grant of Indians and lands.

Life's Work

Perhaps it has his experiences and observations in the Cuban conquest (including the massacre of Caonao) and other military expeditions in Española, or the harsh realities of treatment of the Indians in the mining and agricultural projects throughout the Spanish Antilles, where the number of natives was rapidly being depleted, or perhaps it was his position as priest and land grantee that led Las Casas to begin, at age forty, what would become his life's work. He attributes change of life-style to his meditations on chapter 34 of Ecclesiastes. In any case, he gave his *encomienda* holdings to Diego Columbus and began to preach against the oppression of the Indians, calling for an end to the system of expropriating their land and enslaving them. He returned to Spain to lobby in behalf of the Indians in 1515. The Cardinal Archbishop of Toledo, Francisco Jiménez de Cisneros, supported him in this crusade, naming him priest-procurator of the Indies and appointing him to a commission to investigate the status of the Indians (1516).

Las Casas developed a plan for peaceful colonization and returned to Spain in July, 1517, to recruit farmers and obtain land for the experiment. The Holy Roman Emperor and King of Spain Charles I gave him permission to colonize an estate in Curmána, Venezuela (1510-1521). He later retracted a suggestion that slaves be imported for labor from West Africa. With an expression of shame, he regretted that he came so late to the realization that the natives from Africa had the same human rights as the Indians of the New World. The settlement was a failure, and Las Casas retired from public life to the Dominican monastery at Santo Domingo. It was during this time that he wrote the first draft of *Historia de las Indias* (wr. 1527-1561, pb. 1875-1876; partial translation as *History of the Indies*, 1971).

Las Casas was active in defense of the Indians in Mexico (1532) and in Nicaragua (1535-1536). During these years, he also visited and worked in defense of the Indians in Peru, Puerto Rico, and other settlements in the Spanish New World colonies. After Pope Paul III proclaimed the Indians' rationality and equality with other men to receive instructions and the faith (June 2, 1537), Las Casas renewed his activity to colonize and Christianize the Indians peacefully. His most notable success was in Guatemala.

In 1539, Las Casas returned to Spain. He continued his writings in defense of the Indians. His *Brevísima relación de la destruyción de las Indias occidentales* (1552; partial translation as *A Relation of the First Voyages and Discoveries Made by the Spaniards in America*, 1699) was written during this time although not published until many years later. In this treatise, he placed the desire for gold and material wealth at the center of motivation for all the injustice toward the Indians. Las Casas attributed the continued injustice to the greed of those in power. Because of this greed, those in power did not support just laws; rather, they opposed them in order to continue the system and institutions that would further their material gain.

Las Casas also began his struggle for the passage of the so-called New Laws (1542). These laws reorganized the Council of the Indies and prohibited the oppression of, exploitation of, and cruelty toward the Indians, against which Las Casas had long crusaded. These laws also prohibited the continuation of slavery for Indians of the second generation. Las Casas found support for his position in Spain at court, in the Church, and in the Council of the Indies. In the colonies, however, the New Laws were received with great opposition and were largely unenforced. They were revoked in part, but later the key elements were reinstated.

Las Casas was named Bishop of Chiapas in Guatemala and left Spain in July, 1544, with forty-four Dominicans to establish missions there for the peaceful Christianization of the Indians. He arrived in Guatemala after many interim stops in March, 1545. He proceeded with zeal rather than with practicality to enforce the New Laws, which led to protests and demonstrations against him in the colony. He was forced to return to Spain in 1547.

At the age of seventy-five, Las Casas renounced his bishopric and continued his life of tireless lobbying and protest in the cause of the Indians. He defended the equality and dignity of the Indians against all who were bent on their enslavement and oppression. In 1550 at Valladolid, he engaged in public debate with the Jesuit Juan Ginés de Sepúlveda, who had maintained that the Indians were inferior to the Spaniards. The controversy, which continued through the next year, has been debated anew through the centuries since. Las Casas organized missions to be staffed by learned and religious mendicants, who would Christianize and educate the Indians.

Las Casas continued to write. He also came to be an influential adviser to the Council of the Indies and at court on the many problems related to the colonies of the New World. He was a frequent witness at trials to free Indians, and much of his writing was directed to this end. He died in his early nineties in the Dominican convent of Nuestra Señora de Atocha in Madrid. The King of Spain, Phillip II, had all the works of Las Casas (published and unpublished) collected and preserved.

Summary

Bartolomé de Las Casas lived in the transitional period from the medieval to the modern age. He was traditional in his adherence to doctrine. His writings were based on the Gospel and teachings of the Church. Yet, he had an understanding of and sensitivity to the changing world about him. He was a Christian intellectual who became a prophet in the political and economic climate of his times; his society, however, was not ready and not eager to hear his message. He anticipated many of the principles enunciated in the Charter of the United Nations (1945) and proclaimed by Vatican Council II (1963). His preaching, his planning, his colonial enterprises, and his writings were concerned with reforming the colonial practices of his day, with preaching the Gospel by peaceful persuasion, with abhorrence of violence and oppression, and with individual liberty and self-determination as the right of all peoples. He meant his *History of the Indies* to be a call to social and political change. He clearly inveighed against the injustice and immorality of the colonial system and institutions of the fifteenth and sixteenth centuries. Through his writings, he inspired the nineteenth century revolutionary, Simón Bolívar, and the leaders of the Mexican Revolution in which the independence of that people was won from Spain.

Las Casas' most important writings among the vast works he produced were *Del único modo* (wr. 1539, pb. 1942), which was on the theory of evangelization, *Apologética historia de las Indias* (wr. 1527-1560, pb. 1909), which was an analysis of the Indians' abilities, and his two histories of the Indies. The last of these, according to his instructions, was not to be published for forty years after his death, although the prologue was published in 1562. Nevertheless, a manuscript was circulated even before the publication by the Academy of Madrid, 1875-1876.

His writings, while they exaggerate the plight of the Indians and the cruelty of the Europeans, have fueled the claims about the "Black Legend" of Spanish cruelty in the New World promulgated by Spain's enemies and, in the twentieth century, taken up by nationalists and anticolonialists. His teachings concerning all peoples of the earth (the Indians were not inferior to the Spaniards), all peoples' right to determine their own destiny (self-determination), and all peoples' right to have their basic needs (human rights) satisfied were his most important legacy and have caused his writings to be debated throughout the world for more than four hundred years.

Bibliography

Friede, Juan, and Benjamin Keen, eds. *Bartolomé de Las Casas in History: Toward an Understanding of the Man and His Work*. De Kalb: Northern Illinois University Press, 1971. This is a series of analytical essays on the life and ideology of Las Casas, on his activities and his impact on America and history, and on his writings. The essays are written by authors of different nationalities and ideologies, thus bringing a variety of perspectives to bear on their subject. The text vindicates Las Casas and his ideals in the course that history has taken since his death.

Hanke, Lewis. *Bartolomé de Las Casas: An Interpretation of His Life and Writings*. Philadelphia: University of Pennsylvania Press, 1959. Hanke's scholarly study is a sound biography of the life of Las Casas.

Helps, Arthur. *The Life of Las Casas: The Apostle of the Indies*. London: Bell, and Philadelphia: Lippincott, 1868. Helps writes a standard biography.

Keen, Benjamin. *Essays in the Intellectual History of Colonial Latin America*. Boulder, Colo.: Westview Press, 1998. This is a collection of eleven essays that have been adapted from Keen's writings about Las Casas and related topics. It is an accessible introduction to colonial history and a critical guide to the literature in the field.

Las Casas, Bartolomé de. *History of the Indies*. Edited and translated by Andrée M. Collard. New York: Harper, 1971. Collard's introduction provides helpful analysis of Las Casas the man, the thinker, and the writer. Collard also answers criticisms of Las Casas.

MacNutt, Francis A. *Bartholomew de Las Casas: His Life, His Apostolate, and His Writings*. London and New York: Putnam, 1909. This was the standard biography in English of Las Casas, but it has been superseded by the works of Lewis Hanke.

Wagner, Henry Raup, and Helen Rand Parish. *The Life and Writings of Bartolomé de Las Casas*. Albuquerque: University of New Mexico Press, 1967. This is a critical and detailed documented study of Las Casas. Wagner found much to identify with and to admire in his subject. He presents Las Casas as a prolific writer, and, equally, as a man of action. Las Casas emerges with tremendous stature even among the giants of the sixteenth century. Wagner includes a narrative and critical catalog of Las Casas' writings.

Barbara Ann Barbato

HUGH LATIMER

Born: Between 1485 and 1492; Thurcaston, Leicestershire, England
Died: October 16, 1555; Oxford, England
Area of Achievement: Religion
Contribution: With his powerful preaching, Latimer helped mobilize popular opinion to support the reformation of the English church.

Early Life

Hugh Latimer was born at Thurcaston, Leicestershire, England, sometime between 1485 and 1492. His father, also named Hugh, was a yeoman farmer, and the son who rose to rank and influence in the Church never forgot his humble origins. Latimer's preaching reflected a social and political concern for the well-being of a class which endured the enclosure of its pastures and the pressure of rising rent. In later years, preaching before Edward VI, he would vigorously champion the cause of the oppressed workingman. Latimer was born into a large family. His mother, whose name is unrecorded, had six daughters and several other sons. She also oversaw the milking and care of a large dairy herd. When the father served under Henry VII in putting down an uprising in Cornwall, young Hugh helped buckle on his father's armor. The son also became an accomplished bowman.

Latimer was educated in the common schools and in 1506 went to Cambridge, where in 1510 he was elected a Fellow at Clare Hall and in 1514 received an M.A. Although Erasmus came to Cambridge during Latimer's fellowship, there is no indication that Latimer had any enthusiasm for his insights into the Greek text of the New Testament. Latimer never learned Greek, and like most of his compatriots he shared in the apathy for the new learning of Erasmus that eventually drove the discouraged Dutch scholar back to the Continent. The date of Latimer's ordination to the priesthood is unknown, but in 1522 he became one of twelve preachers licensed by Cambridge University to have the right to preach anywhere in England. A more important honor was his selection to be the cross-keeper to the university, a post that involved his serving as chaplain of New Chapel.

In his early years Latimer seems to have held firmly to Roman Catholic orthodoxy. Although he grew up in an area strongly influenced by the Lollard tradition stemming from the heretical teaching of John Wycliffe, there is no indication of its influence upon Latimer. Since Lollardy especially appealed to the working classes and since Latimer closely identified with this group, it might be surmised that he had at least some acquaintance with the movement. Latimer received a bachelor of divinity degree in 1524 and used the occasion to preach a vigorous sermon denouncing the Lutheran theologian Philip Melancthon. He had also ungraciously maligned George Stafford, a classmate who had deserted the traditions of the church fathers for the study of the New Testament. Latimer preached against Stafford to the people and warned his scholar friends not to hear him. It appeared that Latimer had been unaffected by either Lollardy, Martin Luther's teaching, or the influence of Erasmus.

Latimer's conversion to Protestant theology was in one sense a gradual movement. He was less of a theologian than a preacher, and he only reluctantly modified his views. The beginning of his drift toward Reformation theology began with an encounter with Thomas Bilney, whom Latimer affectionately called "little Bilney." In Latimer's own words, he had been, before his discussion with Bilney, "as obstinate a Papist as any was in England," but after Bilney had brought him to "smell the word of God" he had abandoned the "school-doctors and such fooleries." Bilney's discussion with Latimer occurred on the very day in 1524 that Latimer had made his B.D. oration against Melancthon.

Latimer suffered from toothache and other maladies much of his life. A portrait shows him as a sallow-faced and weary scholar with a huge nose shaped like a parrot's beak. His large eyes look out with penetration but seem tired. Whatever his disabilities, Latimer was a tireless worker. He arose at two in the morning to begin his day's routine. He was also a gifted orator. His messages were emotional appeals couched often in colorful but blunt language. In his famous Sermon of the Plough, Latimer condemned unpreaching prelates for "pampering of their paunches, . . . munching in their mangers, . . . loitering in their lordships."

Life's Work

Bishop West of Ely suspected Latimer of harboring Lutheran ideas and in 1525 ordered him not to preach in the university or the diocese. A nearby

Augustinian monastery, not being under diocesan control, invited Latimer to preach there. The bishop's charges led to a hearing at the court of the papal legate, Thomas Wolsey. Latimer argued before Wolsey's chaplains that he had not become a Lutheran and had not even read Luther's works. He was then again permitted to preach in all England. In 1529, he aroused resentment at the university by his two "sermons on the card" in which he questioned the value of pilgrimages as compared to works of charity. At the same time, he was gaining notice at the court of Henry VIII because of his expressed sympathy with the king's cause in the question of divorcing Catherine of Aragon. In 1530, the king invited Latimer to preach at Windsor during Lent. Latimer did not simply seek to curry favor at any cost. An anonymous letter from this period implored the king to allow Tyndale to print and circulate the Scripture in English translation without restriction. Some scholars believe that the letter was from Latimer. Cranmer's good standing at the court and the favor of Thomas Cromwell, Vicar General of the Church, brought him the living of West Kineton in Wiltshire.

Leaving the court in 1531, Latimer now gave himself to preaching against abuses in the Church. By 1533, he had accepted Luther's doctrine of justification by faith. "If I see the blood of Christ with the eye of my soul," he wrote in that year, "that is true faith that his blood was shed for me." His preaching aroused much opposition, and charges were made that he had denied the doctrines of purgatory, the sinlessness of Mary, and the value of pilgrimages. After appearing before the Bishop of London and then the Convocation of Bishops on these charges, he was finally released upon agreeing to submit to the teachings of the Church. He was made Bishop of Worcester in 1535 but resigned the post four years later because he was unwilling to sign the Six Articles, a conservative expression of theology which indicated that Henry VIII believed that the Reformation had gone far enough and should be checked. Now out of favor, Latimer was held prisoner for nearly a year but was finally released. He was forbidden to preach, to visit the universities, or to return to his old diocese. From 1541 to 1546, his life is nearly a blank, but in the latter year he was sent to the Tower of London because of his association with the condemned preacher Edward Crome. The next year, he was released as part of the general pardon given to prisoners at the accession of Edward VI.

Latimer refused an invitation to return to his old bishopric. Instead, he remained with the Archbishop of Canterbury, Thomas Cranmer. Together they prepared the Book of Homilies. With England now turning strongly toward Reformation doctrines under Edward VI, Latimer in 1548 broke with the doctrine of transubstantiation, accepting instead the doctrine of the real mystical presence of Christ in the sacrament. With Mary Tudor's accession to the throne in 1553 the era of Protestant growth was checked temporarily. It had been clear that the coming of Catherine of Aragon's daughter to the throne would mean a return to papal supremacy in England. Latimer was among the three hundred reformers who perished as heretics during Mary's reign.

Summary

Hugh Latimer's main claim to fame comes not from what he left behind, but from his ability as a shaper of popular opinion. He was not primarily a theologian such as John Calvin, who could leave behind a system of doctrine. His influence was as a preacher, and his effect was primarily upon the people of his own time. He passionately drew their attention both to social injustice and to abuses of the clergy. Many among his hearers had experienced rural life and could identify with his pastoral allusions. He did not spare in his acid criticism the venality of clergymen, the sloth of nonresident bishops, or the hypocrisy of prelates. Latimer was a major influence in creating popular support for Protestant reform in England.

He is also remembered especially for his sacrifice of his own life for the faith he held dear. On September 4, 1553, he was summoned to London, charged with seditious behavior, and confined in the Tower of London. Although his treatment was not especially severe, his advancing age and poor health made the imprisonment very difficult to bear. An intentional warning that the summons was coming had given Latimer several hours to escape for his own life, but he chose to face his accusers. At Oxford, he and Nicholas Ridley and Thomas Cranmer were called upon to argue before the bishops for their doctrine. The trial experienced numerous delays, in part caused by the need of reenacting a capital punishment act for heresy which had been annulled while Edward ruled. With the death penalty for heresy once again the law of England, Latimer finally went to the stake with his friend Ridley, on October 16, 1555. As the torch was being applied to the wood stacked around him, Latimer made the statement that has made him famous. According to John Foxe's *Actes and Monuments* (1563), he turned to his fellow sufferer and said, "Be of good comfort, Master Ridley, and play the man. We shall this day light such a candle, by God's grace, in England, as I trust shall never be put out."

Bibliography

Carlyle, R.M., and A.J. Carlyle. *Hugh Latimer.* London: Methuen, and Boston: Houghton Mifflin, 1899. This is a fairly brief and readable account that is favorable to Latimer. It has no bibliography and little documentation.

Chester, Allan G. *Hugh Latimer: Apostle to the English.* Philadelphia: University of Pennsylvania Press, 1954. Although the author has been criticized for being too meticulous with providing details, this is an exciting and enjoyable book to read. It is also well documented and contains a useful bibliography. The author makes no secret of his admiration for Latimer yet provides a scholarly and cautious account.

Darby, Harold S. *Hugh Latimer.* London: Epworth Press, 1953. A biography written by one who deeply admired Latimer. Darby, himself a pulpiteer, sees Latimer as preeminently a preacher.

Demaus, Robert. *Hugh Latimer: A Biography.* London: Religious Tract Society, and Nashville: Lamar and Barton, 1904. A very laudatory and fairly lengthy work. It was originally published in 1869, then revised slightly in 1881.

Foxe, John. *Actes and Monuments.* London: John Day, 1563. Along with Latimer's sermons the contemporary account by Foxe is a major source of information. Foxe wrote from a pro-Protestant viewpoint at a time when religious viewpoints were expressed in strongly emotional terms.

Latimer, Hugh. *The Works of Hugh Latimer.* Edited by George E. Corrie. Cambridge: Cambridge University Press, 1844-1845. Any serious investigation of Latimer would largely involve the study of his sermons as recorded by Corrie.

Richard L. Niswonger

LEO X
Giovanni de' Medici

Born: December 11, 1475; Florence
Died: December 1, 1521; Rome
Areas of Achievement: Government, politics, religion, and patronage of the arts
Contribution: As a patron of the arts, Leo X turned Rome into the cultural center of the Western world. As pope, he engaged in secular politics and presided over the period in church history that witnessed the outbreak of the Protestant Reformation.

Early Life

Pope Leo X was born Giovanni de' Medici, the second son of Lorenzo (the Magnificent) and his wife, Clarice Orsini. Though brought up in the lap of Renaissance luxury, he was groomed for a career in the Church from an early age. Tonsured at age seven, he was appointed a cardinal at age thirteen, although he did not receive the insignia and the privileges of that office until 1492. As a youth, he was tutored by the famous Humanists Marsilio Ficino, Angelo Poliziano, and Giovanni Pico della Mirandola, who imparted to him a love of literature and the arts, which characterized his entire life. From 1489 until 1491, Giovanni studied theology and canon law at the University of Pisa. Then, in 1492, he moved to Rome and assumed the responsibilities of a cardinal. He served on the conclave, which in that year elected Pope Alexander VI, although Giovanni did not vote for him.

After the death of his father in 1492, Giovanni returned to Florence, where he lived with his elder brother Pietro until the Medici family was exiled from their native city in 1494 during Girolamo Savonarola's "Reign of Virtue." For the next six years, Giovanni traveled in France, the Netherlands, and Germany, and then returned in May of 1500 to Rome, where, for the next several years, he immersed himself in literature, music, and particularly the theater, interests that were the great loves of his life, taking precedence even over hunting, of which he was extremely fond.

When his elder brother died in 1503, Giovanni became the head of the Medici family, and much of his energy and his revenues from his many church benefices was expended in the ensuing years in his efforts to restore his family to prominence in Florence. After a bloodless revolution in that city in September of 1512, the Medicis were allowed to return, and Giovanni became the de facto ruler of Florence, although the nominal ruler would be his younger brother Giuliano. Then, when Pope Julius II died in February of 1513, the seven-day conclave that followed elected Giovanni his successor. Giovanni was crowned Pope Leo X on March 19.

Life's Work

The portrait of Leo by Raphael, which hangs in the Pitti Palace in Florence, depicts the pope as an unattractive man, with a fat, shiny, effeminate countenance and weak, bulging eyes. Yet, according to contemporaries, his kind smile, well-modulated voice, kingly bearing, and sincere friendliness ingratiated him with everyone he met. While his manner of life was worldly, he was unfeignedly religious and strictly fulfilled his spiritual duties—he knew how to enjoy life but not at the expense of piety. He heard Mass and read his Breviary every day and fasted three times a week. Contemporaries report that there was scarcely a work of Christian charity that he did not support, as he contributed more than six thousand ducats per month to worthy causes. He enjoyed banquets and spent lavishly on them but never over-indulged himself. Though his personal morality was impeccable, he sometimes attended scandalous theatrical presentations and seemed to enjoy the absurd and vulgar jokes of buffoons. Even during the very troubled period of 1520-1521, he amused himself during the Roman carnivals with masques, music, and theatrical performances.

Since Leo's love of literature and the arts was well known, soon after his elevation to the Papacy of Rome was flooded with Humanists, poets, musicians, painters, sculptors, and other talented men seeking the pope's patronage. The greatest among them, as well as many of the lesser, were not disappointed. Beneficiaries of his largess as patron were the Humanists Pietro Bembo and Jacopo Sadoleto, the artists Raphael and Michelangelo, the architect Donato Bramante, and hundreds of others. Leo collected books, manuscripts, and gems without regard to price. The construction of St. Peter's Basilica was greatly accelerated. So splendid was the cultural life of Rome during this period that it has been called the Leonine Age, for its patron. Leo is said to have

spent 4.5 million ducats during his reign, leaving the papal treasury a debt of 400,000 ducats.

Although Leo showed little interest in theological matters, he did reconvene the Fifth Lateran Council, which had first opened its doors under Julius II but had adjourned without accomplishment. Its objectives were to promote peace within the Christian world, proclaim a Crusade against the Turks, and reform the Church. The council was poorly attended, and most of the councillors were Italians so that it was not representative of Christendom as a whole. At its conclusion in March, 1517, the council issued decrees calling for stricter regulation of the conduct of cardinals and other members of the Curia and denouncing abuses such as pluralism and absenteeism; these decrees would largely be ignored in practice, however, even by Leo himself. Leo did preach a Crusade against the Turks in 1518, but the monarchs of Europe showed little interest.

As secular ruler of the Papal States and protector of the Medici interests in Florence, Leo found it necessary to engage in the balance-of-power politics characteristic of the age; it is for his political role that he is most severely criticized by modern writers. In this political capacity, he was frequently guilty of treachery and duplicity. For example, when he began his pontificate, he was part of an alliance aimed at thwarting the French king's territorial ambitions in Italy. After Francis I's smashing victory at Marignano (September, 1515), however, Leo secretly deserted his allies, met with Francis, and negotiated the Concordat of Bologna, whereby, in return for guarantees of the integrity of Leo's territory in Italy, Francis was granted the right to nominate all the bishops, abbots, and priors within his realm, a right French kings would retain until the French Revolution.

Leo's capriciousness in political affairs was again demonstrated when Holy Roman Emperor Maximilian I died in January of 1519. The two leading contenders for this position were Francis and Charles I, King of Spain. Leo at first supported Francis, since he feared the territorial ambitions of Charles in both northern and southern Italy; since Francis had similar claims in Italy, however, Leo attempted to persuade Frederick the Wise of Saxony to be a candidate. When Frederick refused, Leo reverted to his support of Francis. When Charles was eventually elected in June of 1519, Leo moved quickly to establish a papal alliance with him. In May of 1521, Leo secretly concluded a treaty with Charles, in which the pope agreed to join Charles in a renewed effort to drive the French from Milan, in return for which Charles promised to close the meeting of the Imperial Diet at Worms with the outlawing of the excommunicate Martin Luther.

Like most Renaissance popes, Leo was guilty of nepotism. In order to provide his nephew Lorenzo with a title, Leo, in 1516, declared the duke of the small papal state of Urbino deposed and conferred the duchy on his nephew. To carry out the deposition, Leo had to raise an army and commit it to an arduous winter campaign against the former ruler. Leo then supported Lorenzo, Duke of Urbino, as the unofficial ruler of Florence. Among Leo's several relatives who enjoyed church appointments under that pontiff was his cousin, Giulio, whom Leo made a cardinal almost as soon as he himself had mounted the papal throne. Giulio would later be elevated to the Papacy as Clement VII.

Despite Leo's irenic disposition, he made enemies, and he did not shrink from retaliation against those who threatened him. In 1517, when a conspiracy aimed at poisoning the pope was uncovered, one of the leaders, Cardinal Petrucci, was executed, several other cardinals were imprisoned and heavily fined, and Leo appointed thirty-one new cardinals in rapid succession so that the pope would have a college in which the majority of cardinals would be loyal to him.

The greatest crisis that Leo faced as pope came toward the end of his pontificate, and he died without really understanding its severity. Leo's predecessor, Julius II, had promulgated a plenary Jubilee indulgence in an effort to raise money for the building of St. Peter's Basilica in Rome. The indulgence had not sold well, and its sale was discontinued until its revival by Leo in March of 1515. Arrangements had been made with Albrecht of Brandenburg for the sale of the indulgence in his archdioceses of Mainz and Magdeburg. When the sale of these indulgences by the Dominican Friar Johann Tetzel began in 1517, it was not long before the matter came to the attention of a young German monk, Martin Luther, who lodged a protest. Pope Leo did not realize the seriousness of the protest and was preoccupied with the preparation for the upcoming imperial election and with his other worldly pursuits, and so the situation was allowed to deteriorate. In June of 1520, Leo issued the bull *Exsurge Domine*, in which Luther was accused of forty-one counts of heresy and ordered to recant on pain of excommunication. Luther's refusal to recant, together with his public burning of the bull, led to his formal excommunication on January 3, 1521. Within a short time after these events, Lutheranism had begun to win adherents among some of the northern German princes as well as in Denmark. Before the extent of the schism could be appreciated, Leo died, on December 1, 1521, from bronchitis.

Summary

In early accounts of Leo X's reign, he was alleged to have remarked at the time of his coronation: "Let us enjoy the Papacy since God has given it to us." While there is strong evidence that Leo never actually said this, this remark does seem to reflect his attitude toward his high office. Within two years in office, Leo had exhausted the full treasury left him by Julius II, and, despite the additional revenues generated by the sale of church offices and papal favors as well as indulgences, Leo's extravagance bequeathed a debt of 400,000 ducats to his successor. While Roman cultural life had never been so splendid as it was during his pontificate, Leo's devil-may-care attitude and his capricious political activities, coupled with his failure to understand the religious intensity of men such as Luther or to respond to it, help to explain Protestantism's early success.

Leo's accession to the papal throne was accompanied by much celebration. Of his passing, a contemporary observed: "Never died Pope in worse repute." While it is no longer contended that he was the victim of poisoning, the circumstances of his burial were severe. The candles used in his obsequies were those left over from another funeral, and no monument was erected to his memory until the time of Paul III. With Leo's death, the age of the Renaissance popes was nearly at an end.

Bibliography

Creighton, Mandell. *A History of the Papacy from the Great Schism to the Sack of Rome*. 6 vols. London and New York: Longman, 1897. Provides a comprehensive survey of the pontificate of Leo. While Creighton gives recognition to Leo's importance as a patron of the arts, he is critical of Leo's reckless spending and his indifference toward spiritual matters. Concludes that Leo left a bitter heritage for his successors. A rather opinionated account.

Mee, Charles L. *White Robe, Black Robe*. New York: Putnam, 1972; London: Harper, 1973. Presents an account of the early Reformation period through an examination of the lives, careers, and ideas of Leo and Luther, vividly contrasting the two protagonists. While it presents little new information on either figure, the work skillfully blends discussion of the political background to the Reformation with that of its theological significance. Contains a useful bibliography.

Pastor, Ludwig. *The History of the Popes from the Close of the Middle Ages*. Vol. 8, *Leo X (1513-1521)*. London: Kegan Paul, and St. Louis, Mo.: Herder, 1924-1953. The entirety of this volume of this classic, monumental study of the modern Papacy is devoted to the pontificate of Leo. Provides an extensive treatment of the cultural life of Rome under Leo's patronage. Includes footnotes and English translations of many previously unpublished documents in the appendices.

Roscoe, William. *The Life and Pontificate of Pope Leo the Tenth*. 5th ed. 2 vols. London: Bohn, 1846; New York: Routledge, 1973. An excellent general history of the period of Leo's pontificate. Includes extensive notes and English translations of numerous documents relevant to the text.

While mainly sympathetic to Leo, Roscoe maintains that criticism of Leo by contemporary and later writers is largely the result of Leo's duplicity and treacherousness as a political figure.

Schevill, Ferdinand. *The Medici*. London: Gollancz, and New York: Harcourt Brace, 1949. The chapter on Leo emphasizes how strongly he was motivated in most of his policies by his desire to advance the fortunes of the Medici family, both in Florence and in Italy as a whole. Schevill is critical of the artistic patronage of Leo, believing that he made poor use of the many talented men in the papal employ.

Vaughan, Herbert M. *The Medici Popes*. London: Methuen, and New York: Putnam, 1908. This work is primarily devoted to an examination of the personal character and the strengths and weaknesses of Leo. The work's attention to unimportant details to the exclusion of the political realities faced by Leo necessitates consulting other works on the pontiff.

Paul E. Gill

LEONARDO DA VINCI

Born: April 15, 1452; Vinci, near Florence

Died: May 2, 1519; Cloux Château, near Amboise, France

Area of Achievement: Art

Contribution: Leonardo da Vinci was the most outstanding painter of the Italian Renaissance; some authorities consider him the best painter and draftsman of all time. In addition, he made a number of discoveries in botany, anatomy, mechanical engineering, and medicine which were unprecedented and unparalleled until the twentieth century.

Early Life

Leonardo da Vinci was born on April 15, 1452, the illegitimate son of Piero da Vinci, descendant of a long line of Florentine minor officials, and a local woman known only as Caterina. Nevertheless, he was reared as a member of his father's household, first in Vinci and then in Florence; a notarized attestation of his birth by his grandfather signifies his family's recognition of him and of its responsibilities toward him. Still, there are few documented facts about his early life. Further, since the first biography of him—by the historian Giorgio Vasari—appeared only some thirty years after his death, conjectural reconstructions have flourished.

Leonardo himself recorded only one event from his childhood, recalled years later, when he was compiling notes on the flight of birds in his notebooks. He simply comments that he was probably fated to write about the flight of kites "because in the earliest memory of my childhood it seemed to me that as I lay in my cradle a kite came down to me and opened my mouth with its tail and struck me with its tail many times between the lips." As open to Freudian reconstruction as this seems to be, it may only document Leonardo's memory of the closeness of the physical environment natural to an upbringing in a Tuscan hill village. This is more likely, since his fascination with horses also seems to date from this period. Both interests continued throughout his life.

There is no evidence earlier than Vasari's biography that Leonardo served an apprenticeship under Andrea del Verrocchio, but legend, as well as some internal evidence, seems to make this likely. Under Verrocchio, Leonardo would have worked with fellow apprentices Perugino, later the teacher of Raphael, and Lorenzo di Credi, both to become masters in their own right.

Of Leonardo's work at this early period little survives, other than some sketches in his notebooks. One page of these, consisting of a series of portraits of the same head—a head which also appears in some of his earlier paintings—seems to record various impressions of himself. If they are self-portraits, they correspond to early reminiscences on the part of his contemporaries of his remarkable beauty and grace; the delicacy of his profile coincides with memories of fluid, dancer-like movement, of a luminous presence and carriage, of an unusually sweet singing voice, of considerable ability as a lutanist, together with quite unexpected physical strength. One early account credits him with contributing the head of an angel to Verrocchio's painting *The Baptism of Christ* (c. 1474-1475), and one head is clearly by a hand subtler and more delicate than Verrocchio's; Vasari reports improbably that Verrochio was so dismayed by the contrast that he refused to paint thereafter, confining himself to sculpture.

A final event from this period deserves mention. While staying at the house of Verrocchio—long after his apprenticeship had come to an end—Leonardo was twice accused of having visited the house of a notorious boy prostitute, which was tantamount to being accused of sodomy, a crime punishable at best by exile, at worst by being burned at the stake. In neither case was the evidence necessary for conviction brought forth, but the incident suggests something about Leonardo's sexual orientation and foreshadows his failure to develop a deep relationship with a woman.

Life's Work

Leonardo remains best known for his painting, even though it is now nearly impossible to restore his works to their original splendor. Yet his qualities announce themselves almost immediately in his first Florentine period (1472-1482). In *The Baptism of Christ* of Verrocchio, for example, his hand can be seen not only in the angel's head long attributed to him but also in the delicate treatment of the watercourse in the foreground and in the fantastic mountain landscape to the rear. Two similar paintings, both called *The Annunciation*—one in the Louvre, one in the Uffizi, both c. 1475—display advances in structure, delicacy of detail, and a

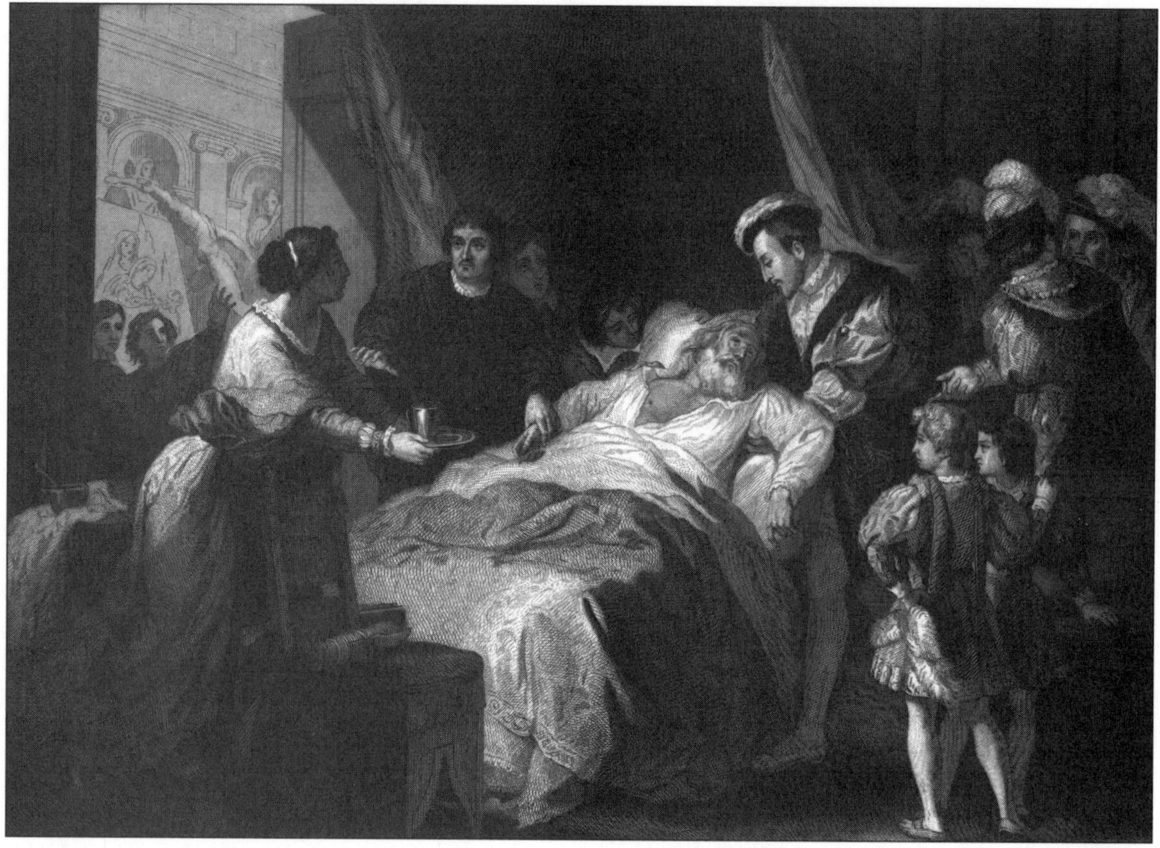

Leonardo at his deathbed

personal iconography unlike that of any previous painter.

Among other masterpieces from this period are a portrait of Ginevra de' Benci (c. 1474), *Head of a Woman* (c. 1475), and the *Madonna Benois* (c. 1478). Here the distinctive element is sensitivity of character, so that the figures rendered seem to take on a life of their own, almost as if establishing eye contact through the pictorial plane. Great as these are, the *Adoration of the Magi* (1481) completely transcends them. This unfinished painting occupied Leonardo's attention for the remainder of his stay in Florence, yet he completed only the preliminary underdrawing. Nevertheless, it displays an absolutely unprecedented sense of fantasy and imagination, all accomplished within the norms of accurate Albertian perspective. With this painting, Leonardo broke free from the confines of traditional Nativity iconography, relegating the ruined stable to the background and replacing it with the powerful symbol of the broken arch. He also regrouped the figures of the traditional scene so that they could appear both as individuals with distinct motives and as participants in a communal activity. Leonardo gives a theological doctrine a real psychological dimension.

Following this stay in Florence, Leonardo resided in Milan for nearly twenty years. Although he apparently hoped to be taken into the service of Duke Ludovico Sforza as military engineer, his principal activities were artistic. His first major work was the *Madonna of the Rocks*, two versions of which survive, one in the Louvre and one in the National Gallery in London, both c. 1485. This work was commissioned by the Convent of the Conception in Milan, and, although the doctrine of the Immaculate Conception had not yet been officially adopted, Leonardo chose to depict it in his painting.

The Last Supper (1495-1497), a fresco, is a true masterwork and a ruin. To get the effects he wanted, Leonardo invented new methods of applying color to wet plaster. At first he seemed to have succeeded, but by 1517 the work had already begun to deteriorate, and by 1566 Vasari pronounced it a jumble of blots. Only in the late twentieth century has restoration recovered the core of the original. What is there is astonishing in itself, but what is lost is irreplaceable. The work at first seems firmly rooted in tradition; the framing derives directly from previous treatments of the subject by Andrea del Castagno and Ghirlandajo. Where they focused on the moment when Christ confronted Judas, Leonardo chose to treat the instant when He revealed the presence of a traitor in the midst of the faithful. Leonardo thus transfixed the immediate response as with a candid lens; all the apostles save one act out their unique forms of the question, "Is it I, Lord?" In this way he reveals their responses both as individuals and as members of a communion. To get the expressions he wanted, he walked the streets for hours, sketching memorable faces on his portable pad, then fitting expression to individual character and working at the combinations until he got the exact effect he wanted. The unveiling of this fresco must have been explosive, for the moment catches the apostles' regrouping after the shock wave has passed. Few spectators would have noted that Leonardo had here also transcended the laws of Albertian perspective.

In 1500, Leonardo left Milan. Thereafter, except for a return lasting from 1508 to 1513, he was a transient. At first this did not keep him from painting. In Florence in 1501, he displayed a preliminary drawing for a *Virgin and Child with Saint Anne and the Infant Saint John*, though he did not complete the painting. The cartoon itself is marvelous in the integrity of the grouping, the revelation of movement in a fixed moment, and the combination of the casual with the intense. An equally celebrated and similar contemporary cartoon for the painting of *Virgin and Child with Saint Anne* (1508-1513) reveals how much has been lost, for this work again shows Leonardo's carrying his ideas one step further. In this painting, he places his subjects against a barren and forbidding backdrop and concentrates on the physical and theological fecundity of the Virgin, who is shown rocking in the lap of her mother while trying to contain her Child, who is evading her to clasp the lamb—the emblem of his sacrifice. Their expressions are joyful, serene, and supernally oblivious to the implications: Leonardo presents a quiet portrait of a family doomed to be ripped asunder to bring life to the world.

This painting, along with a late *Saint John the Baptist*, was among the three works taken by Leonardo when he moved to France in 1515. The third was the *Mona Lisa* (1503), easily the most celebrated and most identifiable painting in the world as well as one of the most controversial. Historians cannot even agree on the subject of the work, so that its proper title is still questioned; critics argue about whether the painting was finished, about the meaning of the famous smile, and about the significance of the background. Yet several points are indisputable. One is that Leonardo created a pose that would dominate portrait painting for the next three centuries. Another is that he made the depiction of arms and hands an indispensable element in the disclosure of character. A third is that the effect of the painting has much to do with the contrast between the savage, uninhabitable background of crag and moor and the ineffable tranquillity of the woman's face. This woman is ascendant over the barren land. That apparently meant everything to the artist as he aged.

For the last ten years of his life Leonardo did little painting, though he was much sought after; instead, he occupied himself with problems in mathematics, botany, optics, anatomy, and mechanics. He left unfinished his last commission, a battle piece for the Palazzo Vecchio in Florence, in which he was in direct competition with Michelangelo. At sixty-three, out of touch with the monumental achievements of his successors Michelangelo and Raphael, he accepted an appointment with the King of France to settle at the château of Cloux, near Amboise, where his only duty was to converse with the king. There he died, still pursuing his research, on May 2, 1519.

Summary

Leonardo da Vinci's achievement was nothing less than the foundation of the High Renaissance in painting, drawing, sculpture, and architecture, in theory or practice or both. His equally significant accomplishments in establishing the groundwork for the scientific study of botany, anatomy, physiology, and medicine fall short only because he did not publish his theories and observations and because his secretive manner of recording kept them from discovery until long after most of them had been superseded. His career presents a unique paradox. He is unique in having accomplished so much during his lifetime—he seems to be a compendium of several men, all of them geniuses. Yet he is also unique in having left so little behind and in having disguised or obscured much of that; some of his legacy was still being rediscovered in the middle of the twentieth century, and much of it will never be restored.

Leonardo's discoveries ranged across the boundaries of art and science, because for him there were no boundaries to the inquiring intellect. The key to opening up these realms of inquiry was the eye, for Leonardo the principal instrument of observation, with which discovery began. In both art and science, Leonardo held that observation had to take precedence over both established authority and established method. What was true to the eye was the supreme truth; the eye alone opened the window to the intellect and to the soul.

Bibliography

Ackerman, James S. "Leonardo da Vinci: Art in Science." *Daedalus* 127 (winter 1998): 207. The author discusses the interaction of science and art as it relates to the works of da Vinci, a former scientist. He includes details on the history of science and on da Vinci's scientific observations.

Brown, David Alan. *Leonardo da Vinci: Origins of a Genius*. New Haven, Conn.: Yale University Press, 1998. This book presents the most complete account ever written of da Vinci's mysterious beginnings as an artist. Brown begins by examining da Vinci's first years in the Florentine workshop of the leading sculptor of the day, Andrea del Verrocchio. Brown shows that da Vinci rapidly outgrew his limited role as Verrocchio's nature specialist.

Clark, Kenneth. *Leonardo da Vinci: An Account of His Development as an Artist*. Rev. ed. London and New York: Viking, 1988. One of the best overall treatments of the technical and compositional qualities of Leonardo's work. Contains excellent plates and good illustrations. Makes fine connections between Leonardo's innovations in optics and anatomy and their effects on his painting techniques.

Foley, Venard. "Leonardo and the Invention of the Wheellock." *Scientific American* 278 (January, 1998): 96. The article provides information on da Vinci and focuses on his wheellock invention. Foley highlights entries from da Vinci's notebooks of original designs and discusses his experimental work.

Goldscheider, Ludwig. *Leonardo da Vinci*. 6th ed. London: Phaidon Press, 1959. Presents a thorough survey of the life and accomplishments of Leonardo, with outstanding plates. Also presents a clear account of Leonardo's relations with other artists and with his patrons.

Hartt, Frederick. *History of Italian Renaissance Art: Painting, Sculpture, Architecture*. 4th ed. London: Thames and Hudson, and New York: Abrams, 1994. Certainly the best-written overall account of its subject, with clear technical exposition, sumptuous illustrations, and finely tuned tracing of the cultural complex. Written by an expert in the iconography of the period.

Heydenreich, Ludwig H. *Leonardo da Vinci*. 2 vols. London: Allen and Unwin, and New York: Macmillan, 1954. This standard scholarly biography abounds in illuminating detail about Leonardo's life, accomplishments, and environment.

Kemp, Martin. *Leonardo da Vinci: The Marvelous Works of Nature and of Man*. London: Dent, and Cambridge, Mass.: Harvard University Press, 1981. Kemp concentrates on the revelations in the published notebooks and in other writings of Leonardo, reproducing the illustrations brilliantly and bringing them to bear on Leonardo's paintings. Kemp also pieces together Leonardo's detached observations into a coherent philosophical system, focusing on the priority of the eye.

Leonardo da Vinci. *Selections from the Notebooks of Leonardo da Vinci*. Edited by Irma Richter. London and New York: Oxford University Press, 1952. The best succinct introduction to the wealth of material contained in Leonardo's notebooks, deciphered and fully published only in the twentieth century. Richter selects the material intelligently and provides the right amount of explanation.

Payne, Robert. *Leonardo*. New York: Doubleday, 1978; London: Hale, 1979. Payne provides an extremely readable and nicely detailed discussion of Leonardo's life and work, avoiding technical jargon and guiding clearly through obscure and confusing material. Some of his judgments are idiosyncratic, but he defends them bravely.

Pedretti, Carlo. *Leonardo: A Study in Chronology and Style*. London: Thames and Hudson, and Berkeley: University of California Press, 1973. The most accessible book of the many on Leonardo by the foremost modern authority. Pedretti is full of insights and useful knowledge, particularly on the relation between the artist's writings and his work.

Wasserman, Jack. *Leonardo da Vinci*. New York: Abrams, 1975; London: Thames and Hudson, 1992. A solid art historian's approach to the life, reflections, and art of Leonardo, this book is more readable than most and provides solid background material as well as illuminating discussion of the paintings. Particularly good on the relationship between written material and art.

James Livingston

PIERRE LESCOT

Born: 1510?; Paris, France
Died: September 10, 1578; Paris, France
Areas of Achievement: Architecture and art
Contribution: Lescot was long regarded as the first of France's great architects, chiefly because of his redesign and reconstruction of the original Louvre. Although modern scholarship modifies this estimate, he remains ranked among the premier French architects and designers of the sixteenth century.

Early Life

Biographical material on Pierre Lescot's early life is limited and often unverifiable. He was probably born in Paris in 1510 into a well-positioned seigneurial family. His father, for whom he was named, was Francis I's crown attorney, an attorney for one of the courts of relief, or assistance, as well as the leader of the Parisian merchant guilds. The elder Lescot held estates at Lissy near Brie, and among others, at Clagny close to the royal residences at Versailles. Originally, the Lescots came to France from Italy, where their connections with the Alessi family affected the younger Lescot's later career.

While a young man, Lescot inherited the paternal estate at Clagny. Favored by Francis and Henry II, Lescot served as their principal chaplain, as their honorary church canon, as an associate abbey at Clermont near Laval, and as a canon at Nôtre Dame in Paris. Advantaged by such royal associations and family position, the younger Lescot began displaying talents as a painter, while at the same time studying mathematics and architecture. Very likely while young, Lescot journeyed to Italy, where, under the auspices of old family friends, he absorbed decorative and architectural concepts later manifested in his work. Unquestionably, he studied Italian architectural writings and examined many of France's Roman ruins many years prior to his official visit to Rome in 1556.

Under absolutist monarchs who were forging France into Europe's first nation-state, Paris during Lescot's lifetime was also changing. Whether engaged in the monarchs' hodgepodge administrative structures or in the small manufacturies producing luxuries for crown and court, most of the 250,000 inhabitants of Paris clustered around the Île de la Cité, the Seine River island which from time immemorial simultaneously offered the people their best opportunities for defense and the first fordbridge linking both riverbanks. During Lescot's lifetime, royalty, its retainers, and courtiers began converting the Marais (swamp), the oldest district on the Seine's north bank, into an aristocratic enclave, where services of architects—builders and artists—were ineluctably drawn.

Life's Work

Lescot's architectural work commenced during a period of brilliance in French Renaissance architecture, translating into its own idiom characteristics of Italian styles, while subduing elements of its own Gothic traditions. Among his contemporaries and colleagues were the great French sculptor Jean Goujon and Philibert Delorme, an innovative engineer. Encouraged by relative domestic peace, the Crown, its court, and other aristocrats not only began new constructions but also planned to redesign buildings and residences that formerly functioned as fortified positions. New or remodeled, these structures were intended as the abodes of men enjoying the money and leisure to live more ostentatiously, surrounded by what they conceived to be the ultimate in style.

Francis' own building obsession, which included several châteaus, was epitomized in 1519 by his redesign of Chambord, initially a feudal strong point, which, upon completion, reflected Italian symmetries imposed upon a functionally banal fortress. Partly a consequence of French and Italian architects and artists crossing one another's borders more frequently, Chambord, as an exemplar, inspired further imaginative, eclectic, and sophisticated architectural design in France.

Francis then turned his attention to the three-hundred-year-old Louvre in Paris, whose pattern closely conformed to other thirteenth century castles, many then still built of wood. It was replete with a strong tower and a donjon, and was surrounded by sturdy masonry walls.

Because the Louvre's poor drainage and *odeurs* made its precincts unfashionable and its proximity to religious houses and the raucous studentry of the Left Bank undesirable, Francis decided in 1526 on the Louvre's modernization, though aside from removing the donjon, nothing was done until 1546. That year, Lescot was selected to construct a new structure on the site of the old château's west wing—the Old Louvre—then lying outside the old city walls. Considering the restricted Parisian work space available, Lescot planned for two floors of detached buildings, with a central pavilion and its staircase. Each side was to be flanked by large public reception rooms. Within five years, however, these plans had been revised, providing for a grander gallery (*salle*) and shifting the staircase to the north wing: in all, requiring construction of two new pavilions at each end with a new staircase for one of them. Moreover, the façade was raised one floor so construction of the King's Pavilion to the southwest would not overpower these two new pavilions.

Monarchs, the times, and styles altered events even as Lescot's revisions were under way. Sometime between 1551 and Henry's death in 1559, Lescot was called upon by the Crown to develop more ambitious plans, which he did. His new plans called for building a court enclosed by blocks double the length of his original wing. The Louvre façade was visually unified with pilasters of the then-preferred Corinthian and Composite orders. Pediments over windows were alternated between triangular and rounded ones: a variety demanding attention. Each of his three pavilions divided into separate bays, differing from the wings uniting them. Ground-floor windows were set inside rounded arches; those windows of the second floor featured open pediments; and attic windows were capped by sculpted crossed torches. All three pavilions, devoid of horizontal lines, were designed to accentuate the vertical: Double columns, among other devices, carried eyes upward. Overall, Lescot (with Goujon) successfully blended classical and traditional French architecture into his own style of French classicism.

Lescot's interior work on the new wing was brilliantly enhanced by Goujon's caryatids—ornamentation unknown in France and rare even in Renaissance Italy—and by the four groups of sixteen richly decorated Doric columns separating—yet affording monumentality—to the southern end of the great gallery. Their genius combined, Lescot's and Goujon's interior collaborations were almost inseparable: Both added distinctions to an architectural masterwork.

Although his career was preempted for years by the Louvre, Lescot managed many other commissions. Again in collaboration with Goujon, he built the Hôtel Carnavalet in 1545, filling the space between the Hôtel de Ville and the Bastille, thereby luring more courtiers and aristocrats into the Marais district. His use at Carnavalet of a wide street flanked by stables and a kitchen in lieu of a plain wall shortly became the rage among wealthy Parisians. Lescot worked on these other projects with great craftsmen. When Henry tired of his bedroom ceiling, Lescot and the Italian wood-carver Scribec di Carpi produced a new ceiling that rivaled any other of the period, including the magnificent ceilings for which Venice was famous.

After Henry's death in 1559, Lescot's personal life disappears from the historical record. Francis, who previously extended him his first commissions, enthusiastically supported him, partially repaying him by designating him the canon of Paris' metropolitan church (with its many perquisites) and by making him the Abbey of Clermont and a royal councillor as well. Francis' successors reconfirmed these prerogatives for him, and throughout his career he maintained his Clagny estate. There is no other substantial knowledge of him, except that his death occurred on September 10, 1578, in Paris.

Summary

For some modern architectural historians, Pierre Lescot has been a source of debate: He was basically an amateur architect, and he was not a critical figure in the development of French architecture, particularly the distinctive Gallic version of Renaissance architecture—French classicism. In addition, many of Lescot's plans and constructions were flawed, and some believe that as a mere overseer he assumed credit for the genius of men such as Jean Goujon. Whatever modicum of credibility may be accorded these views, in the light of the overall evidence available, they fail to diminish significantly his contribution to his singularly imaginative plans and designs combining Italianate Renaissance elements with traditional French elements that produced a uniquely French architectural style. This was no more pronouncedly evident than in the original reconstruction of the Louvre and in the designs and plans that substantially determined the shape of that magnificent structure's future. Moreover, the design and embellishment of this and other of his original work represents a rare conjunction of architectural, engineering, and sculpting genius—that is, the collaboration of Lescot, Goujon, and Scribec di Carpi. In addition to all of their other accomplishments, they produced a nucleus around which, architecturally, one of the world's most visual and magnificent urban cultural centers would develop to the wonderment of many subsequent generations.

Bibliography

Blunt, Anthony. *Art and Architecture in France, 1500-1700.* 5th ed. New Haven, Conn.: Yale University Press, 1998. Excellently and authoritatively written for laymen by a distinguished art critic and historian. Descriptions of Lescot's work on the Louvre are clear and detailed. Contains notes for each chapter and many illustrations and plates.

Gardner, Helen. *Gardner's Art Through the Ages.* 10th ed. Fort Worth, Tex.: Harcourt Brace, 1996. Chapter 14 is especially pertinent to the work of Lescot and his colleagues. The book is beautifully illustrated in both color and black and white and includes plates and schematics. The text is well written for both novitiates and more sophisticated art lovers. Contains a glossary, a bibliography, and an index.

Hamlin, Talbot. *Architecture Through the Ages.* New York: Putnam, 1940. Chapter 16 bears particularly on the Renaissance in France and Italy, and hence on Lescot's work on the Louvre. Older and less critical than Blunt's book, it is still accurate and substantial in its major features. Contains many fine photographs and schematics and an excellent, double-columned index.

Janson, H. W. *History of Art: A Survey of the Major Visual Arts from the Dawn of History to the Present Day.* 3d ed. London: Thames and Hudson, 1977; New York: Abrams, 1986. Clearly written, and authoritatively so, this is a large, lavishly illustrated work with splendid black-and-white and color photographs. Part 3 of the book deals specifically with the Renaissance and Chapter 5, the subject of which is the Renaissance in the North, has excellent materials, including photographs of Lescot's old Louvre.

Ranum, Orest A. *Paris in the Age of Absolutism.* New York: Wiley, 1968. A brief, scholarly work, but readily understandable by laymen, this extended essay is very important to an understanding of the general social, political, and intellectual climate prevalent in Lescot's day. Lescot is mentioned both in connection with the Louvre and other works. Contains prints of local scenes, a fine view of the Louvre front, and portraiture paintings. Includes an excellent select bibliography and an extensive, double-columned index.

Clifton K. Yearley

SIR THOMAS LITTLETON

Born: 1422; Frankley, Worcestershire, England

Died: August 23, 1481; Frankley, Worcestershire, England

Area of Achievement: Law

Contribution: Littleton's fame rests upon a short treatise titled *Tenures*, written toward the end of his life, in which he gives a full and clear account of the several estates, tenures, and doctrines pertaining to landholding that were then known to the English law. *Tenures* is the primary source of the land law of medieval England, and it is considered to be the first great book upon English law not written in Latin and wholly uninfluenced by Roman law.

Early Life

Thomas Littleton was one of four sons and four daughters born to Thomas Westcote of Westcote, near Barnstaple, England, a courtier to the king, and Elizabeth de Littleton, daughter and sole heir of Thomas de Littleton, lord of the manor of Frankley, and esquire of the body to three kings: Richard II, Henry IV, and Henry V. It was agreed at the time of the marriage that, since the estate that would ultimately come to Elizabeth was large and that it was desirable to maintain the Littleton name, the first-born son would have the name Littleton rather than Westcote. Therefore, where the other children of the marriage used the name Westcote, Thomas, the eldest son, was named Thomas de Littleton (spelled Luttleton prior to the reign of Henry VI).

What is known of Littleton's early personal life is very spare. He received his training in law at the Inns of Court, where he was a member of the Inner Temple. Between the years 1440 and 1450, in addition to his marriage to Joan, the widow of Sir Philip Chetwynd, of Ingestrie, Staffordshire, and one of the daughters and coheirs of Sir William Burley of Bromscroft Castle, he started to gain considerable prominence in the county of Worcestershire: His professional services were requested against the famous family of the Pastons; he became in 1444 escheator of the county, undersheriff of that county from 1447 to 1448, and in 1450 recorder of the town of Coventry, who had the honor of receiving Henry VI when that king came to visit in 1450. On his appointment as Reader of the Inner Temple in or about 1450, he began to study and explain the great Statute of Westminster II, otherwise known as *De donis conditionalibus*, which in 1285 had revolutionized the alienation of land, and in 1451 or 1452, he was granted for life, as a result of his great and good counsel, the manor of Sheriff Hales in Staffordshire by Sir William Trussel.

On July 2, 1453, about the time when the Wars of the Roses were beginning in England, Littleton was called to the degree of serjeant of law, and then on May 13, 1455, was appointed Henry VI's serjeant, where he rode the northern circuit as a justice of assize. Although this appointment did not bring him an increase in legal business, it did bring him an advance in dignity and responsibility. The king's serjeants were actually advisers to the Crown, standing at the head of the legal profession, and even outranking, according to the historian Eugene Wambaugh, the attorney general. He was under the protection of Richard of York, one of the contenders for the throne in the Wars of the Roses, and must have been of high repute, for he was placed on a commission under the privy seal for raising funds for the defense of Calais, was one of the commissioners of array for Warwickshire, and was justice of the county palatine of Lancaster. High in favor with Edward IV, who came to the throne in 1461, Littleton was first reappointed as king's serjeant and then raised to the position of Justice of the Court of Common Pleas in Westminster on April 27, 1466, retaining that position until his death. It was in that position that he was drawn particularly close to the matter of land questions, because the Court of Common Pleas largely dealt with real estate issues.

Life's Work

According to Sir John Fortescue, the noted judge of the Court of King's Bench, in his *De laudibus legum Angliæ* (1470), the judges of England sat in the king's courts only about three hours in the day, from eight in the morning until eleven, the courts being closed in the afternoon so that the judges would have time to study the laws, read the Holy Scriptures, and busy themselves with other "innocent amusements," so that the life of a judge appeared to be one of contemplation. Therefore, Littleton's appointment as a judge gave him the opportunity to devote himself to the writing of his work on tenures. Also, the position gave Littleton a certain freedom from care, in view of the fact that although the Crown changed hands two times, the judges of the Courts of

Common Pleas and the Court of the King's Bench were not affected, being given new patents to retain their positions.

Honors came to Littleton fairly rapidly, for he was employed on a commission to arbitrate a dispute between the Bishop of Winchester and several of the bishop's tenants with regard to their services and the quality of their tenure under him; he was chosen to be trier of petitions from Gascony in the parliaments of 1467 and 1472; he was made a Knight of the Bath on April 18, 1475; and he was allowed extensive expenditures for salary and personal expenses. He executed his will on August 22, 1481, died the following day, August 23, 1481, and was interred in the Cathedral Church of Worcester, "under a fair tomb of marble, with his statue or portraiture upon it, together . . . with a memorial of his principal titles," in the words of Sir Edward Coke. Out of the mouth of the statue, which Littleton had finished while yet alive, was inscribed the prayer "Fili Dei miserere mei."

According to Coke, Littleton had a "grave and reverend countenance," as he observed from the figure of Littleton shown kneeling in coif and scarlet robes that adorned the east window of the chancel of the Chapel of St. Leonard, Frankley, and a portrait of him in one of the windows of the church at Halesowen, both of which were destroyed at some point after Coke's observation. There is, however, an engraving of the Frankley portrait in Coke's second (1629) edition of his *The First Part of the Institutes of the Law of England: Or, A Commentary upon Littleton* (1628). One can also view the effigy on his tomb in the nave of Worcester Cathedral, which tomb Littleton erected himself. The chances are that the effigy is more a stereotype of how distinguished men of that time wanted to appear than an actual portrait of Littleton. The portrait of Littleton on the brass plate set on top of his tomb disappeared during the Puritan Revolution in England (1642-1660).

Littleton's work on *Tenures* (c. 1480) is the first of the five great books on the history of English law, the others being those of Ranulf de Glanville, Henry de Bracton, Coke, and William Blackstone. Written originally as a source of information for one of his sons, Richard, a lawyer, it was composed in the law French of Littleton's day and translated into English by John Rastell, an author, printer, and serjeant of law (1514-1533). It must have been accepted as a classic from the very first, because the poet John Skelton, who died in 1529, remarked on one occasion that Littleton was well known in his own time.

Although the book gives little hint of new developments that characterize the land law, such as uses and contingent remainders, it does present a fine summary of the medieval English land law and was so admired by the great English jurist Sir Edward Coke that he referred to Littleton's *Tenures* in the preface to his *Institutes*, in which he wrote a commentary on Littleton, as "a work of as absolute perfection in its kind, and as free from error, as any book that I have known to be written of any humane learning, shall to the diligent and observing reader of these Institutes be made manifest. . . ." Coke also touched upon the real reason for Littleton's fame, claiming that "by this excellent work which [Littleton] had studiously learned of others, he faithfully taught all the professors of the law in succeeding ages." What Littleton did was to make sense and order out of the growing chaos of the land law of the preceding 150 years, thereby giving future generations of lawyers a point of departure from which to develop a land law in conformity with changing social and political conditions.

The work is divided into three books: book 1, dealing with the types of holdings or estates; book 2, with the rights by which these estates are held and their incidents of holding; and book 3, with holdings by more than one person, and miscellaneous items.

Much of what Littleton wrote about at the end of the fifteenth century is no longer valid today, because Littleton's land law was based on the feudal system, a system that no longer operates, but whatever of Littleton pertains to modern practice, such as his doctrines on joint tenancies and tenancies in common, remains generally valid at the core of the land law. As more than one historian has noted, Littleton summed up the medieval land law and passed it on to future generations of lawyers before that land law was altered by the needs of the Industrial Revolution and the rise of equity, just as Blackstone's *Commentaries on the Laws of England* (1765-1769) summed up and passed on the common law as developed up to his time by the work of lawyers before it was remodeled by the direct legislation inspired by the teachings of Jeremy Bentham. No mere collection of decisions, Littleton's *Tenures* is rather a creative work based upon the practical knowledge and needs of the time. Trying to get beneath the surface of the decisions, Littleton studied and assessed the arguments of the lawyers and the reasoning of the judges to construct a coherent body of legal knowledge.

Before Littleton wrote his *Tenures*, the land law, despite its importance as the major portion of the English law during medieval times, had given rise to a small treatise generally known as *The Old Tenures*, probably composed during the preceding, fourteenth century, which gives brief descriptions, among other things, of the various tenures and their incidents, of villeinage, villein tenure, and creditors' rights. Its main claim to fame is that its brevity suggested to Littleton that he might write an expansion of this little treatise.

The exact date when Littleton's book was published is not known, but it is known that during Littleton's lifetime, two complete manuscripts were available. The first edition, or *editio princeps*, of the work is a folio published at London by Lettou and Machlinia without date or title, which was followed by an edition issued by Machlinia alone, also without date or title. Many other editions followed, although Coke's remains the most famous.

Summary

Sir Thomas Littleton provided, in a reasonably easy-to-understand work, a clear and full account of the various estates known to English law through the fifteenth century in England, together with the incidents of ownership and the legal doctrines pertinent to them. The first great book upon English law not written in Latin and generally uninfluenced by Roman law, his *Tenures* served as the foundation upon which, gradually, succeeding generations of lawyers and courts of law fashioned what are today the modern concepts of the land law. Although the book was founded upon the Year Books, which are the law reports of the Middle Ages in England, Littleton's work is not merely a compilation of court decisions. Rather, it is a study of the judicial decisions with interpretations and commentary by its author. There can be no understanding of the development of the English feudal system without an understanding of the land law—as described by Littleton—upon which that feudal system was based.

Bibliography

Coke, Sir Edward. *The First Part of the Institutes of the Law of England: Or, A Commentary upon Littleton*. 19th ed. London: Clarke, 1832; Philadelphia: Small, 1853. Although written in rather florid seventeenth-century style, Coke's preface is an excellent introduction to the life of Littleton. Coke's commentary on Littleton's work is, however, beyond the understanding of most lay readers.

Foss, Edward. *The Judges of England, with Sketches of Their Lives and Miscellaneous Notices Connected with the Courts at Westminster from the Time of the Conquest*. 9 vols. London: Longman, 1848-1864; New York: AMS Press, 1966. Like most of the early sketches of judges of England, Foss's sketch of Littleton is relatively brief, giving only the barest details of his life and no presentation of the material contained in Littleton's book. It does, however, give some information on Littleton's descendants.

Holdsworth, Sir William. *The Mediaeval Common Law*. 3 vols. London: Methuen, and Boston: Little Brown, 1903-1909. Constitutes the first three volumes of Holdsworth's great multivolume *History of English Law*. Both a very readable presentation of the life of Littleton and an excellent digest of the estates, incidents of tenure, and doctrines of law emanating from these estates and tenures, as given by Littleton. At times difficult for the lay reader but with rereading and careful attention it may be readily understood. Probably the best introduction to Littleton.

Littleton, Sir Thomas. *Littleton's Tenures*. Edited by Eugene Wambaugh. Washington, D.C.: Byrne, 1903. This book is most valuable because it gives the most complete presentation of Littleton's life and the editions of his *Tenures*. Also, although it gives no commentary or explanation of Littleton's work, it does give the student the opportunity to read what Littleton himself wrote in as correct a translation as possible, Wambaugh having spared no effort to introduce what he believed to be an accurate translation of the French law of the fifteenth century.

———. *Lyttleton: His Treatise of Tenures in French and English*. Edited by Thomas Ellyne Tomlins. London: Sweet, 1841; New York: Russell and Russell, 1970. This work is important to the lay reader for the editing of Coke's preface. Tomlins annotates the preface with commentary upon Coke's presentation of Littleton's life. Also provides Littleton's will and other documents pertinent to the life of Littleton, and an account of the various editions of *Tenures*.

Robert M. Spector

LOUIS XI

Born: July 3, 1423; Bourges, France
Died: August 30, 1483; Plessis-les-Tours, France
Areas of Achievement: Politics and government
Contribution: Louis XI rebuilt France from the Hundred Years' War, prevented renewed English invasion, demolished Burgundy as a great power within France, ended the era of feudal dominance, restored the extent and influence of the royal domain, and reorganized medieval France as a modern nation-state, with himself as the prototype of Renaissance despotism.

Early Life

When Louis de Valois was born in 1423 to Charles VII and Mary of Anjou, the misfortunes of the Hundred Years' War saw most of France controlled by the English or their Burgundian allies following the 1415 Battle of Agincourt. Louis was reared with middle-class companions at Castle Loches in Touraine and was educated on broad lines, while his father, disinherited by the 1420 Treaty of Troyes, dawdled at Bourges, essentially waiting on events. Joan of Arc's victories in 1429 and 1430 revived confidence in the Valois cause, and, following the Franco-Burgundian alliance of 1435 and the 1436 recapture of Paris, Charles VII felt secure enough to bring the dauphin, Louis, into public affairs.

In 1436, Louis entered an arranged political marriage to eleven-year-old Princess Margaret of Scotland, an unhappy and barren union. His soldiering also began in 1436, and by 1439 he held independent commands. As a general, Louis was energetic, courageous, and moderately successful. As king, he would prefer diplomacy to war from his personal experience that "battles are unpredictable."

From 1436 to 1445, Louis and his father agreed on broad royal policy, but not on specific men and measures, and in 1440 the dauphin was persuaded by powerful magnates to head a rebellion dubbed "the Praguerie." The revolt failed, and reconciliation followed. After his wife's death in 1445, the dauphin resumed his demand for new royal advisers, and in 1447 Charles sent his heir to semibanishment as governor of Dauphiné.

Louis reorganized the government in Dauphiné and took his own line in foreign policy, including his 1451 marriage to Charlotte of Savoy, which Charles refused to accept. The crucial father-and-son quarrel centered on the efforts of each to control or bribe the advisers of the other. In 1456, Charles sent his troops to Dauphiné to enforce his authority, and Louis fled to the court of Burgundy.

Louis spent five years in the Burgundian Netherlands as a guest of Duke Philip the Good and his son, the future Duke Charles the Bold. Louis could see that their wealth, army, and ambition were all organized toward making Burgundy an independent power in France and Europe. Charles VII died on July 22, 1461, and Louis at last came to the throne of France. He was thirty-eight years old.

Life's Work

As king, Louis initially replaced most of his father's advisers but continued basic royal policy. External defense and internal coordination were still the great national problems. Territorial feudalism still defied control by wreaking local havoc, but the feudal levy of lance-wielding knights could not defend France in wars of gunpowder and missiles. Yet the king's expensive, new standing army of middle-class professionals threatened the whole structure of feudal government, and the great magnates resisted in four separate rebellions against Louis.

In the first of these feudal revolts, audaciously advertised as "The League of the Public Weal," Charles led a concerted advance on Paris in 1465. The indecisive Battle at Montlhéry on July 16 left Paris saved by Louis but besieged by Charles and the magnates. To keep Paris, the king was forced to give the rebels territories later expensively regained. The Burgundian settlement was challenged by Charles after his 1467 accession, and Louis was then forced to make humiliating concessions at the Peronne Conference of 1468.

The 1468 marriage alliance of Charles and Margaret of York, sister of Edward IV of England, posed an open threat to Louis of invasion. His bold support of the Lancastrian restoration of 1470 seemed ill-judged when Edward resumed power in 1471. By the time Edward invaded France in June of 1475, however, Charles was preoccupied in a Rhineland siege. Louis came to terms with Edward in the August 29 Treaty of Picquigny, offering him money and a pension; the two monarchs exchanged sardonic compliments through an iron grill.

Charles, meanwhile, pursued his claims in other quarters. In 1476, the duke and his army advanced to Lake Neuchâtel and began a campaign in which he was thrice soundly beaten in unexpected attacks by Swiss infantry—at Grandson, Murten, and Nancy, where Charles died fighting in 1477. His heir was his nineteen-year-old daughter, Mary.

Louis gave the Swiss only money until they began to win and then moved decisively, bringing Nevers, ducal Burgundy, Charolais, Picardy, Artois, Boulogne, and Rethel under the control of France. Mary, to protect Franche-Comté, Luxembourg, and the remaining Burgundian Netherlands, married Maximilian of Habsburg. Louis broke the power of Burgundy in France by being ready and able to invade in the hour of Burgundian defeat.

By inheritance and pressure, Louis acquired Provence, Anjou, Maine, and Bar. The emerging geographic outline of modern France was accompanied by a strategic linkage of royal lands in the Loire and Seine river valleys. With the Duke of Alençon under control, the estates of Armagnac partitioned, the heir of Bourbon married to Louis' daughter Anne, and the elderly Duke of Brittany now harmlessly isolated, Louis was now the feudal master of France, which he had to be in order to change the feudal system.

Externally, Louis managed to gain Roussillon from the aged and wily John II of Aragon, but John's revenge was masterful. His son Ferdinand married Isabella of Castile in 1469, commencing an age of increasing Spanish unity, nationalism, and anti-French sentiment. In Burgundy, Spain, Italy, and elsewhere, the fear of French strength prepared the way for the future Habsburg-Valois wars.

Domestically, Louis replaced the military, administrative, police, tax, and judicial institutions of the territorial lords with agencies of the Crown. The nobles who had ruled fiefs became a privileged class of patriotic military and civilian servants sworn in loyalty to the king. The 1472 concordat with the pope gave Louis somewhat comparable powers in the appointment of new bishops. Significantly, the king's taxes, such as *taille, aides*, and *gabelle*, were now collected without representative consent, and the remaining parlements merely registered the king's laws.

Additionally, Louis invested in and promoted new industries such as silk production and modernized mining as well as many commercial enterprises. A royal messenger system became a sort of postal service, conveying not only government business and privileged letters but also the publications of the new printing industry which Louis helped to develop.

This rebuilding and modernization of French life depended on the safety of commerce and the tranquillity of a country no longer beset by ravaging armies. In the revised order of the new French state, the greatest economic benefit went to the bourgeoisie and the wealthiest peasants, but political power in France was concentrated in the hands of the king. On the whole, Louis governed wisely and well, but he institutionalized despotism.

Great in his accomplishments for France, Louis was not impressive in appearance, being short, fat, bald, and somewhat ugly. His dress and manners were informally bourgeois rather than royal. Louis was witty, garrulous, and even charming in conversation or letters, but he lacked the touch of dignity, heroism, generosity, or even understandable vice that would cause men to overlook the cruelties of which, like his contemporaries, he was sometimes capable.

Apoplexy crippled Louis as early as February, 1481, and eventually killed him. He died at Plessis on August 30, 1483, hopeful that his religious observances, his generosity to the Church, and his sincere faith would gain for him a fair judgment from God. His only son succeeded as Charles VIII with his sister Anne as regent. A younger daughter, Jeanne, became Duchess of Orléans.

Summary

When Louis XI ascended the throne in 1461, the postwar lives of Frenchmen were still dominated by territorial feudal lords whom the king could not control. When Louis died in 1483, a centralized nation-state monarchy was the new great fact for the future of France. The scattered royal domain lands of 1461 were increased in extent, geographic cohesiveness, and economic leadership. Most conspicuously, Louis' policy helped to shatter the Burgundian power which, in alliance with the external foes and internal rivals of the French Crown, had long constituted a threat to the survival of France itself as a nation of consequence.

The nation-state that Louis created gave the country more security, peace, and order, as well as better laws and justice; new industry, production, commerce; and a better life, especially in the towns, than feudal Europe had ever sustained. High taxes were the naturally unpopular price for the benefits. Louis' political system endured basically unchanged for three centuries, until the old regime was swept away in 1789.

Despite the greatness and importance of Louis' achievements, legend, fiction, and even some historians have distorted and diminished his reputation. Most scholars agree that he deserves a better place in public estimation. Apart from the problem of misrepresentation, however, the evidence at hand suggests that, while Louis XI was in his own time respected and feared, he did not, for whatever reason, capture great sympathy and affection.

Bibliography

Bakos, Adrianna E. *Images of Kingship in Early Modern France: Louis XI in Political Thought, 1560-1789*. London and New York: Routledge, 1997. Louis XI was known as "The Spider King" because he wove many intricate plots and is thought of primarily as a villain and a cruel, cunning, rather unscrupulous character. Absolutists fled to his banner while constitutionalists reviled him as a rapacious totalitarian murderer. In this book Bakos uses the changing nature of Louis XI's historical reputation to explore the intellectual and political climate of early modern France, and offers new, more complex interpretations of the ideological landscape of early modern France.

Champion, Pierre. *Louis XI*. Translated by Winifred Stephens Whale. London: Cassell, and New York: Dodd Mead, 1929. Once the standard biography on Louis XI, this work is weakened by its reliance on Philippe de Commynes, sparsity of detail, and lack of footnotes, but it is still a clear and enjoyable account.

Commynes, Philippe de. *The Memoirs of Philippe de Commynes*. Edited by Samuel Kinser. Translated by Isabelle Cazeaux. London: Bohn, 1877; Columbia: University of South Carolina Press, 1969. These readable memoirs are the contemporary source most used by later biographers. The author, an adviser and confidant to Louis for eleven years, combines an intimate and generally favorable account of the king with his own reflections on politics.

Kendall, Paul Murray. *Louis XI*. London: Allen and Unwin, 1971; New York: Norton, 1972. The most useful single volume to consult on Louis XI. Kendall's research is comprehensive. This book is scholarly, informative, and accurate, with an extensive bibliography and footnotes that give the reader the sources for everything consequential. Although it is well written, the complex story is not as easy to follow as in Champion.

Le Roy Ladurie, Emmanuel. *The Royal French State, 1460-1610*. Translated by Juliet Vale. Oxford and Cambridge, Mass.: Blackwell, 1994. In this second volume of the History of France series, Ladurie provides an account of the early modern period. Readers will discover a compelling narrative combined with a broad analysis of events and wider comparisons with European history.

Lewis, D. B. Wyndham. *King Spider*. New York: Coward-McCann, 1929; London: Heinemann, 1930. A popular work, now dated, but useful for the section translating a short selection of Louis' letters from the eleven-volume French edition. The book's title comes from Charles the Bold's description of Louis XI as "the universal spider," a label that has lasted.

Mosher, Orville W., Jr. *Louis XI, King of France*. Toulouse, France: Édouard Privat, 1925. Many biographers complain of the distortion and legend surrounding Louis without adequate explanation. Mosher supplies this, although the work should be read with later works.

K. Fred Gillum

SAINT IGNATIUS OF LOYOLA

Born: 1491; Loyola, Guipúzcoa Province, Spain
Died: July 31, 1556; Rome
Area of Achievement: Religion
Contribution: Founder of the Society of Jesus, better known as the Jesuits, Loyola was a dynamic religious leader whose life and writings strongly influenced his times. His religious order has been particularly notable in the field of education.

Early Life

The youngest son of a family known for its prowess in war, Ignatius was given as an infant into the care of a nearby farm woman. During his childhood and youth, Ignatius was thus divided between his father's house, Casa Torre, and his foster mother's home, giving him a view of life from two sides—that of the rulers and that of the ruled. Of Basque descent, the Loyola family shared the characteristics of being deeply religious as well as hot-tempered. Ignatius' father, Don Beltram, had close connections with the king for services rendered and, in return, received many privileges, both lay and clerical. He had justifiably high aspirations for all of his children.

Ignatius spent his early teens mostly at Casa Torre, taking school lessons from the village priest. At the age of sixteen, he was taken as a page into the house of Juan Velázquez de Cuéllar, a family relative who was treasurer of Castile and royal major domo at the court. In his service, Ignatius learned to sing, dance, and play musical instruments—skills he retained for the remainder of his life. For ten years, he lived as a courtier, traveling with his master and the royal court, visiting all the towns of Castile. Thoroughly trained in formal manners and caught up in court life, Ignatius spent much time reading romances, tales featuring ghosts, dragons, princesses, and heroes engaged in impossible adventures.

Upon the death of King Ferdinand in 1516, Juan Velázquez lost most of his estates and his position at court. He died in 1517, and a bereft Ignatius went to Pamplona, the capital of Navarre, to enlist in the viceroy's army, having decided to become a career soldier. From 1517 to 1521, a captain in the service of the Duke of Najera, Ignatius fought the French, who were attempting to seize all of Navarre by capturing the strategic city of Pamplona. In 1520, Ignatius participated in its defense, and, in a fierce battle lasting six hours, he was struck by a cannon ball, suffering a broken right leg. The victorious French treated him well, returning him to Casa Torre for recuperation.

During his convalescence, a bored Ignatius, lacking his usual romances, read a life of Christ and a book on the lives of the saints. He was attracted by the sanctity of Christ and His saints and wanted to imitate their virtues. Meditating on his past and on the future, he felt a need to do penance, which would culminate in a pilgrimage to Jerusalem. Upon recovery, he set about carrying out this goal.

Life's Work

In the spring of 1522, Ignatius visited Montserrat, the site of a famous shrine to the Black Virgin. From there, he went to Manresa, where he stayed about a year, undertaking a program of prayer and penance. During this period, Ignatius first conceived the idea of founding a "spiritual militia" for the service of the Church. At Manresa, he began writing his *Ejercicios espirituales* (1548; *The Spiritual Exercises*, 1736), for the use of directors of spiritual retreats. This famous book gives methods of freeing the soul to seek and to find the will of God. The practitioner goes through stages of meditation, examination of conscience, and methods of prayer; the exercises require thirty days to be completed. These exercises remain a vital part of the life of Jesuits.

From Manresa, Ignatius went to Barcelona in 1523, a stopover before continuing on to Rome. While in Barcelona, he occupied himself in prayer and good works, visiting hospitals and prisons. In March of 1523, he left for Rome, where he received Pope Adrian VI's blessing on his pilgrimage to Jerusalem. Leaving Venice, he was delayed for two months before finally sailing for Palestine. Ignatius and his fellow pilgrims arrived at Jerusalem in September, 1523, to be guided by Franciscan Friars in their visits to the Holy Places. Although he wanted to stay permanently, converting the Muslims, Ignatius was refused permission by the Franciscan superiors. The pilgrims left Jerusalem and were back in Italy in October, 1523. Ignatius returned to Barcelona, arriving in March, 1524.

Wealthy friends paid for Ignatius' studies at the University of Barcelona, where he studied grammar. In 1526, he switched to Acalá University, studying logic, theology, and physics. Between classes, Ignatius begged alms for the poor and

taught *The Spiritual Exercises* to any willing pupils. He gathered four like-minded companions about him and they went throughout the city teaching Christian doctrine. Thus were sown the seeds of the future Society of Jesus.

In 1528, leaving his companions to follow at a later date, Ignatius went to France to attend the University of Paris. Dominican professors at both Barcelona and Salamanca judged him not ready to be a valid preacher. Needing a good foundation in systematic learning, Ignatius spent the next years studying Latin grammar, classical texts, theology, and philosophy. He obtained his Licentiate in March, 1533, and his master's degree in 1534. In addition to his studies, Ignatius taught *The Spiritual Exercises* to fellow students. Among these was a roommate from Navarre, Francis Xavier, whom Ignatius eventually won to his way of life and who was destined to be the glory of Jesuit missionary work. By 1534, Ignatius had nine companions who agreed to unite in any needed spiritual enterprise.

The band of nine went to Rome in 1537, seeking the pope's approval of their new order. In 1539, Pope Paul III gave verbal approval to the society and in September, 1540, they were granted canonical approval. That June, Ignatius and seven of his companions were ordained priests. They settled in Rome, living on alms and preaching sermons, catechizing children, and attending the sick.

Ignatius intended his Society of Jesus to be at the service of the pope and, thereby, of the universal church. The Renaissance church was in need of reform, being secularized by the prevailing educational and cultural milieu. Ignatius' society took a vow to obey the pope in all things and to go where and when he indicated a need for their services. In 1540, the first Jesuits were sent to the foreign missions. Two of them were chosen to work in India, one being Francis Xavier. From Goa, Xavier traveled to Japan, arriving in 1549. Later, he attempted to work in China but died before that desire could be fulfilled (1553). Jesuits fanned out all over the globe, with a concentration in Europe.

Ignatius and his society focused on education as the chief tool for reform within the Church, establishing many secondary schools and universities. Educated laymen were needed to spread the Christian spirit. Martin Luther's teachings were widespread in Europe in the sixteenth century, and Ignatius' society was in the vanguard of the Church's Counter-Reformation.

In 1541, Ignatius was elected the first general of the Society of Jesus—head for life. He began drafting the *Constitutions* for the society, setting a solid foundation and structure on which his followers could build. The *Constitutions* set down the qualities needed for the Jesuit general, among them a holy life, prayerfulness, humility, charity, and circumspection. There were also rules for admitting or expelling members, for the examination or formation of novices, and regulations for prayers. With some adaptation, *The Spiritual Exercises* and *Constitutions* remain basic to Jesuit life.

In 1553, pressed by his friends, Ignatius began narrating his autobiography, completing it in early 1555. He spent the last year of his life overseeing the work of his far-flung order, which, by that time numbered about one thousand members. Ignatius died in 1556, confident that his society was fulfilling his hopes for it, revitalizing the spiritual life of the Church.

Summary

Although Saint Ignatius of Loyola did not found his society expressly to combat the Protestant Reformation, his Jesuits are credited by his contemporaries and by later historians with having stemmed its tide. They were instrumental in winning back many who had fallen away from the Church and in opening vast new territories to the Church (for example, the Indies, China, Japan, South America, and North America). A contemporary of such giants as Sir Thomas More, Desiderius Erasmus, Niccolò Machiavelli, Ferdinand Magellan, Michelangelo, Martin Luther, and the Tudors, Ignatius helped train and form men who became formidable theologians, lawyers, scientists, and mathematicians and who would be at home in the courts of European and Asian princes as well as around the campfires of American Indians. The society's ultimate goal always remained the greater glory of God.

Because of strong criticism by opponents—chiefly within the Church—the Jesuit Order was suppressed in 1773 by Clement XIV. It dwindled in number but not in fervor and, upon formal restoration in 1814, under Pius VII, it quickly regained its former vitality. Friends and foes alike acknowledge the tremendous effect of the Society of Jesus upon the world, then and now. In 1622, the Catholic Church gave its highest seal of approval to Ignatius Loyola, canonizing him a saint.

Bibliography

Fleischer, Barbara J. "The Ignatian Vision for Higher Education: Practical Theology." *Religious Education* (spring 1993): 255. Fleischer examines Saint Ignatius' vision for religious education in light of contemporary dialogue on practical theology. She discusses the history of practical theology, the personal background of Saint Ignatius of Loyola, and the implications of his vision for higher education.

Loyola, Ignatius. *The Autobiography of Saint Ignatius Loyola*. Edited by John C. Olin. Translated by Joseph F. O'Callaghan. New York: Harper, 1974. Contains an informative introduction. Sets the autobiography in the context of its time and gives a brief biography of Ignatius. The preface is by Father Luis Goncalves da Camara, to whom Ignatius narrated his life story. Contains reproductions of illustrations from a work published in Rome in 1609, footnotes expanding on the text, and appendices. Contains a short annotated bibliography.

Maynard, Theodore. *Saint Ignatius and the Jesuits*. New York: Kenedy, 1956. Examines the life of Ignatius in eight chapters, briefly, and gives the remaining seven to an analysis of the Jesuit Order and its experiences in the following centuries. Focuses on missionary activities, the suppression of the order, Jesuit education, and corporate achievement. Defends and admires the Society of Jesus. Contains a bibliography and an index.

Mitchell, David. *The Jesuits*. London: Macdonald, 1980; New York: Watts, 1981. A balanced, critical but respectful treatment of Ignatius and his Jesuits. Covers beginnings to the late 1970's. Contains several illustrations. Appendices include a list of the generals and general congregations, common words used with reference to Jesuits, and a list of popes. Contains an extensive bibliography and a detailed index.

Purcell, Mary. *The First Jesuit*. Westminister, Md.: Newman Press, 1957. Based on contemporary evidence: the writings of Saint Ignatius and records of the first companions and fathers of the first generation of the Society of Jesus. Contains three appendices, a source list, notes, and an index.

Ravier, André, S. J. *Ignatius Loyola and the Founding of the Society of Jesus*. Translated by Joan Maura and Carson Daly. San Francisco: Ignatian Press, 1987. An interpretation of Ignatius and his society. Begins with a chronology of Ignatius and his followers' activities; ends with an analysis of the message and mission of Ignatius. Based on Ignatius' correspondence and his autobiography, letters of some of his close collaborators, and several volumes of the Monumenta Historica Societatis Jesus. Contains a bibliography (primarily French sources) and an index.

Richter, Friedrich. *Martin Luther and Ignatius Loyola, Spokesmen for Two Worlds of Belief*. Translated by Leonard F. Zwinger. Westminster, Md.: Newman Press, 1960. A comparison/contrast of the careers of Luther and Ignatius. Analysis of Protestant and Catholic thought and teachings. No bibliography, but contains a brief index.

Tylenda, Joseph N., ed. and trans. *A Pilgrim's Journey: The Autobiography of St. Ignatius of Loyola*. Wilmington, Del.: Michael Glazier, 1985. A brief biography of Ignatius in the introduction. Contains a commentary on each page to flesh out allusions in the text. Contains appendices, select bibliography, and notes for each chapter.

S. Carol Berg

ISAAC BEN SOLOMON LURIA

Born: 1534; Jerusalem

Died: August 5, 1572; Safed

Areas of Achievement: Philosophy and religion

Contribution: Luria was the culminating figure in the history of the Jewish mystical tradition known as Cabala, which, originating in southern France in the last quarter of the thirteenth century, reached its height in the sixteenth century. Luria's revision of key Cabalist concepts and his theory of a dynamic creation—catastrophically altered by sin but capable of regeneration and final redemption—had a profound influence on subsequent Jewish thought, including Hasidism, and on messianic movements in both the Jewish and the Christian worlds.

Early Life

Isaac Luria, also known as ha-Ari (the acronym of the Ashkenazic Rabbi Isaac), was born in Jerusalem in 1534. His father was an Ashkenazi who had come from Germany or Poland, and his mother was of Sephardic stock. At his father's death, his mother took him to Egypt, where he grew up in the household of his wealthy uncle, a tax collector. Details of his life are sparse; the principal source is the *Toledot ha-Ari* (life of the Ari), an account written fifteen or twenty years after his death in which fact and legend are freely mingled.

Luria was highly precocious, and his uncle provided him with able tutors, including David ibn Ali Zimrah and Betsal'al Ashkenazi. He collaborated with the latter in producing legal commentaries and wrote a study of the Book of Concealment section of the *Zohar*, the central text of the Cabalist tradition. In later life, he disdained to write, however, preferring personal teaching and communication with his disciples; his mature thought is known only through their accounts, particularly those of Chaim Vital (1543-1620), who claimed to have recorded his master's thoughts verbatim.

Luria married at the age of fifteen and later went into commerce, in which he was engaged to the end of his life. At the age of seventeen, he began an intensive study of the Cabala, focusing on the *Zohar* and on the works of his elder contemporary, Moses Cordovero (1522-1570), the leading figure of the major Cabalist school at Safed in Palestine. In early 1570, he took up residence in Safed with his family and studied briefly with Cordovero himself, who was said to have appointed him his spiritual successor.

Life's Work

At Cordovero's death, Luria became the head of a group known as the Cubs (his own nickname of Ari meant "Holy Lion" in Hebrew), who formed a core of devoted disciples about him. They lived as a community, with quarters for themselves and their families. Luria lectured to them on the Sabbath, after they had donned ritual white garments and marched processionally into the neighboring fields. He also worked with them on an individual basis, imparting the techniques of mystical meditation and elucidating the spiritual ancestry of each in accordance with the Cabalist principle of transmigration.

The impact of Lurianic doctrine may be attributed not only to its intrinsic power as a revision of Cabalist tradition but also to the condition of Jewry in the aftermath of the Spanish expulsion of 1492 and the revived anti-Semitism of Reformation Europe. For Jews seeking a divine meaning in these calamities and thrown back anew upon the painful consciousness of their *Galut*, or exile, Luria's thought had both explicative and consolatory appeal.

Traditional Cabalism described the creation of the universe as a wholly positive event, emanating from God's benevolence and unfolding in orderly stages. Luria, in contrast, described this process as involving an act of privation, a contraction or concentration (*tzimtzum*) of the Godhead into itself to create a space outside itself (the *tehiru*, or void) in which the universe could be formed.

The divine light of creation was released into the void, but some of the forms or vessels (*sefirot*) created to receive it were overwhelmed by its force. This "breaking of the vessels" (the *shevirah*) caused a catastrophic scattering of light. The intact vessels constituted a perfected but incomplete upper realm, while the broken ones (including the highest, Adam Kadmon, or Primal Man, which consisted not only of Adam but of the souls of all of his progeny as well) produced a lower, fallen world, to which, however, many sparks of divine light still clung. The sin of Adam then produced further ruin, increasing the alienation of the fallen world from the Godhead.

Adam having failed, God turned to the people of Israel to accomplish the redemption (*tikkun*) of the fallen world and to liberate the divine sparks from their material prison. Each Jew could advance or retard this process by his ethical conduct; with each pious act, a spark was redeemed, but with each wicked or impious one, a spark of the sinner's own soul was lost to chaos. The individual thus not only sought personal salvation by his acts but also participated in the process of universal redemption.

The most esoteric part of Luria's doctrine concerned the divine motive for creating the world and its abortive realization. Luria suggested that there were elements of disunity within the Godhead itself, although the divine essence was seamless and could be conceptualized only as light. In the act of *tzimtzum*, God differentiated these elements (the *reshimu*), which cleaved to the "surface" of the *tehiru* in the manner of water clinging to a bucket. From this exteriorized residue, the vessels were to be composed, and this formed emptiness, penetrated by retained light from the Godhead. Thus, the creation of the universe was to accomplish the reintegration of the Godhead with itself. The world of evil resulted when the refractory vessels failed (or refused, since they were composed both of and by the *reshimu*) to contain the Godhead's light; yet even that world was penetrated by divine goodness in the form of the sparks.

Luria's explanation of the fallen world may be regarded as an abstract reconceptualization of the story of the rebel angels, filtered through Manichaean and Gnostic thought. His attempt, as with all theodicy, was to account for the presence of evil without imputing it directly to God. Despite its abstract nature, it presented a powerfully compelling picture of creation itself as the process of God's own self-exile and redemption, and the *tikkun* as Israel's opportunity to participate in the completion of His design for the universe. Israel's own exile, and the tribulations heaped on it by the forces of evil, could thus be seen as a mirror of the divine travail. The more closely the final victory of *tikkun* approached, the more violently evil resisted. Thus, the expulsion of the Spanish Jews and the general persecution of Israel were indications not of the weakness of the Jews in the face of their enemies but of their gathering strength against all opposition to the divine will.

Luria's brief ministry ended with his death in August, 1572, during an epidemic in Safed, but such was the force of his personality and doctrine that his teachings were rapidly propagated throughout the Jewish world, where they profoundly influenced both contemporary messianic movements and the theological, liturgical, and literary traditions of Judaism.

The Safed Cabalists believed that the moment of redemption was imminent. Luria may have conceived of himself as the Messiah ben-Joseph, the first of the two messiahs prophesied in Jewish tradition, whose fate was to be slain in the war of Gog and Magog; he was apparently so regarded by his admirers, and his sudden death did nothing to dispel the notion. Messianic expectation, nourished by Lurianic doctrine, flourished widely in the Jewish world for the next hundred years, culminating in an attempted mass migration to Palestine in 1665-1666 under Sabbatai Zevi. Christian chiliasts, who believed that the Jews' return to Palestine was the prelude to the Second Coming of Jesus, were deeply stirred by this ferment, and the Lurianist Menasseh ben Israel paid a state visit to England at the behest of Oliver Cromwell.

Summary

Isaac ben Solomon Luria was the culminating figure in the Cabalist movement, the major tradition of Jewish mysticism and speculative theology in the late medieval and early modern world. Menasseh ben Israel declared that "the wisdom of Rabbi Isaac Luria rises above the highest mountains," and a modern scholar, Joseph Dan, has called the concept of *tikkun* "the most powerful idea ever presented in Jewish thought." After 1620, almost all works of ethics in Hebrew used Lurianic symbolism, and, as Dan further comments, "Lurianism became a national theology for Judaism for several generations." Although Luria's influence reached its apogee in the seventeenth century, it remained important in the eighteenth and nineteenth centuries, and passed directly into Hasidism. Luria's emphasis on the world-altering significance of each believer's acts revitalized Jewish ethics and continued to animate it long after his arcane theology had become, for most, a historical curiosity. The critic Harold Bloom has tried to revive Lurianic Cabalism as a device of literary scholarship, and a current periodical of Jewish American thought calls itself *Tikkun*. Luria thus remains one of the most seminal figures in the past five hundred years of Judaism.

Bibliography

Bloom, Harold. *Kabbalah and Criticism*. New York: Seabury Press, 1975. A modern reinterpretation of Luria's Cabalism as a "psychology of belatedness" that anticipates Freudian doctrine, a philosophy of suffering that anticipates Friedrich Nietzsche, and a system of signs with affinities to Charles Sanders Peirce. Bloom also proposes Luria's thought as a paradigm for literary interpretation.

Fine, Lawrence. *Safed Spirituality: Rules of Mystical Piety, the Beginning of Wisdom.* New York: Paulist Press, 1984. Focuses on the customs and rituals practiced by Luria and his disciples.

Schechter, Solomon. "Safed in the Sixteenth Century: A City of Legists and Mystics." In his *Studies in Judaism.* London and New York: Macmillan, 1905. A classic essay, still valuable, on the Cabalists of Safed and especially Luria.

Scholem, Gershom. *Major Trends in Jewish Mysticism.* London: Thames and Hudson, and New York: Schocken, 1955. Scholem was the foremost twentieth century scholar of Jewish mysticism and the Cabala. His work has been so dominant that it has spawned a major literature of reinterpretation and revision, best summarized in Joseph Dan's *Gershom Scholem and the Mystical Dimension of Jewish History* (1987). Luria's system is treated in the eighth chapter of Scholem's book, which was first published in 1941. Includes an analysis of the textual issues in reconstructing the system from the writings of the disciples, with special emphasis on Joseph ben Tabul.

———. *On the Kabbalah and Its Symbolism.* London: Routledge, and New York: Schocken, 1965. Another of Scholem's major works, indispensable for understanding the Cabalist tradition and containing a chapter on Luria. See also his book-length essay, "Kabbalah," in the *Encyclopedia Judaica* (Jerusalem: Keter Publishing House, 1971).

Tishby, Isaiah. *Torat ha-Ra veha-Kelipah be-Kabbalat ha-Ari.* Jerusalem: Magnes Press, 1983. This important book deals with the problem of Luria's conception of evil and treats, as does Scholem, the textual problems of his system.

Robert Zaller

MARTIN LUTHER

Born: November 10, 1483; Eisleben, Saxony
Died: February 18, 1546; Eisleben, Saxony
Areas of Achievement: Theology, philosophy, religion, and church reform
Contribution: Out of his own personal struggle and his conflict with the Church, Luther developed a theology and a religious movement that rejuvenated the Christian faith and had a profound impact on the social, political, and religious thought of Western society.

Early Life

Martin Luther was born on November 10, 1483, at Eisleben, Saxony, to Hans and Margarethe Luther. Soon after his birth, the family moved to Mansfield, where his father worked in the copper mines, prospering sufficiently to become one of the town's councillors in 1491. Possessing a strong, forceful character, Hans Luther had a great impact on his son. He could be exceptionally stern; years later, Luther stated that his father gave him a sense of inferiority that took years to overcome. Yet, recognizing that his son had a promising intellect, his father sent Luther to Latin school at Mansfield. At age twelve, he spent a year at a school in Magdeburg operated by the Brethren for the Common Life and in 1498 attended a school at Eisenach. In 1501, Luther entered the University of Erfurt, one of the best universities in Germany, obtaining his bachelor's degree in 1502 and his master's degree in 1505.

His father wanted Luther to pursue a legal career. Luther, however, was suffering from depression, a lifelong chronic condition. On July 2, 1505, as he was returning to Erfurt from Mansfield, a lightning bolt knocked him to the ground. Fearful, facing eternity, Luther at that moment vowed to become a monk. Without consulting his father, Luther immediately entered the Augustinian monastery in Erfurt. He was ordained in 1507 and was selected for advanced theological studies, receiving his doctorate in theology from the University of Wittenberg in 1512. Luther then succeeded his mentor, Johann von Staupitz, to the chair of biblical theology at Wittenberg.

Beneath his successful exterior, however, all was not well with Luther. Between 1505 and 1515, Luther underwent an acute personal crisis. Harboring terrible anxieties about sin and his own salvation, Luther believed that no matter how irreproachably he lived, he was unable to satisfy God. Luther was clearly headed for a breakdown. At this juncture, Staupitz interceded and told Luther to abandon the concept of God as judge, to focus on Christ, and simply to love God. This was a revelation for the young monk. While studying Paul's Epistle to the Romans, Luther realized that mankind is saved by faith and not by works. Thus, the essential theology of Protestantism arose to a large extent from Luther's inner, personal struggle.

Life's Work

The issue that ignited Luther's conflict with the Church was the sale of indulgences in Germany by the Dominican friar Johann Tetzel. Indulgences were the remission for money of part of the temporal (priest-assigned) penalties for sin. They were granted on papal authority and sold by licensed agents. While the Church never maintained that divine forgiveness could be obtained through an indulgence, unscrupulous agents such as Tetzel employed such claims with great success. Luther, disturbed that ordinary people were having their salvation endangered by these false claims, authored ninety-five theses attacking indulgences and fastened them to the door of All Saints Church in Wittenberg on October 31, 1517. Contrary to Luther's wishes, the theses were widely circulated, striking a responsive chord among the Germans. What Luther had intended as a local, scholarly debate was becoming a public controversy.

The Archbishop of Mainz, who was profiting directly from the sale of indulgences, forwarded copies of the ninety-five theses to Rome, requesting that Luther be disciplined. Pope Leo X, viewing the dispute as an argument between the Augustinians and Dominicans, simply told the former to deal with Luther. At this point, the scope of the controversy suddenly widened. A colleague of Luther at Wittenberg, Bodenstein von Karlstadt, responding to criticisms of Luther's positions by Johann Eck, published 405 theses, some of which attacked Eck personally. Eck's order, the Dominicans, were outraged, and heresy proceedings against Luther began to move forward in Rome. Luther himself inflamed the situation by publishing a sermon on excommunication which clearly questioned papal authority.

Rome sent a summons for Luther to appear at Rome to Cardinal Thomas Cajetan, who was at Augsburg. For political reasons, however, the pope could not afford to antagonize Frederick II of Sax-

ony, an elector of the Holy Roman Empire and Luther's protector. Luther was instead given a safe-conduct to have a personal interview with the conservative Cajetan.

History will always note the dramatic presentation of the ninety-five theses in 1517 and the even more significant confrontation at Worms in 1521, but the meeting at Augsburg in 1518 probably had more impact than either. In 1517, Luther was insulated by his anonymity; in 1521, he was famous, with possibly half of Germany supporting him. Yet in 1518 Luther was vulnerable, not yet famous and not certain how the Church would deal with him. The Church had an opportunity to silence Luther without suffering severe damage and failed to do so. Cajetan had no intention of hearing Luther's statements, and, although he promised to forward Luther's "explanations" to Rome, he demanded that Luther recant. Luther refused and, in fear for his life, fled Augsburg.

While he had been in Augsburg, Luther had met with Eck and had agreed to a debate at Leipzig in July, 1519. This dispute did not go well for Luther. Eck was able to maneuver him into supporting some Hussite positions and into questioning papal authority as well as the authority of ecclesiastical councils. The Church responded on June 15, 1520, with a papal bull condemning many of Luther's teachings. The papal legate sent to circulate the bull among the German cities was shocked to discover German opinion solidly behind Luther. Luther's friends, aware of his dangerous position, tried to have him moderate his beliefs, but Luther had already moved beyond that point and in 1520 published three of his most famous treatises.

In January, 1521, the Church formally excommunicated Luther. At this juncture, Frederick obtained a promise from Emperor Charles V to provide Luther with an opportunity to defend himself before the Imperial Diet then meeting at Worms. At the meeting, it became clear that Luther had been summoned only to recant. Since his life could depend on his answer, Luther requested time to think. The next day, Luther made a skillful statement, and the Chancellor of Trier made an equally skillful reply from the papal perspective. He concluded with a demand that Luther give a simple answer to the question, "Do you recant, yes or no?" Luther responded with a reply that change the course of history. Unless he were proved wrong on the basis of the Scriptures and sound reason—for popes and councils had erred and might do so again—he was bound by his conscience to the Word of God. He concluded in German, "May God help me. Amen."

There was no doubt that Luther had won a great moral victory, but his enemies also gained something important: the Edict of Worms, which declared Luther an outlaw and proscribed his writings. This edict would dog him all of his days, but while it could restrict his freedom of movement, it could not restrict Luther's ideas. It did mean that his protector, Frederick, could not openly support Luther, so for political reasons and for Luther's own safety, Luther was "kidnapped" to the castle at the Wartburg. He found this enforced inaction tiresome and depressing, but he did use the time to begin the translation of the New Testament from Greek into German. Published in September, 1522, it was a historic work which would have a tremendous influence on German language, life, and religion. Luther remained informed about developments beyond the Wartburg, and when he left in March, 1522, he faced a situation that gravely concerned him.

Religious doctrine can easily have social and political ramifications, and Luther was very alarmed by the political and social unrest his theological cornerstones—justification by faith and the priesthood of all believers—had engendered. Luther, always a conservative, feared that the new radical teaching by Karlstadt and others would lead to revolution. In response, Luther in 1523 postulated the Two Realms theory. There is the spiritual realm, where man exists only in relation to God, and the temporal realm, where man exists as flesh, subject to sin and the needs of the flesh. Since both realms are divinely inspired, man has a duty to obey civil authority, and thus it is sinful to rebel against lawful authority. Freedom for Luther consisted of man's freedom to obey the Gospel. These views help explain Luther's strong condemnation of the Peasants' Revolt of 1524-1525.

The year 1525 was pivotal for Luther and the Protestant Reformation. Luther was married to Katherina von Bora, a former nun, who proved to be a wonderful wife, bringing much-needed stability into his life. Also that year, relations were severed between Luther and Desiderius Erasmus. Early in the Reformation, Erasmus had supported its goals, but he had counseled caution, peace, and change through a reforming council. He feared a catastrophic split in the Church. As Luther's theology evolved and it became clear that the Reformation was no longer a reformation but a religious revolution, Erasmus parted company with Luther and chose the Church.

By the end of 1525, the lines were clearly drawn. From this point, Luther was the leader of a great religious movement—a man of true accomplishment. He would have to deal with doctrinal problems, the more radical Protestant leaders such as John Calvin and Huldrych Zwingli, and, as he grew older, others, especially Philipp Melanchthon, who would share the mantle of leadership with Luther. Early in 1546, Luther traveled to Eisleben to settle a quarrel between two young princes. The weather was awful and cold. On February 17, he suffered a heart attack and died the next day. When news of his death reached Wittenberg, Melanchthon announced to his class, "Alas, gone is the horseman and the chariots of Israel," citing the words spoken by Elisha when Elijah was taken to heaven.

Summary

Martin Luther rejuvenated and restored the Christian faith. Rather than canon law, it was now the Bible that was at the center, leading people to a life of faith, love, and good works. Jesus of Nazareth was once again considered to be a personal savior and not a distant, judgmental God approachable only through priestly mediation. The Church returned to being a community of believers and not a legalistic, bureaucratic institution. In accomplishing these reforms, Luther transformed the face of Europe as radically as Napoleon I or Otto von Bismarck and dramatically changed the course of Western civilization.

Luther himself is more difficult to summarize. He was clearly a man constrained by his love of God and the Scriptures. He was often depressed by the evil he found in the world but was ultimately confident of the salvation and glory that awaited after death. That this attitude gave Luther tremendous courage and confidence in the face of powerful opposition is seen in an incident that occurred early in the Reformation. While at the Wartburg, in hiding from his enemies under the ban of the empire, and with his own future far from certain, Luther wrote, "Our enemies threaten us with death. They would do better to threaten us with life."

Bibliography

Atkinson, James. *Martin Luther and the Birth of Protestantism*. London and Baltimore: Penguin, 1968. This book is essentially a theological account of Luther that is engagingly written and very understandable. Luther comes alive on these pages as a theologian and as a historical figure. Includes a subject index, an index of biblical references, a select bibliography, and a chronological table. Highly recommended.

Boehmer, Heinrich. *Road to Reformation: Martin Luther to the Year 1521*. Translated by John W. Doberstein and Theodore G. Tappert. Philadelphia: Muhlenberg Press, 1946; London: Thames and Hudson, 1957. Based thoroughly on primary sources, the book's detail and insight into Luther's life and thinking to the conclusion of the Diet of Worms are exceptional. Lucid and well written, this work is considered by many Luther scholars to be a classic in the field. Includes an index.

Ebeling, Gerhard. *Luther: An Introduction to His Thought*. Translated by R. A. Wilson. London: Collins, and Philadelphia: Fortress Press, 1970. Although this work is not popular discussion of Luther's thought, it does not assume any special knowledge on the part of the reader. It concentrates on the dynamics of Luther's thought. The discussion of Luther's view of philosophy and theology is particularly insightful.

Schwiebert, Ernest G. *Luther and His Times*. St. Louis, Mo.: Concordia, 1950. Schwiebert lays stress upon the philosophical and sociogeographical factors that contributed to the molding of Luther. The first three chapters give an excellent historical background to the Reformation. This highly impressive, scholarly, yet accessible book should be a standard in any Luther bibliography. Includes an index, chapter notes, bibliographical notes, numerous photographs, and illustrations.

Smith, Preserved. *The Life and Letters of Martin Luther*. London: Murray, and Boston: Houghton Mifflin, 1911. The author is considered one of the great Reformation scholars. This book is an excellent introduction to Luther's letters with comments by the author placing them in historical context. Includes an index, chronological tables, and a detailed bibliography.

Smith, Ralph F. *Luther, Ministry, and Ordination Rites in the Early Reformation Church*. New York: Peter Lang, 1995. Reformation rites for ordination and installation of ministers appeared throughout sixteenth century Germany in official Church Orders. New theological understanding was expressed in these attempts to shape an evangelical rite but not a new theological datum. When the liturgical reforms are studied in context, the continuity between the medieval and early Reformation Church regarding ordination and public ministry becomes clear. Early reformers, including Martin Luther, never abandoned what the inherited rites intended.

Spitz, Lewis W. *Luther and German Humanism.* Aldershot and Brookfield, Vt.: Variorum, 1996. Within the general context of the cultural and intellectual crosscurrents of the Renaissance and Reformation movements, this volume provides essays on Luther and his relationship to German humanism. It discusses the reformer's imposing knowledge of the classics; his promotion of education and support for human studies; the religious and patriotic interests of the humanists; the role of the younger generation of humanists in the Reformation; and the impact of humanism and the Reformation on Western history.

Thompson, W. D. J. Cargill. *The Political Thought of Martin Luther.* Brighton, Sussex: Harvester, and New York: Barnes and Noble, 1948. Thompson was recognized as a leading authority on Luther's political thought. He places Luther's political views in the context of his complete theology. The discussion of the Two Realms theory is outstanding. Includes an index and a select bibliography of secondary sources.

Todd, John M. *Luther: A Life.* London: Hamilton, and New York: Crossroad, 1982. Like all top biographers of Luther, Todd draws heavily from Luther's own writings. This historical and theological account of Luther is lucid, providing an excellent discussion of the historical currents and events that helped to shape the Reformation. Includes an index, an excellent appendix on indulgences, numerous illustrations, and a map of Germany.

Ronald F. Smith

NICCOLÒ MACHIAVELLI

Born: May 3, 1469; Florence
Died: June 21, 1527; Florence
Areas of Achievement: Political science, historiography, and literature
Contribution: Machiavelli's posthumous reputation rests primarily on his having initiated a pragmatic mode of political discourse that is entirely independent of ethical considerations derived from traditional sources of moral authority, such as classical philosophy and Christian theology.

Early Life

The year 1469 has a dual significance in the historical annals of Florence, since it marks both the date of Lorenzo de' Medici's ascension to power and that of Niccolò Machiavelli's birth. The boy was reared in a household consisting of his parents, Bernardo and Bartolomea, along with two older sisters and a younger brother. Bernardo, a tax lawyer and petty landowner of modest means, was a man of pronounced scholarly proclivities with a genuine passion for Roman literature. Machiavelli's own schooling in the principles of Latin grammar and rhetoric began at the age of seven. The study of arithmetic, however, was deferred until several years later. Although the family was too poor to own many books, it did possess a copy of the first three decades of Livy's survey of ancient Roman history. This work must have been a favorite of both father and son, since it was eventually sent to the bindery when Niccolò was seventeen years of age. Little is known for certain about the next decade in Machiavelli's life. There is some evidence which indicates that he may have spent most of the years between 1487 and 1495 in Rome working for a prominent Florence banker.

The political climate in Florence had altered drastically in the years immediately preceding Machiavelli's return from Rome. Lorenzo de' Medici died in 1492 and had been succeeded by his eldest son, Piero, an inept youth barely twenty years of age. Piero was soon confronted with a major crisis when King Charles VIII of France invaded Italy in 1494 to lay claim to Naples, and Piero's feckless conduct vis-à-vis the French monarch met with such revulsion on the part of his fellow citizens that they resolved to banish the entire Medici clan from the city forever. Soon thereafter, control of the Florentine republic fell into the hands of an austere Dominican friar from Ferrara, Girolamo Savonarola.

While Savonarola made considerable headway in mitigating the dissolute moral conditions that pervaded Florence, he had considerably less success with his self-imposed mission to restore Christian virtue to the Roman Catholic church. His adversary in this struggle was the Spaniard Rodrigo Borgia, whose reign as Alexander VI is generally conceded to represent the moral nadir in the history of the Papacy during the Renaissance. Savonarola's persistent challenges to papal authority led to his being formally excommunicated by the Roman pontiff; this event emboldened the friar's political adversaries into taking direct action to destroy him. The climax of this struggle occurred on May 23, 1498, when Savonarola and his two closest confederates in the Dominican Order were escorted to the main square in Florence and hanged atop a pile of brush and logs that was thereupon promptly set ablaze by the hangman. Several hours later, the charred remains of the three men were tossed into the Arno River. Machiavelli witnessed Savonarola's rise and fall at first hand and viewed the episode as an object lesson as to the danger of being "an unarmed prophet."

Life's Work

Savonarola's demise turned out to be highly beneficial with respect to Machiavelli's own personal fortune, for a few months thereafter he was called upon to serve in the newly reconstituted municipal government in several important posts. Its chief executive, Piero Soderini, appointed him both head of the Second Chancery and secretary to the Council of Ten for War. It remains unclear why an inexperienced young man of twenty-nine from an impoverished family should have been elevated to these key offices. Most likely, it was his keen intelligence which recommended him to Soderini, for each of the artists for whom Machiavelli chose to pose has fully captured this character trait. In addition to the bemused cynicism manifested in his facial expression, Machiavelli is depicted as a slender man with thin lips and penetrating eyes. He was, in short, a man whose crafty countenance must have caused others to be on their guard while conducting official business with him.

Despite his initial lack of diplomatic experience, Machiavelli was routinely commissioned to undertake sensitive missions to other Italian states as well as to the courts of Louis XII in France and

Maximilian I in Germany. Diplomatic activities such as these played a vital role in Machiavelli's development as an uncompromising exponent of political pragmatism. Most instructive of all in this context were his extensive contacts with Cesare Borgia in Romagna during 1502-1503. It was this illegitimate son of Pope Alexander VI who best exemplified the quality of manliness (*virtù*) that Machiavelli most admired in a political and military leader. Cesare Borgia's meteoric career was, however, terminated abruptly as a result of the death of his father in 1503. The new pope, Julius II, was an inveterate enemy of the entire Borgia clan and soon sent Borgia into exile, where he later died.

Julius was also responsible for terminating Machiavelli's career as a civil servant. When Louis XII of France invaded Italy and succeeded in establishing control over the Duchy of Milan, Julius proceeded to form a political coalition known as the Holy League, whose aim was to drive the invader from Italian soil. Soderini, despite Machiavelli's advice, refused to permit Florence to join the coalition and insisted on its maintaining strict neutrality throughout the entire conflict. After the expulsion of the French, Julius decided to punish the Florentine republic and compelled its citizenry to accept the return of the Medicis. Both Soderini and Machiavelli were immediately dismissed from office. On February 23, 1513, moreover, Machiavelli was falsely accused of being part of a conspiracy to reestablish the republic and put to torture on the rack. Though lack of evidence compelled the authorities to release him, he feared rearrest and decided to retire to his ancestral villa at Sant' Andrea, near Florence, together with his wife, Marietta Corsini, and their six children.

His premature retirement from public life at age forty-three enabled Machiavelli to study Roman literature and to compose many original works. His major political treatises are *Il principe* (wr. 1513, pb. 1532; *The Prince*, 1640) and *Discorsi sulla prima deca di Tito Livio* (wr. c. 1513-1517, pb. 1531; *Discourses on the First Ten Books of Titus Livius*, 1636). Since Machiavelli focuses upon issues pertaining to the governance of principalities in *The Prince* and of republics in the *Discourses*, these works constitute, in effect, a unified exposition of the author's political theories and should therefore be studied in conjunction with each other. The title of the *Discourses* is, however, misleading to the extent that this work is not really a commentary on Livy's history of ancient Rome. Machiavelli subscribed to a cyclical view of history based on the theories propounded by the Greek historian Polybius, and he used the *Discourses* to draw parallels between the events depicted by Livy and the political situation of his own time. He next tried his hand at writing comedies for a brief period. The most celebrated of his works in this genre is *La Mandragola* (c. 1519; *The Mandrake*, 1911), the other two being adaptations of plays by Terence. Foremost among the other books that Machiavelli wrote at Sant' Andrea are *Libro della arte guerra* (1521; *The Art of War*, 1560) and *Istorie fiorentine* (wr. 1520, pb. 1525; *The Florentine History*, 1595). In *The Art of War*, Machiavelli argues strongly in favor of the greater efficacy of native militias as opposed to mercenary armies, and in *The Florentine History* he chronicles the city's fortune from the fall of the Roman Empire to the death of Lorenzo the Magnificent.

Even though Machiavelli had been an ardent supporter of the republic headed by Soderini, he considered himself to be a professional civil servant above all else and burned with a desire to be of service to his native city. Machiavelli, in fact, wrote *The Prince* for the express purpose of getting the Medici family to recognize his political sagacity and offer him employment in the new regime. Within a few years, the responsibility of governing Florence passed into the lands of Lorenzo de' Medici, to whom Machiavelli decided to dedicate *The Prince*. Lorenzo, however, showed no interest in the treatise. Lorenzo died prematurely in 1519 at the age of twenty-seven and was succeeded by Cardinal Giulio de' Medici, under whose administration of the city's affairs Machiavelli's personal fortunes improved somewhat. He was entrusted with a few minor diplomatic missions on behalf of the Medicis. More important, it was Giulio who commissioned Machiavelli to write *The Florentine History*.

Giulio de' Medici became Pope Clement VII in 1521 when the immediate successor to Pope Leo died after a brief reign of twenty months. A series of diplomatic missteps on the part of Clement led to the horrendous sack of Rome in 1527 by mercenaries in the service of the German Emperor Charles V. The citizens of Florence took advantage of the occasion and expelled the Medicis from their own city for the sake of reestablishing the republic. Machiavelli expected to be reinstated in the posts that he had held under Soderini. The Florentines, however, took a dim view of Machiavelli's previous association with the Medicis and declined to entrust him with any posts in the new regime. Bitterly disappointed, Machiavelli died in Florence a scant few months after the city had regained its liberty. The eclipse of the Medicis turned out to be a short one since Pope Clement and Emperor Charles were quick to reconcile their differences. The Medicis returned to Florence in 1530, but this time they did so as a hereditary nobility. The city's days as an independent republic were thus ended forever.

Summary

Niccolò Machiavelli's political writings have elicited an unusual number of disparate reactions over the course of time. The negative viewpoint was initiated by the Roman Catholic church when it decided to ban open dissemination of Machiavelli's works by placing his entire oeuvre on its Index of Prohibited Books in 1559. Oddly enough, even though an English translation of *The Prince* did not appear until 1640, it was the frequent allusions to Machiavelli which occur in plays by Elizabethan dramatists such as Christopher Marlowe and William Shakespeare that did most to popularize his image as an evil counselor. It is generally assumed that the Elizabethan public had already derived a measure of familiarity with the contents of *The Prince* from earlier French translations of the work. Sir Francis Bacon, on the other hand, took a more favorable view of Machiavelli and hailed him as a fellow empiricist who described "what men do, and not what they ought to do." Jean-Jacques Rousseau went even further in vindicating Machiavelli by contending that the real purpose of *The Prince* was to expose the modus operandi of tyrants and thereby to advance the cause of democracy. In modern times, however, *The Prince* has frequently been called "a handbook for dictators."

Whatever may be said for and against Machiavelli's political doctrines, it is necessary to recognize that he himself was deeply committed to a republican form of government. Even after one concedes Machiavelli's genuine patriotism and his deeply held commitment to republican virtues, there are a number of disquieting elements in his political philosophy that cannot easily be dismissed. There is, for example, his excessive taste for violent and cruel solutions to political problems as reflected in his unabashed admiration for the bloody deeds of Cesare Borgia. Similarly, he held the view that morally reprehensible actions in terms of Christian standards are fully justifiable if perpetrated for what has come to be known as "reasons of state." For these and other reasons, Machiavelli continues to be a disturbing figure in the cultural pantheon of Western culture.

Bibliography

Bock, Gisela, Quentin Skinner, and Maurizio Viroli, eds. *Machiavelli and Republicanism.* Cambridge and New York: Oxford University Press, 1990. This book presents a critical examination of Machiavelli's thought, combining an accessible, historically informed account of his work with a reassessment of his central ideas and arguments. Viroli challenges the accepted interpretations of Machiavelli's work, insisting that his republicanism was based on the ideal of civic life protected by fair laws. His detailed study of the way in which Machiavelli composed *The Prince* offers a number of new interpretations.

Bondanella, Peter E. *Machiavelli and the Art of Renaissance History.* Detroit: Wayne State University Press, 1973. This astute study constitutes a chronological survey of Machiavelli's development as a literary stylist. Focuses on the compositional techniques that he employed in depicting the character and conduct of heroic personages. Lacks a formal bibliography, but there are copious endnotes for each chapter.

Grant, Ruth W. *Hypocrisy and Integrity: Machiavelli, Rousseau and the Ethics of Politics.* Chicago: University of Chicago Press, 1997. Both Machiavelli and Rousseau recognized that the irrationalities of human nature made totally honest and rational politics impossible. Drawing on their insights, Grant shows that the tasks of the politician cannot be accomplished while remaining inflexibly attached to principle. By clarifying the differences between idealism and fanaticism, moderation and rationalization, Grant's inquiry uncovers the moral limits of compromise and reveals new standards for ethical judgment.

Hale, John Rigby. *Machiavelli and Renaissance Italy.* New York: Macmillan, 1960; London: English Universities Press, 1961. Hale's primary objective is to demonstrate the extent to which Machiavelli's writings are a reflection of the political events that were unfolding in Italy during his own lifetime. Generally viewed as the best introduction to the study of Machiavelli and his age. Contains two maps and a brief annotated bibliography.

Machiavelli, Niccolò. *Machiavelli: The Chief Works and Others*. Edited and translated by Allan Gilbert. 3 vols. Durham, N.C.: Duke University Press, 1989. The most extensive collection of Machiavelli's writings currently available in English translation. Although textual annotations are dispensed with, there are succinct introductions to the individual selections as well as an outstanding index to the entire corpus.

Pitkin, Hanna Fenichel. *Fortune Is a Woman: Gender and Politics in the Thought of Niccolò Machiavelli*. Berkeley: University of California Press, 1984. This pioneering study of gender as a factor in political theory depicts Machiavelli as a misogynistic authoritarian. It is particularly useful in clarifying the manner in which Machiavelli employs the concepts of *fortuna* and *virtù*. The text is extensively annotated and supplemented by a highly detailed index and a useful bibliography of works cited.

Ridolfi, Roberto. *The Life of Niccolò Machiavelli*. Translated by Cecil Grayson. London: Routledge, and Chicago: University of Chicago Press, 1963. This biography is generally regarded as superior to the earlier efforts of Pasquale Villari and Oreste Tommassini by virtue of its focus on the course of Machiavelli's life rather than on his ideas or his cultural and historical milieu. Exhaustive documentation of sources.

Strauss, Leo. *Thoughts on Machiavelli*. Glencoe, Ill.: Free Press, 1958. The author, one of the most renowned political scientists of the modern age, argues that Machiavelli was a teacher of wickedness. This work is especially helpful in evaluating the relationship between the ideological content of *The Prince* and the *Discourses*. Minimal index, but each chapter is accompanied by extensive endnotes.

Victor Anthony Rudowski

FERDINAND MAGELLAN

Born: 1480; northern province of Minho, Portugal
Died: April, 1521; Mactan Island, the Philippines
Area of Achievement: Exploration
Contribution: Magellan was the first person to command an expedition that circumnavigated the earth. While doing so, he discovered the southernmost point of South America (later called the Strait of Magellan), was the first to sail across the Pacific Ocean (which he named), and discovered the Philippine Islands. His feat also proved that the earth is indeed round.

Early Life

Ferdinand Magellan was born in the northern Portuguese province of Minho, the third child of Dom Roy and Donha Alda Magalhães. His father was high sheriff of the district and city of Aveiro, located south of the city of Pôrto on the Atlantic coast. Magellan grew up with his siblings—sister Isabel and brother Diogo—in the Torre de Magalhães, the family farmhouse, and had a pleasant childhood in this rustic setting. At the age of seven, he attended school in the nearby monastery of Vila Nova de Mura, where he learned basic arithmetic, Latin, and the importance of harboring a strong faith in the power of Christianity.

When he was twelve, Magellan, with his father's influence, was able to travel to Lisbon and attend Queen Leonora's School of Pages with his brother, Diogo. The King of Portugal, John II, was a great supporter of marine exploration, and the young pages were expected to master such subjects as celestial navigation, cartography, and astronomy as well as the regular court subjects such as court etiquette, hunting, jousting, and swordsmanship.

In March, 1505, Magellan, his brother Diogo, and his cousin, Francisco Serrano, sailed with the fleet of Francisco de Almeida to the Orient, the three young squires having signed for a three-year service with the fleet. Magellan would serve eight years in the Orient, leaving as an extra sea hand and returning as an accomplished captain. During his service in the East, he helped establish major ports from the East African coast all the way to the Malay Peninsula. He was also involved in major confrontations with Muslim and Indian forces and was wounded several times.

Magellan, stocky in height with dark, swarthy features and piercing yet sympathetic eyes, developed strong leadership qualities and a keen appetite for adventure during his years in the East. He was also known as a fair and just man, who many times risked his life for his fellow crewmen. He was a soldier, one who could remain calm and decisive during a crisis, but one who preferred the excitement of discovery to the life of a military officer.

In July, 1511, Magellan captained a Portuguese caravel to a destination that remains unclear but was probably the Moluccas, or Spice Islands, in Indonesia, the ultimate destination of all explorers. Pepper, which was used as a food preservative by all the major countries and was therefore nearly as valuable as gold, was exported largely from the Spice Islands. During his travels, Magellan became convinced that there was an alternate route to the Spice Islands and the Indies, one that could be attained by sailing west from Europe as Christopher Columbus had done. Unlike Columbus, Magellan had knowledge of a passage around the newly discovered South American continent, previously explored by a fellow navigator and friend, John of Lisbon. John had also informed Magellan that an unexplored ocean existed through the South American passage and that the Spice Islands could be reached in a few weeks time by sailing across this ocean.

When Magellan returned to Portugal in 1512, he was anxious to find backing for an expedition to discover the new sea route. He found no support from John II's successor, King Manuel I, who was much less receptive to new exploratory ventures. Rebuffed by Portugal, Magellan sailed to Spain in October, 1517, hoping to present his proposal to King Charles I. Magellan's chief contact in Spain was Diogo Barbosa, a former Portuguese navigator who had made a fortune in the spice trade and who was now the wealthy governor of the Castle of Seville. Magellan married Barbosa's daughter, Beatriz, in December, 1517. The marriage gave Magellan much pleasure, as well as a son, Rodrigo. On March 22, 1518, Magellan secured an audience with Charles. Charles was so impressed with Magellan and his proposal that he approved the expedition that same day. Preparations were then made for what would turn out to be the most epic voyage in the history of exploration.

Life's Work

During the year it took to prepare for the voyage, Magellan dealt with all details, from the rigging and loading of the ships to preventing riots and pilferage caused by spies sent from Portugal and Venice to sabotage the voyage. In the end, Magellan triumphed and finally set sail with 277 crewmen and five ships—the *Victoria*, the *Santiago*, the *Concepcion*, the *San Antonio*, and the *Trinidad*—on September 20, 1519, from San Luca, Spain, for westward passage to the Indies.

Soon after leaving Spain, Magellan's Spanish captains, led by second-in-command Juan de Cartagena, began ridiculing Magellan's authority, attempting to provoke him so that they could justify a mutiny and take command of the voyage. Magellan, however, refused to be provoked.

After suffering major storms along the African coast and disturbing doldrums near the Equator, the ships successfully crossed the Atlantic by early December, 1519. On December 8, the coast around Cape Roque in northern Brazil was sighted. Knowing that this area was under Portuguese domain, Magellan headed south into unclaimed territory and landed in what is modern Rio de Janeiro on December 13. There the crewmen secured provisions and indulged in friendly and amorous relations with the generous natives. Two weeks later, they set sail down the coast, looking for *el paso*, the pathway first revealed to Magellan by his friend John of Lisbon.

Three months later, when no trace of *el paso* had materialized, the crew was at its breaking point. Winter storms, the worst of the expedition, began battering the ships. Magellan gave the command to seek a harbor where the ships and crew would wait out the winter for five months. The Spanish captains thought that he was mad and urged him to sail eastward for Africa's Cape of Good Hope and follow the old route to the Indies. The crew wanted him to return to the idyllic harbor at Rio de Janeiro and spend the winter there. Magellan, however, held firm.

The armada anchored at San Julián in southern Argentina on March 31, 1520. The following evening, the Spanish captains mutined. Under the leadership of Juan de Cartagena, they quickly secured three of the five ships. During a confusing boat exchange of crewmen between mutinous ships, Magellan was able to capture one of the small boatloads of men, substitute his own men for the mutiny sympathizers, and send the boat back to one of the Spanish captains along with another boat load of Magellan's men. While the Spanish captain was dealing with the first boat load, one of Magellan's men suddenly pulled out a knife and stabbed the mutinous captain as the second boat load reached the ship and scrambled on deck, ready to do battle with the rebellious crew. The crew, shocked by the sudden turn of events, became sympathetic to Magellan once more. With three ships in his favor, Magellan surrounded the other two ships and forced the remaining captains to surrender.

A trial was held for the mutineers. Two men were beheaded, and their ringleader, Juan de Cartagena, was set adrift in a small boat, never to be seen again. Through the ordeal of the mutiny, in fact through every ordeal the expedition faced, Magellan remained strong and decisive. The fact that he never doubted his ability to succeed with his mission ultimately inspired his crew to follow him, even when conditions were unbearable.

The expedition spent a total of seven months waiting for the storms to subside, first at San Julián and then farther south at Puerto Santa Cruz, where the *Santiago* was smashed against the shoreline and lost. Finally, on October 18, they set sail once again in search of *el paso*. Three days later, they came to a narrow inlet protected on either side by jagged cliffs. The inlet seemed too dangerous to navigate, but Magellan, by now appearing nearly insane to his crew, ordered the *Concepcion* and the *San Antonio* to explore the inlet. The two ships had just entered the pathway when a storm suddenly rose and swept the ships through the inlet and out of sight, while forcing Magellan's *Trinidad* and the *Victoria* out to sea. For two days, Magellan fought the storm until he was able to return to the inlet where the *Concepcion* and the *San Antonio* had disappeared. Close to panic, fearing that the two ships had been destroyed, Magellan entered the treacherous pathway. The following morning, a cloud of smoke was sighted. Then, miraculously, the two lost ships sailed into view, flags and pennants waving and crewmen cheering excitedly. They had found *el paso*.

Navigation of the strait (which Magellan called the Strait of Desire, but which was later named for him) was not complete until mid-November. During that period, the *San Antonio* disappeared. Magellan searched for the missing ship until it became apparent that the *San Antonio* had deserted and returned to Spain. Because the *San Antonio* was the largest ship and carried the bulk of their provisions, the crew urged Magellan to turn back as well. Magellan, however, would not be deterred. After the three remaining ships had sailed out of the treacherous strait and into the surprisingly calm waters of a new ocean, Magellan spoke to his men: "We are about to stand into an ocean where no ship has ever sailed before. May the ocean be always as calm and benevolent as it is today. In this hope, I name it the Mar Pacifico [peaceful sea]."

No one encountering the Pacific Ocean for the first time could have anticipated its immensity. In the following three months, nearly half of the remaining men died of starvation and scurvy. Magellan was unfortunate in that his course across the Pacific Ocean led him away from all the major groups of islands that would have supplied him with necessary provisions. During the ghastly voyage across the Pacific Ocean, Magellan threw his maps overboard in anguish, knowing that they were uselessly inaccurate. Some of the men began to believe the old superstition that the ocean would lead them not to the other side of the world but to the end of the world. When the food rotted and the water turned to scum, the dying men began eating rats and sawdust. On March 4, 1531, all the food was gone. Two days later, after ninety-eight days and thirteen thousand miles across the mightiest ocean on the planet, they reached Guam and salvation.

Taking on provisions at Guam was made difficult by the weakened state of the men and the hostility of the natives. As quickly as he could, Magellan set sail and, on March 16, found the island of Samar in the Philippines. Magellan had now achieved his personal goal, having discovered a new chain of islands for Spain. Here the expedition rested and the sick were tended, Magellan personally nursing his emaciated men.

On March 28, during the start of Easter weekend, the crew held a pageant to which the natives were invited. Magellan had made friends with the local raja and began encouraging him and his followers to convert to Christianity, which they did by the thousands. Inspired by this enthusiastic acceptance of his religion, Magellan decided not only to claim the island chain for Spain but also to convert as many natives to Christanity as he could. His desire to reach the Spice Islands, always of secondary importance to him, faded as he became more determined to make the Philippines his ultimate destination.

One month later, after exploring more of the Philippines and being favorably accepted, Magellan attempted to force the powerful raja of the island of Mactan to honor Magellan's presence. When the raja refused, Magellan assembled a small army of volunteers and the next morning, on April 27, 1521, led an attack on the raja and his followers. Because of all the hardships he had encountered and con-

quered, and because his expedition had now taken on a divine mission, Magellan must have come to think of himself as invincible. Unfortunately, he realized too late that he was not.

Magellan quickly realized that he and his men were hopelessly outnumbered. When he ordered a retreat, a panic ensued in which his men scrambled to the shoreline and frantically rowed back to the ships, leaving Magellan and a handful of men stranded. For more than an hour, the men defended themselves as the rest of the crew watched from the ships, until finally Magellan was struck down and killed. Antonio Pigafetta, the chronicler of the voyage, was one of the men who fought beside Magellan when he was struck down. Pigafetta was able to escape during the frenzy that followed. Later he wrote: "And so they slew our mirror, our light, our comfort and our true and only guide."

Summary

On September 8, 1522, sixteen months after Ferdinand Magellan's death, a floating wreck of a ship with an emaciated crew of eighteen men sailed into the harbor of Seville, Spain. The ship was the *Vic-*

toria. The men, led by Juan Sebastián de Elcano, a former mutineer, staggered out of the ship and marched barefoot through the streets to the shrine of Santa Maria de la Victoria, Our Lady of Victory, the favorite shrine of their fallen leader. They lit candles and said prayers for their dead comrades, then proceeded through the streets of Seville, shocking the citizens with their wasted appearance. The *Victoria* had returned laden with riches from the Spice Islands, which had indeed been reached on November 8, 1521. As for the fate of the remaining two ships, the *Concepcion* had been burned before reaching the Spice Islands and the *Trinidad* had been captured by the Portuguese, its fifty-two crewmen hanged.

Magellan's reputation was at first defiled and degraded by his contemporaries as they learned about his behavior from the crew of the *San Antonio*, the ship that had deserted in South America. Later, however, the magnitude of his accomplishments could not be denied. He had proved that the Indies could be reached by sailing west, had discovered a pathway around the southern tip of South America, had named and crossed the largest body of ocean on the planet, had discovered a new chain of islands, had accumulated a mountain of new information about navigation, geography, and exploration, and had commanded an expedition which, after three years and forty-two thousand miles, had circumnavigated the world.

Bibliography

Cameron, Ian. *Magellan and the First Circumnavigation of the World*. London: Weidenfeld and Nicolson, and New York: Saturday Review Press, 1973. Generously illustrated with maps, woodcuts, and drawings, this biography of Magellan details his life and his voyage and uses generous quotes from other biographers as well as passages from the journal of Antonio Pigafetta. Includes a selected bibliography.

Craig, Simon. "The Ship that Shrank the World." *Geographical Magazine* 69 (September, 1997): 64. The author focuses on the geographical discoveries of Magellan, detailing the discovery of the Spice Islands, the voyage that located the sea passage now known as the Magellan Strait, and the conversion of the Philippines to Christianity.

Humble, Richard. *The Explorers*. Alexandria, Va.: Time-Life Books, 1978. Contains an overview of the accomplishments of the four most significant Renaissance explorers: Bartolomeu Dias, Christopher Columbus, Vasco da Gama, and Magellan. Nearly a third of the book is devoted to Magellan. Includes excellent maps and charts plus an illustrated section on the ships and navigational instruments used by the explorers, as well as a detailed description of the *Victoria*. Includes a selected bibliography.

Parr, Charles McKew. *So Noble a Captain: The Life and Times of Ferdinand Magellan*. New York: Crowell, 1953; London: Hale, 1955. The definitive biography of Magellan. Traces Magellan's ancestry, details the lives of all the principal men and women who affected or were affected by Magellan, vividly re-creates the time in which he lived, and chronicles his accomplishments in minute detail. Contains an extensive bibliography, including books on such related subjects as the history of Spain and Portugal, sailing-ship construction, navigation, and various locations visited by Magellan.

Pigafetta, Antonio. *Magellan's Voyage: A Narrative Account of the First Circumnavigation*. Translated by R. A. Skelton. New Haven, Conn.: Yale University Press, 1969; London: Folio Society, 1975. This is an English translation from a French text of Pigafetta's Italian journal. It is full of detailed descriptions of the events of the voyage, the lands discovered, the natives encountered and their habits and customs, and the tales told by the natives and examples of their vocabulary.

Sanderlin, George. *First Around the World: A Journal of Magellan's Voyage*. New York: Harper, 1964. An interesting reconstruction of Magellan's life and voyage using letters and journals of Magellan's contemporaries. The early texts are linked by comments from the author. Most of the book is composed of excerpts from Pigafetta's journal. Illustrated, with a selected bibliography.

Zweig, Stefan. *Conqueror of the Seas: The Story of Magellan*. Translated by Eden Paul and Cedar Paul. New York: Viking Press, 1938. A full account of Magellan's life from the time of his first voyage in 1505 to his death, and the results of his epic voyage. Contains maps and illustrations of the principal events taken from early texts.

James Kline

SIR THOMAS MALORY

Born: Early fifteenth century; Warwickshire or Cambridgeshire

Died: 1469 or 1471; Cambridgeshire or London

Area of Achievement: Literature

Contribution: Combining French prose, Arthurian romances, and some English materials with stories of his own invention, Malory set the Arthurian legend in its enduring form in *Le Morte d'Arthur.*

Early Life

The problem in writing the biography of the most famous author of Arthurian stories is that it is not known with any certainty who he was. At one time or another, scholars have championed no fewer than nine Thomas Malorys, but perhaps only three of those men deserve serious attention.

The primary conditions for establishing the author's identity come from the text of *Le Morte d'Arthur* itself. Modern scholars have available to them the first printed edition, produced in 1485 by William Caxton, and also in the late fifteenth century manuscript version, found in the library of Winchester College in 1934 by Walter F. Oakeshott. "Syr Thomas Maleoré, Knyght" tells his readers that he has completed the work in the ninth year of the reign of Edward IV (that is, March 4, 1469, to March 3, 1470) and asks them to pray for his "good delyuerance" from prison. In the "explicit," the formal statement ending the first of the eight tales that make up the whole book in the Winchester manuscript, Malory again suggests that he is a knight prisoner. Thus, one knows that the author was a knight, was of an age to write the work in 1469-1470, and was a prisoner of some sort. That the printer Caxton knew so little about Malory suggests further that Malory had died by the time the book was printed, or before July, 1485.

Throughout most of the twentieth century, the man who was thought to have best met these qualifications was a Thomas Malory of Newbold Revel in Warwickshire. George L. Kittredge had made this identification most forcefully in his influential article "Who Was Sir Thomas Malory?" written in 1896. As Kittredge and other scholars supported this choice of the Warwickshire Malory with further evidence in later publications, the link appeared to become increasingly sound. Some scholars began to treat it as established fact; Sir Thomas Malory was the author and a man by that name and rank could be identified who seemed to meet the qualifications; therefore, Sir Thomas Malory of Newbold Revel had written *Le Morte d'Arthur.* In many ways, he fit the part. This Malory was a member of an old Warwickshire family; he had served for a quarter of a century in the wars in France, following Richard Beauchamp, Earl of Warwick, a mirror of chivalry to his contemporaries; and he had been a Member of Parliament for Warwickshire in 1445-1446.

Yet there were troublesome aspects to this identification, for the Warwickshire Malory was at least accused of committing a remarkable series of crimes between 1450 and 1460. The list of charges included attempted murder, rape (twice, against the same victim), cattle raiding, extortion, and raids on an abbey. He was imprisoned eight times and twice escaped dramatically. Could this man actually have written the great chivalric tale of Arthur and his knights of the Round Table? Could a man who seemed so immoral have produced what many readers considered a moral book? Some scholars tried to excuse Malory, arguing that he had been simply indicted, not convicted. Others merely shrugged off the charges as evidence of the vigorous acts of a man living in a violent age. Eugène Vinaver, the editor of the standard edition of *Le Morte d'Arthur,* frankly stated that the morality of the author was not the same issue as the morality of his artistic work.

Until 1966, those scholars troubled by the "morality issue" or, more generally, by the identification of the Warwickshire knight with the author had no strong opposition candidate. In that year, however, William Matthews criticized the case for the leading candidate and advanced a previously unknown Thomas Malory who came from Hutton Conyers in Yorkshire. He supported this Malory from the north of England by pointing to northern elements in the Winchester text—in vocabulary and usage, in a preference for northern geographical locations, and in a frequent use of northern romances as sources. That this Thomas Malory could not be proved either a knight or a prisoner presented obstacles, but Matthews argued that "knight prisoner" might mean "prisoner of war." Some scholars found these arguments appealing; few found them convincing. Specialists, for example, have cast doubts on the validity of the linguistic evidence. Yet the question of identity, formerly more or less considered settled on the

Warwickshire knight, once again seemed to be a matter for debate.

The likelihood of further debate increased in 1981, when Richard R. Griffith reopened a case for a candidate from Papworth St. Agnes, a tiny village in Cambridgeshire on the border with Huntingdonshire. This Thomas Malory had been considered as long ago as 1897 but had been dismissed ever since. Griffith thinks the dialect, age, and political affiliations of the Cambridgeshire Malory fit the author perfectly. He argues that his candidate was briefly imprisoned before his execution (for reasons of politics, not crime) in September of 1469 (Malory's prayer for good deliverance thus being in vain). Griffith suggests that this Malory had access to the one library in England likely to have contained all the French romances that went into *Le Morte d'Arthur.* Though there is no incontrovertible proof that this Malory was a knight, Griffith makes a plausible case that he possessed the status so crucial to his identification with the author.

Supporters of the traditional author, the Warwickshire knight, have continued to advance and modify their case. P. J. C. Field, for example, having eliminated a claim for a second Warwickshire knight, a Thomas Malory of Fenny Newbold (by proving that Newbold Revel and Fenny Newbold were simply two names for the same place), has clarified the birth date of Malory, altering the chronology for his entire career. Field suggests a birth date of about 1416, putting the Warwickshire Malory in his mid-thirties and early forties when imprisoned and about age fifty-five when he died in 1471. This chronology eliminates the idea of Malory's long wartime service with that great knight, the Earl of Warwick, but it provides a chronology that fits the author quite well.

Life's Work

Whoever Sir Thomas Malory the author was, his enduring achievement was the writing of *Le Morte d'Arthur.* Yet this work has no more been free from controversy than its author. Two issues in particular have attracted attention and generated debate. In the nineteenth century, many scholars concentrated on identifying Malory's sources and began to debate the issue of his originality. By the twentieth century, scholarship on Malory had tended to focus instead on the structure of *Le Morte d'Arthur* and debated the issue of the unity of the work.

The emphasis on Malory's sources focused first on his numerous French sources (such as the Prose *Tristan* and the Vulgate *Queste del Saint Graal*, both written in about 1230) and only later considered his English sources (such as the alliterative *Morte Arthure*, which also dates back to about 1230). The emphasis on sources coincided with the tendency during the nineteenth century to consider Malory a "mere" translator or compiler, rather than an author of much originality. Yet, increasingly, scholars began to describe Malory as a conscious artist, selecting and adapting his sources, creating from their immense diversity and bulk a set of Arthurian stories that above all bear the stamp of his own originality and style. From the complex French tales, with their elaborately interwoven incidents (using a technique called intertwining, or *entrelacement*), Malory wrote a long story of eight sequential, cumulative, major sections (as in the Winchester manuscript, though there are twenty-one books as printed by Caxton), culminating in the dramatic collapse of the fellowship of the Round Table.

The question of originality led to the discussions of unity more common in twentieth century scholarship on Malory: What was the structure of *Le Morte d'Arthur*? Did Malory intend and achieve a unified work of art? Vinaver placed such questions at the forefront of discussion by giving his 1947 edition of the work (based on the Winchester manuscript) the controversial title *The Works of Sir Thomas Malory.* Although Vinaver softened his views in a second edition published in 1967, he considered Malory primarily a translator of French Arthurian tales and argued that he actually adapted eight separate romances, not a single book. This latter contention was hotly debated for at least the following two decades. Robert M. Lumiansky and Charles Moorman vigorously argued that in *Le Morte d'Arthur* Malory shows clear intent of linking the eight tales and that he succeeded in making them a unified book. The views of Vinaver's critics appear most clearly in a volume edited by Lumiansky and significantly titled *Malory's Originality: A Critical Study of Le Morte Darthur* (1964) and in Charles Moorman's *The Book of Kyng Arthur: The Unity of Malory's "Morte Darthur"* (1965).

Summary

The uncertainties and the scholarly debates about Sir Thomas Malory and his work must be considered, but they should not obscure his achievement and importance. It is through Malory and his great book (or books) that English-language readers know the stories of King Arthur, Queen Guinevere, Sir

Lancelot, Sir Gareth, and Sir Tristram, and of the Quest for the Holy Grail, the Round Table, and Camelot. In telling these stories, Malory has delighted his readers for hundreds of years. As Vinaver wrote:

> Perhaps none of this would have seemed real to us if so much of it were not conveyed in a form which in a very true sense creates its own substance, a prose both crisp and resonant, blending the majesty of epic eloquence with the freshness of living speech. How strange and yet how instructive the contrast between the appeal of the work to English readers and the neglect into which the Arthurian legend fell in the country where it found its first poetic expression! . . . [Malory's] magic spell . . . had revived in English prose the quests of Arthurian knights, the epic grandeur of their grim battles, and the "piteous tale" of the fall of Arthur's kingdom.

Bibliography

Bennett, J. A. W., ed. *Essays on Malory.* Oxford: Clarendon Press, 1963. Seven essays by various scholars debating significant aspects of Malory's work.

Field, P. J. C. "Sir Thomas Malory, M.P." *Bulletin of the Institute of Historical Research* 47 (1974): 24-35. Supports the Warwickshire candidate proposed by Kittredge over Matthews' Yorkshire candidate. Shows that there were not two Warwickshire Malorys.

———. "Thomas Malory: The Hutton Documents." *Medium Aevum* 48 (1979): 213-239. Argues that there was only one Sir Thomas Malory alive in 1468-1470, and this is the Warwickshire Malory.

Griffith, Richard R. "The Authorship Question Reconsidered: A Case for Thomas Malory of Papworth St. Agnes, Cambridgeshire." In *Aspects of Malory,* edited by Toshiyuki Takamiya and Derek Brewer. Woodbridge, Suffolk: Brewer, and Totowa, N.J.: Rowman and Littlefield, 1981. Elaborate argument for the Malory from Papworth St. Agnes.

Kittredge, George Lyman. "Who Was Sir Thomas Malory?" *Harvard Studies and Notes in Philology and Literature* 5 (1896): 85-106. The essay which placed the Warwickshire Malory in the front rank among contenders for authorship of *Le Morte d'Arthur.*

Life, Page West. *Sir Thomas Malory and the Morte Darthur: A Survey of Scholarship and Annotated Bibliography.* Charlottesville: University Press of Virginia, 1980. An indispensable guide to all topics concerning Malory and all scholarship before 1980. The annotated bibliography lists nearly one thousand items; the introductory essay provides a highly useful survey of scholarship.

Lumiansky, Robert M. *Malory's Originality: A Critical Study of Le Morte Darthur.* Baltimore: Johns Hopkins University Press, 1964. Eight essays by different authors, each examining the function of an individual tale in Malory's book as a whole.

Malory, Sir Thomas. *The Works of Sir Thomas Malory.* Edited by Eugène Vinaver. 3d ed. Oxford: Clarendon Press, and New York: Oxford University Press, 1990. The standard edition. Oxford also published a one-volume paperback edition in 1971, minus the introduction, critical apparatus, index, and bibliography, but including a revised glossary, summaries of Vinaver's original commentary on each romance, and explanatory notes.

Matthews, William. *The Ill-Framed Knight: A Skeptical Inquiry into the Identity of Sir Thomas Malory.* Berkeley: University of California Press, 1966. Matthews' attack on the Warwickshire Malory as author and his case for the Yorkshire Malory.

Moorman, Charles. *The Book of Kyng Arthur: The Unity of Malory's "Morte Darthur."* Lexington: University Press of Kentucky, 1965. Incorporates a number of his articles published earlier, discussing important aspects of Malory and themes of his work.

Richard W. Kaeuper

ANDREA MANTEGNA

Born: c. 1431; Isola di Cartura, Republic of Venice
Died: September 13, 1506; Mantua
Area of Achievement: Art
Contribution: Mantegna contributed to the growth of Renaissance art in northern Italy while at the same time creating an individual style appreciated for its powers of invention, directness of presentation, illusionism, and detailed realism. His most important contributions were centered in his roles as transmitter of the Florentine Renaissance to his northern Italian contemporaries and as artistic interpreter of antiquity for his own and succeeding generations.

Early Life

Andrea Mantegna was born in Isola di Cartura, near Padua, in northern Italy. His probable birth date of 1431 is based on an inscription, preserved in early documents, from a lost altarpiece of 1448 executed for the Church of Santa Sofia in Padua. It lists his age as seventeen when the project reached completion. Little is known of Mantegna's life before he reached the age of ten. At that time his father, Biagio, a carpenter, gave him up for adoption to the painter Francesco Squarcione, who appears to have acted as adoptive father to several talented boys. In addition to his activities as a painter, collector, and dealer, Squarcione trained his young charges while providing them with a home and the necessities of life. Once their schooling was complete, the master contracted with wealthy patrons for the services of his young protégés.

Mantegna served his apprenticeship in the workshop of his adoptive father from 1442 to 1448. During the 1440's in Padua, Squarcione's *bottega* functioned as an exchange for ideas and methods among important artists and craftsmen. In this ambience, Mantegna was introduced to the best talents and the latest artistic developments of the time. The superior genius of Donatello, the Florentine sculptor, provided a focus for Paduan art from 1443 to 1453. Donatello's works must have been a major topic of conversation among artists and patrons who frequented Squarcione's workshop.

Other Florentine artists influenced Mantegna's development through the agency of Squarcione's *bottega*. In 1447, the master and his apprentices moved to Venice and resided there for several months. Paolo Uccello, Fra Filippo Lippi, and Andrea del Castagno had preceded them by the period of a decade or more, and at different times. These artists had all left the mark of the Florentine Renaissance on the city of canals and lagoons. It should also be noted that Lippi had executed in Padua works that Mantegna would already have seen. Elements peculiar to the individual styles of these artists were transmitted to Mantegna at that formative period in his career.

The atmosphere of Squarcione's shop, with its constant activity and opportunity for dialogue, provided Mantegna with all the conditions necessary for his accelerated development as a painter. Squarcione's own approach to painting appears to have had minimal impact on Mantegna. The importance, however, of Donatello and the new Florentine art in the formation of Mantegna's style is universally recognized and may be clearly distinguished in the young artist's paintings of the 1450's. In addition to providing Mantegna with an entrée into the contemporary art circles, Squarcione instilled in his adopted son a love of antiquity. The influence of classical art and literature appear constantly in Mantegna's earliest and latest work.

Mantegna's early training came to a close in 1448. In January, the young man sued Squarcione over the terms of his adoption and what he considered to be insufficient compensation for his six years as an apprentice. The two men reached a compromise that enabled Mantegna to declare his independence and to take control of his own finances. It seems extraordinary that Mantegna was able to do this at the tender age of seventeen, unless he had made significant contributions as a member of Squarcione's *bottega*, thereby establishing his reputation as a painter of great potential.

Life's Work

Mantegna received his first major independent commission in May, 1448. The plan for decoration of the Ovetari Chapel in the Church of the Eremitani in Padua included provisions for an altar and frescoes with scenes from the lives of Saints James and Christopher, who were patron saints of the church. At the outset, Mantegna shared this work with several other artists. For several reasons, including the death of two participants and withdrawal from the project by the others, Mantegna was left with a large number of scenes to finish by himself. The three standing figures of Saint Peter, Saint Paul, and Saint Christopher in the

vault of the chapel's apse were probably the earliest frescoes that Mantegna completed. If this is true, they were done while Niccolò Pizzolo, a Paduan painter who initially shared Mantegna's half of the commission, was still alive. Modern scholarship supports the conclusion that Pizzolo may have had an even stronger influence on Mantegna's artistic formation than Squarcione. As Mantegna's older associate in the Ovetari venture, Pizzolo may have cemented the connection between the younger artist and the new Florentine art. Mantegna's three saints do not have the strong sculptural quality of Pizzolo's adjacent figures, but the draperies are carefully studied and the poses are harmonious and symmetrically balanced in the new manner.

Saint James Baptizing Hermogenes and *Saint James Before Herod Agrippa* are the first completely mature works by Mantegna in the Ovetari Chapel. The painter's thorough knowledge of Leon Battista Alberti's perspective system, published in *De pictura* (1435; *Of Painting*, 1726), is visible in the precisely measured perspective grid of each fresco as well as in the common vanishing point employed for these two adjacent scenes. The classical derivation of the architectural settings and the sculptural decorations in these works reveal Mantegna's growing love of the antique. Although there is no direct proof, the soldier standing in the right foreground of *Saint James Before Herod Agrippa* is often identified as a self-portrait. The sharp angular features and the distinct frown fit written descriptions of Mantegna's serious and often severe demeanor.

Two other scenes, *Saint James Led to Execution* and *Martyrdom of Saint James*, are impressive in their continued exploration of perspective and figural relationships. Their position on the wall places the lower edge of each composition approximately at eye level, making the figures and architecture appear to move down the picture plane as they recede in the picture space. Several of the figures in the foreground seem to violate the picture plane and project into the viewer's space. By this time, such effects were common in Florentine painting but still quite unusual in northern Italian art. The sculptural, stony quality of Mantegna's figures was very likely a result of his love of ancient sculpture and an appreciation for the work of Donatello. This sculpturesque quality combined with the northern Italian penchant for detailed realism are two of the major components of Mantegna's mature style. During the nine years the painter worked in the Ovetari Chapel, from 1448 to 1457, his formation as a major Renaissance artist occurred.

Between 1457 and 1459, Mantegna was occupied with the commission for a major altarpiece for the Church of San Zeno in Verona. The main part of this polyptych consists of three panels which depict a *Madonna Enthroned with Saints*. The carved and gilded wooden frame with its arched pediment and entablature form a temple format using the Corinthian order. Its design and the general placement of the figures in the painting are thought to reflect the original disposition, now much changed, of the principal elements in Donatello's altar for Sant' Antonio. Mantegna visually attached the columns of the frame to piers in the painting and continued the illusion by creating a square loggia that encompasses the Madonna, the Christ Child, and the saints, while defining the perspective space of the picture. A "classical" frieze of cherubs, clearly Mantegna's own invention, surrounds the level above the piers. The spatially conceived garland of fruit painted at the front of the picture, the crisp detail, and the bright colors show Mantegna at his best. The San Zeno altarpiece sets the tone for a whole group of works of this category in northern Italian art in the fifteenth and sixteenth centuries.

By 1459, Mantegna had accepted the invitation of the Marchese Ludovico Gonzaga, Lord of Mantua, to become his court painter. As one of the first Renaissance artists officially attached to a princely court, Mantegna found himself painting altarpieces, frescoing churches, decorating palaces, and even designing costumes and entertainments for lavish court pageants. The frescoes of the Camera degli Sposi (chamber of the bride and groom) in the Gonzaga Palace were painted between 1465 and 1474, and are considered to be major works in Mantegna's mature style. He covered the walls and ceiling of the square chamber with scenes from the life of the Gonzaga family. The left wall contains a depiction of the meeting between Ludovico Gonzaga and his son, Cardinal Francesco. The Gonzaga court is shown on the right wall, and the ceiling fresco takes the form of a circular architectural opening, the eye, or oculus, of a dome. The intermediate zone, which ties the lower scenes to the oculus, consists of illusionistically painted transverse arches that crisscross a flattened domical ceiling and encompass wreathed medallions containing the busts of Roman emperors. Although there is a wealth of classical allusion juxtaposed with scenes from the life of the Gonzaga family, the exact meaning and relationship of the parts have not yet been satisfactorily explained. The overall design and meticulous detail of the chamber reveal Mantegna's genius as a decorator and his skill with *trompe l'oeil* effects. The oculus in particular is a tour de force of perspective and foreshortening and, when viewed from the proper vantage point beneath, surprises and amuses the viewer with the artist's expertise and gentle sense of humor.

Mantegna continued in the service of the Gonzagas after Ludovico's death in 1478, first for Federico and then for Francesco. Francesco presented Mantegna to Pope Innocent VIII in June, 1488, and this trip to Rome gave Mantegna the opportunity to study the classical antiquities of the Eternal City. In addition, he was commissioned by the pope to paint a small chapel in the Vatican. Upon his return from Rome in 1491, a change occurred in Mantegna's style. The paintings of his late period, such as the *Madonna of the Victory* (1495), are almost overrefined. Linear elements increase in complexity and tend to rob figures and objects of their three-dimensional form. The brilliance of the earlier works is exchanged for softer tones. While still the works of a great painter, the later productions lack the force and vitality of his youth, and instead evoke an idyllic mood of quiet and gentleness.

The *Triumph of Caesar* (begun c. 1486) was the last great series created by Mantegna. These enormous canvases painted in tempera are 274 by 274 centimeters and represent a theme based on Petrarch's description of a triumphal procession. Clearly inspired by Mantegna's trip to Rome, these works are the masterpieces of his late style. They are carefully planned and executed to provide a continuity of atmosphere from one canvas to the next as the procession unfolds. They are also so precisely detailed that they present an unparalleled feeling of truth to nature. Yet, in all of their complexity of line, foreshortening, and changes in scale, designed to portray the noise and clamor of such an event, they exude the same curious quietness and serenity that mark many of Mantegna's late works.

A letter from Mantegna's son to Francesco Gonzaga tells of the artist's death at seven in the evening on Sunday, September 13, 1506. Although Mantegna suffered from recurring ill health and financial problems toward the end of his life, he remained an active and innovative figure in northern Italian art to the end.

Summary

Andrea Mantegna stands forth as a major figure in the history of Renaissance art. For his northern contemporaries, he functioned as an important interpreter of the new Florentine art. He was among the very few artists working in Padua, Venice, or the other princely states of the north who was intellectually prepared to understand and absorb the full meaning and potential of the art of Paolo Uccello, Filippo Lippi, Andrea del Castagno, and Donatello. Mantegna's coherent and consistent vision of the physical world, fostered by his Florentine contacts, became the standard to which his contemporaries conformed. His passion for perspective devices and foreshortening was also born of this connection. Mantegna combined his knowledge of the new Florentine experiments with the native northern Italian tradition of detailed realism and created a style that guided his own generation and the next into a full-fledged Renaissance.

Mantegna was also the principal interpreter of antiquity for his generation. His constant use of classical references, real or invented, resulted in the synthesis of ancient and contemporary forms and ideas central to any definition of the Italian Renaissance. Mantegna had the courage to use his artistic genius to the fullest, to give free rein to his intellectual curiosity about the distant past, and to use his talent to explore the latest contemporary developments in art. He was truly and completely a man of his time and deserves to be remembered as a major contributor to the northern Italian Renaissance.

Bibliography

Camesasca, Ettore. *Mantegna*. New York: Harper, and London: Summerfield, 1981. A well-illustrated survey that contains a discussion of all the major works of the artist and includes reference to the most recent primary evidence that sheds light on the artist's career and production. Presents summaries of many of the scholarly arguments relative to questions about Mantegna's work in an attempt to arrive at a consensus concerning perennial problems in the artist's oeuvre. Includes excellent color reproductions and a good general bibliography.

Carr, Dawson W. *Andrea Mantegna: The Adoration of the Magi*. Los Angeles: J. Paul Getty Trust Museum, 1997. The Getty Museum's magnificent painting by Mantegna, *The Adoration of the Magi*, is based on one of Christianity's most beloved stories: the arrival of the gift-bearing Wise Men at Jesus' crib. Carr explores Andrea Mantegna's life and milieu in fifteenth century Padua, the influence on the artist's career of the revolutionary theoretical ideas of his time, comparable works by Mantegna as well as other artists, and the significance of the subject matter in Christian theology.

Fiocco, Giuseppe. *The Frescoes of Mantegna in the Eremitani Church, Padua*. Introduction by Terisio Pignatti. 2d ed. Oxford and New York: Phaidon Press, 1978. This definitive study of the Ovetari frescoes was first published in 1947, after the destruction of the chapel by stray bombs during World War II. Updated by Pignatti to include all the more recent research, which includes new documentation that confirms Fiocco's original assertions about Mantegna's part in the frescoes and the influences at work on him.

Greenstein, Jack M. *Mantegna and Painting as Historical Narrative*. Chicago: University of Chicago Press, 1992. Interpretation and criticism of one of the most enigmatic and influential works of the Renaissance, the Uffizi "Circumcision of Christ." Greenstein reassesses the nature and goals of high humanist narrative painting.

Hartt, Frederick. *History of Italian Renaissance Art*. 4th ed. London: Thames and Hudson, and Englewood Cliffs, N.J.: Prentice Hall, 1994. The most recent comprehensive survey of Italian Renaissance art, including painting, sculpture, and architecture. Written for the general reader and copiously illustrated with black-and-white and color illustrations.

Kristeller, Paul. *Andrea Mantegna*. London and New York: Longman, 1901. The earliest definitive monograph on Mantegna, marked by a scholarly and thorough use of all available documentary evidence related to the life and work of the artist. This monograph is a valuable and comprehensive study that will reward the serious reader with many insights about Mantegna's contributions to Renaissance painting.

Mantegna, Andrea. *All the Paintings of Mantegna*. Text by Renata Cipriani. Translated by Paul Colacicchi. 2 vols. London: Oldbourne, and New York: Hawthorn, 1964. Illustrates in black-and-white all the known and attributed works of the artist. Contains a general essay on Mantegna's life and work, biographical notes and dates, a brief catalog of works, selected criticism, and a selected bibliography. Good as a quick reference.

John W. Myers

MANUEL I

Born: May 31, 1469; Alcochete, Portugal
Died: December 13, 1521; Lisbon, Portugal
Area of Achievement: Monarchy
Contribution: Manuel I, known as "the Fortunate," is considered one of Portugal's most illustrious monarchs. His reign represents the zenith of Portuguese imperial strength. Continuing the centralizing trends and overseas expansion policies of his predecessors, Manuel brought both to a climax, while presiding over a court remarkable for its splendor.

Early Life

Manuel I of Portugal was born in the town of Alcochete on the east bank of the Tagus River. He came from a prominent family, the youngest of nine children of Prince Fernão, the Duke of Viseu. He was a grandson of King Afonso V, a cousin to King John II, and the younger brother of John's queen Leonor. Despite the prominence of his family, Manuel's upbringing was filled with turmoil. Four of his elder brothers died before he reached adulthood. In 1484, in reaction to the growing threat of royal absolutism, his brother, the Duke of Viseu, became involved, along with other members of the nobility, in a plot against John. The plot was discovered and the duke died by the king's own hand. Yet the intervention of his sister the queen protected Manuel's interests. When John's only legitimate son, Afonso, died in 1491, Leonor was able to block his attempts to have his illegitimate son, Jorge, declared his heir. Instead John was forced to accept Manuel, Leonor's last surviving brother, as the future king. When John died on October 25, 1495, Manuel, Duke of Beja and Master of the Order of Christ, ascended the throne as the fifth monarch from the House of Avis. Historian H. V. Livermore describes the twenty-six-year-old monarch as "fair, rather thin, diligent, sparing in his food and drink, musical, vain, and fond of display." These personal traits would also be characteristic of Manuel's administration.

Life's Work

As king, Manuel continued the centralization of royal power begun by his predecessors. Ironically, he benefited from the results of John's ruthless policy of breaking the independent power of the nobility that had led to his elder brother's death. There was now much greater acceptance of royal authority. Manuel was able to strengthen royal authority further in a number of ways. The three military orders came under the control of the Crown, and memberships were dispensed as rewards for royal service. A system of royal allowances encouraged the nobility to reside at court, where their actions could be more easily monitored while at the same time increasing their financial dependency on the Crown. The system of justice was centralized and the laws codified by the compilation of the first modern legal code, called the Ordinances of King Manuel. Administrative power began to pass from the old privileged groups into the hands of an expanding royal bureaucracy, much of it consisting of university-trained legists dependent on the monarch for their livelihood. Manuel called the Cortes only four times in his twenty-six-year reign, reflecting the Crown's lessening dependence on it as a source of revenue. Weights and measures were standardized after 1499 to facilitate national trade. In the early sixteenth century, Manuel introduced Portugal's first postal system, which helped to link the countryside to Lisbon and the royal court.

The greatest achievements attributed to Manuel's tenure as king came in overseas expansion. After nearly a century of success in exploring and mapping the African coast, as Manuel took the throne, Portuguese navigators were poised to open an all-water trade route to India. Vasco da Gama's groundbreaking voyage (1497-1499) had been authorized and planned before John's death, and it was left to Manuel to implement his predecessor's plans. Following da Gama's triumphal return from India, the king obtained papal confirmation of the discoveries and assembled a huge fleet under Pedro Álvars Cabral to follow up on contacts. On this voyage, Cabral made contact with lands on the western side of the southern Atlantic, thus establishing Portugal's claim to Brazil. He then completed his voyage to India. Portuguese trade contacts in India and other lands bordering the Indian Ocean continued to expand during Manuel's reign. This trade, transacted at enormous profit, made Portugal the richest kingdom in Europe. Manuel maintained the Portuguese presence in North Africa and, during this same time, Portuguese explorers visited Greenland, Labrador, and Nova Scotia, failing to find the fabled Northwest Passage but in the process opening the bountiful waters off Newfoundland to Portuguese fishermen.

Manuel not only sought to enlarge the empire through further exploration but also hoped to increase his dominions by marriage alliances with other royal houses. Yet these dreams came to nothing in the end. Manuel hoped to join the crown of Portugal with those of Ferdinand II and Isabella of Aragon and Castile by producing a joint heir. As this coincided with Ferdinand's own dynastic designs, a marriage was arranged in 1497 between Manuel and their eldest daughter, Princess Isabella, the widow of John's son Afonso and second in the line of royal succession after her brother Juan. Following the death of Juan, Manuel and Isabella were proclaimed heirs of Castile (although not Aragon); Isabella died in childbirth, however, and their son died soon after. Manuel then married a younger daughter of Ferdinand and Isabella, Maria, who produced his heir in 1502.

One major aspect of Manuel's reign that brought him no glory was his vacillating policy toward the Jewish population of Portugal. Prior to Manuel's tenure, the small but significant Jewish community was generally tolerated and allowed to follow its religious and cultural traditions. In fact, many Spanish Jews were allowed to settle in Portugal following their 1492 expulsion from Spain. The Jewish community made important intellectual and economic contributions that served the Crown in a number of important ways in the fifteenth and sixteenth centuries. After continuing this liberal policy of toleration upon his succession, Manuel soon changed his mind. Manuel had wished to marry Isabella for reasons of dynastic union. Under Spanish pressure, as part of that marriage agreement, Manuel promised to expel all unconverted Jews. All were ordered out of the country by October, 1497, the month the marriage took place. This decree proved to have far-reaching economic consequences as large numbers of Jews prepared to liquidate their holdings and move their families out of the country. Faced with financial dislocations, the king settled on a controversial policy of forced conversion as a way to meet his obligations yet preserve for Portugal the Jewish community's financial assets. To soften the blow of forced conversion, Manuel embarked on a policy of gradual assimilation of the so-called New Christians. They were to be given a twenty-year grace period, during which their religious practices and social customs would not be scrutinized. Yet even converted Jews would not be allowed to leave, underscoring the essentially economic rather than religious motivation of this policy. This policy, tied to the trend toward royal centralization, created an atmosphere of resentment against the New Christians, many of whom continued to practice Judaism under the protection of the royal decrees. Only after serious rioting in Lisbon in 1506 and the massacre of thousands of New Christians did Manuel give in to their pleas and again grant permission to leave and reenter Portugal at will. Nevertheless, at the same time Manuel secretly requested from the pope the establishment of the Inquisition (a request only granted in the reign of Manuel's successor) apparently as a means of controlling Judaization among the population he had agreed to protect from such scrutiny.

The fabulous material wealth flooding in from Portugal's overseas trade (estimated at more than one million cruzados a year) created opulence at home. Manuel's court was known for splendor and ostentation. In 1513, for example, Manuel sent to Rome richly bejewelled vestments, an Eastern manuscript, and a selection of exotic animals that included a trained elephant as a gift to the newly elected Pope Leo X. Yet the money went for more than luxury and waste. The wealth pouring in from the empire not only supported a sumptuous court but also financed patronage for artists and intellectuals. The reign of Manuel saw the first blossoming of Humanism in Portugal, which would reach its rather modest peak in the reign of John III. Manuel provided patronage for Portuguese students abroad and undertook the reform of the University of Lisbon in the early sixteenth century. The wealth arriving from the Portuguese Indies provided commissions for buildings, decorative sculptures, and paintings. The buildings were often designed in the late Gothic style (marked by lavish decoration on a basic Gothic structure) called "Manueline" by art historians, although the style remained popular in Portugal long after Manuel's death. The reign of Manuel is also remarkable for the numerous paintings produced on royal commissions.

Manuel died in Lisbon on December 13, 1521. His son John inherited a prosperous kingdom, but one beginning to show the strains of rapid growth, which would lead to a noticeable decline in Portuguese fortunes by the end of John III's reign.

Summary

Manuel I, aptly called "the Fortunate," ruled Portugal at the high point of its imperial fortunes. His reign represents the culmination of several trends begun earlier in the fifteenth century by the Avis monarchs, most notably the growth of royal power and the search for a water route to India, which Manuel completed. His tenure marks the clear emergence of the Renaissance state in Portugal. He was an able administrator, who could build on John II's accomplishments to establish firmly the dominance of royal authority and complete the centralization of administration. Manuel's approach to government was practical. Even his inconsistencies with regard to the Jews are best understood in terms of administrative rather than religious imperatives. It was Manuel's good luck to ascend the throne at the precise moment in which the all-water trade route to India, proved by the voyage of Bartolomeu Dias, was about to be activated. The enormous profits accruing to the Crown ensured the funds to support Manuel's other policies. He is justly credited with generously patronizing intellectuals, artists, and architects and in so doing helping to usher in a golden age in Portugal. Yet his royal absolutism, harsh treatment of the economically important Jewish community, and lavish spending of the Indies wealth on ostentation blocked modern economic development and thus hastened the decline in Portugal's economic fortunes that would follow his reign.

Bibliography

Adil, Janeen R. "Two nations, Two Kings." *Calliope* 8 (April, 1998): 18. Adil focuses on two great sea explorers, King Alfonso X of Spain and King Manuel I, providing details on the success of exploration and discovery during Manuel I's reign.

Diffie, Bailey W., and George D. Winius. *Foundations of the Portuguese Empire, 1415-1580.* Minneapolis: University of Minnesota Press, 1977. The best summary in English of Manuel's involvement in the Portuguese overseas expansion in the late fifteenth and early sixteenth centuries. Voyages of discovery and the evolution of Portuguese policy are both addressed. Includes an extensive bibliography.

Greenlee, William Brooks. *The Voyage of Pedro Álvares Cabral to Brazil and India from Contemporary Documents and Narration.* London: Hakluyt Society, 1938; St. Clair Shores, Mich.: Scholarly Press, 1972. The extensive introduction to this volume of documents gives considerable information on Manuel's involvement in the voyages of discovery undertaken under his auspices. The work is also valuable for its translated documents, which include letters written to Manuel describing the discovery of Brazil and from Manuel to other monarchs concerning Cabral's voyage.

Livermore, H. V. *A New History of Portugal.* 2d ed. Cambridge and New York: Cambridge University Press, 1976. Gives a chapter-long overview that covers the main aspects of Manuel's reign. While royal centralization, the Jewish question, and Manuel's dreams of dynastic union with Spain are all addressed, the greatest attention is given to Portugal's successes in overseas expansion.

Oliveira Marques, A. H. de. *History of Portugal.* 2 vols. 2d ed. New York: Columbia University Press, 1976. Presents a concise description of the development of the Renaissance state under kings John II, Manuel I, and John III. Useful in tracing institutional developments in Manuel's reign. This work covers intellectual and artistic achievements in addition to tracing political and religious change.

Payne, Stanley G. *A History of Spain and Portugal.* 2 vols. Madison: University of Wisconsin Press, 1973. Volume 1 contains an overview describing major political, economic, religious, and cultural aspects of Manuel's reign. Gives attention to fiscal and economic matters as well as social and demographic factors contributing to the rise and eventual decline of Portuguese power in the sixteenth century. Each volume has a bibliography, but most works cited are written in Portuguese or Spanish.

Yerushalmi, Yosef Hayim. *The Lisbon Massacre of 1506 and the Royal Image in the "Shebet Yehudah."* Cincinnati, Ohio: Hebrew Union College-Jewish Institute of Religion, 1976. A critical view of Manuel's relationship with the New Christian community in Portugal and his handling of the 1506 riot in Lisbon. It cites resentment of royal centralization as the real cause of the 1506 pogrom and the New Christians as the convenient targets for pent-up frustration. The notes provide a bibliography on the subject of the Jews in Portugal.

Victoria Hennessey Cummins

MARGUERITE OF NAVARRE
Marguerite D'Angoulême

Born: April 11, 1492; Angoulême, France

Died: December 1, 1549; Tarbes, France

Areas of Achievement: Humanism, monarchy, and religious reform

Contribution: Both as a writer herself and as patroness of reformers and poets, Marguerite helped her brother, the king of France, introduce the new humanism into French culture. Her courts, first at Alençon and later in Navarre, were centers where educated women and men could discuss religion, literature, and politics. Marguerite single-handedly invented the *salon*, as it came to be known in the seventeenth century. She was the first society woman of learning—what the eighteenth century would call a "bluestocking."

Early Life

Marguerite of Angoulême—so called in order to distinguish her from her grand-niece, Marguerite of Valois, who also married a king of Navarre—was the first child of the ambitious and dominating Louise of Savoy. Marguerite was two years older than her brother François (later king of France). Their mother reared the children to become queen and king, insisting that they both master the "new learning" (essentially classical literature, the Bible, and Latin). Tall and fiercely intelligent, Marguerite charmed by her wit rather than her beauty. Until she became a queen in her own right by virtue of her second marriage in 1527, her early life revolved around that of her Valois brother, the glorious King François I (ruled 1515-1547). She would later recollect their childhood and adolescence under the guise of a *roman à clef*, or a story whose characters are known only to readers who have the "key."

In 1509, with her fifteen-year-old brother already betrothed to the ten-year-old princess of France, Marguerite was married by the scheming Louise to the duke of Alençon, a simple nobleman with a pious and unworldly mother. Marguerite took her books with her to Normandy and proceeded to set up at Alençon one of the earliest *salons*, or learned courts, in imitation of the society in which her mother had reared her and François. Her husband the duke left Marguerite to her cultivated guests, preferring his horses and hounds to the new learning. Illiterate himself, he was embarrassed to visit the royal court with a wife who knew how to talk about Dante Alighieri and Giovanni Boccaccio. There began Marguerite's patronage of Clément Marot and other poets, and there she met the great humanist scholar Jacques Lefèvre d'Etaples.

Lefèvre was the French counterpart of Desiderius Erasmus, the famous Dutch humanist, and the teachings of both scholars attracted the strong-minded noblewoman, who was still in her twenties. In this context, one must recall that Martin Luther did not begin the Reformation. The movement to reform the church (which was still the Christian church, with no distinction of Protestant or Catholic) had been underway for a generation by the time Luther nailed his angry "theses" to the church door in 1517. Among the various reform movements that ensued, Catholic reformers outnumbered Protestant by at least three to one. Like Erasmus, Lefèvre wanted to strip the institutional trappings from religious experience so that the believer might communicate more directly with Christ. In particular, these men hoped to "make everyone his or her own theologian," as Erasmus wrote in his preface to the New Testament, which he edited in its original Greek. Educated Christians could pray to God and think for themselves, without the help of priests or doctors of theology. These humanists expressed their hostility to theologians by insisting that the teachings of the great pagan moralists—including Socrates, Plato, and Cicero—were closer to the spirit of biblical Christianity than were the doctrines debated at the Sorbonne in Paris. Erasmus even prayed to "Saint Socrates."

To Marguerite, living with an ignorant husband and his puritanical mother, the humanist teaching came like the dawn of a new epoch. After ten years of marriage, she still had no children, and, knowing herself the intellectual and social equal of any aristocrat in France, she embraced Lefèvre's cause as her life work. He put her in touch with the bishop of Meaux (near Paris), and with her letters in 1521 she began her thoughtful writing on religion and the Scriptures. Without ever condoning Luther's radicalism, Marguerite lent her protection to a number of Catholic reformers and even to Luther's follower, John Calvin. This earned for Marguerite the hatred of the doctors at the Sorbonne, who were determined to root out "Lutheran heretics" and burn them at the stake. When the Sorbonne's activists overstepped their authority and condemned one of Marguerite's religious tracts, her brother the king was furious and banished their ringleader from the country.

Protecting and nourishing the new ideas and encouraging her brother to do likewise were perhaps Marguerite's greatest historical accomplishments. In 1534, following the Affair of the Placards (when overnight all of Paris was plastered with signs denouncing the church's main dogmas, such as the presence of Christ in the host), François was powerless to stop the mob reaction against Protestantism, and the Sorbonne hunted down Lefèvre. Marguerite sheltered the old man and was at his bedside when he died.

Life's Work

The year 1525 was a critical one for Marguerite. She wrote her first serious poem, a discussion of the afterlife conducted in a dialogue with the imaginary spirit of her eight-year-old niece, who had just died. Her brother the king had led an army into Italy, where he was defeated and captured at the Battle of Pavia. Sent to Spain as the prisoner of his archrival the Emperor Charles V, François languished in a cell until his sister came to Madrid to negotiate with the astonished emperor. François was eventually released after promising to cede all of Burgundy to Charles (a promise François never kept). In the meantime, Marguerite's husband, who had run away from the encounter at Pavia, died in disgrace. Charles immediately wrote to Louise (who was governing the country as regent for her imprisoned son) and asked for her daughter's hand in marriage. Marguerite had dealt with the emperor and loathed him; she preferred the handsome Henri d'Albret, king of Navarre and eleven years her junior. They were married in January, 1527. Late in 1528, in her thirty-seventh year, Marguerite gave birth to a daughter, Jeanne d'Albret; later, she would have a son who lived only a few months, as well as twins who died at birth. Her only surviving child, Jeanne, would marry a Bourbon and become the mother of Henri IV, France's most illustrious king between Louis IX (St. Louis) and Louis XIV.

After the Affair of the Placards, Marguerite retired from Paris to her court at Nérac in Navarre (Gascony). There she hosted several evangelical humanists; besides Lefèvre and Calvin, she patronized Maurice Scève, the poet, and her old friend Marot. From Paris, the church doctors complained that she was "accompanied by her Lutheran demons under the name of advisers." It was probably her court at Nérac that served as William Shakespeare's model for his brilliantly witty comedy *Love's Labour's Lost* (pr. c. 1594-1595). During this final decade of her life, Marguerite wrote not only her most profound religious poems and dialogues but also five of her seven comedies, as well as the work for which she is best known, the *Heptameron* (1559). At the same time, she realized that she was losing her power to protect the humanist reformers from the Inquisition, which with her brother's encouragement was then raging in Paris. Marguerite had always felt herself to be part of the intellectual avant-garde. Like Erasmus when Luther challenged him to choose between a corrupt establishment and anarchical reform, Marguerite was now caught between the conservative reaction known as the Counter-Reformation, on the one side, and Calvin's uncompromising Protestantism on the other. Still hopeful, Calvin had dedicated his explosive *Institutes of the Christian Religion* to the king in 1540. Marguerite might have appreciated that gesture, but she must have been dismayed by Calvin's attack on a fellow humanist, François Rabelais, who in 1546 dedicated to Marguerite his *Tiers Livre* (*Third Book*), which ridiculed Calvinism. These fallings-out among her gifted protégés must have greatly discouraged the queen, who had theretofore found her guiding vision in their eager collaboration to harmonize the new learning with true religion.

Marguerite had also grown estranged from her adored brother. Perhaps she experienced some disillusionment when François broke his oath to Charles; however, she could not have expected François to give away Burgundy if he was to remain king of France. François not only ignored the birth of her daughter in 1528, but he also schemed in 1540 to marry Jeanne for his own advantage to a man she detested. Jeanne was a headstrong young woman who was later to win fame as a military leader, a woman able to campaign with her army while taking a day off to give birth to her son Henri. François had removed her from her mother's care when she was two because he was afraid Marguerite would betroth her to Charles V's son, Philip. Marguerite might have been expected to intercede for Jeanne when the king married her against her will; instead, Marguerite chose to fall in with the king's state policy, and she ordered her twelve-year-old daughter to be lashed until she submitted. Jeanne, who had to be forcibly carried to the altar,

never forgave her mother. After Marguerite's death, Jeanne came to admire her abilities and oversaw the publishing of her *Heptameron*, but she could never love her. (Fortunately for Jeanne, when her detested husband allied himself with Charles three years later, the king decided to annul her marriage. That left Jeanne free to marry the man of her choice, Anthony of Bourbon.)

Summary

From his fortieth year, King François, who had been perhaps the most notorious philanderer in Europe—he easily outdid England's uxorious Henry VIII—was afflicted with syphilis. Partly to distract him from his constant pain, his estranged sister began the series of tales modelled on Boccaccio's *Decameron* (1353; the Greek title means "ten days"). She imagined five men and five women stranded at a spa in the Pyrenees and entertaining one another by telling a tale each day. Marguerite left the work unfinished after starting the eighth day—hence the title, meaning "seven days." Unlike Boccaccio, Marguerite—who appears herself as Parlamente, one of the storytellers—stipulates that all the tales are to be true narratives. Despite the stories' factual appearance, however, Marguerite contrives to discuss the political and religious quarrels of her time under the veil of fable, just as Rabelais does. Scholars have only begun to discover the *Heptameron*'s complex art and its hidden meanings.

François's death in 1547 devastated Marguerite. She lived two more years in a monastery in Poitou, completing her finest long poem, *Prisons*. In this six-thousand-line Neoplatonic masterpiece, the queen of Navarre proceeds in her imagination from one prison to another as her soul looks for a way to escape from the dungeon of life. One of the "prisons" is the sun-flooded palace of love, where pleasures blind the soul and keep it from taking flight. The Renaissance humanist in Marguerite had receded into the background, giving way to the medieval ascetic that had always lurked deep in her nature.

Bibliography

Erasmus, Desiderius. *The Paraclesis.* In *Christian Humanism and the Reformation*, edited by John C. Olin. New York: Harper, 1965. Erasmus's brilliant preface to his 1516 version of the New Testament distills the essence of Christian humanism on the threshold of the Lutheran Reformation.

Marguerite de Navarre. *The Heptameron.* Translated by P. A. Chilton. Harmondsworth, England: Penguin Books, 1984. Contains a useful introduction, a key to the characters, and summaries of the seventy-two stories.

More, Thomas. *Utopia.* Edited by Edward Surtz. New Haven, Conn.: Yale University Press, 1964. This classic dialogue, with a prefatory letter from Guillaume Budé, the star of François I's court, is an excellent example of the witty discussions sponsored by Marguerite in her *salons*.

Putnam, Samuel. *Marguerite of Navarre.* New York: Coward-McCann, 1935. The only modern biography in English, by a famous translator of Rabelais and Miguel de Cervantes.

Stone, Donald. *France in the Sixteenth Century: A Medieval Society Transformed.* Englewood Cliffs, N.J.: Prentice Hall, 1969. An accessible overview of French society in Marguerite's day.

David B. Haley

CHRISTOPHER MARLOWE

Born: February 6, 1564; Canterbury, England
Died: May 30, 1593; Deptford, England
Areas of Achievement: Theater and literature
Contribution: An author concerned largely with the question of power and how it affects human beings, Marlowe was complex, lyrical, and frequently erotic in both his dramatic and his poetic writing.

Early Life

Dead at twenty-nine from stab wounds suffered in a tavern brawl, Christopher Marlowe led a life of violence, intrigue, mystery, and remarkable productivity. His dramas and poetry have established him as an Elizabethan dramatist second only to William Shakespeare. It is tempting to speculate on what he might have produced had he lived a normal life span.

The son of John and Catherine Arthur Marlowe, Christopher was born on February 6, 1564, and was thus almost an exact contemporary of Shakespeare, who was born on or near April 23 of the same year. Marlowe was the second child in a family of nine children, six of whom, two boys and four girls, survived infancy. John Marlowe was a leatherworker and a member of an affluent guild in Canterbury, the Kentish cathedral town in southeastern England in which the shrine of St. Thomas à Becket is located.

Despite the prosperity of the guild to which he belonged, John Marlowe was not a wealthy man. His family had gained the reputation of being contentious and litigious. John, judging from court records of the time, followed in his ancestors' footsteps, as did his offspring. John was said to be loud, arrogant, demanding, and profligate.

Marlowe was enrolled in the King's School in Canterbury—a noble institution of which Roger Ascham had been headmaster in the generation before Marlowe—at fifteen, the top age for admitting new students. The school was renowned for its emphasis on theater and was considered one of the best schools in Elizabethan England. The young Marlowe, fair of countenance, with unruly dark hair and the bright eyes of one ever alert to and aware of his surroundings, read selectively in the extensive private library of the headmaster, concentrating on medieval romances, particularly Thomas Malory's versions of the Arthurian legends. Marlowe favored blood-and-thunder romances, indicating that perhaps the legendary Marlowe combativeness had been passed on to this young member of the family. Much of his writing appears to have as its source works from the library available to him during his days at King's School.

In 1581, two years after he had entered King's School, Marlowe became a student at Corpus Christi College of Cambridge University, where he was considered an excellent student and an accomplished poet, writing at that time primarily in Latin. He was named a Canterbury Scholar for his six years at Cambridge, apparently because he had expressed his intention of entering the clergy.

Marlowe's college career was marked by long absences from the university, and it is now assumed that he was engaged in some sort of espionage activities in Europe for the Crown. This assumption is substantiated by the fact that when Cambridge moved to withhold Marlowe's master's degree from him in 1587, Queen Elizabeth's Privy Council intervened to see that Marlowe received his degree, saying in a letter to university officials that his absences from the university had benefited the Crown. It is known that Marlowe worked for Sir Francis Walsingham, the secretary of state for Queen Elizabeth, who was much involved in espionage.

In the early summer of 1591, Marlowe shared a workroom with Thomas Kyd, renowned for his *The Spanish Tragedy* (c. 1585-1589). Marlowe and Kyd were at that time both under the patronage of Thomas Walsingham, cousin of Sir Francis, who provided the workroom. Queen Elizabeth finally knighted Thomas Walsingham.

Life's Work

After he received the master's degree from Cambridge University in 1587, Marlowe rushed to London, England's cultural and theatrical center. By that time, he had already completed two plays, *Dido, Queen of Carthage* (1586-1587) and *Tamburlaine the Great* (c. 1587), as well as translations of Lucan's *Pharsalia* (first century A.D.) and Ovid's *Amores* (c. 20 B.C.).

Tamburlaine the Great traces the life of the powerful Persian conqueror to his conquest of Egypt and his marriage to Zenocrate, daughter of the defeated Egyptian sultan. The Lord Admiral's Company first performed the play in London probably in the fall of 1587, possibly as late as November. Marlowe had not intended to take his drama of

Tamburlaine beyond Tamburlaine's marriage to Zenocrate. The play was so successful, however, that it soon came to be billed as *Tamburlaine the Great, Part 1*, and shortly after its first performances that year, Marlowe followed it with the sequel, *Tamburlaine the Great, Part 2*, which continued the Tamburlaine story through to the death of the Eastern conqueror. Certainly, these two plays established Marlowe's reputation as an important playwright, but they also left him open to charges of atheism by people of established reputation.

Charges of atheism and pederasty, both capital offenses in Elizabeth's England, were to follow Marlowe throughout his brief life. The latter charges stemmed initially from Marlowe's statements that all men who do not love tobacco and boys are fools and later from the fact that his *Edward II* (1592) is about a homosexual king. Because Marlowe reveled in shocking people, it is difficult to know whether he spoke out of conviction or out of a desire to get reactions from his listeners when he made his statements about boys. Certainly, writing a historical play whose protagonist is homosexual does not make the writer homosexual. Marlowe's own sexuality has not been convincingly established. It is interesting, but not surprising, that one of Marlowe's most vigorous attackers, Robert Greene, was also his most fervent imitator.

By 1589, Marlowe was living in Norton Folgate, close to London's theatrical district. In September of that year, Marlowe was involved in a street fight with William Bradley. Marlowe's friend, the poet Thomas Watson, came to Marlowe's assistance and killed Bradley by inflicting stab wounds. Marlowe ran from the scene, but soon Watson was arrested and taken to Newgate Prison. Shortly thereafter, Marlowe was arrested and imprisoned in Newgate for a fortnight. Watson was held until February, when he was exonerated on the grounds of self-defense.

In 1587, *Historia von D. Iohan Fausten* was published in German in Frankfurt. Although Marlowe is not known to have read this seminal book in German and although it was not translated into English until 1592, Marlowe appears to have begun working on his renowned *The Tragicall History of D. Faustus* (known more commonly as *Doctor Faustus*) shortly after his two Tamburlaine plays were produced. The Stationers' Register shows that a play presumed to be *Doctor Faustus* was registered on February 28, 1589, and other dramatists writing before 1592 show evidence in their work of having borrowed heavily from Marlowe's play.

In 1589, the Lord Admiral's Company performed Marlowe's *The Jew of Malta*, a play to which Shakespeare's *The Merchant of Venice* (c. 1596-1597) bears strong resemblances. Marlowe's play, deemed atheistic by many of his contemporaries, should probably be viewed as a biting satire rather than as the tragedy that some critics have considered it to be. Barabas' annihilation of a whole convent full of nuns is the sort of bloody, melodramatic theme that Marlowe liked and that Kyd also exploited in *The Spanish Tragedy*.

The three parts of *Edward II*, which Pembroke's Men first performed in 1592, represent Marlowe's most mature and well-crafted writing. Also, the text for the play is the most reliable extant text of any Marlowe play save *Tamburlaine the Great*. In *Edward II*, Marlowe's chief concern is with the question of civil authority. The fact of Edward's homosexuality is incidental, although Marlowe deals head-on with the king's proclivity. The death scene in this play is among the most affecting death scenes in the whole of Western literature.

Four months after *The Massacre at Paris* was first staged on January 26, 1593, Marlowe was arrested as an atheist, a capital charge in his day. On May 12, Kyd was arrested on a charge of atheism, and on the rack he attributed the documents that had led to his arrest to Marlowe. On May 18, a warrant was issued for Marlowe's arrest, and he was apprehended at the estate of Sir Thomas Walsingham, his patron. On May 20, having answered the charges against him to the Privy Council, he was directed to attend the council daily, a lenient sentence for one charged with a capital offense. Ten days later, on May 30, 1593, Ingram Frizer, Lady Walsingham's business agent, fatally stabbed Marlowe in a tavern in Deptford during a dispute over a bill. Marlowe was interred in the Walsingham tomb in Deptford on June 1, 1593, and Frizer was promptly acquitted of his murder on grounds of self-defense.

Summary

In his short and colorful life, Christopher Marlowe cut a swath in British drama that no other playwright of his time equaled except Shakespeare. Indeed, Calvin Hoffman in *The Murder of the Man Who Was "Shakespeare"* (1955), argues that Marlowe, living under a cloud in 1593, was not actually murdered but, rather, went to the Continent and continued to write, producing before his death many of the plays attributed to Shakespeare. Hoffman's claim has been thoroughly discredited but suggests something of Marlowe's dramatic stature.

After Marlowe's premature death, which many of his contemporaries took to be God's judgment of a man who was atheistic and homosexual, a steady stream of his writing continued to appear. His translation of *Lucan's First Book* (the first part of *Pharsalia*) and his incomplete poem *Hero and Leander* were entered in the Stationers' Register in September, 1593, the former published in 1600, the latter in 1598.

In 1594, *Edward II* and *Dido, Queen of Carthage* were published, and Marlowe's translation of Ovid's *Amores*, to be publicly burned in 1599 as heretical, appears also to have been published in 1594, although it is not dated. *The Massacre at Paris* was probably also published in 1594, followed ten years later by the publication of *Doctor Faustus*.

Marlowe was a literary giant, a genius who wrote some of the most compelling dramas of his day. He had a lyrical gift that showed both in his drama and in his poetry. His full power as a dramatist has yet to be fully recognized, although it is generally conceded that Marlowe's only real peer in Elizabethan drama is Shakespeare, whose dramatic gifts generally exceed those of Marlowe.

Bibliography

Friedenreich, Kenneth, ed. *Christopher Marlowe: An Annotated Bibliography of Criticism Since 1950*. Metuchen, N.J.: Scarecrow Press, 1979. A comprehensive bibliography of almost three decades of Marlowe criticism. The editor is thorough and exhaustive, and his initial essay assesses Marlowe's critical standing.

Hilton, Della. *Who Was Kit Marlowe? The Story of the Poet and Playwright*. London: Weidenfeld and Nicolson, and New York: Taplinger, 1977. This great admirer of Marlowe seeks to explain his alleged atheism and homosexuality and also comments interestingly upon some of his mysterious espionage work. The book is at times lacking in objectivity, and the conjecture that Marlowe committed suicide is not credibly presented.

Hoffman, Calvin. *The Murder of the Man Who Was "Shakespeare."* New York: Messner, 1955. Hoffman's contention that Marlowe was not killed on May 30, 1593, but lived on in Europe to write many of the plays attributed to Shakespeare is a fascinating fiction that has been convincingly disproved by scholars more knowledgeable than the dilettante who wrote this intriguing book.

Knoll, Robert E. *Christopher Marlowe*. New York: Twayne, 1968. Knoll provides a useful overall coverage of Marlowe, dealing forthrightly with interpreting his work and with the controversies surrounding some of its interpretation. The standard Twayne format is useful for beginning readers of Marlowe. Knoll is quite successful in identifying Marlowe's basic themes and in discussing them.

Levin, Harry. *The Overreacher: A Study of Christopher Marlowe*. Cambridge, Mass.: Harvard University Press, 1952; London: Faber, 1954. By far the best assessment of Marlowe to date, this book calls for a less romanticized assessment of the author than most of the treatments of him have been. Levin shows a Marlowe who is deeply intelligent, highly complex, and given to a hyperbole that many critics have taken more seriously than Marlowe apparently intended it.

Marcus, Leah S. *Unediting the Renaissance: Shakespeare, Marlowe, Milton*. London and New York: Routledge, 1996. This work examines the issue of the textual editing of Renaissance works. Marcus focuses on key Renaissance works—*Dr. Faustus*, *The Merry Wives of Windsor*, *The Taming of the Shrew*, and *Hamlet*, as well as poems by Milton, Donne, and Herrick—to re-examine how editorial intervention shapes the texts which are widely accepted as 'definitive.'

Marlowe, Christopher. *The Complete Works of Christopher Marlowe*. 2 vols. Edited by Fredson Bowers. London and New York: Cambridge University Press, 1973. This standard edition of the works of Marlowe includes introductions to each work. It summarizes bibliographical problems associated with the canon and contains detailed notes of help to both the scholar and general reader.

Norman, Charles. *The Muse's Darling; The Life of Christopher Marlowe*. New York: Rinehart, 1946; London: Falcon Press, 1947. A well-written, much reprint-ed biography of Marlowe that gives shrewd appraisals of the man and of his work. A thoroughly readable book that somewhat ro-manticizes its subject.

Nuttall, A. D. *The Alternative Trinity: Gnostic Heresy in Marlowe, Milton, and Blake*. Oxford: Oxford University Press, 1998. Nuttall tracks the subversive theology of an antagonistic creator and Christ from the Gnostics of the second century, through its flickering reappearance in Marlowe and Milton, and to its full development in Blake.

Pinciss, Gerald M. *Christopher Marlowe*. New York: Ungar, 1975. A brief discussion of Elizabethan theater, of Marlowe's life and contributions, and of each of Marlowe's seven plays. This is a good starting point for someone unfamiliar with Marlowe's work.

R. Baird Shuman

MARY, QUEEN OF SCOTS

Born: December 8, 1542; Linlithgow Palace, West Lothian, Scotland

Died: February 8, 1587; Fotheringhay Castle, Northamptonshire, England

Area of Achievement: Government

Contribution: Through the misfortunes of her personal life, Mary precipitated a political and religious struggle in Scotland that ultimately led to her death in England as a Catholic martyr.

Early Life

Mary, Queen of Scots, was born at Linlithgow Palace, West Lothian, on December 8, 1542. Six days later, her father, James V, only thirty years of age, died. His death, hastened by the physical and mental anguish of the English defeat of the Scots at Solway Moss in November, brought to the throne one of the most remarkable and tragic women of the sixteenth century.

Mary's infancy ensured a regency under her French mother, Mary of Guise. In the midst of the war, Henry VIII proposed a marriage between his young son Edward and the infant queen. Ancient Scottish fears of English domination, and the regent's family connections, led to marriage negotiations with France. Thus, at the age of five, Mary Stuart was sent abroad.

Her departure from Scotland was marked by storms and the danger of shipwreck on enemy shores, but despite the perils, Mary landed in France to receive a warm welcome. Her formidable grandmother Antoinette of Guise met the child and introduced her to the French court at Moulin. There, for the first time, Mary met Francis, the Dauphin of France and her future husband. The two children became fast friends. Mary at five was a vivacious, charming, and happy child. Her four-year-old fiancé was frail and shy but affectionate. The French court was enchanted, and Henry II proclaimed Mary the "most perfect child" he had ever seen.

The education of such a child could not be ignored, but Mary's training would be much more conventional and less rigorous than that of her Tudor cousins in England. Fortunately, Renaissance France offered much that could challenge and captivate a bright child. Mary learned the traditional Latin and a smattering of Greek as well as Italian and Spanish. More important socially, she learned how to draw, to sing, to play the lute, and to dance elegantly. Hunting and riding became passions shared with the nobility of Europe. Moreover, she absorbed the Catholic faith of the French court with youthful devoutness. Mary became the very model of a French princess. In April, 1558, she and Francis were married, but because of his ill health the marriage may never have been consummated.

Mary Tudor's death in England in November, 1558, stirred the French court deeply. Mary, like her English cousin Elizabeth, was a Tudor descendant of Henry VII. Mary's blood claim to the English throne was, however, untainted by the questions that surrounded Henry VIII's marriages and children. Indeed, for Catholics, her claim to the throne of England was purer constitutionally than that of Elizabeth. Henry II responded immediately to Elizabeth's accession by having Mary Stuart proclaimed Queen of England, Ireland, and Scotland. It was a decision that would haunt Mary for three decades and would play a role in her death sentence.

Nevertheless, the year 1559 opened joyously. The royal family, despite family rivalries, the stirrings of religious dissent, and the unpopular treaty of Cateau-Cambresis, celebrated a number of royal weddings. The balls and pageants were magnificent enough to obscure the national tensions. Then suddenly it all collapsed.

On June 30, 1559, at the conclusion of a tournament, Henry II, wearing the black-and-white colors of his mistress Diane de Poitiers, was injured in a bizarre accident. The lance of an opponent struck the king viciously, splintering into his eye and throat. Nine days later, he died in agony. With his death, Francis II became king and Mary, Queen of Scots, was now Queen of France as well. For a timid boy of fifteen and a carefree girl of sixteen it must have been a shattering transition.

Not surprisingly, a tug of war ensued between the young king's mother Catherine d'Medici and the powerful Guise family of the young queen. Yet, in this period Catherine's example may have been a great influence upon her daughter-in-law. Mary watched Catherine maneuver, intrigue, and balance quarreling factions, for the sake of the Bourbon dynasty. The lessons were not lost. Mary would never match her mother-in-law's ability as intriguer but it would not be for want of trying.

In November, 1560, Francis returned from a hunting expedition with a terrible earache. Three weeks later, the young king was dead of a massive infection. Mary had lost both her husband and her

closest childhood friend. She was eighteen, and it was time to return to Scotland, a home she had never really known.

Life's Work

Mary arrived at Leith, Scotland, early on a typically damp and dismal day. Her reception would have daunted any but the most obtusely cheerful. Barely a handful of local fisherman were on hand to greet the Queen of Scotland and only the generosity of a local inhabitant provided some shelter until a royal welcoming committee arrived.

Her entry into Edinburgh was, however, a triumph. As crowds poured out to greet her, bonfires were lit, bells rang, and bagpipes played. The queen made a vivid impression on all who saw her. Nearly six feet tall, Mary had a delicate-boned elegance that set off her golden blonde hair, white complexion, and hazel eyes. Her voice was light but commanding, her high forehead deemed a sign of intellect, and her long, thin hands a sign of aristocracy. Her most compelling physical feature was probably her sensual, heavy-lidded eyes. Not classically beautiful, she had an indefinable charisma that drew others to her and earned for her the romantic title "the Queen of Hearts." Certainly, she captured the hearts of those who saw her return to Holyrood Palace in 1561.

Mary was equally pleased with her subjects and was thrilled by the rugged, misty beauty of Scotland. Yet the problems she now faced were daunting. Thirteen years of absence gave her little knowledge of her country. Furthermore, she had little real political or administrative experience. Scotland was beautiful but impoverished. A warring nobility and a feudal governmental structure made it more a relic of the medieval era than a modern emerging nation. Moreover, while Mary was growing up in France, the force and fury of the Protestant Reformation had swept across the land. The fiery Calvinist leader John Knox and other adherents of the new faith viewed the queen's return with alarm.

Despite such problems, Mary's reign began auspiciously. Indeed, with the advice of her illegitimate half brother James, Earl of Moray, her first months of government went well. It was her rash decision to remarry that began a series of crises that would destroy her throne.

In July, 1565, Mary married her cousin Henry Stewart, Earl of Darnley, the son of the fourth Earl of Lennox. Although a love match, it was, nevertheless, a choice which was certain to antagonize Elizabeth, whose support Mary needed. Elizabeth, always hostile to the Scottish Queen and fearful of her claims, was incensed. Darnley, a Tudor descendant, doubly underscored Mary's rights in England. The Earl of Moray despised Darnley personally and hated the Lennox family. He would continually incite other Scottish nobles against the queen.

The real and continuing problem was Darnley himself. Under a tall, thin, elegant, exterior that won Mary's heart if not her mind, Darnley was at best an amiable dolt. At his worst, which was more often the case, he was weak, spoiled, vain, and silly. Unfortunately, he also possessed a cruel, even vicious streak. In March of 1566, he conspired in the brutal murder of David Riccio. Mary's hapless Italian secretary was hacked to death in front of the queen, despite her pleas for his life. Mary, who was expecting her first child in June, never forgave Darnley. After the birth of her son James VI, she turned increasingly for support to a group of powerful nobles under the leadership of James Hepburn, Earl of Bothwell.

On February 9, 1567, the house at Kirk o'Field near Edinburgh where Darnley was staying was destroyed by an explosion. When the crowds came running, Darnley's nearly naked body was found in the garden, where he had apparently been caught and strangled. Whether Mary was privy to the conspiracy, which had been led by James Hepburn, the fourth earl of Bothwell, is unclear. The only evidence ever introduced against Mary as an accomplice was the highly suspect collection of "Casket Letters." The letters, however, are a puzzling mixture of genuine documents and outright forgeries.

Whatever Mary's knowledge of the events, her dependence upon Bothwell and his faction was obvious. Bothwell was acquitted of any involvement in Darnley's death after a farcical hearing. Less than three months later, Mary married Bothwell, after an alleged abduction and rape.

The public was outraged. All over Scotland, placards with the arms of Bothwell went up, depicting the queen as a mermaid, an ancient symbol of prostitution. The implication that she had condoned the murder of Darnley for love of Bothwell was clear. On June 15, 1567, an army led by Mary was defeated at Carberry Hill. The queen was forced to abdicate in favor of her infant son. After nearly a year of incarceration, she escaped and rallied her supporters for a fight at Langside. With Langside lost, Mary fled south. Her advisers agreed that her return to France was essential; there she could appeal to her powerful Guise relatives and to Catholic sentiment to finance a return. At Dundrennan Abbey, she startled her followers by deciding to enter England and seek aid from Elizabeth. Thus, Elizabeth suddenly found herself hostess to the one woman in Europe who might threaten her throne. Mary remained in England for nineteen years under increasingly tight captivity. She proved too valuable a diplomatic prize and too dangerous a rival to set free.

The Rising of the Northern Earls in 1569 was the beginning of a long series of plots to overthrow Elizabeth on Mary's behalf. Over the years, the Norfolk plot, Ridolfi plot, the Babington plot, all financed by Philip of Spain, would exhaust the patience of Elizabeth's government. In late 1586, Mary was sentenced to death for conspiring to assassinate Elizabeth. On February 8, 1587, she was beheaded at Fotheringhay Castle.

Summary

Mary, Queen of Scots, met her death as she had lived her life: with courage and a sense of adventure. A prisoner, she still captivated the hearts of those who knew her and stirred the dreams of those who did not. Her famous motto had been "In My End Is My Beginning." She knew that Elizabeth was aging, barren, and bitter and that Mary's son James would be the logical successor to the English Crown. The Stuarts would triumph in the end. Despite the turbulence of her early years, she had finally found an inner serenity. In an age of martyrs, she would be surely the most royal. Her end, like her beginning, would capture romantic imaginations forever.

Bibliography

Fraser, Antonia. *Mary Queen of Scots*. London: Weidenfeld and Nicolson, and New York: Delacorte Press, 1969. A colorful and sympathetic biography of Mary, written with tremendous zest and extensive research. Fraser is, perhaps, overly antagonistic to Elizabeth's political situation but is so readable that the reader forgives any imbalance.

Froude, J. A. *History of England from the Fall of Wolsey to the Defeat of the Spanish Armada*. London: Parker, 1862; New York: Scribner, 1970. A panoramic work by a distinguished historian, it sets the stage for Anglo-Scottish policies on a national and international scale.

Girouard, Mark. *Robert Smythson and the Architecture of the Elizabethan Era*. London: Country Life, 1966; South Brunswick, N.J.: Barnes, 1967. Interesting for the illustrations of several of the places where Mary was held during her nineteen-year stay in England. In particular, some of the properties of the Earl of Shrewsbury and his formidable wife, Elizabeth, are depicted.

Gore-Browne, R. *Lord Bothwell*. London: Collins, and New York: Doubleday, 1937. Remains the only work to study Bothwell in some detail and is useful if somewhat romanticized on the family background.

Hosack, John. *Mary, Queen of Scots, and Her Accusers*. Edinburgh: Blackwood, 1869. An old but interesting examination of the enemies of the queen, their motives and weapons in attacking her rule and reputation.

MacNalty, Sir Arthur Salusbury. *Mary Queen of Scots: The Daughter of Debate*. London: Johnson, 1960; New York: Ungar, 1961. A good, readable biography of Mary and the attitudes of those who knew her. While interesting, it does not have the depth of interpretation of character that makes Fraser's Mary so vivid.

Phillips, J. E. *Images of a Queen: Mary Stuart in Sixteenth Century Literature*. Berkeley: University of California Press, 1964. An interesting and scholarly work that reflects both the concept of royalty and the life of Mary in the literature of her own times.

Strickland, Agnes. *Lives of the Queens of Scotland.* London: Coburn, and New York: Harper, 1854. A pioneering work in the use of historical sources. Strickland was deeply stirred by the tragedy of Mary's life and devoted considerable energy to understanding the queen's personality and the conflicts within sixteenth century Scotland.

E. Deanne Malpass

MARY I

Born: February 18, 1516; Greenwich, England
Died: November 17, 1558; London, England
Area of Achievement: Government
Contribution: Mary was the first woman to rule England in her own right; she also restored Catholicism to her country.

Early Life

Mary I was the first surviving child of King Henry VIII and his first wife, Catherine of Aragon. Although Henry VIII wanted a male heir and although he could still hope a son would be born, Mary received more than the normal attention due a royal child. Catherine commissioned the Spanish humanist, Juan Vives, to devise an educational program for Mary and employed Thomas Linacre as her daughter's first tutor. Henry often proudly displayed the young princess to foreign ambassadors. She played the expected role in diplomacy as Henry tried to arrange marriages for her with the heir to the French throne as well as with her older cousin, the Holy Roman Emperor, Charles V. In 1524, Henry made her the first princess of Wales with her own household and administrative staff at Ludlow.

The king's "Great Matter," Henry's decision to end his marriage to Catherine in order to marry Anne Boleyn, reversed Mary's fortunes in her teenage years. Henry had every reason to expect a favorable response from Rome, but just as he needed an annulment, the Papacy came under the control of Charles V, Catherine's nephew. Consequently the pope, Clement VII, was not free to dissolve the marriage. Henry was genuinely fond of Mary so her position did not change immediately. Although she was seldom at court while the king and his council struggled to obtain the "divorce" from 1529 to 1533, Mary developed a hatred of Anne and a fierce loyalty to her mother. When the new Archbishop of Canterbury, Thomas Cranmer, declared the marriage to Catherine void in the spring of 1533, Mary became illegitimate. After the birth of Elizabeth, on September 7, Mary's material circumstances changed radically. To punish Mary for her loyalty to Catherine, Henry separated her from her mother, revoked her title, and placed her in the hostile atmosphere of the Princess Elizabeth's household. Despite intense pressure, she refused to accept the separation from Rome and the altered succession to the Crown; as a result of this psychological conflict, she suffered recurring physical ailments. She did not submit until after her mother's death and Anne Boleyn's execution in 1536. After that, her situation improved, but she never regained her former favored position. Mary lived quietly for the rest of Henry's reign, but as a result of her previous experiences, she firmly identified herself with her mother's memory and Catholicism.

The reign of her half brother Edward VI (1547-1553) tested Mary's religious conviction. Mary's position became precarious as Protestantism grew, under the leadership of Edward Seymour, Duke of Somerset, and then John Dudley, Duke of Northumberland. Because she had become a symbol of the old religion, the council challenged her right to hear Mass in her household after the rebellious summer of 1549. Mary consistently resisted. Ultimately, her closest advisers and household servants were sent to the Tower of London, but she was not harmed. In the spring of 1553, as it became obvious that Edward would not live, the young king and the Duke of Northumberland altered the established succession by replacing Mary with Lady Jane Grey, a Protestant, the granddaughter of Henry VIII's younger sister Mary. When Edward died on July 6, Mary was warned in time to escape to Framlingham castle in Suffolk, whence she could either flee to the Continent or resist the new government. Lady Jane was proclaimed queen, but to the surprise of many, the East Anglian nobility and gentry responded to Mary's call for aid. Within nine days, she had a council and an army strong enough to convince the officials in London to proclaim her queen on July 19, 1553.

As she ascended the throne at the age of thirty-seven, Mary's attitudes were shaped by her past experiences. She remained devoted to her mother's religion and continued to rely on the advice of Charles V, whose ambassadors had often been her only consistent support and comfort. Given her history, Mary could have been an embittered, vengeful woman, but she was not. She enjoyed the elegant clothes and jewels that she used to enhance her auburn hair and small stature. Although she loved to gamble, she appeared serious and pious, more like a kindly maiden aunt than a queen regnant.

Life's Work

History has not treated Mary well. Her persecution of Protestants earned for her the epithet "Bloody Mary," and her marriage to Philip II of Spain, the son of Charles V, was a serious mistake. At the beginning of her reign, Mary faced many problems. Her right to rule had been challenged, she had to form a government using the same officials who had supported Lady Jane, and she had to overcome the factionalism and economic distress of the previous reign. Initially, without advisers whom she could trust implicitly, Mary relied on the Spanish ambassador, Simon Renard. She energetically devoted her first months as queen to selecting her councillors, establishing her government, beginning to restore Catholicism, and choosing a husband. Although she had been accepted as the legitimate ruler, most believed a woman was naturally too weak to rule alone, and she had a duty to produce a Catholic heir to the throne. During those first months, she made only one disastrous decision by rejecting the single viable English candidate for her hand, Edward Courtenay, the Earl of Devon, and accepting Philip II of Spain. The choice was not popular from the beginning. It split her council and partially caused Wyatt's rebellion (January-February, 1554), the most serious insurrection of the reign. During the rebellion, Mary showed herself a true Tudor. She resisted Renard's advice to flee. Her speech at the Guildhall, in London, rallied the city to her cause and the rebellion failed.

The initial steps toward reunion with Rome were taken in 1553 by Mary's first Parliament. It repealed all the religious legislation of Edward VI's reign, but papal absolution was required to return England to the Catholic fold. Reginald Cardinal Pole, Mary's cousin, was sent as papal legate to end the schism in the fall of 1554. While he had gained a reputation for wisdom and learning during his twenty-year exile, Pole revealed his ignorance of English conditions by insisting that former monastic lands be returned to the Church. Mary, her councillors, and Charles V persuaded Pole to relent, and in December, he presided over the formal reconciliation. Religion was considered the cement of society in the sixteenth century, so religious diversity could not be tolerated: It would subvert a spiritually healthy commonwealth and an orderly government. In that spirit, Parliament revived the medieval heresy laws. The passage of laws could not ensure a Catholic revival, and Pole's plan for a progressive, reformed English Catholicism did not have time to work. As a result, Mary's reign is remembered for heresy trials and the fires of Smithfield. About 293 heretics were burned at the stake after February, 1555. To varying degrees, Bishop Edmund Bonner of London, Bishop Stephen Gardiner of Winchester, the Lord Chancellor, and Cardinal Pole supported the persecution, but the chief responsibility belongs to Mary. She acted, not out of cruelty, but out of a deep concern for the spiritual health of her realm. Still, her firm conviction, which would have been better tempered with a dose of political consideration as Philip advised, led to failure. Far from eliminating heresy, the Protestants became martyrs associated with courage and national pride.

The marriage to Philip failed to produce an heir. Worse, Philip drew Mary into his foreign entanglements. Ironically, in 1557 Mary agreed to aid Philip against the Papacy and France. The following January, England lost Calais, her last outpost on the Continent, a symbol of England's past military glory. The loss was more symbolic than real. Although Mary has been criticized for entering the war and thus straining her financial resources, it had positive results. The navy was overhauled. A new administrative structure and new men produced a naval policy which defeated Philip's armada in 1588. Mary's death in 1558, ending her reign, was welcomed and celebrated by many of her subjects.

Summary

Accounts of Queen Mary I's reign are still clouded by the liberal Whig vision of history, because England took a more modern direction under Elizabeth I. Mary's accomplishments are often overlooked, and she is unfairly compared to Elizabeth, who ruled forty-five years, not five. In the important area of government finance, the revenue courts were consolidated, austerity measures were employed, and a new book of rates (customs duties) began to increase royal revenue. England's trade position improved when the government recognized that England had been too dependent on trade through Antwerp. Mary and her advisers supported exploration by the Merchant Adventurers and encouraged northern trade though the Muscovy Company. These initiatives outweighed the loss of Calais. Mary's council has traditionally been criticized for being inefficient and factional because of its size. An informal inner ring which functioned with energy and discretion directed policy, and genuine discussion of opposing views on important questions such as religion and her marriage should not be mistaken for factionalism. Parliament showed little organized opposition to the return to Catholicism. Members were more concerned with preserving their monastic lands than with religious issues, and a spirit of compromise and flexi-

bility marked Mary's relationship with them. Mary faced economic and social crises which were a true test of her skill as a ruler, and her solutions compare favorably with Elizabeth's handling of a similar crisis at the end of her reign. After harvest failures in 1555 and 1556, followed by a flu epidemic the next year, the government worked to stimulate the economy. The establishment of London's charitable and welfare institutions, which Mary encouraged, served as models for the whole country. Many of Mary's initiatives bore fruit in Elizabeth's reign. Although personally the most attractive of the Tudors by modern standards, and perhaps the most merciful toward her political enemies, Mary lacked the redeeming political skill of the other Tudors, who instinctively understood and shared the hopes, prejudices, and desires of their subjects. She proved that a woman could rule, if not entirely wisely in terms of policy, at least competently.

Bibliography

Erickson, Carolly. *Bloody Mary.* New York: Doubleday, and London: Dent, 1978. A colorfully written, popular biography which takes a traditional approach and relies on standard sources.

Harbison, E. Harris. *Rival Ambassadors at the Court of Queen Mary.* Princeton, N.J.: Princeton University Press, and London: Oxford University Press, 1940. A classic study of the important role played by the French and Spanish ambassadors in Mary's reign.

Loach, Jennifer. "Mary Tudor and the Re-Catholicisation of England." *History Today* 44 (November, 1994): 1-16. The author presents a reinterpretation of Mary Tudor's re-Catholicization of England. She outlines the survival of Catholicism up to the reign of Elizabeth, and examines the emphasis on the ceremonial and physical aspects of the church and the importance of ceremonies for ordinary parishioners.

———. *Parliament and the Crown in the Reign of Mary Tudor.* Oxford: Clarendon Press, and New York: Oxford University Press, 1986. The only study of Mary's reign from the standpoint of this very important institution of Tudor governance. This study rejects the traditional interpretation of conflict between Crown and Parliament and Catholics and Protestants in her reign.

Loades, David M. *The Oxford Martyrs.* London: Batsford, and New York: Stein and Day, 1970. An objective and scholarly account of the Marian persecution of Protestants.

———. *The Reign of Mary Tudor.* London: Benn, and New York: St. Martin's Press, 1979. The most original, scholarly, and complete account of Mary's reign. It does not include much biographical material, but it does thoroughly analyze the events of the reign.

———. *Two Tudor Conspiracies.* Cambridge: Cambridge University Press, 1965. An account of Wyatt's Rebellion in 1554 and the Dudley Conspiracy in 1555. Some points in the discussion of Wyatt's Rebellion have been disputed, but the book gives invaluable information about some of the discontented.

Prescott, H. M. F. *Mary Tudor.* London: Eyre and Spottiswoode, 1952; New York: Macmillan, 1953. While some aspects of the political and administrative treatment need revision in the light of subsequent scholarship, this is the standard biography.

Richards, Judith M. "Mary Tudor as 'Sole Queen'?: Gendering Tudor Monarchy." *Historical Journal* 40 (December, 1997): 895. Richards argues that the study of Mary Tudor's reign is important in its own right, as well as being a necessary introduction for any wider study of English female monarchy.

Tittler, Robert. *The Reign of Mary I.* 2d ed. London and New York: Longman, 1991. Designed for college students, Tittler's work presents both positive and negative aspects of Mary's reign through a short commentary and documents.

Weikel, Ann. "The Marian Council Revisited." In *The Mid-Tudor Polity: c. 1540-1563*, edited by Jennifer Loach and Robert Tittler. London: Macmillan, and Totowa, N.J.: Rowman and Littlefield, 1980. Contests the traditional view of Marian government through an examination of her council.

Ann Weikel

MASACCIO
Tommaso di Giovanni di Simone Guidi

Born: December 21, 1401; Castel San Giovanni, Republic of Florence

Died: 1428?; Rome

Area of Achievement: Art

Contribution: During a brief career, Masaccio became one of the major creators of the new Renaissance style of painting. His innovations utilizing perspective created a standard of realism admired and imitated by subsequent generations of artists.

Early Life

In contrast to the lives of such prominent Renaissance artists as Leonardo da Vinci and Michelangelo, little is known concerning the life of the Florentine painter Masaccio, who managed during his brief life to revolutionize the world of painting. He was born Tommaso di Giovanni di Simone Guidi in the small Tuscan town of Castel San Giovanni, now known as San Giovanni Valdarno, on Saint Thomas' Day, December 21, 1401.

His grandfather had settled in San Giovanni in the 1380's and established himself as a successful furniture maker. Masaccio's parents, Giovanni di Mone Cassai and Monna Iacopa di Martinozzo, were only twenty and nineteen when their first son was born; they still lived with his grandfather. Masaccio was a nickname derived from Tommaso, meaning "hulking Tom," or "slovenly Tom." In 1406, his parents had another son, Giovanni, who also became an artist and was nicknamed "Lo Scheggia," meaning "the splinter," or "chip." In the same year, Masaccio's father died, and his mother soon remarried. Her second husband was an elderly pharmacist named Tedesco.

The next sixteen years of Masaccio's life are essentially a mystery. Coming from a prosperous family of artisans, he no doubt enjoyed a comfortable childhood. The first specific records of him after 1406 date from January, 1422, when he enrolled in the Florentine guild of physicians and apothecaries, which then included artists in its membership. It remains uncertain under whom he trained, the old theory that he studied under the artist Masolino having been convincingly disproved. He possibly learned some basics about painting from one of the artisans who decorated the painted chests produced in his grandfather's shop. It is also uncertain exactly when Masaccio left San Giovanni for the greater opportunities afforded by Florence. He may have studied there with the painter Mariotto di Cristofano, the husband of one of his stepsisters.

The Florence which became the adolescent Masaccio's new home was then one of the most vibrant and important cities in Europe, on the threshold of its greatest century. One of the chief ways the city fathers expressed their pride in Florence's increasing prominence was by commissioning painters, sculptors, and architects to produce works of art for the city. Masaccio arrived in Florence at exactly the time when monumental artistic projects were making the city the leading artistic center of Europe.

Though the identity of Masaccio's teachers remains a mystery, his revolutionary style was undoubtedly influenced by three key individuals: Giotto, Florence's greatest painter of the previous century; Donatello, the contemporary master sculptor; and Filippo Brunelleschi, the inventive architect and artist. By his early twenties, Masaccio had absorbed the simple dignity of Giotto's composition and solid naturalism of Donatello's sculptures and applied them to Brunelleschi's new laws of linear perspective, so that he was ready to produce some of the most influential paintings and frescoes of the century.

Life's Work

The young Florentine genius enjoyed an active career of less than a decade before his premature death. His earliest known work, a triptych discovered in the obscure Church of San Giovenale in the valley of the Valdarno in 1961, consisted of a Madonna and Child flanked by four saints, a very traditional subject. Already, however, Masaccio was showing signs of a new naturalism and inventiveness in this work. The Christ child was originally completely nude and depicted eating grapes, an iconographical innovation referring to the Eucharist. The triptych's figures clearly mirrored those of Giotto a century earlier and showed a skilled use of foreshortening and light.

Another early work, dating from approximately 1423, was his *Madonna and Child with Saint Anne and Angels*, an altarpiece painted for the Church of Sant'Ambrogio in Florence. Evidently part of this work was painted by Masolino, although scholars disagree on the exact division of work between the two.

One of the few works of Masaccio that can be dated definitively is another altarpiece, a polyptych done for the Church of Santa Maria del Carmine in Pisa. The work was commissioned for a chapel, and Masaccio received eighty florins for his undertaking. The polyptych was dismantled in the eighteenth century and the various pieces scattered. Scholars have subsequently identified eleven of these, and they are now housed in museums in London, Berlin, Naples, Pisa, and Vienna. The only surviving description of the entire work is found in Giorgio Vasari's history. For his centerpiece of the Pisa polyptych, Masaccio again painted the *Madonna and Child*. Surrounding them are four small angels, two of them playing lutes. Another key panel features a dramatic crucifixion scene notable for its rather bulky rendition of Christ and its moving Mary Magdalene. Surviving pieces from the work's predella include a visitation by the Magi and scenes from the lives of various saints.

Works such as the Pisa altarpiece undoubtedly added to the growing reputation of the young painter. Contemporary records reveal little about the details of his life in Florence during this period. The number of known works he produced demonstrates that he was rarely without work and thus reasonably secure financially. Tax returns from July, 1427, indicate that he was living in a house rented for ten florins a year. His younger brother and widowed mother were living with him. He also rented part of a workshop for an additional two florins a year. Donatello and Brunelleschi were among his close friends. Writing more than a century after Masaccio's death, Vasari characterized him as an affable, absent-minded individual unconcerned with worldly goods and careless about his dress.

By the mid-1420's, several key elements combined to produce Masaccio's distinctive style. In obvious rebellion against the delicacy of the International Gothic favored by such successful contemporary Florentine artists as Gentile da Fabriano, Masaccio emphasized solid, monumental figures accompanied by somber and simple backgrounds. His careful study of the human form and the effect of light produced works of revolutionary realism. Although color was not unimportant to him, Masaccio was more clearly dedicated to form. His figures emerged as unique individuals rather than faceless stereotypes. Instead of the elaborate brocades habitually used in International Gothic, Masaccio's biblical figures wore simple, heavy cloaks. Above all, the new laws of perspective enabled the young master to produce works that put his figures in believable space rather than having them float aimlessly against solid gold backgrounds.

The outstanding examples of Masaccio's style are found in his frescoes located in the Brancacci Chapel in the Florentine Church of Santa Maria del Carmine. The exact date of his work there remains unclear, as does the name of the patron, although it was undoubtedly a member of the influential mercantile Brancacci family. Some of the chapel's frescoes were the work of Masolino, who had earlier collaborated with the young artist on the altarpiece for the Church of Sant'Ambrogio. It remains uncertain whether the two worked together in the chapel or whether Masolino began the project and then abandoned it to Masaccio when he left for another commission in Hungary. The chapel remained unfinished at the time of Masaccio's death and was completed only in the 1480's by a third artist, Filippino Lippi.

Scholars generally attribute six of the major scenes and part of another to Masaccio. One of these includes *The Expulsion from Paradise*, a moving work showing Adam and Eve being driven from the Garden of Eden. The figures, depicted against a bleak landscape, almost resemble freestanding sculpture in the new tradition of Donatello. Masaccio's masterful use of atmospheric perspective and emotional expression infuses the scene with drama.

The majority of his Brancacci chapel frescoes, though, depict various scenes from the life of Saint Peter, a rare iconographical theme in Florence during this period. By far the most famous of these, and generally regarded as his masterpiece, is *The Tribute Money*. Inspired by the biblical story found in Matthew 17:24-27, the fresco is a simultaneous narrative in three parts. In the center section, a tax collector confronts Christ and his apostles and demands tribute. On the left, Saint Peter obeys Christ's injunction to cast forth his hook and take a coin out of the mouth of the first fish he catches; on the left, Saint Peter pays the tribute to the tax collector. This fresco was perhaps inspired by a new tax imposed by the Florentine government in 1427. Whatever the inspira-

tion, the figures in *The Tribute Money*, as well as in Masaccio's other frescoes in the chapel, exhibit a convincing realism and individuality.

Masaccio's most unconventional fresco is located in the Church of Santa Maria Novella in Florence. The famous *Holy Trinity with the Virgin and Saint John*, most commonly dated to 1425, again shows his creative genius. It depicts the Trinity within an architectural framework inspired by Brunelleschi, expertly creating an illusion of depth through the barrel vaulted ceiling. To accompany the Trinity, Masaccio painted figures of Mary and John and below them full-size portraits of the donor and his wife. Their identities remain uncertain although it is possible that they were members of the Lenzi family. For the first time, the donors are portrayed on the same scale as the divine figures, a significant innovation. Long covered by a sixteenth century altar, *Holy Trinity with the Virgin and Saint John* was not rediscovered until 1861. When it was cleaned in 1952, restorers discovered a skeleton painted below the donors. Such memento mori were rare in Florence's artistic tradition.

In addition to the previously discussed works, Masaccio produced several others which have been destroyed. These included a "Consecration" fresco for the Carmine Cloisters in Pisa, a fresco of Saint Ives and his wards for Florence's Church of the Badia in 1627, and a Saint Paul fresco for that city's Church of the Carmine. Vasari mentions that Masaccio painted several portraits of eminent Florentines, but these remain lost or have not survived.

Sometime in 1428, the young artist abandoned work on the Brancacci Chapel and left Florence for Rome. The reason remains unclear, although it was possibly a response to a summons from his friend Masolino, who was then in the city. Before the end of the year, Masaccio died, so suddenly and unexpectedly that rumors spread that he had been poisoned. His friend Brunelleschi summarized the impact of the twenty-seven-year-old genius' demise when he remarked that the art world had suffered a most grievous loss.

Summary

The paintings of Masaccio had an influence upon the formation of the Renaissance style equal to the contemporary accomplishments in sculpture by Donatello and in architecture by Brunelleschi. The young Florentine was thus one of the three pivotal influences in establishing Florentine ascendancy in the art world during the fifteenth century, a most remarkable achievement considering the brevity of his career.

His handful of surviving frescoes inspired generations of painters who studied them for their masterful skill in making the human figure come alive. Such prominent artists as Fra Filippo Lippi, Sandro Botticelli, Andrea del Verrocchio, Leonardo da Vinci, Michelangelo, and Raphael all found inspiration for aspects of their style in the work of Masaccio. All made the pilgrimage to the tiny Brancacci Chapel to study his masterly modeling of the human figure.

Influenced by the earlier works of Giotto, as well as by classical sculpture, Masaccio created a brilliant new standard for painting that effectively abandoned medieval two-dimensionality and instead explored the possibilities for realism provided by atmospheric and linear perspective. Masaccio's figures emerged as real individuals, full of emotion and dignity. They symbolized the self-confidence of the Renaissance epoch dawning in Florence and served as models for countless later Renaissance works. The Brancacci Chapel frescoes established artistic standards that endured virtually unchallenged until the nineteenth century. Although the details of his life remain obscure and largely undocumented, Masaccio's importance in art history remains firmly entrenched. Few other painters, if any, have managed to transform the course of painting so decisively in such a short time.

Bibliography

Berti, Luciano. *Masaccio*. University Park: Pennsylvania State University Press, 1967. A lucid and lavishly illustrated biography, meticulously researched, with detailed explanatory footnotes. Contains a chronological bibliography of books and articles written about Masaccio between 1436 and 1964. Includes a catalog of Masaccio's known and lost works and of paintings that have generally been attributed to him.

Cole, Bruce. *Masaccio and the Art of Early Renaissance Florence*. Bloomington: Indiana University Press, 1980. This well-researched monograph contains three chapters on Masaccio, dealing respectively with his life, the Pisa Altarpiece, and his frescoes. The other four chapters discuss the nature of Florentine art in the decades immediately preceding and following his death. The bibliography contains more than sixty books and articles on Masaccio, as well as many others dealing with the period.

Goffen, Rona, ed. *Masaccio's "Trinity."* Cambridge and New York: Cambridge University Press, 1998. This work examines one of the most influential paintings of the Italian Renaissance. Renowned for the grandeur of its characterizations and for the illusion of perspective of its architectural setting, the fresco has been famous from the time it was painted in the 1420s, and is remembered despite its having been hidden from view for nearly two centuries. This volume considers the "Trinity" in its historical and spiritual contexts, and describes the significance of Massacio's innovative depictions of time and space.

Hartt, Frederick. *History of Italian Renaissance Art: Painting, Sculpture, Architecture*. 4th ed. London: Thames and Hudson, and Englewood Cliffs, N.J.: Prentice-Hall, 1994. A standard survey of the major achievements of the era. Hartt's chapter on "Gothic and Renaissance in Florentine Painting" discusses Masaccio's life and works, especially relating them to Masolino. Contains useful introductions and a good bibliography.

Olmert, M., and A. Quattrone. "The New Look of the Brancacci Chapel Discloses Miracles." *Smithsonian* 20 (February, 1990): 94. The authors report on the restoration of the Masaccio frescoes in the Brancacci Chapel in Florence, outlining the restoration technique, the histories of the frescoes, and the basic facts regarding Masaccio's life.

Vasari, Giorgio. *The Lives of the Artists*. Edited by William Gaunt. 4 vols. London: Dent, and New York: Noonday Press, 1963. First published in 1550 and substantially expanded in 1568, Vasari's collection of biographies of famous Renaissance architects, sculptors, and painters provides the earliest secondary information about the life and career of Masaccio. He established many historical traditions about Masaccio and described some of his works that have subsequently been destroyed or lost. Some of his statements have been disproved by modern art historians.

Venturi, Lionello, and Rosabianca Skira-Venturi. *Italian Painting: The Creators of the Renaissance*. Geneva: Skira, 1950; New York: Skira, 1951. This volume deals with the thirteenth through the fifteenth century in Italian painting and includes a brief chapter on Masaccio. Contains large color reproductions of many of his major works and a useful chart on the Brancacci Chapel frescoes.

Tom L. Auffenberg

MATTHIAS I CORVINUS
Mátyás Hunyadi

Born: February 24, 1443; Kolozsvár, Transylvania
Died: April 6, 1490; Vienna, Austria
Areas of Achievement: Monarchy, government, politics, the military, and patronage of the arts
Contribution: Matthias I excelled as soldier, diplomat, and legal reformer. Most important, he moved Hungary from feudal particularism toward a more centralized state and through his lavish patronage promoted a remarkable Humanist literary and artistic achievement on the model of the Italian Renaissance.

Early Life

Matthias I Corvinus was the second son of János Hunyadi, a self-made man of the lesser Hungarian nobility. Hunyadi won great military renown fighting against the Ottoman Turks and in the process had become the largest single landowner in the kingdom, arousing the fear and resentment of the magnates, to Matthias' later detriment. Meanwhile, Matthias as a boy received under his father a rigorous military training. He polished his soldierly skills in battle and was knighted at the age of fourteen during a victorious engagement with the Turks at Belgrade. Matthias' father also provided him with a superior education through private tutors headed by János Vitéz, a man of strong Humanist sympathies. Matthias became fascinated with Italian Renaissance culture.

Upon the sudden death of his father in 1456, Matthias and his elder brother were seized by feudal enemies of the Hunyadi family, with the approval of the impressionable boy-king Ladislas V. Matthias' brother was executed, but Matthias was spared, apparently because of his youth. When Ladislas died without an heir in late 1457, the Diet of Hungarian nobles decided, with some qualms, to elect as king the fifteen-year-old Matthias, preferring him both for his native birth and for the heroic image left by his father. The candidates of assorted Polish, Saxon, and Austrian Habsburg dynasties were passed over. At his accession, Matthias was a blond-haired, vigorous, powerfully built youth. He had a charming manner that belied a sometimes-fiery temper.

The new king faced a desperate situation. The royal treasury was empty while hostile forces pressed from virtually all sides. As Czech marauders and Hungarian rebels plagued much of northern Hungary, Turkish armies to the south held all of Serbia and raided Hungarian territory continually. Meanwhile, to the west the Austrian Habsburg Emperor Frederick III, who coveted the Hungarian crown, plotted Matthias' overthrow with the help of an alienated faction of the Hungarian magnates. Finally, a crippling condition of Matthias' election was that he submit during the first five years of his reign to a regency government under his uncle and a council of state composed mainly of magnates. In meeting these challenges, Matthias soon demonstrated that Hungary had acquired no ordinary monarch.

Life's Work

Matthias I rejected from the outset the authority of the regency council. Within months he had deposed his uncle, the regent, and replaced the magnates on the council with his personal choices. The young king then drew upon his private resources to crush the northern rebellion and clear that region of its roving Czech military bands. By 1462, he had met temporarily the challenge of the Austrian emperor from the west through a skillfully negotiated treaty. That gave Matthias the breathing space to turn finally to the south, where Turkish forces had advanced from Serbian bases to overrun the neighboring Hungarian region of Wallachia. In a series of brilliant campaigns, Matthias recovered northern Serbia and most of Wallachia. He consolidated his gains with a chain of forts.

Matthias' impressive military and diplomatic successes were attributable largely to a complete restructuring of the Hungarian army accomplished during his first years in power. Believing the traditional feudal levy inadequate to his needs, the king recruited an army composed mostly of Czech and German mercenaries, professional soldiers who could be mobilized on short notice. These troops, supplemented by native feudal contingents, he personally trained and maintained with firm discipline and good pay. At its peak, the new standing army numbered some thirty thousand men, about two-thirds of them heavily armed cavalry. Known from their garb as the Black Army, these forces became the chief instrument in carrying out Matthias' foreign policy objectives.

To support his large military establishment, the king had to overhaul the tax system. A decree of 1467 become the cornerstone of a fiscal policy designed to produce the funds not only for the army but also for Matthias' extensive political and cultural projects. Previously inviolate tax exemptions for the magnates were drastically curtailed, while heavy new taxes were imposed on the free peasantry. Old taxes were given new names and expanded in scope. To handle the windfall of revenue, Matthias staffed his treasury office with specialists. Despite widespread protests and occasional tax rebellions, Matthias' fiscal reforms yielded a tenfold increase in royal income over that of his predecessor.

The king pursued other administrative and social reforms. Deeply suspicious of the feudal magnates, Matthias chose to run his government through a professionalized chancellery office staffed by men of humbler social background. He also won the gratitude of many towns through royal grants of autonomous status through the local feudal jurisdictions. To improve the administration of justice generally, Matthias revamped the court system. He installed a new appeals procedure that ran from local jurisdictions through an intermediate level to the royal court itself, at each stage conducted by judges knowledgeable in the law. Also, new laws were decreed that protected the rights of the free peasantry, softening the impact of his taxes by improving their status in relation to the magnates, while other legislation prohibited the tightening of bonds on serfs. Matthias' legal reforms culminated in a royal decree of 1486, in which he sought to provide a synthesis or codification of the best principles of Hungarian jurisprudence, both in criminal and in civil law.

Following his early military and diplomatic victories, Matthias determined to use the Black Army to unite the Czech and Austrian realms with Hungary. Although his long-range policy goals were never clearly stated, it is possible that he contemplated the building of a coalition of central European Christian states to deal decisively with the Muslim Turkish menace in the Balkans, something he felt unable to achieve alone. In any case, from 1468 onward, Matthias began to compete more aggressively for the crown of Bohemia. By 1478, after defeating a combined Czech, Polish, and Austrian force four times the size of the Black Army, Matthias had his prize. Under terms of the Peace of Olomouc, the Hungarian monarch took not only the title of King of Bohemia but also the associated lands of Moravia, Silesia, and Lusatia. Then, between 1477 and 1490, Matthias fought three wars against his old antagonist the Austrian Emperor Frederick III. By 1485, the Black Army had occupied the Habsburg capital of Vienna and most of southern Austria soon afterward. Matthias triumphantly took up residence in Vienna, but the imperial crown itself would elude him, as Frederick III refused to designate Matthias his heir.

The most enduring achievement in Matthias' reign would lie not in his political and military exploits but in the prodigious cultural energies he brought to focus in Hungary. Convinced that cultural distinction was essential to a prince of his eminence in the Renaissance era, Matthias determined early to create a court life that was at once enlightened, elegant, and cosmopolitan. To this end, he gathered Humanist scholars around him, mostly from Italy, and drew many of his officials from their ranks. Further, he subsidized with great generosity the work of painters, sculptors, architects, and goldsmiths. Himself highly educated, the king often was a participant in the lively philosophical and scientific discussions he encouraged at court. His marriage in 1476 to Beatrix, daughter of the

King of Naples, only intensified the impact of the Italian Renaissance on Hungarian elite society.

Resident Italian historians such as Antonio Bonfini now wrote histories of Hungary in which Matthias, to his delight, was hailed as a "second Attila." The same flattering Humanist Bonfini also stretched Matthias' genealogy to include as forebear a distinguished ancient Roman consul whose family crest, a crow (*corvinus*), Matthias promptly made his own. Finally, the king imported art work from Italy and ordered the decoration of his various palaces with appropriate Renaissance paintings and statues.

Matthias' reputation as "friend of the muses" would rest above all on the splendid Corvina library he assembled in his Buda palace. The estimated twenty-five hundred manuscripts of the Corvina at its peak contained some six thousand distinct Greek and Latin works. These titles, by pagan and Christian alike, reflected the breadth of Matthias' interests. The books ranged in subject from military strategy and law through art and theology to Renaissance literature. Matthias also employed transcribers and book illuminators to copy and adorn selected works and emboss them with gems and precious metals. The Corvina would remain his greatest cultural legacy.

Matthias Corvinus died at age forty-seven in Vienna, the victim of a stroke that ended prematurely his grand scheme of a Hungarian empire embracing south-central Europe. He was interred near Budapest. He left only an illegitimate son who was quickly passed over by the Diet of magnates. They elected a Polish youth who seemed malleable enough and who, above all, was not of the house of Corvinus. In the grim generation that followed, the Black Army was disbanded, and Matthias' other major reforms were allowed to lapse. In 1526, an overwhelming Hungarian defeat at Mohács began two centuries of Turkish occupation.

Summary

Most of King Matthias' achievements proved fleeting because of the lack of capable successors. Yet the thirty-two years of his reign remain among the most remarkable in Hungarian history. Against heavy odds, Matthias I Corvinus managed to reverse several generations of feudal anarchy. He did so by remodeling the central government in ways similar to innovations then being ventured in the major Renaissance monarchies of the West. In particular, Matthias' administrative and legal reforms laid the foundations for a regime perceived as more stable and more just in its relations with its citizens generally. The renown of his judicial measures is reflected in the popular lament that followed his passing: "Matthias is dead; justice has fled." In addition to his judicial and economic reforms, Matthias created in the Black Army one of the earliest standing armies in Europe. It made Hungary for a time the major power of central Europe. Yet there is some validity to the criticism that Matthias became so obsessed with the conquest of the Habsburg lands and the imperial crown that he badly neglected the critical problem of the Turks.

Matthias is remembered not only as a warrior, statesman, and lawgiver, but also as an extremely generous patron of arts and letters. The Corvina library ranked with the Vatican and the Medici collections in Italy as the foremost in Europe.

Matthias I, the Renaissance King of Hungary, was inspired by a larger vision than most princes of his time regarding the distinctive values of a civilized society and how to achieve them. A generation of prosperity and promise for his people expired with the man himself.

Bibliography

Csapodi, Csaba. *The Corvinian Library: History and Stock.* Translated by Imre Gombos. Budapest: Akadémiai Kiadó, 1973. The definitive descriptive and historical account of Matthias' library. Provides valuable information on the scribes and illuminators of the books and where manuscripts are to be found. Provides an informed estimate that the Corvina originally contained at least twenty-five hundred manuscripts.

Kosáry, Dominic G. *A History of Hungary.* New York: Benjamin Franklin Bibliophile Society, 1941. Foreword by Julius Szekfü. An admiring but solid account of Matthias' chief policies and achievements. Kosáry argues that Matthias' efforts at erecting a central European empire of Austria and Bohemia, along with Hungary, was intended only as a prelude to ending decisively the Turkish threat in the south.

Kosztolynik, Zoltan J. "Some Hungarian Theologians in the Late Renaissance." *Church History* 57 (1988): 5-18. A good overview of an important segment of intellectual life in Matthias' Hungary, focused especially on the distinguished theologian Pelbart of Temesvar. Valuable for aspects of Matthias' relationship with the Hungarian church, particularly in substantiating the underlying resentment and hostility of leading Hungarian churchmen toward their Renaissance king.

Sinor, Denis. *History of Hungary.* London: Allen and Unwin, and New York: Praeger, 1959. The most balanced, scholarly, and informative account available in English. Provides a careful appraisal of the weaknesses as well as the strengths of Matthias' impressive reign. Sinor argues, contrary to Kosáry, that Matthias' pursuit of an elusive Hungarian empire that would include Austria and Bohemia was an end in itself, not directed toward building an anti-Turkish alliance.

Vámbéry, Arminius, with Louis Heilprin. *The Story of Hungary.* London and New York: Putnam, 1886. Lacking a good modern biography in English, this rather uncritical treatment remains useful for the vivid, extensive detail relating to Matthias himself, especially the earlier years, on which little is available elsewhere.

Varga, Domokos G. *Hungary in Greatness and Decline: The Fourteenth and Fifteenth Centuries.* Translated by Martha S. Liptaks. Atlanta: Hungarian Cultural Foundation, 1982. The most extensive treatment available in English on the core period of Matthias' regime. The main value of this work lies in its extensive citations of original chronicle sources and its excellent illustrations.

Donald D. Sullivan

MAXIMILIAN I

Born: March 22, 1459; Wiener Neustadt, Austria
Died: January 12, 1519; Wels, Austria
Areas of Achievement: Government and politics
Contribution: Maximilian I revived and strengthened both the concept and the actual position of Holy Roman Emperor by a great reform movement. These accomplishments were short-lived, however, and his enduring contribution lies in the development of German and Austrian nationalism.

Early Life

Maximilian was the only son of the emperor Frederick III and Eleanor of Portugal. The varied genetic background of Maximilian (he was also the great-great-grandson of John of Gaunt and had Polish, Lithuanian, and Russian blood from his paternal grandmother) combined to produce a highly interesting character. He was energetic, vivacious, and restless; he was an adventurer, an avid hunter, and a mountaineer; he was friendly, gregarious, and popular because he inspired confidence; and he loved writing, music, and the study of different languages. He was filled with curiosity, a love of learning, and a desire to meet people.

With his dynamic personality, it is not surprising that even before he became emperor, on the death of his father in 1493, Maximilian could boast of an impressive string of accomplishments. On February 16, 1486, he was crowned king at Aix-la-Chapelle, becoming coruler with his father. In 1486, he was also granted the title King of the Romans. Frederick worked patiently with Maximilian to teach him the concepts of governing an empire, a sense of responsibility, and political ethics. Maximilian also gained from his father personal strength and dignity. These lessons would prove valuable when Maximilian assumed full control of the imperial office.

In 1477, with his career just beginning, Maximilian married the heiress of the Burgundian lands, Mary, daughter of Charles the Bold. Charles had just been killed in battle against the Swiss, who, along with the French, moved quickly to appropriate portions of his inheritance, which Charles had carefully and laboriously assembled in the hope of Burgundy's becoming a kingdom. Maximilian, often called "the last knight," arrived just in time to prevent the dismembering of Burgundy. By his marriage to Mary, he added her lands, consisting of the Netherlands, Luxembourg, Artois, and Picardy, to the Habsburg holdings. Maximilian also recovered Franche-Comté and lands in Austria and the Tyrol. By 1491, he had made claim to Hungary and Bohemia. Maximilian not only acquired lands but also emerged as a recognized leader in the field of European politics, giving rise to the power of the house of Habsburg. Thereafter, the Habsburgs retained control of the imperial office, and France was forced to pursue its expansionist policies in Italy.

Maximilian's relationship with Mary resembled a storybook romance. He loved her sincerely, spending much time with her at sporting activities, social events, and government functions. Together they had two children, Philip and Margaret. Mary was killed in 1482, however, as a result of a fall from a horse, causing Maximilian to have to face the resistance of stubborn Netherlanders who did not want to see Mary's children entrusted to his guardianship. In 1488, the citizens of Bruges even took him prisoner, although he was rescued by his father. All the events, however, successful and frustrating, of his involvement with Burgundian politics taught him valuable lessons in statecraft and gave him insights into ethnic characteristics of the Flemish people that he could use later.

Life's Work

Maximilian became Holy Roman Emperor in 1493 after the death of his father. His great popularity, untiring energy, and capacity for work aroused the concern of the electors, who did not want to see the imperial office regain real power. The leader of the opposition was his lifelong enemy, Prince Berthold, Elector of Mainz. Berthold attempted to increase opposition to the emperor and create an administrative machine which would weaken Maximilian's hand and require approval for his acts. Berthold proposed a regency council (*Reichsregiment*), which the emperor bitterly fought. It was adopted in 1500 but failed two years later. Had it continued, it would have represented a great victory for the Electors and the Estates of Germany. Maximilian, trying to sabotage the council, acted independently of it, gaining support from the young princes of Germany, with whom he was highly popular. He also took advantage of the quarrels and dissension among council members.

His need for money to deal with the threat of invasion by the Turks forced him into a meeting with the

electors and princes in 1495. This assembly, the Diet of Worms, marked the real beginning of his reign. Maximilian showed his capability as a ruler by dealing with the demands of the jealous nobility through compromises in which he gained more than the nobility. One of the results was the Common Penny, a tax collected from subjects throughout the realm to provide funds for Maximilian's campaign against the Turks. In return, he allowed the Estates the opportunity to be included in his new bureaucratic offices. As a counterpoise to the proposed *Reichsregiment*, Maximilian established the Imperial Chamber (*Reichskammergericht*), a supreme court of justice with a president appointed by the emperor and sixteen justices appointed by the Estates. The chamber acted as a court of appeals in private cases and as a court to settle disputes among princes. It is important to note that the chamber implemented Roman law and served as a court of the empire rather than of the emperor. It also served as a rival to the regency council and gave the emperor considerable influence in judicial proceedings. Perhaps the most significant accomplishment of the Diet of Worms was the peace (*Landfriede*), which effectively brought an end to personal warfare. With the decline of feudal power and the loss of feudal restraints, private vendettas were rife in Germany. This peace, to be eternal, meant that private disputes would now be settled in a court of law.

In another move to centralize power, Maximilian activated the six administrative circles originally planned by Emperor Albert II in 1438. In 1512, Maximilian added four circles. Each major district of the empire contained the organization for both war and peace as each circle had a military commander and an administrative director. In 1501, Maximilian created the Aulic Council, which had eight members appointed by the emperor. This council allowed the emperor to hear appeals and to exercise supreme jurisdiction, extending the emperor's authority even into Italy.

Maximilian also had a separate financial administration dependent on him alone and a modern chancery with judges whom he appointed. Within a few years, Maximilian was able to replace the old feudal power of the Electors and the Estates of Germany with a new, modern, centralized bureaucracy. By 1505, Berthold was dead, leaving Maximilian with no enemies. He had gained the support of the young leaders, and he had reached the apex of his power and influence. In 1508, Pope Julius II approved for him the title Roman Emperor Elect. Maximilian took very seriously his religious responsibilities, believing that he was born destined to be a new Constantine who would strengthen and extend the borders of Christ's kingdom. He also took quite seriously the concept that he was destined to perpetuate the ancient Roman Empire as a new Augustus.

As important as Maximilian's modernized bureaucracy was to the enhancement of Habsburg power, perhaps more important were the dynastic marriages he arranged. He promoted a double marriage between his son Philip and Joanna, the second daughter of Ferdinand and Isabella of Spain, and between his daughter Margaret and the Spanish prince John. The untimely deaths of the heirs to the Spanish throne placed Philip in a position to inherit the Spanish empire. He later arranged a marriage between his granddaughter and Louis II, son of Ladislas, the King of Hungary and Bohemia, and between his grandson Ferdinand and Louis' sister. These dynastic marriages extended Habsburg control to include an extensive empire.

Maximilian's apparent genius as a leader and his successes attracted the attention of the scholarly community of Europe, who looked to Maximilian to establish an enlightened Christian empire. Humanists, whose vision centered on classical antiquity and the days of imperial Rome, were drawn to the patronage of Maximilian's court. They sincerely believed that Maximilian was destined to restore glory to Germany; Maximilian felt keenly this sense of his own destiny to be the founder of a new world order. At the same time, he found the Humanists useful in spreading the good news of his glorious reign. Maximilian worked hard to upgrade learning in the empire; he turned the University of Vienna into one of the most significant universities in Europe. He also composed works of his own: the *Weisskunig*, an account of his life, *Freydal*, and *Theuerdank*.

The least successful of Maximilian's policies was his involvement in Italian affairs. Maximilian made an alliance with Ludovico, tyrant of Milan, sealing it by marrying Ludovico's niece, Bianca Maria Sforza, in 1494. His purpose was to counteract the growing French influence in Italy, caused to a large degree by Maximilian's expulsion of the French from Burgundian lands. In 1495, he joined the Holy League with the pope, Milan, England, and Aragon to stop the French in Italy. In 1508, he joined the Cambrai League against Venice, and then the new Holy League against the French in 1513. The league forced the French king Louis XII to withdraw, but the French returned later under Francis I. Maximilian's anti-French policy contributed to the protracted war between German and French forces in Italy, which escalated into a series of bloody conflicts over both politics and religion that did not end until 1648. Maximilian also struggled in vain against the Swiss. They fought his forces to a standstill in 1499 during the Swabian War, resulting in the de facto independence of the Swiss, recognized officially at the Peace of Westphalia in 1648. In his declining years, Maximilian spent his time preparing his young grandson Charles to assume the throne. (His son Philip had died in 1506, leaving Charles as heir to the entire Habsburg holdings.) Maximilian died on January 12, 1519, in Wels.

Summary

Maximilian I was able to restore the effectual authority of the emperor and the prestige and prominence of the Holy Roman Empire to its greatest degree of strength since the downfall of the Hohenstaufens. The empire had now at least the appearance of a united state. His own position as a Habsburg ruler was the strongest of any of his family, largely because of his timely dynastic marriages. He was responsible for a more cohesive Germany and for the cultivation of a spirit of national pride within the German people. His *Landfriede* program brought about peace and order, ending the tyranny of robber barons. Maximilian faced political realities and could conceive of modern alternatives to feudal traditions and institutions. He was not an original thinker, but he was able to take ideas from others and make them work, creating an effective political machine. He was an enlightened ruler who showed an interest in church reform and the advancement of learning. He showed a modern adroitness in political propaganda—a politician's skill in disarming his opponents—usually coming out on the winning side.

Maximilian's reform, however, was short-lived. Internally, his power was never more than an uneasy balance between imperial and feudal elements. Although the Aulic Council continued to the end of the empire, generally his efforts to create permanent centralized institutions failed. His efforts probably had more to do with the rise of Austrian and German national states than with the preservation of the empire. Some consider him to be the last ruler of the Holy Roman Empire. Certainly he is a transition figure from the old medieval empire to the modern national states. He had energy and a dedication to work, but he lacked clear objectives and persistence. The death of his wife was not only an emotional catastrophe for him but also a political one. His involvement in Burgundy drove the French to Italy, and his involvement in Italy resulted in war and great distress for Germany. Switzerland was lost to the empire; Burgundy became an area fought over by France and Germany for centuries.

The most important and lasting achievement of Maximilian was the cultivation and the institutionalizing of German nationalism. In years to come, the efforts of this "last knight"—who himself was the bridge to the modern world—contributed to the rise of the nineteenth and twentieth century political realizations of the German Reich.

Bibliography

Bryce, James. *The Holy Roman Empire*. Rev. ed. London: St. Martin's Press, and New York: Macmillan, 1904. Important for the discussion of the transfer of the imperial consciousness from Roman to German and the carrying forth of the concept that the one empire is eternal. Somewhat dated but thorough, especially in the discussion of the relationship of Germany to the Church.

Gilmore, Myron P. *The World of Humanism, 1453-1517*. New York: Harper, 1952. Very valuable source for the study of Humanism, which provides the intellectual context for Maximilian's time. The chapter on dynastic consolidation is interesting, especially as it pertains to Germany. The discussion of Maximilian is highly informative.

Heer, Friedrich. *The Holy Roman Empire*. Translated by Janet Sondheimer. London: Weidenfeld and Nicolson, and New York: Praeger, 1968. A most valuable source for students of medieval German history. Begins with the birth of the Roman Empire and traces the development of imperial consciousness. Excellent discussion of Maximilian and his relationship to the general picture. Good illustrations, an excellent index, and a bibliography.

Holborn, Hajo. *A History of Modern Germany*. Vol. 1, *The Reformation*. New York: Knopf, 1959; London: Eyre and Spottiswoode, 1965. Begins with the German migrations and continues through the history of the empire to the sixteenth century. Very good for setting forth ideas and underlying causes; good analysis. Overview of Maximilian's life is good; main points delineated well.

Maehl, William H. *Germany in Western Civilization*. University: University of Alabama Press, 1979. This critical and very comprehensive work begins with ancient times and follows the history of Germany to the post-World War II era. An excellent index, a bibliography, a glossary, and a chronological list of German rulers. Especially good discussion of Maximilian's dedication to scholarship, his marriage alliances, and his Italian policy.

Stubbs, William. *Germany in the Later Middle Ages, 1200-1500*. Edited by Arthur Hassall. London and New York: Longman, 1908. This work consists of a series of lectures which the author delivered at the University of Oxford. Provides a detailed view of Germany in the thirteenth, fourteenth, and fifteenth centuries.

J. David Lawrence

LORENZO DE' MEDICI

Born: January 1, 1449; Florence

Died: April 8, 1492; Careggi, near Florence

Areas of Achievement: Banking, finance, government, politics, diplomacy, and literature

Contribution: Florence's Lorenzo de' Medici was the most important statesman in Italy during the latter part of the fifteenth century. Lorenzo was also a noted banker, poet, and patron of the arts. He epitomized the concept of the Renaissance man.

Early Life

Lorenzo de' Medici was born in Florence in 1449. His father, Piero, died at age fifty-three in 1469. Lorenzo's grandfather, Cosimo, building on the accomplishments of his father, Giovanni, had established himself as the most powerful individual in the Florentine Republic. Medici influence resulted in the wealth accumulated through banking activities. Financial abilities were joined to political talents and ambitions, which made them the most formidable nonroyal family in fifteenth century Europe.

The Medicis were not unique. By the 1400's, there were other influential families in Florence whose wealth and power also came from banking and commerce. Although a republic, Florence was not a democracy; political rights came from membership in the various guilds which had evolved in the later Middle Ages. At the apex were a small number of Florentines, and it was this wealthy oligarchy which controlled the government. All offices were constitutionally open to all guild members, but through various techniques it was possible to manipulate the system. In Renaissance Florence, however, life was more than simply wealth and power for their own sakes. Civic responsibilities went together with political ambition; one was expected to provide public buildings, sponsor schools, or be a patron of the arts. Participation in politics was also expected, as the Medicis well understood, and other Florentine families matched them in wealth and ambition.

In addition to his banking and political responsibilities, Piero, Lorenzo's father, was a patron of the sculptor Donatello and the painter Sandro Botticelli. Lorenzo's mother, Lucrezia Tornabuoni, was a poet of note. Privately tutored, Lorenzo received a humanistic education through the Latin and Greek classics. Education was not merely intellectual: The body and spirit were equally important. He played the lyre, sang his own songs, and wrote his own verse. He rode well and was an accomplished athlete, and he enjoyed talking to both peasants and popes. Piero arranged for Lorenzo's marriage to Clarice Orsini, from an aristocratic Roman family; political and economic considerations were more important than love. Lorenzo was not handsome, with his dark complexion, irregular features, jutting chin, and misshapen nose which denied him a sense of smell. Yet he had a brilliant mind and a charismatic personality.

Life's Work

Lorenzo was only twenty when Piero died. Given his age, he was reluctant to assume the various political and economic responsibilities, but in fact it was impossible for him not to do so. As he himself noted, it did not bode well for someone of wealth to evade his civic obligations. The same techniques that the Medicis had used to gain influence at the expense of others could equally be used against them; if they wished to maintain their position, they had to participate in the political arena. Not only had Lorenzo been trained by scholars, but also he had been sent upon several diplomatic missions before Piero's death. At that time, modifications were made in the Florentine constitution which assured the continued primacy of the Medici party, both for Lorenzo and for those other oligarchs who had attached their ambitions to the Medici banner. Nevertheless, Florence remained officially a republic and Lorenzo ostensibly a private citizen.

During Lorenzo's lifetime, the Medici banks continued to be influential throughout Europe, but less so than earlier. Lorenzo was not particularly interested in banking. Over time, the Medicis became relatively less powerful in banking matters as other cities and nations of Europe rose to positions of power. During Lorenzo's era, his resources were occasionally put under pressure and he was accused of manipulating the economy of Florence to the benefit of the Medicis. Lorenzo could argue that his position, unofficial as it was, benefited all Florentines and that he deserved to be recompensed. Given the nature of Florentine politics, it was perhaps impossible to separate Lorenzo's private needs from the republic's welfare.

Other Italian city-states and European nations were accustomed to dealing with the head of the Medici family directly instead of through the official

Florentine government. Lorenzo's position of primacy was never officially avowed: He remained merely a citizen, although the most important citizen. While Lorenzo was the unquestioned leader of a banking and merchant oligarchy, he did not always enjoy absolute freedom to commit his city to a particular course of action, freedom such as the hereditary Dukes of Milan or the popes in Rome exercised.

The Medicis had a close relationship with the Kings of France: Louis XI had granted Piero the right to incorporate the three lilies of the French royal house of Valois onto the Medici arms. Lorenzo realized, however, that it was necessary to keep that large kingdom's military might out of Italy. The peninsula was divided by various ministates and their rivalries. To the south lay the Papal States and the Kingdom of Naples, and to the east, the Republic of Venice. To balance those powers, the Medicis relied upon an alliance with the Dukes of Milan.

In 1471, Francesco della Rovere ascended the papal throne as Pope Sixtus IV. Intitially, the relationship between Sixtus and Lorenzo was cordial, but within a few years it soured. The pope had a large family to support, and Lorenzo feared that those needs threatened the security of Florence and of the Medicis. For several decades, the Medicis had been the papal bankers, a connection which was beneficial to both parties, but when Sixtus requested a loan to purchase Imola for one of his nephews, a city which Lorenzo considered to be within the Florentine sphere of influence, Lorenzo refused. Sixtus ended the papal connection with the Medici bank and turned to another Florentine banking family, the Pazzis.

The Pazzis, though connected to the Medicis through marriage, were political and economic rivals. In addition to the Imola loan, other issues combined which led to a plot, known as the Pazzi conspiracy, to remove the Medicis from power. Sixtus stated that while he wished the Medicis to be gone, he did not want it accomplished by murder. It is doubtful, however, that Sixtus truly believed that such an end could be attained without violence. The other conspirators turned to assassination.

The conspirators struck on a Sunday in April, 1477, during the High Mass in the cathedral of Florence. They were partially successful: Giuliano, Lorenzo's brother, was stabbed to death. Lorenzo, however, though injured, survived. Florence rallied to Lorenzo. Most of the conspirators, including leading members of the Pazzi family, were quickly seized and brutally executed. Sixtus responded by accusing Lorenzo and Florence of murder. Lorenzo was excommunicated from the Church, and Florence was placed under an interdict. Because of the animosity toward Sixtus, however, the churches of Florence remained open.

Sixtus also declared war on Florence. As a result of the recent assassination of its duke, Galeazzo Maria Sforza, Milan was of no assistance to Florence, and with King Ferrante of Naples allied to the Papacy, with an economic downturn in part caused by the military situation, and with the onset of plague, life in Florence soon became very difficult. Finally, in an act of calculated courage, Lorenzo journeyed to Naples and placed himself in the hands of Ferrante. Although he had some indication that Naples might be willing to agree to a treaty with Florence, Lorenzo's action was still a gamble. A treaty was agreed to, and Lorenzo was returned to Florence as a hero.

Afterward, Lorenzo took an even greater interest in public affairs. His power in Florence increased, although constitutionally he was still only a private citizen. In 1484, Sixtus died, and his successor, Innocent VIII, developed a close relationship with Lorenzo, sealed with the marriage of one of Lorenzo's daughters to one of Innocent's sons. Lorenzo also concerned himself with the relations of the other Italian states, and until his death major conflict was avoided. To what degree his policies were responsible for peace is impossible to ascertain, but Lorenzo received the credit. As Scipio Ammirato noted, Florence

> remained free of all troubles, to the great reputation of Lorenzo. The Italian princes also enjoyed peace, so that, with everything quiet beyond her frontier and with no disturbances at home, Florence . . . gave herself up to the arts and pleasures of peace.

The arts and pleasures of peace were an integral part of Lorenzo's life and character. He arranged festivals and took part in jousts. He was a patron as well as a colleague of various writers and artists, including Michelangelo. He himself was a poet of considerable ability and a supporter of the Universities of Florence and Pisa. Suitably, on his deathbed, one of his last statements was to express regret that he was not going to live to assist in completing a friend's library.

Summary

Lorenzo de' Medici died in the spring of 1492 at Careggi, one of the family's villas outside Florence.

LAVRENTIVS MEDICES PETRI FILIVS

Inheriting his father's medical maladies, Lorenzo in his last years suffered increasingly from gout and other illnesses. He was only forty-three. Shortly before his death, Lorenzo received Girolamo Savonarola, a Dominican monk who had recently become a notable figure in Florentine life for his vehement condemnations of Renaissance society in general and Lorenzo in particular. Within two years, Savonarola became the ruler of Florence. Lorenzo's son, Piero, had neither his father's abilities nor his luck, and the Medicis were forced into exile.

Yet Medici wealth and influence were not extinguished. Just before Lorenzo's death, one of his sons, Giovanni, age sixteen, had become a cardinal in the Catholic Church. In 1512, the Medicis returned to Florence from exile, and in the following year Giovanni was elected pope as Leo X. He died in 1521, and after a brief hiatus his cousin, Giulio, the illegitimate son of Lorenzo's brother, ascended the papal throne as Clement VII. In 1533, Clement performed the marriage of Catherine de Médicis to the son of King Francis I of France. She became one of the most powerful women of the sixteenth century. In Florence, the Medicis became hereditary dukes. The republic was over.

Lorenzo was a controversial figure in his own era and has remained so ever since. His status is suggested by the epithet that frequently accompanies his name: Il Magnifico (the Magnificent). During his era that appellation was used as an honorary title for various Florentine officials; in time, however, it was applied only to Lorenzo. Fifteenth century Florence epitomizes the civilization of the Renaissance, and Lorenzo the Magnificent remains inseparable from the history of that civilization and that city. His reputation has fluctuated; he has been praised for qualities he perhaps did not possess, and he has been condemned for activities which were not within his responsibility. One of his critics was his fellow Florentine, the historian Francesco Guicciardini, an avid republican in ideology. Still, even Guicciardini had to admit that if Florence was not free under Lorenzo, "it would have been impossible for it to have had a better or more pleasing tyrant."

Bibliography

Ady, Cecilia M. *Lorenzo dei Medici and Renaissance Italy.* London: English Universities Press, and New York: Macmillan, 1952. There has been no major biography of Lorenzo in English in recent decades; Ady's work is the most satisfactory substitute.

Hale, J. R. *Florence and the Medici: The Pattern of Control.* London: Thames and Hudson, 1977. This study of the Medicis traces the family from its earliest days through its decline in the eighteenth century. Hale places Lorenzo within the overall context of Florentine politics.

Hibbert, Christopher. *The House of the Medici: Its Rise and Fall.* New York: Morrow, 1975. The author is a prominent narrative historian who has written many works on English and Italian subjects. A well-written survey of the Medicis.

Rowdon, Maurice. *Lorenzo the Magnificent.* London: Weidenfeld and Nicolson, and Chicago: Regnery, 1974. This brief work traces the story of the Medicis through the fifteenth century to Lorenzo's death in 1492. The author tells the tale adequately and is especially helpful on the broad economic issues affecting the Medicis. Includes many illustrations.

Williamson, Hugh Ross. *Lorenzo the Magnificent.* London: Joseph, and New York: Putnam, 1974. This volume is similar to Rowdon's work although somewhat more extensive. Like Rowdon, Williamson recites the history of Lorenzo and his family. Includes illustrations.

Eugene Larson

MEHMED II

Born: March 30, 1432; Adrianople, Ottoman Empire
Died: May 3, 1481; Hunkârúayırı, Ottoman Empire
Areas of Achievement: Government and the military
Contribution: As Sultan of the Ottoman Empire, Mehmed II commanded armies that captured Constantinople, and under his rule control of the Balkans and Anatolia in substantial portions was extended as the Ottoman state became one of the most important powers of early modern times.

Early Life

Although it is known that, as a prince of the Ottoman Empire, Mehmed was the son of Murad II, the sixth sultan, the identity of the boy's mother has not been established with certainty. It would appear that she was one of the sultan's slave girls, and she may have been from a non-Muslim family in the Balkans. Mehmed was born on March 30, 1432, in Adrianople, the Ottoman capital of that time. At about the age of two, he was sent to a special court at Amasya, in north central Anatolia; later, he was taken to Manisa, near Izmir, where he was educated by tutors who subsequently gained distinction in the academic profession or as government ministers.

For reasons that still remain obscure, and notwithstanding Ottoman reverses of this period during fighting in Europe, in August, 1444, Murad abdicated in favor of Mehmed. A coalition of Christian powers had been formed, under the leadership of Hungary's János Hunyadi, which was also promoted by the Byzantine Empire, the Papacy, and Venice, in an effort to present a common front against the Ottoman state. After attending to conflicts in Asia, and even with his son nominally ruler, Murad returned at the head of a large army, and a major defeat was inflicted upon their opponents at Varna, in Bulgaria, on November 10, 1444. While this major battle served notice to European governments that the Ottomans could not easily be dislodged from the Balkans, other engagements followed; though the position of George Branković, the despot of Serbia, remained problematical, the renowned Skanderbeg (George Kastrioti) of Albania had commenced resistance to the Ottomans. In May, 1446, Murad returned to the throne in the wake of a janissary revolt. Another important battle was fought in October, 1448, at Kosovo in Serbia; while Murad commanded Ottoman troops, Mehmed also took part in actual fighting as Hungarian and other armies were put to flight.

For Mehmed, family concerns arose at a relatively early age. His first son, who later was to become his successor as Bayezid II, was born to him by Gülbahar, a slave girl, in December, 1447, or January, 1448. In 1450, Mehmed's second and favorite son, Mustafa, was born, though the identity of the mother remains unclear. Subsequently a marriage with a woman from a suitable social station was arranged when Mehmed took Sitt Hatun, from a noted family of central Anatolia, as his wife. Mehmed also became the father of six other children, some of whom were born from liaisons or marriages that were concluded after he came to power. Although during Murad's second reign Mehmed may have continued to regard himself as the rightful sultan, a reconciliation of sorts would appear to have taken place; yet Murad died of apoplexy rather unexpectedly. On February 18, 1451, Mehmed ascended to the throne in Adrianople. While in the past Ottoman rulers, including Murad, had eliminated family members for political reasons, Mehmed had two of his brothers executed and sanctioned the practice of fratricide by which, for nearly two centuries, sultans summarily were to remove potential rivals from any struggle for supreme power.

Life's Work

At the outset of his second reign, Mehmed II attended to a flurry of unrest in Anatolia and stirrings of discontent among the janissaries before turning to military planning, which was centered upon a single consuming ambition. The Byzantine Empire had maintained a prolonged and precarious existence even though Constantinople was surrounded by territories under Ottoman control; by virtue of its double line of walled fortifications and its position at the edge of the Bosporus, the imperial city remained difficult of access to armies in the field. While the Byzantine emperor Constantine IX Palaeologus had threatened to support a different claimant to the Ottoman throne, a trade agreement with Venice had been renewed, at the request of Çandarli Halil, the grand vizier, and a treaty was negotiated with Hungary; though Halil advised against precipitous action, it had become evident that the beleaguered city could expect little European assistance. Mehmed commenced preliminary operations with the construction of a major fortress north of Constantinople; a sympathetic Hungarian gunsmith known as Urban helped to cast cannon of a size larger than any that previously had been used. In the face of an Ottoman blockade, Byzantine forces received few reinforcements, apart from a Genoese contingent from Chios; some Venetian and Genoese fighting men already had been stationed nearby. The Ottomans possessed an immense numerical advantage, with possibly eighty thousand men under arms, as opposed to about nine thousand defenders.

The siege began on April 6, 1453, and, following repeated bombardments, Mehmed resolved finally to storm the city. On May 29, after some sharp fighting at many points, Ottoman troops entered Constantinople through a gate to the north and subdued their opponents in short order. Apparently Constantine died at this time. For his military prowess, Mehmed acquired the byname *Faith*, or the Conqueror. The city was pillaged briefly, and some prominent men, including Çandarli Halil, were executed; afterward, to encourage the restoration and development of the new Ottoman capital, which became known as Istanbul, the sultan allowed many original inhabitants to return to their homes. Further settlers, both Muslims and Christians, were recruited from Asia and Europe. As a mark of his toleration for religious communities within the Ottoman Empire, Mehmed recognized Gennadius II Scholarius, a churchman who had opposed union with the Catholics, as the Greek Orthodox patriarch; a Jewish grand rabbi and an Armenian patriarch also were accepted as representatives of their faiths in Mehmed's capital.

Subsequent military endeavors revealed the broad sweep of Mehmed's ambitions and the extent of Ottoman power on two continents. Although in 1456 Ottoman forces failed to take Belgrade after a siege of six weeks when Hunyadi's forces intervened successfully against them, the Hungarian commander died later that year, and shortly thereafter George Branković of Serbia also died. In 1459, the Ottomans annexed what remained of the southern Slavic area, while in 1463 most of Bosnia was occupied as well. During other expeditions, Ottoman forces captured Athens in 1456, and during the next four years much of the Morea was overrun. Some setbacks which were suffered by Mehmed's armies did not have lasting effects. A campaign into Wallachia to enforce a previous tributary relationship, against the infamous Vlad Ţepeş (the Impaler, who was also the historical prototype for the famous horror figure Dracula), resulted in a grisly massacre of Ottoman soldiers. Yet, under pressure from Mehmed, Vlad was deposed in 1462, and when he returned to power much later he met with death in battle.

In Asia Minor, Ottoman forces secured the submission of Trebizond, the last Greek kingdom of the Byzantine era, in 1461. Subsequently a particularly dangerous threat arose when Uzun Hasan, of the Turkmen Ak Koyunlu state that had become established in western Iran, attempted to displace Mehmed's authority in central Anatolia. An entire Ottoman army was mobilized, and, when Mehmed led his troops in person, a convincing victory was obtained at Bashkent near Erzincan, on August 11, 1473. Ottoman control of the area northwest of the Euphrates River thus was consolidated; an important success for Ottoman policy on the northern coast of the Black Sea came in 1475, when the Tatar khanate of the Crimea acknowledged Mehmed's suzerainty. Political complications at several points in the Balkans had led to a prolonged war with Venice, between 1463 and 1479, and during much of his later reign Mehmed was also involved in undertakings of several sorts in Europe. Although the redoubtable Skanderbeg, who was allied with the Venetians, had resisted Ottoman incursions until shortly before his death in 1468, eventually the fortress of Krujë surrendered to Mehmed himself in 1478, and Ottoman forces held most of Albania. In the end, Venice was compelled to make peace on relatively harsh terms. Mehmed evidently was not entirely appeased, and in 1480 an Ottoman army obtained a foothold in Italy by capturing Otranto; a landing at Rhodes, in the eastern Mediterranean, was repelled, however, by the Knights of Saint John.

While Mehmed frequently accompanied his armies during their campaigns, his administrative work brought many reforms, some of which provoked an adverse reaction after his death. His conception of power was along strictly autocratic lines, and often he did not attend meetings of the Divan, or council of state; where he did delegate authority, he exercised some care in maintaining distinctions among offices which were subordinate to his. Mehmed also directed the codification of laws, which were promulgated on his authority and were meant to serve regulatory purposes alongside

Koranic law. Fiscal policies were far-reaching but high-handed. Mehmed instituted the sale of private monopolies in essential goods to augment government revenues; some private estates and religious foundations were confiscated as state lands. Commercial relations with other countries were promoted even as Mehmed had customs duties increased. One of the most widely resented of Mehmed's measures, however, was the repeated reduction in the silver content of Ottoman coinage. In other respects, Mehmed has been regarded as having had an urbane and cosmopolitan outlook. He was a patron of literary men, including Persian poets, and he composed a collection of verse in his own right. In addition to supervising the conversion of Byzantium's most famous church into the Hagia Sophia mosque, he left further architectural monuments, of which the Faith mosque in Istanbul was perhaps the most notable. He had an interest in the visual arts that overcame any religious objections to such forms of representation, and he supported the production of medals and paintings by which his appearance has become known. The most famous portraits of Mehmed, by Sinan Bey, a Turkish artist, and by Gentile Bellini, a Venetian master whom Mehmed commissioned to paint his likeness, show broad, angular features with the eyes set in a stern fixed gaze; a large curved nose was set above thin, taut lips and a small, slightly receding chin. A brown or reddish mustache and full beard suggested somewhat more of an imperious bearing. Sinan's work also depicts Mehmed as having some tendency toward corpulence, which reputedly affected the sultan during his later years. Indeed, when Mehmed died, on May 3, 1481, at a place about fifteen miles east of Istanbul, the effects of gout were cited as a cause; some suspicion has existed, however, that he was poisoned.

Summary

The interpretations that have generally been advanced of Mehmed II's character and aims are of several sorts; while his importance in the expansion of Ottoman power has invariably been acknowledged, some have maintained that he intended essentially to extend his authority over an area roughly corresponding to that of the Byzantine Empire from a much earlier period. It has further been contended, though with some notable exaggerations, that older Byzantine practices served as the model for some of the measures that were implemented during his reign. Other views have emphasized the Turkic elements in his methods of rule and have noted that continuity among Ottoman rulers was stressed in the official court historiography of Mehmed's period. It has been maintained as well that, because primacy with respect to other Islamic states was asserted in many of Mehmed's pronouncements, he regarded his efforts as the fulfillment of aspirations that were at once both religious and political. The conception of Mehmed as a Renaissance ruler who was at home in several cultural milieus, while alluring to certain writers, has been sharply criticized as neglecting the priority he typically assigned to military matters. On the other hand, the notion that Mehmed was unusually cruel and vindictive, or inordinately devoted to conquest as an end in itself, has been challenged by those who would argue, with some justice, that the Ottoman ruler was probably no more severe than other commanders of his age. In all, it would appear that, very much in the way that Ottoman traditions combined political and cultural elements from several sources, the achievements of Mehmed may have arisen from aims and ideas that reflected his various purposes.

Bibliography

Babinger, Franz Carl Heinrich. *Mehmed the Conqueror and His Time*. Edited by William C. Hickman. Translated by Ralph Manheim. Princeton, N.J.: Princeton University Press, 1978. This bulky and imposing work by an important modern scholar is by far the most significant Western study of Mehmed's statecraft. Although some specialists have found Babinger's interpretations idiosyncratic and biased, and the original German edition of 1953 appeared without notes or scholary apparatuses, the English translation provides updated references that summarize scholarly views and research findings.

Ducas. *Decline and Fall of Byzantium to the Ottoman Turks*. Translated by Harry J. Magoulias. Detroit: Wayne State University Press, 1975. A well-informed Greek writer produced this chronicle of which the most useful and detailed portions deal with events from the time of Murad until 1462. In spite of a tendency to criticize Mehmed harshly, the author provides some shrewd insights about political developments of this period.

Gueriguian, John L. "Amirdovlat, Mehmed II, and the Nascent Armenian Community of Constantinople." *Armenian Review* 39, no. 2 (1986): 27-48. Some interesting and little-known facts about one of Mehmed's personal physicians are presented here alongside speculation about Mehmed's physical and psychological condition.

Inalcik, Halil. "Mehmed the Conqueror (1432-1481) and His Time." *Speculum* 35 (1960): 408-427. Shortcomings and lacunae in the original edition of Babinger's work are discussed in this acute, sometimes caustic, article.

———. "The Policy of Mehmed II Toward the Greek Population of Istanbul and the Byzantine Buildings of the City." *Dumbarton Oaks Papers* 23/24 (1969/1970): 231-249. In a solid scholarly study, the author demonstrates the extent of Mehmed's efforts to promote recovery and urban development after the siege of 1453.

Kritovoulos. *History of Mehmed the Conqueror*. Translated by Charles T. Riggs. Princeton, N.J.: Princeton University Press, 1954. The divided sympathies of a Greek writer who became the Governor of Imbros under Mehmed are expressed in this narration of events from 1451 until 1467. The work was dedicated to Mehmed and praises him highly in places, but delivers lamentations for the fate of peoples in formerly Byzantine lands.

Michałowicz, Konstanty. *Memoirs of a Janissary*. Translated by Benjamin Stolz. Ann Arbor: Department of Slavic Languages and Literatures, University of Michigan, 1975. The experiences of a Southern Slav who was taken prisoner and accompanied Mehmed's armies were set down in this account, which is of particular value for the period between the fall of Constantinople and the Bosnian campaign of 1463. Text transcribed from a Czech manuscript, with the translation on facing pages.

Phrantzes, Georgios. *The Fall of the Byzantine Empire*. Translated by Marios Philippides. Amherst: University of Massachusetts Press, 1980. In this autobiographical chronicle by a well-placed Greek observer, who was captured briefly and suffered family losses after the siege of Constantinople, personal impressions are provided of events through 1477.

Raby, Julian. "Pride and Prejudice: Mehmed the Conqueror and the Italian Portrait Medal." *Studies in the History of Art* 21 (1987): 171-194. A noted art historian herein provides some interesting evidence, drawn partly from Venetian archives, about Mehmed's interest in portraiture during various stages of his career.

Runciman, Steven. *The Fall of Constantinople, 1453*. Cambridge, England: Cambridge University Press, 1965. This study, by a distinguished Byzantinist, is probably the standard work in English on the famous siege; attention to scholarly detail does not impede the retelling of enthralling and tragic episodes from the last days of the city's resistance to the Ottomans.

Tursun Beg. *The History of Mehmed the Conqueror*. Edited and translated by Halil Inalcik and Rhoads Murphey. Minneapolis, Minn.: Bibliotheca Islamica, 1978. The work of an important Ottoman writer is presented here in a summary translation followed by a facsimile of an original Turkish manuscript. The author, who participated in a number of Mehmed's campaigns, comments in places on the harsher qualities of Mehmed's character in an account which was meant partly as instruction for Mehmed's successor.

J. R. Broadus

PHILIPP MELANCHTHON

Born: February 16, 1497; Bretten, Baden

Died: April 19, 1560; Wittenberg

Areas of Achievement: Religion, theology, and education

Contribution: Melanchthon was a German Humanist scholar who became a close associate of Martin Luther in the Protestant Reformation. Known for his warm evangelical piety and his irenic, ecumenical spirit, he was the author of the Augsburg Confession of 1530, basically a summary of Luther's teachings, which remains as the fundamental confessional platform of worldwide Lutheranism. Melanchthon also is credited with having established the German school system.

Early Life

Philipp Melanchthon was born in the village of Bretten in the German Rhineland, some twenty miles south of Heidelberg, on February 16, 1497. His real name was Philipp Schwartzerd; his father, Georg Schwartzerd, was an armorer under the Palatinate princes. His mother, Barbara Reuter, was a niece of the great Humanist and Hebrew scholar Johannes Reuchlin, whose influence over Philipp can be seen not only in his early studies but also in his Humanist leanings.

The eldest of five children, Philipp proved himself something of a child prodigy under the direction of his great-uncle Reuchlin, at that time regarded as the best Greek and Hebrew scholar in Germany. It was Reuchlin who first recommended Johann Unger of Pforzheim as Philipp's private tutor and who later caused him to enroll in the Pforzheim Latin school, one of the most celebrated in the Palatinate. At Pforzheim, Philipp came under the influence of Georg Simler and John Hiltebrant, both classicists and excellent scholars of Latin, Hebrew, and Greek. It was there that Reuchlin, in recognition of Philipp's accomplishments in the Greek classics, followed a contemporary custom and declared that such a brilliant young man should no longer be known by the humble name Schwartzerd (meaning "black earth") but should henceforth be called by its Greek equivalent—"Melanchthon."

In October, 1509, Melanchthon followed the advice of Reuchlin and Simler and enrolled in the University of Heidelberg. During his years at Heidelberg, he seems to have pursued his studies for the most part by himself, preferring the Greek classics, such as the orations of Cicero and Demosthenes, to the medieval Scholastic orientation of Heidelberg. There, he also studied the writings of Rodolphus Agricola and the warm devotional sermons of Johann Geiler von Kaysersberg.

In 1511, Melanchthon, not yet fifteen years of age, was awarded the bachelor of arts degree from Heidelberg. Yet after another year of devoted study of Scholastic philosophy, his application for the master of arts degree was denied, primarily because of his youth and boyish appearance. Small for his age, Melanchthon had a somewhat shy and awkward manner about him and suffered from attacks of fever from time to time. Later portraits of him reveal a more serious demeanor, a thoughtful face marked by a very high forehead, penetrating eyes, and an aquiline, craggy nose. When lecturing on a topic of particular interest, he is said to have visibly changed in appearance, with his voice becoming clear and forceful, his actions animated, and his large blue eyes sparkling with delight and excitement.

In the fall of 1512, again at the advice of Reuchlin, Melanchthon left Heidelberg and moved south to Tübingen, Reuchlin's own university, where he would reside as a student and later as professor for the next six years. A much newer university than Heidelberg, Tübingen had been founded in 1477 and was less under the influence of medieval Scholastic philosophy. At Tübingen, Melanchthon heard lectures on Aristotle that fascinated him for years. There, he came under the influence of the great Desiderius Erasmus, as well as certain "reformers before the Reformation," such as John Wessel. He also began serious study of Hebrew and Latin. In 1514, he was awarded the master of arts degree, the first among eleven in his class. He then became a tutor at the university and, two years later, professor of rhetoric and history. During his Tübingen years, he published translations of Plutarch, Pythagoras, Agricola, and Terence Lucidas, as well as a Greek grammar and a handbook of general history, and began major works on Aristotle and Aratus. Melanchthon and his work were highly praised by Erasmus, and at Tübingen he became widely recognized as the finest humanistic scholar in Germany.

Life's Work

In the autumn of 1518, at the age of twenty-one, Melanchthon was called to become professor of Greek at the University of Wittenberg, once again

largely as a result of the highest recommendation of his kinsman Reuchlin. At Wittenberg, he would spend the rest of his career; marry and rear a family; come under the powerful influence of Martin Luther, his closest friend for nearly thirty years; and become intimately involved in the Protestant Reformation and the education of Germany's youth. Only four days after he arrived in Wittenberg, on August 29, 1518, Melanchthon delivered a lecture on the improvement of studies, in which he called for fresh study not only of the Latin and Greek classics but also of Hebrew and the Bible. This was an indication of his early interest in education, which would bear fruit in later years.

Melanchthon began his own lectures in Wittenberg with Homer and the Epistle to Titus. Luther was so inspired by Melanchthon's lectures, some of which attracted as many as two thousand persons, including professors, ministers, and various dignitaries as well as students, that he made much more rapid progress in his translation of Scripture into German than he had made before. Melanchthon assisted Luther in collating the various Greek versions and revising some of his translations.

In November, 1520, Melanchthon married Katharine Krapp, daughter of the Wittenberg burgomaster, apparently primarily because Luther had concluded that it was time for Melanchthon to take a wife. Four children were born of this apparently happy union, which lasted thirty-seven years.

Melanchthon was first drawn into the Reformation controversies when he accompanied Luther and others to Leipzig in June and July of 1519 for the Leipzig Disputation between Luther and Andreas Carlstadt on one side and Johann Eck of Ingolstadt on the other. Melanchthon attended as a spectator but was shortly afterward attacked by Eck for aiding Luther and Carlstadt. Melanchthon replied to Eck in a brief treatise, in which he supported Luther's argument on the supreme authority of Scripture and denied the authority of the Church Fathers on whom Eck had relied so heavily in Leipzig. From that point onward, Melanchthon's die was cast with the Protestant Reformers. Shortly thereafter, at Luther's insistence, Melanchthon was made lecturer in theology in addition to his professorship in Greek. The degree bachelor of divinity was conferred upon him; it was the only theological degree he ever accepted.

In 1521, during Luther's confinement in Wartburg, Melanchthon became the main leader of the Reformation in Wittenberg. At that time, he had chosen Paul's Epistle to the Romans as the subject for his lectures and had compiled from that letter a series of classified statements of scriptural truths that were to become one of the most influential manuals of Protestant theology. He wrote them primarily for his own personal use and called these statements "common places," or *Loci communes rerum theologicarum* (1521; *The Loci Communes*, 1944), following a phrase of Cicero. At the encouragement of others, he allowed them to be published, and this document almost immediately established him in the theological forefront of the Reformation. Luther once even praised *The Loci Communes* as worthy of a place in the canon of Scripture.

For most of the remainder of his career, Melanchthon was greatly occupied with theological controversy and debate, largely in defense of Luther against charges brought by the Roman Catholics. He insisted that Luther was accused of heresy not because of any departure from Scripture but because he opposed the universities, the Fathers, and the councils of the Church in their theological errors. During Luther's absence from Wittenberg in 1521 and 1522, a much more radical group of Reformers took control, primarily under the leadership of Carlstadt. Ecclesiastical vestments were abolished; persons were admitted to communion without confession or repentance; and pastoral oversight was neglected, as were hospitals and prisons. Melanchthon, the scholar, opposed such radical changes but was powerless to check them until Luther's return in March, 1522. After he had restored some semblance of order to the Reformation in Wittenberg, Luther, with Melanchthon's encouragement, completed his translation of the entire Bible into German, in many ways his own most important work and the one which introduced the Reformation to the masses.

After the First Diet of Speyer in 1526, Melanchthon was one of those commissioned to visit the various reformed states and issue regulations for the churches. This resulted in the publication, in 1528, of his *Unterricht der Visitatorn* (visitation articles), which contained not only a statement of evangelical Protestant theology but also an outline of education for the elementary grades. This was shortly thereafter enacted into law, and, as a result, Germany had the first real Protestant public school system, one which was soon copied far and wide. Hundreds of teachers were also trained in Melanchthon's methods and thousands of students instructed by his textbooks. He encouraged the establishment of universities and revised dozens of schools' curricula. All of this earned for him the title "Preceptor of Germany." His influence on German education can hardly be overstated.

A man of moderation and peace, Melanchthon was also present at the Second Diet of Speier, when the protest, from which the name "Protestant" originated, was lodged against the Roman Catholic majority in 1529. He was the leading representative of Protestant theology at the Diet of Augsburg in 1530 and the author of the Augsburg Confession of 1530. This document remains the basic confessional statement of worldwide Lutheranism, which has influenced nearly every subsequent major Protestant creed. Melanchthon tried very hard to be conciliatory in the Augsburg Confession without sacrificing important convictions. He met with papal representatives amid frequent charges of collaboration in an effort to reconcile Protestant-Roman Catholic differences. Eventually, he wrote a spirited defense of the Augsburg Confession entitled *Apologie der Confession aus dem Latin verdeudschet* (1531), or the *Apology*, also generally recognized as one of the best writings of the Reformation.

Melanchthon staunchly held the middle ground between more radical Reformers and the Roman Catholic theologians. He defended the Reformation doctrines of justification by faith and the authority of the Scriptures; yet for the sake of unity he was willing to accept a modified form of the Papacy. After Luther's death in 1546, Melanchthon's later years were marked by poor physical health and major theological disputes, especially the so-called *Adiaphoristic* controversy and arguments concerning the role of humans in salvation.

Adiaphora, religious beliefs and practices of indifference, were areas where flexibility or compromise may be necessary. Melanchthon, however, was unfairly accused of including among the *Adiaphora* such essentials to the Protestant cause as justification by faith. He was, indeed, willing to recognize the necessity of good works for salvation, not as in any way meriting God's favor but as the inevitable fruits of faith. Melanchthon eventually also seems to have rejected the doctrine of predestination, which he earlier shared with Luther. In the *Apology* of 1531, he represented the mercy of God as extended to all; yet he insisted that God draws to Himself only those who are willing to turn to Him. Humans thus have an important role in the process of salvation, although a secondary one of response to God's initiative in the written and preached Word. Melanchthon was unjustly accused of the heresy of Pelagianism as a result of his theological views, and his influence declined during his lifetime. It is only in modern times that his contributions have come to be fully appreciated.

Summary

Philipp Melanchthon is a prominent example of an outstanding theologian and scholar whose works have been neglected. His was a melding of the twin influences of the Renaissance and the Reformation. His services to educational reform in Germany, as well as to classical scholarship and Humanism, were outstanding, but it was as a theologian that he excelled. Throughout his lifetime, he tried to be a reconciler, and his influence was consistently thrown on the side of moderation and peace. Yet he was misunderstood and unappreciated by many of those on both sides of the great theological controversies of his age.

Bibliography

Hildebrandt, Franz. *Melanchthon: Alien or Ally?* Cambridge: Cambridge University Press, 1946; New York: Kraus, 1968. An exploration of the complex relationship between Luther and Melanchthon, this volume is primarily an examination of the five main "concessions" said to have been made by Melanchthon to elements outside the inner circle of Protestant evangelicals. Particularly valuable in highlighting some of the most important doctrinal differences between Luther and Melanchthon.

Kusukawa, Sachiko. *The Transformation of Natural Philosophy: The Case of Philip Melanchthon.* Cambridge and New York: Cambridge University Press, 1995. This book examines the genesis of Lutheran interest in natural philosophical issues by focusing on the reform of natural philosophy initiated by Melanchthon. It suggests that he transformed traditional natural philosophy into a specifically Lutheran viewpoint in an effort to refute civil disobedience and promote Luther's cause.

Manschreck, Clyde L. *Melanchthon: The Quiet Reformer.* New York: Abingdon Press, 1958. One of the most important works on Melanchthon currently available in English. Basically a historical approach. Manschreck also gives a sympathetic and lively description of the doctrinal issues that preoccupied so much of Melanchthon's career. The volume is copiously documented and indexed, with a variety of interesting illustrations.

Melanchthon, Philipp. *Melanchthon on Christian Doctrine: Loci Communes, 1555.* Edited and translated by Clyde L. Manschreck. New York: Oxford University Press, 1965. The first translation into English of the 1555 (final) edition of *The Loci Communes*, this volume is translated and edited by the English-speaking world's foremost Melanchthon scholar. Contains a valuable preface by Manschreck and an introduction by Hans Engelland, a German Melanchthon scholar. Good bibliography and index.

Richard, James W. *Philip Melanchthon: The Protestant Preceptor of Germany, 1497-1560.* London and New York: Putnam, 1898. One of the best nineteenth century biographies of Melanchthon available in English. Richard includes many quotations from Melanchthon's letters and other writings in this volume. Carefully documented and includes a helpful index and many illustrations.

Vajta, Vilmos, ed. *Luther and Melanchthon in the History and Theology of the Reformation.* Philadelphia: Muhlenberg Press, 1961. A series of addresses on the relationship between Luther and Melanchthon delivered before the Luther Research Congress. Most are in German, but among the English contributions of particular interest are "Luther and Melanchthon" by Wilhelm Pauck, in which the inseparability of the two theologians' works is clearly demonstrated, and "Melanchthon in America" by Theodore G. Tappert, in which the revival of interest in Melanchthon during the first half of the nineteenth century in the United States is explored.

Wengert, Timothy J. *Human Freedom, Christian Righteousness: Philip Melanchthon's Exegetical Dispute with Erasmus of Rotterdam.* New York: Oxford University Press, 1998. This book argues that Philip Melanchthon was, at least theologically, not Erasmian at all, but in fact sharply anti-Erasmus; this runs contrary to conventional thought, which placed him as caught between Erasmus and Luther. Wengert draws largely on Melanchthon's *Scholia* on the Epistle of Paul to the Colossians as well as on a range of other contemporary sources. He addresses a number of important questions, including the complicated relationship between humanism and the Reformation, and the issues of proper biblical interpretation of free will, of divine and human righteousness, and of political order.

Wilson, George. *Philip Melanchthon: 1497-1560.* London: Religious Tract Society, 1897. Published after the death of its author, this brief biographical work is a more personal memoir than the volumes by Manschreck and Richard. Wilson had planned a much more complete work on Melanchthon than this but did not live to finish it.

C. Fitzhugh Spragins

PEDRO MENÉNDEZ DE AVILÉS

Born: February 15, 1519; Avilés, Spain
Died: September 17, 1574; Santander, Spain
Area of Achievement: Exploration
Contribution: Menéndez de Avilés developed the Florida peninsula as a colony of the Spanish crown.

Early Life

One of twenty-one brothers and sisters, Pedro Me-néndez de Avilés was born in the seaport town of Avilés on Spain's northern coast. A member of a family with claims to *hidalgo* (minor nobility) status, he was related also by marriage to the important Valdés clan. Like many of his relatives, friends, and contemporaries who lived in this port city, Menéndez turned to the sea in pursuit of a career.

The young seaman served initially with a leading local privateersman, Alvaro Bazán, in battles with French corsairs operating off of the coast of Western Europe. Soon he bought his own small ship with the prize money that he had earned and began the pursuit of French raiders under royal commissions granted by the Spanish crown. His successes led him to expand his operations across the Atlantic to the Indies. He became a captain-general and commander of the Spanish treasure fleets plying the routes between their colonies and the homeland.

His rising reputation as a naval leader caused Spain's Emperor Charles V to assign Menéndez to accompany the emperor's heir, young Prince Philip, to England for the latter's wedding to Mary Tudor, the eldest daughter of King Henry VIII. While the close relationship that he had developed with the heir to the throne during this period helped Menéndez throughout his subsequent career, he incurred also the enmity of the powerful merchant circle in Seville, which had to bear the expense of maintaining the armed fleet needed to protect the sea lanes to Spain's colonies. The merchants saw the young seaman as a potential rival for the profits emanating from the transatlantic trade.

Life's Work

By the middle of the sixteenth century, open hostilities had broken out between Spain and France, exacerbated by the militant Protestant movements that had swept Europe. Philip II, now king of Spain, turned south to stem the Protestant tide both on the European continent and in Spain's colonial empire.

Rumors had reached the Spanish court of French incursions and the establishment of settlements on the coast of Florida, territory claimed by Spain by right of discovery. Loss of control of this strategic area would seriously jeopardize Spanish sovereignty over the whole Caribbean zone. Philip II decided that he had to take strong countermeasures as quickly as possible. Previous attempts by Spain to establish a permanent colony under its explorers Hernando de Soso and Juan Ponce de León had ended in failure.

Philip now turned to his successful, experienced Captain General Menéndez to evaluate and to make recommendations on how to deal with the Florida problem. The veteran sailor replied quickly that the French threat was a real one and that the so-called Protestant heretics, if they were successful in enlisting Florida's Indians in their cause, could threaten the Spanish political and economic status quo throughout the area. Menéndez recommended the dispatch of an expedition immediately to rout the French if they had indeed established bases there, to institute agricultural settlements with Spanish immigrants, and to employ missionaries to convert the indigenous peoples to Catholicism. He estimated the cost of such an expedition, together with a necessary year's supplies after landing, to be in the neighborhood of eighty thousand ducats to the royal treasury.

The king and his advisers countered the proposal by offering to license Menéndez as *adelantado*, or governor, promising him lands, revenues, and titles if he would undertake the expedition largely at his own expense, but with some financial and material support by the Crown. Such an arrangement had become a common practice employed by Spanish royalty at the time, since it reduced the burden on the Crown's own finances. Menéndez accepted this risky venture involving exploration, the probabilities of serious conflict, the transfer of a substantial group of immigrants, and the religious conversion of the native population.

Although the new *adelantado* initially received moral support, military men, supplies, and missionaries to aid him, he encountered resistance from another quarter, the merchants of Seville and the Casa de Contratación—powerful groups that played a major role in the transatlantic trade between Spain and its colonies. They delayed the aid pledged by the Crown in furnishing the ships and supplies Menéndez required to start his enterprise.

Undaunted, Menéndez not only employed all his own personal resources in the project but also secured the support of family and friends in and about Avilés. These loyal comrades became the key personnel on which he depended in building and administering the new colony. The group pledged not only their wealth but also their lives in support of their kinsman and close friend.

Meanwhile, powerful French Huguenot interests had begun assembling a fleet of their own. They did indeed have a colony started at Fort Caroline on the Florida coast, and they planned to reinforce this fledgling operation before Menéndez arrived.

By the time that the Spanish expedition had reached Florida in mid-1565, the enterprising French had already reinforced their settlement at the Caroline location. On September 8, Menéndez landed north of the French fort at a beach that he named St. Augustine and dedicated to the Spanish crown. It became the headquarters for the new *adelantamiento*, or seat of government.

Two weeks later, the Spanish leader marched south, carried out a surprise attack on Fort Caroline, captured it, and killed most of the inhabitants. Later, when some of the survivors of the initial battle who had escaped attempted to surrender, Menéndez executed the majority of them as well. Such massacres of the vanquished were all too common in the bloody encounters among European rivals. In this case, the Spaniards had quickly and forcefully ended the French threat to their control of Florida.

The *adelantado* then proceeded to launch his threefold plan of action for the colony: the establishment of military bases, the preparation for the influx of permanent settlers, and the religious conversion of the indigenous peoples. The progress proved to be slow. Food remained in short supply during the settlement's initial stages, causing low morale within the garrisons, and the local natives proved to be difficult to convert to a new religion.

The relationships between the conquistadores and their Indian charges were tumultuous. The missionaries that accompanied the soldiers insisted that the natives give up their traditional gods and adopt Catholicism exclusively. The friars demanded that the converts discontinue their practices of polygamy, sodomy, and child sacrifice, customs that were accepted traditionally within their culture. The Spanish soldiers also took by force what they wanted from the Indians and abused their women as well. Moreover, when the Spaniards adopted a particular tribe as allies, they immediately incurred the enmity of that group's traditional adversaries.

Vital supplies continued to be a problem for Menéndez's Floridian colonies. Officials both in Cádiz and in Havana either ignored the *adelantado*'s requests or demanded prepayment for goods to be delivered. The scarcity of provisions critical to the settlements' welfare kept the outposts at a bare survival level.

Despite the hazards facing the Spaniards throughout Florida, Menéndez managed to establish a string of forts along the shores of the peninsula. Unfortunately, sporadic raids by Indians, food shortages, and mutinies created problems for the Spanish leader whenever his duties called him away from the peninsula. On many occasions he was forced to punish drastically, and in some cases to execute, malefactors.

The cost involved in establishing and supplying these outposts proved to be much higher than anticipated. The colony's backers lost many ships and cargo in the process of navigating through uncharted waters. Menéndez and his associates also suffered severe financial reverses, because Florida's natural resources offered little in the way of immediate return on investment. Disorder broke out constantly among the unruly soldiery when they came to realize that there was little loot to be acquired from the native population. Menéndez decided to return to Spain and present his problems to the Crown.

Unfortunately for the Spanish colony's leader, Philip II had turned his attention to more pressing difficulties closer to home. Both France and England threatened Spain's control over its spheres of interest on the European continent itself. Accordingly, faraway Florida ranked low on the king's list of priorities.

Nevertheless, a visit to court by Menéndez did produce some favorable results. King Philip added to Menéndez's Florida command the post of governor of Cuba as well. Menéndez acquired command of a newly formed armada to operate as Spain's main line of defense throughout the Caribbean. Recalcitrant Seville and Cádiz merchants received orders from the Crown to furnish Menéndez with overdue money and supplies.

The *adelantado* was not left to govern his Florida enterprises for much longer. Philip recalled him to Europe for a new, somewhat more mysterious, assignment in mid-1573. He gave Menéndez command of a great two-hundred-ship armada, the purpose of which was to launch an attack against English home ports and to cut off supplies to English raiders harassing Spanish shipping in the Americas.

On September 17, 1574, while in the midst of organizing this undertaking, Pedro Menéndez de Avilés suddenly died, perhaps poisoned by English spies. Certainly Spain's outstanding seaman represented a serious threat to the English crown. When Philip attempted an invasion of England some fourteen years later under a less experienced and less successful admiral, the undertaking proved to be a disaster.

Although Philip II had heaped honors of all kinds on his captain general, the huge expenses of the Florida expedition left Menéndez penniless at the time of his death.

Summary

Pedro Menéndez de Avilés has been criticized by some historians for his brutal repression of the French colonists who attempted to secure Florida for their own king. He is credited with being the first European to colonize the peninsula on a permanent basis as well as to found the oldest city in the continental United States, St. Augustine. Although he sustained prohibitive financial losses personally in his attempt to develop the colony, Menéndez never wavered in his loyalty to the Spanish ruler or in his commitment to introduce Catholicism to the indigenous peoples of Florida. He must be recognized as one of Spain's outstanding colonial explorers and military leaders. He lies buried in his hometown of Avilés.

Bibliography

Barrientos, Bartolomé. *Pedro Menéndez de Avilés: Founder of Florida*. Translated by Anthony Kerrigan. Gainesville: University of Florida Press, 1965. Barrientos, a historian, was a contemporary of Menéndez.

Folmer, Henry. *The Franco-Spanish Rivalry in North America, 1524-1723*. Glendale, Calif.: Arthur H. Clark, 1954. The author attributes the Fort Caroline massacre of the French by the Spaniards to direct orders by Philip II to Menéndez to kill all of those he might find in Florida. Folmer also describes the severe reprisals that the French took against the Spaniards during their raid on the Spanish settlement that had replaced Fort Caroline in 1568.

Kenny, Michael. *The Romance of the Floridas*. 1934. New York: AMS Press, 1970. This work is divided into two parts: "The Finding: From Ponce de León to Pedro Menéndez de Avilés, 1512-1565" and "The Founding: The Menéndez-Jesuit Period, 1565-1575." The emphasis is on the Jesuit missionary activity that took place during the Menéndez expeditions.

Lyon, Eugene. *The Enterprise of Florida: Pedro Menéndez de Avilés and the Spanish Conquest of 1565-1568*. Gainesville: University of Florida Press, 1976. An account of the initial era of exploration and settlement of Florida by the Menéndez expeditions.

———, ed. *Pedro Menéndez de Avilés*. New York: Garland, 1995. Volume 24 in the Spanish Borderlands Sourcebooks series, this work includes bibliographical references, illustrations, and maps.

Solís de Merás, Gonzalo. *Pedro Menéndez de Avilés*. Translated by Jeanette Thurber Connor. Gainesville: University of Florida Press, 1964. Solís de Merás was Menéndez's brother-in-law. The writer furnished an intimate knowledge of the explorer and his times.

Carl Henry Marcoux

MENNO SIMONS

Born: 1496; Witmarsum, Friesland

Died: January 31, 1561; Wüstenfeld, Holstein

Areas of Achievement: Church reform, religion, and theology

Contribution: Menno contributed a stabilizing influence to the Anabaptist movement of the sixteenth century and also to a defense of religious toleration. His most lasting contribution has been his emphasis on the Bible as the authority in religion and theology.

Early Life

Menno Simons was born in the Dutch village of Witmarsum, between the cities of Franeker and Bolsward, less than ten miles from the North Sea. His parents were devout Roman Catholics who consecrated their son to the service of their church. Menno's education for the priesthood was most likely at the Franciscan Monastery in Bolsward. While there, he performed the duties of a monk but never took the vows. He studied Roman Catholic theology, learned to read and write Latin, acquired a basic knowledge of Greek, and became familiar with the writings of the early church fathers. Conspicuously absent from Menno's studies was the Bible.

Menno was ordained as a Roman Catholic priest in 1524 and remained faithful to that calling for twelve years. The last five years (1531-1536) he served as parish pastor in his home village of Witmarsum. Outwardly, he was the average country priest of the sixteenth century, performing his duties faithfully but with the least possible effort. With two fellow priests, his leisure time was spent ". . . playing [cards] . . . , drinking, and in such diversions as, alas, is the fashion . . . of such useless people." Inwardly, Menno was troubled by doubts concerning the ceremony of the Mass. He could not escape the thought, which he first attributed to Satan, that the bread and wine were not really transformed into the body and blood of Christ as he had been taught. Menno's doubts may have been prompted by the Sacramentists, a group which denied the physical presence of Christ in the Lord's Supper. Two years after becoming a priest, Menno sought and found his answer in the Bible. He later wrote, "I had not gone very far when I discovered that we were deceived. . . ." Menno then faced the same decision that faced other reformers: Would he rely on his church for authority, or would he take the Bible as his sole authority for doctrine and practice? His decision to accept the latter came in 1528.

Privately rejecting Roman Catholic authority did not mean an immediate break between Menno and the Church. Although not in agreement, he was willing to continue performing the Mass in the traditional way; at the same time, he became more deeply involved in personal Bible study.

Menno's second question concerning the traditions of his church, and the one which eventually led to his departure from it, concerned infant baptism. In 1531, a man was beheaded in nearby Leeuwarden because of Anabaptism (rebaptism based on baptism for believers only). Menno's Bible study soon convinced him that believers' baptism was the biblical position. By this time, small groups of Anabaptists were forming throughout the Netherlands, but Menno did not join any of them, partly because he enjoyed the comfortable life of a priest and partly because of the radical nature of some Anabaptists, such as those who violently captured Münster in 1534.

The greatest change in Menno's life came in April, 1535, when he accepted, as a ". . . sorrowing sinner, the gift of His [God's] grace. . . ." He then rejected both the Roman Catholic Mass and infant baptism. On January 30, 1536, Menno renounced the Roman Catholic Church and joined the Anabaptists.

Life's Work

Following his break with Rome, Menno began a period of wandering that would last about eighteen years, in which he served as an underground evangelist to the scattered Anabaptist communities. In late 1536, he settled briefly in the northern Dutch province of Groningen, where at least a semblance of religious freedom existed. While there, he was baptized with believers' baptism and ordained as an elder in the Anabaptist movement. Soon thereafter, Menno was forced to resume his wandering. His exact points of residence can be traced only by noting those who were executed for sheltering him. On January 8, 1539, Tjard Reynders, a God-fearing Anabaptist in Leeuwarden, was executed solely because he had given a temporary home to Menno.

Until late 1543, Menno's work was concentrated in the Netherlands. The authorities in Leeuwarden, the capital of West Friesland, seemed determined to be rid of Menno, whose hometown of Witmarsum was in their province. In 1541, they offered a pardon to any imprisoned Anabaptist who would betray him, but the offer was not accepted. On December 2, 1542, with the support of Charles V, Emperor of the Holy Roman Empire, as well as ruler of the Netherlands, they offered a reward of one hundred gold guilders, plus a pardon for any past crime, to anyone who would deliver Menno. These efforts testify to the importance ascribed by that time to Menno's leadership of the movement.

The exact time and place when Menno married Geertruydt are not known; in 1544, however, he wrote ". . . to this hour I could not find in all the country . . . a cabin or hut . . . in which my poor wife and our little children could be put up in safety. . . ." Menno continued throughout these years to express concern for his family, all of whom, except one daughter, preceded him in death. From 1541 to 1543, Menno concentrated his labor farther south around Amsterdam, but details of this work are scarce. He evidently baptized many, although the names of only two have been preserved.

The most enduring part of Menno's work is his writing. By 1543, at least seven books from the pen of Menno Simons were circulating throughout the Netherlands, including *Dat fundament des christelycken leers* (1539; *A Foundation of Plain Instruction*, 1835), *Van dat rechte christen ghelooue* (c. 1542; *The True Christian Faith*, 1871), and *Verclaringhe des Christelycken doopsels* (c. 1542; *Christian Baptism*, 1871). Rather than being academic treatises designed for theologians, they are commonsense presentations for the average layman. Precisely because Menno's works were so accessible, church authorities were particularly determined to destroy them.

In the fall of 1543, Menno and his family left the Netherlands, and for the last eighteen years of his life he labored primarily in northwest Germany. His first German refuge was Emden, in East Friesland, ruled by the tolerant Countess Anna of Oldenburg. Menno had visited the province, which had become a haven for all Anabaptists, many times previously. By this time, however, Anna was being pressured by Charles V to suppress all the outlawed sects.

The superintendent of the East Friesland churches, on whose advice Anna relied, was John a'Lasco, a Zwinglian reformer of Polish descent. Although on friendly terms with Menno, a'Lasco's goal was a state-controlled Reformed church. Countess Anna decided to suppress those whom a'Lasco declared to be heretical. To this end, a theological discussion was held on January 28-31, 1544, involving a'Lasco, who hoped to bring the Anabaptists into the state church, and Menno, who hoped to preserve the tolerant spirit in East Friesland. The discussion revealed three irreconcilable differences. First, Menno strongly opposed the concept of a state-controlled church, which he believed always led to compromise and spiritual lethargy. Second, a'Lasco could not reconcile believers' baptism to a state church. The final point concerned Menno's unique understanding of the Incarnation of Christ; he taught that the body of Christ, to be completely sinless, had to be given completely to the Virgin Mary by the Holy Spirit. A'Lasco interpreted this as a denial of the humanity of Christ, weakening His position as the Saviour of mankind; he therefore declared that Menno was guilty of heresy. In 1545, Anna issued a decree that the more radical Anabaptists were subject to execution, while the "Mennisten" were to be examined and, if they did not conform to the state church, were to leave the province. This decree was the first official document to recognize Menno's leadership by applying his name to the peaceful branch of the Anabaptist movement.

Menno Simons left East Friesland in May, 1544, for the lower Rhine area of Cologne and Bonn, where he spent two fruitful years; the last fifteen years of his life were spent in the province of Schleswig-Holstein. There, in 1554, Menno finally found a permanent home for his weary family in Wüstenfelde, between Lübeck and Hamburg.

Menno's final years were productive in that he had time for more writing, including revising some of his earlier books. They were also troublesome years in which Menno had to settle disputes and defend himself within the Anabaptist movement. The most serious dispute concerned the ban and shunning of excommunicated members; Menno took the strict position that all human ties, even those of marriage and family, had to be broken under the ban of the church.

By 1560, Menno's health was failing. The years of hardship and privation, as well as the burden of the church, had taken a heavy toll. He often used a crutch as a result of an injury suffered in Wismar at about 1554. Menno died in his own home on January 31, 1561, exactly twenty-five years after his break with Rome, and was buried in his own garden. Unfortunately, Wüstenfelde was destroyed during the Thirty Years' War, and the site of Menno's grave could only be approximated in the early twentieth century, when a simple memorial was erected.

Summary

The Anabaptist movement began in 1525; for the next eleven years, Menno Simons was a Roman Catholic priest. Therefore, he was only a leader, not the founder, of the church that bears his name. Menno's role in the Reformation is not as obvious as that of his contemporaries, Martin Luther, Huldrych Zwingli, and John Calvin; yet his true significance is revealed in three areas of influence: his character, his message, and his work.

The character of Menno was ingrained with a sensitivity for the truth, an unswerving devotion to his convictions, and a deep trust in God. These traits enabled him to have a steadying influence on the diverse Anabaptist communities of the Netherlands and northern Germany.

The foundation of Menno's message was the Bible. He declared that he ". . . would rather die than to believe and teach my brethren a single word or letter . . . contrary to the plain testimony of the Word of God. . . ." He identified the heart of his message when he said, "I strive after nothing . . . but . . . that all men might be saved . . ."; although as a reward for this message, ". . . we can expect nothing from them (I mean the evil disposed) but the stake, water, fire, wheel, and sword. . . ."

The significance of Menno's work is that he united the northern wing of the Anabaptist movement, thus preventing its disintegration through persecution. Unlike other reformers, he did this without the aid of the state. The endurance of the Mennonite church throughout the centuries is the best testimony that his work was in the providence of God.

Bibliography

Estep, William R. *The Anabaptist Story.* 3d ed. Grand Rapids, Mich.: Eerdmans, 1996. Emphasizes the calming influence of Menno on the diverse Anabaptist groups in the Netherlands. Estep argues that Menno's leadership enabled the movement to survive the persecution, as well as the violent and visionary elements within the movement.

Horsch, John. *Mennonites in Europe.* Scottdale, Pa.: Mennonite Publishing House, 1942. Includes an account of Menno's doubts about Roman Catholic doctrine. Covers his early contacts with the Anabaptist movement. Identifies sources of information about Menno's early labors as an Anabaptist evangelist.

Littell, Franklin H. *A Tribute to Menno Simons.* Scottdale, Pa.: Herald Press, 1961. Written to recognize the historical significance of Menno Simons on the quadricentennial of his death. Emphasis on his contributions to the Anabaptist movement, in particular, and to Protestantism, in general. Author's position is that Menno has great significance to twentieth century Christianity.

Menno Simons. *The Complete Writings of Menno Simons.* Edited by J. C. Wenger. Scottdale, Pa.: Herald Press, 1956. Complete English translation of Menno's literary works. Includes an introduction and a good brief biography. Also includes the location of the writings in other editions. Contains books, tracts, letters, hymns, and all other available writings. Gives direct insight into the philosophy and theology of Menno. Good illustrations.

Roth, John D. "The Mennonites' Dirty Little Secret." *Christianity Today* 40 (October, 1996): 44. Roth discusses how Simons restored stability to the Anabaptist movement after the reign of terror instituted by Jan van Leyden, which included polygamy, the elimination of private property, and forced baptism.

Smith, C. Henry. *The Story of the Mennonites.* Bern, Ind.: Mennonite Book Concern, 1941. Includes a good summary of the inner conflicts experienced by Menno in his relationship to the Roman Catholic Church.

Glenn L. Swygart

GERARDUS MERCATOR
Gerhard Kremer

Born: March 5, 1512; Rupelmonde, Flanders

Died: December 2, 1594; Duisburg, Duchy of Cleves

Areas of Achievement: Cartography and geography

Contribution: Mercator invented a map projection that is particularly useful for ocean navigation. He was the first person to use the name "atlas" for a volume of maps. His maps represented the best geographic knowledge available at his time.

Early Life

Gerardus Mercator was born in Rupelmonde, Flanders, near the modern city of Antwerp, Belgium. He was christened Gerhard Kremer but took, as did many scholars of his day, the Latinized form of his given name and surname. In the process, he upgraded his name. *Kremer* was the German word for "trader," and *mercator* is the Latin word for "world trader." Mercator's parents both died while he was young. He was provided for by his uncle, Gisbert Kremer, who financed his way at the University of Louvain, where he studied philosophy, mathematics, astronomy, and cosmography (geography of the cosmos).

After graduation, he established a workshop in Louvain, where he made globes, sundials, mathematical instruments, armillary spheres, astrolabes, and other measuring instruments. He drew, engraved, and colored maps. His first known map was of the Holy Land. In 1538, he engraved and published his first world map. It was drawn on a double, more or less heart-shaped projection that was interrupted at the equator. The Northern Hemisphere was drawn in the left-hand heart, and the Southern Hemisphere in the right. This map claims the distinction of being the first known map to give two names to the Americas: *Americae pars septemtrionalis* and *Americae pars meridionalis*, North and South America respectively. While in Louvain, he also published a map of Flanders that was based on his own survey rather than being an edited copy of another's map or a compilation of data reported by others. He also made celestial and terrestrial globes, several of which have a certain renown because of their large size and the fact that they belonged respectively to Emperor Charles V and his prime minister.

Mercator lived at the time of the Protestant Reformation and the reactionary Counter-Reformation of the Roman Catholic church. This religious conflict was particularly strong in the Low Countries. For some reason, Mercator was arrested for heresy in 1544. After Mercator was in prison for several months, some influential friends obtained his release, which very possibly may have saved his life. This experience caused Mercator to move his business to Duisburg, Germany, where he spent the rest of his life.

Life's Work

Mercator's 1554 map of Europe was one of the largest maps available at that time. It was enlarged on fifteen copper plates, and, when assembled, it was 132 by 159 centimeters in size. Mercator used italic lettering for the first time on a map drawn in northern Europe. These changes were important but superficial. The map is more important in three items of content that it corrected. A careful study of the accounts of navigators on the Mediterranean Sea and travelers in Eastern Europe led him to shorten the length of the Mediterranean Sea ten degrees of longitude. He increased the distance between the Black and the Baltic seas by several degrees of latitude and made the Black Sea several degrees longer. These corrections made his map of Europe the most accurate of his day.

In 1564, Mercator produced a 129-by-89-centimeter map of the British Isles. This map seems unusual to a modern map-reader in that it was orientated with West instead of North to the top of the map. Mercator is best known for his world map of 1569, which he drew on a projection that he invented and is known by his name. It was another large map in the Mercator tradition measuring 131 by 208 centimeters. It contained the latest geographic information known by 1569. The map showed three land masses, Africo-Eur-Asia, the New Indies (North and South America), and a large southern continent antipodal to Africo-Eur-Asia. In the latter case, Mercator seems to have been perpetuating the belief of ancient philosophers rather than reporting the findings of explorers.

South America is more rectangular on this map than it is in reality, and North America is much wider. Baja California is shown as a peninsula in

this map, correcting other maps of the time that showed it as an island. Little was known of the interior of North America, so Mercator used this space to explain the features of his projection. Mercator drew North America as separated from Asia, which encouraged explorers to mount efforts to find the Northwest Passage to China. Europe, the best-known part of the world to Mercator, was drawn with the most accuracy. The coastline of Africa and Asia is easily recognized, except for eastern India, southeast Asia, and China.

The interior of Asia was not well known. The Caspian Sea is not recognizable except for its general location. This map shows that Mercator was aware that the magnetic north pole was not located at the geographic North Pole. He placed it where the Bering Strait now appears. Mercator inserted items within cartouches placed in what would have been blank spaces in the area occupied by the great southern continent. These items included notes on measuring distances on this projection, a map of the North Polar Region, and the like. Today the map is an important historic document in that it reveals what was known about the world in the mid-sixteenth century.

The projection Mercator invented for this map was a very important cartographic invention that is still being used with modifications today. Yet the importance of this projection was not appreciated until almost one hundred years after his death. The Mercator projection draws the spherical earth within a rectangular frame. It is characterized by equally spaced parallel lines of longitude and parallel lines of latitude that become farther and farther apart as the distance from the equator increases. Since lines of longitude are not parallel and lines of latitude are equally spaced, the projection introduces two errors which magnify each other. The result is that the areas of places located away from the equator are significantly distorted. The Mercator projection is soundly rejected by editors of modern-day textbooks, magazines, and atlases. It must be remembered, however, that Mercator drew this map for navigators, not geographers. The remarkable thing about his map was that every straight line drawn on this map plotted a course of constant compass direction. Thus, if the true locations of two places were known and correctly plotted on this projection, the navigator could connect the two places with a straight line and find the compass direction to follow in order to reach the place at the other end of the line. Mercator knew that this would not be the shortest possible course between two places, but he believed that the ease with which the course could be found fully compensated for the extra distance that would have to be traveled as the result of not following a great circle route.

While Mercator's projection is little used for world maps, several forms or derivations of his projection are still in common use, and his name can still be seen on many large-scale maps of small areas and on many aeronautical maps. When Mercator drew his world map in 1569, he drew it as if a cylinder were placed around the globe, tangent at the equator. Today, it is common to place this cylinder tangent to the earth at the North and South poles. When this is done, it is called a transverse Mercator projection. This form is used for most United States military maps. It is also used for medium-scale topographic maps published by the United States Geological Survey and by the Canadian Department of Mines and Technical Surveys. Aeronautical maps are drawn with the cylinder tangent to the earth along the great circle, connecting the starting place with its destination.

Mercator had what could be called a life's goal. He believed that the world needed a cosmography. His cosmography was made of three parts: The first part was about the beginnings of the world; the second part was the geography of the ancient world; and the third part was about the world geography of his day. The year 1569 marked the publication not only of his world map but also of the first part of his cosmography, *Chronologia* (1569). Mercator tried to establish the beginning of the world and to reconcile the chronologies of the ancient Hebrews, Greeks, Egyptians, and Romans with that of the Christian world.

In 1578, he published his version of Ptolemy's *Geographike hyphegesis* (*Geography*), which contained twenty-seven plates engraved especially for this edition that are generally agreed to be the finest ever prepared for this work. This edition became the second part of his cosmography.

Mercator envisioned that the third part of his cosmography, *Atlas sive cosmographicae meditationes de fabrica mundi et fabricati figura* (1595; *Historia mundi: Or, Mercator's Atlas*, 1635), would include some one hundred maps, and he spent the last sixteen years of his life working on it. Since this work contained many maps bound together in one volume, it has given its name to all other such map collections.

Mercator's atlas was long in coming. In fact, it was published in parts, the first of which covered France, Belgium, and Germany. The second part contained twenty-two maps covering Italy, Yugoslavia, and Greece. The last section, which contained thirty-four maps, twenty-nine drawn by Mercator and five by his son Rumold and two grandsons, was published in the year after his death.

Summary

Gerardus Mercator is renowned for four things: his terrestrial and celestial globes of 1541; his large map of Europe in 1554 and of the British Isles in 1564; his world map of 1569, particularly the projection on which it was drawn; and his three-part cosmography, which included a chronology of the world from creation to his day, an edition of the works of Ptolemy, and his atlas of the then-known world.

Few if any books in English are dedicated to Mercator and his work. What little is known about Mercator's life comes from a very short biography written by a neighbor and fellow mapmaker, who described him as "a man of calm temperament and exceptional candor and sincerity." While little is known about Mercator, much is known about his works, many of which have been preserved in rare-book libraries around the world. Mercator was the leading cartographer of the last half of the sixteenth century. He was more than a skilled engraver and publisher of maps. He was an innovator and geographer as well.

Bibliography

Brown, Lloyd A. *Map Making: The Art That Became a Science*. Boston: Little Brown, 1960. This book contains a portrait of Mercator and a reproduction of his world map that first used separate names for North and South America. It also tells the story about his book of maps.

———. *The Story of Maps*. Boston: Little Brown, 1949; London: Cressett Press, 1951. A scholarly book on the history of cartography that contains information on the life and work of Mercator. It puts Mercator into the historical context of his time. Contains extensive notes, bibliographic data, and several illustrations of Mercator's maps.

Crone, Gerald R. *Maps and Their Makers: An Introduction to the History of Cartography*. 5th ed. Folkestone: Dawson, and Hamden, Conn.: Archon, 1978. This book contains some biographical material. It is more concerned, however, with Mercator's works, particularly the geographic contents of his world map of 1569 and his cosmography. Illustrated, with bibliographic references.

Greenhood, David. *Mapping*. Rev. ed. Chicago: University of Chicago Press, 1964. Contains little information about Mercator himself. Instead, the chapter of projections describes Mercator's projection and how it is constructed in accurate yet not overly technical terms. Well illustrated.

LeGear, C. E. "Gerardus Mercator's Atlas of 1595." In *A La Carte: Selected Papers on Maps and Atlases*, compiled by Walter W. Ristow. Washington, D.C.: Library of Congress, 1972. This chapter is a reprint of an article that originally appeared in the *Library of Congress Quarterly Journal of Acquisitions* in May, 1950. It describes the contents of Mercator's atlas and provides a short biography of Mercator. Contains three reproductions of illustrations that appeared in his atlas, Mercator's portrait, and two of his maps, one of the New World and one of the British Isles.

Mercator, Gerhard. *The Mercator Atlas of Europe: Facsimile of the Maps by Gerardus Mercator*

Contained in the Atlas of Europe, circa 1570-1572. Edited by Marcel Watelet. Pleasant Hill, Ore.: Walking Tree Press, 1998. Reprints of seventeen maps purchased unknowingly in a second-hand store in Belgium in 1967; essays by five leading map scholars place this find in historical perspective.

Stevenson, Edward Luther. *Terrestrial and Celestial Globes: Their History and Construction Including a Consideration of Their Value as Aids in the Study of Geography and Astronomy*. New Haven, Conn.: Yale University Press, 1921. In addition to the usual short biography and the study of Mercator's projection and atlas, this book contains a lengthy description of Mercator's globes.

Thrower, Norman J. W. *Maps and Man*. Englewood Cliffs, N.J.: Prentice-Hall, 1972. A short history of cartography. The unique contribution of the chapter on Renaissance cartography is Thrower's description of Mercator's map rather than the projection on which it is drawn. Contains bibliographic citations.

Vujakovic, Peter, and Brian Dicks. "The Man Who Changed the World." *Geographical Magazine* 66 (December, 1994): 14. The authors assess the contributions of Mercator to cartography, including his greatest work—a bound collection (or atlas) of maps, a concept which was, for his time, revolutionary.

Theodore P. Aufdemberge

MICHELANGELO

Born: March 6, 1475; Caprese, Tuscany
Died: February 18, 1564; Rome
Areas of Achievement: Art and architecture
Contribution: Michelangelo was a true Renaissance man, excelling in sculpture, painting, architecture, and poetry. He was the supreme master of the human body, especially the male nude, and his idealized and expressive treatment of this theme was enormously influential, both in his own day and in subsequent centuries.

Early Life

Michelangelo Buonarroti was the second of five sons of an aristocratic but impoverished Florentine family. He was born in the village of Caprese, near Arezzo, where his father was serving as magistrate, but before he was a month old the family returned to Florence.

From childhood Michelangelo was strongly drawn to the arts, but this inclination was bitterly opposed by his father, who considered artistic activity menial and hence demeaning to the family social status. The boy's determination prevailed, however, and at the age of thirteen he was apprenticed to the popular painter Domenico Ghirlandaio. From Ghirlandaio he presumably learned the technique of fresco painting, but his style was formed on the study of the pioneers of Renaissance painting, Giotto and Masaccio. It was, in fact, while copying a Masaccio fresco that he was punched in the face by another apprentice. The resulting broken nose gave his face its distinctive bent profile for the rest of his life.

About a year after entering his apprenticeship, Michelangelo's precocious talent attracted the notice of Lorenzo de' Medici, the unofficial ruler and leading art patron of Florence, and the boy was invited to join the Medici household. There he had the opportunity to study both classical and modern masterpieces of sculpture and to absorb the humanistic culture and Neoplatonic philosophy that pervaded the Medici court. From this period date Michelangelo's two earliest surviving works, both reliefs, *The Battle of the Centaurs* (c. 1492) and *The Madonna of the Steps* (c. 1492). When Lorenzo died in 1492, Michelangelo left the Medici palace and undertook the study of anatomy based on the dissection of corpses from the Hospital of Santo Spirito, for which he carved a wooden crucifix in gratitude.

In 1494, the populace of Florence, stirred by the puritanical monk Girolamo Savonarola, ousted the Medici family and reestablished a republic. Michelangelo, although he seems to have admired Savonarola and supported the republic, evidently felt threatened because of his close ties to the Medici family and fled the city, staying briefly in Venice and then in Bologna. There he supported himself with relatively minor sculpture commissions.

The year 1496 found him in Rome, where he undertook two important projects, the *Bacchus* (1497), which effectively replicated the Hellenistic style, and the Vatican *Pietà* (1499), an image of the Virgin Mary supporting the dead Christ. In this work Michelangelo minimizes the painful aspect of the subject by showing the Virgin as a lovely, surprisingly youthful woman gazing down serenely at the classically beautiful body of her son. To overcome the awkwardness of balancing an adult male body on the lap of a woman, he enlarges the Virgin but masks her size with billowing drapery and wraps the body of Christ around her to create a compact, pyramidal group. The contract called for the *Pietà* to be "the most beautiful work in marble which exists today in Rome." When, at the age of twenty-five, Michelangelo completed the piece, there was no question that he had met this requirement.

Life's Work

In 1501, Michelangelo returned triumphantly to Florence and to a new challenge. An enormous marble block that had been abandoned decades earlier because its tall, shallow proportions seemed unsuitable for a figure sculpture was assigned to him, and from it he carved the *David* (1501-1504). David was a favorite Florentine subject, but Michelangelo's treatment broke with tradition in representing the shepherd boy as a Herculean nude, twice life-size, before, rather than after, the battle so as to incorporate greater physical and psychic tension. The statue was placed in the square outside the governmental palace, but it has since been moved inside to protect it from the weather. Contemporary with the *David* or slightly later are several powerful representations of the Madonna and Child, including the artist's only unquestioned panel painting, the *Doni Madonna* (c. 1503-1505).

In 1504, the Florentine republic ordered two large battle scenes for its council chamber, one from Leonardo da Vinci and the other from Miche-

langelo. Neither fresco was actually painted, and even Michelangelo's preliminary drawing survives only in a copy. It shows a group of bathing soldiers struggling out of a stream at the battle alarm, and the treatment of the straining, foreshortened bodies was to provide instruction and inspiration to a whole generation of Italian artists.

This painting and a series of sculpted apostles for Florence Cathedral were interrupted when the recently elected pope, Julius II, called Michelangelo to Rome. The pope's first commission was for his tomb, a grandiose, multilevel structure that was to include more than forty figures. Michelangelo had hardly begun this project when the pope changed his mind and ordered the artist instead to paint the ceiling of the Sistine Chapel. Michelangelo vigorously objected that he was a sculptor, not a painter, but in the end he spent the years 1508-1512 covering the surface, approximately fifty-eight hundred square feet, seventy feet above the floor, with scenes from Genesis, enframed by nude youths and surrounded by enthroned prophets and Sibyls. In keeping with his preference for sculpture, emphasis is placed on the monumental figures with rather minimal background. Nevertheless, as cleaning of the fresco has revealed, the coloring is both subtle and brilliant.

Upon completion of the ceiling, Michelangelo resumed his work on the pope's tomb, producing *The Dying Slave* (1513-1516), *The Rebellious Slave* (1513-1516), and *Moses* (1505-1545). Julius, however, died in 1513, and his successors would include two members of the Medici family, both boyhood companions of Michelangelo, Leo X (1513-1521) and Clement VII (1523-1534). Both preferred to keep Michelangelo employed largely on family projects in Florence, so that progress on the Julius tomb was slow and sporadic. The first Medician commission, an elaborate façade for the family church of San Lorenzo, was never executed, but the next, a new sacristry in the same church containing tombs of the Medici dukes, although never finished, was to be the artist's most complete architectural and sculptural ensemble. Probably the most celebrated figures from this complex are the personifications of *Night* and *Day, Dawn* and *Dusk* (1520-1534), which recline uneasily on the curved and sloping sarcophagus lids. Above them sit idealized effigies of the dead dukes, who turn toward a statue of the Madonna and Child, the so-called *Medici Madonna* (1525). There is a noticeable change in Michelangelo's style in the 1520's, the decade of this chapel. His figures become more restless, with spiraling rhythms and sometimes elongated or otherwise distorted proportions, the overall effect of which is disturbing. The same quality is found in the architecture that Michelangelo executed in the same decade, especially the vestibule of the Laurentian Library, which includes a number of unconventional and even bizarre features. This change corresponds to a more general anticlassical and antinaturalistic trend in Italian art at this time which is often characterized as mannerism.

When, in 1527, the Florentines again expelled their Medici rulers and restored the republic, Michelangelo sided against his patrons and supported it. During the ensuing conflict he played a major role in designing the fortifications of the city, and when Medici forces recaptured it in 1530 he went into hiding. Pope Clement amnestied the artist, but Michelangelo felt threatened and estranged under the new autocratic regime and spent increasing amounts of time in Rome. Finally, in 1534, he left Florence forever. Two days after he arrived to settle in Rome, Clement VII died.

Michelangelo expected now to be free to return to the long-delayed and repeatedly scaled-down Julius tomb, but again he was frustrated. The new pope, Paul III, declaring that he had waited thirty years to have Michelangelo work for him, induced Julius' heirs to accept a modest wall tomb featuring *Moses*, from the original project, and two more female figures from Michelangelo's hand. The monument was completed in 1545, and Michelangelo was at last free of what he himself described as "the tragedy of the tomb."

Meanwhile, he was engaged on several major projects for Pope Paul II, beginning with the fresco of the *Last Judgment* on the altar wall of the Sistine Chapel, painted between 1536 and 1541. The expressionist tendency in Michelangelo's art, already noted, is dominant here. Clusters of swirling figures alternate with empty sky and the scale of the figures changes unaccountably, with the more distant becoming larger. A poignant personal note is the inclusion of a grimacing self-portrait of the artist on the discarded skin of one of the saints.

The *Last Judgment* was followed by two more frescoes painted during the 1540's for Paul III's private chapel, *The Conversion of Saint Paul* (1542-1545) and *The Crucifixion of Saint Peter* (1542-1550). The pope also placed Michelangelo in charge of several architectural projects, including the rebuilding of the cupola at St. Peter's Basilica and the remodeling of the Piazza del Campidoglio. Neither, however, was to be completed in the artist's lifetime.

In his last years Michelangelo returned to sculpture with two devotional and deeply personal works. The Florence *Pietà* (1550-1556) was intended for Michelangelo's own tomb and contained his self-portrait. In 1555, however, he attacked and damaged the piece in a fit of frustration. Thereafter he sculpted the Rondanini *Pietà* (1552-1564), on which he was still working six days before his death, in 1564, when he was eighty-eight.

Summary

Michelangelo gave eloquent expression, in sculpture, painting, and poetry, to his own ideals and those of his contemporaries as they moved from the confident Humanism of the High Renaissance to the anxious spirituality of the Counter-Reformation period. His early work seems to harmonize the pagan sensuality of antiquity with Christian themes and to celebrate human beauty as a reflection of divine creation. As his art and thought evolved, however, he increasingly conveyed a tension between spirit and body, form and matter, and he came to depreciate physical perfection in favor of psychological and spiritual expression. In his late Roman years he became associated with the Catholic reform movement, and his growing religious fervor gives a highly personal and sometimes mystical flavor to the art of this period.

Michelangelo's genius was recognized and venerated by his contemporaries, and he exerted enormous influence on generations of younger artists. It was, however, the superficial aspects of his style—serpentine poses and muscular anatomies—that were easiest to assimilate. None of his followers was able to match his profundity of thought and feeling.

Bibliography

Condivi, Ascanio. *The Life of Michelangelo*. Edited with an introduction by Hellmut Wohl. Translated by Alice Sedgwick Wohl. Oxford: Phaidon Press, and Baton Rouge: Louisiana State University Press, 1976. An essential primary source, this biography was written during Michelangelo's lifetime by one of his students and is based on the artist's own recollections. Illustrations and bibliography.

De Tolnay, Charles. *Michelangelo*. 5 vols. Princeton, N.J.: Princeton University Press, 1943-1960. The definitive scholarly study of the artist in five volumes, each devoted to a particular aspect of his life or work. Catalog of works, extensive notes, illustrations, and bibliography.

Hartt, Frederick. *Michelangelo*. London: Thames and Hudson, and New York: Abrams, 1965. Limited to Michelangelo's paintings, which are dealt with in an introductory essay, followed by color plates with interpretive comments. Biographical chronology and bibliography.

———. *Michelangelo, the Complete Sculpture*. New York: Abrams, 1968; London: Thames and Hudson, 1969. Contains lavish illustrations, many in color, with fine interpretive text geared to plates. Includes biographical chronology and bibliography.

Hibbard, Howard. *Michelangelo*. New York: Harper, 1974; London: Lane, 1975. A highly readable, unobtrusively scholarly survey of Michelangelo's life and career. Illustrations and bibliography.

Murray, Linda. *Michelangelo: His Life, Work, and Times*. London and New York: Thames and Hudson, 1984. Focus on the artist's historical setting, with extended quotes from contemporary sources. Numerous illustrations relate both to Michelangelo's works and to his background. Bibliography.

Nagel, Alexander. "Gifts for Michelangelo and Vittoria Colonna." *Art Bulletin* 79 (December, 1997): 647. Nagel interprets Michelangelo's drawing of the "Pietá" for painter Vittorio Colonna as a model for a conception of religious faith and divine grace promoted in the reforming circles of the mid-sixteenth century.

Vasari, Giorgio. "Michelangelo." In *Lives of the Artists*, translated by George Bull. London and New York: Penguin, 1965. A major primary source, this biography by a friend and fellow artist was written shortly after Michelangelo's death and includes firsthand impressions and recollections.

Wallace, William E. "Michelangelo's 'Risen Christ.'" *Sixteenth Century Journal* 28 (winter 1997): 1251. Wallace examines the sculpture titled the "Risen Christ" by restoring it to its original context and assessing its unusual and moving iconography. Information is provided on the sculpture's history, its location, and the reason it is the least known of Michelangelo's works.

Jane Kristof

MOHAMMED I ASKIA

Born: c. 1442; probably near Gao, Songhai Empire

Died: 1538; near Gao, Songhai Empire

Areas of Achievement: Monarchy and statecraft

Contribution: Mohammed I Askia greatly expanded and consolidated the Songhai Empire, which dominated much of West Africa in the fifteenth and sixteenth centuries. His policies resulted in a rapid expansion of trade and the imposition of the stamp of Islamic civilization on Songhai.

Early Life

Mohammed I Askia was born Mohammed Ture ibn Abi Bakr, probably of parents of the Soninke people. Although the Soninke frequently are cited as the source of the royal lineage of ancient Ghana, a large West African kingdom that flourished before A.D. 1000, most Soninke, including Mohammed's clan, were subject in the fifteenth century to the Songhai Empire, centered at the Niger River entrepôt of Gao. Mohammed's family was of a military caste, providing soldiers and officers for the Songhai cavalry regiments. His childhood and education no doubt reflected that experience. He probably received systematic religious instruction in some Islamic institution as a child. In early adulthood, Mohammed became a trusted lieutenant in the service of the Songhai Emperor, Sonni Ali. Mohammed's early years were a time of unprecedented expansion and turmoil for Songhai. Although oral dynastic history of Songhai goes back to the eighth or ninth century, prior to the fifteenth it had been only a small principality.

Sonni Ali's leadership transformed Songhai into a regional influence. Taking advantage of the progressive disintegration of its powerful western neighbor Mali, after 1450, his forces swept westward, capturing the fabled city of Tombouctou, pushing back the Saharan nomads who menaced the river towns, and punishing recalcitrant Mossi chieftains to the south. In the process of forming an empire, however, Sonni Ali revealed a streak of barbaric cruelty. Further, many of the newly conquered areas west of Songhai proper were heavily Islamic and culturally more sophisticated than Songhai itself, and often related more to North African than sub-Saharan ethnic types. Sonni Ali's vicious temperament and cavalier attitude toward Islam set his subjects to plotting. His death in 1492, before consolidation of Songhai's considerable territorial gains could be completed, prepared the way for Mohammed to emerge as a national leader.

Life' Work

In April, 1493, Mohammed allied himself with the Muslim clerics and disaffected Muslim portions of the empire against Sonni Ali's son and would-be successor, whose support lay primarily in the Songhai homeland. Ethnic and religious divisions ran deep in the ranks of the large Songhai army. Mohammed avoided what otherwise might have become a bloody and prolonged civil war by staging a coup, seizing the capital, and forcing Sonni Ali's son into exile. He took the dynastic title of Askia (*askiya*).

Mohammed's first task was to obtain recognition as the legitimate ruler of Songhai. That he achieved, at least initially, by purging or deporting as many members of earlier Songhai dynastic lines as possible. His long-term strategy, however, involved cultivation of tighter alliances with Muslim intellectuals and clerics. Mohammed viewed Islam as the logical counterpoint in Songhai to the power and influence of the traditional priesthood and political leadership. He lavished attention, gifts, and titles upon Muslim notables, particularly those in the newly conquered, western part of the empire. He also strove to develop the city of Tombouctou—already known for its concentration of Muslim clerics and scholars—into a first-rate center of learning, a cultural focus that could rival the traditional religious center of Kukia in the eastern Songhai homeland.

Mohammed must have perceived the enormous advantages of Islam in transforming Songhai from a peripheral state into a partner in what was, in the sixteenth century, the world's most diverse and extensive civilization and commercial network. Songhai, and its predecessors Ghana and Mali, depended upon the export of gold and ivory to North Africa for hard currency and crucial imports such as horses for cavalry. There is evidence too that, by Mohammed's time, the presence of European trading stations on the West African coast was beginning to affect traditional commercial networks in the region.

For these reasons, doubtless also as an expression of his own piety, Mohammed in late 1496 undertook the hajj, or pilgrimage, to Mecca. The expedition was a stupendous effort to eclipse the pomp and splendor of the pilgrimage by Mansa Musa some 175 years earlier. In Egypt, the titular Abbasid caliph bestowed upon Mohammed the title Caliph of the Blacks. In addition to donating enormous amounts of gold to the poor and needy, Mohammed endowed a hostel for future pilgrims from West Africa. Mohammed was away nearly two years, which suggests that he was firmly in control of affairs in Songhai.

Mohammed's hajj was a boon to the fortunes of Islam in West Africa. He established visibility for the kingdom and returned determined to purify the practices of West African Muslims and bring them into line with orthodoxy. The hajj attracted scholars and religious notables from all over the Middle East; many accompanied Mohammed back to Songhai and greatly strengthened the scholarly community there. Tombouctou, in particular, developed an international reputation as an academic and religious center. Farther to the west, amid the serpentine courses of the Niger floodplain, protected from invasion by the annual inundation, the city of Djenné developed a reputation throughout West Africa comparable to that of Tombouctou.

Mohammed continued to expand Songhai's frontiers, often in the cause of a jihad, or holy war. His soldiers battled the Mossi tribes of modern Burkina Fasso to the south and captured most of the important salt mines and oases in the Sahara as far as the frontiers of modern Algeria and Libya. Even some of the powerful Hausa city-states of northern Nigeria fell under Mohammed's sway. The Songhai army featured a mobile cavalry and levies of conscripts, very likely the first such standing army in Africa, supported by a strong riverine navy on the Niger. (Firearms, however, though apparently known, were not used by the Songhai forces.) By the end of Mohammed's active reign, these forces had created what most likely was the largest political entity in African history to that time.

The administrative structure of Songhai shows little of the Islamic influence so pervasive in other facets of the state. It was a simple system of provincial governors responsible to Mohammed. There was a ministerial council of sorts but with little real power and usually dominated by members of the royal family in any case. The court protocol that was reported by foreign travelers—among them the famous Leo Africanus—suggests that Mohammed continued to behave as a traditional West African king, wielding almost absolute power. Despite his commitment to Islam, there is no evidence of persecution of unbelievers. Gao, in fact, became a haven for Jewish refugees from the Saharan oases when persecution broke out there in the early sixteenth century. Many of Mohammed's gestures toward traditionalism may have resulted from the fact that the people of the Songhai capital of Gao continued to resist Islamic influence.

Signs of despotism reappeared in Mohammed's later years. Moreover, the large and unprecedented administrative apparatus of the court and provincial government had to be supported by a growing system of landed aristocrats, a network of royal estates producing food and military supplies through slavery and forced labor. Newly conquered peoples found themselves assigned to the production of weapons and armor or to service to the army. Others plied the Niger to produce fish for the court.

In his declining years, Mohammed lost his grip on the empire. In order to foster the continued growth of Islam, the king had designated a western governor as successor, but his ambitious sons were determined to seize power. In 1528, they deposed Mohammed, who was already blind and infirm, exiling him to an island in the Niger. Nearly a decade of turmoil elapsed before the Askia rivals settled on a system of succession and power sharing.

Summary

Mohammed I Askia belongs to a tradition of warrior-kings who periodically unified and integrated the Niger basin and adjacent areas, beginning perhaps as early as A.D. 800. This periodic unification greatly affected the economic history of lands around the Mediterranean, especially with respect to the export of gold and other precious commodities. In the Niger region itself, it established a level of political order and stability necessary for commerce to thrive. In the period of Mohammed, as well as in earlier decades when Mali was prominent, Islam made important advances, which conferred a measure of cultural unity upon the region and also stimulated interaction with the outside world.

Mohammed himself was among the foremost of the unifiers, administrators, and purveyors of Islam. Evidence from the era of his predecessor, Sonni Ali, strongly suggests that Islam was in decline, actively challenged by pagan and traditional elements in West African society. Given the importance of Muslim merchants in the economic life of the region, it is also likely that the Niger basin was in a state of economic disarray owing to the disintegration of Mali and growing hostility to outsiders. These trends Mohammed dramatically reversed, restoring and greatly expanding commerce and drawing the Niger basin closer than ever before to the world economy. His contributions toward an Islamic cultural order laid the foundations for the eventual emergence of Islam as a mass religion in West Africa.

Mohammed's Askia dynasty continued after his death. His sons ruled ably for fifty years in the mid-sixteenth century, during which time Songhai maintained relations with the newly established Ottoman Empire in North Africa, and Songhai was able to withstand some of the commercial turmoil resulting from increased European activity on the African coast.

On the other hand, the limits of Mohammed's Islamic campaign in Songhai are clear. Neither he nor his successors managed to close the gap between the predominantly Muslim west and the still-pagan Songhai heartland in the eastern part of the empire. Civil war eventually resulted in a disastrous reverse for Mohammed's Islamic edifice in 1588. Three years later, an invasion from Morocco brought the empire crashing down and the Askia dynasty to a humiliating close.

Bibliography

Boahen, A. Adu, Jacob F. Ade Ajayi, and Michael Tidy. *Topics in West African History*. 2d ed. Burnt Mill, Essex: Longman, 1986. An excellent description of Songhai within the wider context of medieval West African history.

Bovill, E. W., and Robin Hallet. *The Golden Trade of the Moors*. 2d ed. London and New York: Oxford University Press, 1968. An excellent treatment of medieval West African history and its connections with European events. Gives a detailed account of the rise of Songhai and the contributions of its major rulers.

Hunwick, J. O. "Religion and State in the Songhay Empire." In *Islam in Tropical Africa*, edited by I. M. Lewis. London: Oxford University Press, 1966. Discusses the tensions between Islamic and pagan religious and philosophical ideas in Songhai and how the major rulers borrowed and elaborated upon ideas from both sources to organize and administer the empire.

Kaba, Lansine. "The Pen, the Sword, and the Crown: Islam and Revolution in Songhay Reconsidered, 1464-1493." *Journal of African History* 25 (1984): 241-256. Traces the rise of Songhai to changing trade patterns and discusses Sonni Ali's antagonism toward Muslim elites which, by contrast, Mohammed supported and used to build his administration.

Pardo, Anne W. "The Songhay Empire Under Sonni Ali and Askia Muhammad: A Study in Comparisons and Contrasts." In *Aspects of West African Islam*, edited by Daniel F. McCall. Boston: Boston University Press, 1971. An unusually critical treatment of chronicles and other sources in an effort to determine the precise ideological and religious attitudes of Sonni Ali and Mohammed.

Saad, Elias. *A Social History of Timbuktu: The Role of Muslim Scholars and Notables, 1400-1900*. Cambridge and New York: Cambridge University Press, 1983. An important study of social and intellectual life in precolonial West Africa. Provides extensive coverage of the zenith of Songhai civilization in the early sixteenth century, using indigenous chronicles and a wide variety of other documentary sources.

Trimingham, J. Spencer. *A History of Islam in West Africa*. London and New York: Oxford University Press, 1962. One of the most painstaking studies of the development of Islamic influence and practices in the region. Particularly harsh on Sonni Ali and critical of other accounts suggesting a high level of Islamic intellectual activity in Songhai and the center of learning in Tombouctou.

Ronald W. Davis

MICHEL DE MONTAIGNE

Born: February 28, 1533; Château de Montaigne, Périgord, France

Died: September 13, 1592; Château de Montaigne, Périgord, France

Areas of Achievement: Philosophy, politics, and literature

Contribution: In an age of violent religious and political struggles, Montaigne mediated for tolerance. His gift to literature was the invention of the essay.

Early Life

Michel Eyquem de Montaigne was born in his father's château in Périgord, a French county east and north of Bordeaux, which became a part of France in 1607. His father, Pierre Eyquem, held many important posts, including that of Mayor of Bordeaux, and afforded an unusual model of religious tolerance by heading a Catholic family that included a Protestant wife of Spanish and Jewish blood and two Protestant children.

Montaigne dearly loved his father, who was responsible for his receiving a gentle and cultured life. At age six, he was sent to the finest school in Bordeaux, where he completed the twelve-year course in seven years. Sometime during the next eight years, he very likely studied law.

From 1557 to 1570, Montaigne was a councillor in the Bordeaux Parlement and took numerous trips to Paris. During this period, he made a close and erudite friend, Étienne de La Boétie, who in the remaining four years of his life came to be more important to Montaigne than anyone else and influenced Montaigne throughout his life. It was La Boétie's stoic acceptance of suffering and his courageous death, at which Montaigne was present despite the danger of contagion, that turned Montaigne toward Stoicism and probably inspired him to begin writing.

In 1565, Montaigne married Françoise de La Chassaigne. He seldom mentions her in his writing. Of his six children, only one, Léonor, survived childhood.

About 1567, Montaigne's father had him translate a work which was strongly opposed to Protestantism and atheism: *Theologia naturalis, sive Liber creaturarum* (1485; the book of creatures: or natural theology), written in medieval Latin by a fifteenth century Spaniard, Raymond Sebond. His father, although terminally ill, arranged for the publication of the translation.

After his father's death, Michel became Lord of Montaigne, owner of the château and the estate, and at thirty-eight years of age retired to what he hoped would be a life of quiet study and composition. Much of his time was spent in the tower, which he asked to be added to his castle, and which even his wife was forbidden to enter. There he wrote his life's work, *Essais* (1580, 1588, 1595; *The Essays*, 1603), which was placed on the Index in 1676 but was viewed favorably by the Vatican in Montaigne's day.

Life's Work

Over a period of thirty years, Montaigne dealt with every conceivable aspect of man's life by describing in detail his own thoughts, beliefs, experiences, and habits of living. Nothing was too abstruse to be tackled or too insignificant to be mentioned. His essay titles range from "Sur des vers de Virgile" ("On Certain Verses of Virgil") to "Des coches" ("Of Coaches"). His early essays were compilations of views followed by a brief moral, often showing the influence of Seneca the Younger or Plutarch, both of whom he admired immensely. These were followed by what is called his skeptical period, during which he coined his motto: "What do I know?" The years from 1578 onward are termed his Epicurean period, wherein he endeavored to find his own nature and to follow its dictates. His hero during this period was Socrates, and life was a great adventure to be lived as happily as possible, with due regard for the rights of others and guided by common sense. He counseled moderation in all things, freedom with self-control, and honesty and courage.

In the essay "De la proesumption" ("About Presumption"), Montaigne describes himself as below average height but strong and well-set, with a face not fat but full. A portrait of him in the Condé Museum at Chantilly depicts a handsome man with regular features, fine eyes, short-cropped hair, a small mustache, and a neat beard. Evidently he was not given to vanity. He enjoyed horseback riding, travel, and conversation with intelligent men. He also enjoyed the company of his "covenant daughter," Marie de Gournay, who became his literary executrix.

After Montaigne's retirement, all of his time was not spent in seclusion: Between 1572 and 1576, he attempted to mediate between his friend Henry of

Navarre (later Henry IV) and the extremist Catholics of the Holy League. At the accession of Henry III in 1576, Montaigne was made a Gentleman of the Bedchamber, an office that gave access to the king without requiring residence at court. His disgust at the excesses of the Wars of Religion gave him a strong distaste for government, and, while he loved the city of Paris, he avoided the royal court.

In 1580, Montaigne journeyed to take the waters at Lucca on the west coast of Italy. He hoped, but probably did not really believe, that the baths could cure his recurring misery caused by a kidney stone. Accompanied by his younger brother, two nobles, and a secretary, he left on horseback with no planned itinerary.

En route to the baths, he visited Paris, Switzerland, and Germany. In Rome, he was declared a citizen of that city, an honor which he greatly coveted. During his second stay in Lucca, he learned to his dismay that he had been elected Mayor of Bordeaux. He tried to refuse the responsibility but finally capitulated and arrived home after an absence of seventeen months.

Montaigne served two terms as mayor, from 1581 to 1585, and without showing undue zeal managed to initiate some reforms that included improving the lot of foundling children and imprisoned women and helping the poor by refusing to allow the rich to be exempt from taxation. He showed his concern for education by improving the Collège des Jésuites and also his own old school, the Collège de Guyenne. He left office somewhat ignominiously, tendering his resignation outside the city, which was at that time stricken by the plague.

Although no longer mayor, Montaigne was unable to avoid for long his involvement in the turbulent political situation. After a peaceful year at home working on *The Essays*, he found his unprotected estate overrun by soldiers and himself suspect to both the Catholics and the Protestants. In early 1588, he was sent to Paris on a secret mission to Henry III from Henry of Navarre. En route, he was detained by Protestants and a few months later found himself briefly imprisoned in the Bastille by the Catholics. After nearly a year spent in following the king from Paris to Chartres to Rouen and attending the Estates-General at Blois, Montaigne returned home and helped to keep Bordeaux loyal to the king. In his remaining years, he continued to add passages to *The Essays*. There is no eyewitness account of his death, but numerous contemporaries claim that he died peacefully while hearing Mass in his room.

Summary

Michel de Montaigne's writing style is vivacious and strong, with unexpected images, picturesque details, and often ironic humor. He reaches his highest level when he discusses the interdependence of mind and matter; modern psychologists and even psychiatrists might well claim him as their forefather. It is said that Sigmund Freud was interested in *The Essays*. Perhaps it is the surprising intimacy that Montaigne creates that is the most novel characteristic of his work: The reader believes that he knows the author better than he knows his closest friends or his family and maybe better than he knows himself. This kind of writing was new to literature.

In politics and in religion, Montaigne was opposed to change; his aim was peace, and he worked toward that end. Despite personal reservations, he remained a loyal subject of the Crown and a practicing Catholic, proclaiming that one ought to accept the government of one's country and its religion.

In education, Montaigne was centuries ahead of his time: In his essay "De l'institution des enfants" (on children's schools), he advocated training a child to be an efficient human being by exposing him not to pedants but to men of all social stations. The child must be taught to observe and to judge for himself.

In literature, Montaigne established the great principle of the seventeenth century: respect for and imitation of the classics. He insisted that the only subject suitable for man's study is man himself. There is no doubt that his essays influenced Francis Bacon, François de La Rochefoucauld, Blaise Pascal, Jean de La Bruyère, and Joseph Addison.

While Montaigne was describing himself in his writings, he was also depicting man in general; in fact, he was dealing with the human condition. In the twentieth century, Albert Camus, André Malraux, Jean-Paul Sartre, and a host of other eminent writers in Europe and the United States have devoted their talents to examining the human condition. Whether they acknowledge it, directly or indirectly, they are all indebted to Montaigne.

Bibliography

Burke, Peter. *Montaigne*. Oxford and New York: Oxford University Press, 1981. Each of the ten chapters is devoted to a special aspect of Montaigne. Each chapter has its own bibliography, and there is an index. The style is straightforward, the information accurate. For students and general readers.

Frame, Donald M. *Montaigne's Discovery of Man: The Humanization of a Humanist*. New York: Columbia University Press, 1955. An account of the life of Montaigne and the development of his thought as conveyed in *The Essays*.

———. *Montaigne's Essais: A Study*. Englewood Cliffs, N.J.: Prentice-Hall, 1969. A detailed study of Montaigne's life and an erudite examination of the evolution of his talent as revealed in *The Essays* as well as an estimate of his impact during the last four centuries. Contains a chronology, a bibliography, and an index.

Melehy, Hassan. *Writing Cogito: Montaigne, Descartes, and the Institution of the Modern Subject*. Albany: State University of New York Press, 1997. Through the work of Montaigne and Rene Descartes, Melehy considers the question of the foundation of the human subject in the context of contemporary debates in literature and philosophy. Montaigne, through writing, examines the many possibilities of subjective experience, and finds that the subject takes shape in writing.

Montaigne, Michel de. *The Essays of Michel de Montaigne*. Translated by George B. Ives. 4 vols. New York: Limited Editions Club, 1946. Introduction by André Gide and an accompanying handbook, which includes notes on the text by the translator and a series of comments on *The Essays* by Grace Norton. Highly readable and informative.

Platt, Michael P. *Freedom over Servitude: Montaigne, La Boetie and "On Voluntary Servitude."* Westport, Conn.: Greenwood, 1998. This volume contains five articles by prominent scholars of French literature and political philosophy that examine the relation between Montaigne's *Essais*, one of the classic works of the French philosophical and literary traditions, and the writings attributed by Montaigne to his friend, the French humanist Etienne de La Boetie. Three contributors to the volume suggest that Montaigne was the real author of the revolutionary tract "On Voluntary Servitude," along with the other works he attributed to La Boetie.

Quint, David. *Montaigne and the Quality of Mercy: Ethical and Political Themes in the* Essais. Princeton, N.J.: Princeton University Press, 1998. In a fresh reading of Montaigne's *Essais*, Quint portrays the great Renaissance writer as both a literary man and a deeply engaged political thinker concerned with the ethical basis of society and civil discourse. From the first essay, Montaigne places the reader in a world of violent political conflict reminiscent of the French Wars of Religion through which he lived and wrote. Quint shows how a group of interrelated essays, including the famous one on the cannibals of Brazil, explores the confrontation between warring adversaries: a clement or vindictive victor and his suppliant or defiant captive.

Sichel, Edith. *Michel de Montaigne*. London: Constable, and New York: Dutton, 1911. Divided into "Montaigne the Man" and "Montaigne the Philosopher," this is a leisurely and rather personal view of his times, his life, and his work based largely on quotations from *The Essays*. Facsimiles of portraits and manuscript and bibliographical notes. Pleasant, easy reading.

Watson, Richard A. *Language and Human Action: Conceptions of Language in the* Essais *of Montaigne*. New York: Peter Lang, 1996. Montaigne's *Essais* presents a subject matter that often discusses and analyzes concepts of language in general as well as language as a vehicle of its own expression. The great Renaissance humanist's depiction of language in the *Essais* is analyzed in this book on the basis of its division among intellectual, moral, and aesthetic aspects.

Dorothy B. Aspinwall

MONTEZUMA II

Born: 1467; Tenochtitlán, Aztec Empire
Died: June 30, 1520; Tenochtitlán, Aztec Empire
Area of Achievement: Monarchy
Contribution: Montezuma II expanded the Aztec Empire to its greatest size and died as his empire crumbled under the pressures of Hernán Cortés.

Early Life

Axayácatl named his fourth son Montezuma, the Younger, after the child's great-grandfather. Montezuma I was the Mexica *Uei Tlatoani* (great speaker, or emperor) of the Aztec Empire, centered in Anahuac, an intermontane valley in central Mexico. At Montezuma the Younger's naming ceremony, held four days after his birth in 1467, the priests dedicated the infant to Quetzalcóatl, that year's patron deity, and prophesied that he would earn greatness as both ruler and priest.

The prophecy was not a guarantee. Young Montezuma was born into an oligarchy called the *Pipiltin* (sons of lords) that was composed of the putative descendants of Acamapichtli, founder of the Mexica state, and a princess of the fading Culhuacán dynasty. The office of emperor was not hereditary. A council of *Pipiltin* elders elected a successor on the basis of merit rather than on degrees of kinship to the deceased emperor. For Montezuma to become emperor when his generation came of age, his accomplishments would have to set him apart from his brothers and cousins.

After spending five years in the *Calmécac*, an elite preparatory school, twelve-year-old Montezuma moved into the barracks for a two-year apprenticeship before joining the warriors in combat. He soon excelled in battle and captured enough enemies to be inducted into the exclusive Order of the Eagle. In 1483, at age sixteen, he resumed religious studies and became a priest of the war god Huitzilopochtli (Blue Hummingbird). The next year, Montezuma had to decide whether to take an oath of celibacy and devote his entire life to the priesthood or to marry and continue his military career.

He chose the middle route and became a warrior-priest. He took, eventually, four legitimate wives and participated in most of the major military campaigns until his installation as emperor in 1503. Through his first wife, he inherited the title *Tlatoani* (speaker, or ruler) of the city-state Ehecatepec. Prowess in war made him an army commander at age thirty, and later he became *Tlacochcalcatl* (prince of the house), one of the four closest advisers to the emperor. He also retained his priestly office and rose through clerical ranks to become high priest of Huitzilopochtli.

Life's Work

This warrior-priest bore the markings of both professions on his body. Among warriors he was a *Tequihua* (master of cuts) and had the sides of his head shaved, leaving on top a stiff tuft bound with a red thong. A sizable plug through his lower lip and large studs through extended ear lobes identified him as an aristocrat. A band of black paint across his face signified his priestly status, as did the streaks of cuts and scars on his ears, arms, and thighs. Montezuma had made these cuts with cactus thorns as he propitiated the deities with his own blood. He was of average height, slight but of wiry build; he had little wisps of hair on his upper lip and chin and a yellowish-brown skin color. In demeanor he was grave, reserved, almost aloof. To his reputation of bravery was added respect for his soft-spoken advice on political and religious affairs of state.

The Aztec Empire was relatively young. The Mexica themselves were the last branch of the Aztec tribe to leave the ancestral home of Aztlán. They had arrived in Anahuac in 1258. Called *Chichimeca* (sons of dogs) by the remnants of the disintegrating Toltec-Culhuacán civilization, the Mexica had been treated as outcasts for a century. In 1375, Acamapichtli had secured recognition as a fellow *tlatoani* from the rulers of the city-states around Lake Texcoco. Having risen from abasement to parity, Acamapichtli and his three successors had forged alliances and waged wars until the Mexica dominated Anahuac.

Montezuma I, the fifth *tlatoani*, had sent conquering armies down the slopes of the central valley in all directions and built an empire that reached the oceans to the east and west, the deserts to the north, and the tropical forests to the south. His next three successors, his grandsons—the father and uncles of Montezuma II—had inherited the title *Uei Tlatoani* and continued the policy of constant expansion.

The Aztec Empire was built by war and sustained by blood. Conquered nations paid annual tributes of young men and women who were sacrificed to gods that consumed human hearts. The victims' beating hearts were ripped out of their chests, heads severed then stacked in enormous pyramids, and bodies butchered for consumption by the victorious Mexica.

When Emperor Ahuitzotl died in 1502, Montezuma's piety and prowess persuaded the council of elders that he was preferable to his elder brother Macuilmalinaltzin. Following his election, Montezuma II spent a brief time in prayer and meditation, and then he led an invasion of two neighboring provinces. He brought back fifty-one hundred prisoners to be sacrificed and eaten as part of the enthronement festivities the following year. As emperor, Montezuma had to let his hair grow to shoulder length, wear a thin gold tube through his nose, and exchange his copper lip and ear plugs for larger, golden plugs. He wore a half-miter crown and gold sandals. Once installed, he launched a series of startling actions.

He purged from all government positions *Pipiltin* supporters of his brother and dissolved the council of elders. He then directed the massacre of Macuilmalinaltzin, two younger brothers, and twenty-eight hundred Texcoco warriors. With his power consolidated, Montezuma turned his attention to the empire's subject states. He required all conquered nations to send their nobles to Tenochtitlán, where they replaced the commoners in Montezuma's palace as servants. Tribute payments were increased, and each nation had to erect its own temples to Huitzilopochtli. He then sent armies to the south to add new territories to the empire and to bring more oblations to Huitzilopochtli. By 1519, Montezuma's empire encompassed about 200,000 square miles and contained more than twenty million people. Montezuma had created a chasm between himself and commoners by surrounding himself with only nobles. He had elevated Huitzilopochtli in importance throughout the empire and had identified himself more closely with Huitzilopochtli. Soon, however, his patron god Quetzalcóatl overtook the war god in importance for Montezuma and his empire.

The principal deities of the primitive Mexica had been their tribal goddess Mexitli and Huitzilopochtli. When the Mexica arrived in Anahuac, the principal Toltec deity was Quetzalcóatl, the god of divine wisdom who had taught humans agriculture and all the other arts of civilization. The Toltecs had an elaborate cosmogony that included a cyclical theory of time and a conviction that quarrelsome gods had created and destroyed the world four times. At a reconciliation, some of the gods had created a fifth world by immolating themselves. Quetzalcóatl traveled to the netherworld and collected the bones of humans who had lived in the previous worlds. He then ground the bones into powder and re-created humanity by mixing his own divine blood into the powder.

In the ninth century, three hundred years before the Mexica began their trek, the Toltecs were ruled by a high priest who had taken Quetzalcóatl as his own name. This Quetzalcóatl introduced radical religious reforms. He ended human sacrifice, took a vow of celibacy, and sought spiritual unity with his divine namesake through prayer, meditation, and penance. When the priest was an old man, three sorcerers gave an intoxicant, which they called a medicine, to Quetzalcóatl. When the priest was inebriated, the sorcerers put him in bed with a princess, who successfully tempted him to break his vow of chastity. Upon awakening, Quetzalcóatl felt his disgrace so keenly that he fled the Toltec nation, which promptly restored human sacrifice. When Quetzalcóatl reached the Gulf of Mexico, he sailed eastward on a magic raft and vowed to return once he found the place of perfect wisdom.

In their cyclical reckoning of time, the Toltecs and their successors calculated the possible return of Quetzalcóatl and the possible destruction of the fifth world. In the third year of Montezuma's reign, 1506, a fifty-two-year cycle of time was completed. A campaign to Oaxaca garnered twenty-three hundred captives, who were sacrificed en masse in a petition for fifty-two more years of life. If Quetzalcóatl were to return in this new cycle, the light-skinned, bearded priest would return from the East on a magic raft in 1519.

While Hernán Cortés and his five hundred Spaniards sailed up the Yucatán coast in early 1519, Montezuma received regular reports of their activities. After consulting with his priests, Montezuma concluded that the Spaniards were either Quetzalcóatl himself and his entourage or emissaries of the fabled priest. The return of Quetzalcóatl not only was predicted by the calendar but also explained the series of fantastic events that had baffled the Mexica since 1489. There had been earthquakes, a solar eclipse, a flood, and comets that appeared both in the day and at night. Grotesque people and wondrous animals mysteriously appeared and magically disappeared. Huitzilopochtli's temple burst spontaneously into flames, and its replacement was struck by lightning. A woman rose from the dead and told Montezuma that he was the last

Aztec Emporer Montezuma graciously receives the Spanish explorer Cortés

emperor, and a disembodied woman's voice frightened residents of Anahuac by wailing in lament at night. To Montezuma, the arrival of Cortés gave meaning to these bizarre events; they foretold the return of Quetzalcóatl, who would reclaim the empire he had left years ago.

Reluctant to face the religious reformer who had ended human sacrifice, the high priest of Huitzilopochtli tried to hold onto the throne without defying Quetzalcóatl. Montezuma sent Cortés rich gifts, pledged his fealty, exaggerated the difficulties of the journey from the coast to Anahuac, and asked the Spaniards to return to the East. When Cortés led his Spaniards and six thousand Indian allies across the mountains, Montezuma desperately tried to have Cortés ambushed. When all efforts failed, Montezuma accepted his fate and on November 8, 1519, greeted Cortés with these words: "Thou hast arrived on earth; thou hast come to thy noble city of Mexico. Thou hast come to occupy thy noble mat and seat, which for a little time I have guarded and watched for thee. . . . [N]ow it is fulfilled: thou hast returned."

Montezuma's advisers were appalled at their emperor's behavior. They regarded the Spaniards as dangerous aliens who should be repulsed rather than welcomed. The Spaniards' Indian allies were the rebellious Cempoalans and the intransigent Tlaxcalans who already had encouraged the subject states to renounce their loyalty to the empire. Sensing danger, Cortés arrested Montezuma and hoped that his royal hostage would guarantee the Spaniards' safety. When the Spaniards massacred the priests of Huitzilopochtli and placed crucifixes in the temples, Montezuma tried to secure his freedom through intrigue, but it was too late. The *Pipiltin* deposed Montezuma, replaced him with his brother Cuitláhuac, and assaulted the Spaniards. When Cortés had Montezuma taken to the rooftop to restore calm, the infuriated warriors threw stones at their former *Uei Tlatoani* and wounded him seriously in the head. Montezuma died three days later, on June 30, 1520. That night, the Spaniards fought their way out of the city and vowed to return. When the *Pipiltin* found Montezuma's body, they first threw it into a sewage canal and then burned it in a trash heap.

Summary

Since the time of the Spanish conquest and the destruction of the Aztec culture, Montezuma II has entered the world of symbolism. For centuries, he was seen as the embodiment of barbarism, cruelty, and evil. His image was rehabilitated by *indigenistas* (admirers of Indian culture) during the Mexican Revolution of 1910, and he has been portrayed as the epitome of an innocent America violated by a corrupt, greedy, ruthless Spain. With the waning of *indigenista* fervor by the mid-twentieth century, the name Montezuma has come to be associated with the concept of "authentic" Mexico.

Bibliography

Brundage, Burr Cartwright. *A Rain of Darts: The Mexica Aztecs*. Austin: University of Texas Press, 1972; London: University of Texas Press, 1987. A careful chronicle of the Aztecs, based on intensive study of the codices. Brundage concludes that Montezuma was insecure, bloodthirsty, and morbidly religious.

Burland, C. A. *Montezuma: Lord of the Aztecs*. London: Weidenfeld and Nicolson, and New York: Putnam, 1973. This biography, richly illustrated with photographs of Mexico and the Aztec codices, is somewhat melodramatic and error prone.

Díaz del Castillo, Bernal. *The Discovery and Conquest of Mexico*. Translated by A. P. Maudslay, with an introduction by Irving A. Leonard. New York: Limited Editions Club, 1942. First written in the 1560's and first published in 1632. Díaz wrote his vivid memories of the conquest of Mexico and his observations of the Aztecs and of Montezuma.

Dollar, Tom, and Kateri Weiss. "Tantalizing Myths Hold That Montezuma's Treasure Lies Buried Somewhere in the Ajo Mountains." *Arizona Highways* 70 (October, 1994): 48. The authors focus on the legend of Montezuma II's treasure, which is believed to be hidden in the Ajo Mountains of the Organ Pipe Cactus National Monument in Arizona; they include information on Montezuma's rule of the Aztec Empire during the Spanish colonization of Mexico.

Fagan, Brian M. *The Aztecs*. New York: Freeman, 1984. This copiously illustrated work is a topical examination of Aztec society that updates older studies by George C. Vaillant, Jacques Soustelle, and Nigel Davies.

Madariaga, Salvador de. *Hernan Cortes: Conqueror of Mexico*. New York: Macmillan, 1941; London: Hodder and Stoughton, 1942. A lively work that is much more than a biography of the Spanish conqueror. Gives extensive, sympathetic treatment to Montezuma.

Padden, R. C. *The Hummingbird and the Hawk: Conquest and Sovereignty in the Valley of Mexico, 1503-1541*. Columbus: Ohio State University Press, 1908; London: Harper, 1970. One of the narratives of the conquest of Mexico. Padden concludes that Montezuma was reaching for divinity and lost his grip on humanity and reality.

Paul E. Kuhl

SIR THOMAS MORE

Born: February 7, 1478; London, England
Died: July 6, 1535; London, England
Areas of Achievement: Literature, government, and religion
Contribution: Devoted to his faith and Renaissance learning, More served as the first lay Lord Chancellor of England, opposed Henry VIII's break with Rome, and forfeited his exalted position and his life rather than swear allegiance to the king as the supreme head of the Church of England.

Early Life

Thomas More was born February 7, 1478, in the Cripplegate neighborhood of London. He was the second of five children born to John More and Agnes Granger. Three siblings apparently died in childhood, and Thomas was the only surviving son. An ambitious and talented man, John More had succeeded his father as butler of Lincoln's Inn but aspired to be a barrister. The benchers of Lincoln's Inn liked the young fellow who managed their meals and approved him for membership; he subsequently was admitted to the bar. His marriage to Agnes Granger advanced his career, for she was the daughter of a prosperous merchant and sheriff of London. John More was appointed judge in the Court of Common Pleas, then promoted to the Court of King's Bench, and was even knighted by the king. Having risen from the working class himself, he had great expectations for his son.

Young More learned Latin at St. Anthony's School in London. He was much influenced by headmaster Nicholas Holt, who had taught John Colet and William Lattimer, both of whom became English humanists and friends of More. At thirteen, More was placed in the household of Thomas Morton, Archbishop of Canterbury and Lord Chancellor, who immediately took a liking to the intelligent boy. In 1492, at Morton's urging, More entered Canterbury Hall (later absorbed by Christ College), Oxford University, where he met and began lasting friendships with Thomas Linacre and William Grocyn, two scholars who had studied in Italy and drunk deeply of the Renaissance literature. Along with the classics, More studied mathematics and history and learned to play the flute and viol. His lifelong love of humanistic learning had been kindled.

Convinced that his son should pursue a legal career, John More recalled Thomas to London in 1494 and enrolled him as a law student at New Inn. Thomas moved to Lincoln's Inn in 1496, began lecturing on the law, and came to be known as an eloquent and insightful student of law. He did not, however, forsake literature. He wrote Latin and English verse, immersed himself in the humanistic writings of Pico della Mirandola, and joined the intellectual circle that included Grocyn, Linacre, William Lily, and John Colet. He especially looked to Colet for direction in both life and learning. He and Lily published epigrams rendered from the Greek anthology into Latin prose. More met and began an enduring friendship with the remarkable Desiderius Erasmus of Rotterdam, undoubtedly the leading Christian humanist. As Erasmus later recounted, More seriously considered devoting his life to the Church. For almost four years, he lived near the Charterhouse in London and followed the discipline of the Carthusian order. Spending much of his time in prayer and fasting, he regularly scourged himself and began a lifelong habit of wearing a hair shirt. He came near to joining the Franciscan Order. During this time, he also lectured, at the request of his friend Grocyn, on Saint Augustine's *City of God* (413-426).

After four years of living much like a monk, More apparently resolved his doubts about what he should do. Although he remained a pious Catholic, he threw himself into the practice of law. Various reasons have been suggested for this abrupt shift to the secular. The corruption of the Church, his own intellectual and material ambitions, and his unwillingness to remain celibate may all have contributed to his decision; he soon gained a reputation as a just and knowledgeable barrister. He also studied politics, adding to what he had learned from his father and Archbishop Morton. At twenty-six, he was elected to Parliament (apparently from the City of London) and quickly emerged as a primary critic of government inefficiency and heavy taxation.

More played a major role in frustrating Henry VII's efforts to extract a hundred thousand pounds from Parliament upon the marriage of his daughter Margaret to the King of Scotland. Henry was so angry with young More that he trumped up charges against his father, John More, had him imprisoned in the Tower of London, and released him only after he had paid a large fine. This lesson on sovereign power was not lost upon Thomas, whose thoughts were concerned with much more than politics. In 1505, More married Jane Colte, the eldest daughter of a

landed gentleman, and together they had four children. Upon her death in 1511, More wasted little time in marrying Alice Middleton, an affable but rather unattractive and unlettered woman who proved to be a fine mother for his children.

Life's Work

By the time of his second marriage, More was emerging as a leading London barrister. In 1509, the same year that Henry VIII ascended the throne, More was elected to Lincoln's Inn, where he became a reader in 1511. The year before, he was appointed undersheriff of London, a position of considerable responsibility in the sheriff's court. Especially well liked by London merchants, More was chosen by King Henry as a member of an English delegation sent to Flanders in 1514 to negotiate a commercial treaty. His contribution was minor, but during those six months abroad, he delighted in the company of Peter Giles, a renowned humanist and friend of Erasmus, and began work on his *Utopia*, published in 1516. His most significant work, *Utopia* was a skillful satire that condemned the poverty, intolerance, ignorance, and brutality of English society by juxtaposing it to the economic communism and political democracy that prevailed among the tolerant and peace-loving Utopians. Although surely attracted by the idealism of *Utopia*, More was always the realist, as his *History of Richard III*, written about the same time, makes clear. Disturbed by the ineptitude and avarice in both church and state, he wanted change for the better, but not revolutionary change.

Over the next few years, More became a favorite of Henry VIII and his Lord Chancellor, Cardinal Thomas Wolsey. They sent him on several diplomatic missions dealing with commercial matters critical to the interests of London merchants. More's skill in arguing the law convinced Henry that he should be an officer of the Crown. In 1517, he was appointed Master of Requests, the official through whom all petitions were passed to the king, and he was elevated to the Privy Council the next year. King Henry appreciated humanistic learning and found in More a delightful intellectual companion. He encouraged More to defend Greek studies against the obscurantist attacks of conservative critics. In his turn, More joined Henry in denouncing the Lutheran heresy. On Wolsey's recommendation, More was appointed Speaker of the House of Commons in 1532 and generally worked smoothly with the powerful cardinal. More surely learned from Wolsey, as he had from Archbishop Morton, and proved to be a fair and effective official, respected by the people as well as his peers. Henry rewarded him with both sinecures and landed estates.

More bought more land in Chelsea in 1523 and built a mansion there with an orchard and spacious garden. It was a happy place, where More delighted in entertaining his many friends and relatives. Illuminati such as Erasmus were frequent guests, and the king himself regularly visited More at Chelsea. As Erasmus portrayed him, More was the epitome of Christian humanism, a wonderfully enlightened public official who nurtured intellectual and scholarly pursuits. More's idyllic existence, however, was not to last. The king's "Great Matter"—his desire to divorce Queen Catherine and marry Anne Boleyn—threatened the kind of revolutionary change that was repugnant to More's conservative temperament. When Pope Clement VII denied Henry's request for an annulment, Wolsey was the first to feel his sovereign's wrath, being deprived of his position as Lord Chancellor, dismissed from the court, and accused of treason. Although Henry knew that More disapproved of his plans for divorce, he nevertheless made him Lord Chancellor, the first layman to hold that august office. Yet the real power in the Privy Council was exercised not by More but by the Duke of Norfolk, Anne Boleyn's uncle.

If Henry thought that by making him Lord Chancellor More would be more pliable, the king was mistaken. More performed his duties admirably enough, but he was increasingly on the fringes of the religious revolution that Henry and Parliament were undertaking. Even as Henry made overtures to leading English Protestants, More was trying his best to root out heresy. He even approved of torture for those who defied Catholic orthodoxy. Ironically, his own day of reckoning was coming. Between 1530 and 1532, Henry gradually extended royal authority over the Church of England, and More was at last compelled to resign as Lord Chancellor when Henry suggested relaxing the laws against heresy. More wanted to withdraw to his Chelsea estate and be left alone, but Henry demanded his assent to the laws taking England out of the Church of Rome. More resisted. He was motivated not by love for the Papacy but by reverence for the unity of the Church. Stripped of his office and stipends, he was confined to the Tower of London in 1534. After more than a year of increasingly harsh treatment, he still refused to yield. In July, 1535, More was convicted of defying the Supremacy Act of November, 1534, and executed. Instantly proclaimed a martyr to the cause of Catholicism, More was beatified in 1886 and canonized in 1935.

Summary

Sir Thomas More was a man pulled in several directions at once. He was a talented royal official, a learned and intelligent humanist, and a devout Catholic. As a lawyer and a judge, he gained a reputation for fairness. As the first lay Lord Chancellor, he personified the growing secularization of both society and government in the sixteenth century. Yet like the prelates who had preceded him, More understood the practical limitations of politics, and as Lord Chancellor, he was not about to embrace the religious and political toleration so idealized in *Utopia*. Indeed, More was basically conservative when it came to religion and politics. He did not hesitate to prosecute religious heretics, regarding them as a threat to both the church and the state.

On the other hand, More found great satisfaction in intellectual and scholarly pursuits. Christian humanism shaped his writings and his relationship with friends and family alike. *Utopia* at once established his international reputation as a leading literary figure. Among his early works were poems, Latin epigrams, and an English translation and adaptation of the biography in Latin of Pico della Mirandola, the brilliant young Italian humanist whose writings More deeply admired. Like Pico, More prized the life of the mind. He carried on a prolific correspondence with fellow intellectuals, performed numerous tasks for friends such as Erasmus, and defended humanist literatures from obscurantist criticism. More was happiest when his family and friends were with him. The children of his household, whether male or female, were educated under More's personal supervision. Friends such as Erasmus celebrated the intellectual exchange and hospitality that they always enjoyed with More. He had a modern devotion to intellectual curiosity.

Yet for all of his reaching toward modernity, More remained tied to the religious faith of the Middle Ages. A part of him always yearned for the monastery. He was a pious man, and his piety was grounded in a fundamental distrust of the human animal. The spiritual realm was very real to him, and very difficult to reach, and in that quest for spiritual understanding, the Church was crucial. It was not the pope, but the Church—its saints, its sacraments, and its history—that More loved and revered. Despite the sordidness of individual priests or even popes, he believed that the Church was pure and spiritual and must not be corrupted by either Martin Luther or Henry VIII. In the end, it was his spiritual side that prevailed. He defied his sovereign and paid for that defiance with his life. He cared more for his king than for any pope, but he truly loved his church best of all.

Bibliography

Chambers, Raymond Wilson. *Thomas More*. London: Cape, and New York: Harcourt Brace, 1935. A Pulitzer Prize-winning biography published in the same year that More was canonized, this scholarly and thoroughly sympathetic study presents More as truly the man for all seasons—the Christian humanist and statesman who opposed the tyrannical Henry VIII.

Fox, Alistair. *Thomas More: History and Providence*. Oxford; Blackwell, 1982; New Haven, Conn.: Yale University Press, 1983. An intellectual biography of More, this work details the evolution of More's thought, delving deep into his views of God and man. Emphasizes the contradictions within the man and makes him more of a tragic figure.

Marius, Richard. *Thomas More*. New York: Knopf, 1984; London: Dent, 1985. The best biography of More to date, this work is a comprehensive study of the man and his thought. It is distinguished by its felicitous prose and its brilliant analysis of a man, torn between the medieval world of faith and the modern world of reason, who ultimately chooses the spirit over the flesh.

More, Thomas. *Saint Thomas More: Selected Letters*. Edited by Elizabeth Frances Rogers. New Haven, Conn.: Yale University Press, 1961. Contains sixty-six letters revealing the many sides of the man—his literary friendships, his concern with politics, his religious views, and especially his concern for his children.

Reynolds, E. E. *Thomas More and Erasmus*. London: Burns and Oates, and New York: Fordham University Press, 1965. A careful study of the relationship between these two dynamic men, so similar in many ways and yet so very different. Besides explaining the influence that Erasmus had on More, Reynolds illuminates the nature of Northern European humanism.

Routh, Enid M. *Sir Thomas More and His Friends*. London: Oxford University Press, 1934; New York: Russell and Russell, 1963. An interesting study that portrays More as a transitional figure between the Renaissance and Reformation. Gives insight into the intellectual life of More and other English humanists and political and religious figures. Demonstrates the connections between English and Continental humanism.

Ronald William Howard

PHILIPPE DE MORNAY
Seigneur du Plessis-Marly

Born: November 5, 1549; Buhy, Normandy, France
Died: November 11, 1623; La Forêt-sur-Sèvre, France
Areas of Achievement: Diplomacy; government and politics; military; religion; theology
Contribution: Mornay was one of the formative influences within the early Huguenot movement in France. As the author of numerous religious and political tracts, he has had a lasting impact on liberal political theory; as a military leader and diplomat, he performed invaluable service toward securing the succession to the French throne for King Henry IV.

Early Life

Philippe de Mornay was born at Buhy, Normandy, into a minor aristocratic family. He converted to Calvinist Protestantism at the age of eighteen, largely, it would appear, through the influence of his mother. He was sent abroad for his education, embarking upon the study of law, jurisprudence, and German at the University of Heidelberg in Germany; he also studied Hebrew and history at the University of Padua in Italy. Prior to 1572, he had traveled extensively through Britain, western Germany, and the Netherlands, and he was fluent in six languages other than French.

Mornay began his career as a man of letters while at Cologne, Germany, in 1571 and 1572, writing a theological tract, *Dissertation sur l'eglise visible* ("a thesis on the visible church") and two well-publicized "remonstrances" justifying and advocating further resistance to Spanish rule among Protestants in the Netherlands. The Spanish Netherlands had been a seething cauldron of conspiracy, subversion, and repression throughout the 1560's and early 1570's. The alienation of the Netherlands' nobility, under the leadership of William of Nassau, prince of Orange, outbreaks of vandalism and destroying of images and statues by Protestant mobs, and the chronic ineffectiveness of the government of the regent, Duchess Margaret of Parma, led to the replacement of Margaret with the Spanish duke of Alba in 1567. Alba soon unleashed a campaign of terror that resulted in the execution or imprisonment of some twelve thousand (mainly Protestant) dissidents. By April, 1572, the Dutch, or northern, Netherlands erupted into open rebellion against Spain when a band of Dutch seamen dubbed "sea beggars" seized the port city of Brill.

Mornay thus came to the notice of the Huguenot leader, Admiral Gaspard de Coligny. Coligny's skillful handling of French Protestant armies during the Third French War of Religion (1568-1570) had forced the royal government to grant a cease-fire (the Edict of Pacification of St. Germain, 1570), and he had subsequently gained great influence over the young king, Charles IX. By June, 1572, Mornay had been called back to France and taken into Coligny's entourage. At the request of the admiral, Mornay composed a memorial to the king urging France to intervene militarily against Spain in support of the Dutch Protestants. The queen mother, Catherine de Médicis, resentful of Coligny's sway over her son and alarmed at the possible disastrous consequences of open conflict with Spain, used the occasion of a royal marriage in Paris during the month of August to eliminate the threat posed by the Huguenot Party. Mornay witnessed an abortive attempt on Coligny's life on August 22, 1572; two days later, he narrowly escaped death during the St. Bartholomew's Day Massacre, in which agents of the queen mother and Catholic followers of the duke of Guise killed the admiral and much of the Huguenot leadership. Mornay sought refuge in England and did not return to France until the following year.

Life's Work

From 1572 to 1574, Mornay acted in support of another prominent Huguenot, François La Noue, at whose request he sailed from England to the port of La Rochelle in 1573. There he composed the first in a series of pamphlets denouncing both the royal Valois family and the Guise family; he returned to England for a few weeks at the end of 1573 on a diplomatic mission for La Noue. In 1574, Mornay broke with La Noue, incensed by the latter's cooperation with the Politiques, a moderate Catholic faction sponsored by the queen mother. He became radical in his views, entering military service in support of the Protestant King Henry of Navarre, a royal cousin whose family (the Bourbons) stood next in line to the French throne after the Valois. In 1575, he was captured by Catholic forces, but he managed to conceal his true identity, and he was quickly ransomed and released into the custody of Henry De La Tour D'Auvergne, duke of Bouillon, at Sedan. It was while he was at the duke's household that he met Charlotte Arbaleste, whom he married the following year.

During the next five years, Mornay went through his most radical phase, advocating the overthrow of the Valois and rejecting compromise with both the Catholics and the Politiques. This phase culminated in his purported writing of *Vindiciae Contra Tyrannos* ("a defense of liberty against tyrants," 1579). Some scholars call into question Mornay's authorship, attributing *Vindiciae* to either Hubert Languet or Johan Junius de Jonge, or to Mornay and Languet in a collaborative effort. It is certain, however, that *Vindiciae* uncannily mirrors both Mornay's style and what is known about his views at the time. *Vindiciae* is widely considered the most significant and influential work of political theory arising out of the French Wars of Religion.

Building upon the theories of Theodore Beza and François Hotman, *Vindiciae* developed the idea of government as a contractual agreement between a people and their sovereign. In the event of a monarch's violation of popular liberties under this unwritten contract, resistance to, rebellion against, and deposition of the tyrannical ruler were justified. *Vindiciae*, however, fell short of advocating total popular revolution by reserving this power for the lesser magistrates (the nobility, judges, and justices) in their representative capacities; this group could include the magistracy from foreign states. It is of significance that the leadership of the Huguenot Party consisted of the lesser magistracy, as defined by the author, and that the door was left open for foreign intervention (the assistance of Queen Elizabeth I of England and the German Protestant princes was actively solicited by the Huguenot Party, and Mornay's diplomatic missions played a crucial role in these efforts). During the 1570's, Mornay also published *Discours sur la Roi Charles* ("a debate concerning King Charles," 1572); *Remonstrances aux estats pour la paix* ("on the conditions necessary to achieve peace," 1576); and *Excellent discours sur la vie et la mort* ("a deep discussion on life and death," 1577).

From 1578 to 1580, Mornay was dispatched on missions to the Netherlands and England several times for Henry of Navarre. He had risen so high in the king's confidence that, in 1581, Henry named him as his chief adviser. Mornay's prestige within the Huguenot community as a philosopher, activist, negotiator, and propagandist had been so enhanced by this time that his opponents labeled him the "Huguenot pope." In the 1580's, Mornay seems to have moderated his political stance to the extent that he could reach agreement and work with the Politique element on Henry's behalf.

Much of Mornay's time was spent on diplomatic missions, preparing briefs for Henry of Navarre and speaking to various estates and parliaments on his master's behalf. His first administrative appointment, as governor of the Huguenot stronghold of Montauban in the Languedoc, 1585-1586, ended in failure. After fifteen months of being frustrated by the independent-minded Montaubanois, who resented Mornay as a northerner, he resigned. The final break occurred after Mornay's wife had been publicly humiliated at church when the pastor and elders refused to allow her to take Holy Communion, citing as the cause her frivolous attire and hairstyle.

The death in 1584 of the heir to the French throne, François, duke of Anjou, placed Henry of Navarre next in succession to his childless cousin, King Henry III. From 1585 to 1589, Henry III engaged in armed conflict with both Navarre and his Huguenot forces, and with those of Henry, duke of Guise, leader of the ultra-Catholic League (the conflict is often referred to as the "War of the Three Henrys"). Mornay directed and composed most of the pro-Navarre propaganda of the period, choosing to concentrate his attacks on the Guise faction in hope of leaving the door open to accommodation with Henry III.

On December 23, 1588, Henry III connived at Guise's assassination, an act that placed the king in a desperate state of political isolation. In July, 1589, in the greatest diplomatic coup of his career, Mornay negotiated an alliance between Henry III and Navarre. On August 1, 1589, Henry III was fatally stabbed by a fanatical monk, Jacques Clemente; on his deathbed, he acknowledged Navarre to be his successor as King Henry IV. Mornay was awarded the governorship of Saumur, and the Huguenot University he founded there became a great seat of Calvinist scholarship.

Henry IV's conversion to Catholicism in 1593 deeply mortified Mornay, who thrice refused his sovereign's request to come to Paris and remained at Saumur, though his loyalty was never in question. The estrangement became complete after the publication of Mornay's 1598 work *De l'institution, usage et doctrine du saint sacrament de l'Eucharistie* ("on the founding, practice, and doctrine of the holy sacrament of the Eucharist"). Mornay intended to prove that the Protestant Eucharist more closely resembled the original Eucharist, as instituted by Jesus Christ and perpetuated within the early Christian church, than did the version practiced by the Catholic church. When challenged, he rashly accepted to debate a skilled theologian, Jacques Davy Du Perron, bishop of Evreux. The debate, approved by the king, took place from May 2 to May 4, 1600, at Fontainebleau. The event proved a disaster for Mornay, who lost on every point; as a result, he blamed the king for engineering his entrapment.

After Henry IV's assassination in 1610 and the succession of his son Louis XIII, the Huguenots' political situation deteriorated. Mornay had to fight to maintain his influence within the Huguenot community against the young, militantly antiroyalist Henry, duke of Rohan. Though successful in fending off Rohan's attempts to precipitate a crisis at the Assembly of Saumur in 1612, Mornay was unable to prevent his rival from launching the Huguenot War against the government in 1621. Reaffirming his loyalty to the crown, he welcomed Louis XIII into Saumur. However, the mistrustful Louis relieved him of the governorship, and Mornay retired to his estate at La Forêt-sur-Sèvre, where he died on November 11, 1623.

Summary

Mornay held the Huguenot Party together and molded it during a pivotal stage in its history, mapping out most of its major initiatives during the 1580's. His assistance to Navarre in facilitating his ascension to the throne was perhaps indispensable, and he certainly participated in the formulation of the Edict of Nantes in 1598, although the extent of his role is the subject of conjecture. It is certain that his polemical skills and command of the written and spoken word publicized and placed in context the issues of obedience and resistance to authority in the name of freedom, and he thus merits recognition as a significant figure in the development of Western political thought.

Mornay, however, failed to gain a firm political base. His censorious moralizing tended to isolate him, and his public berating of Henry IV over the king's sexual promiscuity contributed to their ultimate alienation. Had Mornay shown greater tact in the matters of faith and morals, he might not have been supplanted by the duke of Sully.

Bibliography

Buisseret, David. *Henry IV.* London: Allen and Unwin, 1984. Uses the life of the king to shed light upon the times and the interaction of personalities, including Mornay. Provides the most complete account of the Mornay-Du Perron debate.

Greengrass, Mark. *France in the Age of Henry IV: The Struggle for Stability.* New York: Longman, 1984. Scholarly background treatment that tries to explain Henry's achievement as the restorer of equilibrium as a personal phenomenon, and thus tends to downplay or obscure the role of nonregal participants

Heller, Henry. *Iron and Blood: Civil Wars in Sixteenth Century France.* Montreal: McGill-Queen's University Press, 1991. Provides interesting insights on Calvinist/Huguenot constitutional theory and acknowledges Mornay's crucial behind-the-scenes contributions—as confidante, ghost writer, and go-between—to the eventual eclipse of the Catholic League.

Koenigsberger, H. G., George L. Mosse, and G. Q. Bowker. *Europe in the Sixteenth Century.* New York: Longman, 1989. Detailed overview that includes maps, genealogical tables, chronology, bibliography, an excellent treatment of *Vindiciae Contra Tyrannos*, and a creditable attempt to place the entire French Calvinist movement in its continental perspective.

Thompson, Jack Westfall. *The Wars of Religion in France: 1559-1576.* Chicago: University of Chicago Press, 1909. Discusses events from the death of Henry II to the end of the fifth civil war. Cites significant details on Mornay's early career and associations with Coligny and La Noue.

Raymond Pierre Hylton

NĀNAK
Rāi Bhoi dī Talvandī

Born: 1469; Talwandi, Punjab
Died: 1539; Kartārpur, Punjab, Mughal Empire
Area of Achievement: Religion
Contribution: Nānak was a religious reformer who synthesized the fundamental principles of Islam and the tradition of Hinduism into a new universal religion, Sikhism. His teaching emphasizes equality of all human beings and regards responsible social action as integral to true spiritual practice. Monism and the rejection of excessive ritual are the basic tenets of this religion.

Early Life

The historical facts of Nānak's life can be gleaned only by sifting them carefully from the embellishments of myth and legend. The essential story of his life, however, seems fairly clear. Nānak was born in 1469 in the West Punjab in a small town, Talwandi. His father, Kalu, was a relatively well-to-do person and commanded influence in the area. N3nak was a precocious and gifted child possessing unusual intelligence and an extraordinarily pronounced concern for the well-being of everyone with whom he came into contact. He had a contemplative nature with a strong inclination toward otherworldly preoccupations. Stories about his childhood and the years toward adulthood indicate these qualities. It is said that even when Nānak was an infant his heart would melt at the sight of others' suffering. At play, he would devise games imitating holy men and involving mental concentration to achieve a perception of God.

Nānak's intellectual abilities and spiritual insights had already developed phenomenally before he was old enough to start school, although the story of his questioning the teacher on the first day of school about the significance of the letters of the alphabet and his composing on that occasion an acrostic on each letter is almost certainly apocryphal. The same must be said about his discussion with the family Brahmin when the latter came to invest him with the sacred thread. Nānak rejected the thread, thus refuting the importance of the external trappings of religion. A hymn by Nānak ascribed to this occasion must be of later date.

Nānak was married at a very young age and soon had children, but to his father's dismay he did not settle down to a regular occupation. If Kalu sent him on a trip to buy merchandise for business, Nānak gave away the money to holy mendicants and called it a "true transaction." Asked to work at the family farm, he left things unattended. Stories about this period of his life relate several supernatural occurrences. For example, one hot, sunny day while herding cattle, he fell asleep under the shade of a tree. The shade did not move with the sun's movement. Another time, a cobra was seen shading his head with its hood while he slept in the sun.

Life's Work

At the age of eighteen, Nānak moved to Sultanpur, where his father and brother-in-law procured for him employment as storekeeper and accountant at a government store. He stayed there for about ten years, settling down to a well-regulated life. He maintained his family with only a small portion of his salary, giving the rest away to the poor. He spent his spare time meditating or discussing metaphysics with holy men and continued thus to progress steadily in his spiritual search. One morning, when he went for his daily bath in the Bein, a nearby stream, he disappeared, some thought in the Bein. During his disappearance, he had a spiritual experience. Soon after he reappeared, he proclaimed that he was neither Hindu nor Muslim, left his family and all other worldly belongings, and set out on worldwide travels.

Popular accounts of Nānak's travels are filled with fantastic occurrences. He is described as traveling to distant places, often by a supernatural process of instant self-transportation. These stories do have a basis in history, however, and they are also quite meaningful in another way, for they convey in a veiled manner aspects of his teaching. Primary biographical sources, such as they are, claim that he went as far as Assam in the east, Ceylon (modern Sri Lanka) in the south, Tibet and China in the north, and the Middle Eastern countries and Turkey in the west. On many of these journeys he was accompanied by his Muslim disciple, Mardana. Wherever Nānak went, many people became his followers. Hindus regarded him as their guru and Muslims as their *Pir*, and eventually his followers came to be known as "Sikhs," meaning "disciples." Thus started Sikhism, a new religion transcending the boundaries of the other religions.

The religion that Nānak preached emphasized a monistic metaphysics and the importance of social and moral responsibility. The elements of his teaching are illustrated by various incidents during his peregrinations. According to one account, Nānak pointed out the difference between the wholesomeness of honest living and the corruption of ill-gotten wealth by squeezing in separate hands two morsels of food, one from a hard-working carpenter with whom he stayed and the other from a rich man whose banquet he had refused. From his host's food poured milk and from the rich man's, blood. In another story, Nānak reformed a highway thug whose name, "Sajjan," meant "friend." With his hospitality and show of piety, Sajjan enticed travelers to stay with him and robbed them while they slept. Nānak shocked Sajjan into realizing the true meaning of his name and the karmic consequences of evil deeds. Sajjan mended his ways. At Hardwar, on the banks of the Ganges, Nānak stood in the river and started to splash water toward the west. Asked by the Hindu pilgrims what he was doing, he said that he was watering his fields in the Punjab. When they laughed, he asked how they expected the water they threw up toward the sun to reach the sun, thus pointing out the futility of rituals. Similarly, in a dialogue with a pundit, he expounded on the vanity of learning devoid of the inner experience of true reality. Inner peace, he insisted, is obtained by contemplation, not mere reading. During his sojourn in the Himalayas, he met some yogis. He reprimanded them for hiding from the social and political turmoil of the time, saying that it was their duty to guide and help oppressed humanity. The best-remembered story about Nānak's travels is one about his visit to Mecca. It is said that upon reaching the Kaaba, Nānak lay down with his feet toward the shrine, the holiest in Islam. Outraged, the keepers of the shrine admonished him to move his feet away from the Kaaba. He refused and told them to turn his feet to where there was no God. As they dragged him around, the Kaaba moved in the same direction as his feet, the moral being that God is everywhere. In the turmoil caused by Bābur's invasion of India, Nānak was taken prisoner. It is believed that Bābur, whose interest in religion was deep, heard about Nānak and met with him. Nānak is said to have given him instruction and conveyed to him his concern for people's suffering.

In about 1526, Nānak ended his travels and settled down at Kartarpur, on the bank of the river Ravi in central Punjab. There he consolidated his life's work and laid down the essential organizational bases of the Sikh religion—the institutions of guruship, prayer, *sangat* (congregation), *langar* (communal meal and sharing), and family. He returned to the life of a regular householder, considering it far superior to renunciation as a means of spiritual realization. Before his death, in 1539, he chose his best disciple, Angad, as the next guru in preference to his own sons.

Throughout his life, Nānak regularly recorded his observations about life in poetical compositions which over time added up to a large volume. These compositions, or hymns, articulate with intense feeling Nānak's views on theology and ethics, and on social, political, and economic issues. Used as recitations for prayer from the very time of their creation, Nānak's hymns comprise the nucleus to which the verses of the later Sikh gurus and other saints were added to make the Sikh scripture, the *Ādi Granth*. Nānak's verses contain the essence of the Sikh religion. They are gathered in various sequences. Most important among these sequences is the *Japji*, meaning "recitation," the daily morning prayer. Its recitation is also central to prayers for many other occasions. In a sense, *Japji* contains the gist of the whole scripture. The root mantra of the Sikh religion is *Japji*'s opening verse. Because of its quintessential character, the verse is also a complete prayer by itself and figures at the start of other major compositions. It reads:

> There is one God
> Whose name is Truth
> He is the Creator
> Devoid of fear
> Without rancour
> Of eternal form
> Beyond birth and death.
> Self-existent, By the Guru's grace He is obtained.

The root mantra has its further summation in "There is one God" (*Ek Onkar*)—oneness including all other attributes of divinity.

In Nānak's teachings, as Creator, the divine Self produces creation from within Itself. Creation, therefore, is part of the divine reality, emerging from and merging back into the eternal oneness of Being. There is no duality between the Creator and the created. As creatures, however, human beings suffer from the illusion that they have an existence of their own as separate individuals. This separateness from the source, regardless of whether they know it, causes grief and suffering for them. The state of being an all-encompassing unity is alone a state of unqualified happiness. God is that state; God is perfect bliss. Nānak explained that to free themselves from the sorrows of the endless cycle of birth, death, and rebirth, human beings must regain union with God. One cannot achieve this goal only by the performance of outward acts of piety or by learning. Spiritual realization requires sincere devotion to God and detachment from worldly desires. One must bring to this devotion complete self-surrender to God's will and a total renunciation of the ego. Nānak often described the relation between God and the human soul as one between the bride and the bridegroom. He prescribes the recitation (*simran*) of God's Name (*nam*) as a necessary means for expressing as well as winning the love of God. *Nam* comprehends all compositions (*bani*), such as Nānak's hymns, so that *simran* involves not mere mechanical repetition of words but concentration on their meaning and application of this meaning in one's daily conduct.

The process by which, with *simran*, one overcomes the ego, achieves mental calm, and becomes disciplined in action is slow and gentle (*sahaj*). Nānak rejected extreme asceticism as a means to spiritual development. He rather recommended a life of moderation—one that includes normal worldly activities but shuns attachment to the world. One should be like the lotus, which stays dry amid water. Progress on this path of spiritual growth requires personal guidance by a teacher (guru), the true guru being one who has realized truth. Also necessary for progress is the company (*sangat*) of others who are on the same quest. *Sangat* not only provides mutual mental reinforcement but also is the arena for right social action, without which there can be no spiritual life. It represents the equality, community, and mutual interdependence of all humanity. In Nānak's teaching, God, guru, and humans are one. The road to God realization lies squarely in the human world. A loving acceptance of this world fills Nānak's compositions with such enchanting poetry and music as make the face of the earth a window on the divine.

Summary

Nānak's teaching was part of the religious reform that swept India during the fifteenth and sixteenth centuries. By that time, Muslims had ruled the country for about three hundred years and made a deep impact on it. On one hand, Islam and its social egalitarianism had spread widely, but on the other the strictly defined character of the Muslim religion and the Muslim state's discriminatory policy toward Hindus caused extreme religious conflicts and social strife. Communal antagonism bred bigotry and an excessive preoccupation with the external forms of religion, leading to frequent oppression of non-Muslims. That tended to tear asunder the fabric of society. There was a dire need for a resolution of this conflict, for the creation of unity and harmony. Sufis, the mystics of Islam, who emphasized love of God instead of works of religion, many of whom were active in India, helped prepare the way toward such a resolution. The full answer to the problem came with the rise of the *Bhakti* movement, which spontaneously overwhelmed India on all sides toward the fifteenth century. *Bhakti*, which means "love of God," rejected all outward forms of religion and found the universal meaning of religion in intense devotion to God. It considered the love of God inseparable from the love of humanity and the rest of creation, thus combining the quest for the divine with active involvement in the world.

Indian Sufism and the *Bhakti* movement reached a culmination in Nānak's teaching. He preached a universal religion based on the oneness of God and the sameness of human beings everywhere. Because of the force his message had for unifying people of widely divergent backgrounds, he left a deep imprint on Indian civilization. His picture—a man with a long, white, perfectly rounded beard, his large eyes half closed in quiet bliss, and his whole aspect exuding a deep friendliness and tranquillity—hangs prominently in the homes of Indians, and his image lives in their minds.

Bibliography

Anand, Balwant Singh. *Guru Nānak: His Life Was His Message*. New Delhi, India: Guru Nānak Foundation, 1983. A lucid biographical account.

Banerjee, Anil Chandra. *Guru Nānak and His Times*. 2d ed. Patiala, India: Punjabi University, 1984. About half of the volume is devoted to the historical context of Nānak's life and work.

McLeod, W. H. *Guru Nānak and the Sikh Religion*. Oxford: Clarendon Press, 1968. A major work by a non-Indian. The focus is on Nānak rather than on Sikhism as a whole. The book has aroused some controversy.

Nānak. *Hymns of Guru Nānak*. Translated by Khushwant Singh. New Delhi, India: Orient Longmans, 1969. A judicious selection of hymns from Nānak's works. Translated with literary sensitivity.

———. *Hymns of Guru Nānak.* Translated by S. Manmohan Singh. Patiala, India: Language Department, Punjab, 1972. Contains all of Nānak's compositions. Gives the original in Punjabi, an English translation, and an explanation of the meaning in Punjabi prose.

Singh, Ganda, ed. *Sources of the Life and Teachings of Guru Nānak.* Patiala, India: Punjabi University, Department of Punjab Historical Studies, 1969. Compiled by a foremost scholar of Sikh history, it is a basic work.

Singh, Harbans. *Guru Nānak and Origins of the Sikh Faith.* New York: Asia Publishing House, 1969. Examines Nānak's work as the foundation of Sikhism.

Singh, Kartar. *Guru Nānak Dev: Life and Teachings.* Ludhiana, India: Lahore Book Shop, 1969. Tells the story of the Guru's life and concludes with a review of his teachings.

Singh, Trilochan. *Guru Nānak, Founder of Sikhism: A Biography.* Delhi, India: Gurdwara Parbandhak Committee, 1969. This book is a standard, well-documented work.

Talib, Gurbachan Singh. *Guru Nānak: His Personality and Vision.* Delhi, India: Gur Das Kapur, 1969. A comprehensive and analytical survey of Nānak's thought.

Surjit S. Dulai

JOHN NAPIER

Born: 1550; Merchiston Castle (near Edinburgh), Scotland

Died: April 4, 1617; Merchiston Castle, Scotland

Areas of Achievement: Mathematics; religion and theology

Contribution: Working alone, without the benefit of earlier work and the encouragement of mentors, John Napier invented logarithms, the greatest boon to experimental science produced during the Renaissance.

Early Life

John Napier, eighth lord of Merchiston, was born at Merchiston Castle (near Edinburgh), the son of Sir Archibald Napier by his first wife, Janet Bothwell. He was born into a family notable for several famous soldiers at a time when religious controversy was rife in Scotland.

Little is known of his childhood, but when Napier was thirteen, his mother died. He was subsequently sent to St. Salvator's College, St. Andrews University, a school not noted for its quiet academic environment. Although Napier remained at St. Andrews for only one year, he developed two intense interests that were to continue for the remainder of his life: theology and arithmetic. Because of the nonacademic environment, the bishop of Orkney advised that young John could better pursue an academic career at schools on the continent. Although no direct evidence remains to confirm this, it is highly probable that he followed this course. As young Napier traveled through a Europe divided into warring factions by the Protestant Reformation, he became a strong adherent of the Calvinist movement then sweeping Scotland. He was to remain a fervent and uncompromising believer, active in Protestant politics throughout his life, much of which was spent embroiled in bitter religious dissension aggravated by the embarrassing political activities of his papist father-in-law, Sir James Chisholm.

By 1571, he had returned to Scotland. The following year, he married Elizabeth Stirling and occupied a castle at Gartnes. In 1579, his wife died, leaving two children. Subsequently, Napier married Agnes Chisholm and sired ten additional children. Upon the death of his father in 1608, Napier moved into Merchiston Castle, where he remained for the rest of his life.

As a member of the Scottish landed aristocracy, he had the time and resources to pursue his many interests. These included theology, agricultural improvements, and military science. In the latter field, he anticipated inventions three centuries before they were actually fabricated, and he invented an artillery so powerfully destructive that he refused, in horror, to develop or even to publicize it. Napier also experimented with fertilizers for crops and invented a mechanical device to pump water out of coal pits.

Life's Work

Napier's first literary work, *A Plaine Discovery of the Whole Revelation of St. John*, published in 1593 after five years of toil, was the first important work of biblical interpretation written in Scotland. In the book's introduction, the Scottish King James VI (the future James I of England) is entreated to safeguard the Scottish Protestant church and to purge and punish all of the Roman Catholic nobility. The body of this bitterly anti-Catholic exposition, among other things, identifies the pope as the anti-Christ described in the biblical Book of Revelations. Although from the perspective of history this enterprise may appear to be little more than fruitless theological supposition, it established Napier's reputation as both scholar and theologian. His theological interpretations followed the Greek form of mathematical argument, a form of theological reasoning that would not become popular for several centuries.

Although Napier's public life during these tumultuous times has been amply documented, the development of his mathematical work, conducted alone and almost in secret, is more difficult to trace. It seems as though mathematics was for Napier a solitary pursuit of leisure, while his highly visible public life focused on anti-Catholic pro-clamations meant to keep Catholicism out of Scotland.

An early treatise concerned with arithmetic and algebra was apparently assembled during his first marriage but remained unpublished until 1839. About 1590, he set out to make arithmetic easier; the task required twenty years of labor, but he succeeded by inventing logarithms, a system that simplified the computation of products, quotients, and roots. His fanatical dedication to Calvinist Protestantism shows the same obsessive persistence that enabled him to finish the grueling task of producing a useable set of logarithmic tables.

Logarithms, or "logs," are the exponents of a stated number, the "base," and are used to represent powers (exponents) of the base. Consider, for example, the powers of 2: 21, 22, 23, 24, 25, and so on. These correspond to 2, 4, 8, 16, 32, and so on. The exponents 1, 2, 3, 4, and 5 are the logs of these numbers to the base 2. To multiply any two numbers in the series, it is necessary only to add the exponents (or logs) of the numbers and then find to the antilog of the result, which corresponds to the sum desired. Thus, to multiply 32 by 4, take the log of 32, which is 5, and add it to the log of 4, which is 2, to get 7. The antilog of 7 (that is, the number with a log of 7) is 128, the desired result. Division is performed by subtracting logs.

By extension, numbers not found in the above series can be used if a noninteger number can be found such that when 2 is raised to this power the desired number is produced. For example, since 2 = 21 and 4 = 22 , it follows that 3 = 2x, where x must be a number greater than 1 but less than 2. In fact, x is approximately equal to 1.585. Since any number can be expressed to a good approximation as a power of 2, any arithmetic operations can be performed provided a table of powers of 2 is provided.

Although Napier did not use 2 as the base of his logarithms, the principle is the same. Whereas logs make arithmetic computation considerably easier, Napier set himself the grueling task of computing, by various mathematical means, a complete set of log tables, that is, sufficient powers of the base to generate a complete set of numbers, including decimal fractions. The calculation of the tables occupied Napier for almost twenty years. While not entirely error-free, the calculations were basically accurate, forming the foundation for all subsequent log tables.

In 1614, Napier published the description of his logarithms together with a set of log tables, several uses for them, and rules for the solution of both plane and spherical triangles using the tables. This work, titled *Mirifici Logarithmorum Canonis Descriptio* (*Description of a Marvelous Canon of Logarithms*, 1857), omitted any explanation of his methods of calculation. Although the common folk who were Napier's neighbors had always suspected him of being a warlock who delved into the black arts behind his thick castle walls, his miraculous technique of logarithms, presented unexpectedly without explanation or rationale, seemed like black magic even to the relatively sophisticated people who had the occasion to use them.

A later work, published posthumously in 1619, *Mirifici Logarithmorum Canonis Constructio* (*Construction of a Marvelous Canon of Logarithms*, 1889), provides the explanation of his calculations, an outline of the steps leading to his invention, and the properties of his logarithmic function.

Napier sent a copy of his 1614 work to Henry Briggs, a professor at Gresham College. Briggs had the idea of making the base of the log tables 10, an innovation of which Napier approved because it simplified calculations. In 1624, Briggs published his tables of common logs (base 10 logarithms), but he gave full credit to Napier for the original idea.

Napier also invested considerable time in deriving complicated equations and exponential forms of trigonometric functions, since these played such important roles in astronomical computations. By mathematical manipulation, he was able to reduce the requisite number of spherical trigonometry equations from ten to just two general statements.

Napier's tables of logarithms were greeted with great enthusiasm by astronomers, since it simplified computations and removed some of the drudgery from analyzing data. Johann Kepler (1571-1630), who inherited several decades of extremely accurate data on planetary motions from the great Danish astronomer Tycho Brahe (1546-1601), used Napier's logarithms to simplify the analysis. The results of his work led to Kepler's three laws of planetary motion, the first correct and accurate statement of planetary motion. Later, Isaac Newton (1642-1727) used Kepler's laws in formulating his theory of gravity.

In 1617, Napier published the results of his work on a mechanical system to simplify arithmetic computation, *Rabdologiae, seu Numerationis per Virgulas Libri Duo* (*Study of Divining Rods, or Two Books of Numbering by Means of Rods*, 1667). This involved manipulating a set of small counting rods (later termed "Napier's Bones") to multiply and divide numbers. This device could be considered the precursor of the slide rule (a set of sliding logarithmic scales that enabled rapid multiplication and division), a device widely used by scientists and students until the latter half of the twentieth century. Last but not

least, Napier standardized and popularized the system now universally used for decimal notation, in which a decimal point is used to separate the integer from the fractional part of a number.

Summary

The 1614 publication of Napier's canon of logarithms is one of those extraordinary and exceptional events in the history of science whereby a new invention of great importance appears, seemingly out of thin air, with no obvious precursors foreshadowing its creation. Napier's invention revolutionized arithmetic calculation; it removed much of the drudgery from reducing scientific data, particularly for astronomers attempting to use accurate measurements to predict planetary motions. When Johann Kepler used Tycho Brahe's accurate data to deduce his laws of planetary motion, Napier's logarithms helped make the arduous task possible. In the centuries following their invention, log tables grew more detailed and more accurate, culminating in 1964 with the publication of a table of logarithms accurate to 110 decimal places. Until the 1970's, when inexpensive hand-held calculators and personal computers rendered them obsolete, log tables formed an essential component of college-preparatory secondary education, and no reputable engineer would be without his slide rule, a portable version of the log tables.

As a titled landowner, John Napier, lord of Merchiston, devoted considerable energy to agricultural products to improve his crops and cattle. He tinkered with inventions and was granted a patent for a hydraulic screw to pump water from coal pits, and he outlined plans for (but never constructed) four new weapons of war, including an artillery piece that was designed to kill anything within a one-mile radius. Napier's first literary work, an interpretation of the Book of Revelation, secured his reputation as a scholar and as a theologian, although outside of Scotland this work no longer commands high regard.

Bibliography

Hobson, E. W. *John Napier and the Invention of Logarithms*. Cambridge: Cambridge University Press, 1914. This lecture is the most useful of the various reconstructions of Napier's invention of logarithms. Highly recommended.

Knott, C. G., ed. *Napier Tercentenary Memorial Volume*. London: Dawson's of Pall Mall, 1966. A reprint of a 1915 original. Contains a set of articles detailing different aspects of Napier's accomplishments by experts in various fields of mathematics, as well as some considerable detail on the historical background to his work. Also included is a complete bibliography of books exhibited at the July, 1914, Napier Tercentenary Celebration.

McLeish, John. *Number*. New York: Fawcett Columbine, 1991. Chapter 12, "John Napier: The Rationalization of Arithmetic", details his work on logarithms and Napier's Bones. Included are examples detailing the construction and use of both these inventions.

Napier, John. *Napier's Mathematical Works*. Translated by William F. Hawkins. 3 vols. Auckland, New Zealand: University of Auckland Press, 1982. A translation from Latin of all of Napier's writings on mathematics, including those published posthumously. Volumes 2 and 3 include a commentary on Napier's work and how it fits into the history of mathematics.

Napier, Mark. *Memoirs of John Napier of Merchiston: His Lineage, Life, and Times*. Edinburgh: W.

Blackwood, 1834. Written by a direct descendent of John Napier with direct access to the family's private papers, this carefully researched work provides the original source material from which most later books were derived.

George R. Plitnik

THOMAS NASHE

Born: November, 1567; Lowestoft, Suffolk, England
Died: c. 1601; place unknown
Areas of Achievement: Literature; theater and drama
Contribution: A versatile writer of satiric pamphlets, plays, lyric poetry, and a novel, Thomas Nashe had a marked influence on many of his contemporaries, including William Shakespeare and Ben Jonson, who admired his powers of wit and observation and his inventive use of language.

Early Life

Thomas Nashe was born in Lowestoft, Suffolk, the third son of William Nashe, a clergyman. In 1573, when Thomas was six, the family moved to West Harling, Norfolk, where Thomas's father took up a position as rector. Since the nearest school was seven miles away, it is likely that Nashe received his early schooling from his father.

In October, 1582, Nashe matriculated as a sizar scholar of St. Johns College, Cambridge University, although he may have been in residence at St. Johns for two terms before this. A sizar was a poor student who performed menial tasks such as making beds and serving at table in return for free food rations.

Student life at Cambridge was strict. The academic day began at dawn; students were expected to attend college for all but three weeks a year and were allowed to leave the college only twice a week. Punishments were severe, including whippings and fines; lodgings were crowded, and in winter were damp and cold.

In spite of these privations, Nashe seemed to flourish at Cambridge, and in 1584 he was appointed as a scholar of the Lady Margaret Foundation of the University. In Nashe's later writings, he praised St. John's College highly, although he did lament the strong Puritan influence there, which gave him a lifetime aversion to Puritanism.

While at Cambridge, Nashe was a close friend of the dramatist Christopher Marlowe, and he probably had a hand in producing some satirical plays during his student years. In 1586, Nashe was awarded the degree of bachelor of arts. He continued at St. Johns to work on a master of arts degree, but he never completed it, leaving Cambridge for London in the early fall of 1588. The reason for his departure is not known, but it may have been because his father, who had helped to support him at the university, died the previous year, leaving Nashe without the financial means to continue. Nashe's intention in London was to follow his fellow Cambridge graduate Robert Greene and make a living as a writer. In Elizabethan England, the idea of pursuing a career as a professional writer was a novel one, but Nashe, full of youthful confidence, was prepared to give it a try.

Life's Work

Once Nashe reached London, he registered his first literary piece, a dull pamphlet entitled *The Anatomie of Absurditie*, which he had written during a vacation in 1587. Not published until 1590, it received almost no attention. The following year Nashe wrote a preface to Robert Greene's *Menaphon* (1589); the fact that he was commissioned to write such a piece for an established author suggests that he already had something of a reputation in literary London. Yet it was not until the publication of his pamphlet *An Almond for a Parrat* in the spring of 1590 that Nashe found his true voice, a satirical, colloquial, vivid, journalistic style that was to make him the most popular of the Elizabethan pamphleteers. *Almond* was Nashe's contribution to the controversy surrounding the Puritan pamphlets of "Martin Marprelate," which were attacks on the Church of England written in colloquial language to appeal to public opinion. Nashe's reply successfully imitated the style of the Martin pamphlets and also identified for the first time in print the name of their author.

Armed with his new style, Nashe produced his greatest popular success, the social satire *Pierce Penilesse, His Supplication to the Devil* (1592), which went through at least five editions between 1592 and 1595. In this book, Nashe's persona, Pierce Penilesse, grumbles that his talents go unrewarded and that in the society in which he lives, money goes to those least deserving of it. He therefore decides to send a supplication to the devil, asking him for a loan. The supplication takes up most of the book, in which contemporary social abuses are described in terms of the seven deadly sins. Nashe's purpose appears to have been to entertain rather than to moralize, however, and *Pierce Penilesse* is memorable for its lively anecdotes, the feeling of spontaneity it conveys, the poetic imagery, and the realistic detail taken from the streets of the Elizabethan London that Nashe walked every day. It is notable also for its defense of literature and of the theater.

Thin and long-haired, with a boyish appearance, Nashe was now a well-known figure in London, and his self-cultivated notoriety was only increased by a long-running literary quarrel between himself and Cambridge scholar Gabriel Harvey. It was Harvey who had first attacked Nashe in print, and Nashe responded later in the same year with *Strange Newes of the Intercepting of Certain Letters* (1592). So began an exchange of slanderous pamphlets that showed Nashe at his most boisterous and vituperative.

Strange Newes was written in the country at Croydon, where Nashe, eager to escape the plague that was sweeping London, took refuge as guest of the Archbishop John Whitgift. While in Croydon he also wrote his only surviving play, *Summer's Last Will and Testament* (1600), which was probably performed in Croydon in 1592 but was not published until 1600. After returning to London, Nashe wrote the long *Christe's Tears over Jerusalem* (1593), in which he made a comparison between the sins of the Jews that led to the destruction of Jerusalem and the decayed morals of contemporary London, which, he argued, would bring a similar calamity. A born controversialist, Nashe had much to say about greedy merchants and corrupt public officials, and the outcry was such that he was forced to issue a denial that he was attacking any particular individual. This did not stop the London city council from taking action against him in December; Nashe was extricated from his ensuing difficulties only by the intervention of his influential acquaintance, Sir George Carey. Nashe stayed at the Carey family castle on the Isle of Wight until early 1594.

Returning to London once again, he published *The Unfortunate Traveller: Or, The Life of Jack Wilton* (1594), which he had completed the previous year. Describing the picaresque adventures of its protagonist, this book is sometimes called the first English novel. Later that year Nashe published *The Terrors of the Night* (1594), which he described as an "incredible narration" of a series of visions that came to a man in his last illness. Intended as an attack on superstition, the work discusses dreams and spirits in a rambling and digressive style that is typical of Nashe generally.

During 1595, Nashe worked on his final reply to Harvey, *Have with You to Saffron-Walden* (1596). In this period, he was also trying to write plays, but on his own admission with little success. In 1597, Nashe was again involved in a dangerous controversy when he collaborated with Ben Jonson and others on a satirical play, *The Isle of Dogs*, now lost. When performed in July, the play was declared seditious by the authorities. Nashe's lodgings were searched and his papers confiscated. Nashe claimed to have written only the induction and the first act, the remaining four acts being supplied by the players without his consent. Several of those involved in the play, including Ben Jonson, were imprisoned, a fate Nashe avoided by fleeing to the coastal town of Yarmouth, in Norfolk. He arrived probably in December and remained there for six weeks.

After leaving Yarmouth, Nashe wrote his last pamphlet, *Nashe's Lenten Stuffe* (1599), during Lent. The book arose out of his desire to thank the town of Yarmouth for its hospitality to him. It is not known where Nashe was living at the time, although he does comment that the book was written "in the country." Nashe was certainly back in London by February, 1599, when he wrote the preface to *Lenten Stuffe*.

Several months later, in June, 1599, another disaster struck Nashe. The authorities issued an order confiscating Nashe's books wherever they might be found and banning any further printing of them. The order also applied to Nashe's adversary, Gabriel Harvey, as well as a number of other satirical writers. After the edict, little more is heard of Nashe, and in Charles Fitzgefrey's *Affaniae* (1601), he is referred to as already deceased. No other facts about his death or place of burial are known.

Summary

Perhaps more than any other Elizabethan writer, Thomas Nashe had his finger on the pulse of the times. He kept his eyes and ears close to the chatter and bustle of the London streets, and his writings catch the rawness of life as it was lived in the 1590's. Although Nashe is usually described as a pamphleteer, the term gives little indication of the range of his work; the form in which his writing would have flourished best, journalism, had not yet been invented. Many of his pieces would qualify today as investigative reports or magazine feature articles. Not only did Nashe have a nose for news, he also possessed the ability to write quickly, with a helter-skelter style (which he called his "extemporall veine") that was easily recognizable. Such a rapid style seemed to come naturally to him, but it was also necessitated by the conditions under which he lived. Lacking a wealthy patron, he chose to make a living from the popular press, which yielded small financial rewards and demanded a quick output.

Harassed by poverty and government censors and dying young, Nashe did not achieve all that his talents merited. As a satirist however, he influenced other Elizabethan writers such as Ben Jonson and William Shakespeare. For example, Nashe's distinctive use of language finds an echo in Shakespeare's *The Taming of the Shrew* (pr. c. 1593-1594); the character Moth in *Love's Labours Lost* (pr. c. 1594-1595) is widely believed to be based on Nashe; and Shakespeare also drew extensively, in *Henry IV, Part 1* (pr. c. 1597), on Nashe's observations of the idiosyncrasies of speech and behavior.

Bibliography

Hibbard, G. R. *Thomas Nashe: A Critical Introduction.* Cambridge, Mass.: Harvard University Press, 1962. The most detailed critical study of Nashe, written with the intention of rescuing him from critical neglect. Contains some errors of chronology regarding Nashe's writings, which are corrected in McGinn. Concludes that there was a gap between Nashe's talents and what he was able to achieve with them.

Lewis, C. S. *English Literature in the Sixteenth Century Excluding Drama.* London: Oxford University Press, 1954. Describes Nashe as the greatest of the Elizabethan pamphleteers and one of the most original writers in the English language. Lewis portrays Nashe as a literary showman who could keep a crowd entertained by his sheer virtuosity.

McGinn, Donald J. *Thomas Nashe.* Boston: Twayne, 1981. Probably the best place to start for an overall understanding of Nashe's life and work. McGinn analyzes the works in chronological order and, in a concluding chapter about Nashe's place in English literature, describes him as a sixteenth century H. L. Mencken. Includes a chronology of Nashe's life and an annotated bibliography.

Nicholl, Charles. *A Cup of News: The Life of Thomas Nashe.* London: Routledge, 1984. The only full-length biography of Nashe, this is so comprehensive it is unlikely to be superseded. Meticulous research sheds new light on many episodes in Nashe's life and also gives a picture of London literary life in the last decade of the sixteenth century. Includes ten illustrations and twelve reproductions of documents.

Wells, Stanley, ed. *Thomas Nashe: Selected Writings.* Cambridge, Mass.: Harvard University Press, 1965. Contains four of Nashe's books in their entirety (with spelling modernized) and extracts from five others. Also contains a glossary and an introductory critical essay.

Bryan Aubrey

SAINT PHILIP NERI

Born: July 21, 1515; Florence
Died: May 26, 1595; Rome
Area of Achievement: Religion
Contribution: As a priest living in Rome during the Counter-Reformation, Saint Philip Neri stood apart from the religious politics of his time and influenced countless Catholics to reform their lives and return to traditional spirituality. Called the "Apostle of Rome," he founded the Congregation of the Oratory, which inspired both laymen and clergy to lead lives of holiness and charitable works.

Early Life

Saint Philip Neri was born in a poor section of Florence, ruled at that time by the Medicis. His father, Francesco Neri, was unsuccessful in his career as a notary and thus turned to alchemy, losing the family's financial security through his improvidence. When Philip was five years old, his mother, Lucrezia da Mosciano, died shortly after giving birth to her fourth child. The household, by all reports a happy one, was thereafter managed by a woman who was either the mother-in-law of Francesco, or his second wife.

Young Philip, unlike many other saints, showed no evidence of a precocious interest in religion. Yet even as a child he was noted for his charm and sweetness of disposition, personal qualities which would characterize his relationships with others throughout his life. His nickname was "Pippo Buono" (good little Philip). His formal schooling with the Dominican fathers probably ended when he was about sixteen, and thereafter he was self-educated. In 1532, he went to San Germano to work for his father's cousin Romolo Neri, with the understanding that he would eventually take over the family business. Instead, during a period of intense prayer and meditation, he decided to give his life to God. He had no plans to enter the priesthood but to live in poverty and offer his service to humankind. Accordingly, in 1533 he left San Germano and traveled to Rome, where he lived in the home of Galeotto Caccia, a customs official from Florence, serving as tutor to Caccia's two young sons.

Life's Work

Although Philip would not be ordained a priest until he was thirty-six years old, in 1533 he quietly began the work to which he would dedicate the rest of his life. Philip lived during the Counter-Reformation, thus called by those who consider it to have been a response to the Protestant movement; it is also known as the Catholic Revival by those who consider it to have been an internal revitalization of the Church begun in the previous century in Spain.

Rome, sacked during an invasion by the French in 1527, was noted for its atmosphere of licentiousness and low moral standards, and was ripe for reform. To Catholic observers, the influence of classical, or "pagan," authors was responsible for the weakness of faith in the Church. Abuses within the Church were flagrant, with the Medicis using their political power to control church elections and corrupt clergymen neglecting the spiritual needs of the people. The Council of Trent, meeting from 1545 to 1563, would reform the abuses and clarify church teaching but would be unsuccessful in the attempt to reunite with the Protestants.

Philip, his life newly dedicated to God, became one of the many hermits of the streets of Rome, preaching informally to anyone who would listen. At night, however, he went to the catacombs outside the city to pray and meditate in solitude, beginning his life as a mystic. He also took courses in philosophy and theology at the university but, realizing that he had no calling to the scholarly life, sold his books and gave the money to the poor. He continued to live with the Caccia family, in a small attic room, eating a meager diet of bread and olives.

Soon Philip's gift for influencing others came to public attention. With his good humor, he succeeded in converting many young men who had come at first to mock his preaching. He also took up charitable work in the public hospitals, offering spiritual comfort to the dying. Although he met Saint Ignatius of Loyola during this time, Philip was not attracted to the Jesuit priesthood and had no intention of seeking ordination himself, even though many of the young men he converted became priests.

In 1544, on the eve of Pentecost, Philip underwent an unusual experience while praying in the catacombs. He reported that a ball of fire entered his mouth and lodged in his heart, creating a swelling or malformation that was visible to others. The autopsy report of his death showed an enlarged heart that had broken several ribs. Whatever the explanation for this phenomenon, observers noticed throughout his life that his heartbeat could be heard

across a room and that he would tremble violently when overcome by a mystical experience.

In 1548, Philip laid the foundation for the organization that would eventually become the Congregation of the Oratory. With Father Persiano Rossi, he formed a confraternity of laymen that met at the Church of San Girolomo to pray, read the Scriptures, and discuss the lives of the saints and church history. In 1551, at the insistence of Father Rossi (and probably because the Church disapproved of lay preachers), Philip was ordained. At that time, no special education was required for ordination, although the Council of Trent was to found the system of seminaries that would educate priests in the future.

Given the power to hear confessions, Philip, contrary to the custom of the time, insisted that his followers receive this sacrament frequently. He was noted for his insights as a spiritual adviser, reportedly knowing what the penitent was thinking before any words were spoken. Despite his need for solitude, he made himself available at all hours, even during the night, to those who asked for his guidance.

Philip's meetings became famous in Rome, attracting many followers. After the spiritual exercises, the followers would make the pilgrimage to the Seven Churches, a special devotion in Rome, stopping to eat and drink with the enthusiasm of picnickers. Among his followers were the historian Cesare Baronio, Cardinal (later Saint) Carlo Borromeo of Milan, Pierluigi da Palestrina, and Giovanni Animuccia. These last two composed sacred music for the prayer meetings, originating the musical form of the oratorio, which takes its name from this group.

In 1575, Pope Gregory XIII formally recognized the Congregation of the Oratory. Although Philip had not intended to found a religious congregation, his movement spread to several other cities in Italy. The Congregation of the Oratory differed significantly from other religious organizations in that, although the priests lived in community, they took no vows, kept their personal property, and were free to leave at any time. The pope gave Philip the property of Santa Maria in Vallicella, where he had a new church constructed and lived for the rest of his life. Since he had no wealth of his own, he apparently depended upon contributions from the faithful to carry out his work.

Philip's reputation for clownish behavior might seem at first to contradict his saintly vocation. He often ordered strange penances, such as requiring a follower to sing or dance in the streets or perform humiliating work such as sweeping the church steps while dressed in an outlandish costume. Once, when a penitent asked permission to wear a hair shirt, Philip commanded him to wear it outside his clothing, visible to all. With his belief in the virtue of humility, Philip saw these penances as a way of puncturing the egos of sinners full of self-love. Although he was personally fastidious, his appearance was sometimes laughable. Once he appeared in the streets with half his beard shaved, and sometimes he wore his clothes inside out. When the pope offered him the red hat of a cardinal, Philip took this honor as a joke and tossed the hat around like a ball. This good-humored mockery of his own dignity was taken by Romans as evidence of his saintliness and increased their affection for him.

Throughout his life, Philip wrote poetry, although little remains, as he destroyed his papers before death. As his reputation for sanctity grew, so did stories about his mystical experiences while celebrating Mass. He would often lose himself in contemplation and go into a trancelike state, reportedly rising in the air, then collapse in a state of exhaustion. His followers increased, including not only ordinary people but also cardinals and even several popes.

In his old age, Philip had a luxuriant white beard and bright, childlike blue eyes. His frail appearance became more pronounced; always an ascetic, he ate barely enough to sustain life and in his last years withdrew entirely to a life of contemplation. Philip died in 1595. Popularly acclaimed as a saint during his lifetime, he was canonized by Pope Gregory XV in 1622.

Summary

Saint Philip Neri is an example of the power of a humble man, devoid of any desire for public acclaim or political power, to exert a significant influence on the events of his time. A priest of the Roman Catholic Church during the turbulent years of the Counter-Reformation, his example of personal holiness, balanced with a whimsical (at times eccentric) sense of humor, persuaded countless Romans, from ordinary workers to highly placed churchmen, to reform their lives. He is called the "Apostle of Rome."

The most significant event during Philip's lifetime was the Council of Trent, which clarified the doctrines of the Catholic Church, set down the rules for the reform of the clergy, and called upon the faithful to lead disciplined lives under the spiritual direction of the Church. Although Philip took no part in the deliberations of the council, he founded the Congregation of the Oratory (Oratorians), a loosely organized group of laymen and priests who gathered to pray, read and discuss the Scriptures, and exhort others to a life of holiness. Some of Rome's most notable clerics, public figures, and musicians attended these meetings. The Oratorians, unlike members of other religious orders, took no vows.

As is often the case in reports of saints' lives, controversy arises over the contemporary biographers' records of miraculous occurrences (ecstasies, prophecies, medical cures) as manifestations of Philip's holiness. Interpretation of the meaning of these phenomena is a matter of faith. Yet there can be no question that, in a time when the Church produced both illustrious and notorious public figures, Philip stands out as a man who, through his considerable personal magnetism and holiness, became a model for personal reform for the countless people who sought his spiritual guidance.

Bibliography

Bouyer, Louis. *The Roman Socrates: A Portrait of St. Philip Neri*. Translated by Michael Day. London: Chapman, and Westminster, Md.: Newman Press, 1958. Offers insight into Philip's spiritual life from the viewpoint of a modern French priest who belongs to the Congregation of the Oratory.

Butler, Samuel. "St. Philip Neri." In *Butler's Lives of the Saints*, edited by Herbert Thurston and Donald Atwater. New York: Kenedy, and London: Burns and Oates, 1956. An updated edition of an indispensable reference work, which gives a concise overview of Philip's life and contribution to the history of the Catholic Church.

Daniel-Rops, Henry. *The History of the Church of Christ*. Vol. 5, *The Catholic Reformation*. Translated by John Warrington. London: Dent, and New York: Dutton, 1962. A detailed scholarly study, especially useful in placing Philip's life and work within the framework of the Catholic Revival, which influenced him and was influenced by him, because so many of his followers were church officials.

Harney, Martin P. "Religious Orders, Old and New." In *The Catholic Church Through the Ages*. Boston: Daughters of St. Paul, 1974. A highly readable account of church history for those without scholarly knowledge of the times. Valuable in describing the Congregation of the Oratory against the background of the Council of Trent.

Kerlin, Michael J. "St. Philip Neri and Sixteenth-Century Church Renewal." *America* 172 (May, 1995): 22. Deals with the life of St. Philip Neri as a reference point of Church renewal today, focusing on his childhood, life of service, personal characteristics, influence, and adversaries.

Maynard, Theodore. *Mystic in Motley: The Life of St. Philip Neri*. Milwaukee: Bruce Publishing, 1946. A lucid biography that draws on sources from Philip's own time as well as earlier biographies not generally available. Sifts through the technical accounts of canonization procedures and miracles to provide a readable, balanced explanation for many events in Philip's life.

Schamoni, Wilhelm. "Philip Neri, the Apostle of Rome." In *Face of the Saints*. Translated by

Anne Freemantle. New York: Pantheon Books, 1947; London: Sheed and Ward, 1948. A fascinating collection of death masks and portraits of the saints painted during their lives, along with brief biographies. The introduction has a useful explanation of the canonization process for the lay reader.

Marjorie J. Podolsky

NEZAHUALCÓYOTL

Born: 1402; probably Texcoco
Died: 1472; Texcoco
Area of Achievement: Government
Contribution: Nezahualcóyotl, who was primarily responsible for the creation of the Aztec Empire, was a proponent of a religious vision which, if it had prevailed, might have made possible that empire's survival.

Early Life

Nezahualcóyotl (Hungry Coyote) was the son of Ixtlilxóchitl, King of Texcoco, and therefore a descendant of Xólotl, who led a Chichimec tribe into the northern part of the Valley of Mexico in the mid-thirteenth century and established the Kingdom of Alcolhuacán. Quinatzin, who established his Alcolhuacán capital at Texcoco in 1318, was the great-grandson of Xólotl and the great-grandfather of Nezahualcóyotl, who also had connection with the Mexica Aztecs of Tenochtitlán through his mother, Matlalcihuatzin, who was the daughter of a Tenochtitlán king.

To understand why the childhood of Nezahualcóyotl was a time of great peril for the royal house of Alcolhuacán, the reader must take account of the wars fought in the valley in the period before the rise of the Mexica Aztecs of Tenochtitlán. The arena of these wars was a relatively small area in the vicinity of modern Mexico City, and the powers engaged were all cities on or near the shores of Lake Texcoco or on its islands. Because the various codices upon which one depends for knowledge of these events were written from memory after the Spanish Conquest, they do not agree in detail, but their description of the wars that tore the Valley of Mexico apart in the years before Nezahualcóyotl came to the throne of Texcoco are in agreement on the basic events.

The dominant power on the western shore of the lake was the Tepanecans of Azcapotzalco, whose great King Tezozómoc, though he was himself a grandson of Xólotl, was determined to extend his control over the valley by conquering Texcoco, which dominated the country between the lake and the mountains to the east. In 1412, Tezozómoc launched a three-pronged attack, sending armies against Alcolhuacán around the north and south ends of the lake and sending his Mexican allies from Tenochtitlán directly across the lake in their war canoes. Ixtlilxóchitl repulsed the southern attack and drove off the war canoes; then, in a war that lasted three years, he defeated the armies of Tezozómoc in every battle in the country north of the lake and laid siege to Azcapotzalco itself.

At this point, Tezozómoc sued for peace, and Ixtlilxóchitl, who had virtually won the war, magnanimously chose not to demand unconditional surrender. This stance ensured his own downfall, because Tezozómoc chose not to abide by the terms of the peace treaty, which called for both sides to disarm. In 1418, he launched a treacherous attack, and Ixtlilxóchitl was defeated and forced to flee to the mountains with Nezahualcóyotl. There, hiding in the branches of a tree, the boy saw his father make his last stand before he was cut down by the pursuing Tepanecans. From that moment, apparently, Nezahualcóyotl was determined to have his vengeance on Azcapotzalco.

Though the chronicles may rely only on popular legend, they all suggest that after fleeing across the mountains to Tlaxcala, where he found refuge with relatives, Nezahualcóyotl spent the next few years traveling incognito in Alcolhuacán, preparing his people for the day when he would lead them in a war of liberation against Azcapotzalco. In any case, during this period he was in great peril as a result of a reward posted by Tezozómoc, and he eventually was captured at Chalco, a city on the southeast shore of the lake subject to Tezozómoc. According to the chronicles, Tezozómoc ordered him caged and starved to death, but his guards, remembering the greatness of his father, secretly fed him. Later, when he was to be put to death, one of his guards permitted him to escape and was himself killed in his place.

Eventually—in 1425 according to one account—two of his aunts, related to the royal houses of both Texcoco and Azcapotzalco, persuaded Tezozómoc to permit the young prince to return, and he was allowed to live in Texcoco and with his mother's relatives in Tenochtitlán. In his last days, however, Tezozómoc regretted giving the prince even this limited freedom and sent an assassin to kill him. Again, Nezahualcóyotl survived as a result of the prestige he enjoyed as the son of Ixtlilxóchitl; the assassin warned him of the plot.

In 1426, Tezozómoc died. Nezahualcóyotl, as an Aztec prince related by blood or marriage to all the royal houses of the valley, attended the funeral, apparently keeping his own counsel as he observed the final rites performed for the tyrant against whom he had sworn vengeance. Even then the sons of Tezozómoc were arguing about the succession, and Nezahualcóyotl, whose political instincts were strong, must have been planning the conspiracy by which he would destroy them and their city. The accession of Maxtla to the throne of Azcapotzalco in 1426 set in motion the events which led eventually to the destruction of Azcapotzalco, the rise of Tenochtitlán to prominence, and the return of Nezahualcóyotl to his rightful place on the throne of Texcoco.

Life's Work

In 1420, Tezozómoc had rewarded his allies in Tenochtitlán with suzerainty over Texcoco. Now with Tezozómoc's death, Chimalpopoca, the King of Tenochtitlán, granted the rule of Texcoco to Nezahualcóyotl, who immediately conspired with Chimalpopoca against Azcapotzalco's new king, Maxtla. The plot was a failure, and Nezahualcóyotl was again forced to flee. In 1427, however, Chimalpopoca was killed—either by agents of Maxtla or by the most aggressive elements in Tenochtitlán itself—and Ixtcóatl (or Itzcóatl, as the name is also transliterated) succeeded him on the throne of Tenochtitlán. The way was now prepared for the alliance which would bring Maxtla down.

Though Maxtla's henchmen ruled in Texcoco, Nezahualcóyotl was able to call upon the goodwill he had earned among the people in the other cities east of the lake during his exile. The alliance of these cities now became part of a grander alliance of all those city-states that had grievances against Azcapotzalco. They were a mixed lot. Besides Nezahualcóyotl's cities, the alliance included his allies in Huexotzinco and Tlaxcala beyond the mountains east of the lake, Cuauhtitlán on the northwest shore of the lake, and Tlacopán on the west shore. Above all, it included Tenochtitlán. These Mexica Aztecs had fought against Nezahualcóyotl's father, they had opposed Nezahualcóyotl himself, and they had reduced him for a time to the status of a tribute-paying prince. He knew that the alliance against Azcapotzalco would not succeed without their warriors, however, and the alliance which resulted was primarily the result of his recognition of the political realities of the valley. Tenochtitlán, more or less imprisoned on its island in the lake, needed land, and Nezahualcóyotl used this land-hunger as a means of wreaking vengeance on Azcapotzalco.

As a result, he took a force of his best warriors to Tenochtitlán to aid in its defense. Maxtla's Tepanecans attacked across the causeways which linked Tenochtitlán to the western shore, and the Mexica and Nezahualcóyotl's Acolhua repulsed it. Meanwhile, armies from Huexotzinco and Tlaxcala were advancing on Azcapotzalco from the north. In 1428, the allies laid siege to Azcapotzalco and eventually destroyed it. The primary result of the victory was the ascendancy of Tenochtitlán in the political and military life of the valley and the rise to dominance of the most warlike and aggressive elements in that city.

Nezahualcóyotl remained in Tenochtitlán for several years, even building a palace there, while planning his campaign to regain the throne of Texcoco from the henchmen of Maxtla. The Mexica, keeping their part of the bargain, assisted him from 1429 to 1430 in the recovery of Texcoco. Now firmly allied with Tenochtitlán, he assisted them in their campaigns against the other cities on the shores of the lake, including Coyoacán and Xochimilco. In 1433, the fall of Cuitláhuac ended the Tepaneca War.

In 1431, Nezahualcóyotl was crowned emperor of the three-city league of Texcoco, Tenochtitlán, and Tlacopán, which he, more than anyone, had created. He realized that the kind of empire his ancestor Xólotl had achieved, a single state ruled by a single overlord, was no longer possible. Peace in the Valley of Mexico, therefore, depended on the maintenance of a loose confederation of the Acolhua of Texcoco, the Mexica of Tenochtitlán, and the Tepaneca of Tlacopán. Whatever the faults of this "empire," it endured until the Spanish Conquest.

In 1433, Nezahualcóyotl returned to Texcoco and embarked on a program which inaugurated that city's golden age and made it the most beautiful city in the Valley of Mexico and its intellectual and cultural center. He was a patron of science, industry, art, and literature; he was himself a poet of considerable renown; and he encouraged the creation of historical archives which at the time of the Spanish Conquest were the most extensive in Mexico.

In 1440, when King Itzcóatl of Tenochtitlán died, Nezahualcóyotl rededicated himself to the friendship of the three cities and gave his support in the election of a new king to Moctezuma (or Montezuma) I. Apparently he believed that Moctezuma would be a less ambitious threat than any other candidate to the integrity of Alcolhuacán and was willing to make concessions to ensure this election, which in time proved to be disastrous. The Mexica under Moctezuma's leadership became the dominant power in the valley, though Nezahualcóyotl continued as emperor.

In 1450, when torrential rains raised the level of the lake and flooded Tenochtitlán, Nezahualcóyotl, who was perhaps the most distinguished engineer and builder in Mexico before the Conquest, proposed the great dike which stretched nine miles north to south down the lake and isolated Tenochtitlán from the east side of the lake, which received the heaviest runoff from the mountains. In the next few years, however, the Valley of Mexico was afflicted with a long drought. Nezahualcóyotl distributed food from his own supplies and resisted the charge of some of his subjects that the gods had withheld the rain because Nezahualcóyotl had neglected to maintain the rites of human sacrifice. Characteristically, he preferred to build an extensive irrigation system to bring water from the mountains.

Nezahualcóyotl's antipathy to human sacrifice, which is in itself enough to make him the most remarkable political figure of his time and place, apparently derived from his sympathy with the cult of Tloque Nahuaque. This god, who was assumed to be unfathomable, all-present, and formless, was the one god in the pantheon that did not demand human sacrifice, and in the encouragement of his cult, Nezahualcóyotl seems clearly to have been attempting to lead his people toward a religion based on a benevolent monotheism.

One of Nezahualcóyotl's concessions to Moctezuma was his agreement to assist his ally in future wars of aggression. From 1455 to 1458, therefore, he contributed to the success of Tenochtitlán's war against the Mixtecs, and in 1464 he sent an army that helped Tenochtitlán destroy Chalco.

In 1467, Nezahualcóyotl completed in Texcoco the temple to the war god Huitzilopochtli, which was required as a further concession to the Mexica of Tenochtitlán. In the same year he completed a temple to the peaceful, benevolent Tloque Nahuaque. The coincidence of these two events must be considered an indication of the tragedy inherent both in the life of Nezahualcóyotl and in the history of Mexico. In the next half century, that tragedy would play itself out to its inevitable conclusion as the adherents of Huitzilopochtli, with their doctrine of war, aggression, and human sacrifice, would triumph over the cult of peace and benevolence of which Nezahualcóyotl had been the champion.

Summary

Nezahualcóyotl was a supreme example of the Aztec knight, but he was also a poet, a lawgiver, a skillful politician and diplomat often called upon to mediate disputes, a builder and engineer, and a great patron of culture and learning. When he dedicated the temple to Huitzilopochtli in 1467—which in the Aztec calendar was called One Reed—he predicted that when One Reed returned in fifty-two years, the Aztec Empire would be destroyed. This prediction, along with the popular assumption that the benevolent god Quetzalcóatl would return in One Reed, was part of a complex of fears that haunted the last years of Aztec supremacy in Mexico with visions of the end of their civilization.

The demands of the Aztec war god for ever-increasing gifts of blood caused wars waged to capture sacrificial victims and ultimately dissension within the empire, which an astute conqueror would find easy to exploit. For this reason, Nezahualcóyotl's political decision to make concessions to Tenochtitlán—and thus to the cult of Huitzilopochtli—for the sake of peace within the empire must be considered an unfortunate development in the religious history of Mexico. If he had been able to unite the empire under the protection of a god of brotherhood and benevolence, the Spanish Conquest would undoubtedly have been more difficult. As it happened, however, when One Reed came around again (in 1519), it brought the Spanish and, as Nezahualcóyotl had predicted, the destruction of the civilization of which he was the outstanding representative.

Bibliography

Brundage, Burr C. *A Rain of Darts: The Mexica Aztecs*. Austin: University of Texas Press, 1972. Based on enormous scholarship, this book is the single most important work in English on Aztec history, with a thorough and well-balanced account of the Kingdom of Alcolhuacán and the life and achievements of Nezahualcóyotl.

Gillmor, Frances. *Flute of the Smoking Mirror*. Albuquerque: University of New Mexico Press, 1949. A biography of Nezahualcóyotl, based on extensive scholarship but written in a novelistic style which requires the reader to check the narrative against the thoroughly documented end notes.

Padden, R. C. *The Hummingbird and the Hawk: Conquest and Sovereignty in the Valley of Mexi-*

co, 1503-1541. Columbus: Ohio State University Press, 1908; London: Harper, 1970. Padden treats primarily Aztec affairs during the reign of the last Aztec emperor and the early colonial period, but his book includes a useful account of the religious conflicts in Mexico during Nezahualcóyotl's lifetime.

Peterson, Frederick A. *Ancient Mexico*. New York: Capricorn Books, 1962. A splendid survey of Mexican history and culture before the Spanish Conquest, with a useful discussion of Nezahualcóyotl's achievements and their historical background.

Radin, Paul. "The Sources and Authenticity of the History of the Ancient Mexicans." *University of California Publications in American Anthropology and Ethnology* 17 (1920-1926): 1-150. Includes the text of the Codex Xólotl, the most important original chronicle to discuss Nezahualcóyotl and the history of Texcoco.

Robert L. Berner

NICHOLAS V
Tommaso Parentucelli

Born: November 15, 1397; Sarzana, Republic of Genoa

Died: March 24, 1455; Rome

Areas of Achievement: Diplomacy, church reform, and patronage of the arts

Contribution: Nicholas V restored church unity by ending the schism between the Papacy and the conciliar party in Basel. He initiated serious efforts at church reform, helped bring peace to Italy, and sponsored architectural and literary projects in Rome.

Early Life

Tommaso Parentucelli, the future Pope Nicholas V, was born a physician's son at Sarzana in the Republic of Genoa. Orphaned early, he was forced in his youth to withdraw from the University of Bologna to earn a living as a tutor in Florence. There he met Humanist scholars and artists who enhanced his interest in the classical studies then gaining popularity among the educated classes of northern Italy. In 1419, he was able to return to complete a doctorate in theology. The impressive academic record and serious demeanor of the young priest caught the eye of Niccolò Albergati, the Bishop of Bologna, who offered him a position as his assistant. This association, which lasted twenty years, provided Parentucelli with a valuable apprenticeship in church politics.

He accompanied Albergati on many trips, within Italy and beyond. He visited the papal court under Martin V, the first pontiff to reign unchallenged in Rome in more than a century. Parentucelli used every opportunity on his travels to acquire the classical manuscripts that had become his passion. Then, in 1439, his skills in settling a dispute with Greek churchmen at the Florence Council so impressed Pope Eugene IV that, upon Albergati's death in 1443, the pope named Parentucelli to succeed him as Bishop of Bologna.

In late 1446, the pope elevated Parentucelli to the cardinalate for his performance as papal diplomat among the German princes. Finally, when Eugene died in March, 1447, Parentucelli was elected his successor by the College of Cardinals. He had been only four years a bishop and less than four months a cardinal, but his spirituality and conciliatory temperament seemed most to have recommended him as a compromise candidate. He took the papal name Nicholas V in honor of his patron Niccolò Albergati. The new pope was a small, shomely man of delicate constitution, but he had a driving sense of purpose to confront the problems inherited from Eugene.

The Roman church was in crisis. The Council of Basel, convened half a generation before, continued to reject papal authority, recognizing only its own creation, the antipope Felix V. In Germany, most princes remained either hostile to Rome or neutral in the papal-conciliar struggle. They found effective political leverage in the mutual antagonism of pope and council. In addition, the Church suffered across Europe from scandals and corruptions that went largely unchecked. Simony and concubinage were rife among the clergy, while exotic superstitions beguiled many among the general populace. Some secular lords ruthlessly exploited church property and appointments in their lands. In Italy, the major city-states seemed incapable of peaceful coexistence. Also, the last years of Eugene IV's troubled pontificate had left Rome and the Papal States dangerously vulnerable and in a state of decay. The papal treasury was empty. The extent to which Nicholas met such challenges and the means that he chose would define his place in papal history.

Life's Work

Nicholas intensified at once the negotiations with the German princes begun by Eugene IV. Within a year, the new pope had reached a milestone agreement with Austrian Emperor Frederick III and most of the princes. The Concordat of Vienna of February, 1448, conceded official imperial recognition of Nicholas V as head of the Church and acknowledged specified papal rights to church revenues and appointments in Germany. In return, the pope accepted certain limits to his taxing and investiture privileges in the German church.

By recognizing the Austrian state as an equal in political negotiations, the pope probably surrendered in the long term more than he received. Yet the Concordat of Vienna in effect sounded the death knell of the Basel Council. With the crumbling of its last major political support, the council declared itself dissolved in April, 1449. Nicholas, the skilled diplomat, had already persuaded the antipope Felix to abdicate in exchange for a generous pension and the official rank of cardinal-bishop, second in honor only to Nicholas himself. All spiritual penalties were annulled, and most conciliarists were reconciled with Rome. On the model of the Vienna agreement, the pope proceeded to individual understandings with the kings of Portugal, Castile, and Poland, as well as with lesser princes.

To celebrate the restored unity of the Western church, Pope Nicholas declared 1450 a jubilee year in which Christians everywhere were invited to Rome. They were offered the spiritual benefits of a rich indulgence (a release from penalties for sins) and the opportunity to visit the sacred places there. The donations of the thousands of pilgrims who swarmed to the papal city filled church coffers to overflowing, which provided Nicholas with the financial means to pursue other major policies.

First, to confront the spiritual neglect, corruption, and schism plaguing the Church at large, the pope in 1450 dispatched a number of cardinal-legates. They were instructed to bring the jubilee indulgence to those unable to come to Rome and, above all, to reform in the name of the Papacy such spiritual deformities as they found. Prominent were the missions to France, northern Italy, and the German empire, including Bohemia.

Most extensive of all was the reform legation through the Germanies of Cardinal Nicholas of Cusa; however, the pope's conciliatory style served more to undermine Nicholas of Cusa's efforts than to reinforce them. The legate found his decrees against the most serious abuses, such as the cult of bleeding hosts, modified or rescinded by a pontiff fearful of offending German princes and prelates so recently partisans or sympathizers of the Basel Council. Nicholas of Cusa's legation, the last major reform attempt within the German church before Martin Luther, came to little. The other missions achieved only marginal success.

In providing for the security of Rome and the Papal States, however, Nicholas proved strikingly successful. Recognizing that peace and order at home were the essential preconditions to substantive actions elsewhere, he moved energetically in a number of directions. He built new walls around the city, then dismissed the disruptive mercenaries who had controlled Rome for nearly a decade. They were replaced by strategically located fortifications, manned by new troops under officers chosen for their loyalty and competence. Nicholas imposed similar changes in the Papal States, appointing new governors, usually drawn from the local population. Finally, he granted effective self-government to the city of Rome, conceding rights of taxation and of appointment to civil office to influential local nobles. In such ways, Nicholas peacefully defused the sometimes-furious resentment that the Roman aristocracy had felt toward his predecessor.

With these considerable political and ecclesiastical achievements realized over the first four years of his pontificate, the pope turned full attention to still another realm, the cultural and intellectual. It is for his achievements here that Nicholas would be called the first "Renaissance pope." Nicholas had once commented that, after God, his greatest love lay in buildings and books. Because of the jubilee donations, he now had the funds to pursue his passions.

It was to proclaim in more visible ways the return of greatness and dignity to the papal city that Nicholas commissioned a sweeping program of architectural construction and renovation. He built new bridges and aqueducts and completed the repair of more than forty dilapidated churches. Most impressive, Nicholas put together an elaborate plan for a project of urban renewal that would encompass both the renovation and the new construction of buildings in the Borgo region adjacent to the Vatican palace and within the palace itself.

In the neoclassical style of the designs, including porticoed streets, round towers, triumphal arches, lush gardens, and fountains, there is evident the close influence of the renowned architect Leon Battista Alberti. Although Nicholas was able to complete only the refurbishing of the Vatican Palace, his plan provided the general framework for future projects, including the completion in the early sixteenth century of the new St. Peter's Basilica. Fra Angelico and Piero della Francesca were among the painters commissioned by Nicholas to decorate various Vatican buildings, including the walls of his private chapel.

Nicholas also regarded himself as the patron of all who laid claim to Humanist achievement, and he delighted in the company of scholars. He spared no expense in making the papal court a lively center of the new learning and literature. For example, distinguished Humanists such as Lorenzo Valla and Poggio were amply compensated for translating the Greek classics of Homer and Thucydides, among others, into a fluid Latin for Western readers.

Nicholas was determined as well to restock a papal library that had in the previous century been dispersed beyond recovery by the upheavals of papal exile and schism. He searched for rare manuscripts, had copies made of others, and donated his private collection. Nicholas left some 1,150 manuscripts, both Latin and Greek, patristic as well as classical. He thereby laid the original foundations of the Vatican library, one of the cultural treasures of Western civilization. After 1453, the pope's health deteriorated rapidly, marked by recurring and agonizing attacks of gout. To the end, he remained actively engaged in his various endeavors. He was buried in St. Peter's Basilica, close to the tomb of his predecessor, Eugene IV.

Summary

The pontificate of Nicholas V constitutes something of a turning point in papal history. His diplomatic successes in ending the conciliar threat, regaining the allegiance of the German princes, and bringing peace to much of Italy portended at least a partial recovery of papal authority and prestige. Further, as a Christian Humanist scholar, bibliophile, and patron of the arts, Nicholas enjoyed considerable success in making Rome for a time the center of art, architecture, and literature in the West. He provided a major stimulus to cultural distinction on the model of the classical past.

The greatest disappointment of his pontificate was the failure after the first few years to carry forward the ambitious program of church reform that he had launched. Particularly discouraging to him was the cold response of the Western states to his plea for a crusade to liberate the Byzantine Empire from the Ottoman Turks.

Yet the reign of Nicholas was, overall, a time of peace, prosperity, and promise after generations of conflict and upheaval in the Church. As the peacemaker pope, Nicholas sought to use all the weapons of papal diplomacy and Renaissance culture he could mobilize to signal the restoration of an unchallenged papal monarchy in Rome and the revived glory of the Western church.

Bibliography

Creighton, Mandell. *History of the Papacy During the Period of the Reformation*. Vol. 3, *The Italian Princes, 1464-1518*. London: Longman, and Boston: Houghton Mifflin, 1882. Based largely on published sources of the time. The balanced, even-handed treatment has withstood well the test of subsequent scholarship. Especially enlightening on Nicholas' relations with the Basel Council and with the German Empire, as well as the discussion of the Papacy in its Italian setting.

Pastor, Ludwig von. *History of the Popes from the Close of the Middle Ages*. Vol. 2. Edited and translated by F. I. Antrobus. London: Kegan Paul, and St. Louis, Mo.: Herder, 1891. By far the most detailed study in English of the full range of Nicholas' activities, including his achievements in cultural patronage, political negotiations, and especially in the extensive reform mission of papal legates in the German empire and neighboring lands. Pastor, among the first scholars granted access to the secret Vatican archives, bases his account largely on manuscript evidence. That makes the work indispensable, despite its often highly partisan tone.

Stieber, Joachim W. *Pope Eugenius IV, the Council of Basel and the Secular and Ecclesiastical Authorities in the Empire: The Conflict over Supreme Authority and Power in the Church*. Leiden: Brill, 1978. Shows how Nicholas, over the crucial first two years of his pontificate, continued closely certain policies of his predecessor, Eugene IV. Above all, he sought through major concessions to enlist the support of Europe's secular powers against a conciliar party that sought to reduce the Papacy under the authority of general church councils. In a valuable appendix, Stieber provides a thorough discussion of the main documentary sources for Nicholas' pontificate.

Stinger, Charles L. *The Renaissance in Rome*. Bloomington: Indiana University Press, 1985. Provides in separate segments a clear, recent overview of the main facets of Nicholas' cultural activities. Updates Pastor's standard position not only that Nicholas was the first true Renaissance pope but also that his pontificate represents a major turning point in the recovery of the Papacy.

Vespasiano da Bisticci, Florentino. *Renaissance Princes, Popes, and Prelates*. Translated by William George and Emily Waters, with an introduction by Myron P. Gilmore. New York: Harper, 1963. Contains a lively and very readable short biography of Nicholas by a close friend, the Humanist bibliographer Vespasiano. While the account is invariably laudatory, it offers personal details that provide a vivid sense of the pope's personality.

Westfall, Carroll W. *In This Most Perfect Paradise: Alberti, Nicholas V, and the Invention of Con-*

scious Urban Planning in Rome, 1447-55. University Park: Pennsylvania State University Press, 1974; London: Pennsylvania State University Press, 1975. Contends that Nicholas' vast scheme of renovation for the city of Rome began with the architect Alberti's concept of urban renewal. Westfall suggests that Alberti's general designs were adapted by others to specific projects. In the collaboration of pope and architect, Westfall sees a remarkable breakthrough toward a conscious and comprehensive urban design. The bibliography is excellent.

Donald D. Sullivan

NICHOLAS OF CUSA

Born: 1401; Kues, Upper Lorraine
Died: August 11, 1464; Todi, Papal States
Areas of Achievement: Philosophy and religion
Contribution: Nicholas of Cusa contributed to preserving the hierarchical authority and unity of the Roman church while at the same time advocating Humanism and lay participation in both sacred and secular government during the early years of the Renaissance. His most lasting contribution has been to Western philosophy.

Early Life

Nicholas Kryfts (Krebs) was born in the village of Kues, between Trier and Bernkastel, on the Mosel River in the German Rhineland. His moderately prosperous father operated a barge on the busy river, which served as a major commercial waterway in Northern Europe. Young Nicholas was first sent to a school administered by the Brothers of the Common Life at Deventer on the Lower Rhine. Nicholas was inspired by the new learning that the brothers emphasized, and they also encouraged him in a spirit of church reform centered on the idea of the Roman church as a community of clergy and faithful.

In 1416, at the age of fifteen, Nicholas registered at the University of Heidelberg. Although Nicholas only remained at Heidelberg for one year, here, too, he was exposed to modern learning. Nominalistic philosophy—rejection of universals as myths and a turn toward philosophizing based on individualism—left its mark on young Nicholas. He began to question truths arrived at through pure deduction and based on traditional authority. The Scholasticism of the late Middle Ages was giving way to a Humanistic thinking in both theology and philosophy.

Nicholas of Cusa next enrolled at the University of Padua in Italy. Padua was a major center for the study of canon law in Europe. In its lecture halls, scholars of science, mathematics, astronomy, and the humanities rigorously challenged established sacred and secular dogma. Yet the revival of Neoplatonism—envisioning a hierarchy of knowledge extending from a perfect and infinite God to an imperfect and finite world—also played a crucial role in Nicholas' education. It was at Padua that young Nicholas had an opportunity to observe at first hand the government of Roman city-states, many of which inherited the idea of citizen participation from Greek antiquity. Nicholas studied at Padua for six years, earning a doctorate in canon law in 1423.

Nicholas' early education shaped his later life's work within the Roman Catholic Church; it reflected the change in worldview in the transition years from the late Middle Ages to the early Renaissance years. The medieval notion that God governed the world through unchallenged hierarchical authority was tempered by growing acknowledgment that the Creator provided all of his creatures with freedom and responsibility, subject to divine judgment. The dialectic of God's transcendence and His immanence in the world dominated the thought and life of Nicholas of Cusa; he sought in his philosophy and in his daily life to reconcile these views of God and world.

Life's Work

Nicholas of Cusa returned to Germany in 1425 to embark on his life's work as papal diplomat, theologian, and philosopher. At first he enrolled at the University of Cologne to lecture and to continue his research. There he attracted the attention of Cardinal Giordano Orsini, who was impressed by a legal document prepared by Nicholas at his request. Cardinal Orsini was a noted Humanist and progressive within the Roman church; he played an important role in Nicholas' ordination as a priest in 1426. Orsini's influence was also instrumental in securing an appointment for Nicholas as a legal adviser to the Council of Basel in 1432.

Nicholas' career in church politics began in earnest at the Council of Basel. The debate centered on the issue of the pope's authority. Nicholas sided with those who believed that the Roman church ought to be governed by a general council representing clergy and congregations. The council was to be superior to the pope, who would remain the Church's religious and administrative head but who could be discharged by the council. Nicholas' conviction was that it was through conciliar government that church unity would be best preserved. The congregation ought to be the source of church law, with pope and hierarchy serving the general council.

Nicholas expanded his thinking on church government in a philosophical treatise. This work, *De concordantia catholica* (1433; on unity), sets forth what has been called the conciliar theory of government, based on Nicholas' belief that authority of the ruler must rest on consent granted by the ruled. His main thesis was that this governmental form would bring about unity within the Church.

The controversy over conciliar government continued after the Council of Basel. Subsequently, Nicholas of Cusa modified his antipapal stance. Three reasons have been offered to explain this turnabout. First, Nicholas was displeased with the turmoil between members of the council and the Holy See. Second, Nicholas' highest priority was church unity. Finally, Nicholas was motivated by the opportunities for his own career within the Church hierarchy.

Nicholas was rewarded with a papal appointment. In 1437, Nicholas was a delegate to a meeting between the Roman and Eastern Orthodox Christians in Constantinople. There he invited Greek representatives to attend a scheduled council in Italy on reunification of the Greek and Roman churches. Although his efforts failed, Christian unity and reform continued to motivate Nicholas throughout his life, in his dealings with church politics as well as in his philosophical writings.

Nicholas continued to accept diplomatic posts from the Vatican. From 1438 to 1448, he was a papal delegate to Germany, where he worked for both reform and unity within the Church. As a reward, in 1449 Pope Nicholas V made Nicholas of Cusa a cardinal of the titular Church of Saint Peter in Chains in Rome. In 1450, he was named Bishop of Brixen, in Austria. During his tenure as bishop, Nicholas encountered the growing conflict between the Church and secular politics. It was a difficult phase in his life.

His later years were spent in a bitter struggle with the secular ruler of Austria, Archduke Sigismund. Nicholas set out to reform corrupt practices among the priests and monks of his diocese, but his efforts met with apathy and hostility among the clergy. At one point, he sought to reform a convent at Sonneburg, and there Bishop Nicholas ran into bitter opposition from secular authorities because many of the nuns had been recruited from noble families. Archduke Sigismund assumed the role of protector of the nuns.

Added to this controversy was one which concerned ecclesiastical appointments. Sigismund was unhappy over several of Nicholas' choices for church posts; the bishop had bypassed candidates supported by the duke. Open conflict between the bishop and the duke resulted in negotiations, appeals to the Vatican, and, ultimately, compromise. Nicholas was recalled in 1459 to Rome.

As a reward for his services to the Holy See, Nicholas was appointed to the high post of vicar-general for temporal affairs; he was Governor of Rome and the papal territories. It was Nicholas of Cusa's last and highest office. Unfortunately, Cardinal Cusa was not freed from conflict with the Austrian duke. Now the controversy turned into a dispute between Sigismund and the Church over certain property rights in Austria. Claims and counterclaims intensified.

On one occasion, the duke's soldiers surrounded and fired their guns upon a castle in Austria in which Nicholas was temporarily residing as the pope's representative in the dispute. The cardinal surrendered and was put under house arrest. Pope Pius II, humiliated by this treatment of his representative, intervened directly and sought to punish the duke. Nicholas was extricated from the affair. He returned to Italy to live his final days in relative peace and contemplation.

During his many years of church diplomacy, Nicholas of Cusa continued his theological and philosophical research and writing. He wrote about forty-six books and manuscripts. In addition, he was an enthusiastic collector of literary and philosophical works. His two most influential works are *De docta ignorantia* (1440; *Of Learned Ignorance*, 1954) and *De coniecturis* (1442; on conjecture); together they make up a complete outline of his philosophy.

In *On Learned Ignorance*, Nicholas sets forth the doctrine that man knows God only through whatever God chooses to reveal and through human experience. Human reason reaches its limitations in its knowledge of God, for man is finite and God is infinite. Reason is applicable to this finite world, but it is a stumbling block to knowing God. Man will be the more learned the more he grasps his own ignorance of the unknown God. The infinite God is not accessible through reason, but His awareness is present in men's minds. Through man's recognition of reason's limits, a realization which is itself reached through reason, the wisdom of learned ignorance is achieved. For Nicholas' speculative metaphysics, man's highest stage of knowledge is his recognition that he cannot attain a comprehensive knowledge of God.

In *De coniecturis*, Nicholas expands his philosophy of learned ignorance. Here Nicholas argues that God is prior to the opposition of being and nonbeing. God is unity transcending the coincidence of all opposites; He transcends and confines in Himself all distinctions and oppositions. God is thus the unity of opposites, of the finite and the infinite. He transcends man's understanding, and thus man cannot form a full and accurate concept of His nature. God transcends the world, but the world is His mirror. God is the unity of world and cosmos. These statements lead into Nicholas' theology, which concludes that because God is beyond human intellect, learned ignorance opens the way to Christian faith.

Nicholas of Cusa died in 1464. He is buried in the Church of Saint Peter in Chains in Rome. Inside the church there is a statue of Nicholas kneeling before Saint Peter. His best monument, however, is the home and hospital for the poor that he and his family founded in his native Kues. The attached library contains many of Nicholas' original manuscripts and his collection of books. It remains in operation as a center for scholarly research.

Summary

Nicholas of Cusa is an outstanding example of a philosopher who was active in practical affairs; he combined a life of contemplation with one of action. Throughout his life, Nicholas attempted to resolve the conflict between old and new views of God and mankind while he remained an obedient member of the Church hierarchy. His later writings and practical work reflected his moderation: He sought reform within the context of order and continuation. In philosophy and ecclesiastical politics, Nicholas advocated gradual development and progress, not rebellion and revolution. Nicholas lived his life according to the fundamental principles of his thought; he remains an exemplar of the unity of thought and practice in a human being's life. As such, his life captured the spirit of the Golden Rule. Above all, Nicholas' life reflected his deep devotion to the ideal of the unity of all being in God, of harmony between reason and faith, theology and philosophy, church and state.

Scholars do not agree on whether Nicholas of Cusa was the first modern thinker or a transitional figure standing between the Middle Ages and the Renaissance. It is clear that he combined traditional elements of Neoplatonism and the Scholastic tradition with postmedieval nominalism and Humanism. Evidence is inconclusive as to whether Nicholas contributed original ideas or dressed the thought of Plato, Saint Augustine, and others in the modes of his era. It is certain, however, that Nicholas of Cusa must be included in any list of the world's great philosophers. He forged a speculative metaphysics that influenced Gottfried Wilhelm Leibniz, G. W. F. Hegel, Martin Heidegger, and the existential philosophers. Nicholas' philosophical legacy remains his enduring contribution to Western civilization.

Bibliography

Bett, Henry. *Nicholas of Cusa*. London: Methuen, 1932; Merrick, N.Y.: Richwood, 1976. Standard biography, presenting detailed account of Nicholas' life coupled with a discussion of his writings and a critique of his philosophy. Stresses Nicholas' consistent thought throughout his political, philosophical, and theological writings; this thought culminates in the unity of all existence in the hidden God.

Cassirer, Ernst. *The Individual and the Cosmos in Renaissance Philosophy*. Translated with an introduction by Mario Domandi. Oxford: Blackwell, and New York: Harper, 1963. An advanced critique of Nicholas' philosophy. Argues that he was a systematic thinker who presented a totally new philosophical orientation and that the beginning of modern philosophy cannot be understood without a consideration of Nicholas' work. Nicholas offered the foundations for a new theory of knowledge and history; his greatness is enhanced because he achieved this major contribution to Renaissance philosophy from within the religious ideas of the Middle Ages.

Copleston, Frederick Charles. "Nicholas of Cusa." In *A History of Philosophy*, vol. 3. London: Burnes and Oates, and Paramus, N.J.: Newman Press, 1946. Concise treatment of Nicholas of Cusa's philosophy from the perspective of the contemporary Roman Catholic Church. Author's theme is that Nicholas' work and writings aimed at reconciliation, harmony, and unity in difference.

Hopkins, Jasper. *A Concise Introduction to the Philosophy of Nicholas of Cusa*. 3d ed. Minneapolis, Minn.: Arthur J. Banning Press, 1986. Includes a text in Latin and English of Nicholas' *De possest* (1460; *On Actualized-Possibility*, 1978). Hopkins contends that this short essay contains an excellent summation of Nicholas of Cusa's philosophy; he recommends that first-time students begin here. The long introductory interpretation serves as a useful reader's guide. Excellent bibliography containing a list of the

English translations of Nicholas' works as well as a list of secondary interpretations.

Jaspers, Karl. "Nicholas of Cusa." In *The Great Philosophers*, edited by Hannah Arendt and translated by Ralph Manheim, vol. 2. New York: Harcourt Brace, and London: Hart-Davis, 1962. A detailed critique of the metaphysics of Nicholas of Cusa. Jaspers considers Nicholas' philosophical writings from the perspective of his own existentialist philosophy. He finds Nicholas' major contribution in keeping alive the idea of individual freedom in human relations and in relation to God.

McDermott, Peter L. "Nicholas of Cusa: Continuity and Conciliation at the Council of Basel." *Church History* 67 (June, 1998): 254. McDermott presents an essay focusing on the collapse of the conciliar movement, highlighting the stance taken by Nicholas of Cusa that led to the discord at the Council of Basel. Details are given of Cusa's education and career, his role in the discussion about the reunification of the Christian church, and his affiliation with the Council of Basel.

Nicholas of Cusa. *Unity and Reform: Selected Writings of Nicholas de Cusa*. Edited with an introduction by John P. Dolan. Notre Dame, Ind.: University of Notre Dame Press, 1962. Selected excerpts from Nicholas' major philosophical and theological writings. Text is supplemented by editor's informative introduction, which serves as an excellent reader's guide.

Sigmund, Paul E. *Nicholas of Cusa and Medieval Political Thought*. Cambridge, Mass.: Harvard University Press, 1963. Concentrates on Nicholas' political theory, emphasizing the foundational principle of government by consent. The philosophical and legal antecedents of Nicholas' political philosophy are traced. Good bibliography of secondary sources from the political philosophy perspective.

Smirnov, Andrey V. "Nicholas of Cusa and Ibn' Arabi: Two Philosophies of Mysticism." *Philosophy East and West* 43 (January, 1993): 65. The author investigates the way in which the mystical outlook was rationalized in the philosophies of Nicholas of Cusa and Ibn' Arabi and deals with the relation of God to the world and the role of humanity in the world.

Gil L. Gunderson

NOSTRADAMUS

Born: December 23 or 24, 1503; St. Rémy de Provence, France

Died: July 1 or 2, 1566; Salon de Provence, France

Areas of Achievement: Astronomy; government and politics; literature; medicine

Contribution: A prominent physician and political adviser, Nostradamus achieved widest fame with collections of veiled prophecies in poetical form.

Early Life

Nostradamus was born Michel Notredame (or Nostredame, the Provençal spelling) near the end of 1503 in St. Rémy de Provence in southern France. Although he would later claim that his father and grandfather were physicians, it appears more likely that they were in fact prosperous grain merchants. What is certain is that the family had recently converted from Judaism to Christianity and dropped its original name in order to remain in Catholic France.

The young Michel received his earliest education from his grandfathers, who found him a promising student. He was then able to continue his studies at two nearby cities renowned for their intellectual and cultural life, Avignon and Montpellier. Michel began secondary school at the former in 1517, where the prescribed course of study included grammar, rhetoric, logic, music, mathematics, and astronomy (which encompassed astrology as well). At the time, Avignon was under direct control of the Catholic Church; there, as in all seats of learning, classes were taught in Latin.

Michel went on to study medicine at the University of Montpellier in 1522, where once again astrology played a role alongside such subjects as anatomy and surgery. Tradition has it that he concentrated upon pharmacology and various methods of treating the plague. When he was graduated in 1525 at the age of twenty-two, he followed the custom of signaling his accomplishment by Latinizing his last name, thus adopting the form by which he is best known today.

Life's Work

Nostradamus (as he would henceforth be known) was now fully qualified to practice medicine, and did so for several years, but he undertook further study and teaching at the University of Montpellier, from which he received an advanced medical degree. He eventually apprenticed himself to eminent physician and scholar Jules-César Scaliger of Agen in 1532. Soon afterward he married, and the couple bore two children.

However, Nostradamus' family were to die of the plague in 1537 while he was traveling to treat other victims. He subsequently quarreled with the notoriously irascible Scaliger and was accused of making heretical remarks, events that were to lead to his quitting Agen. After ten more years of travel, practice, and teaching in France and Italy, Nostradamus met and married Anna Ponce Gemelle of Salon de Provence, a town not far from his birthplace. The couple eventually produced six children.

Nostradamus began compiling astrological almanacs—popular and highly salable publications—in 1550. He followed with two collections of medical and cosmetic formulas in 1552, *Traicté des fardemens* and *Vray et parfaict embellissement de la face*. These were combined in 1555 as *Excellent et moult utile Opuscule à touts necessaire qui desirent auoir cognoissance de plusiers exquises Receptes* ("excellent and very useful treatise necessary for all those who desire to have knowledge of several exquisite recipes"). Nostradamus also published *Orus Apollo, fils de Osiris, roi de Ægipte niliacque* ("the book of Orus Apollo, son of Osiris, king of Egypt"), a collection of maxims of dubious origin. More important was his translation from Galen, the classical Greek physician, *Paraphrase de C. Galen sur l'exortation de Menodote*, in 1557. This translation was criticized as inaccurate, although Nostradamus may have been working from an imperfect manuscript.

Nostradamus' most famous works, however, were his *Centuries*, originally published in French as *Les Prophéties de M. Michel Nostradamus*, a series of ambiguously worded prophecies. Unlike his almanacs, which forecast events one year at a time, these new works predicted events to the year 3797, although in no particular order. The first three series appeared in 1555; by 1558, seven more had been published, although their exact dates are not certain. Referred to as "centuries" because each ostensibly included one hundred verses, their total actually comes to somewhat less than one thousand. A complete collection seems to have been published in 1558, but no copies of this edition are known to survive.

Cast in quatrains (stanzas of four lines), the *Centuries* are notoriously obscure. They mix local allusions, references to France's unsettled political situation, and generalized predictions of disasters and calamities—as cynics have noted, always a safe bet. Although claims have been made for Nostradamus' skills as a poet, his work is oddly punctuated and his grammar and syntax wayward. It has never been clearly established what Nostradamus intended to express in these writings, nor whether profit was his motive in publishing them.

Public reaction to the *Centuries* varied, with the wide range of responses illustrating the intellectual and social ferment of the times. Wealthier (and arguably vainer) readers found the verses' daunting obscurity both a compliment and a challenge to their erudition. The masses, on the other hand, seem to have disliked and distrusted Nostradamus, partly because of his growing wealth and partly because of his presumed league with supernatural powers. Two other groups openly ridiculed him: those who dismissed astrology as nonsense and, ironically enough, astrologers themselves, who protested that the astrological content of the *Centuries* was defective. Despite—or, more likely, because of—such opposition, Nostradamus' works sold well and were routinely reprinted and pirated.

In any case, Nostradamus' fame spread quickly, and he soon found an important and suitably superstitious reader in the French court. So impressed was Catherine de Médicis, the queen of France, that she invited Nostradamus to Paris. He subsequently visited the city in mid-1556 (a trip of a month in those days) and was asked by the queen to cast the horoscopes of her sons. He seems to have remarked in guarded terms that her sons would be kings—a prediction both gratifying and not, after all, unlikely—and returned to Salon more famous still. When the French court visited southern France nearly a decade later, they made a point of visiting Nostradamus and bestowing official honors upon him.

Throughout the latter part of his life, Nostradamus seems to have increased his income by money-lending, which in at least one instance had long-lasting consequences. Approached by an entrepreneur anxious to link the Rhône and Durance rivers with a canal and thus irrigate the surrounding region, Nostradamus helped finance the project, which was completed in 1559.

Nostradamus has routinely been portrayed as both an astrologer and an orthodox Catholic, roles not regarded as necessarily contradictory during his lifetime. However, a cache of letters discovered by scholar Jean Dupèbe has revealed that Nostradamus' sympathies were Protestant—a fact that could easily have led to his execution in passionately Catholic France had the letters fallen into the wrong hands.

Nostradamus was described in his prime by an apprentice as being slightly shorter and stockier than average, heavily bearded, energetic, and short-tempered. The same source praised his quick intelligence, keen memory, and outstanding generosity, although the ascription of such qualities may strike modern readers as being somewhat generalized and formulaic. He is traditionally pictured wearing the four-cornered cap typical of a medical doctor of his time.

Nostradamus suffered from arthritis, gout, and dropsy toward the end of his life, and by 1566 was confined to his house, where he died in early July. One of his predictions had suggested that his body would be found near his bed and bench. Nostradamus had placed a bench in such a way as to help himself into bed, and he was indeed found sprawled near or upon it after death—another example of a prophecy both tantalizingly suggestive and yet far from unlikely.

Summary

Nostradamus lived during a period torn between two divergent systems of thought. One was the occult, which strove to interpret the world supernaturally and which was even then falling out of favor. The other was the scientific, which has increasingly but never totally predominated in Western civilization.

It was a time of enormous upheaval. France's political situation was chaotic, and Protestantism vied with Catholicism for supremacy throughout Europe. The plague ravaged southwestern Europe several times during Nostradamus' lifetime, and although he seems to have established a reputation as an effective plague doctor, he lost his own family to the dreadful disease. Thus his preoccupation as expressed throughout the *Centuries* with disaster of all kinds is easy to understand, and may have been fueled by fears for his own safety as a Protestant sympathizer.

Neither is it difficult to understand the keen interest that subsequent generations have taken in Nostradamus. Although Europe has experienced periods of stability since his day, the desire to know the future seems to be a constant. Scholars have demonstrated that Nostradamus filled his many prophecies with topical and contemporary references—a great many of them lost to modern readers—but the poet's allusive style lends his work mystery and ambiguity. Thanks to these characteristics, later readers have discovered "references" to such leaders and tyrants as Napoleon and Adolf Hitler and have been able to make persuasive arguments for their discoveries. The mirror that Nostradamus holds up to his readers is so clouded, it seems, that almost anything for which one looks may be found there.

Bibliography

Gould, Rupert T. "Nostradamus." In *Oddities: A Book of Unexplained Facts*. New York: Frederick A. Stokes, 1928. A noted but skeptical student of anomalies, Gould compares Nostradamus with other "prophets" and astrologers. He concludes that Nostradamus produced puzzlingly accurate prophecies in a few cases.

Laver, James. *Nostradamus: Or, The Future Foretold*. London: Collins, 1942. An influential historian of art and fashion, Laver summarizes Nostradamus' life and devotes most of his attention to the prophecies, which he argues are valid.

Leoni, Edgar. *Nostradamus: Life and Literature*. New York: Exposition Press, 1961. The most thorough study of the *Centuries* to have appeared in English, Leoni's book was originally submitted to Harvard as his B.A. thesis. It contains complete texts and translations of the *Centuries* and a survey of all pertinent literature. Reprinted as *Nostradamus and His Prophecies* in 1982.

LeVert, Liberté E. (pseudonym of Everett Bleiler). *The Prophecies and Enigmas of Nostradamus*. Glen Rock, N.J.: Firebell Books, 1979. An acknowledged expert in the field of speculative fiction, Bleiler argues that Nostradamus was a fascinating personality and a skillful, though not great, poet, and that the *Centuries* repay careful study for these reasons alone. Objective and evenhanded.

Randi, James. *The Mask of Nostradamus: The Prophecies of the World's Most Famous Seer*. Buffalo, N.Y.: Prometheus Books, 1993. Intensely skeptical and at times annoyingly sarcastic, Randi surveys Nostradamus' life, examines the early editions of his works, analyzes the mindset of those he calls the "Nostradamians," and places the *Centuries* within a framework of similar prophecies.

Shumaker, Wayne. *The Occult Sciences in the Renaissance: A Study in Intellectual Patterns*. Berkeley: University of California Press, 1972. Shumaker outlines five occult systems of thought and practice common to the Renaissance, including astrology. The works of Shumaker and Lynn Thorndike are the best sources for locating Nostradamus and his writings within the intellectual context of his time. Good bibliography.

Thorndike, Lynn. *A History of Magic and Experimental Science*. New York: Macmillan, 1923-1958. Thorndike's vast survey complements Shumaker's narrower study. Especially pertinent are Volumes 5 and 6 (*The Sixteenth Century*) and Volumes 7 and 8 (*The Seventeenth Century*), in all of which Nostradamus is discussed. Extensive bibliographical references.

Ward, Charles A. *Oracles of Nostradamus*. New York: C. Scribner and Welford, 1891. Ward opens with a biography of Nostradamus drawn from the first translator of the writer into English. Arguing that Nostradamus foresaw the future, he explicates the prophecies that he believes relate to subsequent events. A good example of the involved literature produced by believers in Nostradamus' occult powers. Frequently reprinted.

Wilson, Colin. "The World of the Kabbalists." In *The Occult: A History*. New York: Random House, 1971. This chapter from a standard work on the subject compares Nostradamus with two roughly contemporary figures in the occult tradition, Cornelius Agrippa and Philippus Aureolus Paracelsus.

Grove Koger

ODA NOBUNAGA

Born: June, 1534; Owari Province, Japan
Died: June 21, 1582; Kyōto, Japan
Areas of Achievement: The military, government, and politics
Contribution: The greatest soldier of his time, Oda started a process through diplomacy and war that put an end to political fragmentation in Japan and paved the way for the unique feudal system that governed Japan during the Tokugawa period (1602-1867).

Early Life

Oda Nobunaga lived during the Sengoku Jidai, or Age of the Country at War (sixteenth century), when both the shogun and the emperor were figureheads and a multitude of warlords, known as daimyo, held sway over the provinces. In addition to the secular warlords, there were militant Buddhist organizations with standing armies often allied to some of the daimyo. The country may thus be viewed as a patchwork quilt of power centers.

Oda was born in Nagoya Castle in Owari Province. His father, Oda Nobuhide, was a lesser official of the Shiba family serving in Owari. Nobunaga's original name was Kitsubōshi, but it was changed at age thirteen. While still a teenager, Nobunaga began to adopt eccentric dress and behavior, which earned for him the nicknames "Great Fool" and "Idiot." It has been suggested by some scholars that he chose to play the fool as part of a ploy for surviving the pending fratricidal struggle that ensued upon the death of his father in 1551, when Nobunaga was seventeen years old. Despite the fact that he learned to use firearms from a very early age and that much of his military reputation hinged on guns, he was alleged to have favored the spear.

Among those who served the young Nobunaga was his sandal-bearer Kinoshita Tokichiro, who is more popularly remembered as Toyotomi Hideyoshi and who became Nobunaga's most valuable military follower; ultimately Toyotomi took over the reins of power. From 1551 until 1560, Oda fought a series of campaigns to gain control of his home province of Owari. As many members of the Oda clan were reluctant to follow him because of his youth, he used a band of one thousand low-ranking soldiers to gain a foothold in the initial period of clan infighting. In 1556, Oda managed to displace a number of his rivals in Kiyosu, which became his first "capital." Oda's younger brother posed a challenge when he gained support from some of his father's retainers. The rivalry ended with the death of the younger brother. In the year 1560, Oda became daimyo of Owari Province.

Oda was quite adept at splitting his opponents' defensive efforts. For example, he would try to make an alliance with daimyo whose territory bordered on that of an enemy of Oda. In that manner, the enemy was then compelled to divide his forces to deal with an attack on two fronts. One of the most expedient tools for cementing diplomatic and political alliances was the arranged marriage. Marriages were often used to facilitate alliances, but they remained fragile agreements at the best of times. Oda himself married the daughter of Saitō Dōsan, the daimyo of neighboring Mino Province, which lay between Owari and the capital. In 1556, while Oda was still trying to consolidate his own power in Owari, Saitō was killed by his son Tatsuoki, Oda's brother-in-law. The murder gave Oda the pretext for invasion on the grounds of avenging his father-in-law's death.

Life's Work

During June of 1560, Oda had a chance to prove his mettle to other daimyo. Imagawa Yoshimoto, the daimyo of Suruga, Totomi, and Mikawa Provinces, was on his way through Owari to Kyōto at the head of a vast army of twenty-five thousand. Although Oda could muster no more than eighteen hundred men, he nevertheless decided to give battle. His opportunity came when his enemy was encamped in a narrow sheltered valley. Taking advantage of a violent rainstorm, he launched a surprise attack, routing his enemy in the furious but brief Battle of Okehazama.

In contrast, the operations against Saitō Tatsuoki, for control of Mino, dragged on for years. Nevertheless, by 1564, Oda had reduced Saitō's fortress of Inabayama, and, by 1567, at the age of thirty-three, he had finally defeated Saitō. He decided to use Inabayama as his own capital and renamed it Giōu. At the same time, he adopted the motto *Tenka fubu*, incorporating it into his personal seal. *Tenka fubu* is translated variously as "the realm covered in military glory," "the realm subjected to the military," or "rule the realm by force." Alarmed by Oda's increasing strength, his enemies banded together to form an anti-Oda league. To bolster his position, Oda decided to espouse the cause of Ashikaga Yoshiaki, heir to the Ashikaga shogunate. After defeating limited opposition, Oda entered Kyōto with Ashikaga on November 9, 1568. The latter was installed as the shogun, the last of the Ashikaga line. The stormy relationship between Oda and the shogun was to last five years.

Much of Oda's energy during the last ten years of his life was absorbed in attempts to suppress the military power of the Buddhists. Various Buddhist groups had evolved powers that paralleled those of the daimyo, and their temples became centers of political, economic, and military activity. First, Oda dealt with the Enryakuji, the temple of the Heian school on Mount Hiei, which had been labeled "The Indestructible Light of the [Buddhist] Law." In 1571, Oda's forces stormed their stronghold and the mountainside became a killing ground as men, women, and children were killed, and the temple complex put to the torch. Between three and four thousand priests were killed; the orgy of bloodletting lasted a week.

Then Oda turned his attention to the Shinshu Buddhists (also known as Ikkō), whose sectarian strongholds were strewn across the land. Their headquarters was located at Hongan-ji, an impregnable fortress situated on highly defensible terrain and ringed by more than fifty forts and outposts. In seeking to reduce the Hongan-ji, Oda found that he had first to dispose of the threat of the shogun and the powerful daimyo Takeda Shingen. In July, 1574, Oda laid siege to the Ikkō stronghold of Nagashima, located on an estuary of the Kiso-gawa. The captive population tried to surrender but to no avail. Oda ordered the fortress to be burned to the ground, and anyone who sought to escape was shot. It is estimated that as many as twenty thousand people died inside the burning fort.

The Battle of Nagashino, against Takeda Katsuyori (Shingen's son), in 1575, demonstrated Oda's military insight. The battle grew out of Oda's efforts to relieve the siege of Nagashino Castle in Mikawa Province. The Takeda forces had surrounded the castle, which was within the territory of Oda's trusted follower Tokugawa Ieyasu. Oda had a combined force of up to thirty-eight thousand troops, of which ten thousand were armed with match-locks. From those troops, three thousand of the best sharpshooters were selected for deployment. The Takeda clan relied on mounted samurai, which epitomized the art of the cavalry, but Oda denied the enemy a chance to utilize his horsemen effectively. Oda's men were arranged behind wooden barriers, or a palisade, which served to channel the Takeda attack. The lack of a single clear-cut objective meant that the horsemen had to thread their way through the deadly obstacles that concealed the sharpshooters. The peasant footsoldiers, or *ashigaru*, were trained to fire in ranks, which allowed a steady rate of fire as the weapons were fired and loaded in sequence.

Although the majority of sixteenth century Japanese wars were the domain of the samurai, there were also naval operations involved in Oda's rise to power. The siege of the Hongan-ji fortress was prolonged for years, because Kennyo Kōsa, who commanded the Hongan-ji force, had arranged for resupply to be provided by the Mōri clan, who shipped men and supplies from fsaka up the Inland Sea. Oda ordered his vassal daimyo to prepare a fleet to intercept the Mōri navy. The three-hundred-ship force assembled for Oda was outnumbered by more than two to one by the Mōri vessels. The destruction of Oda's fleet in August, 1576, compelled him to build a new navy. This naval reconstruction program resulted in the delivery of seven ironclads, complete with cannons, in July, 1578. The new navy sailed into Ōsaka and effectively cut Hongan-ji from its supply line when it destroyed the six-hundred-vessel Mōri fleet on December 4, 1578. Despite all the time and effort to reduce the Hongan-ji temple, the affair ended in a rather anticlimactic fashion, when the emperor negotiated a peace to end the Ishiyama Hongan-ji War in 1580.

Toyotomi, who had been assigned to pacify western Japan, had become bogged down, and he was compelled to request assistance from his superior. Oda dispatched the bulk of his troops to Toyotomi's aid. With a small band of only two to three hundred men, Oda took shelter at the Honnoji temple in Kyōto before joining the main force. While there, he was attacked by thirteen thousand troops led by one of his most trusted vassal daimyo, Akechi Mitsuhide. The death of Oda on June 21, 1582, at the hands of the renegade Akechi is known as the "Honnoji Incident." Toyotomi made peace with his opponents almost immediately, and thirteen days later he avenged his master's death by defeating Akechi at the Battle of Yamazaki. Akechi is referred to in some texts as the "Thirteen Day Shogun." Toyotomi eventually prevailed as the heir to Oda's efforts, and he also inherited the conquest of the Buddhist armies.

Summary

Despite Oda Nobunaga's reputation as a warlord, he did make contributions to other aspects of Japanese life and culture. Oda declared a number of free trade centers, which helped to break up the economic stagnation of a tradition-bound economy. He also sought to alter the role played by guilds in market centers. There was no blanket policy but rather a series of adjustments made to derive greater economic benefit. In some cases, guilds were abolished, while in other circumstances they were established. Oda also sought to modernize the economy by banning barter trade and replacing it with currency exchange to promote a true money economy. To prevent unfair practice, he also established currency regulations that set official standards for exchange and for the value of copper, silver, and gold. Oda took steps to simplify land ownership and encourage single-party control of estates. That went hand in hand with his implementation of cadastral surveys, which were designed to expedite administration, taxation, and assessment of land productivity.

Oda's policies had the effect of altering the role of Buddhism in Japanese society. The changes evoked include the elimination of military power, the limitation of economic power, and the subjugation of religious authorities to the central administration. Despite the tremendous amount of energy and resources expended against the Buddhists, Oda was not anti-Buddhist. Oda patronized certain temples, had Buddhist military allies, and had even relied on Zen priests as military advisers on occasion.

The Sengoku period was dominated by a warlord society, and even Oda's followers feuded. On occasion, there was treachery, and Oda had to execute some of those daimyo who sought to betray him. Yet such action was not particularly abnormal in a warlord society. The fact that Oda indulged in such behavior did not prove that he was more bloodthirsty than any other daimyo. Oda was responsible for the initial military operations that altered the balance of power and led to the centralization of power in Japan. Eventually, the process culminated in the Tokugawa shogunate, which lasted until the nineteenth century, a period of Japanese modernization known as the Meiji Restoration.

Bibliography

Hall, John Whitney. *Government and Local Power in Japan, 500 to 1700: A Study Based on the Bizen Province*. Princeton, N.J.: Princeton University Press, 1966. This study actually focuses on Bizen Province. Yet chapter 10 has relevant information on Oda. This book establishes Oda's efforts within the realm of the evolving political scene and is useful as a brief overview for those new to the subject.

Hall, John Whitney. Nagahara Keiji, and Kozo Yamamura, eds. *Japan Before Tokugawa: Political Consolidation in Economic Growth, 1500 to 1600*. Princeton, N.J. and Guildford: Princeton University Press, 1981. Although the entire volume is worthwhile from the standpoint of historical context, there are two specific chapters of interest: chapter 5, "The Political Posture of Oda Nobunaga and Toyotomi Hideyoshi." The work gives opportunity to focus on the nonmilitary side of the warlord.

McMullin, Neil. *Buddhism and the State in Sixteenth-Century Japan*. Princeton, N.J.: Princeton University Press, 1984. An advanced examination of the relationship between Oda and the Buddhists. Despite the omission of Oda's name from the title, the work is to a large degree centered on him. This volume used by far the greatest number of original documents from which to draw information. Central to the thesis is the concept that Oda does not deserve the heinous reputation he has received.

Perrin, Noel. *Giving Up the Gun: Japan's Reversion to the Sword, 1543-1879*. Boston: Godine, 1979. Primarily concerned with Japan's adoption and then later rejection of firearms. Although the chapters concerning Oda are few, this book is excellent for those seeking to understand the cultural implications of Oda's use of firearms. The author also used a number of historic Japanese texts for his research, so his bibliography is noteworthy for those studying the history of technology.

Reynolds, Mark E. "The Mighty Shogun." *Calliope* 3 (January/February, 1993): 29. This article discusses Nobunaga, Toyotomi Hideyoshi, and Tokugawa Leyasu; the rigid social class system of the period; Nobunaga's inherited position as 'daimyo'; and Hideyoshi as assistant general of Nobunaga.

Sansom, George. *A History of Japan, 1334-1615*. Stanford, Calif.: Stanford University Press, 1961. This remains one of the standards in the field. The chapters devoted to Oda are 17, 18, and 19. It remains the best single volume for those attempting to deal with this warlord on a one-time basis. The author, however, remains firm in his conviction that Oda was a brute. An effective balance between chronology and analysis.

Turnbull, Stephen. *Samurai Warriors*. London: Blandford Press, and New York: Sterling, 1987. Chapter 5 is the most relevant. As the title implies, this is a study of Oda the warlord. The emphasis is on military achievements, and the chronology of battles, combined with technical information, is useful. Although somewhat explicit, the illustrations serve to make this the most colorful of the works listed.

Randolf G. S. Cooper

JOHAN VAN OLDENBARNEVELT

Born: September 14, 1547; Amersfoort, Bishopric of Utrecht

Died: May 13, 1619; The Hague, United Provinces

Areas of Achievement: Government and statesmanship

Contribution: Oldenbarnevelt was the founder-lawgiver of the United Provinces of the Netherlands, whose statesmanship set the constitutional libertarian course that the modern Netherlands has followed. He was one of the greatest statesmen and diplomats in early modern Europe and in all Dutch history. Oldenbarnevelt served the United Provinces as Pensionary of Rotterdam and Advocate of Holland.

Early Life

Johan Gerrit Reyerszoon van Oldenbarnevelt was born on September 14, 1547, in Amersfoort, the second town in the Bishopric of Utrecht, one of seventeen Netherlandic provinces in the possession of the Habsburg dynasty; thus, he was born a subject of Emperor Charles V. Johan belonged to the regent class, the burgher-oligarchy and provincial nobility of the Netherlands who governed locally by hereditary right on town councils and provincial representative assemblies that were called the states, or estates. The regent class was jealous of its position and privileges, and defended them against both the populace below and the Habsburgs and their lieutenants, called stadtholders, above.

Johan inherited the traditions of both his father's family and his mother's, the Weedes, traditions of burgher-oligarchy and provincial nobility, but he would not proceed directly to eminence. His father appears to have suffered mental incapacitation, and therefore he never served on the Amersfoort town council let alone on a council of the States of Utrecht, Holland, and Zealand, which were in very close political relations, or for the States-General of the Netherlands, the representative assembly of all the provinces. Because of this family crisis, Johan did not go directly from the Amersfoort Latin school to university or on the customary grand tour of France, Germany, and Italy. Instead, in 1563, Johan served a sort of apprenticeship with a lawyer at The Hague. Between 1566 and 1570, Johan combined university study and grand tour and traveled through Louvain, Bourges, Cologne, Heidelberg, Italy, and perhaps Padua, studying arts and the law.

When Oldenbarnevelt returned to The Hague in 1570, the Duke of Alva for the Spanish Habsburgs tyrannized the Netherlands, which had begun the War of Independence in 1569. Oldenbarnevelt established law practice in the courts at The Hague, where he specialized in feudal law and law concerning dykes, drainage, and land reclamation. Because much of the Netherlands, the polders, had been reclaimed from the sea, and questions about title, responsibility for maintaining dykes, and similar matters were many, Oldenbarnevelt's practice grew quickly and soon became very lucrative. The Revolt of the Netherlands swept up Oldenbarnevelt. Though he had become a moderate Calvinist while a university student at Heidelberg, at The Hague he became a partisan of William the Silent.

War interrupted Oldenbarnevelt's legal practice and brought him onto the battlefield in the cause of Netherlandic independence. He saw action as a soldier in the disastrous attempt to relieve the Siege of Haarlem in 1573 and as supervisor of breaching the dykes in order to flood the polders for the celebrated relief of the Siege of Leiden in 1574. He also served William the Silent and his family in a legal capacity at this time.

In 1575, Oldenbarnevelt was married to Maria van Utrecht, the illegitimate daughter of a noble family, who had become a wealthy heiress when Oldenbarnevelt's legal shrewdness secured her legitimation. His courtship of Maria seems not to have been entirely mercenary, for they remained happily married for forty-three years, until his execution, and had two daughters, two sons, and grandchildren. Meanwhile Oldenbarnevelt had regained his rightful place in the regent class, demonstrated considerable legal ability, gained a fortune by his law practice and marriage, and made important friends in the House of Orange. Oldenbarnevelt was a moderate in religion and politics, a believer in liberty of conscience, and a constitutionalist who saw the necessity of balancing particularism and centralism in order to secure freedoms. He shared William the Silent's vision of an independent, united Netherlands.

Life's Work

In 1576, Oldenbarnevelt became Pensionary of Rotterdam, the legal representative and political secretary of the town, and entered the politics of Holland. Because Holland was the leading province, he thus became prominent in Netherlandic politics. Oldenbarnevelt promoted the Union of Utrecht of 1579 and the Act of Abjuration of 1581, which together became the declaration of independence and the constitution of the seven United Provinces of the Netherlands. Tensions between centralism and particularism remained, and at first the States-General thought to confer the sovereignty, which Spain had forfeited by its bloody tyranny, on the Duke of Anjou and then the Earl of Leicester, an action that would have made the United Provinces a satellite of France or England. Oldenbarnevelt led the States of Holland in opposition to such centralizing policies and in 1585 secured the appointment of Maurice of Nassau, son of William the Silent, who had been assassinated in 1584, as stadtholder and captain general. So long as the war against Spain continued, the advocate and the stadtholder collaborated in harmony—Oldenbarnevelt strengthened the United Provinces politically and diplomatically, and supported Maurice with revenue and political cooperation, and Maurice won military victories. Oldenbarnevelt led the United Provinces during the celebrated "Ten Years" (1588-1598), when the provinces achieved full self-government, balancing centralism among the States-General, the stadtholder and captain-general, and the councils, with particularism in the provincial states and the town councils, thus transforming the loose defensive alliance of seven sovereign provinces into the United Provinces of the Netherlands. It was in this that Oldenbarnevelt's leadership proved decisive. He scored the diplomatic triumph of the Triple Alliance in 1596 with France and England against Spain and thus gained international recognition of the independent United Provinces.

In 1598, France made peace with Spain, in 1604 England did the same, so in 1605 Oldenbarnevelt decided to make peace. Spain was exhausted and wanted peace, and Oldenbarnevelt knew that a peace treaty would mean at least de facto recognition by Spain and the Spanish Netherlands (the ten provinces not in the Union of Utrecht) of the independence of the United Provinces. Oldenbarnevelt's peace policy was opposed by Maurice and by his war party, which distrusted Spain's intentions, by the orthodox Calvinists who saw the war in apocalyptic terms, and by commercial interests who wanted economically to penetrate the West Indies. Oldenbarnevelt himself had an energetic commercial policy. He had in 1602 chartered the Dutch East India Company, but he was reluctant to charter a Dutch West India Company, which would jeopardize the peace with Spain. In the face of such opposition to make peace with Spain, Oldenbarnevelt characteristically compromised and negotiated the Twelve Years' Truce. Yet the truce was disturbed by religious conflict within the United Provinces. This conflict had originated in an academic theological debate between two professors at the University of Leiden, the strict Calvinist Franciscus Gomarus and the revisionist Jacob Arminius, over the Calvinist doctrine of predestination. The orthodox Calvinist Gomarists regarded the moderate Arminians, whom Oldenbarnevelt favored, as religious traitors worse than papists.

In 1617, Maurice declared for the Gomarists and rallied all parties that opposed Oldenbarnevelt over the Twelve Years' Truce. Oldenbarnevelt responded with the Sharp Resolution of August 4, 1617, which attempted to remove the military in Holland from the stadtholder and captain-general and to place it under control of the States of Holland and towns of the province. Maurice mobilized the other six provinces in the union against Holland and moved quickly and decisively. On August 28, 1618, the States-General conferred dictatorial powers on Maurice, and on August 29, 1618, Maurice ordered the arrest of Oldenbarnevelt and a few of his followers. In February, 1619, the States-General created an extraordinary tribunal to try Oldenbarnevelt and three codefendants, who included his protégé the great jurist and political philosopher Hugo Grotius.

Oldenbarnevelt's trial lasted from November, 1618, to May, 1619, but he was given neither writing materials nor access to books, documents, witnesses, or counsel. Yet he conducted an eloquent and dignified defense. The judges that were picked were his personal and political enemies, and the tribunal found Oldenbarnevelt guilty of vaguely defined capital crimes, despite his age and long service to the United Provinces. From the scaffold on May 13, 1619, Oldenbarnevelt addressed the crowd, "Men, do not think me a traitor; I have acted honestly and religiously, like a good patriot, and as such I die." After the headsman had done his work, the crowd pressed forward and, for relics of the martyred Oldenbarnevelt, dipped handkerchiefs in his blood.

Summary

Johan van Oldenbarnevelt founded the United Provinces of the Netherlands and its traditions of constitutionalism and libertarianism. While William the Silent and his sons won Dutch independence on the battlefields of the Eight Years' War

against Spain, Oldenbarnevelt preserved independence through lawgiving, statesmanship, and diplomacy. He spent his long life serving his country, and he died an old man beheaded in 1619 by a Dutch special tribunal, a martyr for his vision of Dutch republican liberty. As Pensionary of Rotterdam and Advocate of Holland, Oldenbarnevelt was architect of the United Provinces of the Netherlands, which lasted until 1795, and the Dutch libertarianism which has thrived since. His leadership fostered moderation, freedom, enterprise, toleration, peace, and prosperity, and began the great cultural florescence of the United Provinces during the seventeenth century. The United Provinces became a refuge for intellectual freedom in an age of persecution. Oldenbarnevelt's diplomatic triumphs were the Triple Alliance with France and England in 1596 and the Twelve Years' Truce with Spain and the Spanish Netherlands, which gave the new United Provinces both a respite from war and international recognition. Ironically, it was Oldenbarnevelt's peace policy and religious moderation that led to his fall in 1618, and in 1619 his Dutch political enemies sentenced him to execution on very vague and unfounded charges of official misconduct and treason. On the scaffold at The Hague, the venerable statesman died as he had lived—brave and proud for the cause of liberty.

Bibliography

Geyl, Pieter. *History of the Low Countries: Episodes and Problems*. London: Macmillan, and New York: St. Martin's Press, 1964. An important collection of essays, several of which supply very useful background on Oldenbarnevelt; contentious in tone.

———. *The Revolt of the Netherlands, 1555-1609*. London: Williams and Norgate, 1932; New York: Barnes and Noble, 1958. An admirably clear and cogent narrative, somewhat tendentious about the historical contingency of the divided Netherlands and hence inevitably ambivalent about Oldenbarnevelt's founding of the United Provinces.

Motley, John Lothrop. *The Life and Death of John of Barneveld*. 2 vols. New York and London: Harper, 1874. A classic history, despite its strong Protestant and liberal bias, that is still well worth reading for its drama, eloquence, and insights into Oldenbarnevelt.

Rowen, Herbert H., ed. *The Low Countries in Early Modern Times*. London: Macmillan, and New York: Harper, 1972. Includes well-selected key documents that are edited, translated, and commented upon judiciously. Sections 4 and 6 present such texts as the Union of Utrecht, the Act of Abjuration, the Treaty of the Twelve Years' Truce, and several of Oldenbarnevelt's letters.

Tex, Jan den. *Oldenbarnevelt*. Translated by R. B. Powell. 2 vols. Cambridge: Cambridge University Press, 1973. The standard scholarly biography, this work is appreciative of the great statesman but not uncritically so. Better on the public than on the private man. The book makes a peculiar defense of the special court that condemned Oldenbarnevelt.

Terence R. Murphy

PACHACUTI

Born: c. 1391; probably Cuzco, Peru
Died: 1471; near Cuzco, Peru
Areas of Achievement: Government and warfare
Contribution: Pachacuti, through personal courage, brilliant political sense, and administrative genius, was primarily responsible for the creation of the Inca Empire in its final form.

Early Life

Pachacuti (Cusi Inca Yupanqui), the ninth emperor of the Inca in a direct line from the perhaps legendary Manco Capac, who founded the dynasty about the year 1200, was, with his son Topa Inca Yupanqui and his grandson Huayna Capac, one of the three greatest Inca emperors. Since he was said to have been about eighty years of age when he died in 1471, he presumably was born in Cuzco, the capital, about 1391, the son of Viracocha Inca and Runtu Coya. As the son of the emperor, Pachacuti was thoroughly educated in military science and the art of administration, but almost nothing is known about his life before the dramatic events of 1437-1438 brought him to the throne.

The Inca had no written historical records, and what is known of their origins is to be found in chronicles written after the Spanish Conquest. These were based on the memory of native historians, however, who used the *quipu*, knotted ropes which served as memory devices, to recall the events of Inca history. Certainly from the beginnings of Pachacuti's reign the chronicles must be considered generally reliable, though it is possible that he may have dictated an account of his accession in order to justify the legitimacy of his claim to the throne.

During the reign of Viracocha, the Inca Empire, an area from the country north of Cuzco to the shores of Lake Titicaca, was threatened by various tribes on its borders to the north and west. In 1437, the Chanca, a warrior tribe in the Apurimac Valley northwest of Cuzco, defeated the Quechua, thus upsetting the balance of power which the Inca had maintained among their enemies, and pushed through the Quechua country to the Inca frontier. Viracocha, apparently assuming that Cuzco could not be held, fled the city, while Pachacuti became the leader of a cabal which was determined to defend Cuzco and to put Pachacuti on the throne. He organized the city's defenses, and, even though the Chanca actually broke into the city itself, he drove them out. In one account he is described as wearing a lionskin as he personally led his troops in battle. Later he won a great victory over the Chanca at their stronghold of Ichupampa, west of Cuzco, virtually destroying them as a tribe, and in 1438 he became emperor. At this time, by one account, his father gave him the name Pachacuti, translated variously as "cataclysm" or "Earth upside down," which suggests that even at that time he was determined to change the Inca Empire completely.

Life's Work

The chronicles do not agree on the exact nature of Pachacuti's claim to the throne. According to some, he was Viracocha's eldest son and thus his legitimate heir but was, in effect, disinherited by his father on behalf of Inca Urcon, a younger brother. By another account he was a younger son, and when Viracocha resigned the throne to Inca Urcon the latter made Pachacuti governor of Cuzco while he retired to the enjoyment of his vices. What is certain is that Pachacuti, after his victory in the Chanca War, made Viracocha his virtual prisoner, was given his blessing, and, by methods which are not clear, brought about the death of Inca Urcon. Viracocha died soon after.

Pachacuti spent the first three years of his reign in Cuzco, consolidating power and creating an entirely new leadership; then, in 1441, he embarked on a three-year tour of inspection of the empire and the reconquest of the territory of those tribes which had rebelled against Inca rule during the Chanca incursion. Only then did he undertake the military campaigns which made him the most remarkable conqueror of any American Indian leader.

His first campaign, in 1444, took him into the Urupampa Valley, in an area now called Vilcapampa, north of Cuzco, and then west into Vilcas. Later he conquered the Huanca tribe in Huanmanca (the modern departments of Junín and Huancavelica) and the provinces of Tarma, Pumpu, Yauyu, and Huarochiri. When Hastu Huaraca, the defeated Chanca leader, organized opposition to the Inca in the Apurimac Valley, Pachacuti again defeated him in battle and achieved his submission and a grant of warriors for the Inca army. Later he won a great victory at Corampa, and in a campaign against the Soras, which culminated in a successful two-year siege of Challomarca, their capital, he achieved virtual control of all central Peru south of Ecuador.

He then sent his Chanca auxiliaries south into Collao, followed with his main army, defeated the Canas at Ayavire, at the end of Lake Titicaca, and in a decisive battle at Pucara eliminated Collao power. This military victory was probably in 1450.

Pachacuti's firm control of the imperial administration and of the armies by which it was maintained is indicated by the fact that when he dispatched his general Capac Yapanqui into the province of Chucurpu and then learned that Capac had exceeded his orders and had advanced farther into the lands beyond Chucurpu, he ordered him back to Cuzco and had him executed for disobedience, even though the expedition had added more land to the empire than he had anticipated.

By 1457, Pachacuti had conquered all the territory between the coastal range of Peru and the valley of the Marañón. In 1463, he gave command of the army to his son (and heir), Topa Inca. This force of forty thousand men began in 1464 the subjugation of Chimor, an advanced civilization on the northern Peruvian coast which was, in a sense, Greece to Cuzco's Rome. By 1470, with the fall of the Chimor capital of Chanchan (modern-day Trujillo), this conquest was complete. Other commanders under Pachacuti's orders conquered the territory beyond Lake Titicaca and as far south as the Atacama Desert in northern Chile. In all, these conquests created an empire of sixteen million people, extending from Ecuador to northern Chile and Bolivia.

If Pachacuti were only a conqueror he would be less remarkable. In fact, his supreme achievement was the creation of a political structure which survived with great stability until the civil war which broke out over the question of imperial succession shortly before the arrival of the Spanish. It was Pachacuti who inaugurated the system of populating conquered lands with colonists who eventually intermarried with the local population and gave them identity as Inca, and he created the *mitimaes* system, by which dissident elements in a conquered territory would be moved as colonists to another region where Inca rule had been accepted. He also instituted a system of runners to carry royal messages, which gave the empire the kind of coherence that only rapid communication could make possible.

In religious matters, Pachacuti simplified and redefined the rites of the Incas and incorporated the deities of conquered peoples into the Inca pantheon. Above all, he was determined to make each conquered nation an organic part of a larger whole. Often after conquering a nation he would take its king to Cuzco, bestow upon him lavish gifts and hospitality, and then send him home to rule as his proconsul. He also completely reorganized the imperial school in Cuzco, where not only the sons of the Inca caste but also those of conquered lords studied economics, government, military science, the arts and sciences of the Inca, and Quechua, the language of the empire.

Many of the engineering achievements of Pachacuti are still seen in Peru. In 1440, he began the complete rebuilding of Cuzco, and at about the same time the great fortress of Sacsahuaman, the "house of the sun" north of the city, was begun by twenty thousand laborers, a monument so massive that it was not completed until 1508, during the reign of his grandson. Though scholars no longer agree whether Pachacuti ordered the construction of Machu Picchu, it is probable that he was responsible for its later development as a bastion of Inca defense. He also encouraged terracing to take advantage of the steep Andean terrain for agriculture and is credited with the development of the greatest Inca irrigation systems.

When Topa Inca returned from his conquest of Chimor and Ecuador, Pachacuti partially resigned the throne to him, serving until his death in 1471 as a kind of coregent. This arrangement ensured a smooth transfer of power and enabled Topa to embark on his further conquests when he became emperor, though some accounts suggest that as a result of Pachacuti's declining physical powers, he had no choice but to share power with his son.

Summary

Pachacuti was not only a valiant warrior but also a statesman with a clear understanding of the requirements of imperial administration. The laws and the political structure which he created survived almost a century until his descendants, forgetting the need for imperial unity in their quarrels over the succession to the throne, weakened the empire at precisely the moment that the soldiers of Pizarro landed on the Peruvian coast in 1532. It seems unlikely, in fact, that the Spanish conquest of Peru would have been possible, at least with Pizarro's small force, if it had been attempted when Pachacuti was at the height of his power.

Though Pachacuti's wars with those immediate neighbors who had conspired against the Inca were fought to the death and often culminated in massacre, his conquests through the rest of his empire were followed by liberal treatment of his subjects. For Pachacuti, war was a necessary evil, the last application of political methods to achieve Inca hegemony and the order which, under his leadership, accompanied it. If war in the reigns of his predecessors was a means of personal aggrandizement not unlike hunting or sport, it was for Pachacuti the work of trained professionals and an instrument of public policy. His armies fought aggressively, but their success was in large part a result of Pachacuti's attention to logistic detail. When their victories had been achieved, he directed their energies to the administration of the conquered territory and the creation of those public works that would make them more productive.

For these reasons, Pachacuti must be considered not only the greatest conqueror among all American Indian leaders but also the most brilliant ruler.

Bibliography

Brundage, Burr Cartwright. *Empire of the Inca.* Norman: University of Oklahoma Press, 1963. A thorough discussion of Inca civilization from its origins until the arrival of the Spanish, this study synthesizes all the chronicles and scholarship to provide the most probable account of these events.

Cieza de León, Pedro de. *The Incas.* Edited and translated by Harriet de Onis. Norman: University of Oklahoma Press, 1959. Cieza's account, first published in 1553, is the most objective early account of the Incas. This objectivity and annotations by Victor Wolfgang von Hagen make it a basic text for understanding Inca history.

Cobo, Bernabé. *History of the Inca Empire.* Edited and translated by Roland Hamilton. Austin: University of Texas Press, 1979. Cobo was a Jesuit priest who went to Peru in 1599 as a missionary to the Indians. Most of his manuscript was lost; what remained, published in 1653, was largely concerned with pre-Columbian America. It is based on Cobo's archival research in Mexico City and Lima and on interviews with descendants of the Inca royal dynasty.

Garcilaso de la Vega. *Royal Commentaries of the Incas and General History of Peru.* Translated by Harold V. Livermore. 2 vols. Austin: University of Texas Press, 1966. Complete in 1604 and first published in 1609 as *Primera parte de los comentarios reales*, Garcilaso's history of Peru cannot be ignored but must be used with caution and corrected by reference to Cobo and Cieza de León.

Hyams, Edward, and George Ordish. *The Last of the Incas.* London: Longman, and New York: Simon and Schuster, 1963. This work is primarily concerned with the Spanish conquest of Peru and the events which immediately preceded it, but its second chapter is a thorough discussion of Inca civilization and the events of the reign of Pachacuti.

Means, Philip Ainsworth. *Ancient Civilizations of the Andes.* London and New York: Scribner, 1931. A thorough study of all the cultures and civilizations of Peru from the earliest prehistoric times to the Spanish Conquest. Means devotes two chapters to Inca history which are valuable, though partially superseded by later scholarship.

Rowe, John Howland. "Inca Culture at the Time of the Spanish Conquest." In *Handbook of South American Indians*, edited by Julian H. Steward, vol. 2. Washington, D.C.: Government Printing Office, 1949-1959. Rowe's seven-volume study is primarily concerned with social and cultural aspects of Inca civilization, but it is important for the dating of pre-Conquest events generally accepted by later scholars.

Robert L. Berner

ANDREA PALLADIO
Andrea di Pietro della Gondola

Born: November 30, 1508; Padua, Republic of Venice

Died: August, 1580; Vicenza, Republic of Venice

Area of Achievement: Architecture

Contribution: Palladio was the first great professional architect and one of the most influential the world has ever known. Possibly the most imitated architect in history, he was responsible for fusing classical proportions and harmony with Renaissance exuberance, thus creating an architectural manner that has endured into the twentieth century.

Early Life

Andrea Palladio was born in Padua to Piero, a miller, and donna Marta, called "the cripple." Very little is known of his early years; the record of his activities begins with his apprenticeship in 1521 to a stone carver in the local trade corporation of bricklayers and stonemasons. His master at the corporation of Mount Berico has been identified as Bartolomeo Cavazza de Sossano, the artist responsible for the altar in the Church of Santa Maria dei Carmini in Padua. In 1523, Andrea ran away to Vicenza, where he was followed by Cavazza, who forced him to return to Padua to serve out the rest of his apprenticeship. A year later, the sixteen-year-old Andrea broke his bond and returned to Vicenza, where for the next fourteen years he was first apprentice and then assistant to two sculptors, Giovanni da Porlezza and Girolamo Pittoni, both of the Pedemuro workshop, who had a near-monopoly on commissions, both private and public, to create many of Vicenza's monuments and ornamental sculptures in the then-popular mannerist style. Records show that in 1534 Andrea married Allegradonna, the daughter of a carpenter; the union produced five children. Working with the Pedemuro masters gave Andrea a thorough grounding in the techniques of stonework and sculpture, and he might have remained a craftsman for the rest of his life had he not, at age thirty, met Count Gian Giorgio Trissino.

Trissino hired the young stonecarver to work on a new loggia and a few additions he had designed for his Villa Cricoli on the outskirts of Vicenza. Trissino took Andrea under his wing, housing and educating him with a group of young aristocrats who studied mathematics, philosophy, music, and classical literature. During this period, Andrea was given the appropriately classical name of Palladio by Trissino. Under Trissino's tutelage, the newly christened Palladio embarked on a far-reaching study of architecture—especially that of Vitruvius—and engineering, as well as ancient topography.

Palladio may have joined Trissino on an extended stay in Padua in the late 1530's; perhaps it was then that Palladio encountered the work of Alvise Cornaro, whose influence is evident in Palladio's elegantly simple and clear writing style and in the economy of ornamentation in his designs. In 1541 and in 1545, Palladio visited Rome with Trissino. During these journeys, Palladio acquired a firsthand knowledge of classical architecture by sketching and measuring the ancient buildings—baths, arches, bridges, temples—whose remains could be seen above ground, and by studying and copying from the sketchbooks of other architects.

Shortly after Palladio returned to Vicenza, he won a commission to refurbish the Palazzo della Ragione, a vast Gothic structure that served as the meeting hall of Vicenza's Council of the Four Hundred. Whatever the council's reasons, their choice of Palladio in 1549 brought him instant recognition, and thereafter he was kept busy with commissions for palaces, villas, and churches.

Trissino died in 1550—a loss not only to Palladio but also to Vicenza's intellectual and artistic community—but by then Palladio was firmly established as an architect with several villas and public buildings under commission. Furthermore, in 1554 he published the results of his study tours in *L'antichità di Roma* (the antiquities of Rome), a small but reliable guidebook to the ancient ruins of Rome which became the standard guidebook to Roman antiquities for two centuries.

Life's Work

Ever an active student of architecture, Palladio published his ideas and theories in several works issued throughout his career. In 1556, he collaborated with Daniele Barbaro in an edition of Vitruvius. Palladio's greatest piece of writing, *I quattro libri dell'architettura* (1570), was published late in his career, after he had devoted two decades to design and building. Using many drawings of his own buildings to exemplify the principles of design to which he tried to adhere, Palladio created an architectural pattern book that dictated building practice throughout Western civilization for four centuries. His last book, *I commentari di C. Givlio Cesare* (1575), is an edition of Julius Caesar's *Commentaries*, with illustrations by Palladio's sons Leonida and Orazio.

Palladio's architectural legacy can be classified loosely into three categories: villas, palaces and public buildings, and ecclesiastical buildings. Contrary to a popular misconception, there is no such thing as a typical Palladian villa. Palladio was far too innovative an architect to rely on one standard design, and his villas display the variety and inventiveness of his work. All the villas, however, share, as James Ackerman writes, "a common conception of architectural harmony and composition" and a fusion of the practical and the ornamental, the commonplace and the luxurious, modernity and antiquity. Unlike the typical villas of the day, Palladio's villas were nearly all built for gentlemen farmers, men of wealth, culture, and sophistication. In the mid-sixteenth century, many of the great families moved inland to their vast estates to supervise their new ventures. These families needed homes for themselves and for their workers, shelter for their livestock, and storage for their crops. Palladio, already committed to the blending of the utilitarian and the majestic, was the perfect architect to create the new style which had no single architectural ancestry but which would integrate the traditional, the classical, and the innovative.

Palladio believed in a hierarchy of functions in design and architecture, and in one of his most famous metaphors he compared a well-designed building to the human body: In both, the noble and beautiful parts are exposed and the unattractive but essential portions are hidden. Accordingly, his villas are completely functional structures or structural complexes, created both to accommodate the day-to-day business of a large agricultural venture and to disguise that practicality with a grand design drawn from classical architecture. In another departure from common practice, these villas were situated not in walled gardens but central to the activities of the great estates. Palladio's signature element, which appeared on all the villas except Sarego (c. 1568-1569), is a pedimented temple front that appears in some buildings as a porch, in others as a relief. Although this feature appeared in classical architecture only on religious structures, Palladio incorporated it into nearly all of his domestic buildings.

None of the palaces for which Palladio created designs was completed; in some cases, only the façades and entrances were built. Only one public building was ever completed. The Veneto region in the mid-sixteenth century was subject to much financial and political instability which hampered the building of the grand structures envisioned by Palladio's patrons in Vicenza. Modern knowledge of Palladio's intentions comes from the finished façades and sections and from the detailed illustrations of specific designs in *I quattro libri dell'architettura*. Produced between about 1540 and the early 1570's—with a break of a few years in the late 1560's—the palace designs share with the villas Palladio's distinctive combination of mannerist elements with classical proportion and repose; indeed, four of the palace designs in *I quattro libri dell'architettura*, of which only the Palazzo Antonini (c. 1556) was even partially built, resemble nothing so much as Palladian villas adapted to narrow city building sites and already crowded streets.

While Palladio's villas and palaces are all in the Veneto region, his churches are all in Venice, in which he was increasingly spending much of his time. It is clear that he traveled often in the 1560's: to Turin, to Provence, to Florence, where he became a member of the Academy of Design, and to Venice, where he met Giorgio Vasari, who became his friend. In 1568, Palladio was so busy that he was forced to decline an invitation to visit the Imperial Court of Vienna.

In his fifties by the time he began to design churches, Palladio believed strongly that church architecture should both glorify God and ornament the city. His commissions—private or civic or monastic, rather than from the Church—reflected his belief that religious architecture, like secular design, should surpass the achievement of earlier builders. Palladio, as well as two contemporaries, Galeazzo Alessi and Giacomo Barozzi da Vignola, developed a church design that took into account both the needs of the liturgical revival and the demands of architectural unity. This new ecclesiastical space combined a substantial nave with large side chapels, all joined but not restricted or blocked by a majestic central space that rose to a dome.

In 1558, Palladio's first ecclesiastical commission (which does not survive) was a design for the façade of San Pietro di Castello in Venice. During the next decade, he worked on a cloister for Santa

Maria della Carita; the refectory and cloister and then the Church of San Giorgio Maggiore; and the façade of San Francesco della Vigna, all in Venice. In the decade before his death, Palladio produced four more designs: the Zitelle church (c. 1570) in Venice, considerably altered by the architects who finished it after Palladio's death; a chapel for the Villa Valmarana in Vicenza (c. 1576); Il Redentore in Venice (c. 1576-1577); and the Tempietto at the Villa Maser (c. 1579-1580). In the Tempietto, Palladio found his opportunity to design a central-plan church, modeled on his ideas for reconstructing the Pantheon in a modern idiom. The Tempietto retains the symbolic cross structure, which is integrated with a unified interior space enclosed by wall masses that support a dome. Palladio's last project was the Teatro Olimpico in Vicenza. Commissioned by the members of the Accademia Olimpica for their regular and elaborate stage performances, the theater is an interpretive reconstruction of an ancient Roman theater in France. Palladio did not live to see the theater completed, although most of the construction was done by the time he died in August, 1580.

Summary

Appealing more to austere Protestant sensibilities than to Catholic preferences, which favored the exuberance of the Baroque, the restrained Palladian style enjoyed its greatest popularity in the northern European cultural centers. Andrea Palladio's ideas and designs first traveled to England through the work of Inigo Jones in the seventeenth century, although the true flowering of the Palladian style had to wait for the eighteenth century and Lord Burlington, who was responsible for the popularization of Palladianism in England. The style spread to Ireland and then to the American Colonies, where the simple lines and harmonic proportions of Palladianism dominated in both domestic and public architecture. Not until the classical and Gothic revivals of the nineteenth century would the Palladian style be challenged, but its popularity remained high even in the twentieth century.

Palladianism has been interpreted variously. To some it means restraint and simplicity; to others it signals correct proportions and cool detachment; to the great majority of people it denotes a pediment plus a portico on a public building. Basically, the Palladian style is symmetrical, harmonically proportioned, majestic, and based on reason. At the same time, it is classical in its form and in its use of ornamentation. It conforms to Palladio's goals of composition: hierarchy, or the movement of subordinate elements to a dominant focal point; integration of part to part, and part to the whole; coordination between the exterior design and interior structure; and consistency of proportion.

Bibliography

Ackerman, James S. *Palladio*. London amd Baltimore: Penguin, 1966. A good general study detailing both Palladio's uniqueness and his borrowings from the past and from his contemporaries. Describes his education, his era, and the physical and cultural environment in which he worked. Provides brief critical introductions to Palladio's major buildings. The text is copiously illustrated with both photographs and line drawings.

Bock, Gordon. "Andrea Palladio." *Old House Journal* 22 (January/February, 1994): 18. Bock focuses on Palladio, detailing his education, his influence on Roman architecture, and his villa, palace, and church designs.

Boucher, Bruce. *Andrea Palladio: The Architect in His Time*. Rev. ed. New York: Abbeville Press,

1998. Boucher combines analysis of Palladio's works within the context of the historical, social, and cultural events of his time. The book includes color photographs of structures still standing, illustrations of plans and drawings, and a chronology of major events.

Constant, Caroline. *The Palladio Guide*. Princeton, N.J.: Princeton Architectural Press, 1985; London: Architectural Press, 1987. Although technically belonging to the genre of the architectural guidebook, this volume is a presentation of the theory that Palladio's buildings share an integral relationship with and a spatial attitude to the site. Begins with a brief biography and introduction, followed by a chronological listing of the buildings. The body of the book is a series of articles, each devoted to a single villa and arranged chronologically. Features a selected bibliography and maps. Probably too confusing to be used as a guidebook, but the interpretive commentary is most informative.

Guinness, Desmond, and Julius Torusdale Sadler, Jr. *Palladio: A Western Progress*. New York: Viking Press, 1976; as *The Palladian Style in England, Ireland, and America*, London: Thames and Hudson, 1976. A brief account of Palladio's life and achievement, followed by several chapters describing the influence of Palladianism on architecture in England, Ireland, North America, and the West Indies. Very informative; profusely illustrated, primarily with photographs.

Kaufmann, Emil. *Architecture in the Age of Reason: Baroque and Post-Baroque in England, Italy, and France*. Cambridge, Mass.: Harvard University Press, 1955. The first chapter, "English Baroque and English Palladianism," offers a good introduction to Palladio's principles of design and their application in the architecture of eighteenth century England. An extensive bibliography is provided for each chapter.

Palladio, Andrea. *The Four Books of Architecture*. Translated by Robert Tavernor and Richard Schofield. Cambridge, Mass.: MIT Press, 1997. Of even greater significance than Palladio's buildings is his treatise *I quattro libri dell'architettura* (*The Four Books on Architecture*); it was the most successful architectural treatise of the Renaissance and is one of the two or three most important books in the literature of architecture. First published in Italian in 1570, it has been translated into every major Western language. This is the first English translation of Palladio in more than 250 years, making it the only translation available in modern English.

Puppi, Lionello. *Andrea Palladio*. London: Phaidon Press, and Boston: New York Graphic Society, 1975. An extensive, exhaustive, and profusely illustrated critical study of Palladio's life and work. The detailed and well-documented catalog of works makes up half of the volume and provides a thorough introduction to Palladio's achievement. An excellent bibliography includes works by Palladio and commentators on his work and covers material from the sixteenth century to the 1970's.

Wittkower, Rudolf. *Architectural Principles in the Age of Humanism*. 4th ed. London: Academy, and New York: St. Martin's Press, 1988. An essential work that laid the foundations of modern Palladian criticism. Discusses Palladio's cultural development, analyzes style in the villas and the ecclesiastical buildings, and provides analyses of Palladian principles.

Edelma Huntley

PARACELSUS
Philippus Aureolus Theophrastus Bombast von Hohenheim

Born: November 11 or December 17, 1493; Einsiedeln, Swiss Confederation

Died: September 24, 1541; Salzburg, Austria

Areas of Achievement: Biochemistry, chemistry, medicine, and philosophy

Contribution: Paracelsus has been hailed as the founder of biochemistry. He also made major contributions to the development of modern chemistry and made revolutionary changes in Renaissance medical theory and practice.

Early Life

Philippus Aureolus Theophrastus Bombast von Hohenheim, known to the world as Paracelsus, was born in 1493 in the village of Einsiedeln, Swiss Confederation. He was the only son of a physician, Wilhelm of Hohenheim, who came from a noble Swabian family whose original seat was at Hohenheim, near Stuttgart in northern Germany. Paracelsus' mother, Els Ochsner, came from a family of peasants living on land belonging to the local Benedictine Abbey, and she worked as a nurse's aid. Because his illegitimate father had no legal right to the family heritage, Paracelsus was reared in poverty. Yet he said that his home environment was quiet and peaceful, although his mother apparently suffered from manic depression and committed suicide when he was nine.

Following his wife's death, Wilhelm and his son moved to Villach, Austria. Paracelsus probably attended the mining school of the Fuggers at nearby Hutenberg, where his father was a tutor. In Paracelsus' writings, he pays generous tribute to his father, who played a large part in his son's education. Paracelsus also states that he learned from experts, including bishops and an abbot. It is therefore likely that he received what was considered to be a universal education, including cabalistic, alchemical, and magical traditions, as well as orthodox religion and philosophy. It is clear, however, that Paracelsus neglected many of the formal aspects of his education. His Latin was not good, and he never acquired elegance in either speech or writing.

In 1507, at the age of fourteen, Paracelsus became a traveling student, attending universities in Germany, Italy, France, and Spain. He studied for a bachelor's degree at Vienna between 1509 and 1511, and between 1513 and 1516 he traveled and studied medicine in Italy, notably at Ferrara. Yet he was a restless, pugnacious, and rebellious student, and he soon found himself completely dissatisfied with the education that was offered by the universities he attended. From 1517 to 1524, he again traveled extensively throughout Europe. He was employed as a military surgeon in Venice and was involved in three wars of the period. He traveled to Moscow when the Grand Duke Basil invited Western physicians and Humanists to the Russian court, accompanied a Tatar prince on a diplomatic mission to Constantinople, and visited the Holy Land and Alexandria. In all of his journeys, Paracelsus was building the knowledge that would enable him to revolutionize many aspects of Renaissance medicine.

Life's Work

With his fame spreading rapidly and many of his cures being regarded as miraculous, Paracelsus reached Salzburg in 1524. Yet the following year he was arrested for siding with the peasants in the Peasants' War of 1524-1526 and was forced to flee. In 1526, he arrived in Strasbourg and was entered in the city register as a surgeon. He apparently enjoyed great popularity there and was consulted by many prominent men. Yet he left after less than a year, for unknown reasons. During this period, he wrote eleven treatises on various diseases, ranging from tuberculosis to gout.

From Strasbourg, he traveled to Basel, where he cured the famous and influential printer Johann Froben. Through Froben, he was introduced to the intellectual elite of Basel, the result being his appointment as municipal physician and professor of medicine at Basel in March, 1527. This influential position proved to be the highlight of Paracelsus' professional life. Yet he made no attempt to moderate his habitually aggressive and combative manner. He challenged the established medical system by saying that he would not accept the authority of Hippocrates or Galen. Instead, he would form his theories from his direct experience in dealing with the sick. In a famous incident, he put Avicenna's classical works on medicine to the bonfire. The authorities retaliated by refusing him the right to lecture and disputing his medical qualifications. Yet Paracelsus continued his work. Defying all tradition, he lectured in German rather than Latin, and he drew large and appreciative audiences. Many were attracted by his credo: "The patients are your textbook, the sickbed is your study."

Yet having made so many enemies, Paracelsus' fortunes soon took a turn for the worse. His benefactor, Froben, died suddenly in October, and shortly afterward a malicious lampoon of Paracelsus appeared. He counterattacked in typical fashion, denouncing past authorities and his colleagues in extreme language: They were all liars, cheats, and fakes, according to him. The situation came to a head when Paracelsus accused the town magistrate of ignorance and bias after a legal suit in which Paracelsus had attempted to collect a promised fee from a patient he had cured. Facing arrest and severe punishment for insulting a high official and with most of the town against him, Paracelsus fled in February, 1528.

After this debacle, he embarked on a new set of journeys, to Alsace, Germany, Switzerland, Bohemia, and Austria, rarely staying more than a few months in one place. In 1529, he was in Nürnberg, but professional doors were closed to him. He responded by proposing to cure any patient who had been declared incurable, and he is reported to have succeeded in nine out of fifteen cases involving lepers. In Nürnberg, he also wrote much, particularly on the disease of syphilis, the most pressing medical problem of the day.

In 1530, he was in Beratzhausen, where he again wrote copiously, including one of his best-known works, the brief *Paragranum* (1530; *Against the Grain*, 1894), in which he claimed that medicine should be based on four pillars: natural philosophy, astronomy, alchemy, and virtue. In 1531, he reached Saint Gall, where he wrote *Opus paramirum* (1531), which contains the fundamentals of his medical doctrine. During this period, he also focused strongly on the inner life, writing more than one hundred religious tracts, and he also took to religious preaching.

Facing poverty and adversity wherever he went, he came in 1533 to Appenzell, Switzerland, and to the mining districts of Hall and Schwaz, where he wrote a treatise on the miner's disease—the first ever written on an occupational disease. From Switzerland, he went again to Austria and in 1534 to Sterzing and Meran, living all the time like a beggar and rarely sleeping two nights in the same bed. In 1536, he was in Ulm and Augsburg, where his book on surgery, *Grosse Wundarzney* (1536; *Great Surgery Book*, 1894), was first printed; it said far more about how to avoid surgery than about surgery itself. In 1537, Paracelsus reached Munich and Bohemia, where he began work on his philosophical magnum opus, the *Astronomia magna* (1537-1538; *Great Astronomy*, 1894), which was an attempt to write a comprehensive system of natural philosophy. Highly eclectic but disorderly and inconsistent, it covers a vast range of topics, including man and the universe, salvation, magical lore, such as the healing power of stones, physiognomy, phrenology, meteorology, and Paracelsus' vision of the development of new technologies.

The best-known and most reliable likeness of Paracelsus, in a portrait by Augustin Hirschvogel, dates from 1537. It shows him clean-shaven and bald on the top of his head, with long unruly hair at the sides. Stern-faced, with deep-set eyes, his solemn expression tells the story of a hard but determined life. Of Paracelsus' last three years, little is known. From August, 1540, he was again in Salzburg, summoned by Archbishop Prince Ernst of Bavaria. On September 21, 1541, he suffered a stroke and died three days later.

Summary

From Paracelsus' own day to the present, a fierce debate has raged about his contribution to the development of Western science. Some people in his time denounced him as a charlatan, and his modern detractors have argued that his fame is more the result of his colorful and controversial life than any original contributions he made to human thought. On the other hand, his supporters argue that he was a great medical reformer who made substantial achievements in the development of modern chemistry, that he was the founder of biochemistry, and that he also made contributions to gynecology, psychiatry, and even psychotherapy.

In chemistry, it can certainly be said that he worked toward a systematic classification of all known chemical substances and that he devised a method of detoxifying dangerous chemical compounds, which he was then able to use for therapeutic purposes. He also introduced new laboratory methods. The methods of early chemists such as Andreas Libavius, Oswald Croll, and Jan Baptista van Helmont are clearly linked to those of Paracelsus. In medicine, he left accurate descriptions of diseases and had much success in the treating of wounds and chronic ulcers.

Yet if his contributions to modern knowledge are overemphasized, the picture of his work as a whole becomes distorted. He belongs firmly in the Renaissance. His belief in the correspondence between the microcosm and the macrocosm was a commonplace of the period, but it has been rejected by the modern world. Without it, however, much of Paracelsus' work would become unintelligible. He always viewed man in terms of man's relationship with nature and the cosmos as a whole, believing that everything in the inner world corresponded to something in the outer world and that knowledge of this relationship was vital for the healer. The philosophical bases of his views were the esoteric systems of Gnosticism and Neoplatonism. It is this unique coexistence of contradictory elements in his thought, the ancient and the modern, that makes Paracelsus a man of such enduring fascination.

Bibliography

Debus, Allen G. *The French Paracelsians: The Chemical Challenge to Medical and Scientific Tradition in Early Modern France*. Cambridge and New York: Cambridge University Press, 1991. Shortly after the medical authority of Galen had been reestablished in the Renaissance, Paracelsus proposed a new approach to natural philosophy and medicine utilizing chemistry. The resulting arguments between Paracelsians and Galenists lasted for more than a century and affected the medical establishments of every European country. The author discusses these issues with respect not only to pharmaceutical chemistry and the chemical cosmology of the Paracelsians, but also to the development of chemical physiology and its struggle with the brand of medicine influenced by the mechanical philosophy of the seventeenth century.

Feder, Gene. "Paradigm Lost: A Celebration of Paracelsus on His Quincentenary." *Lancet* 341 (May, 1993): 1396. Feder discusses the life and work of Paracelsus, including his work as a physician and surgeon; his attacks on the rich in his political and theological writings; and his belief in a relationship between bodily and spiritual forces. The author makes a case for the Paracelsian paradigm and the perspective it offers on the abuse of technology and environmental degradation.

Guggenheim, Karl Y. "Paracelsus and the Science of Nutrition in the Renaissance." *Journal of Nutrition* 123 (July, 1993): 1189. The author discusses the role of Paracelsus during the Renaissance. The article covers his opposition to Galenic medicine, his methods of direct observation, and his introduction of chemical thinking into medicine and nutrition.

Jung, Carl G. "Paracelsus" and "Paracelsus the Physician." In *The Spirit in Man, Art, and Literature*. Translated by R. F. C. Hull. New York: Pantheon Books, 1966. The first essay is the text of an address delivered by Jung in 1929 at the house in Einsiedeln where Paracelsus was born. Some of the biographical information is inaccurate, but Jung's insights into the essence of Paracelsus, although full of broad generalizations, remain valuable. The second, longer essay, originally given as a lecture in 1941, is one of the best short introductions in English to Paracelsus' thought.

Pachter, Henry M. *Magic into Science: The Story of Paracelsus*. New York: Henry Schuman, 1951. A lively and very readable biography. Pachter tries to rescue Paracelsus from what he sees as an attempt by esoteric groups, including faith healers, mystics, occultists, and homeopaths, to claim Paracelsus as one of their own. Instead, Pachter gives most prominence to those aspects of Paracelsus' work that show his contribution to the development of modern science, including chemistry, chemotherapy, biochemistry, gynecology, and psychiatry.

Pagel, Walter. *Paracelsus: An Introduction to Philosophical Medicine in the Era of the Renaissance*. 2nd ed. Basel and New York: Karger, 1982. One of the best and most comprehensive examinations in English of Paracelsus' work. Excellent on his philosophy, his medical theories and practice, and his sources. Resists viewing Paracelsus exclusively as a forerunner of modern science and medicine, and as a result serves as a useful corrective to Pachter, above. Instead, shows how Paracelsus forged mystical, magical, and scientific elements into a new synthesis based on personal experience.

Paracelsus. *Selected Writings*. Edited with an introduction by Jolande Jacobi. Translated by Norbert Guterman. New York: Pantheon, 1958. One of the best anthologies in English of Paracelsus' writings. Extracts from his works are arranged under thematic headings; references are comprehensive, although only German titles of the works are given. Jacobi's introduction to Paracelsus' life and work, from a Jungian point of view, contains valuable insights. The detailed glossary of Paracelsan terms is an exceptionally valuable aid to study. Includes many illustrations and a bibliography of primary and secondary sources.

Shumaker, Wayne. *The Occult Sciences in the Renaissance: A Study in Intellectual Patterns*. Berkeley: University of California Press, 1972. Extremely useful for understanding the intellectual and cultural milieu in which Paracelsus lived. Shumaker examines five areas of Renaissance thought: astrology, natural or white magic, witchcraft, alchemy, and the body of occult writings associated with the name Hermes Trismegistus. Includes extensive quotations from primary sources, many of which are unavailable in translation elsewhere, many illustrations, and an annotated bibliography.

Bryan Aubrey

MATTHEW PARKER

Born: August 6, 1504; Norwich, Norfolk, England
Died: May 17, 1575; London, England
Area of Achievement: Religion
Contribution: As the first Archbishop of Canterbury under Elizabeth I, Matthew Parker helped the queen achieve a truly national church, whose doctrine, ritual, and organization would be determined by Scripture, church tradition, and royal supremacy. Under Parker's archbishopric the Anglican church continued as a reformed branch of the Catholic Church rather than as a separate Protestant sect, maintaining religious peace in England.

Early Life

Matthew Parker was born August 6, 1504, in the parish of St. Saviour in Norwich, Norfolk, England. He was the eldest son of William Parker, a merchant, and his wife, Alice (née Monins). When Matthew Parker was twelve years old, his father died; his mother then married John Baker, a wealthy gentleman who became an excellent stepfather to Parker. Parker was close to all of his siblings, especially his brother Thomas, later a mayor of Norwich, and his stepbrother, John, a future benefactor to Corpus Christi College, Cambridge.

Parker was educated at the local grammar school, and in September, 1522, he entered Corpus Christi College, where, in 1525, he achieved a B.A. degree. On December 22, 1526, he became a subdeacon; on April 20, 1527, a deacon; and on June 15, 1527, a priest. In 1528, he achieved an M.A. degree, and he was soon singled out as a promising theologian and scholar, although of a moderately reforming interest. He was a member of the Cambridge Reformers, a group that included such notable reformation figures as Hugh Latimer. Parker was even charged with heresy in 1539, although the charges were dismissed as being "frivolous."

Parker's popular and dynamic preaching style, however, brought him favor. In 1533, he was licensed to preach through the southern province of England, and on March 30, 1533, he agreed to be chaplain to Anne Boleyn. With this chaplaincy came a deanery at the college of St. John the Baptist at Stoke in Suffolk. In 1535, he received a bachelor of divinity degree at Cambridge and, in 1538, a doctor of divinity degree. In March, 1537, he had also been appointed chaplain to Henry VIII. On December 4, 1544, he was elected master of Corpus Christi College, Cambridge, and a short time later he became vice-chancellor of the university. On June 24, 1547, he was married to Margaret Harlestone, the daughter of Robert Harlestone of Mattis Hall, Norfolk. Throughout the reign of Edward VI, Parker was valued for his moderate reforms, and on October 7, 1552, he received the rich deanery of Lincoln.

Upon the accession of Mary Tudor, Parker supported the cause of Lady Jane Grey. This support, along with his marriage and earlier friendships with reformers, resulted in the loss of his church preferments. Throughout Mary's reign Parker lived in fear and concealment. His health, never good, deteriorated even more rapidly after a fall from a horse. He thus devoted his time to theological studies and writing. Upon the accession of Elizabeth I, his continued poor health prevented him from working on a revision of the prayer book (in 1558), and although Parker preferred a quiet theological life, his virtues recommended him to Elizabeth I. Despite protests because of his poor health, he became Archbishop of Canterbury in 1559. For Elizabeth, Parker combined scholarship, administrative experience, loyalty, and moderation; he was free of any taint of Calvinism or Continental exile.

Life's Work

As the Archbishop of Canterbury, Parker faced tremendous difficulties. The negotiation of the Elizabethan church settlement had involved unwilling concessions by both the queen and the more radical Protestant reformers. Elizabeth's liturgy contained as wide a selection of sixteenth century doctrinal matter as possible, but for Anglican doctrine to be so comprehensive it necessarily had to remain vague rather than explicit. The emphasis on the Church of England's continuity with the medieval church, the deletion of black rubric on kneeling, the maintenance of vestments, and the inclusion of sentences within the Communion service (implying a belief in real presence) only alienated many Protestant reformers. In addition, clerical ignorance, minor corruption, and liturgical irregularities abounded. It is, therefore, much to Parker's credit that he so diligently sought to establish this fledgling Anglican church on a firm foundation of Scripture, tradition, and reason.

Deeply conscious of the importance of his own consecration as archbishop to the whole question of episcopal succession in the Church of England, Parker caused an account of the rites and ceremonies to be drawn up and deposited at Corpus Christi College. This account was essential because the Roman ritual was not observed. Indeed, on March 26, 1560, in answer to a letter from deprived bishops denouncing the theory of the new episcopate as subversive of papal authority, Parker drew up a statement declaring the equality of all bishops since the time of the Apostles. This statement has remained a cornerstone of Anglican theology.

After England's refusal to attend the Council of Trent, the Roman Catholic party believed that England's breach with Rome was irreparable. Meanwhile, the more radical British groups expanded their reforms to include the removal of bishops, the elimination of the prayer book, vestments, saints' days, and wedding rings.

Faced with these difficulties and with a queen who would not tolerate any changes, Parker followed a path of what he called, not innovation, but restoration to the times of the more primitive Catholic Church. He reduced the Forty-two Articles of religion to thirty-nine articles while continuing a policy of no explicit definitions. For use in the universities, he issued a new edition of the prayer book which had large numbers of traditional feasts and saints' days. He saw to it that a new translation of the Bible, which became known as the Bishop's Bible, was undertaken in order that the Geneva Bible's Calvinist influence would be reduced.

By 1563, however, disorders concerning ceremonies and vestments so concerned Elizabeth I that Parker was ordered to exact uniformity. In 1566, Parker's *Advertisements* laid down fixed rules for public service and vestments. Elizabeth urged Parker to use his church courts and rites of visitation more. Much to Parker's horror, his moderate statement only inflamed the Puritan reformers backed by the powerful Earl of Leicester. Thirty-seven percent of the London clergy refused to conform and left the church to form the foundation of English Nonconformity.

Meanwhile, at Cambridge University, the assertiveness of the Puritans led by Dr. Thomas Cartwright (1535-1603) grew. Cartwright represented undiluted Calvinism. A brilliant and determined leader, he advocated sweeping reforms stating that Anglicanism, like Roman Catholicism, was in error for its dependence on church tradition and the early church fathers. Cartwright favored abolishing the episcopal system in favor of Presbyterianism, the election of ministers by congregations, and the elimination of the prayer book along with vestments, crosses, statues, painted glass windows, and organs. Both William Cecil and Parker agreed, however, that no concessions could be made. In 1570, Parker was deprived of his professorship, in 1574 he lost his fellowship at Trinity College, and as a result of a summons by the ecclesiastical commission for his arrest, he fled abroad. Cartwright's writings became the foundation of Presbyterian Nonconformity and represented the most comprehensive attack on everything for which the Anglican church stood.

As a result of all these controversies, a new code was compiled for the universities which modified their constitutions in order to prevent future innovations. In his later years, therefore, though Parker was personally and financially dedicated to the universities, his relations with them were not cordial.

Parker's defense of the Anglican church against the Puritans earned for him the title "the Pope of Lambeth." Parker persisted against the Puritans. He removed the Puritan Thomas Aldrich from the mastership of Corpus Christi College, prohibited prophesying on biblical texts in the diocese of Norwich, and saw to it that church patronage and appointments, previously impartial, were now aimed at advancing the careers of those opposed to the Puritan-Calvinist doctrine.

After 1573, Parker withdrew to a more scholarly life. The death of his wife on August 17, 1570, had deeply troubled him. The church controversies made him withdraw from court despite Elizabeth's support. Then in December of 1574, his son Matthew died at the age of twenty-three. Thereafter, Parker's health declined rapidly. He died on May 17, 1575, from kidney disease. He was buried in his private chapel at Lambeth. The Puritans' resentment against him was long-lived, and in 1648, his body was disinterred and buried under a dunghill. At the Restoration, in 1660, his remains and a monument were restored.

Parker died wealthy; many of his bequests were to Corpus Christi College and its library. The library received numerous manuscripts from the monasteries, Anglo-Saxon documents, and thousands of volumes on theology. His preservation of such documents was an invaluable service to future Anglican theologians.

Summary

Despite Matthew Parker's own hesitation about accepting the appointment as Archbishop of Canterbury, he proved to be an excellent leader for the foundation of the Church of England under Elizabeth I. With his own preference for moderation and tolerance, he stood firm against the early Puritan attack and oversaw the establishment of an Anglican church that would eventually view itself as absolute and infallible in its interpretations of tradition, Scripture, and history, as did Rome. The importance of Parker's years as archbishop are emphasized even more by the fact that the church was to survive despite the difficulties of its next archbishop, Edmund Grindal. Grindal, who favored Puritan ideas, was sequestered from office in May, 1577, leaving the church without a Primate until his death in July, 1583. Grindal's successor, Archbishop John Whitgift, for the most part followed Parker's policies.

Parker's legacy is most visible in the fact that the Anglican church which he helped to establish remained uniquely English in its rites, rituals, traditions, and doctrine of a clerical hierarchy. His firm stance against the Puritans, combined with his own broad views, led to the survival of a Church of England accommodating both a High and a Low Church view in one church body on a relatively peaceful basis. The magnitude of this accomplishment becomes clear when England's religious peace is compared with the Continent's religious upheavals and wars.

Bibliography

Brook, Victor J. K. *A Life of Archbishop Parker.* Oxford: Clarendon Press, 1962. This detailed biography provides a careful if not minute examination of every event in which Parker was even marginally involved.

Dickens, Arthur G. *The English Reformation.* 2d ed. London: Batsford, 1989; University Park: Pennsylvania State University Press, 1991. Dickens' book stresses the creation of an Anglican church poised between Protestant and Catholic ideals. It shows the complexity and difficulty of working out a compromise between the contending forces. In its emphasis on the unique accomplishments of Anglicanism it reveals—if unconsciously—that inherent feeling of superiority that Anglicanism came to possess.

Grimm, Harold J. *The Reformation Era, 1500-1650.* 2d ed. London and New York: Macmillan, 1974. This is a standard account of the Continental Reformation, the English Reformation, and the Catholic Counter-Reformation. Excellent for the factual record but not an interpretive history.

Kennedy, William Paul McClure. *Archbishop Parker.* London: Pitman, 1908. This biography is old, but still useful; biographies of Parker are in short supply. The emphasis of this book, which is supported by current works in the field, is that Parker played a crucial role in laying the foundation for Anglicanism.

Perry, Edith Weir. *Under Four Tudors: Being the Story of Matthew Parker, Sometime Archbishop of Canterbury.* London: Allen and Unwin, 1940. Perry sees Parker as the vital figure in the creation of an Anglican church. She attributes to Parker's influence, backed by Elizabeth I, the fact that the Church of England continued as a branch of the Catholic Church instead of becoming a separate Protestant sect. Perry also is very revealing on Parker's wife.

Reardon, Bernard M. G. *Religious Thought in the Reformation.* 2d ed. London and New York: Longman, 1995. This is a detailed theological examination of the Reformation period. Chapters 10 and 11 discuss the complex theological issues of the English Reformation; a reading of these chapters gives an understanding of why problems developed in the Church of England with Puritans, Separatists, and so on.

Williams, Neville. *Elizabeth the First, Queen of England.* New York: Dutton, 1968; London: Sphere, 1971. This biography provides a vivid portrait of Elizabeth I as a woman of strong opinions. Unlike many biographies of Elizabeth, it is informative concerning the relationship between Parker and his queen.

Rose Ethel Althaus Meza

CATHERINE PARR

Born: c. 1512; London, England

Died: September 5, 1548; Sudeley Castle, Gloucestershire, England

Area of Achievement: Monarchy

Contribution: Catherine Parr was the sixth and last wife of King Henry VIII of Great Britain.

Early Life

Catherine (variously spelled Katherine, Katharine, and Catharine) Parr was the daughter of Sir Thomas Parr, a man of considerable distinction and social prominence who served Britain's royal family. Her mother, Maud Greene, was an heiress from Northamptonshire. The exact date of Catherine's birth remains uncertain. In all likelihood, she was born in 1512. She was married twice before her union with King Henry VIII on July 12, 1543. Henry had already been king of England for some years before Catherine's birth, having ascended to the throne in 1509 to begin his thirty-eight-year reign.

Catherine's first marriage was to Edward Borough, who died in 1529, about a year after their marriage. Catherine next married John Neville, Lord Latimer, who died on March 2, 1543. Neither marriage produced children. Edward Borough, about Catherine's age, was the son of Thomas, Lord Borough, chamberlain to Queen Anne Boleyn, Henry VIII's second wife, who was beheaded as an adulteress. During her marriage to Borough, Catherine resided mostly on the family estates in Lincolnshire. Following her husband's death, Catherine lived on a small income derived from some estates in Kent. She was only twenty years old and living at a time when widows had little status; thus her remarriage, which occurred in 1533, was inevitable.

When Catherine married Lord Latimer, he was about forty years old, twice Catherine's age. He had lost two previous wives and was left with two children, John and Margaret. The marriage took place at about the time of Anne Boleyn's coronation. Catherine, through her husband's official connection with the queen, began to form strong social and political connections at Court.

Catherine was highly competent and unquestionably intelligent, although she lacked the coveted classical education available to members of the nobility who became an increasing part of her life. At twenty-one, she was mistress of a large household and a stepmother.

A sensitive person, well attuned to the feelings of those around her, Catherine quickly gained the admiration and love of Margaret Neville, who more than a decade later wrote an encomium to her stepmother in her last will and testament. Catherine's most salient personal characteristic was tact. She had an unerring ability to put people at ease and to understand implicitly their points of view.

Living through England's rift with the Roman Catholic church, Catherine was a committed humanist who valued the sentiments of the evangelical Protestant reformers. Respected not only for her tact and compassion, Catherine was also valued for her practical intelligence and devoutness.

Catherine gained a further connection with the Court when her sister Anne became a lady-in-waiting for Queen Catherine Howard, the king's fifth wife. The king knew Catherine Parr and apparently had designs on her even before her husband died. He gave her a gift on February 16, 1543. Catherine, who was due to come into a great deal of money on Lord Latimer's death, had fallen in love with Thomas Seymour in the preceding year, during which she faithfully attended her dying husband. Despite her attentions to Lord Latimer, Catherine planned to marry Thomas, for whom she felt considerable passion, when Lord Latimer died.

Life's Work

Catherine Parr is remembered chiefly as the sixth and last wife of King Henry VIII. Her marriage to him lasted for the last three and a half years of the king's life.

Despite his prominence as king of England, Henry VIII had gained an unsavory reputation by the time he was ready to marry for the sixth time. He had shed by divorce or annulment two of his wives, Catherine of Aragon and Anne of Cleves, whose marriage to him was never consummated and lasted less than six months. Two other of his wives, Anne Boleyn and Catherine Howard, were beheaded after being convicted of adultery, and one wife, Jane Seymour, died from complications twelve days after bearing Henry's son, Edward.

The king was devastated by Jane Seymour's death after only a year of marriage. Despite his devastation, Henry knew that he would be expected to remarry, and he soon took Catherine Howard as his fifth wife. When her adultery was uncovered, he had her beheaded to save face, but hopelessness engulfed him. Ill and overweight, overbearing and dangerously imperial, Henry was far from the sort of person one would choose to marry. He faced the prospect of living his remaining years without a mate.

Shortly before Catherine Howard's execution, Henry had enacted the 1542 Act of Attainder. The act stipulated that if anyone presented a prospective bride to the king and, upon marrying her, the king deemed her not to be a virgin, the bride, her family, and the person who first presented her to the king would be guilty of treason, an offense punishable by death. Understandably, the king, seeking to remarry, received few recommendations of prospective brides.

Catherine Parr emerged as one of the few viable candidates to marry Henry VIII and become queen of England. Because she had been married twice before, the question of her virginity was moot. The only obstacle was that Catherine was in love with someone else whom she hoped to marry.

As the king intensified his pursuit of Catherine, however, Catherine was more responsive to the call of duty than to the inclinations of her heart. Therefore, on July 12, 1543, four months after the death of her husband, Lord Latimer, Catherine married the ailing king and became much the sort of wife/nurse she had been to Lord Latimer.

Catherine did everything she could to make Henry happy and comfortable. She sought out medicines that she could apply to his painfully swollen, gout-ravished legs. She was diligent in being a good stepmother to his three children, all of whom responded well to her. From all accounts, it was difficult for people not to like the new queen.

A year after Catherine married him, Henry went on a campaign to France. Having recently arranged for his daughters, Mary and Elizabeth, to be in line for the throne after Prince Edward and his male offspring, Henry now arranged officially for any male child he might have by Catherine to come before Mary and Elizabeth in the line of succession. On July 7, 1544, the minutes of the Privy Council declared Catherine Parr regent to serve in the king's stead during his absence, a responsibility that had been granted previously only to Catherine of Aragon.

During Henry's three months in France, with guidance from Thomas Cranmer, archbishop of Canterbury, Catherine reigned over England. She was the model of a conscientious regent and faithful wife, writing frequently to Henry with proclamations of how much she and England missed him. During his absence, Catherine's signature appeared on all official documents.

Catherine's marriage to Henry was low-key. The new queen was not beautiful, but Henry needed a compassionate nurse more than a passionate bed partner. In Catherine Parr, he found just such a person. Considerable trust existed between the two despite Henry's history of deception by women.

As a result of her close association with Thomas Cranmer during her husband's absence, Catherine began to refine some of her own religious views, which had always been slightly subversive. At about this time, Catherine also formed a close relationship with Katherine, duchess of Suffolk, a woman not yet thirty, the death of whose sixty-five-year-old husband left her with considerable wealth and prestige.

The duchess had close ties with religious reformers of her day and sided emphatically with those who wanted everyone to be able to read Scripture rather than have it interpreted for them through a priest. Catherine shared this view, although it is doubtful that Henry agreed with it. She is known to have read and been influenced by Thomas à Kempis' *The Imitation of Christ* (c. 1526) and by Marguerite of Navarre's *Le miroir de l'âme pércheresse* (c. 1540, *The Mirror of the Sinful Soul*), which her eleven-year-old step-daughter, Elizabeth, had translated into English for her as a New Year's gift in 1544.

Partly as a result of these readings, Catherine published her *Prayers and Meditations* (1545), which went through nineteen editions in the next half century. Catherine was one of only eight women to publish during the reigns of Henry VII and Henry VIII. Her book was derivative and obviously was published largely because she was queen. That it reached an audience as large as it did and remained popular for as long as it did clearly suggests that it was well received.

Catherine also published *A Lamentation or Complaynt of a Sinner* (1547) shortly after Henry's death. This book was in part an antipapist attack on the Roman Catholic church, something that would have disturbed Henry. Its most salient plea was for biblical translation so that people could be their own interpreters of Scripture. Henry's daughter Elizabeth, later queen of England, translated Catherine's first book into French, Latin, and Italian when she was a mere eleven years old.

During the king's final year, Catherine frequently entertained the religious reformers of her day in the royal residence. Although Henry was unsympathetic to their cause, he endured their presence because of his regard for Catherine. Some of Henry's conservative followers tried to undermine the queen and went so far as to attempt to arrest her, but the king struck out against the forty guards who tried to carry out the arrest, and the queen's position was assured.

The king's health declined precipitously in December of 1546. On January 28, 1547, he died. By the end of May in the same year, Catherine, her passion for Thomas Lord Seymour reignited, married him. On August 30, 1548, Catherine bore a daughter, Mary. Barely a week afterwards, on September 7, she died from complications associated with childbirth. Ironically, Catherine, considered barren because she had remained childless through three marriages, proved herself capable of motherhood but did not survive it.

Summary

Living in an era when men ruled and women obeyed, Catherine Parr, although compassionate and acquiescent, was a complex woman capable of considerable passion and independence. She embraced many of the humanistic elements of the New Life, considered quite radical by the conservative ruling class in England during her lifetime.

King Henry VIII seemed truly to have appreciated Catherine, although it was clear that his first love was Jane Seymour, beside whom he is buried. Catherine's first real love after three marriages appears to have been Thomas Seymour, whom she wed shortly after Henry's death.

Catherine in her day was an emancipated woman. The very fact that she published set her apart, but the sentiments in her second book, *A Lamentation or Complaynt of a Sinner*, were extremely radical for her day.

Bibliography

Beilen, Elaine. *Redeeming Eve: Women Writers of the English Renaissance*. Princeton, N.J.: Princeton University Press, 1987. This study presents Catherine Parr in the context of her writing.

Fraser, Antonia. *The Wives of Henry VIII*. New York: Knopf, 1992. Fraser's book is thorough, carefully researched, and eminently readable, devoting some sixty fact-filled pages to Catherine Parr.

Lindsey, Karen. *Divorced, Beheaded, Survived: A Feminist Reinterpretation of the Wives of Henry VIII*. New York: Addison-Wesley, 1995. Lindsey's feminist assessment of Henry's wives is particularly lucid in its discussion of the plot in Henry's court to discredit Catherine shortly before Henry's death. Also contains good discussions of Elizabeth's love for Catherine and of Catherine's emotional involvement with Thomas Seymour.

Martienssen, Anthony. *Queen Katherine Parr*. New York: McGraw-Hill, 1974. Dated and in some particulars inaccurate, as new information has been unearthed since its publication. Nevertheless, as the only modern full-length study of Catherine Parr, it makes a significant contribution to the scholarship on her.

Plowden, Allison. *Tudor Women: Queens and Commoners*. New York: Atheneum, 1979. Despite its age, this readable book places Catherine Parr in an interesting context that reveals much about the social standing of women in the sixteenth century.

Weir, Alison. *The Six Wives of Henry VIII*. London: Pimlico, 1991. Weir offers succinct and penetrating insights into Catherine Parr and her ability to manage a marriage relationship with a man whose marital record was questionable.

R. Baird Shuman

PAUL III
Alessandro Farnese

Born: February 29, 1468; Canino, Papal States
Died: November 10, 1549; Rome
Area of Achievement: Religion
Contribution: Pope Paul III was the last of the Renaissance popes, aristocratic, educated in the classics, with the concerns of his family often paramount. Yet he was also the first pope of the Catholic or Counter-Reformation, and it was he who summoned the Cosuncil of Trent, whose decisions governed the Church in subsequent centuries.

Early Life

Alessandro Farnese was born in 1468 into an old aristocratic family whose lands in central Italy were located between Rome and Florence. Generally supportive of the Papacy in its struggles with the Holy Roman Empire, over time the family owned a large amount of land. Yet it was not until early in the fifteenth century that the Farneses succeeded in becoming important in Rome, an event occasioned by a successful marriage. Educated in classical studies in Florence in the establishment of Lorenzo de' Medici, Farnese entered the Church, and inasmuch as it was the era of Renaissance Humanism, the choice was probably more for social than for spiritual reasons.

His sister Giulia, the favorite mistress of Alexander VI, head of the Borgia family, was able to further Farnese's career, and when he became a cardinal in the Church at the age of twenty-five, many claimed that it was a result of her influence. He well might have succeeded anyway; members of his class often rose to the highest positions in the Church during that era. He was properly educated; he was intelligent and shrewd; and his manner was pleasing. After becoming a cardinal, he maintained one of the most opulent palaces in Rome. Although as a cleric he could not marry, he did father several children out of wedlock, which was not unusual among the clergy at that time. He subsequently supervised their upbringing and furthered their careers.

Although Farnese had been a cardinal for many years, it was not until he was about fifty that he took holy orders and became a priest. His abilities and ambition had long been recognized. In 1521, he was one of the alternative candidates to Clement VII, and afterward Farnese became Clement's chief adviser. It was predicted that he would succeed to the papal throne after Clement, and he did so in 1534, against little opposition, at the advanced age of sixty-seven. He took the name Paul III.

Life's Work

Paul's accession was acclaimed among most factions in Christendom. Because of his age, many believed that his reign would be brief and his impact upon events slight. As a Roman, he was popular among the city's populace. As he was an aristocrat, his selection was no threat to the hierarchical social order. Because of his humanistic education, many felt assured that those values would be maintained. Unlike many previous popes, Paul was not tainted with much of the corruption associated with the papal office, this in spite of his own illegitimate children.

It was a complex and difficult time. Paul would probably have preferred to continue in the tradition of most then-recent popes, focusing mainly on secular concerns and pleasures. In 1517, however, Martin Luther began his public criticism of the Catholic Church, and by 1534 the demands of the Protestant Reformers were threatening to tear apart the fabric of the Church and the unity of Christendom. In addition, there were military and political struggles which often impinged upon the security of Italy and the Papal States, and even, it seemed, the survival of the Church itself. In 1527, the forces of Emperor Charles V had captured and sacked Rome, a traumatic event not only for the Romans but also for the Papacy. It is probable that Paul was chosen pope as much for his diplomatic and political abilities as for his spiritual commitments. If so, it was a good choice; in the years which followed Paul succeeded in maintaining his, and the Church's, independence, and the Papacy did not become merely a pawn in the game of power politics, a possibility which seemed likely at the time of his accession.

Paul believed that, in order to resist the various religious and political threats to the Catholic Church, it was necessary to make changes in the papal court itself. The transitional nature of Paul's reign can be seen by his choice of new cardinals. Two were his teenage grandsons, but others, such

as John Fisher, Reginald Pole, Gasparo Contarini, and Gian Pietro Caraffa, proved to be significant selections. Pope Paul also appointed a commission of cardinals to make recommendations regarding possible reforms. When the report was submitted in 1537, it was critical of many past clerical appointments. The buying and selling of church offices and legal decisions from the various church courts was condemned, as were the abuses in the sale of indulgences. It was argued that even the absolute authority of the popes needed to be changed and that Rome itself should be cleansed of corruption. Paul refused to have the report published, but soon unauthorized editions were circulating throughout Europe. Most Protestants were in the process of weakening the authority of the clergy, but the cardinals, and Paul, were more concerned with strengthening the clergy through reform.

Progress was slow. Paul, cautious and conservative, was unwilling to alter the existing system radically, but in 1540 he ordered the banishment of numerous church officials who were improperly residing in Rome. Paul also entertained the possibility of summoning a general church council to reform the Catholic Church, but he was opposed to any weakening of papal authority, and in the past councils had often attempted to place limits upon the Papacy. There was no unity on the matter of a council outside the Church. The Protestants were as reluctant to accept a council's authority and its decisions as to follow papal demands. Various European rulers, in an age of rising nationalism, were unwilling to compromise their freedom of action to any supranational body such as the Church had been in the Middle Ages. Charles V was especially in a difficult position. He was a loyal Catholic, but by the 1530's many of his German subjects had become fervent Protestants. His need for peace within Germany and for support against both Francis I of France and the invasion by Muslim Turks, however, meant that he had to make peace with his Protestant citizens. He desired compromise in a world of increasing polarization. An attempt was made in 1541, at Ratisbon, but little was accomplished. The differences between the two factions was already too great.

Many doubted Paul's own commitment to reform. He had, against considerable opposition, made his illegitimate son a duke from lands of the Papal States, and he continued to further the private interests of his own family, including negotiating the marriage of a grandson to the illegitimate daughter of Charles V. Could such a figure of Renaissance Rome be taken seriously as a religious reformer? He was committed, but only under the condition that the council remain under the firm leadership of the Papacy. Finally Paul called for a general council to meet in northern Italy at Trent, a compromise location not too far from Rome but also within the lands of the Holy Roman Empire. For a number of reasons—military, political, diplomatic, and personal—the council was postponed and did not formally begin until December, 1545. Although meeting only sporadically over many years, it was to prove to be a momentous event in the furthering of the religious reformation of the Catholic Church itself as well as countering the accomplishments and appeals of Luther, John Calvin, and other Protestants.

Paul also gave his support to two other significant events of the Counter-Reformation. In 1540, he gave his consent to the formation of a new religious order, the Society of Jesus, under the leadership of Ignatius Loyola. Loyola had been a controversial figure and had been imprisoned by Catholic officials in Spain before moving to Paris and then to Rome in 1538. Initially Paul was reluctant to grant Loyola's request: Too much fanatical enthusiasm was suspect by the Farnese aristocrat. Yet one of his own cardinals, Gasparo Contarini, convinced him to charter the Jesuits, who then owed allegiance directly to the Papacy itself. Under Loyola and his successors, the order, in its commitment to missionary activity and to the teaching of approved Catholic doctrine, became one of the most important elements in the Counter-Reformation.

In 1542, Paul granted to Cardinal Gian Pietro Caraffa, another of his appointments to the curia, the office of Inquisitor-General of the Inquisition, giving Caraffa full authority in Italy. Influenced by the earlier Spanish Inquisition, Caraffa soon made his mark in rooting out Lutherans and other heretics within and without the clergy. Under Paul, a man of the Renaissance, Caraffa's Inquisition was somewhat limited, but when Caraffa was elected pope as Paul IV in 1554, the Inquisition became more threatening to the unorthodox in religious belief and practice.

Paul reigned as pope for fifteen years in spite of his advanced age. In 1545, somewhat reluctantly, he gave Parma and Piacenza to his illegitimate son, Pier Luigi. The lands belonged to the Papal States, but it was argued that they could be better defended by their own ruler. It was an extravagant example of papal nepotism. Pier Luigi became the first duke. The decision was not popular, and Pier Luigi was assassinated in 1547. The Emperor Charles V demanded the cession of Parma, and when Paul considered instead making a member of the Orsini family the new Duke of Parma, his own grandchildren, fearing a loss of their recently achieved patrimony, began negotiations with the emperor. The rebellion of his family was too much for the eighty-one-year-old pope, and he died in Rome on November 10, 1549.

Summary

In 1543, Titian painted the portrait of Paul III. The pope was then in his mid-seventies, a formidable age. In the artist's rendition, however, Paul still shows his qualities of authority and perseverance. His white beard and aged wrinkles are countered by the focus of his eyes, which appear to be concentrating upon one of his many concerns—Charles V, Francis I, Loyola, or Caraffa. His years as pope were as momentous as any in the long history of the Catholic Church. A man of the Renaissance, he was forced to confront an era of spiritual renewal that was perhaps foreign to his essential nature. As leader of the Church universal, he faced a world of rising nationalism. Nevertheless, Paul, while remaining a product of his immediate past, also transcended it.

By cautiously committing himself to the reform of the Church, he helped pave the way for its rehabilitation. At one time, it seemed as if the Protestants would totally replace the Roman church with a reformed church, or churches, but that was not to be. For his support of change within the papal curia, his willingness to countenance the activities of new Catholic reformers such as Loyola, his support of the Inquisition under Caraffa, and most of all his summoning of the Church council which met at Trent, Paul, in spite of his secular background, his family concerns, and his conservative nature, must rank among the most important of the popes during the early modern period.

Bibliography

Burns, Edward McNall. *The Counter Reformation*. Princeton, N.J.: Van Nostrand, 1964. The author has combined a brief narrative of the events and figures of the era with a selection of documents. There is no biography of Paul III in English, but Burns gives a succinct account of his life and activities.

Dickens, A. G. *The Counter Reformation*. London: Thames and Hudson, 1968; New York: Harcourt Brace, 1969. Dickens, an English academic, is one of the most influential historians of religion in the sixteenth century. This volume is an excellent survey, with many illustrations, of the era of the Counter-Reformation.

Gleason, Elizabeth G. "Who Was the First Counter-Reformation Pope?" *Catholic Historical Review* 81 (April, 1995): 173. The author argues that Paul III was the first pope of the Counter-Reformation. The article defines the Counter-Reformation movement, outlines Paul III's outstanding contributions to the reform, and covers the limits to his commitment to it.

Mullett, Michael A. *The Counter-Reformation and the Catholic Reformation in Early Modern Europe*. London and New York: Methuen, 1984. This brief pamphlet not only covers the major events but also provides a bibliographical account of the various interpretations by historians of the Catholic Reformation and the era of Paul III.

Ranke, Leopold von. *The History of the Popes During the Last Four Centuries*. Translated by E. Foster. London: Bell, 1907. Ranke, the great German historian of the nineteenth century and the father of scientific history, portrays Paul III as a secular figure, diplomatically and politically astute, whose support for the religious reform of the Catholic Church had little to do with any deeply felt spiritual concerns.

Solari, Giovanna R. *The House of Farnese*. Translated by Simona Morini and Frederic Tuten. New York: Doubleday, 1968. The author has written a popular history of the Farnese family, beginning with the life of Alessandro Farnese, Paul III. The volume focuses primarily upon personalities and family activities.

Eugene Larson

PHILIP II

Born: May 21, 1527; Valladolid, Spain

Died: September 13, 1598; El Escorial Palace, Spain

Areas of Achievement: Government, politics, and religion

Contribution: Philip II was one of the most dominant monarchs in Europe during the late sixteenth century. Guided by his deep religious faith, Philip was involved in virtually every major event in the last half of the sixteenth century.

Early Life

Philip was born into the most influential family in sixteenth century Europe—the Habsburgs. His father, Charles V (Charles I of Spain), was the most powerful Holy Roman Emperor to that date. Philip's first years were spent under the guidance of his mother, Isabel of Portugal, as Charles traveled on imperial business. Isabel's religious and serious nature had a pronounced effect on her son. In 1535, Charles established a separate household for Philip, who was taught such arts as riding and hunting. In addition, Philip received a formal education, excelling in language skills. He could speak and write Latin, understand French and Italian, and speak French, but he was most comfortable with the language of his homeland.

Philip's physical appearance was similar to that of his ancestors. Having the famous Habsburg jaw, a large protruding under jaw and lip, he wore a short and pointed beard early in life and allowed it to grow longer and wider as he grew older.

Philip had an unusual married life. He had four wives, and he outlived each of them. At age eighteen, he married Maria of Portugal, the mother of a son who died later under questionable circumstances. Philip's next wife was the English queen Mary I. In 1558, Mary died without heirs, and that broke all connections Philip had with England. His third wife was Elizabeth of Valois, who bore him two daughters before dying in 1568. His last marriage was to Anne of Austria, the daughter of his cousin, Emperor Maximilian II. Anne bore Philip four sons and one daughter before she died in 1580.

Life's Work

Philip ruled many lands. Although Charles V gave the Austrian lands to his brother, Ferdinand, he reserved for Philip the Spanish lands in the New World and Europe. The New World lands were most important as sources of revenue. Among his holdings, however, Philip loved Spain best. Indeed, he never left his homeland after his return from Northern Europe in 1559. He built for himself a palace, El Escorial, which became a monument to his reign; some called it a monastery.

One of the most disturbing problems Philip faced throughout his rule was the Protestant Reformation. Indeed, the fight against the heretics colored almost every aspect of his reign. He had been reared as a Catholic and was devoted to the Church. When the Council of Trent finished its work, he attempted to enforce its decisions. He believed that it was his duty to restore Europe to the true Church. He did not always agree, however, with the popes and often fought with them over authority in church-state issues. In turn, the popes resented Philip's control over the Spanish church. The Spanish clergy, however, supported Philip.

Philip's reign was usually dominated by affairs outside the Iberian Peninsula. The situation in the Netherlands created much difficulty. The Dutch were growing wealthy and were gaining a sizable Protestant population. Although they had been restless under Charles V, they did not create major problems for him; they paid their taxes and, as a result, were low in funds when Philip assumed control. Philip expected the Dutch not only to pay their taxes but also to maintain a defense against his northern enemies, while promoting the Roman Catholic Church.

Philip attempted several different approaches to the Netherlands. He first tried to rule through a regent, his half sister Margaret, and a close adviser, Antoine Perrenot de Granvelle, Bishop of Arras (after 1561, Cardinal Granvelle). The cardinal actually controlled the government and attempted to carry out Philip's orders. The Dutch Protestants, led by William the Silent, insisted that they had certain privileges that had to be respected. William finally forced Philip's recall of Granvelle, only to discover that Granvelle had been following orders. When the Protestant militants began to destroy churches and other property, Philip sent troops to end the rebellion. Several thousand people were executed for heresy. Taking control of the northern provinces, William demanded religious freedom, along with the removal of troops and restoration of rights. Philip could never allow religious freedom, so this civil war continued throughout his reign. While there were a few periods of Spanish success, the northern provinces gained their independence, although Spain refused to recognize the loss until 1648.

England prevented Philip from pursuing the revolt in the Netherlands as actively as he might have wished. Throughout the sixteenth century, Anglo-Spanish relations had seen peaks and valleys. When Philip married Mary in 1554, it had only been after careful consideration. Many in the English Parliament opposed the marriage and relented only after ensuring that Philip would have little to do with English government. Philip was unhappy about the situation but accepted his father's advice to rule England through Mary. Unfortunately for this goal, Mary died soon after the marriage.

Problems constantly beset the two countries during the Elizabethan years. One of the most vexing was the English "Sea Dogs" (privateers), who preyed on Spanish New World trade. Although Philip beseeched Elizabeth to control her sea captains, she never did. She also angered Philip by providing English troops to aid the Protestant cause in the Netherlands.

Convinced that diplomacy was not going to control the English, Philip plotted an invasion. His plans originally called for assembling a large armada and sending it to the Netherlands, where it would board troops and cross the Channel to capture England. This Spanish Armada quickly ran into problems. In 1587, an English sea captain, Francis Drake, surprised the Spanish fleet in port and inflicted considerable damage. Determined, even at great financial costs and administrative difficulties, Philip repaired the Armada and sent it to sea in 1588. As it arrived in the Channel, a combination of English ships and Channel weather seriously crippled the fleet, and only a small portion managed to limp back to Spain. While Philip never gave up the idea of conquering England, the idea remained only a dream.

Spain was in the middle of a war with France when Philip assumed the mantle of leadership from his father in 1555-1556. It was not until 1559 that the Treaty of Cateau-Cambrésis was negotiated with the King of France, Henry II, ending the conflict. After the death of Henry II, there was a struggle for control of the French throne. The French Huguenots demanded their religious rights as well as certain political ones. Wars frequently raged between the Catholic and Huguenot factions. Philip carefully watched the situation and in December, 1584, signed the secret Treaty of Joinville with the Catholic League. The goals of the treaty were to keep a Huguenot off the throne and to suppress heresy in France. When the next in line to the throne seemed to be Henry of Navarre, a Huguenot, Philip forced the reigning King Henry III to proclaim an elderly uncle, Charles, Cardinal of Bourbon, as his successor. When Charles died in 1591, Philip advanced his daughter, Isabella Clara Eugenia, by Elizabeth of Valois, the eldest daughter of Henry II's eldest daughter. These claims failed, and Henry of Navarre assumed his place on the French throne; Philip could not dislodge him.

During the last few years of his life, Philip suffered from crippling arthritis and usually had to be carried from place to place. He accepted what comfort he could from his religion. He was a man of faith, and his religious beliefs, which carried him throughout his life, were with him when he died.

Summary

Philip II was one of the most dominant forces in the second half of the sixteenth century. He touched the lives of many both in the New World and in Europe. In his own fashion, he established a Spanish colonial governance that lasted well into the nineteenth century. In Europe, he fought with his fellow monarchs for control, even seizing the Portuguese crown when it became vacant in 1580. He rarely retreated from any position, because he was usually convinced that God had ordained him to undertake a mission.

Philip would not make decisions quickly. Some argue that he was being prudent, while others say that he was timid. Perhaps his procrastination was caused by his lack of funds. Despite the riches of the New World, Philip had such staggering debts that his reign was bankrupt in 1557, 1575, and 1596. He collected money from every possible source to meet his needs. Another reason for his procrastination could have been his habit of employing ministers with widely varying views, even ones opposed to his own, and then demanding that they express themselves. Council meetings, such as the Council of State, often became battlegrounds for rival factions.

Because of his absolute faith and strong convictions, Philip became part of the Black Legend, or anti-Spanish view, that surfaced in the English-speaking world. Philip's connection with the legend began when William the Silent, deep in battle over the Netherlands, branded Philip a murderer. Two major contributions to the Black Legend's

growth were books by Antonio Perez and John Lothrop Motley. Perez, who had been close to Philip and had fallen from power, tried to destroy Philip's name to avenge himself. Motley, a noted Protestant historian, used the distorted documents of Perez and others to paint Philip as evil. More balanced accounts have since emerged, and Philip has been placed in a more appropriate perspective.

Bibliography

Conklin, James. "The Theory of Sovereign Debt and Spain under Philip II." *Journal of Political Economy* 106 (June, 1998): 483. This article examines the theory of sovereign debt in connection with Spain during the reign of Philip II and provides a history of sovereign lending over the last 500 years.

Mattingly, Garrett. *The Armada.* Boston: Houghton Mifflin, 1959. A readable book about one of the major issues of Philip's reign—the defeat of the Spanish Armada. Contains a good, but outdated, bibliography. This work is considered a classic.

Merriman, Roger Bigelow. *The Rise of the Spanish Empire in the Old World and the New.* Vol. 4, *Philip the Prudent.* New York: Macmillan, 1918. While Merriman's work might be considered an old source, it is still excellent for information on Philip's life. This is a balanced account and a good starting point for a serious study of Philip. Contains bibliographic information.

Parker, Geoffrey. *Philip II.* London: Hutchinson, and Boston: Little Brown, 1978. While the documentation herein is not what many historians would like to see, the book still presents a good view of Philip.

———. "Philip II of Spain: A Reappraisal." *History Today* 19 (1979): 800-847. Parker, who has written several articles on Philip, provides the reader with a close examination of Philip in this short article. Contains comments on the physical problems that Philip had toward the end of his life and addresses the problem of the Black Legend, briefly explaining Philip's role in it.

Pierson, Peter. *Philip II of Spain.* London: Thames and Hudson, 1975. A superb short biography. Pierson covers each major section of Philip's life and work. He tries to make the point that Philip thought in terms of dynasty and religion and not of nation state.

Riginos, Alice Swift. "The Wounding of Philip II of Macedon: Fact and Fabrication." *Journal of Hellenic Studies* 114 (1994): 103. The author focuses on ancient biographers' accounts of the wounding of Philip II, including the changes that have occurred in the biographical facts over the centuries. Information is offered on injuries in general, including wounds to the eye, broken collarbones, and a wound in the leg. Several categories of falsified biographical data are discussed.

Rule, John C., and John J. TePaske, eds. *The Character of Philip II.* Boston: Heath, 1963. An excellent source for trying to determine what Philip was really like. Includes selections from authors representing several nationalities.

Eric L. Wake

PHILIP THE MAGNANIMOUS

Born: November 13, 1504; Marburg, Hesse
Died: March 31, 1567; Cassel, Hesse
Areas of Achievement: Monarchy and church reform
Contribution: Philip the Magnanimous was perhaps the most significant single political supporter of the Protestant Reformation during the critical early years of the movement in the sixteenth century.

Early Life

Philip succeeded his father, Landgrave William II, on the throne of Hesse in 1509, when he was not yet five years of age. For half a century, the principality of Hesse had been riven by dynastic feuds and minority administrations, which had allowed the estates to obtain considerable influence. In 1509, a conflict for control of the regency erupted between the mother of young Philip, Anne of Mecklenburg, and the estates, which resulted in civil war and the intervention of neighboring princes, especially the rival Ernestine and Albertine branches of the House of Saxony.

These conflicts continued throughout the minority of Philip, providing an extremely strife-filled youth for the prince, who was often the object of contention and was shuffled about from one faction to another. Anne was supported by the Albertine Duke George the Bearded of Saxony and arranged for the marriage of Philip to George's daughter, Christine. The Ernestine Elector Frederick the Wise of Saxony, on the other hand, supported Anne's opposition. In 1518, when Philip was but fourteen years old, Emperor Maximilian I proclaimed Philip of age in an effort to restore peace, but the landgrave's mother continued to dominate the government, and civil conflict would continue until Philip assumed personal control of the Hesse throne in the mid-1520's.

In 1521, Philip attended the Diet of Worms, at which Martin Luther's teachings were condemned, and left with a strong attachment to the Wittenberg professor. During the following years, he took part in suppressing the uprising of imperial knights led by Franz von Sickingen and Ulrich von Hutten, and the peasant uprising led by Thomas Münzer.

Philip was a prince of considerable personal charm, with a handsome physique. At least during his youth, he was dynamic and outspoken, even to a fault. At the Diet of Speyer in 1526, for example, he was so eager to testify publicly to his new faith that he dined on an ox on a Friday. His activist nature, joined to the caution of his Saxon allies, often led to divided command in the Protestant camp. Despite the obvious sincerity of his adherence to the Reformation, Philip had strong sensual desires which would lead him into bigamy in 1540. On May 12, 1525, his mother died, and Philip became, for the first time, master of his own house.

Life's Work

By the time of his mother's death, Philip was effectively master of his principality and was committed to the Lutheran Reformation. During the winter of 1525-1526, Philip reached an agreement with the elector John of Saxony, cousin and rival of his mother's supporter, to pursue a common policy in defense of the Reformation at the upcoming Diet of Speyer. At that meeting, the princes, led by John and Philip, were able to prevent the enforcement of the decrees against Lutheranism, obtaining instead an agreement that each prince would act in his own lands "in such a way as everyone trusted to justify before God and the Imperial Majesty." This gave the princes a free hand in their own territories, setting the precedent for the later principle of state supremacy—*cuius regio, eius religio*—adopted by the Peace of Augsburg in 1555.

With this mandate, Philip called a synod of the Hessian church at Homburg in October, 1526, which adopted the *Reformatio ecclesiarum Hassiae*. This plan, primarily the work of François Lambert of Avignon, a Franciscan friar trained at Wittenberg, would have provided the Hessian church with a democratic structure, consisting of elected clergy and annual synods. On the advice of Luther, this model was rejected in favor of that being developed in neighboring Saxony, under which Philip became the effective head of the new church administration.

Twelve months later, Philip summoned the estates of Hesse for the first time in nine years to consider the disposition to be made of the confiscated monastic properties. This parliament agreed that 41 percent of these revenues were to be used by the prince, while the remaining 59 percent were to serve pious, educational, and ecclesiastical purposes, including the foundation of the University of Marburg to train future clergymen and officials. It was Philip's liberal endowment of the new university and various pious and charitable institutions which earned for him the sobriquet "the Magnanimous."

In the atmosphere of mutual suspicion following the rapprochement between Emperor Charles V and Pope Clement VII in 1528, Philip fell prey to the forgeries of Otto von Pack, a discredited councillor of Duke George. Pack persuaded him that Catholic forces were assembling to exterminate the new heresy, whereupon Philip formed an alliance with John, sent feelers to the emperor's enemies in France and Hungary, and assembled a significant armed force. Although no actual fighting ensued, Philip's precipitate action in appealing to the enemies of the emperor weakened the Protestant cause at the next diet, also held at Speyer, where in April, 1529, a new law revoked the concessions made three years earlier, halting all ecclesiastical innovations and restoring the jurisdiction of Catholic bishops. Philip joined with six other princes and fourteen cities in the Protest of Speyer in rejecting this decision, from which the adherents of Luther were known as "Protestants."

By this time, voices other than Luther's had been raised demanding the reform of the Church, resulting in divided councils among the Protestants. The major controversy was between Luther and Huldrych Zwingli over the doctrine of the Eucharist. Believing that a common front was necessary to defend the Protestant cause, Philip sponsored the Marburg Colloquy from October 1 to 3, 1529, in an effort to promote harmony. The disputants agreed on fourteen points, but their failure to achieve full agreement on the fifteenth article, on the Lord's Supper, was also the failure of the Protestant movement to achieve unity.

In 1530, Philip took part in the Diet of Augsburg, where an attempt was made to reach agreement between the Lutherans and the Catholics, and was one of the seven princes to subscribe to the Augsburg Confession presented there. With the failure of these negotiations, the emperor ordered the complete restoration of Catholicism. To defend themselves against this threat, the Protestant princes and the cities of Magdeburg and Bremen formed the military League of Schmalkalden in February, 1531. This league became the major political expression of German Protestantism for a generation.

Philip became the leading spirit in the Schmalkaldic League, overshadowing his more cautious cousin Elector John Frederick of Saxony. With French support, in 1534 Philip made the first significant territorial gain for Lutheranism in southern Germany when he conquered Württemberg from the Habsburgs, restoring the previous ruler, the Lutheran Duke Ulrich. Philip then gave support to the Prince-Bishop of Münster in his conflict with the radical Anabaptists, assisting in the siege of the city, which fell on June 25, 1535. Thus, during the 1530's, Philip was at the height of his influence.

At the age of nineteen, Philip had married Christine of Saxony, a daughter of his mother's ally, Duke George. The marriage was not successful. Influenced by Luther's statement that bigamy was not as serious an offense as divorce, he entered into a second union with Margaret von der Saal, which was soon made public. This not only caused dissension among the members of the league but also, because bigamy was a crime against imperial law as well, gave the emperor considerable leverage with Philip.

A confrontation in Germany had been avoided since 1530, largely because of the emperor's desire to obtain the support of the princes in his wars with the French and the Turks, and because of disagreements with the Papacy. In 1544, with the Treaty of Crépy, peace was concluded with France, and in 1545 the Council of Trent began its deliberations. After failing to convince the Lutherans to attend the council, Charles determined on war. At the Diet of Regensburg in 1546, Philip and John Frederick were placed under the ban of the empire.

In the War of the League of Schmalkalden, the dynamic Philip and the cautious John Frederick shared the command with other allies, which was the major cause of their defeat at Mühlberg on April 24, 1547. John Frederick was captured, and Philip was summoned to surrender, with the promise that his life would be spared; he would not suffer perpetual imprisonment, but he would have to pay a substantial fine of 150,000 gulden. Philip consulted his estates, which advised accepting, and they pledged their loyalty to their prince. A regency under Philip's eldest son was established, which governed during his five-year imprisonment. Taken to the Netherlands, he was not released until after the Truce of Passau in 1552.

The Peace of Augsburg (1555) ended the wars of religion in Germany for this generation. Chief among its provisions was the principle of *cuius regio, eius religio*, confirming the authority of the German princes over the Church in their lands. During the remaining years of his life, Philip devoted himself primarily to the governance of Hesse, but he strove to promote unity among the

Protestants of Germany and to support the Huguenots of France. After his death in 1567, his lands were partitioned among the four sons of his first marriage.

Summary

Philip the Magnanimous, building on the foundations laid during the regency of his mother, broke the power of the estates of Hesse, creating the strong princely authority which would allow his descendants to play an important role in German affairs into the nineteenth century. More important, his early, ardent, and consistent support for the Protestant cause contributed to its spread and eventual acceptance in large parts of Germany. Although the sincerity of his religious convictions is manifest, so also are the limitations placed upon his contributions by the strength of his emotions. His precipitate action in the Pack affair contributed to the Protestant setback at the Diet of Speyer in 1529. His bigamous marriage in 1540 caused scandal for and within the Protestant forces, while politically neutralizing him for a time. His inability to work in harmony with the more cautious John Frederick contributed to the Protestant defeat in 1547.

Despite these failures, Philip undoubtedly contributed significantly to the success of the Lutheran movement. The Protest of Speyer of 1529, the Augsburg Confession of 1530, and the League of Schmalkalden of 1531 were signed by only seven princes. Other than Philip, the only significant signatory was John Frederick. Without Philip's support, the Lutheran movement in Germany might have been overwhelmed at this critical time in its development. This, alone, is sufficient to justify the inclusion of Philip the Magnanimous among the leading figures of the Reformation.

Bibliography

Bainton, Roland H. *The Reformation of the Sixteenth Century.* Boston: Beacon Press, 1952; London: Hodder and Stoughton, 1953. This work by one of the premier twentieth century scholars of the Reformation is a significant contribution to the interpretation of the Protestant movement. It contains a brief but insightful discussion of the impact of Philip's actions on the Diet of Speyer in 1529, and of his bigamy.

Carsten, Francis Ludwig. *Princes and Parliaments in Germany, from the Fifteenth to the Eighteenth Century.* Oxford: Clarendon Press, 1959. This seminal work on the estates of the lesser German principalities contains an extremely useful discussion of the troubled regency period in Hesse, of the relations of Philip with his subjects, and of the unilateral actions of the landgrave in introducing the Reformation into his principality.

Grimm, Harold J. *The Reformation Era, 1500-1650.* 2d ed. New York: Macmillan, 1973; London: Macmillan, 1974. Grimm's masterful study of the Reformation remains unsurpassed among traditional interpretations for its breadth and objectivity. Contains excellent analyses of the character of Philip, his role in the political events of the age, the Sacramentarian controversy and Marburg Colloquy, and the impact of his bigamous marriage.

Holborn, Hajo. *A History of Modern Germany.* Vol. 1, *The Reformation.* New York: Knopf, 1959; London: Eyre and Spottiswoode, 1965. This classical study of German history is especially useful in placing Philip in his historical context and in developing the influence of individual political actions on the course of the Reformation.

Wright, William John. *Capitalism, the State, and the Lutheran Reformation: Sixteenth Century Hesse.* Athens: Ohio State University Press, 1988. This more recent work utilizes developments in modern historiography to place both the individual prince and the Protestant movement as a whole securely in their socioeconomic setting.

William C. Schrader

PIERO DELLA FRANCESCA

Born: c. 1420; Borgo San Sepulcro

Died: October 12, 1492; Sansepulcro, Tuscany

Areas of Achievement: Art and mathematics

Contribution: Though admired selectively for centuries, Piero della Francesca's paintings were not placed among the world's masterpieces until the twentieth century. His *Baptism of Christ, Resurrection, Legend of the True Cross*, and *Nativity* are now seen as crucial to the development of the characteristic forms and methods of Italian Renaissance painting.

Early Life

Partly because of his being born and reared—and later choosing largely to remain—in a provincial Tuscan market town, almost nothing is known of Piero della Francesca's life up to the age of about twenty. For this reason, the date of his birth, and consequently his age at the time of his dated works, have been subjects of considerable debate. This debate is more significant than such things normally are, for Piero was active during the formative period of the high Italian Renaissance. For a long time, his role in this development was obscured by ignorance, and influences originating in him were attributed to others; later, the pendulum swung the other way. Now his genius is firmly established.

He was born into the Dei Franceschi family (della Francesca is a feminine variant of the name), locally prominent leather merchants, dyers, and farm owners, in Borgo San Sepulcro (modern Sansepulcro, Italy), near Arezzo. The first notice of him appears on September 7, 1439, as an assistant to Domenico Veneziano in a series of now-ruined frescoes in the Church of Sant'Egidio in Florence. Later, in 1442, Piero became one of the Priori (town councilmen) of San Sepulcro, an office he kept for the remainder of his life, though he did leave the town periodically to work in Florence, Milan, and Urbino.

This provincial, rustic upbringing supplied an essential element in Piero's mature technique, for the arid, desolate masses of the Apennine foothills provide the brooding, static backgrounds of his scenes of secular and religious history. In this respect, he adapted the scene-framing techniques of Fra Angelico and his master Domenico Veneziano, going beyond them in using natural settings to shape the emotional and iconological contexts of the foreground subjects. That is, he was one of the first to create thematically integrated compositions, in which every detail contributed to the dominant effect. He undoubtedly received the initial impetus toward this totally unified vision during his apprenticeship to Veneziano in Florence, at a time when the dominant artists were, besides his master, Leon Battista Alberti, Luca della Robbia, Lorenzo Ghiberti, Fra Angelico, Masaccio, and Andrea del Castagno. Piero had the good fortune to mature at the very moment that advances in perspective theory, form, light, and color seemed to call for fusion in a new technique. In the course of his career, Piero forged that technique.

Life's Work

Piero's first known work, an altarpiece commissioned in 1445 for the charitable company known as the Misericordia in his hometown, at first seems to show little evidence of this fusion. This commission, intended to replace an existing work in several segments of different sizes, required him to use the existing panels and frames, thus limiting him to what was by then an antique format. This format dominates the work; at first viewing, the observer is likely to believe that the painting dates from the preceding century, so stiff and compartmentalized do the figures represented appear. Fire damage and overpainting during attempted restorations do not correct the impression. Further study, however, reveals that Piero is here experimenting with novel treatments of light as a means of defining and disclosing form. His light is flushed with color, subtly varied from surface to surface, pervading even the shadows from which it emerges. This is the light of Angelico and Veneziano, but immensely refined in that it takes on and projects texture, in the process inhabiting form. His figures, the clothes they wear, and the volumes they create become tactile, almost palpable. Further, the whole breathes an appropriate, and characteristic, solemnity.

Around 1450, Piero created his first masterwork, *Baptism of Christ*, for a priory in San Sepulcro. The large panel centers on Christ standing in the ankle-deep flow of a translucent stream winding its way down a Tuscan hillside; John strides out from the right to perform his ministry, while three angels watch from the left, under the arch of a small poplar springing improbably from the very bank of the stream, and a postulant in the middle distance pulls off his tunic to become the next candidate. The painting is an arresting combination of strength and subtlety. The Christ is severe, stark, almost repulsive; his features are harsh, peasantlike, rather brutal, certainly common. He stands resolute, firm, determined to take what is coming to him, even if against or beyond his will. The angels lounge idly yet ceremonially, as if they were paid attendants, early altar boys. The event may inaugurate a revolutionary mission, yet no one is paying much attention to it; it is simply another baptism, and even John seems to be merely resigned to it, going through a formality.

Still, this Christ is as vulnerable as he is determined. His contours swell softly: His skin would quiver to the touch, and his transparent loincloth reveals his essential humanity. Further, his white, columnar body precisely parallels the trunk of the poplar, as if the two were of one kind, two manifestations of the same spirit, sprung from the same root. Similarly, the dove centered above the vessel from which John pours, representing the Third Person of the Trinity, is almost indistinguishable from the adjacent clouds. More remarkable, and in defiance of artistic tradition, God the Father does not appear, not even by disembodied hand. Piero seems to suggest that the Father, nevertheless, is there, as much as Son and Holy Spirit. He is simply more immanent than they, as the Son is also in the tree and the Spirit in the clouds. This revelation of theme in seemingly accidental yet completely integrated detail is the signature of Piero. Typically, every naturalistic detail—like the inverted reflection of landscape in the stream—is rendered with the utmost fidelity to the natural phenomena.

The *Resurrection* fresco (c. 1453) is Piero's best-known work. The subject was the official symbol of the town—hence its name—and Piero deliberately represents the event as taking place while the sun rises in the rocky hills above the town. Christ mounts the sarcophagus with his left foot, grasping a red-cross standard which unfolds above him. His pale rose-colored robe opens to expose the spear wound. The face is as compelling as that in the *Baptism of Christ*, but these eyes are simultaneously harrowing—they have experienced everything—and compassionate, probing into the soul of the viewer. Four soldiers sprawl in front of the tomb, dozing, the back of one resting against the frontal plane of the painting. Though apparently disposed at random, the figures combine with that of the risen Christ in a pattern of interlocking and embedded triangles, creating an impression of great strength and endurance.

In the middle background, the landscape on the left—luminous in the shimmering light of dawn—is withered and barren, while that on the right is in full leaf. This is the iconographic equivalent of Christ's remark on the way to Calvary: "If they do these things in a green tree, what shall be done in the dry?" (Luke 23:31), referring to the persecution that would follow upon his execution. There was a further association of green and withered trees with the Trees of Life and of Knowledge in the Garden of Eden, the second of which in legend became both symbolically and actually the agent of human redemption, by furnishing the wood for Christ's cross. In this painting, Piero created an image in which all of the details fuse in a vision of total integrity, in which psychological intensity and doctrinal content reinforce each other.

Piero's only major fresco cycle, the *Legend of the True Cross* (1452-1457), is the most ambitious project he attempted: a series of twelve frescoes setting forth a pious medieval legend of complex, and improbable, fantasy. Unfortunately, the entire chancel, on which the frescoes were done, has suffered from water seepage over the ensuing centuries, and much of the surface has been lost and ineptly restored. These restorations have recently been removed, so that what remains of the original can now be seen.

What is there is astonishing. The panels narrate major episodes in the legend, from the fetching of a branch from Eden by Seth to cure his father Adam through Solomon's burying of a beam and Helena's discovery of the cross fashioned from it to its recovery from Chosroes by the Emperor Heraclius. Piero arranged them not chronologically but in order to focus on visual, symbolic, and thematic resonances. Thus, for example, scenes dominated by women are set on opposite walls, as are those of battles and those involving visions of the Cross. Further, each panel consists of two paired scenes representing two incidents within a single episode. Independently, these paintings serve as illustrations of rhythmic group composition, Albertian perspective, and visual and thematic integration; together, they constitute one of the most magnificent sequences of painting ever composed, truly remarkable especially for the fidelity of its coloring, so that the landscapes and people represented take on tangible reality.

In the middle of his career, Piero occasionally left San Sepulcro to do some of his most significant work at Urbino, Milan, and Florence. In Urbino, for example, he painted a mysterious *Flagellation of Christ* (probably 1463-1464), the thematic content of which has only recently been convincingly interpreted. The dignity of his figures, however, the delicacy of light and color, and the austere sincerity of the work have never been in doubt. Also in Urbino, Piero composed complementary portraits of *Count Federico da Montefeltro* and his wife, *Battista Sforza* (after 1474), which bear allegorical triumph scenes on their reverses. The portraits show to the highest degree Piero's fusion of austerity of vision and revelation of character, and the triumphs disclose a blend of imaginative landscape with mythological content. His last known painting, *Nativity* (1480), reveals modulations of color and light that have never been surpassed; Piero almost makes the air visible.

Though he lived on for some twenty years, he seems not to have returned to painting, busying himself instead in theoretical studies, which included the first Renaissance treatise on perspective and a book on geometry. According to legend, he became blind in the last years of his life.

Summary

Up to the twentieth century Piero della Francesca and his work were believed to be remote and somewhat primitive; at best, he was considered a "provincial master" and treated somewhat condescendingly. At this point, it is difficult to understand that neglect. His work is always compelling, particularly in his rare union of force and subtlety. Even when disfigured by time or made to appear crude by clumsy overpainting, his scenes are honest, direct, forthright, and sincere. Further study always reveals what can only be called marvelous hidden harmonies underlying fully integrated compositions. It is almost as if Piero thought out each painting completely and then executed what he saw in his mind's eye. Every detail falls into its necessary place, supporting and subordinated to the whole.

Probably the most striking aspect of Piero's painting is a quality not immediately perceptible, since the underlying unity and harmony of his work is accomplished by means of subtle geometric patterns; abstract shapes—triangles, parallelograms, rhomboids—emerge through the living figures of the surface. These anchor his compositions, creating weight and mass, imparting a solid dignity rivaled only by Masaccio and Castagno. These geometrical patterns contribute to the formal emphasis of his work, giving it almost palpable substance, as if his scenes have more body than real life. It is easy to understand why the abstract painters and formalists of the early twentieth century should have made a hero out of Piero; he anticipated many of their interests.

Other qualities of his work also had to wait until the twentieth century for proper appreciation. Among them is his creation of human characters who, though outwardly commonplace, even crude, are absolutely convincing in their individuality and humanity. For this reason, reproductions of his incidental figures became favorites of painters and art students during the ascendancy of Georges Braque and Pablo Picasso. Still, there are elements in Piero's work that stand independent of such fashionable revivals. The lyricism of his colors, for example, is a pure joy, transcending the accomplishments of everyone before Leonardo da Vinci. Coincident with that is his use of light, especially in the way he combines the two to bring out the solidity and mass of his figures. Finally, there is his use of landscape to integrate the composition of his paintings and to unify them thematically. No one had done this kind of thing before him; no one ever did it better.

Bibliography

Battisti, Eugenio. *Piero della Francesca*. University Park: Pennsylvania State University Press, 1972. This text is the standard academic study of Piero, fully documented, with excellent reproductions, a complete bibliography, and thorough discussions of the paintings and their artistic and historical contexts. The explanations of the paintings are outstanding, particularly because the quality of the plates is so high.

Baxandall, Michael. *Painting and Experience in Fifteenth Century Italy: A Primer in the Social History of Pictorial Style*. Oxford: Clarendon Press, and New York: Oxford University Press, 1974. One of the standard reference works for Quattrocento art, this offers a particularly incisive account of Piero's pivotal role in the development of painting. Also contains useful insights into his failure to attract general appreciation until the twentieth century.

Clark, Kenneth. *Piero della Francesca*. London and New York: Phaidon Press, 1951. An early account of Piero's work and development, this is perhaps the most accessible study of the paintings. Some of the material and the plates are dated, requiring correction and amplification in later studies.

Gilbert, Creighton. *Change in Piero della Francesca*. Locust Valley, N.Y.: Augustin, 1968. This is a groundbreaking account of Piero's stylistic development, offering a more thorough technical analysis of his methods than any other source. Some of the arguments seem forced, but in general this is an indispensable work for an appreciation of what Piero really accomplished.

Hartt, Frederick. *History of Italian Renaissance Art: Painting, Architecture, Sculpture*. 4th ed. London: Thames and Hudson, and New York: Abrams, 1994. Hartt gives an excellent account of Piero's position in the development of Italian Renaissance art; in short space, he sketches the essential qualities of his work, focusing on formal and thematic integrity. His writing is eminently readable, making this the best available introduction.

Kemp, Martin. "Piero's Perspective." *Nature* 390 (November, 1997): 128. Kemp examines Piero's unique artistic perspective, focusing on his book *The Perspective of Painting*, which deals with practical mathematics and simple algebra.

Longhi, Roberto. *Piero della Francesca*. 2d ed. Milan, Italy: Hoepli, 1946. One of the first revisionist studies of Piero's formal qualities and of his role in the evolution of Italian painting. It is still vital and convincing, but the reproductions are inferior and many of the interpretations need to be updated

Peterson, Mark A. "The Geometry of Piero della Francesca." *Mathematical Intelligencer* 19 (summer 1997): 33. This article looks back on the life of Francesca, providing background information covering his career achievements and his contributions to mathematics.

Vasari, Giorgio. *Lives of the Most Eminent Painters, Sculptors, and Architects*. 10 vols. Translated by Gaston du C. De Vere. London and New York: Macmillan, 1912-1914. In this edition of a famous volume of biographical sketches by a near-contemporary of Piero, Vasari includes many details which would otherwise have been unrecorded; he is thus the source of most of what is known, though much is based on hearsay. Vasari also shows what was thought of Piero during the sixteenth century.

James Livingston

THE PINZÓN BROTHERS

Martín Alonso Pinzón

Born: c. 1440; probably near Palos, Spain
Died: March, 20, 1493; Palos, Spain

Vicente Yáñez Pinzón

Born: c. 1462; Palos, Spain
Died: c. 1523; probably Spain
Area of Achievement: Exploration
Contribution: The two Pinzón brothers provided crucial assistance for Christopher Columbus' first voyage to the New World. The brothers helped Columbus obtain and outfit his three ships and served as captains of the *Pinta* and the *Niña*.

Early Life

Martín Alonso and Vicente Yáñez Pinzón were brothers in a family of wealthy shipowners and navigators in the Spanish port city of Palos. Martín, the elder of the two men, had spent most of his life since the age of fifteen at sea. He had sailed throughout the Mediterranean and along the northwest coast of Africa, serving Spain in a war against Portugal. He was widely recognized as an expert seaman, navigator, and captain. His younger brother, Vicente, about whom less is known, also spent most of his life at sea, learning the practical arts of seamanship and navigation.

The Pinzón family was one of the three leading shipping families in the important port city of Palos, on Spain's southwest coast. The enthusiastic support of the Pinzóns for Christopher Columbus' first voyage to the New World greatly helped Columbus to secure the skilled seamen, ships, material, and leaders necessary for success. In the summer of 1491, Columbus arrived in Palos to consult with a Franciscan friar and astronomer who supported his claims of the possibility of a trans-Atlantic trade route to Asia. This friar, Fray Antonio de Marchena, introduced Columbus to the leading families of Palos, including Martín Alonso of the Pinzóns.

Following the initial visit of Columbus, de Marchena and others communicated their support to the Spanish royal court. Columbus was then called to meet with Queen Isabella. When she decided to support Columbus' voyage, Martín Alonso Pinzón and his family in Palos helped Columbus to obtain the use of two ships, the *Pinta* and the *Niña*, for the voyage. Martín Pinzón also assisted Columbus in recruiting the necessary skilled hands for the expedition's three vessels, helped to calm fears of a voyage into the unknown, and offered his services and that of his brother as captains of the two ships provided by the city of Palos. Columbus himself captained the third ship, the *Santa Maria*. By the late summer of 1492, the small fleet had finished preparations for the historic journey.

Life's Work

On Friday, August 3, 1492, the three ships departed Palos, heading south toward the Canary Islands off the northwest coast of Africa. The fleet left the Canaries in early September and set a course due west in search of a trade route to Asia. Columbus had chosen a more southern course to avoid difficult and heavy seas in the North Atlantic. He hoped to find the mythical island of Antilla halfway to Japan where he could restock his ships with water, and possibly food. Martín and Vicente Pinzón, captains of the Pinta and the *Niña*, followed this course diligently. The fleet made more than 1,100 miles in its first nine days, pushed onward by easterly winds.

In last week of September, the fleet made less than four hundred miles. Columbus never found the island of Antilla, and the ships' water began to go bad. Under this stress, the crews of all three ships began to grumble. No man in any crew had been so distant from land before. Grievances formed, fights had to be broken up, and the men began to fear for their lives. There were rumors of mutiny. Then, in October, things turned better for Columbus and the Pinzóns. Rainstorms replenished the ships' water supplies, and the wind increased. By October 6, the fleet had traveled more than 2,400 miles. That day, Martín Alonso Pinzón told Columbus that the ships should alter their course to the southwest, because he feared that they had missed Japan. Columbus, though, held true to his westerly course.

The next day, great flocks of birds passed over the ships, heading to the southwest. Columbus decided to follow Martín Pinzón's advice and changed course. This was fortunate for the fleet, because this was the shortest course to the nearest land. Yet mutiny reared its head again, as the crewmen began to once more question Columbus; they had sailed much farther west than anyone had expected. Columbus's resolve was heartened by the complete support of both Martín and Vicente Pinzón. On October 11, signs of land began to appear, as tree branches and flowers drifted by on the ocean. The mutterings of mutiny died away as all expected a quick landfall.

At two o'clock in the morning of October 12, a lookout on the *Pinta* spotted what looked like white cliffs shining in the moonlight. Martín Pinzón checked and verified the landfall, firing a gun as the agreed signal. Columbus, in the *Santa Maria*, caught up to Pinzón and shouted across the water that he would pay a large bonus to his captain. The fleet had found one of the Bahamas in the Caribbean Sea. The next afternoon, the expedition found a shallow bay and anchored offshore. Columbus and the Pinzóns went ashore, and the Columbus gave the island the name San Salvador, or "holy savior."

In the next month, the fleet cruised about the eastern Caribbean Sea, exploring about the Bahamas and discovering Cuba and the island of Hispaniola. Columbus found fine harbors, beautiful beaches, and virgin forests, excellent for the construction of ships, but there was no gold. He could not find Japan or China either. The fever for gold was so great that Martín Pinzón left the fleet on November 21 and sailed for the mythical island of Babeque without asking Columbus for permission. The *Santa Maria* and *Niña*, captained by the more loyal Vicente Pinzón, continued on without him. They found generally friendly natives, ripe for exploitation, as Columbus wrote in his journal.

Very early on December 25, 1492, disaster struck. The *Santa Maria* ran into a coral reef off the north coast of the island of Hispaniola. Despite Columbus' best efforts, the ship's hull filled with water, and the *Santa Maria* had to be abandoned. Columbus and his crew moved to join Vicente Pinzón on the *Niña*. On January 2, 1493, the *Niña* departed for home. Sixteen men were left behind to build a fort, look for gold, and explore the area. Two days later, Columbus sighted the *Pinta*. Martín Pinzón explained his six-week absence as a successful one of both exploration and a search for gold. Columbus, glad to have company on the long voyage back to Spain, decided to forgive Martín Pinzón.

The return trip was rough, as the two ships ran into contrary winds and made little headway eastward. In mid-February, the *Pinta* and the *Niña* encountered a tremendous storm that almost sank both vessels. The two ships were separated sometime during the night of February 13-14, and the *Niña*'s crew almost gave up hope on Valentine's Day. Fearing that both ships would be lost, Columbus threw a summary of his journey overboard in a bottle. The *Niña* survived and finally beat its way back to Spain after surviving another great tempest that almost drove the ship onto Portugal's rocky western coast.

On March 15, 1493, the *Niña* reached Palos. Finally back home, Columbus discovered that the *Pinta* had survived and that Martín Pinzón had sent a message to Queen Isabella announcing his arrival. Pinzón had reached Spain's northwest coast in February. He had then begged for permission to tell the Spanish queen about the voyage, but she told him to wait. The *Pinta* arrived in Palos shortly after Columbus on March 15. Martín Alonso Pinzón, older than Columbus, exhausted from his journey and snubbed by the Spanish royalty, went directly to his home near Palos and died there on March 20.

Vicente Yáñez Pinzón made important discoveries on his own after his return with Columbus in 1493. In late 1499, he sailed from Spain and discovered South America on February 7, 1500, three months before the first Portuguese discovery. He also discovered the Amazon River and continued northwest along the South American coast at least as far north as present-day Costa Rica. In 1507, he returned again to explore the coast of Central America. Two years later, Vicente Pinzón explored southward along the Argentinean coast. All traces of Vicente Yáñez Pinzón's life after 1523 are lost.

Summary

While the support of the Pinzóns and other families in Palos proved critical to the successes of Columbus' voyage, the exploration could likely have continued without their support, if necessary. It is quite possible, however, that without the assistance of the Pinzóns, Columbus first voyage would not have been as successful as it was.

The loyalty and material assistance provided by the Pinzóns allowed Columbus to proceed with his first voyage as planned. Despite Martín Alonso's insubordination in November and his attempt to steal Columbus' glory upon his return to Spain in 1493, Martín's assistance greatly helped the expedition. His suggestion to change to a southwesterly course on October 6 allowed Columbus to make a landfall earlier than expected and may have helped to avert further difficulties with their crews. His death on March 20, 1493, was a major loss to history, for there has never been a reliable account of the first voyage other than that of Columbus.

Vicente Yáñez Pinzón's role in history is also nearly forgotten. His primary importance to the early exploration of the New World lies with his discovery of South America and with his explorations in Central America and of the Amazon River. Unfortunately for Vicente, the Portuguese explorer Pedro Cabral, who actually arrived in South America later, has been given historical credit for the European discovery of the continent.

While it would be a historical fallacy to claim that the assistance of the Pinzóns ensured Columbus' successes, their importance should be neither overlooked or forgotten. Men such as the Pinzóns provided the foundation for the accomplishments of explorers such as Christopher Columbus.

Bibliography

Bradford, Ernie. *Christopher Columbus.* New York: Viking Press, 1973. Gives the best explanation of how Columbus first encountered Martín Pinzón but does not provide much biographical information on the two brothers. Surpassed by Samuel Eliot Morison's work on Columbus, even though this work is more recent.

Collis, John Stewart. *Christopher Columbus.* New York: Stein and Day, 1976. This biography includes good information on preparations and plans for the voyage, as well as some brief background on the two Pinzóns.

De Madariaga, Salvador. *Christopher Columbus.* New York: Frederick Ungar, 1940. An outdated and overly enthusiastic endorsement of Columbus and his historical role; however, this book does provide one of the best biographical outlines of Martín Alonso's early life.

Fernadez-Armesio, Felipe. *Columbus.* New York: Oxford University Press, 1991. An excellent overview of Columbus' entire life, with an especially good treatment of the role of both Pinzóns in the first voyage. The work is rather broad in its scope, however, and it dedicates less than thirty pages to the first voyage.

Fyre, John. *Los Otros: Columbus and the Three Who Made His Enterprise of the Indies Succeed.* Lewiston, N.Y.: Mellen Press, 1992. The only biography that provides a detailed history of the Pinzóns. A short but accurate work that summarizes what is known about Martín Alonso and Vicente Yáñez Pinzón.

McKee, Alexander. *A World Too Vast: The Four Voyages of Columbus.* London: Souvenir Press, 1990. A well-written and thorough summary of Columbus' voyages that, however, contains little biographical material on either Pinzón.

Morison, Samuel Eliot. *Admiral of the Ocean Sea: A Life of Christopher Columbus.* Boston: Little Brown, 1942. One of the best biographies of Columbus. The tenth chapter, on officers and men, contains brief but useful biographical information on both Pinzóns.

———. *The Great Explorers: The European Discovery of America.* New York: Oxford University Press, 1978. Morison is one of the greatest of maritime historians, and his chapters on Columbus' voyage and the roles of Martín Alonso and Vicente Yáñez Pinzón are unmatched.

Jeff R. Bremer

PIUS II
Enea Silvio Piccolomini

Born: October 18, 1405; Corsignano, Republic of Siena
Died: August 14/15, 1464; Ancona
Areas of Achievement: Religion and politics
Contribution: Through his elegant rhetoric and skilled diplomacy, Pius II reconciled differences among Christians to bring some peace to Western Christendom and tried vainly to mobilize a crusade to liberate Constantinople from the Turks.

Early Life

Enea Silvio Piccolomini—better known by the Latin version of his name, Aeneas Silvius Piccolomini—was born in the village of Corsignano (which changed its name to Pienza when its most famous son was elected to the Papacy), near Siena, of a noble but poor family. Piccolomini left home to begin his studies at the University of Siena in 1423, but he really began his career in 1431, when he accompanied Domenico Capranica to the Council of Basel. For the next four years, Enea learned his trade, polishing his rhetorical skills in speaking and writing and earning the trust of others, for whom he conducted many diplomatic errands. On one of his missions to Scotland, he fulfilled a vow to walk barefoot for ten miles to a shrine; as a result, he froze his feet so badly that he was a semi-invalid for the rest of his life.

In 1436, he obtained a seat on the Council of Basel, which soon moved to Florence. At Florence he participated in the election of Amadeus VIII of Savoy as Pope Felix V. As ecclesiastical conflicts raged and Felix was declared an antipope, Piccolomini left Rome in 1442 to enter into the diplomatic service of Emperor Frederick III. Welcomed by this Holy Roman Emperor, who promptly named him poet laureate, Piccolomini wrote most of his pagan poetry and prose during this time. Writing in the style of Giovanni Boccaccio's *Decameron: O, Prencipe Galeotto* (1349-1351; *The Decameron*, 1620), Piccolomini wrote a play, *Chrysis* (1444), and a more substantial prose romance, *De duobus amantibus Eurialo et Lucresia* (1444; *The Tale of Two Lovers*, 1560), which endeared him to the literary Humanists of the Italian Renaissance.

All this activity ended, to the skepticism of his peers, when in 1446, Piccolomini announced that he was "forsaking Venus for Bacchus," by which he meant that he was renouncing sexual license for the wine of the Eucharist. He took holy orders as a deacon and was reconciled to the church hierarchy by Pope Eugene IV. After that, ascent was swift. Pope Nicholas V appointed him Bishop of Trieste in 1447 and promoted him to the bishopric of Siena in 1449. Callistus III made him cardinal in 1456. Finally, on August 19, 1458, a sharply divided College of Cardinals looked for a peacemaker and elected Aeneas Silvius Piccolomini pope; he boldly chose the name of a second century saint, Pius, to be "reminiscent of pious Aeneas."

Life's Work

Pius II faced an enormous challenge. Surrounded on all sides by rivals and enemies, he would need all of his diplomatic skills to play his enemies against one another. From the northeast there was the Papacy's oldest rival, the empire—which people had long since declared to be neither "holy" nor "Roman" nor an "empire," but which remained powerful. Pius relied upon his previously congenial diplomatic service with Frederick to defuse this threat. From the northwest there was the Papacy's most dangerous enemy, the kingdom of France, which nearly fifty years earlier had been forced to give up its Avignon antipope and which, a half century hence, would invade Italy. Pius would fight his fiercest battle with King Louis XI. On the Italian peninsula itself, in the north the commercial city-state republics of Venice, Florence, and others defied papal pretensions; in the south, the shaky throne of Naples was attracting the covetous attention of both Spanish Aragon and French Anjou. Pius could ignore the northern threat; he tried to mediate between the latter claimants. Overriding all other threats for the leader of Western Christendom, however, were two supreme challenges: one from within—conciliarism—and one from without—the calamitous fall of the capital of Eastern Christianity, Constantinople, to the Turks in 1453.

During the first four years of his reign, Pius persuaded France's new king, Louis XI, to withdraw his support for the Pragmatic Sanction in order to gain papal support for the French claim to the kingdom of Naples. This diplomatic coup was designed to nullify simultaneously the conciliarism and the enmity of France. The Pragmatic Sanction of 1438

represented the high point of the conciliar movement, the ecclesiastical movement to subordinate the pope to the church councils. The French kings and most French clergy had supported the sanction because they hated the clerical power of Rome. Pius had inherited his predecessors' policy, which supported the Aragonese claim to Naples, but he suggested to the French king that he could back the Angevin claim in exchange for some concessions. This diplomatic feat was Pius' only political success, and he was unable to capitalize on it.

The diplomatic situation was complicated because there were other players in the game. In fact, Louis' repudiation of the conciliar movement stemmed more from his fear of his own clergy in France (called "Gallicans") than from any foreign policy consideration. The Gallican clergy opposed many aspects of monarchical rule. Louis was also fighting the Burgundian duke who claimed the French throne. Unfortunately, Pius was unable to follow through on his bargain with Louis. Finding that he needed Spanish support for his greater enterprise, the pope was compelled to turn to Burgundy, making concessions which solidified French hostility. The conciliar movement, however, was mortally wounded, and Pius deserves partial credit for administering its *coup de grâce*.

For the last two years of his reign, Pius prepared for the Crusade to liberate Constantinople from the Ottoman Turks. Eight centuries of fighting had culminated in the city's capture only five years before Pius' election. In his eyes, a crusade was essential to vindicate his life, his career, and his faith. At the personal level, a crusade was the only way that Pius could prove to his public, to his skeptical Humanist peers—who were angry at his desertion—and to the anxious religious constituents who were not yet convinced of his piety and faith, that he was what he professed to be: a true Christian. At the political level, this was the best way that Pius could protect the Papacy from its internal enemies. In *Commentarii* (1464; *The Commentaries of Pius II*, 1936-1937), which he wrote in the last years of his life, Pius had four themes, which are largely political. On the Italian peninsula, to recover papal territory and support the anti-French candidate to the throne of Naples, Sigismondo Malasta of Rimini must be fought. On the Continent, the pope must not only curb France but also intervene judiciously in the turmoil of the empire, where Frederick III is embattled. In the moral realm, there is the nonreligious materialism of the Venetians, Florentines, and even Sienese—as dangerous as the outright heresy of the Hussites in Bohemia. Finally, there is the greatest menace of all: the Turk.

Pope Pius' Crusade was a failure. Providentially finding alum mines in Italy to help raise money, he decided to lead the crusade himself. Carried on a litter because of his ruined feet, he embarked on June 18, 1464. Accompanied by a handful of loyal troops from Rome, Pius crossed to the shores of the Adriatic Sea. At the rendezvous, there were virtually no Italians. Louis XI from France did not come; the Aragonese from Spain and Naples, the Burgundians, and Emperor Frederick III did not come. During the night of August 14/15, at Ancona on the Adriatic Sea, far from Constantinople, Pius died.

Summary

The question still lingers: Who was dominant? Aeneas Silvio Piccolomini, Renaissance Humanist and man of letters, or Pope Pius II, Crusader and would-be martyr? The man was not a mystic like Joan of Arc, whose accomplishments and martyrdom streaked across the European landscape when he was in his twenties. He was not a poet or scholar like his idols and peers, whose literary achievements were transforming Europe throughout his lifetime. He was not a charismatic reformer capable of cleansing the Church from the inside. All he had learned from his formal education was to write elegantly and speak persuasively to educated people. All he had inherited from his medieval profession was the desire to protect the papal office and to start a crusade.

History has not remembered either the Humanist or the pope, and scholars who study him in the context of other pursuits have not been kind. In a speech to a group of cardinals, Pius frankly observed that the Europe of his day had rejected the medieval concept of a crusade without having yet awakened to the Turkish threat to Western civilization. When he said this in 1462 (before he was committed to his futile project), he was aware of his own variety of motives, both practical and idealistic. Nevertheless, he did decide to mobilize the gigantic defense operation necessary to save Christian Europe from the Turk—although he did not know how to proceed. All he could manage was to be carried in the direction of the battle and wait for either natural or supernatural intervention. He waited in vain.

What remains, then, are his writings. Although he ranks as a second-rate writer of the Italian Renaissance, being neither as good a storyteller as Boccaccio nor as incisive politically as Niccolò Machiavelli nor as philosophically profound as Giovanni Pico della Mirandola, he was adept enough to rise from poverty in a world of elegant Humanists. In addition, he was concerned enough to perceive that the greatest peril of the day emanated not from antipopes but from materialism in the West and the Turks from the East. He was brave enough to act upon his observations with courage and commitment to the very end.

Bibliography

Ady, Cecilia M. *Pius II (Aeneas Silvius Piccolomini) the Humanist Pope*. London: Methuen, 1913. This older study was written by an authority on late medieval and Renaissance Italy. It is favorable and sympathetic to a man caught in the predicament of being both a Humanist intellectual and a political leader of an institution not respected by Humanist intellectuals. Outdated.

Gragg, Florence A., and Leona C. Gabel. *Memoirs of a Renaissance Pope*. New York: Putnam, 1959; London: Allen and Unwin, 1960. Gragg and Gabel delineate four major themes in the introduction to this abridged translation of *The Commen-taries of Pius II:* Italian political conflicts, both between the pope and secular opponents and between two factions for the throne of Naples; France's malevolent presence; the disintegration of the amorphous Holy Roman Empire; and the planned Crusade against the Ottoman Turks, who had conquered Constantinople in 1453.

Rowe, John Gordon. "The Tragedy of Aeneas Silvius Piccolomini." *Church History* 30 (1961): 288-313. A savage critique of the man as a Humanist and as pope. This review is valuable to balance the usually positive view of Pius II. Unless the pope was spectacularly villainous—as many were in this period—most are sympathetically treated by both popular and academic critics. Since the literature in English on Pius is limited, this critique must serve. Ample bibliography.

Woodward, William Harrison. *Vittorino da Feltre and Other Humanist Educators: Essays and Versions*. Cambridge: Cambridge University Press, 1897; New York: Columbia Uni-versity Press, 1964. Woodward devotes most of his attention to Vittorino da Feltre. Although Pius is fitted into his historical context, he is portrayed as not very important. Woodward's pedagogical moralism will strike most students as old-fashioned. No bibliography.

David R. Stevenson

PIUS V
Antonio Ghislieri

Born: January 17, 1504; Bosco, Duchy of Milan
Died: May 1, 1572; Rome
Areas of Achievement: Religion and church reform
Contribution: Pius V effected the reforms dictated by the Council of Trent, attempted to stem the spread of Protestantism, participated in the Inquisition, and was largely responsible for the naval defeat of the Ottoman Empire at Lepanto. His piety, religious zeal, and dedication to the Church eventually resulted in his canonization.

Early Life

Antonio Ghislieri, who would become Pope Pius V, was born in Bosco, a small town near Alessandria, in the Duchy of Milan. His parents, Paolo and Dominica (née Augeria), were poor, and the future pope worked as a shepherd as a youth. Through the generosity of a more prosperous neighbor, he was put under the tutelage of the Dominican friars at Bosco; two years later, at fourteen, he was sent to the Dominican convent at Voghera. After beginning his novitiate at the Convent of Vigevano, he received his Dominican habit in 1520 and assumed his religious name, Michael, the following year. During this time, he developed his scholarly talent and practiced the monastic ideals of austerity, simplicity, and self-denial. His character and conduct as a pope were shaped in large part by his early life in the monastery.

An avid student, Ghislieri attended the University of Bologna, and he later became an equally successful teacher of philosophy and theology, which he taught at several Dominican friaries. In 1528, he was raised to the priesthood at Genoa and for the next several years served at various Dominican convents, where his piety, humility, and dedication won for him the respect of his colleagues—he was elected prior at four of the friaries. During this time, he also became confessor to many important people, among them the Governor of Milan, yet he remained humble and, unlike many of his clerical peers, traveled everywhere by foot.

In 1542, the humble priest's life was changed by an act which ultimately led to his elevation to the Papacy. As a result of religious schism, notably the spread of Martin Luther's doctrine, a papal bull instituted the Roman Inquisition. Because of Ghislieri's skill at refuting the Lutheran "heresies"—he had been summoned to Parma in 1543 to combat Lutheran doctrine and attacks on pontifical authority—he became inquisitor in the diocese of Patvia in 1543. It was his zealous role in the Inquisition that brought him to the attention of church leaders and his eventual election as Pope Pius V.

Life's Work

Although he was almost forty years old when he began his inquisitorial career, Pius' life's work and place in history are inextricably related not only to his pontificate but also to the Inquisition. In the relentless pursuit of his duties, he was often embroiled in disputes with a populace, including clergy, that was sympathetic to Luther. After he confiscated twelve bales of "heretical" books and excommunicated the guilty parties in Como, he barely escaped an enraged crowd. He was vindicated in Rome and as Inquisitor of Bergamo dealt severely with a Luther supporter, Bishop Vittorio Soranzo, who was subsequently imprisoned, convicted, deposed as bishop, and exiled to Venice. In 1551, he became, despite his objections, Prefect of the Palace of the Inquisition, and in 1558 he became the first and the only Grand Inquisitor of the Roman Catholic Church. Ecclesiastical advancement accompanied his increasing role in the Inquisition. In 1556, he became Bishop of Sutri and Nepi, then Bishop of Mondovi; in 1557, he was named Cardinal Alessandrino (after the large city near his birthplace). So secure was his position that the 1559 election of Pope Pius IV, which adversely affected other cardinals, left him untouched. In fact, he demonstrated that his principles were more important than politics when he opposed Pius IV's elevation of a relative youngster to a position of authority in the Church.

Upon Pius IV's death, Cardinal Alessandrino became, through the efforts of Cardinal Borromeo, Pope Pius V. While his papacy lasted only six years (1566-1572), he presided over a church under siege from without and undermined from within. The Turks of the Ottoman Empire were a constant threat, and the Reformation sects in Germany, France, England, and the Lowlands were rapidly gaining converts, a disturbing development since church and state were one in the sixteenth century. Unfortunately, the Catholic princes—Philip II of

Spain, Maximilian II of Germany, and Sigismund Augustus of Poland—were protective of their own power, unwilling to offend powerful Protestants, or bent on achieving their own ends. Pius also had to contend with clergy who did not share his enthusiasm for the reforms of the recently concluded Council of Trent (1545-1563) and with clergy who had been tainted by Lutheran doctrine.

Pius moved quickly to effect the reforms dictated by the Council of Trent, reforms that were consistent with his monastic life, his idealism, and his piety. During his papacy, the *Catechismus Romanus* (for pastoral use) appeared, the reform of the Breviary was completed, the *Missale Romanum* was printed, and three new masses were composed. Besides the liturgical reforms, he brought about an improvement in public morals in a Rome accustomed to the luxury-loving Renaissance popes. His internal reforms, which can be seen as a Counter-Reformation or reaction to Reformation inroads, can also be regarded as the Church's efforts to reform itself, efforts that had begun before Luther's break with the Church.

In Germany, where the Reformation was solidly established, Pius' efforts to influence Maximilian II (who was also the Holy Roman Emperor) were unsuccessful, for the emperor pursued a policy of conciliating the Catholics without alienating the Protestants. Despite the efforts of Commendone, the pope's nuncio (representative) to Germany, Maximilian was unwilling to move beyond the Augsburg Confession of 1555, which was unacceptable to the pontiff, and the emperor continued to let his Protestant subjects practice their religion. When his numerous concessions to Maximilian proved fruitless, Pius responded with an action that angered the emperor because it encroached on political matters. In an attempt to recapture the ancient rights of papal authority, which had been diminished by his predecessors, Pius crowned Cosimo I as Grand Duke of Tuscany in 1569.

The same erosion of papal authority had occurred in Spain, where Philip II shared Maximilian's concern about the threat to "Caesaropapistical" rights, rights that political rulers had gained at the expense of the Papacy. Philip II was reluctant to have the imprisoned Archbishop Carranza moved to Rome for his heresy trial, and Pius succeeded in moving Carranza only after making financial concessions and conducting protracted negotiations with Philip. Though, like Maximilian II, Philip vowed his support of Pius, the Spanish king was equally reluctant

to grant the pope's request that he send his troops to subdue the rebellious Netherlanders. The political/ecclesiastical conflict was heightened by Pius' unpopular papal bull prohibiting bullfighting, but Philip was also guilty of making civil inroads on papal authority. When Pius attempted to curb civil authority in his papal bull of 1568, *In Coena Domini*, Philip essentially ignored it and never really relinquished his regal rights to Pius V.

Even in Poland, a Catholic stronghold, there were problems. Although the Catholics were able to prevail over the Protestants at the 1570 Diet in Warsaw, Pius' nuncio to Poland could not persuade Sigismund Augustus to reform the monasteries or to join the league against the Turkish threat. The Polish monarch's recalcitrance was caused in part by the pope's unwillingness to grant him a divorce from Queen Catherine.

In England, where Henry VIII's divorce had caused a break with Rome, Pius failed in his attempt to return the country to the Catholic faith. Unsuccessful in gaining support for Mary, Queen of Scotland, from Philip or from the Duke of Alba, Pius excommunicated Elizabeth in 1570. His *Regnans in Excelsis*, which also freed Catholics from the obligation to obey her, was countered by Elizabeth's repressive anti-Catholic measures. Elizabeth was the last monarch to be excommunicated by a pope.

Only in the Netherlands and in France did Pius win convincing victories for the Church. Philip finally dispatched the Duke of Alba to crush the revolt in the Netherlands; the duke was only partly successful, and his brutality was notable even when judged by sixteenth century standards. In France, the civil war was ended in 1569 at Jarnac, where the Catholics won a decisive victory.

The pope's greatest achievement, however, was the defeat of the Turkish forces at Lepanto in 1571. Although the Ottoman Empire had invaded Hungary and threatened not only Venice but also Italy, only Pius seemed aware of the danger. Through the pope's negotiating skills and his financial commitment to the cause, Philip was persuaded to join Venice against the Turks. Under the command of Don Juan of Austria, the Christian fleet sailed to battle against the Ottoman forces, which had already overrun Nicosia and Famagusta in Cyprus. The Christian victory at Lepanto marked the high point of Pius' efforts for the Catholic Church.

Soon after the battle the pope's health, which had never been good, deteriorated, and he died on May 1, 1572. One hundred years later, Pope Clement X beatified Pius V, and on May 22, 1712, he was canonized by Pope Clement XI.

Summary

The fact that no pope had been canonized in the 350 years that preceded Pius' canonization vividly demonstrates the esteem that he enjoyed within the Catholic Church. His efforts to effect the reforms dictated by the Council of Trent, his own monastic piety, his missionary zeal (during his papacy many missionaries were sent to South America, especially Brazil), and his lack of personal ambition—these traits reflect the saintliness of the pope known as "The Pope of the Holy Rosary." History, however, has not been kind to the "Inquisition Pope," whose redemption of Sixtus of Siena must be measured against the strict censorship and the brutal torture of the Inquisition he endorsed and supported.

Pius was motivated by his ambition for the Catholic Church, threatened by the Turks and the Protestant Reformers, beset by internal apathy, and undermined by the political ambitions of rulers whose expanding powers eroded traditional papal authority. From the Church's perspective, church and state were the same, and political threats were religious threats (England, the Ottoman Empire, the Protestant German states) that ultimately threatened a civilization synonymous with the Church. Given the besieged condition of such an integrated world, Pius' extreme measures can be understood, if not justified.

The Western world was, however, irrevocably fragmented politically and theologically, and Pius' attempts to return to an earlier unified age were futile. In fact, his efforts to restore lost papal authority were not realistic, given the religious ferment and the political ambitions of rulers. Philip ignored Pius' papal bull of 1568, and Elizabeth's response to her excommunication revealed that weapon to be futile and obsolete. The world was effectively divided between the temporal and spiritual realms, and even the glorious victory at Lepanto was followed by apathy and dissension among the Catholic allies. Although he did not restore the Church's power and did not prevent the spread of Protestantism, Pius did achieve some success at reforming the Church and did enhance the image of the Papacy, which had been in decline.

Bibliography

Browne-Olf, Lillian. *The Sword of Saint Michael: Saint Pius V, 1504-1572*. Milwaukee: Bruce, 1943. One of the few biographies in English, the book vindicates Pius and suffers from such a Roman Catholic bias that it equates World War II with the Reformation and Adolf Hitler with Martin Luther. Nevertheless, the book is helpful at showing the Reformation in context. Contains a select bibliography.

Daniel-Rops, H. *The Catholic Reformation*. Translated by John Warrington. New York: Dutton, 1955; London: Dent, 1962. An evenhanded evaluation of Pius that praises his reforms, summarizes his relations with Maximilian and Elizabeth, and discusses his "draconian orders for the hunting down of heresy, free thinking, and the faintest scent of Protestant sympathies." Daniel-Rops describes Pius' outlook as "largely medieval."

Seppelt, Francis X., and Clement Löffler. *A Short History of the Popes: Based on the Latest Researches*. London and St. Louis, Mo.: Herder, 1932. A short overview of the pope's most important achievements, which are seen as church reform and monastic life. His role in the Inquisition is virtually ignored except for an observation that he could be "harsh and severe when offenses were committed against ecclesiastical discipline."

Von Ranke, Leopold. *The History of the Popes During the Last Four Centuries*. 3 vols. London: Bell, 1912. The first volume contains an overview of Pius from the perspective of a German Protestant. While granting the pope's achievements, the author does portray Pius as an obstinate zealot who insisted on obedience and as a persecutor of innocence and purity. Consequently, Pius' role in the Inquisition is stressed, and his sainthood is not mentioned.

Walsh, William Thomas. *Characters of the Inquisition*. New York: Kenedy, 1940. Examines the inquisitorial spirit from the time of Moses to the twentieth century. Walsh focuses on the relationship between Philip and Pius, discusses the Carranza affair, and concludes that Spain ruthlessly trampled on the rights of the Catholic Church.

Woodcock, Catherine M. A. *Saint Pius V: Pope of the Holy Rosary*. London and New York: Longman, 1911. A short biography from a Roman Catholic perspective, the book was one of the sources for Browne-Olf's *The Sword of St. Michael* (1943). The book is rich in anecdotes and provides information about the details of the pope's canonization.

Thomas L. Erskine

FRANCISCO PIZARRO

Born: c. 1495; Trujillo, Spain
Died: June 26, 1541; Lima, Peru
Area of Achievement: Exploration
Contribution: Pizarro was a sixteenth century Spanish conquistador who experienced many frustrating years in the New World in search of fame and fortune before discovering and conquering the Incan Empire of Peru.

Early Life

The details of Francisco Pizarro's early life are not clear. He was probably born around 1495 in Trujillo, a city in the province of Estremadura, Spain, from which came many of the famous conquistadores. Pizarro was one of several illegitimate sons of Gonzalo Pizarro, an infantry officer. His mother, Francisca Morales, was a woman of plebeian origin about whom little is known. He received little attention from his parents and was, apparently, abandoned in his early years. He could neither read nor write, so he became a swineherd and was so destitute that, like the prodigal son, he was reduced to eating the swill thrown out for the pigs. He probably needed little encouragement to abandon this ignoble profession to go to Seville, gateway to the New World and fame and fortune.

The circumstances under which Pizarro made his way across the Atlantic Ocean to the island of Hispaniola in the early years of the sixteenth century are not known. By then in his thirties, Pizarro was in his prime, yet his most productive years lay ahead. Contemporary portraits depict him as tall and well built with broad shoulders and the characteristic forked beard of the period. He possessed a noble countenance, was an expert swordsman, and had great physical strength. In 1510, he joined Alonso de Ojeda's expedition to Uraba in Terra Firma, where, at the new colony of San Sebastian, Pizarro gained knowledge of jungle warfare. When the colony foundered and Ojeda was forced to return for supplies to the islands, Pizarro was left in charge. He remained in the doomed colony for two months before death thinned the ranks sufficiently to allow the survivors to make their way back to civilization on the one remaining vessel. Shortly thereafter, Pizarro entered the service of Vasco Núñez de Balboa and shared in the glory of founding a settlement at Darien and the subsequent discovery of the Pacific Ocean in 1513. Yet when Balboa fell from favor and was accused of treason by the governor of Panama, Pedrarias, Pizarro was the arresting officer. In the service of Pedrarias, there were new adventures, but, approaching fifty, old for that day, Pizarro had only a little land and a few Indians to show for his years of labor in the New World.

Life's Work

In 1515, Pizarro crossed the Isthmus and traded with the natives on the Pacific coast. There he probably heard tales of a mysterious land to the south rich beyond belief in gold and silver. The subsequent exploits of Hernán Cortés in 1519-1521 and an expedition by Pascual de Andagoya in 1522, which brought news of wealthy kingdoms, gave impetus to further exploration and greatly excited the cupidity of the Spaniards. To finance an expedition, Pizarro formed a business triumvirate with Diego de Almagro, a solider of fortune, and Hernando de Luque, a learned ecclesiastic.

Pizarro's first foray, launched in December, 1524, took him down the coast of modern Colombia, where he encountered every hardship imaginable and soon returned quietly to Panama. Under the guidance of Bartolomé Ruiz, a famous navigator and explorer, Pizarro's second expedition set sail in early 1526. The voyage took them beyond modern-day Ecuador into the waters south of the equator, where they found evidence of an advanced Indian civilization. An inadequate number of men, dwindling provisions, and hostile natives forced Pizarro and part of the company to take refuge first on the island of Gallo and later on Gorgona while Almagro returned to Panama to seek assistance. The governor, however, refused further help and sent a ship to collect the survivors. Audaciously, Pizarro and thirteen others refused to return. They endured seven months of starvation, foul weather, and ravenous insects until Almagro returned with provisions and the expedition was resumed. At length, they discovered the great and wealthy Incan city of Tumbes on the fringes of the Peruvian Empire. After a cordial stay with the natives, Pizarro returned to Panama with some gold, llamas, and Indians to gain support for an even greater expedition. The governor remained uninterested, so the business partners decided to send Pizarro to Spain to plead their case.

Charles V and his queen were sufficiently impressed with Pizarro's exploits and gifts to underwrite another expedition. In July, 1529, Pizarro

*Ille ego quâ propria famam virtute parau
Pizardus patri nothus, at notißimus Orbi;
Armis namque meis olim ampla Peruuia ceßit,
Omnis vt Hispano, duce me, sit sit subdita sceptro:
Pluraque fecißem numeroso carmine digna,
Indigna si non sublatus morte fuißem.*

was given extensive powers and privileges in the new lands, among them the titles of governor and captain-general with a generous salary. Almagro received substantially less, which caused a rift between the two friends. Before leaving Spain, Pizarro recruited his four brothers from Estremadura for the adventures ahead.

In January, 1531, Pizarro embarked on his third and last expedition to Peru. With no more than 180 men and three vessels, the expedition charted a course to Tumbes, which, because of a great civil war in the country, they found much less hospitable. Even so, the Spaniards' arrival was fortuitous in that the victor, Atahualpa, had not yet consolidated his conquests and was now recuperating at the ancient city of Cajamarca. In September, 1532, Pizarro began his march into the heart of the Incan Empire. After a difficult trek through the Andes, during which they encountered little resistance, they entered Cajamarca on November 15, 1532. Finding the Incan king at rest with only a portion of his army, Pizarro, pretending friendship, seized Atahualpa after a great slaughter of Indians. Atahualpa struck a bargain with his captors. In return for his release, he promised to fill a large room with gold. A second, smaller room was to be filled with silver. Fearing revolt, however, the captors carried out a summary trial, and the Inca was condemned to death.

Meanwhile, Almagro and his men had arrived in February, 1533, and loudly demanded a share of the wealth. The gold and silver vessels were melted down and distributed among the conquerors, while Almagro's men received a lesser amount and the promise of riches to come. Hernando Pizarro, Francisco's only legitimate brother, was sent to Spain with the royal one-fifth portion. From Cajamarca, Pizarro and his company pushed on to Cuzco. After encountering some resistance in the coutryside, the conquistadores entered the city on November 15, 1533, where the scenes of rapine were repeated again.

After the conquest of Cuzco, Pizarro settled down to consolidate and rule his new dominion, now given legitimacy and the name of New Castile in royal documents brought back from Spain by Hernando Pizarro. A new Inca, Manco Capac II, was placed on the throne, and a municipal government was organized after the fashion of those in Iberia. Most of Pizarro's time, however, was consumed with the founding of a new capital, Lima, which was closer to the coast and had greater economic potential. These were difficult years. In 1536, the Manco Capac grew tired of his ignominious status as a puppet emperor and led the Peruvians in a great revolt. For more than a year, the Incas besieged Cuzco. After great loss of life and much destruction throughout the country, the siege ended, although the Incas would remain restive for most of the sixteenth century.

In the meantime, a power struggle had developed between Almagro, who had returned from a fruitless expedition into New Toledo, the lands assigned him by the Crown, and Pizarro for control of Cuzco. On April 6, 1538, Almagro's forces were defeated in a great battle at Las Salinas. Almagro was condemned to death. In the three years that followed, Pizarro became something of a tyrant. On June 26, 1541, the Almagrists broke into Pizarro's palace in Lima and slew the venturesome conquistador.

Summary

There are, perhaps, two possible ways in which the career of Francisco Pizarro might be evaluated. On the one hand, it is easy to regard him as one of many sixteenth century Spaniards, called conquistadores, whose cupidity sent them in search of fame and fortune, specifically gold and silver, in the New World. In a relatively short period of time, Incas everywhere were conquered, tortured, murdered, and systematically stripped of their lands, families, and provisions. Pizarro played a major role in the rapacious conduct of the Castilians. Although this view is not without some merit, it must be understood within the context of Pizarro's world. He was not unlike a medieval crusader who sallied forth against the enemy with the blessings of Crown and Church. The Crown was interested in precious metals and new territorial possessions, while the Church was concerned about lost souls. When his opportunity for fame and fortune finally presented itself, Pizarro had to overcome seemingly insurmountable odds—financial difficulties, hostile natives, harsh weather and terrain, and later the enmity of other conquistadores—to create a Spanish empire in South America. Although his methods cannot be condoned, the empires of Alexander the Great, Charlemagne, and other conquerors were fashioned in much the same way.

Bibliography

Birney, Hoffman. *Brothers of Doom: The Story of the Pizarros of Peru.* New York: Putnam, 1942. A well-written study of Pizarro and his brothers from the opening of the age of exploration to the death of Gonzalo Pizarro in 1548. The author purposely eschews footnotes and lengthy bibliographical references. A good introductory work.

Hemming, John. *The Conquest of the Incas.* London: Macmillan, and New York: Harcourt Brace, 1970. A history of the conquest from Balboa's discovery of the Pacific Ocean in 1513 through the disintegration of the Inca Empire, with reference to the life of Pizarro. Includes chronological and genealogical tables plus an excellent bibliography.

Hemming, J., and S. Franklin. "Pizarro." *National Geographic* 181 (February, 1992): 90. Hemming profiles Pizarro, detailing his conquest. The article is highlighted with modern photos of Peru's Sun Festival and other celebrations.

Howard, Cecil, and J. H. Perry. *Pizarro and the Conquest of Peru.* New York: American Heritage, 1968; London: Cassell, 1970. A well-illustrated history of the conquest and the civil wars which followed. Excellent for a younger reading audience.

Kirkpatrick, F. A. *The Spanish Conquistadores.* London: Black, 1934; New York: Barnes and Noble, 1946. A survey of Spanish exploration, conquest, and settlement of the New World beginning with the voyages of Christopher Columbus. Provides a good overview of Pizarro's career.

Means, Philip Ainsworth. *Fall of the Inca Empire and the Spanish Rule in Peru: 1530-1780.* London and New York: Scribner, 1932. A history of the last years of the Inca Empire and Spanish dominion to 1780. Most of the important events of Pizarro's life are mentioned. Includes a scholarly bibliography plus a helpful index and glossary.

Prescott, William H. *The Conquest of Peru.* Revised with an introduction by Victor W. von Hagen. New York: New American Library, 1961. After more than a century and many editions, still one of the best works on the subject. Prescott's style will appeal to readers at all levels.

Larry W. Usilton

LA PLÉIADE

Guillaume des Autels (1529-1581)

Joachim du Bellay (c. 1522-1560)

Jean Dorat (1508-1588)

Jacques Peletier du Mans (1517-1582)

Pierre de Ronsard (1524-1585)

Antoine de Baïf (1532-1589)

Rémy Belleau (1528-1577)

Étienne Jodelle (1532-1573)

Jean de la Peruse (1529-1554)

Pontus de Tyard (c. 1522-1605)

Flourished: 1549-1589; Paris, France
Area of Achievement: Literature
Contribution: The Pléiade is a name given to a group of loosely organized poets dedicated to raising the level of sophistication of the French language by adding words and genres derived from classical literature. Led by Pierre de Ronsard and Joachim du Bellay, they developed a new form of poetry based on forms such as the sonnet, the ode, epic, and elegy. They also worked to elevate the level of the poet to a position as an intermediary between humanity and the heavens.

Early Life

The most famous member of the Pléiade, Pierre de Ronsard, was born in 1524 in what is now the département of Loire-et-Cher. He came from a prominent family, and his father, Louis de Ronsard, was a gentleman of the court. As a youth, he was trained for a diplomatic or military career, and at the age of twelve he became a page at the royal court of France assigned to serve the children of Francis I. After the marriage of the woman he served, Madeline, to James Stuart of Scotland, he moved to the Scottish court. He accompanied the ambassador Lazare de Baïf on an assignment to Alsace in 1540 and later to Turin. He became ill shortly after his return, and he lost most of his hearing in 1553. He abandoned what was a promising diplomatic career and devoted himself to scholarship and poetry.

Lazare de Baïf had employed the master hellenist Jean Dorat to tutor his son, Jean-Antoine de Baïf. Although Dorat fancied himself a great poet and wrote innumerable poems that have never been published as a collection, his main contribution to the development of the Pléiade was in his role as a master teacher. He was able to inspire his students with a love of Greek and Latin and the literature available in these languages. Ronsard studied with Dorat in the Baïf home.

In 1547, Dorat was named the principal of the Collège de Coqueret in Paris, and the three men went to Paris together. Other young men soon joined them—Joachim du Bellay (who had spent four years working for the cardinal Jean du Bellay in Rome, where he had become fascinated with the history and culture of the old capital), Étienne Jodelle, Rémy Belleau, Pontus de Tyard—and soon became part of the group. These young men of letters at first called themselves the Brigade and devoted themselves to the study of poetry.

Life's Work

The Pléiade rejected the poets of the Middle Ages who had generally thought of poetry as a kind of game that had the amusement of the reader as its main goal. The poets of the Renaissance had a different conception. Inspired by their Greek and Roman heroes, they wanted to make poetry a more vibrant and essential part of life. They believed that the purpose of poetry was to inspire and move the reader by depicting the glories of love, heroism, sacrifice, and religion. Above all, they believed that the poet was an exalted being who occupied a privileged place in society and who deserved this place because of his dedication to his art.

Dorat, Ronsard, du Bellay, and their friends gathered frequently to discuss these new ideas. The result of these discussions was a remarkable work that reflected their collective thought. Although written by both Ronsard and du Bellay, *La Défense et illustration de la langue française* (1549) appeared under du Bellay's name because of the prominence of his family. The main premise of the

Défense was that all languages were basically equal, since they were all the creation of the human mind. Even if Greek and Latin seemed to be superior to others, that was simply because they had been enriched through use. Other languages, they argued, and especially French, could be made as rich and versatile as Greek or Latin by using them to express complex ideas.

Thus, they argued, it was necessary to "defend" French against Latin and free it from Latin domination by using it to create masterpieces, and especially masterpieces in verse. This was not an easy assignment. They called for poets to reject the formulas of the middle ages and adopt the newly discovered forms used in Greek and Roman classics, such as the ode, the elegy, satire, and the sonnet, a form they borrowed from Italian literature. Poets should address great and serious subjects so as to prove their importance as exalted personages. Poets should also be prepared to write comedies and tragedies, but should only do this with royal support.

Ronsard and du Bellay also argued that it should be the poet's task to "illustrate" the French language and enrich it by adding words garnered from many sources. Poets could look to the language of craftsmen or of the country people, for example. They could bring archaic words back to the living language and even invent words by combining word roots.

The innovators wanted to break with the past, so as to give France an infinitely better poetry. In truth, the Pléiade continued some of the work of Clément Marot (1496-1554), whose translations of two books of the *Metamorphoses* provided new and fresh vision of classical texts. Thus, to a certain degree, the work of the Pléiade poets was based on ideas that were already current. What was new in the *Défense* was its call for enthusiasm on the part of the poet, which was called a "divine madness." The poet was supposed to be an interpreter of divine secrets and mysteries and an intermediary who could explain these things to humankind. This exalted conception of the poet inspired and brought forth masterpieces, of which the *Défense* itself was the first. The *Défense* was not poetry but a literary manifesto, the first in French. Because of its almost complete rejection of established traditions in poetry, the *Défense* was roundly attacked from all sides after its publication.

At about the same time as the publication of the *Défense*, Ronsard began to think of his loose-knit "brigade" of friends in more exalted terms. Since there were seven of them that collaborated most closely, they began to become known in the minds of their admirers as the Pléiade, and they began to apply this term to themselves. The Pléiade was a term firmly based in classical scholarship. It had been variously applied to a group of sixth century B.C. philosophers and to the seven poets who worked in Alexandria, Egypt, in the third century B.C. under Ptolemy Philadelphia. In classical literature, the term also refers to the seven daughters of Atlas and Pleionne who were so devastated by the suffering of their father that they killed themselves and were changed into stars. A small constellation of seven stars in the Northern Hemisphere is named after them.

There is some controversy about which poets really constituted the Pléiade. The group changed somewhat over time. Ronsard's closest allies were always there—Joachim Du Bellay, Pontus de Tyard, Jean-Antoine De Baïf, and Étienne Jodelle were always included in the Pléiade—but others joined as members died or were replaced. In 1553, Jean des Autels and Jean de la Péruse became members of the seven, as did Jacques Peletier du Mans and Rémy Belleau in 1555 and 1556. Nevertheless, scholars specializing in studies of the Pléiade have come to agree on the names of Ronsard, Dorat, du Bellay, de Baïf, Belleau, Jodelle, and Tyard as defining the group.

The *Défense* recommended that the poet take inspiration from the classics by borrowing from the "sacred treasures of the Delphic temple." The first products of the new method were the Petrarchan sonnet and the classical ode. One of the most important contributions of the Pléiade was the combination of the sonnet, the style of Petrarch, and the Italian *canzonieri* (love songs addressed to a single mistress). The Pléiade poets did not invent any of these genres, but their fusion resulted in a new type of poem that still is remarkably fresh and direct. Examples are du Bellay's *l'Olive* (1549-50) and *Trieze sonnets de l'honnête amour* (1552) and Ronsard's *Amours* (1552). The odes of the Pléiade poets imitated the ancients, especially Horace, to describe sentiments such as love, heroism, and glory. Ronsard's *Quatres premiers livres des Odes* (1550) is important, and the ode to *Michel de L'Hôpital* is the masterpiece of the genre.

The Pléiade poets believed that the poet should collaborate with the ruling class. Since 1549, Ronsard, du Bellay, Jodelle, and Belleau had served as court poets and had composed a number of poems celebrating royal events. This included such things as victory chants (*Prise de Calais*, 1558), celebrations of peace (*Trêve de Vaucelles*, 1556), and celebrations of marriage (*Marriage du dauphin François avec Marie Stuart*, 1558).

In 1558, Ronsard was named a counselor to the king. He received many awards and honors for his royal work. After the death of Charles IX in 1574, however, Ronsard fell out of royal favor, and he spent most of his time on his estates until his death from a lengthy illness on December 27, 1585. In spite of the fact that he had fallen out of favor with the court, a royal decree ordered that he be provided a splendid funeral. This funeral showed how important the role of the poet in the life of the state had become. The hope expressed in *Défense* that the poet would achieve a position of prestige and prominence in French life had come true.

Summary

The achievements of the Pléiade were numerous. They incorporated several genres of poetry into the French language that, while not new, had not been available to French poets. Their emphasis on making French equal to Latin in its power and versatility contributed to the emergence of French as a premier literary language. They were instrumental in incorporating classical styles of the epic, the ode, the satire, and the Italian sonnet and love song into French. Their innovations in stylistic matters brought about modernizing changes in poetic rhyme, meter, and verse. They also elevated the poet/scholar to a new level of prominence in France. Although Pléiade poetry has undergone criticism in modern times for what seems to be excessive erudition and complexity, much of it has withstood the test of time, and Ronsard is generally acclaimed as France's greatest premodern poet.

Bibliography

Armstrong, Elizabeth. *Ronsard and the Age of Gold.* Cambridge, England: Cambridge University Press, 1968. A standard work that places Ronsard in the milieu of the Renaissance and discusses how his work was influenced by that of Clément Marot and Maurice Scève.

Castor, Graham. *Pléiade Poetics: A Study in Sixteenth Century Thought and Terminology.* Cambridge, England: Cambridge University Press, 1964. A formal study of the influence of the Pléiade and other Renaissance poets on the structure of poetry. A good study for advanced students of poetry and its technical aspects.

Cave, Terence, ed. *Ronsard the Poet.* London: Metheuen, 1973. A collection of seven essays on Ronsard that range from an examination of the role of music in his poetry to a study of neoplatonism.

Clements, John Robert. *Critical Theory and Practice of the Pléiade.* Cambridge, Mass.: Harvard University Press, 1942. Primarily for serious students of poetry, but a classic work on the Pléiade. Reissued in 1970 by Octagon Books.

Silver, Isadore. *The Intellectual Evolution of Ronsard.* St. Louis: Washington University Press, 1969. A good study of the early years of Ronsard's intellectual life and how his association with Dorat and the accompanying introduction to the classics of ancient Greece prepared him for a life as a poet.

C. James Haug

POGGIO

Born: February 11, 1380; Terranuova, near Arezzo

Died: October 30, 1459; Florence

Area of Achievement: Literature

Contribution: Through his tireless efforts, Poggio discovered and copied manuscripts of classical Latin authors that had been lost for centuries and which, if not for him, might have remained lost forever.

Early Life

Giovanni Francesco Poggio Bracciolini, better known as Poggio, was born in Terranuova, part of the Republic of Florence, in 1380. He received his earliest education in nearby Arezzo, but at the age of sixteen or seventeen moved to Florence to complete his studies and train for the profession of notary. He was taught Latin by John of Ravenna and may have been a student in Greek under Manuel Chrysoloras, although this is disputable because Poggio never gained mastery of Greek. Since he was from a poor family, Poggio copied manuscripts for the book trade to support himself in these endeavors in Florence.

Poggio's knowledge of Latin caught the attention of Coluccio Salutati, a student of Petrarch and Florence's first Humanist chancellor. It was probably at this time that Salutati nurtured in the young Poggio a love for the classics and the determination to search for lost manuscripts. Also at this time, Poggio met and became a close friend of Niccolò Niccoli, a wealthy Florentine with whom he shared a lifelong passion for classical artifacts and classical manuscripts. These two men, along with Leonardo Bruni, Ambrogio Traversari, and Leon Battista Alberti, carried on the intellectual movement begun by Petrarch in the late 1300's and continued by Salutati in the early 1400's.

In 1403, Poggio entered the Papal Curia as a *scriptor* (scribe). He soon advanced to the post of apostolic secretary and, except for an unhappy interlude from 1418 to 1422, when he served Henry Beaufort, Bishop of Winchester, in England, spent the next fifty years in service to five different popes.

During the early years of his career in the Curia, Poggio developed the Humanist style of writing. The letters of this hand, simpler and rounder in formation and easier to read than Gothic, directly imitated the Carolingian script of the eleventh century. The earliest example of Humanist script is in a manuscript of Cicero's letters to Titus Pomponius Atticus in Poggio's own hand and dated 1408.

Life's Work

Poggio's main interest throughout his lifetime was in the area of classical studies—including archaeology, architecture, coins, epigraphy, and statues, as well as manuscripts. Upon entering Rome for the first time in 1403, Poggio was struck by the decay of the once-noble city. He was the first to use a truly scientific approach to the study of the city's ruins. Comparing the sights with descriptions from Livy (Titus Livius), Marcus Vitruvius Pollio, and Sextus Julius Frontinus, Poggio was able to catalog in part the remains of ancient Rome. He accurately assigned to the Republican era a bridge, an arch, a tomb, and a temple. Among the buildings dating to the Empire, he described several temples, two theaters (including the theater of Pompey the Great), the Colosseum, the Column of Trajan, and the mausoleums of the emperors Augustus and Hadrian. His treatise, *De varietate fortunae* (1431-1438;

on the vicissitude of fortune), is the most important document for the physical state of Rome in the fifteenth century. Many artifacts which he discovered on his travels were used to decorate his villa outside Florence.

Poggio's most significant contribution to classical scholarship came in the area of ancient manuscripts. It is reported that as early as 1407 Poggio was in the monastery of Monte Cassino looking for lost texts. The Council of Constance in 1414, however, opened up the monastic libraries of the transalpine countries to Italian scholars. The council meetings, designed to establish one single pope in Rome, afforded the apostolic secretary much leisure time in which to explore the monasteries in search of ancient Latin manuscripts.

From 1415 to 1417, Poggio made his most important and most numerous discoveries in the monasteries of France, Germany, and Switzerland. In 1415, at Cluny, Poggio unearthed two previously unknown orations of Cicero. At Saint Gall the next year came his astounding discovery of the entire *Institutio oratoria* (c. A.D. 95; *On the Education of an Orator*, better known as *Institutio oratoria*) by Quintilian, which had previously been known only from a mutilated copy found in Florence by Petrarch in 1350. In the same expedition, Poggio also found most of the first half of Gaius Valerius Flaccus' *Argonautica* (c. A.D. 90) and a ninth century manuscript of Asconius Pedianus' commentaries on Cicero's orations. On other trips in 1417 he unearthed Sextus Pompeius Festus' *De significatu verborum* (second or third century A.D.), Lucretius' *De rerum natura* (c. 60 B.C.; *On the Nature of Things*), Marcus Manilius' *Astronomica* (c. A.D. 14-27), Silius Italicus' *Punica* (first century A.D.), Ammianus Marcellinus' *Res gestae* (c. A.D. 378), Apicius' *De re coquinaria* (late fourth century A.D.; *The Roman Cookery Book*, 1817), and Statius' *Silvae* (c. A.D. 91-95). Also in 1417, Poggio found a manuscript of Cicero's oration on behalf of Caecina, a Roman general.

After his reinstatement as secretary in the Papal Curia in 1423, Poggio brought to light manuscripts of Sextus Julius Frontinus' *De aquaeductibus* (c. A.D. 97) and Firmicus Maternus' *Matheseos libri* (c. A.D. 354). Other ancient authors rediscovered by Poggio included Columella, Vitruvius Pollio, Nonius Marcellus, Marcus Valerius Probus, and Eutyches. In Poggio's mind, the end justified the means, and he was not above stealing to appropriate manuscripts, as he makes clear in his letters.

Poggio is not without his critics in the area of manuscripts. The seeker of lost texts was not especially careful with his discoveries after he had copied them, and many of his manuscripts disappeared shortly after they were found. Manilius' *Argonautica* was copied, then the original was lost. Asconius Pedianus is only preserved in copies made from the manuscript found by Poggio. The codex of Gaius Valerius Flaccus disappeared shortly after it was copied, and Cicero's work on the comedian Quintius Roscius is known only from an apograph of the recovered text. This carelessness has caused great anguish, even anger, among modern paleographers and textual critics who are more interested in the contents of ninth century texts than they are in Poggio's fifteenth century copy.

Poggio's own writings reveal a multitude of interests and range from moral dialogues to indecent satires on clergy and friars. Two of his more important moral essays are *De avaritia* (1428-1429; on greed) and *De varietate fortunae. Facetiae* (1438-1452; *The Fables of Poge the Florentyn*, 1484, 1879) paints humorous, often obscene, vignettes of priests, monks, and rival Humanists. Of most historical value are Poggio's letters, published in three separate works. Addressed to 172 correspondents, the nearly six hundred epistles reveal not only Poggio's own life but also the activities of a number of popes and various rulers throughout Europe, and especially in Italy.

In 1435, at the age of fifty-five, Poggio married the eighteen-year-old Vaggia Buondelmonti. He seems to have been quite happy with his wellborn bride, even though the marriage forced him to forsake his mistress, with whom he had had fourteen children. In 1453, he left the papal court to become Chancellor of Florence and devoted the rest of his life to continuing Leonardo Bruni's *Historiarum, Florentini populi* (c. 1415; history of the Florentine republic). Poggio died in 1459 and was buried in the Church of Santa Croce, where a statue by the artist Donatello commemorates him.

Summary

Poggio's contribution to classical studies is three-fold. His development of the Humanist script, which was refined by the succeeding generation of scribes, became the prototype for the Roman font when the art of printing was introduced into Italy from Germany. The Roman type, which was easier to read, gradually supplanted the Gothic. Because of Poggio's calligraphic efforts, books became more legible. His collection of Latin inscriptions, which he compiled in 1429, evolved over centuries into the modern *Corpus inscriptionum Latinarum*, an ongoing reference work listing all known Latin inscriptions. This reference work provides Latin linguists, Roman historians, Latin philologists, and other scholars with crucial information about early, even pre-Republican, Rome.

Poggio's most lasting achievements, however, lie in the area of manuscript recovery. Petrarch, initiating the intellectual movement called Humanism, had begun the efforts to find and copy ancient texts, and his work had been carried on by Giovanni Boccaccio. In the next generation, Salutati, who espoused the same philosophy of the importance of the classics, continued their work. In addition, he transmitted his beliefs to a number of his most gifted students, Poggio among them.

Poggio, however, eclipsed both predecessors and contemporaries in the amount and importance of his discoveries. In continuing activities begun by Petrarch, he was advancing the Humanist movement, but, more important, he preserved for posterity classical works which might have disappeared forever. Although succeeding centuries have produced far fewer revelations of ancient manuscripts, scholars continue to devote their lives to searching for lost texts. It is in part because of Poggio's successes that they do so.

Bibliography

Baron, Hans. *The Crisis of the Early Italian Renaissance: Civic Humanism and Republican Liberty in an Age of Classicism and Tyranny.* 2 vols. Princeton, N.J.: Princeton University Press, 1955. Still-useful portrayal of the political, intellectual, and cultural atmosphere of the early 1400's. Includes exhaustive notes probably useful only to the advanced reader.

Bracciolini, Poggio. *Two Renaissance Book Hunters: The Letters of Poggius Bracciolini to Nicolaus de Niccolis.* Edited by Phyllis Walter Goodhart Gordon. New York: Columbia University Press, 1974; London: Columbia University Press, 1975. This English translation of the Latin reveals Poggio's excitement and problems at finding and copying old manuscripts. The introduction chronicles Poggio's life. Includes copious notes (though in places incorrect) and an extensive bibliography.

Holmes, George. *The Florentine Enlightenment: 1400-50.* London: Weidenfeld and Nicolson, and New York: Pegasus, 1969. The author, writing in a straightforward style, provides a clear picture of the social, political, and religious atmosphere of Florence before, during, and after Poggio's time. There is no bibliography, and the footnotes are of limited help. Illustrated.

Salemi, Joseph S., trans. "Selections from the *Facetiae* of Poggio Bracciolini." *Allegorica* 8 (1983): 77-183. Published in a bilingual format, this study is a translation of forty of Poggio's fables, as well as the introduction and conclusion. Provides insight into Poggio's cynical view toward most of humanity. The footnotes are helpful. Illustrated.

Symonds, John Addington. *Renaissance in Italy, Part II: The Revival of Learning.* London: Smith Elder, and New York: Holt, 1877. The research is dated, but the lively anecdotes of Poggio's feuds will entertain and educate.

Trinkhaus, Charles. *The Scope of Renaissance Humanism.* Ann Arbor: University of Michigan Press, 1983. Contains a careful survey of Humanists, how they interacted, and what they contributed. The abundant notes, often in a foreign language, will be useful mainly to the advanced reader.

Ullman, Berthold L. *Ancient Writing and Its Influence.* London: Harrap, and New York: Longman, 1932. Ullman discusses Poggio only as the developer of the Humanistic script, but the photograph of a manuscript in Poggio's own hand makes the book worthwhile.

Joan E. Carr

JUAN PONCE DE LÉON

Born: c. 1474; probably Santervás de Campos, Spain
Died: July, 1521; Havana, Cuba
Area of Achievement: Exploration
Contribution: Ponce de Léon discovered Florida and, more important, the Bahama Channel and the Gulf Stream, which proved invaluable to Spanish treasure ships making the passage from Mexico to Spain.

Early Life

Historical facts about Juan Ponce de Léon's early life are limited. Born of uncertain parentage, Ponce may have been one of twenty-one illegitimate children acknowledged by Count Juan Ponce de Léon, a noble of Seville. Ponce probably served as a page to the knight Pedro Núñez de Guzmán, mastering sword and combat skills, the social graces, and religious instructions. During the late 1480's, Ponce probably participated in the campaign to drive the Moors out of Spain, which succeeded in 1492. With the wars over, Ponce would have been at loose ends when Christopher Columbus returned triumphantly to Spain in the spring of 1493, boldly claiming the discovery of a New World filled with spices and gold, exhibiting its gold-ornamented native Indians and exotic animals, and promising quick fortunes. When Columbus organized his second voyage to colonize the new lands in late 1493, foot-soldier Ponce was among the eager volunteers.

On September 25, 1493, according to Fernández de Oviedo *Historia general de las Indias* (c. 1535-1557), Ponce left with Columbus's expeditionary force of seventeen ships, 1,200 men, and six priests, bound for the island of Hispaniola (present-day Haiti and the Dominican Republic). Arriving in late October or early November, Ponce and the other volunteers followed Columbus's orders of establishing the new settlement of Isabella. Ponce survived the bad food and drink, the malarial swamps, and the unfamiliar climate that afflicted the volunteers. He and the others were expected to press the local Indians into slavery, forcing them under threat of torture to clear and plant fields, tend cattle, or mine for gold.

Between 1494 and 1502, Ponce most likely returned to Spain but came back to Hispaniola, living in Santo Domingo from 1502 to 1504 and in Salvaléon from 1505 to 1508. During these years, Ponce's soldiering abilities and his rising social status on the island made him a favorite of Governor Nicolás de Ovando. He married a prominent innkeeper's daughter named Leonor, secured an impressive dowry from his father-in-law, and fathered three daughters and a son. When the Indians of the eastern province of Hispaniola rebelled and massacred Spaniards in 1504 because of cruel Spanish treatment, Ponce helped put down the rebellion and hanged its leader. Governor Ovando then appointed Ponce as deputy governor of the rebel province.

Finding little gold in the rebel province, Ponce developed farms, equitably distributing land grants and Indian slaves, building permanent stone buildings for defense, and creating a long-term commitment to developing the island's economy. Now in his thirties, the dauntless conquistador was also a devout Christian and an honest administrator, with a pleasing, ruddy-hued face. Still, he wanted more than financial success from agricultural endeavors. He looked eastward, toward the nearby island of Borinquén, a legendary cache of gold.

Life's Work

Between 1506 and 1508, Ponce sent Governor Ovando coded information about the possibility of gold on Borinquén (present-day Puerto Rico) and secretly led a preliminary exploration of the island. Ponce, as captain of the militia, made friendly contact with the natives of Borinquén, who helped him to find gold deposits and led him to an excellent harbor for his ships. In 1508, Ponce claimed Borinquén for the Spanish crown, establishing farms that later produced casava bread and other staples.

In 1509, King Ferdinand appointed Ponce acting governor of Borinquén. Ponce became a wealthy and powerful man, encouraging Spanish settlers and gold seekers to make their fortunes on the island. He controlled the distribution of land grants, licensed the Indian-slave trade, and mined for gold. At the harbor near Caparra (present-day San Juan), he built warehouses, a causeway, docks, roads, and some fortifications. On October 26, 1510, he opened a foundry for smelting and refining precious metals.

Ponce's island became increasingly popular with Spanish settlers from 1509 to 1511 because of his administration, the abundant food supply, and the availability of Indian slaves. Yet the native Indians suffered terrible abuses and torture. Some

Indians resigned themselves to a hopeless future; others did not resist because they believed the Spanish were immortal and godlike. This belief persisted until the Indians drowned a lone Spaniard and allowed his body to decompose. Once convinced that the Spaniards were mortal, the natives planned a bloody uprising. While Ponce was away from the island in early 1511, rebel Indians wiped out the most notorious abuser of Indians, Cristóbal de Sotomayor, and his settlement. Ponce, commanded to put down the spreading rebellion, gathered an army that fell upon the rebellious Indians, killing many in a series of skirmishes and returning others to slavery. Although Ponce was more lenient in his treatment of the natives than most Spaniards of his time, he did not hesitate to destroy Indian rebels or to kidnap natives from other islands to serve as laborers.

Also in 1511, political enemies in Spain forced an ailing King Ferdinand to replace Ponce as governor of Borinquén with Diego Columbus, nephew of the discoverer of America. For a time, Ponce and his supporters found themselves under house arrest, and their properties were confiscated by the Columbus faction. Upon hearing what had happened, Ferdinand insisted that restitution be made to Ponce and his followers. After dismissing Ponce as governor, the king curiously sent messages to Ponce in June or July, 1511, urging him to negotiate a contract to discover and settle new lands to the north, such as the legendary island of Bimini, which promised much gold and a fabulous fountain that made the old young again.

No historical evidence exists that Ponce actually sought the "fountain of youth" during his voyage to discover Bimini in 1513. The first mention of the marvelous fountain in Bimini may be found in Antonio de Herrera's account of Ponce's voyage *Historia general de los hechos de los castellanos* (c. 1549-1625). Historians have speculated that perhaps Ponce simply reported the Indian legends; that he may have wished to inflame the passions of those whose support he needed to make his voyage successful; and that perhaps the aged Ferdinand wanted the fountain's curative powers to restore his health and enable him to father a son. At any rate, Ferdinand issued a contract on February 23, 1512, appointing Ponce as *adelantado*, or supreme governor over all lands he discovered. Ponce agreed to pay all expenses of the venture, build a settlement, and provide the king his usual one-fifth share of the proceeds.

On March 3, 1513, Ponce and his followers sailed to the present-day Bahama Islands, finding the Bahama Channel but not Bimini or its fabled riches. They reached the eastern coast of present-day Florida on April 2, probably going ashore the next week somewhere between present-day Saint Augustine and the St. Johns River to claim possession of the land for Spain. Believing his discovery an island, Ponce named it *La Florida* (meaning "land of flowers") to honor the Catholic observance of Easter. By late April, Ponce's ships sailed southward until they ran into the strong current of the Gulf Stream, which forced them back toward land. Landing, the voyagers encountered several ferocious attacks by native Indians. Proceeding to the tip of Florida, Ponce's ships moved through the Florida Keys, then sailed up the west shore, doing some trading with Indians who wore palm-leaf loincloths.

By late May or early June, Ponce and his voyagers anchored probably near present-day Charlotte Bay, only to be driven off by a hissing cloud of arrows and hordes of fierce Indians in canoes. Ponce ordered his other ship to continue the exploration while he returned to Puerto Rico by mid-October, 1513. While Ponce failed to find the promised gold or the fountain of youth, he had discovered Florida and, more important, the Bahama Channel and the Gulf Stream, which later expedited the movement of Spanish treasures from the Caribbean to Spain.

During the early part of 1514, Ponce sailed to Spain, reporting his discoveries to Ferdinand and seeking approval for his colonization plans. After giving the king five thousand gold pesos, Ponce on September 27, 1514, received his contract, which called for him to colonize the lands; convert the natives to Catholicism; captain an armada to destroy the cannibalistic Carib Indians; and pay all expenses for the venture.

From 1515 to 1521, Ponce spent much of his time and energy in wiping out the marauding Caribs, who threatened Spanish dominance in the Caribbean by preying on Spaniards and their Indian allies. During the interim, Ponce also busied himself with domestic matters, such as arranging the marriages of his daughters to prominent men on Borinquén; remarrying upon his first wife's death and then burying his second wife; and devoting much of his increasing wealth to religious and charitable purposes. As an influential politician, Ponce became involved in the intense power struggle after the death of Ferdinand in 1516 and the accession of Charles I of Spain.

Ponce postponed his earlier plans for settling Florida until late February, 1521. Little is known about his second expedition other than he took equipment and supplies for establishing a self-sufficient colony. Somewhere on the west coast of Florida, probably on one of the islands in Charlotte Harbor, he and his followers unloaded their gear and constructed some dwellings and a chapel. Unfortunately for the Spaniards, they misjudged the reception of the indomitable Caloosa Indians and went ashore with too small a force of soldiers. In the ensuing battle, the Indians used fire-hardened reed arrows to pierce the Spaniards' chain armor, causing many deaths. Ponce received a severe arrow wound in the thigh and bled heavily. He and the other battered survivors made their way to Havana, Cuba, where Ponce died of his infected wounds. He was buried at San Juan, Puerto Rico. Ponce's heirs did not seek to continue his efforts in settling Florida. His son became a friar, while his daughters' descendants became prominent in Puerto Rico and Central America.

Summary

After his death, Ponce de Léon's achievements tended to be forgotten in the wake of public acclaim for other conquistadors' exploits and their fabulous discoveries of gold and treasure in the New World. Ponce's name mistakenly became associated with the fruitless search for the fountain of youth. Yet Ponce's exploration of the Caribbean resulted in the colonization of and creation of economic prosperity on the islands. As a noted farmer, he became instrumental in raising self-sufficient food supplies for all Spanish-maintained islands in the Caribbean. As a negotiator skilled in working with various Indian chieftains, Ponce left a legacy of relatively humane treatment of the Indians, a legacy the priests on the islands continued by pressuring Spaniards who treated the Indians cruelly to mend their ways.

Although other explorers such as John Cabot and Amerigo Vespucci claimed to have discovered Florida earlier, Ponce de Léon received official credit because his 1513 voyage was made under Spanish auspices and officially recorded. Ponce's discovery of Florida laid the foundation of a Spanish heritage in Florida, linking it culturally to the Caribbean and Latin America. More important, Ponce's exploration of Florida's coastlines resulted in his marking both the Gulf Stream and the Bahama Channel, allowing expedient passage of Spanish treasure ships from Mexico to Cuba to Spain itself. Ponce de Léon's discoveries helped Spain maintain its dominance over other European powers during the ensuing era of conquest.

Bibliography

Devereux, Anthony Q. *Juan Ponce de Léon, King Ferdinand, and the Fountain of Youth*. Spartanburg, S.C.: Reprint Company, 1993. Draws upon Spanish archival information about Ponce's life, filling in the historical gaps.

Dolan, Sean. *Juan Ponce de Léon*. New York: Chelsea House, 1995. A highly readable biography with vivid illustrations of life in the New World.

Kenny, Michael. *The Romance of the Floridas: The Finding and the Founding*. New York: AMS Press, 1970. Part 1 covers Ponce's contributions to later Spanish settlements in Florida. Defends the Catholic Church's role in the Spaniards' enslavement of the Indians.

Kerby, Elizabeth P. *The Conquistadors*. New York: Putnam, 1969. Compares Ponce de Léon's contributions to those of such conquistadors as Hernán Cortez, Francisco Pizarro, and others.

Rienits, Rex, and Thea Rienits. *The Voyages of Columbus*. London: Hamlin, 1970. Provides information on the political times in which Ponce lived. Richly illustrated.

Richard Whitworth

FRANÇOIS RABELAIS

Born: c. 1494; La Devinière, near Chinon, France
Died: April, 1553; Paris, France
Area of Achievement: Literature
Contribution: Rabelais, although a physician by trade, is best known for his writings, which satirize the Church and its officials while capturing the spirit of the Renaissance through grandiose characters who have an insatiable thirst for knowledge. Rabelais' strong challenge to spiritual authority is representative of a new period in literary thought and action.

Early Life

François Rabelais was most likely born in 1494 or 1495 in the Loire valley of France, at La Devinière, near Chinon, in the province of Touraine. His father was a lawyer, a prominent member of the landowning middle class. Little is known of his youth and, in fact, scarcely a date in his biography is beyond dispute. At some point, he entered the Franciscan monastery of La Baumette at Angers as a novice. Since his subsequent actions and especially his writings suggest the opposite of the stereotypical monastic temperament, Rabelais, the scholars surmise, entered the order so that he might study ancient texts. By the age of twenty-seven, Rabelais is known to have been a monk in the monastery of Puy-Saint-Martin at Fontenay-le-Comte, where he was immersed in Greek and other "new" humanistic studies. The faculty of theology at the Sorbonne was opposed to the study of Greek (eventually proscribing such study in France), and the head of the monastery was hostile to it as well. As a result, Rabelais petitioned Pope Clement VII for a transfer to the more liberal and scholarly Benedictine Order. His request was granted in 1524, and the rest of his life was a step-by-step return to a secular status.

Little is known about the next six years of Rabelais' life. He must have found even the Benedictine monastery unsatisfactory, for he left it in 1527 or 1528. It is believed that he did considerable traveling over the next three years or so, principally because his books would later show evidence of wide travel. In September, 1530, he entered the University of Montpellier as a medical student and earned a bachelor's degree in medicine; the extreme brevity of his residence and his knowledge of Parisian student types, as exhibited in his writings, suggest that he had previously studied medicine in Paris. Early the next year, Rabelais was giving public lectures on Galen and Hippocrates, the ancient Greek physicians. In 1532, he moved to Lyons and was appointed a physician in the city hospital of the Pont-du-Rhône. Henceforward, medicine was Rabelais' trade. The Church did not object, so long as he retained his priestly garb and abstained from the practice of surgery.

Life's Work

Rabelais was an outstanding Greek scholar. He was a lecturer on anatomy, using the original Greek treatises. He received his doctorate of medicine at Montpellier in 1537 and for the last two decades of his life was highly regarded as a skilled physician. He was an intimate of the learned and powerful. It was not until he began his literary career at almost forty years of age, however, that he won lasting fame.

In 1532, Rabelais was working for a Lyons printer, editing Greek medical texts. During that summer, he read *Grandes et inestimables cronicques du grant et énorme géant Gargantua* (1532; great and inestimable chronicles of the great and enormous giant Gargantua), a newly published book by an anonymous author. This crude tale was an adjunct to the Arthurian legends, employing a character who had been present in French folklore for centuries. Rabelais was moved to write a sequel, greatly superior to the original in both style and content. *Pantagruel* (English translation, 1653), the literal meaning of which is "all-thirsty," was published in the autumn of 1532. It is the story of Gargantua's son, a boisterous and jovial drunkard, who is the gross personification of the tippler's burning thirst. A visit by Rabelais to his home province during a time of severe drought also may have been an inspiration for the book. *Pantagruel's* author was identified as Alcofribas Nasier, which was an anagram of François Rabelais. The book was an immediate success with the public but was censured by the theological faculty of the Sorbonne as obscene. Also in 1532, Rabelais published a tongue-in-cheek almanac, *Pantagruéline Prognostication*, which survives only in fragments.

Rabelais met Jean du Bellay, Bishop of Paris and subsequently a cardinal, in 1533. By the next year, Rabelais was the bishop's personal physician and was attending him during a trip to Rome. In Rome, Rabelais requested absolution for leaving the Benedictine monastery without permission, but the pope declined to grant it. Later in 1534, back in France and still under the protection of his powerful patron, he published *Gargantua* (English translation, 1653), the main episode of which (concerning the Picrocholine War) was based upon his father's dispute with a neighbor over fishing rights. The events of *Gargantua* precede those of *Pantagruel; Gargantua* would eventually become book 1 of the combined work. This volume was more satiric than the first, and Rabelais made his enemies, the theologians at the Sorbonne, the objects of scorn and derision.

Rabelais' satire of Scholasticism, the Church's official intellectual system for the previous two hundred years, roused such prejudice against him that he went into hiding for a time. By 1536, however, he was back in Rome, again traveling as a member of Jean du Bellay's party. This time, his petition was successful. The pope granted him absolution, and later in the year, after his return to France, he gained the status of a secular priest. For the rest of his life, Rabelais avoided the official censure of the Church. He continued to travel during the years that followed, and he acquired further protection from his academic enemies by winning a minor post at the court of King Francis I. In all, Rabelais made four documented visits to Italy, under the protection either of Jean du Bellay or Jean's older brother Guillaume. The third sojourn in Rome lasted until 1541 and put Rabelais in frequent contact with the most learned and powerful men at the courts of the French ambassador and the pope. During these years, Rabelais was regarded as a greater physician than writer—he was famed for his dissection of cadavers and for the number of amazing cures he had effected.

Also in 1541, a new edition of Rabelais' work, *Gargantua and Pantagruel* (which combined the two earlier publications), appeared. Rabelais edited the work so as to soften somewhat its satirical treatment of theologians. The Sorbonne was not, however, in the least mollified; it forbade the sale or possession of the book.

During the 1540's, relations between the temporal and spiritual authorities were severely strained in France as elsewhere, so Rabelais maintained a low profile. Eventually, Rabelais used his court connections to publish the next installment of the giants' adventures. Book 3 of *Gargantua and Pantagruel* (1546) was dedicated to Queen Marguerite of Navarre, sister to the king. In fact, in 1545, Rabelais had secured official permission from the king to publish the book. Still, the faculty of theology at the Sorbonne condemned book 3. In this volume, the central character is really Panurge. In the loose narrative of the earlier works, Gargantua has sent Pantagruel to Paris to be educated. There the giant falls into the company of Panurge, who is about thirty-five years of age at the time they meet. Panurge (literally "all-doer" or "knave") is the stereotypical perennial college student: He lives by his wits and is sly, mischievous, lascivious, and debauched.

Rabelais made his fourth and final visit to Rome in 1548, and in his absence opposition to *Gargantua and Pantagruel* grew steadily. Nevertheless, in 1550 he again obtained the king's permission to publish further. In 1552, he brought out book 4, as well as revised and corrected versions of the first three books. Not unexpectedly, the Sorbonne banned book 4 immediately upon its publication. In 1551, Rabelais had been appointed to the two curacies of Saint-Martin-de-Meudon and Saint-Cristophe-de-Jambet. He resigned both appointments early in 1553. Some scholars believe that he was forced to give up the curacies as a result of having published book 4; others speculate that poor health was his motivation. According to tradition, Rabelais died in April, 1553, in the rue des Jardins, Paris.

From 1562 through 1564, a fifth book was assembled. Few accept book 5 as being totally the work of Rabelais. Critical opinion ranges from the belief that it includes only sketches and fragments by Rabelais to the belief that it is essentially his work, edited and expanded by the hand of another.

Summary

François Rabelais has been afforded the greatest honor which can be bestowed upon any literary man or woman—his name has become an adjective. The term Rabelaisian is often applied too narrowly, to mean simply a story which graphically features copulation and the bodily functions. Still, the origination of that adjective is an acknowledgment that Rabelais' work is so singular as to be described only on its own terms.

It has been suggested that no writer better captures the spirit of the Renaissance. His giants represent the grandiosity of his age. Their appetite for life is as huge as their bodies, and they thirst for knowledge as well as wine. Few passages in literature contrast the medieval and the Renaissance attitudes so strikingly as do chapters 21 through 24 of book 1. Gargantua's tutor, Ponocrates, an advocate of the "new learning," saves the giant from the slothful and

ineffective instruction of his former teachers, the worst of whom is the Sophist and Scholastic master, Tubal Holofernes. The demanding regimen of Ponocrates turns Gargantua into a complete man, physically, mentally, and spiritually—what the moderns have come to call the Renaissance man.

Also, few examples of the Humanist ideal can match Rabelais' utopian Abbey of Thélème (book 1, chapters 52 through 57). The rule of Thélème is the obverse of that of Saint Benedict, which Rabelais himself had finally fled. Only the brightest and most beautiful are admitted to the abbey. There, members of both sexes freely mingle, wearing beautiful clothes and engaging in exhilarating conversation. Their behavior is virtuous not because of codes and admonitions but because of their natural high-mindedness. The only rule at Thélème could serve as the motto of the Renaissance: "Fay ce que vou dras" (do what you wish).

Bibliography

Bakhtin, Mikhail. *Rabelais and His World*. Translated by Hélène Iswolsky. Cambridge, Mass.: MIT Press, 1968. Bakhtin's widely influential study considers Rabelais in the context of the "carnival" tradition: a rich and subversive vein of folk humor and comic festivities evident throughout the Middle Ages and the Renaissance.

Brown, Huntington. *Rabelais in English Literature*. Cambridge, Mass.: Harvard University Press, 1933; London: Cass, 1967. Argues that since the Renaissance, Rabelais has been better appreciated in England than in his own country and that his influence upon English literature has been very marked. Brown traces this influence in Ben Jonson, Sir Thomas Browne, Jonathan Swift, Laurence Stern, Tobias Smollett, and others.

Carron, Jean-Claude, ed. *Francois Rabelais: Critical Assessments*. Baltimore: Johns Hopkins University Press, 1995. Carron brings together a distinguished group of senior scholars who have found themselves at the center of an ongoing debate about historical context and interpretive strategies. Chapters explore such issues as the "design" and composition of the text, Rabelais as humanist, his anti-feminism, his religious position as revealed by biblical or evangelical references, and particular aspects of low early-modern culture. A chapter on Rabelais and Erasmus draws essential differences between the two "giants of European humanism."

Coleman, Dorothy Gabe. *Rabelais: A Critical Study in Prose Fiction*. Cambridge: Cambridge University Press, 1971. This study examines the first four books of *Gargantua and Pantagruel* in nine chapters and some 230 pages of text. The author excludes discussion of book 5 on the grounds that its authenticity has not been established in four hundred years and may never be. She has used the English version (a very free interpretation) of Sir Thomas Urquhart of Cromarty (1611-1660) for the first three books and that of Peter le Motteux for the fourth. She quotes Rabelais directly when a more accurate rendering is required. Contains a chronology and a select bibliography.

Harp, Margaret B. *The Portrayal of Community in Rabelais's* Quart Livre. New York: Peter Lang, 1997. This book analyzes Rabelais' presentation of alternately comical and grotesque insular communities in the *Quart Livre*. Harp considers all the work's episodes, demonstrating that Rabelais' final work maintains the optimistic and evangelical traits of early French Renaissance writings while still revealing the concern and despair provoked by the impending Religious Wars. It further examines the text's central themes of utopia and exile.

Kaiser, Walter. *Praisers of Folly: Erasmus, Rabelais, Shakespeare*. Cambridge, Mass.: Harvard University Press, 1963; London: Gollancz, 1964. Begins with a prologue, discussing the fool in Renaissance literature. Part 2 is devoted to Rabelais' Panurge. He is compared to Desiderius Erasmus' Stultitia (part 1) and to William Shakespeare's Falstaff (part 3). Includes an extensive bibliography.

Rabelais, François. *Rabelais: A Dramatic Game in Two Parts*. Edited by Jean-Louis Barrault. Translated by Robert Baldick. London: Faber, and New York: Hill and Wang, 1971. A play adapted from the five books of Rabelais. The playwright attempts to capture and project Rabelais' essential psychic health and love of life. Part (act) 1 is devoted to Gargantua and Pantagruel; part (act) 2 is devoted largely to Panurge. Each of the famous incidents is dramatized: part 1, scene 5, "Medieval Education"; part 1, scene 6, "Humanist Education"; part 1, scene 7, "Picrochole"; part 1, scene 8, "The Abbey of Thelema"; and the epilogue, "The Death of Rabelais." Includes nine photographs from the play in performance.

Randall, Michael. *Building Resemblance: Analogical Imagery in the Early French Renaissance*.

Baltimore: Johns Hopkins University Press, 1996. In this book, Randall examines the complex development of analogical imagery, linking the imperfect human to the perfect divine in the poetry and prose of Jean Molinet and Jean Lemaire de Belges (two official historiographers working at the court of Burgundy), and in the novels of Rabelais. Randall identifies a movement from Molinet's works, which feature a conflicted relationship of resemblance and difference, to Lemaire's, in which resemblance flourishes, and finally to Rabelais' *Quart Livre*, in which difference triumphs.

Tilley, Arthur Augustus. *Studies in the French Renaissance*. Cambridge: Cambridge University Press, 1922; New York: Barnes and Noble Books, 1968. Three chapters are devoted exclusively to Rabelais: chapter 3, "Rabelais and Geographical Discovery," chapter 4, "Rabelais and Henry II," and chapter 5, "Rabelais and the Fifth Book." Fully indexed.

Patrick Adcock

SIR WALTER RALEIGH

Born: 1552 or 1554; Hayes Barton, Devon, England
Died: October 29, 1618; London, England
Areas of Achievement: Exploration, politics, and literature
Contribution: Raleigh's vision and enterprise paved the way for English settlement in North America.

Early Life

Walter Raleigh's birth date is even more uncertain than that of his contemporary William Shakespeare, but the dates of their deaths are precisely recorded, because by then they were among the most famous men of their time. Similarly, their family names are spelled in various ways. More than seventy spellings are recorded for Raleigh, the form he preferred in the second half of his life.

Raleigh is often designated as having been born in 1552, though 1554 accords with depositions he made in lawsuits. In any case, his birth occurred in the farm, or Barton, of Hayes, near East Budleigh on the south coast of Devon. His father was a gentleman farmer, who, like some of his relatives and other adventurous men of southwestern England, made money from maritime ventures, including privateering. Young Walter assuredly learned much about seafaring, as imaginatively depicted in Sir John Everett Millais' famous painting of Walter and another boy sitting on the beach, listening enthralled to a sailor's tale. Famous as he was to become by seafaring, however, Walter first made his mark as a soldier on land. At the end of the 1560's, he was campaigning in France as one of the volunteers fighting for the Protestant Huguenots against the Catholics, an experience which helped to shape his anti-Catholic attitude for the rest of his life. By 1572, he was an undergraduate at Oriel College in Oxford University, but within two years he left without taking a degree, a common practice then. In 1575, he enrolled in the Middle Temple, one of the Inns of Court in London, though he did not complete his legal education. No doubt he acquired knowledge of city and court ways.

Life's Work

In 1578, Raleigh sailed from Plymouth in Devon as captain of one of the ships under the command of his half brother, Sir Humphrey Gilbert, who held the charter to settle new lands for the Crown. The expedition aimed to explore and colonize the coast of North America. Bad weather drove the other ships back to England, but Raleigh persevered and reached the Cape Verde Islands, four hundred miles west of Africa.

After obtaining a minor post at court, in 1580 he was given command of a company of soldiers sent to help suppress rebellion in Ireland. He was involved in savage fighting, he befriended the poet Edmund Spenser, and he got Alice Gould pregnant. (He provided in his will for their illegitimate daughter and found Alice a well-to-do husband.) According to one account, "Raleigh coming out of Ireland to the English Court in good habit (his clothes then being a considerable part of his estate) found the Queen walking [in] a plashy place." He immediately "spread his new plush cloak on the ground, whereon the Queen trod gently, rewarding him afterward." This story, reported some eighty years later in Thomas Fuller's *The History of the Worthies of England* (1662), may be apocryphal, but it contains two indisputable truths: paintings and miniatures of Raleigh show that he dressed in the most opulent styles of the period, and he quickly became one of Queen Elizabeth I's favorite courtiers. In 1583, she gave him Durham House, a mansion on the north bank of the Thames, east of Westminster Abbey, and in 1584 the profitable monopolies of "the farm of wines" (by which he was authorized to charge every vintner in the realm one pound a year to sell wine) and the license to export woolen broadcloths. Also in 1584, he became a Member of Parliament for Devon and soon afterward Vice Admiral of Devon and Cornwall, Lord Lieutenant of Cornwall, and Lord Warden of the Stannaries (the tin mines of Cornwall). In January, 1585, the queen bestowed a knighthood on him and later made him captain of her guard.

Raleigh was adept at flattering the queen in Petrarchan poems praising her beauty, power, and influence. More tangibly, he would present to her the new lands of "Virginia," now North Carolina, where the expedition he equipped had landed in 1584. The following year, he sent about one hundred men to Roanoke Island on its coast, but they returned after the hardships of the first winter proved too severe for them. In 1587, a third expedition brought more than one hundred men and women to the site. The first child was born to the colonists on August 18 and christened Virginia Dare. Dealing with the Spanish Armada prevented a relief expedition from coming out until 1590, by which time the colonists had vanished. Although this lost colony was Raleigh's last colonizing attempt in North America, his efforts paved the way for the establishment there of an English-speaking empire in the early seventeenth century and prevented the northward spread of the Spanish Empire.

By the end of the 1580's, Raleigh could have been more than satisfied both by his personal advancement and by England's success at Spain's expense. Yet his fortunes were being undermined. The dashing and ambitious Robert Devereux, Earl of Essex, arrived at court and soon became the aging queen's latest favorite. Meanwhile, Raleigh became involved with one of her ladies-in-waiting, Elizabeth Throckmorton, who was a dozen years younger than he and some thirty years younger than the queen. By November, 1591, if not earlier, Raleigh was secretly married to Throckmorton. A son was born in March, 1592, but seems not to have survived for long. A second son, Walter, was born in 1593 and a third, Carew, in 1604.

In 1592, Queen Elizabeth had put Raleigh in command of an expedition against Panama, though forbidding him to sail beyond Spain. While he was at sea, she learned of his secret marriage, and on his return she had him and his wife imprisoned separately in the Tower of London. When the expedition returned with a captured Portuguese galleon laden with riches from the East Indies, Raleigh was sent to Dartmouth to make sure that the queen's share of the booty—and his share, which she appropriated—were not looted. In effect, he was obliged to buy his pardon.

Released from prison but banished from court, Raleigh and his wife withdrew to the Dorset estate of Sherborne, which he had begged from the queen while still in favor and which he now set about rebuilding. This activity, however, did not satisfy his ambitions. After Sir Humphrey Gilbert drowned on the voyage home from Newfoundland in 1583, Raleigh had acquired Gilbert's charter to explore and settle new lands. He now focused on South America, source of the wealth carried to Spain in the ships which Sir Francis Drake, Raleigh, and others captured at sea. In one such action Sir Richard Grenville lost his life in a heroic (though perhaps ill-judged) rearguard action at the Azores in 1591; Raleigh glorified this event in *A Report of the Truth of the Fight About the Isles of Açores This Last Summer* (1591; also known as *The Last Fight of the Revenge*), his first published book. (Individual poems by or attributed to him were published from 1576 onward, but he never published a collection of his poems.) Raleigh was convinced that in the hinterlands of Guiana, now Venezuela, lay the fabulously rich empire of El Dorado. In 1595, he led an expedition to Guiana and on his return promptly wrote and published *The Discovery of the Large, Rich, and Beautiful Empire of Guiana . . .* (1596), in which he argued that abundant gold could be found there, and that friendly Indians were eager to overthrow their cruel Spanish oppressors and welcome the benign rule of Elizabeth.

Whatever the queen thought of this argument, Raleigh was soon employed on a different venture. He was given command of a squadron in the 1596 expedition against Cadiz, under the leadership of Lord Admiral Howard and Essex. Raleigh boldly led his ships against the harbor defenses and suffered a leg wound which left him using a cane for the rest of his life. His spirited initiative was not shared by the commanders, whose temporizing failed to secure the fullest spoils possible.

The following year, he and Essex led another expedition to seize a Spanish treasure fleet off the Azores. Again, Essex's inadequacies and Raleigh's courage were revealed, the only gain being the temporary capture of the port of Fayal, which Raleigh achieved by leading his men ashore under fire. These events did nothing to assuage the rivalry between the two courtiers. When the irrationally ambitious Essex raised his abortive rebellion against the queen in 1601 and was executed for doing so, suspicion that Raleigh had contributed to his doom was widespread.

While Essex was ruining himself, Raleigh was improving the trade and fortifications of the isle of Jersey, of which the queen made him governor in 1600. This was to be his last advancement, however, because with her death in 1603 his fortunes plummeted. The new sovereign, James I, was strongly biased against Raleigh, reportedly greeting him with the words, "I have heard rawly of thee" and soon depriving him of his positions. Rumored to be discontented, as he might well have been, Raleigh was suspected of treasonous conspiracies against the new king from Scotland. In 1593, he had been exonerated when tried for atheism for his association with the "School of Night," a group of skeptics and freethinkers which included Christopher Marlowe. In 1603, the charges were to be even more implausible but more far-reaching. Raleigh was accused of being in Spanish pay to seek a new policy of peace toward Spain and to be

part of a conspiracy to depose James and replace him with his cousin Arabella Stuart. Though Raleigh's position on these matters is not entirely clear, his trial was conducted with appalling injustice and venom, and in spite of the splendid speeches he made in his defense, a rigged jury guaranteed that he would be found guilty and sentenced to death.

Perhaps because executing the "last Elizabethan" hero was deemed to be impolitic, Raleigh was not put to death but imprisoned in the Tower of London again, this time for almost thirteen years. Again refusing simply to languish in royal disfavor, Raleigh wrote letters containing exaggerated professions of regard for James and humiliating pleas for pardon. He had hundreds of books brought in and embarked on writing *The History of the World* (1614). This monumental undertaking went as far as 133 B.C., and although Raleigh does not refer to the sovereigns he served, James denounced the book as "too saucy in censuring princes" and tried to suppress its publication. James's enmity was not shared by his queen, Anne of Denmark, and their son Prince Henry, both of whom often visited Raleigh in the Tower. Raleigh served as tutor to Prince Henry, for whom he wrote *The History of the World* and whose premature death in 1612 at the age of eighteen caused Raleigh to stop work on the book. The death was a double blow to Raleigh, not only because of the prince's announcement that "No one but my father would keep such a bird in a cage," but also because the manly and chivalric prince seemed likely to be the inspiring monarch that James was not.

James's attempts to secure a substantial dowry from a proposed marriage between his younger son Charles and a Spanish princess had been frustrated by 1616. Hearkening to Raleigh's continual claim that gold could be extracted from Guiana, James released Raleigh to organize and lead an expedition there. At the same time James secretly assured the Spaniards that if Raleigh came into conflict with them, his life would be forfeit. Raleigh was now in his sixties and had suffered several strokes. By the time the expedition neared Guiana in late 1617 he was so ill with fever that he had to delegate command of the party that went up the river Orinoco to his trusted second-in-command, Lawrence Keymis. At the fort of San Thomé, the party got into a fight with the Spaniards, during which Raleigh's son Walter was killed. No gold was found; after returning to the ships, Keymis committed suicide.

Raleigh returned to England a shattered man and was soon imprisoned yet again in the Tower. After having been condemned to death in 1603 on the charge of conspiring to make peace with Spain, he was now to be executed for making war with Spain. The sentence of fifteen years earlier was carried out on October 29, 1618. A huge crowd gathered in the Old Palace Yard at Westminster and Raleigh, elegantly dressed, delivered a speech of nearly an hour in which he defended himself against the charges brought against him and committed himself to the mercy of God. Declining a blindfold, he laid his head on the block and told the hesitant executioner, "What dost thou fear? Strike man, strike!" The headsman needed two blows to sever Raleigh's head, which was carried away by his widow, while his body was buried in the nearby church of St. Margaret's, Westminster.

Summary

Often disliked as a proud, ambitious upstart during his rise, Sir Walter Raleigh, by the courage and grace with which he faced his end, won widespread sympathy as a political martyr. Among those who witnessed his execution were some of the men who would lead the Great Rebellion of the 1640's against the autocratic despotism of the Stuart monarchy. Ironically, therefore, the beheaded victim of King James became an influence on those who would behead James's son King Charles I thirty years and three months later.

Raleigh's life has an aura of mystery to it. He had the characteristics of both a hero and a scoundrel. Further, his vision of the possibilities of empire for England in the Americas, although persuasively supported by his gift as a writer and his daring as an explorer and soldier, would not be realized in his lifetime. Still, he captured the imagination of the English people, and his enterprises and plans were brought to completion by others. Thus, Raleigh can be seen as a colorful, gifted person who failed to be the historical force he might have become.

Bibliography

Adamson, J.H., and H.F. Folland. *The Shepherd of the Ocean: An Account of Sir Walter Ralegh and His Times*. London: Bodley Head, and Boston: Gambit, 1969. Sets Raleigh's life in its historical and political contexts and devotes ample space to summarizing his literary work and relationships.

Armitage, Christopher M. *Sir Walter Ralegh: An Annotated Bibliography*. Chapel Hill: University of North Carolina Press, 1987. Contains nearly two thousand items by and about Raleigh, from 1576 to 1986.

Hammond, Peter. *Sir Walter Ralegh*. London: Pitkin Pictorials, 1978. A concise biography, with abundant pictures of people and places of significance in Ralegh's life.

Jones, H.G., ed. *Raleigh and Quinn: The Explorer and His Boswell*. Chapel Hill: North Caroliniana Society, 1987. A wide-ranging set of papers from the 1987 International Conference on Raleigh, at which David Beers Quinn, emeritus professor at the University of Liverpool, was honored for his many publications in the field.

Lefranc, Pierre. *Sir Walter Ralegh, écrivain: L'Oeuvre et les idées*. Quebec: Presses de l'Université Laval, 1968. Considers Raleigh's mind and art, analyzes the evidence for his authorship of the poems and prose attributed to him, and evaluates his development as a writer.

Mills, Jerry Leath. *Sir Walter Ralegh*. Boston: Hall, 1986. A year-by-year listing, from 1901 to 1984, of books and articles about Raleigh, with often extensive annotation by the compiler.

Nicholl, Charles. *The Creature in the Map: A Journey to El Dorado*. London: Cape, and Chicago: University of Chicago Press, 1997. By combining scholarship and travelogue, Nicholl reconstructs Sir Walter Raleigh's 1595 South American journey, bringing the six-week expedition to life.

Raleigh, Sir Walter. *The History of the World*. Edited by C.A. Patrides. London: Macmillan, and Philadelphia: Temple University Press, 1971. The most substantial modern selection from this huge work, with an analysis of Raleigh's achievement as a writer of history.

———. *Selected Prose and Poetry*. Edited by Agnes M.C. Latham. London: University of London Athlone Press, 1965. A selection by the editor of the standard edition of *The Poems of Sir Walter Ralegh* (1929).

———. *Selected Writings*. Edited by Gerald Hammond. Manchester: Carcanet, 1984: New York: Penguin, 1986. A convenient modern selection of Raleigh's poems, prose works, and letters.

Raleigh, Sir Walter, William Oldys, and Thomas Birch. *The Works of Sir Walter Ralegh*. Oxford: Oxford University Press, and New York: Franklin, 1829. 8 vols. Volume 1 contains the early biographies of Raleigh by W. Oldys and T. Birch; volumes 2-7 contain *The History of the World*; and volume 8 contains miscellaneous essays, poems, and letters, many now considered to have been foisted on Raleigh after his death.

Roberts, Linda. "Setting Sail." *Cobblestone* 15 (April, 1994): 4. This article recounts attempts by Sir Walter Raleigh to colonize a new land in North America during the 1500s and outlines why England needed colonies. Roberts discusses Raleigh's cousin, Sir Richard Grenville; the colonizing of Roanoke Island; John White; and Virginia Dare, the first English child born in America.

Wallace, Willard M. *Sir Walter Ralegh*. London: Oxford University Press, and Princeton, N.J.: Princeton University Press, 1959. Covers Raleigh's life and pays considerable attention to his literary work.

Christopher Armitage

RAPHAEL
Raffaello Sanzio

Born: April 6, 1483; Urbino, Tuscany, Italy
Died: April 6, 1520; Rome
Areas of Achievement: Art, architecture, and archaeology
Contribution: With Leonardo da Vinci and Michelangelo, Raphael was part of the great trio of High Renaissance masters. He became the most prolific and most widely celebrated painter of his time.

Early Life

Raffaello Sanzio, known as Raphael, had the good fortune to be born in the mountain town of Urbino, where Federico da Montefeltro maintained a ducal court manifesting splendor, pomp, elegance, and the new learning. Raphael's father, Giovanni, a minor painter and versifier, had access to the court; from his youth, Raphael was introduced to the ongoing works of Piero della Francesca, Sandro Botticelli, Paolo Uccello, and other contemporary masters. Giovanni died, however, when Raphael was eleven; at this age, he may already have been apprenticed to Perugino in Perugia. There he rapidly moved to the head of that artist's busy workshop, which won so many commissions that the master had to develop an elaborate atelier system, in which assistants did much of the preliminary work on projects. By the age of sixteen, Raphael was already influencing local artists, and from this time his hand is detectable in Perugino's works.

Raphael's earliest independent paintings both date from 1504. The first, *Marriage of the Virgin*, shows both his indebtedness to Perugino—the disposal of figures, the use of a temple as background, and an array of colors are all drawn from him—and the introduction of what are to become signature characteristics—the supple, resilient posture of the figures, their unearthly serenity of expression, and the rhythmic organization of the composition. The second, *Saint George and the Dragon*, is a small panel that was commissioned by the Duke of Urbino to present to Henry VII of England. The influence of Leonardo da Vinci's *Battle of Anghiari* (1503) is evident here, as it is in all subsequent mounted battle paintings. Again the dominant element is rhythmic organization: The mounted knight on his diagonally placed steed intersects the massed landscape, so that all the tension of the painting drives through the lance, pinning the wriggling monster to the earth. The spiral coil of the horse's body generates much of the accumulated tension; yet the animal itself is surprisingly static, betraying the artist's inexperience. The painting abounds in finely observed, meticulously rendered details; the young artist seems to be showing off the facility of his technique. These two paintings constitute the auspicious beginning of an ambitious career.

Life's Work

Raphael's fifteen-year career falls into two phases, Florence and Rome. He settled in Florence in 1505, stepping into a void created by the withdrawal of both Leonardo and Michelangelo, at a time when the appetite for painting had been stimulated by their examples. Raphael's facility soon proved prosperous. Within three years, he finished seventeen still-extant Madonnas and Holy Families, besides several other major works. That kind of activity makes both Michelangelo, productive as he was, and Leonardo, who failed to complete one painting during that period, look like monuments of indolence. Part of the reason for this difference derives from Raphael's method of working. Unlike either of his fellow giants, Raphael did not approach painting as a series of solutions to technical problems of representation. Instead, he made preliminary sketches—many of them preserved—which show him testing variables in the relationship of forms. Only in the the painting itself would he settle on one moment in the flow of forms. That allowed him to produce paintings that merely glossed over problems which would have hamstrung either of the other two. That is, Raphael painted for his patrons, not for his peers.

The *Madonna of the Meadows* (1505) is one of the best of the markedly similar items in the series. As before, much of the design and the framing landscape derives from Leonardo's examples, and much of the iconography, from Michelangelo's. Yet the rhythmical organization, the sinuous upward coiling, is distinctly Raphael, as is the countermovement in the downward glance of the Virgin. Yet the truly astonishing feature is the Virgin's face. Though both Fra Angelico and Fra Filippo Lippi had anticipated this clarity of line and simplicity of form, the viewer is still struck almost dumb by this representation of incarnate grace and superhuman serenity.

Raphael also produced for his patrons a remarkable series of portraits, in the process raising the portrait to a new level. At the same time that he was idealizing the features of his sacred work, he reversed the practice with his portraits. With them, he became the dispassionate observer, coolly recording the essential character of his subjects. The result is a gallery of distinct personalities, caught in moments of self-revelation. In doing this, he became the most successful portraitist of all time.

Around 1509, the twenty-six-year-old Raphael was called to Rome by Pope Julius II to embark on the major phase of his career, which would last for eleven years. His first commission from the pope was to take over the official decorations of the Vatican apartments (called *Stanze*, or rooms) from Sodoma. He started with the Stanza della Segnatura; in it, he determined to depict the ideals of the new pope's regime and, in the act, create frescoes of unprecedented refinement and harmony of form. His plan included two major wall frescoes facing each other and a complementary lunette: the *Dispute over the Sacrament* (1510-1511), the misnamed *School of Athens* (1510-1511), and the *Cardinal Virtues* (1511). The first is an attempt to represent the entire doctrine of the Eucharist, from its origin in Heaven to its veneration by the people. In the cloud scene above, Raphael portrays the ordered harmony of divine Providence, in sharp contrast to the fierce contention of theologians from various disciplines on the earth below. The grandeur and rhythmic energy of the composition surpass anything yet attempted in art—or would, if Michelangelo were not simultaneously at work on the Sistine Chapel ceiling a few barricaded corridors away. Even so, the scene is colossal.

The medallion inset above the *Dispute over the Sacrament* depicts Theology; opposite it is that for Philosophy. The fresco below, the *School of Athens*, attempts to do for that field what the *Dispute over the Sacrament* does for theology—that is, represent all the leading figures in classical philosophy engaged in debate. This painting is Raphael's best-known work; it provides the textbook example of the High Renaissance ideals of integral unity and spatial harmony. The figures circulate in depth around the central figures of Plato and Aristotle, all set within a great vaulted dome in the classical manner, impractical but magnificently proportioned. This beautifully rational frame establishes the perfect setting for the debate of abstract problems; the figures surge beneath the stable, solid dome. The philosophers themselves are wonderfully individualized, yet each is playing an ensemble role in the total composition. The only modern figure slumps prominently in the foreground, dressed in stonecutter's work clothes: He turns out to be Michelangelo, the single man alive whom Raphael considered worthy of a place in the company of the ancients. The painting thus constitutes Raphael's statement of the relationship of the Renaissance to antiquity. Further, the lunette of the *Cardinal Virtues* demonstrates what Raphael had learned from Michelangelo; for his figures there suddenly take on the monumentality of that master, though transformed by Raphael's characteristic sweetness, organic rhythm, and grace.

This transition in style, from balanced serenity to dramatic expressiveness, culminates in the second apartment, the Stanza d'Eliodoro, which contains two full-wall frescoes and two window surrounds: the *Expulsion of Heliodorus* (1512), the *Expulsion of Attila* (1513-1514), the *Mass of Bolsena* (1512), and the *Liberation of Saint Peter from Prison* (1512). These combine harmony of organization with new, vibrant coloring and dramatic tension, so that the images seem almost to seethe with motion and sing with color. They show Raphael raising his unique style of spiral rhythmic organization to a new height: His figures gain weight and tension, and energy explodes in their dynamic interconnection. The artist seems to be moving toward a mode of representation beyond the capacity of the High Renaissance. His work here has been termed proto-Baroque for this reason. The *Expulsion of Heliodorus* is typical of this new sense of the dramatic. In it Raphael shows that he was secure enough in his habits of rational organization to test them to their limits. His figures take on the mass and muscle of Michelangelo's; they vibrate with energies that threaten to tear apart his rationally organized scheme. Everything still harmonizes, but only barely.

Raphael's *Sistine Madonna* (1513) created a vision of the Madonna which totally eclipsed all of his former efforts. If any painting crystallizes the essence of the High Renaissance, this one does. This work defines rhythmic organization: Its broad spiral curves and delicately balanced masses, counterpointed by the two often-excerpted putti at the bottom of the frame, almost look like a demonstration piece for a painting class. Furthermore, the Virgin is the quintessential Virgin, perhaps the loveliest woman ever painted. Among other por-

traits of this period which confirm his reputation as a portraitist are those of *Baldassare Castiglione* and *Pope Leo X with Cardinals*. They have never been excelled.

Raphael's most ambitious pictorial project was to design ten massive tapestries, for which he produced full-size watercolor cartoons as models. These were intended to continue the iconographic cycle on Christian religious history begun by Michelangelo. This is Raphael's largest work, and it exhibits his dramatic intensity raised to its highest power. At the same time, Raphael was busy with architectural projects, the grandest of which is the Villa Madama in Rome; though unfinished at his death and never completed, the fragment is exquisite in design and proportion and elegant in its imaginative detail. His final great painting, completed by assistants, is the *Transfiguration of Christ* (1517). Here Raphael matches the level he had reached in the *Expulsion of Heliodorus*; color, design, and rhythm fuse in a drama that swirls off the canvas, and the figures pulse with real breath and warmth. Moreover, this painting generates a religious intensity far removed from the serene, rational indifference of the early Madonnas. Unfortunately, Raphael had little time to develop this mystical strain, for he died after a brief illness on April 6, 1520.

Summary

Raphael is the Renaissance artist ideal, or at least the embodiment of one half of the Renaissance standard of excellence. In his *Il cortegiano* (1528; the courtier), Raphael's friend Baldassare Castiglione had defined the essential quality of the refined gentleman as *sprezzatura*, an untranslatable term which means something like making difficult things look easy. Raphael certainly had the technical facility for that. Perhaps no other painter possessed equal talent. Raphael could do things effortlessly with brush or pen that artists of normal ability could produce only with monumental labor. Moreover, this effortlessness comes through in his work: Everything he does looks easy, natural, right; his figures seem not to be figures but simply themselves. In many ways, he taught his viewers what it meant to see. In the paintings, this ease of technique translates itself into ineffable grace.

Yet in his early works Raphael pays a price for this facility. He produced so much so easily that it is possible to accuse him of creating by mechanical formula. Further, instead of solving technical problems, he merely brushes by them; in this respect, he falls short of another Renaissance ideal, to make human intelligence the norm by which everything knowable was to be measured. As a result, a premium was placed on meeting the difficult head-on; problems were meant to be solved, and the man of true genius used reason to find a solution. Raphael's talent was so great that he ran the risk of becoming merely facile.

His encounters with Leonardo and Michelangelo changed that. Not that he became a great innovator, though much of his work did establish formal precedents, especially in portraits and in group narratives. Rembrandt, for example, copied Raphael's canvases with care and imitated his poses, and Nicolas Poussin and Jean-Auguste-Dominique Ingres are almost unimaginable without his examples. His work for the Vatican, however, clearly ranks with the greatest paintings of all time. In them, the early grace and serenity take on weight, mass, and energy, and a dynamic intelligence informs the whole. In these respects, Raphael becomes the incarnation of the High Renaissance ideal. As a portraitist he is supreme; his perfectly balanced, perfectly poised figures seem to occupy a moment in time, so that one can imagine a gallery of them carrying on civilized conversation when no one is in the room. His real genius, however, appears in the Vatican group compositions, in which he seems to create his own heroic universe, electric with its own energy and populated with entirely plausible though larger-than-life characters. There Raphael seems to reach the limits of the natural. It is small wonder that painters succeeding him were forced to grotesque distortions to represent superabundant energy; only Raphael could cage such forces within his cosmos of radiant and dynamic calm.

Bibliography

Beck, James. *Raphael*. New York: Abrams, 1976. This is an excellent, thorough study of Raphael and his times, with much technical information. Intended mainly for specialists, it is surprisingly approachable and packed with a wealth of detail and good reproductions.

Fischel, Oskar. *Raphael*. Translated by B. Rackham. 2 vols. London: Kegan Paul, 1948. Fischel presents the authoritative, old-fashioned account of Raphael's life and works. Though somewhat dated, Fischel is indispensable, partly because critical opinion on Raphael has not changed much since the publication of this work.

Freedberg, Sydney J. *Painting in Italy, 1500-1600*. 3d ed. New Haven: Conn.: Yale University Press, 1993. The reproductions in this small-format book do little justice to Raphael's large-scale works, but then no reproductions can. The text, intended for the general reader, is appealingly informative and nontechnical, making this a useful general reference.

Hall, Marcia, ed. *Raphael's "School of Athens."* Cambridge and New York: Cambridge University Press, 1997. This book examines one of the masterpieces of the Italian Renaissance and the artist's best known work. The "School of Athens" represents the gathering of the philosophers of the ancient world around the central figures of Plato and Aristotle. Presented in this volume are the early criticisms of the fresco, along with new interpretations of its iconography in relation to the other frescoes in the Stanza and in the context of the humanism and rhetorical tradition of the papal court.

Hartt, Frederick. *History of Italian Renaissance Art: Painting, Sculpture, Architecture*. 4th ed. London: Thames and Hudson, and New York: Abrams, 1994. Hartt provides the most accessible brief introduction to the work of Raphael, in clear, nontechnical language and with good reproductions, though mostly in black and white. He is particularly good at summarizing iconography and analyzing formal qualities.

Hersey, George L. *High Renaissance Art in St. Peter's and the Vatican: An Interpretive Guide*. Chicago: University of Chicago Press, 1993. Before discussing individual works, Hersey describes how the shifting political and religious alliances of sixteenth century Italy, France, and Spain played themselves out in Rome. He offers vivid accounts of the lives and personalities of four popes, each a great patron of art and architecture: Julius II, Leo X, Clement VII, and Paul III. Having set the historical scene, Hersey explores the Vatican's magnificent Renaissance art and architecture, giving the story behind the work, and outlining themes important to the artist, the papacy, and the church.

Jones, Roger, and Nicholas Penny. *Raphael*. New Haven, Conn.: Yale University Press, 1983; London: Yale University Press, 1987. This nonspecialist text is a fine source for the general reader, placing Raphael squarely in his historical and social setting and including brilliant reproductions of entire works as well as blow-ups of details.

Raphael. *The Complete Work of Raphael*. Edited by Mario Salmi et al. New York: Reynal, 1969. As the title indicates, this is the only work available which attempts to catalog and reproduce everything that Raphael accomplished. Yet, since he produced so much work which has been preserved, it is impossible to reproduce everything in one volume, so the title misleads somewhat. Still, this volume offers more than any other, and the documentation is thorough.

Vasari, Giorgio. *Lives of the Most Eminent Painters, Sculptors, and Architects*. 10 vols. Translated by Gaston du C. de Vere. London and New York: Macmillan, 1912-1914. Though not always accurate, Vasari is the best near-contemporary source for Raphael's life and his contemporary reception and reputation. Vasari's work is full of entertaining anecdotes and much miscellaneous information, all gathered at second hand. He is better on Raphael than on some, perhaps because he identified so closely with him.

James Livingston

RICHARD III

Born: October 2, 1452; Fotheringay Castle, Northamptonshire, England

Died: August 22, 1485; Bosworth Field, Leicestershire, England

Areas of Achievement: Government and politics

Contribution: England's most maligned monarch, Richard III, in his attempt to restore order and dynastic stability to a nation torn by three decades of civil war by first serving his brother, Edward IV, loyally and then by accepting the throne himself, fell victim to the intrigues of those who were jealous of his loyalty and abilities and who coveted the Crown.

Early Life

Richard Plantagenet was born on October 2, 1452, at Fotheringay Castle, the youngest of nine children of Richard, Duke of York, and Cicely (née Neville), Duchess of York. He had two sisters—Anne, Duchess of Exeter, and Margaret (later Duchess of Burgundy)—and three brothers—Edmund, Earl of Rutland, Edward (later Edward IV), and George (later Duke of Clarence)—who survived to adulthood. Young Richard's father had a claim to the throne, which was then occupied by the third king of the House of Lancaster, Henry VI. Although Richard, Duke of York, secretly aspired to the throne, he made no formal claim until 1459, four years after the outbreak of the dynastic struggle between the houses of York and Lancaster known as the Wars of the Roses. In the 1450's, young Richard was nothing more than a junior cadet of a leading aristocratic family. None would have anticipated that within three decades he would become England's most controversial monarch.

Richard's attitudes and actions throughout his life were determined by the violence and chaos which became endemic among the great noble families during the Wars of the Roses, lasting from 1455 until Richard's death thirty years later. The immediate background of the wars can be traced to the mental incapacitation of Henry VI in the summer of 1453. Henry's wife, Margaret of Anjou, to whom a son, the future Edward, Prince of Wales, was born in October, 1453, desired a regency for herself. Richard of York was named protector, however, and served capably until Henry regained his sanity in 1455. Then, under the influence of York's enemies, the restored king not only demanded and secured the duke's resignation but also threatened his life. It was at this time that the Duke of York and his supporters, chiefly his cousin Richard Neville, Earl of Warwick, rose in rebellion. The first phase of the Wars of the Roses was decided at the Battle of St. Albans. Henry was defeated and taken prisoner by Richard, but the Duke of York did not take the throne, remaining temporarily satisfied to control the government indirectly. Queen Margaret was displeased, however, with York's unofficial supremacy. Determined that her son should eventually succeed his father, she made her move in late 1460. At the Battle of Wakefield, on December 30, 1460, the Yorkists suffered a seemingly disastrous defeat. The Duke of York and his oldest surviving son, Edmund, Earl of Rutland, were killed. Warwick did not arrive from France fast enough to save his cousin, and the Lancastrians had regained unchallenged control.

The revival of Lancastrian power did not, however, last long. The leadership of the Yorkist cause was now assumed by the dead duke's oldest surviving son and Richard's oldest brother, Edward. Joining his forces with those of Warwick, Edward defeated the Lancastrian forces at Towton Moor on March 29, 1461. Henry VI and Queen Margaret fled, and Edward of York marched on London, claiming the throne as Edward IV by right of descent from Edward III. Soon after his coronation in June, 1461, his brothers George and Richard were admitted to the Order of the Garter. At this time also George was created Duke of Clarence and Richard Duke of Gloucester.

The first years of Edward's reign went well, and primarily with the aid of Warwick, he succeeded in restoring order to the realm. In 1463, Queen Margaret again raised the standard of revolt for the House of Lancaster. Again defeated, she fled with her son Edward into exile in France. Henry VI was captured and imprisoned in the Tower of London. At this point, Richard was only eleven years old. Already in his short life he had witnessed extreme violence and had been its indirect victim. His father and brother and various relatives and friends had been killed in battle or executed, and he had been forced into exile with his mother. The impressionable boy had learned that immorality and duplicity were rewarded often with success. Soon, he himself was to play a leading role in the tumultuous course of events.

Little is known about Richard's life during the 1460's. He, his brother Clarence, and his unmarried sister Margaret probably were quartered at the royal palace at Greenwich from 1461 to 1465. From 1465 until at least 1468, Richard alone was placed in the custody of the Earl of Warwick, then the most powerful magnate in England with extensive landholdings throughout England and especially in the north. Richard spent those years at Warwick's castles of Middleham and Sheriff Hutton, where he became acquainted with his future wife, Warwick's younger daughter, Anne Neville (the Duke of Clarence married Warwick's older daughter, Isabel), and with one of his closest lifelong friends and supporters, Francis, Lord Lovell. Richard also became acquainted at this time with many of the northern noblemen and gentry who were attached to Warwick. Through marriage, Richard would later become Warwick's principal heir in the north, and this region became his base of popularity and power. His connections there were later helpful in his securing the throne and in his brief reign.

During the 1460's, relations between Edward IV and Warwick began to sour. Warwick, who had played a key role in advancing the Yorkist cause, assumed the right to advise the king unofficially and direct his policy. One of his major goals was to arrange a fortuitous marriage alliance for the young Edward in order to establish greater stability for the House of York's dynastic future. Several royal alliances were considered, but Edward, strong-willed, impetuous, and amorous, secretly married an Englishwoman of his own choosing, Elizabeth Woodville, the daughter of Richard Woodville, Baron Rivers, a former Lancastrian ally, and the widow of Sir John Grey, a Lancastrian retainer who had been killed at St. Albans. Edward kept his marriage, which was to doom his dynasty, secret for several months. When he was finally forced to reveal it to Warwick, the latter was incensed, as were many of Edward's other supporters who resented his marriage into a Lancastrian family, and who were especially alienated by the preferments the king showed to members of his wife's family. In 1468, Warwick and his supporters, which a year later came to include his new son-in-law, Edward's brother the Duke of Clarence, struck against the king. Taken by surprise at Northampton, Edward was imprisoned at Middleham. Warwick thus acquired the nickname "the Kingmaker," for he had two kings as prisoner: Edward at Middleham and Henry in the Tower. Although Warwick soon restored Edward to his throne, the king, infuriated by Warwick's execution of his wife's father and brother, refused to accept permanent subservience to the earl. In March, 1470, Warwick was accused of treason. The earl escaped to France, taking Clarence with him. Joining forces with Queen Margaret and her son Edward of Lancaster, and aided by a subsidy from Louis XI of France, Warwick planned to return to England, restore Henry VI to the throne, and marry his daughter Anne (later Richard III's wife) to Edward of Lancaster. They then crossed the Channel to England in September, 1470, raised the banner of rebellion against Edward, and forced him to flee across the Channel to his ally, his brother-in-law the Duke of Burgundy, taking with him his loyal younger brother, Richard of Gloucester.

Life's Work

While abroad, Richard began to play an active role in the affairs of his family and the realm. In his late teens, those physical features distorted by later pro-Tudor detractors, especially by William Shakespeare, had developed. Physically, he resembled his father. Darker and shorter than Edward and George, who had inherited the Neville fairness and height, Richard was not the deformed "crookback" as he was later portrayed in order to enhance his villainy. Perhaps one arm and shoulder were larger than the other, but this was probably more because of its use with a sword in the practice of the martial arts than because of a deformity. Richard was held in exceptionally high regard by his brother Edward because of his loyalty, martial abilities, and intelligence. In March, 1471, Edward and Richard set sail for England. Within three months the king and his younger brother had met Warwick in battle at Barnet, where the mighty earl was killed, and had defeated the main Lancastrian army at Tewkesbury, where Edward of Lancaster was slain. Most of the Lancastrians were killed at Tewkesbury. A few escaped, however, including the young Henry Tudor, Earl of Richmond, who was later to become Richard's most inveterate foe. Edward IV now resumed the throne, and soon after, Henry VI died in the Tower under mysterious circumstances. In the summer of 1471, it appeared that the last Lancastrian threat had been removed, and England looked forward to many years of peace and enlightened rule by its young king. The Duke of Clarence had been temporarily reconciled with the king, and Richard was rewarded by the king for his loyalty and services at Barnet and Tewkesbury. Richard received large grants of land and offices and was married in 1472 to Edward of Lancaster's young widow and the companion of his youth, Warwick's daughter Anne Neville.

The marriage to Anne brought to Richard half of the Warwick inheritance. The Duke of Clarence, however, resented having to split the inheritance with his brother. The estrangement that had already developed between the brothers as a result of Clarence's treachery toward Edward widened and was never to be resolved. As a result, historians have been unable to determine the extent of Richard's involvement in Clarence's conviction on the charge of treason in 1478 and his subsequent private execution, according to tradition in a butt of Malmsey wine. Certainly, Clarence's fall was primarily the work of the Woodvilles, whom he continued to resent. Nevertheless, although some defenders of Richard have argued that Richard intervened unsuccessfully to save his brother's life, certainly they were on very poor terms personally by 1478, and Richard was not overly saddened by his duplicitous brother's demise.

Richard spent the remaining years of Edward's reign primarily in the north, where he had his base of power and wealth. Eventually, in 1480, he was made Edward's lieutenant general in the north and, in 1483, hereditary warden of the western marches. In his viceregal position, he exercised his authority effectively and scrupulously and became much loved in that section. In 1482, he also undertook a successful military expedition to recapture Berwick-upon-Tweed from the Scots. Most important, after 1478 Richard was seldom at court and thus not directly involved in the intrigues that revolved around the feud over the succession between the king's closest friend and adviser, Lord Chamberlain William Lord Hastings, and the queen, her two sons by her first marriage (the Marquess of Dorset and Lord Richard Gray), and their ally John Morton, Bishop of Ely. Edward, with Hastings' support, decided that in the event of his premature death his brother Richard should head a regency for his oldest son, Prince Edward. The Woodvilles opposed a protectorate by Richard, fearing that they would be supplanted in positions of importance by Richard's supporters. They wanted a Woodville regency, or at least the authority to hold the young king and thus control his actions, both of which were vehemently opposed by many of the most powerful families, who regarded the Woodvilles as dangerously ambitious upstarts. Although Edward IV succeeded in effecting a reconciliation between Hastings and the Woodville faction at the time of his death in April, 1483, the succession question arose again immediately thereafter.

Richard, motivated by both personal ambition and a desire to avert a return to the factionalism of the 1450's and 1460's, then made his move and became intimately involved in a series of events which formed the foundation of the later Tudor defamation of the last Yorkist king. In a letter from Hastings, Richard (still in the north) received the news of his brother's death and his appointment as Lord Protector. He then wrote the proper letters of condolence and set out for London. During the course of his journey, he received additional letters from Hastings telling of the Woodville machinations. At Stony Stratford, Richard joined forces with his main ally, Henry, Duke of Buckingham, took the young king, Edward V, away from his uncles and half brothers, and placed Edward under his own protection. Richard Woodville (the young king's uncle) and his half brother Richard Grey were executed soon after, the queen mother sought sanctuary with her younger son, Richard, and her daughters at Westminster, and Dorset fled to France. The Woodville's attempted coup had been thwarted, and the young king and the Lord Protector arrived in London on May 4, 1483. By the middle of May, Edward V had taken up residence in the Tower of London, where he was joined in mid-June by his brother Richard. This was by no means unusual during the period before a coronation. What happened at this point is unclear. Apparently, the queen mother was continuing her intrigues against Richard and was accused of conspiring with one of her husband's former mistresses and Hastings' present mistress, Jane Shore. Whatever the case, during a Council meeting in the Tower on June 13, Richard accused his old friend Hastings, as well as John Morton, Bishop of Ely, and Thomas, Lord Stanley, the stepfather of Henry Tudor, of plotting against his authority and life. Hastings was beheaded immediately on Tower Green, Stanley was briefly imprisoned, and Morton was placed in Buckingham's custody.

Although the coronation of Edward was postponed, it was becoming clear that Richard's position as Lord Protector was precarious. Increasingly, he became convinced that he must take the throne. Several more years of divided loyalties and conspiracies under a regency was politically untenable. On June 22, one Dr. Shaw in a sermon at St. Paul's Cross accused Edward IV of bigamy, thus questioning the legitimacy of his children by Elizabeth Woodville. Four days later, with the assistance and prodding of Buckingham, a petition was drafted which set aside the claims of Edward IV's children, reduced their mother from queen and wife to Dame Elizabeth Grey, mistress of the late king, and prevailed upon Richard, as Edward IV's nearest legitimate heir, to take the crown. Richard agreed and, in so doing, regardless of his motives, undoubtedly helped to avert another civil war. On July 6, 1483, Richard was crowned king and his wife, Anne, queen.

Richard's coronation proved to be the personal apex of his reign. Although he attempted to govern well by enacting financial reforms, reducing taxes, building churches, patronizing learning, and instituting reforms to aid petitioners, he was plagued almost from the beginning by rumors and plottings. To discredit him, the Woodville faction complained that Edward IV's sons were in danger, thus laying the foundations for the most vicious accusation soon leveled against Richard: that he had ordered the murder of the little princes in the Tower. Ostensibly sickened by these rumors, Richard undertook a royal progress to York and was most enthusiastically received wherever he stopped. Buckingham accompanied him as far as Gloucester, where he left the royal train to go to his castle of Brecknock, where he met with Morton, the crypto-Lancastrian he had been holding captive since the crucial meeting in the Tower. Richard, who had made a fatal mistake by temporarily abandoning his capital and the south, was enthusiastically welcomed at York, where he knighted his nine-year-old son, Edward. When he left York in mid-September to return south, he soon received word that his most trusted supporter, Buckingham, had assumed the leadership of an uprising against him.

The motive for the duke's defection has never been clear, but the prime movers in the plot appear to have been Morton, Lord Stanley, and his wife, Margaret Beaufort, Lady Stanley, who advanced a dubious claim to the throne through the Lancastrian line for her son Henry Tudor, Earl of Richmond. Morton, who held great influence over Buckingham, was apparently convinced to support the Stanley-Tudor connection because of the fall of the Woodville faction which had originally provided his hope for advancement. Although Richard defeated and captured Buckingham and had him executed, he failed to deal sufficiently harshly with the other rebels. Most portentously, Lady Stanley's life was spared, and Morton escaped to join Henry Tudor. In April, 1484, Richard's only son and heir, Edward, Prince of Wales, died at Middleham. A year later, in March, 1485, Richard's wife Anne succumbed to tuberculosis.

Within a period of less than two years, Richard had had his royal authority seriously challenged and had lost his wife and only child. Within less than six months, he was to lose his crown and his life. In August, 1484, Henry Tudor crossed from Brittany and landed at Milford Haven with a motley army composed primarily of mercenaries paid for by his mother, Lady Stanley. Although Lord Stanley and his brother Sir William Stanley professed their loyalty to Richard, they, along with the equally duplicitous Earl of Northumberland, on whom Richard had depended, defected at the beginning of the Battle of Bosworth, where the armies of Richard and Henry Tudor met on August 22, 1485. Abandoned by most of his friends, with the notable exception of Lord Lovell, who had remained a faithful friend since childhood, Richard fought valiantly but was finally killed. Stripped naked and thrown across the back of a pack horse, his body was taken to nearby Leicester, where it was buried in the church of the Grey Friars. With the dissolution of the monasteries during Henry VIII's reign, the grave was opened and the remains were scattered. Henry Tudor, the last indirect remnant of the Lancastrian line, now took the throne as Henry VII and inaugurated the Tudor dynasty. The Yorkist line and the Wars of the Roses were effectively at an end.

Summary

Although the historical Richard III died on the battlefield of Bosworth, the legendary Richard was born there with Henry Tudor's assumption of a throne to which he had a highly dubious claim. Immediately, Henry found it necessary to blacken the name and reputation of his predecessor as a means of enhancing his own and to provide a justification for his unsurpation. He and his son, Henry VIII, remained acutely insecure about the stability of the Tudor dynasty and as a result welcomed accounts critical of the last Plantagenet. Unfortunately, many of Richard's actions, regardless of their motivation, made him suspect.

Two individuals were particularly responsible for the creation of the myth that has made Richard

III the most controversial English monarch. The first, Polydore Vergil of Urbino, was an Italian humanist who came to England in 1502 as a deputy of his Italian patron and collector of papal taxes, Cardinal Adriano Castelli. Under Henry VII's encouragement, Vergil wrote a history of England, his *Anglicae Historia Libri XXVI*, completed in 1513 but not published until 1534. Vergil was not rewarded by the king for his labors; thus, he was not a lackey of Henry. It was nevertheless he who first portrayed Richard as the consummate villain. The second, and best-known, creator of the Tudor tradition of Richard III historiography was Sir Thomas More, whose *History of King Richard III* (written c. 1513) first appeared in 1543. More's history may have been influenced, or some have suggested even written, by John Morton, Bishop of Ely, the traitor to Richard in whose household More served as a page in his youth. Vergil's and More's histories portray Richard as a monster in physical appearance and deeds.

It is this image of Richard that has come down to the present through two of Shakespeare's historical plays, *Henry VI, Part III* (c. 1590-1591) and *Richard III* (c. 1592-1593). This is the Richard who has been accused of a catalog of crimes of gargantuan proportions. It was Shakespeare's Richard who not only murdered the little princes in the Tower but also slew Henry VI in that same mysterious building and his son, Edward, Prince of Wales, at Tewkesbury. It was this Richard who tricked his brother Edward IV into ordering the execution of the Duke of Clarence. Shakespeare's Richard even gloated over the death of his own wife, Anne, and perhaps even ordered it to enable himself to effect a more beneficial marriage alliance with his niece and Henry Tudor's later bride. Although Shakespeare intended his play to be good theater rather than sound history, the popularity of his dramatic works, especially *Richard III*, and the appeal of the Bard's Richard to actors, who revel in his cleverness and villainy, have assured that Shakespeare's portrayal of Richard will remain foremost in the popular imagination.

Fortunately, Richard's defenders and supporters have also vigorously advanced their argument that he was the innocent victim of Tudor vilification. The first major exponent of the revisionist school of Richard historiography was the man of letters Horace Walpole, whose *Historic Doubts on the Life and Reign of Richard III* was published in 1768. Since then, the debate has raged on unabated. Indeed, it has been suggested that something has been written about Richard in every single generation since his death. The Richard III Society, an international organization dedicated to his rehabilitation, remains very active. Although most of the questions about Richard's actions will never be definitively answered, the continuation of the great debate about the last Plantagenet promises to attract curious and passionate detractors and defenders long into the future.

Bibliography

Kendall, Paul Murray. *Richard III*. New York: Norton, 1955. This account was the definitive biography of Richard III until Charles Ross's publication. Although Kendall occasionally romanticizes his subject, his biography is still valuable to the scholar and the best-written of all, thus providing an ideal introduction to this fascinating subject.

———. *Richard III: The Great Debate*. New York: Norton, and London: Folio Society, 1965. This volume includes the texts of the two key conflicting arguments in the great debate over Richard III's character and deeds: More's *History of King Richard III* and Walpole's *Historic Doubts on the Life and Reign of King Richard III*. Edited and with a useful introduction by one of the two leading twentieth century authorities on the subject.

———. *The Yorkist Age: Daily Life During the Wars of the Roses*. London: Allen and Unwin, and New York: Norton, 1962. An extremely evocative social history of the era in which Richard lived by a scholar who has immersed himself in the period he has chosen for study. This is a marvelously detailed, eminently readable companion piece to Kendall's biography of Richard.

Lamb, Vivien B. *The Betrayal of Richard III*. 4th ed. London: Mitre Press, 1972. This small volume has been included as a good example of the continued intensity of the great debate over Richard. This book, as its title indicates, is a defense of the maligned king and discounts, or at least seriously questions, most of the charges of Richard's detractors.

Ross, Charles. *Richard III*. London: Methuen, and Berkeley: University of California Press, 1981. This is the indispensable study of Richard and of the historic debate that has arisen about him. Exhaustively researched and scholarly, yet well written and readable, Ross's biography is scrupulously objective. It is one of the few books on the subject which deals fairly, but critically, with both Richard's detractors and his defenders.

Tey, Josephine. *The Daughter of Time*. London: Davies, 1951; New York: Macmillan, 1952. This novel by one of England's best-known mystery writers centers on an amateur sleuth's attempt to solve the mysteries associated with Richard III while temporarily confined to a hospital. Although the work is fictional, the material dealing with Richard is sound history. There is no better introduction to the subject for the curious but superficially informed reader.

Wilson, Derek. *The Tower: The Tumultuous History of the Tower of London from 1078*. London: Hamilton, 1978; New York: Scribner, 1979. Although the historical time frame covered by this volume is far broader than the era of Richard III, it is nevertheless a fascinating study and provides interesting insights into those dark events associated with the Tower during the Wars of the Roses, especially the fate of the little princes, Edward and Richard.

Wood, Charles T. *Joan of Arc and Richard III: Sex, Saints, and Government in the Middle Ages*. New York: Oxford University Press, 1988. Professor Wood's study of French and English history invites readers to reconsider their notions on a variety of usually controversial subjects.

J. Stewart Alverson

NICHOLAS RIDLEY

Born: c. 1500; probably at Willimotiswick Castle, South Tynedale, Northumberland, England

Died: October 16, 1555; Oxford, England

Areas of Achievement: Church reform; religion and theology

Contribution: The English bishop and Protestant reformer Nicholas Ridley worked closely with Archbishop Thomas Cranmer to consolidate the reformation of the Church of England. Through his theological writings and by his martyrdom under Queen Mary Tudor, Ridley helped to further the development of the Anglican Church.

Early Life

Nicholas Ridley was born in Northumberland (modern Northumbria), probably at Willimotiswick, South Tynedale, around the year 1500. He was the younger son of Christopher Ridley of Unthank Hall and Ann Blenkinsop. Nicholas had an older brother, Hugh, and two sisters, Elizabeth and Alice. The Ridley family had lived in the South Tynedale area, near the Scottish border, for three centuries prior to Nicholas' birth. In addition to Willimotiswick Castle, the Ridley family possessed several family homes in northern England, including that of Nicholas' father. When Nicholas was born, Tynedale was a dangerous and backward area, and the residents were subjected to frequent raids by the Scots as well as by numerous local bandits.

Nicholas' uncle, Robert Ridley, a priest and conservative humanist scholar at Cambridge University, most likely urged his nephew Nicholas to enter the church. Considering the role that Nicholas was to play in the Reformation of the English church, it is interesting to note that his uncle not only worked against the English translation of the Bible by William Tynedale but also publicly supported the condemnation of the German reformer Martin Luther in 1521. At Cambridge, moreover, Robert Ridley was a teacher who helped to shape the philosophical outlook of Thomas Cranmer, the future archbishop of Canterbury, who, together with Nicholas, would later help to move the English church into the Reformation. Nicholas was first educated at Newcastle; in 1518, at his uncle Robert's expense, he went to Cambridge to study at Pembroke Hall. There, in addition to his other studies, he read Greek and Latin.

In 1522, he received his bachelor's degree. His uncle provided for his further study at Pembroke, where he read philosophy and theology. Nicholas was ordained a priest sometime prior to April, 1524, and he then received a fellowship at Pembroke Hall. In July, 1525, Nicholas received his master's degree. At his uncle's expense, Nicholas continued his studies at the Sorbonne in Paris and later at Louvain in Brabant. By 1530, Nicholas had returned to Cambridge, where in 1533 he was elected senior proctor of Cambridge University. There, he would soon be drawn into the work of the English Reformation.

Life's Work

In order to facilitate his divorce from Catherine of Aragon, the English king Henry VIII appointed the reformed-minded Thomas Cranmer as archbishop of Canterbury and primate of all England. The pope, unaware of Henry's plan, agreed to Cranmer's appointment in 1533. After Henry's excommunication in the fall of 1533, Henry enlisted the help of the English universities to uphold his position that the pope had no ecclesiastical jurisdiction in England. In May, 1534, Cambridge University officially approved Henry VIII's position on the Papacy. The pope was to be recognized only as the bishop of Rome, with no right to interfere in the ecclesiastical affairs of England. Along with his Cambridge colleagues, Nicholas approved of Henry's break with Rome. This was not a hard decision, for by 1534 Nicholas Ridley had become a convinced Protestant.

Beginning in 1534, the Oaths of Succession and Supremacy were required of the clergy and those in the political sphere. By these oaths, Henry consolidated his leadership in matters political and ecclesiastical. Henry's reform of the church was somewhat along Lutheran lines and was conservative in nature. Monasteries were dissolved, and an English Bible based on Tynedale's translation was published by royal order. A large number of relics and shrines of saints were destroyed or removed from churches and sold. Still, the traditional ordering of bishops, priests, and deacons continued. The traditional vestments, language (Latin), and even understanding of the mass (transubstantiation) were retained.

As the English Reformation progressed, so did Nicholas's ecclesiastical career. In 1537, Nicholas received the bachelor of divinity degree and became chaplain for Archbishop Cranmer. The next year, Cranmer appointed Ridley vicar of Herne, in Kent. By that time, Ridley had come to more radical Protestant views, holding that confession was not necessary for salvation and that the services of the church should be sung in English rather than Latin. By the end of 1546, Ridley had given up his belief in transubstantiation and in any form of corporal presence of Jesus Christ in the holy communion, coming to this position through his reading of the ninth century eucharistic controversy and the work of Ratramnus of Corbie. Shortly before his death, in his 1554 *Treatise Against the Error of Transubstantiation*, Ridley articulated his developed views on the holy communion in a definite Reformed manner, holding that holy communion is only a memorial of Christ's suffering. It was specifically for these views on holy communion that he was burned at Oxford in 1555.

In 1539, the movement of the English Reformation was slowed with the publication of Henry VIII's Six Articles, which among other things set forth transubstantiation as the official understanding of holy communion. The Catholic party within the English church was now in the ascendancy. Publicly preaching or teaching contrary to the articles was made a capital offense. The king allowed Archbishop Cranmer and those such as Ridley with Protestant leanings to continue their livings as long as they supported the Six Articles.

In July, 1540, Ridley became a doctor of divinity at Pembroke. Later that year, he was elected master of Pembroke. He soon received a further honor: He was appointed a royal chaplain. In this capacity, he would have presided at a number of royal masses and heard the private confession of the king. Even though he had to fend off charges of heresy from the Catholic party, Ridley's preferments continued. In April, 1541, Cranmer appointed him as a prebendary of Canterbury Cathedral, and in October, 1545, Ridley was appointed a prebendary of Westminster.

In 1547, Henry VIII died. Shortly before his death, Henry had turned the ecclesiastical tide back toward the Protestants. With the accession of Henry's son Edward VI as king, the English Reformation picked up where it had left off. In that same year, Ridley was made bishop of Rochester, and in February, 1550, after the deposition of Bishop Bonner, Ridley was appointed bishop of London. A brief physical description of Ridley at this period was made by John Foxe in his 1563 *Actes and Monuments of These Latter and Perillous Dayes*,

often known as *Foxe's Book of Martyrs*: "He was a man right comely and well proportioned in all points, both in complexion and lineaments of the body." In terms of his personal life, Ridley was recognized by all sides as possessing a morally upright character. Furthermore, his generosity was widely acknowledged. While he defended the marriage of the clergy, Ridley never married.

Ridley influenced the development of both the 1548 and 1552 editions of the *Book of Common Prayer*. He had more impact on the production of the 1552 version, as by then he had persuaded Cranmer into coming to a more Reformed understanding of the eucharist. As bishop of London, Ridley rapidly spread Protestant practices throughout his diocese. He caused controversy by removing altars and replacing them with unadorned communion tables. He also wrote *A Treatise on the Worship of Images*, which condemned the use of religious images in churches.

On July 6, 1553, Edward VI died; shortly thereafter, the Catholic Mary Tudor became queen. Later that month, Ridley and other Protestants were placed in prison in the Tower of London. In March,

1554, Ridley was sent to Oxford with Cranmer and Bishop Hugh Latimer for a disputation with Catholic theologians on the presence of Christ's body in holy communion. They were imprisoned in the Bocardo jail, above Oxford's North Gate, and eventually kept in separate quarters. Ridley and the others refused to give up their faith, despite numerous attempts to convert them. After being ceremonially degraded from their clerical status, Ridley and Latimer were burned together on October 16, 1555. They were led in chains outside what was then the city wall and were martyred on a spot that today is on Oxford's Broad Street. As the fire was lit, Latimer reportedly said to Ridley: "Be of good comfort, Master Ridley, and play the man; we shall this day by God's grace light such a candle in England, as I trust shall never be put out." Latimer, being a good deal older than Ridley, died quickly, but Ridley took some time to die, suffering greatly. He finally succumbed only when a bag of gunpowder, tied round his neck by his brother-in-law in an effort to shorten Ridley's suffering, exploded.

Summary

The Protestant reforms for which Nicholas Ridley worked and died for were soon restored when Elizabeth I became queen in 1558. Supporters of the established Church of England and those dissenters who formed the Puritan party both looked on the Oxford martyrs as martyrs for their cause. Ridley's legacy was remembered in different ways by his ecclesiastical heirs. His work with Cranmer in consolidating the Anglican Reformation was upheld within the established church, while his protest unto death against the Catholic party was upheld by the Puritan party.

The spot where Ridley died is marked today in the road with a black cross and a wall plaque nearby. Around the corner from this spot, on St. Giles Street, stands the 1841 Martyrs Memorial honoring Cranmer, Ridley, and Latimer. This monument was erected by the evangelical wing of the Church of England and caused embarrassment to the Anglo-Catholics of the Oxford Movement, who sought to defend the theological and liturgical connectedness of the Anglican Reformation with the Anglican Church's Catholic past.

Despite the sixteenth and nineteenth century controversies over Ridley's ecclesiastical legacy, he was a man who was able to rise above the barbarity of his native Tynedale to become both a respected scholar and an able and dedicated churchman. As a bishop and as a theologian, he played an important role in the development of the Anglican tradition.

Bibliography

Foxe, John. *The Actes and Monuments of these Latter and Perillous Dayes*. Eight vols. Edited by Stephen Reed Cattley. London: R. B. Seeley and W. Burnside, 1888. Popularly known as *Foxe's Book of Martyrs*, this volume, originally published in 1563, has been reprinted numerous times, frequently in abbreviated form. It provides a significant sixteenth century account of the events surrounding the English Reformation and the life and work of Bishop Ridley.

MacCulloch, Diarmaid. *Thomas Cranmer*. New Haven, Conn.: Yale University Press, 1996. A useful account of the development of the English Reformation, offering insight into Ridley's collaboration with Cranmer in shaping the Anglican tradition as well as the social and political implications of the Reformation in England.

Ridley, Glocester. *The Life of Dr. Nicholas Ridley*. London: 1763. A helpful source of information on Ridley's family history by one of Nicholas's descendants. The volume offers particulars of Nicholas's personal development as well as details of his role as a church reformer.

Ridley, Jasper. *Nicholas Ridley: A Biography*. London: Longman, 1957. The most complete biography, also by one of Nicholas's descendants. Contains details of Nicholas's personal and intellectual development. Treats his life and work primarily from a historical perspective yet offers insight into the religious dimensions of his thought. Includes a detailed bibliography of secondary sources.

Ridley, Nicholas. *The Works of Nicholas Ridley*, edited by Henry Christmas. Cambridge: Cambridge University Press, 1841. A collection of Ridley's major and minor writings, covering a wide range of theological and practical issues. Includes accounts of his disputation at Oxford and other correspondence demonstrating Ridley's perspective on the development of the English Reformation.

Ryle, J. C. *Five English Reformers*. London: The Banner of Truth Trust, 1960. A brief popular account of Ridley's life and work from a decidedly Protestant perspective. Offers brief excerpts from Ridley's writings plus a shortened version from Foxe's account of Ridley's death.

J. Francis Watson

PIERRE DE RONSARD

Born: September 11, 1524; near Couture, Vendômois, France

Died: December 27, 1585; Saint-Cosme, France

Area of Achievement: Poetry

Contribution: Ronsard enriched French poetry by adapting classical genres and styles to his native language. He wrote historically significant odes, hymns, and lyrics and one of the most important sonnet sequences in the history of literature.

Early Life

Pierre de Ronsard was born into a noble family in the Vendômois area of France. His father, Louis, was made a chevalier by Louis XII a few years before the poet was born. At the age of twelve, Ronsard was placed as a page in the French court, which put him in a position to become an important courtier or functionary in the royal household. His father wanted him to pursue a legal career, then the path to preferment, but Ronsard performed poorly at each school he attended. He was bored with the subjects that were taught but fascinated by the Latin poetry he read, and he nurtured the ambition of becoming a poet.

After the death of his father in 1544, Ronsard took a crucial step in becoming a poet. He placed himself under the tutelage of Jean Dorat, an early French Humanist. He studied Latin and Greek language and literature under Dorat with his friend Jean-Antoine de Baïf. This rigorous training provided him with classical models in form, genre, and style that he believed were superior to the existing medieval models, which were primarily romances and religious works. Ronsard and his friends Joachim du Bellay, Baïf, and others, formed a group that supported the aims of the new poetry and became known as the Pléiade. Ronsard was determined to become not merely another poet but also the poet who would change the tradition by incorporating classical models, elegance, and rigor into French literature. In 1550, three years after completing his studies with Dorat, he published *Odes* and was hailed as the French Pindar.

Life's Work

Ronsard's *Odes* were well received at the time, but later criticism has tended to disparage them, and a nineteenth century critic, Charles-Augustin Sainte-Beuve, called them unreadable. They were historically important in introducing classical forms and myths into French literature, and some can still affect readers today. One of the problems later readers faced was that Ronsard followed the metrical and stanzaic patterns of Pindar—primarily a short poetic line and stanzas grouped into triads—and he transferred some of the subject matter from Pindar directly into poems that seemed distant from sixteenth century France. The odes that imitated Horace were more successful; Horace's structure was looser, the style more urbane, and the world they represented had some analogies to those of Ronsard.

The first poem of the third book of odes, in which he announces his vocation as a poet, is a good example of Ronsard's celebration of his classical models. After announcing that he has become "the gods' mortal companion" because the Greek Muse of poetry, Euterpe, has lifted him up to that state, he now can scorn common pretenders since the "Muse loves me. . . ." At the end of the poem, he describes his poetic position as directly linked to Greece and Rome: "Making me part of high Athens' glory,/Part of the ancient wisdom of the Romans." The common pretenders would be those still mired in the older forms of poetry or those writing merely love lyrics, while Ronsard has become one of the ancients.

Ronsard's next major work was *Les Amours* (1552). Petrarch, who was Ronsard's poetic model for this work, was closer in time. Ronsard wrote sonnets that followed and varied the Petrarchan structure and metaphors. These poems have remained popular through the years and to most people are the quintessential Ronsard. The first part of *Les Amours* deals with the poet's love for Cassandra. In poem 20, he desires to be rain that falls "one golden drop after another/ Into Cassandra's lovely lap. . . ." He then metamorphoses into a white bull who will take her when she passes. Finally, he becomes a narcissus and she a spring so he can plunge into her. After suggesting metaphorical and mythical ways to unite, the last three lines speak of a union at night with a desire to suspend the approach of dawn. The poem varies slightly from Petrarchan conventions, since it speaks directly about the union with the beloved.

In 1554, Ronsard offered a less ambitious but delightful collection, *Le Bocage*. These poems deal more directly with the countryside, nature, and contemporary events. There is, for example, a poem on the frog "La Grenouille"; Ronsard cele-

brates the ordinary frog above other animals and even calls her a goddess. In addition, the frog is not subject, as man is, to hard times. He also asks, in a personal touch, that the frog not disturb "the bed or study/ Of my good friend Remy Belleau." The tone is playful and clearly different from the *Odes*. The most interesting poem from that collection, however, is on famine. It asks God to relieve His people and compares the situation of the French to the Israelites. Near the end, he asks that this hardship be visited on barbarians, Scyths, Tartars, and Turks. The last request is the only classical allusion in the poem; the poet asks for a return to the age of precious gold, a common allusion in Ronsard, where people lived naturally and freely.

Also in 1554, Ronsard began the frustrating attempt to produce a national epic of France, *La Franciade* (1572). The poem was to be modeled after Vergil's *Aeneid* and deal with the legendary founding of France. He published fragments of the poem over the years and one book for the royal family; however, even though he wished to master all poetic forms including the epic, as the greatest poets did, the ambitious work was never completed and seems to have been alien to Ronsard's genius. His gift was for the lyric, not the epic.

In 1555, Ronsard found a form midway between the lyric and the epic in the first book of *Les Hymnes* (1555-1556). The subjects for these poems were lofty and general. For example, there is a hymn to eternity and one on philosophy. Later, he wrote a sequence on the four seasons. The most interesting poem in this collection is, perhaps, "Hymne des astres," a long poem on the mythic history of the stars.

In 1556, he published the *Nouvelle continuation des amours* and the second book of hymns. In the new *Nouvelle continuation des amours*, Ronsard wrote poems on a mysterious rural woman called Marie. These poems use many of the familiar strategies of the sonnet tradition, including the *carpe diem* motif. They are, however, more immediate and intense in their approach to the beloved. For example, in one poem Ronsard urges Marie to rise and join nature, which is already active. At the end, the poet states that he will teach her through kisses on her eyes and breast. There is no Petrarchan coyness here.

In 1559, Ronsard finally achieved the preferment for which he had wished in order to make his life less precarious. He was appointed *counseiller* to King Henry II, and he dropped *Nouvelle continuation des Amours* for poems on political and religious subjects. He defended the royal cause and the Catholics against the Protestants. In 1561, he wrote *Discours des misères de ce temps*, appealing to Catherine de Médicis to heal the division within the country. Yet the religious conflict continued, and, although Ronsard defended the Catholic cause, he was moderate and always counseled peace and toleration. In 1563, he wrote *Remonstrance au peuple de France*, scolding his countrymen for their failure to be reasonable and preserve peace. He also tried to influence the new king Charles IX by writing a plan for his education and training. Ronsard's strong desire for harmony is a reflection of the structure and themes of his poems.

Ronsard also continued his sonnet writing during this period and created one of his finest works, *Sonnets pour Hélène* (1578; *Sonnets for Helen*, 1932). The poems have an intensity and feeling about the experience of love that goes beyond the mythic approach of the Cassandra sonnets. In "Quand vous serez bien veille" ("When You Are Old"), he warns Hélène that she will grow old and live only in the memory and blessing Ronsard's poems will give, an important theme in William

Shakespeare's sonnets. The final lines turn from a warning to a plea, "take me, living, now."

In 1574, after the triumph of *Sonnets for Helen*, Ronsard completed *Les Derniers Vers*, which marked a change in tone and approach. They do not speak of love but of a rejection of the body. Appropriately, one of his last poems is to his soul; his soul, which had been his body's hostess, at death will be purged of remorse and rancor. The last lines are a farewell: "Ladies and gentlemen, my talk/ Is finished: follow your/ Fortune. Don't trouble/ My rest. I will sleep now."

In his last years, Ronsard's health failed. He suffered from a variety of ailments, including gout. He died at Saint-Cosme in 1585, at the age of sixty-one.

Summary

Pierre de Ronsard remains an important historical figure in the development of European literature. He transformed the rediscovered texts and myths of the Greeks and Romans into new French poems. The poetic tradition and the range of allusion and reference could not be the same after his poems. He wrote extensively in every available poetic genre of his time. In addition, he wrote some of the finest lyrics and one of the most influential sonnet sequences of the period. French and European poetry would not have been the same without Ronsard.

There is no doubt that Ronsard wrote too much; there are a huge number of poems, and many are of interest only to students of the period. In addition, he tended to lean on classical mythology to do the work of structuring many of his poems. The job of a critic or reader is to separate the poems that are permanent and valuable from those that are ephemeral or dated, so that we might once more see the value of a poet who was exalted in his own lifetime and still deserves careful and proper attention.

Bibliography

Bishop, Morris. *Ronsard, Prince of Poets*. London and New York: Oxford University Press, 1940. An old-fashioned but readable biography of the poet. The author can be annoying by claiming knowledge of Ronsard's inmost thoughts, but he does provide some important background information.

Campo, Roberto. *Ronsard's Contentious Sisters: The Paragone Between Poetry and Painting in the Works of Pierre de Ronsard*. Chapel Hill: University of North Carolina Press, 1998. This book examines Ronsard's participation in the heated paragone debate between poets and painters: the Renaissance contest for superiority in the ranking of the arts that emerged in counterpoint to the parity-centered principle of *ut pictura poesis* ("as is painting, so is poetry"). The book explores issues that have remained largely unnoticed. In broadest terms, it investigates the poet's notions about the differences between poems and pictures.

Cave, Terence, ed. *Ronsard the Poet*. London: Methuen, 1973. An excellent collection of essays on Ronsard's poetic art. Cave's essay "Ronsard's Mythological Universe" is especially good. There are useful essays on Ronsard's conception of beauty and on the last poems.

Jones, K. R. W. *Pierre de Ronsard*. New York: Twayne, 1970. An excellent introduction to the life and works of Ronsard. Jones places more emphasis on the poems than the life, but he does give the necessary facts. Contains a chronology and a bibliography.

McGowan, Margaret M. *Ideal Forms in the Age of Ronsard*. Berkeley: University of California Press, 1985. McGowan connects the poetry of Ronsard to structures found in the art of the period. This is an excellent interdisciplinary study with illustrations of paintings and sculpture. The book is learned but not leaden.

Wilson, D. B. *Ronsard: Poet of Nature*. Manchester: Manchester University Press, 1961. Deals fully with one of the most important subjects of Ronsard and connects Ronsard to the tradition of the descriptive poem in that period. Good discussion of Ronsard's use of landscape and his typical strategies in using nature as subject and context.

James Sullivan

FIRST EARL OF SALISBURY
Robert Cecil

Born: June 1, 1563; Westminster, England

Died: May 24, 1612; Marlborough, Wiltshire, England

Areas of Achievement: Politics and diplomacy

Contribution: As the principal secretary to both Queen Elizabeth and King James I, Cecil managed Parliament, supervised the peaceful transition from Tudor to Stuart rule, and negotiated a peace treaty with Spain.

Early Life

Robert Cecil was the second son born to Queen Elizabeth's Lord Treasurer, William Cecil, Lord Burghley, by his second wife, Mildred, the daughter of Sir Anthony Cooke. A frail child, Cecil grew up with a twisted foot, a bent back, a short stature, and a keen mind. His education was closely supervised by his father, who recognized in his younger son qualities lacking in his heir, Thomas. He provided Robert with a number of fine tutors who cultivated in him the skills needed for a career in public life. The young Cecil won a degree of affection and support from his parents which they never gave to his older brother, and his father took time to teach Robert some of the valuable political skills and lessons he had learned at court.

Cecil's formal education is not well recorded. He entered St. John's College, Cambridge, in 1579 or 1580, several years later in life than did most of his contemporaries. In 1580, he was among those "specially admitted" to study law at Gray's Inn, London, though he seems to have returned to Cambridge later that fall. In 1580, he sat in Parliament (the third session of 1576) through his father's patronage. He continued his studies, and in 1581, Vice Chancellor Perne wrote to his father and commended Cecil for his piety, diligence, and industry. Cecil appeared to have learned the importance of hard work, prudence, and caution as well as a mastery of foreign languages, which served him well throughout his career. Despite his success as an undergraduate, Robert was prepared for a career in public life and sent abroad to expand his education.

After the parliamentary session of 1584, Cecil traveled to France, where he spent the greater part of the next two years, returning in 1586 to represent Westminster as he had in 1584. While on the Continent, Cecil accompanied Lord Derby's mission to the Netherlands to negotiate peace terms with the Spanish. He was chosen for several tasks because of his excellent facility with foreign languages as well as his growing reputation for handling matters with tact and prudence.

Cecil returned to England before the victory over the Spanish Armada, and he may have been employed by Queen Elizabeth to write a pamphlet in her defense. He was elected to Parliament as a Knight of the Shire for Hertford in the February, 1589, session and was appointed High Sheriff of the county later in that year.

On August 31, 1589, four months after his mother's death, Cecil married Elizabeth Brook, the daughter of Lord Cobbam. She died on January 24, 1596, from the complications of delivering her third child, Catherine, having provided Cecil with an heir, William, and another daughter, Frances.

Life's Work

In the aftermath of the execution of Mary, Queen of Scots and the defeat of the Spanish Armada, as the rivalry between the factions led by Robert Devereux, second Earl of Essex, and Lord Burghley intensified, Cecil began to gain influence and experience at court. After the death of Secretary Walsingham in 1590, Burghley convinced Elizabeth to allow him to assume the duties of the secretary's office, which he then delegated to his son Cecil. On May 20, 1591, while Elizabeth was visiting Burghley at Theobalds, Burghley was made chief secretary and Cecil was knighted. Three months later, Cecil was made a member of the privy council, but he was not made secretary until July, 1596, though he increasingly exercised the duties of the office as a result of his father's declining health.

As a member of the council, Cecil helped to convict Sir John Perrot, sat in the Parliaments of 1592, 1597, and 1601, and served the queen in a variety of ways. In 1593, he became the functional leader of the Crown's supporters in the Commons, with little prior speaking experience. Despite some initial difficulties, Cecil quickly learned to manage the government's business with great effectiveness. In one session, he secured a large bounty for the queen and assistance for the poor despite a severe economic depression.

As he worked to gain the trust and confidence of the queen, Cecil experienced a period of personal and political difficulties. His wife's death in 1596 left him depressed, gray-haired, and heavily burdened. Despite his wife's advice to remarry, Cecil remained a widower and devoted himself to the service of his royal mistress to a degree which left little room for shared affections. Cecil's isolation increased when his cousins, Francis and Anthony Bacon, joined his rival, Essex, and even further intensified with the death of his father in July, 1698, shortly after Cecil's return from a diplomatic mission to France.

While Thomas received his father's title and the bulk of his estate, Robert received Theobalds, land in Hertfordshire and Middlesex, and a network of political associates who had served his father. In 1608, Cecil exchanged Theobalds with King James VI of Scotland and received Hatfield House, which still survives as one of the better examples of early Stuart interior decoration. He also succeeded his father as Master of the Court of Wards, a lucrative position which he supervised with unusual skillfulness.

In the final years of the queen's reign, Cecil replaced his father as one of the queen's most trusted councillors. His sagacity, prudence, and leadership were severely tested by the political difficulties in Parliament, the troubles in Ireland, Essex's rebellion, and the misadventures of Sir Walter Raleigh. Through all these difficult trials, conspiracies, and rivalries, Cecil effectively safeguarded the Crown's interests and his own. He skillfully defended himself against Essex's slanders, maintained his control of the machinery of government, and kept the esteem of the queen, who called him her little "elf."

Only after Essex's execution did Cecil initiate a secret correspondence with King James VI of Scotland which helped James gain Elizabeth's favor and privy council support for his ascension to the English throne after Elizabeth's death on March 24, 1603. Cecil dispelled the doubts that his rivals had planted and gained James's confidence by his good advice, which spared Elizabeth from embarrassment and allowed James to ascend the throne unopposed.

In appreciation for Cecil's management of the peaceful transition, King James I of England kept Cecil as his principal secretary of state. The government discovered a conspiracy led by Henry, Lord Cobbam, his brother George, and Sir Walter Raleigh, in 1603, known as the Bye and Main Plots. As a reward for his efficacious handling of the conspirators, Cecil was made Lord of Essendine, Rutland, on May 13, 1603. In October, he was appointed Lord High Steward to Queen Anne, whose interests he also supervised with notable success.

After negotiating a peace with Spain in 1604, Cecil was made Viscount Cranborne in August of that year, and on May 4, 1605, he was elevated to become the first Earl of Salisbury. A year later, he was made a Knight of the Garter after becoming lord-lieutenant of Hertfordshire. On May 6, 1608, after the death of Thomas, Earl of Dorset, Cecil became Lord Treasurer, an office once held by his father.

Cecil served King James I with the same devotion and sagacity with which he had served Queen Elizabeth I. He urged moderation in the treatment of Puritan ministers and supported conciliation efforts which resulted in the Hampton Court Conference and the King James version of the Bible, published in 1611. He supervised a series of negotiations with France and played a small role in the diplomacy which ended hostilities in the Netherlands in 1609.

While King James poked fun at his "little beagle" who labored at home while all the good hounds were at the hunt, the king recognized Cecil's immense talents and left most domestic and foreign affairs in his capable hands. From his seat in the House of Lords, James had difficulties managing business in the House of Commons.

Cecil was able to frustrate Puritan initiatives in all five sessions of James's first Parliament, secure new tax revenues, and guide the government through the dangerous Gunpowder Plot of 1605, without allowing it to become an anti-Catholic crusade. The event is celebrated by Guy Fawkes Day, a holiday named after the chief conspirator in this plot to kill the king and destroy Parliament.

Cecil expanded tariff revenues with the imposition of a new book of rates in 1608, despite parliamentary opposition, which had earlier defeated his effort to unify England and Scotland. In the fourth session, Cecil worked diligently to stabilize and restructure royal finances by negotiating the Great Contract of 1610. While royal extravagance, the king's unwillingness to compromise, and the suspicions of the Commons combined to frustrate the negotiations in the fall of 1610, Cecil's long hours of hard work and dedicated service took their toll on his frail constitution. Despite Cecil's increasing medical problems and the king's disappointment with the failure of the Great Contract, James continued to grant favors to Cecil's friends and solicit Cecil's advice on all major government business in the following two years.

Cecil not only supervised the administration of government in England but also was chiefly responsible for supervising Scottish affairs from London. If James ruled Scotland "by pen," as one historian asserts, then it is clear that the penmanship was Cecil's. Despite his strong efforts and the work of a commission to settle disputes, Cecil was not able to secure passage in Parliament of an Act of Union to unite James's two kingdoms. Given their long history of animosity, Cecil wisely abandoned the project as harmony existed without it.

The unsuccessful effort to unite the two realms, the rise of a royal favorite, Robert Carr, and the failure of the Great Contract were events which, to some degree, worked to limit Cecil's effectiveness. As he became ill and weary in the last years of his life, it seemed to some that he lost political control and royal favor after 1610. Scholarship has shown that he maintained his influence, the support of the king, and his ability to aid office seekers, including Carr. He was given new honors in August, 1611, and all the members of the royal family visited him when he suffered his final illness, a stomach tumor.

Summary

Robert Cecil was an immensely hardworking politician and statesman who successfully served two monarchs with great wisdom and effectiveness. While he was not always correct in his political assessments or an advocate of reform, he survived and kept the confidence and support of his monarch despite many challenges and crises. In a hectic and economically troubled era, Cecil provided the domestic stability and external peace which enabled Queen Elizabeth I to retire gracefully and allowed King James I to establish a new dynasty with popular support.

Bibliography

Cecil, Algernon. *A Life of Robert Cecil, First Earl of Salisbury.* London: John Murray, 1915; Westport, Conn.: Greenwood Press, 1971. A dated, apologetic, and occasionally inaccurate biography, it is still the best picture of the "public" man.

Cecil, David. *The Cecils of Hatfield House.* London: Constable, and Boston: Houghton Mifflin, 1973. A popular portrayal of the family's founder by a descendant; includes an account of the house that Cecil spent five years and thirty-eight thousand pounds to restore.

Coakley, Thomas M. "Robert Cecil in Power: Elizabethan Politics in Two Reigns." In *Early Stuart Studies: Essays in Honor of David Harris Willson.* Edited by Howard S. Reinmuth. Minneapolis: University of Minnesota Press, 1970. A balanced assessment of the style and consequences of Cecil's managerial and political activities.

Croft, Pauline. "The Reputation of Robert Cecil." *History Today* 43 (November, 1993): 41. Croft comments on historians' disagreements about Cecil, at once attacked for his cunning, duplicity, and corruption, and praised for his devoted service to stem the crown's growing deficit.

Handover, P. M. *The Second Cecil.* London: Eyre and Spottiswoode, 1959. A detailed biography of Cecil's rise to power which corrects factual errors in Algernon Cecil's account; contains a weak assessment of Cecil's career.

Hurstfield, Joel. *The Queen's Wards: Wardship and Marriage Under Elizabeth I.* London and New York: Longman, 1958. A valuable description of the activities of the court with a defense of Cecil's activities as its Master.

———. "The Succession Struggle in Late Elizabethan England." In *Freedom, Corruption, and Government in Elizabethan England.* Cambridge, Mass.: Harvard University Press, and London: Cape, 1973. A realistic evaluation of Cecil's contribution to the negotiations which produced an orderly transition of power.

Lindquist, Eric N. "The Last Years of the First Earl of Salisbury, 1610-1612." *Albion* 18 (Spring, 1986): 33-41. A solid refutation of the assertion that Cecil fell from favor after the failure of the Great Contract of 1610.

Wilson, David Harris. *King James VI and I.* Oxford: Oxford University Press, 1956; New York: Oxford University Press, 1967. The definitive biography; includes a detailed account of Cecil's activities during James's reign.

Sheldon Hanft

JACOPO SANSOVINO
Jacopo Tatti

Born: July 2, 1486; Florence
Died: November 27, 1570; Venice
Areas of Achievement: Art and architecture
Contribution: Sansovino was the first architect to bring Renaissance classical ideas of architecture into a successful conjunction with the Venetian Byzantine-Gothic style, resulting in buildings in the Piazza San Marco which were to confirm its reputation as one of the greatest architectural developments in the world.

Early Life

Jacopo Sansovino was born in Florence. His original name was Jacopo Tatti, but he later took the name Sansovino in honor of his master, the sculptor Andrea Sansovino, whose wall tombs were deeply admired and imitated throughout the sixteenth century. Jacopo Sansovino's early training was, therefore, as a sculptor, and his early reputation was confined to that discipline. He worked in Florence and, particularly, in Rome and was a close associate of many of the great artists of the high Renaissance, many of whom were adept in more than one artistic discipline. It was not, in fact, unusual at the time for an artist to work with considerable distinction at painting, sculpture, and architecture, and Sansovino's contemporaries, who included Raphael, Michelangelo, and Donato Bramante, would provide the model for a young sculptor eager to try his hand at other forms of artistic expression. Sansovino had done some architectural work in Florence at the Duomo in 1515, but it was only for a temporary, decorative façade to mark the visit of Pope Leo X to the city. In Rome, he began two churches, San Marcello al Corso and San Giovanni di Fiorentini, but he did not finish either of them. He completed one important private residence, the Palazzo Gaddi, and showed considerable skill in handling Renaissance architectural ideas. The site for the Palazzo was not an easy one with which to work, but Sansovino solved the problems with elegance and style, anticipating the way in which he would deal with architectural troubles in his Venetian career.

In 1527, at the time of the sack of Rome, Sansovino went to Venice, intending to return to the south when political turmoil had eased. He was forty-one years old, and his reputation was mainly as a sculptor. He gained a commission to restore the domes of St. Mark's Basilica, and he did so with marked competence. His appointment as the *proto*, the supervising architect for the Procurators of St. Mark, a body of prominent Venetian citizens responsible for the maintenance of the buildings in St. Mark's Square, was the factor that kept him in Venice. He joined them on April 7, 1529, and held that office until his death in 1570.

Life's Work

Architecture is, perhaps, the least independent kind of art form, and Sansovino's work as the *proto* was not confined to keeping existing structures repaired; he was to provide a complete renewal of one side of the Piazza San Marco to extend around the corner of the piazza into the smaller piazzetta facing the Doge's Palace, immediately to the south of the basilica. This was a task of major urban renewal, all the more important because the piazza, the piazzetta, the basilica, and the Doge's Palace were, together, the center of Venetian religious and political life. Any changes or additions had to reflect that sense of importance. It was decided that the buildings on the south side of the square were to be razed and a library built to house the world-famous Venetian collection of Greek and Latin manuscripts; the building would also house the procurators. This project continued throughout Sansovino's life, and parts of it were not finished until after his death. It was the major test of his skill, not only as an architect but also as a negotiator, compromiser, and manager. The main difficulty was designing a building which would be both a visual exemplification of Venetian power and grandeur and a residence for important local politicians, while remaining commercially viable. Long-term leases with merchants in the existing buildings had to be renegotiated, and the new structure had to be able to accommodate shops which would provide income for the procuracy.

Sansovino managed to overcome all the complications to produce what Giorgio Vasari called a building without parallel; Andrea Palladio, the greatest architect of the period, proclaimed it the richest and most ornate building since antiquity. Venice had longed to make the piazza something that Rome would envy. Sansovino gave it to them in a building which makes ample use of Renaissance architectural ideas but lightens them, opens them up to the Venetian tradition of lavish encrustation and lively sculptural decoration. The use of the local Istrian stone, easy to carve, responding in its bright whiteness to the sparkling light flashing off the lagoon, makes the building typically Venetian, while the use of the classical orders, Doric below, Ionic on the second floor, topped by a balustrade upon which sculptural figures seem to float in the air, gives it a sense of both majestic solidity and ethereal lightness. The library was to be Sansovino's greatest work.

Sansovino completed two other projects in the San Marco complex. The campanile had, until Sansovino's time, been tucked into a corner of the buildings, losing much of its visual power in a jumble of shops and commercial structures. Sansovino adjusted the line of the library to allow space around the tower, giving it the sight line from all sides which makes it one of the major points of interest in the piazza. He also rebuilt the loggia, a small meetinghouse at the base of the campanile. Prior to his work, the building had no particular aesthetic appeal; when Sansovino was done, it had become a tiny gem of rich red-and-white marble, appropriate for its place at the base of the tower. It is, as Deborah Howard has suggested, not so much a building as a piece of sculpture.

On the lagoon side of the library, Sansovino had another problem, the rebuilding of the Venetian Mint, or Zecca, and again he displayed a capacity for compromise which allowed him to make art out of impossible situations. Something had to be provided for the cheese merchants who had always had shops immediately in front of the proposed site. The multiple bays of the ground floor, heavily rusticated in the Renaissance tradition of acknowledging the classical heritage of Italian architecture, provide an appropriate fortresslike base for a building in which the coin of the realm was cast and stored. The Zecca has become part of the library; in its time, the bays led into the separate shops of the cheese sellers without compromising visually the importance or aesthetic unity of the structure. The upper stories, Doric on the second floor, Ionic on the third, are formidable in their use of column, lintel, and window surround. The Zecca reflects the practice of mirroring a building's function in its façade—the lower floor suggesting its impregnability, the upper levels, particularly the second floor, with its massive protruding lintels, exaggerating the same idea of sudden closure.

Sansovino's career was not confined to the piazza. He was allowed to take private commissions, and he provided an interesting building for the Rialto market area, still extant and still used in the twentieth century. The Fabbriche Nuove again incorporates the Renaissance use of the orders into the long, three-storied building. Sansovino also undertook the more modest problem of a residence for destitute women; the success of the inexpensive stucco building lies in its tasteful proportions and some very witty chimney pots.

Sansovino also designed several churches, probably six in all, but only three of them survive, one of them with a façade by Palladio. The façades of the other two, San Martino and San Giuliano, have interesting mannerist inclinations. San Giuliano in particular manifests the mannerist tendency to eccentric manipulation of architectural motifs. Sansovino usually eschewed variations that were too idiosyncratic in his use of the Renaissance architectural vocabulary, but the narrow site of San Giuliano, and the determination of his patron to be publicly recognized, led to the mounting of a statue of the patron, seated on a sarcophagus, on the front of the church. The statue reminds one of Sansovino's beginnings as a pupil of Andrea Sansovino, the master of tomb sculpture (sculptures usually only mounted on the interior of a church). It is a stunning façade, clearly original in conception and execution.

Sansovino also designed two palazzos of considerable distinction. The Venetian palazzo was used not only as a residence but also as a place of business, since so many of the great Venetian families were traders. Their palazzos were proof of business success, but they were also used as warehouses and offices and often sheltered several generations of the family at once. The first floor was, therefore, designed not only to store goods but also to take in and distribute the goods from the door facing immediately onto the canals. Other floors housed the extended family, and the façades of the buildings, often right on the canal, were required to be as handsome as money could make them. Palazzos were usually in an established style that was partly Byzantine, partly Gothic. Sansovino's Palazzo Dolfin was built to serve in the old way as a home and place of business, but there was no need for a large central entrance on the canal, since there was a small stream down one side of the building which could be used to enter the residential areas of the palace.

That allowed Sansovino to use on the ground level six Doric arches in a regularized Renaissance pattern leading to six separate warehouses. The second and third floors made use of Ionic and Corinthian decoration, but Sansovino kept the common Venetian arrangement of windows to achieve another successful mix of the old and the new.

Sansovino's second, grander commission was for a family of political consequence, and again, on a much larger scale, Sansovino put the classical orders into play, especially in a generous inner courtyard. Vasari called it the finest palace in Italy in its time, and it displayed the sense of amplitude and richness of design that Sansovino seemed peculiarly able to manipulate without vulgarity.

Sansovino remained active until his death. Vasari writes that he was a handsome and charming young man, well-built and red-bearded. In his old age, he retained his charm, but the beard was white. Tintoretto painted him, bright-eyed and wary, and Vasari notes that in old age he dressed elegantly, kept himself well-groomed, and took pleasure in the company of women.

Summary

Jacopo Sansovino was not a great architect, but he was a very good one, and he produced a handful of major projects which are as good as anything produced in Venice. He was able to break the hold that the Byzantine-Gothic tradition had on Venetian architecture and develop a new kind of style which was thoroughly modern and committed to the dignity and calm weight of Renaissance classicism, yet also retained the lively, decorative lightness of the island mode. He showed other architects how to bring Venice forward into the Renaissance without repudiating the peculiar history or virtues of the old style.

Sansovino was also able to make architectural compromise work without debasement of standards; he worked with the complicated Venetian committees, demanding a certain amount of tradition within a mercurial political and economic climate. He was, in a sense, the ideal architect—learned, modestly imaginative, sensitive to local prejudices, capable of playing the game, able to nurse major projects along despite constant threats of setbacks and changes of mind. His contributions to the Piazza San Marco alone entitle him to be considered one of the finest architects of urban renewal.

Bibliography

Boucher, Bruce. *The Sculpture of Jacopo Sansovino*. New Haven, Conn.: Yale University Press, 1991. Boucher provides an elaborate and admirable documented monograph on the Venetian High Renaissance sculptures of Sansovino that urges students of his work to revisit them from a new perspective.

Fletcher, Sir Banister. *Sir Banister Fletcher's History of Architecture*. London: Athlone, and New York: Scribner, 1975. The architecture student's basic reference text. Provides good illustrations and puts Venetian architecture, Renaissance Italian architecture, and Sansovino's version of both in context.

Howard, Deborah. *Jacopo Sansovino: Architecture and Patronage in Renaissance Venice*. New Haven, Conn.: Yale University Press, 1975; London: Yale University Press, 1987. A very sensible and easily understood study of how Sansovino went about making art in the context of a social and political structure that foiled many lesser men. Howard is good on the history of Venice and its architecture and shows how Sansovino adjusted to the rules.

Lowry, Bates. *Renaissance Architecture*. London: Prentice-Hall, and New York: Braziller, 1962. A substantial essay on the subject of Renaissance architecture. Includes a generous selection of photographs.

McCarthy, Mary. *Venice Observed*. New York: Harcourt Brace, 1956; London: Heinemann, 1961. A famous essay by one of America's finest writers. Venice is a work of art and should be understood as such. McCarthy and other literary figures, such as Hugh Honour, Jan Morris, and Henry James, are able to make that phenomenon sensible.

Norberg-Schulz, Christian. *Meaning in Western Architecture*. London: Studio Vista, and New York: Praeger, 1975. This text does not speak directly of Sansovino but examines how architects make buildings illustrate the ideals of a society, a skill at which Sansovino was particularly good.

Charles Pullen

GIROLAMO SAVONAROLA

Born: September 21, 1452; Ferrara

Died: May 23, 1498; Florence

Areas of Achievement: Religion and government

Contribution: Savonarola set in motion the greatest religious revival of his day, turning a materialistic and worldly city into a democratic theocracy. He inspired many Florentines with a new, simple faith. He began the tide of Reformation soon to sweep over Europe.

Early Life

Girolamo Savonarola was the third son of Niccolò di Michele della Savonarola and Elena Bonacossi. His mother was a descendant of the Bonacossi family who had been lords of Mantua. The Savonarolas were a merchant family with an aristocratic-military background. The boy's grandfather, Michele, had been a well-known physician and teacher at the University of Padua, and had become personal physician to Niccolò III d'Este. This grandfather was the primary influence on the boy—a pious, ascetic, aged, and scholarly man, he had much of the medieval schoolman in him, and passed this characteristic along to his grandson, who became, partly because of this influence, somewhat out of his time.

Savonarola's family intended that he become a doctor, but he studied many disciplines, including art, music, poetry, and philosophy (Aristotelian and Thomist). Savonarola did study the sciences and medicine, but he eventually turned instead to theology and close study of the Bible.

Pious and inflexible, from a very early age, Savonarola seemed wounded by the corruption of the time. On April 24, 1475, he left home and his medical studies, which he had begun after taking his degree in the liberal arts, and entered the Dominican Order at Bologna, which had a famous school of theology. At the monastery, Savonarola wished to live humbly as one of the brothers, to rid himself of his philosophy, and to be obedient and at peace. The superiors of the order, however, did not wish to waste such a fine education and wanted him to become a priest. His theological studies began in 1476. In 1479, he was sent to complete his studies in Ferrara. Sustaining a disputation there, Savonarola impressed his superiors sufficiently to be elected to the office of lecturer at the Convent of San Marco in Florence. He first arrived in that city on foot that May. Florence was at that time in the hands of Lorenzo de' Medici, patron and poet of the Humanism so hated by Savonarola.

Life's Work

Arriving at Florence in 1482, Savonarola took up his post of lecturer at San Marco. A great biblical scholar, he taught the Bible to novices at the monastery. The Old Testament was his specialty, especially the canonical books. He was a very learned teacher but was primarily concerned to move his students. He inspired a quiet religious revival at San Marco during his tenure there. His first sermons in Florence, preached at small churches such as the Murate and Orsanmichele, were not successful. His sermons were not to the sophistical taste of the Florentines, who admired the art of rhetoric, and they also found his Ferrarese accent laughable. Nevertheless, in 1484, he preached at one of the main churches in the city, San Lorenzo, the parish church of the Medicis. He had no more success there. It was not until he began preaching sermons based on his apocalyptic revelations, at the Church of San Gimignano during Lent of 1485 and 1486, that he began to wield influence as a preacher. Perhaps the reason for his success then was that the theme of his sermons—the need for church reform, his prophecy that the Church would be scourged and renewed—struck an urgent chord after the election of the pope with the ironical name of Innocent VIII. On August 12, 1484, Sixtus IV had died. He had not been a virtuous pope, but his successor was far worse.

In 1487, Savonarola left Florence, having been appointed master of studies at the Studium Generale of San Domenico in Bologna, his own illustrious school. After the year of his appointment was over, he was sent to preach in various cities. In 1488, he went to Ferrara to see his mother and sisters (his father had died during Lent in 1485); he stayed two years at the convent of Santa Maria degli Angeli in that city and traveled to other towns on foot preaching. By this time, Count Giovanni Pico della Mirandola, a famed scholar and linguist, had become a great admirer of Savonarola and requested of his patron and friend Lorenzo de' Medici that he use his influence to bring Savonarola back to Florence. This Lorenzo did, and in 1490, Savonarola was back again in Florence, at the request of the very family to whom he was to be such a scourge. In August of that year, Savonarola began preaching his sermons on the Apocalypse, which continued until 1491. His rough style began to gain favor with the people, though his adherents were the pious, the poor, and the malcontents, not the city's elite. His themes were based on real abuses: the confiscatory taxes and corruption of the Medicis, and their looting of the dowry foundations (the *monte del doti*) set up for the marriages of poor girls. In 1491, he preached the Lenten sermons at Santa Maria del Fiori, the principal church of the city.

Lorenzo began to awake to the danger that these revolutionary sermons posed and warned Savonarola not to prophesy or stir up unrest. Savonarola did not take this advice and continued to vilify Lorenzo and the city government for abuses. His popularity continued to increase as Lorenzo's health failed. In 1491, Savonarola was elected Prior of San Marco. He began to be seen as a saint. Poets, philosophers, and artists became his adherents at about this time. His Lenten sermons of 1492 had a more markedly prophetic tone than ever before. Soon after this, Lorenzo lay dying and sent for Savonarola to ask his blessing. Contrary to an apocryphal story, eyewitness accounts have it that Savonarola did indeed give his blessing to the dying man and that Lorenzo was greatly consoled by it. Medici rule did not long survive Lorenzo, largely because his son and successor, Piero, was not a competent leader.

In 1492, Pope Innocent VIII died, fulfilling one of Savonarola's prophecies. His successor was the notorious Borgia pope Alexander VI, who was almost certainly an atheist, had droves of children whose fortunes he aggrandized, had reportedly committed incest with two of his daughters, and had openly purchased the Papacy. At this time, Savonarola had a vision: An arm with a sword appeared to him. A voice spoke, inviting conversion, speaking with "holy love," warning that a time was coming when conversion would no longer be possible. Clouds of angels appeared, dressed in white, carrying red crosses, offering the same accountrements to all. Some accepted, some did not, and some prevented others from accepting. The sword then turned down, and thunder, lighting, darkness, plague, war, and famine began.

During this time, Savonarola had been engaged in the reform of cloistered life. He told his monks of San Marco that he had had a vision wherein it had been revealed to him that of the twenty-eight monks who had died in the last few years, twenty-five were eternally damned for love of possessions. The monks then brought him all their private goods, which were sold for the benefit of the poor. He changed the dress and diet of the monks, and wanted to found a new, very austere convent outside Florence. He also battled to separate San Marco from the Lombard Congregation and to start a new congregation along with the Convents of Fiesole and Pisa. Savonarola eventually accomplished this goal.

The French invasion of Italy, the event that proved the end, for the time, of Medici administration in Florence, occurred in 1494. The French were opposed by the Aragonese of Naples and the pope; Piero de' Medici sided with them against Florence's traditional ally, France. In 1492, Savonarola had predicted the French invasion and its success; now, with the approach of Charles VIII and his army, Piero's administration was imperiled. It did not help that he was arrogant, openly tyrannical, and a less-than-clever politician. Piero panicked when it became obvious that he could not raise funds for the defense of the city, and he went to treat directly, on his own authority and not that of the Signoria (the Florentine Senate), with the French king. He conceded all the Florentine strong points to the French, and the French entered the city and began to mark houses for the billeting of troops. The citizens were angry, and a group was appointed, among them Savonarola, to negotiate with Charles. All during this time, Savonarola had been preaching apocalyptic sermons on the theme of Noah's Ark and invoking his earlier prophecy. He now played an important part in negotiations with Charles, hailing Charles as a prophesied deliverer, but warning him to be careful of Florence and admonishing him not to abuse the city.

When Piero de' Medici returned to Florence after his disastrous private embassy, he was baited and ridiculed. He fled; Florence became a republic once more, with Savonarola as its de facto ruler. Savonarola advocated the republican form of government and was not personally ambitious. His goal was to found the City of God in Florence which would then act as a model for reform throughout Italy. In the difficult days after the end of Medici rule, with the French occupying the city and the citizens beginning to align along traditional factional lines, Savonarola's constant preaching of moderation, forgiveness, and calm prevented any outbreaks which could have set off civil war. He rejected vengeance against Medici adherents and rebuked the people for executing a particularly hated tool of the Medicis, Antonio Bernardo. There were no more executions, and Savonarola's government grew in popularity.

Nevertheless, there were opponents. The Arrabbiata (the enraged), the opposition faction, began to ally themselves with the opponents of the King of France: the Duke of Milan, the pope, and the other members of the Holy League, the Italian anti-French alliance. The Holy League saw Savonarola as the main obstacle preventing Florence's joining them, and the pope began to use his authority over Savonarola as head of the Church to bring him to heel. He summoned Savonarola to Rome, praising him for his wonderful works; Savonarola was justly suspicious and pleaded illness as an excuse for not going. Alexander sent a second brief vilifying him and ordered him to Bologna under threat of excommunication. Savonarola replied respectfully to this brief but did not comply, pointing out mistakes in its formulation. A third brief arrived a month later, forbidding him to preach. Several months later, admitting the political reason behind the ban on Savonarola's preaching, which Savonarola had obeyed, Alexander gave a Florentine embassy a verbal revocation of the ban. Savonarola then preached his 1496 Lenten sermons on Amos, in which he continued to criticize the Church and vilified Alexander's private life. Despite this impolitic behavior, a college of theologians convened to examine the propriety of Savonarola's preaching found nothing to criticize in it. He was allowed to continue.

The pope, however, tried other angles: He offered a cardinal's hat as a bribe and tried to incorporate San Marco into another congregation, in which Savonarola would have no authority. The incorporation was ordered on pain of excommunication. Savonarola protested but obeyed—and the order was not put into effect; he could continue his course. Just before Lent in 1497, during Carnival season, Savonarola's authority and popularity reached a kind of peak with "the burning of the vanities," when bonfires were made of those possessions deemed sinful by the new regime. Bands of children went about the city encouraging the destruction of these "vain things." Soon afterward, Savonarola's grip on the city began to fail. His own faction, the Frateschi, or brothers (termed pejoratively "the Piagnoni" or the weepers), lost control of the government to the Arrabbiata, who bought a bull of excommunication from Alexander VI. It was secret, and marred by errors; the pope himself disowned it. Nevertheless, it was not withdrawn. The Arrabbiata began to foment riots against Savonarola. The Florentine government tried to get the bull of excommunication revoked; Rome offered to do it if Florence joined the Holy League. At this point, Savonarola took a hand in his own

defense and began to preach on Exodus; these Lenten sermons of 1498 were to be his last. The city was threatened with an interdict, and Savonarola was forced to stop preaching.

His final downfall was caused, indirectly, by one of his own supporters in a rather ludicrous episode of failed heroism. A Franciscan monk had challenged to an ordeal by fire anyone who maintained that the pope was not correct in excommunicating Savonarola. A loyal adherent, Fra Domenico da Pescia, took up this challenge. The Franciscan did not show up. Even though, by the terms of the trial, this meant that Savonarola's team had won, the city was disappointed in the lack of a miracle, and the following day Savonarola and two followers were arrested.

His trial for heresy was marked by confessions extracted under torture. His testimony is very touching in its frankness, and it is evident that the verdict was unjust. He was found guilty by the papal commissioners and was hanged and burned by the civil authorities. He received the pope's absolution and plenary indulgence before his death. A cult soon grew up around him, and until the nineteenth century flowers were found on the spot of his execution every May 23, left by devotees in the night. Miracles that he performed were recorded, and occasionally his name was brought up as a candidate for sainthood.

Summary

Girolamo Savonarola's primary importance was as a reformer. In a time that had become corrupt, he reawakened the possibility of virtue, both in religion and in civic life. His remarkably direct and simple approach to right action brought together the life of the spirit and the life of the body, religious life and civil life, in a time when these aspects of life were becoming more separate—when life was becoming, actually, what one would recognize as modern.

That, after all, is the oddity of his life. He was a reformer, a voice of the new, a revolutionary even; yet the source of his ideas was archaic. In living out perhaps the last medieval life in Renaissance Italy, in resisting the alienation of personal life from the eternal that marked the beginning of the modern, he opened the door to attacks on the centralized authority of the Church. Reared in the aura of his grandfather's fourteenth century education and finding his own time too relativistic, too "advanced," he revolutionized his society in the attempt to archaize it. The life of Savonarola shows the difficulty, for interpreters of history, in the consistent application of the idea of "progress." He is remembered now for his incorruptibility and for his championing of the humble against the great, for his devotion to the Church and his opposition to its human incarnation, and for his effect on certain of the thinkers and artists of his day, such as Michelangelo and Pico della Mirandola.

Bibliography

Butters, H. C. *Governors and Government in Early Sixteenth-Century Florence, 1502-1519*. Oxford: Clarendon Press, and New York: Oxford University Press, 1985. A thorough examination of the political aftermath of Savonarola's rule of Florence. Chapter 1, "Florentine Politics and Society at the End of the Fifteenth Century," covers the period of transition and reorganization. The details of political and economic life ignored by nineteenth century Romantic historians are here included. Good index and an appendix of principal actors in the various aspects of the state.

Lucas, Herbert. *Fra Girolamo Savonarola*. London: Sands, and St. Louis, Mo.: Herder, 1906. An account of Savonarola's life, copious but rather dry, in which special attention is paid by its Jesuit author to points of theology and canon law. The author takes great pains to present a balanced view of both Savonarola and his enemies. Contains an index.

Ridolfi, Roberto. *The Life of Girolamo Savonarola*. Translated by Cecil Grayson. London: Routledge, and New York: Knopf, 1959. Probably the best general life of Savonarola. Written with grace and scope, this is an account of the events that strives for balance. The author has a wide, cultured grasp of the Florentine spirit and history.

Rocca, Francis X. "Saint Savonarola?" *Wall Street Journal: Eastern Edition* 232 (July, 1998): W11. Rocca's editorial speculates on the canonization of Savonarola and details the activities of a commission named by the Cardinal Archbishop of Florence to accumulate information on him. The author advances the view that controversy may arise from the efforts to rehabilitate Savonarola, who was eventually burned at the stake.

Rowdon, Maurice. *Lorenzo the Magnificent*. London: Weidenfeld and Nicolson, and Chicago: Regnery, 1974. A chatty, heavily illustrated look at the Florence of Lorenzo, which includes material on Savonarola's career. His earlier life as a prophet and reformer of influence in the days of Lorenzo is fairly well covered; his three-year period of rule is cursorily dismissed. Many maps, paintings, and photographs. Offers a sound introduction to the period for a not-too-demanding student. An index is provided, as well as a bibliography for further study and a list of illustrations.

Villari, Pasquale. *Life and Times of Girolamo Savonarola*. Translated by Linda Villari. New York: Scribner, and London: Unwin, 1888. This is the commonly cited authoritative biography before the Ridolfi work. A copious but outdated treatment. It has perpetuated some factual errors. A sort of apology for Savonarola, it tells what has become the classic account of his life, heroicizing it in opposition to the wickedness of the times. A thorough index is provided.

Weinsten, D. "Savonarola—Preacher or Patriot?" *History Today* (November, 1989): 30. This article examines the career of Savonarola, focusing on the Florentines' convictions that Savonarola was a prophet of God, the friar's emphasis on penitence and reform, and his ultimate downfall.

Ann Klefstad

JOSEPH JUSTUS SCALIGER

Born: August 5, 1540; Agen, France
Died: January 21, 1609; Leiden, United Provinces
Areas of Achievement: Literature and historiography
Contribution: Educated by a learned father and through study with leading scholars, Scaliger became the foremost scholar of Greek and Latin in his time. His editions of Latin authors set high critical standards; his research on ancient chronology established the study of ancient history on a firm foundation and introduced to Europe the literature and history of Byzantium.

Early Life

In 1525, the physician Julius Caesar Scaliger accompanied the Italian nobleman M. A. de la Rovère to Agen, a small town in western France, where the nobleman would serve as bishop. The physician claimed a remarkable record. Julius Caesar Scaliger was descended from the family (the della Scala) that once had ruled Verona. He had studied art (with Albrecht Dürer), medicine, theology, natural history, and classical literature. He had earned military distinction during seventeen years of service under his kinsman the Holy Roman Emperor Maximilian I. Now the physician devoted himself to other pursuits. His medical practice at Agen flourished, and in 1528 he married an adolescent orphan of a noble family, Andiette de Roques Lobejac. From this union came fifteen children.

The physician studied Greek and Latin in his leisure. He circulated a brilliant (if misguided) polemic against Desiderius Erasmus' criticism of contemporary Latin in 1531, from 1533 to 1547 wrote volumes of his own Latin verse, which would be critically disparaged but read widely and reprinted often, and composed his own Latin grammar in 1540 and a notable treatise on Latin poetry (published in 1561 after his death). His major work was a massive commentary on the ancient Greek tradition of natural history as understood by Hippocrates, Aristotle, and Theophrastus. This great study was completed in 1538 but not published until after the author's death, when Gottfried Wilhelm Leibniz praised it as the best contemporary guide to Aristotle.

Julius Caesar Scaliger's love of classical learning bore its greatest fruit in his third son (and tenth child), Joseph Justus. Educated at home to age twelve, Joseph was then sent, with his brothers Leonard and John, to the College of Guyenne at Bordeaux. There they read standard Latin authors and learned Greek by using the fashionable new grammar of the Protestant educator Philipp Melanchthon. Plague erupted in Bordeaux in 1555, and the three boys returned to Agen to be educated again by their father. The elder Scaliger required of his sons daily composition and declamation in Latin—studies in which Joseph excelled: By age seventeen, he had composed an original Latin drama (*Oedipus*), of which his father approved and of which he himself remained proud in his old age.

His father, however, did not instruct his son in Greek. Therefore, after Julius Caesar's death in 1558, Joseph Scaliger set out for the University of Paris. There he attended the lectures of a contemporary master of Greek, Adrian Turnèbe, but soon realized that he knew insufficient Greek to profit from the course. Scaliger thereupon dedicated two years to reading basic Greek authors and, in the process, compiled his own Greek grammar. He then went on to study Hebrew and Arabic to a good level of proficiency. Scaliger's formal education at Paris ended in 1563, when another Greek professor, Jean Dorat, was sufficiently impressed by Scaliger's learning to recommend him successfully as companion to the young nobleman Louis de Chastaigner.

Life's Work

Scaliger's position as companion to Chastaigner provided secure employment and other advantages: extensive travel, access to learned men and to scholarly collections throughout Europe, and, what was of especial importance in an age of turmoil (for these were the years of religious and dynastic wars in France), freedom to study and write. Thus, in 1564, Scaliger published his first work, *Coniectanea in M. Terentium Varronem de lingua latina*, a wide-ranging discussion of textual problems and the etymologies of Latin words in the *De lingua latina* (first century B.C.; *On the Latin Language*, 1938) by the Roman scholar Marcus Terentius Varro. The book attracted scholarly attention, because here Scaliger demonstrated his profound knowledge of classical and Near Eastern languages and revealed what would become a deep interest in archaic (before 100 B.C.) Latin. Thus, as well, Scaliger accompanied Chastaigner on several journeys to Italy, where he met the great French Humanist and textual critic Marc-Antoine Muret, who introduced Scaliger to Italian scholars and their li-

braries. Chastaigner and his companion next traveled to England and Scotland, where Scaliger disliked the insularity, ignorance, and vulgarity of the scholars he encountered but found time to continue his studies on Varro and record his impressions of Mary, Queen of Scots (negative), and Queen Elizabeth (positive). The years from 1567 through 1570 Scaliger spent with the Chastaigner family, moving from place to place in France to avoid the ravages of civil war.

From 1570, Scaliger lived for two and a half years at Valence with the great scholar of Roman law Jacques Cujas. Cujas provided an introduction to a wide range of scholars (with whom Scaliger would correspond in years to come), expert instruction in the study of Roman legal texts, and a library of more than two hundred Greek and Latin manuscripts and instruction in how to discriminate among them. Cujas' influence and the texts he placed at Scaliger's disposal encouraged Scaliger to concentrate his energies on the manuscript sources for individual ancient authors and the ancient sources for specific topics. Thus, in 1573, Scaliger published an edition of the late, difficult Latin poet Ausonius, based on his own scrutiny of an important ninth century manuscript that Cujas possessed.

The Saint Bartholomew's Day Massacre—the slaughter of Huguenots in France in 1572—caught Scaliger en route to Poland on a diplomatic mission. Scaliger had been reared as a Roman Catholic, but in Paris he had taken instruction from Calvinists and, by the time of his sojourn in England, had declared himself a Protestant. He therefore fled to Calvinist Geneva, where he was given a professorship of philosophy. He lectured on Aristotle and Cicero but did not enjoy his subjects. His private tutorials were more successful.

At the first opportunity, in 1574, Scaliger returned to France to live with Chastaigner. Intermittent wars made the next twenty years far from comfortable; Scaliger several times had to serve in the military. Nevertheless, with the financial support of Chastaigner, Scaliger produced important studies of individual Latin authors in which he demonstrated his skill at textual emendation (the correction of the received text of an author). Scaliger's breadth of knowledge and technical skill at evaluating manuscripts changed emendation from a common and popular practice of haphazard guesses to a rational procedure founded on principles consistently applied.

In this same period (1574-1594), Scaliger produced works that established the study of ancient chronology on a solid basis. Scaliger's 1579 edition of the poetry of the Latin astrologer Manilius was in fact a treatise on astronomy as understood by the ancients and served as preface to Scaliger's *De emendatione temporum* (1583; on the correction of chronologies), in which Scaliger argued that a correct understanding of ancient history must be based on a comparative, critical, and analytic study of the surviving fragments of ancient chronological systems (king-lists, calendars, and the like) and a correct understanding of how the ancients reckoned the passage of time. Furthermore, Scaliger in a sense here created a new discipline, ancient history, by establishing comparative chronologies not only for Greek and Roman civilization but also for the societies of the ancient Near East (Egypt, Mesopotamia, Judaea). These studies were the foundations of Scaliger's most important work: *Thesaurus temporum* (1606; treasure of chronologies), a collection of the known Greek and Latin fragments on chronology and a reconstruction of the great *Chronicon* (fourth century A.D.) of Eusebius. Eusebius had compiled a comparative chronology of Greek, Roman, Christian, and Jewish events back to the time of Abraham, but his chronicle was known only from Saint Jerome's and other Latin versions. Scaliger's reconstruction of Eusebius was so good that some later scholars have mistaken Scaliger's work for Eusebius' own text. Later study and discovery of other manuscripts confirmed the accuracy of Scaliger's reconstruction.

In 1594, Scaliger accepted a position at the University of Leiden, where, with no teaching responsibilities, he dedicated his time to scholarly correspondence and encouraging a new generation of scholars who, in their own ways, would carry on his work. He enjoyed complaining of his accommodations and the climate at Leiden but enjoyed even more the honor in which he was held at this Protestant university. His energies, however, were sapped by dispute. Leiden recognized his claim of descent from the Princes of Verona. Assorted Jesuits and lay scholars, for whom Scaliger's historical and textual criticism was perceived as a threat, did not. They attacked Scaliger's scholarship and religious beliefs by questioning his ancestral pedigree. A few months after completing a pamphlet in his own defense, the embittered scholar died at Leiden, on January 21, 1609, in the company of his colleague and student Daniel Heinz. Scaliger was buried four days later in Saint Mary's, the church of the Huguenots in Leiden.

Summary

A typical scholarly production of Joseph Justus Scaliger's time was the *Adversaria*: a miscellany volume wherein an author offered his observations, argued his criticism, and proposed his emendations on a variety of classical texts. Scaliger often affirmed that, while he could have written volumes of *Adversaria*, he preferred to work on complete scholarly editions of classical authors. Indeed, when his contemporaries saluted Scaliger as among the most learned of any age, they cited as evidence his skill at emendation exhibited in his editions of, for example, Catullus and Manilius. Later generations acknowledged the worth of those editions but recognized that Scaliger's studies of ancient chronology were more significant. Furthermore, the breadth of his chronological studies was the manifestation of Scaliger's firm belief that as broad a knowledge of antiquity as possible was the prerequisite for a proper understanding of ancient texts. Scaliger thus anticipated the nineteenth century German scholarly ideal of *Altertumswissenschaft*—"a science of (all of) antiquity." In addition, Scaliger's study of the sources for ancient chronology drew attention to an entire field of history and literature previously unrecognized in Western Europe. In the nineteenth century, students of Byzantine history and literature looked back to Scaliger as their master and as the founder of their discipline.

In retrospect, Scaliger may be recognized as the first of a new breed of scholar. That scholarship ought to impart skills and values was a basic principle of Renaissance Humanism. That principle, in turn, was founded on a tradition stretching back to the Greek historian Polybius and beyond: The ideal historian was the man of political involvement who brought to his studies the experience of life; those studies would then instruct others to lead more effective lives. Scaliger's father was a man of this mold. Scaliger, however, thought otherwise: "Scholars should not teach practical politics." The scholar should, in Scaliger's estimate, devote himself to scientific study; knowledge should be pursued for purely intellectual, not practical, ends. In this emphasis on "value-free" studies, Scaliger asserted an educational and academic principle that would not be widely recognized until two centuries later and still remains a topic of considerable debate.

Bibliography

Grafton, Anthony. *Joseph Scaliger: A Study in the History of Classical Scholarship*. Vol. 1, *Textual Criticism and Exegesis*. Oxford: Clarendon Press, 1983; New York: Oxford University Press, 1993. This study (the first of a projected two-volume biography) takes its subject up to 1579. Grafton treats well Scaliger's early education and assesses Scaliger's early writings in their contemporary context. Detailed notes, no bibliography; adequate index. This study should be supplemented with the following item.

Grafton, Anthony, and Lisa Jardine. *From Humanism to the Humanities*. London: Duckworth, and Cambridge, Mass.: Harvard University Press, 1986. A fine study of education and the emergence of scholarly disciplines in Europe during the fifteenth and sixteenth centuries. Documents and discusses the education that Scaliger and his brothers received at Bordeaux. An excellent index and full bibliographic footnotes compensate for the lack of a bibliography.

Hall, Vernon, Jr. *Life of Julius Caesar Scaliger (1484-1558)*. Philadelphia: American Philosophical Society, 1950. This is the best single discussion of the elder Scaliger's life and literary works. Contains information on the education the Scaliger sons received at home and at Bordeaux. Includes reference notes, a bibliography, and a full index. Hall's discussion of the elder Scaliger's early (pre-1525) career should be supplemented with Paul Oskar Kristeller's discussion in *American Historical Review* 57 (1952): 394-396.

Pattison, Mark. *Essays by the Late Mark Pattison.* 2 vols. Edited by Henry Nettleship. Oxford: Clarendon Press, 1889; New York: Franklin, 1964. Volume 1 contains two essays that constitute an excellent sketch of Scaliger. Pattison emphasizes both Scaliger's scholarly work and the circumstances of his life. Volume 2 contains a brief index.

Pfeiffer, Rudolf. *History of Classical Scholarship from 1300 to 1850.* Oxford: Clarendon Press, 1968; New York: Oxford University Press, 1976. A standard discussion, with emphasis on Scaliger's place in the history of classical philology. Pfeiffer offers sound critical judgments on Scaliger's scholarly works and places those works in their contemporary intellectual context. Contains bibliographic footnotes and a full index.

Sandys, John Edwin. *History of Classical Scholarship*. Vol. 2, *From the Revival of Learning to the End of the Eighteenth Century.* Cambridge: Cambridge University Press, 1908; New York: Hafner, 1964. Features a straightforward, brief literary biography of Scaliger, with little analysis. Contains bibliographic footnotes and a full index.

Scaliger, Joseph Justus. *Autobiography of Joseph Scaliger with Autobiographical Selections from His Letters, His Testament, and the Funeral Orations by Daniel Heinsius and Dominicus Baudius.* Edited and translated by George W. Robinson. Cambridge, Mass.: Harvard University Press, 1927. The brief (five-page) autobiography takes Scaliger to Leiden in 1594; the selection of letters illustrates Scaliger's personality; the will offers information on the scholar's family, library, and other worldly goods. Contains an adequate index, a fine bibliographical introduction by Robinson, and two contemporary portraits of Scaliger.

Paul B. Harvey, Jr.

MICHAEL SERVETUS

Born: 1511?; Villanueva de Sixena, Spain
Died: October 27, 1553; Geneva
Areas of Achievement: Religion and medicine
Contribution: Servetus was the first to provide a systematic account of Unitarian ideas. As a doctor, Servetus' greatest achievement was the discovery of the pulmonary circulation of the blood.

Early Life

Michael Servetus was born probably in 1511 in Villanueva de Sixena, Spain. His parents, Antonio Serveto, alias Reves, and Catalina Conesa, were locally prominent; his father was raised to the nobility in 1529. Little, however, is known about Servetus' childhood. It is evident, however, that the young Michael was given a good education. During the years of his youth, Spain was in a period of relative toleration and admiration of Renaissance learning. The works of Humanists such as Thomas More and Desiderius Erasmus were in circulation. The mixed heritage of Spain meant that both Jewish and Islamic literatures were also available, and Servetus had become well acquainted with the Koran before reaching maturity. His writing suggests that Jewish and Muslim criticisms of the Trinity as polytheistic influenced his own opinion.

Upon completing his primary education, Servetus studied law at Toulouse in 1528-1529. It was here, in all probability, that he first saw a complete copy of the Bible (the Catholic tradition was that priests studied the Bible and then told communicants about it). Eagerly perusing the scriptures, he concluded that there was no biblical basis for the doctrine of the Trinity.

Meanwhile, his academic talents led to a position in the service of Juan de Quintana, confessor to Charles V, King of Spain and Holy Roman Emperor. As a servant of Quintana, Servetus was taken to Italy, where emperor and pope were meeting to settle their differences. His observation of the veneration and obeisance paid to the pope and other church officials during the ceremony in Bologna left a deeply negative impression on the young Servetus.

After leaving Quintana's employ in late 1529 or early 1530, Servetus visited Johannes Oecolampadius in Basel. Although Servetus was inclined toward the Protestant movement, Reformers such as Oecolampadius, fighting desperately to establish their own sects, were little more tolerant of deviation than were papal authorities. The newcomer's forthrightness about his Unitarian beliefs led to agreement among the leading Reformers in Switzerland—including Huldrych Zwingli, Martin Bucer, and Oecolampadius—that if he would not convert to the true faith, he should be suppressed.

Life's Work

During his time in Switzerland, Servetus wrote his first book, *De trinitatis erroribus libri septem* (1531). Although his Latin was crude, Servetus' discussion of the Trinity was erudite, and the work's publication marked his emergence from obscurity. Later, wishing to respond to some of his critics, Servetus revised and expanded his views in *Dialogorum de trinitate libri duo, de justicia regni Christi capitual quatuor* (1532).

Trinitarian doctrine, which the Church had adopted as orthodox, was far from simple. God, it stated, had a single essence but existed in three coequal, eternal forms: Father, Word or Son, and Holy Spirit. The Son had both human and divine natures, each of which had all the properties of the other. Despite all of these forms and natures, God—that is, the single essence—was One.

Servetus, who believed that the Church's teachings should be understandable to all the faithful, regarded Trinitarian thought as a disguised polytheism with no scriptural warrant. Father, Son, and Holy Spirit, according to Servetus, were simply the various manifestations of God and not separate entities at all. The Holy Spirit was God's spirit, which enters all men and has no independent existence. The biblical Jesus was purely human, though specially infused with the Holy Spirit, as shown by his supernatural origins. He was sent by God, as the prophets had been. Although Servetus never made a clear distinction between the human Jesus and Logos, the Word (he applied the term "Christ" to both), some might judge his Unitarian doctrine simpler and easier to understand than Trinitarian orthodoxy.

Although some Protestants of Servetus' time were apparently troubled by Trinitarian ideas, they preferred to avoid debate on that point, and Servetus' assertion that God as the Holy Spirit was in all things sounded too much like pantheism. Accordingly, in 1532 Oecolampadius and Bucer repudiated him, and he fled to France. He was welcomed to his new country by an arrest order from the Inquisition. Warned of the danger, he flirted with the idea of emigrating to the New World, but instead enrolled at the University of Paris as Michel de Villeneuve. Though he made himself unpopular with his haughty behavior and even challenged John Calvin, himself a fugitive, to a debate (Servetus did not appear), Villeneuve was not unmasked. Increasing hostility toward heretics, however, made discretion the better part of valor, and in 1534, still as Villeneuve, Servetus moved to Vienne, just outside Lyons.

Many people around Lyons favored religious reform, and the leading cleric, Archbishop Pierre Palmier, was as liberal as any ecclesiastic of the time. Publishing flourished in the area, and Servetus was quickly employed as editor and corrector for the firm of Trechsel. His first project was a new edition of Ptolemy's study of geography; he was to correct errors made by previous editors and to update the work, incorporating new discoveries. The 1535 edition was so successful that he was commissioned to do an even more completely revised version that was published in 1541.

Servetus quickly developed a friendship with Symphorien Champier, a local Humanist and doctor. In 1537, presumably on Champier's advice, Servetus returned to the University of Paris to study medicine. He supported himself by publishing medical pamphlets and lecturing on geography, but when he added astrology, he was soon in trouble. Because of a remark by Saint Augustine that the stars influence the body but not the will, the Church had permitted the use of astrology in medical treatment. It did, however, condemn efforts to foretell the future. Although apparently moderate in his espousal of astrological influence, Servetus was greatly annoyed by criticism of his ideas and wrote *Apologetica disceptatio pro astrologia* (1538) in response. He was brought before the Parlement of Paris to answer charges that included heresy. Although the court ordered confiscation of all copies of his apology for astrological study, it went no further than to read him a lecture on respect for his university's faculty. Soon Servetus left Paris, apparently without taking a degree.

Although he did not publish the information until 1553, it was probably in Paris that Servetus made the medical discovery that is most commonly associated with his name: the concept of the pulmonary circulation of the blood. Galen, the second century Greek physician whose ideas still dominated Western medicine, had asserted that blood was created in the liver and consumed as part of the body's nutritive process. Servetus accepted these ideas but also recognized the blood's purification in the lungs and return to the heart. The fact that this discovery was published in a theological tract is explained by Servetus' adoption of the idea that the soul is in the blood. Galen spoke of a vital spirit that flowed through and vivified humans; for Servetus, that spirit was clearly the Holy Spirit. Although Matteo Realdo Colombo is known to have made the same discovery during this period, an unpublished manuscript of Servetus seems to predate Colombo's work, and it is certain that Servetus published first.

After two or three years at Charlieu, in late 1540 or early 1541 Servetus returned to Vienne; he spent the next twelve years working as physician and editor. He had the patronage of Palmier and aristocratic friends and patients. His second edition on Ptolemy appeared in 1541. The next four years were spent editing the Bible.

Perhaps hoping that Calvin might still be induced to reconsider his doctrine, Servetus initiated a correspondence, but he was haughty and didactic. He enclosed copies of his earlier works on theology, and in 1546, a draft of what would become *Christianismi restitutio* (1553). Calvin, increasingly exasperated, eventually stopped replying and, despite requests, did not return the books and manuscripts to their author. He did send a copy of his own book, *Christianae religionis institutio* (1536; *Institutes of the Christian Religion*, 1561), which Servetus inscribed with sarcastic and critical annotations and returned. Whether out of rage at being ignored or simply out of excessive zeal, Servetus drifted off into apocalyptic prophecy.

In *Christianismi restitutio*, Servetus attempts to restore the Church to its original nature—a common theme for him and most Christian Reformers. Although the Protestants had made a beginning on one of the central tenets that had to be reformed—the means of redemption—they had done nothing to improve church doctrine concerning the Incarnation. Servetus expanded his earlier idea that God is manifest in all things, skirting but not quite embracing pantheism. He called for adult baptism, suggesting that the ritual represented a process of redemption and spiritual rebirth that could not occur until the individual was mature in his knowledge of good and evil; such maturity was not possible before age twenty. After all, Servetus noted, Jesus deferred baptism until the age of thirty. His position on baptism was much like that of the Anabaptists, but he rejected the social radicalism that marked that group.

Soon after the anonymous publication of *Christianismi restitutio* in January, 1553, Servetus was betrayed to the Inquisition. Although he did not write the letters of betrayal, Calvin supplied evidence from the correspondence of a few years earlier. Arrested and questioned, Servetus escaped. His whereabouts were unknown until he was arrested by Genevan authorities in August.

Calvin, who argued that Protestants should be no less ruthless than Catholics in the fight against heresy, worked to have Servetus prosecuted. The trial, which was highlighted by direct, though mostly written, confrontation between the two theologians, was also a battleground in the confrontation between Calvin and the Libertine Party for control of the city. The outcome was a triumph for Calvin. Servetus was condemned for heresy and sentenced to the stake. He was burned, dying in agony, on October 27, 1553. Two months later, the Catholic authorities in Vienne burned his effigy. Calvin was never again challenged for control of Geneva.

Summary

Michael Servetus is an example of the Renaissance man, for his intellect penetrated divergent areas of thought. Servetus knew classical and modern languages, theology, mathematics, and medical science. His discovery of the pulmonary circulation of the blood was a significant advance in physiology, and he practiced successfully as a physician. Although not the first to advance a Unitarian theory, Servetus was a key figure in pulling such ideas together and stating them systematically. As such, he is an important forerunner of modern Unitarianism.

Servetus' failures came in the areas of politics and human relations. He was so convinced that his views were correct that he had no patience with those who disagreed. He died a martyr not only to his faith but also to tolerance and free speech, yet he probably could have avoided that martyrdom by leaving Calvin alone. His ego drove him to proselytize and to become infuriated when his ideas were rejected. His career, then, reflects the best and worst of the Renaissance and Reformation era. As Humanist and scientist, he had great breadth and depth of knowledge. His condemnation to a hideous death by both Protestants and Catholics exemplifies the tension and fear produced by the zealously held religious convictions of the Reformation.

Photo courtesy of National Library of Medicine

Bibliography

Bainton, Roland H. *Hunted Heretic: The Life and Death of Michael Servetus, 1511-1553.* Boston: Beacon Press, 1953. A valuable biography, containing a thorough description of Servetus' life as well as an analysis of his theology. The account is balanced, well documented, and easy to read. An extensive bibliography is also included.

———. "Michael Servetus and the Pulmonary Transit." *Bulletin of the History of Medicine* 7 (1938): 1-7. A short but helpful discussion of the major medical discovery made by Servetus. This article will be most useful for those interested in Servetus as a doctor.

Durant, Will. *The Story of Civilization.* Vol. 6, *The Reformation.* New York: Simon and Schuster, 1935. Colorful writing and effective storytelling are the hallmarks of Durant's monumental series about civilization. This volume and its concise biography of Servetus are no exceptions. For the general reader seeking information about Servetus and his era, Durant is a delight. Unfortunately, his work is marked by rather too-frequent factual errors and should be used with care.

Friedman, Jerome. *Michael Servetus: A Case Study in Total Heresy.* Geneva: Droz, 1978. A biography with an emphasis on the religious elements in Servetus' career and a tendency to be hostile toward its subject. The analysis of Servetus' theology and his problems with the Church is interesting but not always convincing.

Fulton, John F., and Madeline E. Stanton. *Michael Servetus: Humanist and Martyr.* New York: Reichner, 1953. A biography that is rather favorable to Servetus. The authors make an effort to establish Servetus' place in Renaissance Humanism, and the book is most useful for setting that context.

Pettegree, A. "Michael Servetus and the Limits of Tolerance." *History Today* 40 (February, 1990): 40. The article profiles Servetus and his controversial theology that challenged the doctrine of the Trinity. Pettegree details his persecution and arrest on charges of heresy, his conflict with reformer John Calvin, and his eventual execution.

Sill, Geoffrey M. "The Authorship of an Impartial History of Michael Servetus." *Papers of the Bibliographical Society of America* 887 (September, 1993): 303. The author examines the origin and indeterminate authorship of the book *An Impartial History of Michael Servetus*, arguing that the book is the work of many authors. Sill provides literary analysis of the book, suggests possible authors, and cites existing commentaries on the book.

Wilbur, Earl Morse. *A History of Unitarianism.* Vol. 1, *Socinianism and Its Antecedents.* Cambridge, Mass.: Harvard University Press, 1947. This standard work on Unitarianism devotes five chapters to the career of Servetus. The focus is on theology and Servetus' importance in the development of the Unitarian position. Much biographical information is included.

Wilcox, Donald J. *In Search of God and Self: Renaissance and Reformation Thought.* Boston: Houghton Mifflin, 1975. Although Servetus is not discussed at length in this book, it provides an excellent background for an understanding of his life and theology. The emphasis is on intellectual history, particularly religion, and the major themes of the era are clearly presented.

Fred R. van Hartesveldt

SESSHŪ

Born: 1420; Akahama, Bitchu Province, Japan
Died: 1506; Yamaguchi, Suho Province, Japan
Area of Achievement: Art
Contribution: Sesshū is considered the greatest of Japanese landscape painters and a major ink painter whose genius pushed Japanese art toward its apex at the beginning of the sixteenth century.

Early Life

Sesshū was born in a rural village, Akahama on the Inland Sea, and was placed while very young in the Hofukuji, a large temple in the city of Soja nearby, to undergo religious training. Still in his early years, Sesshū entered a monastery in Kyōto as a novice. He acted as attendant to a priest, Shunrin Shuto, who eventually became chief abbot. He also studied painting with the monk-painter Tensho Shubun, who later was welcomed by the Ashikaga Shogunate as a master of the official academy. Both Shunrin and Shubun had a tremendous influence on Sesshū's life. Sesshū became a monk and practiced Zen discipline under the tutelage of the Zen master Shunrin, who was highly respected for his piety and truthfulness. Sesshū's career was determined by Shubun, whom Sesshū called "my painting master," and who was the first Japanese artist to rise to the full power and grasp of Chinese art.

Already enjoying great renown as a painter and past the age of forty, Sesshū left the monastery in 1462, for nothing could satisfy him short of studying in China. He moved west in the hope of making his way to China and established himself in a studio in Yamaguchi, which was under the control and patronage of the Ouchi family. Japan was going through a time of civil disturbance which culminated in the Onin Wars (1467-1477), which devastated Kyōto and dispersed its culture to the provinces; Yamaguchi thrived as a "Little Kyōto." In 1467, Sesshū traveled to China with a shogunal commercial fleet to study Chinese ink painting at first hand. His trip, which took him by land from Ningpo to Peking, gave him numerous opportunities to see not only some famous Chinese scenery but also many Chinese paintings, including those by Ming Dynasty painters still unknown in Japan. Sesshū had gone to China in search of a good painting master and found only mediocre ones who were weighed down with academic formalism. The grandiose landscape of the continent, however, revealed to him the secret composition in Chinese painting. Wherever he went, he drew landscapes and scenes of popular life which display the essential qualities of his art: solid construction and concise brushwork. He traveled especially to all the famous scenes where the great Sung landscapists had painted from nature. His style of sketching was so rapid and incisive that he brought back to Japan in 1469 thousands of fresh impressions of all the most noted places in Chinese scenery and history, along with accurate studies of costumes worn by famous individuals and of portrait types.

Life's Work

After returning to Japan in 1469 with his invaluable raw materials from China, Sesshū moved from place to place in northern Kyushu in order to avoid the disorder of civil war. He finally settled in Oita, under the patronage of the Otomo family. There he opened a studio which he named "Tenkai Togaro" and which was situated high on the side of a hill overlooking town, water, and mountains. Sesshū would often begin his work by gazing out upon the beautiful broad landscape that lay beneath his window. After a drink of sake, he would pick up his bamboo flute and play a sonorous, lingering melody to establish the right mood. Only then would he take up his brush and begin to paint. He was truly prolific; his floor was constantly covered with scattered pieces of used and unused paper. His monk friend Bofu Ryoshin, after visiting him in 1476, commented that everyone in the town, from the nobility to the common people, admired Sesshū's art and asked for a piece of his work. It seems that Sesshū never grew weary of depicting his private world, communing from time to time with the great world of nature outstretched beneath his balcony.

His practice of *zazen* (meditation) and his custom of making leisurely pilgrimages to various Buddhist temples and monasteries seem to have given him a strong body and robust health; he was able to travel on foot to various parts of the country, painting realistic pictures of the places he visited along the way. Sesshū always kept his clerical name and his Buddhist robe, which allowed him to travel through districts that were dangerous or that were barred to others.

Between 1481 and 1484, Sesshū made a long journey throughout Japan, making landscape drawings along the way. This artistic pilgrimage deepened his ability to capture the essential features of Japanese landscapes in his wash drawings. The Sung tradition of Chinese wash drawing had been fully assimilated in Japan, thanks to Shubun's talents and common sense, but it was Sesshū who first succeeded in giving a deeply personal and national expression to the new technique. Moreover, Sesshū's style is remarkable for its clear departure from the lyrical mode associated with his teacher Shubun. Dynamic brushwork and structured composition dominate Sesshū's works. He thoroughly developed and perfected a style of his own, and throughout his career he pushed back the limits of expression. Sesshū was completely wrapped up in his art. Upon returning to the west, he set up his Tenkai Togaro studio in Yamaguchi.

Sesshū's studio became a place of pilgrimage as people requested a token from his brush. He painted the walls of many monasteries (unfortunately long-since destroyed) and hundreds of six-fold screens, of which many have moldered away or been burned. An enormous amount of his work remains, however, though it is so zealously prized and guarded that few have seen many of his great masterpieces.

Among his compositions that are available to public view and representative of his work are *Autumn and Winter Landscapes*, a pair of hanging scrolls which must have belonged to a sequence of four seasons, a traditional theme for a set of landscapes, and *Landscapes of the Four Seasons* (1486), a long picture sequence illustrating the transition from spring to winter, done in a horizontal hand scroll format and representing the synthesis of his art. *Haboku Landscape* (1495), his best-known work, is a landscape in cursive style. It was given to his disciple Josui Soen, a painter-monk of the Enkakuji, when he took leave of Sesshū to return to Kamakura after a long course of study in his studio. The landscape, with a few rapid wash strokes accentuated with dark black lines, skillfully represents a tiny segment of nature lacking neither grandeur nor stability. *Amanohashidate* (1502-1505; bridge of heaven), drawn on the spot during a visit to the famous place on the Sea of Japan, represents the climax of his art. In this panoramic view of a pilgrimage site, all the details are represented with clean-cut lines, accompanied even by the names of the localities. Sesshū succeeded in capturing the innermost qualities of the famous place; to the technique of wash painting, he gave a highly personal expression.

Sesshū's versatility extended to other genres such as bird and flower painting—numerous sets of screens on this subject have been attributed to him. Moreover, noteworthy examples of portraits and other figure subjects including *Huike Severing His Arm*, a large, deeply moving composition executed in 1496 in which Huike (Hui-k'o) is cutting off his arm to show his will power to Bodhidharma.

Sesshū died shortly after painting *Amanohashidate*; he was vigorously healthy right up to the end of his life. During his lifetime, Sesshū was the host of many pupils, mostly Zen priests, of whom the greatest is Sesson Shukei. Among other acknowledged masters of this Sesshū school were Shugetsu Tokan, Umpo Toetsu, Kaiho Yusho, and Soga Chokuan. The Sesshū school continued on into the seventeenth century before melding with other schools. Its decline and death was not surprising, for no school of Japanese pictorial art so entirely depended on the skill of its delineator.

Summary

The style of Sesshū is central in the whole range of Asian art. Its primary vigor lies in its line—Sesshū's conceptions are thought out in terms of dominant lines. The line is hard, rough, and splintery, as if his brush were intentionally made of hog bristles irregularly set. Sesshū is a great master of straight line and angle. Moreover, he perfected the Chinese *suiboku* style of painting, making it typically Japanese by using the *haboku* technique, literally "flung ink," which employs a freely handled wash. *Suiboku* was monochrome work using black ink on a brush, which emphasized skilled brush work in place of a balance of color. Sesshū was the master of this style.

Sesshū loved painting landscapes because the landscape remains personal. It is the man who selects its elements, stamps them with his seal, infuses them with his strength, his will, his impetus. The genius clings throughout to human values, imposes them on the world, and victoriously refashions a world of his own. Sesshū's primary achievements can be easily categorized. He was preeminently skillful in landscape and figure painting. He excelled in the portrayal of birds, animals, and flowers. His manner was distinguished by the rapidity and certainty of its brushwork. He cultivated the habit of capturing as much of the subject as possible with one stroke. The effects of details such as leaves, feathers, and the like were almost invariably done at the single application of the brush, controlled by an unerring but perfectly free hand.

Many of the finest artists of the sixteenth century claimed to be his successor. The competition became so fierce that Unkoku Togan and Hasegawa Tohaku became embroiled in a legal dispute over the right to claim artistic descent from Sesshū.

Bibliography

Akiyama, Terukaza. *Japanese Painting*. Cleveland: World Publishing, 1961. A beautiful volume with illustrations covering the whole range of Japanese painting according to their genre. Chapter 6 emphasizes the influence of Chinese art and the development of monochrome painting, at the heart of which is Sesshū.

Binyon, Laurence. *Painting in the Far East*. 4th ed. London: Arnold, and New York: Longman, 1934. An interesting analysis of Sesshū's paintings appears in chapter 11.

Fenollosa, Ernest F. *Epochs of Chinese and Japanese Art*. London: Heinemann, and New York: Stokes, 1912. One of the first interpreters of note on Japanese and Chinese art. Reviews Sesshū's accomplishments and their significance. Provides a unique perspective of Sesshū.

Paine, Robert Treat, and Alexander Soper. *The Art and Architecture of Japan*. 3d ed. New Haven, Conn.: Yale University Press, and London: Penguin, 1981. Part 1 deals with the broad sweep of Japanese painting through history. Chapters 9 and 10 emphasize Sesshū, his compatriots, and his influence on successors. The 1981 revised third edition contains an updated, invaluable bibliography by W. D. Waterhouse.

Tanaka, Ichimatsu. *Japanese Ink Painting: Shubun to Sesshū*. Translated by Bruce Darling. New York: Weatherhill, 1972. A standard work on Sesshū and his master Shubun which places them in historic perspective in the development of Japanese painting. Chapter 4 is devoted exclusively to Sesshū.

Warner, Langdon. *The Enduring Art of Japan*. New York: Grove Press, 1952. A classic analysis of Japanese art trends in a historical perspective. Chapter 5 emphasizes the Ashikaga period, into which fit Sesshū and ink painting.

Edwin L. Neville, Jr.

LUDOVICO SFORZA

Born: July 27, 1452; Vigevano, Republic of Milan
Died: May 27, 1508; Loches, Toubrenne, France
Areas of Achievement: Government and patronage of the arts
Contribution: One of the most spectacular and significant statesmen and political manipulators of the High Renaissance in Italy, Sforza directed the Duchy of Milan during a crucial period of European history. His political maneuvers determined the following century of Italian affairs.

Early Life

The fourth legitimate son of Francesco Sforza, first Duke of Milan, and Bianca Maria Visconti, Ludovico Sforza was born into two of the most powerful families of the fourteenth century. At birth, his mother gave him the surname Maurus, which she later changed to Maria. By that time, however, "Maurus" had evolved into the nickname "Il Moro" (the Moor), which Ludovico liked, not only because it suited his dark complexion but also because it conjured up images of romance and adventure. Thereafter, the name stuck; Ludovico even used puns on that name to provide the metaphorical basis of some of his favorite personal devices and symbols, a Moor's head (*moro*) and a mulberry tree (*mora*). He became his mother's favorite while still young, remaining devoted to her his entire life. Discovering that he was bright, she directed his early education and eventually hired the Humanist Francesco Filelfo as his tutor. Sforza received a thorough grounding in the new learning of the Renaissance, becoming adept in both ancient languages and literature and the intellectual and technical innovations of the time. As a result of this background, he would later take his responsibilities as patron of the arts and literature and as commissioner of public buildings seriously, though he apparently had little confidence in the consistency or accuracy of his taste and judgment.

When the twenty-four-year-old Sforza was visiting France, his brother Galeazzo Maria, who had succeeded their father as Duke of Milan ten years earlier, was assassinated on December 24, 1476, leaving the seven-year-old Gian Galeazzo as heir. The child's mother, Bona of Savoy, assumed the regency, with Cicco Simonetta as principal adviser. Intrigues seemed to occur overnight, prompted chiefly by older Sforza relatives. When a plot implicated Ludovico and his brothers, all three were exiled. Eventually, however, Ludovico persuaded Bona to pardon him. On his return to Milan, he learned that Bona had taken a young servant, Tamino, as her lover. He used both his privileged position and his inside knowledge to gain control, having Simonetta murdered, driving Tamino away, discrediting Bona, and getting the nominal duke to appoint him chief counselor. From that time—November, 1480—he was virtual duke.

Life's Work

Sforza's life was the governing of Milan. At first, that meant making his rule legitimate, but eventually it would mean making it both legitimate and secure; neither was easy. Sforza's opening move was to ally himself with Ferdinand I, King of Naples. This eventually led to a marriage arrangement between Isabella of Aragon, granddaughter of Ferdinand, and the teenage Gian Galeazzo; in confirming the marriage, Sforza probably outsmarted himself, failing to realize that this articulate and ambitious woman would not accept the title of duchess without the power. At any rate, he refused to relinquish control after the wedding, thereby precipitating his ultimate downfall. Isabella immediately began conspiring to turn her Aragonese kinsmen against him, especially after January, 1491, when he married the young and equally spirited Beatrice d'Este of Ferrara, who was also of the family of Aragon. The Aragonese listened to Isabella.

Desperate for allies, Sforza turned to Charles VIII of France, establishing a mutual defense compact with him in 1492. Later that year, Alexander VI became pope with the support of Sforza's brother, the Cardinal Ascanio; this gave Sforza hope of papal support. Temporarily safe, Sforza attempted to maintain security by constructing a tenuous web of secret alliances and counteralliances. Once again he was too subtle for his own good: Charles VIII, who claimed the throne of Naples in his own right, and who had become obsessed with establishing a base in Italy for mounting a crusade, seized upon a pretext of perceived danger to invade Italy in 1494. During this campaign, Charles visited Gian Galeazzo at Pavia; the next day, the young man became ill and died, in circumstances that looked suspiciously like poisoning.

Meanwhile, Sforza was also carrying on surreptitious negotiations with the Emperor Maximilian I, who needed both money and a wife. In exchange for accepting a well-dowried niece of Sforza, Maximilian agreed to legitimate him as Duke of Milan. Gian Galeazzo's death occurred before this could happen. To divert public accusation, Sforza immediately summoned the Milanese Council, proposing that the duke's infant son be named his successor. Since he had packed the council, he knew in advance that its recommendation would be in favor of strength and experience, not rule by children. Thus, Sforza finally became Duke of Milan in name as well as in fact.

In the meantime, Charles pushed on through Italy and subjugated Naples. His success unsettled the states of Italy; Sforza feared that he had given Charles a foothold from which he would not budge—a fear intensified by the presence in Charles's army of the Duc d'Orléans, himself a claimant to the throne of Milan through his mother. Quickly Sforza withdrew his troops from the alliance and opened talks with Venice. The various Italian states joined forces to trap Charles in the peninsula, but he evaded them, withdrawing from Italy in October, 1495. Sforza took credit for forcing the retreat; he bragged at the time that the pope was his chaplain, the emperor his *condotierre* (military commander), Venice his chamberlain, and the King of France his courier. This was at best wishful thinking; Sforza was more likely a master in the art of self-deception.

He did not have much leisure to indulge such delusions. Maximilian came for a visit but proved too poor and vacillating to provide any real assistance. Shortly thereafter, the pope changed his strategy, Venice asserted its independence, the Aragonese recovered Naples, and Charles VIII died, to be succeeded by Sforza's antagonist, the Duc d'Orléans, now Louis XII, who had himself crowned both King of France and Duke of Milan. Far from manipulating his enemies, Sforza was now hemmed in on all sides. Sforza tried the desperate expedient of urging the Turks to invade Venice. Instead, Maximilian abandoned him, and the pope, France, and Venice formed a common league. Louis XII invaded the outlying districts, seizing the mountain strongholds. Sforza had no recourse but to flee. With his fortress at Milan in the hands of his chosen commandant, he packed his treasury in an immense mule train and escaped to Maximilian's court at Innsbruck. The emperor had probably never dreamed of such a windfall; Sforza's coffers went a long way toward solving Maximilian's financial problems.

In the meantime, rather than defending the castle to the death as instructed, in September, 1499, Sforza's commandant surrendered it to the French for 150,000 ducats. Sforza's cause was almost lost. He used what remained of his treasure to hire an army of Swiss and Burgundian mercenaries. At first, his campaign was successful; the people rallied behind him, since the high-handed methods of the French had alienated them. Yet Sforza did not have the opportunity to bring his opponents to battle. The Swiss were bribed to surrender him to the French, which they did on April 5, 1500. Taken to France as a prisoner, he was confined to the fortress at Loches in Touraine, where he remained in captivity until his death eight years later.

Sforza's lifetime marked the high point of Italy's greatness. At the beginning of his life, Italy was the paragon of Europe, the leader in the new civilization of the Renaissance, setting the pace of innovation in painting, music, sculpture, literature, philosophy, and all the arts of civilization. At the beginning of Sforza's career, Italy was considered a superior civilization, impregnable, almost sacrosanct, a region populated by a higher race. By his end, it had become a playground for petty princes and their mercenaries, stamped with fraud, corruption, greed, and venality. Worse, its vulnerability to external aggression had been exposed. Henceforth, it would become merely a collection of victims for plundering.

Summary

Like many other notable Renaissance princes, Ludovico Sforza has not been given the attention by contemporary historians that he received from previous generations.

Yet Sforza was celebrated in his time for the splendor of his court and his patronage of the arts. He set a standard of living that has rarely been equaled for style and taste. His center lacked the strenuous intellectualism and the learned grace of his great predecessor, Federigo da Montefeltro of Urbino; yet that gathering of learning, beauty, and wit, the fantasy of all academics since, could never be duplicated, and Sforza did not try. He wanted to build not a haven for intellectuals but a model of harmonious living for all of his citizens. This did not mean conspicuous consumption of luxury for the sake of ostentation, though there was plenty of that. It did mean that general prosperity and enlightened regulation were fundamental to his plan—ideals which unfortunately often conflicted with his political and military operations. Along these lines, he built a model farm to test new agricultural methods; for it and others near it, he devised a new system of irrigation by canal. He had his hometown and favorite retreat of Vigevano completely rebuilt. He promoted art, literature, science, and trade.

Yet his reputation for courtly living derived more from his dreams and plans than from what he actually was able to bring into being. Sympathetic contemporary biographers contributed largely to his legend. Thus Sforza is widely credited with patronage of Leonardo da Vinci and Donato Bramante. Yet the encouragement he gave them was often more verbal than financial. Ludovico commissioned the astonishing *Last Supper* (1495), which he also had almost completely reconstructed; he also did much to make both art and learning more available to the community. The final judgment on his patronage is aptly symbolized in the fate of the great statue of Francesco Sforza, which, like so many of Ludovico's dreams, never materialized. The brass for its casting was diverted during the French invasion to be made into cannons, and the model itself was shattered by French soldiers, who used it for target practice, after the fall of the castle.

Finally, Sforza is perhaps best seen as a man who dreamed grandly but could not control the forces, social and political, in which he found himself. It is hard to imagine what might have happened had he not seized power when he did. He failed to accomplish what he intended. The temporary security he provided made the destruction following him seem that much more devastating. In his subtlety he outmaneuvered himself. His extravagance was financed by increasing and unpopular taxation. Yet for his time he was magnificent. If he, with his intensity, intelligence, and force, failed, what would have happened under Gian Galeazzo? He has been blamed for the dissolution of Italian self-rule that followed him, but it is likely that it would have taken place anyway. His career is ultimately tragic, for he tried much and failed grandly. His attempt remains impressive.

Bibliography

Breisach, Ernst. *Caterina Sforza: A Renaissance Virago*. Chicago: University of Chicago Press, 1967. In this scholarly biography of one of the most remarkable women of the fifteenth century, Breisach includes much incidental information about Sforza since his focus is properly on his subject. He does emphasize the interrelationship of the two, which was not of primary importance for Sforza. The bibliography is helpful in locating material on Sforza, most of which is in Italian.

Burckhardt, Jacob. *The Civilization of the Renaissance in Italy.* Translated by S. G. C. Middlemore. London: Allen and Unwin, and New York: Macmillan, 1914. In this classic study, Burckhardt may be said to have invented the idea of the Renaissance as a cultural entity. Since one of his focal points is the development of the individual personality, he shows insight into all the major personalities of the period, as he does with Sforza. His material is dated, however, and he does not present a unified treatment.

Larner, Joseph. *The Lords of Romagna: Romagnol Society and the Origins of the Signorie*. London: Macmillan, and Ithaca, N.Y.: Cornell University Press, 1965. Larner presents a balanced view of Sforza with extensive information and provocative points of view. His portrait is somewhat revisionist, in that he rejects the once-conventional notion that Sforza was simply a subtle schemer with dreams of glory. He presents Sforza as a progressive for his time, concerned with the welfare of the state as a whole.

Plumb, J. H. *The Italian Renaissance: A Concise Survey of Its History and Culture*. New York: Harper, 1965. Though not known as an authority on the Italian Renaissance, Plumb here presents a brilliant synthesis of the basis of that culture. His account of Sforza is lucid, readable, and packed with detail. This is easily the best source for the general reader.

Potter, G. R., ed. *The New Cambridge Modern History.* Vol. 1, *The Renaissance*. Cambridge: Cambridge University Press, 1957. Includes a general account of Sforza in relation to the historical events of his time.

James Livingston

WILLIAM SHAKESPEARE

Born: April 23, 1564; Stratford-upon-Avon, Warwickshire, England

Died: April 23, 1616; Stratford-upon-Avon, Warwickshire, England

Area of Achievement: Literature

Contribution: The leading playwright in the great flowering of Renaissance English drama, Shakespeare created some of the world's most enduring literary and dramatic masterpieces.

Early Life

William Shakespeare was descended from tenant farmers and landed gentry; one of his grandfathers, Richard Shakespeare of Snitterfield, rented land from the other, Robert Arden of Wilmcote. Shakespeare's father, John, moved to nearby Stratford-upon-Avon, became a prosperous shop owner (dealing in leather goods) and municipal officeholder, and married his former landlord's youngest daughter, Mary Arden. Thus Shakespeare—the third of eight children, but the first to survive infancy—was born into a solidly middle-class family in a provincial market town.

During Shakespeare's infancy, his father was one of the town's leading citizens. In 1557, John Shakespeare had become a member of the town council and subsequently held such offices as constable, affeeror, and chamberlain; in 1568, he became bailiff (mayor) and justice of the peace. As the son of a municipal officer, the young Shakespeare was entitled to a free education in the town's grammar school, which he probably entered around the age of seven. The school's main subject was Latin studies—grammar and readings drilled into the schoolboys year after year. The Avon River, the surrounding farmlands, and the nearby Forest of Arden offered plenty of opportunities for childhood recreations.

When Shakespeare was a teenager, his family fell on hard times. His father stopped attending town council meetings in 1577, and the family's fortunes began declining. Matters were not improved in 1582 when Shakespeare, at the age of eighteen, hastily married Anne Hathaway, the twenty-six-year-old daughter of a farmer from the nearby village of Shottery; she presented him with a daughter, named Susanna, approximately five months later. In 1585, the couple also became the parents of twins, Hamnet and Judith. As was then customary, the young couple probably lived in his parents' home, which must have seemed increasingly crowded.

The next mention of Shakespeare is in 1592, when he was an actor and playwright in London. His actions during the seven-year interim have been a matter of much curious speculation, including unproved stories of deer poaching, soldiering, and teaching. It may have taken him those seven years simply to break into and advance in the London theater. His early connections with the theater are unknown, although he was an actor before he became a playwright. He might have joined one of the touring companies that occasionally performed in Stratford-upon-Avon, or he might have gone directly to London to make his fortune, in either the theater or some other trade. Shakespeare was a venturesome and able young man who had good reasons to travel—his confining family circumstances, tinged with just enough disgrace to qualify him to join the disreputable players. The theater was his escape to freedom; he therefore had strong motivation to succeed.

Life's Work

The London theater, in Shakespeare's day, was composed of companies of men and boys (women were not allowed on the Renaissance English stage but were played by young men or boys) who performed in public playhouses roughly modeled on old innyards. The theaters were open to the air, had balconies surrounding the pit and stage, and held from two to three thousand people. A group known as the University Wits—John Lyly, George Peele, Thomas Lodge, Robert Greene, Thomas Nashe, and Christopher Marlowe—dominated the drama. Shakespeare learned his art by imitating these Oxford and Cambridge men, but for him they were a difficult group to join. They looked down on most actors and on playwrights, such as Thomas Kyd, who had not attended a university. Shakespeare offended on both counts, and Robert Greene expressed his resentment in the posthumously published book *Greene's Groatsworth of Wit* (1592), which included a famous warning to three fellow "gentlemen" playwrights:

> Yes, trust them [the players] not: for there is an upstart crow, beautified with our feathers, that with his *Tiger's heart wrapt in a player's hide*, supposes he is as well

> able to bombast out a blank verse as the best of you: and being an absolute *Johannes Factotum*, is in his own conceit the only Shake-scene in a country.

Greene's literary executor, Henry Chettle, later printed an apology for this slur on Shakespeare, with its pun on his name and its parody of a line from *Henry VI, Part III*. Upon meeting him, Chettle found Shakespeare's "demeanor no less civil than he, excellent in the quality he professes. Besides, divers of worship have reported his uprightness of dealing, which argues his honesty, and his facetious grace in writing, that approves his art."

Actually, Greene's judgment of Shakespeare's early work is more accurate. The early plays are far from excellent; they include some of the most slavish imitations in Renaissance English drama, as Shakespeare tried his hand at the various popular modes. The interminable three-part history play *Henry VI* (1589-1592) makes, as Greene notes, bombastic attempts at Marlowe's powerful blank verse. In *The Comedy of Errors* (c. 1592-1594), based on Plautus' *Menaechmi*, and in the Senecan tragedy *Titus Andronicus* (c. 1593-1594), Shakespeare showed his ability to copy Roman models down to the smallest detail, even if he did lack a university degree. Apparently, he also lacked confidence in his own imagination and learned slowly. *Richard III* (c. 1592-1593), however, showed promise in the malignant character of Richard, while *The Taming of the Shrew* (c. 1593-1594) offered its rambunctious love-fight.

Despite their imitative nature and many other faults, Shakespeare's early plays—notably *Henry VI*—were popular onstage, but his greatest early popularity came from two long narrative poems, *Venus and Adonis* (1593) and *The Rape of Lucrece* (1594). Shakespeare wrote these two poems during the two years that the plague closed down the London theaters. He dedicated the poems to a patron, the young Henry Wriothesley, third Earl of Southampton, who may have granted him a substantial monetary reward in return. In any event, when the theaters reopened in 1594 the acting companies were almost decimated financially, but Shakespeare was in a position to buy or otherwise acquire a partnership in one of the newly reorganized companies, the Lord Chamberlain's Men. Henceforth, Shakespeare earned money not only from the plays he had written or in which he acted but also from a share of the profits of every company performance. The financial arrangement seemed to inspire his creative efforts, for he set about writing the plays that made him famous, beginning with *Romeo and Juliet* (c. 1595-1596) and going on to the great history plays and comedies, including *Richard II* (c. 1595-1596), the two-part *Henry IV* (c. 1597-1598), *Henry V* (c. 1598-1599), *A Midsummer Night's Dream* (c. 1595-1596), *The Merchant of Venice* (c. 1596-1597), *Much Ado About Nothing* (c. 1598-1599), *As You Like It* (c. 1599-1600), and *Twelfth Night: Or, What You Will* (c. 1601-1602).

At about the time Shakespeare wrote *Romeo and Juliet* and *Richard II*, he probably also began his great sonnet sequence, not published until 1609. The 154 sonnets, tracing a friendship with a young man and a romance with a "dark lady," raise the question of how Shakespeare lived when he was away from Stratford, where his wife and children presumably remained. The young man might be a patron—perhaps Wriothesley, though other names have also been proposed—and the "dark lady" strictly imaginary, created to overturn the sonnets' trite Petrarchan conventions. Other speculations favor a more personal interpretation, seeing an actual *ménage à trois* of the poet, the young man, and the "dark lady." All the questions raised by the sonnets remain open, and the only evidence about how Shakespeare spent his spare time in London indicates that he sometimes frequented taverns (notably the Mermaid) with his fellow playwrights and players.

Evidence also indicates that he remained in close contact with Stratford-upon-Avon, to which he probably returned as frequently as possible. He used his earnings from the theater to install himself as the town's leading citizen, buying New Place as a family residence in 1597 and thereafter steadily amassing other land and property. In 1596, his father was granted a hereditary coat of arms and thus became a gentleman, a status he had never achieved on his own. Unfortunately, also in 1596, Shakespeare suffered a setback when his son, Hamnet, died at the age of eleven. His affection for his two remaining children, Susanna and Judith, may be reflected in the witty, saucy, but lovable heroines of his great comedies.

Shakespeare's company in London prospered. In 1599, it stopped renting theaters and built its own, the Globe, which increased company profits. The company was a favorite of the reigning monarchs, who paid well for special performances at court—first Elizabeth I, then after 1603, James I, who loved the theater even more and renamed Shakespeare's company the King's Men. The company

also began performing most of the plays of Ben Jonson, who ranked second only to Shakespeare and who excelled at satiric comedy. Shakespeare turned to tragedy, first writing *Julius Caesar* (c. 1599-1600) and *Hamlet, Prince of Denmark* (c. 1600-1601) and then—one after another—*Othello, the Moor of Venice* (c. 1604-1605), *King Lear* (c. 1605-1606), *Macbeth* (c. 1605-1606), and *Antony and Cleopatra* (c. 1606-1607).

Yet even during this period—perhaps the high point in the history of world drama—Shakespeare's company had its problems. One was the competition of the boys' companies which performed in the private theaters—small indoor theaters that charged higher admission and appealed to a more exclusive audience than the public theaters. In 1608, the King's Men acquired one of the private theaters, the Blackfriars, plus the services of two playwrights who wrote for it, the collaborators Francis Beaumont and John Fletcher. With their light, witty comedy and melodramatic tragicomedy, represented by such plays as *The Knight of the Burning Pestle* (1607), *Philaster: Or, Love Lies A-Bleeding* (1608-1610), and *A King and No King* (1611), Beaumont and Fletcher introduced a new cavalier style into Renaissance English drama that ultimately eclipsed even Shakespeare's popularity and perhaps hurried his retirement. It is uncertain whether they or Shakespeare introduced tragicomedy, but Shakespeare's final complete plays are in this fashionable new mode: *Pericles, Prince of Tyre* (c. 1608-1609), *Cymbeline* (c. 1609-1610), *The Winter's Tale* (c. 1610-1611), and *The Tempest* (c. 1611-1612). After Beaumont married an heiress and stopped writing plays in 1612 or 1613, Shakespeare collaborated with Fletcher, and possibly others, on *Henry VIII, The Two Noble Kinsmen*, and *Cardenio* (now lost), all performed during 1612-1613.

By 1608, when his productivity dropped to one play per year, Shakespeare may have spent part of each year in Stratford-upon-Avon. In 1607, his elder daughter had married Dr. John Hall, the local physician, and in 1608, with the birth of their daughter, Elizabeth, Shakespeare became a grandfather. Around 1613, he retired completely to Stratford-upon-Avon, though he also joined John Heminge, a partner in the King's Men, and William Johnson, the host of the Mermaid Tavern, in purchasing the gatehouse of the Blackfriars priory, probably for London visits. On February 10, 1616, his younger daughter, Judith, at the age of thirty-one, married Thomas Quiney, a member of another prominent Stratford family. On March 25, 1616, Shakespeare made out his last will and testament, leaving most of his estate to Susanna, a substantial amount of money to Judith, and his "second best bed" to Anne. He died on April 23, 1616, and was buried in Holy Trinity Church, Stratford-upon-Avon.

In 1623, Shakespeare's surviving partners in the King's Men, John Hemings and Henry Condell, published the First Folio collection of his plays. The portrait included in the First Folio depicts Shakespeare with a short mustache, large staring eyes, and an oval face accentuated by his high, balding forehead and the remaining hair that almost covers his ears. The bust erected above his grave is similar, except that he has a goatee and the balding has progressed further. The First Folio portrait resembles a soulful intellectual, while the Stratford bust suggests a prominent burgher.

Summary

The two portraits of William Shakespeare portray the two parts of his nature. On the one hand, he possessed immense intellectual curiosity about the motives and actions of people. This curiosity, plus his facility with language, enabled him to write his masterpieces and to create characters who are better known than some important figures in world history. On the other hand, reflecting his middle-class background, Shakespeare was himself motivated by strictly bourgeois instincts; he was more concerned with acquiring property and cementing his social position in Stratford than he was with preserving his plays for posterity. If his partners had not published the First Folio, there would be no Shakespeare as he is known today: still acted and enjoyed, the most widely studied and translated writer, the greatest poet and dramatist in the English and perhaps any language.

Besides his ability to create a variety of unforgettable characters, there are at least two other qualities that account for Shakespeare's achievement. One of these is his love of play with language, ranging from the lowest pun to some of the world's best poetry. His love of language sometimes makes him difficult to read, particularly for young students, but frequently the meaning becomes clear in a well-acted version. The second quality is his openness, his lack of any restrictive point of view, ideology, or morality. Shakespeare was able to embrace, identify with, and depict an enormous range of human behavior, from the good to the bad to the indifferent. The capaciousness of his language and vision thus help account for the universality of his appeal.

Shakespeare's lack of commitment to any didactic point of view has often been deplored. Yet he is not entirely uncommitted; rather, he is committed to what is human. Underlying his broad outlook is Renaissance Humanism, a synthesis of Christianity and classicism that is perhaps the best development of the Western mind and finds its best expression in his work. This same generous outlook was apparently expressed in Shakespeare's personality, which, like his bourgeois instincts, defies the Romantic myth of the artist. He was often praised by his fellows, but friendly rival and ferocious satirist Ben Jonson said it best: "He was, indeed, honest, and of an open and free nature," and "He was not of an age, but for all time."

Bibliography

Alexander, Peter. *Shakespeare's Life and Art.* London: Nisbet, 1939; New York: New York University Press, 1961. A short but much-admired critical biography, treating Shakespeare's life in relation to his work.

Bate, Jonathan. *The Genius of Shakespeare.* London: Picador, 1997; New York: Oxford University Press, 1998. Bate, one of Britain's most acclaimed Shakespeare scholars, explores the extraordinary staying power of Shakespeare's work. He opens by addressing questions of authorship (what works are attributable to Shakespeare) and of Christopher Marlowe's influence on his work. This book provides an inquiry into the nature of genius and ponders the legacy of a talent unequaled in English letters.

Bradbrook, Muriel C. *Shakespeare, the Poet in His World.* London: Weidenfeld and Nicolson, and New York: Columbia University Press, 1978. An excellent study by one of the leading scholars and critics of Renaissance English drama.

Chute, Marchette. *Shakespeare of London.* New York: Dutton, 1949; London: Secker and Warburg, 1951. The most readable and accurate of the popular biographies. Based on documents contemporary to Shakespeare.

Frye, Roland Mushat. *Shakespeare's Life and Times: A Pictorial Record.* Princeton, N.J.: Princeton University Press, 1967; London: Faber, 1968. Introduces the most important information about Shakespeare through 114 illustrations and captions of one to three paragraphs each.

Halliday, F.E. *Shakespeare and His World.* New York: Scribner, 1956; London: Thames and Hudson, 1970. Another short introduction containing the essential facts and 151 illustrations.

Quennell, Peter. *Shakespeare: A Biography.* London: Weidenfeld and Nicolson, and Cleveland, Ohio: World, 1963. Another fine critical biography, scholarly and readable.

Reese, M.M. *Shakespeare: His World and His Work.* Rev. ed. London: Arnold, and New York: St. Martin's Press, 1980. A full, well-written introduction to Shakespeare's life, the drama which preceded his, the Elizabethan stage, and his art.

Schoenbaum, Samuel. *Shakespeare's Lives.* Oxford: Clarendon Press, and New York: Oxford University Press, 1970. Not a biography per se, but rather an evaluation of the portraits of Shakespeare, the contemporary references, the legends, and the many biographies written about him up to 1970. Fascinating but dense reading. An important scholarly reference work.

———. *William Shakespeare: A Compact Documentary Life.* Oxford: Clarendon Press, and New York: Oxford University Press, 1977. A scholarly biography that scrupulously examines the facts, documents, and myths of Shakespeare's life, supported by the author's considerable knowledge of previous biographies.

Smith, Molly. *Breaking Boundaries: Politics and Play in the Drama of Shakespeare and His Contemporaries.* Aldershot and Brookfield, Vt.: Ashgate, 1998. The period 1585-1649 was rich in innovative drama that challenged the boundaries between social, political, and cultural activities of various kinds. In this book, Smith examines ways in which texts by Renaissance authors reflect, question, and influence their society's ideological concerns. In the drama of Kyd, Shakespeare, Beaumont and Fletcher, Webster, Middleton, Massinger, and Ford, she identifies the simultaneously serious and playful appropriation of popular cultural practices.

Harold Branam

SIR PHILIP SIDNEY

Born: November 30, 1554; Penshurst, England
Died: October 17, 1586; Arnhem, the Netherlands
Areas of Achievement: Literature, government, and the military
Contribution: Known during his lifetime as the perfect example of a Renaissance courtier because of his learning, nobility, and chivalry, Sidney was also a poet of the first rank whose sonnet sequence *Astrophel and Stella* is a classic of English literature.

Early Life

From his birth, Philip Sidney was associated with the court of England. His godfather was Philip II of Spain, husband of Queen Mary, and his godmother (his grandmother) was the Duchess of Northumberland. Philip's father, Sir Henry Sidney, was active in government affairs in Wales and Ireland. Sidney's early years were spent at Penshurst, the family estate. In 1564, he began attending Shrewsbury School, where he met the future writer Fulke Greville, who would later compose the first biography of Sidney.

In 1568, Sidney entered Christ Church, Oxford, where he impressed his teachers and fellows with his intelligence and character. His circle of friends grew to include such notables as Richard Carew, who would become known as a poet, and Richard Hakluyt, who would win fame as an explorer and writer.

His stay at Oxford was cut short in 1571 when he left the university because of the plague; Sidney never received a degree. In 1572, he began a two-year tour of the Continent, ostensibly to improve his knowledge of foreign languages, but also to serve in a quasi-diplomatic function for Elizabeth I. It was during this visit that Sidney met a number of Protestant leaders in Europe and became a firm and vocal champion of their cause. This belief was strengthened during his stay in France by the St. Bartholomew's Eve massacre of Protestants on August 23, 1572.

During his extensive travels, Sidney met and befriended Hubert Languet, who accompanied Sidney to Vienna and the court of Maximilian II, and later to Poland. Languet had a great influence on Sidney and further confirmed for the young Englishman the truth of the Protestant cause. Sidney also visited Hungary, spent time in Venice studying astronomy, music, and Italian literature, and, upon his return to Vienna, learned horsemanship under John Peter Pugliano, the foremost equestrian of the age. Later, in his *Defence of Poesie* (1580), published in another edition as *Apologie for Poetry*, Sidney gave a vivid description of these lessons.

In June, 1575, Sidney returned to England. His education was now complete, and he was ready to embark on his service to England and the court of Elizabeth. He was already known for his intelligence and his serious nature, and his contemporaries universally acknowledged him as a paragon of virtues. In appearance, he was quite handsome, with light hair, a fair complexion, and fine features. The numerous portraits which survive testify to his refined but not overly elegant presence.

Life's Work

As a member of the court, Sidney met Walter Devereaux, first Earl of Essex, and his daughter, Penelope, who would later become the "Stella" of Sidney's sonnet sequence. Although there was discussion of marriage, the death of Essex in 1576 and Sidney's attention to political matters at court allowed the desultory courtship to lapse. At the time, Sidney composed verses inspired more by literary models than Penelope herself; his earlier sonnets are clearly patterned after those of the Earl of Surrey to his love, Geraldine. It was only after 1581, when Penelope had married Lord Rich, that Sidney seemed to have been moved by real passion toward her. By then, he could only vent his feelings in the sonnets of *Astrophel and Stella* (1591).

In the meantime, however, Sidney was occupied with political and diplomatic affairs at court. In 1577, he was dispatched with messages for the newly crowned Elector Palatine and to the Emperor Rudolf II, who had also recently succeeded to the throne. While in Prague, Sidney boldly lectured the new emperor on the need to combat the threat of Spanish domination of Europe. While returning to England, he traveled through the Low Countries, where he met and was captivated by William of Orange, leader of the Protestant cause in northern Europe.

Back in England, Sidney wrote a defense of his father's conduct of Irish affairs to counter criticism. Sidney also turned to more creative work, composing a masque called *The Lady of May* (1578) to celebrate Elizabeth's May Day visit to one of her subjects. Such visits were, under Eliza-

beth, elaborate state occasions of considerable importance, and their ceremonies were often expressions of political significance. Increasingly, Sidney was to be found in association with scholars and writers, such as Gabriel Harvey and Edmund Spenser. Sidney and Spenser met in 1578; the next year, Spenser dedicated to Sidney his important work, *The Shepherd's Calendar.*

Sidney recognized Spenser's talent and contribution, but another work dedicated to him that year pleased him not at all: Stephen Gosson's *Schoole of Abuse* (1579), a virulent attack on the theater and the quickly developing English drama. Sidney composed and circulated in manuscript his *Defence of Poesie* as a reply to Gosson's charges.

The *Defence of Poesie* is one of the earliest and most important pieces of English literary theory, and formed the standard defense of literature that would be used against Puritans and others who decried the art as being at best, trivial, at worst, sinful. In his spirited and vigorous defense, Sidney used the argument that poetry (by which he meant all forms of literature, including drama) teaches virtue more vividly, and therefore more profoundly, than do history or philosophy. Through its creative powers, poetry instills in its audience a lasting love of proper actions, and so makes them better persons. To bolster his argument, Sidney used as examples such English writers as Geoffrey Chaucer, the Earl of Surrey, and Edmund Spenser.

Sidney published none of his literary works during his lifetime, but he was much less discreet with the distribution of his political writings. In January, 1580, he dared to send Queen Elizabeth a lengthy, well-reasoned, but highly improper essay which argued against her possible marriage to the Duke of Anjou, the Roman Catholic heir to the French throne. Sidney's reproach to his sovereign was based on the grounds of loyal patriotism and Protestantism, but the queen was so angered that she banished Sidney from her presence for months. During this interlude, Sidney wrote his romance, *Arcadia* (1590), to amuse his sister.

Sidney's talents and abilities, as well as his reputation and his many admirers, regained him favor at court. In 1581, he was elected to Parliament; that spring he took a major part in a festive tournament and other ceremonies honoring a French embassy; and on January 13, 1583, he was knighted. He was also given a more practical post as joint master of the queen's ordnance.

The income from the ordnance position and other funds he had been granted from fines paid to the Crown, were necessary, for a marriage had been arranged by Sidney's father and Sir Francis Walsingham, whose daughter Frances was then only fourteen. The two were married on September 20, 1593. Although Sidney seems to have felt genuine affection for his wife, he continued his devotion to Penelope. These emotions, deep as they appear to have been, found expression only in his collection of sonnets which were given the title *Astrophel and Stella* ("star lover" and "star," the poetical names Sidney devised for himself and Penelope).

Sidney's desire for service found little outlet during these months. Frustrated, he considered joining voyages of exploration or colonization. In Parliament, he sat on a committee setting boundaries for the projected Virginia colony, and his interest in this topic was well enough known that Hakluyt, his friend from Oxford, dedicated his own celebrated work, *Divers Voyages, Touching the Discovery of America* (1582), to Sidney.

A more urgent call to action lay closer to home. In 1584, the assassination of William of Orange shocked Protestant Europe, and made Sidney more determined than ever to insist on England's resistance to Spanish actions in the Low Countries. Elizabeth, anxious to avoid open conflict with the powerful Spanish, was finally convinced to send an army to the Netherlands in the summer of 1585, but her commitment was tentative and hesitant.

Sidney, craving a more active part, attempted to join Sir Francis Drake, who was then preparing a raid on the Spanish coast. Sidney's arrival at Plymouth was secret, but Drake promptly and prudently informed Elizabeth, who summoned Sidney to court. Once again, however, peace was restored between monarch and subject, and on November 7, Sidney was appointed governor of Flushing, a town in the Low Countries garrisoned by the English. He sailed on November 16, 1585.

The English army was small and its supplies poor. Operations with the Dutch were hampered by language barriers and mutual suspicion. Contact with the Spanish forces consisted mainly of raids and skirmishes, rather than full battles, which the English could not afford and the Dutch did not desire. On July 6, 1586, Sidney was part of a daring raid on Axel, a small village twenty miles from Flushing. Conducted at night and by boat, the assault took the town's garrison by surprise. Later that year, Sidney participated in the assault of Doesburg, a small citadel near the town of Arnhem.

The English commander, the Earl of Leicester, was embarked on a policy of systematically reducing the Spanish strong points. The next one he attacked was at Zutphen. Leicester brought his army up to Zutphen on September 13 and was soon engaged in a running series of skirmishes with the defenders. On September 22, Sidney joined the earl with about five hundred English cavalry in an attack on the Spanish lines. Meeting a friend who was wearing no leg armor, Sidney gallantly but rashly removed his own.

In the battle, Sidney had one horse killed under him, mounted another, and charged through the enemy line. On his return to the English forces, a bullet struck him in the left leg just above the knee. He was able to ride back to camp, and was carried by barge to Arnhem. His wife had joined him earlier, in March, and, although pregnant, remained to care for him. The wound became infected, and on October 17, Sidney died.

Summary

The grief which was felt throughout England at Sir Philip Sidney's death was profound and sincere. His funeral on February 16 brought mourners from all social classes to St. Paul's Cathedral. Both Oxford and Cambridge published collections of elegies in his honor, and more than two hundred other poetic memorials were printed, among them eight elegies in Spenser's *Colin Clout's Come Home Again* (1595).

It was appropriate that Sidney's passing be marked by poetic tributes, because he himself is best known as a poet and writer. His three major works were important influences on English literature, and one has attained the status of a classic.

Sidney's *Arcadia*—composed primarily to amuse his sister, and therefore sometimes called *The Countess of Pembroke's Arcadia*—is an elaborate chivalric romance, with verse interludes. The language, highly patterned and deliberately ornate, is typical of the genre, which was established by John Lyly's *Euphues, The Anatomy of Wit* (1578) and which captivated an entire generation of Renaissance readers.

The plot is a rambling account of two princes' pursuit of their two princesses, and there are numerous episodes of disguises, mistaken identities, battles, tournaments, and philosophical speeches. Pastoral eclogues are scattered throughout the work. *Arcadia* was first published in 1590, but the edition of 1593, which was prepared by Sidney's sister, provides the first reliable text. Although very popular during the sixteenth and seventeenth centuries, the romance has since declined in reputation and influence.

The *Defence of Poesie*, which was widely circulated in manuscript during the author's life, remains an important document of the English Renaissance and provides an interesting insight into the critical views of the time. When Gosson dedicated his work, *The Schoole of Abuse*, to Sidney without permission, Sidney was moved to prepare his rebuttal. Gosson attacked plays, poems, and all other forms of fiction as being vain and sinful. Sidney sought to refute these charges in his reply, which consists of three parts. The first justifies poetry as a source of virtue; the second reviews the forms of poetry; and the third offers an optimistic prediction of the future of English writing. Interestingly, Sidney seems to have been unaware of the forthcoming achievements English drama was about to make.

By far the most important of Sidney's literary creations was his sonnet sequence *Astrophel and Stella*, in which he chronicles his long, passionate, and ultimately unhappy relationship with Penelope

Rich. The collection consists of 108 sonnets, which use the familiar "Shakespearean" form of three quatrains and a concluding couplet. There are also eleven songs in the sequence.

Sidney's powers as a poet grew as he composed the series; the earlier poems often seem flat or contrived, but the later sonnets are both technically proficient and poetically powerful. He made particularly good use of metaphors and allusions from military and political affairs, as was fitting for a courtier poet. The influence of these poems on other writers, including Shakespeare, is clear.

Because of Sidney's personal appeal, and the success of the *Arcadia*, unauthorized editions of *Astrophel and Stella* began appearing in the early 1590's, with the first being prepared by the noted Elizabethan writer, Thomas Nashe (1591). The 1598 edition of *Arcadia* contains the most complete version of the sequence, and presents it in an order probably close to that which Sidney intended.

Although he was loved and admired in his own time as an outstanding individual, a defender of the Protestant cause, and an English patriot, Sidney's enduring legacy consists of his place among the first rank of poets who created the English Renaissance.

Bibliography

Buxton, John. *Sir Philip Sidney and the English Renaissance*. London: Macmillan, and New York: St. Martin's Press, 1954. A solid study of Sidney and his place within the Elizabethan period, concentrating on his literary works, but also providing background on his life and activities as a courtier and soldier.

Garrett, Martin, ed. *Sidney: The Critical Heritage*. London and New York: Routledge, 1991. This work gathers together a large body of critical soures on major figures in literature, including Sir Philip Sidney. Each volume presents contemporary responses to a writer's work, enabling students and researchers to read these sources directly.

Greville, Sir Fulke (First Baron Brooke). *The Life of the Renowned Sir Philip Sidney*. Edited by N. Smith. Oxford: Clarendon Press, 1907: as *Sir Fulke Greville's Life of Sir Philip Sidney*, Folcroft, Pa.: Folcroft Library, 1971. The original biography, written by Sidney's longtime friend. First published in 1652, this work is the primary source for Sidney's life. It also sheds light on the thoughts and perspectives of his contemporaries.

Hamilton, A. C. *Sir Philip Sidney: A Study of His Life and Works*. Cambridge and New York: Cambridge University Press, 1977. A well-written, well-balanced overview of Sidney's life and writings, especially helpful for showing how the two relate in many areas.

Howell, Roger. *Sir Philip Sidney: The Shepherd Knight*. London: Hutchinson, and Boston: Little Brown, 1968. Concentrates on Sidney's political and diplomatic activities, placing his writings within the historical context of the times, particularly his patriotism and intense devotion to the Protestant cause.

Kimbrough, Robert. *Sir Philip Sidney*. New York: Twayne, 1971. Good introductory overview of Sidney the man and writer, and Kimbrough takes special care to provide a quick but adequate sketch of the turbulent period of the late sixteenth century. A good place for the beginning student to start.

Parker, Tom. *Proportional Form in the Sonnets of the Sidney Circle: Loving in Truth*. Oxford: Clarendon Press, and New York: Oxford University Press, 1998. Sir Philip Sidney's "Astrophil and Stella" initiated the vogue for sonnet sequences in the 1590s , and Parker examines its purpose. Focusing on the sonnet sequences of Philip and Robert Sidney, Fulke Frevill, Giordano Bruno, Mary Worth, Henry Constable, Barnabe Barnes, and Michael Drayton, this book reveals a previously unrecognized pattern in their arrangements that ties these most popular hymns of love to broader cosmological concerns.

Sidney, Sir Philip. *The Poems of Sir Philip Sidney*. Edited by William A. Ringler, Jr. Oxford: Clarendon Press, 1962. Since Sidney is best known today for his sonnets, a thorough study of him must include *Astrophel and Stella*. This edition is textually impeccable, and contains a fine introduction useful to literary and nonliterary readers alike.

———. *Selected Prose and Poetry*. Edited by Robert Kimbrough. New York: Holt Rinehart, 1969. A handy one-volume collection of Sidney's major writings, very helpful for those readers who want at least a sample of the *Arcadia* or *Defence of Poesie*. Kimbrough's introduction is useful in placing Sidney within the context of his times.

Woudhuysen, H.R. *Sir Philip and the Circulation of Manuscripts, 1558-1640*. Oxford: Clarendon Press, and New York: Oxford University Press, 1996. This is the first modern study of the production and circulation of manuscripts during the English Renaissance. Woudhuysen examines the relationship between manuscript and print, looks at people who lived by their pens, and surveys authorial and scribal manuscripts. In particular, he examines Sir Philip Sydney's works, discussing all of Sidney's important manuscripts, and seeking to assess Sidney's part in the circulation of his works and his role in the promotion of a scribal culture. A detailed examination of the manuscripts and early prints of his poems sheds new light on their composition, evolution, and dissemination, as well as on Sidney's friends and admirers.

Michael Witkoski

DIEGO DE SILOÉ

Born: c. 1495; near Burgos, Spain
Died: October 22, 1563; Granada, Spain
Areas of Achievement: Architecture and art
Contribution: Siloé ranks as one of Spain's greatest architects for his exquisite translations and combinations of Roman, Moorish, and High Renaissance Italian style into a Spanish idiom, most evident, despite his many other works, in the great Cathedral of Granada.

Early Life

While the artistic and intellectual achievements of fifteenth and sixteenth century Renaissance figures are often well documented, this is rarely true of their early lives. Of Diego de Siloé, it is known that about 1495 he was born in Old Castile in or near Burgos, Spain. Founded in the eighth century, Burgos had served as an important commercial center, as the seat of the monarch for many years, and more important for Siloé, as a town famed for its architects and architecture, all markedly influenced by northern Gothic styles and very little by those of Mediterranean origins.

Burgos was also the home of the wealthy and cultivated Bartholome Ordóñez, who, breaking with local tradition, between 1490 and 1500 studied with the great Florentine and Neapolitan sculptors and artists, absorbing the best of his Italian masters and becoming familiar with Michelangelo's work.

In Naples, Ordóñez befriended Diego, the son of Gil de Siloé. Apparently a migrant from Orléans, France, to Burgos, Gil had earned esteem in his adopted town as a specialist in late Gothic carving. Diego and Ordóñez collaborated to perfect their craftsmanship. Given his Catholic artistic convictions, Ordóñez, like Siloé, was a devotee of Michelangelo's Florentine style and a spiritual disciple of Donatello. Each man's influence upon the other was beneficial. Siloé's sculpture of *Saint George Slaying the Dragon* (c. 1514-1515) for the renowned Caraccioli Altar and his *Virgin and Child*, a relief for a chapel of the Naples Cathedral, amply demonstrate this stylistic affinity.

Returning to Burgos in 1519, Siloé immediately was selected by the cathedral to design an alabaster monument to a bishop. With restrained, High Renaissance, three-dimensional realism, the monument's face was made from the bishop's death mask and was soon recognized as the most convincing of Spain's integrated effigies, even exceeding similar works by Ordóñez. Only twenty-four years old, Siloé next designed a masterpiece in the Escalera Dorado's iron balustrade, with painted and gilded bas-reliefs, varied grotesques, and delightful nudes. Between 1523 and 1526, he collaborated on the Constable Chapel at Burgos Cathedral. There his mastery of polychrome wood sculpture, the *Presentation* in particular, as well as his *Pietà* at Saint Anne's Altar, represented the best of Renaissance elements, establishing him as Burgos' undisputed master of his field.

Such creativity led in 1528 to his completion of an unfinished church in Granada, marking it with traditional heraldic devices evocative of proud Spanish lineages and with heroic figures, both ancient and biblical. For a Granadan bishop he designed a monument of Almería marble, while in the late 1520's he carved for San Jeronimo the choir stalls and the prior's seat. In that same church, the bust of the Virgin and Child beneath a bust of God is comparable to the finest Italian Renaissance work of its genre.

Collectively, such commissions expressed the maturing characteristics of Siloé's youthful style: joyous and passionate yet restrained Catholicity; meticulous and imaginative execution; lively and gently rhythmic lines. With remarkable chasteness and clarity, Siloé combined the vestiges of Spanish Gothic with *mudéjar*, a style developed during the Moors' domination of Spain. These stylistic signatures, and his eclecticism, uniquely identified him with the best of High Renaissance art.

Life's Work

Siloé's crowning efforts were invested from approximately 1528 until the late 1530's in the design, erection, and embellishment of the great Cathedral of Granada. Siloé's role in the cathedral's origins for years divided architectural and art historians, blurring an accurate understanding of the cathedral's architectural evolution and a full appreciation of Siloé's contributions. Modern scholarship generally acknowledges that the credit for the cathedral belongs more to Siloé than to anyone else. He did employ the peripheral walls of the original foundations, but within that arc the foundations for the chevet (the apse or termination of the apse—that upper portion of a church, which usually consists of several smaller, secondary apses radiating from the main apse) were of Siloé's design. Moreover, the nave's proportions are solely attributable to him.

Contrary to allegations that he enclosed the cathedral's rotunda sanctuary by copying a fashion common in other Spanish churches, Siloé opened it not only to the transept but also to the ambulatory. Most such criticisms reflected efforts to place the cathedral's development entirely within the Spanish architectural tradition, while in fact, Siloé's experiences were broader. Because of his years of working in Italy, more of his inspiration and stylistic conceptions flowed from the Tuscan-Roman Italy of the High Renaissance than from northern Europe. Siloé, however, did not employ pure Italian Renaissance architecture in the vocabulary of the Cathedral of Granada. No Italian church featured a prototype of the rotunda of the Granada Cathedral. Granada's dome roofed a high, cylindrical shaft of space, opened by tunnels as its base. The normal Latin cross that characterized Italian churches was replaced by Siloé's siting the choir in the central aisle as well as by a cruciform arrangement of the nave around a central lantern. Unlike Italian architectural idioms, the Granadan dome did not dominate. Siloé's conjunction of a domed rotunda with a basilican nave was unprecedented in medieval Europe.

Though Siloé's design was always under the scrutiny of communal and church officials and though it was without traditional models, whether from the Gothic, *mudéjar*, or Italian Renaissance, Siloé's cathedral was very much a distinctive hybrid. It owes perhaps more to ancient Roman architecture and Vitruvius than to the modern Roman style, which he imitated in many other designs.

Siloé's combination of the mausoleum with the cathedral's ambulatory was also novel. Other Renaissance churches had been planned to include the mausoleum with ambulatory, but they were never constructed. Nor did earlier European models of the apse have such central openness as Siloé's did. The cathedral's huge rotunda rises from two stages of Corinthian columns with a Roman grandeur, but it is well proportioned to its space. Siloé made the chevet, the cathedral's spiritual center, the cynosure of his design.

As Siloé designed the cathedral, he planned to have more than one hundred windows and whitewashed walls to create a luminous interior; the church was to be capped by a lantern of glass located over the nave's central bay. Such a light-flooded interior comported fully with a general Renaissance ideal. Unfortunately, this effect was never achieved.

In 1559, Siloé carefully designed a floor plan in which each section of the pavement was to be distinguished from other units by different colors and patterns. This practice was as ancient as buildings in Pompeii and Herculaneum and was even relatively common in classical households. It remained spectacularly effective. Black-and-white marble squares were to cover the sanctuary; black marble would floor the transept; and white marble was to cover the ambulatory pavement. Siloé probably also sought to accentuate the central aisle with a cross of black marble within the white flooring of the square nave, emphasizing the cruciform shape dramatically.

The cathedral's upper structure was supported by multiple cruciform piers: Gothic vaults with well-proportioned Roman ribs rose from Roman piers. Construction of basilican churches during the Renaissance—structures consisting of naves and aisles with a clerestory and a large, high transept from which an apse projected—had presented previous architects with almost insurmountable problems. Siloé managed with his combination of ancient orders of columns with barrel vaults to resolve these problems with great ingenuity. No less ingenuity was demonstrated in his distinctive styling and decoration of the cathedral's four portals. A finishing touch, a twin-towered façade that was to rise above the roof, was never completed. Nevertheless, the Cathedral of Granada stands as one of Renaissance Europe's great processional churches.

Summary

The liberation of Spain following centuries of Moorish domination, along with the restoration of both secular and Christian authority, lent special inspiration to national religious celebration. This fact helps to explain the communal and religious support that drew Diego de Siloé and other artists, sculptors, and architects to Granada as well as to numerous other Spanish communities during the first sixty years of the sixteenth century. His association with Ordóñez in Italy and his collaboration with him and others in Spain as well as his many commissions filled a substantial catalog by the time he had reached his mid-twenties, establishing him as a master who seems to have been in constant demand.

Despite years of confusion and critical debate about his role in designing, building, and embellishing the Cathedral of Granada, modern scholarship appears to confirm that while he deserves less credit than once was accorded him on minor points, the great cathedral is nevertheless his premier achievement. Siloé ingeniously, joyously hybridized elements of Gothic, Moorish, and Renaissance architecture with the essentials of ancient Roman structures. Siloé's extraordinary, versatile talent produced what has since been exalted as a unique architectural-artistic monument. Principal elements of its design and construction reached across to Spain's overseas empire and cultural enclaves in the sixteenth and seventeenth centuries.

Bibliography

Byne, Arthur, and Mildred Stapley. *Spanish Architecture in the Sixteenth Century.* New York and London: Putnam, 1917. An informative work. Though somewhat technical, the writing is clear and sufficiently authoritative to inform lay readers. It has good photographs, schematics, and plates. There are notes, a bibliography, and an index.

Hamlin, Talbot. *Architecture Through the Ages.* New York: Putnam, 1940. A well-written, richly illustrated survey for the lay reader. Superb photographs and numerous schematic drawings. Possesses an extensive, useful index.

Kubler, George, and Martin Soria. *Art and Architecture in Spain and Portugal and Their American Dominions, 1500 to 1800.* London and Baltimore: Penguin, 1959. This authoritative and ambitious work is superb for an understanding of Siloé's achievements. The writing is scholarly and somewhat uncompromising, but there are extensive chapter notes and scores of excellent photographs, schematics, and plates. Also includes a superb index.

Rosenthal, Earl. *The Cathedral of Granada: A Study in the Spanish Renaissance.* Princeton, N.J.: Princeton University Press, 1961. This is perhaps the definitive work on the cathedral. Covers all that is known about Siloé, his colleagues, the debates about the evolution of the cathedral, its technical construction, its setting, and its meaning. The terminology is scholarly, but the work is immensely informative. There are hundreds of photographs, illustrations, schematics, and plates. Contains a lengthy appendix, a very extensive bibliography, and an excellent index.

———. "Changing Interpretations of the Renaissance in Art History." In *The Renaissance: A Reconsideration of Theories and Interpretations of the Age*, edited by Tinsley Helton. Madison: University of Wisconsin Press, 1961. Rosenthal is a preeminent authority on Spanish Renaissance architecture, particularly on Ordóñez, Siloé, and the Cathedral of Granada. Essential reading for an understanding of Siloé. The book has plates, notes, and a useful index.

Clifton K. Yearley

HERNANDO DE SOTO

Born: c. 1496; Jérez de los Caballeros?, Spain
Died: May 21, 1542; near modern Ferriday, Louisiana
Areas of Achievement: Exploration and conquest
Contribution: After playing a prominent role in the conquest of Nicaragua and Peru, de Soto led the 1539-1542 expedition which explored what became the southeastern United States and discovered the Mississippi River.

Early Life

Hernando de Soto was born around 1496, probably in Jérez de los Caballeros in southwestern Spain. He was the second son of Francisco Méndez de Soto and Leonor Arias Tinoco (the proper family name is Soto but the English-speaking world calls him de Soto). The family was lower nobility, and Hernando received some education, although he was always by temperament a soldier and adventurer.

De Soto could expect to inherit little from his father's small estate and thus sailed to Central America in 1513-1514 with Pedro Arias Dávila (called Pedrarias), the new governor of Panama. Pedrarias allowed his followers to ravage Central America as long as they respected his authority. In these lawless conditions, de Soto flourished. Above average in height, bearded, and darkly handsome, he was vigorous, brave, and aggressive, always in the vanguard. His spoils in land and Indian workers made him wealthy.

By 1517, de Soto was a captain. He soon formed a partnership with Hernán Ponce de León and Francisco Campañón to share equally in the booty which fortune might bring them. They helped conquer Nicaragua in 1524. Campañón died in 1527, but de Soto and Ponce de León stayed on in Nicaragua. De Soto served a year as magistrate of León, although temperamentally unsuited to administration. He also became ambitious for his own governorship, but Pedrarias blocked those aspirations in Nicaragua.

Life's Work

In 1530, de Soto agreed to join forces with Francisco Pizarro in the conquest of Peru. When he met Pizarro at Puná Island in late 1531, de Soto had two ships, one hundred men, and some horses. He expected to be Pizarro's second in command and to receive an independent governorship. Pizarro gave de Soto charge of the vanguard. On a scouting foray inland to Cajas, de Soto seized several hundred Indian women and turned them over to his female-starved men. The Spaniards also learned at Cajas that the Inca empire had been torn apart by a great civil war and that Atahualpa, leader of the victorious faction, was encamped with his army at Cajamarca not too far away.

When the Spaniards arrived at Cajamarca, Pizarro sent de Soto with a small detachment to greet Atahualpa. A great horseman, de Soto tried unsuccessfully to frighten the emperor, who had never seen a horse before, by riding right up to him: Atahualpa accepted Pizarro's invitation to visit the Spaniards in Cajamarca the next day. Once he was inside the city walls, they took him captive. While a hostage, Atahualpa became close to de Soto and gave him valuable gifts. De Soto was on a scouting expedition when Pizarro executed Atahualpa. Upon his return, de Soto criticized the execution, arguing that Atahualpa should have been sent to Spain as a prisoner rather than killed. Always punctilious about keeping bargains, de Soto was also upset that Pizarro had killed the emperor after Atahualpa had filled rooms with gold and silver, as his agreed-upon ransom.

On the march from Cajamarca to the Inca capital, Cuzco, during the second half of 1533, de Soto again led the vanguard. As they neared Cuzco, he disregarded orders and rushed ahead with his small force to claim credit for occupying the city. The Indians ambushed his party at Vilcaconga, however, and only the timely arrival of reinforcements saved him. Pizarro appointed de Soto lieutenant governor of Cuzco in 1534 but replaced him by that year's end. Convinced that Pizarro would never give him an independent command in Peru, de Soto headed for Spain. He left behind Leonor Curuilloi, an Inca princess and his mistress, and their daughter Leonor. Ponce de León came from Nicaragua to manage de Soto's property.

In Spain by 1536, de Soto had 100,000 pesos with him, a reputation as a great conqueror and explorer, and a hunger to lead a new expedition. He petitioned the king. On April 20, 1537, Charles V made him governor and captain general of Cuba and Florida and gave him authority to explore and conquer the New Land at his own expense. Álvar Núñez Cabeza de Vaca, a survivor of the disastrous Panfilo de Narváez expedition to Florida, had come to Spain with tales of great riches in the New

Land. De Soto tried but failed to persuade him to join the expedition. Hundreds of young adventurers rushed to enlist, however, assuming that Florida would make them rich and famous. His wife, Doña Isabel de Bobadilla (Pedrarias' daughter, whom he had married in 1536), and about seven hundred carefully chosen soldiers of fortune sailed with him to Cuba in 1538.

De Soto spent a year in Cuba to train his men and gather provisions. The expedition departed for Florida in May, 1539, with de Soto's wife remaining behind to govern Cuba. It landed at Espiritu Santo (Tampa) Bay on May 30. At the outset, de Soto discovered Juan Ortiz, a survivor of the Narváez expedition who had lived with the Indians for twelve years. Ortiz became de Soto's interpreter.

De Soto had made his fortune in Central America and Peru by plundering the Indians. He intended to do the same in Florida. When the expedition came to an Indian settlement, de Soto took the chief hostage so that the Indians would serve the Spaniards while they ravaged the village. When the expedition was ready to move on, de Soto forced the hostage chieftain to provide porters (he took neck irons and chains to Florida with this aim in mind). De Soto released the porters and chief at the next village, where new hostages where seized. Those who resisted were mutilated, burned alive, or thrown to the dogs.

The Spaniards wandered through what later became Florida, Georgia, South Carolina, North Carolina, Tennessee, Alabama, Mississippi, Arkansas, Louisiana, and Texas. De Soto knew nothing of the land, nor did he have a destination in mind. He simply assumed that the Indians of the New Land would have riches to plunder. The expedition proceeded north from Tampa Bay and soon exhausted its supplies. From then on, the explorers lived off the land and Indian agriculture, plus a herd of swine which de Soto had brought in the fleet. Turning west, they reached the rich agricultural lands of the Apalachees in the Florida panhandle and stayed from October to March, 1540.

Then they marched northeast toward Cofitachequi, on the Savannah River near what became Augusta, Georgia. Their porters had died during the winter, and the Apalachees had run away before they could be enslaved. Thus, the Spaniards had to carry their own food and equipment. At Cofitachequi, they found large quantities of freshwater pearls, and de Soto himself obtained a chestful after plundering the village and burial grounds. Taking the queen hostage and thus provided with porters, de Soto headed northwest through Cherokee land in the Carolina piedmont and then turned west toward the Tennessee River. The Spanish learned about tribes rich in gold somewhere farther on but could never find them. De Soto cared nothing about mining; only plunder interested him.

In July, 1540, de Soto marched south, having learned of a rich people called Coosa (Creek territory). They were moving through Alabama, toward Mobile Bay. Disappointed by Coosa, they continued southwest and came to the Mabilas (Choctaws). At Mabila, the Indians revolted, killed twenty-two Spaniards, and burned much of the equipment, including de Soto's pearls. By then, more than one hundred of the men who had started with de Soto at Tampa Bay were dead. Although not too far north of Mobile Bay, de Soto refused to push on to the coast, fearful that his men would desert. Instead, he turned north again and occupied a Chickasaw village for winter quarters. After enduring the Spaniards for several months, the Chickasaws revolted on March 4, 1541. They set fire to the village and killed a dozen Spaniards, fifty horses, and many of the pigs. The Spanish escaped annihilation only because a sudden storm prevented the Indians from immediately renewing their attack.

Pushing westward, de Soto discovered the Rio Grande (Mississippi) on May 8, 1541, built barges, and crossed the mighty river on June 18 a little above its junction with the Arkansas. The Spaniards wandered for two months through central Arkansas. De Soto sent a scouting party to the Ozarks after rumors of gold there. They spent the severe winter of 1541-1542 at Utiangue in south-central Arkansas.

Battered and discouraged, the expedition left Utiangue on March 6, 1542, and followed the Ouachita River south through Louisiana to the Mississippi. De Soto fell ill with a fever. Realizing that his end was near, he named Luis de Moscoso, another veteran of Peru, to succeed him. The great explorer died on May 21, 1542, to the relief of those who wanted to abandon the quest. His men sank his body in the Mississippi to hide it from the Indians.

The men decided to march overland to Mexico and traveled several hundred miles into Texas. After four months and no sign of Mexico, they turned back. They spent their last winter near the Mississippi at Aminoya (northwest of Natchez). In the spring of 1543, they built barges, and, floating down the river to the Gulf of Mexico in July, they then sailed west. Clad in rags and animal skins when they arrived in Mexico in September, 1543, about one third survived of those who had started at Tampa Bay.

Summary

De Soto evokes conflicting impressions. On the one hand, he was certainly one of the bravest Spaniards of his time. He was gallant and courageous, the epitome of the explorer and conquistador. On any expedition, he was always in the vanguard; in any battle, he was in the front ranks. He amassed a huge fortune in Nicaragua and Peru, and he failed to do so in North America only because there were no rich Indian cities to plunder. Yet adventure, danger, and the unknown seemed to attract him more than riches. His expedition was extremely well organized. He recruited not only soldiers but also artisans, who could build boats and bridges. He raised a herd of pigs on the march so that the expedition would have meat later. Despite rugged terrain and many attacks from fierce Indians, he held the expedition together.

On the other hand, de Soto was a plunderer, not a builder. His expedition made no effort to settle or colonize; nor did it even attempt to exploit the natural resources of the region. De Soto had learned too well the lessons under Pedrarias, and the experiences in Peru reinforced them. Perhaps he took less delight in butchery than some Spaniards, but he was ready to torture and kill in his quest for the riches of Florida. Indians' lives were worth little to him. Although he considered Christianization of the Indians one of his expedition's responsibilities, he did little to achieve it. Moreover, he was too stubborn and proud to end the foray despite its obvious failure to find the booty for which the Spaniards hunted.

The Spanish atrocities should not, however, obscure the achievements of the expedition. It was the first major European penetration of the North American interior and left valuable information about the Indians and geography of the region. De Soto and his men left a legacy of courage, ambition, and perseverance rarely equaled as they opened the region to European expansion. The great river they discovered eventually proved to be a natural treasure more valuable than the booty de Soto sought.

Bibliography

Bourne, Edward Gaylord, ed. *Narratives of the Career of Hernando de Soto*. 2 vols. New York: Allerton, 1904; London; Nutt, 1905. Contains English translations of the three most important chronicles of de Soto's expedition by Luis Hernández de Biedma, factor of the expedition, Rodrigo Ranjel, de Soto's secretary, and an unidentified Portuguese gentleman from Elva.

Garcilaso de la Vega, The Inca. *The Florida of the Inca*. Translated and edited by John Grier Varner and Jeannette Johnson Varner. Austin: University of Texas Press, 1951. The most famous of the four early chronicles of de Soto's expedition. Unlike the others, it was not written by an eyewitness and is thus more problematical.

Hemming, John. *The Conquest of the Incas*. London: Macmillan, and New York: Harcourt Brace, 1970. An excellent, well-written account of the conquest of Peru, with information about de Soto's role in it.

Maynard, Theodore. *De Soto and the Conquistadores*. London and New York: Longman, 1930. The best biography of de Soto, although marred by inaccuracies and omissions.

Ober, Frederick A. *Ferdinand de Soto and the Invasion of Florida*. New York and London: Harper, 1906. Based extensively on Garcilaso's narrative and aimed primarily at younger readers.

Sauer, Carl Ortwin. *Sixteenth Century North America: The Land and the People as Seen by the Europeans*. Berkeley: University of California Press, 1971. Contains a chapter on de Soto's expedition by the leading historical geographer of sixteenth century North America. Critical of de Soto's motives and behavior.

United States de Soto Expedition Commission. *Final Report of the United States De Soto Expedition Commission*. Washington, D.C.: Government Printing Office, 1939. A scholarly, definitive study of the route followed by the de Soto expedition.

Kendall W. Brown

EDMUND SPENSER

Born: c. 1552; London, England
Died: January 13, 1599; London, England
Area of Achievement: Literature
Contribution: Reflecting both Renaissance and Reformation ideals in his Christian humanism, Spenser incorporated classical, Continental, and native English poetic traditions to create in his epic *The Faerie Queene*, the quintessential statement of Elizabethan national and moral consciousness.

Early Life

Little is known about Edmund Spenser's life. He was born about 1552, one of the three children of Elizabeth and John Spenser (a Lancashire gentleman by birth who had settled in London and become a free journeyman of the Merchant Taylors' Company). The family's income must have been limited, because a wealthy Lancashire family assisted with Edmund's education. At the Merchant Taylors' School from 1561-1569, he was influenced by the famous humanist educator Richard Mulcaster, who imparted to Spenser the notion that a man must use his learning in the service of the public good (usually as a courtier advising his prince). During this period, Spenser demonstrated his Reformation sympathies by contributing several verse translations to *A Theater for Worldlings* (1569), a strongly anti-Catholic work.

Spenser matriculated at Pembroke Hall, Cambridge University, in 1569 as a "sizar," or poor scholar; there he continued his study of the Greek and Latin classics and contemporary French and Italian literature. Spenser was also fascinated by the mystical elements in Plato and the writings of the Italian Neoplatonists Pietro Bembo and Marsilio Ficino. Spenser's Neoplatonism was always blended with staunch Protestantism, which was strengthened by Cambridge's Puritan environment. While at Cambridge, Spenser formed a friendship with Gabriel Harvey, a university don; the two shared a concern with poetic theory and hoped for a revival of English verse.

After receiving his B.A. in 1573 and his M.A. in 1576, Spenser, in true Renaissance fashion, became a man of action as well as of letters. He served as secretary to John Young, Bishop of Rochester, and was later employed by Robert Dudley, the Earl of Leicester, whose nephew Sir Philip Sidney was well known for his promotion of English poetry (his famous *Defence of Poesie* was published posthumously in 1595).

It is to Sidney that Spenser's first major work, *The Shepheardes Calender* (1579), is dedicated. Heralding a new movement in English verse, *The Shepheardes Calender* consists of twelve pastoral eclogues, one for each month. The classical eclogue records shepherds' songs and conversations about their simple lives. Vergil had established the form as a preparation for the greater genre of epic, dealing with war instead of love and with the founding of a great civilization. Spenser thus identified himself as England's epic poet, who would sing the praises of the nation and its sovereign: In the April Eclogue, Colin Clout (Spenser's shepherd persona) sings the beauties of the shepherdess Elisa (Elizabeth I).

Moreover, Colin Clout is a shepherd (*pastor* in Latin) in the spiritual sense; the eclogues can be read as a satiric critique of contemporary ecclesiastical practices, and the poet-shepherd, like Moses and Christ, is also a prophet. Spenser thus established himself within both classical and Christian contexts. He also proclaimed himself truly English by deliberately using archaic language, which provides a rustic "native English" tone and, more important, identifies Spenser as the heir of Geoffrey Chaucer. Spenser was eminently qualified for this role: *The Shepheardes Calender* displays both his humanist learning and his technical skill (he experimented with thirteen different meters in the work). In an age that encouraged self-fashioning, Spenser firmly established himself as Elizabeth's "poet laureate."

Life's Work

In 1580, Spenser was appointed secretary to Lord Grey of Wilton, the Lord Deputy of Ireland; with the exception of a few visits to England, Spenser lived the rest of his life in Ireland, and his love of the Irish countryside is evident in his poetry. In 1588, Spenser was granted a three-thousand-acre estate, Kilcolman, between Limerick and Cork in Munster. There, while serving in various official capacities, he practiced his poetic craft.

Most Elizabethan poets engaged in the fashionable practice of sonnet writing, and Spenser was no exception: His sonnet sequence *Amoretti* was published in 1595. Always the innovator who transformed his models, Spenser combined the Italian

and English sonnet forms to create the Spenserian sonnet: three linked quatrains and a couplet, rhyming *ababbcbccdcdee*. Spenser also imbued the Petrarchan sonnet with his own Christian, Neoplatonic sensibility. Sonnet 79, for example, celebrates the "true beautie" of his mistress, which is not physical but spiritual and proceeds from God, the source of beauty. It is thus "free from frayle corruption." The sequence's structure is loosely based on the Christian liturgical cycle (reflecting the concern with time's movement introduced in *The Shepheardes Calender*).

Spenser had married Elizabeth Boyle in 1594; by publishing his *Epithalamion* (a poem celebrating the wedding day) at the conclusion of the *Amoretti* in 1595, he reverses the Petrarchan tradition: His courtship, unlike the never-ending frustrated yearning of Petrarchan lovers, would be consummated in a fruitful marriage. The *Epithalamion* is one of Spenser's most beautiful and intricate works. Typically eclectic, it combines the Italian *canzone* form with numerous allusions to classical mythology and descriptive details drawn from the Irish countryside. The poem is numerologically significant in that it contains twenty-four stanzas and 365 long lines, symbolizing not only the wedding day and night but also the year and ultimately man's entire life in its movement from birth through death to heaven. Highly formal and intensely personal, the poem creates an "endlesse moniment" to love and the power of poetry.

Spenser's syncretism culminated in his greatest work, *The Faerie Queene*. The first three books were published in 1590, with an introductory letter to Sir Walter Raleigh; books I-VI were published in 1596, and books I-VI, combined with the *Cantos of Mutabilitie*, presumably fragments from an unfinished seventh book, were published in 1609. Fortunately, Spenser's letter to Raleigh provides readers with clues to interpret his "continued Allegory, or dark conceit." The work's purpose, according to Spenser, is "to fashion a gentleman or noble person in vertuous and gentle discipline." *The Faerie Queene* thus functions as a courtesy or conduct book used to train a perfect courtier. Each of the six books is devoted to the exploits of a knight who represents a particular virtue: holiness, temperance, chastity, friendship, justice, and courtesy.

In writing this courtesy book, Spenser drew on several literary sources: the classical epics of Homer and Vergil (the poem began *in medias res* with the well-known line, "A Gentle Knight was pricking on the plaine. . . ."); the medieval tradition of allegory; the "matter of Britain," or Arthurian legend; sixteenth century Italian epic romance (such as Ludovico Ariosto's *Orlando Furioso*, 1532, and Torquato Tasso's *Gerusalemme Liberata*, 1581); and the Bible. The use of allegory was typical of Elizabethan thought, given the fourfold method of biblical exegesis inherited from the medieval period and the common habit of allegorizing classical authors such as Homer, Vergil, and Ovid. *The Faerie Queene* operates on several allegorical levels, though not always simultaneously. Narrative events can be interpreted literally, historically (the character Sir Calidore, for example, was modeled on Sir Philip Sidney), morally, or theologically.

The work's verse form, the Spenserian stanza (eight lines of iambic pentameter followed by an Alexandrine, rhyming *ababbcbcc*), is both unique and challenging. The demanding rhyme scheme gives Spenser an opportunity to show off the poetic suppleness of vernacular English, as well as establish a stanzaic unity of thought. Simultaneously active and static, the stanza continues the narrative flow of events (and Spenser uses inversion to create rhythmical effects that imitate the canter of a horse or the seductive charm of an enchantress) while also standing as a discrete unit. In this sense, the stanza operates as a stationary picture or emblem, which the Alexandrine at its end explains or summarizes. The reader is thus forced to be active and contemplative, involved and detached, simultaneously.

Read as the great English epic of the Elizabethan age, *The Faerie Queene* is an intensely nationalistic poem, celebrating the person of Gloriana, the fairy queen (Elizabeth I). The poem is not, however, merely an effusive compliment which Spenser wrote to gain patronage; it was intended to reflect Elizabethan England in its idealized form, so that in reading or gazing into the textual mirror and imitating the vision, the sovereign, her courtiers, and ultimately the country would be transformed. Spenser re-created England's past, present, and future in an intricate overlapping of plot and life; he unites the fairy-tale world—replete with knights, ladies, magicians, castles, giants, and dragons—with the temptations and emotions of everyday experience.

Except for an annual pension of fifty pounds granted in 1591, Spenser was not rewarded by his queen for singing England's praises. When Kilcolman was sacked in 1598 by Irish forces rebelling against English domination, Spenser and his wife fled to London. Spenser died in 1599 in forlorn and diminished, if not penurious, circumstances and was buried, appropriately, near Geoffrey Chaucer in what is now known as the poets' corner of Westminster Abbey. Always fascinated by time's cyclical ability to move forward and yet stay the same, Spenser ended his life very much as he began it.

Summary

Edmund Spenser was perhaps the most articulate spoksman for the values and attitudes of the Elizabethan age. His life reflects the dual Renaissance commitment to action and thought, and his works reflect the exuberant eclecticism of humanist learning. Manifesting the period's eagerness to discover new worlds, Spenser's imagination simply created them and, in so doing, forged a national identity and revitalized English prosody. His technical innovations attested the powers of the English language in an age which celebrated the vernacular. The Spenserian stanza was used by Percy Bysshe Shelley, John Keats, and George Gordon, Lord Byron. Spenser also profoundly influenced John Milton, who considered himself a descendant of Spenser as a Christian humanist poet-prophet to the English nation.

As the father of English pastoral, Spenser united classical and native traditions to celebrate a past, present, and future golden age. Concerned with the transience of life's beauty and the devastating effects of time, Spenser reflected the Elizabethan vogue for pleasurable, cultivated melancholy yet affirmed the permanence of Christian glory. His poetry exemplifies Elizabethan literary theory in its endeavor to teach and delight, but at the same time it possesses an unfading psychological relevance. *The Faerie Queene*'s episodic structure and its vast narrative scope, its portrayal of determined questing interrupted by moments of vision, directly reflect human experience. Though rooted unmistakably in the Elizabethan age, Spenser's poetry is, paradoxically, "eterne in mutabilitie."

Bibliography

Alpers, Paul J. *The Poetry of "The Faerie Queene."* Princeton, N.J.: Princeton University Press, 1967. Alpers' goal is to "bring *The Faerie Queene* into focus." He analyzes verse and narrative, emphasizing Spenser's manipulation of reader response; he also considers historical and iconographical sources and provides a detailed reading of books I and III.

Baker, David J. *Between Nations: Shakespeare, Spenser, Marvell, and the Question of Britain.* Stanford, Calif.: Stanford University Press, 1998. Fusing historiography with literary criticism, Baker's book produces an array of unexpected readings of early modern texts. Starting from the premise that England has never been able to emerge or define itself in isolation from its neighbors on the British Isles, this book places Renaissance England and its literature at a meeting of English, Irish, Scottish, and Welsh histories.

Frye, Northrop. "The Structure of Imagery in *The Faerie Queene*." *University of Toronto Quarterly* 30 (1961): 109-127. Frye focuses on imagery rather than allegory to demonstrate the work's unity and sees the six books as a unified structure. Private and public education are discussed as central themes.

Hamilton, A. C. *The Structure of Allegory in "The Faerie Queene."* Oxford: Clarendon Press, 1961. One of the foremost Spenser critics, Hamilton argues for reading the poem simultaneously on the literal and allegorical levels and shows how book I prefigures the remaining books. Hamilton has also edited an excellent annotated edition of *The Faerie Queene*, published by Longman.

Hankins, John Erskine. *Source and Meaning in Spenser's Allegory: A Study of "The Faerie Queene."* Oxford: Clarendon Press, 1971. As the title suggests, Hankins focuses on a possible source in a work by Francesco Piccolomini. Emphasizes internal allegory as *psychomachia*. An informative discussion of all six books follows his analysis of the poem's allegorical basis, method, quest, and landscape.

Highley, Christopher. *Shakespeare, Spenser, and the Crisis in Ireland.* Cambridge and New York: Cambridge University Press, 1997. Highley's book explores the most serious crisis the Elizabethan regime faced: its attempts to subdue and colonize the native Irish. Through a range of literary representations from Shakespeare and Spenser, and contemporaries such as John Hooker, John Derricke, George Peele, and Thomas Churchyard, he shows how these writers produced a complex discourse about Ireland that cannot be reduced to a simple ethnic opposition. Highley argues that the confrontation between an English imperial presence and a Gaelic 'other' was a profound factor in the definition of an English poetic self.

Lewis, C. S. *Spenser's Images of Life*. Edited by Alastair Fowler. Cambridge: Cambridge University Press, 1967. A brief 144 pages, the work expands Lewis' Cambridge lecture notes. Views *The Faerie Queene* as a series of masques, pageants, and emblems, which results in simple fairy-tale pleasure made sophisticated by polyphonic technique. Somewhat disjointed (Lewis died before completing the book) but delightfully written, it conveys a genuine love of Spenser.

MacCaffrey, Isabel G. "Allegory and Pastoral in *The Shepheardes Calender*." *English Literary History* 36 (1969): 88-109. Shows how *The Shepheardes Calender* prefigures the technique and theme of *The Faerie Queene* in its encyclopedic nature, concern with the nature of human life, and simultaneously linear and cyclical structures.

Nohrnberg, James. *The Analogy of "The Faerie Queene."* Princeton, N.J.: Princeton University Press, 1976; Guildford: Princeton University Press, 1977. An incredibly detailed commentary (791 pages) on Spenser's allegory, mythography, and sources. Citations not always accurate.

Woodhouse, A. S. P. "Nature and Grace in *The Faerie Queene*." *English Literary History* 16 (1949): 194-228. Analyzes major characters and key incidents in the light of grace's superiority to nature. Good comparison of books I and II.

Caroline McManus

SÜLEYMAN THE MAGNIFICENT

Born: 1494 or 1495; probably in Istanbul, Ottoman Empire

Died: September 5 or 6, 1566; near Sziget, Hungary

Areas of Achievement: Government, politics, and law

Contribution: Süleyman I was undoubtedly the best-known Ottoman Turkish sultan: He extended the domains of the Ottoman Empire eastward, establishing a long-lasting border between the Sunni Turks and the Shi'ite realm under the Safavid shahs. His reign marked a period of internal stability, primarily through an ordered system of laws.

Early Life

Süleyman I, tenth in the line of Ottoman Turkish sultans, was the son of Sultan Selim I (ruled 1512-1520) by his wife Aisha Sultan. Aisha Sultan was herself the daughter of a prestigious Islamic ruler, Menghli Giray, the head of the Black Sea Crimean khanate. Little is known about Süleyman's early education in the palace environment of Istanbul. The young prince received practical training, first as governor of the district, or *sancak*, of Kaffa, during the sultanate of his grandfather Bayezid II, and later, under Selim, as governor of the province of Manisa (ancient Lydia, in Asia Minor).

Possibly because Selim was such a dominant sultanic authority, his son's succession at the time of Selim's death seems to have come automatically, without the necessity of advance preparation to avert internal intrigues between rival pretenders. Once on the Ottoman throne, Süleyman proved that he was more than worthy of Selim's confidence in his administrative as well as his military capacities.

Life's Work

The Ottoman sultan whose reputation is symbolized by the Western epithet, "the Magnificent," carried a different title in Ottoman tradition. The nearly half-century rule of Süleyman (from 1520 to 1566) earned for him the Ottoman epithet *Qanuni*, or law giver. This honor resulted largely from the fact that he systematized imperial Turkish rule over diverse provinces conquered by his predecessors in Christian Europe and in the Arab Islamic zone. Süleyman's reign was also marked by repeatedly spectacular demonstrations of Turkish strength. Süleyman personally commanded thirteen major Ottoman military campaigns, ten against European adversaries and three in Asia against Islamic rivals.

Süleyman's reputation for military leadership began in the first two years of his reign, when he captured the city of Belgrade (1521) and the island fortress of Rhodes (1522). From then on, Ottoman armies would play an important role in the international game of influence between the French Valois king Francis I and the Austrian Habsburg emperor and Spanish king Charles V. The latter was a natural rival of Süleyman because the Habsburg and Ottoman empires were both tempted to expand claims over the territory of weaker Danubian neighbors.

First, at the battle of Mohács in 1526, when the Ottomans toppled the last medieval Hungarian dynasty, killing King Louis II, and again in the spectacular campaign of 1529, the future of Hungary was the object of Habsburg-Ottoman struggles. These ended, at least temporarily, when Süleyman laid siege to Vienna itself in September, 1529. After this extraordinary show of force, Süleyman was

able to ensure recognition of his protégé-king John Zápolya in Buda.

From the Danubian valley, the focus of Ottoman imperial pretensions spread to North Africa. Here again, despite Habsburg efforts to stop the sultan's expansionist diplomacy, Ottoman domination would become increasingly imminent in the 1530's. An important sign of Süleyman's intention to bring the North African areas into closer dependence on the Ottoman Empire was his appointment of Khayr ad-Dīn (known in the West as Barbarossa), perhaps the dominant renegade corsair leader along the North African coast, to the post of *kapudan pasha* (Ottoman high admiral) in 1533.

In 1534, Süleyman also succeeded in annexing Iraq to the empire—defeating the Safavid Persian shah's claims. From their southernmost bases in Iraq, the Ottoman navy could proceed to dominate the Persian Gulf, entering the Indian Ocean at the height of Süleyman's reign. Süleyman took great interest in the newly annexed Ottoman province of Iraq. He built an important mausoleum in Baghdad for Abu Hanifah, founder of the Hanifite school of Islamic law (the "official" school followed by the Ottomans). He also personally visited the most important Islamic shrines of Iraq, including the holy Shi'a sites of Nedjef and Karbala.

By the 1540's and 1550's, it was quite clear that, with the exception of the westernmost area of North Africa (the independent sultanate of Morocco), all major Arab zones of the eastern and southern Mediterranean would fall under the suzerainty of Süleyman or his immediate successors. Only the borders of the Danubian west and eastern Anatolia, where the struggle with the Safavid shah went on until the Treaty of Amasia in 1555, were still in question. It might have been possible to gain a comparable treaty with Süleyman's Habsburg rival, Emperor Ferdinand I, who had never abandoned hopes of dominating Hungary. Apparently Süleyman's Grand Vizier Rustem (who was also his son-in-law) made this impossible until his death in 1561. No sooner had Süleyman signed a treaty (1561) than, with the advent of a new Habsburg monarch (Emperor Maximilian), new hostilities erupted.

The last five years of Süleyman's long reign seemed to be marked with signs of both personal and political decline. The death of his wife Khurram demoralized the sultan. Two of his sons, Princes Bayezid and Selim, began a bitter rivalry. The tragic outcome of this split, which ended with the execution of Bayezid, not only shook the sultanic family itself but also affected the interests of contending political groups who could no longer be certain how to organize support for the future sultan, Selim II. Nevertheless, Süleyman's visible strength was enhanced by his choice of a new grand vizier, Mehmed Sokollu. Süleyman accompanied his armies, now virtually under Sokollu's command, one more time, to the Hungarian battlefield of Szigetköz. Although the Ottomans were successful in this confrontation with their perennial Christian enemies, Süleyman died during the campaign, presumably without knowledge of his army's victory.

Summary

The reign of Süleyman the Magnificent can be considered representative of the golden age of the Ottoman Empire, which ran roughly from 1450 to about 1600: The empire at that time was politically, militarily, and culturally strong. Probably the outstanding example of the strength of Ottoman political and military organization was the Janissary (literally, new army) corps. Although this military corps had arisen at least a century before Süleyman's sultanate, it seems to have reached the zenith of its efficiency in the first half of the sixteenth century. What the Janissaries represented militarily was characteristic of the entire structure of Ottoman rule under Süleyman: absolute loyalty and individual subservience to the sultan.

Süleyman was careful to maintain and control the Ottoman institution that could provide for such a system of unquestionable loyalty; this was the *devshirme*, or levy of non-Turkish conscripts, who were mainly Christian youths "contributed" by subjects populations in the Balkan zone or raided areas beyond Ottoman frontiers. Such conscripts, called *kapi kullar* (slaves of the imperial gate), were brought into the special schools of Istanbul and given special training to prepare them for very select service, either as military elites or bureaucratic officials—such high-ranking officers as the grand vizier could be drawn from these men. Since their sole source of sponsorship was the palace at Istanbul, such elites could be sent to any area of the empire at the sultan's will.

In Süleyman's time, the practical results of such centralization were still quite visible: There were very few acts of insubordination, either within the formal imperial administration or on the part of provincial populations under Ottoman rule. In this respect, Ottoman governing institutions under Süleyman represented a considerably more efficient substructure for monarchical authority than could be found anywhere else, either in Europe or in the immediately adjacent areas of western Asia under the Ottomans' neighbors, the Safavid shahs of Iran. The unquestioned authority of the sultanate probably contributed to other symbols of self-assurance in the Ottoman Empire under Süleyman I. There are suggestions, in the form of the great *ganunnahmes*, or "books of law" prepared under the sultan's supervision for each major province of the empire, of a pervading sense of social and economic order that would have affected not only elite but also all classes of governed populations, whether Christian, Jewish, or Islamic. One may still observe, in the splendid architectural monuments (especially mosques and schools, or *medreses*) erected by Süleyman's chief architect, Sinan Pasha, models of structural support and harmony which, in purely aesthetic terms, reflected the assurance of imperial supremacy.

Bibliography

Fisher, Sydney N. *The Middle East: A History.* 5th ed. New York: McGraw-Hill, 1897. Chapter 17 of this well-known general history is entitled "The Ottoman Empire as a World Power." In addition to providing a comprehensive review of the major events of Süleyman's reign, Fisher covers a number of cultural topics including Ottoman literature and architecture of the period.

Gibb, H. A. R., and Harold Bowen. *Islamic Society and the West: A Study of the Impact of Western Civilization on Moslem Culture in the Near East.* Vol. 1, *Islamic Society in the Eighteenth Century.* London: Oxford University Press, 1950; New York: Oxford University Press, 1957. Although the joint authors of this work dedicate the majority of their analysis to Islamic society in the eighteenth century, chapters 2 and 3 ("Caliphate and Sultanate" and "The Ruling Institution") provide essential details of the internal organization of the Ottoman Empire in the age of Süleyman I. These include discussions of the army and central administration, both originally recruited by means of the *devshirme* system.

Hodgson, Marshall G. S. *The Venture of Islam: Conscience and History in a World Civilization.* Vol. 2, *The Gunpowder Empires and Modern Times.* Chicago: University of Chicago Press, 1974. Chapter 3 of this volume is entitled "The Ottoman Empire: *Shari'ah*—Military Alliance, 1517-1718." In this section dealing with the strongest period of Ottoman history, the author provides an analytical framework for comparing prototypes of government and society in several geographical areas of Islamic civilization. The Ottoman model represented by Süleyman is compared with that of the Safavid shahs in Iran and the "Indo-Timuri" (Mughal) empire of India.

Houghteling, Lawrence. "Suleyman the Magnificent." *Calliope* 6 (January/February, 1996): 9. The author examines the fortune of young Suleyman on becoming Sultan in 1520 and provides personal background on his life.

Inalcik, Halil. "The Heyday and Decline of the Ottoman Empire." In *The Further Islamic Lands, Islamic Society and Civilizations.* Vol. 2 in *The Cambridge History of Islam*, edited by P. M. Holt, Ann K. S. Lambton, and Bernard Lewis. Cambridge: Cambridge University Press, 1970; New York: Cambridge University Press, 1978. This is the most concise history of the Ottoman Empire in the age of Süleyman. Like most other political histories dealing with the reign of Süleyman, it turns very quickly to a discussion of decline under his immediate successors, particularly under Selim.

Lybyer, Albert H. *The Government of the Ottoman Empire in the Time of Suleiman the Magnificent.* Cambridge, Mass.: Harvard University Press, 1913. This is one of the earliest attempts by a Western historian to provide a comprehensive history of Süleyman's reign. Nevertheless it provides basic facts and the beginnings of an analytical framework for discussing the structures of the Ottoman "ruling institution," a term and concept taken over and developed in much greater detail by H. A. R. Gibb and Harold Bowen in the 1950's.

Byron D. Cannon

TORQUATO TASSO

Born: March 11, 1544; Sorrento, Kingdom of Naples
Died: April 25, 1595; Rome
Area of Achievement: Literature
Contribution: Tasso—considered to be one of the greatest Italian poets—reflects the crisis of his age, and his writings seek to reconcile classical ideals with the renewed religious fervor arising from the Counter-Reformation. In this attempt to synthesize the vision of perfection and human dignity of the classics with Christian spiritual values lies the significance of his major works.

Early Life

Torquato Tasso was born in the coastal village of Sorrento, just south of Naples. His mother came from a noble Neapolitan family, while his father, originally from the northern town of Bergamo, was a diplomat and an accomplished man of letters who wrote a well-known chivalric poem entitled *Amadigi* in 1560. Although Tasso's first years were spent in the serene and idyllic atmosphere of the Mediterranean Sea, they were soon disturbed by a sudden and unexpected turbulence: His father, caught in the political misfortunes of his protector, the Prince of Salerno, was forced into exile, and all of his goods were confiscated. At the age of ten, Tasso was taken from the Jesuit school in Naples, where for two years he had studied Latin and Greek and had received a thorough religious training, and sent to Rome to be with his father. Thus began the agitated and roaming existence that was to mark his entire life, first by necessity and later as a tormented vocation. This abrupt separation from his mother, whom he was never to see again (she died prematurely a year later in 1556), left in the young Tasso an indelible impression that was to influence his lyrical production and reinforce his pessimistic view of the human condition. In 1557, he was at the court of Urbino; his father had just entered in the service of the duke, who was aware of Torquato's penchant for poetry and wanted the precocious young man to be a study companion to his own son. It was at Urbino that Torquato first came into contact with the splendid yet treacherous courtly environment that was to influence his life and writings deeply. At the age of fifteen, he relocated to Venice, and it was there, where the presence of the Turks was most felt and feared, that he began a rough draft of his famous epic poem on the First Crusade. The next five years were spent studying at the University of Padua, first law, according to his father's wishes, and then his own chosen fields of philosophy and letters. There, he met and frequented one of the most celebrated literary figures of the Renaissance, Sperone Speroni, and other famous scholars who stirred in him the ardent desire for lyrical expression.

At Padua, Tasso joined the Accademia degli Eterei and in 1562 published a chivalric poem in octaves, *Rinaldo* (English translation, 1792). This is a significant work in that it contains many of the themes that were to characterize his later production: the thirst for glory, adventure, and love and the yearning for chivalric ideals. It was during this time that Tasso's first doubts on religious matters surfaced—a lifelong spiritual struggle that would culminate in his later years in a complete revision of his famous epic, using orthodox religious teachings, and a dedication of the final years of his life to religious didactic works. Finally, it was at Padua that his love for Lucrezia Bendidio blossomed, and it was to her that many of his love poems would be dedicated.

Life's Work

In 1565, Tasso entered the service of Cardinal Luigi d'Este at the court of Ferrara and began the happiest and most fruitful period of his career; for the next ten years, he lived the ideal life of the man of letters for which he had longed. In 1567, he was given a literary stipend by Duke Alfonso II, and in this serene and refined courtly environment he was able to cultivate his genius and produce his most important works. Ferrara had been the home of the famous Renaissance poet, Ludovico Ariosto, and this for Tasso was both a source of inspiration and a spur to competition. Although the court of Ferrara was flourishing only in appearance and in reality was following Italy toward its political downfall, Tasso saw in its pomp and false grandeur the last vestiges of the ideals of the Renaissance, and he felt compelled to sing its praises.

Even though he composed many of his most beautiful poems during this period, dedicated to the ladies of the court, it was with the *Aminta* (1573; English translation, 1591) that Tasso established his reputation as a poet and playwright. This pastoral drama in five acts was first represented in the presence of Alfonso II on the island of Belvedere, the lovely summer residence of the Estensi, and was an immediate success. In his depiction of the world of the classical shepherd-poets, so rich in literary tradition, Tasso projected his ideals of a genteel and serene existence devoid in its primordial innocence of the sense of evil and sin. It also becomes for the poet an allegory of courtly life seen as a point of encounter for poets, sensitive souls, and fervent lovers. Although there are elements of tragedy in *Aminta*, all negativism is dissolved in the atmosphere of myth in which the drama evolves, and Tasso arrives at a perfect Renaissance unity of tone, rhythm, and style.

Only two years later, Tasso completed his most famous work and the one that established his poetic immortality, *Gerusalemme liberata* (1581; *Jerusalem Delivered*, 1600). The poem is divided into twenty cantos, in octaves, and follows the traditional hendecasyllabic scheme. While the subject matter is the historical conquest of Jerusalem by the First Crusade and therefore conforms to the rules of the epic, which Tasso had intended to follow as he states in *Discorsi del poema eroico* (1594; *Discourses on the Heroic Poem*, 1973), within the narration there are numerous secondary episodes that betray the poet's ambivalent feelings. It is in *Jerusalem Delivered* that the crisis of the Counter-Reformation is most strongly reflected. It is clear, especially in the love stories of Erminia, Clorinda, and Tancredi, that Tasso tries to recuperate the ideals of the Renaissance. Yet in the depiction of the struggle between good and evil, in the veiled sensuality and the sense of guilt found in the description of the garden of Armida, and in the tragic deaths of Solimano and Clorinda, a melancholy and pessimistic mood becomes apparent that reflects the crisis of the Baroque era.

Technically, *Jerusalem Delivered* tries to solve the debate concerning the relative merits of the chivalric and epic traditions. To the multiform variety of Ludovico Ariosto's chivalric poem, Tasso opposes the Aristotelian unity of action, and to the use of classical mythology he opposes the Christian supernatural. Yet the true value of the work lies in its depiction of the human condition; the main characters appear to be victims of a cruel fate that places them in utter solitude and renders them incapable of appeasing their desires. Even the surroundings are arid and desolate and seem to symbolize mankind's frailty and impotence.

This sense of tragic isolation was also felt in Tasso's personal experiences. Immediately after the completion of the epic, Tasso was haunted by religious scruples and personal self-doubt. On a literary plane, he revised the work along orthodox lines, culminating in the appearance of *Gerusalemme conquistata* (1593; *Jerusalem Conquered*, 1907), and he dedicated the rest of his life to religious writings such as *Le sette giornate del mondo creato* (1607; *Creation of the World*, 1982), in which he was able to meditate on Christian mysteries. On a personal level, he began a life of roaming marked by bizarre behavior and psychic disequilibrium. Torn by religious doubts (on more than one occasion he asked to be examined by the Inquisition) and haunted by a sense of persecution, he traveled throughout Italy only to return to Ferrara in 1579 on the occasion of the duke's marriage. Believing that he was slighted since little note was taken of his return, Tasso provoked a scandal by criticizing the duke, was declared mad, and was incarcerated in Sant' Anna.

After seven years of incarceration (much has been written concerning his presumed madness during this period), Tasso was freed through the intercession of the Prince of Mantua, but he could not find peace and continued to wander throughout Italy until his death on April 25, 1595.

Summary

Torquato Tasso is a prime example of the man of genius caught up in a period of transition, of change and upheaval. His major works reflect the conflict of the age of the Counter-Reformation and betray a nostalgic homage to the splendid literary revival of the Renaissance. Critics disagree as to whether Tasso was the last major poet of the Renaissance or the first great poet of the Baroque. Many consider him to be a transitional figure between the two periods, and indeed characteristic elements of both can be found in his writings. There is no disagreement, however, that Tasso belongs on the list of the world's greatest poets—from John Milton to Voltaire, from Lord Byron to T. S. Eliot, the poetry of Tasso has been praised and imitated, contemplated and enjoyed.

The melancholy and pessimistic mood that pervades much of his literary production can be attributed to the rapid changes that were taking place during his lifetime in the areas of religion, science, and politics. Amid such changes, Tasso attempted to reconcile the classical ideals that he cherished with contemporary reality. It is not surprising, therefore, that he was a favorite of the Romantic poets and still has much to offer to the contemporary reader.

Bibliography

Boulting, William. *Tasso and His Times*. London: Methuen, and New York: Putnam, 1907. The classic biography of Tasso. Details the life of the author from both a factual and, at times, romantic point of view, with little critical analysis of his works. Although later scholarship has rejected its romanticized view of Tasso's life, Boulting's book is still fascinating reading and offers valuable insights into the author's age and the courtly environment that influenced his writings. Includes illustrations.

Brand, C. P. *Torquato Tasso*. Cambridge: Cambridge University Press, 1965. The standard English biographical and critical work on Tasso. Discusses the author's use of historical sources, gives a detailed account of his life, and analyzes his major works. Includes an interesting essay on the legend of Tasso's life and presumed madness, and ends with a lengthy chapter on the poet's contribution to English literature. Bibliographic references are included in the notes.

Cody, Richard. *The Landscape of the Mind*. Oxford: Clarendon Press, 1969. The first half of the book discusses the pastoral and Platonic theories in Tasso's *Aminta*. Also studies the play from the point of view of theater and makes references to it in the second half, where William Shakespeare's early comedies are analyzed.

Giamatti, A. Bartlett. *The Earthly Paradise and the Renaissance Epic*. Princeton, N.J.: Princeton University Press, 1966. Contains an interesting chapter on Armida's garden, with references to classical antecedents. Argues that *Jerusalem Delivered* was one of the most concentrated efforts of the sixteenth century to incorporate classical and chivalric materials into a Christian view of the world.

Greene, Thomas. *The Descent from Heaven: A Study in Epic Continuity*. New Haven, Conn.: Yale University Press, 1963; London: Yale University Press, 1975. Presents a concise introduction to the epic from Homer to Vergil to Ludovico Ariosto's failed attempt. Proposes that Tasso does not produce a true epic since *Jerusalem Delivered* is too close to the romance tradition and much of the tragic potential is subordinated to the calls of the Counter-Reformation. Work includes a thorough bibliography.

Kates, Judith A. *Tasso and Milton: The Problem of Christian Epic*. London: Associated University Presses, and Lewisburg, Pa.: Bucknell University Press, 1983. Following a discussion of the critical content of *Jerusalem Delivered*, this work analyzes *Discorsi dell' arte poetica* (1587), which is seen as a primer for the epic poem. The central chapter discusses *Jerusalem Delivered* in terms of the classical heroic and the modern romance. Concludes with Tasso's influence on John Milton's *Paradise Lost* (1667) and a lengthy bibliography.

Saez, Richard. *Theodicy in Baroque Literature*. New York: Garland, 1985. Places Tasso's work within a Baroque framework and uses religion as a critical guide. Of major importance is the bibliography that follows.

Tasso, Torquato. *Jerusalem Delivered*. Translated and edited by Ralph Nash. Detroit: Wayne State University Press, 1987. Easily the most readable translation in prose of *Gerusalemme liberata*. Includes a very useful glossary of names and places and an index of characters.

Victor A. Santi

SAINT TERESA OF ÁVILA

Born: March 28, 1515; Ávila, Spain
Died: October 4, 1582; Alba, Spain
Areas of Achievement: Church reform and theology
Contribution: This patron saint of Spain and doctor of the Church was active in reforming monasticism in Spain. She is also known for her mystic writings, which describe how mental prayer can bring the soul through successive stages to union with God.

Early Life

In the sixteenth century, in the aftermath of the victory over the Muslims and of the expulsion of the Jews, religious fervor, controversy, and fanaticism dominated Spain. The Inquisition was established to impose purity of thought on the peninsula. In this atmosphere of religious zeal, the Inquisition forced Teresa de Cepeda y Ahumada's Jewish grandfather, Juan Sánchez, and his two sons (including Teresa's father) to accept public humiliation to prove that they were sincere converts to Christanity. Such demonstrations did not necessarily preserve converted Jews from future abuse, so Sánchez took his wife's name, de Cepeda, and left his home in Toledo to begin a new life free from the scrutiny of the Inquisition. Teresa's father, Alonso de Cepeda, settled in Ávila, where he worked as a merchant and tax collector. There he married his second wife, Beatriz Ahumada, Teresa's mother.

Teresa was born on March 28, 1515, in Ávila. She was a cheerful, vivacious child who loved friends and conversation. She was very pretty, plump with white skin and curly black hair. Her looks and personality made her a favorite of her father and her nine siblings, and throughout her life she continued to charm all who knew her. As a child, she enjoyed reading, from her father's serious books to her mother's light romances.

The carefree childhood years ended when Teresa was thirteen and her mother died. For three years, Teresa indulged in behavior that she recalled could have damaged her reputation. Her father removed her from danger by sending her to study at the Augustinian convent. In 1536, she overcame her father's objections and entered the Carmelite Convent of the Incarnation in Ávila, where she took her vows the following year.

The Convent of the Incarnation observed a mitigated Rule of Mount Carmel, which meant that it was not very strict. For almost twenty years in the convent, Teresa was torn between her conflicting desires. She yearned for a spiritual life, reading mystic books and practicing mental prayer. At the same time, she desired a secular life, enjoying the admiration of her many visitors. In later years, Teresa wrote against lax convents that permitted nuns to indulge in such vanities, and her experience as a young nun shaped her reform movement. During this time, perhaps partly because of her internal turmoil, she became ill and suffered pain and temporary partial paralysis. For the rest of her life, she endured recurring illness. When she was thirty-nine years old, she had a vision of Christ and then began to have other mystic experiences that finally let her free herself from her worldly temptations and begin her spiritual life as a mystic and church reformer.

Life's Work

Teresa's first visible manifestations of spirituality were raptures, during which she became rigid and cold with no discernible pulse. During these rap-

tures, Teresa also was reputed to have experienced levitation, floating up uncontrollably, much to her embarrassment. These external manifestations of her spiritual state did not end her struggles with the Spanish hierarchy. Her grandfather's Jewish past was not forgotten, and it made some religious leaders look at her experiences with suspicion.

By 1557, the Catholic Reformation was well under way. The Council of Trent was meeting to defend doctrine against the challenge of Protestants. Spanish Catholics such as Teresa seemed to fear Lutherans as much as they feared appearances of the Devil. As part of the Church's rigorous reform, Pope Paul IV issued a new Index of forbidden books that censored many of the mystical writings that had guided Teresa's mental prayers. Religious authorities searched convents and confiscated books. In 1559, the Inquisition increased its efforts to protect the peninsula from unorthodox thought, often focusing on converted Jews, whom they believed were susceptible to secret nonconformity often expressed through mystic theology. Church authorities assigned Teresa a series of confessors to examine her raptures, and her confessors' doubts caused her much turmoil. In 1559, she received her most famous vision, seeing and feeling an angel piercing her heart with a spear. This vision settled her doubts; she no longer feared confessors or inquisitors. Thus spiritually at ease, she began her active life as a reformer of the Carmelite Order.

In 1560, Teresa and a small group of nuns at the Convent of the Incarnation made a vow to follow the more rigorous unmitigated rule of the original Carmelites. Her desire to move out of her unreformed convent into a new one in Ávila raised an outcry. Many monks and nuns objected to Teresa's dedication, because such a reform represented an implicit criticism of their own lives. Further objection came from the population of Ávila. In the mid-sixteenth century, almost one-fourth of the population in Spain was ecclesiastical, either clerical or monastic. The lay public had to finance this religious population, and the people of Ávila were reluctant to support another convent within their city walls. Opposition from both of these groups, monastic and lay, plagued the reform movement that represented much of Teresa's life's work.

Two years after Teresa began her efforts at reform, she received permission to establish a new convent in Ávila. In August of 1562, she founded the reform convent of San José, and became its prioress the following year. As a symbolic gesture of her new reform, she and the novices removed their shoes to wear rough sandals. This act gave her reform movement the name Discalced (without shoes), and writers describe the subsequent struggles within the Carmelite movement as between the Calced and Discalced groups.

Teresa's notoriety brought her again to the attention of the Inquisition, which ordered her to write an account of her life for its review. In 1562, Teresa completed the first version of her autobiography, which she later expanded. The Inquisition found this *Libro de su vida* (wr. 1565, pb. 1611; *The Life of the Mother Teresa of Jesus*, 1611) acceptable. This work is a major source of information about the saint's early life. It also opens a new and influential side of Teresa's active life, her writings. In addition to her autobiography, Teresa wrote four books, six shorter works (including a collection of verses), and many letters, of which 458 survive. Her most famous mystical works are *El camino de perfección* (wr. 1565, pb. 1583; *The Way of Perfection*, 1852), written to guide the nuns in her newly reformed convents, and *El castillo interior: O, Tratado de las moradas* (wr. 1577, pb. 1588; *The Interior Castle: Or, The Mansions*, 1852). In these and other works, Teresa described her techniques of mental prayer, which had been so important in her own spiritual growth.

From 1567 to 1576, Teresa expanded the Discalced Reform by establishing new convents throughout most of Spain. Teresa, frequently ill, traveled throughout the countryside to bring enclosed convents, erected in poverty, to many parts of the kingdom. The indefatigable founder overcame problems of opposition and financing to found seventeen reform convents for women. During her travels, Teresa met John of the Cross, a Carmelite and priest, who became her confessor, friend, and supporter in establishing two Discalced monasteries for men.

Between 1576 and 1578, the expansion of the reform movement was stopped by increasing pressure from the opposition. The Calced Carmelites kidnapped leaders of the Discalceds to force them back into observance of the Mitigated Rule of Carmel. Calced monks imprisoned John of the Cross in Toledo for eight months during these times of troubles. The turmoil reached Teresa herself; once again, the Inquisition summoned her to respond to its interrogations. Throughout this period, Teresa wrote many letters to gather support for her movement and was able to win the support of influential patrons, including King Philip II of Spain.

Finally, in 1580, her reform movement was victorious. Pope Gregory XIII officially separated the Calced from the Discalced Carmelites, sanctioning the reform and creating its independent administration. Teresa's favorite, Jerome Gracián, was made the first leader of the Discalceds, and John of the Cross became an administrator of the movement. Teresa was content that papal authority had safeguarded her reform, and she spent the last two years of her life establishing three more foundations and writing many letters. She became ill as she journeyed to the reform convent in Alba and died there on October 4, 1582. (The day after her death, the Gregorian reform calendar was adopted, and her feast day is celebrated on October 15 because of the changed calendar.)

Summary

Nine months after Teresa of Ávila's death, her followers exhumed her body and allegedly found that it had not decayed. Her supporters used this discovery to forward her cause for sanctity, and her immediate popularity led to repeated dismemberments of the body and distribution of her relics to many churches. In 1614, Pope Paul V declared her blessed, and the Spanish parliament proclaimed her the patroness of Spain in 1617. In 1622, Pope Gregory XV pronounced Teresa a saint.

One of Teresa's enduring accomplishments was her reform of Spanish monasticism, which was part of the Catholic Reformation's response to the growth of Protestantism. The Discalced Reform she began continued and spread after her death to remain a force in Spanish life. Teresa is probably most widely remembered for her mystical experiences and for her written articulation of spiritual doctrine. The sculptor Gian Lorenzo Bernini popularized the piercing of Teresa's heart in his statue, *The Ecstasy of Saint Teresa*, made in 1645 for the Church of Santa Maria della Vittoria in Rome. Reverence for this ecstasy grew in the eighteenth century, when churchmen examined Teresa's heart and discovered that it bore a hole as evidence of the angel's piercing arrow. In 1726, Pope Benedict XIII instituted the Feast of the Transverberation of Teresa's heart to commemorate this mystical event.

In 1970, Pope Paul VI declared Teresa to be a doctor of the Church and her works worthy of study. All Teresa's major spiritual writings include discussions of her mystic theology, but the most sophisticated expression of her theology is found in *The Interior Castle*. Teresa wrote this book while in a trance, and it discusses the soul's capacity to move progressively through the rooms of itself to reach God, who dwells at the center. By locating God at the center of the soul, Teresa expressed God's presence and accessibility to searching believers.

The Interior Castle mirrors the life of the saint herself. Teresa had to cut herself off from her past, which in Counter-Reformation Spain marked her as a converted Jew; she called herself Teresa of Jesus, renouncing her family name. She had to transcend the temptations that bound her for twenty years in feelings of sin, and she fought against a monastic system that she believed had grown too lax for spiritual safety. She did all of these things by retreating to a strength inside herself, where she found God. Through this strength, she changed her world and wrote to tell others how to change theirs.

Bibliography

Clissold, Stephen. *St. Teresa of Ávila*. London: Sheldon, 1979; New York: Harper, 1982. A fine, easy-to-read short biography that brings Teresa's world and accomplishments to life. Provides a sensitive balance between the reputation of the saint, with her raptures and levitations, and the woman, who worked hard in her reform movement. Contains an index.

Gross, Francis L., Jr., and Toni Perior Gross. *The Making of a Mystic: Seasons in the Life of Teresa of Avila*. Albany: State University of New York Press, 1993. This is a passionate book about a gifted woman. It is written from a psychological viewpoint using the developmental point of view of a number of contemporary developmental psychologists, both men and women.

Lincoln, Victoria. *Teresa: A Woman*. Albany: State University of New York Press, 1984. A thorough, well-researched, and readable biography of Teresa with details on all aspects of her life and work. Stresses the woman rather than the saint. Contains a useful index and a brief bibliography.

O'Brien, Kate. *Teresa of Ávila*. London: Parrish, and New York: Sheed and Ward, 1951. A short book describing Teresa's life and work. Rambling at times, but provides background on the Carmelite Order and Teresa's reform work.

Peers, E. Allison. *Saint Teresa of Jesus, and Other Essays and Addresses*. London: Faber, 1953. A collection of essays by the preeminent Teresan scholar. Contains an index.

Sackville-West, Victoria. *The Eagle and the Dove*. London: Joseph, and New York: Doubleday, 1944. A comparison of the life of Saint Teresa with that of Thérèse de Lisieux. The section on Teresa of Ávila offers a short account of her mystic experiences, written from within the Catholic tradition.

Whalen, James. *The Spiritual Teachings of Teresa of Ávila and Adrian Van Kaam: Formative Spirituality*. Lanham, Md.: University Press of America, 1984. Offers a sophisticated description of Teresa's theology and compares it with a twentieth century existential philosopher. Useful for those who want to explore the complexities of Teresa's thought and its relevance for modern times, but it is too complicated for the casual reader. Contains a full annotated bibliography.

Joyce E. Salisbury

TINTORETTO
Jacopo Robusti

Born: c. 1518-1519; Venice

Died: May 31, 1594; Venice

Area of Achievement: Art

Contribution: Tintoretto was a leading exponent of the mannerist movement in painting, a style which parted with the rational symmetry of the Renaissance and moved toward dramatic imbalance and tension and the creation of mysterious moods by means of chiaroscuro, radical foreshortening, and unorthodox brushwork.

Early Life

Jacopo Robusti derived his artistic pseudonym, "Tintoretto," from his father's trade as a dyer (*tintore*). He left Venice only once or twice in his lifetime, for a visit to Mantua and the Gonzaga court in 1580 and a probable trip to Rome in 1547. His marriage at age thirty-six produced eight children, of whom four, most notably Domenico and Marietta, were painters.

Tintoretto may have studied under Bonifazio de' Pitati (Bonifazio Veronese). Almost uniquely among Renaissance artists, however, he was largely self-taught, copying available models of Michelangelo's works and devising his own clay or wax models, dressing them, arranging them in different attitudes in cardboard houses, and introducing light through tiny windows in order to study the effect of lights and shadow on the figures. He also suspended the models from above to learn their chiaroscuro effects and foreshortenings when seen from below. As early as 1545, the letters of Pietro Aretino, Tintoretto's first important patron (for whom he painted *Apollo and Marsyas* in 1545), criticize his arrogance and apparent hasty sketchiness (which stemmed from the artist's early work in fresco but was also a genuine factor in his inventive style).

In his own lifetime, Tintoretto's biography was written by Giorgio Vasari. In 1642, Carlo Ridolfi's adulatory biography reported that Tintoretto had served an apprenticeship with Titian which ended within days because of Titian's jealousy of his pupil's talent coupled with Tintoretto's youthful pride. The real reason for the dismissal, however, may have been Tintoretto's careless style. The combined judgment of Titian and Aretino were, in any case, costly in terms of artistic patronage, as they were the arbiters of taste in Venice. Nevertheless, Tintoretto reputedly hung in his studio the motto (coined by Paolo Pino in his *Dialogo della pittura*, 1548), "The drawing of Michelangelo, the color of Titian."

As Tintoretto began his career, however, the Tuscano-Roman style and the colorful, horizontal Venetian style of these two masters were locked in a losing struggle with the new mannerist impulse throughout Italy; in Venice, the carriers were Andrea Schiavone, Veronese, and, eventually, Tintoretto.

Tintoretto's earliest works (1539-1540) are standard *sacre conversazioni* (Virgin and Child with saints), in the warm reds, golds, and whites expected of a painter of a Venice dominated by Titian. They contain almost nothing of the conscious artificialities of emergent mannerism. His early *Last Supper* (1545-1547) is marked by emotional restraint and horizontal symmetry; only the violent foreshortening of the floor is a mannerist device.

Tintoretto's reputed visit to Rome and his first masterpiece culminate this early period of laborious experimentation. His *Saint Mark Rescuing a Slave* (1548) indeed evinces the muscular forms of Michelangelo and the rich color of Titian. The large monument forecasts the dramatic use of light so prominent in Tintoretto's narrative style.

Life's Work

During the 1550's, the chief elements of Tintoretto's unique style found their place in his voluminous output. *Susanna and the Elders* (1550) manifests the use of strong diagonals. In the Genesis scenes for the Scuola della Trinitá (1550-1553), the colors are less brilliant as Tintoretto first joined color, light, and form to create the mood dictated by the subject matter. The Old Testament scenes (1554-1555) brought to Madrid by Diego Velázquez mark an important moment in Tintoretto's evolving mannerism: The six ceiling paintings feature color that is subtle but sparkling with light and an almost improvisational sketchiness. In the later 1550's, the artist began to use crowds in procession to accentuate space. In *Saint Ursula and Her Virgins* and the *Miracle of the Loaves and Fishes*, the processions fade away into the depths of the paintings, dissolving in the distance in a *non finito* (unfinished) diaphanous sketchiness.

Between 1552 and 1562, Tintoretto contributed, for the cost of materials alone (he was disliked in the artistic community for frequently underpricing his art or working free), several paintings to his beloved parish church, Madonna dell' Orto. One was his famous *Presentation of the Virgin in the Temple*. On either side of the high altar, his *Laws and Golden Calf* and *Last Judgment* rose fifty feet high.

During the 1560's, Tintoretto's work became increasingly dramatic, psychological, and artistically sophisticated. He achieved these effects by using a less diffuse, more immediate light source allowing more pronounced chiaroscuro, increased use of diagonal composition, and vast panoramic scenes. He continued to be prolific. In the *Finding of the Body of Saint Mark*, the radically oblique, sharply receding vault of the church and the stark chiaroscuro enhance the miraculous event taking place in the foreground. Similarly, the ominous storm lightening the edge of the clouds is the focus of the *Translation of the Body of Saint Mark* (both were painted for the Scuola di S. Marco in 1562-1566). Tintoretto concurrently painted for S. Trovaso Church a *Crucifixion* with massive diagonals and a *Last Supper.*

In 1564, Tintoretto started his work in the Scuola di S. Rocco, which was to span twenty-three years. The Scuola was an asymmetrical building, worthy of Tintoretto's bold designs. There followed a series of large scenes of Christ's Passion, including an immense and profoundly moving *Crucifixion*, which John Ruskin pronounced "above all praise." Tintoretto was made a member of the Scuola, a sort of civic-service lodge, and later a lifetime officer.

Contemporaneously (1564-1568), Tintoretto produced a *Crucifixion*, a *Resurrection*, and a *Descent of Christ into Limbo* for S. Cassiano Church, a *Last Judgment* for the Sala del Scrutinio in the Doges' Palace, and for the Church of S. Rocco, a great *Saint Roche in Prison*. Between 1576 and 1581, Tintoretto resumed his work in the upper hall of the Scuola di S. Rocco. There, the ceiling received twenty-one Old Testament scenes, while the walls were decorated with ten events from the life of Christ, of which the *Baptism* and *Ascension* are noteworthy.

Meanwhile, Tintoretto's trip to Mantua in 1580 bore fruit in the eight battle scenes completed with the help of assistants. From 1577 to 1584, too, the artist painted, with less enthusiasm, the four small allegories of classical mythology in the Sala del' Anticollegio of the Doges' Palace. He also executed important scenes from Venice's history in the Sala del Senato, and in the imposing Sala del Maggior Consiglio, an enormous *Paradise* occupying the years 1584-1587. It was the largest oil painting ever done until that time.

In 1583, Tintoretto returned to the Scuola di S. Rocco, this time producing scenes from the life of the Madonna in the lower hall. His conception was consummate: His space opens out dynamically in all directions and his perspectives are limitless; light dominates and dissolves volume and color, rendering his figures incorporeal and unfinished. The entire project in Scuola di S. Rocco has been compared to the Sistine Chapel and the Raphael stanze. Tintoretto finally put down his brush in 1587 and painted no more for the Scuola di S. Rocco.

Among Tintoretto's approximately three hundred paintings are dozens of portraits. In these, he aimed to capture the inner spirit or personality of the subject more than his clothing or background. Notable is his self-portrait at age seventy. Additionally, about one hundred drawings survive; they are mainly practice sets by which Tintoretto perfected his chiaroscuro and foreshortening skills and cartoons for mosaics in San Marco Church.

His last works include two large oils for the presbytery of S. Giorgio Maggiore. Of these, the *Last Supper* epitomized all of his earlier achievements and effects and attained a new level of psychological impact: The darkened room is lit by a lamp striking the disciples from behind and by an unnatural glow radiating from the halo of Christ, who intently administers communion; the table thrusts diagonally into the canvas; angels hovering above add their mystical presence. All of this is in stark contrast to the realism of the Venetian pitchers on the table, a cat drinking from the water cistern, and the everyday activities of servants taking place in the same room.

Tintoretto's last work, the *Entombment* for the chapel of S. Giorgio Maggiore (1594), also employs a double illumination, one the natural sunset, the other artificial, or rather spiritual, which divides the groups of figures by their separate lighting.

Summary

The legendary rivalry between the older Titian and Tintoretto has occasioned an ongoing division among art critics. Both are truly representative of Venetian artistic tradition, but Titian had known the glorious time of Venice; his art reflects the sensuous richness of the city. Tintoretto, however, was born in a Venice humbled by the League of Cambrai (1508); he grew up in a Counter-Reformation atmosphere of religious revival. Thus, a religious mysticism pervades his art.

Contemporaries also took sides. Vasari and Aretino favored Titian. In the seventeenth century, the age of the Baroque, the tide moved to Tintoretto, who was much admired by El Greco and Ridolfi. The eighteenth century saw Tintoretto unfavorably, through the neoclassical eyes of the Age of Reason. Ruskin represents the nineteenth century preference for Tintoretto over Titian and even over Michelangelo. Jakob Burckhardt, however, regarded Tintoretto as crude, barbaric, and artistically immoral, "abandoning himself to the most shameless superficiality."

To the twentieth century, Tintoretto is a giant; he has been regarded variously as one who succeeded in spiritualizing reality, a forerunner of modern illusionism or of German Expressionism. The theatrical quality of his later works comports well with modern artistic sensibilities, which share his delight in foreshortening, his artificial use of lighting to emphasize action or suggest spirituality, his penchant for oblique composition, his use of subdued subaqueous color, his *non finito* sketchiness, and his preoccupation with the human body caught unfolding and poised in mid-action.

Bibliography

Berenson, Bernard. *Italian Pictures of the Renaissance: A List of the Principal Artists and Their Works, with an Index of Places, Venetian School.* 2 vols. London and New York: Phaidon Press, 1957. Volume 1 includes a complete list of Tintoretto's works and their locations; volume 2 contains seventy-six black-and-white plates. These volumes present a list of all the principal Venetian artists, their works and their locations, and 1,334 representative plates.

Honour, Hugh. *The Companion Guide to Venice.* 4th ed. Woodbridge, Suffolk: Companion Guides, 1997. Tintoretto's art is affectionately discussed as discovered by the visitor to the churches and galleries of Venice. En route, the reader is exposed to the cultural and political history of Venice in its living stones and works of art and in its relationship to the rest of Italy. Street plans and museum layouts bring the world of Tintoretto into clarity.

Newton, Eric. *Tintoretto.* London and New York: Longman, 1952. A superlative biography with details not found elsewhere. Throughout, Newton draws from Ridolfi and urges caution in accepting Ridolfi's interpretations. Includes a chronological list of Tintoretto's paintings and seventy-six black-and-white plates.

Rosand, David. *Painting in Sixteenth-Century Venice: Titian, Veronese, Tintoretto.* Rev. ed. Cambridge and New York: Cambridge University Press, 1997. This work uses a study of three masters—Titian, Veronese, and Tintoretto—to explore the visual tradition of one of the most important centers of the Italian Renaissance; these artists dominated and shaped the traditions of Venetian painting in the High and Late Renaissance. Rosand also explores the formal principles and technical procedures that determined the uniqueness of painting in Venice—above all, the development of oil painting on canvas.

Tintoretto. *Tintoretto: The Paintings and Drawings.* Edited by Hans Tietze. London: Phaidon Press, and New York: Oxford University Press, 1948. A short biography and appreciation of Tintoretto. Especially useful for its three hundred black-and-white illustrations and excellent detailed commentary on each plate.

Daniel C. Scavone

TITIAN
Tiziano Vecellio

Born: c. 1490; Pieve di Cadore, Venetian Republic
Died: August 27, 1576; Venice
Area of Achievement: Art
Contribution: Titian is considered one of the greatest artists of the Italian High Renaissance. During his long and prolific career, he developed an oil-painting technique of successive glazes and broad paint application which influenced generations of future artists.

Early Life

Titian was born Tiziano Vecellio in the northern Italian town of Pieve di Cadore. Over the centuries, there has been considerable confusion concerning his birth date, as a result of a misprint in his biography by sixteenth century art historian Giorgio Vasari, who recorded it as 1480. The progress of Titian's career, along with other documentary evidence, indicates instead that Titian was born sometime between 1488 and 1490.

According to the 1557 biography of Titian's life written by his friend Lodovico Dolce, it is known that Titian arrived in Venice, in the company of his brother Francesco, when he was only eight years old. He first worked for the mosaicist Sebastiano Zuccato but soon entered the workshop of the aging painter Gentile Bellini. Unhappy with Gentile's old-fashioned style, he moved to the studio of Gentile's brother, Giovanni, and it is there that Titian learned the current Venetian style and techniques. He also met the short-lived but magnificent painter Giorgione. By 1508, Titian had left Bellini's studio and was working with Giorgione, perhaps as his assistant, on exterior frescoes for the Fondaco dei Tedeschi (German Commercial Headquarters) in Venice.

Until around 1515, Titian's style would remain very close to that of Giorgione. In fact, scholars have difficulty distinguishing between the two hands when their paintings from this period are unsigned. The most famous example of this attribution problem is the so-called *Fête Champêtre* of around 1510, now in the Louvre. The lush pastoral setting, soft lighting, and strong atmospheric qualities characterize the styles of both artists at this time.

In 1511, Titian completed his first dated work, a series of three frescoes in the Scuola di San Antonio at Padua. This commission established his career. Within the next decade, his independent, mature style found expression.

Life's Work

In 1518, Titian's *Assumption of the Virgin* was unveiled at the Church of the Frari in Venice. In this dynamic, monumental composition, Titian seemed suddenly to assimilate the achievements of the Roman High Renaissance style. Since there is no evidence that he had yet traveled beyond the region near Venice, it is assumed that he learned these stylistic lessons through visiting artists, drawings, and reproductive engravings. The painting reflects the harmony and delineation of forms typical of High Renaissance classicism, and an energetic movement similar to that found in Raphael's Vatican murals and Michelangelo's Sistine Chapel ceiling. To this Titian added his distinctive brilliant colors, unified by successive layers of glazes.

During the succeeding decades, Titian's reputation grew until he was, along with Michelangelo, the most famous artist in Europe. His patrons included some of the most powerful men and families of the age. For Alfonso I d'Este of Ferrara he created, among other works, three famous mythological paintings, *The Bacchanal of the Andrians* (c. 1520), *The Worship of Venus* (1518-1519), and *Bacchus and Ariadne* (1522-1523), which were installed in Alfonso's alabaster *studiolo.* He also worked for the Gonzaga of Mantua and several popes. His most important patrons, however, were the Spanish Habsburgs. In 1533, Titian was summoned to Bologna for the first of several meetings with the emperor Charles V, who became one of his greatest admirers. The emperor made him a count and brought him to Augsburg two times as court painter. When Charles died in 1558, his son Philip II continued the relationship.

These prestigious patrons brought Titian fame, wealth, and social position. A shrewd businessman, he invested wisely and by the 1530's was living in luxury. Sometime in the early 1520's he began a relationship with a woman named Cecilia, by whom he had four children, two before they married in 1525. Cecilia died in 1530, and the next year Titian moved his family to a palace which came to be known as the Casa Grande. There he lived a princely existence far removed from the

craftsmen status which artists had held only one hundred years earlier.

Titian's compositions were often revolutionary as he freed Renaissance classicism from its planar symmetry. He exploited the dramatic possibilities of diagonal placings and perspectives, and set up unusual spectator viewpoints. In this way he could give traditional subjects a fresh look. This predisposition to creative compositions was evident very early in his career. *The Gypsy Madonna* (1510-1515) is a variation of the half-length Madonna and Child popular with Giovanni Bellini. Yet Titian has moved all the major forms off center and encouraged the viewer to look diagonally into a landscape to the left of the Madonna. *The Madonna of the Pesaro Family* (1519-1526) shows a more radical alteration of a traditional subject. The pyramidal grouping of figures, with the enthroned Madonna at the apex, has been shifted so that it is placed diagonally to the frontal plane.

Titian's style never stagnated. Over the years, his brushwork loosened and forms were increasingly defined by color and light instead of line. In 1546, he returned from an eight-month visit to Rome, and from this point on his broad handling of paint increased. The result was a type of optical realism, in which the structures of objects were built up through a free application of paint. Details that the human eye does not see without close inspection were not delineated with precise drawing but rather indicated with freely manipulated color and light. In the hands of a master such as Titian, the result was one of startling reality since he had essentially reproduced with paint the reality which the human eye actually absorbs. An example of this loosely painted style was *The Rape of Europa* (1559-1562), in which textures of fur, skin, cloth, and water were faithfully rendered through broad relationships of color and light. Titian's development of this technique, which would influence artists throughout forthcoming centuries, played no small part in his fame.

Toward the end of his long career, Titian's technique loosened still further, and a certain dematerialization of form took place in his paintings. Especially in his religious works, which reflected his own growing awareness of mortality, physicality was overcome by mystical light and emotional expression. Like the late works of Michelangelo, Titian's final paintings seemed more concerned with spirituality than with the substance of the natural world.

Summary

Titian's career was a watershed in the evolution of artistic status within society. Well traveled and well respected, he was a friend of princes and intellectuals. Collectors clamored for his works and, despite a large workshop and numerous assistants, he could not satisfy them all. The laws of supply and demand were in his favor and provided a degree of freedom for artistic development rarely seen before. He became the first artist to achieve the status of gentleman.

As early as the middle of the sixteenth century, artists and intellectuals argued over whether Titian or Michelangelo was the greater painter. At the center of this discussion was Titian's emphasis on color, versus Michelangelo's preference for line, in creating forms. Some art historians see a dualism of technique and expression beginning with these two artists which can be traced through Baroque art to the theories and practices of the later European art academies. To be sure, sixteenth century Italian painters formulated a tradition which would serve as a reference point for art until the middle of the nineteenth century. Titian's style was an essential option within that tradition.

Bibliography

Freedberg, Sidney J. *Painting in Italy: 1500-1600.* 3d ed. New Haven, Conn.: Yale University Press, 1993. An extensive chronological survey of painting in sixteenth century Italy, this volume discusses the various stages of Titian's career as they relate to contemporary artistic developments in Venice and the rest of Italy. A solid introduction to Titian's art, with an emphasis on stylistic issues. Contains limited but pertinent photographs and a basic bibliography.

Goffen, Rona. *Titian's Women.* New Haven, Conn.: Yale University Press, 1997. Richly illustrated with paintings by Titian, this book examines the artist's enduring fascination with the theme of the beautiful woman. Goffen offers a new interpretation of Titian's secular paintings of women, setting them in the context of life in sixteenth century Venice. Without denying the erotic appeal of Titian's women, Goffen argues that an exclusively sensuous view diminishes both the artist's achievement and an appreciation of his art and empathy for women. To characterize Titian's paintings of women as pornographic, as many have, is to confuse modern response with the historical realities of Venetian Renaissance culture, including beliefs about sex and sexuality.

Panofsky, Erwin. *Problems in Titian, Mostly Iconographic*. London: Phaidon Press, and New York: New York University Press, 1969. Examines the subjects of a number of Titian's paintings and how they connect with medieval and Renaissance iconographic traditions. Shows how Titian drew upon both popular imagery and high philosophical ideas in devising his symbolism. Contains numerous photographs. There is no bibliography, but as with all Panofsky's work, the extensive citations in the footnotes serve as the equivalent.

Rosand, David. *Painting in Sixteenth-Century Venice: Titian, Veronese, Tintoretto*. Rev. ed. Cambridge and New York: Cambridge University Press, 1997. Contains several innovative articles which place Titian's compositions within the pictorial and theatrical traditions of Venice. Lengthy analysis of *The Madonna of the Pesaro Family* and *The Presentation of the Virgin*. Contains excellent illustrations, photographs, and bibliography.

Rosand, David, and Michelangelo Muraro. *Titian and the Venetian Woodcut*. Washington, D.C.: International Exhibitions Foundation, 1976. Discusses Titian's involvement with the graphic media, especially woodcuts. Extensive illustrations of woodcuts by Titian and other artists influenced by his imagery or technique. Expansive catalog entries on the prints, with excellent illustrations and insightful art historical analysis. Includes a topically limited bibliography.

Wethey, Harold E. *The Paintings of Titian*. 3 vols. London and New York: Phaidon Press, 1969-1975. The standard reference in English and the most recent catalogue raisonné of Titian's paintings. Each volume contains general essays surveying the artist's biography, chronology, stylistic development, and handling of themes. Extensive catalog entries on every known or attributed painting, with photographic reproductions (black-and-white) of the complete works. Wethey's attributions of some early and minor works are not universally accepted, and his analysis of influence can at times be narrow-minded; yet this still remains the most complete source on Titian.

Madeline Cirillo Archer

TOMÁS DE TORQUEMADA

Born: 1420; Torquemada, Spain
Died: September 16, 1498; Avila, Spain
Areas of Achievement: Church reform; government and politics; religion and theology
Contribution: More than any other individual, Torquemada shaped the Spanish Inquisition, which led ultimately to the expulsion of the Jews from Spain in 1492.

Early Life

Tomás de Torquemada was born in the small town of Torquemada (a name derived from the Latin phrase *torre cremata*, "burnt tower"), near the city of Valladolid in northern Castile. The only son of the nobleman Pero Fernández de Torquemada, Tomás was a nephew of Juan de Torquemada, cardinal of San Sisto, who had gained a reputation among his contemporaries for his theological works, including early defenses of the doctrines of papal infallibility and the Immaculate Conception.

Little is known of Tomás' early life. While still a boy, he entered the Dominican order, later taking his vows at the Convent of St. Paul in Valladolid. He completed a doctorate in philosophy and divinity, soon gaining a reputation both for his scholarship and for the extreme austerity in which he lived. For the rest of his life, Torquemada never ate meat or permitted linen to be used in either his clothing or bedding. As a means of mortifying his flesh, he wore a rough hair shirt against his skin regardless of the weather and denied himself even the slightest appearance of luxury. This asceticism was extended even to other members of his family. After his father died and his sister came of age, Torquemada limited her, his sole surviving close relative, to a dowry no larger than that sufficient to permit entrance into the Tertiary Order of Dominican nuns.

The grave and austere young man soon came to the attention of his superiors, and in 1452 Torquemada became prior of the Dominican monastery of Santa Cruz in Segovia. It is possible that this would have been the extent of his rise to power had he not been given the opportunity to serve as confessor to the Castilian monarch Isabella I in 1474. Five years earlier, Isabella had married Ferdinand V of Aragon, and together these two monarchs ruled kingdoms that would become the core of the modern nation of Spain. As confessor to Isabella, and soon to Ferdinand as well, Torquemada obtained precisely the right position in which to have a profound impact upon the direction that Spanish religion would take throughout the early years of the Renaissance.

Life's Work

In 1482, as Torquemada was supervising the construction of a new monastery of St. Thomas Aquinas in the city of Avila, he was informed that Ferdinand's campaign against the Moors near the city of Loja was about to fail. The king's army was suffering from disease, and supplies of both food and weapons were running low. Torquemada immediately ordered that twenty-four pitchers be filled with gold he had painstakingly acquired to pay for the fabric and vestments of his new monastery. These pitchers were then covered with a layer of cloth and leaves and carried by mule to Isabella. Torquemada's instructions were that the queen should use the gold in whatever way might best assist the king in his siege of Loja. Torquemada's gold arrived too late to be of much use; the siege had to be lifted and the army recalled. Nevertheless, the young priest's swift action proved his loyalty to the crown in a manner that would soon be repaid by Ferdinand and Isabella.

In 1483, conservative elements of the church, alarmed by tales (many of them false) of Jewish converts to Christianity who had reverted to their ancestral faith or lapsed into heretical doctrines, persuaded Pope Sixtus IV to reorganize a board of inquisition that had been established in Spain five years earlier. This original board had taken a largely passive role, lending support to a plan of Cardinal Mendoza, the archbishop of Seville, to combat instances of heresy through the issuance of a new catechism. Now, with papal blessing—and the strong support of Isabella—the conservative faction saw to it that Torquemada was appointed the first inquisitor general of Castile on October 2, 1483. Fifteen days later, Torquemada's appointment was also extended into Aragon. Torquemada's Dominican Order, the "Order of Preachers" most fervently devoted to combating heresy, remained in charge of the Inquisition for the rest of its history. In 1487, Pope Innocent VIII expanded Torquemada's position still further by appointing him grand inquisitor of all Spain.

In theory, the newly reorganized Inquisition was charged only with investigating Christians who were accused of unorthodox views. It was never intended to prosecute unconverted Jews or even to punish Christians who were guilty of heresy. The stated goal of the Inquisition was to return sinners to the "true faith" and, if this proved impossible, to surrender them to the Spanish government for "condign punishment" (a phrase used for "appropriate penalties" that were supposed to be merciful and to stop short of injury, torture, or death). In reality, however, the Spanish Inquisition was responsible for as many as two thousand deaths by fire, the imprisonment of at least 100,000 people, countless acts of torture and, indirectly, the expulsion of all Jews from Spain.

Torquemada's procedure was to investigate any charge of heresy made by two or more witnesses. The accused were informed of the charges against them and, if they were reluctant to confess, threatened with torture. Often this threat alone was enough to compel a confession; if the defendant refused to cooperate, however, Torquemada permitted the use of force. The most common tortures used by the Spanish Inquisition were the rack and a variety of water torture in which a long cloth was forced down the victim's throat and drenched in water until the person began to choke and nearly drown.

Those who were found guilty of the charges brought against them could be fined, have their property confiscated, or forced to undergo a public penance before being surrendered to the government for further punishment. True to his ascetic habits, Torquemada kept none of the goods confiscated for himself but used them both to advance his religious order and to enrich the government's coffers. Ferdinand, whose religious zealotry seems to have been less intense than Isabella's, was attracted to the Inquisition at least as much for its economic advantages as for its suppression of heresy. Once in the hands of the state, the most recalcitrant of the convicted—largely former Jews found guilty of false conversion—were subjected to a highly public final punishment. Though the Inquisition always kept true to its charge by making a perfunctory request that the state show mercy, the convicted were usually executed. In a public spectacle known as the *auto da fé* (Portuguese for "act of faith"), victims were subjected to a lengthy sermon detailing their faults, led in a procession to the place of execution (during which they were often dressed in the *sanbenito*, a yellow tunic bearing images of infernal torment specially revived by Torquemada), bound, and burned at the stake, with the burning wood occasionally dampened to prolong their agony. In extreme cases, before the fires were lit, the bodies of the victims were torn by pincers or otherwise mutilated. Those convicted *in absentia* were sometimes burned in effigy, a symbol of the fate awaiting them if they ever returned to Spanish territory.

Torquemada's first *auto da fé* took place in May, 1485, with a second following in June. Later that same year, the deaths of Torquemada's fellow inquisitors, Pedro Arbues and Gaspar Juglar—Arbues was assassinated and Juglar died of illness, though his death widely suspected at the time to be the result of poisoning—led the Inquisition to be even more severe in its oppression of Jewish converts to Christianity. In 1486, Saragossa was the site of no fewer than fourteen *autos da fé*, with forty-two victims executed and an additional 134 imprisoned, flogged, or subjected to public penance. Those who were convicted of Arbues' murder were castrated and had their hands cut off before they were hung; while still alive, they were cut down from the gibbet and killed by having their bodies quartered and burned.

Torquemada's reputation as a religious figure grew after he predicted a dire fate for the king of Naples. The grand inquisitor had been attempting to prosecute a political appointee of Ferrantino, king of Naples, when the pope agreed to a special dispensation protecting the accused. A Neapolitan ambassador presented Torquemada with the documents, which he accepted only after remarking that he would now need to contact Rome so as to be certain that the papers were genuine. When the ambassador expressed shock at such an insult, Torquemada replied that he had a greater right to be amazed, as the king of Naples wished to protect a heretic. "In any case," Torquemada is reported to have continued, "it matters little, since Ferrantino will soon die without an heir." Remarkably, Ferrantino's only son did die soon thereafter and, at the king's death, the throne of Naples passed to his uncle.

Perhaps the most infamous prosecution undertaken by Torquemada was the so-called La Gardia (or La Guardia) Trial of 1490-1491. Torquemada was informed that, in a travesty of Good Friday, a four-year-old Christian boy had been crucified by false Jewish converts to Christianity. A lengthy investigation began, and it is unclear whether the confessions that were finally received resulted from exhaustion following extensive torture or an actual instance of necromantic rite. In any case, eight converted Jews were burned. Three who repented at the last moment were strangled as a sign of "mercy." Three others who had cheated the executioner by their earlier deaths were burned in effigy. Two Jews implicated in the plot were tortured and then burned. The crucified four-year-old boy, who may never have existed at all, was later canonized as San Cristobal, or the *santo niño* ("holy infant") of La Gardia.

The public outcry resulting from the La Gardia trial led to the expulsion of the Jews from Spain in 1492. Shortly thereafter, Torquemada resigned his positions as grand inquisitor and royal confessor. He spent the rest of his life overseeing the monastery of St. Thomas Aquinas in Avila, and he died peacefully after receiving the last rites of the Catholic Church in September, 1498.

Summary

Without the persistence of Torquemada, the Spanish Inquisition might never have occurred. At the very least, Torquemada must be held accountable for the brutality of many of the prosecutions undertaken by the Inquisition. Although many have argued that other courts of the day, whether religious or secular, resorted to torture and summary judgment even more frequently than that established by Torquemada, the grand inquisitor's single-minded hatred of Jews and Jewish converts to Christianity was responsible for the deaths of hundreds, the torture of thousands, and the impoverishment of numerous others.

So completely did the Inquisition rid Torquemada's country of opposition to Catholic orthodoxy that Spain was almost the only nation in Europe unaffected by the Reformation during the 1500's. Torquemada's legacy was to leave Spain arguably the most homogeneously Catholic country in Europe, a status that may have led to later conflicts, including the launch of the Spanish Armada against England in May and June of 1588.

Bibliography

Hope, Thomas. *Torquemada: Scourge of the Jews.* London: Allen and Unwin, 1939. A concise introduction for the general reader. Marred by a few strained comparisons of Torquemada and the Inquisition to Hitler and Nazism.

Longhurst, John Edward. *The Age of Torquemada.* Lawrence, Kans.: Coronado Press, 1964. A short survey both of Torquemada's life and of the principal events of his period.

Perez Galdos, Benito. *Torquemada.* Translated by Frances M. Lopez-Morillas. New York: Columbia University Press, 1986. Unquestionably the most thorough source on Torquemada. Suited primarily to the serious academic reader.

Sabatini, Rafael. *Torquemada and the Spanish Inquisition: A History.* New York: Houghton Mifflin, 1924. A still-useful source that has the advantage of providing information on the history of the Inquisition both before and after Torquemada and the disadvantage of a flowery, tendentious style.

Jeffrey L. Buller

TOYOTOMI HIDEYOSHI

Born: February 6, 1537; Nakamura, Owari Province, Japan

Died: August 18, 1598; Fushimi, Yamashiro Prefecture, Japan

Areas of Achievement: Government, politics, and the military

Contribution: Hideyoshi was one of the pivotal figures in the unification of Japan out of a welter of competing feudal domains at the end of the sixteenth century. As an astute general and canny power broker and lawgiver, Hideyoshi was to go a long way toward establishing the political foundations that brought Japan from the middle ages into its early modern period.

Early Life

Toyotomi Hideyoshi was born on February 6, 1537, at Nakamura, Owari Province, near what is the modern city of Nagoya. His father was a retired foot soldier in the service of Oda Nobuhide, the father of Oda Nobunaga, who was to be Hideyoshi's overlord during the early phases of his military career. Legends surrounding Hideyoshi's birth recount that his mother dreamed that a ray of sunshine entered her womb and he was thus conceived. Hideyoshi perhaps himself perpetrated this fable to embellish his otherwise humble beginnings. The only picture extant of Hideyoshi shows a deeply lined, narrow, ascetic face with cold haughty eyes and a sour mouth set atop a squat body. Singularly ugly, he was later jokingly referred to by Nobunaga as a "bald rat" or a "monkey."

Hideyoshi came of age in the latter part of Japan's Warring States period, during which local lords jockeyed constantly for advantage with growing armies of samurai and musket-wielding foot soldiers. The Ashikaga family of shoguns maintained only nominal sovereignty over this patchwork of local power centers, able to exert influence only through shifting military alliances. It is small wonder, therefore, that Hideyoshi chose a military career. A family tradition, it was also virtually the only means of advancement for those of humble birth.

In 1558, Hideyoshi, having already served in the army of another lord, presented himself to Nobunaga, a fast-rising star who was master of Hideyoshi's home area. Nobunaga quickly took a liking to Hideyoshi, whose military talents began to bloom as Nobunaga began the campaigns that were to conquer the heartland of Japan around the ancient imperial capital of Kyoto. Through military conquest, Nobunaga was to set in motion the process of pacification of contending power blocs which is known in Japanese history as the unification. Fundamentally more ruthless than Hideyoshi in his approach to military matters, Nobunaga moved to defeat feudal coalitions in central Japan and also besieged and laid waste to armed Buddhist monasteries with a cruelty reminiscent of Genghis Khan.

As Hideyoshi demonstrated his military talents, his position in Nobunaga's command structure rose. It was Hideyoshi who, in 1566-1567, secured a victory over Tatsuoki Saito at Inabayama by constructing at night a fortress facing the enemy. Hideyoshi was rewarded with lands seized from Nobunaga's enemies. In these lands, Hideyoshi exercised an enlightened administrative policy of easing taxation in order to encourage economic development.

In 1575, Nobunaga, with Hideyoshi leading one of two wings of his army, pushed westward to challenge the formidable Mōri clan. Hideyoshi here made siege craft his specialty by taking the massive and strategic Himeji Castle and two other fortresses by imaginative engineering (including flooding) and by clever psychological warfare. In 1582, Nobunaga was treacherously assassinated. Hideyoshi hastily made peace with the Mōri clan, then returned to confront and defeat Nobunaga's murderer. At the council of vassals, Hideyoshi successfully presented himself as Nobunaga's avenger and overrode opposition to sponsor the infant grandson of Nobunaga as heir. He thus became, at age forty-five, the master of five provinces and primary councillor at the head of the mightiest military coalition yet seen in Japan.

Life's Work

Hideyoshi had now inherited the mission of completing unification, and he embarked upon a carrot-and-stick strategy of combining massive attacks on those who actively opposed him with generous land rewards to win over potential rivals as well as keep faithful supporters. In 1582, he defeated the Shibata family, who had opposed him within the coalition, then used Shibata lands to reward his supporters. By 1584, he came to an uneasy settlement with Tokugawa Ieyasu (who was later to complete the unification after Hideyoshi's death). In 1587, he undertook a difficult campaign to subdue the southern island of Kyushu. The defeated were treated generously, but loyal supporters were placed strategically, in the center, and his erstwhile opponents, the Mōri, were given generous tracts in the north. At the conclusion of the Kyushu campaign, he issued his famous eleven-point edict against Christianity, denouncing it as subversive and calling for expulsion of Jesuit missionaries. Although the edict was not enforced for some years, it was clear that Hideyoshi was interested in European contact only for trade. It is possible that he used this as a gesture in support of his hegemony, since he issued the ban on behalf of the entire nation.

Military force was not the only implement used by Hideyoshi in his creation of a national hegemony. Any combination of forces could always undo any purely military arrangement. Therefore, he started to build political power out of his military position. First, he amplified his status as military hegemon through oaths of allegiance and the requiring of hostages from nominal subordinates. In 1585, he secured an appointment from the figurehead emperor to the office of imperial regent as a means of bolstering his legitimacy as a national leader. Realizing that the most solid basis for national power was the capacity to control the right to land proprietorships, Hideyoshi undertook a systematic program of redistributing landholdings aimed at reducing the powers of some lords, placing trustworthy ones in strategic locations, and appeasing potential rivals. It was mainly the smaller lords who were moved around, but gradually the idea solidified that the lords held their land in trust and not absolutely. Acceptance of this growth of central power might have been difficult except that it was recognized that Hideyoshi was merely doing at a national level what the lords had to do locally to hold their territory. They were willing to give up some autonomy to safeguard their domains under Hideyoshi's seal of approval. Never again after 1590 could individual lords acquire land rights not permitted by a national hegemon.

Between 1587 and 1590, Hideyoshi instituted administrative measures that were to be his most far-reaching legacies. He ordered the land survey begun by Nobunaga to be extended and improved. Uniform units of measurement were used. For the first time, Japan's leadership, both local and national, had an accurate plot-by-plot estimate of the productive capacity. This allowed a tax base to be determined, and it revolutionized the tax structure

by allowing the lords greater access to the taxable product and standardized accounting. Once Hideyoshi determined the feudal lord's status in relation to productive capacity, he could more easily shift the lords around, since they were tied more to status than to a particular geographic place. In 1588, he ordered a mass confiscation of all weapons from peasants. That had the double aim of reducing the likelihood of armed rebellion and of separating the warrior classes from all unarmed commoners. In 1590, an accurate population census froze the social classes into samurai, farmers, artisans, and merchants and bound peasants to their land. Samurai were gradually pulled into castle garrisons and, rather than collecting their own taxes, were paid by fixed stipends.

In 1590-1591, Hideyoshi crushed his final remaining challengers in the east of Japan. Now that he was the undisputed master of Japan, he considered the conquest of Korea and China. The first Korean expedition in 1592 ended in a draw after the Japanese encountered determined resistance from the Koreans. The second, in 1597, ended with Hideyoshi's death. Surrounded by magnificent gardens and artworks, pleading for loyalty to his heir from his coalition vassals, he died on August 18, 1598.

Summary

Toyotomi Hideyoshi's military unification of Japan represents only one facet of a diverse life. In his own time, his primary impact seemed to be that he, more than any other individual, acted the role of central figure. He restored the imperial dignity, rebuilt the capital and other cities, enforced peaceful symbols upon the popular mind by parades, theatricals, and tea ceremonies for thousands of commoners. He encouraged new building and patronized new, flamboyant, and colorful artistic fashions. Ostentation became a tool of statecraft. Even the megalomania of the Korean expeditions seemed to bring personal destiny together with national destiny.

Hideyoshi's last appeals for loyalty to his five-year-old son failed. His plans for succession were aborted by the wily Ieyasu, who asserted his supremacy in one final battle, took the title of shogun, and went on to complete Japan's unification by taming feudalism into a stable, peaceful system for the next 250 years. He did so by making full use of the existing legal and administrative structure of census roles, frozen class structure, surveys, and tax procedures and by shifting lords around, assuring loyalty through hostages, closing off Japan from the outside, and the like. That Ieyasu built upon the existing legal, political, and social foundations is proof of Hideyoshi's enduring legacy.

Bibliography

Berry, Mary Elizabeth. *Hideyoshi*. Cambridge, Mass.: Harvard University Press, 1982; London: Harvard University Press, 1989. Clearly the primary biographical source in English on Hideyoshi's life and a thoroughly modern treatment. Save for artistic matters, Berry is comprehensive in her coverage. Gives a complete background and then exhaustively analyzes developments in economics, military affairs, and administrative and political arrangements. Based almost entirely on Japanese sources but, surprisingly, lacks a bibliography.

Coats, Bruce Arthur. "The Arts of the Momoyama Period in Japan." *Magazine Antiques* 150 (September, 1996): 324. Coats discusses different works of art in Japan during the reign of Hideyoshi, detailing his military campaigns, tea ceremony preferences, and study of and performance in the theater. The article also examines the impact of Europeans traders on Japanese architecture and weaponry.

Dening, Walter. *The Life of Toyotomi Hideyoshi*. London: Kegan Paul, 1930; New York: AMS Press, 1971. The first edition of this biography was published in 1888 and not much was added in later editions. A classic Victorian biography, rich with anecdotes and extensive detail about Hideyoshi the man. Contains extensive quotes of conversations without footnote citation; while it is true that Hideyoshi left much correspondence, it is probably that most is the product of the imagination of an author overanxious to paint a vivid personal picture. There is not much analysis on Hideyoshi nor much about the period as a whole.

Elison, George. "Hideyoshi, the Bountiful Master." In *Warlords, Artists, and Commoners: Japan in the Sixteenth Century*, edited by George Elison and Bardwell Smith. Honolulu: University of Hawaii Press, 1981. This essay sheds some light on Hideyoshi's genealogy by focusing on his search for legitimacy as a leader. Elison draws a theoretical comparison between Hideyoshi as a charismatic leader—drawing legitimacy from his accomplishments and through invented mythology about a supernatural birth and miraculous deeds—and Hideyoshi as one who sought traditional legitimacy by inventing a conventional pedigree and taking on court titles.

Hall, John W. *Government and Local Power in Japan, 500 to 1700: A Study Based on Bizen Province*. Princeton, N.J.: Princeton University Press, 1966. Hall offers many general historical comments and insights. His powers of summary are acute, so the book is valuable as an overview. His treatment of Hideyoshi in chapters 9, 10, and 11 shows the impact of some of the central decisions on this one region in western Honshu.

Hall, John W., Nagahara Keiji, and Kozo Yamamura, eds. *Japan Before Tokugawa: Political Consolidation and Economic Growth, 1500-1650*. Princeton, N.J. and Guildford: Princeton University Press, 1981. This collection is the product of a binational conference on the Warring States and gives an overview of the whole period, focusing on historiographical questions. Hall's chapter on Hideyoshi's domestic policies attempts to draw out his contribution to the political scene as Japan moved out of its middle ages into its early modern condition. Hall summarizes specific measures devised by Hideyoshi, most of which were to survive as the basis for government for the next 250 years.

Murdoch, James. *A History of Japan During the Century of Early Foreign Intercourts, 1542-1651*. Vol. 2. Maps by Isoh Yamagata. Kobe, Japan: Kobe Chronicle, 1903. The second of a massive three-volume history. Murdoch, a Scot who spent many years teaching in Japan, is rather stilted in his prose, idiosyncratic in his approach, and often opinionated. Still, this work is occasionally extremely valuable. Modern works seldom offer such lavish detail. Hideyoshi is covered in chapters 8, 9, 12, and 13. Murdoch, who is ordinarily disdainful of feudalism as such, is more positive in his treatment of Hideyoshi. Although he ignores economic considerations, he offers a fuller picture of the range of administrative problems addressed by Hideyoshi.

Reynolds, Mark E. "The Mighty Shogun." *Calliope* 3 (January/February, 1993): 29. This article discusses Toyotomi, Oda Nobunaga, and Tokugawa Leyasu; the rigid social class system of the period; and Hideyoshi as assistant general of Nobunaga.

Sansom, George B. *A History of Japan, 1334-1615*. Stanford, Calif.: Stanford University Press, 1961. This is the second volume in a three-volume history of Japan which is arguably the most complete general history of premodern Japan available in English. This well-illustrated and readable work, based entirely on Japanese sources, is indispensable as a reference work. Hideyoshi's life and career are covered in chapters 19 through 24, including a chapter on the artistic scene. Although less adequate for economic matters than more modern works, Sansom's history as a whole comes close to striking the perfect balance between lively prose and a wealth of detail. His bibliography is annotated, his appendices pertinent, his index meticulous. This is a full-service history to which all students of pre-1867 Japan should come first.

Toyotomi, Hideyoshi. *101 Letters of Hideyoshi: The Private Correspondence of Toyotomi Hideyoshi*. Edited and translated by Adriana Boscaro. Tokyo: Sophia University Press, 1975. Boscaro gives an extensive introduction and then intersperses the graceful translations with editorial comment and explanation of the letters. She explains some of the problems of dealing with this kind of documentation. Contains appendices, a catalog of letters with a photoreproduction of a sample letter, and notes on people and places.

David G. Egler

THE TUDOR FAMILY

Ruled: 1485-1603

Areas of Achievement: Monarchy

Contribution: The Tudor monarchs dominated the politics of their time, moving England into the modern era.

Background

The accomplishments of the Tudors must be measured against the challenges occurring during the Renaissance era. The disaster of the Black Death, the decline of the Roman Catholic Church and the breakdown of Christian unity resulting from the Protestant Reformation, the Hundred Years War between England and France, the development of the printing press, and the voyages of discovery to Asia and the Western Hemisphere were factors that weakened the medieval fabric of earlier centuries.

England suffered during the 1400's. The forced abdication of Richard II in 1399 placed the throne under a cloud. Henry V arguably hurt rather than helped his kingdom with his military victories over the French, which resulted in the unification of the French and English thrones. England was overextended on the Continent. When Henry V died in 1422, his son, Henry VI, was only a year old; when he came of age, moreover, he showed that he had inherited the mental instability of his French grandfather, Charles VI. After England's defeat and withdrawal from France in 1453, various factions in England turned on each other in the so-called War of the Roses, and with a weak king, anarchy and violence was the result, particularly at the upper levels of society. By the 1470's, stability seemed to have returned under the leadership of Edward IV, but during the reign of Richard III (1482-1485) the crown was under siege again, ending only at the Battle of Bosworth. The victor and new king, the first of the Tudor dynasty, was Henry VII.

The Tudors were impoverished Welsh nobility. Owen ap Meredith ap Tudor, a minor member of Henry V's court, married Henry's widow, Catherine of France, after the king's death. Through this marriage, the children of Owen Tudor were by blood tied to the rule of the unstable Henry VI, their half-brother. During the War of the Roses, the Tudors sided with the crown. Owen Tudor was captured and beheaded in 1461. Owen's son, Edmund, earl of Richmond, died in 1456; Edmund's only son, Henry, was born three months later, in January, 1457. After the deaths of Henry VI and his heir in 1471, Henry Tudor became the Red Rose faction's candidate for the throne; he was supported by the opponents of Edward IV and the White Rose faction, which endorsed the House of York. Henry Tudor was an opportunistic survivor; with French assistance, he landed a small army in south Wales in August, 1485, and three weeks later defeated Richard III at Bosworth.

Dynastic Accomplishments

Victory did not guarantee survival. During the rest of Henry VII's reign, there were various claimants to the throne, but the stratagems and plots against him failed. Consolidating his rule was paramount, and he married Elizabeth of York, sister to Edward IV and Richard III, in an attempt of reconcile the Yorkists. In often controversial ways, Henry VII increased the financial resources of the crown, and he left a surplus in the royal treasury when he died, an unusual accomplishment in those times. His concern for money gave him the reputation of a miser, governed by avarice only, but he spent money generously on his court, believing that royal pomp not only was his due but also reinforced his royal authority.

Concerned with the survival of his dynasty, Henry often focused his diplomacy upon matrimonial matters. After the death of his queen, he offered himself as a groom to prospective royal candidates from the Continent. In addition, his eldest son, Arthur, was married to Catherine of Aragon, a princess from one of the most powerful royal families in Europe. Arthur died shortly after the marriage, but with Catherine already in England, Henry VII arranged that Catherine marry his remaining son, Henry. When the king died in 1509, the survival of the dynasty seemed ensured. Henry VII was not loved by many, but he was respected.

Henry VIII epitomized the Renaissance prince. Young, athletic, charismatic, he was well read, not least in religious matters. His marriage to Catherine was consummated, and in 1516 she gave birth to their only child, Mary. Henry attempted to establish his fame, and English power, through military actions, but in the rivalries between the Valois monarchs of France and the Hapsburgs of Spain, Henry VIII was unable to achieve parity with his continental rivals. Instead, his dynastic concerns and the accompanying religious issues made him the larger-than-life figure he desired to be.

Catherine of Aragon, several years older than Henry, lost her physical charms, and Henry found solace with younger, more attractive women. Compounding his lack of sexual interest in Catherine was her failure to produce a male heir to the throne, a seeming necessity in a society that assumed male superiority, in part because of the military valor associated with monarchy. By the end of the 1520's, Henry had fallen in love with Anne Boleyn and wished to be legally rid of Catherine in order to remarry. In the Catholic Church, marriage was a sacrament. Marriages, particularly among royalty, could be dissolved, but only through the Church's auspices. Pope Clement VII was probably willing to annul the marriage, but he and Rome were under the control of Charles V, ruler of Spain and the Germanies, and Catherine's nephew. Yet Henry found another alternative.

In 1517, Martin Luther had set off the spark that led to the Protestant Reformation and the division of Christendom. With Thomas Cromwell as chancellor, the English Parliament, claiming that there was no higher authority than national sovereignty, passed legislation ending Henry's marriage to Catherine. Henry immediately married Anne, who soon gave birth—but to a daughter, Elizabeth. Although Henry was well into middle age, his romantic eye continued to wander, and he contrived to have Anne executed. Henry then married again, this time to Jane Seymour, who did her royal duty by presenting Henry a son, Edward, but who died in childbirth. Three more royal marriages followed: Anne of Cleves, whom Henry divorced, Catherine Howard, who was executed for adultery, and Catherine Parr, who survived his death.

More important than Henry's matrimonial failures was the impact he had upon government and religion. Using Parliament, Henry and Cromwell engineered a revolution in increasing the powers of Parliament as the fount of law. Because of his divorce, Henry inadvertently became the founder of the Protestant Church of England, or the Anglican Church. His own religious beliefs have been described as being essentially Catholic but without veneration of the Papacy, although he veered at times in a Protestant direction.

With Henry VIII's death in 1547, Protestantism quickly triumphed in England, at least temporarily. The new king, Edward VI, Henry's youngest child but sole son, was only nine years of age; however, he was precocious. Surrounded by royal uncles, Edward was a convinced Protestant. He could hardly have been anything else, in that his own legitimacy depended upon the legality of Henry's divorce from Catherine of Aragon. Edward's reign was brief, however, and he died at the age of fifteen in 1553. During those years, however, the Anglican Church established deep roots, particularly under the leadership of Thomas Cranmer, the archbishop of Canterbury.

Edward's oldest half-sister, Mary, ascended the throne. Ignored by her father and believing that she had the obligation to restore her mother's reputation and religion, Mary was a staunch Catholic. Not alone in the violent sixteenth century, she was willing to use force to achieve her religious aims, which were to bring England back to Catholicism. Her reign was a disaster. Her religious persecutions gained her the nickname "Bloody Mary," and, in an era of rising national consciousness, her marriage to Philip of Spain was equally controversial. The mourners were few when she died in 1558.

Elizabeth, the second of Henry VIII's three children, was twenty-five when she became queen, and she exhibited the survival qualities of the earlier Tudors. Historians have debated her motives, some claiming that her actions were determined by her psychological experiences under her father and her sister, and some arguing that it was her intellect that guided her decisions. She moved cautiously, and given that she was Anne Boleyn's daughter, had little alternative but to keep England Protestant. She stated that she was not interested in looking into her subjects' souls, but she did demand outward adherence to the Anglican faith. Well-educated, she had her father's charisma, and she used both her mind and her charm to good effect, steering a middle way between the Catholic monarchs on the Continent and the radical Protestants—the Puritans—in England.

To the north ruled Mary Stuart, queen of Scots, distantly related to Elizabeth. Scotland was riven by religious concerns, with Mary representing the Catholic interest and John Knox the Protestant cause. Mary fled Scotland for England, where she was placed under close confinement. The eternal schemer, Mary hoped to eliminate Elizabeth, become queen of England, and restore Catholicism; nevertheless, it was with considerable reluctance that Elizabeth ordered Mary executed in 1587. With Mary's death, Philip II of Spain launched a great naval armada against England. When it failed in 1588, the English surmised that God must truly be a Protestant.

Elizabeth never married, perhaps associating marriage with death and possibly unwilling to share her position with a male who might, because of the times, become the dominant figure; as a result, she was referred to as the "virgin queen." With her death in 1603, the Tudor dynasty came to an end; ironically it was James, the son of Mary, queen of Scots, who became the next English monarch.

Summary

The Tudors are the most famous dynasty in English history, both for their accomplishments and for their powerful personalities. Henry VIII and Elizabeth I were larger-than-life figures. "Bloody Mary," because of her religion and marriage, became one of the chief villainesses in English history. Even the young Edward VI was memorable, perhaps because of his youthful death. The monarch who left the least mark on subsequent historical imagination was Henry VII, arguably the most able of the Tudors.

This was an important era in English history, and the Tudors were at the center. Henry VII restored the position of the monarchy, ending the endemic ruling-class violence. Henry VIII, intentionally or not, strengthened Parliament and established the Anglican Church. Even Edward and Mary affected the politics and religion of the time. And Elizabeth—hailed as "Gloriana" and "Good Queen Bess"—also successfully ruled England for a long time, ending in the Age of Shakespeare and the English Renaissance.

The Tudor accomplishments can be contrasted with those of the monarchs who preceded them and those of the dynasty which followed. Between 1399 and 1485, the throne was frequently in dispute. The Stuart dynasty of the seventeenth century was also a story of royal failure. The Tudors have been defined as despotic rulers, but "Tudor despotism" incorporated Parliament into the decision- and law-making process, even if only as a secondary factor. By making use of Parliament to advance their own aims, moreover, the Tudors so strengthened Parliament that within a century of their passing, England had become a constitutional monarchy, with Parliament more powerful than the monarchs.

Bibliography

Chimes, S. B. *Henry VII*. Berkeley: University of California, 1972. Scholarly but readable, this is an excellent biography of perhaps the most important but least known Tudor.

Elton, G. R. *England Under the Tudors*. New York: Barnes and Noble, 1962. An excellent survey of Tudor England by a premier historian. Especially good on Henry VIII's revolution in government.

Erickson, Carolly. *Bloody Mary*. New York: Doubleday, 1978. A sympathetic and entertaining account of Mary. Erickson is a popular biographer of many historical characters.

Scarisbrick, J. J. *Henry VIII*. Berkeley: University of California Press, 1968. The best biography of Henry VIII, both critical and sympathetic to England's most famous king.

Slavin, Arthur Joseph. *The Precarious Balance*. New York: Knopf, 1973. Energetically written, this volume is challenging and insightful, with the additional value that includes a discussion of both the pre- and post-Tudor centuries.

Smith, Lacey Baldwin. *Elizabeth Tudor: Portrait of a Queen*. Boston: Little Brown, 1975. Written by a distinguished authority of the Tudor era, this is a brief, exciting, and readable biography.

Eugene Larson

WILLIAM TYNDALE

Born: c. 1494; probably Gloucestershire, England
Died: October 6, 1536; Vilvorde, Belgium
Areas of Achievement: Religion and literature
Contribution: During the Reformation, Tyndale translated the New Testament and the first five books of the Old Testament into English.

Early Life

William Tyndale was born near the border between Wales and England, probably in Gloucestershire, around 1494. He was also known as William Hutchins; the family moved from the north and took the name Hutchins to avoid detection during an unsettled period of war. Nothing is known about either his childhood or his family except that he had a brother named John and possibly another one named Edward.

Tyndale entered the University of Oxford around 1508. While there, he abandoned the teachings of the Church and instructed students in scriptural truths. About 1516, after receiving his master's degree, Tyndale entered the University of Cambridge, where he remained until 1521. Tyndale's friends loved and respected him, and even his enemies acknowledged his learning and his irreproachable integrity. Neither proud nor selfish, he was zealous in his work, courageous, and faithful throughout his life.

Life's Work

From 1521 to 1523, Tyndale served as schoolmaster to the children of Sir John Walsh, a knight of Gloucestershire, at the manor house of Little Sodbury. He also began to preach in nearby villages and to crowds that gathered around him in Bristol. When Thomas Parker, a man of violent temper who vigorously prosecuted accusations of heresy, was appointed chancellor of the district, Tyndale was accused of heretical teaching and summoned to appear before him. He was threatened and reviled, but because no witnesses would testify against him, he was given no punishment. This was the only time, aside from his last trial, that Tyndale was brought before any church officer on charges of heresy.

Tyndale realized that the clergy of his day opposed his doctrine because they did not know Latin, the language of their Bible, and consequently could not know what Scripture actually taught. Concerned more with ritual than with truth, their ignorance was indicative of the spirit of the church rulers. When a friend told him that the pope was the Antichrist of Scripture, Tyndale concluded that, as Antichrist, the pope would strive to keep the Holy Writ from the people. Tyndale had come to know Christ through his study of Scripture, and he believed that if others had that opportunity they would also choose Christ over the Church. He decided that the only remedy would be an English translation of the Bible distributed to the people so that they could study it for themselves.

Tyndale resolved that he would be the translator. While still at Little Sodbury, he began the New Testament, working from the original Greek and not from the Latin Vulgate as John Wycliffe had done in the 1300's. Because of his sympathy with the religious reformers, Gloucestershire was unsafe for him and he moved to London in 1523. He had hoped that Cuthbert Tunstall, the new bishop, would grant him patronage, which would support him while he studied and wrote. This was not to be

the case; when Tyndale was granted an interview, Tunstall coldly refused to help.

Fortunately, while preaching at St. Dunstan's-in-the-West in London, Tyndale met Humphrey Monmouth, a wealthy cloth merchant and patron of needy scholars. Monmouth invited Tyndale to stay with him and paid him to pray for his parents and other saints. In Monmouth's home, Tyndale was free to work on his translation, and he heard men discuss the history of King Henry VIII's reign and the progress of the Reformation in Germany, France, and Switzerland.

Deciding that the English version of the New Testament would be impossible to print in England, Tyndale sailed for Germany in May of 1524, never to set foot in his native land again. Upon his arrival in Hamburg, he visited Martin Luther in Wittenberg and remained there until April, 1525. While at Wittenberg, he worked on his translation with the help of a secretary, William Roye. In the spring of 1525, Tyndale returned to Hamburg to collect some money he had left with Monmouth. He and Roye then traveled to Cologne and arranged for the printing of the New Testament. Johannes Cochlaeus, dean of St. Mary's Church at Frankfurt, discovered the plan and obtained an order from the Cologne Senate which prohibited the printers from proceeding with the work. In addition, Cochlaeus warned Henry VIII to watch the British seaports in order to prevent the translation's arrival in England.

Before Cochlaeus could confiscate the papers, Tyndale and Roye escaped to Worms in October of 1525, taking the already printed sheets with them. They hired Peter Schoeffer, a printer with Lutheran sympathies, to complete a new printing of the New Testament. In spite of the precautions taken by the king and the bishops, the copies of the Testament were smuggled into England early in 1526 by enterprising merchants and were widely circulated and sold.

When the translation was discovered in London in the early fall of 1526, the church authorities met to discuss possible courses of action. Tunstall recommended prohibition, and the prelates unanimously agreed to burn all copies of the book which were found. Acting on their decision, Tunstall denounced and burned the work at Paul's Cross. People were warned to rid themselves of all copies of the Testament or face excommunication. The prelates' goal was to cleanse England of all Tyndale's translations; the Archbishop of Canterbury bought copies simply to destroy them. After the bishops learned that Tyndale was the source of the translation, he was forced to leave Worms to escape arrest. Roye had left earlier for Strasbourg, so Tyndale went alone to Marburg in 1527. He was able to write there under the protection of the Landgrave of Hesse-Cassel and probably visited other cities as well. Near the end of 1529, he moved to Antwerp.

During this same period, Tyndale published *The Parable of the Wicked Mammon* (1527), which discusses the parable of the unjust steward and justification by faith, and *The Obedience of a Christian Man, and How Christian Rulers Ought to Govern* (1528), his most important original work, intended as a defense of the reformers against charges of encouraging disobedience of the government. He also finished translating the first five books of the Old Testament, and the Pentateuch was printed in January, 1530, probably at Marburg. This edition of the Pentateuch included a general preface, a preface to each book, a glossary, and marginal notes.

The Practice of Prelates, printed in 1530, criticized both the English government and the Church's practices; unfortunately, however, Tyndale could not accurately judge the political revolution in England from his place of refuge on the Continent. Nevertheless, the book described the ways in which the pope and clergy had gone from poverty and humility to universal supremacy, a topic with which Tyndale was most familiar. In *The Practice of Prelates*, Tyndale also spoke out against the king's attempts to obtain a divorce from Catharine of Aragon, and Tyndale's fierce stand on this controversial issue made for him many enemies. Displeased with Tyndale's criticism of the Church, Sir Thomas More, a layman and Member of Parliament, wrote an essay in 1529, defending the doctrines and practices of the Church. In 1531, Tyndale's answer appeared as a clear argument for reform and a sharp criticism of More's work. This controversy continued for several years; More asserted the authority of the Church, and Tyndale replied by quoting Scripture; their discussion defined the issues but brought no agreement.

In 1531, Thomas Cromwell became a privy councillor, and he sent Stephen Vaughan, an English envoy in the Netherlands, to find Tyndale and offer him safe conduct back to England. Cromwell advocated a "one king, one law" policy which Tyndale also recommended; Cromwell probably wanted Tyndale to help him wage a literary war in support of this policy. Tyndale, however, refused to return, as he feared for his safety. This proved to be a wise decision; during the following year, Henry commissioned Sir Thomas Elyot to find and apprehend Tyndale. Tyndale left Antwerp as a consequence, returning in 1533 when the situation again seemed safe. In 1534, he moved into the home of Thomas Poyntz, an English merchant, and worked on his revised translations of the Pentateuch and the New Testament, which were issued in 1534.

In 1535, Tyndale met a young Englishman, Henry Phillips, who falsely declared himself a supporter of religious reform. Phillips posed as an admirer and friend of Tyndale and then betrayed him to the Belgian imperial officers. Tyndale was arrested in May, 1535, and imprisoned at the castle of Vilvorde. Poyntz zealously worked for his release but failed and was also imprisoned. In 1536, Tyndale was tried for heresy, condemned, and sentenced to death. On October 6, 1536, at Vilvorde, Tyndale was strangled and burned at the stake.

Summary

Although William Tyndale left England and lived in exile for twelve years before his death, his name became well known in his native land because of his work on the Bible. His translations of the New Testament and Pentateuch from their original languages into English were endorsed by the translators of the King James Version in 1611 for their accuracy and style. His work set the standard for later versions because of its simplicity, forcefulness, and lack of Latinized expressions. His literary style also influenced future English writers encouraging the use of simple, ordinary language and idioms.

Tyndale was one of the most important English reformers. Although Tyndale was not a public figure, his writings are scholarly expositions of the reformist views. His Bible translations and treatises were important factors in promoting the Reformation in England, and his writings give the reformist perceptions of the ecclesiastical and royal governments.

Before Tyndale was executed, he prayed aloud that God would open the eyes of the King of England. Within a year, a version of the English Bible, based largely on Tyndale's work, circulated in England with the king's permission. Within two years, the English Bible was set up in every English church so that all could come and read it for themselves. Thus, Tyndale's vision of a Bible for the people was realized.

Bibliography

Bainton, Ronald H. *Here I Stand: A Life of Martin Luther.* New York: New American Library, 1950; London: Hodder and Stoughton, 1951. The most popular biography of Luther, comprehensive in its details. Useful in understanding the man who was so highly esteemed by Tyndale.

Bruce, F.F. *History of the Bible in English.* 3d ed. New York: Oxford University Press, 1978; London: Lutterworth, 1979. A scholarly work which traces the English Bible from its beginnings in picture form to the many versions available in the 1970's. Includes some English history, biography, and comparisons of excerpts from different translations.

Daniell, David. *William Tyndale: A Biography.* New Haven, Conn.: Yale University Press, 1994. This important book is the first major biography of Tyndale in sixty years. It sets the story of his life in the intellectual and literary contexts of his immense achievement and explores his influence on the theology, literature, and humanism of Renaissance and Reformation Europe. Daniell discusses Tyndale's achievement as biblical translator and expositor, analyzes his writing, examines his stylistic influence on writers from Shakespeare to those of the twentieth century, and explores the reasons why he has not been more highly regarded.

Demaus, Robert. *William Tyndale.* Revised by Richard Lovett. London: Religious Tract Society, 1886. Considered to be the standard authority on Tyndale. Gives an accurate account of his life and works as well as the historical details of that era.

Durant, Will. *The Reformation: A History of European Civilization from Wyclif to Calvin, 1300-1564.* New York: Simon and Schuster, 1957. Considers religion in general and explores the problems and conditions of the Catholic Church, particularly after 1300. Discusses the Reformation in relation to politics, economics, art, and the social revolution.

Elton, G. R. *Reform and Reformation: England, 1509-1558.* London: Arnold, and Cambridge, Mass.: Harvard University Press, 1977. A study of the reigns of Tudor rulers Henry VIII, Edward VI, and Mary I and the ways in which reform shaped English politics, religion, and behavior. Gives no facts on Tyndale, but the background information on this period of time is helpful.

Mozley, J.F. *William Tyndale.* London: SPCK, and New York: Macmillan, 1937. A good biography that covers some material not included in Demaus' original work. Includes a chapter on Tyndale's translation of the New Testament.

Spitz, Lewis W. *The Protestant Reformation: 1517-1559*. New York: Harper, 1985. Emphasizes the Reformation as the outstanding achievement of the age but includes the significant developments in other areas of life throughout Europe. Argues that the Reformation was of even more critical importance to history than the Renaissance.

Elaine Mathiasen

LORENZO VALLA

Born: 1407; Rome
Died: August 1, 1457; Rome
Areas of Achievement: Religion and philosophy
Contribution: By means of his careful scholarship, Valla helped to legitimize Renaissance Humanism, reorganize philosophical methodology, and expose certain prevalent Roman Catholic beliefs and practices to critical scrutiny, thus helping to prepare the way for the rise of Protestantism.

Early Life

Few important details have survived concerning the early life of Lorenzo Valla, one of the greatest of the Italian Renaissance Humanists. It is known that he was born in Rome in 1407, to a pious, upper-class family that traced its roots back to Piacenza, in the Italian Alps. The advantages he enjoyed by birth were magnified by his education, for Valla was extremely fortunate in his instructors, sitting at the feet not only of Vittorino da Feltre, one of the premier scholars at the University of Rome, but also Leonardo Bruni, who taught Valla Latin, and Giovanni Aurispa, who taught him Greek. Under their tutelage Valla became a superb linguist. He became so proficient, in fact, that he often was commissioned by the pope for official translations. Ironically, the same linguistic proficiency which brought him papal attention and commendation would eventually call forth the pope's ire.

While still in his early twenties, Valla was appointed to the "chair of eloquence" at the University of Pavia, an appointment that required him to teach rhetoric, Latin, and Greek. It was during his tenure at Pavia that Valla, in 1431, was ordained a Roman Catholic priest.

The same year he was ordained, Valla published *De voluptate* (1431), later revised under the title *De vero bono* (1433; *On Pleasure*, 1977). In it, he searches for the highest human good. This search is conducted as a comparative exposition, in dialogue form, between Leonardus, Antonius, and Nicolaus, Valla's imaginary representatives of Stoicism, Epicureanism, and Christianity, respectively. According to Leonardus, the highest human good is moral virtue, which must be pursued at all costs, even the cost of one's life and happiness, if need be. Antonius counters this assertion by identifying pleasure (which he closely ties to utility), as the highest good. Nicolaus, whose views are probably to be seen as Valla's own, says that Christanity is the highest good because it combines the best of Stoicism and Epicureanism without any of their shortcomings. To him, whoever serves God gladly does best (that is, has virtue) and is happiest (that is, has pleasure). To Nicolaus, Christianity is our glad service for God and, because it is, it is the highest human good.

Valla's service at the University of Pavia lasted for about three years until, in 1433, his public letter attacking a notable local jurist aroused such a tempest that he was forced to resign his academic post. For the next three years, in true Renaissance fashion, he followed the ancient peripatetic model for scholars, moving from Pavia to Milan, to Genoa, and to Mantua, before settling finally in Naples, where he became private secretary to King Alfonso, a post from which he rose to public prominence.

Life's Work

At about the same time that Valla enlisted in the service of the king, he published *De libero arbitrio* (c. 1436; *On Free Will*, 1948), an influential work that examines the relationship between divine foreknowledge and election, on the one hand, and human free will and responsibility, on the other. It also examines the relationship between reason and religion. In it, Valla argues that human beings cannot shun their responsibility to do good and they cannot blame God for their shortcomings, as if He were the cause of their evil and not they themselves. To Valla, because God is omniscient, He knows what a person will do even before he does it. That person, nevertheless, cannot say that God caused his action, because prior knowledge is not a cause. The verb "to know" is an intransitive verb. That is, it has no external effect. Simply to know that one will deposit money in one's bank account will neither make one richer nor cause the deposit to occur. Only going to the bank and leaving money in the account can do that, and that is a human responsibility. It also is something one is free to do or to leave undone. The fact that God knows what will happen does not alter the action or relieve a person of the responsibility to get it done. Nor does it vitiate the freedom to do so. Thus, divine foreknowledge and human freedom are compatible concepts. Infallible prediction is not the same as predeterminism.

Valla goes on to explain that while the human mind can comprehend such difficult problems, and even offer plausible solutions to them, religion is not reducible merely to reason. Some things in religion exceed reason's grasp. As a pious Renaissance Humanist, Valla believed that religion, rhetoric, and reason form a hierarchy. Religion, so to speak, is king; rhetoric is queen, and reason is their servant. Thus, while good theology and good philosophy are complementary, religion takes precedence over reason. Valla is not opposed to philosophy. He is opposed to bad philosophy and to philosophy that does not keep to its proper place or role. God's revelation is understandable to reason, but it is not subject to reason. Reason is subject to it.

At about the same time that Valla published *On Free Will*, he began work on what was perhaps his most popular work, *Elegantiae linguae latinae* (1444). This book is Valla's effort to restore Latin usage to its ancient purity, a purity he believed was lost at the hands of medieval Latinists, whom he called "barbarians." This book, therefore, is a Humanist handbook on how to achieve graceful style and verbal precision. Because it was the first great effort at Humanistic philology, it was the first work to place the study of Latin usage on a somewhat scientific basis. It soon became the standard textbook for Humanists interested in verbal accuracy and verbal art.

Dialecticae disputationes (c. 1439) is Valla's attempt to restore and restructure medieval philosophy by rearranging its arguments. In this book, Valla tried to simplify logic and to rearrange it according to the discipline of rhetoric. By allying philosophical clarity with rhetorical flourish, Valla was trying to teach scholars not only how to speak sense (logic) but also how to speak sense beautifully and compellingly (rhetoric). Reason (ratio) must be combined with eloquence (oratio). Valla, in other words, tried to modify the prevailing Aristotelianism of his day by showing that metaphysical truth could be clarified by linguistic criticism, literary analysis, and rhetorical emphasis. To Valla, Aristotle's philosophical language was unsound. *Dialecticae disputationes* is Valla's effort to correct this shortcoming with a philosophy that was rhetorically a better description of reality.

Easily Valla's most sensational work, *De falso credita et ementita Constantini donatione declamatio* (1440; *The Treatise of Lorenzo Valla on the Donation of Constantine*, 1922), revealed the fraudulent nature of the document upon which medieval popes based their claim for political and military power. Written while he was still in the pay of King Alfonso (an adversary of the pope), and probably written at the king's suggestion, this book resulted in Valla's trial on charges of heresy, a trial that was stymied by the king's intervention. The spurious Donation of Constantine, supposedly written by the ancient Roman emperor himself, gave the entire western region of the Empire to Pope Sylvester because the pope allegedly had cured the emperor of leprosy. As a result, Constantine withdrew himself and his court from Rome to Constantinople because he did not feel worthy to live in the same city as such a holy man as Sylvester. In gratitude for his healing, the emperor granted the pope political and military charge over the West.

Valla's critical analysis, both linguistic and historical, overturned the integrity of the document. By means of his own philological expertise, Valla showed that this document could not have been written in the fourth century, as it purports to have been. Instead, by exposing many of its anachronisms, he showed it to be an eighth century forgery, perhaps from Paris. Thus, while he was not the first to question this document's authenticity—Dante and John Wyclif had done so before him—he was the first to establish his objection on the basis of sound historical and linguistic judgment.

Having to some extent debunked papal claims to civil power, Valla next took aim at traditional Roman Catholic piety. *De professione religiosorum* (1442; on monastic views) is his effort to prove that religious people, such as priests, monks, and nuns, are not necessarily the best. Ostensibly a dialogue between Frater, a traditional Roman Catholic, and Lorenzo, whose views represent Valla's own, this book is a courageous and outspoken challenge to prevalent views on Christian life. In it, Valla denies, as the Protestant reformers do later, that any special spiritual status attaches to members of the clergy or of the religious orders. To Valla, all Christians are on equal footing. One must not be called religious simply because one has taken vows. Vows, he believes, are worthless if one does not lead a godly life. If one can lead a godly life without vows, why are they necessary? True sanctity comes from being acceptable to God, not to one's ecclesiastical superiors. Vows, in fact, are inimical to spirituality because virtue begins with pious inner attitudes, not obedience to external rules. On this point Valla believed the laity actually to be superior because when they obey they do so out of their own good will, not because of pressure imposed upon them from the outside. In addition to vows, Valla opposes the exaltation of poverty. To be wealthy, he said, is not the same as being sinful, nor is being poor synonymous with being pious. Christ taught us to be poor in spirit, not poor in goods. The monkish practice of giving all one's money to the poor so that one too may become a beggar is, to Valla, a perversion of Christianity, which is faith in Christ and love to God and humanity.

In 1448, Valla left the service of King Alfonso in order to assume the dual role of apostolic secretary to Pope Nicholas V and professor at the University of Rome, tasks that allowed him plenty of time to engage in scholarly pursuit. That he was employed by the pope, even after the attack on the Donation of Constantine was published, is a tribute to the pope's tolerance, to his confidence in himself and his office, and to Valla's prestige and worth as a scholar.

Valla's final major work, one published posthumously by Desiderius Erasmus, was his *Adnotationes in Novum Testamentum* (1505). This book deals with the Latin translation of the Bible (the Vulgate) in the light of Valla's knowledge of Greek. In it, he attempts to correct some of the Vulgate's mistakes, which he evaluated on grammatical, stylistic, and philosophical grounds. The first assesses the strict accuracy of the Vulgate's vocabulary and syntax, the second how well the Vulgate captured the eloquence and power of the original, and the third how fully the philosophical and theological content have been preserved. It was by these tests, Valla believed, that one could best aid the cause of theological restoration and the recovery of the fundamentals of Christianity.

After nearly a decade in Rome, Valla died, in 1457, after suffering an unidentified illness.

Summary

Lorenzo Valla was one of the most original and influential scholars of the Italian Renaissance. His work demonstrates most clearly the effect that accurate historical perspective and careful literary analysis could have on the various fields of knowledge, especially theology and philosophy. In that light, he was one of the leading critical minds of his age. He succeeded in establishing the new study of philology as a respectable and useful academic discipline.

Thus, Valla was a groundbreaker and a pioneer. His work served as a guide and inspiration for later Humanists such as Erasmus, who also desired to restore theology by means of the humanities. Valla also enjoyed a measure of success in reorganizing philosophical inquiry by freeing it from the control of medieval Scholastic methods. In this he anticipated later European thinkers such as Peter Ramus. By Protestants such as Martin Luther, Valla was considered a theological forerunner and a kindred spirit. Like them, he believed that faith was the basis of Christian living, not any external actions. Like them, he also denied the spiritual superiority of the monastic life-style, and he attacked the validity of some papal claims to authority. It is wrong, nevertheless, to see Valla as a Protestant. Although he was a protesting Catholic, he was not a Protestant. He never thought of himself as outside the Roman fold. Whenever he differed from the Church, he considered himself not un-Catholic, but "more orthodox than the orthodox."

Bibliography

Cassirer, Ernst, Paul O. Kristeller, and John Herman Randall, Jr., eds. *The Renaissance Philosophy of Man*. Chicago: University of Chicago Press, 1948. Chapter 2, "Lorenzo Valla," contains the best available English translation of *On Free Will*. The introduction to this chapter, by Charles Trinkaus, although it contains very little biographical detail, is an excellent entry into Valla's beliefs and intellectual methods. This chapter is enhanced by a useful annotated bibliography.

Kristeller, Paul O. *Eight Philosophers of the Italian Renaissance*. Stanford, Calif.: Stanford University Press, 1964; London: Chatto and Windus, 1965. Although it recounts the biographical details of Valla's life only briefly, chapter 2, "Valla," provides a succinct yet lucid introduction to his thought and its historical background. This chapter pays special attention to Valla's *On Free Will, On Pleasure*, and *Dialecticae disputationes*.

Spitz, Lewis W. *The Renaissance and Reformation Movements*. 2 vols. Chicago: Rand McNally, 1971. One of the finest and most accessible introductions to the period, the first volume of this set describes the various intellectual elements of Renaissance Humanism. Each chapter is well organized, readable, and accurate. Chapter 6, "Renaissance Humanism," contains a brief but excellent introduction to the life, background, and contribution of Lorenzo Valla. Though each chapter contains bibliographical references throughout, and though each chapter concludes with a useful bibliography, the titles listed concerning Valla are few.

Trinkaus, Charles. *In Our Image and Likeness: Humanity and Divinity in Italian Humanist Thought.* 2 vols. London: Constable, and Chicago: University of Chicago Press, 1970. Chapter 3, "Lorenzo Valla: Voluptas et Fruitio, Verba et Res," is a well-documented, closely argued, seventy-page account of Valla's moral and religious thought. Trinkaus traces several key motifs through Valla's most important books, from which, in his footnotes, he quotes at length in the original Latin.

———. "Lorenzo Valla on the Problem of Speaking about the Trinity." *Journal of the History of Ideas* 57 (January, 1996): 27. The author examines Valla's application of humanistic theology to the Christian doctrine of the Trinity, the disastrous result of the "Repastinatio dialectice et philosophie." He cites Augustine's discussion of the three members of the Trinity.

Valla, Lorenzo. *On Pleasure: De Voluptate.* Edited and translated by A. Kent Hieatt and Maristella Lorch. New York: Abaris Books, 1977. This excellent volume contains both the Latin original of Valla's book and an accurate, readable English translation on facing pages. The book is prefaced by a forty-page introduction that describes Valla's personality, his polemics, his Humanist background, and his *On Pleasure*. The volume concludes with twenty-five pages of notes and appendices. Though many works are alluded to in the process, no separate bibliography is given.

Michael Bauman

GIORGIO VASARI

Born: July 30, 1511; Arezzo, Republic of Florence
Died: June 27, 1574; Florence
Areas of Achievement: Literature, art, and architecture
Contribution: Modern knowledge of the lives and works of the principal, as well as a number of lesser, artists of the Renaissance derives almost exclusively from Vasari's *Lives of the Most Eminent Painters, Sculptors, and Architects*. Vasari was also a minor painter and architect.

Early Life

Giorgio Vasari, from ancient Arezzo, a hill town dating from Etruscan times and rich in mementos of the Middle Ages and the early Renaissance, was born into a family numbering several local artists among its antecedents. His father, Antonio, a tradesman, compensated for his own lack of creativity and financial success by maintaining close contact with men of consequence within the Church and in artistic circles and was particularly proud of his kinship with Luca Signorelli, a major figure in mid-Renaissance art, who provided the young Vasari with his first lessons in drawing. His formal training, however, began under the guidance of a Frenchman resident in Arezzo, Guglielmo di Marsillac, now remembered as a major stained-glass artist. Yet it is likely that Vasari learned much more from his daily exposure to local art treasures; he claimed, in fact, to have spent his early youth copying "all the good pictures to be found in the churches of Arezzo."

At age fifteen, as a result of his father's splendid contacts, Vasari was taken to Florence by Cardinal Silvio Passerini of Cortona, who brought him to the studios of Andrea del Sarto and Michelangelo. This initial contact with Michelangelo marked the beginning of a close relationship destined to last for forty years, and no single artist in Vasari's vast knowledge of Renaissance creativity was more admired by him than Michelangelo: "I courted Michelangelo assiduously and consulted him about all my affairs, and he was good enough to show me great friendship."

Cardinal Passerini also introduced him to members of the Medici family, in whose favor Vasari would remain for the duration of his career. At this particular time, however, such contact was of little consequence, for the Medicis were soon driven from the city, and Vasari, fearful for his own safety in the ensuing anti-Medici atmosphere, fled back to Arezzo, only to find his hometown ridden with a plague that had already taken his father's life. His uncle, as guardian of the family, advised him not to go home and expose himself to such peril and instead arranged for him to live in nearby villages, where he made a meager living doing decorative work in small churches. The following year, the plague having run its course, he joined his family in Arezzo, once more relishing the opportunity to observe and copy local artworks and also finishing his first commission, a painting for the Church of San Piero.

Yet, when Florence again appeared safe for a Medici protégé, he returned, this time in the hope of making a reasonable living for his family, whose welfare was now his responsibility. He entered into an apprenticeship with a goldsmith. Once more his plans were disrupted by political upheaval, now in the form of the 1529 siege of Florence. Vasari, never one to court danger, made his way to Pisa, where he abandoned his new craft and returned to painting, quickly making a name for himself as a reli-

able, competent, hardworking artist. His patrons were not Pisans but exiled Florentines, members of the distinguished Pitti and Guicciardini families.

Still not yet twenty years old and driven by the restlessness of youth, Vasari soon left Pisa, traveling a circuitous route via Modena and Bologna back to Arezzo, where he completed his first fresco, a representation of the four evangelists with God the Father and some life-size figures. From that time on, he was never lacking in distinguished patronage. Working on commissions for local rulers, princes of the Church, and the pope, he completed, always in record time, major fresco projects in Siena, Rome, Arezzo, and Florence. His works in this medium, most notably those in Rome's Palazza della Cancelleria, the interior of Filippo Brunelleschi's monumental dome in Florence's cathedral, and the splendidly reconstructed rooms in the Palazzo Vecchio were viewed as masterpieces in their day, and Vasari was richly rewarded. Yet despite their great contemporary appeal, posterity has dealt harshly with Vasari's decorative works, viewing his efforts as superficial and flamboyant, devoid of intellectual clarity and spiritual depth.

Life's Work

Although Vasari described himself as a painter and architect and clearly exerted a major portion of his time and energy on works in these fields, he made his principal contribution with *Le vite de' più eccellenti architetti, pittori, et scultori italiani, da cimabue insino a' tempi nostri* (1550; *Lives of the Most Eminent Painters, Sculptors, and Architects*, 1855-1885), a prodigious compendium of information on art and artists gradually accumulated throughout his mature years. Wherever he happened to be—and he traveled widely—and whatever the primary purpose of his journey, he always devoted a significant portion of his time to the observation of works by other artists, making sketches and taking notes and, whenever the opportunity was there, acquiring original sketches and drawings for his steadily mounting collection to which in his work he refers time and again and invariably with great pride.

It is quite possible that without the prodding of others, in particular his Rome patron Cardinal Farnese, the *Lives of the Most Eminent Painters, Sculptors, and Architects* would have remained the writer's private, unpublished notes on the arts of the Renaissance. The subject of compiling all of his material into a published account, Vasari reports, was brought up at a dinner party in the home of the cardinal in 1546, when Paolo Giovio, already a renowned collector of portraits and a biographer but not an artist, expressed the wish for having available "a treatise discussing all illustrious artists from the time of Cimabue to the present." Considering that the first manuscript was ready for the scribe in 154s8, it stands to reason that Vasari must have had most of the material on hand by the time the subject of·a book was broached, and that the two ensuing years must have been spent organizing the vast body of notes into a logical entity.

Not everything in the work represents the writer's original thoughts. Vasari borrowed liberally from all available sources—written observations by Brunelleschi, Lorenzo Ghiberti, Ghirlandajo, Raphael, and many others—as a rule acknowledging his indebtedness. Such secondary aspects of the work, however, are far less important than Vasari's own meticulous, often pedantic, descriptions of thousands of works of art in terms of structure, form, color, and purpose. To facilitate the reader's comprehension and establish a degree of unity in his flood of observations, he puts forth a set of criteria which in his opinion form the basis on which a work of art should be judged. First in this hierarchy of values is *disegno*, or word design, by which Vasari implies not only the total layout of a particular work but also the actual skill of drawing that must precede the finished product. With *natura*, true to the Renaissance spirit, he claims that excellence in art derives from careful observation and faithful re-creation of nature, or even, in the Neoplatonic consciousness so prevalent at the time, an improvement on nature. *Decoro* refers to the appropriateness, the decorum, or dignity, that should always be part of all visual creativity, stressing that the representation must befit the subject at hand. *Iudizio*, a less tangible term, is a criterion applied to the evaluation of an artist's sense of sound judgment relative to his combining all the separate elements that go into the evolvement and completion of his work. Last in Vasari's listing is *maniera*, an overall consideration referring either to a single artist's unique style and approach or to the style, the manner, of an entire school, for example, the Sienese or the Florentine.

Vasari's own style of writing ranges from the matter-of-fact listing of data and descriptive details to a florid gushing of superlatives. In his discussion of Masaccio, he describes the *Pisa Madonna* in this straightforward way:

> In the Carmelite church at Pisa, inside a chapel in the transept, there is a panel painting by Masaccio showing the Virgin and Child, and some little angels at her feet, who are playing instruments and one of whom is sounding a lute and inclining his ear very attentively to listen to the music he is making. Surrounding Our Lady are St. Peter, St. John the Baptist, St. Julian, St. Nicholas, all very vivacious and animated.

Entirely different and far more elevated are his comments on Leonardo da Vinci:

> The excellent productions of this divine artist had so greatly increased and extended his fame that all men who delighted in the arts (nay, the whole city of Florence) were anxious that he should leave behind him some memorial of himself; and there was much discussion everywhere in respect to some great and important work to be executed by him, to the end that the commonwealth might have glory, and the city the ornament, imparted by the genius, grace, and judgment of Leonardo to all that he did.

While the weight and importance placed on Vasari's descriptions and evaluations in subsequent times have shifted, his approach to artistic biography remained the unchallenged standard for the next three hundred years. Even in modern times any study of the artists of the Italian Renaissance tends to have Vasari's *Lives of the Most Eminent Painters, Sculptors, and Architects* as its point of departure. It is to a considerable extent to his particular credit that neglect was not to be the destiny of the multitude of artists active on the Italian peninsula in those two hundred years he designated as the Renaissance.

Summary

In *Lives of the Most Eminent Painters, Sculptors, and Architects*, Giorgio Vasari devotes much space to a detailed description of his own numerous works carried out on commission in various parts of Italy, and to the lofty sociocultural standings of the many who sought to employ his talent and fame. It is therefore quite evident that he would have preferred to be remembered as a significant painter. Even so, he never succeeded in making a lasting impact in that field. Even his major commission, the challenging decorations in the most auspicious rooms in the Palazzo Vacchio, did not in retrospect come up to the standards set by his Florentine predecessors in the art of fresco painting, let alone those by artists much closer to his own time, Michelangelo and Raphael, whom he so deeply admired and whose works he so eloquently described. In the final analysis, he failed by his own standards as well, for most of his frescos are hopelessly congested, pompously rhetorical, wearisome to the eye, and clearly lacking the visual mellowness, the decorum and sound judgment set forth in his work as prerequisites for true artistic accomplishment.

None of this detracts in the least from the pioneering importance of his written work. Modern research carried out under circumstances far more favorable than those under which Vasari labored may have brought to light certain inaccuracies in his findings, and some of his evaluations have not withstood the test of time. More often than not, however, new research has simply resulted in a validation of his findings and observations. Furthermore, his minute descriptions of works of art constitute not only the basis on which the field of art history has been built but also provide the pattern for the process of attribution of works of art of the past, so important for the development of collections, private and public.

Bibliography

Burckhardt, Jacob. *The Altarpiece in Renaissance Italy.* Edited and translated by Peter Humfrey. Cambridge and New York: Cambridge University Press, 1988. Swiss scholar Burckhardt's nineteenth century works on the Italian Renaissance are considered classics in the field. Originally published in 1894 with two other essays, "The Collectors" and "The Portrait," the original edition was entirely without illustrations, whereas in this first English edition the accompanying illustrations, in color and black and white, greatly enhance the discussion. While Burckhardt based his studies on personal probing of the subject, his principal documentation is rooted in Vasari's *Lives of the Most Eminent Painters, Sculptors, and Architects.*

Decker, Heinrich. *The Renaissance in Italy: Architecture, Frescoes, Sculpture.* London: Thames and Hudson, and New York: Viking Press, 1969. A profusely illustrated volume containing meaningful references to Vasari. Although this and other statements tend to reinforce some of the negative criticism so often aimed at Vasari, Decker also stresses the importance of his contribution and actually judges his frescos more favorably than do other writers.

Robert, Carden W. *The Life of Giorgio Vasari: A Study of the Later Renaissance in Italy.* London:

Warner, 1910; New York: Holt, 1911. Drawing on Vasari's own accounts and on other sources, the author discusses Vasari's contribution as an artist and a writer in the perspective of the creative spirit of the waning years of the Renaissance and the early period of mannerism. Because Vasari's own detailed description of his life and activities has made it less urgent to write on that subject, Robert's work still remains the only comprehensive study available in English.

Satkowski, Leon G. *Giorgio Vasari: Architect and Courtier.* Princeton, N.J.: Princeton University Press, 1993. Satkowski presents the first book in any language to survey the architecture of Vasari. By focusing on the architect's service to his distinguished patrons and his collaboration with other architects, Satkowski reveals how Vasari combined imaginative design, political meaning, and a clear sense of history to create buildings that are appealing to modern students of architecture.

Wackernagel, Martin. *The World of the Florentine Renaissance Artist: Projects and Patrons, Workshop and Art Market.* Translated by Alison Luchs. Princeton, N.J.: Princeton University Press, 1938. Wackernagel's book, a pioneering study, examines the relationship between the arts and the immediate sociopolitical and economic conditions under which artists worked. Vasari's documentations and judgment, as well as his relationship with patrons, receive good coverage.

Wittkower, Rudolf. *Idea and Image: Studies in the Italian Renaissance.* London and New York: Thames and Hudson, 1978. The last volume in the author's collected essays contains extensive references to *Lives of the Most Eminent Painters, Sculptors, and Architects*, always cited with great respect for the authority of the document. Particularly interesting is Wittkower's discussion of the evolvement of Michelangelo's dome of St. Peter's in the Vatican, of which, Wittkower states, Vasari provided "detailed and reliable description," in turn totally ignored by subsequent builders. Equally positive is Wittkower's estimation of Vasari's perspicacity relative to the development of Raphael's talent.

Reidar Dittmann

PAOLO VERONESE
Paolo Caliari

Born: 1528; Verona, Republic of Venice
Died: 1588; Venice
Area of Achievement: Art
Contribution: Veronese was one of the greatest painters in sixteenth century Venice and, along with Titian and Tintoretto, was responsible for the countermannerism which characterized the style of that school of art. His luminous colors and dynamic, decorative compositions foreshadow the artistic concerns of the next century's painters.

Early Life

Paolo Veronese was born Paolo Caliari in 1528 in Verona, Republic of Venice. His father, Gabriele di Piero Caliari, was a sculptor and stonecutter in that city, and in all likelihood Veronese received his earliest artistic instruction in his father's studio, perhaps learning to model in clay. Further training came in the painting workshop of his uncle, Antonio Badile, and he may also have worked for a time with the painter and architect Giovanni Caroto.

Veronese appears to have remained in Verona until around 1552, when he left to execute commissions in various northern Italian cities, including Mantua, where he worked on an altarpiece for the cathedral with several other painters. It is not clear exactly when he first settled in Venice, but in 1553 he was given work at the Venetian Ducal Palace. This important commission, also a collaboration, involved painting the ceiling of the room where the Council of Ten met for deliberations (Sala del Consiglio dei Dieci).

Veronese's style during his earliest period was in line with the sophisticated mannerism popular in Italy during the middle of the sixteenth century. In particular, his early work shows the influence of Emilian artists such as Parmigianino. As he matured, however, his style evolved a more classical handling of space and form. A natural predisposition for pictorial compositions, along with the influence of Titian's style, seemed to account for this countermannerist development.

Life's Work

Veronese is generally considered, along with Titian and Tintoretto, one of the greatest painters of sixteenth century Venice. His paintings, frequently of immense size and crowded with figures, are like tapestries filled with color and light. The sumptuous textures, details, and colors create patterns which emphasize the decorative qualities of what is, emphatically, a joyful, aristocratic art. Veronese's colors are pure and clear, a combination of pale and vivid tones, unsubdued by shadows or glazes such as those of Titian and Tintoretto.

Within a few years of his arrival in Venice, Veronese was given a commission which, along with his work in the Ducal Palace, established his reputation as one of Venice's preeminent painters. For the Church of San Sebastiano, he executed, around 1556, a series of frescoed murals and canvas ceiling paintings. The ceiling paintings in particular demonstrate dramatic compositional arrangements. Exploiting the position of the paintings above the viewer's head, Veronese employed perspective to create the illusion that the ceiling had opened up and that the scenes being depicted were in fact happening while the viewer looked up from below. In *The Triumph of Mordecai*, horses shy at the edge of an abyss in which, spatially speaking, the viewer stands. Lords and ladies look directly down from a balcony. Veronese was not the first artist to use this illusionistic device (called *di sotto in su*). Andrea Mantegna had employed it in the fifteenth century, and Corregio had explored its possibilities. Veronese, however, developed its full pictorial and atmospheric potential and served as a reference for Baroque artists of the seventeenth century.

Veronese appears to have spent most of his mature career in and around Venice. He did visit Rome sometime between 1555 and 1560, where he saw the work of the High Renaissance masters, but most of his travels took him to cities near Venice. Around 1561, he executed a series of frescoes at the Villa Barbaro in Maser, and in 1575 he is documented as working in Padua on a *Martyrdom of Saint Justina* and *An Ascension of Christ.* In the late 1570's, Veronese received one of his most important commissions. A 1577 fire had destroyed the painted decorations in the Hall of the Great Council (Sala del Maggior Consiglio) of the Ducal Palace, and Veronese was hired to repaint the ceiling. His central allegorical scene, *The Triumph of Venice*, combines the illusionism of the San Sebas-

tiano ceiling paintings with a new spatial expansiveness full of strong, almost unearthly highlights and pure color.

Veronese's personal life was fairly uneventful. He married Elena Badile, the daughter of his teacher, in 1566 and had two sons. By all accounts he was a religious, morally strict man. It is ironic, then, that his name has been immortalized not only for his art but also for the fact that he was called before the Inquisition to defend one of his paintings.

In April of 1573, Veronese completed a painting depicting the Last Supper for the refectory of Saints Giovanni and Paolo in Venice, to replace a work of the same subject by Titian which had been destroyed by fire in 1571. Three months later, he was summoned to appear before the Holy Tribunal, or Inquisition, to answer complaints against the work. Specifically, the church hierarchy was concerned by what it perceived as a lack of decorum in the composition. The crowded painting showed, in addition to the traditional Christ and apostles, dwarfs, buffoons, drunkards, and Germans. These superfluous figures, added for picturesque and decorative effects, violated the decrees of the Council of Trent, which, in its codification of the tenets of the Counter-Reformation, had stated that religious paintings should contain no distortions or distractions which might interfere with the moral message. The transcript of Veronese's interview with the tribunal survives and shows him deflecting the criticism with naïveté, claiming that he added the excess figures for compositional, or artistic, purposes. The tribunal decided that Veronese was to make corrections at his own expense. Instead, he changed the title of the painting to *The Feast in the House of Levi*, and left it as he had painted it with only the most minor alterations.

Summary

Paolo Veronese is sometimes described by art historians as a proto-Baroque artist. His essentially naturalistic and illusionistic handling of form and space was certainly not in keeping with the mannerist taste which dominated Italian painting during the middle of the sixteenth century. Some of his mature works do, in fact, demonstrate expansive views of space, theatrical compositions, and decorative arrangements of color and light which point to the styles of the next two centuries. At the same time, other of his paintings look back to the pictorial traditions of fifteenth century Venice. In particular, his use of the old tableau composition, with figures lined along a shallow plane before a descriptive Venetian backdrop, hark back to the works of Vittore Carpaccio and Gentile Bellini.

Of the three great masters of sixteenth century Venetian painting (Titian, Tintoretto, and Veronese), Veronese's reputation has suffered the most in recent centuries. Critics often find his decorative compositions lacking in profundity. The perceived deficiencies are not those of talent or technique, but rather in the area of expression. This attitude may say more about the expectations of art in the modern world than about Veronese's intentions and accomplishments.

Bibliography

Cocke, Richard. "The Development of Veronese's Critical Reputation." *Arte Veneta* 34 (1980): 96-111. Discusses the critical attitudes toward Veronese over the centuries and the extent of his influence in each period of art. Especially valuable in describing Veronese's influence on Baroque artists.

———. *Veronese*. London: Jupiter, 1980. A monographic overview of Veronese's life and career, this book is a useful introduction to the artist. Particular emphasis is placed on stylistic issues, although biographic information is also included. Contains one hundred illustrations, with some in color, and a bibliography.

———. *Veronese's Drawings, with a "Catalogue Raisonné."* London: Sotheby, and Ithaca, N.Y.: Cornell University Press, 1984. A thorough analysis of Veronese's drawings and how they relate stylistically and programatically to their related paintings. Includes a chronology of documentable activities, a bibliography, and illustrations and catalog entries for each drawing. Useful as a supplement to Cocke's monograph cited above.

Danto, A. C. "The Gorgeousness of Life." *Art News* (January, 1989): 108. The author discusses the paintings of Veronese that, at the time the article was written, were on exhibit at the National Gallery of Art in Washington, D.C.

Fehl, Philipp. "Veronese and the Inquisition: A Study of the Subject Matter of the So-Called *Feast in the House of Levi.*" *Gazette des Beaux-Arts* 58 (1961): 325-354. Discusses the iconography of Veronese's famous painting and the events surrounding the confrontation with the Inquisition.

Goldwater, Robert, and Marco Treves, eds. *Artists on Art.* New York: Pantheon, 1958; London: Murray, 1956. A translation of the examination of Veronese by the Holy Tribunal regarding his *Last Supper*, later retitled *The Feast in the House of Levi.* The original record is preserved in the Archives in Venice. Most other anthologies of art-historical documents also include this transcript.

Rosand, David. *Painting in Sixteenth-Century Venice: Titian, Veronese, Tintoretto.* Rev. ed. Cambridge and New York: Cambridge University Press, 1997. This work contains readable, scholarly articles investigating the sources and influences on Veronese's compositions, including fifteenth century traditions and contemporary theater designs. Also provides an analysis of Veronese's waning reputation and a synopsis of the examination by the Inquisition. Contains excellent black-and-white photographs and a bibliography.

Madeline Cirillo Archer

ANDREA DEL VERROCCHIO
Andrea di Michele Cione

Born: 1435; Florence

Died: October 7, 1488; Venice

Area of Achievement: Art

Contribution: Verrocchio was one of the best sculptors of the later part of the fifteenth century and a great favorite of the Medici family. He was able to work in silver, bronze, and terracotta as well as marble and was also active as a painter. It was in Verrocchio's workshop that Leonardo da Vinci received his first training.

Early Life

Andrea di Michele Cione, best known to his contemporaries by his nickname "Verrocchio," was the son of Michele Cione and his first wife, Gemma. He was born in Florence, where he grew up and where he spent most of his life. His father, who was in his fifties when Andrea, his first child, was born, worked as a tilemaker or brickmaker and was a member of the Stoneworkers' Guild. He owned a home on the Via dell'Angolo in the parish of San Ambrogio as well as some land outside the city. Andrea's mother evidently died while he was young, for his father remarried and Andrea was reared by his stepmother. In 1452, his father died. The following year, the eighteen-year-old Verrocchio was involved in an incident in which a man was killed in a scuffle outside the walls of the city. Verrocchio had thrown a stone which hit a young wool worker, who subsequently died of his injuries. Verrocchio was brought before the authorities and charged with homicide, but he was acquitted and the cause of the death was determined to be accidental.

According to his sixteenth century biographer, Giorgio Vasari, Verrocchio was largely self-taught; historians have no certain knowledge of when he received his early training or who his teachers may have been. From 1467 onward, his name appears in the surviving contemporary documents as "del Verrocchio," and while a seventeenth century source reports that he received his first training in the shop of a goldsmith named Giuliano da Verrocchi, it is now known that he owed his nickname to the fact that in his youth he was a protégé of an ecclesiastic named Verrocchio. In the tax return which he and his younger brother Tommaso filed for the year 1457, he does state that he has been working as a goldsmith but complains that there is no work in this craft and that he has been forced to abandon it. One early source implies that he was trained by Donatello, and while that is possible, modern critics have also suggested that he may have studied or worked with Desiderio da Settignano or Bernardo Rossellino. In 1461, Verrocchio was one of a number of Florentine artists who were asked to furnish designs for the construction of a chapel in the cathedral at Orvieto, but none of the Florentines received the commission.

Life's Work

Verrocchio emerges as an important artist only in the late 1460's. His earliest authenticated works are decorative or architectural, and two of them were commissioned by the Medicis, marking the beginning of his long association with that family. The marble, brass, and porphery tombstone for Cosimo de' Medici in the Church of S. Lorenzo, Florence, was completed in 1467. By 1472, the year in which he was listed as a painter and carver in the records of the Florentine artists' professional association, the Guild of Saint Luke, he had completed his first major work and one of his most important ones: the tomb of Piero and Giovanni de' Medici in the Church of S. Lorenzo. Verrocchio employed virtually no figural decoration and no Christian symbolism, but the tomb has a solemn majesty which derives from his characteristic combination of simplicity of design and great richness of detail.

Verrocchio's famous bronze *David* in the Museo Nazionale di Bargello in Florence was probably commissioned in the early 1470's and is certainly one of the earliest of his figural compositions. Like Donatello's bronze *David*, it was a Medici commission, but there is an embellishment of the forms that signals the change in Florentine taste toward the richer and more sumptuous taste that marks the late fifteenth century. At about the same time, Verrocchio completed his most popular work, the wonderful bronze *Putto with a Dolphin* that was part of a fountain in the Medici villa at Careggi. This is a work of great importance for the history of Renaissance sculpture, for it is the first sculpture since antiquity to present equally pleasing views from all sides.

In January of 1467, Verrocchio received the first payments for one of his finest works, the bronze group of *Christ and Saint Thomas* in the central niche on the east front of the Or San Michele in Florence. The niche had originally been designed for a single figure, and the creation of a two-figure, more than life-size group for the narrow space presented unusual difficulties. Verrocchio was able to solve these problems by making the figures very shallow, a fact of which the spectator is unaware, and by letting the figure of Saint Thomas extend out of the niche toward the viewer. It is possible that the creation and execution of these figures may have occupied him for as long as eighteen years, for they were not placed in the niche until June of 1483.

Verrocchio also carried out several important commissions in marble, of which one of his finest is the half-length *Portrait of a Woman*, a work that bears a strong resemblance to Leonardo's *Portrait of Ginevra dei Benci*. None of his monumental marble works, though, remains in its original condition. The earliest of these was the monument to Francesca Tornabuoni, which was set up in the Church of S. Maria sopra Minerva in Rome, where the Tornabuoni family of Florence had a chapel. It may have been executed in the late 1470's, but very little of it remains. Of the monument to Cardinal Niccolò Forteguerri, there are at least some substantial remains and the original appearance of the work can be partially reconstructed from the large terracotta sketch held in the Victoria and Albert Museum in London. In May of 1476, Verrocchio's model was chosen from among five competitors by the council of Pistoia, the cardinal's native city. The monument was to be erected in the Cathedral of Pistoia, but the execution dragged on and several figures and some of the architectural framework were still not finished when Verrocchio died. The monument was given its present form in the mid-eighteenth century. Verrocchio also was responsible for some of the decoration of the huge silver altar frontal for the altar in the Florentine Baptistery. This masterpiece of the goldsmith's art had been begun in the fourteenth century, and generations of artists had contributed to it. In 1480, Verrocchio completed the silver relief representing *The Beheading of Saint John the Baptist*, which was placed on the lower right side of the altar.

Verrocchio and his studio regularly produced paintings as well as sculpture, but very few paintings can now be identified as his with any certainty. Of the many half-length Madonnas which have been attributed to him, there is little agreement as to which, if any, may be actually by him. The *Madonna Enthroned with Saints John the Baptist and Donatus* was commissioned from Verrocchio not long before 1478, but much of the execution seems to be by Lorenzo di Credi, who worked with Verrocchio and often collaborated with him. Verrocchio's best painting, and the only one which is universally agreed to be his, is the *Baptism of Christ*, which probably dates from the mid-1470's. Vasari's statement that one of the kneeling angels is by Leonardo, who was in Verrocchio's studio in 1476, is generally accepted. What is clear is that Verrocchio depended heavily on pupils, members of his workshop, and collaborators to produce the paintings which were commissioned from him.

The last years of Verrocchio's life were devoted to the design of what was to become his masterpiece: the over life-size *Equestrian Statue of Colleoni* in Venice. The noted Renaissance soldier Bartolommeo Colleoni of Bergamo had died in 1475 and in his will left funds for a commemorative equestrian statue to be erected in his honor in

Venice. Verrocchio's full-scale model was completed in the summer of 1481, and in 1483 Verrocchio moved to Venice, where he remained until his death in 1488. At the time of his death, no parts of the work had yet been cast and it was not until 1496 that the work was completed and installed on a high pedestal in the Piazza of SS. Giovanni e Paolo. Although he never lived to see its completion, it is in every way the supreme achievement of his artistic genius.

Summary

Andrea del Verrocchio's contribution to the development of monumental sculpture during the Renaissance is a major one. Only Donatello ranks with him. Verrocchio's workshop was one of the largest and most active in Florence, and in his mastery of all facets of the visual arts he provided a role model for his greatest pupil, Leonardo da Vinci. Leonardo's conception of the artist as a man of science, versed in all aspects of engineering and anatomy as well as design, owes much to Verrocchio's example. It would be unfair, however, to see Verrocchio's achievement primarily in terms of the accomplishments of his best pupil. In his own right, he is one of the most characteristic artists of the Florentine Renaissance. The naturalistic element in his work is very strong, and in this he reflects the dominant ideal of the Florentine artist of his day: fidelity to nature. All aspects of the natural were to be studied and understood, but for Verrocchio this naturalism was never an end in itself. Instead, it was the means by which he could create a perfect and untarnished world of forms and ideal types. Verrocchio's contemporaries fully appreciated this aspect of his work. One of them noted that his head of Christ in the group of *Christ and Saint Thomas* was thought to be "the most beautiful head of the Saviour that has yet been made."

His masterpiece, the monument to Colleoni, shows how effectively he was able to balance these two tendencies. It is a work of enormous power, and the violent and aggressive twist of the rider's body gives a sense of tremendous energy waiting to be unleashed. To achieve this effect, Verrocchio has twisted the figure to the limits of human possibility. Similarly, the brutal face is an unflinching delineation of a type, not an individual, but it is rendered so plausibly that it seems more vital than any portrait. No fifteenth century artist better exemplified the artistic ideals of the era.

Bibliography

Butterfield, Andrew. *The Sculptures of Andrea del Verrocchio*. New Haven, Conn.: Yale University Press, 1997. This catalog is the first comprehensive and detailed study of Verrocchio's sculptures. Butterfield has combined careful visual analysis of the sculptures with research into their function, iconography, and historical context. In order to explain Verrocchio's contributions to the different genres of Renaissance sculpture, Butterfield provides important information on a broad range of issues such as the typology and social history of Florentine tombs, the theoretical problems in the production of perspectival reliefs, and the origins of the *Figura serpentinata*.

Covi, Dario A. "Four New Documents Concerning Andrea del Verrocchio." *The Art Bulletin* 48 (1966): 97-103. New and important documents dealing with the life of the artist and his work.

Passavant, Günter. *Verrocchio: Sculptures, Paintings, and Drawings: Complete Edition*. Translated by Katherine Watson. London: Phaidon Press, 1969. The best general modern survey. The text covers all aspects of Verrocchio's work, and there is a catalog of the sculptures, paintings, and drawings, which the author believes to be authentic, as well as information on rejected works.

Pope-Hennessy, John. *Italian Renaissance Sculpture*. 4th ed. London: Phaidon Press, 1996. The best general introduction to the field of Italian Renaissance sculpture, with extensive coverage of the major masters. The short article on Verrocchio is an excellent summary of his work as a sculptor and there are catalog entries of his major works.

Seymour, Charles, Jr. *The Sculpture of Verrocchio*. London: Studio Vista, and Greenwich, Conn.: New York Graphic Society, 1971. The best catalog of Verrocchio's sculpture. Contains notes on the principal works, an appendix of documents with translations, and a partial translation, with some explanatory notes, of Vasari's 1568 biography of the artist.

Vasari, Giorgio. *Lives of the Most Eminent Painters, Sculptors, and Architects*. Translated by Gaston du C. de Vere. Vol. 3. London: Medici Society, 1912; New York: AMS Press, 1976. The standard translation of the second edition of Vasari's biography of the artist, first published in 1568. This is the only nearly contemporary biography of the artist, written by a man who was born more than twenty years after Verrocchio died. While it is not a reliable source for dates or attributions, it contains a wealth of information available in no other source.

Wilder, Elizabeth. *The Unfinished Monument by Andrea del Verrocchio to the Cardinal Niccolò Forteguerri at Pistoia*. Vol. 7 of *Studies in the History and Criticism of Sculpture*. Northampton, Mass.: Smith College, 1932. Photographs by Clarence Kennedy and appendix of documents by Peleo Bacci. The most thorough study of any of Verrocchio's works. Includes complete documentation and excellent photographs.

Eric Van Schaack

ANDREAS VESALIUS

Born: December 31, 1514; Brussels

Died: October 15, 1564; Zacynthus (modern Zante), Greece

Areas of Achievement: Medicine and physiology

Contribution: Vesalius, a physician and anatomist of the Renaissance, was one of the most important figures in the history of medicine. He published the first modern comprehensive text of human anatomy. His accurate description of the structure of the human body, the result of firsthand dissection, is the basis of the modern scientific study of human anatomy.

Early Life

Andreas Vesalius was descended from a long line of physicians, of whom he belonged to the fifth generation. The family combined scholarly and humanistic interests (several had written medical treatises or commentaries on Arabic and Hippocratic works) with medical ability and ambition, having served the courts of Burgundy and the Habsburgs. Although the family had long lived in Flanders, it had come originally from Wesel on the lower Rhine River, hence the family's name, of which Vesalius is the Latin form. Vesalius' father was apothecary to the court of the Habsburg Emperor Charles V. As a boy, Vesalius dissected dogs, cats, moles, mice, and rats. He attended the University of Louvain from 1529 to 1533, where he studied Latin and Greek. He then went to the University of Paris to study medicine, remaining there from 1533 to 1536. The medical faculty at Paris was under the influence of Galen, the great second century Greek medical writer, whose authority in anatomical matters was unchallenged. Vesalius found that there was little practical teaching of anatomy. Human corpses were dissected only twice a year, but Vesalius found the procedure disappointing. The professor of anatomy never performed the dissection himself but merely read passages from Galen as an assistant dissected the cadaver. In most cases pigs or dogs were dissected. Eager to obtain human skeletons, Vesalius sought them from cemeteries and gallows outside the city, where he obtained corpses of criminals in various states of decay. He became skilled at dissection and gained a firsthand knowledge of human anatomy. He began to acquire a reputation as an anatomist and even conducted a public dissection.

Vesalius left Paris in 1536 upon the outbreak of war between France and the Holy Roman Empire. He returned to Louvain, where he completed his baccalaureate degree in the following year. Thereupon he traveled to Italy and enrolled in the University of Padua, which enjoyed an outstanding reputation. On December 5, 1537, Vesalius received his medical degree with highest distinction. On the following day, he was appointed professor of surgery, which entailed the teaching of anatomy as well. He was only twenty-three years of age.

Life's Work

The young professor was enormously successful at Padua, where he lectured to some five hundred students, professors, and physicians. Dispensing with an assistant, he personally descended from his academic chair to dissect cadavers. He prepared four large anatomical charts to illustrate his lectures. In 1538, he published three of them and three skeletal views, which have come to be known as *Tabulae anatomicae sex (Six Anatomical Tables*, 1874). The publication of these accurate and detailed plates marked a major advance in anatomical illustration. In the same year, he published a dissection manual based on Galen, *Institutiones anatomicae* (1538), and in the following year he published *Epistola, docens venam axillarem dextri cubiti in dolore laterali secandam* (1539; *The Bloodletting Letter of 1539*, 1946), in which he argued for the importance of the direct observation of the body.

As a result of his publications and success in teaching, Vesalius began to acquire more than an ordinary reputation. He was reappointed to the medical faculty in 1539 at an increase in salary. In his lectures on anatomy, Vesalius had, as was then customary, expounded the views of Galen, whose authority was accepted in virtually every medical faculty in Europe. In dissections he performed, however, he began to notice discrepancies between what he observed and what Galen had described. At first, so few cadavers were available that there was only limited opportunity for dissection. Beginning in 1539, however, corpses of executed criminals were made available to him. Repeated dissections made it increasingly apparent to Vesalius that Galen's descriptions were erroneous and that Galen had based his descriptions on the anatomy of animals, primarily apes, pigs, and dogs. He expounded his discoveries first at Padua (in his fourth public dissection, at which he ceased to use Galen as a text), then, in 1540, at Bologna, where he was invited to lecture.

As early as 1538, Vesalius had apparently contemplated a major work on anatomy. As his dissections revealed many discrepancies between Galen's anatomy and his own discoveries, he recognized the need for a new and comprehensive text to replace Galen. After his return to Padua from Bologna, he commenced work on one in earnest. Vesalius had woodcut illustrations for the work prepared in Venice, probably in Titian's studio. To produce at least some of the illustrations, he chose a compatriot, Jan Stepfan van Calcar, who belonged to the school of Titian and had drawn the skeletal figures for the plates in *Six Anatomical Tables*. Other painters associated with the school of Titian almost certainly had a hand in the illustrations as well. Vesalius selected a firm in Basel to print the work, and the wood blocks for the illustrations were transported by donkey. In the summer of 1542, Vesalius went to Basel to oversee printing of *De humani corporis fabrica libri septem* (seven books on the structure of the human body; best known as *De fabrica*), which was published in August, 1543. *De fabrica* was one of the most outstanding examples of the bookmaker's art in the sixteenth century. Every detail had been personally supervised by Vesalius: the paper, woodcuts, typography, and famous frontispiece. The woodcuts, showing skeletons and flayed human figures, represented the culmination of Italian painting and the scientific study of human anatomy. They were meant to be studied closely with the text and were so successful that they were frequently plagiarized; they set the standard for all subsquent anatomical illustrators.

In *De fabrica*, Vesalius corrected more than two hundred errors of Galenic anatomy and described certain features that were either previously unknown or had been only partially described. He was not the first to find mistakes in Galen, but he went beyond mere correction by insisting that the only reliable basis of anatomical study was dissection and personal observation. *De fabrica* was the first modern treatise on human anatomy that was not based on Galen or drawn from dissected animals. The most extensive and accurate description of human anatomy that had yet appeared, it surpassed all previous books on the subject. Its publication revolutionized the study of anatomy, not least of all by its outstanding use of illustrations. Vesalius was only twenty-eight years of age when the book appeared, less than a week after the publication of Nicolaus Copernicus' *De revolutionibus orbium coelestium* (1543; *On the Revolutions of the Celestial Spheres*, 1939), which challenged the dominant geocentric theory of Ptolemy as *De fabrica* challenged the anatomy of Galen. Both books aroused violent controversy. Vesalius' fame spread rapidly, and many Italian physicians came to accept his views. Yet Galen's supporters reacted with strong attacks. Jacobus Sylvius, the leading authority on anatomy in Europe and Vesalius' former teacher, published a vitriolic pamphlet against Vesalius, perhaps angered at his attacks on the deficiencies of training in anatomy. Disappointed by the opposition of the Galenists, he abandoned his anatomical studies, burned all of his manuscripts, resigned his chair at Padua, and left Italy to accept the position of third court physician to the Holy Roman Emperor Charles V.

Vesalius was to spend some thirteen years in the service of the emperor, following a family tradition of service to titled houses. In 1544, his father, who had been an apothecary to Charles, died and left a substantial inheritance to Vesalius, who then was married to Anne van Hamme. About a year later, a daughter, his only child, was born. Vesalius spent much of his time traveling with the emperor, who suffered from gout and gastrointestinal disorders. He served as a military surgeon as well, during which time he introduced several new procedures, the most notable of which was the surgical drainage of the chest in empyema. Vesalius enjoyed the full confidence of the emperor, and his professional reputation continued to grow. Upon Charles's abdication from the Spanish throne in 1556 (he had abdicated as Holy Roman Emperor in 1555), he granted Vesalius a pension for life.

In 1546, Vesalius found time to write a short work, *Epistola, rationem modumque propinandi radicis Chynae* (China root letter), in response to a friend who sought his opinion of a fashionable remedy called the China root. In 1552, he began work on a second edition of *De fabrica*, which was issued a few months after Charles's abdication in 1555, though, like the first edition, it was dedicated to the emperor. The new edition was even more sumptuous than the first. Vesalius took the opportunity to revise and correct the text and make a number of additions. In 1556, he took up residence in Madrid as one of the physicians in the service of Philip II, who had succeeded his father, Charles, as

King of Spain. Vesalius' reputation was sufficiently outstanding that in 1559, when King Henry II of France was severely wounded in the head during a tournament, he was summoned to Paris, where he joined the distinguished French surgeon Ambroise Paré in treating the king. The wound proved fatal, however, and the king died ten days later. Vesalius' reputation as one of the greatest physicians of the age was secure, and his opinion was repeatedly sought. In 1562, Don Carlos, heir to the throne of Spain, received a severe head injury as the result of a fall. As his condition grew worse, the king summoned Vesalius to join several Spanish physicians in attendance on the infante. Although they distrusted him from the beginning, the Spanish physicians eventually allowed Vesalius to administer a treatment that resulted in a rapid improvement of the prince, who recovered.

In the spring of 1564, Vesalius embarked on a trip to the Holy Land by way of Venice. There is reason to believe that he did not intend to return to Spain. He seems to have been regarded with hostility by the Spanish physicians at court. He was probably motivated as well by a desire to return to an academic position, inspired by reading Gabriello Fallopio's *Observationes anatomicae*, which had been published in 1561. He was offered the vacant chair at Padua of his pupil Fallopio, who had recently died, and he signified his intention to take the position upon his return. He proceeded to Palestine by way of Cyprus, but he became ill on the return journey and died on October 15, 1564. He was buried on the island of Zacynthus.

Summary

The product of a long line of distinguished physicians and Humanists, Andreas Vesalius received a fine Renaissance education, had an excellent Latin style, and excelled in philological scholarship. He was trained in the Galenic system, which was taught in all European medical faculties. Only gradually did he come to see why Galen's anatomical descriptions, based on the dissection of animals, needed correction. Even then he was not wholly able to escape Galen's influence, for he sometimes reproduced his errors. His great contribution to medicine was his insistence that anatomical study be based on repeated dissection and first-hand observation of the human body.

The personality of Vesalius remains somewhat enigmatic. He appears to have been a man of considerable dynastic and personal ambition, who possessed great energy and desire to succeed. A man of genius, he enjoyed an enviable reputation in his own time but was nevertheless sensitive; he resented the attacks that were made on him by former teachers and jealous colleagues. Independent, unafraid of challenging authority, and confident of his own opinions, he combined great powers of observation with a reputation for remarkably accurate prognosis. He defended himself and his opinions when attacked but was willing to accept correction of his own errors.

Vesalius may be called the founder of modern anatomy. The importance that he placed on the systematic investigation of the human body led to dissection's becoming a routine part of the medical curriculum. His *De fabrica* revolutionized the study of anatomy, and its anatomical illustrations became the model for subsequent medical illustrators. Its publication marked the beginning of modern observational science and encouraged the work of other anatomists. Vesalius' ideas spread rapidly throughout Italy and Europe and came to be widely accepted within a half-century, in spite of the continuing influence of Galen. In his remarkable genius and his influence, Vesalius deserves to be ranked among the most distinguished contributors to medical science.

Bibliography

Cushing, Harvey. *A Bio-Bibliography of Andreas Vesalius*. New York: Schuman's, 1943. Contains an excellent bibliography of the various editions of Vesalius' writings and secondary literature about him.

Kemp, Martin "Vesalius's Veracity." *Nature* 393 (June, 1998): 421. Kemp examines the work of Vesalius; he includes depictions of his surgical instruments and compares him with Greek physician Galen.

Lambert, Samuel W., Willy Wiegand, and William M. Ivins, Jr. *Three Vesalian Essays*. New York: Macmillan, 1952. These essays deal with aspects of the printing and illustrations of *De fabrica*.

O'Malley, C. D. *Andreas Vesalius of Brussels, 1514-1564*. Berkeley: University of California Press, 1964. The definitive biography of Vesalius, which replaces that of Moritz Roth (Berlin, 1892).

Raju, Tonse N. K. "The First True Anatomist." *Hippocrates* 12 (June, 1998): 74. This article profiles Vesalius and provides background information on his life and medical career, and cites his book *De humani corporis fabrica*.

Singer, Charles, and C. Rabin. *A Prelude to Modern Science*. Cambridge: Cambridge University Press, 1946. A discussion of the history of *Six Anatomical Tables* and its sources.

Vesalius, Andreas. *The Illustrations from the Works of Andreas Vesalius of Brussels*. Introduction and annotations by J. B. de C. M. Saunders and Charles D. O'Malley. Cleveland: World Publishing, 1950. Contains a lengthy introduction describing the life and career of Vesalius and reproduces the woodcuts from *De fabrica* and other works of Vesalius.

Gary B. Ferngren

AMERIGO VESPUCCI

Born: March 14, 1454; Florence
Died: February 22, 1512; Seville, Spain
Areas of Achievement: Exploration and cartography
Contribution: The first European credited with persuading his contemporaries that what Christopher Columbus had discovered was a "New World," Vespucci revolutionized geographic thinking when he argued that this region now bearing his name was a continent distinct from Asia.

Early Life

Amerigo Vespucci was the third son of a Florentine family of five children. His father, Stagio Vespucci, was a modestly prosperous notary and a member of a respected and learned clan that cultivated good relations with Florence's intellectual and artistic elite. The fortunes of the family improved during Amerigo's lifetime, and his father would twice occupy positions of fiscal responsibility in the Florentine government.

Unlike his older brothers, who attended the University of Pisa, Amerigo received his education at home under the tutelage of a paternal uncle, Giorgio Antonio, a Dominican friar. The youth became proficient in Latin and developed an interest in mathematics and geography, an interest which he was able to indulge in his tutor's extensive library. In his uncle's circle, Amerigo also became acquainted with the theories of Paolo Toscanelli dal Pozzo, a Florentine physician and cosmographer who first suggested the possibility of a westward voyage as an alternative route to the Orient, an idea that Columbus and others eventually borrowed.

The study of geography was considered useful for anyone interested in a career in commerce, the profession chosen for Amerigo by his parents. Travel was also considered suitable training for businessmen, and Amerigo accepted the first opportunity when another uncle, Guido Antonio Vespucci, a lawyer, invited the twenty-four-year-old to Paris. The elder Vespucci had been appointed Florentine ambassador to the court of Louix XI in 1478 and had asked his young relative to join him as his private secretary.

In 1482, two years after Amerigo's return to Florence from France, his father died, making Amerigo responsible for the support of the family. The following year, Amerigo became manager of the household of one of the branches of the ruling Medici family, and he performed his task loyally for the next sixteen years. In this capacity, he traveled to Spain at least once to look after the financial interests of the Medicis. He was in Spain again toward the end of 1491 and settled permanently in the city of Seville, where he established financial relations with the city's active Italian merchant community. He would eventually marry María Cerezo, a native of Seville. The couple had no children.

At the close of the fifteenth century, the port city of Seville was the hub of commercial activity and the center of overseas travel and exploration. The Portuguese had taken the lead in the search for a new route to India by reaching the Orient circumnavigating Africa. Confirmation of the accuracy of their vision came with news that Bartolomeu Dias' expedition had reached the Cape of Good Hope (the southernmost tip of Africa) in 1488. The Spanish lagged behind their Portuguese neighbors until Columbus' triumphant return from his first voyage. The Crown had paid Columbus' expenses, and he was expected to search for yet another alternate route to the East. Following the theories of Toscanelli, Columbus sailed in 1492 and returned to Spain early the following year.

Columbus' initial optimistic reports that he had found a new route to Asia ensured greater interest and opportunities for investment on the part of all who knew of his trip, and Vespucci would soon be involved in several of the many maritime enterprises that mushroomed in Seville in the wake of Columbus' success. Vespucci, as a subaltern of the Italian merchant Giannetto Berardi, assisted Columbus in financing and outfitting a second voyage of discovery, which sailed in 1493. Berardi died before the provisioning of the fleet was complete, and Vespucci assumed the task. It is highly likely that Vespucci and Columbus had many opportunities to meet during this period and that the Florentine's early interest in geography and cosmography was revived as a result of these contacts. The lure of the sea and the prospects of discovery would soon prove irresistible. By 1499, Vespucci had decided to change professions from businessman to explorer.

Life's Work

Much controversy surrounds certain facts about Vespucci's life between the years 1497 and

1499—the period immediately prior to his first generally acknowledged ocean voyage—especially because some of his biographers assert that he, not Columbus, was the first European to discover the American mainland along the coast of northern South America. In order for this assertion to be valid, Vespucci would have had to undertake this voyage before Columbus' third—during which Columbus sailed along the coast of Venezuela—that is, before June, 1498. Vespucci was an inveterate letter writer. The most compelling evidence that he might have gone on this trip appears in a document of dubious authenticity attributed to Vespucci himself, the *Lettera di Amerigo Vespucci delle isole nouvamente trovate in quattro suoi viaggi* (c. 1505; *The First Four Voyages of Amerigo Vespucci,* 1885). This long letter is addressed to the head of the Florentine republic, the gonfalonier Piero Soderini. In this document, the author purports to have made four voyages overseas, the first of which, circa 1497, took him along the Caribbean coast of the American mainland—that is, to Venezuela, Central America, the Yucatán Peninsula, and the Gulf of Mexico, well in advance of Columbus. Since there is little independent evidence to corroborate information about this voyage, many scholars dismiss this episode as a fiction propagated by the letter, which could have been a forgery published by an overzealous and unscrupulous printer eager to cash in on a reading public thirsty for news of and reports from the New World. The fourth voyage described in the letter is also believed to be apocryphal.

What is universally accepted is the fact that Vespucci sailed for the New World as a member of a three-ship expedition under the command of the Spaniard Alonso de Ojeda in the spring of 1499. Two of the ships had been outfitted by Vespucci, at his own expense, in the hope of reaching India. Vespucci's expectations were founded on a set of maps drawn from the calculations of Ptolemy, the Egyptian mathematician and astronomer of the second century, whose work *Geōgraphikē hyphēgēsis* (*Geography*) was the foremost authority to fifteenth century Europeans on matters related to the size and shape of the world.

Ptolemy had concluded that the world was made up of three continents: Europe, Africa, and Asia. When Vespucci set out on his voyage in 1499, he expected to reach the Cape of Cattigara, the southernmost point of Asia on Ptolemy's map. Instead, his expedition reached the northern coast of Brazil and the mouth of the Amazon River. From there, Vespucci's ship proceeded southward to the equatorial zone, after which it turned northward to the Caribbean, navigating along the northeastern coast of South America. Seeing houses on stilts that reminded the crew of Venice, they named the area "Venezuela" (little Venice). The entire expedition returned to Spain, with a cargo of pearls and slaves and not the hoped-for Asian spices.

Back in Seville, Vespucci planned a second expedition that would take him farther south along the Brazilian coastal route, but his license to travel was suddenly revoked, on the grounds that he was a foreigner, when the Spanish crown, in competition with the Portuguese, began to treat geographical knowledge as secrets of state. When the ships that made up the expedition sailed in August, 1500, they carried only Spaniards. A Portuguese explorer, Pedro Álvars Cabral, had already claimed Brazil for the Portuguese crown in 1500 and, perhaps because of this fact, Vespucci's knowledge of its northern coast might have been of interest to Portugal. He was summoned to appear before King Manuel I. The monarch commissioned the Florentine to undertake a new voyage of discovery along the coast of Brazil, following Cabral's and Vespucci's own original intentions. Vespucci sailed from Lisbon in the spring of 1501.

This second independently verifiable voyage of Vespucci followed the coast of Brazil, crossed the equator, and proceeded south to Patagonia. Experiences during this last stage convinced Vespucci that Ptolemy's calculations had been mistaken, that the Cape of Cattigara and Asia were not where they were expected to be, and that the landmass before his eyes was more likely a new continent, separate and distinct from Asia. Upon his return to Lisbon, Vespucci, along with geographers and mapmakers, began to redraw and redesign Ptolemy's world to accommodate this new insight. The Atlantic coast of this region began to be detailed in maps that circulated throughout Europe, the first of which appeared in 1502.

Vespucci's employment by the Portuguese did not last long. He returned to Seville in 1502, disappointed that his plans for the exploitation of the new lands were not accepted by Manuel. In Spain, Vespucci's efforts and considerable geographical and navigational knowledge were finally recognized, and in 1505 he was granted citizenship by King Ferdinand II, who appointed him pilot major of the country's board of trade, the Casa de Con-

AMERICUS VESPUTIUS

tratación de las Indias. Vespucci held this position until his death in 1512.

Vespucci is believed to have been short of stature, with an aquiline nose, brown eyes, and wavy hair. This description comes from a family portrait painted by the Florentine muralist Ghirlandajo. Vespucci has also been described as deceitful, self-promoting, and cunning. His reputation suffered after the publication of two letters attributed to him, *The First Four Voyages of Amerigo Vespucci,* mentioned earlier, and *Mundus Novus* (c. 1503; English translation, 1916), an account of Vespucci's 1501 expedition addressed to Lorenzo de' Medici, his Florentine employer. In this second letter, the author argues that the lands he had recently visited (the Atlantic coast of South America) could only be part of a new world.

The ideas contained in the disputed letters, published in many editions and languages shortly after their initial printing, inspired a German mapmaker, Martin Waldseemüller, at Saint-Dié in Lorraine, to draw a new map to accompany narrative descriptions of this new world. The map, which was published in 1507, more closely resembles the geography of the American continent than earlier efforts, separates America from Asia, and assigns to the new land the name America in honor of its presumed discoverer Americus (Amerigo). The feminine version of Amerigo was selected to be consistent with the feminine names of the other continents, Europe, Africa, and Asia. This is the first known example of the use of America as the name of the new continent. The word was quickly accepted by northern Europeans as the rightful name for South America, but it would take some fifty years before southern Europe adopted the name and applied it to the entire American landmass, north and south.

Vespucci's complicity in this matter has never been fully established; some believe that he contributed to his own mythology by making himself the center of attention in all of his correspondence, never mentioning others in his circle under whose direction he might have worked. He is accused of taking credit for the deeds of his collaborators. Defenders of Columbus, the bulk of Vespucci's critics, argue that the new continent should have been named for Columbus rather than for Vespucci the impostor. Columbus, however, was never quite convinced that the lands he had reached were not in Asia and did not live long enough to experience the historical slight in favor of Vespucci.

Summary

Amerigo Vespucci, in spite of the fact that he has been seriously criticized by a number of eminent and revered figures, deserves much of the credit for revolutionizing geographic thinking in Europe. His travels, especially his vain search for Asia following a Ptolemaic map, convinced him that the accepted authority on things geographical was mistaken. To challenge Ptolemy and a scientific tradition of such long standing in sixteenth century Europe was an act of great intellectual and moral courage. While Europeans were slow in accepting the full implications of Vespucci's discoveries, his insights nevertheless received much immediate publicity. Vespucci's ideas captivated the imagination of cartographers and publishers, and a steady stream of historical literature filled the minds of Europe's growing reading public. These accounts fired readers' imaginations. Vespucci's conclusions stimulated the growing community of cartographers, navigators, and geographers. He described his experiences in detail, kept careful records of astronomical, navigational, and geographical observations, and made it possible for his contemporaries to accept the idea of America long before additional eyewitness evidence would confirm the wisdom of his insights.

Bibliography

Arciniegas, Germán. *Amerigo and the New World: The Life and Times of Amerigo Vespucci.* New York: Knopf, 1955. A most admiring biography, which argues vehemently in favor of the authenticity of Vespucci's four voyages. The author dismisses some of the criticism of Vespucci as nationalistic propaganda.

Parry, J. H. *The Discovery of South America.* London: Elek, and New York: Taplinger, 1979. An informative and panoramic account of European expansion in America by one of North America's most respected historians. This work is filled with replicas of contemporary maps and charts and is a serious and objective treatment of the period. Parry disputes the authenticity of *The First Four Voyages of Amerigo Vespucci* but credits Vespucci with having contributed to Europe's knowledge of geography and navigation.

Pohl, Frederick J. *Amerigo Vespucci, Pilot Major.* New York: Columbia University Press, 1944; London: Cass, 1966. The author devotes much attention to Vespucci's mature years, the period of his life that coincides with his voyages overseas. Pohl believes that Vespucci was a most deserving individual and that his fame was legitimately earned. Contains a complete English version of two of Vespucci's letters and two informative appendices.

Vigneras, Louis-André. *The Discovery of South America and the Andalusian Voyages*. Chicago: University of Chicago Press, 1976. A carefully constructed survey of the separate expeditions from Spain to America beginning with Columbus' first voyage in 1492. A separate appendix is devoted to Vespucci's Portuguese voyage. The author's treatment of Vespucci echoes the consensus of contemporary scholarship about him by doubting the authenticity of two of the four voyages.

Zweig, Stefan. *Amerigo: A Comedy of Errors in History*. Translated by Andrew St. James. New York: Viking Press, 1942. An account by the popular Austrian writer who at one point resided in Brazil. Zweig believes that America received its name because of an error, and he argues that Vespucci's letters are filled with serious factual mistakes and coincidences. For Zweig, Vespucci's great fame rests on a false foundation.

Clara Estow

FRANÇOIS VILLON

Born: 1431; Paris, France
Died: 1463?; place unknown
Area of Achievement: Literature
Contribution: In his intensely personal, forthright verse, sordidly realistic yet devout, Villon was the greatest poet of medieval France.

Early Life

Born in Paris in 1431, François Villon was originally named François de Montcorbier et des Loges. Apparently his father died when the child was quite young, for François was sent to live with Guillaume de Villon, a priest who was chaplain to the church of Saint-Benoît-le-Bientourné, near the University of Paris. His protector gave the boy a home and an education; the grateful François adopted his name, Villon, and several times wrote fondly of him in his verse, calling him "more than father . . . who has been to me more tender than a mother and raised me from swaddling-clothes." Nothing is known of his real father, not even his first name; Villon called himself "of poor and obscure extraction." His mother, for whom he wrote "Ballade to Our Lady," he describes at the time as a poor old woman who knew nothing of letters.

Nothing is known of Villon's boyhood. Joan of Arc was burned at the stake the year he was born, and for the first five years of his life, Paris was in the hands of the English conquerors, while the ineffectual Charles VII nominally ruled the unoccupied part of France. Most of the country had been ravaged by the Hundred Years' War, and bands of freebooters were plundering whatever of value remained in the countryside or the capital. In 1434, there was the coldest winter in memory, followed in 1436 by a famine, which was succeeded in 1438 by an epidemic of smallpox that claimed some fifty thousand victims. Starving wolves invaded Paris and preyed upon children and the weak. It was a grim, harsh era, and as a child, Villon must have seen violence and famine and been surrounded by death.

When he was about twelve, Villon was enrolled at the University of Paris, from which he was graduated in March, 1449, as a bachelor of arts. He was tonsured and received minor holy orders, affording him some protection from the police—which he needed, as he was involved in student escapades that were typical of the medieval conflict between town and gown, including stealing boundary stones and house signs that were then carried off to the student quarter, which in turn was raided by the police. Despite his peccadilloes, Villon received a master of arts degree in August of 1452.

Life's Work

Despite his education and the opportunities that it might have provided him, Villon fell in with a group of criminals known as "Coquillards" and began a life of crime. Among his cronies, who are featured in his poems, were Colin des Cayeulx, described by the authorities as a thief and picklock, and Regnier de Montigny, a thief, murderer, and church robber. Both of them were hanged, and Villon wrote their epitaphs. Villon also prowled around Paris with Guy Tabarie, Jehan the Wolf, and Casin Cholet, all of them thieves, and spent much time at brothels and taverns such as the Mule and the Pomme de Pin, whose proprietor, Robin Turgis, was often a target of Villon's humor.

According to a poem of the time entitled "Repues Franches," thought to be by Friar Baulde de la Mare, Villon and his rascally friends had a genius for conning free fish, meat, bread, and wine from gullible victims. Soon Villon's picaresque career became more sinister. In the evening of June 5, 1455, the Feast of Corpus Christi, Villon was seated under the clock of Saint-Benoît-le-Bientourné, in company with a priest and a woman named Ysabeau, when another priest, Philip Chermoye, who had apparently been harboring a grudge, started a quarrel with Villon, drew a dagger, and slashed his upper lip. Bleeding copiously, Villon drew his own dagger and stabbed Chermoye in the groin; when Chermoye still attempted to injure him, Villon threw a rock that struck him in the face. After having his wound dressed, Villon fled from the city. Chermoye was taken to the Hôtel-Dieu, where he died after a few days. According to one account, Chermoye on his deathbed confessed that he had started the fight and forgave Villon. Thus Villon's friends were able to get him a pardon in January of 1456, and he then returned to Paris. There, he fell in love with Katherine de Vausselles, who may have been a kinswoman of a colleague of Guillaume de Villon. At any rate, she teased and tormented Villon and eventually left him for Noël Joliz, who beat him in her presence. Heartsick and purse poor, Villon resolved to leave Paris at the end of 1456 and wrote for the occasion his first important work of poetry, *Le Lais* (1489; *The Legacy*, 1878, also known as *Le*

Petit Testament, *The Little Testament*), in which he bids an ironic farewell to his friends and mockingly bequeaths them his worldly goods.

Before departing, he and four of his Coquillard cronies, probably on Christmas Eve, climbed over the wall into the College of Navarre, broke into the sacristy, and stole five hundred gold crowns from the faculty of theology. With his one-fifth share, Villon left the city, going first to Angers and thence wandering for the next four and a half years. In the meantime, Guy Tabarie boasted of the crime, was arrested and tortured, and confessed the details. A wanted man, Villon stayed on the run, going at one time to the court of Blois, where he associated with the courtly poet Charles d'Orléans, to whose daughter Marie he wrote a poetic epistle. Otherwise, except for a few clues that he drops in his verse, his activities are unknown until the summer of 1460, when he was in a dungeon at Orléans under sentence of death, from which he was pardoned during the passage through the city of the Princess Marie. A year later, at Meung-sur-Loire, he was tried at the ecclesiastical court of Thibault d'Aussigny, Bishop of Orléans, who chained him in a dungeon under the moat and inflicted the water torture on him. Villon's health was broken, but he once more received a pardon when King Louis XI made a royal progress through the town and freed the prisoners.

Hiding near Paris, during the winter of 1461, Villon wrote his major work, aside from some of the ballades, *Le Grand Testament* (1489; *The Great Testament*, 1878), which follows the form of the earlier *The Legacy* but has far more depth and texture and which also incorporates a number of ballades, chansons, and rondeaux. Back in Paris itself, he was arrested in November, 1462, for petty theft; before he was released, the authorities made him sign a bond promising to repay the money that was stolen from the College of Navarre. Shortly thereafter, following an evening of revelry, one of Villon's companions got into a brawl with a papal scribe and wounded the man with a dagger thrust. Though Villon had left at the first sign of trouble, he was identified, arrested as an accomplice, and imprisoned in the Châtelet, where he was tortured and sentenced to the gallows. While awaiting execution, he wrote an ironic "Quatrain" and his great "L'Épitaphe Villon," otherwise known as "Ballade of the Hanged," in which he imagines himself and six others rotting on the gibbet and prays to God to absolve them all. Yet once more Villon cheated the gallows. He appealed to Parliament, and since he had not taken part in the fight and the victim had not died, his sentence was annulled and changed to ten years' exile from Paris. In response, Villon wrote his "Panegyric to the Court of Parliament" requesting three days to prepare for his departure and his sardonic "Question to the Clerk of the Prison Gate." In January, 1463, he left Paris and vanished from history and into legend. Though only thirty-two years old, he may have died from the lasting effects of imprisonment and torture. In *The Great Testament*, he speaks of having the worn-out body of an old man and of "spitting white"—a hint that he may have had a lung disease, perhaps tuberculosis. A century later, François Rabelais recounts Villon's having gone to England and received the protection of Edward V; Rabelais also tells of Villon's having retired in his old age to Poitou. Without any corroborating evidence, however, Rabelais' accounts are probably fiction. At any rate, no more of Villon's poetry is recorded after he left Paris.

The Legacy is made up of forty octaves or *huitains* of octosyllabic lines; *The Great Testament* has 175 such octaves, among which are interspersed sixteen ballades, a triple ballade, three rondels, and *Belle Leçon*; in addition, there is Villon's codicil, containing other ballades, the quatrain written after his being sentenced to death, and a number of poems in thieves' jargon. The standard ballade consists of three stanzas of eight octosyllabic lines each, followed by a four-line *envoi* generally beginning with the vocative "Prince!"—though Villon's may be addressed to Fortune, a mistress, a fellow poet, or God. The rhyme scheme is invariably *ababbcbc* in the octave and *bcbc* in the *envoi*. A difficult verse form with only three rhymes, the ballade went out of favor after Villon's time and was not revived until nineteenth century imitations of Villon.

The Legacy is minor apprentice work, but after his career of crime, five years of vagabondage, and several ordeals under torture, Villon emerged as a great poet in *The Great Testament*. In it, he re-creates with vivid intensity the underworld of medieval Paris—the same setting as Victor Hugo's *Nôtre-Dame de Paris* (1831; *The Hunchback of Notre Dame*, 1833). Writing sometimes in thieves' jargon, Villon takes the reader through the taverns, brothels, thieves' dens, and prisons. His is a world of ribald bawdry, crime, revelry, profanity, prostitution, disease, and the dance of death, but it is redeemed by sardonic wit, by an intense relish for life, and despite Villon's sacrilege, by a devout reverence for medieval Christianity and an awareness of the vanity of his riotous life. Outstanding among his poems are his "Ballade of Fat Margot"; "Lament of the Belle Heaulmière" (the beautiful armoress), about an aging prostitute; the ballades to the ladies and lords of bygone times, the first with its haunting refrain, "But where are the snows of yesteryear?"; the "Ballade of the Hanged"; the "Ballade as a Prayer to Our Lady," which he put into the mouth of his aged mother; the "Ballade Against the Enemies of France"; and "The Dialogue Between the Heart and Body of Villon."

Summary

The first critical edition of François Villon's poems was made in 1533 by Clément Marot, himself a major poet of the Renaissance. Thereafter, Villon's life and works fell into obscurity for the next three centuries. Not until the 1830's did Villon resurface, when Théophile Gautier began to write about him as a precursor to the Romantics and bohemians and to praise Villon's defiance of bourgeois values. In England, Villon was quite unknown until the 1860's, but during the rest of the century he received a considerable amount of attention, his work appearing in numerous translations, most notably by Dante Gabriel Rossetti and Algernon Charles Swinburne, both of whom tried to make the French poet fit into their Pre-Raphaelite aesthetic and who portrayed him as a rebel against middle-class morality. Following them, a number of lesser poets—Andrew Lang, Edmund Gosse, Walter Besant—did routine translations of some of Villon's poems as well as imitations of him. In 1878, John Payne published the first complete translation of Villon's work, issued to subscribers called "The Villon Society" to circumvent Victorian censorship. An edition for the public three years later was bowdlerized and expurgated of Villon's frank realism.

In 1877, Auguste Longnon published the first biography of Villon, following which a number of articles appeared in British periodicals providing a condensed account of Villon's life and exploiting the sensationalism of Longnon's discoveries. Several used Villon as a cautionary example to condemn bohemianism and aestheticism. Despite his own genteel bohemianism, Robert Louis Stevenson, in an article in 1877, presented Villon as an example of dissipation and degradation, one lacking the dignity of a Victorian gentleman, and condemned his "way of looking upon the sordid and ugly aspects of life," which he found becoming prominent in the work of such nineteenth century French writers as Émile Zola. Stevenson believed that one should bear one's sufferings stoically and complained that "Villon, who had not the courage to be poor with honesty, now whiningly implores our sympathy, now shows his teeth upon the dung-heap with an ugly snarl." In the same year, Stevenson published his first short story, "A Lodging for the Night," about Villon's supposedly whining, cowardly behavior after his friend de Montigny murdered a priest. All the nineteenth century writers who saw in Villon a reflection of certain features of their own time oversimplify the man and his works and ignore the complexity of the medieval Christian not only indulging in debauchery, theft, murder, and sacrilege but also repenting and expressing a profound faith.

Reversing the portrayal by Stevenson and other nineteenth century writers, twentieth century fiction transformed Villon into the dashing and noble hero of swashbuckling romance. In 1901, Justin Huntly McCarthy's novel and play *If I Were King* turn Villon into a king of vagabonds who then becomes grand constable of France for a week and saves Paris from the invading Burgundians. The narrative is melodramatic and posturing; the characters speak what W. S. Gilbert calls "platitudes in stained-glass attitudes." The title poem, the best-known "verses" of Villon, are not by Villon at all but by McCarthy. *If I Were King* was turned into the popular operetta *The Vagabond King* (1925), with music by Rudolf Friml, which has been filmed twice, and a variation on the novel has been filmed three times, with William Farnum, John Barrymore, and Ronald Colman, respectively, playing Villon. It sounds an essentially false note but has colored the popular impression of Villon.

In a more serious vein, Villon influenced Ezra Pound, who wrote an opera about him, *The Testament of François Villon* (1926), an appreciative essay, "Montcorbier, alias Villon," and several "Villonaud" poems. Pound and T. S. Eliot also borrow for their own work the opening line of *The Great Testament*. Among Villon's other modern admirers was William Carlos Williams, who praised Villon's "intensity of consciousness," his psychological forthrightness and artistic integrity, his wit and daring realism, the immediacy and modernism of his personal note, so that of all the poets of the Middle Ages, Villon speaks most forthrightly to modern readers.

Bibliography

Anacker, Robert H. *François Villon*. New York: Twayne, 1968. A critical survey in the Twayne World Authors series, Anacker's work follows the standard format for that series, with a chronology, a brief account of Villon's world and of his life, chapters analyzing *The Legacy*, *The Great Testament*, and other works, and an annotated bibliography. Dismisses the simplistic view of Villon as a "carefree vagabond," a "tavern minstrel," a bohemian, a Romantic lover, a forerunner of beatniks and hippies; tries to see him in the context of his times.

Daniel, Robert R. *The Poetry of Villon and Baudelaire: Two Worlds, One Human Condition*. New York: Peter Lang, 1997. This book is a comparative reading of François Villon's and Charles Baudelaire's poetry. Despite the intervening centuries, these works are analogous in a number of ways. This study elucidates the affinities by examining the poets' treatments of certain themes: temporality, physical constraint, deterioration, death, putrefaction, and the *danse macabre*.

Fein, David A. *A Reading of Villon's Testament*. Birmingham, Ala.: Summa Publications, 1984. Fein reads the poetry on three levels: surface value, "that which Villon appears to be saying"; travesty, when Villon praises or blesses his enemies; and symbolic meaning. Quotes extensively from Villon, using Galway Kinnel's translation of the Longnon-Foulet text.

Hunt, Tony. *Villon's Last Will: Language and Authority in the* Testament. Oxford: Clarendon Press, and New York: Oxford University Press, 1996. Traditionally, scholars have scoured Villon's *Testament* for details about life in fifteenth century Paris; few have shown why it is interesting as literature. Hunt puts aside historic references to concentrate exclusively on the textual strategies of the work, in particular its rhetorical techniques involving dialogue and irony. He views the *Testament* as ironic from start to finish, revealing how the poet's technique results in the dissolution of meaning, authority, and authorial identity.

Lewis, D. B. Wyndham. *François Villon: A Documented Survey*. London: Peter Davies, and New York: Coward-McCann, 1928. The best biographical and critical study in English, Lewis' volume reconstructs in vivid detail the life of fifteenth century Paris. The biographical section is sometimes conjectural, as the author, writing in the first person, imagines the character of some of Villon's associates and dramatizes some of his escapades. Lewis also provides commentary on the works, followed by a variety of translations and an extensive bibliography of French sources.

Morsberger, Robert E. "Villon and the Victorians." *Bulletin of the Rocky Mountain Modern Language Association* 23 (December, 1969): 189-196. A study of the rediscovery of Villon, his influence upon such nineteenth century writers as Dante Gabriel Rossetti, Charles Algernon Swinburne, Robert Louis Stevenson, the interpretations and misinterpretations of him by the Victorian decadents and aesthetes, and his transformation in twentieth century fiction and films into a noble hero of romance.

Stevenson, Robert Louis. "François Villon, Student, Poet, and Housebreaker." In *Familiar Studies of Men and Books*. London: Chatto and Windus, and New York: Scribner, 1905. A sometimes biased study, Stevenson's article condemns Villon for not having the traits of a Victorian gentleman but is important for showing the reaction of a leading Victorian writer. The article led to and parallels Stevenson's first short story, "A Lodging for the Night."

———. "A Lodging for the Night." In *The Complete Short Stories of Robert Louis Stevenson*. Edited by Charles Neider. New York: Doubleday, 1969. The first treatment of Villon in fiction, it presents Villon as a whining, cowardly equivocator. The biased portrait of Villon is distorted by Stevenson's advocacy of the strenuous and stoical life and of noblesse oblige, which he thought Villon failed to exemplify.

Villon, François. *The Complete Works of François Villon*. Translated by Anthony Bonner. New York: Bantam, 1960. This edition gives the works in their original French, with Bonner's unrhymed translation on the facing page. The introductory material includes an appreciative essay by William Carlos Williams and a brief biography. The thirty-seven pages of notes are extremely thorough, identifying all the poems' characters, allusions, and historical details. A brief bibliography refers the reader chiefly to sources in French.

———. *Poems*. Translated by John Heron Lepper. New York: Horace Liveright, 1926. A complete translation, following Villon's rhyme scheme, with an introduction by Lepper. Includes as well the first complete and unabridged translation by John Payne (also in Villon's rhyme scheme), as well as Payne's introduction to his 1883 edition and translations by Swinburne, Rossetti, Arthur Symons, and Ezra Pound.

Vitz, Evelyn Birge. *The Crossroads of Intentions: A Study of Symbolic Expression in the Poetry of François Villon*. The Hague: Mouton, 1974. Vitz studies the symbolic expression in Villon's poetry—the process by which places, people, and things become symbolic. Considers the sexual symbolism, the symbolism in writing a will, and the contrast between Villon's self and the symbolic persona he assumes. Analyzes the medieval concept of psychology and cosmography.

Robert E. Morsberger

FRANCISCO DE VITORIA

Born: c. 1483; Vitoria, Álava, Spain
Died: August 12, 1546; Salamanca, Spain
Areas of Achievement: Philosophy, theology, and law
Contribution: Vitoria was a Spanish theologian and pioneer in the field of international law. He is principally associated with his idea that the nations of the world constitute a community based on natural law.

Early Life

Francisco de Vitoria was born in the small town of Vitoria in the Basque province of Álava. The exact date of his birth is uncertain, but scholars generally place it between 1480 and 1486, with 1483 being the year most often mentioned. When still very young, Vitoria entered the Dominican Order, of which his elder brother Diego was also a member. He went to San Pablo in Burgos for his education, and, because he showed promise as a scholar in the classics, he was sent to the College of the Dominicans in Paris for further study. While in Paris, he also attended classes at the Sorbonne. His education equipped him as a Humanist versed in Greek and Latin texts, and Vitoria is also said to have met the great Humanist Desiderius Erasmus during those years.

Vitoria arrived in Paris around 1506 and studied first at the Dominican College of Saint Jacques, becoming well versed in the classics before occupying the chair of theology there. He was influenced by nominalist teachers, who helped revive the study of the *Summa theologiae* (c. 1265-1273; *Summa Theologica*, 1911-1921) of Saint Thomas Aquinas in addition to, or sometimes instead of, the previous standard Dominican text, *Sententiarum libri IV* (1148-1151; four books of sentences) by Peter Lombard. He even became involved in the preparations of editions of Aquinas' work that appeared in the period of 1514-1519. Before returning to Spain, he completed his degree of licentiate in theology at the Sorbonne on March 24, 1522.

Life's Work

Vitoria embarked on his life's work upon his return to Spain after earning his degree in theology. He had attained a good reputation among his colleagues and was able to serve at the College of Saint Gregory in Valladolid from 1523 to 1526 before being appointed to the chair of theology at the University of Salamanca. He would remain at the university until his death.

Vitoria made his first mark on history as he lectured on theology. He impressed a new character on this field of study, as his discussions were full of ideas, and drew other areas of learning into the consideration of theological questions. Such questions were not to be considered intellectual exercises but rather areas of legitimate practical concern in the real world. That such discussions and proposed solutions could actually produce serious consequences was shown in many lectures: notably those discussions on the rights and treatment of Native Americans in the newly discovered hemisphere and those on the question of what constitutes a just war. His teaching incorporated a desire for justice in world affairs and a strong belief that moral questions have an impact on all phases of life.

One of the greatest influences on Vitoria was his contact with the great Humanists, including Erasmus. Vitoria's defense of the Indians and his humanitarian principles in relation to war bear the stamp of this influence. Vitoria distinguished himself as a professor and helped increase the reputation of the University of Salamanca. At first he was compelled to lecture on the *Sententiarum libri IV* of Peter Lombard while he preferred Saint Thomas Aquinas, but it later became the rule to discuss the *Summa Theologica* with references to Lombard—a practice which better suited Vitoria's thinking. His courses soon met with favorable reactions as he combined solid doctrine with a clear, elegant style of exposition. Among his students were Melchor Cano, Domingo Soto, and Bartolomé de Medina. Although Vitoria did not publish his lectures, his students gathered many of them and published them after his death, as a tribute to him. Vitoria's reputation for applying theology to practical matters and his broad knowledge were such that Charles V consulted him on a number of questions, including the arguments by Henry VIII of England for annulling his marriage to Catherine of Aragon.

In 1532, Vitoria discussed the justifications for Spanish domination in the New World. In 1539 and 1540, Charles V consulted him about several matters relating to the conquest of the Indies. Then, in 1541, Vitoria was consulted on the question of baptizing Native Americans without religious instruction, a question brought to the Council of the

Indies by Bartolomé de las Casas, in whose favor Vitoria argued. In 1545, Vitoria was invited to attend the Council of Trent; however, because of illness, other representatives were sent instead.

Vitoria's tenure at Salamanca lasted from 1526 to 1546. The last two years of his life, he suffered from rheumatic pain, and a substitute lecturer, Juan Gil Fernández de Nava, had to be called in. Vitoria died on August 12, 1546. The efforts of his students assured that his influence continued long after that.

Some of Vitoria's lectures were collected for publication by his former students in *Relectiones theologicae* (1557; English translation, 1934). Vitoria's guiding premise was that theology or questions of morality extend over the entire field of human activity. He particularly believed that the question of the treatment of the Native Americans as a barbarian race, not subject to an established human law, must be viewed from the point of view of divine law. The Native Americans had been reduced to servitude on the large land-holdings or to slavery in the mines. Compulsory labor and separation of families was the norm. Bartolomé de las Casas became a famous defender of the Native Americans at this time, and Vitoria himself defended a humanitarian view. Using his considerable skill in reasoning and argumentation, he contradicted proposed theories that allowed for the subjugation of Native Americans based on the right to convert them to Christianity, on the right to punish idolatry, or on the (supposed) superiority of Christians over so-called barbarians.

Vitoria also refuted the argument that Spain had title to the land based on discovery. He resorted to the Law of Nations, which allows such title only if the regions are uninhabited—which these clearly were not. He also argued that Spaniards could travel in these new lands on condition that they did not harm the inhabitants and that, where there was common property, Spaniards might also profit. Vitoria's concept of a just war included the idea that it was lawful for the Spaniards to defend themselves against Native American attacks, while always showing generosity and moderation to the defeated. If the Native Americans persisted with their attacks, however, the Spaniards were allowed recourse to the rights of war, including plunder and captivity, which were seen as the right to punish wrongdoing according to law.

Because of his many students and his participation in the important discussions of his time, Vitoria's influence was widespread. With the publication of his lectures, that influence continued after his death.

Summary

During the period when the rules of international law were being formulated, the two main schools of thought included positivists and naturalists. Hugo Grotius, the leading Dutch naturalist writer, is often regarded as the founder of modern international law. For other scholars, however, this title should go to Vitoria, who based his arguments as well on natural law. Vitoria's argument was that the basic principles of all laws are derived from principles of justice with universal validity. He believed that such principles were part of a natural, divine law, not a man-made one.

Vitoria spoke often on the question of war. To Vitoria, war was justified to assure free trade and communication when other means of persuasion had failed. The violation of a right was the essential condition for a just war. Defensive wars protected the individual or nation from tyranny; offensive wars might punish a nation guilty of injustice. In any case, he believed that the defeated should always be treated with moderation once the purpose has been achieved. Furthermore, a just war must always promote the common good of the world community over the advantage of an individual state.

When Vitoria has been called the founder of modern international law by scholars, it has been based particularly on *De Indis* and *De jure belli relectiones*, lectures given in 1532, published in 1557, and translated into English in 1917. In *De Indis*, he first defined international law as a natural law binding all states of the world, and he applied it to the treatment of the Native Americans in the New World. In visualizing an international society, he applied Saint Thomas Aquinas' principles to the concept of state and built a theory of international society as well on his principles. His guiding principle was that an international society was based on a natural association of equal states. In the areas of philosophy and theology, his contributions were recognized within his lifetime; Vitoria's contribution in the area of law, especially international law, are equally indisputable.

Bibliography

Benkert, Gerald Francis. *The Thomistic Conception of an International Society.* Washington, D.C.: Catholic University of America Press,

1942. Examines the writings of Thomas Aquinas and from his philosophical principles delineates the basis for constructing an international society. Particular emphasis is given to the views of Vitoria in the Spanish revival of Thomistic thought. Includes an extensive bibliography.

Delos, Joseph Thomas. *International Relations from a Catholic Standpoint.* Edited and translated by Stephen J. Brown. Dublin: Browne and Nolan, 1932. Contains a discussion of the Catholic viewpoint on natural law and international relations. Particularly useful in defining the Catholic attitude and contributions to peaceful international relations throughout history and particularly the contributions of various theologians, Vitoria among them.

Francisco de Vitoria. *Francisci de Victoria De Indis et De Ivre Belli Relectiones*, edited by Ernest Nys. Vol. 7, *The Classics of International Law*, edited by James Brown Scott. Washington, D.C.: Carnegie Institution of Washington, 1917; London: Wildy, 1964. Includes a translation by John Pawley Bate of the two *Relectiones theologicae* by Vitoria, along with the full Latin text. Marginal notes and summary of the major points are maintained from the original. Helpful introduction by Ernest Nys includes biographical information and a discussion of some of Vitoria's principal arguments.

Hamilton, Bernice. *Political Thought in Sixteenth-Century Spain: A Study of the Political Ideas of Vitoria, De Soto, Suárez, and Molina.* Oxford: Clarendon Press, 1963. A discussion of the political ideas of four Spanish thinkers on natural-law theory, political communities, war, New World colonization, law of nations, and relative powers of Church and state. Contains bibliographies.

Reidy, Stephen J. *Civil Authority According to Francis de Vitoria.* River Forest, Ill.: Aquinas Library, 1959. A specialized study of Vitoria's teaching on the nature and causes of civil authority with a discussion of his position on the ancient scholastic teaching. Contains a bibliography of books and periodicals in several languages.

Scott, James Brown. *The Spanish Origin of International Law: Francisco de Vitoria and His Law of Nations.* Oxford: Clarendon Press, 1932. A thorough discussion of Vitoria's life, putting his accomplishments in the context of the "era of discoveries" and the thinking of the Spanish School. Appendices include translations of six important *relectiones.*

Susan L. Piepke

WANG YANG-MING

Born: November 30, 1472; Yu-yao, Chekiang, China

Died: January 9, 1529; Nan-en, Kiangsi, China

Areas of Achievement: Philosophy and politics

Contribution: As a high official, holding many governmental offices from magistrate to governor, Wang suppressed rebellions and created a reign of peace in China that lasted a century. As a Neo-Confucian philosopher, he exercised tremendous influence in both China and Japan for 150 years.

Early Life

Wang Yang-ming was born on November 30, 1472, in Yu-yao, Chekiang Province, the son of a minister of civil personnel in Nanking. He was renamed Wang Yang-ming by his students, but his private name was Shou-jen and his courtesy name was Po-an. According to legend, he could not speak until he was given a name at the age of five. He soon began reading his grandfather's books and reciting their contents. When he was eleven years old, he went to live with his father at Peking. At the age of twelve, Wang announced to a fortune-teller that the greatest occupation was that of a sage, not that of a government official. His mother, Madame Cheng, died when he was thirteen. At fifteen, he visited the Chu-yung Mountain passes, where he first became interested both in archery and in the frontier.

Wang was married at the age of seventeen, but he was so absorbed in a conversation he was having with a Taoist priest on his wedding night that he forgot to go home until he was sent for the next morning. As he and his wife were passing through Kuang-hsin the next year, he had another important discussion, this time with a prominent scholar named Lou Liang. Lou was so impressed with Wang that he predicted that Wang could become a sage if he studied diligently. Wang, however, devoted his nineteenth year to the study of archery and military tactics.

During the next ten years, Wang was torn between pursuing a career in the military, in politics, in literature, and in philosophy. After receiving his civil service degree, he delved deeply into the works of Chu Hsi. While visiting his father in Peking, he spent seven days sitting quietly in front of some bamboos in an attempt to discern the principles of Chu Hsi embodied within them. The stress was too much for Wang, however, and he became very ill. Thoroughly disillusioned with philosophy, he spent his time writing flowery compositions instead of studying for his civil service examinations. Consequently, he failed his examinations in 1493 and again 1496, and he shifted his interest back to military crafts and to the Taoist philosophy.

Wang finally settled on one career choice after passing his civil service examinations in 1499, at the age of twenty-seven. He was appointed to the Ministry of Public Works, where he impressed his superiors with a method for defending China against invasion. Though his proposal was rejected, Wang was made minister of justice in Yunan in the following year. In 1501, Wang reversed the convictions of many prisoners after checking the prison records near Nanking. Ill health forced Wang to retreat to the Yang-ming ravine to recuperate. He built a house in the ravine and began calling himself "Philosopher of Yang-ming." Wang soon became very skeptical of some of the teachings of Taoism and Buddhism and of his literary pursuits.

Having fully recovered from his illness, Wang returned to Peking in 1504, where he was appointed director of the provincial examinations in Shantung. That same year, he became a secretary in the Ministry of War. In 1505, members of his large student following convinced him that he was better suited as a philosopher, and he began lecturing on the importance of becoming a sage. His attacks of the practice of reciting classics and writing flowery compositions alienated him from the more conservative scholars, who accused him of trying to build a reputation for himself. Only one scholar, the honored academician Chan Jo-shui, appreciated his merits. Not only did he befriend Wang but also he helped him spread the true doctrine of Confucius.

A year later, Wang's career as a lecturer was dramatically interrupted. In 1506, he came to the defense of a group of supervising censors who had been imprisoned by a corrupt eunuch, Liu Chin. Wang wrote a memorial that so angered Liu Chin that he ordered Wang to be beaten, imprisoned, and banished to Lung ch'ang, a place inhabited primarily by barbarian tribes. Wang was demoted to head of a dispatch station. He began his journey in 1507 and arrived at Lung ch'ang a year later. During his trip, he barely escaped an assassination attempt by Liu's agents.

The three years that he spent living among the aborigines were the turning point of his life. Hav-

ing to scavenge for food and water for himself and his subordinates in a desolate land and to build houses for the Miao aborigines took its toll on Wang's health. Yet the isolation was beneficial, for his privations forced him to look inward. One night, he suddenly realized that one need only look into one's own mind to find the eternal principles of life instead of searching for these principles in objects. In 1509, he developed a theory that held that knowledge and action are one. Monogamy, for example, can only be fully understood when it is practiced. With these theories, Wang was revising Idealist Neo-Confucianism, as it had been pronounced by Lu Hsiang-shan. In addition, Wang was directly opposing the rationalistic Neo-Confucianism of Chu Hsi.

Life's Work

As soon as Wang's term as head of the dispatch station had ended in 1510, he was made magistrate of Lu-ling. During his seven-month stay in office, he carried out a number of reforms. As the result of an audience with the emperor, Wang was promoted to Secretary of the Ministry of Justice and Director of the Ministry of Personnel in 1511, Vice Minister of Imperial Stables in 1512, and Minister of State Ceremonials in 1514.

Wang enjoyed his greatest military successes at Kiangsi. When he first arrived there in 1517 as the new senior censor and governor, Kiangsi was the scene of repeated insurrections by rebels and bandits. Two months after his arrival, he suppressed the rebellion and initiated the rehabilitation of the rebels. In 1518, he conducted tax reform, established schools, carried out reconstruction, and instituted the Community Compact, which improved unity as well as community morals.

Wang reached the pinnacle of his political career in 1519. On his way to suppress a rebellion in Fukien, he discovered that the Prince of Ning, Ch'en-hao, had declared himself head of state. Wang surrounded the prince's base, Nan ch'ang, and captured him. Rumors had surfaced as a result of his contact with Ch'en-hao, and Wang was accused by a jealous official of conspiring with the prince, resulting in the imprisonment of one of Wang's pupils. Nevertheless, Wang was appointed Governor of Kiangsi by the end of the year. In 1520, he instituted more reforms.

Wang's achievements were not viewed as a cause for celebration by everyone in the kingdom. The emperor tried to claim credit for the victory at Nanking by leading the expedition himself. Wang also embarrassed the emperor, first by capturing the prince and then by giving credit to the department of military affairs. Most damaging of all, though, was the fact that Wang and the prince had exchanged messengers before the rebellion took place. Wang's political enemies were so incensed by his correspondence with the prince that Wang's messenger, Chi Yuan-heng, was tortured to death.

Wang was exonerated of all charges in 1521 when the Chia-ching emperor ascended the throne. After his father died in 1522, Wang went into virtual retirement at Yu-yao for five years, where he attracted hundreds of disciples from all over China, even though his critics escalated their attacks against him. During this period, he developed his philosophy to full maturity with his doctrine of the extension of innate knowledge. With this theory, Wang turned psychology into ethics, suggesting that the human mind possesses an innate capacity for distinguishing between good and evil. Wang's conversations with his students were collected in his major work, *Ch'uan-hsi lu* (1572; *Instructions for Practical Living*, 1963).

In 1522, Wang was called upon to suppress a rebellion in Kwangsi, a feat which he accomplished in only six months. The coughing that had bothered him for years became so pronounced during the fighting that he had to conduct the battles from carriages. On his return home, he died in Nan-en, Kiangsi, on January 9, 1529. After his death, a political enemy of Wang, senior academician Kuei O, vented his anger against Wang by revoking his earldom and all of his hereditary privileges, thereby disinheriting Wang's sons. In 1567, though, a new emperor bestowed on Wang the posthumous title of Marquis of Hsin-chien. In 1584, he was accorded the highest honor of all by the offering of sacrifice to him in the Confucian temple.

Summary

Wang Yang-ming will be remembered as the scholar-official who brought a lasting peace to China. Under the leadership of such corrupt eunuchs as Liu Chin, fifteenth century China was a chaotic country, overrun with rebels and bandits. Wang rose to power through the civil service examination system, which had been the traditional avenue to fame and political authority for more than one thousand years. Although he had many political enemies, Wang used his various offices to quell the rebellions. Consequently, a large portion of China enjoyed a century of peace.

Wang's contributions to Neo-Confucian philosophy also had a tremendous effect on China. In the fifteenth century, the Confucian classics, such as the works of Chu Hsi, were being used by the rulers to restrict freedom of thought. Wang arrived at this conclusion through a three-step learning process that began with the writing of flowery compositions, proceeded to intense study of Chu Hsi's works, and culminated in his revolutionary pronouncements. His doctrine of unity of action and knowledge and his doctrine of innate knowledge invigorated the Confucian system. After his death, Wang's philosophy would become a potent force in China and Japan for 150 years, producing a number of brilliant reformers.

Bibliography

Chang Carson. "Wang Yang-ming's Philosophy." In *Philosophy East and West*, vol. 5. Honolulu: University of Hawaii Press, 1955. A short introduction to Wang's life and work. Useful primarily for its clear, concise explanation of Wang's philosophy.

Cua, A. S. "Between Commitment and Realization: Wang Yang-Ming's Vision of the Universe as a Moral Community." *Philosophy East and West* 43 (1993): 611. This article provides a critical introduction to the basics of Wang Yang-Ming's philosophy, including the vision of *jen* as an object of ethical commitment; the nature of self-confidence; and the concept of *liang-chih* as a meditation between the ideal jen and the actual world.

Feng, Yu-lan. *A History of Chinese Philosophy.* Translated by Derk Bodde. Vol. 2. Princeton, N.J.: Princeton University Press, and London: Allen and Unwin, 1953. An introduction to Wang's philosophy. Although the entry relies heavily on quotations from Wang's works, it does offer commentary at the beginning and ending of each section.

Wang Yang-ming. *Instructions for Practical Living and Other Neo-Confucian Writings.* Translated by Wing-tsit Chan. New York: Columbia University Press, 1963. The introduction is a comprehensive account of Wang's achievements as a politician and as a philosopher, based on standard Chinese sources. This text is an indispensable biography for the English-speaking reader.

———. *The Philosophy of Wang Yang-ming.* Translated by Frederick Goodrich Henke. London and Chicago: Open Court, 1916. An uncritical translation, which is based largely on such legends as Wang's escape by boat from assassins. Omits some essential material, but it does provide a good overview of Wang's early life.

Zehou, Li. "Thoughts on Ming-Quing Neo-Confucianism." In *Chu Hsi and Neo-Confucianism*, edited by Wing-tsit Chan. Honolulu: University of Hawaii Press, 1986. Clarifies Wang's philosophy by contrasting it with the work of Wang's precursor, Chu Hsi.

Alan Brown

EARL OF WARWICK
Richard Neville

Born: November 22, 1428; probably Wessex, England

Died: April 14, 1471; Barnet, Hertfordshire, England

Area of Achievement: The military

Contribution: Warwick's activities during the Wars of the Roses proved that the accumulation of wealth and power in the hands of the nobles led only to chaos and destruction. New techniques of government—nationalism and diplomacy—were needed in a more modern world.

Early Life

Richard Neville was born on November 22, 1428; he was the eldest son of Richard Neville, the fifth Earl of Salisbury, and his wife, Alice (née Montacute). The Nevilles were one of the oldest, most important, and wealthiest families in England and were descended from and related to kings. Cecily Neville, Neville's aunt, was married to Richard, the Duke of York, who was heir to the English throne. Shortly before Neville's birth, his mother's father, the fourth Earl of Salisbury, had been killed while fighting in France. In his wife's name, Neville's father inherited Salisbury's lands and title. As a consequence, Neville was reared to wealth and power.

As a child, Richard was married to Anne Beauchamp, the only daughter of the Earl of Warwick. In June, 1449, following the death of his wife's brother, Richard inherited his father-in-law's title and lands, making him the most powerful earl in England, with precedence over even his father. Not that his father minded; both his father and his grandfather had provided astutely for their numerous children. (Richard's father had twenty-two full or half siblings.) They intended to make their family the most powerful in England, and for a short while they were successful. Of thirty-five members of the House of Lords, eleven were Nevilles. Richard Neville expected to play an important role in his country's politics.

The influence of this small number of very powerful nobles was one reason mid-fifteenth century England was both prosperous and chaotic. Henry VI, born during the Hundred Years' War while England was victorious, ruled both England and France. Governed by others, he never learned to rule well and was a weak king. When the war with France was lost, the English people blamed Henry's ministers, especially those responsible for the king's marriage to Margaret of Anjou, the niece of Charles VII of France. The war's end brought not only popular discontent but also hosts of disbanded mercenaries. These soldiers swelled the private armies of the powerful barons, including the Nevilles.

Fifteenth century England was not isolated from international politics. Richard's childhood was spent in the shadow of these events, as the country negotiated with France and continued its friendship with France's enemy, Burgundy. Scotland, Ireland, and Wales were also areas of concern; Neville's father was Henry VI's Warden of the West Marches near Scotland.

In 1450, these national and international influences resulted in the Wars of the Roses. The Duke of York, supported by popular agitation to punish the ministers responsible for the mismanagement of the French war, began to demand reforms in government. Supporting those ministers, Queen Margaret excluded York from the King's Council. The populace protested, and the barons began to choose sides. In August, 1453, when Henry VI was declared insane, the Duke of York, as heir, was named regent in spite of Margaret's animosity. The Earl of Salisbury went to London to serve on the Council of Regency, and Warwick went with him. It was not until 1455, however, that Richard Neville, Earl of Warwick, began his own life's work.

Life's Work

Having regained his senses, Henry VI summoned a Royal Council in 1455 and once again excluded the Duke of York and his followers. York, Salisbury, and Warwick, with their thousands of retainers, rode to meet the king and his army at St. Albans. Discussion failed to settle the matter, and the opening battle of the Wars of the Roses between Henry's Lancastrians and the Yorkists was fought there on May 22, 1455. York and Warwick were victorious; they captured the king, only to release him when he agreed to appoint Yorkists to government positions.

Warwick gained a military reputation at St. Albans. His chief talent, however, was administrative, and, when he was named governor of Calais in 1455, he was given the perfect setting for his talents. On the coast of France, adjacent to both Burgundy and Flanders, Calais was constantly threatened by the French because of its strategic importance. Calais also controlled the trade route between Flanders and Burgundy. Even though it was an important Continental outpost, the garrison was seldom paid adequately or on time. Consequently, Warwick's creativity and talent for management made him a popular commander, as he became a pirate to pay his soldiers. Seizing Spanish, French, Burgundian, and even some Hanseatic vessels en route to London, Warwick plundered them for his men, regardless of the king's policy. All the men serving at Calais wore the Warwick badge out of admiration for their swashbuckling leader.

In 1459, at the moment when Margaret of Anjou believed herself secure enough to challenge the Yorkists, Warwick made a lightning raid on England to rescue his cousin, Edward, and his father. When Margaret's representative attempted to seize Calais, Warwick was in control, and when the queen sent arms to her men, they fell into Warwick's hands. To retrieve his ships from royal control, Warwick and his men slipped into the borough of Sandwich, seized them, and returned to Calais. In 1460, Warwick sailed to Ireland, conferred with the Duke of York, and returned to Calais. Margaret's naval forces offered battle; Warwick, without hesitating, bore down directly on the English fleet, as it turned and fled. Mutinous English sailors refused to fight Warwick.

These years before 1460 may well have been some of Warwick's best. Calais gave him the necessary scope for his courage, love of action, administrative skill, and vanity. Young, strong, friendly, generous, and fair, Warwick was well loved by the Calais garrison. He punished only those men who had turned against him and those nobles who had wronged him. The common people he spared. This ability to manage men and to excite their loyalty, first apparent at Calais, appeared again and again in Warwick's dealings with individuals, Parliament, military retainers, and foreign rulers.

Calais held for Warwick in spirit, if not in fact, until he died. He returned often to Calais between battles, but after 1460 the earl's attention shifted to England. In June, 1460, Warwick and his father landed at Sandwich after distributing throughout the country a proclamation of grievances against the king. Joining the Duke of York, they defeated the Lancastrians at Northampton, and again captured the king. The Duke of York with difficulty resisted the temptation to claim the throne and resumed his place as regent.

In January, 1461, Margaret momentarily reclaimed the initiative at the second Battle of St. Albans—a battle that cost the Duke of York and Warwick's father their lives. By the end of February, Edward of York, succeeding to his father's title and ambition, had won the Battle of Mortimer's Cross, claimed the throne as Edward IV, and routed the Lancastrians at Towton at a cost of thirty thousand lives, though only eight thousand of them were Yorkists. On May 1, 1461, Edward IV, Warwick's cousin and protégé, entered London. Warwick "the Kingmaker" remained in the north to pacify the English and Scottish rebels.

Wary of Margaret's negotiations to secure French or Burgundian assistance and of her efforts to stir up Scottish and Lancastrian rebellion, the Yorkists fought sporadically until May, 1464, when the Lancastrians were finally subdued and the civil wars temporarily ended. In September, Warwick appeared before Parliament to propose a treaty with the French which would permanently prevent aid to Margaret and her supporters. To seal the treaty, he urged a marriage between the sister-in-law of Louis XI of France and Edward, only to be told that Edward had secretly married Elizabeth Woodville, a widow with a family as prolific, if not as noble, as the Nevilles.

During the spring of 1465, Warwick traveled to Burgundy and France to negotiate a truce. Burgundy vowed to continue its aid to Margaret; France quickly agreed to a truce. In 1467, Warwick returned to France to make that peace permanent. Diplomatic negotiation, like the command at Calais, was work which suited Warwick well. In England, between 1465 and 1467, Warwick spent more time on his own estates than he had during the previous ten years. The Nevilles were being replaced by Woodvilles. Edward's dependence on Warwick waned, and the cousins grew apart. The king refused to allow his brother, the Duke of Clarence, to marry Warwick's daughter, Isabella, and dismissed Warwick's friends and kinsmen from office. When Warwick brought the French delegates to London to conclude the peace with Edward, the king treated them coldly, having already concluded an agreement with Burgundy. The French were humiliated; more important for England, Warwick, who had placed Edward on the throne, was humiliated. These actions demonstrated foolish ingratitude on Edward's part: Warwick was popular and seen as a

friend of the people; the Woodvilles, on the other hand, were disliked as renegade Lancastrians.

At Christmas, 1467, Warwick refused to attend a Royal Council while his enemies surrounded the king. In January, 1468, popular leaders threatened to rise against the king and called on Warwick for leadership, but Warwick sent them home. In the spring, Edward attempted to reconcile with Warwick by consulting him about a planned attack against France. Warwick hid his dissatisfaction and waited. In April, 1469, he took his wife and daughters to Calais, where the Duke of Clarence married Isabella. Meanwhile, riots broke out again in York. Clarence and Warwick landed in Kent with the Calais guard after the ritual demand for reforms. At Olney, Edward was outfought and captured. His capture provided the opportunity for an outbreak of private wars and the resurgence of Lancastrian rebellions. In order to restore order to the realm, Warwick was forced to bargain with Edward.

A cautious peace continued between the two, with Warwick supporters in office and Woodvilles out, until March, 1470, when Edward claimed that rebels in Lincolnshire had implicated Warwick and Clarence in their rebellion. Branded as traitors, Warwick, his family, and his son-in-law fled south to Kent, where the seafaring people helped them acquire ships. The Warwick party sailed to Calais, where the garrison reluctantly refused to admit them. Having captured a Burgundian fleet en route to France, Warwick was welcomed by Louis XI. Happy to avenge himself against Edward's threat, Louis encouraged Warwick to reconcile with Margaret of Anjou, sealing the bargain with a marriage between Warwick's daughter and Margaret's son.

In September, Warwick again landed in England and declared himself for Henry VI. Quickly defeated by Warwick's forces, Edward fled to Burgundy. From October, 1470, to February, 1471, Henry VI ruled with Warwick—kingmaker for the second time—as his chief minister. Through Parliament, Warwick inaugurated a new reign of tolerance and amnesty, and concluded a treaty with France against Burgundy. Popular with some, Warwick had acquired enemies: the London merchants, the Yorkist nobles allied to the Woodvilles, and the Duke of Clarence.

By March, 1471, Edward had gathered support in Burgundy and landed at Ravenspur in the north. By strategy and guile, proclaiming his loyalty to King Henry VI, Edward was able to marshal his troops, reach his wife and son in London, and reclaim the throne. Warwick, unable to unite his own forces, met Edward at Barnet on a foggy Easter morning. Warwick's army could not defeat Edward's troops, and the Kingmaker fell in battle, at the age of forty-two. Soon after, Margaret of Anjou's son Edward fell at Tewkesbury.

Summary

Richard Neville, Earl of Warwick and Salisbury, was the last of the great English nobles to oppose the Crown. His death ended the possibility that any noble family would ever again be able to dominate the throne. The Lancastrians were killed, as were many of the Woodvilles. By the end of the fifteenth century, Henry VII, a king neither Yorkist nor Lancastrian, ruled. His primary goal was to be wealthier and more powerful than all of his nobles put together. He fought few wars, balanced the budget, and strengthened the gentry and merchant classes. A new world was dawning.

Warwick was the last of a dying breed. He was also, by his ability and interest, the first of a new kind of government manager much like those who later served Henry VIII. As a leader, he realized the importance of popularity with the ordinary man and soldier. As a statesman, he was a skillful speaker and diplomat. His negotiations with France and Burgundy were for England as a nation rather than for himself. In this sense, Warwick was a man of the future, more committed to solving problems than to fighting wars.

Bibliography

Gillingham, John. *The Wars of the Roses: Peace and Conflict in Fifteenth-Century England*. London: Weidenfeld and Nicholson, and Baton Rouge: Louisiana State University Press, 1981. Debunks the Shakespearean myth of the Wars of the Roses with its cruel bloodshed and long-term conflict. A military history.

Jacob, E.F. *The Fifteenth Century, 1399-1485*. Oxford: Clarendon Press, 1961; New York: Oxford University Press, 1978. The sixth volume of the Oxford History of England series presents the traditional view of the Kingmaker and his king. Portrays the problem between them as one of policy: Warwick wanted to control foreign policy with a French alliance, while Edward wanted to recover the French lands lost in 1450.

Kendall, Paul Murray. *Warwick the Kingmaker*. London: Allen and Unwin, and New York: Norton, 1957. A well-written, dramatic biography enlivened by inferences and reconstructions. Portrays Warwick as a precursor of sixteenth century statesmen.

Lander, J.R. *Government and Community: England, 1450-1509*. London: Arnold, and Cambridge, Mass.: Harvard University Press, 1980. Identifies the Yorkist party only in 1460; sees no conspiracy against Henry VI. Depicts Warwick as greedy and Edward as a more competent ruler than usually portrayed.

Oman, Charles W. *Warwick the Kingmaker*. London and New York: Macmillan, 1891. A standard laudatory biography by a military historian. Emphasizes battles and generalship.

Ross, Charles. *Edward IV*. London: Methuen, and Berkeley: University of California Press, 1974. Adds to the traditional assessment that the Woodvilles had kin in Burgundy to help to explain Edward's insistence on the Burgundian alliance.

Wolffe, Bertram. *Henry VI*. London: Methuen, 1981. This view of Henry downplays the role of Margaret of Anjou and concedes that Edward was restored without opposition in 1471. A standard biography.

Loretta Turner Johnson

ROGIER VAN DER WEYDEN

Born: 1399 or 1400; Tournai, the Netherlands
Died: c. June 18, 1464; Brussels
Area of Achievement: Art
Contribution: One of the greatest of the fifteenth century Netherlandish painters, Rogier influenced other painters of the Christian altarpiece, stylistically and tonally, and dominated northern European painting throughout the period.

Early Life

Although Rogier van der Weyden was presumably born in the French-speaking, southern region of the Netherlands, there is no specific knowledge of his ethnic background. Indeed, scholarly controversy continues to surround his life and his work. No single painting by him is confirmed by his signature, and the documentary evidence is also very slight. It is known that one Rogier van der Weyden entered an apprenticeship with the painter Robert Campin in 1427 in Tournai and fulfilled his service, getting his patent as Master in 1432. Yet the facts are complicated by the name Rogier van der Weyden appearing on Tournai documents in 1426, already denoted a Master.

It may be that Rogier had been previously trained in another trade, perhaps sculpture, since the modeling in his paintings has distinct affinities to that art, which has led to speculation that his father might have been a sculptor. He also seems to have come to his apprenticeship as a painter relatively late in life; there is evidence that he had a son, eight years old in 1435, which suggests that he must have been married sometime in the mid-1420's.

Even his apprenticeship to Campin is conjectural. Stylistically, his work is very close to that of Campin, and it is presumed that he is the "Rogelet de le Pasture" who was taken into training by Campin. If so, he was the son of Henry de le Pasture, whose family can be traced back in Tournai as far as 1260. Whatever the truth may be concerning his early years, he was, by 1436, firmly established in Brussels, married to a Brussels native, Elisabeth Goffaerts, and employed as the official town painter.

Life's Work

The three most important Netherlandish painters of the late Gothic period are Jan van Eyck, the Master of Flémalle, and Rogier van der Weyden. Jan van Eyck has emerged in the long run as the most admired of the three, but that was not the case in the fifteenth century. In truth, Rogier had considerably more influence on other contemporary painters than either of the other two. The difficulty in speaking of his career, however, lies in the peculiar fact that there is no work clearly identified as an example of his early career as a painter. Only the great works of his maturity (although the greatest, his *Descent from the Cross*, may be fairly early) are extant, a situation which has produced one of the most interesting scholarly puzzles in art history: Where are the works of his early career?

Like van Eyck, Rogier was primarily a painter of altarpieces—that is, paintings specifically ordered to be hung above the altar used in Roman Catholic churches to celebrate the Mass. They tend, as a result, to be large and connected to a specific church, and their original function was religious rather than aesthetic. The twentieth century preference for van Eyck's works over the paintings of Rogier is directly related to the fact that van Eyck, who is often credited with developing, sometimes with inventing, oil painting, anticipat-

ed Renaissance Humanist realism in his works. There is some slight influence of his work in Rogier, but Rogier seems deliberately to eschew the splendid technical leap forward into recording the real world in favor of the more static representation of humans and nature which characterized the medieval style. Rogier refused to abandon the last stages of Gothic art; thus, Rogier's work was not only distinct from that of van Eyck but also more popular in his own century.

The painter Rogier seems to resemble most is the Master of Flémalle, the shadowy figure whose altarpieces seem to have been produced in the 1430's. Touches of van Eyckian naturalism and a close relationship to Rogier's mature works distinguish the Master's painting. The Master's identity remains a mystery, but it is often suggested that he was an associate of Rogier's Master, Robert Campin, or that he was, in fact, Campin. There is also an intriguing suggestion that the very paintings ascribed to the Master of Flémalle are Rogier's missing early work—that is, that Rogier is, in short, the Master of Flémalle, or at least the creator of some of the paintings now identified with the Master. Given the present lack of signed works and limited documentation, the question falls into the slippery area of style, technique, and connoisseurship, in which the eye of the critic dominates. Aside from the historical importance of the question, and the rather piquant nature of the problem, the arguments themselves cut to the heart of the nature of Rogier as a painter.

It is believed that much of Rogier's work has been lost. He produced a major work for the Brussels town hall, four variations on the theme of justice, but it was lost in a fire in 1695. There exist, however, several examples of his work as an altarpiece painter and some of his portraits which clearly show why he had such a long and prosperous career, not only as a painter but also as the head of a busy workshop. His best work is *The Descent from the Cross* (it is also his most popular), displayed at the Prado in Madrid. It features all those aspects of his talent which not only distinguished him from van Eyck but also established him as the most influential painter of his time in the Netherlands. The subject is the common one of the lifting of the dead Christ from the Cross; yet where other painters of van Eyckian inclination might try to portray this scene with some sense of the physical, realistic surrounding of the act of pity and awe, Rogier packs ten figures into a flat, shallow niche which reminds one of the tomb itself—with the figures spread out (though densely impinging one another) in a line across the front, similar to a sculptural frieze. The fall of the draperies and the sharply contorted poses are Gothic; yet the colors are bright and hard, almost enamelized, and the faces are charged by Rogier's greatest gift, the ability to convey a sense of spiritual suffering.

There is in Rogier not only a mannered, stylized way with composition, structures, and nature (all of which run contrary to van Eyck's warm naturalism) but also a capacity to express emotions, usually spiritual, which are quite beyond anything attempted by van Eyck. Rogier's work as a portrait painter (the lovely *Portrait of a Woman* is a good example) draws back from the particulars of realism into a kind of introverted world of religious dream.

Scholars surmise that Rogier made a trip to Italy, perhaps in 1450, and that he must have visited both Florence and Rome. His *Entombment* in the Uffizi shows that he was not entirely obdurate in his approach to his art, since it shows signs of the influence of Fra Angelico. Further, his *Madonna with Four Saints* in Frankfurt, which contains in its panels the Florentine coat of arms, contains elements of the Italian *sacra conversazione*.

Rogier's career seems to have prospered from beginning to end, and his large studio employed a group of painters who carried on in his style a type of altar painting which was to dominate during the late medieval period in the Netherlands. He died in Brussels in June of 1464.

Summary

If van Eyck is the twentieth century's painter of choice for the late Gothic period, then Rogier van der Weyden, with his stiffer, somewhat monumental seriousness and lyric, almost mystic intensity was the choice not only of the public but also of the painters who came to maturity in the same period. Rogier's way of telling the eternal story, ascetically restrained, physically desiccated (although in glowing color), was deeply admired and unabashedly imitated. It was as if Rogier read the sensibility of the age and knew that people still clung to the old imperatives, subordinating the particular, the individual, to the general, the idealized; he knew that society was not yet ready to break with the safety of the collectivized, church-centered world of religious submission to the mystery of Christianity.

The inclination today is to read Rogier's paintings through the strangely vibrant colors, the ambiguous intensities of the portrait heads, and to find his stylized draperies, his dispositions of the human body, as somewhat quaint in their Gothic awkwardness. Yet an understanding of what Rogier was doing and when he was doing it allows for a deeper appreciation of his greatness as a painter, of the imploded power, the sonority, and the graceful, dramatic timelessness of his best work.

Bibliography

Friedlaender, Max J. *Early Netherlandish Painting: From Van Eyck to Bruegel.* London and New York: Phaidon Press, 1956. This popular volume contains a chapter on Rogier, in addition to helpful chapters on van Eyck and the painting of the period in general.

———. *Early Netherlandish Painting: Rogier van Weyden and the Master of Flémalle.* Translated by Heinz Norden. New York: Praeger, and Brussels: Éditions de la Connaissance, 1967. Not to be confused with the previous title, this volume is a scholarly work. Yet it is so delightfully and reasonably written that it is thoroughly accessible to the lay reader. Not only does Friedlaender deal with the mystery of Rogier and the Master, but he also handles the entire career and makes pertinent assessments of Rogier's style and influence.

Fuchs, R. H. *Dutch Painting.* London: Thames and Hudson, and New York: Oxford University Press, 1978. A popular, well-illustrated history of painting in the Netherlands region. Chapter 1 is a simple and direct discussion of the period in which Rogier worked. Somewhat simplistic, but a useful introduction.

Lane, Barbara G. *The Altar and the Altarpiece: Sacramental Themes in Early Netherlandish Painting.* New York: Harper, 1984. The problem of fully understanding the quality of Rogier's work, given the limited knowledge and understanding of the deeply religious sensibility, is met with care, attention, and careful argument in this short book. Rogier's work figures substantially in Lane's text.

Panofsky, E. *Early Netherlandish Painting: Its Origins and Character.* 2 vols. Cambridge, Mass.: Harvard University Press, 1953. By a master of iconography, intriguing essays on how to read the secret language of the religious painting.

Charles Pullen

WILLIAM THE SILENT

Born: April 24, 1533; Dillenburg Castle, Nassau

Died: July 10, 1584; Delft, Holland

Areas of Achievement: Government and politics

Contribution: William, Prince of Orange and Count of Nassau, led the revolt of the Netherlands against Spain despite overwhelming difficulties. His leadership proved decisive to the Dutch independence movement at its crucial beginnings in the late sixteenth century.

Early Life

William, the eldest son of Count William of Nassau-Dillenburg and his second wife, Juliana von Stolberg, was born on April 24, 1533, at Dillenburg Castle. The family was large, and the young heir's prospects not particularly remarkable until 1544, when, at the age of eleven, he inherited the titles and possessions of an elder cousin, René of Orange, who was killed during the siege of Saint Dizier. Because of the wealth and importance of his new estates, as well as the fact that William's parents had become Lutherans, the Habsburg emperor Charles V determined that the boy should be brought up at his court and educated in the Roman Catholic faith.

William's pleasant manners and appearance and genial personality soon made him a general favorite at court. The aging emperor became very fond of the young man and arranged an advantageous marriage for him with a pretty heiress, Anne of Egmond-Buren; this union would produce a son, Philip William, and a daughter. Anne died in 1558 and does not appear to have played a very important part in her husband's emotional life.

William had fulfilled a number of social and military duties at the court before the abdication of Charles V in 1555 in favor of his son Philip II. It was perhaps ironic that the emperor chose to lean upon the shoulder of the young Prince of Orange as he passed the sovereignty of Spain and his Burgundian territories to the man who would become Orange's most bitter enemy. Yet for a while the relationship between William and Philip was amicable, if not warm. Philip was godfather to Philip William, and William would be given new responsibilities. Now in his middle twenties, William's career as a loyal servant of the new monarch seemed assured.

Life's Work

There is a traditional story that Philip and William disliked each other on sight; if that were so, their mutual antagonism took time to mature. William was named a Councillor of State and a Knight of the Golden Fleece by the new king. In 1559, William was chosen to be one of three chief negotiators concluding the Treaty of Cateau-Cambrésis between France and Spain. His associates, Antoine Perrenot de Granvelle, Bishop of Arras, and Fernando Álvarez de Toledo, Duke of Alva, would also play crucial roles in the revolt of the Netherlands. It was during this stay in France that William began to acquire his reputation for being discreet, but "taciturn" or even "sly" are better descriptive terms than the misleading nickname "silent." William was a career diplomat, fond of company and never at a loss for words.

With the conclusion of this diplomatic mission, William was appointed stadtholder (governor and military commander) in Zeeland, Utrecht, Holland, and later (1561) Franche-Comté. On the eve of Philip's departure for Spain in August, 1559, however, the nobility and people of the Netherlands were beginning to complain. Spanish troops had not been withdrawn despite the peace, Spanish courtiers were being made Councillors of State, and sterner measures were being authorized against Protestants. William and other important nobles protested, and Philip seemed willing to make concessions regarding Spanish troops and politicians—but not heretics. He appointed his half-sister Margaret, Duchess of Parma, as regent, with Granvelle (now a cardinal) as her adviser.

William was anxious to marry again, but his choice of wives was not a fortunate one. Anne of Saxony, a well-born heiress, was erratic and quarrelsome, her family had traditionally opposed the Habsburgs, and, worse, she was a Lutheran. William made vague promises about his wife's conformity when they were married in 1561, but Philip was not pleased.

As Granvelle's influence increased (he created more than a dozen new bishoprics), the nobility of the Netherlands felt their traditional leadership threatened. Snobbery also played a role in the nobility's dislike for Granvelle, who was said to be the grandson of a blacksmith. Toleration of Calvinists was initially less important than the replacement of the hated minister with one more to their liking. In

letters to Philip, however, the nobles, led by William and the Counts of Egmond and Hoorne, were careful to avoid direct criticism of royal policies.

In the spring of 1564, it seemed that the anti-Granvelle faction had won; Margaret had also decided that Granvelle was a political liability, and he was withdrawn. Yet Philip, however preoccupied with the Turks and the administration of his vast empire, was unyielding in matters of faith. Catholicism was to be imposed upon the Netherlands and Protestant heresy rooted out.

William and his associates tried to support Margaret while attempting to promote a policy that would allow liberty of conscience, if not public worship, for Protestants. Efforts at a reasonable compromise were doomed to failure by both sides. A number of the lesser nobility and their supporters advocated violence to intimidate the regent and the Catholics. These men became known as the "Beggars" (*les Gueux*), from a slighting reference made about them by one of Margaret's advisers. Riots erupted in the summer of 1566. Fanatical Calvinist mobs sacked churches, even turning some of them into Protestant meetinghouses. By the end of the year, an angry Philip appointed the Duke of Alva as his general to pacify the Netherlands at any cost.

William hesitated; he refused to command the rebels, protested his loyalty to the king, and then declined to take the oath of unconditional obedience that Margaret demanded. In April, 1567, he retired to his family estates at Dillenburg. Other prudent men fled the country, but Hoorne and Egmond remained, only to be betrayed, arrested, and executed. The Duke of Alva's methods for maintaining order were so brutal that eventually Margaret resigned. A reign of terror instituted by a special commission, the Council of Troubles—soon nicknamed the Council of Blood—filled the land with fear, as thousands of victims were arrested and executed. When William refused to return, he was declared a rebel, his property in the Netherlands was sequestered, and his son, a student at the University of Louvain, was carried off to Spain, never again to see his father.

With few choices remaining save armed rebellion, William and his brothers raised an army to expel the Duke of Alva. Two invasions were launched in April, 1568, but the people did not rise; both attempts were badly defeated. William and his few supporters took refuge in France. William was entering the most difficult period of his life. Impoverished, outlawed, and peripatetic, he was made miserable by Anne of Saxony's irrational behavior. She was flagrantly unfaithful, and at last he divorced her in 1571.

Meanwhile, William continued to look for allies. Elizabeth I of England was not encouraging. The German Protestant princes had provided little support. His best hopes seemed to lie with the Calvinists, whose faith he would adopt in 1573. Another area of resistance lay with the "Sea Beggars," an irregular band of nobles, merchants, patriots, and pirates. In April, 1572, they seized the town of Brielle, which triggered a popular uprising, and soon most of Holland, Zeeland, and Friesland declared William their stadtholder.

To strengthen his advantage, William's brother Louis of Nassau launched an attack from France but was eventually blockaded at Mons. As William moved to aid him, his support among the French Huguenots was undercut by the Massacre of Saint Bartholomew's Day (August 24, 1572). Again William's forces were obliged to disband, and he retreated to Holland to lead the resistance there for four more frustrating years (1572-1576).

In June, 1575, William married his third wife, Charlotte de Bourbon, a former nun who had fled her convent, escaped to Germany, and converted to Calvinism. Catholics were outraged at this union, but it proved to be both happy and successful, as Charlotte won the trust and affection of her husband's countrymen by her devotion to their cause.

By 1576, even Philip was becoming aware of the costs of this seemingly endless war. The rebellion was not crushed, and his own troops began to mutiny for lack of pay. William's status rose with the Pacification of Ghent (November 8, 1576), in which the seventeen provinces agreed to a common cause against Spain. This was followed in January, 1577, by the short-lived Union of Brussels, in which both Catholics and Protestants joined in demanding the withdrawal of Spanish troops, the southerners reserving the right to remain Catholics. At this point, William was at the height of his power and influence, but he was unable to maintain this fragile alliance, despite his natural toleration and his talents as a diplomat.

Believing that he must have the support of another ruling dynasty against Spain, William again turned to France and proposed the unlikely candidacy of the feckless Duke of Anjou, brother of Henry III of France, as sovereign of the Netherlands. Philip riposted in March, 1581, with a ban proclaiming William a traitor and offering a considerable reward for his assassination. The first attempt on his life a year later failed, but his wife died of a fever and the strain of nursing her husband.

The Duke of Anjou's double-dealing and ambitions made him unacceptable to his new subjects, few of whom would mourn his death in June, 1583. Two months before, William had married Louise de Coligny, a daughter of the famous Huguenot leader Gaspard II de Coligny, killed on Saint Bartholomew's Day. Of his twelve children, it would be her son Frederick Henry who would leave heirs to carry on the Nassau name. With Louise, William lived simply and quietly in Delft, a father figure beloved by the people, until July 10, 1584, when he was fatally shot by a Catholic fanatic. William's dying words were a prayer for his poor country. He was given a state funeral by the city and buried in the New Church at Delft.

Summary

The sequence of events following the murder of William the Silent was a study in vengeance and intolerance by all parties. William's friends and supporters relieved their outraged feelings by torturing and slowly executing the young assassin Balthazar Gérard. When the murder became known, William's enemies, who included Philip and Granvelle, expressed triumphant satisfaction at what they considered to be divine justice. The reconquest of the entire Netherlands appeared a certainty, but such was not to be.

Philip's dream of a Catholic Netherlands as the obedient handmaiden of Spain faded before the realities of Dutch determination, his own financial mismanagement, and the defeat of his grand armada by England in 1588. Yet William's dream of a united Netherlands would not become a reality. The depths of distrust between Protestants and Catholics, middle-class merchants and the nobility, north and south were too great to be bridged. William invested his fortune, his family (three of his brothers would die on campaigns), and finally his own life for the cause in which he so strongly believed. Yet not even his personal popularity and his diplomatic skills could hold the provinces together for long. William's cause failed, but he had dared greatly and became the heart and symbol of the Dutch independence movement.

Bibliography

Geyl, Pieter. *The Revolt of the Netherlands, 1555-1609.* 2d ed. London: Benn, and New York: Barnes and Noble, 1958. This is the first chronologically in a series of three books by Geyl that deals with the Netherlands from 1555 to 1715. As a Dutch historian, Geyl has a special perspective on the revolt. This book places William in his historical context. Includes maps, an extensive index, and a short bibliography.

Harrison, Frederic. *William the Silent.* London and New York: Macmillan, 1897. The style and interpretation of this biography are of necessity somewhat dated, but the lack of a standard biography of William in English makes it useful. Contains a bibliography and useful information on William's family and descendants.

Kossman, E. H., and A. F. Mellink, eds. *Texts Concerning the Revolt of the Netherlands.* London and New York: Cambridge University Press, 1974. This book introduces the reader to letters and documents related to the revolt. Several letters by William are included. Contains a short bibliography and an index.

Parker, Geoffrey. *The Dutch Revolt.* Rev. ed. London: Penguin, 1985; New York: Penguin, 1990.

Parker makes the valid point that there was not one Dutch revolt but several. This study attempts to balance the majority of treatments, which are pro-Dutch, with attention to the Spanish viewpoint. Contains maps, diagrams, tables, and an extensive bibliography.

Putnam, Ruth. *William the Silent, Prince of Orange (1533-1584) and the Revolt of the Netherlands*. New York and London: Putnam, 1895. The character of William the Silent is at times overly idealized, but this book is a useful beginning to a study of William and his times. Pictures, maps, and facsimiles of letters make it interesting to the general reader. Includes a detailed bibliography and an index.

Swart, K. W. *William the Silent and the Revolt of the Netherlands*. London: Historical Association, 1978. This work is one of a series on a wide range of historical topics. Though brief, it is a clear and unromantic portrait of William. Contains a useful annotated bibliography.

Wedgwood, C. V. *William the Silent, William of Nassau, Prince of Orange*. London: Cape, and New Haven, Conn.: Yale University Press, 1944. Well written and detailed but continues the trend of older studies in idealizing William's motives and character. For the general reader.

Wilson, Charles. *Queen Elizabeth and the Revolt of the Netherlands*. London: Macmillan, and Berkeley: University of California Press, 1970. The English view of the Netherlands as well as the role played by Elizabeth I is the focus of this useful study, but there is good background material on William also. Includes detailed notes on sources.

Dorothy Turner Potter

CARDINAL THOMAS WOLSEY

Born: 1471 or 1472; Ipswich, Suffolk, England
Died: November 29, 1530; Leicester Abbey, Leicester, England
Areas of Achievement: Government and politics
Contribution: By combining in himself the highest lay administrative post of chancellor and the religious position of papal legate *a latere*, Wolsey paved the way for the combining of church and state under Henry VIII.

Early Life

Thomas Wolsey was the child of Robert Wulcy, a butcher, from Ipswich, Suffolk, and his wife, Joan. Sent at an early age to Oxford, he received his B.A. at the age of fifteen. He became a Fellow at Magdalen College in 1497, soon after receiving his M.A. and becoming first junior and then senior bursar there. Forced to resign as bursar for using funds without authorization in order to complete the building of the great tower there, he became a priest in 1498. Subsequently, Wolsey became chaplain to Sir Richard Nanfan, the deputy lieutenant of Calais, and Nanfan recommended him to Henry VII. The king appointed Wolsey as one of his chaplains and occasionally used him on royal business. With the accession of Henry VIII in April, 1509, and the death of his grandmother, who did not like Wolsey, Wolsey came into his own. He became Henry's almoner in November and was advanced to councillor in late 1511.

Life's Work

From 1512 until his fall from power in 1529, Wolsey controlled the government of England, by acquiescing to the desires of his sovereign. Wolsey satisfied Henry's appetite for glory with the successful French campaign of 1513, in which Henry's forces won the Battle of Spurs and captured the French towns of Tournai and Thérouanne. In return for this success, Henry rewarded Wolsey by securing for him several clerical appointments—the bishopric of Tournai, the bishopric of Lincoln, the archbishopric of York, and the cardinalate. Later, Wolsey would add legate *a latere*, the bishopric of Bath and Wells, the abbacy of St. Albans, the bishopric of Durham, and the bishopric of Winchester to his titles. Though only Archbishop of York and thus theoretically under the Archbishop of Canterbury, Thomas Warham, Wolsey surpassed Warham and the entire English church by virtue of his status as papal legate *a latere*. Moreover, when Warham resigned as chancellor in December, 1515, Henry appointed Wolsey to the post. Thus, Wolsey united in himself the supreme lay post of chancellor and the supreme clerical post of legate *a latere*, making him the most important man in the kingdom second only to the king. As Henry's chief minister, Wolsey expended most of his energies on diplomacy. Whenever he saw either Charles V, the Holy Roman Emperor, or Francis I, the King of France, growing stronger, Wolsey sided with the other, trying to maintain a balance of power on the Continent. His greatest successes included the 1513 campaign against the French; the Anglo-French treaty of 1514; the 1518 peace treaty of Noyon, which involved England, France, and the Holy Roman Empire; and the magnificent Field of Cloth of Gold of 1520, when Henry and Francis met in a glorious spectacle of amity. His failures included the refusal of the East Anglians to agree to the Amicable Grant of 1525 and the pope's re-

fusal to annual Henry's marriage to Catherine of Aragon so that he could marry Anne Boleyn.

In 1527, Henry began to worry about his lack of a male heir and about the legality of his marriage to Catherine, who had previously been married for nearly five months to his elder brother, Arthur. Wolsey, with Warham, in May, 1527, examined the king about the marriage but came to no conclusion. Instead Wolsey decided to use his influence to secure a decree of nullity from Pope Clement VII. Clement was unwilling to antagonize Charles V, whose troops had sacked Rome in 1527 and briefly imprisoned the pope. Charles was Catherine's nephew, and he had sworn to help her. Nevertheless, the pope sent his legate to England but instructed him to do nothing without papal permission. Wolsey and the papal legate heard the marriage case from June 18 to July 23, 1529, when the case was called back to Rome because the planned Peace of Cambrai between Charles and Francis soon made it unnecessary for Clement to give Henry what he wanted. Earlier in the year, when Clement had been gravely ill, Wolsey had desperately tried to accumulate enough votes in the college of cardinals for his own candidacy, in the event of Clement's death. Twice before, in 1522 and in 1523, Wolsey had thought of himself as a papal candidate, but in 1522, Charles's tutor became Adrian VI, and in 1523, Giulio de' Medici became Clement VII. Perhaps it was unrealistic for a man such as Wolsey, who had never been to Rome and had not developed his Italian contacts, to think of himself as a viable candidate. Wolsey expended most of his energies on serving Henry and advancing his own interests.

Failure to secure the decree of nullity led to Wolsey's fall from power. He was indicted on October 9, 1529, under the statute of *praemunire*, which said that no ecclesiastical causes could be taken outside England for settlement, for his having overstepped his authority as legate. Wolsey lost his post as chancellor on October 18, 1529, to Sir Thomas More and signed a confession of his wrongdoing three days later. On November 3, he answered forty-six parliamentary charges against him (he was ably defended by Thomas Cromwell). In February, 1530, Henry restored him as Archbishop of York, and Wolsey went to that city in the spring. Once there, he endeared himself to the people by singing masses in parish churches and adopting a more religious way of life, even to the wearing of a hair shirt. Questions, however, arose about his correspondence with foreign powers after his fall, and the king had him arrested for treason. As Wolsey made his way to London, he stopped at Leicester Abbey, where he died on November 29, 1530. He was buried in the abbey chapel, next to Richard III.

Summary

Money from Thomas Wolsey's various ecclesiastical posts, combined with his fees from chancery and foreign pensions, made him the wealthiest man in the kingdom, wealthier even than the king in personal income. Wolsey was a great builder. He constructed York Place; his palace in Westminster, which later became the palace of Whitehall when Henry took it over; and Hampton Court, which Wolsey gave to Henry in 1525 to appease the king's jealousy. Although Wolsey was given the power as papal legate to reform the English church, he failed to do so. He was anti-Lutheran and, in 1521, had presided over the burning of Martin Luther's books. Nevertheless, Wolsey had a reputation for fairness in his dealings in the Court of the King's Council and in the Star Chamber.

Wolsey's private life, arrogance, and pluralism made for him many enemies, including the poets William Roy and John Skelton, who viciously satirized him in their poetry. Possibly Wolsey's example fed the anticlericalism that enabled Henry and Thomas Cromwell to reform the English church in the Reformation Parliament of 1529-1536. Moreover, Wolsey's practice of dissolving decaying monasteries in order to use the revenue to found colleges at Ipswich and Oxford was not lost on Cromwell, who dissolved all the English monasteries and nunneries to feed Henry's coffers. Thus, Wolsey's example of uniting lay and clerical power in himself paved the way for the extension of Henry's power over the church as well as the state. Wolsey served Henry well, but financially, he served himself better. At his death he was scarcely mourned, except by the good people of York, who, in the few months that he spent with them, saw him as their spiritual father.

Bibliography

Bindhoff, S. T. *Tudor England*. London and Baltimore: Penguin, 1950. A classic. Has a fine section on Wolsey showing the extent to which Wolsey served himself while serving Henry.

Cavendish, George. *The Life and Death of Cardinal Wolsey*, in *Two Early Tudor Lives*. Edited by Richard S. Sylvester and Davis P. Harding. New Haven, Conn.: Yale University Press, 1962. One of the earliest of English biographies, written in 1557 by Wolsey's gentleman usher.

Elton, G. R. *Reform and Reformation: England, 1509-1558.* London: Arnold, and Cambridge, Mass.: Harvard University Press, 1979. Notes the ephemeral nature of Wolsey's achievements. The real administrative revolution awaited the energy, efficiency, and work of Thomas Cromwell.

Erickson, Carolly. *Great Harry: The Extravagant Life of Henry VIII.* New York: Summit Books, 1980. Fascinating insights into both Wolsey and Henry VIII.

Ferguson, Charles W. *Naked to Mine Enemies: The Life of Cardinal Wolsey.* London: Longman, and Boston: Little Brown, 1958. Dramatic, readable retelling of Wolsey's life by the former editor of *Reader's Digest.*

Gunn, S.J., and P.G. Lindley, eds. *Cardinal Wolsey: Church, State and Art.* Cambridge and New York: Cambridge University Press, 1991. This lavishly illustrated book combines essays by eleven experts with a broad introduction to examine every aspect of Wolsey's career. It sets him in his English and European context as a politician, international and domestic statesman, ecclesiastical reformer, power-broker, and also as patron of the arts. This rounded appreciation of the range and scale of Wolsey's activities accounts easily for his dramatic impact on his contemporaries, and provides a fuller and fairer judgment of his achievements and historical significance.

Guy, J.A. *The Cardinal's Court: The Impact of Thomas Wolsey in Star Chamber.* Hassocks: Harvester Press, and Totowa, N.J.: Rowman and Littlefield, 1977. Based extensively on documents in the Public Record Office, this study notes Wolsey's innovative use of Star Chamber but concludes that the court was used more extensively and more practically by Thomas Cromwell. Challenging, but well worth reading.

Harvey, Nancy Lenz. *Thomas Cardinal Wolsey.* London and New York: Macmillan, 1980. A brief, readable account. Follows the judgments of Wolsey's gentleman usher and Wolsey's other contemporaries.

Pollard, A.F. *Wolsey.* London and New York: Longman, 1929. This is Pollard's masterpiece. Revised by works of Erickson, Williams, and Elton, but still worth reading.

Skelton, John. *John Skelton: The Complete English Poems.* Edited by John Scattergood. London: Penguin, and New Haven, Conn.: Yale University Press, 1983. Skelton's poems critical of Wolsey give a contemporary flavor of how much Wolsey was hated and despised. Scattergood's notes to the poems are especially useful.

Smith, Lacey Baldwin. *A History of England.* Vol. 2, *This Realm of England, 1399-1688.* 7th ed. Lexington, Mass.: Heath, 1996. A wonderfully written tour de force. The sort of history that cannot fail to excite the reader.

Thornton, Tim. "Cardinal Wolsey and the Abbot of Chester." *History Today* 45 (August, 1995): 12. The author examines the role played by Wolsey and the abbot of St. Werburgh's monastery in Chester, England. Thornton disputes history's tale of a centralized state and advances the opinion that strong, independent jurisdictions were still present in fifteenth century England.

Williams, Neville. *The Cardinal and the Secretary: Thomas Wolsey and Thomas Cromwell.* London: Weidenfeld and Nicolson, 1975; New York: Macmillan, 1976. A fascinating dual biography of two men, Wolsey and Cromwell, who were at the center of English public events for nearly thirty years. Shrewd insights from a master historian.

M. J. Tucker

SAINT FRANCIS XAVIER

Born: April 7, 1506; the Castle of Xavier, Navarre
Died: December 3, 1552; Island of Sancian, China
Area of Achievement: Religion
Contribution: Francis, who suffered many physical and mental hardships in order to bring the Christian message to countries of the Far East, was one of the first seven members of the Roman Catholic Church's Jesuit Order as well as its most successful missionary.

Early Life

The youngest of a family of several children, Francis Xavier was born to a prosperous nobleman, Don Juan de Jasso of Navarre, and a mother whose connection with the Xavier family brought property into her marriage. Francis' parents focused on his education early in his life, and, since they determined he had a real love for learning, he was allowed to go to the College of Saint Barbara at the University of Paris, where, in 1530, he received a master of arts degree. After being graduated, Francis taught Aristotelian philosophy at the same institution. Francis was known to be a generous, helpful, and stirring lecturer, having a thorough knowledge of his subject. Yet it was his sense of adventure, combined with a serious, searching, and scholarly nature, that drew students to him and made him ready to embark on daring journeys to little-known or unknown lands.

It was Ignatius Loyola (Later Saint Ignatius of Loyola), a fellow student of Francis at the University of Paris, who helped Francis find his calling—that of Christian missionary work. For three years, Ignatius prodded Francis to dedicate his life to God rather than to the vain pursuits of the worldly minded; yet Francis ignored the summons. Finally, however, Francis' resistance broke down, and he decided to serve God rather than scholarship. Together, Francis and Ignatius, along with five other idealistic youths, pledged themselves to Church service at Montmartre in Paris, their group becoming the Society of Jesus (Jesuits). Six of the original seven members went on to become ordained into the priesthood at Venice, Italy.

Francis and Ignatius then went to Rome and informed Pope Paul III that they would do whatever he asked of them. The pope, impressed by their youthful vigor and intellectual gifts, eventually gave official approval to the Society of Jesus. When the time came, the young men—Ignatius, Francis, Peter Faber, Nicholas Bobadilla, Diego Laínez, Alfonso Salmeron, and Simon Rodriguez—not only took traditional monastic vows of perpetual poverty and chastity but also pledged total obedience to the pope's wishes, going wherever he might find it necessary to send them.

From inauspicious beginnings in 1534, the society would help evangelize many nations and bring countless converts to the Church, while performing humanitarian deeds for the people converted and battling any heresy, vice, and spiritual lethargy they might encounter. Francis' name would become forever intertwined with that of the society, for he came to exemplify all that was positive in it.

Life's Work

After being ordained in the priesthood in 1537, Francis, in the company of Ignatius and the other Jesuits, worked long days to make the society into a successful venture, enthusiastically spreading the news about it to potential recruits. In 1540, the Portuguese king John III instructed his Vatican emissary to petition the pope to allow Jesuits the right to propagate the Christian faith within the new Portuguese possessions overseas. An opportunity for missionary work came after a vision of Ignatius, in which God told him to ask the pope a second time for a chance to do missionary tasks. In Ignatius' vision, God said that He would make certain that the permission would be granted.

With Ignatius elected the general of the society and with orders from Paul to convert pagans in Portugal's expanding empire, Francis joined fellow priest Rodriguez in Lisbon; then, with two trusted aides, he sailed on to Goa, a Portuguese colony in India, situated on the coast. While on board the ship taking him to Goa, Francis showed characteristic love for his fellow passengers by assisting those sickened by scurvy and other diseases, by saying Mass regularly, and by arbitrating arguments among the sailors. Once in Goa, which had been a Portuguese possession for only thirty years, Francis noted with dismay that the Europeans within the colony were dissipated by debauchery of all kinds and thus provided the native people with a terrible example of Christian conduct.

Taking upon himself the same selfless activities that he had performed on ship—caring for the sick, comforting the dying, advising those in difficult situations, teaching the Catechism, and saying

Masses—Francis slowly created order out of the Goan chaos, giving by precept as well as example a measure of self-discipline to the unruly inhabitants. Because he taught the residents of Goa the principles of the Catholic religion and put those principles directly into practice, Francis gained the residents' complete trust and high regard.

In 1542, having done much for Goa, Francis decided to journey to Cape Cormorin in southern India in order to teach a group of half-converted natives, called the Paravas, Christian values and beliefs; his message was well received by the poorest Paravas, who gathered in large numbers to hear him deliver his inspiring sermons. The love Francis had for the people of India was evident to almost everyone, even if his message sometimes became garbled or was incomprehensible. Once more, Francis' actions did more persuading than did his eloquent words.

After working with the Paravas, Francis decided to return to Goa in order to find new priests for the Society of Jesus. Again he was forced to deal with the immoral behavior and often outright hostility of Portuguese traders, who found his preaching an affront to a libertine way of life. This time, he worked alongside two Goanese priests and a lay catechist, helping the Goanese people by protecting them from European harassment.

At Travancore, Francis founded many churches, but at the same time he tore down the natives' ancestral places of worship and idols. He was said to have brought the dead back to life in the manner of Jesus Christ. Francis' exploits and his miracles led to his being hated by the Hindu Brahmans as well as local Muslims, who on occasion massacred Christian converts. As for his mission at Goa, Francis often wrote in letters to John III about how difficult an endeavor the mission had been for him and his followers. Fighting the immorality of the Portuguese residents at Goa demanded so much of Francis' time that he admitted to chronic weariness and, upon more than one occasion, a sense of defeat.

It may well have been his exasperation with fellow Europeans that led to Francis' departure from Goa in 1545, when he sailed to a city on the Malaysian peninsula called Malacca. There people who had previously been hostile to Christianity converted enthusiastically after Francis worked his miracles. He journeyed on to the southern Pacific Ocean, where he spent time on the Molucca Islands. There Francis once more battled the hardened, sinning Portuguese traders, some of whom would have liked to kill him.

From the Moluccas, Francis returned to Goa, this time by way of Ceylon, but wanted to journey on to the little-known secretive country of Japan. He traveled to Kagoshima on the island of Kyūshū, where he and his band were given permission to learn the Japanese language and to preach Christian doctrine to the city's inhabitants; unfortunately, this budding mission was almost destroyed when the prince who gave permission for Francis' evangelistic efforts became irate with him over the fact that Francis had dared use a base of Japanese operations other than his own city of Kagoshima.

Nevertheless, the converts that Francis had made remained faithful to the Church established in Japan. He made still more converts when he moved to the town of Hirado near Kagoshima. Other attempts at reaching the Japanese at the port city of Yamaguchi in 1549 were unsuccessful. At Kyōto, the imperial city itself, Francis found himself at another impasse, this time because he was so poorly dressed that the emperor believed that Francis could not possibly be an important Western dignitary and thus would not deign to see him. Francis, ever able to rise to a challenge, decided to purchase luxurious clothing for himself and for his fellow adventures. Dressing as extravagantly as he could, he presented himself to Oshindono, Prince of Nagote, who, after having been impressed by the splendor of Francis' party, decided to allow him to preach the Gospel in his realm. This opening allowed Francis to baptize many in the Christian faith.

Still other missionary ventures opened at Bungo in Kyūshū province, where the ruler was friendly to Francis and his followers and friends. When Francis left Japan in 1551, he could look back on a considerable achievement: He had singlehandedly converted more than seven hundred Japanese people to the Christian faith without bloodshed or turmoil.

Francis' last major challenge was to find a way to establish a mission in the forbidding country of China, long closed to all outsiders on the pain of death. Encouraged solely by the fact that so many missions had already been established in places once thought to be totally inhospitable to Christianity, Francis believed that God wanted him to open China to his faith and gain many converts there. Yet from the outset, the venture proved impossible. Francis dreamed of being the first priest to enter China. After he had done much exhausting work for the lepers at Malacca, he asked the new governor, Don Alvaro d'Ataide, to provide him with a ship and supplies so that he might sail to China. The governor, knowing well that China remained closed to outsiders, at first refused the request but then, after reconsidering, grudgingly allowed it.

Francis' plan was to sail to Japan in company with a Christian brother and a Chinese Christian, and then to travel secretly to China in the hope of somehow gaining entry. In the late summer of 1552, he landed at the port of Shang-ch'uen, where he hired a merchant to take him by night into Canton province. At a time when he needed all the strength he could find, Francis fell ill with a raging fever and was summarily left alone by most of the Portuguese on the island, who made a precarious living trading with mainlanders. Although one ship would have taken him home to Europe, Francis could not bear the ship's motion as it made its way out to sea, and he begged the captain to take him back to Shang-ch'uen, where he died asking God's forgiveness and praising Him.

Summary

Saint Francis Xavier, canonized by Pope Gregory XV in 1622 at the same time as was his great friend Ignatius, was one of the Catholic Church's most daring, astute, and productive leaders. He used his fine intellectual gifts and his ability to deliver powerful speeches and sermons to glorify God when he very well might have pursued far less arduous and far more lucrative careers than that of a missionary.

Francis was fortunate to have been born during Spain and Portugal's "Golden Age" of the sixteenth century, when empire-building was the pursuit of the Hispanic nations and their kings. Both countries, out to counter the Reformation brought on by followers of Martin Luther and to add to national coffers, needed able priests to subdue through conversion the natives of conquered lands. Thus, Francis found the kind of support he needed for his missionary efforts.

Without Francis and his fellow Jesuits, India, Japan, and other places in the Orient would have remained untouched by the Church's message and, without Francis' support, Ignatius might not have been able to found and properly organize the Jesuit Order. Today, with a debt owed to its founders, the society remains the preeminent scholarly order of the Catholic Church as well as its greatest supplier of educators, who teach children in secondary schools, colleges, and universities around the world. Appropriately, Francis remains the patron saint of all involved in missionary work and the guiding influence of multitudes of priests who have served their God in foreign places.

Bibliography

Aveling, J. C. H. "The Dangerous Missions." In *The Jesuits*. London: Blond and Briggs, 1981; New York: Stein and Day, 1982. This superb study of the Society of Jesus and its dynamic of faith, though it chooses not to dwell for long on Francis, does a fine job of discussing the magnitude of his opening the Far East to the Christian faith.

Barthel, Manfred. "The Light of the World: The Jesuit as Missionary." In *The Jesuits: History and Legend of the Society of Jesus*. Translated by Mark Howson. New York: Morrow, 1984. Explains Francis' contribution to the founding of the Society of Jesus and to its early mission work, and how he is to be remembered. For those readers wishing to have a grounding in the Jesuit Order's history and Francis' place in it. The general bibliography is useful.

Bartoli, Daniello, and J. P. Maffei. *The Life of St. Francis Xavier, Apostle of the Indies and Japan*. London: Jones, 1958; Baltimore: Murphy, 1959. Bartoli's account is one of the handful of studies of the saint in English translation. Serves as a basic guide to the subject of Francis' travels.

Clarke, C. P. S. "St. Francis Xavier." In *Everyman's Book of Saints*. London: Mowbray, and Milwaukee, Wis.: Young Churchman, 1914. Elementary but helpful introduction to Francis' place in the canon of saints.

Foss, Michael. "Reform of the Church and the Life of Renewal." In *The Founding of the Jesuits*. London: Hamilton, and New York: Weybright and Talley, 1969. Foss traces the society from its inception to the modern era. Francis is given credit for his pioneering work.

Maynard, Theodore. *The Odyssey of Francis Xavier*. London and New York: Longman, 1936. Compelling study of Francis and his importance to the Catholic Church's missionary outreach.

John D. Raymer

HULDRYCH ZWINGLI

Born: January 1, 1484; Wildhaus, Swiss Confederation

Died: October 11, 1531; near Kappel, Swiss Confederation

Areas of Achievement: Church reform and theology

Contribution: Zwingli led the Swiss Reformation against Roman Catholic ecclesiastical abuses, sharing both the rhetoric and the theology of Germany's own reformer, Martin Luther, until the two disagreed over the nature of the Eucharist. Overshadowed in church history by both Luther and John Calvin, Zwingli's most lasting contribution to Church history is his incipient Reformed theology and his recognition of the role that secular government might play in ecclesiastical matters.

Early Life

Huldrych Zwingli was born in Wildhaus, Swiss Confederation, to wealthy, devout parents. Zwingli's father served as a village magistrate and sought early to train his son in the ways of his Catholic faith—a Catholic faith invigorated by the new Humanism, which recognized and bestowed upon mankind more human responsibility and involvement in divine affairs. His father earnestly desired that Zwingli be educated as a priest and sent the boy at age ten to a Latin school in Basel, where he excelled in grammar, music, and dialectics. In 1498, Zwingli entered college study at Berne, where he came under the tutelage of Heinrich Wölflin, an influential Humanist scholar, who planted the initial seeds of intellectual independence in Zwingli. At Berne, Zwingli, now called Ulrich, distinguished himself as a musician and singer and was urged by the Dominican Order in Berne to join their choir and study music further. Zwingli initially accepted their invitation but abruptly withdrew. He chose instead to continue his theological education and entered in 1500 the University of Vienna, where he spent two years studying Scholastic philosophy, astronomy, and physics.

In 1502, Zwingli returned to the University of Basel, where he continued his classical studies while teaching Latin in the school of Saint Martin. He completed his bachelor's degree in 1504 and his master of arts degree in 1506 and became known officially as "Master Ulrich." At Basel, he became friends with Leo Jud, who would later become a chief associate in the reformation efforts in Zurich. Both studied under the famous Thomas Wyttenbach, professor of theology at Basel, whom Zwingli credits with opening his eyes to evils and abuses of the contemporary Church, especially its trafficking in indulgences—the sale of divine favors, such as forgiveness of or license to sin, or immediate entrance into heaven upon death.

Zwingli was ordained in the priesthood by the Bishop of Constance in 1506 and appointed pastor of Glarus, the capital city of the canton of the same name. Zwingli spent ten years in Glarus, occupied by preaching and pastoral duties as well as continuing to advance his knowledge of biblical languages, Greek and Roman philosophy, and the church fathers. Unlike Martin Luther, Zwingli did not in this fallow period seek a doctor of divinity degree, content with work in local pastorates and aiming at no higher church office. In the spring of 1515, Zwingli met the great Humanist scholar Desiderius Erasmus, whose writings he had been studying, and was deeply impressed by both his learning and his moderate theological views on inherited sin and his emerging symbolic reinterpretation of the Lord's Supper. Both Wyttenbach and Erasmus had helped remove the theological naïveté from Zwingli, infusing the spirit of Humanism into his own understanding and response to traditional Catholic teaching and a spirit of skepticism in his relationship with the Church hierarchy.

During this time, Zwingli also served as chaplain to the Glarus mercenaries who served the pope—devout men who he believed were being exploited by an illegitimate foreign power. This experience fueled his Swiss patriotism and compelled him to oppose publicly the mercenary system itself so vociferously that he was forced out of his pastorate in 1516. He subsequently moved to Einsiedeln, where he served as parish priest for three years, continuing his inquiry into the Greek New Testament and the church fathers. There Zwingli crystallized his views on salvation by faith, memorizing the New Testament letters of the apostle Paul and meshing his patriotic fervor with Erasmus' radical pacifism to take both a theological and a political stance against Rome. In his preaching, Zwingli began to oppose the use of relics in worship and pilgrimages to holy shrines as acts of devotion, regarding them as needless and idolatrous concessions to a religion that had left its eternal moorings.

Life's Work

Zwingli thus emerged from his early adult life as a clergyman emancipated from blind trust in the wisdom and infallibility of the Church hierarchy and its magisterium—the accumulated body of interpretation of Scripture used as an authority in disputes over the meaning of the Bible. In his slow but inexorable independence from established Christendom, he began to place great value upon his classical learning and great emphasis upon the need for individuals to exercise their faith in God directly—without the help of intermediaries such as relics and images, priests and departed saints. This intellectual ferment prepared him for the greatest task of his life: the reformation of Swiss Catholicism.

In the biographies of all the activists within the Protestant Reformation, the most important aspects of their lives rest as much on their intellectual efforts as on their dramatic deeds. This is the case with Zwingli, although his willingness to engage in armed warfare on behalf of his faith distinguishes him from some of his fellows. Nevertheless, Zwingli is most prominent for his contribution to the theological ferment of his times as well as to the realignments and associations forged in his native land of Switzerland and his adopted city, Zurich. As Luther had Wittenberg and Calvin Geneva, so Zwingli had Zurich, a city in which his great ideals would find incarnation not only in its cathedrals but also in its government structures. His beliefs eventually led him into local and canton politics, as he sought to move the secular city and the City of God into a more symbiotic, merciful status with each other.

In 1518, Zwingli was nominated for the position of people's priest at the Great Minister Church in Zurich, a prestigious and powerful pastorate. His candidacy was at first opposed in view of Zwingli's admittedly broken vow of celibacy; a friend intervened, however, and Zwingli assumed his new post on January 1, 1519. His early sermons were practical and ethical rather than doctrinal and divisive. From an unassuming beginning, Zwingli's pulpit became famous and extremely popular in Zurich; his down-to-earth expositions of biblical texts—as opposed to the dense, allegorical sermons common to the time—opened up the Scriptures to his flock and made Christianity seem present and vital rather than otherworldly and detached. This fresh emphasis on the Bible as an authoritative document that could speak directly to the hearts of people became the scaffolding for the Reformation everywhere, including Switzerland.

As Luther's reform movement began to shake the Church in Germany, Zwingli could not help but take notice. The war over indulgences that Luther had valiantly won in the German church became only a minor skirmish in Zurich, as the Roman church moved quickly to rectify abuses in Switzerland in an effort to stall the wholesale revolution it feared. Zwingli would engage the war on a different front: the authority of the Bible against the authority of the papal hierarchy. Zwingli's active involvement in the reform movement may well be located in August, 1519, when a plague broke out in Zurich and swept away one-third of the population and nearly took Zwingli's life. His experience in ministry to the sick and bereaved brought him renewed faith in God and emboldened him to speak out about the responsibility of the Church to offer grace, not law, to its members. Zwingli suggested that this would be accomplished by restoring Scripture to its rightful place in the authority of the Church and by dismantling the elaborate liturgy of the Mass, replacing it with a more homely and accessible kind of personal worship that would focus on God, not man.

Zwingli also began to see the civil government as an ally in his reform effort. Actively campaigning in the city council, Zwingli persuaded its members to take action against nonbiblically centered preaching in Zurich. In December, 1520, the council ordered the priests in the city and country to preach only from the Bible—the first time a secular authority had intervened in the affairs of the Church. Zwingli himself was elected to the council in 1521, and, within a month, the council repudiated its citizens' participation in the mercenary system he had long opposed. Renouncing his papal salary, Zwingli parlayed his alliance with local government into greater dominion and influence, as his pulpit became a sharp weapon against Rome. During the season of Lent in 1522, Zwingli openly called for his parishioners to ignore prohibitions against eating meat and to practice their liberty. In addition, he called for the end of forced celibacy for clergy, having entered the same year into a secret marriage himself with Anna Reinhard, a widow with three children.

These radical demands brought on direct opposition from Rome, and the civil authorities called for two public debates on the matter. Threatened with assassination, Zwingli defended his stance vigorously both in public and in print. His *Artikel* (1523; sixty-seven conclusions)—parallel to the famous ninety-five theses that Luther nailed to the Wittenberg Cathedral door—boldly repudiated papal authority, forced celibacy, the veneration of the saints, the transubstantiation view of the Eucharist, the existence of purgatory, and the necessity of fasting. In January, 1523, the Council of Zurich declared Zwingli the victor in the disputation, and Zurich became a firm canton of the Reformation.

Most of Zwingli's writings were born of conflict, including his *De vera ac falsa religione* (commentary on true and false religion), published in 1525, which may be regarded as the first Protestant systematic theology—a thoroughgoing treatise explaining the Protestant view of key doctrines such as salvation, the nature of Christ, the authority of the Scriptures, and the role of the Church. With his co-Reformer, Leo Jud, he also translated the Scriptures into German-Swiss as the Swiss reform quickly spread to other German and Italian cantons. Zwingli's radical departure from received Catholic doctrine reached its zenith in 1525. Preceding it were months of organized purges of pictures, crucifixes, altars, candles, and any other images from the churches of the city—all on the principle that the Second Commandment forbade the making of any artistic image of God or Christ as idolatry. Then, during Holy Week of April, 1525, Zwingli formally displaced the traditional Catholic Mass with the first great Reformed communion service in the Great Minister Church, the bread and the wine celebrated as "representations" and not the "real presence" of Christ.

The reformation of Zwingli's Zurich was substantially complete by 1525, as both secular and ecclesiastical institutions united in iconoclastic spirit to create a uniquely Swiss Protestant church. Yet the controversy over the roles of each institution in the lives of Christians continued from a right flank, as a group of Reformers known as the Anabaptists, or "re-baptizers," began to oppose Zwingli's accommodations with Rome and the council. A split had occurred in 1523 during an intense debate over the Zurich city council's refusal to bring about certain religious changes called for by Anabaptist theologians. Zwingli's view that the civil authorities should be persuaded by patient preaching rather than violent social action differed from the even more radical Anabaptists, who believed that Scripture alone—not the wisdom or political machinations of a secular government—should determine the course of the Reformation. Over two years, the gap widened, as the Anabaptists pressed their opposition to the baptism of infants and to any jurisdiction of the civil government in their Church life. In spring, 1525, a complete rupture occurred when the Zurich city council, led by Zwingli, forbade the Anabaptists to assemble or to disseminate their views. Those who refused the order were tortured, incarcerated, and, in a few prominent instances, put to death by drowning. There is no indication that Zwingli opposed the latter.

From 1526 to 1531, the Reformation spread to other cantons, and intolerance of opposing views accompanied it as Protestant Switzerland was internally beset by both military and theological challenges from Rome and by doctrinal challenges from Lutheran comrades in the Reformation. In October, 1529, the Colloquy of Marburg occurred, bringing together Zwingli and Luther, and their colleagues, to reconcile their differing views on the Lord's Supper. Zwingli held firmly to his view that the transubstantiation taking place at the Lord's Supper was not in the bread and wine but in the living saints who are gathered in the congregation to celebrate it. Unable to find common ground, the Reformers and their followers went their separate ways.

Meanwhile, tensions continued to build between those cantons that had joined the Reformation, notably Basel, Berne, and Zurich, and those that remained staunchly Catholic. In 1529, a modest peace had been negotiated at Kappel that would allow for mutual toleration and the freedom of a canton to be either Catholic or Protestant. By 1531, relationships had again deteriorated as a Catholic alliance, fearing the eventual domination of Protestant Christianity over them, launched a virtual civil war, an offensive designed to bring them final relief from their aggressors. In October 9, 1531, a Catholic militia, aided by papal mercenaries, marched to the borders of Zurich at Kappel, which was unprepared. Zwingli, who had warned the city council of the impending danger that the Catholic cantons presented, accompanied the small army gathered for defense and was himself killed. His body was recovered by the victorious Catholic militia and then quartered for treason and burnt for heresy, his ashes scattered to the winds. Zwingli's mantle of leadership then fell on Heinrich Bullinger, a friend of John Calvin, who continued to fight for Zwingli's theological and political principles.

Summary

Huldrych Zwingli's legacy to history takes the form of his unique contribution to Protestantism, particularly his dissenting views on the Lord's Supper and the proper relationship between the Church and civil authority. Zwingli had much in common with Luther and Calvin, particularly with their high view of Scriptural authority and their opposition to the legalistic theology of salvation commonly preached by contemporary Roman Catholic clerics. The Reformers, however, parted company significantly in their views of the Church, the nature of the Lord's Supper, and the relationship between the Church and civil authority. While Lutheran and Calvinistic Protestantism emphasized the Church's responsibility to preach the Word and its authority to administer the Sacraments, Zwingli understood the Church less as an institution than as a relationship called into being by Christ, a relationship resting upon the loyalty of the members of a local body of Christ to one another. What binds them together in his view is not hierarchical authority but commitment to the Bible as sole spiritual authority and to one another as functioning members of the body of Christ. Thus, Zwingli promoted the Lord's Supper as an activity to unite the Church in recognition of a common calling, not as a reenactment of the death of Christ proffered by an authoritative Church hierarchy.

Zwingli thus emerges from the sixteenth century as a much more modern, even liberal, theologian when compared with Luther and Calvin. His advocacy of an activist role in Church matters by a godly civil state sets him apart from his fellow Protestants in Germany, France, and Britain, who bitterly opposed secular intrusion into their theological and ecclesiastical dealings. Believing that God ordained the civil government as a coequal community with the Church to provide peace and order so that Christians could minister grace and salvation to the world, Zwingli offered a compromise position that established the kingdom of God in the politics of mankind. Despite the flaws of intolerance that crept into his own social and theological practice in times of tension, Zwingli's beliefs serve as a precursor to much liberation theology of the late twentieth century and certainly foreshadow the Civil Rights movement headed by Martin Luther King, Jr., in the United States of the 1950's and 1960's.

Bibliography

Bromiley, Geoffrey W., ed. *Zwingli and Bullinger.* London: SCM Press, and Philadelphia: Westminster Press, 1953. Contains selected texts of Zwingli—and his successor Bullinger—translated into English with a good, short introduction to the life, writings, and Reformed theology of Zwingli. This is the most accessible English source for Zwingli's primary texts.

Davies, Rupert E. *The Problem of Authority in the Continental Reformers: A Study in Luther, Zwingli, and Calvin.* London: Epworth Press, 1946; Westport, Conn.: Greenwood Press, 1978. This monograph has a single focus: How did the Reformers resolve issues of religious authority in their efforts to reform Roman Christianity? Davies documents with admirable clarity—in a lengthy chapter devoted entirely to Zwingli—Zwingli's attempt to place biblical authority at the center of the Reformation, while recognizing a proper sphere for ecclesiastical authority within the life of an individual Christian. The author's comparative study of the three Reformers illuminates the answers of each to this vexing question.

Farner, Oskar. *Zwingli the Reformer: His Life and Work.* Translated by D. G. Sear. London: Lutterworth Press, and New York: Philosophical Library, 1952. A brief, very readable overview of the life, times, and theology of Zwingli by the most prominent German scholar of Zwingli in the twentieth century. Farner's main intention is to acquaint the novice reader with the broad outlines of Zwingli's thought rather than to offer an interpretive, scholarly context for understanding. In this it is primarily a helpful primer on Zwingli's contribution to the Swiss Reformation rather than a comprehensive treatise.

Furcha, E. J., and H. Wayne Pipkin, eds. *Prophet, Pastor, Protestant: The World of Huldrych Zwingli After Five Hundred Years.* Pittsburgh: Pickwick, 1984. An anthology of essays by ten prominent contemporary Zwingli scholars, who have evaluated the historical impact of Zwingli's Reformation efforts on Church history on the occasion of the five hundredth anniversary of Zwingli's birth. A compendium of wise scholarship on various aspects of Zwingli's political and theological thought, valuable for its corrective reassessment of earlier Zwingli scholarship.

Garside, Charles, Jr. *Zwingli and the Arts.* New Haven, Conn.: Yale University Press, 1966. A unique work of Zwingli scholarship that attempts to assess the nature and impact of Zwingli's views of art and creativity on sixteenth century Christian worship, particularly in the visual and musical arts. Skillfully juxtaposing Zwingli's views to those of Calvin and Luther, Garside reveals Zwingli's austere devotion to an "invisible" God who could not and should not be captured in art; thus, there was for Zwinglian Christianity no place in the Church for the Christian artist seeking an outlet for expression.

Potter, G. R. *Zwingli.* Cambridge and New York: Cambridge University Press, 1976. This volume is the standard scholarly work on Zwingli, breathtaking in its scope and coverage of Zwingli's personality, theology, and politics. Its author, an emeritus professor of medieval history at the University of Sheffield, sets a high standard for readable scholarly biography in this work, which should be the first volume consulted for serious inquiry into Zwingli's impact on the Swiss culture and the European church history. Zwingli emerges as a man more welcome in the twentieth century than in his own.

Rilliet, Jean. *Zwingli: Third Man of the Reformation.* Translated by Harold Knight. London: Lutterworth Press, and Philadelphia: Westminster Press, 1964. Rilliet regards Zwingli as the least known and appreciated of the three famous reformers and orients his study toward rehabilitating Zwingli's place in Reformation history and bringing him out of the shadow of Calvin and Luther. Rilliet highlights both the unique emphases and truths Zwingli discovered and the errors he unwittingly promoted. The book's chief value lies in its extensive treatment of the Eucharistic controversy and of Zwingli's denial of the common Catholic and Lutheran understanding of transubstantiation.

Schaff, Philip. *History of the Christian Church.* Vol. 8, *Modern Christianity: The Swiss Reformation.* Grand Rapids, Mich.: Eerdmans, 1910. This volume focuses entirely on the Swiss Reformation and Zwingli's dominant contribution to it. The main advantage of Schaff's text, as an earlier—and formerly standard—Church history, is that it presents with its wider angle a holistic, comprehensive overview of Church history through the centuries and labors to present a less provincial treatment of the isues raised by the Swiss version of the Reformation.

Walton, Robert C. *Zwingli's Theocracy.* Toronto: University of Toronto Press, 1967. This work helpfully clarifies a long-standing controversy regarding Zwingli's conception of the role and relationship of the clergy and royalty in the governance of a Christian state. Walton argues that, when one attends to Zwingli's later writings in comparison with his more often quoted, better-known earlier works, one finds that Zwingli did not, in fact, advocate a "theocracy" but rather a state in which authority is shared in a cooperative government operated by both sacred and secular officials.

Bruce L. Edwards

Dictionary of World Biography

The Renaissance

Indices

AREA OF ACHIEVEMENT

GEOGRAPHICAL LOCATION

NAME INDEX

PHOTO CREDITS

Unless individually credited, all photos in this volume are courtesy of the Library of Congress except for the following:

Courtesy of Archive Photos: 37, 71, 75, 87, 106, 156, 170, 216, 291, 316, 394, 417, 420, 469, 488, 546, 552, 614, 617, 658, 669, 672, 722, 729, 778.

The Institute of Texan Cultures: 189

National Library of Medicine: 677